TOTAL PENGUINS

The Definitive Encyclopedia of the Pittsburgh Penguins

Rick Buker

TRIUMPH
BOOKS

Total Penguins is dedicated with loving memory to my late grandmother, Miriam Arbuthnot. She was a lovely woman who lived a life of giving and self-sacrifice. Miriam taught me the value of life's simplest and yet greatest virtues—love, kindness, loyalty, and patience. She was my "Badger Bob" Johnson.

Library of Congress Cataloging-in-Publication Data

Buker, Rick, 1957–
  Total Penguins : the definitive encyclopedia of the Pittsburgh Penguins / Rick Buker.
    p. cm.
  ISBN 978-1-60078-397-5
  1. Pittsburgh Penguins (Hockey team)—History. I. Title.
  GV848.P58B85 2010
  796.9620974886—dc22
                        2010009705

This book is available in quantity at special discounts for your group or organization. For further information, contact:
  Triumph Books
  542 South Dearborn Street
  Suite 750
  Chicago, Illinois 60605
  (312) 939-3330
  Fax (312) 663-3557
  www.triumphbooks.com

Printed in U.S.A.
ISBN: 978-1-60078-397-5
Design by Patricia Frey
Photos courtesy of the *Pittsburgh-Post Gazette* unless otherwise indicated

Contents

Acknowledgments

The idea to write a book about the Penguins originally came to me in 1991. An avid hockey fan since my early teens, I realized that no one had ever written a comprehensive book about the team.

Inspired by the thought of telling the Penguins' story, I began to do research. I spent my weekends combing through microfilm files of the *Pittsburgh Post-Gazette* and *Pittsburgh Press* at the Carnegie Library. During my free time I began to craft what eventually became a piece of the "Down Through the Seasons" chapter. Little did I realize at the time that this book would be 19 years in the making!

Over the next several years I wrote in fits and starts, adding seasons and player profiles here and there. As the team's fortunes took a turn for the worse in the early part of this decade, I stopped writing altogether. Around 2006, however, I pulled the book out of mothballs. Determined to finish what I started, I once more began to work on it in earnest.

When Tom Bast of Triumph Books responded to my query about a publishing deal in the fall of 2009, I had a mini-version of what would ultimately become *Total Penguins* in place. It was his vision to do the book on a grander scale. Tom's willingness to take a chance on a first-time author, and Adam Motin's invaluable assistance and continual support throughout the project, helped to make my lifelong dream of authoring a book about the Penguins come true.

I'd like to thank Dave Molinari of the *Pittsburgh Post-Gazette* for graciously contributing the foreword. The author of his own book about the Penguins—*Best in the Game*—Dave has covered the team for more than 25 years with a masterful blend of insight and humor. In 2009 he received the Elmer Ferguson Memorial Award from the Hockey Hall of Fame. I'm honored that he was willing to contribute to *Total Penguins*.

So many people offered encouragement throughout this process. It goes without saying that without the love and support of my family, *Total Penguins* would not have been possible. I wish to acknowledge Connor Buker, Dan Buker, Joshua Buker, Karen Buker, Kyle Buker, Laurie Buker, Linda Buker, Alexander Costello, Chase Costello, Roger Costello, Bonnie Faucheux, the late Susan Haley, and John and Linda Tinnemeyer for their support and indulgence.

Friends played a big part, too. I'd like to thank Rich Arthurs, Ric Drake, Dave Karpinski, Kathryn Kluk, Stasi Longo, Mike Shullo, Debbie Stockdale, Mike Verdello, Shelby Whaley, and Dave Yelich, and fellow "hockey nuts" Rob Black, Tom Blanciak, Evan Freshwater, Ryan Kish, and Paul Sarknas for their steadfast encouragement. A special word of thanks goes to Stasi, who provided much-needed insight and guidance along the way.

I owe a large debt of gratitude to Melanie Blaser, my friend and supervisor at my former employer, Consolidated Natural Gas Company. Melanie mentored me for countless hours and did so much to nurture and develop the skills required for *Total Penguins*.

My sincere appreciation goes to my boss, Dave Wright, and my coworkers at Wright's Gym in Pittsburgh. Although we operate with a lean staff, Dave allowed me to work part-time during the height of our busy season. Travis Gracey selflessly picked up two of my shifts—often putting in 50- to 60-hour weeks—while I did the lion's share of the writing. Bob Mazuer assumed extra duties and volunteered to work during his off hours. Their sacrifices enabled me to complete the book in a timely fashion, while easing my burden.

Likewise, I wish to acknowledge Allison Alexander, Shari Smedley, Angelika Kane, and the marketing staff at the *Pittsburgh Post-Gazette* for their help and support during the photo selection process. They graciously shared their office with me while providing training and other resources.

A special thanks to everyone who has played for or been a part of the Penguins organization over the years, from Mario Lemieux to the locker-room attendees. Without their supreme effort and sacrifice, there would be no story to tell.

Last but not least, I wish to thank my Lord and Savior Jesus Christ. Through Him, all things are possible.

Foreword

The Pittsburgh Penguins have been a lot of things since they entered the National Hockey League in 1967. Controversial. Combative. Endangered. Entertaining. Woefully inept. Wildly successful. During the franchise's first four-plus decades—and there were several times when there was little reason to believe it would last that long—it won three Stanley Cups, survived two bankruptcies, produced 13 NHL scoring champions, fended off threats to transplant it to such diverse locales as Hamilton, Ontario, and Kansas City, and sent no fewer than 17 players, coaches, and executives to the Hockey Hall of Fame.

All of that is chronicled in *Total Penguins*, a comprehensive look at the story, with all its brilliance and blemishes, of a franchise that has experienced the highest highs and lowest lows imaginable. It covers the triumphs of their championships and the off-ice tragedies, like the untimely death of Michel Briere in an auto accident after his rookie season.

Hundreds of players, from Ramzi Abid to Sergei Zubov, have pulled on a Penguins sweater—whatever colors it happened to be at the time—since 1967, and many of them aren't household names beyond the confines of their backyards. Others, though, are among the most storied and celebrated figures in hockey history. The headliner since 1984 has, of course, been Mario Lemieux, who became the cornerstone of the franchise when he was the first player selected in that year's draft. He went on to lead the Penguins to their first two Stanley Cups, being honored as the most valuable performer in the playoffs both times. Little more than a year after retiring as a player in 1997, he brought the team out of bankruptcy.

Lemieux, though, didn't settle for having the view from the owner's box, and revived his playing career late in 2000, remaining on active duty until 2005, when a heart ailment finally caused him to hang up his skates for good. Just a few years later, however, his protégé, Sidney Crosby, captained the Penguins to their first championship with Lemieux as the boss.

Lemieux hardly is the only world-class talent who has passed through Pittsburgh. Jaromir Jagr had his most productive seasons with the Penguins. Ron Francis was a key member of their first two Cup-winning squads. So was Joe Mullen, who was a member of the Penguins when he became the first U.S.-born player to score 500 goals. Hall of Famer Paul Coffey added to his Cup collection while playing for the Penguins, too.

Although the Penguins didn't win their first championship until 1991, there were some pretty special players who passed through Pittsburgh before that, and *Total Penguins* doesn't neglect them. While the franchise struggled to find its footing and a niche in the city's sports hierarchy during its early years, by the mid-1970s, its lineup featured the gifted likes of Pierre Larouche and the "Century Line" of Syl Apps, Jean Pronovost, and Lowell MacDonald. Those with an appreciation for good defense admired the shot-blocking ability of Dave Burrows, and fans of give-no-quarter hockey—and there's never been a shortage of those in Pittsburgh—roared their support for Bob "Battleship" Kelly and Steve "Demolition Durby" Durbano.

For years, the Penguins' most memorable moments came in defeat, and the 1975 squad that was built around those players suffered one of the most epic setbacks in hockey history, as the New York Islanders became just the second NHL team ever to rally from a 3–0 deficit to win a best-of-seven playoff series. That devastating loss was followed in short order by a plunge into receivership, and highlights and happy moments during the late 1970s and early 1980s were all too rare for Penguins fans. And again, there were heartbreaking playoff defeats by superior opponents—to St. Louis in double overtime in 1981, to the Islanders in overtime a year later—that continued to define the franchise as star-crossed.

The Penguins bottomed out in 1983–84, when they earned a mere 38 points, but their fortunes took a dramatic turn for the better in June 1984 when Lemieux was put on the payroll. There still were tough times and frustrations to be endured, but at that point, the Penguins began the metamorphosis into the top-shelf operation they are today.

Some key pieces still had to be put in place—hiring Craig Patrick as general manager in 1989 was another critical moment in the Penguins' evolution—but it was clear the cornerstone was in place from the moment Lemieux scored a goal on his first professional shift. The Penguins' fortunes began to pick up. So did their victories total. And the crowds at the Civic Arena. Long before they won their first Stanley Cup, they had cemented their place as a major force on the city's sporting landscape and when that championship did arrive, their fans celebrated with a pent-up exuberance born of all those years of defeat and disappointment.

And now, nearly 20 years later, Lemieux and Francis and Jagr have given way to the likes of Crosby, Evgeni Malkin, and Marc-Andre Fleury as cultural icons in Western Pennslyvania, players whose popularity rivals, or surpasses, that of any athletes in the city. The years of ownership that were less than stable are way in the rearview mirror, and the Penguins are moving into the new arena they believe will give them the resources to remain competitive for decades to come.

Of course, the Penguins aren't the only pro hockey team that has called Pittsburgh its home, and *Total Penguins* doesn't ignore their predecessors. Fans interested in just how deep the game's roots run in Western Pennsylvania will find a chapter detailing clubs like the Pirates, Yellow Jackets, and, of course, the Hornets, the American Hockey League club that was the primary tenant at the Civic Arena before the Penguins moved in.

The story of hockey in Pittsburgh is a rich and long one. And *Total Penguins* tells it all.

—Dave Molinari, *Pittsburgh Post-Gazette*

TOTAL
PENGUINS

Down Through the Seasons

After operating as a tightly knit six-team organization for nearly 25 years, the National Hockey League stunned the sports world in 1965 by unveiling plans to double in size for the 1967–68 season.

The announcement drew the attention of a pair of former law school classmates, Pennsylvania senator Jack McGregor and attorney Peter Block. Determined to bring big-league hockey back to Pittsburgh, they began to line up investors and gather information on the bidding process.

McGregor and Block soon learned the NHL's expansion plan was based on geography. The league planned to add two teams from the West Coast, two from the Midwest, and two from the East. With Philadelphia already earmarked as one of the eastern clubs, Pittsburgh faced some stiff competition.

"Our closest competition was Buffalo," McGregor recalled. "The Buffalo group went all out to pick off the sixth franchise. Two half brothers, Bruce Norris, owner of the Detroit Red Wings, and Jim Norris, owner of the Chicago Black Hawks, began leaning toward Buffalo."

Fortunately, McGregor had an ace in the hole. He enlisted the help of Pittsburgh Steelers owner Art Rooney Sr., who had connections to the Norris brothers through the horse-racing business.

"I'll never forget Art calling each from his New York City hotel room, in my presence," McGregor recalled. "He said to each: 'You owe this to me. You cannot put Buffalo ahead of Pittsburgh. It would be personally embarrassing to me if you did.'"

A short time later the NHL awarded a franchise to McGregor's 21-man syndicate, which included Rooney and some of the most prominent names in Pittsburgh business society. The other franchises were awarded to Los Angeles, Minneapolis–St. Paul, Philadelphia, St. Louis, and San Francisco–Oakland.

Senator McGregor's first order of business was to select a general manager. In May of 1966 he chose Jack Riley to fill the post. A man with vast hockey experience, the 46-year-old Riley had served as the general manager for the Rochester Americans and later as president of the American Hockey League.

Riley immediately hired 36-year-old George James "Red" Sullivan to coach the club. A former captain of the New York Rangers, Sullivan starred in the NHL for nine seasons. After hanging up his skates he coached the Rangers for three seasons.

With the management team in place, attention shifted to choosing a name. As suggestions poured in, McGregor decided to sponsor a "Name the Team" contest. After accepting 26,400 entries, McGregor announced that the team would be called the Penguins.

"Most fans wanted to keep the Hornets name," Jack Riley recalled. "I certainly wasn't in favor of the name Penguins at the time, but it caught on."

Indeed, the Hornets would cast a large shadow over the fledgling franchise. While Riley and Sullivan were busy preparing for the upcoming Expansion Draft, the Hornets were tearing up the AHL. Arguably one of the most powerful minor league teams ever assembled, they steamrollered the competition en route to the Calder Cup.

For Riley and Sullivan, the timing couldn't have been worse. The Hornets' success pushed them to build a team that could compete right away. They consciously emphasized experience, an approach that led them to bypass younger players.

Still, the duo did their homework. In the fall of 1966 Riley unearthed a gem by signing goaltender Les Binkley. A vastly underrated performer, Binkley had never been given a shot by the established NHL clubs because he wore contact lenses.

"The contact lenses, that's what kept me back," Binkley said. "[The managers] knew I had good reflexes, but they were afraid I couldn't see."

Craig Simpson is congratulated by Mario Lemieux after scoring a big goal.

1967–68

Record: 27–34–13
Points: 67
Goals For: 195
Goals Against: 216
Finish: Fifth (West)
Coach: Red Sullivan
General Manager: Jack Riley

On June 5, 1967, Senator McGregor signed a check for $2 million and the Penguins became official members of the National Hockey League. The following day he and his staff gathered at the Queen Elizabeth Hotel in Montreal for the Expansion Draft. Since the established teams were allowed to protect 11 skaters and a goaltender, the talent pool consisted mainly of former stars and fringe players.

Staying true to their "win now" philosophy, the Penguins' brass selected mostly veterans. As a result, the team averaged a creaking 32 years of age.

The Pens' first pick was Joe Daley, a 24-year-old goaltender from the Red Wings' system. Conscious of making the team strong down the middle, Riley chose New York center Earl Ingarfield as his first position player.

After 12 rounds were completed, McGregor got a strong endorsement from Montreal general manager Sam Pollock. A keen judge of talent, Pollock told the Penguins owner that his club—along with Oakland—had done the best job of drafting. Some of the Pens' top picks came from the Detroit Red Wings. They included husky winger Ab McDonald and stocky Leo Boivin, a rock 'em, sock 'em defenseman. But the best pick was yet to come.

"Going into the 17th round I noticed that Andy Bathgate was still available. He was expensive [$75,000], another reason why he had not been selected. But I felt he had a year or two left in him and should be worth the investment," McGregor said. "I told Jack Riley, our general manager, 'Let's go for Andy Bathgate.'"

The Penguins promptly snatched up the former Hart Trophy winner, who would serve as a major gate attraction.

In an effort to boost fan support even further, Riley picked as many former Hornets as possible. Indeed, the Penguins roster boasted no fewer than nine onetime Wasps, including Bathgate, Boivin, McDonald, Bob Dillabough, Val Fonteyne, Dick Mattiussi, Art Stratton, Gene Ubriaco, and popular goaltender Hank Bassen.

Dubbed "Sully's Skaters" by the local press, the Pens posted an impressive 4–1–1 mark in exhibition play. With proven veterans like Bathgate, Ingarfield, and Boivin leading the way, many experts felt the new Pittsburgh entry was a cinch to capture the West Division crown.

The first meeting between an established club and an expansion team took place on October 11, 1967, pitting the Penguins against the powerhouse Montreal Canadiens at the Civic Arena.

Hall of Famer Andy Bathgate led the club in scoring in 1967–68.

A healthy crowd of 9,307 fans turned out to watch the Canadiens nip the Pens 2–1 in a tight defensive struggle. Bathgate scored the first Penguins goal, while legendary Montreal center Jean Beliveau reached a milestone by notching his 400th career goal.

"[Goalie Rogie] Vachon saved the game for us," Habs coach Toe Blake said. "On a given night, with everybody playing well, Pittsburgh is going to win some games against the old clubs."

Led by Bathgate, who exploded for six goals in the first seven games, the Pens zoomed into second place. However, Ingarfield was felled by a knee injury and the club began a gradual fade, while Minnesota and St. Louis gained ground.

By the end of January the Penguins had tumbled to fifth place. To make matters worse, key performers Ken Schinkel and Les Binkley were sidelined with injuries.

The team rebounded to win its last four games, but it was too little too late. The Pens finished a scant two points behind fourth-place Minnesota and missed the playoffs. In the fiercely competitive West Division, the team trailed the first-place Philadelphia Flyers by only six points.

On an individual level the ruggedly handsome Bathgate was every bit the marquee player the club had hoped for. He had a wonderful season, leading all West Division players with 59 points, including 20 goals.

"He was the best 17th-round draft choice in sports history," Riley said.

Captain Ab McDonald also had a fine year, notching a team-high 22 goals, while rookie Gene Ubriaco chipped in with 18. Ingarfield, Schinkel, and Boivin contributed with solid campaigns.

The most pleasant surprise was Binkley. The 33-year-old rookie justified Riley's faith in him by posting a sparkling 2.88 goals-against average and six shutouts, the latter a club record that stood for 30 years.

Unfortunately, the team did not fare well at the box office. Steel City fans were used to cheering for a winner. They did not warm easily to a team with a losing record.

At the end of the season the Penguins received a sorely needed infusion of cash when a group of nine Michigan businessmen headed by Detroit bank executive Donald Parsons purchased an 80 percent interest in the club. Parsons replaced McGregor on the board of governors, while the latter continued to serve as team president.

	GP	G	A	PTS	PM	+/-
Andy Bathgate	74	20	39	59	55	- 11
Ab McDonald	74	22	21	43	38	- 4
Ken Schinkel	57	14	25	39	19	- 10
Art Stratton	58	16	21	37	16	- 6
Earl Ingarfield	50	15	22	37	12	- 7
Val Fonteyne	69	6	28	34	0	- 23
Gene Ubriaco	65	18	15	33	16	- 13
Noel Price	70	6	27	33	48	- 7
Paul Andrea	65	11	21	32	2	- 2
Billy Dea	73	16	12	28	6	- 15
Keith McCreary	70	14	12	26	44	- 3
Leo Boivin	73	9	13	22	74	- 15
Bob Dillabough	47	7	12	19	18	- 7
Bob Rivard	27	5	12	17	4	0
Bill Speer	68	3	13	16	44	- 14
George Konik	52	7	8	15	26	- 9
Al MacNeil	74	2	10	12	58	- 6
Wayne Hicks	15	4	7	11	2	2
Dunc McCallum	32	0	2	2	36	- 2
Dick Mattiussi	32	0	2	2	18	- 9
Mel Pearson	2	0	1	1	0	- 1
Ted Lanyon	5	0	0	0	4	1
Hank Bassen	25	0	0	0	8	0
Les Binkley	54	0	0	0	0	0

	GP	MINS	GA	SH	AVG	W	L	T
Hank Bassen	25	1299	62	1	2.86	7	10	3
Les Binkley	54	3141	151	6	2.88	20	24	10
	74	4440	216	7	2.92	27	34	13

Bygone Era

There's no denying that player salaries have skyrocketed since the Penguins joined the NHL in 1967. According to former general manager Jack Riley, the payroll for the inaugural Pens team totaled around $315,000—a mere pittance when compared to today's salaries.

Fast-forward to the 2009–10 season when the NHL salary cap was set at $56.8 million. The lowest-paid Penguin—backup goalie Brent Johnson—earned $525,000.

1968–69

Record: 20-45-11
Points: 51
Goals For: 189
Goals Against: 252
Finish: Fifth (West)
Coach: Red Sullivan
General Manager: Jack Riley

The team's philosophy of drafting veterans had failed to produce a winner. With a roster packed with 16 players aged 30 years or older, Donald Parsons wisely recognized the need for a farm system. Taking his cue from the front-running Flyers and Kings, who had each purchased a minor league team, he struck a working agreement with Amarillo of the Central Hockey League. Riley brought in Jack Button, a trusted lieutenant from his American Hockey League days, to manage the new club.

Riley gave the team a facelift during the off-season with an emphasis on improving the club down the middle, where it was paper thin. He dealt Ab McDonald to St. Louis in a three-team trade that netted center Lou Angotti, the captain of the division-champion Flyers.

In one of his best deals ever, Riley picked up a young French Canadian right wing named Jean Pronovost from Boston for a first-round draft pick. The addition of Pronovost helped ease the loss of Bathgate, who abruptly called it quits before the end of training camp.

Despite the new faces, the Penguins faded quickly. Although the club had a modicum of talent, they were a passive team that didn't like the rough going, a trait that galled the combative Sullivan to no end.

"Some of these guys feel all they've got to do is throw their sticks on the ice," he fumed. "They better get on the ball, I tell you that."

The 1968–69 Penguins are ready for action.

	GP	G	A	PTS	PM	+/-
Ken Schinkel	76	18	34	52	18	- 39
Charlie Burns	76	13	38	51	22	- 9
Keith McCreary	70	25	23	48	42	- 23
Jean Pronovost	76	16	25	41	41	- 4
Lou Angotti	71	17	20	37	36	- 21
Val Fonteyne	74	12	17	29	2	- 25
Wally Boyer	62	10	19	29	17	- 21
Bob Woytowich	71	9	20	29	62	- 26
Gene Ubriaco	49	15	11	26	14	0
Earl Ingarfield	40	8	15	23	4	- 17
Billy Harris	54	7	13	20	8	- 18
Noel Price	73	2	18	20	61	- 30
Billy Dea	66	10	8	18	4	- 32
Leo Boivin	41	5	13	18	26	- 6
Dunc McCallum	62	5	13	18	81	- 35
Paul Andrea	25	7	6	13	2	- 10
Duane Rupp	30	3	10	13	24	- 13
George Swarbrick	19	1	6	7	28	- 4
Bill Speer	34	1	4	5	27	- 16
Tracy Pratt	18	0	5	5	34	6
Ron Snell	4	3	1	4	6	4
Bryan Watson	18	0	4	4	35	- 11
Doug Barrie	8	1	1	2	8	- 2
Gary Swain	9	1	1	2	0	- 1
Dick Mattiussi	12	0	2	2	14	- 2
John Arbour	17	0	2	2	35	- 14
Jean-Guy Lagace	17	0	1	1	14	- 8
Marv Edwards	1	0	0	0	0	0
Bill Lecaine	4	0	0	0	0	0
Bob Dillabough	14	0	0	0	2	- 6
Joe Daley	29	0	0	0	2	0
Les Binkley	50	0	0	0	0	0

	GP	MINS	GA	SH	AVG	W	L	T
Marv Edwards	1	60	3	0	3.00	0	1	0
Joe Daley	29	1615	87	2	3.23	10	13	3
Les Binkley	50	2885	158	0	3.29	10	31	8
	76	4560	252	2	3.32	20	45	11

In late January, with the club mired in last place and floundering in the midst of a nine-game winless streak, Riley made some drastic changes. He dealt aging Leo Boivin to Minnesota for veteran defenseman Duane Rupp.

The following week Riley pulled off a blockbuster six-player trade with Oakland. He sent two of the team's top scorers, Ingarfield and Ubriaco, along with defenseman Dick Mattiussi to the Seals for forward George Swarbrick, utility player Bryan Watson, and minor league defenseman Tracy Pratt.

Riley was roundly criticized for giving up too much for three players who had scored a combined total of five goals. But he knew his club lacked the snarl that Swarbrick, Watson, and Pratt would supply.

The key player in the deal was Watson. Nicknamed "Bugsy" for his irritating style of play, he made a name for himself by checking Chicago great Bobby Hull to a standstill during the 1966 Stanley Cup Playoffs. Indeed, Watson had taken to the daunting task of shadowing the Chicago superman with such fervor that he immediately became known as "the Boy on Bobby's Back."

Although the Penguins finished in a fifth-place tie with the North Stars, there were a few bright spots. The newcomers pumped some badly needed life into the club. The Pens finished with a respectable 10–13–4 record in the final two months, including a team-record six-game unbeaten streak to end the season.

Schinkel led the club in scoring with 52 points. For the second year in a row the Johnny Unitas look-alike played in the All-Star Game. Gritty Keith McCreary enjoyed the best season of his career with 25 goals. The speedy Pronovost had a fine rookie campaign, rolling up 16 goals and 41 points.

1969–70

Record: 26–38–12
Points: 64
Goals For: 182
Goals Against: 238
Finish: Second (West)
Coach: Red Kelly
General Manager: Jack Riley

The Penguins continued to make changes during the off-season. Sullivan was replaced behind the bench by another redhead, Leonard "Red" Kelly. A former Hall of Fame player and a member of eight Stanley Cup championship teams, Kelly had guided the Los Angeles Kings into the playoffs the previous two seasons.

On the ice, Jack Riley gave the team a major overhaul. He claimed former All-Star winger Dean Prentice and bolstered the lineup with tough forwards Glen "Slats" Sather and Bryan Hextall. In a big trade with St. Louis, the Penguins GM swapped Angotti for hardworking center Ron Schock. To help Binkley in goal, he plucked colorful Al Smith from Toronto.

The best addition came through the Amateur Draft. On the recommendation of Quebec scout Dick Coss, the Penguins selected a small center of French Canadian heritage named Michel Briere. Although reed thin, he was a smooth skater, a wonderful playmaker, and a fierce competitor. Briere blossomed into the team's best player, finishing third on the club in scoring while leading the way with 32 assists.

An intriguing team to say the least, the Penguins averaged barely two goals per game and were shutout a whopping 14 times. But they employed a scrappy, defensive style that earned them the nickname "Pesky Pens." The ringleader was Watson, who was establishing himself as one of the toughest players in the league while piling up 189 penalty minutes. Sather, a terrific agitator, and big Tracy Pratt also joined the "century club."

The Pens had some talent to go with the toughness. Prentice made Riley look like a genius by leading the club with 26 goals and 51 points. Schinkel finished second in the team scoring race with 45 points, including 20 goals. Pronovost reached the 20-goal plateau as a sophomore while teaming up with Briere and Val Fonteyne on the speedy "Jet Line." Defenseman Bob Woytowich—a favorite of the team's Polish fans—tallied 33 points and was named to the West Division All-Star team.

Despite the mixture of muscle and ability, the Penguins started slowly. The turning point came on January 31 during a contest with the division-leading St. Louis Blues. Like the Pens, the Blues' lineup bristled with rugged skaters, including the notorious Plager brothers, Barclay and Bob.

Goaltender Les Binkley starred for the Pens from 1967 to 1972.

Early in the second period Barclay Plager jousted with Watson. Later in the frame the St. Louis bad boy took another run at the spunky Penguins defenseman. This time Sather intervened before Plager could reach his intended target, so they dropped their sticks and gloves and started swinging. As the battle intensified, Tracy Pratt led a charge off the Penguins' bench, and Bob Plager and the Blues followed suit. When order was finally restored the Pens triumphed 2–1.

Afterward, Sather drew the ire of Blues coach Scotty Bowman for his part in the melee.

"He [Sather] couldn't lick his lips," Bowman fumed. "He's all mouth. What a little [expletive]."

The Penguins had a different reaction. Ignited by the big win, they reeled off nine victories in their next 14 games to catapult into second place. Although they cooled in March, the Pens earned their first-ever berth in the Stanley Cup Playoffs.

For his superb coaching job, Kelly was named Coach of the Year by the *Hockey News*. Following the playoffs, he was appointed to the dual role of coach and general manager. Jack Riley was promoted to club president.

Woyto's Polish Army

Defenseman Bob Woytowich wasn't the most talented player to ever don a Penguins jersey. He did, however, have something in common with Western Pennsylvania's most celebrated athlete, golf great Arnold Palmer. He had an Army of his own.

After discovering Woytowich was of Polish descent, Tom Niemiec began to organize the Polish Army. Its ranks soon swelled to nearly 70 full-fledged members and hundreds of sympathizers. The Army camped in the cheap seats, up near the Civic Arena roof. On Saturday nights in the late 1960s and early 1970s they often filled an entire section.

Despite its origins, one didn't have to be Polish to join the Army. The entry requirements were simple: prospective members were required to purchase a general admission ticket and root like crazy for Woytowich and the Penguins. Under no circumstances was a member allowed to say anything complimentary about the opposing team.

According to John Patterson of the *Pittsburgh Press*, the Army even had scripted cheers. For example, Bobby Hull and his Chicago teammates were serenaded by the following diddie:

"Clap your hands/Stomp your feet/Chicago Black Hawks have flat feet."

	GP	G	A	PTS	PM	+/-
Dean Prentice	75	26	25	51	14	- 20
Ken Schinkel	72	20	25	45	19	- 26
Michel Briere	76	12	32	44	20	- 15
Jean Pronovost	72	20	21	41	45	- 2
Bob Woytowich	68	8	25	33	49	- 12
Bryan Hextall	66	12	19	31	87	- 22
Ron Schock	76	8	21	29	40	- 7
Keith McCreary	60	18	8	26	67	- 6
Glen Sather	76	12	14	26	114	- 13
Val Fonteyne	68	11	15	26	2	- 4
Wally Boyer	72	11	12	23	34	- 5
Nick Harbaruk	74	5	17	22	56	- 7
Jim Morrison	59	5	15	20	40	- 20
Duane Rupp	64	2	14	16	18	- 11
Tracy Pratt	65	5	7	12	124	- 29
Bob Blackburn	60	4	7	11	51	- 14
Bryan Watson	61	1	9	10	189	- 1
Mike McMahon	12	1	3	4	19	2
Rick Kessell	8	1	2	3	0	0
Ron Snell	3	0	1	1	0	- 2
George Swarbrick	12	0	1	1	8	0
Les Binkley	27	0	1	1	0	0
Joe Daley	9	0	0	0	0	0
Dunc McCallum	14	0	0	0	16	- 4
Al Smith	46	0	0	0	20	0

	GP	MINS	GA	SH	AVG	W	L	T
Joe Daley	9	528	26	0	2.95	1	5	3
Al Smith	46	2555	129	2	3.03	15	20	8
Les Binkley	27	1477	79	3	3.21	10	13	1
	76	4560	238	5	3.13	26	38	12

1970–71

Record: 21–37–20
Points: 62
Goals For: 221
Goals Against: 240
Finish: Sixth (West)
Coach: Red Kelly
General Manager: Red Kelly

On May 15, 1970, fate intervened and dealt the Penguins a crushing blow. While driving with two friends on a rainy evening near his hometown of Malartic, Quebec, Michel Briere was involved in a terrible automobile accident. When emergency crews arrived on the scene, they found him lying unconscious a short distance from the car. Although he had been thrown from the vehicle, there wasn't a mark on him.

While he showed no obvious signs of injury, Briere had suffered brain damage in the accident. After lapsing into a

coma for seven weeks, he spent much of the next year in a twilight condition, alternating between consciousness and unconsciousness. His loss would have a devastating effect on the team.

Stunned by the horrendous twist of fate, the club made few moves over the off-season. The only significant additions were first-round draft pick Greg Polis, a high-scoring left wing, and Andy Bathgate, who returned after a two-year hiatus.

In December the team absorbed yet another cruel blow when owner Donald Parsons announced that he could no longer pay his debts. The league assumed control of the troubled franchise for the remainder of the season.

On the ice, the Penguins plodded into the new year tied for fourth place. As if the team hadn't been plagued by enough misfortune, McCreary, Rupp, Schinkel, and Watson were felled by injuries within the span of a week.

Remarkably, the club responded with a superb effort over the next month to move into a tie for third place. However, the wear and tear of playing without so many key performers eventually took its toll. In a dismal finish, the Penguins won only three of their last 23 games and subsided to sixth. They were a terrible team away from the Civic Arena, winning just three road games all season long.

Still, the club made some progress, most notably through a savvy trade Riley engineered with New York GM Emile Francis. Desperate for muscle, the Rangers shipped promising youngsters Syl Apps and Sheldon Kannegiesser to Pittsburgh for Glen Sather, who was arguably the team's most popular player.

At the time of the deal Apps had scored only one goal in 31 games, while Kannegiesser was playing defense for the Rangers' farm team in Omaha. The swap was derided by the Penguins faithful, who hung a banner at the Civic Arena imploring "Why Slats?"

Apps quickly silenced the critics. In his first game as a Penguin he scored a spectacular breakaway goal against

Coach Red Kelly makes a point with newcomers (left to right) John Stewart, Lowell MacDonald, and Greg Polis.

Toronto's legendary netminder, Jacques Plante. The gifted young center went on to register nine goals and 16 assists in 31 games.

After undergoing a series of operations to relieve pressure on his brain, Michel Briere passed away from his injuries on April 13, 1971. To honor their fallen teammate, his number 21 was retired, never to be worn again.

"His death left a big hole on the club," Red Kelly said. "We just couldn't fill it."

	GP	G	A	PTS	PM	+/-
Bryan Hextall	76	16	32	48	133	- 23
Jean Pronovost	78	21	24	45	35	8
Andy Bathgate	76	15	29	44	34	- 11
Wally Boyer	68	11	30	41	30	10
Ron Schock	71	14	26	40	20	2
Dean Prentice	69	21	17	38	18	- 8
Ken Schinkel	50	15	19	34	6	- 19
Keith McCreary	59	21	12	33	24	7
Greg Polis	61	18	15	33	40	- 6
Duane Rupp	59	5	28	33	34	- 10
Dunc McCallum	77	9	20	29	95	- 13
Bob Woytowich	78	4	22	26	30	8
Nick Harbaruk	78	13	12	25	108	- 9
Syl Apps	31	9	16	25	21	3
Rod Zaine	37	8	5	13	21	- 8
Val Fonteyne	70	4	9	13	0	- 8
Glen Sather	46	8	3	11	96	0
Jim Morrison	73	0	10	10	32	- 12
Bob Blackburn	64	4	5	9	54	0
Bryan Watson	43	2	6	8	119	- 5
John Stewart	15	2	1	3	9	- 9
Robin Burns	10	0	3	3	4	1
Yvon Labre	21	1	1	2	19	2
Rick Kessell	6	0	2	2	2	1
Sheldon Kannegiesser	18	0	2	2	29	- 9
Steve Cardwell	5	0	1	1	15	- 4
Lowell MacDonald	10	0	1	1	0	- 6
Paul Hoganson	2	0	0	0	0	0
Cam Newton	5	0	0	0	4	0
Les Binkley	34	0	0	0	0	0
Al Smith	46	0	0	0	41	0

	GP	MINS	GA	SH	AVG	W	L	T
Les Binkley	34	1870	89	2	2.86	11	11	10
Al Smith	46	2472	128	2	3.11	9	22	9
Cam Newton	5	281	16	0	3.42	1	3	1
Paul Hoganson	2	57	7	0	7.37	0	1	0
	78	4680	240	4	3.08	21	37	20

1971–72

Record: 26–38–14
Points: 66
Goals For: 220
Goals Against: 258
Finish: Fourth (West)
Coach: Red Kelly
General Manager: Red Kelly–Jack Riley

As the memory of the bitter 1970–71 season faded away, the Penguins began to rebuild. The club was purchased by a group of Pittsburgh investors headed by Thayer "Tad" Potter, Peter Burchfield, Elmore Keener, and former club secretary Peter Block. The new owners immediately gave Red Kelly a vote of confidence, signing him to a lucrative five-year contract with an annual salary of $50,000.

Believing a youth movement was in order, Kelly replaced many of his grizzled veterans with fresh legs. This was particularly evident on defense, where he made sweeping changes. He plucked 22-year-old Dave Burrows from Chicago in the Intra-League Draft and promoted promising youngsters Kannegiesser and Darryl Edestrand from Hershey. Twenty-year-old Joe Noris, the club's second pick in the Amateur Draft, also made the squad.

To serve as unofficial playing coach for his kiddie corps of defensemen, Kelly claimed Tim Horton, a former teammate on Toronto's great Stanley Cup champions. Although 41 years old, Horton had long been regarded as one of the strongest players in the league. The perennial All-Star was just the man to provide on-ice instruction and leadership for his youthful teammates.

Kelly continued to shuffle the deck by claiming speedy young center Rene Robert in the Intra-League Draft. When the Red Wings selected hard-luck Al Smith, he snapped up 22-year-old goalie Jim Rutherford.

Buoyed by the infusion of new blood, the Penguins won five of their first six games, including a club-record three straight on the road. However, Horton sustained a broken ankle and the young defensive corps struggled during his absence.

The Pens soon fell back into the pack. They spent most of the season chasing St. Louis and Philadelphia for the final playoff spot.

As the season wore on, Kelly began to rely more heavily on his veterans. Horton returned to the lineup at midseason, and steady Duane Rupp was recalled from Hershey. Jack Riley reassumed the GM duties in January and promptly dealt Robert to Buffalo for another former teammate of Kelly's, winger Eddie Shack.

With the defense stabilized and the rugged Shack providing a much-needed spark, the Penguins rallied sharply down the homestretch, compiling a 5–1–5 record in their last 11 games.

Keith McCreary is bloodied but unbowed after a battle with Vancouver's John Schella.

	GP	G	A	PTS	PM	+/-
Syl Apps	72	15	44	59	78	18
Jean Pronovost	68	30	23	53	12	15
Greg Polis	76	30	19	49	38	- 4
Ron Schock	77	17	29	46	22	- 10
Ken Schinkel	74	15	30	45	8	- 10
Bryan Hextall	78	20	24	44	126	- 26
Darryl Edestrand	77	10	23	33	52	- 12
Bob Leiter	78	14	17	31	18	- 25
Nick Harbaruk	78	12	17	29	46	- 13
Duane Rupp	34	4	18	22	32	0
Bryan Watson	75	3	17	20	212	5
Val Fonteyne	68	6	13	19	0	- 1
Al McDonough	37	7	11	18	8	- 6
Rene Robert	49	7	11	18	42	- 11
Steve Cardwell	28	7	8	15	18	0
Eddie Shack	18	5	9	14	12	5
Dave Burrows	77	2	10	12	48	- 7
Tim Horton	44	2	9	11	40	5
John Stewart	25	2	8	10	23	- 6
Keith McCreary	33	4	4	8	22	- 10
Joe Noris	35	2	5	7	20	- 8
Sheldon Kannegiesser	54	2	4	6	47	- 14
Bob Woytowich	31	1	4	5	8	- 19
Bill Hicke	12	2	0	2	6	- 6
Brian McKenzie	6	1	1	2	4	- 2
Wally Boyer	1	0	1	1	0	- 1
Rick Kessell	3	0	1	1	0	- 1
Roy Edwards	15	0	1	1	0	0
Robin Burns	5	0	0	0	8	- 4
Les Binkley	31	0	0	0	2	0
Jim Rutherford	40	0	0	0	16	0

	GP	MINS	GA	SH	AVG	W	L	T
Roy Edwards	15	847	36	0	2.55	2	8	4
Jim Rutherford	40	2160	116	1	3.22	17	15	5
Les Binkley	31	1673	98	0	3.51	7	15	5
	78	4680	258	1	3.31	26	38	14

1972–73

Record: 32–37–9
Points: 73
Goals For: 257
Goals Against: 265
Finish: Fifth (West)
Coach: Red Kelly–Ken Schinkel
General Manager: Jack Riley

The chase for the fourth and final playoff spot came down to the final night of the season. Needing a victory over St. Louis coupled with a Philadelphia loss, the Pens rose to the occasion and clobbered the Blues at the Civic Arena 6–2.

Meanwhile, at the Memorial Auditorium in Buffalo, the Flyers appeared to be skating to a tie with the Sabres. But with only four seconds left on the clock Gerry Meehan uncorked a 60-foot slap shot that sailed past Philly goaltender Doug Favell. Suddenly the Penguins were in the playoffs.

There were many bright spots. The young line of Apps, Pronovost, and West Division All-Star Greg Polis developed into an offensive force. Pronovost and Polis set a club record with 30 goals apiece, while Apps established new highs for assists and points. Rugged Bryan Hextall reached the 20-goal plateau and continued to develop into a solid player.

On defense, rookie Dave Burrows displayed the poise of a seasoned veteran. Bugsy Watson, as cantankerous as ever, led the league with 212 penalty minutes. Young Jim Rutherford emerged as the team's goaltender of the future.

Encouraged by the team's progress, Jack Riley continued to promote the Penguins' youth movement. Defenseman Jack Lynch—the club's top draft pick—and 22-year-old Al McDonough were given considerable ice time.

Riley and Kelly firmly believed the team was on its way to becoming a contender. The club boasted three solid forward lines and promising youngsters Burrows and Rutherford on defense and in goal.

"They have spirit and drive, and can go as far as they want," Kelly said.

With strong production from their forwards, the Penguins got off to a quick start. On November 22, they erupted for the fastest five goals in NHL history en route to a 10–4 destruction of St. Louis. The Pens reached their peak on December 16 with a victory over Atlanta to gain sole possession of fourth place.

Things began to sour when Jean Pronovost was forced from the lineup with a badly broken nose, upsetting the club's delicate offensive balance. The team suffered through an eight-game winless streak, managing a paltry 16 goals during the slide.

By the time the Pens snapped out of the doldrums with a victory over Chicago, Red Kelly's job was in jeopardy. In January Riley replaced him with Ken Schinkel, who promptly retired as the team's all-time leading scorer to take over the helm.

Under Schinkel the Penguins bobbed along at a .500 clip. The club had its best season to date, posting a 32–37–9 mark, but failed to qualify for the playoffs by three points.

Singing the Blues

While the 1972–73 Penguins weren't the most talented bunch in franchise history, they did possess some firepower. On the night of November 22, 1972, they put it on display against archrival St. Louis before a hometown crowd at the Civic Arena.

The eruption began innocently enough, when Bryan Hextall struck for a power-play goal at the 12-minute mark of the third period. Eighteen seconds later, Jean Pronovost beat Blues goalie Wayne Stephenson again. After a brief respite, Al McDonough lit the lamp at 13:40, followed in short order by Ken Schinkel (13:49) and Ron Schock (14:07).

The sudden outburst set a new NHL record—five goals in a scorching two minutes and seven seconds!

Despite the disappointment of missing the postseason for the fourth time in six years, several players enjoyed outstanding seasons. Syl Apps blossomed into the team's first superstar, shattering his own club records with 56 assists and 85 points. Named after his father, a Hall of Fame center with

Red Kelly offers Syl Apps (26) tips on winning face-offs, while Jean Pronovost (19) and Lowell MacDonald observe.

Toronto during the 1930s and '40s, the darkly handsome Apps was a splendid skater and a superb playmaker.

He was complemented beautifully by a pair of former Los Angeles Kings, Al McDonough and Lowell MacDonald. Nicknamed "the Mad Hatter" for his penchant for scoring hat tricks, McDonough set a new club standard with 35 goals.

MacDonald enjoyed a truly remarkable season. He scored 34 goals and led the team with a sterling plus/minus rating of plus 37. The fact that the 31-year-old was still playing was a testimony to his grit and determination. The soft-spoken veteran had missed nearly two full seasons while recuperating from knee surgery, a dark art at best in the days before arthroscopic procedures. It was only fitting that he was awarded the Masterton Trophy for his Lazarus-like performance.

	GP	G	A	PTS	PM	+/-
Syl Apps	77	29	56	85	18	25
Al McDonough	78	35	41	76	26	20
Lowell MacDonald	78	34	41	75	8	37
Bryan Hextall	78	21	33	54	113	- 23
Greg Polis	78	26	23	49	36	- 32
Ron Schock	78	13	36	49	23	- 12
Eddie Shack	74	25	20	45	84	- 10
Jean Pronovost	66	21	22	43	16	- 15
Darryl Edestrand	78	15	24	39	88	3
Dave Burrows	78	3	24	27	42	- 4
Nick Harbaruk	78	10	15	25	47	- 11
Ken Schinkel	42	11	10	21	16	- 10
Duane Rupp	78	7	13	20	62	- 3
Jack Lynch	47	1	18	19	40	- 21
Bryan Watson	69	1	17	18	179	18
Rick Kessell	67	1	13	14	0	- 9
Jean-Guy Lagace	31	1	5	6	32	- 8
Steve Cardwell	20	2	2	4	2	- 2
Jim Shires	18	1	2	3	2	- 8
Robin Burns	26	0	2	2	20	- 6
Jim Wiley	4	0	1	1	0	1
Cam Newton	11	0	1	1	2	0
Denis Herron	18	0	1	1	0	0
Sheldon Kannegiesser	3	0	0	0	0	- 1
Andy Brown	9	0	0	0	2	0
Ron Lalonde	9	0	0	0	2	0
Jim Rutherford	49	0	0	0	0	0

	GP	MINS	GA	SH	AVG	W	L	T
Jim Rutherford	49	2660	129	3	2.91	20	22	5
Denis Herron	18	967	55	2	3.41	6	7	2
Cam Newton	11	533	35	0	3.94	3	4	0
Andy Brown	9	520	41	0	4.73	3	4	2
	78	4680	265	5	3.40	32	37	9

1973–74

Record: 28–41–9
Points: 65
Goals For: 242
Goals Against: 273
Finish: Fifth (West)
Coach: Ken Schinkel–Marc Boileau
General Manager: Jack Riley–Jack Button

The Penguins' high command continued to bolster the team through the draft. Several youngsters were being counted on to make an impact, including top picks Blaine Stoughton and Wayne Bianchin. The club also had high hopes for Jim Wiley, a big free-agent center who had produced well at Hershey, and Ron Jones, a defenseman culled from the Bruins in the Intra-League Draft.

Although Bryan Watson was still, pound for pound, one of the toughest players in the league, the Pens had been intimidated the previous season by big, physical teams like Philadelphia, Boston, and St. Louis.

The tone was set in a preseason game against the Blues. Early in the contest Bob Plager chopped down Bianchin. A full-scale brawl erupted in the second period when Barclay Plager attacked Watson in the penalty box. At one point Bugsy fended off Plager and several other Blues while big Steve Durbano, who had just beaten the daylights out of Watson in a lopsided fight, threatened to vault the Plexiglas partition that separated the penalty boxes.

Across the way, Bryan Hextall could see that Watson was in big trouble. He motioned to the Penguins' bench for help. No one budged. Finally, Hextall charged across the ice to rescue his teammate. He was intercepted and pummeled by one of the Blues.

Emasculated by St. Louis, the Penguins began the season in a tailspin. Their reputation as the 98-pound weaklings of the league was well deserved. Most of the team wanted no

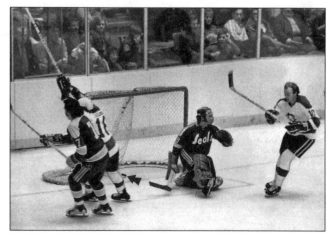

Ron Lalonde and Ted Snell (10) celebrate a goal versus the California Golden Seals.

Don't Forget to Duck

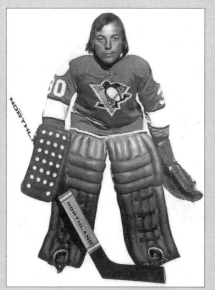

Feisty Andy Brown was the last goalie in the NHL to play without a mask.

The 1973–74 Penguins were loaded with characters, including Bryan "Bugsy" Watson, Steve Durbano, and Battleship Kelly to name just a few. But by far the most colorful was goaltender Andy Brown.

A journeyman of modest abilities, Brown had the distinction of being the last NHL goalie to play without a mask. Perhaps as a way of protecting his exposed mug, he became proficient at using his big goaltender's blade as a deterrent, whacking and hacking his way to 60 penalty minutes—a league record for netminders.

During a late-season contest against Chicago, the combative Brown took a huge swipe at Black Hawks defenseman Phil Russell. Fortunately, the rugged rearguard's self-preservation instincts took over. He ducked out of harm's way in the nick of time, saving him from becoming an on-ice version of the Headless Horseman.

Brown's taste for danger wasn't confined to the hockey rink. He loved fast cars, and even had aspirations of qualifying for the Indy 500. It was fitting that he finished his professional career with the Indianapolis Racers in the World Hockey Association.

part of the puck if it meant taking a hit. So few of the players seemed to be putting forth an effort that one rival general manager suggested that Riley and Schinkel check jerseys to see who was breaking a sweat. The Pens plummeted toward the bottom of the standings.

Riley seemed genuinely stunned by the team's poor showing. Despite the club's terrible start, MacDonald, McDonough, and Burrows were named to the West Division All-Star team. Apps, Pronovost, and Polis were All-Star-caliber players. It was an impressive array of talent for a next-to-last place team.

Early in the new year the Penguins' GM finally made a bold move. He traded the club's leading scorer, Al McDonough, to the Atlanta Flames for forward Chuck Arnason and defenseman Bob Paradise.

The trade didn't have much impact. Paradise was big, strong, and tough as nails, but he wasn't a policeman. While Arnason displayed a blistering shot, he had difficulty getting it on net. The club continued to sag.

Time finally ran out on Jack Riley. On January 13 owner Tad Potter accepted his resignation and promoted director of player personnel Jack Button.

Four days later Potter worked out a blockbuster five-player trade with St. Louis. He shipped Polis, Watson, and a second-round draft pick to the Blues for Steve Durbano, left wing Bob "Battleship" Kelly, and defenseman Ab DeMarco. Hours after the big trade with St. Louis, Button swung his first deal, sending Rutherford and Jack Lynch to Detroit for giant defenseman Ron Stackhouse.

The shake-up had a dramatic effect on the team. Standing 6'1" and weighing 210 pounds, the 22-year-old

Durbano was a larger-than-life character straight from the movie *Slap Shot*.

Aptly described by a local sportswriter as a "hard fist of a defenseman," his appetite for mayhem had already reached legendary proportions. While skating for the Rangers' top farm team in Omaha in 1971–72 he set a professional hockey record with an astronomical 402 penalty minutes. Hockey fans in London, Ontario, still spoke with disbelief about the night Durbano had speared three of their star players on the opening shift of a playoff game.

The bluster of his physical play obscured the fact that Durbano was a talented defenseman. His heavy shot and surprisingly soft hands made him an ideal point man on the power play.

Like Durbano, Kelly was coveted for his muscle. After all, he wasn't nicknamed "Battleship" for nothing. The tall, rangy winger had earned a reputation as one of the most fearsome fighters in hockey. His victims included Philly's notorious bad man, Dave "the Hammer" Schultz.

It was as if Wyatt Earp and Bat Masterton had suddenly ridden into town. With Durbano and Kelly riding shotgun, the Penguins' skill players flourished once more. During a 6–2 triumph over Vancouver, Durbano scored the first goal of the game and broke Dave Dunn's nose with a roundhouse right.

Next, the Pens visited Philadelphia to take on the pugnacious Flyers. Prior to the game, Kelly was interviewed on camera by a local sportscaster.

"You can play this interview in their locker room," Kelly said. "I don't care. I'm not afraid of anyone."

The Penguins won 5–3.

When the team began to sputter again, Button reassigned Schinkel and promoted Marc Boileau, who was coaching the club's International League affiliate at Fort Wayne.

Nicknamed "Popeye" for his fiery nature, Boileau had no NHL coaching experience. However, the Pens jelled under his leadership, compiling a 14–10–4 mark down the home-stretch. They had fallen too far behind to make the playoffs. But they had transformed from one of the worst teams in the division into one of the best by season's end.

	GP	G	A	PTS	PM	+/-
Syl Apps	75	24	61	85	37	21
Lowell MacDonald	78	43	39	82	14	17
Jean Pronovost	77	40	32	72	22	9
Ron Schock	77	14	29	43	22	- 27
Al McDonough	37	14	22	36	12	- 3
Greg Polis	41	14	13	27	32	- 18
Ron Lalonde	73	10	17	27	14	2
Wayne Bianchin	69	12	13	25	38	- 15
Bernie Lukowich	53	9	10	19	32	- 4
Ab DeMarco	34	7	12	19	4	5
Bob McManama	47	5	14	19	18	- 12
Ron Stackhouse	36	4	15	19	33	12
Chuck Arnason	41	13	5	18	4	- 2
Steve Durbano	33	4	14	18	138	17
Bob Kelly	30	7	10	17	78	- 5
Dave Burrows	71	3	14	17	30	- 13
Ted Snell	55	4	12	16	8	- 22
Nick Beverley	67	2	14	16	21	- 16
Blaine Stoughton	34	5	6	11	8	- 12
Bryan Hextall	37	2	7	9	39	- 13
Bob Paradise	38	2	7	9	39	- 3
Jean-Guy Lagace	31	2	6	8	34	- 12
Jack Lynch	17	0	7	7	21	- 15
Bryan Watson	38	1	4	5	137	- 12
Yvon Labre	16	1	2	3	13	- 7
Larry Bignell	20	0	3	3	2	- 3
Jim Wiley	22	0	3	3	2	- 4
Ron Jones	25	0	3	3	15	- 14
Jim Rutherford	26	0	1	1	2	0
Darryl Edestrand	3	0	0	0	0	- 2
Denis Herron	5	0	0	0	0	0
Hank Nowak	13	0	0	0	11	- 14
Gary Inness	20	0	0	0	0	0
Andy Brown	36	0	0	0	60	0

	GP	MINS	GA	SH	AVG	W	L	T
Gary Inness	20	1032	56	0	3.26	7	10	1
Jim Rutherford	26	1432	82	0	3.44	7	12	4
Andy Brown	36	1956	115	1	3.53	13	16	4
Denis Herron	5	260	18	0	4.15	1	3	0
	78	4680	273	1	3.50	28	41	9

1974–75

Record: 37–28–15
Points: 89
Goals For: 326
Goals Against: 289
Finish: Third (Norris)
Coach: Marc Boileau
General Manager: Jack Button

Much to his credit, Jack Button refused to rest on his laurels. Realizing the Penguins relied too heavily on the "Century Line" of Apps, MacDonald, and Pronovost, he made two major trades over the summer to add some offensive punch. First, he took advantage of a fire sale by the Rangers and landed onetime 50-goal scorer Vic Hadfield. Then he acquired young sniper Rick Kehoe from Toronto for talented but unproven Blaine Stoughton.

The Pens bolstered their offense even further by selecting 19-year-old center Pierre Larouche with their first pick in the Amateur Draft. Small and shifty, the enormously gifted Larouche had tallied 94 goals and 251 points the previous season with Sorel of the Quebec League.

On defense Button added a pair of rugged rookies, Colin "Soupy" Campbell and hard-hitting Dennis Owchar.

Steel City fans were buzzing about the team's chances as the much-improved Penguins opened the season with a 4–2 victory over Minnesota. But after clobbering Detroit in their home opener, the Pens fell to defending Stanley Cup champion Philadelphia.

As if losing to the hated Flyers wasn't bad enough, Steve Durbano shattered his left wrist in a collision with Andre Dupont. At first he was expected to miss only six weeks, but the injury was career-threatening. It would take several surgeries to repair the damage.

With Durbano on the shelf, weaknesses in the Penguins' defense were quickly exposed. In November Button shipped Ab DeMarco to Vancouver for veteran Barry Wilkins, a tough, steady rearguard. Owchar, who was aptly nicknamed "Owch," replaced Jean-Guy Lagace and responded with a slew of thundering hits. Lagace was sent to Kansas City for Michel Plasse, a solid backup goalie. Plasse's presence lit a fire under incumbent Gary Inness, who performed brilliantly in the second half of the season.

Rejuvenated by the trades, the team finally began to jell during a five-game home stand over the holidays. Following ties with St. Louis and Atlanta, the Pens heated up with consecutive victories over Toronto, Minnesota, and Vancouver.

They were even better in the new year. Paced by a record-tying six-assist performance by Ron Stackhouse, the Penguins thrashed the Flyers 8–2 on March 8. They rode a 20-game unbeaten streak on home ice to a third-place finish in the newly formed Norris Division.

Boasting three strong lines, the team was an offensive juggernaut. The Pens lit the lamp a whopping 326 times—the

Pete Laframboise and Jean Pronovost hunt for the puck while Montreal goalie Ken Dryden scrambles back to the net. Future Pen Don Awrey is tending goal.

watering holes. They constantly teased him about his age. In the war of words the fresh-faced rookie gave as good as he got. During one such exchange Lucky Pierre needled elder statesman Vic Hadfield: "When I was a little kid, Vic, I used to watch you on television."

The stage was set for a strong postseason run. But after sweeping aside archrival St. Louis in the Preliminary Round, the Penguins suffered a crushing defeat at the hands of the upstart New York Islanders.

The disappointing loss undermined the team's fragile finances. In June, principal owner Tad Potter was forced to enter into receivership.

fourth-highest total in the league. Nine players topped the 20-goal mark. The Century Line combined for 94 goals, including a team-leading 43 by Pronovost. The second unit of Hadfield, Kehoe, and Ron Schock was nearly as potent, scoring 86 times.

Perhaps the most pleasant surprise was the play of the third line, which featured Larouche skating between Battleship Kelly and Chuck Arnason. Oozing charisma and extremely popular with the fans, "Lucky Pierre" set new team rookie scoring records with 31 goals, 37 assists, and 68 points.

The 19-year-old Larouche became a talisman of sorts to his fun-loving teammates, who dragged him to their favorite

Lucky Pierre

Even as a fresh-faced 19-year-old center straight from the junior ranks, Pierre Larouche didn't lack for confidence. When the storied Montreal Canadiens promised to make him a first-round pick in the 1974 Entry Draft, Larouche told them not to bother.

"If you draft me, you'll send me right to the minor leagues," he said. "I'm good enough to play in the NHL now. If you draft me, I'll sign with the World Hockey Association."

Rebuffed, the Canadiens passed on Larouche. Penguins general manager Jack Button promptly snatched up the cocky youngster with the eighth overall pick.

Days later Button received a telegram, which said: "You are invited to attend the first annual Pierre Larouche Invitational Golf Tournament in Amos, Quebec. Bring your own clubs. Pierre."

	GP	G	A	PTS	PM	+/-
Ron Schock	80	23	63	86	36	22
Syl Apps	79	24	55	79	43	8
Jean Pronovost	78	43	32	75	37	13
Vic Hadfield	78	31	42	73	72	5
Pierre Larouche	79	31	37	68	52	2
Rick Kehoe	76	32	31	63	22	18
Lowell MacDonald	71	27	33	60	24	16
Ron Stackhouse	72	15	45	60	52	13
Chuck Arnason	78	26	32	58	32	0
Bob Kelly	69	27	24	51	120	6
Barry Wilkins	59	5	29	34	97	29
Colin Campbell	59	4	15	19	172	28
Pete Laframboise	35	5	13	18	8	3
Bob Paradise	78	3	15	18	109	- 2
Dennis Owchar	46	6	11	17	67	12
Dave Burrows	78	2	15	17	49	3
Bob McManama	40	5	9	14	6	6
Lew Morrison	52	7	5	12	4	- 5
Nelson Debenedet	31	6	3	9	11	- 3
Jean-Guy Lagace	27	1	8	9	39	5
Kelly Pratt	22	0	6	6	15	1
Ab DeMarco	8	2	1	3	4	- 4
Ron Lalonde	24	0	3	3	0	1
Gary Inness	57	0	2	2	2	0
Mario Faubert	10	1	0	1	6	- 2
Steve Durbano	1	0	1	1	10	0
Michel Plasse	20	0	1	1	6	0
Yves Bergeron	2	0	0	0	0	- 3
Wayne Bianchin	2	0	0	0	0	- 1
Denis Herron	3	0	0	0	0	0
Bob Stumpf	3	0	0	0	4	- 4
Harvey Bennett	7	0	0	0	0	- 2
Bob Johnson	12	0	0	0	6	0

	GP	MINS	GA	SH	AVG	W	L	T
Gary Inness	57	3122	161	2	3.09	24	18	10
Michel Plasse	20	1094	73	0	4.00	9	5	4
Bob Johnson	12	476	40	0	5.04	3	4	1
Denis Herron	3	108	11	0	6.11	1	1	0
	80	4800	289	2	3.61	37	28	15

1975–76

Record: 35–33–12
Points: 82
Goals For: 339
Goals Against: 303
Finish: Third (Norris)
Coach: Marc Boileau–Ken Schinkel
General Manager: Wren Blair

Despite the grim set of circumstances, the club was purchased within a month by a group headed by Albert Savill, Otto Frenzel, and former Minnesota GM Wren Blair for the bargain-basement price of $3.8 million. Blair assumed the dual role of president and general manager, which meant that Jack Button—one of the most capable executives in club history—was out of a job. Marc Boileau was retained as coach.

While the new owners hardly had deep pockets, the financial situation was stabilized. Players and fans alike began to look forward to the upcoming season. The Penguins had loads of offensive talent. With the return of tough guy Steve Durbano, who had missed virtually the entire 1974–75 season with a severe wrist injury, some felt they might even be a dark-horse challenger for the Stanley Cup.

It was not to be the Penguins' year. After opening the season on a high note with four victories, they slipped into a 2–9–2 tailspin. The club briefly righted itself at the end of November with four straight wins, but it proved to be a last gasp. In December the Pens collapsed and fell into a deep slump. Although still an offensive powerhouse, the defense was atrocious and the transition game was in shambles.

Blair pulled the trigger on several trades in an effort to shake the team out of the doldrums. He shipped Bob Paradise and hulking Harvey Bennett to Washington for versatile forward Stan Gilbertson and a draft choice. Early in the new year Durbano and Chuck Arnason were sent packing to Kansas City for veteran winger Simon Nolet and youngster Ed Gilbert.

While the trades added even more skill to a talent-laden lineup, they cost the team a huge chunk of muscle. It was a shortcoming that would quickly be exposed in the heyday of goon-squad hockey. Although Battleship Kelly was still a commanding presence, most opponents avoided him like the plague.

When the club continued to sputter, Blair relieved Boileau of the coaching duties and handed the reins back to Ken Schinkel, who had remained in the organization as a scout. The team had logged a dismal 15–23–5 record under Boileau. Morale was at an all-time low.

Under Schinkel's steady hand the Pens began an immediate turnaround. They soon ran off an 11-game unbeaten streak, a club record that stood for 17 years. The hot streak propelled the team into the playoffs for the second year in a row.

Despite the team's Jekyll and Hyde play, it was a season filled with brilliant individual achievements. Second-year pro Pierre Larouche burst into stardom, becoming the youngest player in NHL history to score 50 goals. He finished fifth in the league scoring race and established club records with 53 goals and 111 points.

Only slightly off Larouche's torrid pace was Jean Pronovost, who also cracked the 100-point barrier. On March 24 "Prony" became the first player in franchise history to tally 50 goals. Silky smooth Syl Apps joined his teammates among the league's top-10 scorers while establishing career highs with 32 goals, 67 assists, and 99 points.

On the blue line, Ron Stackhouse and Dave Burrows were far and away the team's top performers. Stackhouse

Syl Apps (26) and Barry Wilkins (5) look on as Montreal's Bob Gainey (23) beats goalie Gary Inness.

had another big year offensively, setting new team records for a defenseman with 60 assists and 71 points to go with a plus 19 rating. Burrows enjoyed the best season of his career with seven goals and 22 assists and a team-leading plus 27 rating.

A mobile rearguard who could skate faster backward than most players could skate forward, Burrows was especially brilliant. Opponents who tried to go around him were cleanly but firmly ridden off the puck and into the boards. The quiet-tough defender was nearly impregnable to an inside move as well.

	GP	G	A	PTS	PM	+/-
Pierre Larouche	76	53	58	111	33	4
Jean Pronovost	80	52	52	104	24	16
Syl Apps	80	32	67	99	24	17
Rick Kehoe	71	29	47	76	6	9
Lowell MacDonald	69	30	43	73	12	14
Ron Stackhouse	80	11	60	71	76	19
Vic Hadfield	76	30	35	65	46	-3
Ron Schock	80	18	44	62	28	2
Bob Kelly	77	25	30	55	149	4
Dave Burrows	80	7	22	29	51	27
Barry Wilkins	75	0	27	27	106	-1
Stan Gilbertson	48	13	8	21	6	-3
Simon Nolet	39	9	8	17	2	7
Colin Campbell	64	7	10	17	105	-4
Dennis Owchar	54	5	12	17	19	13
Chuck Arnason	30	7	3	10	14	-4
Lew Morrison	78	4	5	9	8	7
Mario Faubert	21	1	8	9	10	6
Steve Durbano	32	0	8	8	161	9
Harvey Bennett	25	3	3	6	53	4
Wayne Bianchin	14	1	5	6	4	-4
Ed Van Impe	12	0	5	5	16	4
Bob McManama	12	1	2	3	4	0
Ed Gilbert	38	1	1	2	0	-1
Jacques Cossette	7	0	2	2	9	-2
Michel Plasse	55	0	2	2	18	0
Bob Taylor	2	0	0	0	0	0
Gord Laxton	8	0	0	0	0	0
Bob Paradise	9	0	0	0	4	-7
Gary Inness	23	0	0	0	2	0

	GP	MINS	GA	SH	AVG	W	L	T
Michel Plasse	55	3096	178	2	3.45	24	19	10
Gary Inness	23	1212	82	0	4.06	8	9	2
Gord Laxton	8	414	31	0	4.49	3	4	0
Bob Taylor	2	78	7	0	5.38	0	1	0
	80	4800	303	2	3.79	35	33	12

1976–77

Record: 34–33–13
Points: 81
Goals For: 240
Goals Against: 252
Finish: Third (Norris)
Coach: Ken Schinkel
General Manager: Wren Blair–Baz Bastien

On June 3 Wren Blair ushered in a new era in Penguins hockey when he appointed Aldege "Baz" Bastien to the post of assistant general manager. The move was very well received among the local fans and press. An old-school executive who had worked his way up through the ranks, Bastien was a folk hero of sorts in Pittsburgh. Once a promising young goaltender, he'd lost an eye while playing for the Hornets, which served to cement his popularity with the hardscrabble, steel-working Pittsburgh fans. After becoming the club's coach in 1966, he led the Hornets to a Calder Cup title.

The team's top priority in the off-season was to shore up the porous defense. The Pens obtained seasoned pro Don Awrey from Montreal and added a strapping American-born rookie from the University of Minnesota named Russ Anderson.

Blair also made wholesale changes in goal. In a savvy move he signed free agent Denis Herron, who had played brilliantly for a terrible Kansas City team, while shipping spare parts Campbell, Nolet, and Plasse to the Scouts as compensation.

The club had one of its finest Amateur Drafts in 1976. Blair had shrewdly exchanged first-round draft positions in his deal with Kansas City the year before. With the second choice overall he selected Saskatoon Blades scoring ace Blair Chapman, a sharp-shooting right wing who was universally hailed as an impact player. The Penguins followed up by grabbing husky center Greg Malone.

In the third round they chose Morris Lukowich, a tough, speedy little winger from Medicine Hat who would prove to be the best of the bunch. Unfortunately the bidding war with the fledgling World Hockey Association had reached its zenith. Operating on a shoestring budget, Blair couldn't come to terms with Lukowich, who went on to score a whopping 65 goals in 1978–79 as a member of the Winnipeg Jets.

With Chapman and Malone adding fresh legs up front, the Penguins blasted Vancouver in the season opener. The victory came with a steep price, however, as Herron went down with a broken arm. The plan to use unproven Gordie Laxton in goal lasted one game—a 10–1 shellacking at the hands of Montreal.

Desperate to plug the dyke, Blair scurried to find an experienced netminder. Only too happy to oblige, the Rangers offered up problem child Dunc Wilson.

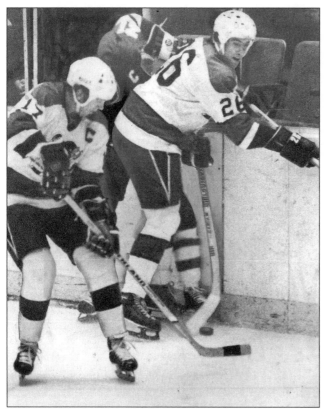

Ron Schock (17) and Syl Apps (26) battle for a loose puck against the Flames.

	GP	G	A	PTS	PM	+/-
Jean Pronovost	79	33	31	64	24	8
Pierre Larouche	65	29	34	63	14	- 10
Syl Apps	72	18	43	61	20	2
Rick Kehoe	80	30	27	57	10	- 5
Ron Schock	80	17	32	49	10	- 6
Mike Corrigan	73	14	27	41	36	- 13
Ron Stackhouse	80	7	34	41	72	11
Greg Malone	66	18	19	37	43	3
Blair Chapman	80	14	23	37	16	- 12
Wayne Bianchin	79	28	6	34	28	- 1
Bob Kelly	74	10	21	31	115	13
Dennis Owchar	46	5	18	23	37	- 7
Stan Gilbertson	67	6	9	15	13	- 9
Mario Faubert	47	2	11	13	32	- 4
Russ Anderson	66	2	11	13	81	5
Don Awrey	79	1	12	13	40	- 2
Dave Burrows	69	3	6	9	29	- 15
Lew Morrison	76	2	1	3	0	- 6
Ed Van Impe	10	0	3	3	6	- 2
Lowell MacDonald	3	1	1	2	0	- 1
Tom Price	7	0	2	2	4	0
Vic Hadfield	9	0	2	2	0	1
Denis Herron	34	0	1	1	4	0
Dunc Wilson	45	0	1	1	21	0
Yves Bergeron	1	0	0	0	0	0
Steve Lyon	3	0	0	0	2	0
Gord Laxton	6	0	0	0	0	0
Ed Gilbert	7	0	0	0	0	- 3

	GP	MINS	GA	SH	AVG	W	L	T
Denis Herron	34	1920	94	1	2.94	15	11	5
Dunc Wilson	45	2627	129	5	2.95	18	19	8
Gord Laxton	6	253	26	0	6.17	1	3	0
	80	4800	252	6	3.15	34	33	13

For one year at least, the free-spirited Wilson proved to be a terrific acquisition. Sporting a distinctive rebel mask and moving to the beat of his own drum, he was extraordinary, winning 18 games while posting a 2.95 goals-against average and five shutouts.

Misfortune continued to dog the Pens through the early going as top scorers Hadfield and MacDonald were felled by injuries. The situation grew worse in November when the team's brass suspended Larouche for two games for a myriad of sins.

Everyone involved tried to downplay the suspension. "I don't know why the press made such a big deal of it," coach Ken Schinkel said. But it was a harbinger of things to come.

With so many key performers either hobbled or on the shelf, the team's production plummeted. Gone were the days of fire-wagon hockey and 6–5 victories. To his credit, Schinkel encouraged a more defensive style of play and the Pens pared down their goals against. It was a stunning reversal of form for a team that had been such an offensive force.

Still, defensive hockey had its merits. For the third year in a row, the Penguins placed third in the Norris Division to qualify for the Stanley Cup Playoffs.

1977–78

Record: 25–37–18
Points: 68
Goals For: 254
Goals Against: 321
Finish: Fourth (Norris)
Coach: Johnny Wilson
General Manager: Baz Bastien

With the near miss against the Islanders and disappointing opening-round losses to Toronto as a backdrop, the aging Penguins were ripe for a retooling. The rebuilding effort would be led by Baz Bastien, who had been promoted to the post of general manager.

The Penguins and the Black Hawks brawl. Russ Anderson is at the center of the melee.

In terms of management style, Bastien operated in much the same manner as Raymond "Buddy" Parker, the impulsive Pittsburgh Steelers coach of the late 1950s and early '60s. Parker, a fiery Texan who won a pair of NFL championships with the Detroit Lions, was a free-wheeling sort who traded draft picks for veterans at the drop of a hat.

Like Parker, Bastien was a master of the short-term fix. He also had little regard for the Amateur Draft, a point that was driven home in his first major trade. The new Penguins GM astounded the hockey world by dealing the club's first pick in the 1979 draft to Washington for Hartland Monahan, a rather ordinary checking forward who was coming off a career year. Monahan would play all of seven games with the team before he, too, was traded away.

Bastien faced some daunting challenges. Veteran Vic Hadfield had retired and penalty-killing ace Stan Gilbertson tragically lost a leg in an automobile accident. Thirty-six-year-old Lowell MacDonald was a huge question mark as well—he had suffered yet another career-threatening injury. Other key departures included free agents Battleship Kelly and Don Awrey.

Pierre Larouche was clearly unhappy in Pittsburgh. He postured throughout the summer for a trade. To Bastien's credit, he lined up a beauty with the Cleveland Barons that would have netted high-scoring center Dennis Maruk and hard-nosed winger Al MacAdam. Unwilling to play for a franchise that was struggling even more than the Penguins, Larouche killed the deal by invoking a no-trade clause in his contract.

Unfazed, Bastien continued to reshape the team. In an effort to add some muscle and spirit he reacquired rugged Bob Paradise and shipped aging captain Ron Schock to Buffalo for rambunctious winger Brian "Spinner" Spencer. Scrappy Colin Campbell rejoined the team after spending a season with Colorado.

Hoping to instill a sense of discipline, Bastien promoted Ken Schinkel to director of player personnel and brought in his old friend and former coach with the Rockies, NHL iron man Johnny Wilson. It was anything but a match made in heaven.

Predictably, the Penguins slogged out of the starting gate. Dismayed by his team's dismal showing, Al Savill sought out the opinion of ex-Bruins star Derek Sanderson at a party. Sanderson, who staged a brief and unsuccessful comeback with the Penguins later in the season, advised Savill that the club lacked aggression.

"You have no real big, tough guy," the former Boston bad boy said. "You should get Dave Schultz. You've got a lot of right-handed center-men. Get rid of one of your centers."

The Penguins did just that. In a stunning trade, Bastien shipped popular but declining Syl Apps and the recently acquired Monahan to the Los Angeles Kings for Schultz and center Gene Carr.

"The Hammer" lived up to his press clippings. Although no longer the NHL's undisputed heavyweight champ, he dropped the mitts a whopping 20 times. Meanwhile, Carr added some dash and color to the mix with his blazing speed.

Bastien soon followed up with a second blockbuster deal. He sent Larouche, who had become a cancer in the locker room, to Montreal for hulking center Pete Mahovlich and prospect Peter Lee. Bastien was well acquainted with Mahovlich, who had briefly played for the old Hornets. Lee was a speedy little winger who scored 81 goals in his final year of junior hockey.

While it was debatable whether the trades made the club better, it certainly gave the team more heart and spirit. Backed by Schultz's bare-knuckled, brawling style, the Pens began to hustle and hit.

The newcomers made significant contributions. Mahovlich averaged better than a point per game and electrified the fans with his patented end-to-end rushes. Carr and Tom Edur—nicknamed "the Gold Dust Twins" for their flowing blond locks—gave the club a pair of competent point men on the power play. Lee didn't score many goals, but he endeared himself to teammates and fans with his diligent play.

The Penguins gradually closed in on the .500 mark and entered March a scant two points behind second-place Los Angeles. Just as they appeared to be gathering momentum, the wheels fell off the wagon. They collapsed down the homestretch, winning just five of 20 games.

There were few individual performances of note. Once again, Pronovost paced the attack with 40 goals and 65 points, while Kehoe, Chapman, and Wayne Bianchin reached the 20-goal mark. Mahovlich gave a great effort, at times trying to lift the team into the playoffs single-handed.

Fortunately, the team's fragile finances received a considerable boost when Edward DeBartolo Sr. took control. DeBartolo, who amassed a fortune through his construction and real estate ventures, would provide the Penguins with the stable ownership they had always lacked.

	GP	G	A	PTS	PM	+/-
Jean Pronovost	79	40	25	65	50	- 16
Pete Mahovlich	57	25	36	61	37	4
Greg Malone	78	18	43	61	80	- 16
Gene Carr	70	17	37	54	76	- 15
Rick Kehoe	70	29	21	50	10	- 18
Blair Chapman	75	24	20	44	37	- 11
Tom Edur	58	5	38	43	18	- 9
Dave Schultz	66	9	25	34	378	- 9
Wayne Bianchin	61	20	13	33	40	- 14
Brian Spencer	79	9	11	20	81	- 18
Mike Corrigan	25	8	12	20	10	- 7
Ron Stackhouse	50	5	15	20	36	- 16
Dave Burrows	67	4	15	19	24	- 30
Peter Lee	60	5	13	18	19	- 11
Russ Anderson	74	2	16	18	150	- 5
Lowell MacDonald	19	5	8	13	2	0
John Flesch	29	7	5	12	19	- 7
Bob Paradise	64	2	10	12	53	- 30
Pierre Larouche	20	6	5	11	0	- 13
Dennis Owchar	22	2	8	10	23	- 12
Colin Campbell	55	1	9	10	103	- 19
Tom Cassidy	26	3	4	7	15	- 4
Syl Apps	9	0	7	7	0	0
Jim Hamilton	25	2	4	6	2	- 3
Mario Faubert	18	0	6	6	11	2
Derek Sanderson	13	3	1	4	0	- 6
Jacques Cossette	19	1	2	3	4	- 5
Hartland Monahan	7	2	0	2	2	- 7
Lew Morrison	8	0	2	2	0	3
Dunc Wilson	21	0	1	1	0	0
Denis Herron	60	0	1	1	6	0
Kim Davis	1	0	0	0	0	0
Greg Redquest	1	0	0	0	0	0
Gord Laxton	2	0	0	0	0	0
Tom Price	10	0	0	0	0	- 4

	GP	MINS	GA	SH	AVG	W	L	T
Denis Herron	60	3534	210	0	3.57	20	25	15
Dunc Wilson	21	1180	95	0	4.83	5	11	3
Gord Laxton	2	73	9	0	7.40	0	1	0
Greg Redquest	1	13	3	0	13.85	0	0	0
	80	4800	321	0	4.01	25	37	18

1978–79

Record: 36–31–13
Points: 85
Goals For: 281
Goals Against: 279
Finish: Second (Norris)
Coach: Johnny Wilson
General Manager: Baz Bastien

Baz Bastien faced a major rebuilding job in the off-season. Convinced that his team needed an infusion of new blood, he engineered a series of deals that were designed to instill a winning attitude.

For the second year in a row Bastien traded away the Pens' first-round draft choice. This time he received three proven veterans from the Flyers in return—Orest Kindrachuk, Ross Lonsberry, and Tom Bladon.

In one of his best trades, he acquired speedy forward George Ferguson and husky young defenseman Randy Carlyle from Toronto in exchange for Dave Burrows. A few days into the season Bastien dealt yet another first-round pick to Montreal for left wing Rod Schutt.

"I just got Schutt from Montreal," he crowed to the press corps. Folklore has it that he believed he had acquired *Steve Shutt*, the brilliant left wing who'd scored 60 goals during the 1976–77 season.

Although the club seemed to be headed in the right direction, Jean Pronovost was unwilling to endure another rebuilding program. Bastien did his best to accommodate the club's career scoring leader, sending him to Atlanta in a three-way deal that netted Gregg Sheppard, a badly needed center.

Thanks to Bastien's bold maneuvering, the Penguins were vastly improved. They started slowly, but caught fire in December and rambled through the month with a 9–2–4 record. The Pens capped off one of the most successful stretches in club history with a rousing come-from-behind victory over Detroit on New Year's Eve. Trailing the Red Wings by four goals late in the second period, they struck for five straight goals, including the game winner by Randy Carlyle with just seven seconds remaining.

The Pens continued to play solid hockey in the second half. The team finished with a record of 36–31–13, good for second place in the Norris Division and a slot in the Stanley Cup Playoffs.

Youngsters Greg Malone and Peter Lee blossomed into 30-goal scorers—Malone in particular seemed destined for stardom. Newcomers Ferguson, Lonsberry, and Schutt each topped the 20-goal mark, as did holdover Rick Kehoe. Team captain Orest Kindrachuk played gritty, inspired hockey while providing sterling leadership.

The club was tremendously improved on defense. Stackhouse rebounded to have a solid year. Randy Carlyle exceeded all expectations by scoring 13 goals and 47 points. Colin Campbell had his finest season and played particularly well down the homestretch. Bladon and Dale Tallon added much-needed experience and mobility at the blue line, while Russ Anderson supplied the muscle.

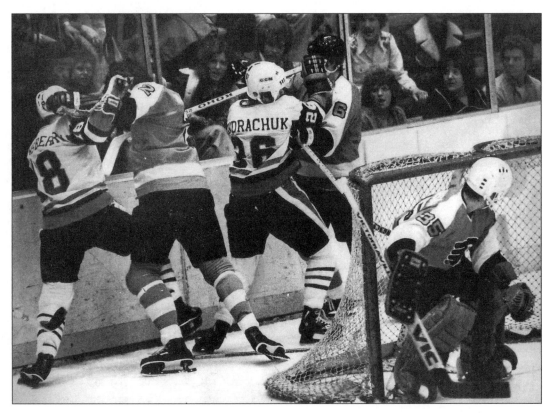

Ex-Flyers Ross Lonsberry and Orest Kindrachuk battle against their former team.

Between the pipes, Denis Herron and Greg Millen posted winning records and identical 3.37 goals-against averages. A 21-year-old rookie who possessed cat-like reflexes, Millen showed flashes of brilliance.

For his outstanding rebuilding job, Bastien was honored as the NHL's Executive of the Year.

	GP	G	A	PTS	PM	+/-
Greg Malone	80	35	30	65	52	6
Orest Kindrachuk	79	18	42	60	84	3
Peter Lee	80	32	26	58	24	- 13
Pete Mahovlich	60	14	39	53	39	- 11
George Ferguson	80	21	29	50	37	10
Randy Carlyle	70	13	34	47	78	4
Ross Lonsberry	80	24	22	46	38	7
Rick Kehoe	57	27	18	45	2	14
Rod Schutt	74	24	21	45	33	- 9
Ron Stackhouse	75	10	33	43	54	21
Gregg Sheppard	60	15	22	37	9	8
Dale Tallon	63	5	24	29	35	- 15
Tom Bladon	78	4	23	27	64	- 17
Colin Campbell	65	2	18	20	137	14
Blair Chapman	71	10	8	18	18	- 12
Russ Anderson	72	3	13	16	93	1
Gary McAdam	28	5	9	14	2	4
Dave Schultz	47	4	9	13	157	- 2
Wayne Bianchin	40	7	4	11	20	- 2
Jacques Cossette	38	7	2	9	16	- 1
Denis Herron	56	0	2	2	18	0
Kim Davis	1	1	0	1	0	0
Bob Paradise	14	0	1	1	4	- 4
Gord Laxton	1	0	0	0	0	0
Tom Price	2	0	0	0	4	- 2
Jim Hamilton	2	0	0	0	0	0
Lex Hudson	2	0	0	0	0	0
Mike Meeker	4	0	0	0	5	- 1
Brian Spencer	7	0	0	0	0	0
Greg Millen	28	0	0	0	0	0

	GP	MINS	GA	SH	AVG	W	L	T
Denis Herron	56	3208	180	0	3.37	22	19	12
Greg Millen	28	1532	86	2	3.37	14	11	1
Gord Laxton	1	60	8	0	8.00	0	1	0
	80	4800	279	2	3.49	36	31	13

1979–80

Record: 30–37–13
Points: 73
Goals For: 251
Goals Against: 303
Finish: Third (Norris)
Coach: Johnny Wilson
General Manager: Baz Bastien

The long-awaited merger of the NHL and the World Hockey Association finally took place over the summer of 1979. Under the agreement hammered out between the rival leagues, the cream of the WHA crop—the Edmonton Oilers, Hartford Whalers, Quebec Nordiques, and Winnipeg Jets—joined the NHL.

The merger came at a steep price for the former WHA teams. In addition to paying a $10 million entry fee, each club was allowed to protect only two skaters and two goalies. The rest of their players would be offered to the NHL teams that held their rights through a special "reclaim" draft. The new teams would then be restocked through an Expansion Draft.

Pens goalie Greg Millen keeps his eyes on the puck.

Groundhog Day

In the 1993 movie *Groundhog Day*, comedian Bill Murray plays a weatherman who keeps reliving the same day. Fourteen years earlier the Penguins experienced a real-life "groundhog week" of their own.

Beginning on December 8, 1979, the Pens played to four consecutive 3–3 ties over a seven-day stretch. Even more remarkably, three days prior to commencing the streak the Penguins skated to a 3–3 deadlock with Vancouver. Their eerie dance with déjà vu was suspended—but only temporarily—by a 5–3 victory over the Capitals on December 7.

Murray's movie character escapes his predicament by using the recurring day to improve himself. Alas, the Penguins had no such luck. They snapped their string of cookie-cutter ties with a dismal 4–1 loss to Quebec.

Bastien coveted Winnipeg's high-scoring winger Morris Lukowich and Quebec's Paul Baxter, a rugged defenseman. As fate would have it, they were among the players protected by their respective teams. The Penguins settled for Kim Clackson, a fierce blue-liner and onetime WHA penalty king. The club lost Wayne Bianchin and Colin Campbell along with the rights to Tom Edur. All three were claimed by Edmonton.

Never satisfied with the return he'd gotten in the Larouche deal, Bastien swung his third major trade with the Canadiens in three years. This time he shipped starting goaltender Denis Herron to Montreal for unproven netminder Rob Holland and Pat Hughes—the man he'd wanted all along.

The Penguins' GM was ecstatic. He was convinced that the husky, blond-haired winger would become a star. He also believed that Gary McAdam, nicknamed "Wheels" for his blazing speed, would develop into a big-time offensive threat.

The team performed remarkably well through the first half of the season. Early in the new year they beat the Islanders to gain sole possession of first place for the first time in franchise history.

In an effort to reinforce the winning tradition established by Pittsburgh's other big-league sports teams, the Penguins lobbied to change their colors from columbia blue, navy blue, and white to black and gold. The Boston Bruins, who also wore black and gold, immediately filed a protest. The league sided with the Penguins, citing that the original Pittsburgh entry—the Pirates—had sported the colors back in the 1920s.

Although they were now birds of a different color, the Penguins weren't a very good team. The club tumbled from its lofty perch as injuries to Malone and Kindrachuk took away precious scoring and leadership. McAdam scored 18 goals by the end of December, but in a complete reversal of form tallied only one more the rest of the way. Mark Johnson, fresh from his heroic gold-medal performance in the Olympic Games, joined the club in February but failed to provide a spark. Johnny Wilson was exposed as an unimaginitive coach who relied too heavily on his veterans.

By the end of the season the Pens had slipped to a record of 30–37–13, although it was good enough for third place in the mediocre Norris Division and a playoff berth.

	GP	G	A	PTS	PM	+/-
Rick Kehoe	79	30	30	60	4	- 3
Greg Malone	51	19	32	51	46	4
George Ferguson	73	21	28	49	36	0
Orest Kindrachuk	52	17	29	46	63	4
Peter Lee	74	16	29	45	20	- 13
Gary McAdam	78	19	22	41	63	- 17
Rod Schutt	73	18	21	39	43	- 8
Gregg Sheppard	76	13	24	37	20	- 22
Randy Carlyle	67	8	28	36	45	- 23
Ross Lonsberry	76	15	18	33	36	- 4
Ron Stackhouse	78	6	27	33	36	16
Pat Hughes	76	18	14	32	78	- 38
Russ Anderson	76	5	22	27	150	11
Nick Libett	78	14	12	26	14	- 19
Paul Marshall	46	9	12	21	9	- 2
Mario Faubert	49	5	13	18	31	- 19
Dale Tallon	32	5	9	14	18	- 4
Kim Davis	24	3	7	10	43	- 7
Bob Stewart	65	3	7	10	52	- 27
Mark Johnson	17	3	5	8	4	- 4
Tom Bladon	57	2	6	8	35	- 25
Greg Millen	44	0	3	3	14	0
Kim Clackson	45	0	3	3	166	- 8
Jim Hamilton	10	2	0	2	0	- 6
Blair Chapman	1	0	0	0	0	0
Nick Ricci	4	0	0	0	0	0
Rob Holland	34	0	0	0	2	0

	GP	MINS	GA	SH	AVG	W	L	T
Nick Ricci	4	240	14	0	3.50	2	2	0
Greg Millen	44	2586	157	2	3.64	18	18	7
Rob Holland	34	1974	126	1	3.83	10	17	6
	80	4800	303	3	3.79	30	37	13

1980–81

Record: 30–37–13
Points: 73
Goals For: 302
Goals Against: 345
Finish: Third (Norris)
Coach: Eddie Johnston
General Manager: Baz Bastien

Belying his reputation as a wheeler-dealer, Bastien made few moves over the off-season to bolster a team that was in obvious disarray. Once again, his primary concern was shoring up the defensive corps, which was thinned by the losses of Tom Bladon and Dale Tallon to free agency.

For the first time in years the Penguins had a first-round pick in the Entry Draft. They hoped to land speedy defenseman Paul Coffey, an offensive whiz. The Edmonton Oilers snatched up Coffey, so the Pens selected Brantford Alexander scoring ace Mike Bullard. Bastien also signed coveted free agent Paul Baxter, sending the gritty Kim Clackson to Quebec as compensation.

To no one's surprise, Johnny Wilson got the axe. Bastien replaced his old friend with former Chicago coach Eddie Johnston, who had guided the Black Hawks to the Smythe Division title. Johnston, a long-time Bruins mainstay, brought with him the blueprint for Boston's imposing power play.

Upon his arrival, "EJ" was shocked by the dearth of big-league talent at his disposal.

"When I first got here as coach, we only had 23 players on the roster," he said. "Every guy at camp made the team. Our extra guy was a kid named Jim Hamilton."

The lack of depth would soon come back to haunt them. From the opening face-off the Penguins were beset by injuries. Key players Anderson, Baxter, Kindrachuk, and Sheppard went down in rapid-fire succession. When Mark Johnson suffered a hand injury to leave the club with just one healthy center, Bastien sprang to action. He acquired Paul Gardner and former Pen Dave Burrows from Toronto for youngsters Paul Marshall and Kim Davis.

It was one of his finest trades. Gardner was a proven sniper who had scored 30 goals in each of his first three seasons. Although fading, Burrows still was a capable defender.

Bastien continued to stir the pot. He dealt the unproductive McAdam to Detroit for Errol Thompson and acquired scrappy winger Gary Rissling from the Capitals. In March he sent struggling Pat Hughes to Edmonton for edgy defenseman Pat Price.

After nearly tumbling into the cellar in mid-January, the club finally began to jell. Combative newcomers Price and Rissling added an aggression and fire that had been sorely lacking. Thanks to Johnston's renewed emphasis on offense, the team boasted one of the league's most dangerous power plays.

"The only reason we made the playoffs that year was the power play," Johnston would recall. "I used the pick play. I learned that from [Boston Celtics Hall of Famer] Tommy Heinsohn."

Several players enjoyed standout seasons. Utilizing his puck savvy and lightning-quick release to full advantage,

Ross Lonsberry rips off a shot against Dave Parro while Pierre Bouchard (26) closes in.

Rick Kehoe exploded for a club-record 55 goals. Paul Gardner planted himself in the crease and collected garbage goals on rebounds and deflections, an approach that paid off handsomely. He racked up 34 goals and 74 points in just 62 games, while becoming the first Penguin ever to score four goals in one game.

Among the rearguards, Randy Carlyle blossomed into a Norris Trophy winner. He finished second to Kehoe in scoring with 83 points and was the first Penguin ever named to the postseason All-Star team.

	GP	G	A	PTS	PM	+/-
Rick Kehoe	80	55	33	88	6	- 9
Randy Carlyle	76	16	67	83	136	- 16
Paul Gardner	62	34	40	74	59	- 5
Peter Lee	80	30	34	64	86	0
Rod Schutt	80	25	35	60	55	- 13
Mario Faubert	72	8	44	52	118	- 18
Greg Malone	62	21	29	50	68	- 14
Ross Lonsberry	80	17	33	50	76	- 3
George Ferguson	79	25	18	43	42	- 30
Ron Stackhouse	74	6	29	35	86	- 11
Mark Johnson	73	10	23	33	50	4
Gregg Sheppard	47	11	17	28	49	- 13
Pat Hughes	58	10	9	19	161	- 9
Paul Baxter	51	5	14	19	204	- 11
Russ Anderson	34	3	14	17	112	12
Errol Thompson	34	6	8	14	12	- 9
Nick Libett	43	6	6	12	4	2
Orest Kindrachuk	13	3	9	12	34	3
Gary McAdam	34	3	9	12	30	- 16
Pat Price	13	0	10	10	33	2
Marc Chorney	8	1	6	7	14	1
Jim Hamilton	20	1	6	7	18	2
Paul Marshall	13	3	0	3	4	- 7
Mike Bullard	15	1	2	3	19	- 1
Dave Burrows	53	0	2	2	28	- 13
Greg Millen	63	0	2	2	6	0
Kim Davis	8	1	0	1	4	- 3
Gary Rissling	25	1	0	1	143	- 4
Bennett Wolf	24	0	1	1	94	- 1
Gilles Lupien	31	0	1	1	34	- 15
Tony Feltrin	2	0	0	0	0	- 3
Nick Ricci	9	0	0	0	2	0
Rob Holland	10	0	0	0	0	0

	GP	MINS	GA	SH	AVG	W	L	T
Nick Ricci	9	540	35	0	3.89	4	5	0
Greg Millen	63	3721	258	0	4.16	25	27	10
Rob Holland	10	539	45	0	5.01	1	5	3
	80	4800	345	0	4.31	30	37	13

1981–82

Record: 31–36–13
Points: 75
Goals For: 310
Goals Against: 337
Finish: Fourth (Patrick)
Coach: Eddie Johnston
General Manager: Baz Bastien

Buoyed by an inspired effort against the Blues in the previous year's playoffs, the Penguins were looking forward to the new season with high expectations. However, the league had realigned, placing them in the tough Patrick Division alongside the Islanders, Rangers, Flyers, and Capitals. The team would have to improve a great deal in order to keep pace with its new brethren.

In one of the most highly publicized moves of the summer, the Hartford Whalers signed goaltender Greg Millen to a lucrative deal. Since the Penguins still held his rights, Hartford was required to compensate them. The Whalers offered two of their lesser lights, winger Jordy Douglas and veteran goalie John Garrett.

Bastien and Johnston shrugged off the Whalers' offer and boldly went for the jugular. They demanded left wing Pat Boutette—an 80-point scorer—and promising junior player Kevin McClelland. Arbitrator Joe Kane sided with the Penguins.

To plug the pronounced gap in goal, Bastien inked low-profile free agent Michel Dion to a deal. He added more muscle by acquiring giant winger Paul Mulvey from the Capitals for Orest Kindrachuk.

Bastien had assembled the most physical Penguins team in years. Baxter, Price, and Anderson formed the hub of a rough and ready defense, while Mulvey, Boutette, and Rissling provided toughness up front.

The club's aggressive attitude was contagious. In a game against Quebec, gentle giant Ron Stackhouse shocked his teammates by instigating a fight with pugnacious Dale Hunter.

With their new espirit de corps, the team played excellent hockey through the early going. Backed by the red-hot Dion, who electrified the fans with his acrobatic style, the Pens stormed through a 12-game stretch in November and early December at a 9–1–2 clip to close to within two points of the division-leading Islanders.

When the team began to falter, Johnston and Bastien shuffled the lineup in an effort to rekindle the fire. However, most of their moves backfired. Anderson was shipped off to Hartford for former Flyers star Rick MacLeish, who was clearly on the downside of a distinguished career. Rookie Doug Shedden—a capable scorer—was sent to the minors

Michel Dion searches for the puck while Randy Carlyle (25) and Vancouver's Dave "Tiger" Williams fight for position.

	GP	G	A	PTS	PM	+/-
Rick Kehoe	71	33	52	85	8	- 27
Randy Carlyle	73	11	64	75	131	- 16
Pat Boutette	80	23	51	74	230	- 23
Paul Gardner	59	36	33	69	28	- 7
Mike Bullard	75	36	27	63	91	- 1
George Ferguson	71	22	31	53	45	- 6
Paul Baxter	76	9	34	43	409	- 9
Greg Malone	78	15	24	39	125	- 24
Pat Price	77	7	31	38	322	2
Peter Lee	74	18	16	34	98	- 8
Rick MacLeish	40	13	12	25	28	- 7
Doug Shedden	38	10	15	25	12	- 2
Gregg Sheppard	58	11	10	21	35	9
Mark Johnson	46	10	11	21	30	- 14
Rod Schutt	35	9	12	21	42	3
Ron Stackhouse	76	2	19	21	102	- 11
Bobby Simpson	26	9	9	18	4	- 3
Steve Gatzos	16	6	8	14	14	0
Pat Graham	42	6	8	14	55	- 1
Andre St. Laurent	18	8	5	13	4	5
Mario Faubert	14	4	8	12	14	- 2
Greg Hotham	25	4	6	10	16	- 6
Jim Hamilton	11	5	3	8	2	2
Paul Mulvey	27	1	7	8	76	- 7
Marc Chorney	60	1	6	7	63	- 11
Kevin McClelland	10	1	4	5	4	6
Randy Boyd	23	0	2	2	49	- 5
Russ Anderson	31	0	1	1	98	- 4
Michel Dion	62	0	1	1	4	0
Dave Hannan	1	0	0	0	0	- 2
Bennett Wolf	1	0	0	0	2	0
Nick Ricci	3	0	0	0	0	0
Tony Feltrin	4	0	0	0	4	- 3
Gary Edwards	6	0	0	0	2	0
Paul Harrison	13	0	0	0	0	0
Gary Rissling	16	0	0	0	55	- 2

	GP	MINS	GA	SH	AVG	W	L	T
Gary Edwards	6	360	22	1	3.67	3	2	1
Michel Dion	62	3580	226	0	3.79	25	24	12
Nick Ricci	3	160	14	0	5.25	0	3	0
Paul Harrison	13	700	64	0	5.49	3	7	0
	80	4800	337	1	4.21	31	36	13

to make room for MacLeish. Mulvey failed to pass through waivers and was claimed by the Kings.

The club never regained its early momentum and chugged home in fourth place. The Pens did manage to finish the campaign on a mild upswing by going undefeated in their final five games. In the season finale they rolled to a 7–2 triumph over their first-round playoff opponent, the two-time Stanley Cup champion Islanders.

Offensively, the team still possessed plenty of firepower. Rick Kehoe slipped a bit to 33 goals, but led the way with 85 points. Paul Gardner and rookie Mike Bullard paced the attack with 36 goals apiece. Feisty Pat Boutette tallied 23 goals and 74 points while serving 230 minutes in the sin bin.

On the blue line, Randy Carlyle enjoyed another splendid season, piling up 11 goals and 64 assists. Paul Baxter registered 43 points while playing a tough, physical brand of defense. He and his partner, hot-tempered Pat Price, combined for an astounding total of 731 penalty minutes.

1982–83

Record: 18–53–9
Points: 45
Goals For: 257
Goals Against: 394
Finish: Sixth (Patrick)
Coach: Eddie Johnston
General Manager: Baz Bastien

Entering the 1982–83 campaign, the Penguins felt good about their chances. Justifiably proud of a strong effort against the Islanders the previous postseason, the club possessed a core of solid veterans reinforced by what appeared to be a group of talented youngsters.

Eddie Johnston summed up the prevailing belief that the team was on the verge of becoming a contender. "We are about four hockey players away," he asserted.

Ron Stackhouse retired during the off-season, ending the career of perhaps the most maligned and underappreciated player in franchise history. The club had high hopes that Randy Boyd, winner of the Max Kaminsky Trophy as the Ontario League's top defenseman, would fill his slot.

One of the team's top defensive forwards, Gregg Sheppard, also hung up his skates. With Andre St. Laurent and scrappy rookie Dave Hannan waiting in the wings, the Penguins' brass wasn't overly concerned.

For insurance Bastien picked up former All-Star defenseman Ian Turnbull from Los Angeles and reacquired Denis Herron from Montreal for a third-round draft pick. It was the veteran goalie's third tour of duty with the team.

The Pens' top choice in the Entry Draft that year was Lethbridge Bronco right wing Rich Sutter, the youngest (along with twin brother Ron) of the famous hockey-playing family from Viking, Alberta. Although undersized, Sutter had been a productive offensive player in junior hockey while displaying the tenacity and grit that had become a family trademark. But Sutter showed surprisingly little in training camp, leaving the Penguins no choice but to return him to Lethbridge for one more year of junior hockey.

When the Penguins sputtered out of the starting gate, Boyd, Schutt, and Turnbull were immediately dispatched to the minors. The club also lost the services of veteran Rick MacLeish, who secured his release after a handful of games in order to rejoin the Flyers.

Alarmed by the team's sluggish start, Bastien pushed the panic button. He sent the popular but slumping George Ferguson to Minnesota for left wing Anders Hakansson, defenseman Ron Meighan, and an exchange of first-round picks in the 1983 Entry Draft.

On the surface the Pens appeared to have made out pretty well. Hakansson was big and fast, and Meighan was a highly touted young defenseman. Little did Bastien realize that he had traded away the top pick in the Entry Draft—a pick that could have netted Peterborough scoring sensation Steve Yzerman.

Nothing Johnston or Bastien did seemed to help. The Penguins GM tried to add some muscle and leadership by acquiring Stan Jonathan from Boston, but the hard-nosed little winger had lost his competitive edge. The situation worsened in December when Price was released following a dressing room squabble with Johnston.

As the season wore on, the team became mired in a deep slump from which it would not escape. In early January the Penguins embarked on a month-long, 18-game winless streak that assured them of a last-place finish. They limped home with a horrendous record of 18–53–9, surrendering a mind-boggling 394 goals in the process.

In a final exclamation point to one of the most dismal seasons in franchise history, Bastien tragically lost his life in an automobile accident on March 15.

Although it was hard to believe, the worst was yet to come.

Mike Bullard skates away from the Oilers' Jari Kurri. "The Bullet" scored 51 goals in 1983–84.

	GP	G	A	PTS	PM	+/-
Doug Shedden	80	24	43	67	54	- 20
Rick Kehoe	75	29	36	65	12	- 45
Greg Malone	80	17	44	61	82	- 29
Pat Boutette	80	27	29	56	152	- 33
Randy Carlyle	61	15	41	56	110	- 26
Paul Gardner	70	28	27	55	12	- 23
Mike Bullard	57	22	22	44	60	- 21
Dave Hannan	74	11	22	33	127	- 28
Paul Baxter	75	11	21	32	238	- 49
Greg Hotham	58	2	30	32	39	- 14
Peter Lee	63	13	13	26	10	- 9
Andre St. Laurent	70	13	9	22	105	- 15
Anders Hakansson	62	9	12	21	26	- 11
Randy Boyd	56	4	14	18	71	- 36
Steve Gatzos	44	6	7	13	52	- 16
Pat Price	38	1	11	12	104	- 19
Kevin McClelland	38	5	4	9	73	- 18
Gary Rissling	40	5	4	9	128	- 17
Marc Chorney	67	3	5	8	66	- 30
Ron Meighan	41	2	6	8	16	- 10
Tony Feltrin	32	3	3	6	40	- 11
Pat Graham	20	1	5	6	16	- 6
Tim Hrynewich	30	2	3	5	48	- 6
Doug Lecuyer	12	1	4	5	12	- 2
Rick MacLeish	6	0	5	5	2	- 5
Rod Buskas	41	2	2	4	102	- 15
Stan Jonathan	19	0	3	3	13	- 8
Jim Hamilton	5	0	2	2	2	- 2
Michel Dion	49	0	2	2	8	0
Bobby Simpson	4	1	0	1	0	- 1
Denis Herron	31	0	1	1	14	0
Rob Garner	1	0	0	0	0	0
Brian Lundberg	1	0	0	0	2	- 1
Nick Ricci	3	0	0	0	0	0
Roberto Romano	3	0	0	0	0	0
Rich Sutter	4	0	0	0	0	- 2
Rod Schutt	5	0	0	0	0	- 2
Bennett Wolf	5	0	0	0	37	- 2
Ian Turnbull	6	0	0	0	4	- 3
George Ferguson	7	0	0	0	2	- 7

	GP	MINS	GA	SH	AVG	W	L	T
Michel Dion	49	2791	198	0	4.26	12	30	4
Denis Herron	31	1707	151	1	5.31	5	18	5
Nick Ricci	3	147	16	0	6.53	1	2	0
Roberto Romano	3	155	18	0	6.97	0	3	0
	80	4800	394	1	4.93	18	53	9

1983–84

Record: 16–58–6
Points: 38
Goals For: 254
Goals Against: 390
Finish: Sixth (Patrick)
Coach: Lou Angotti
General Manager: Eddie Johnston

The Penguins entered the off-season of 1983 in a state of flux. The club's first order of business was to fill the general manager's post that had been vacant since Baz Bastien's tragic and untimely death. The front-runner was Flyers coach Bob McCammon, but he spurned the Penguins' offer. With few viable options, the DeBartolos turned the job over to Eddie Johnston.

The new GM vowed to break with the club's tradition of trading away draft choices for veterans—a destructive legacy that reached its peak during the Bastien era, when the Pens dealt four first-round picks, as well as a second- and third-round choice. Although his decision received little fanfare, Johnston's commitment to youth was largely responsible for saving the franchise.

Johnston began to rebuild in an unusual fashion. He released Paul Baxter, arguably the club's second-best defenseman, and dealt the still useful Greg Malone to Hartford for a draft pick.

Most of the newcomers were added at bargain-basement prices. Veteran forward Rocky Saganiuk was acquired from

Pac Man

Perhaps no player better symbolized the motley, ragamuffin 1983–84 "Boys of Winter" than its most colorful player, Gary Rissling.

Nicknamed "Pac Man" after the popular video game, the tough little winger had a lumpy, scar-laden mug that only a mother could love. He often took to the ice without his dentures and sporting a heavy five o'clock shadow, ideal for snarling at the opposition in the heat of battle.

Unfortunately, Rissling wasn't nearly as proficient with his dukes as he was with his facial expressions, which were more often comical than frightening. Arguably the losingest fighter in the league, he suffered the ignominy of once coming out on the short end of a scuffle with the Devils' Jan Ludvig, a European with no known reputation for fisticuffs.

While Rissling's pugilistic skills were of questionable pedigree, his heart and soul were not. He kept answering the bell, almost always against bigger and stronger opponents.

Penguins fans had little to cheer about during the dismal 1983–84 season.

Toronto for youngster Pat Graham. Ted Bulley, Warren Young, and Marty McSorley signed on as free agents. Tiny 5'6" Mitch Lamoureux, a 57-goal scorer at Baltimore, and defenseman Phil Bourque were promoted from the minors. Nineteen-year-old Bob Errey, selected with the first-round pick acquired from Minnesota, also made the squad.

The Penguins wisely switched their marketing theme from "We Have a Hockey Team" to the more appropriate "Boys of Winter." Indeed, there would be many nights during the upcoming season when the Pens appeared to be a collection of boys attempting to compete in a man's game.

With a lineup that consisted mainly of aging veterans, minor league retreads, and inexperienced youngsters, the team flopped out of the starting blocks.

In a desperate attempt to add some big-league talent, Johnston pulled off a blockbuster deal with the Flyers, swapping the disappointing Rich Sutter for forwards Ron Flockhart, Mark Taylor, and Andy Brickley.

Still, the club showed little improvement. In an effort to protect the younger players, Johnston and coach Lou Angotti shuffled the lineup at a maddening pace. In total, the Penguins would use a mind-boggling 48 players.

Attendance dwindled along with the club's on-ice fortunes. Rumors circulated that the team would be moved to Hamilton, Ontario, following the season.

As the sad-sack Pens stumbled along, Johnston seemed to weaken the club on purpose—with good reason. The team that finished with the worst record would be in a position to draft Mario Lemieux, the most highly touted player to come out of junior hockey since Wayne Gretzky. Johnston knew the only way the franchise would survive was for the Penguins to land the Laval wonder.

In a shrewd trade that stirred quite a bit of controversy, Johnston dealt former Norris Trophy winner Randy Carlyle to Winnipeg for a first-round pick and future considerations. Under the guise of evaluating talent, he recalled Vincent Tremblay and watched as the overmatched goalie allowed a staggering 24 goals in four games.

"EJ sent down Roberto Romano, who was not great, but good," future play-by-play announcer Paul Steigerwald explained. "Vincent Tremblay wasn't very good."

Predictably, the Pens finished the season in a death spiral. Posting a dismal record of 16–58–6—the worst in the league for the second straight season—they were unquestionably among the most hapless teams of all time.

Few individual performers stood out. All-Star center Mike Bullard shone through the wreckage with a remarkable 51-goal, 92-point season. Marty McSorley established himself as one of the league's toughest and most determined fighters while playing in more games than any other Pens rookie.

The Penguins had survived their darkest hour, but there was barely a pulse. They were in desperate need of a savior—someone who could literally set the franchise on his shoulders and carry it to respectability. This enormous task would fall upon a shy, soft-spoken 18-year-old named Lemieux.

	GP	G	A	PTS	PM	+/-
Mike Bullard	76	51	41	92	57	- 33
Doug Shedden	67	22	35	57	20	- 38
Mark Taylor	59	24	31	55	24	- 20
Ron Flockhart	68	27	18	45	40	- 19
Rick Kehoe	57	18	27	45	8	- 20
Pat Boutette	73	14	26	40	142	- 58
Andy Brickley	50	18	20	38	9	- 7
Greg Hotham	76	5	25	30	59	- 25
Tom Roulston	53	11	17	28	8	- 31
Randy Carlyle	50	3	23	26	82	- 25
Bob Errey	65	9	13	22	29	- 20
Kevin McCarthy	31	4	16	20	52	- 32
Norm Schmidt	34	6	12	18	12	- 1
Gary Rissling	47	4	13	17	297	- 9
Bryan Maxwell	45	3	12	15	84	2
Tom O'Regan	51	4	10	14	8	- 22
Tim Hrynewich	25	4	5	9	34	- 10
Marty McSorley	72	2	7	9	224	- 39
Tom Thornbury	14	1	8	9	16	- 19
Warren Young	15	1	7	8	19	- 2
Greg Fox	49	2	5	7	66	- 42
Steve Gatzos	23	3	3	6	15	- 9
Kevin McClelland	24	2	4	6	62	- 7
Rod Buskas	47	2	4	6	60	- 18
Bob Gladney	13	1	5	6	2	- 1
Ted Bulley	26	3	2	5	12	- 14
Dave Hannan	24	2	3	5	33	- 2
Paul Gardner	16	0	5	5	6	- 4
Jim Hamilton	11	2	2	4	4	2
Rod Schutt	11	1	3	4	4	0
Rocky Saganiuk	29	1	3	4	37	- 12
Darren Lowe	8	1	2	3	0	- 5
Andre St. Laurent	8	2	0	2	21	- 3
Mitch Lamoureux	8	1	1	2	6	- 6
Tim Tookey	8	0	2	2	2	- 2
Dean Defazio	22	0	2	2	28	- 11
Greg Tebbutt	24	0	2	2	31	- 26
Marc Chorney	4	0	1	1	8	- 4
Phil Bourque	5	0	1	1	12	- 2
Randy Boyd	5	0	1	1	6	- 2
Michel Dion	30	0	1	1	2	0
Grant Sasser	3	0	0	0	0	- 2
Vince Tremblay	4	0	0	0	2	0
Rich Sutter	5	0	0	0	0	- 2
Todd Charlesworth	10	0	0	0	8	- 7
Troy Loney	13	0	0	0	9	- 7
Roberto Romano	18	0	0	0	0	0
Denis Herron	38	0	0	0	21	0

	GP	MINS	GA	SH	AVG	W	L	T
Denis Herron	38	2028	138	1	4.08	8	24	2
Roberto Romano	18	1020	78	1	4.59	6	11	0
Michel Dion	30	1553	138	0	5.33	2	19	4
Vince Tremblay	4	240	24	0	6.00	0	4	0
	80	4841	390	2	4.83	16	58	6

1984–85

Record: 24–51–5
Points: 53
Goals For: 276
Goals Against: 385
Finish: Sixth (Patrick)
Coach: Bob Berry
General Manager: Eddie Johnston

Mario Lemieux had captured the imagination of the entire hockey world. As a member of the Laval Voison of the Quebec League, the phenom had shattered junior hockey scoring records, amassing the astronomical totals of 133 goals, 149 assists, and 282 points.

Scouts who watched the rangy 6'4", 200-pound center in action were awestruck. Never before had they seen a player who possessed such a rare combination of attributes and skills—size, reach, quickness, vision, playmaking ability, and scoring touch—in one complete package.

"No one who's come out of junior hockey has ever shown as much potential as Mario—ever," said the Pens' new coach, Bob Berry.

There was an incredible feeling of excitement and tension in the months leading up to the Entry Draft. Other clubs did their best to pry the coveted No. 1 pick from Eddie Johnston's grasp by wooing him with jaw-dropping packages of draft picks and veterans.

Perhaps the most astounding proposal came from the Quebec Nordiques, who reportedly offered their All-Star forward line of Peter, Anton, and Marian Stastny for the chance to draft Lemieux.

The Penguins' GM never wavered. On draft day he proudly strode to the podium and announced in halting

Rookies Warren Young (35) and Mario Lemieux (66) reached the 40-goal mark in 1984–85.

French that the Penguins had selected "No. 66 of the Laval Voison" with their first choice. The team had its savior.

Eddie Johnston was understandably elated. In addition to drafting Lemieux, who was universally hailed as a franchise player, the Pens also had the luxury of two additional first-round selections. With their second pick they chose 18-year-old Doug Bodger, a talented offensive defenseman who had topped 90 points in each of his junior seasons. Then they selected another teenager—body-banging forward Roger Belanger.

Johnston also added a veteran presence to the mix. Moe Mantha, a smooth-skating defenseman, arrived from Winnipeg to complete the Carlyle deal. In the Waiver Draft he picked up Wayne Babych, a former 50-goal scorer with St. Louis.

The Penguins opened the season against the always-tough Bruins in the Boston Garden. While the Pens dropped a close decision, they were clearly much improved. Lemieux wasted little time in establishing himself by scoring on his first shot on goal—undressing All-Star defenseman Ray Bourque in the process. A few nights later he showed that he could handle the rough stuff by thumping Vancouver pest Gary Lupul in his first fight.

Johnston continued to tinker with the lineup through the early going. He dispatched Pat Boutette to Hartford for the rights to young Finnish defenseman Ville Siren and acquired rearguard Randy Hillier from Boston. In early November he sent Ron Flockhart to Montreal in exchange for John Chabot, a big, rangy center who possessed good puck-handling skills. Slumping Mark Taylor was peddled to the Capitals for former junior hockey scoring champ Jim McGeough.

Rejuvenated, the Penguins played surprisingly respectable hockey. By midseason they had climbed to within two wins of the .500 mark on the heels of a 4–3 triumph over Edmonton. Not only was Lemieux enjoying a sensational rookie season, he was largely responsible for turning fellow first-year player Warren Young into an offensive force. Johnston was heaped with praise for filling so many holes so quickly.

Unfortunately, the magic dust soon wore off. The Pens followed up with a miserable second half that cast a pall over their early performance.

Despite the second-half collapse, it was an immensely satisfying season in many ways. Lemieux became only the third rookie in the history of the NHL to score 100 points. He easily captured the Calder Memorial Trophy as the league's top rookie.

Perhaps even more astonishing was the performance of Young, the vagabond left wing who had banged around the minors for years while waiting for an opportunity to play in the NHL. The 28-year-old rookie surprised everyone—including himself—by knocking in 40 goals.

"The reason he didn't make it early was skating," said Gene Ubriaco, Young's minor league coach. "He was a little

Mr. Magoo

In the spring of 1985 Penguins general manager Eddie Johnston was trying to upgrade his struggling young team. So on March 12 he traded Mark Taylor to the Capitals for Jim McGeough (pronounced *Ma-goo*).

A former junior hockey scoring ace, the 21-year-old winger had impressive credentials. He'd racked up an astonishing 169 goals during his final two seasons of junior hockey and potted 40 more as a first-year pro with the Hershey Bears.

McGeough could really fly. One of the fastest players ever to lace on a pair of skates, the 5'8", 168-pound water bug darted around the ice at warp speed.

"If we opened the doors to the Civic Arena he'd skate down Center Avenue," Johnston quipped.

Understandably enamored of his new acquisition, Johnston couldn't wait to team him with rookie phenom Mario Lemieux. Alas, it soon became apparent that McGeough's hands couldn't keep pace with his feet. He flubbed scoring chances with such mind-numbing regularity that he soon earned the nickname "Mr. Magoo."

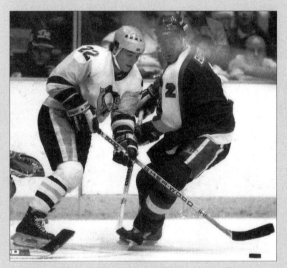

Speedy Jim McGeough (22) bursts around Winnipeg's Dave Ellett.

slow, but he was really smart at reading the play, and also very tough."

Defense was still a soft spot as the club leaked for 385 goals—an abhorrence to the defensive-minded Berry. But several newcomers made positive impressions. Big Moe Mantha turned in a fine 51-point season. Bodger played well for an 18-year-old while flashing enough offensive skill to tally 31 points. Rugged Rod Buskas earned a permanent spot after two seasons of part-time play.

	GP	G	A	PTS	PM	+/-
Mario Lemieux	73	43	57	100	54	- 35
Warren Young	80	40	32	72	174	- 20
Doug Shedden	80	35	32	67	30	- 51
Mike Bullard	68	32	31	63	75	- 43
Wayne Babych	65	20	34	54	35	- 7
John Chabot	67	8	45	53	12	- 37
Moe Mantha	71	11	40	51	54	- 35
Doug Bodger	65	5	26	31	67	- 24
Andy Brickley	45	7	15	22	10	- 14
Randy Hillier	45	2	19	21	56	- 12
Gary Rissling	56	10	9	19	209	- 6
Kevin McCarthy	64	9	10	19	30	- 20
Troy Loney	46	10	8	18	59	- 11
Mitch Lamoureux	62	10	8	18	53	- 9
Mark Taylor	47	7	10	17	19	- 7
Dave Hannan	30	6	7	13	43	- 8
Bruce Crowder	26	4	7	11	23	- 9
Joe McDonnell	40	2	9	11	20	- 19
Rod Buskas	69	2	7	9	191	- 21
Todd Charlesworth	67	1	8	9	31	- 23
Roger Belanger	44	3	5	8	32	- 13
Bryan Maxwell	44	0	8	8	57	- 23
Greg Fox	26	2	5	7	26	- 6
Arto Javanainen	14	4	1	5	2	1
Ron Flockhart	12	0	5	5	4	4
Pat Boutette	14	1	3	4	24	- 5
Jim McGeough	14	0	4	4	4	- 4
Jim Hamilton	11	2	1	3	0	- 6
Wally Weir	14	0	3	3	34	1
Rick Kehoe	6	0	2	2	0	0
Steve Gatzos	6	0	2	2	2	- 6
Greg Hotham	11	0	2	2	4	- 3
Bob Errey	16	0	2	2	7	- 8
Michel Dion	10	0	1	1	0	0
Bob Geale	1	0	0	0	2	- 1
Tom O'Regan	1	0	0	0	0	- 1
Petteri Lehto	6	0	0	0	4	- 4
Mike Rowe	6	0	0	0	7	- 7
Brian Ford	8	0	0	0	0	0
Marty McSorley	15	0	0	0	15	- 3
Roberto Romano	31	0	0	0	2	0
Denis Herron	42	0	0	0	4	0

	GP	MINS	GA	SH	AVG	W	L	T
Roberto Romano	31	1629	120	1	4.42	9	17	2
Denis Herron	42	2193	170	1	4.65	10	22	3
Michel Dion	10	553	43	0	4.67	3	6	0
Brian Ford	8	457	48	0	6.30	2	6	0
	80	4832	385	2	4.78	24	51	5

1985–86

Record: 34–38–8
Points: 76
Goals For: 313
Goals Against: 305
Finish: Fifth (Patrick)
Coach: Bob Berry
General Manager: Eddie Johnston

Heading into the 1985–86 season the Penguins brass faced two major obstacles. First, Johnston still had many holes to fill, particularly on the wings—a problem that was compounded when free agent Warren Young signed a lucrative contract with Detroit. Second, Berry had to find a way to coax the club into playing better defense.

Johnston did a masterful job of taking care of the first need, once again performing the task without sacrificing the team's future. To fill Young's spot he courted free agent Terry Ruskowski and made the gritty little winger an offer he couldn't refuse.

"Eddie Johnston offered me a longer-term deal and a chance, if I did well, to play with Mario," Ruskowski recalled. "I said, 'Where's the dotted line?'"

To shore up the Pens' paper-thin goaltending, Johnston sent Marty McSorley to Edmonton for veteran netminder

"Super Mario" and "the Great One" follow the action.

Gilles Meloche. The team received another boost when Roberto Romano, who'd abruptly quit during the spring, reported to training camp.

In an effort to reinforce the team's porous defense, the Pens' GM signed collegiate defensemen Chris Dahlquist and Jim Johnson, while persuading Finnish rearguard Ville Siren to join the team.

By virtue of their poor finish the Penguins once again held one of the top selections in the Entry Draft. They chose 18-year-old center Craig Simpson from Michigan State. A finalist for the Hobey Baker Award, Simpson led the Central Collegiate Hockey Association in scoring as a sophomore. Although by no means a great skater, Simpson was big and rawboned. He would gladly take a hit to score a goal.

With the newcomers playing significant roles, the Penguins were dramatically improved. Executing Bob Berry's tight-checking system to a T, the club surged above the .500 mark. When the Pens opened the month of March with a 5–1 victory over Hartford, they seemed a shoo-in to make the playoffs.

But once more the team caved in during the final month of the season, winning just three of 16 games.

Johnston and Berry searched desperately for ways to stop the skid. While the veteran coach shuffled the lineup, EJ pulled off a big trade with Detroit. He dealt 30-goal scorer Doug Shedden to the Red Wings for former All-Star Ron Duguay, a seasoned veteran with a proven track record.

Although the tousle-haired Duguay was an instant hit with the female fans, he failed to click with Mario. The Pens finished in fifth place and out of playoff contention again. Posting an impressive 23-point improvement did little to take the sting out of missing the postseason for the fourth year in a row.

Fortunately, Lemieux proved that the spectacular success he enjoyed as a rookie was no fluke. He posted some remarkable numbers, finishing second to Wayne Gretzky in the league scoring race with 48 goals, 93 assists, and 141 points. His accomplishments included a 28-game point-scoring streak. Even more gratifying, the big center received the Lester B. Pearson Award—the NHL Players' Association MVP award.

Other performances of note included a snappy 41-goal, 42-assist campaign from team captain Mike Bullard. Ruskowski notched 26 goals while providing some much-needed toughness and leadership. On the blue line, Moe Mantha tallied 15 goals and 52 assists, with 41 of his 67 points coming on the power play.

	GP	G	A	PTS	PM	+/-
Mario Lemieux	79	48	93	141	43	- 6
Mike Bullard	77	41	42	83	69	- 16
Moe Mantha	78	15	52	67	102	- 4
Doug Shedden	67	32	34	66	32	- 7
Terry Ruskowski	73	26	37	63	162	10
Randy Cunneyworth	75	15	30	45	74	12
John Chabot	77	14	31	45	6	- 1
Doug Bodger	79	4	33	37	63	3
Dave Hannan	75	17	18	35	91	- 4
Willy Lindstrom	71	14	17	31	30	0
Mike Blaisdell	66	15	14	29	36	15
Norm Schmidt	66	15	14	29	57	7
Jim Johnson	80	3	26	29	115	12
Craig Simpson	76	11	17	28	49	1
Dan Frawley	69	10	11	21	174	- 19
Bob Errey	37	11	6	17	8	1
Ron Duguay	13	6	7	13	6	- 14
Ville Siren	60	4	8	12	32	- 8
Troy Loney	47	3	9	12	95	- 8
Rod Buskas	72	2	7	9	159	- 9
Jim McGeough	17	3	2	5	8	- 4
Chris Dahlquist	5	1	2	3	2	1
Tom O'Regan	9	1	2	3	2	1
Randy Hillier	28	0	3	3	53	- 3
Ted Nolan	18	1	1	2	34	- 1
Dwight Mathiasen	4	1	0	1	2	- 4
Todd Charlesworth	2	0	1	1	0	- 1
Gilles Meloche	34	0	1	1	2	0
Roberto Romano	46	0	1	1	4	0
Wayne Babych	2	0	0	0	0	- 1
Denis Herron	3	0	0	0	0	0
Mike Rowe	3	0	0	0	4	- 1
Joe McDonnell	3	0	0	0	2	- 3
Phil Bourque	4	0	0	0	2	- 2
Tom Roulston	5	0	0	0	2	- 2

	GP	MINS	GA	SH	AVG	W	L	T
Roberto Romano	46	2684	159	2	3.55	21	20	3
Gilles Meloche	34	1989	119	0	3.59	13	15	5
Denis Herron	3	180	14	0	4.67	0	3	0
	80	4853	305	2	3.77	34	38	8

1986–87

Record: 30–38–12
Points: 72
Goals For: 297
Goals Against: 290
Finish: Fifth (Patrick)
Coach: Bob Berry
General Manager: Eddie Johnston

The Penguins entered the 1986–87 campaign with a single purpose in mind—to make the playoffs. Once again, Eddie Johnston scoured the free-agent market for help. He signed winger Kevin LaVallee in hopes that the former 30-goal scorer would mesh with Lemieux and add some punch to an underachieving power play. On the eve of the season opener the Penguins' GM reacquired Warren Young—a disappointment with Detroit.

Under Johnston's watchful eye, the team had one of its best Entry Drafts ever. With the club's first selection he chose a blue-chip prospect, offensive defenseman Zarley Zalapski. Scoring sensation Rob Brown, a slow-skating but highly productive forward from Kamloops, was taken in the fourth round. In the ninth round Pittsburgh grabbed speedy center Dave McLlwain.

The Penguins rallied from a three-goal deficit to beat Washington in the season opener. Following up with their finest start ever, they won seven consecutive games to vault to the top of the Patrick Division. Leading the way was

Doug Bodger, Mario Lemieux, Terry Ruskowski, and Moe Mantha celebrate a goal.

Lemieux, who was gaining confidence with every shift. The big center zoomed to the top of the NHL scoring race with 15 goals and 29 points in just 11 games.

Despite Mario's brilliance, cracks soon appeared in the team's armor. His linemates, Ruskowski and Duguay, struggled to find the net. With few viable options, Berry experimented with Craig Simpson on Mario's right wing. Warren Young was given a brief trial on Lemieux's left flank, but the old magic was long gone.

The Penguins' playoff hopes were dealt a crippling blow in December when Mario suffered a sprained right knee. During his month-long absence they tumbled to fifth place.

Johnston turned to trades for help. He sent slumping Mike Bullard to Calgary for creative center Dan Quinn. Faltering Ron Duguay went to the Rangers for Chris Kontos, an underachieving former first-round pick. In a surprising exchange of netminders, Johnston dealt the youthful Romano to Boston for Pat Riggin, a former Jennings Trophy winner who was past his prime.

The Penguins made a last-ditch effort to turn their season around during a road trip in early March. They got off to a rousing start by walloping Quebec, but sank like a stone during a lackluster loss to the Maple Leafs. His nerves frayed over the team's maddening inconsistency and impending collapse, Berry railed at his players.

"Win one 8–1, lose one 7–2," he barked. "Easy come, easy go. That's the attitude."

"They don't have the intestinal fortitude," he continued. "Big shots. Circus performers...Good show, bad show—doesn't matter. They get paid anyway."

The Pens responded by winning the final two games of the road trip, but it was a last gasp. They stumbled through a miserable stretch run to miss the playoffs for the fifth year in a row.

Slowed by the sprained knee and a bout with bronchitis, Lemieux dipped to 107 points. It was a great season by most players' standards but not for Mario—a fact that did not escape his growing legion of detractors. Because he skated so smoothly and effortlessly, they accused him of malingering, particularly on defense. It was a rap that would stick for many years.

Still, there were signs of improvement among the supporting cast. Quinn performed extremely well after coming over from the Flames, rolling up 28 goals and 43 assists in just 64 games. Second-year man Randy Cunneyworth was a pleasant surprise, scoring 26 goals while tying Quinn for the team lead in plus/minus rating.

Nineteen-year-old Craig Simpson also scored 26 goals. He was one of the few players to elevate his game while Lemieux was out of the lineup.

Shortly after the season ended, Johnston had the difficult task of dismissing Bob Berry. Although EJ still thought highly of Berry, the veteran coach had clearly lost the support of the DeBartolos.

	GP	G	A	PTS	PM	+/-
Mario Lemieux	63	54	53	107	57	13
Dan Quinn	64	28	43	71	40	14
Randy Cunneyworth	79	26	27	53	142	14
Craig Simpson	72	26	25	51	57	11
Terry Ruskowski	70	14	37	51	145	8
Doug Bodger	76	11	38	49	52	6
Moe Mantha	62	9	31	40	44	-6
John Chabot	72	14	22	36	8	-7
Bob Errey	72	16	18	34	46	-5
Jim Johnson	80	5	25	30	116	-6
Dan Frawley	78	14	14	28	218	-10
Kevin LaVallee	33	8	20	28	4	-2
Dave Hannan	58	10	15	25	56	-2
Willy Lindstrom	60	10	13	23	6	9
Ville Siren	69	5	17	22	50	8
Warren Young	50	8	13	21	103	-5
Ron Duguay	40	5	13	18	30	-8
Rod Buskas	68	3	15	18	123	2
Chris Kontos	31	8	9	17	6	-6
Troy Loney	23	8	7	15	22	0
Randy Hillier	55	4	8	12	97	12
Mike Bullard	14	2	10	12	17	-6
Dwight Schofield	25	1	6	7	59	4
Norm Schmidt	20	1	5	6	4	-8
Phil Bourque	22	2	3	5	32	-2
Jim McGeough	11	1	4	5	8	-5
Mitch Wilson	17	2	1	3	83	-3
Lee Giffin	8	1	1	2	0	2
Mike Blaisdell	10	1	1	2	2	2
Neil Belland	3	0	1	1	0	0
Dwight Mathiasen	6	0	1	1	2	-1
Pat Riggin	17	0	1	1	2	0
Chris Dahlquist	19	0	1	1	20	-2
Gilles Meloche	43	0	1	1	20	0
Todd Charlesworth	1	0	0	0	0	0
Alain Lemieux	1	0	0	0	0	-1
Steve Guenette	2	0	0	0	0	0
Mike Rowe	2	0	0	0	0	-2
Carl Mokosak	3	0	0	0	4	-4
Roberto Romano	25	0	0	0	0	0

	GP	MINS	GA	SH	AVG	W	L	T
Pat Riggin	17	988	55	0	3.34	8	6	3
Gilles Meloche	43	2343	134	0	3.43	13	19	7
Roberto Romano	25	1438	87	0	3.63	9	11	2
Steve Guenette	2	113	8	0	4.25	0	2	0
	80	4882	290	1	3.56	30	38	12

(Meloche and Romano shared 1 shutout)

Mario the Magician

Terry Ruskowski was already accustomed to playing with legends when he signed on as a free agent with the Penguins in the summer of 1985. After all, he had cut his hockey teeth in the old WHA skating alongside "Mr. Hockey" himself, Gordie Howe. But that was nothing compared to the thrills he would experience as Mario Lemieux's linemate.

"I remember one time there was a face-off on the goalie's left side and Mario called me out of the circle," Ruskowski recalled in an interview with *Sports Illustrated*. "He said, 'Terry, spin off your defenseman when the puck is dropped and go to the net with your stick on the ice.' I said, 'Huh?' And he said, 'Just do it.' So when the puck was dropped I spun and went to the net, and before I looked to see where the puck was, it hit my stick and went in the net. I was so stunned I forgot to raise my arms."

1987–88

Record: 36–35–9
Points: 81
Goals For: 319
Goals Against: 316
Finish: Sixth (Patrick)
Coach: Pierre Creamer
General Manager: Eddie Johnston

The 1987–88 season would prove to be a pivotal one for Eddie Johnston. By all accounts he had done a wonderful job of rebuilding a team that was virtually bereft of talent. However, the fans and ownership were frustrated by the team's disappointing finishes. They were expecting Johnston to produce a playoff team. Anything less would be considered an abject failure.

His first order of business was to find a new coach. With pressure mounting from all sides to produce a winner, it was imperative that Johnston choose the right man for the job. Unfortunately, at a time when he needed to make his best decision, he made one of his worst. After interviewing several candidates, Johnston hired Pierre Creamer.

At first glance Creamer appeared to have all the necessary qualifications. He had coached with a great deal of success in the Quebec League and the Canadiens' minor league system, where he developed a reputation as a good communicator who was especially popular with younger players.

Unfortunately the choice proved to be an unmitigated disaster. A genuinely nice man who spoke fractured English,

Creamer quickly became the butt of jokes among the players, who cruelly nicknamed him "Fred Flintstone."

Aside from his dubious selection of Creamer, Johnston worked hard to upgrade the team's talent level and toughness. Acutely aware of the club's soft reputation, he lured former NHL penalty king Jimmy "Bam Bam" Mann out of retirement. He also signed veteran right wing Wilf Paiement, who combined muscle with scoring ability. Johnston nearly worked out a trade with Quebec for high-scoring winger John Ogrodnick, but at the last minute the deal fell through. He settled for 33-year-old Charlie Simmer, a former All-Star and 50-goal scorer.

Other newcomers included 18-year-old defenseman Chris Joseph, the club's first-round pick, and rookie forwards Dave McLlwain and Rob Brown. The Canadian Major Junior Player of the Year, Brown had set the Western League on its ear while racking up 76 goals and 212 points.

Prior to the season Lemieux participated in the Canada Cup Tournament and caused an unbelievable stir. Thrust into the spotlight on hockey's center stage, his star shone brighter than ever. Playing on a line with fellow supernova Wayne Gretzky, Lemieux was the talk of the tournament. He led all scorers with 11 goals, including four game winners.

Mario clearly benefited from the time he spent with Gretzky and the other NHL stars. Perhaps there had been some lingering doubts in the back of his mind about whether he truly belonged. Now he was ready to take his rightful place among the game's elite.

"He was a different person when he came back from that," teammate Phil Bourque said.

While Lemieux began the season playing the best hockey of his young career, the rest of the team limped along in his vapor trail. His new bargain-basement linemates, Simmer and Paiement, were on their last legs. With nowhere else to turn, the Pens called up career minor leaguer Jock Callander to replace Paiement. It was painfully clear that the team needed another superstar to help Mario develop his extraordinary talents to their fullest measure.

Eddie Johnston knew just the player who could help. Edmonton defenseman Paul Coffey, a perennial All-Star and two-time Norris Trophy winner, was in the midst of a contract dispute with the Oilers. A cornerstone of the Edmonton dynasty, Coffey was one of the top hockey players in the world.

Johnston began negotiating with Oilers GM Glen Sather to acquire the services of the high-scoring defenseman. After weeks of discussions and rumors, a trade was finally announced on November 24. The Pens received Coffey, along with veteran winger Dave Hunter and giant enforcer Wayne Van Dorp, in exchange for Craig Simpson, Moe Mantha, Chris Joseph, and Dave Hannan.

It was a watershed event for Pittsburgh hockey. While Coffey did not come cheaply, the Pens finally had a superstar to team with Lemieux. The quicksilver defenseman immediately made his presence felt with his blazing speed and pinpoint passing.

After arriving in a big trade with Edmonton, Paul Coffey helped Mario Lemieux win the scoring title.

Coffey also instilled qualities that were in short supply in the locker room, including leadership and a winning attitude.

"Hockey's a funny game," he would say. "You have to prove yourself every shift, every game. It's not up to anybody else. You have to take pride in yourself."

Late in the season Johnston had all but announced a second blockbuster deal with the Oilers. The Penguins would have received goaltender Andy Moog in exchange for young goalie Steve Guenette and a first-round pick. But the DeBartolos, concerned that Johnston was suddenly mortgaging the team's future in order to save his job, stepped in to block the deal. It was hardly a vote of confidence.

Still, the Pens improved in the final weeks, winning 11 of their last 16 games. They had a chance to make the playoffs until the very end, but they were eliminated on the final night of the season. Although the team registered its first winning season since 1978–79, it was of little solace to the playoff-starved fans.

The players were quick to fix the lion's share of the blame on Creamer. They openly accused him of playing for a tie in a critical late-season game against the Capitals when the Penguins clearly needed a victory to stay in playoff contention. Unfairly or not, Creamer became the scapegoat.

"They were looking for a big dummy, and they chose me," he remarked, cementing the notion that he was unfit to lead the team.

Amid all the ugliness, one fact was clear: Mario Lemieux had become the most dominant force in the game. Playing with a grab-bag collection of wingers, he led the league with 70 goals and 168 points while capturing the Art Ross and Hart trophies. For the second time in his young career he won the Lester B. Pearson Award. As his confidence grew he became a truly awesome one-on-one player. Facing Lemieux on a breakaway was every goaltender's worst nightmare.

Paul Coffey was magnificent. Serving as the igniter for the Pens' suddenly potent transition game, he bagged a remarkable 15 goals and 52 assists in just 46 games. He became a master at springing Mario loose on breakaways.

Other key contributors were Dan Quinn, who netted 40 goals, and Cunneyworth, who scored 35 goals while blossoming into one of the league's top left wings.

Although the team had taken a quantum leap forward, time had run out on Eddie Johnston. Tethered to the unfortunate Creamer hiring and his failure to produce a playoff team, he was demoted to the post of assistant GM.

Tony Esposito, a Hall of Fame goaltender in his playing days with the Black Hawks, was named as the club's vice president and general manager. It was rumored that the DeBartolos had consulted with him before quashing the Andy Moog trade—a deal that might have propelled the Penguins into postseason play.

	GP	G	A	PTS	PM	+/-
Mario Lemieux	77	70	98	168	92	23
Dan Quinn	70	40	39	79	50	- 8
Randy Cunneyworth	71	35	39	74	141	13
Paul Coffey	46	15	52	67	93	- 1
Doug Bodger	69	14	31	45	103	- 4
Rob Brown	51	24	20	44	56	8
Dave Hunter	59	11	18	29	77	8
Charlie Simmer	50	11	17	28	24	6
John Callander	41	11	16	27	45	- 13
Craig Simpson	21	13	13	26	34	5
Ville Siren	58	1	20	21	62	14
Dave McLlwain	66	11	8	19	40	- 1
Troy Loney	65	5	13	18	151	- 3
Phil Bourque	21	4	12	16	20	3
Dan Frawley	47	6	8	14	152	0
Randy Hillier	55	1	12	13	144	- 6
Jim Johnson	55	1	12	13	87	- 4
Rod Buskas	76	4	8	12	206	6
Steve Gotaas	36	5	6	11	45	- 11
Zarley Zalapski	15	3	8	11	7	10
Moe Mantha	21	2	8	10	23	6
Bob Errey	17	3	6	9	18	6
Chris Dahlquist	44	3	6	9	69	3
Mark Kachowski	38	5	3	8	126	1
Wilf Paiement	23	2	6	8	39	- 4
Chris Kontos	36	1	7	8	12	- 3
Kevin Stevens	16	5	2	7	8	- 6
Dave Hannan	21	4	3	7	23	- 2
Perry Ganchar	30	2	5	7	36	0
Dwight Mathiasen	23	0	6	6	14	- 7
Bryan Erickson	11	1	4	5	0	2
Wayne Van Dorp	25	1	3	4	75	2
Chris Joseph	17	0	4	4	12	2
Norm Schmidt	5	1	2	3	0	1
Todd Charlesworth	6	2	0	2	2	0
Brad Aitken	5	1	1	2	0	1
Lee Giffin	19	0	2	2	9	- 2
Frank Pietrangelo	21	0	2	2	2	0
Scott Gruhl	6	1	0	1	0	0
Pat Mayer	1	0	0	0	4	0
Dave Goertz	2	0	0	0	2	- 1
Warren Young	7	0	0	0	15	- 4
Jimmy Mann	9	0	0	0	53	0
Steve Guenette	19	0	0	0	2	0
Pat Riggin	22	0	0	0	12	0
Gilles Meloche	27	0	0	0	0	0

	GP	MINS	GA	SH	AVG	W	L	T
Steve Guenette	19	1092	61	1	3.35	12	7	0
Pat Riggin	22	1169	76	0	3.90	7	8	4
Frank Pietrangelo	21	1207	80	1	3.98	9	11	0
Gilles Meloche	27	1394	95	0	4.09	8	9	5
	80	4863	316	2	3.90	36	35	9

1988–89

Record: 40–33–7
Points: 87
Goals For: 347
Goals Against: 349
Finish: Second (Patrick)
Coach: Gene Ubriaco
General Manager: Tony Esposito

Slowly but surely the Penguins were coming of age. Mario Lemieux was firmly entrenched as the heir apparent to succeed Wayne Gretzky as hockey's preeminent player. The presence of Paul Coffey would serve to elevate Mario's game to even greater heights. Several other youngsters, including Doug Bodger, Randy Cunneyworth, and Dan Quinn, had blossomed into fine players as well.

Still, there was a fly in the ointment. Tony Esposito's appointment to the post of general manager was received with mixed reviews. Although "Tony O" had once served as president of the NHL Players' Association, he had no previous management experience. Indeed, his hiring was based almost solely on the favorable impression he'd made on Edward DeBartolo Sr. at a sports banquet.

Esposito wasted little time putting his stamp on the team. He dismissed embattled Pierre Creamer and handed the coaching reins to Gene Ubriaco, a member of the original Penguins team.

A gregarious, back-slapping sort who liked to buddy up to his players and give them nicknames (Mario's was "Ace"), Ubriaco had coached the Pens' top farm club for several seasons with moderate success. Although he wasn't Esposito's first choice for the job, the DeBartolos liked him and pushed for the promotion.

While Ubriaco may not have been the man Esposito had in mind for a bench boss, they agreed on one thing—the paperweight Penguins needed to be considerably tougher to compete in the rough-and-tumble Patrick Division.

The new GM went about the task of adding muscle to complement the team's burgeoning stable of skill players. He picked up massive 6'4", 237-pound strongman Jay Caufield and rugged defenseman Steve Dykstra in the Waiver Draft. Twenty-three-year-old Kevin Stevens, a bear of a winger, also made the team.

Other new faces included feisty free-agent center John Cullen, the 1987–88 Minor League Player of the Year. Popular Dave Hannan was reacquired from Edmonton, adding a capable checking center to the mix.

With the facelift complete the Penguins opened the season playing tough, spirited hockey. Ubriaco found a pair of linemates for Lemieux in speedy Bob Errey and Rob Brown.

The trio immediately clicked. With Errey handling the defensive chores and Brown scoring goals in bunches, Lemieux tallied a whopping 41 points in just 12 games—the fastest start in NHL history.

"If he only gets three or four points [in a game], you ask if he has a broken leg or something," Brown quipped.

The Pens met the Rangers in Madison Square Garden on October 30 in a showdown for Patrick Division supremacy. The red-hot Rangers—winners of seven in a row—quickly charged to a 4–0 lead while holding the sluggish Penguins without a shot on goal.

Dan Quinn finally got Pittsburgh on the scoreboard with a power-play goal at 11:30 of the first period. But by the midway point of the second frame the New Yorkers had built an insurmountable seven-goal advantage.

The game turned ugly in the final period when David Shaw clubbed Lemieux across the side of the head. The normally placid Quinn rushed to his teammate's aid and tried to skewer Shaw with the blade of his stick.

The contest quickly degenerated into a no-holds-barred brawl. Embattled referee Andy van Hellemond issued 16 fighting majors and 252 penalty minutes in the third period alone. Thoroughly outclassed, the Pens lost 9–2.

Although Lemieux wasn't seriously hurt, he missed the next two games with a bruised chest and a sore wrist. With their leader on the sideline the Penguins began to sputter, losing four out of six games to tumble into third place. The team's most glaring weakness was in goal, where Steve Guenette, Frank Pietrangelo, and newcomer Wendell Young alternated without much success.

A Hall of Fame goalie, Esposito knew only too well that his team would never climb into contention without a quality netminder. On November 12 he moved boldly to correct the problem. In his signature trade, he sent Bodger and No. 1 pick Darrin Shannon to Buffalo for former Calder and Vezina Trophy winner Tom Barrasso.

Already a seasoned veteran at age 23, Barrasso was regarded as one of the most talented young goaltenders in the league. However, the trade didn't pay immediate dividends. Even with the newcomer between the pipes the Penguins continued to hemorrhage goals by the bushel.

A return match with New York proved to be all the inspiration they needed. Despite the bad blood between the two teams there were no major incidents. Mario collected a

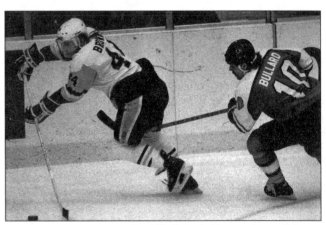

Rob Brown pulls away from ex-Pen Mike Bullard with an uncharacteristic burst of speed. Brown scored 49 goals in 1988–89.

goal and four assists to spark an 8–2 victory. It was truly a team effort as eight different players scored, while Barrasso stopped 32 shots in a virtuoso performance.

Suddenly, the club began to fire on all cylinders. The Pens raced through a 16-game stretch at a phenomenal 12–1–3 clip. In mid-December they hammered the Islanders to claim sole possession of first place.

Lemieux continued to score at an incendiary pace. During a wild 8–6 victory over New Jersey on New Year's Eve, he became the first NHL player ever to tally five goals in a game in five different ways. Mario struck at even strength, short handed, on the power play, on a penalty shot, and capped off his astounding evening with an empty netter. With 104 points in just 36 games, the high-flying center was on a pace to obliterate Wayne Gretzky's single-season record of 215 points.

In early February the Penguins reached a milestone of a different kind. They defeated the Flyers in the Spectrum, snapping a horrific 42-game winless streak in the "City of Brotherly Shove" that had spanned 15 agonizing years.

Following the epic win over the Flyers, the team began to fade. On February 21 the Penguins slipped out of first place with a 2–1 loss to the North Stars, their fifth defeat in six games. The swoon intensified two nights later when they blew a six-goal lead against Detroit and barely held on for a tie.

While never in serious danger of missing the playoffs, the Pens continued to flounder. They were a prolific offensive team—capable of exploding on any given night—but they were much too soft defensively. Although Ubriaco tried to encourage better defensive play, his message seemed to fall on deaf ears. Rumors surfaced that the team had already tuned out the rookie coach.

The Penguins didn't awaken from their slumber until the final weeks of the season. Winning four of their last five games, they secured second place and at long last captured a berth in the Stanley Cup Playoffs.

The club had made enormous strides. At the callow age of 23, Lemieux had reached the very pinnacle of his sport. The numbers spoke for themselves—an astounding 85 goals, 114 assists, and 199 points—and a second straight scoring title. Only Wayne Gretzky had ever posted higher totals.

However, the hockey writers still had an axe to grind with Mario. Inexplicably, he finished second to Gretzky in the voting for the Hart Trophy, despite outscoring "the Great One" by a whopping 31 points.

It didn't matter. In English, Mario's surname translated to "the Best." And he was, plain and simply, the best.

So accomplished was Lemieux that he was a threat to score every time he stepped onto the ice. Most opponents routinely took to fouling him but nothing worked. During a game against Washington, Larry Murphy hogtied Mario at the blue line in a desperate attempt to slow him down. Like a bull shrugging off a flea, Lemieux dragged the exasperated defenseman to the net and scored.

Other players contributed mightily to the Penguins' sudden ascent. Rob Brown became firmly entrenched as

Mario's right wing, scoring 49 goals while silencing the critics who claimed that he was too slow. Dan Quinn quietly rang up 34 goals and 94 points, while Errey and Cunneyworth chipped in with 26 and 25 goals, respectively. An early disappointment, Kevin Stevens returned from Muskegon to help spark the team's playoff drive.

On the blue line, Paul Coffey returned to Norris Trophy form. He tallied 30 goals and 83 assists while keying the Pens' deadly power play.

	GP	G	A	PTS	PM	+/-
Mario Lemieux	76	85	114	199	100	41
Rob Brown	68	49	66	115	118	27
Paul Coffey	75	30	83	113	195	-10
Dan Quinn	79	34	60	94	102	-37
Bob Errey	76	26	32	58	124	40
John Cullen	79	12	37	49	112	-25
Zarley Zalapski	58	12	33	45	57	9
Randy Cunneyworth	70	25	19	44	156	-22
Phil Bourque	80	17	26	43	97	-22
Dave Hannan	72	10	20	30	157	-12
Randy Hillier	68	1	23	24	141	-4
Troy Loney	69	10	6	16	165	-5
Jim Johnson	76	2	14	16	163	7
Kevin Stevens	24	12	3	15	19	-8
John Callander	30	6	5	11	20	-3
Dan Frawley	46	3	4	7	66	-1
Steve Dykstra	65	1	6	7	126	-12
Chris Dahlquist	43	1	5	6	42	-8
Rod Buskas	52	1	5	6	105	-2
Doug Bodger	10	1	4	5	7	6
Jay Caufield	58	1	4	5	285	-4
Tom Barrasso	44	0	5	5	49	0
Scott Bjugstad	24	3	0	3	4	-12
Dave McLlwain	24	1	2	3	4	-11
Gord Dineen	38	1	2	3	42	-5
Mark Kachowski	12	1	1	2	43	1
Mark Recchi	15	1	1	2	0	-2
Wendell Young	22	0	2	2	4	0
Ville Siren	12	1	0	1	14	0
Steve Guenette	11	0	1	1	0	0
Rich Tabaracci	1	0	0	0	2	0
Perry Ganchar	3	0	0	0	0	-3
Frank Pietrangelo	15	0	0	0	2	0
Richard Zemlak	31	0	0	0	135	-4

	GP	MINS	GA	SH	AVG	W	L	T
Tom Barrasso	44	2406	162	0	4.04	18	15	7
Frank Pietrangelo	15	669	45	0	4.04	5	3	0
Steve Guenette	11	574	41	0	4.29	5	6	0
Wendell Young	22	1150	92	0	4.80	12	9	0
Rick Tabaracci	1	33	4	0	7.27	0	0	0
	80	4843	349	0	4.32	40	33	7

1989–90

Record: 32–40–8
Points: 72
Goals For: 318
Goals Against: 359
Finish: Fifth (Patrick)
Coach: Gene Ubriaco–Craig Patrick
General Manager: Tony Esposito–Craig Patrick

Entering the 1989–90 campaign the Penguins were favored by many experts to win the Patrick Division. With Mario Lemieux and Paul Coffey pacing the attack, some felt they might even be a legitimate contender for the Stanley Cup.

In many ways the Penguins resembled the Pittsburgh Pirates of the late 1950s. Just two years before their improbable triumph in the 1960 World Series, the Buccos were the weak sisters of baseball. Struggling to emerge from a dry spell that had lasted 12 long years, they shocked the experts with a second-place finish in 1958.

Led by rising young stars Roberto Clemente and Bill Mazeroski, the Pirates were expected to contend for the pennant in 1959. But weaknesses were exposed and the team stumbled. The Penguins would follow an eerily similar path.

Although Eddie Johnston departed to take the general manager's job at Hartford, Tony Esposito now had a full season in the front office under his belt. He felt the club lacked two key ingredients—a high-scoring winger to provide more balance up front, and a tough, stay-at-home defenseman who could match up with opposing power forwards like the Flyers' mammoth Tim Kerr.

Moving decisively to fill the voids, Esposito peddled Randy Cunneyworth and promising youngsters Dave McLlwain and Rick Tabaracci to Winnipeg for Andrew McBain, Jim Kyte, and Randy Gilhen.

A power-play specialist and former No. 1 pick of the Jets, McBain was coming off consecutive 30-goal seasons. In Kyte, Esposito had acquired a hulking 6'5" defenseman who played with a chip on his shoulder. The energetic Gilhen was a defensive whiz who had impressed the Penguins with his checking performances against Lemieux. He had such a strong training camp that Esposito decided to expose popular Dave Hannan in the Waiver Draft.

Other new faces included promising youngster Mark Recchi and hard-hitting defenseman Gilbert Delorme. For the first time in years the club actually appeared to have a surplus of talent.

But all was not well. Lemieux's contract was up for renewal. Esposito bungled the negotiations so badly that Edward DeBartolo Jr. had to step in to smooth things over. Rumors resurfaced that the players did not like or respect Ubriaco. An air of tension hung over the team.

The Pens opened the season with a 3–2–1 spurt, including an impressive overtime victory over the Canadiens. However, the club soon hit the skids and staggered through a six-game winless streak.

To make matters worse, Mario was suffering through a rare dry spell. The big center failed to register a goal until the fifth game of the season. He had only 20 points after a

Coach Gene Ubriaco offers Mario Lemieux some advice. Rob Brown (right) seems amused, but Mario isn't smiling.

dozen games, a splendid total for most players but well off his expected pace.

It was only the tip of the iceberg. Starting goalie Tom Barrasso went down with a broken wrist and John Cullen contracted hepatitis. Upset over a lack of playing time, veteran defenseman Rod Buskas requested a trade. He was promptly barred from practicing with the team, causing several players to don makeshift armbands in protest.

It quickly became apparent that the Penguins were a troubled team. Ex-teammate Dave Hannan told the *Toronto Globe and Mail* that the club had a morale problem. Following an embarrassing loss to Montreal, commentator Don Cherry said the Penguins played as if they were trying to get Ubriaco fired. The fact that Lemieux was openly critical of his coach did little to help Ubriaco's tenuous position.

Flush with frustration, Ubriaco snapped off a bitter retort. "You can't teach a shark table manners," he said.

Although the Penguins enjoyed a brief turnaround in November, Lemieux continued to feel poorly. He was tested for a variety of ailments, including mononucleosis. While all of the tests were negative, it did not explain his mysterious lack of energy.

When the club stumbled again, the DeBartolos came to town, presumably to dismiss Esposito and Ubriaco. The GM and coach were granted a reprieve when the Pens blanked the Rangers and followed up with impressive victories over Quebec and the Islanders.

Their stay of execution was a short one. On December 5, Edward DeBartolo Jr. handed the ill-fated pair their walking papers and hired Craig Patrick, who would handle the dual roles of coach and general manager.

For once the team's high command had chosen wisely. Hockey was in the 43-year-old Patrick's blood. He was the grandson of the legendary Lester Patrick and the son of former Bruins and Blues GM Lynn Patrick—Hall of Famers both.

Regarded as one of the brightest young executives in hockey, Patrick had served as the Rangers' general manager for five years, where he earned a reputation as an outstanding judge of talent. He also was the top assistant coach to Herb Brooks on the gold medal 1980 U.S. Olympic team.

The Penguins immediately responded to Patrick's calm, low-key coaching style. In mid-January they reached the .500 mark with an impressive 4–3 victory over the Flyers.

However, tragedy struck just when the team was on the verge of turning the season around. Tom Barrasso was granted a leave of absence to care for his daughter Ashley, who was stricken with cancer.

The club was dealt another severe blow on Valentine's Day when Lemieux, who had rolled up a stunning 46-game scoring streak, had to remove himself from a game because of excruciating lower back pain.

Examinations revealed that Mario had suffered a herniated disc. Although No. 66 opted for physical therapy rather than risk an operation, it was doubtful whether he would return before the playoffs.

The Penguins gamely pulled together. They entered March with a firm hold on second place, but the strain of playing without "Super Mario" finally took its toll. Mired in an ugly eight-game winless streak going into their season finale, the Pens needed at least a tie with Buffalo to clinch a playoff berth.

In an effort to end his team's horrifying tailspin, Lemieux decided to suit up, bad back and all. When he stepped onto the ice he received one of the longest and loudest ovations of his storied career.

Although the big center had been out of action for two months, he dramatically scored one goal and set up another.

Despite Mario's heroic effort, the Sabres prevailed on an overtime goal by low-scoring defenseman Uwe Krupp. In a little more than a month the Penguins had tumbled all the way to fifth place and missed the playoffs.

In the locker room following the crushing defeat, a local sportswriter suggested to Craig Patrick that the franchise was cursed. Patrick took exception.

"We'll never miss the playoffs again on my watch," he vowed.

For 11 years he was true to his word.

Comic Relief

The late and legendary sportscaster Myron Cope is generally associated with the Pittsburgh Steelers. In the fall of 1989, however, the impish announcer teamed up with newly acquired Penguins enforcer Jim Kyte to film a commercial for Hombre Tire Center. The diminutive Cope proved to be the perfect foil for the towering 6'5" defenseman.

"There's a new tough guy in town," Cope growled as the camera panned to a scowling Kyte.

The quintessential Mutt-and-Jeff combination proceeded to perform a slapstick routine on the ice that rivaled the Three Stooges. The mere sight of Myron decked out in hockey garb was enough to elicit a gut laugh as he scrambled and flopped his way around the rink.

At the climax, Cope staggered toward the net wearing one of his patented screwball expressions while Kyte stood ominously in his path. Cope sprawled headfirst to the ice and slid between the big blue-liner's legs.

"It's a goal," Kyte wailed, barely able to keep a straight face.

	GP	G	A	PTS	PM	+/-
Mario Lemieux	59	45	78	123	78	- 18
Paul Coffey	80	29	74	103	95	- 25
John Cullen	72	32	60	92	138	- 13
Rob Brown	80	33	47	80	102	- 10
Kevin Stevens	76	29	41	70	171	- 13
Mark Recchi	74	30	37	67	44	6
Phil Bourque	76	22	17	39	108	- 7
Bob Errey	78	20	19	39	109	3
Tony Tanti	37	14	18	32	22	- 11
Zarley Zalapski	51	6	25	31	37	- 14
Dan Quinn	41	9	20	29	22	- 15
Troy Loney	67	11	16	27	168	- 9
Barry Pederson	38	4	18	22	29	- 10
Randy Gilhen	61	5	11	16	54	- 8
Jim Johnson	75	3	13	16	154	- 20
Randy Hillier	61	3	12	15	71	11
Andrew McBain	41	5	9	14	51	- 8
Chris Dahlquist	62	4	10	14	56	- 2
John Callander	30	4	7	11	49	0
Gilbert Delorme	54	3	7	10	44	3
Gord Dineen	69	1	8	9	125	6
Richard Zemlak	19	1	5	6	43	- 6
Jim Kyte	56	3	1	4	125	- 10
Wendell Young	43	0	4	4	8	0
Jay Caufield	37	1	2	3	123	0
Jamie Leach	10	0	3	3	0	3
Doug Smith	10	1	1	2	25	- 2
Alain Chevrier	3	0	1	1	2	0
Mark Kachowski	14	0	1	1	40	1
Rod Buskas	6	0	0	0	13	- 4
Dave Capuano	6	0	0	0	2	0
Frank Pietrangelo	21	0	0	0	2	0
Tom Barrasso	24	0	0	0	8	0

	GP	MINS	GA	SH	AVG	W	L	T
Wendell Young	43	2318	161	1	4.17	16	20	3
Frank Pietrangelo	21	1066	77	0	4.33	8	6	2
Tom Barrasso	24	1294	101	0	4.68	7	12	3
Alain Chevrier	3	166	14	0	5.06	1	2	0
	80	4856	359	1	4.44	32	40	8

1990–91

Record: 41–33–6
Points: 88
Goals For: 342
Goals Against: 305
Finish: First (Patrick)
Coach: Bob Johnson
General Manager: Craig Patrick

Despite their disappointing finish in 1989–90, the Penguins were clearly an up-and-coming team. However, some reshaping was required before they could be regarded as a legitimate Stanley Cup contender. They were in desperate need of a veteran leader or two and a strong coach to guide them to the promised land.

With a single-minded purpose, Craig Patrick moved quickly to fill the voids. He shrewdly dealt the club's second-round choice in the Entry Draft to Calgary for 33-year-old right wing Joey Mullen, a proven 40-goal scorer who had won a Stanley Cup with the Flames. Later in the summer he signed future Hall of Famer Bryan Trottier, the linchpin of the great Islanders dynasty.

Patrick's work was far from over. In a stroke of genius he lured hockey legend Bob Johnson away from his position as executive director of USA Hockey to serve as coach. "Badger Bob" had gained a reputation as one of the game's most enthusiastic and innovative coaches during his long tenure at Wisconsin and later with Calgary, where he led the Flames to the Stanley Cup Finals in 1986. For the first time since the days of Red Kelly, the Pens would have an established bench boss at the helm.

The Penguins' GM solidified the organization even further by hiring Scotty Bowman—the winningest coach in NHL history—to serve as director of player personnel.

There was one lingering concern that Patrick couldn't address—the condition of Mario Lemieux's back. After much deliberation, the Penguins' captain opted for surgery in mid-July. While the operation was initially deemed a success, his back pain flared up with a vengeance during a preseason trip to Texas.

The prognosis wasn't good. A follow-up examination revealed a rare bone infection around the surgically repaired disc. Lemieux would start the season on the disabled list.

It was a dark time for Mario. Bedridden for nearly three months, he wondered if his playing career was over.

The 1990–91 campaign would prove to be a roller-coaster ride, filled with desperate lows and equally dizzying heights. Propelled by the streaking Cullen-Recchi-Stevens line, the Pens jumped out to a respectable 10–7–2 start. Nicknamed the "Option Line" because each would soon be eligible for free agency, the trio quickly moved into the league's top 10 scorers with Cullen leading the way.

Thanks in no small part to Bob Johnson's teaching and upbeat attitude the Penguins were much improved.

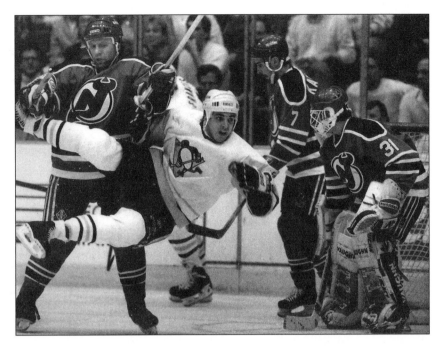

Big Kevin Stevens is upended by the Devils' Slava Fetisov. One of the league's premier power forwards, Stevens scored 40 goals in 1990–91.

But the team began to sputter in mid-November when top guns Mullen and Tony Tanti cooled after blazing starts. Inconsistent goaltending also plagued the club as Johnson shuffled Barrasso, Frank Pietrangelo, and Wendell Young.

To his credit, Craig Patrick refused to accept a losing team. Belying his "stand Pat" reputation, he shook the Pens up after they sank to their eighth loss in 11 games.

In his first trade, Patrick peddled defensemen Jim Johnson and Chris Dahlquist to Minnesota for banger Peter Taglianetti and offensive defenseman Larry Murphy.

Patrick's second deal was made partly for psychological reasons. After a quick start, prized rookie Jaromir Jagr had fallen into a severe funk. Despite the best efforts of veterans like Trottier and Coffey to make him feel at home, the gifted youngster was having a terrible time learning English and adjusting to the North American lifestyle. To remedy the situation, Patrick swapped spare part Jim Kyte to the Calgary Flames for 32-year-old forward Jiri Hrdina, a solid citizen and former captain of the Czech National Team.

The trade paid immediate dividends. Hrdina took Jagr under his wing and the rookie's attitude and level of play improved dramatically. The veteran center proved to be more than just a babysitter as he teamed with Jagr and Phil Bourque to give the club a potent third line.

Suddenly, the Penguins reeled off six straight wins. Bolstered by the additions of Murphy, Taglianetti, and veteran Gordie Roberts, the rebuilt defensive corps performed brilliantly. Barrasso re-emerged as the team's No. 1 goaltender.

Craig Patrick wasn't done tinkering. Just before Christmas he shipped scoring ace Rob Brown off to Hartford for Scott Young. A mild disappointment with the Whalers, Young had all the tools. He could skate like the wind, play right wing or defense, and he possessed one of the hardest shots in the league.

As the holidays approached, the rejuvenated Penguins had a firm hold on fourth place in the tough Patrick Division. The team received a special Christmas gift when Mario began skating again.

News of his imminent return energized the club. The Pens promptly went on a tear and won five of eight games leading up to the All-Star break, including blowouts of perennial powerhouses Edmonton and Calgary.

The long-awaited "Lemieux debut" took place in Quebec on January 26. Although he was not yet in game shape, the Pens' captain collected three assists to earn the No. 1 star.

Despite Mario's triumphant return, dark clouds soon formed on the horizon. The Penguins had been one of the league's top road teams during the first half of the season, but they were reverting back to their old, losing ways. During a western swing in early March they were trounced by Los Angeles, Vancouver, and Calgary to run their road winless streak to 10 games. They wobbled home a thoroughly beaten team.

Even eternal optimist Bob Johnson was alarmed. "We need more pieces to the puzzle," he said. "I don't know what's going to happen…but we need more pieces."

Patrick heeded the veteran coach's cry for help. Once more he belied his no-trade reputation by hooking up with Hartford GM Eddie Johnston on a blockbuster six-player deal. In exchange for leading scoring John Cullen, talented Zarley Zalapski, and minor league forward Jeff Parker, he acquired center Ron Francis and defensemen Ulf Samuelsson and Grant Jennings.

The team was stunned to the core. Cullen was immensely popular and deserved much of the credit for keeping the team afloat during Mario's absence. Zalapski had been regarded as the heir to Coffey's throne as the club's top defenseman, although his role had diminished since the arrival of Larry Murphy.

Francis was a perfect fit. An accomplished player at both ends of the rink, the Whalers' long-time captain and all-time leading scorer was more than capable of filling the role of top-line center should Mario's tender back flare up.

"He was in Hartford for 10 years scoring 80, 90, 100 points a year," Lemieux said. "He was one of the best two-way center-men in the league, and he still is."

The Swedish-born Samuelsson also was a special player. Sporting extra-wide shoulder pads, a face shield, and a sneer, he resembled an on-ice version of the lead character from *Robocop*.

When asked to describe his style of play, he said, "I just go right for the body. I really don't hold back much at all. A lot of people don't appreciate that."

The big trade ignited the team. Francis made an immediate splash with his diligent two-way play, while Samuelsson thumped every opposing forward in sight. The latter became an instant folk hero with his in-your-face style. Color analyst Paul Steigerwald dubbed him "Jack Lambert on skates."

While the resurgent Penguins were gathering steam, the division-leading Rangers had lost five games in a row to set up a showdown for first place on St. Patrick's Day.

Armed with newly acquired enforcer Joey Kocur, the league's most feared fighter, the Rangers tried to run the Penguins right out of Madison Square Garden. Thirty-three seconds into the game Kocur rammed a gloved fist into Samuelsson's face. On his next shift the pugnacious winger collided with Jay Caufield.

Although always willing to tangle, big Jay lacked the balance on his skates to be a truly effective fighter. However, Caufield used his Promethean strength to tie up Kocur, neutralizing the Ranger's fearsome right hand.

"I thought that was the difference in the game," Paul Coffey said. "Jay gave us a big lift. If Kocur had really given it to him there, I'm not sure how we would have responded."

Far from being intimidated, the fight lit a fire under the Penguins. Lemieux and red-hot Kevin Stevens pumped in two goals apiece, while Barrasso kicked out 24 shots. The big win catapulted the team past the Rangers and into first place.

For the title-starved Penguins, the finish line was finally within reach. They buried the Red Wings to snatch the Patrick Division crown—the first title in the team's 24-year history.

"This means a great deal," a euphoric Bob Errey said. "You don't really realize how much it means until you reflect on past years, all the struggles that the team's gone through."

Individually, hustling Mark Recchi took the club scoring honors with 40 goals and 113 points—the first time since Lemieux's arrival that he failed to lead the team. Kevin Stevens burst into prominence as one of the league's top power forwards on the strength of a 40-goal season. After a sluggish start, Jaromir Jagr averaged a point per game in the second half to finish with 27 goals.

On the blue line, Coffey led the way with 93 points. He received strong support from Murphy, who registered a respectable 28 points in 44 games. Rookie Paul Stanton quietly contributed 23 points along with a solid plus/minus rating of plus 11.

	GP	G	A	PTS	PM	+/-
Mark Recchi	78	40	73	113	48	0
John Cullen	65	31	63	94	83	0
Paul Coffey	76	24	69	93	128	- 18
Kevin Stevens	80	40	46	86	133	- 1
Jaromir Jagr	80	27	30	57	42	- 4
Zarley Zalapski	66	12	36	48	59	15
Mario Lemieux	26	19	26	45	30	8
Bob Errey	79	20	22	42	115	11
Joe Mullen	47	17	22	39	6	9
Phil Bourque	78	20	14	34	106	7
Bryan Trottier	52	9	19	28	24	5
Larry Murphy	44	5	23	28	30	2
Scott Young	43	11	16	27	33	3
Randy Gilhen	72	15	10	25	51	3
Paul Stanton	75	5	18	23	40	11
Jiri Hrdina	37	6	14	20	13	- 2
Tony Tanti	46	6	12	18	44	1
Troy Loney	44	7	9	16	85	10
Rob Brown	25	6	10	16	31	0
Gordie Roberts	61	3	12	15	70	18
Barry Pederson	46	6	8	14	21	2
Peter Taglianetti	39	3	8	11	93	16
Ron Francis	14	2	9	11	21	0
Ulf Samuelsson	14	1	4	5	37	4
Jim Johnson	24	0	5	5	23	- 3
Tom Barrasso	48	0	5	5	40	0
Randy Hillier	31	2	2	4	32	- 3
Grant Jennings	13	1	3	4	26	2
Chris Dahlquist	22	1	2	3	30	0
Jamie Leach	7	2	0	2	0	- 1
Jay Caufield	23	1	1	2	71	- 2
Jeff Daniels	11	0	2	2	2	0
Ken Priestlay	2	0	1	1	0	0
Brad Aitken	6	0	1	1	25	- 2
Wendell Young	18	0	1	1	0	0
Frank Pietrangelo	25	0	1	1	24	0
Jim Kyte	1	0	0	0	2	0
Jim Paek	3	0	0	0	9	2
Gord Dineen	9	0	0	0	6	- 4

	GP	MINS	GA	SH	AVG	W	L	T
Tom Barrasso	48	2754	165	1	3.59	27	16	3
Frank Pietrangelo	25	1311	86	0	3.94	10	11	1
Wendell Young	18	773	52	0	4.04	4	6	2
	80	4843	305	1	3.78	41	33	6

1991–92

Record: 39–32–9
Points: 87
Goals For: 343
Goals Against: 308
Finish: Third (Patrick)
Coach: Scotty Bowman
General Manager: Craig Patrick

The Penguins barely had time to celebrate their hard-earned 1991 Stanley Cup victory. After 14 years of quiet and steady leadership, Edward DeBartolo Sr., a reluctant owner from the start, decided to sell the team. To complicate matters, key forwards Ron Francis, Mark Recchi, and Kevin Stevens were eligible to become free agents. Exacerbated by the impending sale, their contract negotiations bogged down as the summer passed. However, these were minor distractions compared to the tragedy that was soon to follow.

While preparing to coach Team USA in the Canada Cup Tournament, Bob Johnson began to experience slurred speech. Initially he thought his difficulties stemmed from some faulty dental work, but the root of the problem was far more severe. On the evening of August 23, Johnson's condition worsened dramatically. He was rushed to the hospital, where emergency surgery was performed to remove a malignant brain tumor.

The team was stunned to the core. The most shaken of all was Craig Patrick, who had forged a deep friendship with Johnson during their time together. An air of heaviness hung over the club as training camp opened without the beloved coach.

With the regular season fast approaching and Bob Johnson's condition worsening with each passing day, Patrick had to select a new head coach. It was a relatively simple choice. He wanted the club's director of player personnel and the winningest coach in NHL history, Scotty Bowman, to step behind the bench.

But Bowman was reluctant to rejoin the coaching ranks. For all of his success, he had failed to produce a winner in his previous stint at Buffalo, where he had come under fire for his gruff, abrasive style. After some coaxing from Patrick, Bowman agreed to take over the coaching duties on an interim basis.

Despite the tragic circumstances, Patrick made some progress when he signed Recchi to a contract in late September. A short time later, Stevens, frustrated by the lack of progress in his own negotiations, signed an offer sheet from the Boston Bruins for over $1 million per year. The Penguins had a week to match the offer or lose the big winger. Seven nerve-wracking days passed before Patrick inked Stevens to a new deal.

The club was finally sold to former Hartford owners Howard Baldwin and Morris Belzberg, who were

Jaromir's Weather

During the Pens' halcyon days in the early 1990s, several players became local celebrities of sorts. Candid and colorful Phil Bourque was a frequent guest on the *WDVE Morning Show*, a hip local radio program. So was Jaromir Jagr.

Show hosts Jimmy Krenn and Scott Paulsen were so enamored of Jagr that they set up a special segment for the popular Pens winger called "Jaromir's Weather."

Jagr was still struggling to learn the language, so the spots were limited to about 10 seconds.

Aficionados who tuned in at the right time were treated to, "Eez cloudy…30 degrees," in their hero's fractured but charming English.

immediately engulfed in controversy. Rumors surfaced that the new owners had considered selling off some of the team's high-priced stars to help finance the deal. Baldwin and Belzberg emphatically denied the accusations, but the league withheld final approval until they convinced the NHL brass that they did not intend to auction off any players.

As the Penguins struggled to maintain a .500 pace through the early going, it was apparent that their thoughts were elsewhere. It became increasingly difficult to focus on a hockey game when their coach was lying in a hospital bed, waging a courageous battle for his life.

On November 26 the players received the heartbreaking news that Bob Johnson had passed away. They had precious little time to regroup. The following night they squared off with New Jersey in a key Patrick Division matchup. In an atmosphere thick with emotion they stood with their heads bowed at center ice as the fans paid homage to the fallen coach.

"It's a shock when we're all sitting out there and they're playing those songs, and the fans are all sitting there, and everyone's thinking about Bob and what he did for us," Kevin Stevens said in an interview for the team's highlight video, *Against the Odds*. "It was an amazing situation because everyone's sitting there with tears in their eyes and all of a sudden the lights come on and we've got to drop the puck and play hockey. It just didn't feel right to go out and try and play a hockey game after that."

In a truly inspired performance the Penguins choked back their emotions and routed New Jersey. Days later the players and staff paid their last respects to Badger Bob at a funeral service in Colorado Springs.

With the passing of their beloved mentor the Penguins began to resemble Stanley Cup champions again. In a frightful burst of offensive fury, they hammered the expansion San Jose Sharks 10–2 and annihilated hapless Toronto 12–1.

Tom Barrasso, Paul Coffey, and Peter Taglianetti repel the Rangers.

During the final weekend of 1991 the Penguins squared off against the Capitals and the Rangers in a pair of crucial Patrick Division contests. They arrived in Landover on December 28 with something to prove. Pittsburgh had virtually owned the Caps since 1987, but Washington had turned the tables and throttled the Pens in their first three meetings of the season by a combined score of 21–4. Traditionally a defensive-oriented team that employed a clutch-and-grab style, the Capitals were energized by the spectacular play of a trio of young forwards from Eastern Europe—Michal Pivonka, Dimitri Khristich, and Peter Bondra.

From the opening face-off the contest had the feel of a playoff game. This time the Penguins got on the board first and forced the Capitals to play catch up. Instead of outskating their rival as they had done in the previous encounters, the Caps employed a more physical approach. With Dale Hunter and Alan May drawing penalty after penalty, Washington rarely got a chance to play at even strength. Taking full advantage, the Pens coasted to a lopsided 6–2 win.

The following night the Penguins took on the Rangers in Madison Square Garden. Led by their new captain, Mark Messier, New York had stunned the Pens with a come-from-behind victory in Pittsburgh a week earlier.

Midway through the opening period boisterous Joey Kocur flattened Troy Loney. Brimming with confidence, the Rangers soon grabbed the lead. Following a second goal by pesky Paul Broten, Kocur went looking for more action. Once again he found a willing combatant in Jay Caufield.

Pumping his vaunted right fist like a piston, the Rangers' enforcer tore into Caufield with a barrage of sledgehammer blows. The big Penguins winger clearly lost the battle, but he gave his team an enormous lift by standing up to Kocur. When the Rangers carelessly drew a pair of penalties a short time later, the Penguins burned them with two power-play goals. The Rangers briefly recaptured the lead, but the momentum was now firmly with the Pens. They exploded for four unanswered goals to pull away.

Thanks to their impressive victories over Washington and New York, the Penguins stood a scant three points out of first place. Little did anyone realize that the team was about to slip into a tailspin that would severely jeopardize its chances of winning another Stanley Cup.

The second-half slump began on New Year's Eve with a lackadaisical effort against New Jersey. Emotionally drained after their big victories over the Capitals and Rangers, the Pens dropped a 7–4 decision to the Devils. The club had a chance for revenge a couple of nights later, but New Jersey manhandled them again.

The All-Star break offered a welcome respite. For the first time in club history five Penguins were named to the All-Star team, including Lemieux, Stevens, Jagr, Coffey, and Bryan Trottier, a special veteran's selection. While "Trots" scored a nifty goal, his teammates looked lethargic. It was an omen of things to come.

In their first game following the break the Penguins blew a big lead and succumbed to Buffalo. The club was now in a full-fledged slump. To make matters worse Lemieux's cranky back acted up, forcing him to miss six games. Meanwhile, Jagr was suspended for 10 games for bumping referee Ron Hoggarth.

With the Islanders and the Flyers rapidly gaining ground, the Penguins finally displayed some intensity. On February 18 they routed their favorite patsies, the Maple Leafs. Perhaps the prettiest goal was scored by Paul Coffey, who streaked around the Toronto defense and snapped a wrist shot past goalie Rick Wamsley. It would be his last tally in the black and gold.

The next day Craig Patrick sent Coffey to Los Angeles as part of a huge three-team deal that was more stunning than his blockbuster the previous spring. The Pens received defensemen Brian Benning and Jeff Chychrun along with a first-round pick from the Kings. Patrick then packaged Benning, Mark Recchi, and the draft pick to Philadelphia for right wing Rick Tocchet, defenseman Kjell Samuelsson, and goaltender Ken Wregget.

The Penguins had parted with a tremendous amount of talent, but the return was also great. Blessed with a huge wingspan, the 6'6" Samuelsson played a smothering style that made life miserable for opposing forwards. Wregget was widely regarded as the best backup goalie in the league. But the key player in the deal was Tocchet.

From his first shift in the NHL, the rugged winger had carved out a reputation as a mean, relentless fighter in the true "Broad Street Bullies" tradition. Yet Tocchet also was a diamond in the rough. Possessing enormous heart and character, he willed himself into becoming one of the game's premier power forwards. When Tocchet ventured into hockey's trenches he rarely emerged without the puck.

"He said all he wanted was a chance to win," the departed Coffey said. "He'll have that in Pittsburgh. He's a good player who won't disappoint anyone in this city. He has the heart the size of a building. He'll do what it takes to win."

One fact had become abundantly clear: Scotty Bowman was not Bob Johnson. In an interview for a Fox Sports Network special that aired in 2008, Bob Errey explained the difference between the legendary coaches.

"Bob Johnson would ask you if you ate your oatmeal for breakfast," he said. "Scotty Bowman wasn't going to ask if you'd had your oatmeal."

As the tension between Bowman and the players grew more palpable with each passing day, the captains suggested a team meeting to Craig Patrick, who was traveling with the club on a western road trip.

"We were frustrated with him," Bryan Trottier said.

Phil Bourque took things a step further.

"I told Craig that we couldn't win with Scotty Bowman," he recalled.

While acknowledging Bowman's shortcomings, Patrick defended the veteran coach.

"We can and *will* win with Scotty," he said.

With the air finally cleared, the club's fortunes took a dramatic turn for the better. The Pens looked impressive in a win

over Calgary, as speedy U.S. Olympian Shawn McEachern made his debut. Rick Tocchet erupted for a hat trick in a 7–3 victory over San Jose, boosting the club's winning streak to three.

Despite a brief strike by the NHL Players' Association, the Penguins were jelling at just the right time. In the season finale they dumped Washington, the team they would face in the first round of the playoffs.

	GP	G	A	PTS	PM	+/-
Mario Lemieux	64	44	87	131	94	27
Kevin Stevens	80	54	69	123	254	8
Joe Mullen	77	42	45	87	30	12
Larry Murphy	77	21	56	77	48	33
Mark Recchi	58	33	37	70	78	- 16
Jaromir Jagr	70	32	37	69	34	12
Paul Coffey	54	10	54	64	62	4
Ron Francis	70	21	33	54	30	- 7
Bob Errey	78	19	16	35	119	1
Rick Tocchet	19	14	16	30	49	12
Bryan Trottier	63	11	18	29	54	- 11
Phil Bourque	58	10	16	26	58	- 6
Troy Loney	76	10	16	26	127	- 5
Gordie Roberts	73	2	22	24	87	19
Jiri Hrdina	56	3	13	16	16	4
Ulf Samuelsson	62	1	14	15	206	2
Ken Priestlay	49	2	8	10	4	5
Paul Stanton	54	2	8	10	62	- 8
Jamie Leach	38	5	4	9	8	- 2
Grant Jennings	53	4	5	9	104	- 1
Jim Paek	49	1	7	8	36	0
Peter Taglianetti	44	1	3	4	57	7
Shawn McEachern	15	0	4	4	0	1
Tom Barrasso	57	0	4	4	30	0
Kjell Samuelsson	20	1	2	3	34	0
Jeff Chychrun	17	0	1	1	35	- 8
Gord Dineen	1	0	0	0	0	- 2
Glenn Mulvenna	1	0	0	0	2	- 1
Todd Nelson	1	0	0	0	0	0
Jeff Daniels	2	0	0	0	0	0
Frank Pietrangelo	5	0	0	0	0	0
Ken Wregget	9	0	0	0	2	0
Wendell Young	18	0	0	0	0	0
Jay Caufield	50	0	0	0	175	- 6

	GP	MINS	GA	SH	AVG	W	L	T
Tom Barrasso	57	3329	196	1	3.53	25	22	9
Wendell Young	18	838	53	0	3.79	7	6	0
Ken Wregget	9	448	31	0	4.15	5	3	0
Frank Pietrangelo	5	225	20	0	5.33	2	1	0
	80	4854	308	1	3.81	39	32	9

1992–93

Record: 56–21–7
Points: 119
Goals For: 367
Goals Against: 268
Finish: First (Patrick)
Coach: Scotty Bowman
General Manager: Craig Patrick

The Penguins entered the summer of 1992 as the toast of the hockey world. Armed with one of the most brilliant collections of skill players ever assembled, they inspired talk of a new dynasty—one that could rival the great Islanders and Oilers teams of the 1970s and '80s.

However, a gradual erosion of the club's tremendous depth had begun. In June, the expansion Tampa Bay Lightning plucked Peter Taglianetti and Wendell Young off the Pens' unprotected list. Free agent Gordie Roberts left for greener pastures in Boston, while popular Phil Bourque defected to the much-hated Rangers. On August 17, Bryan Trottier tearfully announced his retirement, stripping away one the team's most respected and beloved players.

Nonplussed, Craig Patrick moved boldly to plug the dyke. He signed defensive specialists Mike Stapleton and Dave Tippett to boost the club's penalty-killing unit. With the delicate condition of Mario's back a constant concern,

he selected Martin Straka, an explosive little center, in the Entry Draft.

Despite the off-season changes the club opened the regular season looking every bit like two-time Stanley Cup champions. Sparked by Lemieux, the Pens stormed through the first half of the season. Stevens and Tocchet contributed mightily to the club's scorching pace, as did the newly formed second line of Ron Francis, Jaromir Jagr, and Shawn McEachern. The defense, anchored by Larry Murphy and the Samuelssons, provided solid protection for Tom Barrasso.

Meanwhile, Mario took aim at the consecutive-game goal-scoring mark established by "Punch" Broadbent seven decades earlier. Although his bid for the record was halted at a dozen games, the big center was on pace to smash Wayne Gretzky's single-season record of 215 points.

Even the most veteran observers were awed. "Mario Lemieux, to me, is a combination of elegance and power," columnist and commentator Al Morganti said. "An impossible creature to try to defend. I don't know if the sport's ever seen this kind of force, with all this kind of physical ability, all built into one powerful player."

Once again, Mario had climbed to the very pinnacle of his sport. But once more adversity struck just as he reached the summit. On January 13 it was revealed that Lemieux was suffering from Hodgkin's disease, a form of cancer that attacks the lymph nodes.

"Just the word *cancer* scares you a lot," the Pens captain recalled. "I didn't cry right at the time I was at the doctor's, but when I got in my car I actually started crying the whole

A young fan signs a giant get-well card for Mario Lemieux. The Pens' captain missed 24 games with Hodgkin's disease—and remarkably won the scoring title.

A Bitter Pill

Perhaps no one was more shaken by the announcement that Mario Lemieux had Hodgkin's disease than Craig Patrick.

Barely 14 months earlier he'd watched helplessly as his dear friend, Bob Johnson, lost his courageous battle with cancer. Mario's diagnosis was yet another bitter pill.

"I was amazed when the doctors sat in my office and told me what they'd found," he confessed. "Then the more we learned about it, the more we heard about it, the more we understood about the disease, things were a little easier to swallow."

The Penguins general manager had high hopes that Mario would make a full recovery. What No. 66 accomplished in just a few short months was beyond his wildest dreams. Lemieux finished the season with 160 points, including an eye-popping 51 points over an incendiary 16-game stretch.

way down to my house. That was probably the toughest day of my life."

Following surgery to remove an infected lymph node, Mario immediately began a battery of radiation treatments. While the prognosis for a full recovery was favorable, the news hit his teammates with the force of a sledgehammer.

"We're a team that can hardly lose a game, and all of a sudden the word *cancer* is involved," Ulf Samuelsson said. "People lose lives for that."

"I was scared for him, and scared for what's next—what lies ahead," Rick Tocchet added.

Although deeply shaken by the loss of their beloved superstar, the Pens once more displayed their remarkable character. Barely missing a beat, they emerged from the All-Star break with the best record in the league. As if to punctuate their stunning dominance the Penguins crunched the revenge-minded Blackhawks in a brawl-filled engagement on February 13.

It was an impressive victory over a team that many experts touted as a legitimate threat to the Pens' throne. Even the Penguins seemed to be astonished by their mind-boggling success.

"This is by far the best team we've had in Pittsburgh," Kevin Stevens said. "It's a confident team, it's got great leaders, and it's got 25 guys pretty much on the same page. It's just a great team to play for. I don't know how we got this good."

Displaying recuperative powers bordering on the super-human, Mario returned to the lineup on March 2, two full weeks ahead of schedule.

"At that point, all you want to do is prove to yourself that you're fine, that the cancer is behind you," he recalled.

"That's why I came back [so quickly]. Maybe it was foolish, but that's what I felt I had to do."

Although the contest was played in Philadelphia, the big center received a rousing five-minute ovation from the Flyers' fans. After appearing tentative in the early going, he registered a goal and an assist to jump-start the Pens' flagging power play.

Next came Mario's triumphant return to the Civic Arena, where he received a hero's welcome. "I don't even know who we played, I can't even remember the score, but I'm never gonna forget those minutes where the place was going bananas," Ulf Samuelsson said.

Unfortunately, Lemieux's back problems—all but forgotten during his bout with Hodgkin's disease—flared up again. With big No. 66 relegated to spot duty on the power play the offense foundered like a rudderless ship.

In an effort to cure the Penguins' sudden offensive malaise Bowman dusted off tapes of their Stanley Cup triumph over the Blackhawks. Having relearned some valuable lessons they throttled the Capitals, as Mario erupted for four goals. Then, as if to put league scoring leader Pat LaFontaine on notice, Lemieux connected four more times during a 9–3 demolition of the Flyers.

Meanwhile, Craig Patrick was working hard to acquire some additional defensive help. Rumors had circulated for months that he was pursuing Edmonton's Craig Muni, a tough and sturdy defenseman. Patrick crossed up the experts and swung deals for ex-Pen Peter Taglianetti and hard-hitting Mike Ramsey, a favorite of Scotty Bowman's.

With their lineup firmly set, the Penguins embarked on a winning streak that would reach epic proportions. On April 7 they tied the Islanders' mark of 15 consecutive wins with a pulsating overtime victory against Montreal.

Paced by Mario, who steamed past LaFontaine in the scoring race, the Penguins routed the Rangers 10–4 to establish a new standard. They extended their streak to 17 games before settling for a tie in the season finale against New Jersey. It was an exhilarating finish to the most spectacular season in club history.

The Penguins closed out the campaign with a stunning record of 56–21–7, far and away the best mark in franchise history. An offensive powerhouse, they ranked second in goal scoring and placed a stingy third in team defense.

It was a season of truly remarkable individual achievements. Mario Lemieux's courageous battle with Hodgkin's disease and subsequent comeback was a story for the ages. The big center led the league in plus/minus rating and captured his fourth Art Ross Trophy with 160 points. Only Wayne Gretzky ever topped his scoring rate of 2.67 points per game.

Mario won his second Hart Trophy and, for good measure, annexed the Bill Masterton Trophy and the Lester Pearson Award. The mountain of silverware confirmed that he was, indeed, the greatest hockey player in the world.

"He played so wonderfully that it makes you forget why he was out," Tom McMillan said. "In comparison to the

NBA, if Michael Jordan missed a third of the season would he win the scoring title? No."

The 1992–93 Penguins were much more than a one-man show. The ensemble cast included 55-goal scorer Kevin Stevens and 48-goal man Rick Tocchet. Ever the unsung hero, Ron Francis reached the 100-point plateau while performing his defensive duties as diligently as ever.

Tenacious Joey Mullen bounced back from knee surgery to top the 30-goal mark for the ninth time in his illustrious career. Jaromir Jagr set new career highs with 34 goals, 60 assists, and 94 points, while making enormous strides as an all-around player. Speedy Shawn McEachern placed sixth among an elite group of NHL rookies with 61 points. On the blue line, Norris Trophy candidate Larry Murphy rolled up 85 points. Ulf Samuelsson had a terrific year, placing fourth in the league with a plus/minus rating of plus 36. Mario's astounding comeback aside, the story of the year was Tom Barrasso. From start to finish the veteran goaltender was routinely brilliant. He posted a sparkling 3.01 goals-against average and 43 victories, tops in the league.

	GP	G	A	PTS	PM	+/-
Mario Lemieux	60	69	91	160	38	55
Kevin Stevens	72	55	56	111	177	17
Rick Tocchet	80	48	61	109	252	28
Ron Francis	84	24	76	100	68	6
Jaromir Jagr	81	34	60	94	61	30
Larry Murphy	83	22	63	85	73	45
Joe Mullen	72	33	37	70	14	19
Shawn McEachern	84	28	33	61	46	21
Ulf Samuelsson	77	3	26	29	249	36
Dave Tippett	74	6	19	25	56	5
Troy Loney	82	5	16	21	99	1
Jim Paek	77	3	15	18	64	13
Paul Stanton	77	4	12	16	97	7
Martin Straka	42	3	13	16	29	2
Bob Errey	54	8	6	14	76	- 2
Mike Needham	56	8	5	13	14	- 1
Mike Stapleton	78	4	9	13	10	- 8
Jeff Daniels	58	5	4	9	14	- 5
Kjell Samuelsson	63	3	6	9	106	25
Tom Barrasso	63	0	8	8	24	0
Peter Taglianetti	11	1	4	5	34	4
Grant Jennings	58	0	5	5	65	6
Bryan Fogarty	12	0	4	4	4	- 3
Mike Ramsey	12	1	2	3	8	13
Peter Ahola	22	0	1	1	14	- 2
Ken Wregget	25	0	1	1	6	0
Jeff Chychrun	1	0	0	0	2	1
Jamie Leach	5	0	0	0	2	- 2
Jay Caufield	26	0	0	0	60	- 1

	GP	MINS	GA	SH	AVG	W	L	T
Tom Barrasso	63	3702	186	4	3.01	43	14	5
Ken Wregget	25	1368	78	0	3.42	13	7	2
	84	5083	268	5	3.16	56	21	7

(Barrasso and Wregget shared 1 shutout)

1993–94

Record: 44–27–13
Points: 101
Goals For: 299
Goals Against: 285
Finish: First (Northeast)
Coach: Eddie Johnston
General Manager: Craig Patrick

In 1973 Roy Blount Jr. penned a popular book chronicling the season of the up-and-coming Pittsburgh Steelers. The Steelers were on the cusp of becoming arguably the greatest team in NFL history. But that year they fell short of Super Bowl glory, losing a first-round playoff game to archrival Oakland. Blount titled his book, *About Three Bricks Shy…and the Load Filled Up.*

It also was an apt description of the next era in Penguins hockey. For several seasons the Pens were perennial contenders to reclaim the coveted Stanley Cup. However, they lacked a few key ingredients, be it a big checking center or a quality defenseman or two. They were always, it seemed, about three bricks shy.

The failure to win a third straight Stanley Cup set off a power struggle that would have a huge impact on the club. Many of the players had chafed under Scotty Bowman's old-school methods, forcing Craig Patrick to broker an uneasy peace by arranging to have assistant coach Barry Smith run the team's practices.

In the wake of Bob Johnson's untimely death, Bowman had grudgingly accepted the arrangement in order to ease the transition. However, he was less than thrilled. He now demanded more input into practices and personnel decisions, along with a boost in pay.

Patrick was looking for a way out. He'd had his eyes on former coach and general manager Eddie Johnston since the previous summer, when EJ was dismissed by the Whalers. When Bowman entertained a coaching offer from Detroit, Patrick saw his opening. He pressed the veteran coach for a commitment. Bowman balked, and the Pens' GM quickly cut off negotiations.

"He is not prepared to make a decision on whether he wants to coach our team or not," Patrick said. "For that reason, we're going in another direction."

Within weeks Patrick announced that Johnston was returning as the new coach. Bryan Trottier also rejoined the club in the dual role of player and assistant coach, with a plan to groom him as Johnston's eventual successor.

One can only guess at the long-term effect of this changing of the guard. Although the more moderate Johnston was a proven coach and a popular choice among the players, Bowman would guide the Red Wings to three Stanley Cups.

Rugged Rick Tocchet bulls his way to the net.

Palace intrigue aside, the biggest story of the summer was Mario Lemieux's cranky back. In late July he underwent successful surgery to repair a herniated muscle that had plagued him during the playoffs the previous spring.

Meanwhile, Patrick looked for ways to improve a team that most experts felt was a lock to recapture the Stanley Cup. Convinced that his club had been pushed around by the Islanders, he pulled the trigger on yet another stunning deal, peddling playoff disappointment Shawn McEachern to the Kings for onetime Penguins defenseman Marty McSorley.

Once described as a "walking five-minute-major cruising for a penalty box," the burly 225-pounder had evolved from an enforcer into a dependable heavyweight defenseman who could still swap punches with the best of them. With "Marty Mac" and Rick Tocchet on board the Penguins boasted a physical one-two punch they hadn't enjoyed since the days of Steve Durbano and Battleship Kelly.

News on the medical front was mixed. On the plus side, Kevin Stevens quickly recovered from surgery to repair the gruesome facial injuries he'd suffered during the 1993 playoffs. However, Mario's recovery from back surgery was coming along more slowly than hoped. To make matters worse, Tocchet suffered a back injury while lifting weights.

Now competing in the Northeast Division along with Boston, Buffalo, Hartford, Montreal, and Quebec, the Pens stumbled to an uneven start. The club flashed its championship form in victories over the Rangers and Montreal, but appeared to be in complete disarray in losses to Quebec and Tampa Bay. Favoring a free-flowing style of hockey, Eddie Johnston encouraged his defensemen to join the attack. However, with the notable exception of Larry Murphy, the team's plodding rearguards seemed woefully out of their element.

With the tone set, the Penguins lurched through an up-and-down campaign. The fact that Mario was playing at less than 100 percent only added to the team's troubles. In addition to his ailing back, he was suffering from a debilitating case of anemia—a lingering effect from his radiation treatments. Patrick and Johnston had little choice but to rest the big center until he was fully recovered.

After enduring an endless succession of hot streaks and dry spells, Craig Patrick made a decisive move. Although not for a lack of effort, Marty McSorley had failed to find his niche. On February 16 Patrick shipped the rugged blueliner back to Los Angeles along with Jim Paek for Shawn McEachern and right wing Tomas Sandstrom—effectively reversing the trade he'd made during the summer.

The deal provided the boost the Pens so desperately needed. McEachern and Sandstrom added some much needed speed and scoring punch. The team soon reclaimed the top spot in the Northeast Division.

With Mario on the shelf for huge chunks of the season, Jaromir Jagr stepped forward to pace the attack. The brilliant young winger fell one point shy of the century mark with 32 goals and 67 assists. Following close behind was Ron Francis, who tallied 93 points to capture the team MVP honors. Second-year pro Martin Straka improved by leaps and bounds to score 30 goals, while ageless wonder Joey Mullen notched 38. Veteran Larry Murphy was superb, piling up 73 points.

The injury bug bit hard. Tocchet gutted it out and played with back pain, but his production plummeted. Mario's season was virtually ruined by health problems as well. Remarkably, Kevin Stevens managed to score a team-leading 41 goals. However, the big winger had been unable to train properly during the summer and it severely affected his overall performance.

	GP	G	A	PTS	PM	+/-
Jaromir Jagr	80	32	67	99	61	15
Ron Francis	82	27	66	93	62	- 3
Kevin Stevens	83	41	47	88	155	- 24
Larry Murphy	84	17	56	73	44	10
Joe Mullen	84	38	32	70	41	9
Martin Straka	84	30	34	64	24	24
Doug Brown	77	18	37	55	18	19
Rick Tocchet	51	14	26	40	134	- 15
Mario Lemieux	22	17	20	37	32	- 2
Ulf Samuelsson	80	5	24	29	199	23
Shawn McEachern	27	12	9	21	10	13
Marty McSorley	47	3	18	21	139	- 9
Tomas Sandstrom	27	6	11	17	24	5
Bryan Trottier	41	4	11	15	36	- 12
Peter Taglianetti	60	2	12	14	142	5
Kjell Samuelsson	59	5	8	13	118	18
Mike Stapleton	58	7	4	11	18	- 4
Markus Naslund	71	4	7	11	27	- 3
Greg Brown	36	3	8	11	28	1
Jeff Daniels	63	3	5	8	20	- 1
Grant Jennings	61	2	4	6	126	- 10
Ed Patterson	27	3	1	4	10	- 5
Mike Ramsey	65	2	2	4	22	- 4
Jim Paek	41	0	4	4	8	- 7
Greg Hawgood	12	1	2	3	8	- 1
Pat Neaton	9	1	1	2	12	3
Larry DePalma	7	1	0	1	5	1
Mike Needham	25	1	0	1	2	0
Ken Wregget	42	0	1	1	8	0
Tom Barrasso	44	0	1	1	42	0
Rob Dopson	2	0	0	0	0	0
Roberto Romano	2	0	0	0	0	0
Greg Andrusak	3	0	0	0	2	- 1
Justin Duberman	4	0	0	0	0	0
Ladislav Karabin	9	0	0	0	2	0
Jim McKenzie	11	0	0	0	16	- 5
Chris Tamer	12	0	0	0	9	3

	GP	MINS	GA	SH	AVG	W	L	T
Roberto Romano	2	125	3	0	1.44	1	0	1
Tom Barrasso	44	2482	139	2	3.36	22	15	5
Ken Wregget	42	2456	138	1	3.37	21	12	7
Rob Dopson	2	45	3	0	4.00	0	0	0
	84	5118	285	3	3.34	44	27	13

1994–95

Record: 29–16–3
Points: 61
Goals For: 181
Goals Against: 158
Finish: Second (Northeast)
Coach: Eddie Johnston
General Manager: Craig Patrick

A disappointing playoff loss to the Capitals in the spring of 1994 set off a firestorm of criticism among fans and the local press. Many demanded a full-scale rebuilding job—including the appointment of a new coach.

Craig Patrick had other ideas. He believed the club's subpar showing was due in no small part to injuries that forced Eddie Johnston to rely too heavily on a handful of key veterans. Convinced the team would rebound, Patrick gave his cast of champions one last chance to recapture the Stanley Cup.

He defied prevailing wisdom by re-signing 37-year-old Joey Mullen and 36-year-old Kjell Samuelsson. In late July, he pulled the trigger on his third major trade with Los Angeles in less than a year, shipping popular Rick Tocchet and a second-round pick to the Kings for All-Star sniper Luc Robitaille. Patrick continued to stockpile offensive talent by inking free agent Tomas Sandstrom to a new contract and adding former Pen John Cullen, who performed brilliantly during Mario Lemieux's absence in 1990–91.

The deals for additional firepower gave the team renewed hope, but they also had a deeper purpose. In an effort to overcome the anemia that had plagued him since his bout with Hodgkin's disease, Lemieux announced that he would sit out the upcoming season.

Young gun Jaromir Jagr emerged from Mario Lemieux's shadow to win the scoring title in 1994–95.

Although Mario's decision was hardly welcome, the club did its best to take the news in stride. Thanks to Craig Patrick, the Pens still boasted a core of established stars. Even without No. 66 to lead the way, scoring goals would not be a problem.

Preventing them was another matter. Behind the big three of Larry Murphy and the Samuelssons, there was little depth.

A more pressing issue loomed as the start of the regular season approached. Led by Bob Goodenow, the NHL Players' Association was stonewalling efforts by ownership to implement a salary cap or a payroll tax to slow skyrocketing player salaries. With the full support of NHL commissioner Gary Bettman, the owners decided to play hardball by imposing a lockout.

The impasse dragged on into the new year with no end in sight. With the season hanging in the balance, the two sides finally reached an agreement in mid-January. Because the lockout had lasted so long, the schedule was pared to 48 games, the shortest since 1941–42. The season would in effect be a sprint to the finish line—a race that suited the veteran Penguins to a T.

Opening the season on a roll, the Pens won seven straight games. Boasting four productive lines, they possessed mind-boggling depth that was the envy of every team in the league. The defense, bolstered by rugged rookie Chris Tamer and waiver-draft pickups Chris Joseph and Francois Leroux, was holding up well.

On February 21 the Penguins squared off against the equally hot Quebec Nordiques in a battle for Northeast Division supremacy. Led by veteran Wendel Clark and a bevy of talented youngsters, the Nordiques had blazed to a 13–2 start to tie the 12–1–2 Pens for first place.

Played before a packed house at the Civic Arena, the game had the feel of a Stanley Cup Finals matchup. In a see-saw affair that featured four lead changes, the Penguins eclipsed Quebec 5–4 on Jaromir Jagr's sixth game-winning goal of the young campaign.

A week later the two rivals hooked up for a rematch in Quebec. Powered by a six-goal second-period outburst, the Pens blew past the Nordiques to grab the top spot in the division.

The team was flying high. Everyone in the organization was giddy about their chances of recapturing Lord Stanley's coveted silverware. But a knee injury to the hard-shooting Joseph signaled the end of the spectacular early-season run.

Suddenly, the club's fortunes took a turn for the worse. Old weaknesses that weren't apparent during the glorious start began to resurface. The patchwork defense broke down with alarming regularity, while the forwards struggled to hold their own in the trenches. Injuries gnawed away at the team's depth, forcing Cullen, Kevin Stevens, and Ulf Samuelsson from the lineup for extended stretches.

The Penguins managed a second-place finish in the Northeast Division, but there was ample cause for concern. Following its red-hot start the club had struggled to maintain a .500 clip.

Hold the Fries

When Mario Lemieux reported for training camp in the fall of 1995, the first thing his teammates noticed was his newly sculpted physique.

While no one would ever mistake Mario for Arnold Schwarzenegger, the Pens' captain had added nearly 10 pounds of muscle to his 6'4" frame.

Pressed for details about his conditioning program, he quipped, "I don't order fries with my club sandwich."

	GP	G	A	PTS	PM	+/-
Jaromir Jagr	48	32	38	70	37	23
Ron Francis	44	11	48	59	18	30
Tomas Sandstrom	47	21	23	44	42	1
Luc Robitaille	46	23	19	42	37	10
Larry Murphy	48	13	25	38	18	12
Joe Mullen	45	16	21	37	6	15
John Cullen	46	13	24	37	66	- 4
Kevin Stevens	27	15	12	27	51	0
Shawn McEachern	44	13	13	26	22	4
Martin Straka	31	4	12	16	16	0
Ulf Samuelsson	44	1	15	16	113	11
Chris Joseph	33	5	10	15	46	3
Len Barrie	48	3	11	14	66	- 4
Mike Hudson	40	2	9	11	34	- 1
Norm Maciver	13	0	9	9	6	7
Kjell Samuelsson	41	1	6	7	54	8
Greg Hawgood	21	1	4	5	25	2
Markus Naslund	14	2	2	4	2	0
Greg Andrusak	7	0	4	4	6	- 1
Grant Jennings	25	0	4	4	36	2
Jim McKenzie	39	2	1	3	63	- 7
Chris Tamer	36	2	0	2	82	0
Troy Murray	13	0	2	2	23	- 1
Francois Leroux	40	0	2	2	114	7
Rusty Fitzgerald	4	1	0	1	0	2
Richard Park	1	0	1	1	2	1
Peter Taglianetti	13	0	1	1	12	1
Jeff Christian	1	0	0	0	0	0
Philippe DeRouville	1	0	0	0	0	0
Tom Barrasso	2	0	0	0	0	0
Drake Berehowsky	4	0	0	0	13	1
Wendell Young	10	0	0	0	2	0
Ken Wregget	38	0	0	0	14	0

	GP	MINS	GA	SH	AVG	W	L	T
Philippe DeRouville	1	60	3	0	3.00	1	0	0
Ken Wregget	38	2208	118	0	3.21	25	9	2
Wendell Young	10	497	27	0	3.26	3	6	0
Tom Barrasso	2	125	8	0	3.84	0	1	1
	48	2901	158	0	3.27	29	16	3

1995–96

Record: 49–29–4
Points: 102
Goals For: 362
Goals Against: 284
Finish: First (Northeast)
Coach: Eddie Johnston
General Manager: Craig Patrick

For the second time in a decade Mario Lemieux held the Penguins' destiny in his gifted hands. The team breathed a collective sigh of relief on June 20 when Mario announced that he would play again. Hockey fans would see a different man wearing the familiar No. 66. He was bigger and stronger, and his upper body development was particularly impressive.

With the cornerstone set firmly in place, Patrick proceeded to fill in the missing pieces. He welcomed Eddie Johnston back for another season behind the bench. It was one of the few moves Patrick made during that turbulent off-season that didn't raise eyebrows.

Like a scythe cutting through a field of ripened wheat, he jettisoned many of the splendid old warriors who had served the club so well. Joey Mullen, Kjell Samuelsson, and John Cullen were released soon after the season ended. At the NHL Entry Draft he dealt high-priced veteran Larry Murphy to the Maple Leafs for defenseman Dmitri Mironov.

With an eye toward further paring the club's burgeoning payroll, Patrick pulled off two stunning deals. First he peddled Boston natives Kevin Stevens and Shawn McEachern to the division-rival Bruins for promising forwards Bryan Smolinski and Glen Murray. Then, in his most shocking trade of all, he shipped Luc Robitaille and defensive stalwart Ulf Samuelsson to the Rangers for defenseman Sergei Zubov and center Petr Nedved.

Patrick had done his homework. Smolinski and Murray were rising young stars. The former Rangers were likewise budding talents. A superb skater whose puck-handling skills and instincts rivaled those of the departed Murphy, Zubov had played an integral role in the Rangers' 1994 Stanley Cup victory.

Nedved was more of a reach. Drafted in the same class as friend and countryman Jaromir Jagr, he was a gifted offensive performer who possessed great speed along with a laser beam of a wrist shot. However, Nedved's career had been pock-marked by contract squabbles and inconsistency. His only season in New York—where he served as a whipping boy for Mark Messier—had been a dismal failure. Patrick believed a change in scenery would help the talented youngster reach his considerable potential.

Resembling a shiny new sports car that was itching for the road, the Pens raced through the early going. Playing as if he'd never missed a game, Mario amassed a staggering 40 points in only 12 games.

Goalie Ken Wregget teams up with J.J. Daigneault and Tomas Sandstrom to stop the Rangers' Adam Graves.

In late November the streaking Penguins ran into a brick wall, dropping a pair of decisions to the battle-hardened Rangers. Following the losses to New York the club began a mild slide.

As the team continued to stumble in the new year, rumors swirled that yet another blockbuster deal was in the works. Although former first-round pick Markus Naslund had improved by leaps and bounds, it wasn't enough to satisfy Eddie Johnston. Reports out of Edmonton had the 22-year-old winger heading to the Oilers along with rookie Chris Wells for hard-hitting defenseman Bryan Marchment and rugged forward Scott Thornton.

The big trade with Edmonton never materialized. In what would become an enormous stain on his previously sterling record, Craig Patrick peddled Naslund to Vancouver for Alek Stojanov, a tough but plodding winger who had collected one lone assist in 58 games.

The battle for the top spot in the Eastern Conference came down to the final day of the season, but a loss to Boston dropped the Pens into the second slot.

Still, it was a remarkably successful campaign. Few who witnessed the mass exodus of veterans over the off-season dared to dream that the team would be so competitive. With the glaring exception of the Naslund deal, nearly all of Patrick's trades reaped significant dividends. The club responded with a record of 49–29–4, the third-best in franchise history.

For Mario, it was a season to behold. The Pens' captain culminated perhaps the most stunning comeback in the history of the sport, capturing his fifth Art Ross Trophy on the strength a 69-goal, 92-assist campaign. Jaromir Jagr's 149 points shattered league scoring records for right wings and foreign-born players. He matured into arguably the best all-around player in the game.

Ron Francis finished fourth in the NHL scoring race with 119 points while tying Mario for the league lead in assists. Sergei Zubov struggled at times to blend in with the rest of the power-play unit, yet he harnessed enough of his wondrous abilities to produce 11 goals and 55 assists.

Perhaps the most pleasant surprise was Nedved. He caught fire in the second half to tally 45 goals and 99 points while leading the club with a plus 37.

	GP	G	A	PTS	PM	+/-
Mario Lemieux	70	69	92	161	54	10
Jaromir Jagr	82	62	87	149	96	31
Ron Francis	77	27	92	119	56	25
Petr Nedved	80	45	54	99	68	37
Tomas Sandstrom	58	35	35	70	69	4
Sergei Zubov	64	11	55	66	22	28
Bryan Smolinski	81	24	40	64	69	6
Markus Naslund	66	19	33	52	36	17
Dmitri Mironov	72	3	31	34	88	19
Glen Murray	69	14	15	29	57	4
Norm Maciver	32	2	21	23	32	12
Chris Joseph	70	5	14	19	71	6
Dave Roche	71	7	7	14	130	- 5
Chris Tamer	70	4	10	14	153	20
Neil Wilkinson	41	2	10	12	87	12
Kevin Miller	13	6	5	11	4	4
Francois Leroux	66	2	9	11	161	2
Joe Dziedzic	69	5	5	10	68	- 5
Richard Park	56	4	6	10	36	3
J.J. Daigneault	13	3	3	6	23	0
Dave McLlwain	18	2	4	6	4	- 5
Brad Lauer	21	4	1	5	6	- 5
Corey Foster	11	2	2	4	2	- 2
Chris Wells	54	2	2	4	59	- 6
Rusty Fitzgerald	21	1	2	3	12	7
Tom Barrasso	49	0	3	3	18	0
Ian Moran	51	1	1	2	47	- 1
Ed Patterson	35	0	2	2	38	- 5
Ken Wregget	37	0	2	2	8	0
Alek Stojanov	10	1	0	1	7	- 1
Drake Berehowsky	1	0	0	0	0	1
Greg Andrusak	2	0	0	0	0	- 1
Stefan Bergkvist	2	0	0	0	2	0
Jeff Christian	3	0	0	0	2	0
Len Barrie	5	0	0	0	18	- 1
Peter Allen	8	0	0	0	8	2

	GP	MINS	GA	SH	AVG	W	L	T
Ken Wregget	37	2132	115	3	3.24	20	13	2
Tom Barrasso	49	2799	160	2	3.43	29	16	2
	82	4948	284	5	3.44	49	29	4

1996–97

Record: 38–36–8
Points: 84
Goals For: 285
Goals Against: 280
Finish: Second (Northeast)
Coach: Eddie Johnston–Craig Patrick
General Manager: Craig Patrick

Despite a heartbreaking loss to Florida in the Eastern Conference Finals, the Penguins appeared to be in good shape for the 1996–97 season. They possessed a deep and talented group of forwards backed by a serviceable if unspectacular defensive corps.

Mario Lemieux thought otherwise. While accepting his third Hart Trophy at the postseason awards banquet, he dropped a shocking ultimatum on the Pens' brass.

"If the team wants to go in a direction where they have another shot at the Cup, I'd love to be a part of it," he said. "If not, I would weigh that in my decision [to retire]."

"I'm going to be watching at the draft," he added. "I'm sure they're going to be making some big moves at the draft and I'll be watching for a couple of weeks and see what happens."

Caught off guard by Mario's emotional remarks, Craig Patrick began an emergency retooling process that he had not planned to undertake. Indeed, some of the personnel decisions seemed to be heavily influenced if not downright directed by Lemieux. Whatever the reasons, for the first time since taking over the helm the Pens' GM made a spate of moves that were of dubious pedigree.

He pulled off a surprising swap of high-profile defensemen at the Entry Draft, shipping Sergei Zubov to Dallas in exchange for big Kevin Hatcher. Hatcher would give the club three solid seasons but he was far outshone by Zubov, who emerged as a world-class defenseman.

In another move that had Lemieux's fingerprints all over it, Patrick signed the much-traveled Dan Quinn to a contract. Hockey's foremost gypsy, Quinn had virtually lived out of a suitcase since leaving Pittsburgh, changing uniforms no less than nine times in seven years. He remained a close personal friend and golfing buddy of Mario's, a fact that undoubtedly helped to seal the deal.

The Penguins teetered through the early part of the season like drunken sailors. Due to injuries and contract squabbles, many of the players had barely touched the ice during the preseason and it showed. Not only was the club suffering from defensive breakdowns at an alarming rate, but the offense was failing as well.

After the Pens were flattened by the Rangers in mid-November, Howard Baldwin called a meeting with Patrick and Johnston to voice his concern over the club's deplorable play.

Armed with a mandate to shake up the team, Patrick dealt holdout Bryan Smolinski to the Islanders for versatile forward Andreas Johansson and wrecking-ball defenseman Darius Kasparaitis. The brash Lithuanian promised to provide the feistiness and bite that had been lacking since the departure of Ulf Samuelsson.

Beloved in the 'Burgh, Mario Lemieux retired following the 1996–97 season.

"He's got an element that only two or three other guys in the league have with the open-ice hit," Pens defenseman Ian Moran said. "When you see he's out there, you really have to pay attention."

Continuing to wheel and deal, Patrick pulled off a pair of trades with Florida and Anaheim. In stark contrast to his uninspired moves over the summer, the Penguins' GM regained his Midas touch. He parlayed the disappointing Chris Wells into two solid pros—speedy center Stu Barnes and offensive-minded rearguard Jason Woolley.

Patrick's trade with the Mighty Ducks was equally brilliant. He peddled free-agent enforcer Shawn Antoski and Dmitri Mironov to Anaheim for gritty winger Alex Hicks and ultra-smooth defenseman Fredrik Olausson.

Backed by the exceptional goaltending of rookie sensation Patrick Lalime, the rejuvenated Pens rolled through a 28-game stretch at an incendiary 21–3–4 clip. However, the schedule-makers had been kind. The Penguins had enjoyed the extreme good fortune of avoiding the NHL's elite teams during their hot streak. Their luck came to a screeching halt in late January when they were crunched by Colorado and the Rangers.

A team that had been playing like a well-oiled machine suddenly degenerated into a sagging wreck. The defense soured, and neither Lalime nor Ken Wregget could cover up for the mistakes being committed in front of them. Jaromir Jagr injured his already tender groin, forcing him from the lineup for an extended stretch.

Finally, after the Penguins were embarrassed by the streaking Devils for their eighth loss in nine games, Patrick relieved Eddie Johnston of the coaching duties and assigned him to the post of assistant general manager. As he had done in his first year with the team, Patrick stepped behind the bench in an attempt to right the club's foundering fortunes.

He continued his astonishing overhaul by swinging three more deals at the trade deadline. None would have the impact of his midseason moves. The most prominent involved the disappointing Glen Murray, who was sent to Los Angeles for veteran Eddie Olczyk. Like Markus Naslund before him, Murray would blossom into an All-Star.

With the return of Jagr, Wregget, and several other wounded warriors, the Penguins finally began a modest turnaround in time for the stretch run. Despite their bipolar play, the Pens clinched their seventh consecutive playoff berth with a ragged 5–5 tie against the Whalers.

	GP	G	A	PTS	PM	+/-
Mario Lemieux	76	50	72	122	65	27
Jaromir Jagr	63	47	48	95	40	22
Ron Francis	81	27	63	90	20	7
Petr Nedved	74	33	38	71	66	- 2
Kevin Hatcher	80	15	39	54	103	11
Stu Barnes	62	17	22	39	16	- 20
Jason Woolley	57	6	30	36	28	3
Fredrik Olausson	51	7	20	27	24	21
Tomas Sandstrom	40	9	15	24	33	4
Glen Murray	66	11	11	22	24	- 19
Joey Mullen	54	7	15	22	4	0
Alex Hicks	55	5	15	20	76	- 6
Joe Dziedzic	59	9	9	18	63	- 4
Darius Kasparaitis	57	2	16	18	84	24
J.J. Daigneault	53	3	14	17	36	- 5
Greg Johnson	32	7	9	16	14	- 13
Ed Olczyk	12	4	7	11	6	8
Dave Roche	61	5	5	10	155	- 13
Ian Moran	36	4	5	9	22	- 11
Andreas Johansson	27	2	7	9	20	- 6
Garry Valk	17	3	4	7	25	- 6
Chris Tamer	45	2	4	6	131	- 25
Dmitri Mironov	15	1	5	6	24	- 4
Alek Stojanov	35	1	4	5	79	3
Josef Beranek	8	3	1	4	4	- 1
Jeff Christian	11	2	2	4	13	- 3
Tyler Wright	45	2	2	4	70	- 7
Petr Klima	9	1	3	4	4	- 4
Craig Muni	64	0	4	4	36	- 6
Dan Quinn	16	0	3	3	10	- 6
Francois Leroux	59	0	3	3	81	- 3
Ken Wregget	46	0	1	1	6	0
Richard Park	1	0	0	0	0	- 1
Domenic Pittis	1	0	0	0	0	- 1
Philippe DeRouville	2	0	0	0	0	0
Tom Barrasso	5	0	0	0	0	0
Stefan Bergkvist	5	0	0	0	7	- 1
Ed Patterson	6	0	0	0	8	0
Roman Oksiuta	7	0	0	0	4	- 4
Shawn Antoski	13	0	0	0	49	0
Neil Wilkinson	23	0	0	0	36	- 12
Patrick Lalime	39	0	0	0	0	0

	GP	MINS	GA	SH	AVG	W	L	T
Patrick Lalime	39	2058	101	3	2.94	21	12	2
Philippe DeRouville	2	111	6	0	3.24	0	2	0
Ken Wregget	46	2514	136	2	3.25	17	17	6
Tom Barrasso	5	270	26	0	5.78	0	5	0
	82	4969	280	5	3.38	38	36	8

1997–98

Record: 40–24–18
Points: 98
Goals For: 228
Goals Against: 188
Finish: First (Northeast)
Coach: Kevin Constantine
General Manager: Craig Patrick

When Mario Lemieux hung up his skates following the 1997 playoffs, the last vestige of the Pens' great Stanley Cup champions was stripped away. With the notable exceptions of Jaromir Jagr, Petr Nedved, and an aging Ron Francis, the Penguins were now a team of questionable pedigree.

There were other problems as well. The club was losing money at an alarming rate. While well-intentioned, most of Howard Baldwin's attempts to increase revenues—including the installation of luxury boxes and a TV deal with the Fox network—had failed miserably.

Desperate for a fresh influx of cash, Baldwin's prayers appeared to be answered when Roger Marino purchased a 50 percent interest in the team. A successful entrepreneur in his own right, the well-heeled Marino had made a fortune through the company he had founded—data storage giant EMC.

It was an uneasy marriage from the start. While the enterprising Baldwin tended to shoot from the hip, Marino felt the team should be run like a business. Aghast at the money he was losing and clearly at odds with Baldwin's free-spending ways, the hard-nosed Bostonian began to squeeze his partner out of the picture.

Dictated by Mario's retirement, a dwindling pool of upper-echelon talent, and the new financial constraints, the Penguins would need to embrace a totally new philosophy in order to remain competitive. The balance of power had shifted from free-flowing teams like the Pens to clubs that employed a grittier, more disciplined brand of hockey such as New Jersey and Dallas.

Craig Patrick's top priority was to find a coach who could mold what had become a very fragmented and disjointed group into a competitive hockey club. While for the most part necessary, the flurry of trades the previous season had all but shredded any semblance of team unity. Thankfully, the timing couldn't have been better. Several bright young coaches were available, including Ron Wilson, who was unceremoniously dumped by the Mighty Ducks, and Coach of the Year Ted Nolan, who was let go by the Sabres in a power struggle.

From the start there was little doubt about who would become the next Penguins bench boss. Patrick had his eyes on former San Jose coach Kevin Constantine.

The appointment was considered a very large feather in the Penguins' cap. During his first year with San Jose,

Constantine led a modestly talented Sharks team to an NHL-record 58-point improvement. In the playoffs that spring, he outfoxed coaching legend Scotty Bowman to lead the eighth-seeded Sharks to a stunning upset over the President's Trophy–winning Red Wings.

For a time, Constantine would live up to his billing as one of the best coaches ever to set foot behind the Penguins' bench.

With the new skipper in place, Craig Patrick set about completing the overhaul he had started. Under the club's newly minted austerity program, he was unable to pursue any high-priced free agents—including his own. When Petr Nedved held out for a more lucrative contract, Patrick was in no position to renegotiate. The talented center would sit out the entire season.

Forced to scour the waiver wire and the minor leagues for talent, the Penguins' GM rose to the occasion with some of his finest moves. A few were nothing short of brilliant.

Leaving no stone unturned, he culled former Pens Martin Straka and Rob Brown from the scrap heap. Other reclamation projects included Czech-mates Robert Lang and Jiri Slegr.

The most important addition of all was not a new face but an old one. Tom Barrasso returned after missing virtually the entire 1996–97 season. Flashing the form that helped pave the way to a pair of Stanley Cups, he reclaimed the starting job and provided the stellar goaltending that was so crucial to Constantine's defense-first system.

The retooled Penguins took to Constantine's instruction like ducks to water. They led the Northeast Division virtually wire to wire, easily outpacing the competition en route to a sparkling record of 40–24–18.

Stepping out from the long shadow cast by No. 66, Jaromir Jagr proved that he was more than talented enough to carry the team. The husky winger was the runaway league leader in scoring with 102 points. Ron Francis continued to provide

quiet, steady leadership. He had yet another marvelous year, notching 25 goals and 62 assists. Scrappy Stu Barnes also enjoyed a terrific season, contributing 30 goals. Combined, the trio accounted for a whopping 40 percent of the team's production.

Perhaps the finest performance was turned in by Barrasso. He tied or established career highs in games played (63), shutouts (7), goals-against average (2.07), and save percentage (.922).

The season had been an artistic success, but the same could not be said financially. Roger Marino made no secret of his desire to escape the hideous lease agreement with SMG—the Civic Arena management company. The white knight had become a dark prince, hinting at the possibility of moving the team to a new city or selling it outright.

Shortly after the playoffs ended he came up with another solution. The Penguins filed for bankruptcy.

	GP	G	A	PTS	PM	+/-
Jaromir Jagr	77	35	67	102	64	17
Ron Francis	81	25	62	87	20	12
Stu Barnes	78	30	35	65	30	15
Kevin Hatcher	74	19	29	48	66	- 3
Martin Straka	75	19	23	42	28	- 1
Rob Brown	82	15	25	40	59	- 1
Fredrik Olausson	76	6	27	33	42	13
Aleksey Morozov	76	13	13	26	8	- 4
Ed Olczyk	56	11	11	22	35	- 9
Robert Lang	51	9	13	22	14	6
Alex Hicks	58	7	13	20	54	4
Brad Werenka	71	3	15	18	46	15
Jiri Slegr	73	5	12	17	109	10
Andreas Johansson	50	5	10	15	20	4
Darius Kasparaitis	81	4	8	12	127	3
Robert Dome	30	5	2	7	12	- 1
Peter Ferraro	29	3	4	7	12	- 2
Chris Ferraro	46	3	4	7	43	- 2
Tyler Wright	82	3	4	7	112	- 3
Ian Moran	37	1	6	7	19	0
Chris Tamer	79	0	7	7	181	4
Neil Wilkinson	34	2	4	6	24	0
Garry Valk	39	2	1	3	33	- 3
Tuomas Gronman	22	1	2	3	25	3
Tom Barrasso	63	0	2	2	14	0
Greg Johnson	5	1	0	1	2	0
Sean Pronger	5	1	0	1	2	- 1
Peter Skudra	17	0	1	1	2	0
Ken Wregget	15	0	0	0	6	0
Sven Butenschon	8	0	0	0	6	- 1

	GP	MINS	GA	SH	AVG	W	L	T
Peter Skudra	17	851	26	0	1.83	6	4	3
Tom Barrasso	63	3542	122	7	2.07	31	14	13
Ken Wregget	15	611	28	0	2.75	3	6	2
	82	5022	188	7	2.25	40	24	18

After missing nearly all of the 1996–97 season, Tom Barrasso returned with fire in his eyes.

1998–99

Record: 38–30–14
Points: 90
Goals For: 242
Goals Against: 225
Finish: Third (Atlantic)
Coach: Kevin Constantine
General Manager: Craig Patrick

With financial considerations looming larger than ever, the cash-strapped Penguins suffered their first big loss through free agency. Thirty-five-year-old Ron Francis, the club's heart and soul, signed with the Carolina Hurricanes. Although the future Hall of Famer preferred to remain in Pittsburgh, Craig Patrick simply couldn't make him a competitive offer.

Francis' departure affected the club in many ways. In addition to his wonderfully consistent two-way play, he was a strong, dignified force in the locker room. The mantle of leadership would be turned over to Jaromir Jagr, the team's reigning superstar. Whether No. 68 was ready to assume the role was another story.

He certainly looked the part when he reported to training camp. Gone were the long, boyish locks that had been as much a part of his persona as highlight-reel goals. Indeed, he seemed more focused and serious than ever before.

Patrick was able to swing one major deal over the off-season, sending Ken Wregget and Dave Roche to the Flames for forwards German Titov and Todd Hlushko.

On paper, the trade looked like a good one. Wregget had served the Pens extremely well, but the reemergence of Barrasso made him expendable. Titov was a highly skilled and underrated performer who could play wing or center.

In a major development, the Penguins joined the Atlantic Division, which included old Patrick Division rivals such as the Devils, Rangers, Flyers, and Islanders. The move would certainly help boost attendance: the Pens never developed the same sense of rivalry with their Northeast Division brethren. But it also represented a step up in competition.

Unlike the previous season when the Penguins led their division virtually from start to finish, the 1998–99 campaign was a dogfight. The Devils pulled away from the pack early, leaving the Pens to slug it out with the Flyers for second place.

Patrick made a bold move to add some star power in November when he dispatched holdout Petr Nedved to the Rangers for enigmatic Alexei Kovalev.

The trade energized the team. The addition of Kovalev added a level of volatility to the attack that had been stripped away through Mario Lemieux's retirement and the departure of Francis. Titov, Robert Lang, and rookie center Jan

A disappointment with the Rangers, Alexei Kovalev blossomed into a star in Pittsburgh.

Hrdina provided the scoring depth that was lacking the previous year. In his first season as captain, Jagr ran away with the scoring title. He was complimented by Straka, who suddenly burst into prominence as one of the league's most dangerous players.

The only veteran to struggle was Stu Barnes, a streaky scorer who turned ice cold after a red-hot start. Patrick dispatched him to Buffalo at the trade deadline for hyper-aggressive winger Matthew Barnaby.

Although the Penguins dipped to a third-place finish they were clearly improved, particularly up front. Jagr made a mockery of the scoring race by capturing his second straight Art Ross Trophy on the strength of a 44-goal, 127-point campaign.

If Jagr's scintillating performance came as no great surprise, Martin Straka's certainly did. He tallied 35 goals and 48 assists, an incredible achievement for a player who was on the junk pile just two years earlier.

Unquestionably the team's most courageous performer was Darius Kasparaitis. Playing with torn knee ligaments sustained during a preseason contest, the gritty defenseman refused to compromise his marauding style, even though one misstep could have led to a career-threatening injury.

Yet once more, the team's tepid finances undermined its accomplishments on the ice. From his roost in the club's front office Roger Marino continued to project gloom and doom. No longer merely hinting at selling the team, he was actively seeking a buyer. He made it clear that keeping the Penguins in Pittsburgh was of little or no concern.

	GP	G	A	PTS	PM	+/-
Jaromir Jagr	81	44	83	127	66	17
Martin Straka	80	35	48	83	26	12
German Titov	72	11	45	56	34	18
Alexei Kovalev	63	20	26	46	37	8
Robert Lang	72	21	23	44	24	- 10
Kip Miller	77	19	23	42	22	1
Jan Hrdina	82	13	29	42	40	- 2
Kevin Hatcher	66	11	27	38	24	11
Stu Barnes	64	20	12	32	20	- 12
Rob Brown	58	13	11	24	16	- 15
Brad Werenka	81	6	18	24	93	17
Jiri Slegr	63	3	20	23	86	13
Aleksey Morozov	67	9	10	19	14	5
Dan Kesa	67	2	8	10	27	- 9
Bobby Dollas	70	2	8	10	60	- 3
Ian Moran	62	4	5	9	37	1
Maxim Galanov	51	4	3	7	14	- 8
Jeff Serowik	26	0	6	6	16	- 4
Darius Kasparaitis	48	1	4	5	70	12
Matthew Barnaby	18	2	2	4	34	- 10
Tom Barrasso	43	0	3	3	20	0
Martin Sonnenberg	44	1	1	2	19	- 2
Patrick Lebeau	8	1	0	1	2	- 2
Greg Andrusak	7	0	1	1	4	4
Victor Ignatjev	11	0	1	1	6	- 3
Sean Pronger	2	0	0	0	0	0
Harry York	2	0	0	0	0	0
Ryan Savoia	3	0	0	0	0	- 1
Pavel Skrbek	4	0	0	0	2	2
Brian Bonin	5	0	0	0	0	- 2
Chris Tamer	11	0	0	0	32	- 2
Jean-Sebastien Aubin	17	0	0	0	0	0
Sven Butenschon	17	0	0	0	6	- 7
Neil Wilkinson	24	0	0	0	22	- 2
Peter Skudra	37	0	0	0	2	0
Tyler Wright	61	0	0	0	90	- 2

	GP	MINS	GA	SH	AVG	W	L	T
Jean-Sebastien Aubin	17	756	28	2	2.22	4	3	6
Tom Barrasso	43	2306	98	4	2.55	19	16	3
Peter Skudra	37	1914	89	3	2.79	15	11	5
	82	5011	225	9	2.69	38	30	14

1999–2000

Record: 37–31–8–6
Points: 88
Goals For: 241
Goals Against: 236
Finish: Third (Atlantic)
Coach: Kevin Constantine–Herb Brooks
General Manager: Craig Patrick

As the Penguins' financial fortunes sank to rock bottom, Mario Lemieux grew increasing perplexed. Shortly after filing for bankruptcy Roger Marino abruptly halted payments on the $32 million of deferred compensation owed to the former Pens luminary, further cementing his status among local hockey fans as Public Enemy No. 1. Mario had little choice but to file a lawsuit against his former employer.

While Marino waged a pitched battle to wrench control from Howard Baldwin, Lemieux began to gather a group of investors to help him buy the team. When Marino submitted a reorganization plan to the bankruptcy court, Lemieux countered with a plan of his own.

Mario had truly been a miracle worker as a player; what he accomplished as a prospective buyer was sheer wizardry. With the blessing of the NHL Board of Governors, ownership of the Penguins was officially turned over to Lemieux on September 3. For the second time in 15 years Mario had almost single-handedly rescued the franchise from ruin.

With a friendly face in the owner's box, the focus shifted to the team's on-ice prospects. Fresh from their strong showing the previous spring, the Penguins' outlook appeared rosy. The club had adapted well to Kevin Constantine's disciplined system. Despite significant losses to retirement and free agency, the Pens still possessed two strong forward lines.

It was a quiet off-season for Craig Patrick, who made relatively few moves. In his one significant trade he shipped high-priced Kevin Hatcher to the Rangers for Peter Popovic, the giant Swedish defenseman who had stymied Jaromir Jagr in the 1998 playoffs.

With the addition of Popovic, the team boasted no fewer than 14 European-born players, including six Czechs, three Russians, two Swedes, a Lithuanian, a Slovak, and a Latvian. Resembling a meeting of the United Nations, the Penguins had such a strong international flavor that they soon became known as "the Euro-Pens."

To the surprise of many, the Penguins did not roll out of the starting gate like a well-oiled machine. In fact, the 1999–2000 model resembled more of a sputtering, coughing wreck. Twenty-nine games into the season, the team was mired in last place and showing few signs of improvement.

"Some players were kind of not having fun anymore," Darius Kasparaitis explained. "Hockey is all about working hard and having fun."

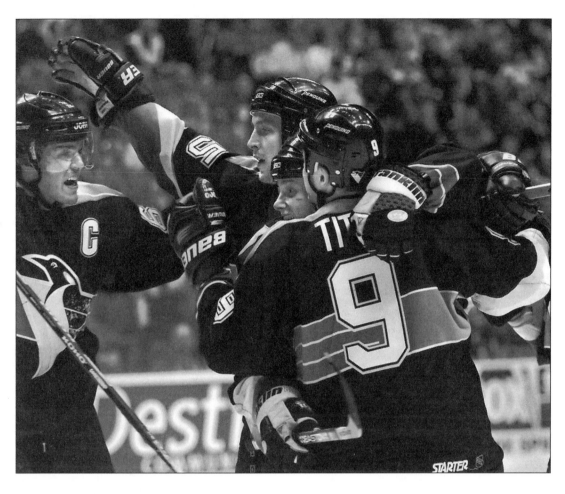

"Euro-Pens" Jaromir Jagr (left), Martin Straka, and German Titov celebrate a goal with Brad Werenka (5).

Craig Patrick had seen enough. On December 9, with the season in danger of slipping away, he dismissed Constantine and installed Herb Brooks as interim coach.

"We agree on a lot of philosophies, and I believe [Brooks] is a better fit for what we have on the ice," Patrick said. "I believe he can get the best out of what we have."

The patron saint of United States hockey, Brooks was like a breath of fresh air. No fan of systematic hockey, he immediately loosened the reins that had been cinched so tightly under Constantine.

"The idea is to give the game to the players," Brooks said. "Not to suffocate them. Not to treat them like a bunch of robots and say 'You do this and you do this.' We want to try and provide an environment that brings out their talents."

Brooks opened the door for players who had mysteriously fallen from grace with the former coach. He recalled feisty Tyler Wright from Wilkes-Barre and gave him a prominent role. Matthew Barnaby, who likewise was relegated to the shadows under Constantine, joined Wright and Aleksey Morozov on what proved to be a very effective third line.

While the Penguins' turnaround under Brooks was gradual, it was obvious the team enjoyed playing for him. Soon they were climbing toward a playoff berth. In February, Patrick made a surprise addition to the coaching staff by adding Czech legend Ivan Hlinka—the heir apparent to succeed Brooks—to an already crowded bench. Unsure at times of who was running the ship, the club briefly floundered. After a short adjustment period, Brooks took charge and the Pens settled down once more.

Patrick did some of his finest work at the trade deadline, including a couple of deals that bordered on grand larceny. First, he pirated veteran defenseman Bob Boughner away from Nashville for Pavel Skrbek, a former high draft pick who had proven to be more suspect than prospect. Although average in size and ordinary with his dukes, Boughner was a tough customer who kept opponents on their toes and the front of the net clear.

In his second steal of a deal, he duped Ottawa GM Marshall Johnston into accepting Tom Barrasso, whose best days were clearly behind him, in exchange for goaltender Ron Tugnutt and defenseman Janne Laukkanen.

The antithesis of the prickly Barrasso, Tugnutt was a seasoned pro and all-around good guy who served as a mentor for the team's younger goaltenders. A steady veteran defender who played with an edge, Laukkanen was regarded as a poor man's Ulf Samuelsson.

With the newcomers filling key roles, the Pens closed with a rush to grab third place in the Atlantic Division.

	GP	G	A	PTS	PM	+/-
Jaromir Jagr	63	42	54	96	50	25
Alexei Kovalev	82	26	40	66	94	- 3
Robert Lang	78	23	42	65	14	- 9
Martin Straka	71	20	39	59	26	24
Jan Hrdina	70	13	33	46	43	13
German Titov	63	17	25	42	34	- 3
Aleksey Morozov	68	12	19	31	14	12
Jiri Slegr	74	11	20	31	82	20
Matthew Barnaby	64	12	12	24	197	3
Rob Brown	50	10	13	23	10	- 13
Tyler Wright	50	12	10	22	45	4
Michal Rozsival	75	4	17	21	48	11
Kip Miller	44	4	15	19	10	- 1
Darius Kasparaitis	73	3	12	15	146	- 12
Hans Jonsson	68	3	11	14	12	- 5
Pat Falloon	30	4	9	13	10	- 2
Ian Moran	73	4	8	12	28	- 10
Brad Werenka	61	3	8	11	69	15
Josef Beranek	13	4	4	8	18	- 6
Janne Laukkanen	11	1	7	8	12	3
Robert Dome	22	2	5	7	0	1
Andrew Ference	30	2	4	6	20	3
Tom Chorske	33	1	5	6	2	- 2
Peter Popovic	54	1	5	6	30	- 8
Steven Leach	56	2	3	5	24	- 11
John Slaney	29	1	4	5	10	- 10
Martin Sonnenberg	14	1	2	3	0	0
Dan Trebil	3	1	0	1	0	2
Rene Corbet	4	1	0	1	0	- 4
Bob Boughner	11	1	0	1	69	2
Jean-Sebastien Aubin	51	0	1	1	2	0
Sven Butenschon	3	0	0	0	0	3
Ron Tugnutt	7	0	0	0	0	0
Tom Barrasso	18	0	0	0	6	0
Peter Skudra	20	0	0	0	0	0
Dennis Bonvie	28	0	0	0	80	- 2

	GP	MINS	GA	SH	AVG	W	L	OT
Ron Tugnutt	7	374	15	0	2.41	4	2	0
Jean-Sebastien Aubin	51	2789	120	2	2.58	23	21	3
Peter Skudra	20	922	48	1	3.12	5	7	3
Tom Barrasso	18	870	46	1	3.17	5	7	2
	82	4984	236	4	2.84	37	37	8

2000–01

Record: 42–28–9–3
Points: 96
Goals For: 281
Goals Against: 256
Finish: Third (Atlantic)
Coach: Ivan Hlinka
General Manager: Craig Patrick

Craig Patrick spent the early part of the summer in a quandary. A few months earlier he'd hired Ivan Hlinka with the understanding that the Czech coaching legend would succeed interim coach Herb Brooks. However, Brooks had done a splendid job of steering the Pens to a playoff berth. He was so beloved and respected by the players that Patrick hoped he would stay on as coach.

In many ways Brooks was like the second coming of Bob Johnson. Not only was he wise as an owl and wholly capable, he and Patrick worked well together and shared a mutual esteem. They fit together hand in glove.

But Brooks also was a doting grandfather. Weary of life on the road, the 63-year-old coach wanted to spend more time at home in suburban Minneapolis. He decided to return to his role as scout, which paved the way for Patrick to promote Hlinka.

It was a grand and noble experiment to say the least, and not one without merit. The team's roster was packed with players from the Czech Republic, where Hlinka was revered as a hockey god. A star center during his playing days, he was among the first wave of foreign-born skaters to successfully make the transition to the NHL.

After returning to his homeland, Hlinka became the coach of the Czech National Team. In his crowning achievement, he led his countrymen to a stunning gold-medal triumph in the 1998 Olympics, an accomplishment that brought him universal acclaim.

While the veteran Czech skipper possessed a keen hockey mind, there was a fly in the ointment: Hlinka spoke only halting English. He often had to take a moment to translate his thoughts before barking out instructions.

For Patrick, it was the first in a series of questionable hires that would contribute to his eventual downfall.

With the notable exception of free agent Ron Tugnutt, who signed a lucrative deal with the expansion Columbus Blue Jackets, the Penguins remained relatively intact over the summer. They entered the season with a star-studded lineup that included four-time scoring champion Jaromir Jagr and emerging stars Alexei Kovalev, Martin Straka, and Robert Lang. Although the defensive corps featured no such luminaries, Jiri Slegr, Janne Laukkanen, and Darius Kasparaitis spearheaded a quietly effective group.

In November hockey fans the world over were given a special treat when Mario Lemieux laced on his skates to

Owner Mario Lemieux is all smiles as he celebrates a goal with Martin Straka and Michal Rozsival.

film a segment of ESPN's *Stars on Ice* with Jaromir Jagr. The dynamic duo took great delight in torturing goaltender-turned-announcer Darren Pang on a series of two-on-nones and breakaways.

It paled in comparison to the surprise that was in store. On December 8, Lemieux announced that he would return to the ice as an active player. Training for weeks under the guidance of former teammate Jay Caufield, he now packed 230 pounds of muscle onto his newly sculpted 6'4" frame.

Mario made his triumphant return two days after Christmas before a standing-room-only crowd at the Mellon Arena. In an emotionally charged pregame ceremony Lemieux received a thunderous two-minute ovation. Then, as if he had a special gift for making time stand still, Mario assisted on a goal by Jagr just 33 seconds into the game. For the evening, the 35-year-old wonder collected a goal and two assists to pace a 5–0 rout of Toronto.

"I'm not sure I can describe what we just watched," offered an elated Craig Patrick.

"I didn't know what was going to happen," Jagr added. "But I didn't expect anything like that."

Prior to Lemieux's return, the Pens were hovering in third place in the Atlantic Division, a handful of games above the .500 mark. With Mario in the lineup the club suddenly had the look of a Stanley Cup contender. The top line of Lemieux, Jagr, and Jan Hrdina was clicking on all cylinders, and the second unit of Kovalev, Straka, and Lang had developed into arguably the most lethal combination in the league.

With the skill players in place, Patrick set about adding another element to the team—intimidation. At the urging of Lemieux, the Pens toughened up by acquiring gargantuan 6'8" winger Steve McKenna. It was only the beginning

of the team's muscle-building spree. In rapid-fire succession Patrick swung deals that netted a trio of burly 230-pounders, including ex-Pen Kevin Stevens, center Wayne Primeau, and Polish hammer Krzysztof Oliwa.

However, the biggest addition came not in the form of a brawny forward but of a "Moose." The Pens had received only so-so netminding from the tandem of Jean-Sebastien Aubin and veteran Garth Snow. Patrick remedied the situation by acquiring Johan Hedberg, who was toiling for the Manitoba Moose in the AHL.

The ultra-competitive Hedberg quickly became the darling of the fans. The team rallied around him, posting an impressive 7–1–1 mark down the homestretch with the rookie in goal.

It was a thrilling season, highlighted by Mario's remarkable comeback. No. 66 amassed an amazing 35 goals and 76 points in just 43 games, while Kovalev (44 goals), Straka (95 points), and Lang (32 goals) emerged as bona fide stars.

The most prominent player of all was conspicuously absent from the honor roll. Although Jaromir Jagr had breezed to his fourth straight scoring title, he was a changed man—and not for the better. Fueled in part by uncertainty over his future with the team and off-ice problems, he had become a morose and sullen presence in the locker room.

Mario admitted to being shocked by his old protégé's attitude. He tried his best to buoy Jagr's sagging spirits, to no avail. The sheer joy that had once been a hallmark of No. 68's play had all but evaporated.

Following the playoffs the situation worsened. During a farewell meeting at the club's training facility, Jagr took Craig Patrick aside.

"What's going on with me?" he asked.

When the Penguins GM began to explain that he needed to meet with the owners to discuss the possibility of a contract extension, Jagr cut him off.

"No, no, you don't understand," Jagr said. "I don't want to be here."

	GP	G	A	PTS	PM	+/-
Jaromir Jagr	81	52	69	121	42	19
Alexei Kovalev	79	44	51	95	96	12
Martin Straka	82	27	68	95	38	19
Robert Lang	82	32	48	80	28	20
Mario Lemieux	43	35	41	76	18	15
Jan Hrdina	78	15	28	43	48	19
Josef Beranek	70	9	14	23	43	- 7
Kevin Stevens	32	8	15	23	55	- 4
Hans Jonsson	58	4	18	22	22	11
Janne Laukkanen	50	3	17	20	34	9
Aleksey Morozov	66	5	14	19	6	- 8
Darius Kasparaitis	77	3	16	19	111	11
Rene Corbet	43	8	9	17	57	- 3
Jiri Slegr	42	5	10	15	60	- 9
Andrew Ference	36	4	11	15	28	6
Milan Kraft	42	7	7	14	8	- 6
Jeff Norton	32	2	10	12	20	8
Kip Miller	33	3	8	11	6	0
Roman Simicek	29	3	6	9	30	- 5
Toby Petersen	12	2	6	8	4	3
Ian Moran	40	3	4	7	28	5
Wayne Primeau	28	1	6	7	54	0
Michal Rozsival	30	1	4	5	26	3
Marc Bergevin	36	1	4	5	26	5
Matthew Barnaby	47	1	4	5	168	- 7
Bob Boughner	58	1	3	4	147	18
Krzysztof Oliwa	26	1	2	3	131	- 4
Billy Tibbetts	29	1	2	3	79	- 2
Frantisek Kucera	7	0	2	2	0	- 2
Josef Melichar	18	0	2	2	21	- 5
Sven Butenschon	5	0	1	1	2	1
Jean-Sebastien Aubin	36	0	1	1	4	0
Greg Crozier	1	0	0	0	0	0
Dennis Bonvie	3	0	0	0	0	- 1
Bobby Dollas	5	0	0	0	4	0
Rich Parent	7	0	0	0	0	0
Johan Hedberg	9	0	0	0	0	0
Dan LaCouture	11	0	0	0	14	0
Dan Trebil	16	0	0	0	7	- 1
Steve McKenna	34	0	0	0	100	- 4
Garth Snow	35	0	0	0	8	0

	GP	MINS	GA	SH	AVG	W	L	OT
Johan Hedberg	9	545	24	0	2.64	7	1	1
Garth Snow	35	2032	101	3	2.98	14	15	4
Rich Parent	7	332	17	0	3.07	1	1	3
Jean-Sebastien Aubin	36	2050	107	0	3.13	20	14	1
	82	4978	256	3	3.09	42	31	9

2001–02

Record: 28–41–8–5
Points: 69
Goals For: 198
Goals Against: 249
Finish: Fifth (Atlantic)
Coach: Ivan Hlinka–Rick Kehoe
General Manager: Craig Patrick

Heading into the off-season, one fact was abundantly clear. Jaromir Jagr, the second-greatest player ever to don the black and gold, had played his last game in a Penguins uniform. Entering the final two years of his contract, Jagr was due for a hefty raise. Combined with the fact that his act had finally worn thin, there was no turning back.

Craig Patrick was consumed over the early part of the summer with finding a taker for the superstar. While trading Jagr would provide Patrick with a golden opportunity to restock the team with an infusion of young talent, finding a suitor would be a challenge. Only a handful of clubs—including Detroit, Toronto, Philadelphia, and the Rangers—had deep enough pockets to afford him.

By the early part of July the rumor mill was running full tilt, with New York or Toronto pegged as the most likely destinations. However, when the trade was finally announced on July 11, it was the Washington Capitals who acquired Jagr and not the Rangers or the Maple Leafs.

The return for the five-time scoring champion was hardly overwhelming. In exchange for one of the greatest offensive talents in the history of the game, the Pens received three raw prospects—defenseman Ross Lupaschuk and forwards Kris Beech and Michal Sivek.

While Patrick seemed genuinely relieved that the deal was finally done, the rest of the hockey world expressed stunned disbelief. Stung by the criticism, he staunchly defended the deal.

"We got great value in return," he said. "Time will show us that, but I can't convince people of that right now. All three of these guys are going to be big contributors here for a long time."

Time would prove the critics right. Beech developed into a serviceable player, but only after returning to the Capitals a few years down the road. Lupaschuk and Sivek were flops. Patrick had basically given Jagr away.

The trade also signaled a dramatic downturn in Patrick's overall performance. Long regarded as one of the top executives in hockey, he had excelled when making deals from a position of strength. Shackled by financial constraints and the team's spotty record in drafting and player development, he now seemed to be operating from behind the eight ball.

The summer of 2001 continued to sour on the embattled general manager. In addition to the considerable fallout over the Jagr trade, he drew heat from the Penguins faithful for allowing tough-as-nails defenseman Bob Boughner to escape through free agency.

Enigmatic Aleksey Morozov beats Flyers goalie Brian Boucher, while John LeClair (10) and Eric Desjardins (37) look on.

To plug the gap, Patrick signed hulking Mike Wilson to a two-year pact. When he entered the league, the 6'6", 229-pound rearguard was favorably compared to Chris Pronger, which was high praise indeed. Unfortunately, the comparison would prove totally unwarranted. Wilson slogged through his 21 games with the team as if he was skating in mud.

Patrick also had problems with Ivan Hlinka. Although the venerable Czech skipper had led the Penguins to the Eastern Conference Finals, they were a talent-laden team that required very little coaching. With Jagr gone, the players would need more instruction and leadership from their coach.

But Hlinka still wasn't fluent enough in English to communicate effectively with the team—particularly during the heat of battle. Patrick urged him to enroll in English classes over the off-season. Apparently something was lost in the translation, because Hlinka opted only to listen to some language tapes.

The pall that hung over the organization extended into the regular season as the Pens belly flopped to an ugly 0–4 start. With the team playing progressively worse with each passing game, Patrick pulled the plug on "l'faire Hlinka."

After initially offering the job to old friend Herb Brooks, Patrick handed the reins to long-time assistant coach Rick Kehoe. While Kehoe wasn't a great deal more demonstrative than the poker-faced Hlinka, at least he spoke the language.

The Penguins began a gradual turnaround, registering a 4–2–1 mark in Kehoe's first seven games at the helm. But the club's problems were only beginning. Superstars Alexei Kovalev (knee), Mario Lemieux (hip), and Martin Straka (broken leg) went down in rapid-fire succession, ripping the offensive guts from the team. Reeling from the injuries, the Pens pressed green youngsters Beech, Milan Kraft, and Toby Petersen into the breach.

As the trade deadline approached the Penguins were well out of range of a playoff spot. For the first time in more than a decade they would be sellers rather than buyers. Robert Lang and hard-hitting Darius Kasparaitis would soon be eligible for free agency. They were high on every contender's wish list.

Despite strong interest from several clubs Patrick failed to move the high-scoring Lang, who was sidelined with an injury. He had better luck with "Kaspar," shipping the spirited blue-liner to the defending-Cup-champion Colorado Avalanche for whirling-dervish winger Ville Nieminen and rugged defenseman Rick Berry.

In other minor deals Patrick plucked checkers Shean Donovan and Jeff Toms off the waiver wire and acquired solid citizens Kent Manderville and Jamie Pushor.

While Patrick felt he had addressed the team's greatest weakness—a lack of veteran depth on the third and fourth lines—the new contingent of foot soldiers failed to mask an ever-shrinking pool of elite talent. The Pens went a miserable 0–9–1 down the homestretch to miss the playoffs for the first time in 12 years.

	GP	G	A	PTS	PM	+/-
Alexei Kovalev	67	32	44	76	80	2
Jan Hrdina	79	24	33	57	50	- 7
Robert Lang	62	18	32	50	16	9
Aleksey Morozov	72	20	29	49	16	- 7
Mario Lemieux	24	6	25	31	14	0
Randy Robitaille	40	10	20	30	16	- 14
Michal Rozsival	79	9	20	29	47	- 6
Stephane Richer	58	13	12	25	14	- 8
Kris Beech	79	10	15	25	45	- 25
Toby Petersen	79	8	10	18	4	- 15
Dan LaCouture	82	6	11	17	71	- 19
Milan Kraft	68	8	8	16	16	- 9
Darius Kasparaitis	69	2	12	14	123	- 1
Janne Laukkanen	47	6	7	13	28	- 18
Andrew Ference	75	4	7	11	73	- 12
Wayne Primeau	33	3	7	10	18	- 1
Ian Moran	64	2	8	10	54	- 11
Martin Straka	13	5	4	9	0	3
Hans Jonsson	53	2	5	7	22	- 12
Billy Tibbetts	33	1	5	6	109	- 13
Kevin Stevens	32	1	4	5	25	- 9
John Jakopin	19	0	4	4	42	2
Shean Donovan	13	2	1	3	4	- 5
Jeff Toms	14	2	1	3	4	- 5
Tom Kostopoulos	11	1	2	3	9	- 1
Ville Nieminen	13	1	2	3	8	- 2
Josef Melichar	60	0	3	3	68	- 1
Mike Wilson	21	1	1	2	17	- 12
Rick Berry	13	0	2	2	21	- 4
Jamie Pushor	15	0	2	2	30	- 3
Krzysztof Oliwa	57	0	2	2	150	- 5
Kent Manderville	4	1	0	1	4	1
Shane Endicott	4	0	1	1	4	- 1
Eric Meloche	23	0	1	1	8	- 7
Johan Hedberg	66	0	1	1	22	0
Jean-Sebastien Aubin	21	0	0	0	0	0

	GP	MINS	GA	SH	AVG	W	L	OT
Johan Hedberg	66	3877	178	6	2.75	25	34	7
Jean-Sebastien Aubin	21	1094	65	0	3.56	3	12	1
	82	4994	249	6	2.99	28	46	8

2002–03

Record: 27–44–6–5
Points: 65
Goals For: 189
Goals Against: 255
Finish: Fifth (Atlantic)
Coach: Rick Kehoe
General Manager: Craig Patrick

After reaching the Eastern Conference Finals in 2001, the team's failure to qualify for postseason play sent shock waves through the organization. Stung by mounting criticism over the club's stunning collapse, Craig Patrick vowed that the Pens would return to the playoffs in short order.

He was counting heavily on veterans Mario Lemieux and Martin Straka to lead the team back to the promised land. Their return took on added significance when the club hemorrhaged yet another star—Robert Lang—to free agency.

While the Pens failed to land any big-name free agents, they did add some intriguing ones. Alexandre Daigle, a speedy former No. 1 pick of Ottawa, was invited to training camp on a tryout basis.

Other additions included popular enforcer Steve McKenna and low-profile free agent Marc Bergevin. Patrick also picked up 28-year-old Swedish defenseman Dick Tarnstrom. He would prove to be a most pleasant surprise.

Echoing the sentiments of Craig Patrick, the players insisted that the team's dismal performance in 2001–02 had been a fluke. Yet in the season opener the Pens resembled anything but contenders as they were walloped by the powerful Maple Leafs 6–0.

Coach Rick Kehoe wasted little time in shuffling the deck. He inserted Tarnstrom and Bergevin on defense in

Although he scored 91 points, Mario Lemieux couldn't lead the undermanned Penguins to a playoff spot in 2002–03.

place of Hans Jonsson and Janne Laukkanen, who were atrocious in the opening-game loss. In a dramatic turnaround, the Penguins flattened the Rangers 6–0 as Aleksey Morozov tallied four points. Two nights later the Pens avenged their opening-night drubbing at the hands of Toronto by defeating the Maple Leafs.

The Penguins confounded the experts through the early going, many of whom had picked them to finish out of the money. Fans who glanced at the NHL scoring leaders saw a familiar name at the top of the list—Mario Lemieux. Incredibly, old No. 66 not only played in all but one of the team's first 22 games, but he racked up 11 goals and 34 assists in the process. Linemates Morozov and Alexei Kovalev joined their captain among the league's elite scorers. By late November the club was perched atop the Atlantic Division.

It would prove to be the high-water mark for a team in transition. The piping-hot power play cooled when Tarnstrom suffered a broken foot. Morozov's breakout season ended with a wrist injury. The Penguins plummeted back to earth and stumbled through a 10-game winless streak.

Despite their dismal showing, they remained within striking distance of a playoff spot until February 10, when Patrick pulled the trigger on perhaps the most shocking trade in team history. In a huge eight-player swap he peddled the supremely gifted Kovalev, gritty Dan LaCouture, and spare defensemen Laukkanen and Mike Wilson to the Rangers for a cast of unknowns, including wingers Rico Fata and Mikael Samuelsson and defensemen Joel Bouchard and Richard Lintner.

Initially, Patrick tried to put a positive spin on the trade. "This is the best deal we can make for what we think we need in our lineup right now to make the playoffs," he said. "Based on that, we believe we made a deal that will enable us to make the playoffs and have a good run."

However, it was painfully clear that the move was little more than a salary dump. Indeed, Rangers GM Glen Sather had relieved the Penguins of two high-priced albatrosses by accepting the injury-prone Laukkanen and the enormously disappointing Wilson, perhaps the biggest free-agent bust in team history.

The talent-challenged Pens put on a brave front and managed to split their next six contests. But on February 23, the club slipped into its second long winless streak of the season—this one spanning 16 games.

With all hopes of a turnaround dashed, Patrick gutted the team at the trade deadline. Predictably, the losses continued to mount. However, on March 26, the club gained a measure of revenge by snuffing out the Rangers' flickering playoff hopes with a rousing 3–1 victory at Madison Square Garden.

Amid the wreckage, there were few bright spots. Lemieux made yet another astonishing comeback to tally 91 points. But at 37 years of age "Super Mario" could no longer carry the team on his broad shoulders.

Deeply frustrated by the team's dismal performance, Mario made it clear that the days of the country-club atmosphere that permeated the organization were over.

He ushered in a new era of accountability and insisted that everyone—including long-time GM Craig Patrick—would be reevaluated.

	GP	G	A	PTS	PM	+/-
Mario Lemieux	67	28	63	91	43	-25
Alexei Kovalev	54	27	37	64	50	-11
Martin Straka	60	18	28	46	12	-18
Dick Tarnstrom	61	7	34	41	50	-11
Jan Hrdina	57	14	25	39	34	1
Aleksey Morozov	27	9	16	25	16	-3
Ville Nieminen	75	9	12	21	93	-25
Randy Robitaille	41	5	12	17	8	5
Wayne Primeau	70	5	11	16	55	-30
Rico Fata	27	5	8	13	10	-6
Milan Kraft	31	7	5	12	10	-8
Tomas Surovy	26	4	7	11	10	0
Steve McKenna	79	9	1	10	128	-18
Michal Rozsival	53	4	6	10	40	-5
Shean Donovan	52	4	5	9	30	-6
Alexandre Daigle	33	4	3	7	8	-10
Marc Bergevin	69	2	5	7	36	-9
Kent Manderville	82	2	5	7	46	-22
Janne Laukkanen	17	1	6	7	8	-3
Ian Moran	70	0	7	7	46	-17
Eric Meloche	13	5	1	6	4	-2
Michal Sivek	38	3	3	6	14	-5
Guillaume Lefebvre	12	2	4	6	0	1
Mathias Johansson	12	1	5	6	4	1
Richard Lintner	19	3	2	5	10	-9
Hans Jonsson	63	1	4	5	36	-23
Jamie Pushor	76	3	1	4	76	-28
Dan LaCouture	44	2	2	4	72	-8
Andrew Ference	22	1	3	4	36	-16
Brian Holzinger	9	1	2	3	6	-6
Dan Focht	12	0	3	3	19	-7
Mikael Samuelsson	22	2	0	2	8	-21
Shawn Heins	27	1	1	2	33	-2
Johan Hedberg	41	0	2	2	18	0
Vladimir Vujtek	5	0	1	1	0	-4
Joel Bouchard	7	0	1	1	0	-6
Tom Kostopoulos	8	0	1	1	0	-4
Kris Beech	12	0	1	1	6	-3
Jean-Sebastien Aubin	21	0	1	1	2	0
Konstantin Koltsov	2	0	0	0	0	-2
Ramzi Abid	3	0	0	0	2	-5
Ross Lupaschuk	3	0	0	0	4	-3
Brooks Orpik	6	0	0	0	2	-5
Josef Melichar	8	0	0	0	2	-2
Sebastien Caron	24	0	0	0	6	0

	GP	MINS	GA	SH	AVG	W	L	OT
Sebastien Caron	24	1408	62	2	2.64	7	14	2
Jean-Sebastien Aubin	21	1132	59	1	3.13	6	13	0
Johan Hedberg	41	2410	126	1	3.14	14	22	4
	82	4972	255	4	3.08	27	49	6

2003–04

Record: 23–47–8–4
Points: 58
Goals For: 190
Goals Against: 303
Finish: Fifth (Atlantic)
Coach: Ed Olczyk
General Manager: Craig Patrick

Charles Dickens opened his classic novel, *A Tale of Two Cities*, with the passage, "It was the best of times, it was the worst of times." Indeed, the 2003–04 campaign could be summed up as a tale of two seasons.

With a lineup stripped of high-priced talent, Craig Patrick began to rebuild. On draft day he boldly swapped positions with Florida and grabbed 18-year-old goaltending phenom Marc-Andre Fleury. However, in an equally surprising move, he gave only cursory consideration to a number of experienced coaches—including highly regarded Larry Robinson—before replacing Rick Kehoe with former NHL star turned broadcaster Eddie Olczyk.

The choice raised eyebrows and generated mounds of criticism. While extremely popular with players and fans alike, "Edzo" had never coached on a professional level.

In another significant change, Patrick relieved his brother Glenn of the coaching duties at Wilkes-Barre. He installed former Montreal coach Michel Therrien, who had squeezed the most out of a modestly talented Canadiens team. The fiery Therrien had earned a reputation for being an excellent teacher, something the Penguins desperately needed for their growing stable of young players.

With a mandate to keep the payroll as low as possible, Patrick was once again unable to pursue any upper-echelon free agents. Instead, he concentrated on reinforcing his young team with a veteran presence. He signed several battle-hardened veterans to bargain-basement contracts, including tough winger Kelly Buchberger, center Mike Eastwood, and onetime Penguins defenseman Drake Berehowsky.

Stocked with a cast of over-the-hill veterans and not-ready-for-prime-time players, most experts picked the "X Generation" Penguins to finish dead last. But the team had a few surprises in store. Playing Olczyk's hustling, defense-first style, the club pulled off a few shockers in the early going, including a stunning 4–3 victory over powerhouse Detroit and an equally impressive overtime conquest of Boston.

No. 1 pick Marc-Andre Fleury flashes his form against the Islanders.

Leading the way were the past and future of the franchise—38-year-old Mario Lemieux and 18-year-old Marc-Andre Fleury. While Mario served as an on-ice coach for his young charges, the unflappable rookie electrified the fans with his acrobatic style. He easily captured Rookie of the Month honors for October, while helping the team post a surprising 3–4–3 mark.

After peaking with back-to-back wins over Columbus and Buffalo in mid-December, the wheels fell off the wagon. Lemieux re-injured his balky hip and grudgingly submitted to season-ending surgery. Playing behind a woeful defensive corps, Fleury showed signs of mortality after his meteoric start. Concerned that his confidence might wilt, the team loaned him to Team Canada for the World Cup Tournament.

On the heels of an impressive 2–1 victory over the division-leading Flyers on January 12, the Pens descended into a nightmarish 18-game winless streak—one short of the league record. They narrowly avoided tying the dubious mark for futility on February 25 with a gritty, come-from-behind overtime victory against Phoenix.

The game winner was scored by newly acquired defenseman Ric Jackman. A former No. 1 pick of the Dallas Stars, Jackman was like the little girl with the curl. Possessing decent skills and a blistering shot, he could be very good offensively and just as bad on defense. He was mostly good with the Penguins, racking up 24 points in just 25 games.

So began the Penguins' second season. Buoyed by the brilliance of Jackman and the strong play of rookies Ryan Malone, Brooks Orpik, and Rob Scuderi, they began an abrupt and dramatic turnaround. Using the victory over the Coyotes as a springboard, the Pens became one of the hottest teams in the league. Patsies no more, they reeled off a remarkable 12–5–3 record down the homestretch, including stunning victories over elite teams Dallas and Toronto.

Despite their late-season surge the Penguins finished last in the overall standings, thus earning a 50-50 chance of landing the No. 1 position in the Entry Draft lottery. As fate would have it, a special player would be available. Alexander Ovechkin, a tall, bullish Russian winger of impeccable pedigree, was hailed as the most gifted performer to enter the league since Mario Lemieux.

The hockey gods failed to smile on the Penguins at the draft lottery. The woebegone Capitals earned the right to pick first and proceeded to snag the supremely gifted Ovechkin.

Fortunately, there was a second standout player available—a rangy 18-year-old Russian center named Evgeni Malkin. Many scouts considered Malkin to be a better all-around player than his more heralded countryman.

Although they lost out on the top pick, nothing could dim the luster of what the Penguins had accomplished through the most trying—and yet, perhaps most rewarding—of seasons. Taking their cue from Olczyk—who did a

Bucky

Perhaps the most heartwarming story of the difficult 2003–04 season involved 37-year-old Kelly Buchberger. A former Stanley Cup winner with the Oilers who had served as captain for several teams, he was brought to Pittsburgh to add leadership and toughness.

Although nearing the end of the line, "Bucky" set the tone by giving his all on every shift and dropping the gloves when necessary to defend a teammate. When he suffered the ignominy of going 58 games without tallying a point, he bore it with grace and dignity.

While Buchberger wasn't scoring, he was making a strong impression on his young teammates and the coaching staff. Appreciative of the veteran winger's sterling attitude and leadership, coach Ed Olczyk gave him extra duty in the final week, including a slot on the power play.

In the penultimate game of the season, lightning finally struck. Buchberger fired his first marker past startled Atlanta goalie Pasi Nurminen to set off a riotous celebration on the Penguins' bench.

Kelly Buchberger corrals a loose puck.

marvelous job of holding the team together—they never quit even through the bleakest of times.

While the Penguins had high hopes for better days to come, a large shadow loomed on the horizon. The collective bargaining agreement between the owners and players union was up for renewal, and the two sides were worlds apart. The impasse would threaten the very survival of the league.

	GP	G	A	PTS	PM	+/-
Dick Tarnstrom	80	16	36	52	38	- 37
Aleksey Morozov	75	16	34	50	24	- 24
Ryan Malone	81	22	21	43	64	- 23
Milan Kraft	66	19	21	40	18	- 22
Rico Fata	73	16	18	34	54	- 46
Konstantin Koltsov	82	9	20	29	30	- 30
Ric Jackman	25	7	17	24	14	- 5
Tomas Surovy	47	11	12	23	16	- 8
Tom Kostopoulos	60	9	13	22	67	- 14
Brian Holzinger	61	6	15	21	38	- 27
Drake Berehowsky	47	5	16	21	50	- 16
Mike Eastwood	82	4	15	19	40	- 18
Matt Bradley	82	7	9	16	65	- 27
Martin Strbak	44	3	11	14	38	- 11
Lasse Pirjeta	13	6	6	12	0	3
Martin Straka	22	4	8	12	16	- 16
Eric Meloche	25	3	7	10	20	- 6
Brooks Orpik	79	1	9	10	127	- 36
Mario Lemieux	10	1	8	9	6	- 2
Marc Bergevin	52	1	8	9	27	- 8
Josef Melichar	82	3	5	8	62	- 17
Patrick Boileau	16	3	4	7	8	- 16
Landon Wilson	19	5	1	6	31	0
Ramzi Abid	16	3	2	5	27	- 5
Jon Sim	15	2	3	5	6	- 4
Dan Focht	52	2	3	5	105	- 23
Kelly Buchberger	71	1	3	4	109	- 19
Matt Hussey	3	2	1	3	0	-1
Rob Scuderi	13	1	2	3	4	2
Steve McKenna	49	1	2	3	85	- 10
Matt Murley	18	1	1	2	14	- 6
Kris Beech	4	0	1	1	6	0
Martin Brochu	1	0	0	0	0	0
Reid Simpson	2	0	0	0	17	0
Nolan Baumgartner	5	0	0	0	2	-7
Steve Webb	5	0	0	0	2	- 3
Andy Chiodo	8	0	0	0	0	0
Marc-Andre Fleury	21	0	0	0	0	0
Jean-Sebastien Aubin	22	0	0	0	2	0
Sebastien Caron	40	0	0	0	6	0

	GP	MINS	GA	SH	AVG	W	L	OT
Martin Brochu	1	33	1	0	1.82	0	0	0
Jean-Sebastien Aubin	22	1067	53	1	2.98	7	9	0
Andy Chiodo	8	486	28	0	3.46	3	4	1
Marc-Andre Fleury	21	1154	70	1	3.64	4	14	2
Sebastien Caron	40	2213	138	1	3.74	9	24	5
	82	4984	303	3	3.65	23	51	8

2004–05

The 2004–05 season would prove to be one of enormous significance for the National Hockey League. Unfortunately, it wasn't due to any glorious on-ice achievements. Indeed, not a single NHL game would be contested.

Instead, a pitched battle was waged between the owners and the NHL Players' Association over the new collective bargaining agreement. With the full support of NHL commissioner Gary Bettman, the owners insisted that a salary cap be included as the centerpiece of the new agreement—a condition that was vehemently opposed by players' union boss Bob Goodenow.

The owners had done their homework. They commissioned consultant Arthur Levitt to conduct an independent study of the league's finances. The results were shocking. The study revealed that nearly two-thirds of the teams were hemorrhaging money, and that 75 percent of all revenues generated went to pay players' salaries.

This grim reality was especially true for small-market teams like the cash-strapped Penguins, who had been forced to divest themselves of high-priced talent for the sake of fiscal sanity. While the Pens' austerity program had kept the books balanced, it did little to help ice a competitive team. It was clear that changes needed to be made.

Goodenow and the players' union scoffed at the study, claiming the results were deliberately skewed in an obvious attempt to support the owners' position. The NHLPA dug in its heels, and the owners did likewise. With the battle lines drawn, Bettman announced that the players were locked out of training camp.

In December 2004, with nearly two months of the season gone and nary a puck dropped, Goodenow approached the NHL owners with a surprising concession. He offered a 24 percent rollback in players' salaries if the owners would agree to drop their demand for a salary cap.

As tempting as the offer was, the NHL high command held firm. They were willing to forfeit the entire season if need be. The salary cap, which had helped right the financial fortunes of the National Football League and the National Basketball Association, was a must.

In mid-February, with the hopes of salvaging even a portion of the season slipping away, the two sides met for a last-ditch round of talks. Again, the players' union gave ground, offering to agree to a salary cap of $49 million for each team. But the owners were playing hardball. They claimed that the NHLPA number was too high, and countered with a cap of $42.5 million. With neither side budging an inch, Bettman announced on February 16, 2005, that the season was officially cancelled.

The lockout affected each player in a unique and individual way. For greybeard veterans such as Mario Lemieux, it provided a chance to recuperate from old injuries. Established players such as Aleksey Morozov and team

MVP Dick Tarnstrom had little choice but to sign on with European teams.

The work stoppage had the most severe impact on youngsters like Ryan Malone and Brooks Orpik. Because they had "one-way" contacts to play in the NHL, they weren't eligible to skate for the Pens' farm team in Wilkes-Barre. For Malone (who suffered a fractured jaw while playing in Switzerland), and Orpik (who opted to finish his studies at Boston College), it would prove to be a lost season.

Still, players with two-way contracts benefited greatly from additional seasoning in the minors. The Baby Penguins got strong seasons from future hopefuls Colby Armstrong, Michel Ouellet, and Ryan Whitney. Although somewhat inconsistent, Marc-Andre Fleury posted 26 wins, five shutouts, and a 2.52 goals-against average.

Craig Patrick had not been idle either. Prior to the lockout, he inked veteran free agent Mark Recchi to a deal, bringing back one of the most popular players ever to don the black and gold.

On July 13, 2005, the longest strike in professional sports history mercifully came to an end. The NHLPA agreed to accept a collective bargaining agreement that included a 24 percent reduction in players' salaries and a $39-million salary cap. Once more, cries of "Game on!" would be heard in arenas throughout North America.

2005–06

Record: 22–46–8–6
Points: 58
Goals For: 244
Goals Against: 316
Finish: Fifth (Atlantic)
Coach: Ed Olczyk–Michel Therrien
General Manager: Craig Patrick

The new collective bargaining agreement was a watershed event for the NHL. Not only would the new CBA provide firm financial footing for the league, but it had a more basic impact as well. Teams such as the Penguins would once again be able to compete for talent on even terms with big-market clubs.

Much to their credit, the NHL owners didn't stop with the new agreement. In the seasons preceding the lockout, hockey had been dying a slow, lingering death. Dominated by teams that employed a defense-first style, NHL games were as exciting to watch as rush-hour gridlock. Players were bigger and faster than ever, which meant there was less room to make plays. Goaltenders' pads and equipment had grown to such obscene dimensions that many resembled the Michelin tire man, taking up virtually every inch of the net simply by standing still.

What was once a beautiful game of ebb-and-flow, crisp passing, and crashing bodies had degenerated into a quagmire of clutching and grabbing. Offense was being choked out of the game. It turned off even the most die-hard fans, to say nothing of the casual observer. Predictably, TV ratings had plummeted to the point where hockey was no longer regarded as a major sport.

In an effort to breathe new life into the game, the owners approved several farsighted rule changes. Perhaps the most significant was sanctioning two-line "home run" passes, which would serve to increase speed and flow while busting the trap. Nets were moved two feet closer to the end boards to increase space in the attacking zone. The old pre-1986 "touch-up" rule on offsides was reinstated. This meant that if an attacking player skated back to the blue line on an offsides play, the puck was live.

To help staunch the endless flow of ties brought about by defensive-oriented, conservative coaching, the shootout was adopted. If games were still knotted up after five minutes of four-on-four overtime, they would be decided by a shootout—a change that would further shine a spotlight on the league's skill players. The shootout was already employed by the American Hockey League as a way of settling ties and was extremely popular with the fans.

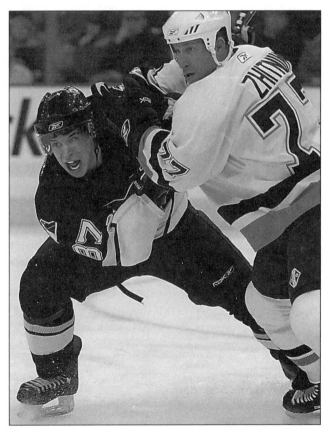

Phenom Sidney Crosby broke Mario Lemieux's rookie scoring record with 102 points.

The new rules hit goaltenders the hardest. In addition to reducing the size of their equipment, the league placed severe restrictions on where goalies could handle the puck.

The NHL ratcheted the excitement factor to even greater heights when it announced that an open lottery would be held for the first pick in the upcoming Entry Draft. The hullabaloo was understandable, for yet another franchise player would be available—phenom Sidney Crosby. Every team in the NHL would have a shot at drafting him, including the Penguins.

Like Alexander Ovechkin the year before, Crosby was considered a true blue-chipper. As a callow 17-year-old, he had lifted a moribund Rimouski team all the way to the Memorial Cup Finals on the strength of a sensational 168-point season. The 5'11", 193-pound center possessed an incredible array of skills, including Lemieux-like instincts and touch, blazing speed, and a willingness to dig in the corners.

Along with fellow bottom-feeders Buffalo, Columbus, and the Rangers, the low-flying Penguins were given two extra balls in the draft lottery. Unlike the previous season, when the hockey gods snubbed the Pens in favor of the Capitals, this time they smiled—and smiled broadly. The Penguins won the rights to draft Crosby. On July 30 a beaming Craig Patrick made it official by selecting him at the Entry Draft.

"People have said he's got the vision of a Wayne Gretzky and the goal-scoring ability and playmaking ability of Mario Lemieux," Patrick offered. "They all say he's a wonderful human being. Very well-spoken. Very humble. A perfect fit for our city, and our fans, and our organization. It's a very lucky day."

Almost immediately, fans began flooding the team office with ticket requests—a welcome change from the 2003–04 season when the club scraped along with a league-low average attendance of 11,877. Reaction was so positive that principal owners Lemieux and Ron Burkle pulled back an offer to sell a majority interest in the team to Californian William DelBiaggio.

Thanks to previous cost-cutting moves, the Penguins were positioned to thrive in the new NHL. With plenty of room under the salary cap, Patrick immediately went about the task of adding proven talent to augment the team's budding core of youngsters.

In rapid-fire succession he inked a bevy of high-profile free agents to deals, including All-Star defenseman Sergei Gonchar and high-scoring wingers Zigmund Palffy and John LeClair. Mindful of the club's need for an experienced goaltender to serve as a mentor for Marc-Andre Fleury, Patrick imported veteran Jocelyn Thibault.

The revamped Penguins faced off against nettlesome New Jersey in the season opener. As the trap-oriented Devils tried to adapt to the new rule changes, the Pens attacked in waves. However, Martin Brodeur repelled shot after shot in a dazzling goaltending display, while Thibault—still on the mend from a chronic hip injury—turned in a weak performance.

With the Penguins' defense touching nary a soul, the Devils rolled to an easy 5–1 victory.

The loss was a harbinger of things to come. Struggling to mesh into a cohesive unit, the club opened the season on a dismal 0–4–5 slide. Sluggish starts by big-name free agents Gonchar and LeClair didn't help matters.

It quickly became apparent that Craig Patrick had missed the mark. Although skill was indeed at a premium in the new-look NHL, he had badly miscalculated the need for speed. Compared to teams like Carolina and Buffalo, the lead-footed Penguins appeared to be anchored to the ice.

Fortunately, one player was thriving. Thoroughbred rookie Sidney Crosby bolted from the starting gate like a Kentucky Derby racehorse to pace the team in points and assists. His brilliant play earned him NHL Rookie of the Month honors for October.

On November 22 the Pens squared off against Washington in the first meeting between Crosby and the Capitals' equally gifted Alexander Ovechkin. It was apparent the two super rookies enjoyed a mutual admiration.

"He's got great hands and he's a powerful skater," Crosby gushed when describing Ovechkin. "He can do it all...he's really dangerous."

His counterpart was equally generous in his praise of Sid the Kid. "He's a great passer, like Gretzky," Ovechkin said, "and he can see the ice...he's a great player."

Round 1 of the clash of the Young Turks went to Crosby. He scored a beautiful breakaway goal and set up Palffy with an equally brilliant backhand pass to lead the Pens to a thrilling 5–4 victory. The two-point effort gave him 27 points in just 22 games, putting him on a pace to tie Mario's rookie record of 100 points.

However, dark days loomed just around the corner. An offense that had been marginally productive completely evaporated when Palffy retired due to a recurring shoulder injury. The Penguins dropped eight of nine games to fade from playoff contention.

Following an embarrassing 3–0 loss to lowly St. Louis in mid-December, Patrick relieved Eddie Olczyk of the coaching duties. In stark contrast to his first season behind the bench—when he'd done a wonderful job of guiding an undermanned team—Olczyk appeared to be in way over his head. It was obvious that he missed his top assistant and mentor, Lorne Molleken, who had departed over the off-season.

Patrick handed the reins over to Michel Therrien, who had led the Baby Pens to a stunning 21–1–2–1 start. The 42-year-old Therrien had carved out a reputation as an in-your-face type of leader. He would have plenty of fodder on an underachieving team that rarely seemed to break a sweat.

After initially responding well to Therrien's firm hand, the Penguins swooned again in January, winning just two of 14 games. The club played so poorly that it evoked memories of the worst Penguins team of all time—the putrid 1983–84 "Boys of Winter."

"It was hell," rookie Maxime Talbot recalled.

Therrien was clearly disappointed. His made no bones about his feelings, ripping into his charges following a lackluster loss to Edmonton.

"I'm not impressed," he said in disgust. "It's a pathetic performance. Half the team doesn't care. These guys would see if we take 50 percent of their salaries because they only play 50 percent of the time."

With a season that began with so much promise rapidly slip-sliding away, Lemieux again put the club up for sale. Despite a proposal to build a badly needed new arena that would not require public funding—hinging instead on a state-granted slots license—politicians were dragging their feet. Once more, the team's future in Pittsburgh was in doubt.

On January 24, Lemieux made a second announcement that deeply saddened the sports world. Suffering from the effects of atrial fibrillation, he announced his retirement. The greatest player in team history was leaving hockey's center stage for the final time.

Shorn of their beloved leader, the Penguins responded with an inspired effort and bombed Washington 8–1. Crosby once more outshone Ovechkin in a head-to-head matchup with a sparkling four-point performance.

The stirring victory over the Caps signaled an upswing in the team's play. Although it wasn't evident by the results, Therrien was working hard to break bad habits, while getting his young charges to trust in his system. He also improved the team's deplorable conditioning.

Meanwhile, Craig Patrick continued to reshape the team. In separate deals, he traded away disappointments Dick Tarnstrom and Ric Jackman. Mark Recchi, who scored 24 goals while giving his all, went to Cup contender Carolina.

Suddenly, the Penguins began to win. Over the final two months they posted a respectable record of 8–9–1–1, including impressive victories over playoff contenders New Jersey, Philadelphia, and Montreal.

Unlike their strong stretch run of the previous season, this one was spearheaded by the kids. Dynamic Sidney Crosby closed with a rush to break Mario's record for rookie scoring with 102 points. Ryan Malone overcame a horrendous start to top the 20-goal mark for the second year in a row. Former first-round pick Colby Armstrong also shone, notching 16 goals in just 47 games.

Marc-Andre Fleury was far and away the team's most effective goalie, posting a 3.25 goals-against average behind a porous team. The defense, led by a resurgent Gonchar and bolstered by the solid play of rookie Ryan Whitney and Brooks Orpik, was much improved by season's end.

Once more, the Penguins qualified for one of the top picks in the Entry Draft. Yet Therrien reflected the growing sense of optimism in the organization when he asserted, "It will be the last time."

	GP	G	A	PTS	PM	+/-
Sidney Crosby	81	39	63	102	110	- 1
Sergei Gonchar	75	12	46	58	100	- 13
Mark Recchi	63	24	33	57	56	- 28
John LeClair	73	22	29	51	61	- 24
Ryan Malone	77	22	22	44	63	- 22
Zigmund Palffy	42	11	31	42	12	5
Colby Armstrong	47	16	24	40	58	15
Ryan Whitney	68	6	32	38	85	- 7
Michel Ouellet	50	16	16	32	16	- 13
Ric Jackman	49	6	22	28	46	- 20
Tomas Surovy	53	12	13	25	45	- 13
Mario Lemieux	26	7	15	22	16	- 16
Andy Hilbert	19	7	11	18	16	8
Josef Melichar	72	3	12	15	66	- 2
Erik Christensen	33	6	7	13	34	- 3
Eric Boguniecki	38	5	6	11	29	- 2
Dick Tarnstrom	33	5	5	10	52	- 10
Konstantin Koltsov	60	3	6	9	20	- 10
Brooks Orpik	64	2	7	9	124	- 3
Maxime Talbot	48	5	3	8	59	- 12
Lasse Pirjeta	25	4	3	7	18	4
Jani Rita	30	3	4	7	4	- 6
Matt Murley	41	1	5	6	24	- 9
Noah Welch	5	1	3	4	2	0
Steve Poapst	21	0	4	4	10	- 5
Rob Scuderi	57	0	4	4	36	- 18
Andre Roy	42	2	1	3	116	- 3
Shane Endicott	41	1	1	2	43	- 9
Ryan VandenBussche	20	1	0	1	42	0
Eric Cairns	27	1	0	1	87	0
Cory Cross	6	0	1	1	6	- 1
Matt Hussey	13	0	1	1	0	- 5
Sebastien Caron	26	0	1	1	0	0
Lyle Odelein	27	0	1	1	50	- 10
Marc-Andre Fleury	50	0	1	1	0	0
Dany Sabourin	1	0	0	0	0	0
Alain Nasreddine	6	0	0	0	8	2
Guillaume Lefebvre	9	0	0	0	9	- 3
Niklas Nordgren	15	0	0	0	4	- 4
Jocelyn Thibault	16	0	0	0	2	0
Rico Fata	20	0	0	0	10	- 5

	GP	MINS	GA	SH	AVG	W	L	OT
Marc-Andre Fleury	50	2809	152	1	3.25	13	27	6
Sebastien Caron	26	1312	87	1	3.98	8	9	5
Jocelyn Thibault	16	807	60	0	4.46	1	9	3
Dany Sabourin	1	21	4	0	11.43	0	1	0
	82	4985	316	2	3.73	22	46	14

2006–07

Record: 47–24–5–6
Points: 105
Goals For: 277
Goals Against: 246
Finish: Second (Atlantic)
Coach: Michel Therrien
General Manager: Ray Shero

Shortly after the 2005–06 season ended, club president and CEO Ken Sawyer dropped a bombshell when he dismissed Hall of Fame general manager Craig Patrick.

"Craig did a great job during his 17 years here, but sometimes you need to make a change," Mario Lemieux said. "The game is a lot different now and you have to be a lot more involved with scouting and knowing the young players, and we thought we needed to make a change there."

Following a month-long search, Sawyer announced on May 26 that Ray Shero would succeed Patrick as the Pens' general manager. Like his predecessor, the 43-year-old Shero was descended from a family with a rich hockey pedigree. His father, the late Fred Shero, had coached the Flyers to back-to-back Stanley Cups in the mid-1970s.

Regarded as one of the top young executives in hockey, Shero served a long apprenticeship, first as the assistant GM in Ottawa and then in Nashville. During his tenure, both clubs improved dramatically while building primarily through the draft. An experienced hand in scouting and

player development, the bright and personable Shero seemed a perfect fit for the up-and-coming Penguins.

He made an immediate impact at the Entry Draft, entertaining a myriad of trade offers before grabbing another plum—talented 6'4", 215-pound center Jordan Staal—with the second overall pick.

Shero continued to put his stamp on the team throughout the summer, releasing a host of players while adding veteran defenseman Mark Eaton and feisty wingers Jarkko Ruutu and Ronald Petrovicky to the mix. He also signed free agent Mark Recchi to provide scoring punch and leadership.

With a full off-season to work with, Michel Therrien began to prepare the Penguins for the upcoming season. Mindful of the need to mold his young charges into a cohesive unit, he arranged for the team to spend four days at the United States Military Academy at West Point. The players were led through a series of team-building and leadership-training exercises by army personnel, including classroom and field demonstrations.

"I think it's going to be phenomenal just before the season starts to be able to get the chance to go there with the quality of the people who will be at West Point to surround our players," Therrien said.

It was obvious from the opening face-off that the 2006–07 Penguins were birds of a different feather. Displaying an abundance of speed and grit, they walloped the formerly fearsome Flyers 4–0 in the season opener.

Paced by piping-hot rookie Evgeni Malkin, who had defected from Russia over the summer, the Pens raced to an impressive 7–3 start to challenge for the Atlantic Division lead.

Calder Trophy winner Evgeni Malkin and veteran Mark Recchi celebrate a big goal.

However, an injury to free-agent defensive stalwart Mark Eaton and a dearth of scoring punch on the wings undermined the club's otherwise sterling play. Following a tough stretch of games that pitted them against some of the league's elite teams, the young Penguins slid back into the pack and soon found themselves scrapping to stay in contention for a playoff spot.

The turning point came during a January 20 showdown with Toronto. Playing before a packed house at the Mellon Arena, the Pens exploded for eight goals.

More importantly, they went toe-to-toe with the Maple Leafs, who were out for blood once the game got out of hand. Rugged rookie Chris Thorburn showed tons of heart by battling Bryan McCabe and towering Hal Gill to standoffs. Brooks Orpik bulldozed McCabe to the ice for taking liberties with Malkin.

The message was loud and clear. Unlike so many Penguins teams, this one refused to be bullied.

Using the victory over the Leafs as a springboard, the Pens went on an incredible 14–0–1–1 tear to vault back into the thick of the playoff picture.

In addition to the brilliant play of Sidney Crosby—who was making a mockery of the league scoring race—18-year-old Jordan Staal emerged as a terrific player. Affectionately nicknamed "Gronk" by Crosby, the tall, blond-haired rookie with the ever-present mouthpiece had developed into a scoring threat and top-notch penalty killer while playing the unfamiliar position of left wing.

As it became apparent that the Penguins would not only make the playoffs but perhaps make some significant noise once they got there, general manager Ray Shero began to look for ways to improve the club. Noting that other teams had begun to target his young stars for abuse, Shero added some muscle by acquiring tough wingers Gary Roberts and Georges Laraque at the trade deadline.

Although a bit long in the tooth at 40 years of age, Roberts still employed the bristling, hard-driving style that had earned him a spot among the league's elite power forwards. He proved to be an excellent acquisition, banging home seven goals in just 19 games, while adding leadership and a physical presence.

"Everyone was saying how much of a warrior he was," Crosby said. "Now, you see it firsthand. Everybody feeds off the way he plays, the way he battles, the way he prepares."

Standing 6'3" and weighing 243 pounds, the imposing Laraque had long been regarded as the NHL's heavyweight champ. He did nothing to tarnish that reputation, besting fellow heavies Colton Orr and Donald Brashear while serving as an effective deterrent.

Despite a brutal slate that included 17 games in March, the Pens continued their strong play down the homestretch. They closed out the campaign with hard-fought, playoff-style victories over Ottawa and the Rangers—two of the hottest teams in the league—and finished the year with a record of 47–24–5–6.

Jark the Spark

When Ray Shero was hired as the Penguins' general manager, one of his first priorities was to make the team more difficult to play against.

Enter Jarkko Ruutu, a free-agent forward from Vancouver. Regarded with equal parts fear and loathing by opposing players, he quickly made his presence felt with his agitating, in-your-face style. While hardly a threat to win the Art Ross Trophy, he occasionally contributed on the score sheet as well.

In 2007–08 Ruutu got off to a slow start, even by his modest standards. Yet on February 16, Shero went out of his way to praise the rugged winger.

"He might be the best zero-goal scorer in the league," the Pens' GM said.

As fate would have it, Ruutu got off the schneid that night with a pretty tally against Buffalo.

"So what does he become now?" a teammate pondered. "The worst one-goal scorer in the league?"

Ruutu would soon have the last laugh. After scoring goals in three straight games he quipped, "My back is sore from carrying the team so much."

The turnaround was nothing short of remarkable. The Penguins registered 105 points—good for a stunning 47-point improvement—the fourth-highest jump in league history.

Fueling the Pens' fire was Sidney Crosby. Aptly labeled by a hockey commentator as "the most skilled grinder the league has ever seen," he set a wonderful example for his mates by giving his all on every shift.

"I wouldn't be surprised if he walks on water one of these days," center Erik Christensen said following a particularly brilliant goal against Montreal. "An amazing goal...it was ridiculous to watch."

Sid the Kid piled up 120 points to become the youngest scoring champion in the history of major pro sports. He made a clean sweep of the league's major awards by capturing the Art Ross and Hart trophies, as well as the Lester B. Pearson Award.

Fellow wonder boys Evgeni Malkin and Jordan Staal also enjoyed spectacular seasons. Displaying the mercurial brilliance of a Rachmaninoff concerto, Malkin scored 33 goals and 85 points to earn the Calder Trophy.

"Every time I turn on the TV, I see Malkin doing something for Pittsburgh," hockey analyst Darren Pang said. "And he's so good without the puck. He just has great instincts."

Staal narrowly missed the 30-goal plateau, knocking in 29 while leading the league with seven shorthanded tallies. On February 10 he became the youngest player in NHL history to score a hat trick, accomplishing the feat during a pulsating 6–5 triumph over the Maple Leafs.

Meanwhile, at the other end of the ice, Marc-Andre Fleury quietly turned in a solid season. In his first full campaign he won 40 games—the second-highest total in club history—while improving his positional play and puck control.

	GP	G	A	PTS	PM	+/-
Sidney Crosby	79	36	84	120	60	10
Evgeni Malkin	78	33	52	85	80	2
Mark Recchi	82	24	44	68	62	1
Sergei Gonchar	82	13	54	67	72	-5
Ryan Whitney	81	14	45	59	77	9
Michel Ouellet	73	19	29	48	30	-3
Jordan Staal	81	29	13	42	24	16
Colby Armstrong	80	12	22	34	67	2
Erik Christensen	61	18	15	33	26	-3
Ryan Malone	64	16	15	31	71	4
Maxime Talbot	75	13	11	24	53	-2
Jarkko Ruutu	81	7	9	16	125	0
Nils Ekman	34	6	9	15	24	-14
Dominic Moore	59	6	9	15	46	1
Gary Roberts	19	7	6	13	26	-5
Josef Melichar	70	1	11	12	44	1
Rob Scuderi	78	1	10	11	28	3
John LeClair	21	2	5	7	12	-2
Ronald Petrovicky	31	3	3	6	28	4
Brooks Orpik	70	0	6	6	82	4
Chris Thorburn	39	3	2	5	69	1
Alain Nasreddine	44	1	4	5	18	12
Mark Eaton	35	0	3	3	16	-6
Marc-Andre Fleury	67	0	3	3	4	0
Kristopher Letang	7	2	0	2	4	-3
Noah Welch	22	1	1	2	22	1
Georges Laraque	17	0	2	2	18	-3
Micki DuPont	3	0	1	1	4	-3
Eric Cairns	1	0	0	0	5	0
Joel Kwiatkowski	1	0	0	0	0	-1
Karl Stewart	3	0	0	0	2	-1
Andre Roy	5	0	0	0	12	-1
Jocelyn Thibault	22	0	0	0	0	0

	GP	MINS	GA	SH	AVG	W	L	OT
Marc-Andre Fleury	67	3905	184	5	2.83	40	16	9
Jocelyn Thibault	22	1101	52	1	2.83	7	8	2
	82	5032	246	6	2.86	47	24	11

2007–08

Record: 47–27–4–4
Points: 102
Goals For: 247
Goals Against: 216
Finish: First (Atlantic)
Coach: Michel Therrien
General Manager: Ray Shero

Refusing to rest on his laurels, GM Ray Shero continued to reshape his exciting young team. In an effort to reinforce the club with a veteran presence, he inked greybeards Mark Recchi and Gary Roberts to new one-year deals and signed thirtysomething free agents Petr Sykora and Darryl Sydor.

Shero also signed Michel Therrien to a contract extension, ending speculation that he might bring in a hand-picked coach to guide the team.

"He's got a lot of the intangibles I was looking for in a coach," Shero said. "I'm a big believer in loyalty and communication. So is he. The loyalty and communication is there both ways."

The Pens' GM took a huge step toward securing the team's talented young core in July by signing Hart Trophy winner Sidney Crosby to a five-year contract extension worth $43.5 million. In a typically unselfish act, Sid the Kid settled for less than the going rate for a player of his magnitude.

A happy bunch of Penguins: (left to right) Mark Eaton, Jordan Staal, and Sergei Gonchar.

Indeed, sacrifice would become the theme for the coming season. The watchword was printed on T-shirts in five different languages—Czech, English, French, Finnish, and Russian—representing the different nationalities on the team. The players wore them under their uniforms as a constant reminder of the effort it would take to become a champion.

Despite the lofty expectations, the Penguins stumbled out of the starting gate. Following a so-so opening month, the club swooned in November. Young guns Colby Armstrong, Erik Christensen, and Jordan Staal struggled to find the net, while Marc-Andre Fleury performed erratically in goal. Recchi also failed to produce and was claimed on waivers by Atlanta.

By Thanksgiving, the Penguins had skidded to an unsightly record of 8–11–1–1. To make matters worse, they were scheduled to face red-hot Ottawa, the team that had schooled them in the playoffs the previous spring.

Instead of pushing the panic button, Ray Shero made a statement that lifted the pressure off of his young team.

"Maybe our success last year came too easily," he said. "Every good team has to face adversity in order to improve. I need this, the coaching staff needs this, and the players need this."

Paced by a pair of goals from Ryan Malone and Jarkko Ruutu's game winner in the shootout, the Penguins rallied from a two-goal deficit to stun the Senators 6–5.

With the monkey off their backs, the Pens reeled off five victories in six games to vault back into the playoff hunt. Reinforced by rookie call-ups Tyler Kennedy and Kris Letang, the team continued to surge in the new year, despite losing Fleury to a high-ankle sprain. Unheralded Ty Conklin, who'd been toiling in Wilkes-Barre, stepped between the pipes and sparked the team with his sensational play.

Just as the Pens were settling into a groove, disaster struck. On January 18, while chasing down a loose puck against Tampa Bay, Crosby slid awkwardly into the boards and was forced to leave the game.

The prognosis wasn't good. The league's scoring leader had suffered a high-ankle sprain and would miss six to eight weeks. Adding to the Pens' injury woes, key players such as Mark Eaton, Gary Roberts, and Max Talbot were sidelined as well.

Faced with the daunting task of surviving without their captain, the Penguins rose to the occasion. Stepping out from Crosby's shadow, Evgeni Malkin grabbed the leadership reins and emerged as one of the premier players in the world. Teamed with Malone and Petr Sykora on the devastating "Steel City Line," he tallied a whopping 20 goals and 28 assists during Crosby's 29-game absence.

Incredibly, the team barely missed a beat, compiling an astonishing record of 16–9–2–2 sans Sid.

"This team has really come a long way," Gary Roberts observed. "They've grown together."

As the February 26 trade deadline approached, most observers felt the Penguins would make a minor deal or

The Ice Bowl

The Penguins made history on New Year's Day 2008 when they participated in the NHL's second-ever outdoor game. Skating before a howling mob of 71,000 fans at Buffalo's Ralph Wilson Stadium, the Pens and the Sabres battled each other and the elements, including 30-degree temperatures and a healthy dose of wind, sleet, and snow.

Despite numerous stops in play to clear the ice, the Winter Classic (a.k.a. "Ice Bowl") was a rousing success. Colby Armstrong struck on the opening shift of the game, but the Sabres evened the score in the second period on a Brian Campbell rocket.

From that point on, the game belonged to the goalies. Ty Conklin—who also played in the NHL's first outdoor game—and his counterpart Ryan Miller made save after save to force the game to a shootout.

The stage was set for a dramatic finish. With the shootout knotted at 1–1, Sidney Crosby stickhandled through the driving snow and snapped the puck between Miller's pads to set off a wild victory celebration.

two, or perhaps stand pat. They were in for a shock. In the biggest blockbuster of the day, Shero shipped Armstrong, Christensen, first-round pick Angelo Esposito, and the team's top pick in the upcoming Entry Draft to Atlanta for All-Star winger Marian Hossa and defensive specialist Pascal Dupuis. The Pens' GM bolstered the defense as well by acquiring behemoth defenseman Hal Gill from Toronto.

It was a stunning shift in philosophy for a team that seemed committed to building slowly over time. But the Pens' stellar play convinced Shero that the club had a legitimate chance to capture the Stanley Cup.

Unfortunately, adversity continued to rear its ugly head as Hossa sprained a knee during his Penguins debut. Remarkably, the team continued to roll. Led by the piping-hot Steel City Line, the Pens exploded for three seven-goal games during a five-game span in March. With Crosby and Hossa returning for the stretch run, they nailed down the Atlantic Division crown with a sterling record of 47–27–4–4.

While the Pens' incredible march through an injury-plagued season was truly a team effort, several players stood above the rest. Malkin erupted for 47 goals and 106 points—a total topped only by his countryman Alex Ovechkin. After years of unfulfilled promise, Ryan Malone blossomed into one of the league's top power forwards, setting career highs with 27 goals and 51 points. Free-agent sniper Petr Sykora was sensational, ripping home 28 goals, including 15 on the power play. Crosby was his usual dominant self when healthy, piling up 72 points in just 53 games.

Serving as the bulwark for a wonderfully balanced defensive corps, Sergei Gonchar enjoyed a Norris Trophy–type season. He registered 65 points—second among NHL defensemen—and logged a solid plus/minus rating of plus 13. Conklin and Fleury provided spectacular goaltending, finishing second and fourth, respectively, in save percentage.

	GP	G	A	PTS	PM	+/-
Evgeni Malkin	82	47	59	106	78	16
Sidney Crosby	53	24	48	72	39	18
Sergei Gonchar	78	12	53	65	66	13
Petr Sykora	81	28	35	63	41	1
Ryan Malone	77	27	24	51	103	14
Ryan Whitney	76	12	28	40	45	- 2
Jordan Staal	82	12	16	28	55	- 5
Maxime Talbot	63	12	14	26	53	8
Colby Armstrong	54	9	15	24	50	6
Erik Christensen	49	9	11	20	28	- 3
Tyler Kennedy	55	10	9	19	35	2
Kristopher Letang	63	6	11	17	23	- 1
Jarkko Ruutu	71	6	10	16	138	3
Gary Roberts	38	3	12	15	40	- 3
Georges Laraque	71	4	9	13	141	0
Darryl Sydor	74	1	12	13	26	1
Jeff Taffe	45	5	7	12	8	2
Pascal Dupuis	16	2	10	12	8	4
Brooks Orpik	78	1	10	11	57	11
Marian Hossa	12	3	7	10	6	0
Mark Recchi	19	2	6	8	12	- 2
Adam Hall	46	2	4	6	24	- 2
Rob Scuderi	71	0	5	5	26	3
Hal Gill	18	1	3	4	16	6
Mark Eaton	36	0	3	3	4	6
Chris Minard	15	1	1	2	10	- 1
Alex Goligoski	3	0	2	2	2	2
Connor James	13	1	0	1	2	- 2
Ryan Stone	6	0	1	1	5	- 1
Ty Conklin	33	0	1	1	4	0
Marc-Andre Fleury	35	0	1	1	0	0
Tim Brent	1	0	0	0	0	- 1
Kris Beech	5	0	0	0	2	- 1
Jonathan Filewich	5	0	0	0	0	- 2
Alain Nasreddine	6	0	0	0	4	- 4
Nathan Smith	13	0	0	0	2	0
Dany Sabourin	24	0	0	0	2	0

	GP	MINS	GA	SH	AVG	W	L	OT
Marc-Andre Fleury	35	1857	72	4	2.33	19	10	2
Ty Conklin	33	1866	78	2	2.51	18	8	5
Dany Sabourin	24	1242	57	2	2.75	10	9	1
	82	4986	216	8	2.55	47	27	8

Scary Gary

The 2007–08 season wasn't especially kind to Gary Roberts. He opened the campaign with a nagging lung infection that severely curtailed his effectiveness.

Still, the tough old pro found ways to contribute. During a brawl-filled engagement with Philadelphia, he stood up for the team by pummeling Flyers tough guy Ben Eager, a man 18 years his junior.

Unfortunately, his run of bad lack continued. Shortly after recording his 900th career point, Roberts suffered a fractured fibula and a high-ankle sprain in a collision with Buffalo's Tim Connolly.

Remarkably, the 42-year-old winger recovered from his injuries in time for the playoffs. Barely a minute into the series opener against Ottawa, Roberts scored the crucial first goal on a pretty backhander from the slot.

"Scary Gary" proceeded to bang any Senator within striking distance before notching a second goal.

"Everyone was really happy to see him get those two goals," Brooks Orpik said.

Inspired by their old warrior, the Penguins swept the Senators in four straight games.

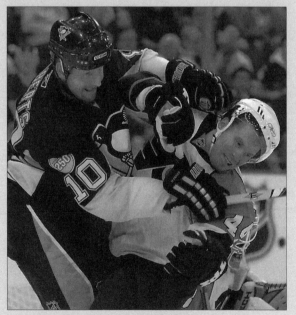

Gary Roberts makes roadkill of the Flyers' Kimmo Timonen.

2008–09

Record: 45–28–3–6
Points: 99
Goals For: 264
Goals Against: 239
Finish: Second (Atlantic)
Coach: Michel Therrien–Dan Bylsma
General Manager: Ray Shero

The Penguins' crushing defeat at the hands of the Red Wings in the Stanley Cup Finals the previous season was matched in magnitude by a series of stunning defections over the summer. Playoff hero Marian Hossa spurned a long-term offer to sign a one-year deal with Detroit. Tampa Bay inked Ryan Malone to a seven-year contract worth $31.5 million. Key role players such as Gary Roberts, Jarkko Ruutu, Georges Laraque, Adam Hall, and Ty Conklin signed on with other teams as well, leaving Ray Shero with some gaping holes to fill.

With barely a four-week window between the end of the playoffs and the start of free agency, the Penguins' GM had little time to react. Mining the free-agent market, he signed a trio of established forwards—high-scoring Miroslav Satan, Ruslan Fedotenko, and feisty Matt Cooke. Rugged winger Eric Godard was imported from Calgary to replace the departed Laraque.

In his most significant moves, Shero signed Evgeni Malkin to a five-year contract extension and inked Marc-Andre Fleury to a new seven-year pact. Bruising Brooks Orpik signed a six-year deal.

After splitting a pair of games with archrival Ottawa in Sweden, the Pens sputtered through an uneven opening month. Losing key defenders Sergei Gonchar (dislocated shoulder) and Ryan Whitney (foot surgery) crippled the power play, and it was obvious the team missed the toughness and leadership provided by the departed trio of Malone, Roberts, and Ruutu.

A rematch with the Red Wings on November 11 proved to be just the right tonic. Trailing by three goals early in the final period, the Pens turned the tide with a blistering rally to force overtime. At 3:49 of the extra stanza, Jordan Staal—who registered a third-period hat trick—set up Fedotenko for the game winner.

"A team like that doesn't panic too often," Staal said afterward. "But we kept putting pucks on the net, and if you keep doing that, some will go in. Once we got the first one, it set them back a bit."

Suitably inspired, the Pens ran off a six-game winning streak to reclaim the top spot in the Atlantic Division. Fueling the Pens' fire was Malkin, who snatched the lead in the NHL scoring race, and Fleury, who continued his hot hand from the playoffs. The new third line of Staal, Cooke, and Tyler Kennedy meshed into a highly effective unit that provided timely scoring and gritty, energetic play.

Unfortunately, a rash of injuries soon derailed "the Penguins Express." Fleury was felled by a groin injury in late November, thrusting erratic Dany Sabourin into the spotlight. Kennedy and newcomer Mike Zigomanis, a speedy checking center, were sidelined early in December. To make matters worse, the streaky Satan turned ice-cold after a jackrabbit start, while displaying precious little chemistry with Crosby.

Lacking the quality depth of previous seasons, the Pens began to struggle. They staggered through December and January at an alarming 10–16–2 pace. Hard-pressed to come up with tactical solutions for the team's poor play, Michel Therrien juggled lines at a frenetic pace, which had an unsettling effect. Even the returns of Fleury and Whitney did little to stem the mounting tide of losses.

Chronicling the team's woes, Michael Farber penned an article for *Sports Illustrated* aptly titled, "Stimulus Needed." "The Penguins have the best player in hockey," he wrote, "as well as its leading scorer, yet last year's Stanley Cup runner-up is still in desperate need of a rescue plan."

The Pens' shocking collapse reached its nadir in Toronto on Valentine's Day. After gaining an early two-goal lead, the

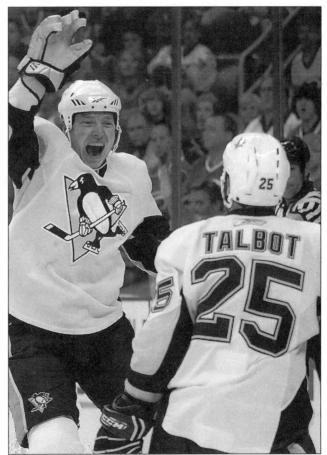

Free agent Ruslan Fedotenko (left) scored 16 goals for the Pens in 2008–09.

team fell into a zombie-like trance while the Maple Leafs stormed back to snatch a 6–2 victory.

"We just fell apart," a glum Crosby said afterward.

Ray Shero had seen enough. With the team teetering in 10th place in the Eastern Conference and on the brink of falling out of the playoff hunt, he fired Therrien and replaced him with Wilkes-Barre coach Dan Bylsma.

"I didn't like the direction the team was headed," Shero said. "I've watched for a number of weeks and, at the end of the day, the direction is not what I wanted to have here. I wasn't comfortable, and that's why the change was made."

The 38-year-old Bylsma proved to be a breath of fresh air in a locker room that had grown decidedly stale. A former NHL player who had carved out a career as a gritty defensive specialist, Bylsma was bright and communicative. In stark contrast to Therrien's trap-oriented system that at times left the Penguins flat-footed and vulnerable, the new coach unveiled plans for the team to play a style that emphasized speed and puck possession.

"With the strengths we have, we should be able to go into buildings and make teams deal with the quality of players we have at every position," he said.

While Bylsma was teaching the finer points of his up-tempo game, Shero gave the lineup a much-needed overhaul. On February 26 he sent Whitney to Anaheim for gritty winger Chris Kunitz and top prospect Eric Tangradi, a strapping young forward.

Then, at the March 4 trade deadline, he shrewdly swapped a conditional draft pick to the Islanders for veteran power forward Bill Guerin. The same age as his new coach, Guerin would fill the leadership vacuum created by the departure of Gary Roberts.

With a pair of brand-new wingers for Crosby and a new, upbeat attitude, the Pens began a turnaround that was every bit as remarkable as their midseason collapse. Suddenly one of the hottest teams in the league, they tore through the homestretch at a remarkable 18–3–4 clip to nail down second place in the Atlantic Division.

Pacing the attack was Malkin, who rang up 35 goals and 113 points to capture his first Art Ross Trophy. After struggling for much of the season, Crosby closed with a rush to score 33 goals and 103 points. Fellow young-gun Jordan Staal bounced back from a disappointing sophomore campaign to tally 22 goals while developing into a top-notch third-line center.

On the blue line, 21-year-old Kris Letang topped the team's defenders with 10 goals. Sergei Gonchar returned to help lead the team's resurgence, piling up 19 points in only 25 games. The quartet of Mark Eaton, Hal Gill, Brooks Orpik, and Rob Scuderi provided rock-steady defensive play in front of Fleury, who enjoyed another fine season.

	GP	G	A	PTS	PM	+/-
Evgeni Malkin	82	35	78	113	80	17
Sidney Crosby	77	33	70	103	76	3
Jordan Staal	82	22	27	49	37	5
Petr Sykora	76	25	21	46	36	3
Ruslan Fedotenko	65	16	23	39	44	18
Miroslav Satan	65	17	19	36	36	3
Tyler Kennedy	67	15	20	35	30	15
Kristopher Letang	74	10	23	33	24	-7
Matt Cooke	76	13	18	31	101	0
Pascal Dupuis	71	12	16	28	30	1
Maxime Talbot	75	12	10	22	63	-9
Alex Goligoski	45	6	14	20	16	5
Sergei Gonchar	25	6	13	19	26	6
Brooks Orpik	79	2	17	19	73	10
Chris Kunitz	20	7	11	18	16	3
Rob Scuderi	81	1	15	16	18	23
Ryan Whitney	28	2	11	13	16	-15
Bill Guerin	17	5	7	12	18	3
Hall Gill	62	2	8	10	53	11
Mark Eaton	68	4	5	9	36	3
Philippe Boucher	25	3	3	6	24	10
Mike Zigomanis	22	2	4	6	27	-2
Eric Godard	71	2	2	4	171	-3
Bill Thomas	16	2	1	3	2	-4
Dustin Jeffrey	14	1	2	3	0	4
Chris Minard	20	1	2	3	4	0
Darryl Sydor	8	1	1	2	2	5
Jeff Taffe	8	0	2	2	2	-4
Tim Wallace	16	0	2	2	7	2
Luca Caputi	5	1	0	1	4	-1
Craig Adams	9	0	1	1	0	0
Paul Bissonnette	15	0	1	1	22	-1
Marc-Andre Fleury	62	0	1	1	8	0
Connor James	1	0	0	0	0	0
Ben Lovejoy	2	0	0	0	0	0
Ryan Stone	2	0	0	0	2	1
John Curry	3	0	0	0	0	0
Mathieu Garon	4	0	0	0	0	0
Janne Pesonen	7	0	0	0	0	-3
Dany Sabourin	19	0	0	0	2	0

	GP	MINS	GA	SH	AVG	W	L	OT
John Curry	3	150	6	0	2.40	2	1	0
Marc-Andre Fleury	62	3641	162	4	2.67	35	18	7
Dany Sabourin	19	989	47	0	2.85	6	8	2
Mathieu Garon	4	206	10	0	2.91	2	1	0
	82	5010	239	4	2.79	45	28	9

2009–10

Record: 47–28–5–2
Points: 101
Goals For: 257
Goals Against: 237
Finish: Second (Atlantic)
Coach: Dan Bylsma
General Manager: Ray Shero

Thanks to their thrilling Stanley Cup victory over Detroit, the Penguins entered the 2009–10 season on a high. Unlike the previous off-season when the team lost six key free agents, the summer of 2009 was comparatively kind. The club's only significant defectors were defensive stalwarts Hal Gill and Rob Scuderi. Free-agent winger Petr Sykora also found a new home, but he had faded badly in the second half before giving way to Miroslav Satan, who likewise was not re-signed.

General manager Ray Shero plugged the gaps with rugged winger Mike Rupp and shot-blocking blue-liner Jay McKee. Thirty-two-year-old Brent Johnson signed a free-agent deal, providing an experienced and capable backup for Marc-Andre Fleury. Veteran Martin Skoula replaced the retired Philippe Boucher as the club's spare defenseman.

Determined to reaffirm their status as the best team in hockey, the Pens tore through October at an incendiary 11–3 clip. The team played so well, it invoked memories of the powerhouse 1992–93 President's Trophy–winning squad. After opening November with a crisp 4–3 victory over Anaheim, however, the wheels fell off the wagon. With big-name stars Sergei Gonchar and Evgeni Malkin sidelined with injuries, the Pens sagged to four straight losses.

Despite Malkin's return, they seemed well on their way to a fifth consecutive defeat during a November 14 contest with the Bruins. But with 0.4 seconds left in regulation play, Bill Guerin beat Boston goalie Tim Thomas with a scorching shot to send the game into overtime. Just over a minute into the extra stanza Pascal Dupuis pounced on a Thomas miscue to notch the game winner.

Buoyed by the dramatic win over Boston, the Penguins resumed their winning ways. Despite a rash of injuries to the blue-line corps, the club reeled off 13 wins in their next 18 games to reclaim the top spot in the Eastern Conference. Just when the Pens appeared to be gathering steam, however, they dropped five in a row over the holidays.

The malaise continued through January and February as the club stumbled along at a .500 pace. Following a disappointing overtime loss to the Rangers on February 12, the players were clearly frustrated.

Good as Gold

The Penguins were well represented at the 2010 Winter Olympics in Vancouver. Sidney Crosby and Marc-Andre Fleury were selected to play for Team Canada. Sergei Gonchar and Evgeni Malkin earned spots on the Russian Federation team, while Brooks Orpik made the United States squad.

With Crosby leading the way, the Canadians were heavy favorites to capture the gold. After dismantling Norway in their opening game, however, Team Canada stumbled. They squeaked by Switzerland on Sid's shootout winner, but dropped an embarrassing 5–3 decision to Team USA.

Meanwhile, the powerful Russians quickly faded from medal contention. After an uneven 2–1 showing in the Preliminary Round, they fell to Team Canada 7–3.

On February 28 Canada and USA squared off in the gold-medal matchup. With their national pride on the line, the resurgent Canadians dominated the Americans for two periods while grabbing a 2–0 lead. But the plucky Americans, paced by the brilliant goaltending of Ryan Miller, mounted a third-period rally. With 24.4 seconds remaining, Zach Parise beat Roberto Luongo to send the game into overtime.

The stage was set for a dramatic finish. Seven minutes into the extra frame, Crosby attempted to split the Americans' defense, only to be turned aside. In his typical hustling fashion, Sid chased the loose puck to the sideboards. After nudging a short pass to linemate Jerome Iginla, Crosby spun and skated toward the net. Iginla found him with a perfect pass, and Sid snapped the puck between Miller's pads to capture the gold for Canada.

In an instant Crosby became a national hero.

"Every kid dreams of this opportunity, of being the one to score that goal for his country," he said. "It's a pretty unbelievable thing."

While proud of their effort, Team USA was understandably downcast.

"Maybe when you're a little older and, when your career's over, this will feel nice," said former Pen Ryan Malone, the first Pittsburgh native to play in the Olympics. "But we came here for the gold, and we were right there. We're disappointed."

"You never want to lose," Orpik added. "But, if you're going to lose, I'm happy Sid had success."

An outstanding two-way center, Jordan Staal slices through the Atlanta Thrashers.

"We haven't really been playing like we should for a long time," Jordan Staal said. "It really shows in our game. It gives other teams hope when they're playing us, and we don't want to play like that."

The Olympic break offered a welcome respite. While Sidney Crosby, Brooks Orpik, Fleury, Gonchar, and Malkin jetted off to Vancouver to represent their countries, the rest of the club received a much-needed break.

It proved to be just the right tonic. Following the Olympics the refreshed Penguins rolled to four straight wins. Shero attempted to bolster the team by acquiring defenseman Jordan Leopold and hulking winger Alexei Ponikarovsky at the trade deadline. The swift-skating Leopold performed well, notching four goals. Ponikarovsky, however, failed to click with Malkin.

Inconsistency continued to rear its ugly head. Following the hot streak, the Pens skidded through a dismal 4–7 stretch in late March. To make matters worse, Malkin suffered a foot injury that severely hampered the team's offensive output.

Hoping to gather momentum during the final regular-season homestand at venerable Mellon Arena, the Penguins clipped Atlanta, thanks to Leopold's overtime winner. But a galling 6–3 loss to Washington knocked them out of first place and gave the high-flying Capitals a sweep of the season series.

"Yeah, it's disappointing," Staal said, "but you've got to move forward. Hopefully, we'll see these guys again."

Taking advantage of a soft schedule, the Pens closed out the regular season with a pair of victories over the Islanders, sandwiched around a shutout loss to Atlanta. Despite their frequent lapses they finished with a record of 47–28–7, good for 101 points and second place in the Atlantic Division.

The team's unquestioned MVP was Sidney Crosby. Determined to provide more offense, Crosby worked long and hard over the summer to improve his shot. The result was a career-high 51 goals and a share of the Maurice Richard Trophy. In shootouts Sid was extraordinary, converting on eight of 10 chances. The 22-year-old captain emerged as a demon on face-offs as well, winning 56 percent of his draws.

Unfortunately, there were many nights when Crosby was the only player performing at the highest level. Fellow superstar Evgeni Malkin was unable to duplicate his Art Ross Trophy performance of 2008–09. Sitting out 15 games due to assorted ailments, Geno sagged to 77 points. Likewise, Sergei Gonchar missed huge chunks of time, although he managed an impressive 50 points in 62 games. Marc-Andre Fleury won 37 games but struggled with his consistency.

Among the supporting cast, veteran Bill Guerin notched 21 goals. Selke Trophy finalist Jordan Staal and rock-solid Brooks Orpik emerged as All-Star-caliber players. Role players Dupuis, Rupp, and Matt Cooke combined to tally 46 goals while picking up the slack for Ponikarovsky and snake bitten Ruslan Fedotenko.

For playoff hero Max Talbot it proved to be a lost season. Laboring to get his game in sync following off-season shoulder surgery, the plucky forward scored only two goals.

	GP	G	A	PTS	PM	+/-
Sidney Crosby	81	51	58	109	71	15
Evgeni Malkin	67	28	49	77	100	-6
Sergei Gonchar	62	11	39	50	49	-4
Jordan Staal	82	21	28	49	57	19
Bill Guerin	78	21	24	45	75	-9
Pascal Dupuis	81	18	20	38	16	5
Alex Goligoski	69	8	29	37	22	7
Chris Kunitz	50	13	19	32	39	3
Matt Cooke	79	15	15	30	106	17
Ruslan Fedotenko	80	11	19	30	50	-17
Kristopher Letang	73	3	24	27	51	1
Tyler Kennedy	64	13	12	25	31	10
Brooks Orpik	73	2	23	25	64	6
Mike Rupp	81	13	6	19	120	5
Mark Eaton	79	3	13	16	26	5
Jay McKee	62	1	9	10	54	6
Craig Adams	82	0	10	10	72	-5
Alexei Ponikarovsky	16	2	7	9	17	-6
Jordan Leopold	20	4	4	8	6	5
Martin Skoula	33	3	5	8	6	-4
Maxime Talbot	45	2	5	7	30	-9
Chris Conner	8	2	1	3	0	-1
Eric Godard	45	1	2	3	76	2
Ben Lovejoy	12	0	3	3	2	8
Chris Bourque	20	0	3	3	10	-4
Luca Caputi	4	1	1	2	2	-1
Nick Johnson	6	1	1	2	2	-2
Deryk Engelland	9	0	2	2	17	-2
Mark Letestu	10	1	0	1	2	-2
Brent Johnson	23	0	1	1	0	0
Marc-Andre Fleury	67	0	1	1	10	0
John Curry	1	0	0	0	0	0
Dustin Jeffrey	1	0	0	0	0	0
Alexander Pechurski	1	0	0	0	0	0
Eric Tangradi	1	0	0	0	0	0
Tim Wallace	1	0	0	0	0	0
Nate Guenin	2	0	0	0	0	-2

	GP	MINS	GA	SH	AVG	W	L	OT
Alexander Pechurski	1	36	1	0	1.67	0	0	0
Marc-Andre Fleury	67	3798	168	1	2.65	37	21	6
Brent Johnson	23	1108	51	0	2.76	10	6	1
John Curry	1	24	5	0	12.50	0	1	0
	82	4998	237	1	2.82	47	28	7

All the Team's Men

Since the Penguins' inaugural season in 1967–68—when the National Hockey League expanded from the "Original Six" to 12 teams—589 men appeared in one or more games for the team through the 2009–10 season. Of that total, 533 have played forward or defense, while 56 have tended goal.

Players with surnames ranging from A to Z have skated for the Penguins, from Ramzi Abid to Sergei Zubov. The most common surname is Johnson (Bob, Brent, Greg, Jim, and Mark). Following close behind are Brown and Wilson (four players each), and Edwards, Price, Samuelsson, Simpson, Smith, Stewart, and Young (three players each).

Nicknames cover every letter of the alphabet as well. Among the more colorful are Ace, Army, Artie, Bam Bam, Bibs, Bugsy, Chico, Durby, Edzo, Flower, Hammer, Kayo, Moose, Prony, Owch, Rammer, Sarge, Spinner, Soupy, Tree, Ubie, Zemmer, Ziggy, and Zubie.

There's "Battleship" for tough guy Bob Kelly and "Rifleman" for hard-shooting Chuck Arnason. Jean-Sebastien Aubin and Sebastien Caron answered to "Sea Bass." Among the tongue twisters, the "Schink-Schock-Shack" line of the early 1970s rates among the all-time greats.

Geographically, 508 Penguins have hailed from North America, including 414 Canadians and 94 players from the United States. Among the 81 non–North Americans, the former Czechoslovakia has produced the most Penguins (28), followed by Sweden (16), the former Soviet Union (16), and Finland (12).

Three Penguins have hailed from Pittsburgh—Nate Guenin, Ryan Malone, and Bill Thomas. Without a doubt Craig Adams boasts the most exotic birthplace (Seria, Brunei Darussalam). Following close behind are Jim Paek and Richard Park (Seoul, Republic of Korea), and Nelson Debenedet (Cordeno, Italy).

From a genetic point of view, the Pens have been blessed with four father-son combinations. Greg Malone and his son Ryan combined to tally 533 points in 794 games for Pittsburgh. Goaltending coach Gilles Meloche and his son Eric each played three seasons with the club. Bob and Brent Johnson served as backup goalies some 25 years apart. Wayne Hicks, the team's first American-born player, was acquired in a late-season trade in 1968. His son Alex joined the team 20 years later.

A fifth father-son duo, Bob Johnson and his son Mark (no relation to Bob and Brent), is perhaps the most famous. "Badger Bob" guided the Penguins to their first Stanley Cup, while Mark—who spent parts of three seasons with the Pens—was a hero on Team USA's "Miracle on Ice" squad.

Three sets of brothers have graced the ice together at the "Big Igloo." Mario Lemieux and big brother Alain played one game together on February 17, 1987. Including the playoffs, Doug and Greg Brown shared the ice for 42 games during the 1993–94 campaign. Chris and Peter Ferraro—the only twins ever to wear the black and gold—skated together on the 1997 team, often as linemates.

Kevin and Kip Miller missed playing together by two seasons. A fifth set of siblings, Rico and Drew Fata, were on the team's depth chart from 2003 to 2006. However, Drew never appeared in a regular-season game for the Pens. Mark Moore was a Penguins draft pick in 1997. His brother, Dominic, skated for the team during the 2006–07 campaign.

While they did not share the ice, two other brother combos enjoyed overlapping careers. Matt Recchi was hired as a scout when his more-famous sibling Mark joined the team for a second tour of duty. Glenn Patrick served as a minor league coach under his younger brother Craig.

The Penguins also boast four sons of Hockey Hall of Famers: Syl Apps, Chris Bourque, Bryan Hextall Jr., and Tracy Pratt.

Statistics in **bold** indicate league-leading totals.

Colorful Ron Duguay (10) celebrates a goal with Craig Simpson and Rod Buskas (7).

A

ABID, RAMZI

Left Wing   **Ht:** 6-2 **Wt:** 210   **Shoots:** left
B: March 24, 1980, Montreal, Quebec

YR	Regular Season					Playoffs				
	GP	G	A	PTS	PM	GP	G	A	PTS	PM
2002-03	3	0	0	0	2	-	-	-	-	-
2003-04	16	3	2	5	27	-	-	-	-	-
Pitt. Totals	19	3	2	5	29	-	-	-	-	-
NHL Totals	68	14	16	30	78	2	0	0	0	0

Acquired from Phoenix with Dan Focht and Guillaume Lefebvre for Jan Hrdina and Francois Leroux, March 11, 2003

Signed as a free agent by Atlanta, August 8, 2005

ADAMS, CRAIG

Right Wing   **Ht:** 6-0 **Wt:** 200   **Shoots:** right
B: April 26, 1977, Seria, Brunei Darussalam

YR	Regular Season					Playoffs				
	GP	G	A	PTS	PM	GP	G	A	PTS	PM
2008-09	9	0	1	1	0	24	3	2	5	16
2009-10	82	0	10	10	72	13	2	1	3	15
Pitt. Totals	91	0	11	11	72	37	5	3	8	31
NHL Totals	589	37	63	100	455	66	5	3	8	41

Claimed on waivers from Chicago, March 4, 2009

AHOLA, PETER KRISTIAN

Defense   **Ht:** 6-3 **Wt:** 205   **Shoots:** left
B: May 14, 1968, Espoo, Finland

YR	Regular Season					Playoffs				
	GP	G	A	PTS	PM	GP	G	A	PTS	PM
1992-93	22	0	1	1	14	-	-	-	-	-
Pitt. Totals	22	0	1	1	14	-	-	-	-	-
NHL Totals	123	10	17	27	137	6	0	0	0	2

Acquired from Los Angeles for Jeff Chychrun, November 6, 1992

Traded to San Jose for future considerations, February 26, 1993

AITKEN, BRADLEY (Brad)

Left Wing   **Ht:** 6-2 **Wt:** 200   **Shoots:** left
B: October 30, 1967, Scarborough, Ontario

YR	Regular Season					Playoffs				
	GP	G	A	PTS	PM	GP	G	A	PTS	PM
1987-88	5	1	1	2	0	-	-	-	-	-
1990-91	6	0	1	1	25	-	-	-	-	-
Pitt. Totals	11	1	2	3	25	-	-	-	-	-
NHL Totals	14	1	3	4	25	-	-	-	-	-

Selected in the 1986 Entry Draft, 3rd choice, 46th overall

Traded to Edmonton for Kim Issel, March 5, 1991

ALLEN, PETER

Defense   **Ht:** 6-2 **Wt:** 200   **Shoots:** right
B: March 6, 1970, Calgary, Alberta

YR	Regular Season					Playoffs				
	GP	G	A	PTS	PM	GP	G	A	PTS	PM
1995-96	8	0	0	0	8	-	-	-	-	-
Pitt. Totals	8	0	0	0	8	-	-	-	-	-
NHL Totals	8	0	0	0	8	-	-	-	-	-

Signed as a free agent, August 10, 1995

Signed as a free agent by San Jose, August 19, 1997

ANDERSON, RUSSELL VINCENT (Russ)

Defense   **Ht:** 6-3 **Wt:** 210   **Shoots:** left
B: February 12, 1955, Minneapolis, Minnesota

YR	Regular Season					Playoffs				
	GP	G	A	PTS	PM	GP	G	A	PTS	PM
1976-77	66	2	11	13	81	3	0	1	1	14
1977-78	74	2	16	18	150	-	-	-	-	-
1978-79	72	3	13	16	93	2	0	0	0	0
1979-80	76	5	22	27	150	5	0	2	2	14
1980-81	34	3	14	17	112	-	-	-	-	-
1981-82	31	0	1	1	98	-	-	-	-	-
Pitt. Totals	353	15	77	92	684	10	0	3	3	28
NHL Totals	519	22	99	121	1086	10	0	3	3	28

Selected in the 1975 Amateur Draft, 2nd choice, 31st overall

Traded to Hartford with 8th round choice in 1983 Entry Draft for Rick MacLeish, December 29, 1981

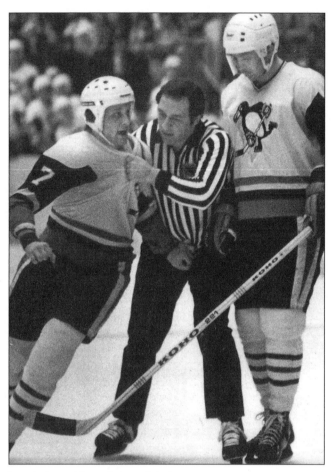

Russ Anderson (7) supplied muscle in the 1970s.

ANDREA, PAUL LAWRENCE

Right Wing   **Ht:** 5-10 **Wt:** 174   **Shoots:** left
B: July 31, 1941, North Sydney, Nova Scotia

	Regular Season					Playoffs				
YR	GP	G	A	PTS	PM	GP	G	A	PTS	PM
1967-68	65	11	21	32	2	-	-	-	-	-
1968-69	25	7	6	13	2	-	-	-	-	-
Pitt. Totals	90	18	27	45	4	-	-	-	-	-
NHL Totals	150	31	49	80	10	-	-	-	-	-
WHA Totals	135	36	48	84	26	14	3	8	11	2

Acquired from NY Rangers with Frank Francis, George Konik, and Dunc McCallum for Larry Jeffrey, June 6, 1967

Traded to Vancouver (WHL) with John Arbour and the loan of Andy Bathgate for the 1969-70 season for Bryan Hextall, May 20, 1969

ANDRUSAK, GREG FREDERICK

Defense   **Ht:** 6-1 **Wt:** 195   **Shoots:** right
B: November 14, 1969, Cranbrook, British Columbia

	Regular Season					Playoffs				
YR	GP	G	A	PTS	PM	GP	G	A	PTS	PM
1993-94	3	0	0	0	2	-	-	-	-	-
1994-95	7	0	4	4	6	-	-	-	-	-
1995-96	2	0	0	0	0	-	-	-	-	-
1998-99	7	0	1	1	4	12	1	0	1	6
Pitt. Totals	19	0	5	5	12	12	1	0	1	6
NHL Totals	28	0	6	6	16	15	1	0	1	8

Selected in the 1988 Entry Draft, 5th choice, 88th overall

Signed as a free agent, March 19, 1999

Signed as a free agent by Toronto, July 19, 1999

ANGOTTI, LOUIS FREDERICK (Lou)

Center/Right Wing   **Ht:** 5-9 **Wt:** 170   **Shoots:** right
B: January 16, 1938, Toronto, Ontario

	Regular Season					Playoffs				
YR	GP	G	A	PTS	PM	GP	G	A	PTS	PM
1968-69	71	17	20	37	36	-	-	-	-	-
Pitt. Totals	71	17	20	37	36	-	-	-	-	-
NHL Totals	653	103	186	289	228	65	8	8	16	17
WHA Totals	26	2	5	7	9	-	-	-	-	-

Acquired from St. Louis for Ab McDonald, June 11, 1968

Traded to St. Louis with a 1st round choice in the 1971 Amateur Draft for Craig Cameron, Ron Schock, and a 2nd round choice in the 1971 Amateur Draft, June 6, 1969

ANTOSKI, SHAWN

Left Wing   **Ht:** 6-4 **Wt:** 235   **Shoots:** left
B: March 25, 1970, Brantford, Ontario

	Regular Season					Playoffs				
YR	GP	G	A	PTS	PM	GP	G	A	PTS	PM
1996-97	13	0	0	0	49	-	-	-	-	-
Pitt. Totals	13	0	0	0	49	-	-	-	-	-
NHL Totals	183	3	5	8	599	36	1	3	4	74

Signed as a free agent, July 31, 1996

Traded to Anaheim with Dmitri Mironov for Alex Hicks and Fredrik Olausson, November 19, 1996

APPS, SYLVANUS MARSHALL (Syl)

Center   Ht: 6-0 **Wt:** 185   **Shoots:** right
B: August 1, 1947, Toronto, Ontario

YR	Regular Season					Playoffs				
	GP	G	A	PTS	PM	GP	G	A	PTS	PM
1970-71	31	9	16	25	21	-	-	-	-	-
1971-72	72	15	44	59	78	4	1	0	1	2
1972-73	77	29	56	85	18	-	-	-	-	-
1973-74	75	24	61	85	37	-	-	-	-	-
1974-75	79	24	55	79	43	9	2	3	5	9
1975-76	**80**	32	67	99	24	3	0	1	1	0
1976-77	72	18	43	61	20	3	1	0	1	12
1977-78	9	0	7	7	0	-	-	-	-	-
Pitt. Totals	**495**	**151**	**349**	**500**	**241**	**19**	**4**	**4**	**8**	**23**
NHL Totals	**727**	**183**	**423**	**606**	**311**	**23**	**5**	**5**	**10**	**23**

Acquired from NY Rangers with Sheldon Kannegiesser for Glen Sather, January 26, 1971

Traded to Los Angeles with Hartland Monahan for Gene Carr, Dave Schultz, and a 4th round choice in the 1978 Amateur Draft, November 2, 1977

Prince of Wales Conference All-Star 1974-75

All-Star Game MVP 1975

Penguins Hall of Fame, 1994

ARBOUR, JOHN GILBERT (Jack)

Defense   Ht: 5-11 **Wt:** 195   **Shoots:** left
B: September 28, 1945, Niagara Falls, Ontario

YR	Regular Season					Playoffs				
	GP	G	A	PTS	PM	GP	G	A	PTS	PM
1968-69	17	0	2	2	35	-	-	-	-	-
Pitt. Totals	**17**	**0**	**2**	**2**	**35**	**-**	**-**	**-**	**-**	**-**
NHL Totals	**106**	**1**	**9**	**10**	**149**	**5**	**0**	**0**	**0**	**0**
WHA Totals	**335**	**30**	**164**	**194**	**568**	**28**	**3**	**13**	**16**	**62**

Acquired from Boston with Jean Pronovost for a 1st round choice in the 1969 Amateur Draft and cash, May 21, 1968

Traded to Vancouver (WHL) with Paul Andrea and the loan of Andy Bathgate for the 1969-70 season for Bryan Hextall, May 20, 1969

Popular Colby Armstrong (right) shares a laugh with Sidney Crosby.

ARMSTRONG, COLBY (Army)

Right Wing   Ht: 6-2 **Wt:** 190   **Shoots:** right
B: November 23, 1982, Lloydminster, Saskatchewan

YR	Regular Season					Playoffs				
	GP	G	A	PTS	PM	GP	G	A	PTS	PM
2005-06	47	16	24	40	58	-	-	-	-	-
2006-07	80	12	22	34	67	5	0	1	1	11
2007-08	54	9	15	24	50	-	-	-	-	-
Pitt. Totals	**181**	**37**	**61**	**98**	**175**	**5**	**0**	**1**	**1**	**11**
NHL Totals	**360**	**78**	**100**	**178**	**317**	**5**	**0**	**1**	**1**	**11**

Selected in the 2001 Entry Draft, 1st choice, 21st overall

Traded to Atlanta with Erik Christensen, Angelo Esposito, and a 1st round choice in the 2008 Entry Draft for Pascal Dupuis and Marian Hossa, February 26, 2008

ARNASON, CHARLES (Chuck, the Rifleman)

Right Wing **Ht:** 5-10 **Wt:** 183 **Shoots:** right
B: July 15, 1951, Ashburn, Manitoba

YR	GP	G	A	PTS	PM	GP	G	A	PTS	PM
	Regular Season					Playoffs				
1973-74	41	13	5	18	4	-	-	-	-	-
1974-75	78	26	32	58	32	9	2	4	6	4
1975-76	30	7	3	10	14	-	-	-	-	-
Pitt. Totals	149	46	40	86	50	9	2	4	6	4
NHL Totals	401	109	90	199	122	9	2	4	6	4

Acquired from Atlanta with Bob Paradise for Al McDonough, January 4, 1974

Traded to Kansas City with Steve Durbano for Ed Gilbert, Simon Nolet, and an exchange of 1st round choices in the 1976 Amateur Draft, January 9, 1976

AUBIN, JEAN-SEBASTIEN

Goaltender **Ht:** 5-11 **Wt:** 180 **Catches:** right
B: July 19, 1977, Montreal, Quebec

YR	GP	MINS	GA	SH	AVE	GP	MINS	GA	SH	AVE
	Regular Season					Playoffs				
1998-99	17	756	28	2	2.22	-	-	-	-	-
1999-00	51	2789	120	2	2.58	-	-	-	-	-
2000-01	36	2050	107	0	3.13	1	1	0	0	0.00
2001-02	21	1094	65	0	3.56	-	-	-	-	-
2002-03	21	1132	59	1	3.13	-	-	-	-	-
2003-04	22	1067	53	1	2.98	-	-	-	-	-
Pitt. Totals	168	8888	432	6	2.92	1	1	0	0	0.00
NHL Totals	218	11197	547	7	2.93	1	1	0	0	0.00

Selected in the 1995 Entry Draft, 2nd choice, 76th overall

Signed as a free agent by Toronto, August 18, 2005

Don Awrey (24) battles to keep the Flames from scoring.

AWREY, DONALD WILLIAM (Don)

Defense **Ht:** 6-0 **Wt:** 175 **Shoots:** left
B: July 18, 1943, Kitchener, Ontario

YR	GP	G	A	PTS	PM	GP	G	A	PTS	PM
	Regular Season					Playoffs				
1976-77	79	1	12	13	40	3	0	1	1	0
Pitt. Totals	79	1	12	13	40	3	0	1	1	0
NHL Totals	979	31	158	189	1065	71	0	18	18	150

Acquired from Montreal for a 3rd round choice in the 1978 Amateur Draft, August 11, 1976

Rights traded to Washington for Bob Paradise, October 1, 1977

B

BABYCH, WAYNE JOSEPH

Right Wing **Ht:** 5-11 **Wt:** 191 **Shoots:** right
B: June 6, 1958, Edmonton, Alberta

YR	GP	G	A	PTS	PM	GP	G	A	PTS	PM
	Regular Season					Playoffs				
1984-85	65	20	34	54	35	-	-	-	-	-
1985-86	2	0	0	0	0	-	-	-	-	-
Pitt. Totals	67	20	34	54	35	-	-	-	-	-
NHL Totals	519	192	246	438	498	41	7	9	16	24

Claimed from St. Louis in the Waiver Draft, October 9, 1984

Traded to Quebec for future considerations, October 20, 1985

BARNABY, MATTHEW

Right Wing **Ht:** 6-0 **Wt:** 189 **Shoots:** left
B: May 4, 1973, Ottawa, Ontario

YR	GP	G	A	PTS	PM	GP	G	A	PTS	PM
	Regular Season					Playoffs				
1998-99	18	2	2	4	34	13	0	0	0	35
1999-00	64	12	12	24	197	11	0	2	2	29
2000-01	47	1	4	5	168	-	-	-	-	-
Pitt. Totals	129	15	18	33	399	24	0	2	2	64
NHL Totals	834	113	187	300	2562	62	7	15	22	170

Acquired from Buffalo for Stu Barnes, March 11, 1999

Traded to Tampa Bay for Wayne Primeau, February 1, 2001

BARNES, STU

Center/Left Wing   **Ht:** 5-11 **Wt:** 182   **Shoots:** right
B: December 25, 1970, Spruce Grove, Alberta

	Regular Season					Playoffs				
YR	GP	G	A	PTS	PM	GP	G	A	PTS	PM
1996-97	62	17	22	39	16	5	0	1	1	0
1997-98	78	30	35	65	30	6	3	3	6	2
1998-99	64	20	12	32	20	-	-	-	-	-
Pitt. Totals	204	67	69	136	66	11	3	4	7	2
NHL Totals	1136	261	336	597	438	116	30	32	62	24

Acquired from Florida with Jason Woolley for Chris Wells, November 19, 1996

Traded to Buffalo for Matthew Barnaby, March 11, 1999

BARRASSO, THOMAS (Tom)

Goaltender   **Ht:** 6-3 **Wt:** 210   **Catches:** right
B: March 31, 1965, Boston, Massachusetts

	Regular Season					Playoffs				
YR	GP	MINS	GA	SH	AVE	GP	MINS	GA	SH	AVE
1988-89	44	2406	162	0	4.04	11	631	40	0	3.80
1989-90	24	1294	101	0	4.68	-	-	-	-	-
1990-91	48	2754	165	1	3.59	20	1175	51	1	2.60
1991-92	57	3329	196	1	3.53	21	1233	58	1	2.82
1992-93	63	3702	186	4	3.01	12	722	35	2	2.91
1993-94	44	2482	139	2	3.36	6	356	17	0	2.87
1994-95	2	125	8	0	3.84	2	80	8	0	6.00
1995-96	49	2799	160	2	3.43	10	558	26	1	2.80
1996-97	5	270	26	0	5.78	-	-	-	-	-
1997-98	63	3542	122	7	2.07	6	376	17	0	2.71
1998-99	43	2306	98	4	2.55	13	787	35	1	2.67
1999-00	18	870	46	1	3.17	-	-	-	-	-
Pitt. Totals	460	25879	1409	22	3.27	101	5918	287	6	2.91
NHL Totals	777	44180	2385	38	3.24	119	6953	349	6	3.01

Acquired from Buffalo with a 3rd round choice in the 1990 Entry Draft for Doug Bodger and Darrin Shannon, November 12, 1988

Traded to Ottawa for Janne Laukkanen and Ron Tugnutt, March 14, 2000

Signed as a free agent, June 18, 2003

Second Team NHL All-Star 1992-93

BARRIE, DOUGLAS ROBERT (Doug)

Defense   **Ht:** 5-9 **Wt:** 175   **Shoots:** right
B: October 2, 1946, Edmonton, Alberta

	Regular Season					Playoffs				
YR	GP	G	A	PTS	PM	GP	G	A	PTS	PM
1968-69	8	1	1	2	8	-	-	-	-	-
Pitt. Totals	8	1	1	2	8	-	-	-	-	-
NHL Totals	158	10	42	52	268	-	-	-	-	-
WHA Totals	350	37	122	159	620	12	1	1	2	31

Purchased from Detroit, October 1968

Claimed in the 1970 Expansion Draft by Buffalo, June 10, 1970

BARRIE, LEN

Center   **Ht:** 6-0 **Wt:** 200   **Shoots:** left
B: June 4, 1969, Kimberley, British Columbia

	Regular Season					Playoffs				
YR	GP	G	A	PTS	PM	GP	G	A	PTS	PM
1994-95	48	3	11	14	66	4	1	0	1	8
1995-96	5	0	0	0	18	-	-	-	-	-
Pitt. Totals	53	3	11	14	84	4	1	0	1	8
NHL Totals	184	19	45	64	290	8	1	0	1	8

Signed as a free agent, August 15, 1994

Signed as a free agent by Los Angeles, July 9, 1999

BASSEN, HENRY (Hank)

Goaltender   **Ht:** 5-10 **Wt:** 180   **Catches:** left
B: December 6, 1932, Calgary, Alberta
D: May 29, 2009

	Regular Season					Playoffs				
YR	GP	MINS	GA	SH	AVE	GP	MINS	GA	SH	AVE
1967-68	25	1299	62	1	2.86	-	-	-	-	-
Pitt. Totals	25	1299	62	1	2.86	-	-	-	-	-
NHL Totals	156	8759	434	5	2.97	5	274	11	0	2.41

Acquired from Detroit for Roy Edwards, September 7, 1967

BATHGATE, ANDREW JAMES (Andy)

Right Wing   **Ht:** 6-0 **Wt:** 180   **Shoots:** right
B: August 28, 1932, Winnipeg, Manitoba

	Regular Season					Playoffs				
YR	GP	G	A	PTS	PM	GP	G	A	PTS	PM
1967-68	74	20	39	59	55	-	-	-	-	-
1970-71	76	15	29	44	34	-	-	-	-	-
Pitt. Totals	150	35	68	103	89	-	-	-	-	-
NHL Totals	1069	349	624	973	624	54	21	14	35	76
WHA Totals	11	1	6	7	2	-	-	-	-	-

Selected from Detroit in the 1967 Expansion Draft, June 6, 1967

Loaned to Vancouver (WHL) for the 1968-69 season for future considerations, October 1968

Loaned to Vancouver (WHL) for the 1969-70 season with the trade of Paul Andrea and John Arbour for Bryan Hextall, May 20, 1969

Claimed by Providence (AHL) in the Reverse Draft, June 10, 1971

Hockey Hall of Fame (Player), 1978

BAUMGARTNER, NOLAN

Defense   **Ht:** 6-2 **Wt:** 205   **Shoots:** right
B: March 23, 1976, Calgary, Alberta

	Regular Season					Playoffs				
YR	GP	G	A	PTS	PM	GP	G	A	PTS	PM
2003-04	5	0	0	0	2	-	-	-	-	-
Pitt. Totals	5	0	0	0	2	-	-	-	-	-
NHL Totals	143	7	40	47	69	4	0	0	0	10

Claimed from Vancouver in the Waiver Draft, October 3, 2003

Claimed on waivers by Vancouver, November 1, 2003

BAXTER, PAUL GORDON

Defense   **Ht:** 5-11 **Wt:** 200   **Shoots:** right
B: October 28, 1955, Winnipeg, Manitoba

	Regular Season					Playoffs				
YR	GP	G	A	PTS	PM	GP	G	A	PTS	PM
1980-81	51	5	14	19	204	5	0	1	1	28
1981-82	76	9	34	43	**409**	5	0	0	0	14
1982-83	75	11	21	32	238	-	-	-	-	-
Pitt. Totals	202	25	69	94	851	10	0	1	1	42
NHL Totals	472	48	121	169	1564	40	0	5	5	162
WHA Totals	290	25	89	114	962	30	6	11	17	94

Selected in the 1975 Amateur Draft, 3rd choice, 49th overall

Signed as a free agent, August 7, 1980

Signed as a free agent by Calgary, September 29, 1983

BEECH, KRIS

Center   **Ht:** 6-3 **Wt:** 211   **Shoots:** left
B: February 5, 1981, Salmon Arm, British Columbia

	Regular Season					Playoffs				
YR	GP	G	A	PTS	PM	GP	G	A	PTS	PM
2001-02	79	10	15	25	45	-	-	-	-	-
2002-03	12	0	1	1	6	-	-	-	-	-
2003-04	4	0	1	1	6	-	-	-	-	-
2007-08	5	0	0	0	2	-	-	-	-	-
Pitt. Totals	100	10	17	27	59	-	-	-	-	-
NHL Totals	198	25	42	67	113	-	-	-	-	-

Acquired from Washington with Ross Lupaschuk, Michal Sivek, and future considerations for Jaromir Jagr and Frantisek Kucera, July 11, 2001

Traded to Nashville for a 4th round choice in the 2006 Entry Draft, September 9, 2005

Claimed on waivers from Washington, January 26, 2008

Signed as a free agent by HV 71 Jonkoping (Sweden), October 13, 2008

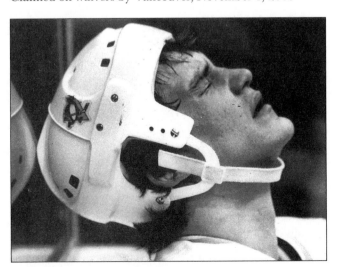

Paul Baxter clears the cobwebs in the sin bin.

BELANGER, ROGER

Center   **Ht:** 6-0   **Wt:** 190   **Shoots:** right
B: December 1, 1965, St. Catharines, Ontario

YR	Regular Season GP	G	A	PTS	PM	Playoffs GP	G	A	PTS	PM
1984-85	44	3	5	8	32	-	-	-	-	-
Pitt. Totals	**44**	**3**	**5**	**8**	**32**	**-**	**-**	**-**	**-**	**-**
NHL Totals	**44**	**3**	**5**	**8**	**32**	**-**	**-**	**-**	**-**	**-**

Selected in the 1984 Entry Draft, 3rd choice, 16th overall

BELLAND, NEIL

Defense   **Ht:** 5-11   **Wt:** 180   **Shoots:** left
B: April 3, 1961, Parry Sound, Ontario

YR	Regular Season GP	G	A	PTS	PM	Playoffs GP	G	A	PTS	PM
1986-87	3	0	1	1	0	-	-	-	-	-
Pitt. Totals	**3**	**0**	**1**	**1**	**0**	**-**	**-**	**-**	**-**	**-**
NHL Totals	**109**	**13**	**32**	**45**	**54**	**21**	**2**	**9**	**11**	**23**

Signed as a free agent, September 29, 1986

BENNETT, HARVEY A., Jr.

Left Wing/Center   **Ht:** 6-4   **Wt:** 215   **Shoots:** left
B: August 9, 1952, Cranston, Rhode Island

YR	Regular Season GP	G	A	PTS	PM	Playoffs GP	G	A	PTS	PM
1974-75	7	0	0	0	0	-	-	-	-	-
1975-76	25	3	3	6	53	-	-	-	-	-
Pitt. Totals	**32**	**3**	**3**	**6**	**53**	**-**	**-**	**-**	**-**	**-**
NHL Totals	**268**	**44**	**46**	**90**	**347**	**4**	**0**	**0**	**0**	**2**

Signed as a free agent, June 25, 1974

Traded to Washington for Stan Gilbertson, December 16, 1975

BERANEK, JOSEF

Left Wing/Center   **Ht:** 6-2   **Wt:** 195   **Shoots:** left
B: October 25, 1969, Litvinov, Czechoslovakia

YR	Regular Season GP	G	A	PTS	PM	Playoffs GP	G	A	PTS	PM
1996-97	8	3	1	4	4	5	0	0	0	2
1999-00	13	4	4	8	18	11	0	3	3	4
2000-01	70	9	14	23	43	13	0	2	2	2
Pitt. Totals	**91**	**16**	**19**	**35**	**65**	**29**	**0**	**5**	**5**	**8**
NHL Totals	**531**	**118**	**144**	**262**	**398**	**57**	**5**	**8**	**13**	**24**

Acquired from Vancouver for future considerations, March 18, 1997

Traded to Edmonton for Bobby Dollas and Tony Hrkac, June 16, 1998

Acquired from Edmonton for German Titov, March 14, 2000

BEREHOWSKY, DRAKE

Defense   **Ht:** 6-2   **Wt:** 225   **Shoots:** right
B: January 3, 1972, Toronto, Ontario

YR	Regular Season GP	G	A	PTS	PM	Playoffs GP	G	A	PTS	PM
1994-95	4	0	0	0	13	1	0	0	0	0
1995-96	1	0	0	0	0	-	-	-	-	-
2003-04	47	5	16	21	50	-	-	-	-	-
Pitt. Totals	**52**	**5**	**16**	**21**	**63**	**1**	**0**	**0**	**0**	**0**
NHL Totals	**549**	**37**	**112**	**149**	**848**	**22**	**1**	**3**	**4**	**30**

Acquired from Toronto for Grant Jennings, April 7, 1995

Signed as a free agent by Edmonton, September 30, 1997

Signed as a free agent, August 29, 2003

Traded to Toronto for Ric Jackman, February 11, 2004

BERGERON, YVES

Right Wing   **Ht:** 5-9   **Wt:** 165   **Shoots:** right
B: January 11, 1952, Malartic, Quebec

YR	Regular Season GP	G	A	PTS	PM	Playoffs GP	G	A	PTS	PM
1974-75	2	0	0	0	0	-	-	-	-	-
1976-77	1	0	0	0	0	-	-	-	-	-
Pitt. Totals	**3**	**0**	**0**	**0**	**0**	**-**	**-**	**-**	**-**	**-**
NHL Totals	**3**	**0**	**0**	**0**	**0**	**-**	**-**	**-**	**-**	**-**
WHA Totals	**65**	**14**	**19**	**33**	**32**	**-**	**-**	**-**	**-**	**-**

Selected in the 1972 Amateur Draft, 8th choice, 120th overall

Selected by Quebec in the 1972 WHA General Player Draft, February 12, 1972

BERGEVIN, MARC

Defense **Ht:** 6-1 **Wt:** 209 **Shoots:** left
B: August 11, 1965, Montreal, Quebec

YR	Regular Season					Playoffs				
	GP	G	A	PTS	PM	GP	G	A	PTS	PM
2000-01	36	1	4	5	26	12	0	1	1	2
2002-03	69	2	5	7	36	-	-	-	-	-
2003-04	52	1	8	9	27	-	-	-	-	-
Pitt. Totals	157	4	17	21	89	12	0	1	1	2
NHL Totals	1191	36	145	181	1090	80	3	6	9	52

Acquired from St. Louis for Dan Trebil, December 28, 2000

Signed as a free agent by St. Louis, November 6, 2001

Signed as a free agent, July 18, 2002

Traded to Tampa Bay for Brian Holzinger, March 11, 2003

Acquired from Tampa Bay for a 9th round choice in the 2003 Entry Draft, May 12, 2003

Traded to Vancouver for a 7th round choice in the 2004 Entry Draft, March 9, 2004

BERGKVIST, STEFAN

Defense **Ht:** 6-2 **Wt:** 224 **Shoots:** left
B: March 10, 1975, Leksand, Sweden

YR	Regular Season					Playoffs				
	GP	G	A	PTS	PM	GP	G	A	PTS	PM
1995-96	2	0	0	0	2	4	0	0	0	2
1996-97	5	0	0	0	7	-	-	-	-	-
Pitt. Totals	7	0	0	0	9	4	0	0	0	2
NHL Totals	7	0	0	0	9	4	0	0	0	2

Selected in the 1993 Entry Draft, 1st choice, 26th overall

BERRY, RICK

Defense **Ht:** 6-2 **Wt:** 210 **Shoots:** left
B: November 4, 1978, Birtle, Manitoba

YR	Regular Season					Playoffs				
	GP	G	A	PTS	PM	GP	G	A	PTS	PM
2001-02	13	0	2	2	21	-	-	-	-	-
Pitt. Totals	13	0	2	2	21	-	-	-	-	-
NHL Totals	197	2	13	15	314	-	-	-	-	-

Acquired from Colorado with Ville Nieminen for Darius Kasparaitis, March 19, 2002

Claimed by Washington in the Waiver Draft, October 4, 2002

BEVERLEY, NICHOLAS GERALD (Nick)

Defense **Ht:** 6-2 **Wt:** 185 **Shoots:** right
B: April 21, 1947, Toronto, Ontario

YR	Regular Season					Playoffs				
	GP	G	A	PTS	PM	GP	G	A	PTS	PM
1973-74	67	2	14	16	21	-	-	-	-	-
Pitt. Totals	67	2	14	16	21	-	-	-	-	-
NHL Totals	502	18	94	112	156	7	0	1	1	0

Acquired from Boston for Darryl Edestrand, October 25, 1973

Traded to NY Rangers for Vic Hadfield, May 27, 1974

BIANCHIN, WAYNE RICHARD

Left Wing **Ht:** 5-10 **Wt:** 180 **Shoots:** left
B: September 6, 1953, Nanaimo, British Columbia

YR	Regular Season					Playoffs				
	GP	G	A	PTS	PM	GP	G	A	PTS	PM
1973-74	69	12	13	25	38	-	-	-	-	-
1974-75	2	0	0	0	0	-	-	-	-	-
1975-76	14	1	5	6	4	-	-	-	-	-
1976-77	79	28	6	34	28	3	0	1	1	6
1977-78	61	20	13	33	40	-	-	-	-	-
1978-79	40	7	4	11	20	-	-	-	-	-
Pitt. Totals	265	68	41	109	130	3	0	1	1	6
NHL Totals	276	68	41	109	137	3	0	1	1	6

Selected in the 1973 Amateur Draft, 2nd choice, 23rd overall

Selected by Edmonton in the 1979 Expansion Draft, June 13, 1979

BIGNELL, LARRY IRVIN

Defense **Ht:** 6-0 **Wt:** 175 **Shoots:** left
B: January 7, 1950, Edmonton, Alberta

YR	Regular Season					Playoffs				
	GP	G	A	PTS	PM	GP	G	A	PTS	PM
1973-74	20	0	3	3	2	-	-	-	-	-
1974-75	-	-	-	-	-	3	0	0	0	2
Pitt. Totals	20	0	3	3	2	3	0	0	0	2
NHL Totals	20	0	3	3	2	3	0	0	0	2
WHA Totals	41	5	5	10	43	-	-	-	-	-

Selected in the 1970 Amateur Draft, 3rd choice, 35th overall

Selected by Vancouver in the 1973 WHA Professional Player Draft, June 1973

BINKLEY, LESLIE JOHN (Les)

Goaltender **Ht:** 6-0 **Wt:** 175 **Catches:** right
B: June 6, 1934, Owen Sound, Ontario

	Regular Season					Playoffs				
YR	GP	MINS	GA	SH	AVE	GP	MINS	GA	SH	AVE
1967-68	54	3141	151	6	2.88	-	-	-	-	-
1968-69	50	2885	158	0	3.29	-	-	-	-	-
1969-70	27	1477	79	3	3.21	7	428	15	0	2.10
1970-71	34	1870	89	2	2.86	-	-	-	-	-
1971-72	31	1673	98	0	3.51	-	-	-	-	-
Pitt. Totals	196	11046	575	11	3.12	7	428	15	0	2.10
NHL Totals	196	11046	575	11	3.12	7	428	15	0	2.10
WHA Totals	81	4228	262	1	3.72	10	464	40	0	5.17

Acquired from San Diego (WHL), October 1967

Selected by Ottawa in the 1972 WHA General Player Draft, February 12, 1972

Penguins Hall of Fame, 2003

BISSONNETTE, PAUL (Bizz Nasty)

Left Wing **Ht:** 6-2 **Wt:** 211 **Shoots:** left
B: March 11, 1985, Welland, Ontario

	Regular Season					Playoffs				
YR	GP	G	A	PTS	PM	GP	G	A	PTS	PM
2008-09	15	0	1	1	22	-	-	-	-	-
Pitt. Totals	15	0	1	1	22	-	-	-	-	-
NHL Totals	56	3	3	6	139	-	-	-	-	-

Selected in the 2003 Entry Draft, 5th choice, 121st overall

Claimed on waivers by Phoenix, September 30, 2009

BJUGSTAD, SCOTT

Right Wing **Ht:** 6-1 **Wt:** 185 **Shoots:** left
B: June 2, 1961, St. Paul, Minnesota

	Regular Season					Playoffs				
YR	GP	G	A	PTS	PM	GP	G	A	PTS	PM
1988-89	24	3	0	3	4	-	-	-	-	-
Pitt. Totals	24	3	0	3	4	-	-	-	-	-
NHL Totals	317	76	68	144	144	9	0	1	1	2

Acquired from Minnesota with Gord Dineen for Steve Gotaas and Ville Siren, December 17, 1988

Signed as a free agent by Los Angeles, August 24, 1989

BLACKBURN, ROBERT JOHN (Bob)

Defense **Ht:** 5-11 **Wt:** 198 **Shoots:** left
B: February 1, 1938, Rouyn, Quebec

	Regular Season					Playoffs				
YR	GP	G	A	PTS	PM	GP	G	A	PTS	PM
1969-70	60	4	7	11	51	6	0	0	0	4
1970-71	64	4	5	9	54	-	-	-	-	-
Pitt. Totals	124	8	12	20	105	6	0	0	0	4
NHL Totals	135	8	12	20	105	6	0	0	0	4

Claimed from NY Rangers in the Intra-League Draft, June 11, 1969

Sold to Vancouver, October 3, 1971

BLADON, TOM

Defense **Ht:** 6-1 **Wt:** 195 **Shoots:** right
B: December 29, 1952, Edmonton, Alberta

	Regular Season					Playoffs				
YR	GP	G	A	PTS	PM	GP	G	A	PTS	PM
1978-79	78	4	23	27	64	7	0	4	4	2
1979-80	57	2	6	8	35	1	0	1	1	0
Pitt. Totals	135	6	29	35	99	8	0	5	5	2
NHL Totals	610	73	197	270	392	86	8	29	37	70

Acquired from Philadelphia with Orest Kindrachuk and Ross Lonsberry for a 1st round choice in the 1978 Amateur Draft, June 14, 1978

Signed as a free agent by Edmonton, July 10, 1980

BLAISDELL, MICHAEL WALTER (Mike)

Right Wing **Ht:** 6-1 **Wt:** 196 **Shoots:** right
B: January 18, 1960, Moose Jaw, Saskatchewan

	Regular Season					Playoffs				
YR	GP	G	A	PTS	PM	GP	G	A	PTS	PM
1985-86	66	15	14	29	36	-	-	-	-	-
1986-87	10	1	1	2	2	-	-	-	-	-
Pitt. Totals	76	16	15	31	38	-	-	-	-	-
NHL Totals	343	70	84	154	166	6	1	2	3	10

Claimed from NY Rangers in the Waiver Draft, October 7, 1985

Signed as a free agent by Toronto, July 10, 1987

Doug Bodger (in white) was a first-round pick in 1984.

BODGER, DOUG

Defense   **Ht:** 6-2   **Wt:** 210   **Shoots:** left
B: June 18, 1966, Chemainus, British Columbia

YR	Regular Season					Playoffs				
	GP	G	A	PTS	PM	GP	G	A	PTS	PM
1984-85	65	5	26	31	67	-	-	-	-	-
1985-86	79	4	33	37	63	-	-	-	-	-
1986-87	76	11	38	49	52	-	-	-	-	-
1987-88	69	14	31	45	103	-	-	-	-	-
1988-89	10	1	4	5	7	-	-	-	-	-
Pitt. Totals	299	35	132	167	292	-	-	-	-	-
NHL Totals	1071	106	422	528	1007	47	6	18	24	25

Selected in the 1984 Entry Draft, 2nd choice, 9th overall

Traded to Buffalo with Darrin Shannon for Tom Barrasso and a 3rd round choice in the 1990 Entry Draft, November 12, 1988

BOGUNIECKI, ERIC

Center/Right Wing   **Ht:** 5-8   **Wt:** 192   **Shoots:** right
B: May 6, 1975, New Haven, Connecticut

YR	Regular Season					Playoffs				
	GP	G	A	PTS	PM	GP	G	A	PTS	PM
2005-06	38	5	6	11	29	-	-	-	-	-
Pitt. Totals	38	5	6	11	29	-	-	-	-	-
NHL Totals	178	34	42	76	105	9	1	3	4	2

Acquired from St. Louis for Steve Poapst, December 9, 2005

Signed as a free agent by Columbus, August 22, 2006

BOILEAU, PATRICK

Defense   **Ht:** 6-0   **Wt:** 202   **Shoots:** right
B: February 22, 1975, Montreal, Quebec

YR	Regular Season					Playoffs				
	GP	G	A	PTS	PM	GP	G	A	PTS	PM
2003-04	16	3	4	7	8	-	-	-	-	-
Pitt. Totals	16	3	4	7	8	-	-	-	-	-
NHL Totals	48	5	11	16	26	-	-	-	-	-

Signed as a free agent, August 28, 2003

Signed as a free agent by Lausanne (Switzerland), May 13, 2004

BOIVIN, LEO JOSEPH

Defense   **Ht:** 5-8   **Wt:** 183   **Shoots:** left
B: August 2, 1932, Prescott, Ontario

YR	Regular Season					Playoffs				
	GP	G	A	PTS	PM	GP	G	A	PTS	PM
1967-68	73	9	13	22	74	-	-	-	-	-
1968-69	41	5	13	18	26	-	-	-	-	-
Pitt. Totals	114	14	26	40	100	-	-	-	-	-
NHL Totals	1150	72	250	322	1192	54	3	10	13	59

Selected from Detroit in the 1967 Expansion Draft, June 6, 1967

Traded to Minnesota for Duane Rupp, January 24, 1969

Hockey Hall of Fame (Player), 1986

BONIN, BRIAN

Center   **Ht:** 5-10   **Wt:** 186   **Shoots:** left
B: November 28, 1973, St. Paul, Minnesota

YR	Regular Season					Playoffs				
	GP	G	A	PTS	PM	GP	G	A	PTS	PM
1998-99	5	0	0	0	0	3	0	0	0	0
Pitt. Totals	5	0	0	0	0	3	0	0	0	0
NHL Totals	12	0	0	0	0	-	-	-	-	-

Selected in the 1992 Entry Draft, 9th choice, 211th overall

Signed as a free agent by Vancouver, September 9, 1999

BONVIE, DENNIS

Right Wing   Ht: 5-11 **Wt:** 205   **Shoots:** right
B: July 23, 1973, Antigonish, Nova Scotia

YR	Regular Season					Playoffs				
	GP	G	A	PTS	PM	GP	G	A	PTS	PM
1999-00	28	0	0	0	80	-	-	-	-	-
2000-01	3	0	0	0	0	-	-	-	-	-
Pitt. Totals	31	0	0	0	80	-	-	-	-	-
NHL Totals	92	1	2	3	311	1	0	0	0	0

Signed as a free agent, September 20, 1999

Signed as a free agent by Boston, October 5, 2001

BOUCHARD, JOEL

Defense   Ht: 6-1 **Wt:** 209   **Shoots:** left
B: January 23, 1974, Montreal, Quebec

YR	Regular Season					Playoffs				
	GP	G	A	PTS	PM	GP	G	A	PTS	PM
2002-03	7	0	1	1	0	-	-	-	-	-
Pitt. Totals	7	0	1	1	0	-	-	-	-	-
NHL Totals	364	22	53	75	264	-	-	-	-	-

Acquired from NY Rangers with Rico Fata, Richard Lintner, and Mikael Samuelsson for Alexei Kovalev, Dan LaCouture, Janne Laukkanen, and Mike Wilson, February 10, 2003

Signed as a free agent by Buffalo, July 14, 2003

BOUCHER, PHILIPPE

Defense   Ht: 6-3 **Wt:** 218   **Shoots:** right
B: March 24, 1973, Ste. Apollinaire, Quebec

YR	Regular Season					Playoffs				
	GP	G	A	PTS	PM	GP	G	A	PTS	PM
2008-09	25	3	3	6	24	9	1	3	4	4
Pitt. Totals	25	3	3	6	24	9	1	3	4	4
NHL Totals	748	94	206	300	702	65	4	10	14	39

Acquired from Dallas for Darryl Sydor, November 16, 2008

BOUGHNER, BOB

Defense   Ht: 6-0 **Wt:** 203   **Shoots:** right
B: March 8, 1971, Windsor, Ontario

YR	Regular Season					Playoffs				
	GP	G	A	PTS	PM	GP	G	A	PTS	PM
1999-00	11	1	0	1	69	11	0	2	2	15
2000-01	58	1	3	4	147	18	0	1	1	22
Pitt. Totals	69	2	3	5	216	29	0	3	3	37
NHL Totals	630	15	57	72	1382	65	0	12	12	67

Acquired from Nashville for Pavel Skrbek, March 13, 2000

Signed as a free agent by Calgary, July 2, 2001

BOURQUE, CHRIS

Center   Ht: 5-8 **Wt:** 180   **Shoots:** left
B: January 29, 1986, Boston, Massachusetts

YR	Regular Season					Playoffs				
	GP	G	A	PTS	PM	GP	G	A	PTS	PM
2009-10	20	0	3	3	10	-	-	-	-	-
Pitt. Totals	20	0	3	3	10	-	-	-	-	-
NHL Totals	33	1	3	4	12	-	-	-	-	-

Claimed on waivers from Washington, September 30, 2009

Claimed on waivers by Washington, December 5, 2009

BOURQUE, PHILLIPPE RICHARD (Phil)

Left Wing/Defense   Ht: 6-1 **Wt:** 196   **Shoots:** left
B: June 8, 1962, Chelmsford, Massachusetts

YR	Regular Season					Playoffs				
	GP	G	A	PTS	PM	GP	G	A	PTS	PM
1983-84	5	0	1	1	12	-	-	-	-	-
1985-86	4	0	0	0	2	-	-	-	-	-
1986-87	22	2	3	5	32	-	-	-	-	-
1987-88	21	4	12	16	20	-	-	-	-	-
1988-89	80	17	26	43	97	11	4	1	5	66
1989-90	76	22	17	39	108	-	-	-	-	-
1990-91	78	20	14	34	106	24	6	7	13	16
1991-92	58	10	16	26	58	21	3	4	7	25
Pitt. Totals	344	75	89	164	435	56	13	12	25	107
NHL Totals	477	88	111	199	516	56	13	12	25	107

Signed as a free agent, October 4, 1982

Signed as a free agent by NY Rangers, August 31, 1992

Scrappy Pat Boutette turns to follow the play.

BOUTETTE, PATRICK MICHAEL (Pat)

Left Wing/Center   **Ht:** 5-8 **Wt:** 175   **Shoots:** left
B: March 1, 1952, Windsor, Ontario

	Regular Season					Playoffs				
YR	GP	G	A	PTS	PM	GP	G	A	PTS	PM
1981-82	80	23	51	74	230	5	3	1	4	8
1982-83	**80**	27	29	58	152	-	-	-	-	-
1983-84	73	14	26	40	142	-	-	-	-	-
1984-85	14	1	3	4	24	-	-	-	-	-
Pitt. Totals	247	65	109	174	548	5	3	1	4	8
NHL Totals	756	171	282	453	1354	46	10	14	24	109

Acquired from Hartford with Kevin McClelland as compensation for Hartford's signing of Greg Millen, June 29, 1981

Traded to Hartford for rights to Ville Siren, November 16, 1984

BOYD, RANDY KEITH

Defense   **Ht:** 5-11 **Wt:** 190   **Shoots:** left
B: January 23, 1962, Coniston, Ontario

	Regular Season					Playoffs				
YR	GP	G	A	PTS	PM	GP	G	A	PTS	PM
1981-82	23	0	2	2	49	3	0	0	0	11
1982-83	56	4	14	18	71	-	-	-	-	-
1983-84	5	0	1	1	6	-	-	-	-	-
Pitt. Totals	84	4	17	21	126	3	0	0	0	11
NHL Totals	257	20	67	87	328	13	0	2	2	26

Selected in the 1980 Entry Draft, 2nd choice, 51st overall

Traded to Chicago for Greg Fox, December 6, 1983

BOYER, WALTER (Wally)

Center   **Ht:** 5-8 **Wt:** 165   **Shoots:** left
B: September 27, 1937, Cowan, Manitoba

	Regular Season					Playoffs				
YR	GP	G	A	PTS	PM	GP	G	A	PTS	PM
1968-69	62	10	19	29	17	-	-	-	-	-
1969-70	72	11	12	23	34	10	1	2	3	0
1970-71	68	11	30	41	30	-	-	-	-	-
1971-72	1	0	1	1	0	-	-	-	-	-
Pitt. Totals	203	32	62	94	81	10	1	2	3	0
NHL Totals	365	54	105	159	163	15	1	3	4	0
WHA Totals	69	6	28	34	27	14	4	2	6	4

Acquired from Montreal for Al MacNeil, June 12, 1968

Selected by Winnipeg in the WHA General Player Draft, February 12, 1972

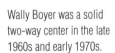

Wally Boyer was a solid two-way center in the late 1960s and early 1970s.

BRADLEY, MATT

Right Wing   Ht: 6-3 **Wt:** 210   **Shoots:** right
B: June 13, 1978, Stittsville, Ontario

YR	Regular Season					Playoffs				
	GP	G	A	PTS	PM	GP	G	A	PTS	PM
2003-04	82	7	9	16	65	-	-	-	-	-
Pitt. Totals	82	7	9	16	65	-	-	-	-	-
NHL Totals	569	52	78	130	463	38	3	8	11	4

Acquired from San Jose for Wayne Primeau, March 11, 2003

Signed as a free agent by Washington, August 18, 2005

BRENT, TIM

Center   Ht: 6-0 **Wt:** 197   **Shoots:** right
B: March 10, 1984, Cambridge, Ontario

YR	Regular Season					Playoffs				
	GP	G	A	PTS	PM	GP	G	A	PTS	PM
2007-08	1	0	0	0	0	-	-	-	-	-
Pitt. Totals	1	0	0	0	0	-	-	-	-	-
NHL Totals	19	1	0	1	8	-	-	-	-	-

Acquired from Anaheim for Stephen Dixon, June 23, 2007

Traded to Chicago for Danny Richmond, July 17, 2008

BRICKLEY, ANDREW (Andy)

Left Wing/Center   Ht: 5-11 **Wt:** 200   **Shoots:** left
B: August 9, 1961, Melrose, Massachusetts

YR	Regular Season					Playoffs				
	GP	G	A	PTS	PM	GP	G	A	PTS	PM
1983-84	50	18	20	38	9	-	-	-	-	-
1984-85	45	7	15	22	10	-	-	-	-	-
Pitt. Totals	95	25	35	60	19	-	-	-	-	-
NHL Totals	385	82	140	222	81	17	1	4	5	4

Acquired from Philadelphia with Ron Flockhart, Mark Taylor, and 1st and 3rd round choices in the 1984 Entry Draft for Rich Sutter and 2nd and 3rd round choices in the 1984 Entry Draft, October 23, 1983

Signed as a free agent by New Jersey, July 8, 1986

BRIERE, MICHEL EDOUARD

Center   Ht: 5-10 **Wt:** 165   **Shoots:** left
B: October 21, 1949, Malartic, Quebec
D: April 13, 1971

YR	Regular Season					Playoffs				
	GP	G	A	PTS	PM	GP	G	A	PTS	PM
1969-70	76	12	32	44	20	10	5	3	8	17
Pitt. Totals	76	12	32	44	20	10	5	3	8	17
NHL Totals	76	12	32	44	20	10	5	3	8	17

Selected in the 1969 Amateur Draft, 2nd choice, 26th overall

BROCHU, MARTIN

Goaltender   Ht: 6-0 **Wt:** 199   **Catches:** left
B: March 10, 1973, Anjou, Quebec

YR	Regular Season					Playoffs				
	GP	MINS	GA	SH	AVE	GP	MINS	GA	SH	AVE
2003-04	1	33	1	0	1.82	-	-	-	-	-
Pitt. Totals	1	33	1	0	1.82	-	-	-	-	-
NHL Totals	9	369	22	0	3.58	-	-	-	-	-

Signed as a free agent, August 22, 2003

BROWN, ANDREW CONRAD (Andy)

Goaltender   Ht: 6-0 **Wt:** 185   **Catches:** left
B: February 15, 1944, Hamilton, Ontario

YR	Regular Season					Playoffs				
	GP	MINS	GA	SH	AVE	GP	MINS	GA	SH	AVE
1972-73	9	520	41	0	4.73	-	-	-	-	-
1973-74	36	1956	115	1	3.53	-	-	-	-	-
Pitt. Totals	45	2476	156	1	3.78	-	-	-	-	-
NHL Totals	62	3373	213	1	3.79	-	-	-	-	-
WHA Totals	86	4777	314	3	3.94	-	-	-	-	-

Acquired from Detroit for a 3rd round choice in the 1973 Amateur Draft, February 25, 1973

Signed as a free agent with Indianapolis (WHA), July 31, 1974

BROWN, DOUGLAS ALLEN (Doug)

Right Wing   Ht: 5-10 **Wt:** 185   **Shoots:** right
B: June 12, 1964, Southborough, Massachusetts

YR	Regular Season					Playoffs				
	GP	G	A	PTS	PM	GP	G	A	PTS	PM
1993-94	77	18	37	55	18	6	0	0	0	2
Pitt. Totals	77	18	37	55	18	6	0	0	0	2
NHL Totals	854	160	214	374	210	109	23	23	46	26

Signed as a free agent, September 28, 1993

Claimed by Detroit in the Waiver Draft, January 18, 1995

BROWN, GREG

Defense **Ht:** 6-0 **Wt:** 185 **Shoots:** right
B: March 7, 1968, Hartford, Connecticut

YR	Regular Season					Playoffs				
	GP	G	A	PTS	PM	GP	G	A	PTS	PM
1993-94	36	3	8	11	28	6	0	1	1	4
Pitt. Totals	36	3	8	11	28	6	0	1	1	4
NHL Totals	94	4	14	18	86	6	0	1	1	4

Signed as a free agent, September 29, 1993

Traded to Winnipeg for cash, April 7, 1995

BROWN, ROBERT (Rob)

Right Wing **Ht:** 5-10 **Wt:** 177 **Shoots:** left
B: April 10, 1968, Kingston, Ontario

YR	Regular Season					Playoffs				
	GP	G	A	PTS	PM	GP	G	A	PTS	PM
1987-88	51	24	20	44	56	-	-	-	-	-
1988-89	68	49	66	115	118	11	5	3	8	22
1989-90	80	33	47	80	102	-	-	-	-	-
1990-91	25	6	10	16	31	-	-	-	-	-
1997-98	82	15	25	40	59	6	1	0	1	4
1998-99	58	13	11	24	16	13	2	5	7	8
1999-00	50	10	13	23	10	11	1	2	3	0
Pitt. Totals	414	150	192	342	392	41	9	10	19	34
NHL Totals	543	190	248	438	599	54	12	14	26	45

Selected in the 1986 Entry Draft, 4th choice, 67th overall

Traded to Hartford for Scott Young, December 21, 1990

Signed as a free agent, October 1, 1997

Prince of Wales Conference All-Star 1988-89

BUCHBERGER, KELLY

Right Wing **Ht:** 6-2 **Wt:** 210 **Shoots:** left
B: December 2, 1966, Langenburg, Saskatchewan

YR	Regular Season					Playoffs				
	GP	G	A	PTS	PM	GP	G	A	PTS	PM
2003-04	71	1	3	4	109	-	-	-	-	-
Pitt. Totals	71	1	3	4	109	-	-	-	-	-
NHL Totals	1182	105	204	309	2297	97	10	15	25	129

Signed as a free agent, July 31, 2003

BULLARD, MICHAEL BRIAN (Mike)

Center **Ht:** 6-0 **Wt:** 195 **Shoots:** left
B: March 10, 1961, Ottawa, Ontario

YR	Regular Season					Playoffs				
	GP	G	A	PTS	PM	GP	G	A	PTS	PM
1980-81	15	1	2	3	19	4	3	3	6	0
1981-82	75	36	27	63	91	5	1	1	2	4
1982-83	57	22	22	44	60	-	-	-	-	-
1983-84	76	51	41	92	57	-	-	-	-	-
1984-85	68	32	31	63	75	-	-	-	-	-
1985-86	77	41	42	83	69	-	-	-	-	-
1986-87	14	2	10	12	17	-	-	-	-	-
Pitt. Totals	382	185	175	360	388	9	4	4	8	4
NHL Totals	727	329	345	674	703	40	11	18	29	44

Selected in the 1980 Entry Draft, 1st choice, 9th overall

Traded to Calgary for Dan Quinn, November 12, 1986

Prince of Wales Conference All-Star 1983-84

BULLEY, EDWARD H. (Ted)

Left Wing **Ht:** 6-1 **Wt:** 192 **Shoots:** left
B: March 25, 1955, Windsor, Ontario

YR	Regular Season					Playoffs				
	GP	G	A	PTS	PM	GP	G	A	PTS	PM
1983-84	26	3	2	5	12	-	-	-	-	-
Pitt. Totals	26	3	2	5	12	-	-	-	-	-
NHL Totals	414	101	113	214	704	29	5	5	10	24

Signed as a free agent, September 30, 1983

BURNS, CHARLES FREDERICK (Charlie)

Center **Ht:** 5-11 **Wt:** 170 **Shoots:** left
B: February 14, 1936, Detroit, Michigan

YR	Regular Season					Playoffs				
	GP	G	A	PTS	PM	GP	G	A	PTS	PM
1968-69	76	13	38	51	22	-	-	-	-	-
Pitt. Totals	76	13	38	51	22	-	-	-	-	-
NHL Totals	749	106	198	304	252	31	5	4	9	6

Claimed from Oakland in the Intra-League Draft, June 12, 1968

Claimed by Minnesota in the Intra-League Draft, June 11, 1969

BURNS, ROBERT ARTHUR (Robin)

Left Wing   **Ht:** 6-0   **Wt:** 195   **Shoots:** left
B: August 27, 1946, Montreal, Quebec

YR	Regular Season					Playoffs				
	GP	G	A	PTS	PM	GP	G	A	PTS	PM
1970-71	10	0	3	3	4	-	-	-	-	-
1971-72	5	0	0	0	8	-	-	-	-	-
1972-73	26	0	2	2	20	-	-	-	-	-
Pitt. Totals	41	0	5	5	32	-	-	-	-	-
NHL Totals	190	31	38	69	139	-	-	-	-	-

Acquired from Montreal, October 2, 1970

Selected by Kansas City in the 1974 Expansion Draft, June 12, 1974

BURROWS, DAVID JAMES (Dave)

Defense   **Ht:** 6-1   **Wt:** 190   **Shoots:** left
B: January 11, 1949, Toronto, Ontario

YR	Regular Season					Playoffs				
	GP	G	A	PTS	PM	GP	G	A	PTS	PM
1971-72	77	2	10	12	48	4	0	0	0	4
1972-73	78	3	24	27	42	-	-	-	-	-
1973-74	71	3	14	17	30	-	-	-	-	-
1974-75	78	2	15	17	49	9	1	1	2	12
1975-76	80	7	22	29	51	3	0	0	0	0
1976-77	69	3	6	9	29	3	0	2	2	0
1977-78	67	4	15	19	24	-	-	-	-	-
1980-81	53	0	2	2	28	1	0	0	0	0
Pitt. Totals	573	24	108	132	301	20	1	3	4	16
NHL Totals	724	29	135	164	373	29	1	5	6	25

Claimed from Chicago in the Intra-League Draft, June 8, 1971

Traded to Toronto for Randy Carlyle and George Ferguson, June 14, 1978

Acquired from Toronto with Paul Gardner for Kim Davis and Paul Marshall, November 18, 1980

West Division All-Star 1973-74

Prince of Wales Conference All-Star 1975-76

Penguins Hall of Fame, 1996

Rugged Rod Buskas led the team with 206 penalty minutes in 1987–88.

BUSKAS, ROD DALE

Defense   **Ht:** 6-1   **Wt:** 206   **Shoots:** right
B: January 7, 1961, Wetaskiwin, Alberta

YR	Regular Season					Playoffs				
	GP	G	A	PTS	PM	GP	G	A	PTS	PM
1982-83	41	2	2	4	102	-	-	-	-	-
1983-84	47	2	4	6	60	-	-	-	-	-
1984-85	69	2	7	9	191	-	-	-	-	-
1985-86	72	2	7	9	159	-	-	-	-	-
1986-87	68	3	15	18	123	-	-	-	-	-
1987-88	76	4	8	12	206	-	-	-	-	-
1988-89	52	1	5	6	105	10	0	0	0	23
1989-90	6	0	0	0	13	-	-	-	-	-
Pitt. Totals	431	16	48	64	959	10	0	0	0	23
NHL Totals	556	19	63	82	1294	18	0	3	3	45

Selected in the 1981 Entry Draft, 5th choice, 112th overall

Traded to Vancouver for a 6th round choice in the 1990 Entry Draft, October 24, 1989

Acquired from Vancouver with Barry Pederson and Tony Tanti for Dave Capuano, Andrew McBain, and Dan Quinn, January 8, 1990

Claimed by Los Angeles in the Waiver Draft, October 1, 1990

BUTENSCHON, SVEN

Defense   **Ht:** 6-4   **Wt:** 215   **Shoots:** left
B: March 22, 1976, Itzehoe, West Germany

YR	Regular Season					Playoffs				
	GP	G	A	PTS	PM	GP	G	A	PTS	PM
1997-98	8	0	0	0	6	-	-	-	-	-
1998-99	17	0	0	0	6	-	-	-	-	-
1999-00	3	0	0	0	0	-	-	-	-	-
2000-01	5	0	1	1	2	-	-	-	-	-
Pitt. Totals	33	0	1	1	14	-	-	-	-	-
NHL Totals	140	2	12	14	86	4	0	0	0	0

Selected in the 1994 Entry Draft, 3rd choice, 57th overall

Traded to Edmonton for Dan LaCouture, March 13, 2001

C

CAIRNS, ERIC

Defense   **Ht:** 6-6   **Wt:** 230   **Shoots:** left
B: June 27, 1974, Oakville, Ontario

YR	Regular Season					Playoffs				
	GP	G	A	PTS	PM	GP	G	A	PTS	PM
2005-06	27	1	0	1	87	-	-	-	-	-
2006-07	1	0	0	0	5	-	-	-	-	-
Pitt. Totals	28	1	0	1	92	-	-	-	-	-
NHL Totals	457	10	32	42	1182	16	0	0	0	28

Acquired from Florida for a 6th round choice in the 2006 Entry Draft, January 18, 2006

CALLANDER, JOHN (Jock)

Right Wing   **Ht:** 6-1   **Wt:** 188   **Shoots:** right
B: April 23, 1961, Regina, Saskatchewan

YR	Regular Season					Playoffs				
	GP	G	A	PTS	PM	GP	G	A	PTS	PM
1987-88	41	11	16	27	45	-	-	-	-	-
1988-89	30	6	5	11	20	10	2	5	7	10
1989-90	30	4	7	11	49	-	-	-	-	-
1991-92	-	-	-	-	-	12	1	3	4	2
Pitt. Totals	101	21	28	49	114	22	3	8	11	12
NHL Totals	109	22	29	51	116	22	3	8	11	12

Signed as a free agent, July 31, 1987

Signed as a free agent by Tampa Bay, July 29, 1992

Long before he became the NHL's czar of discipline, Colin Campbell was a feisty defenseman for the Pens.

CAMPBELL, COLIN JOHN (Soupy)

Defense   **Ht:** 5-9   **Wt:** 190   **Shoots:** left
B: January 28, 1953, London, Ontario

YR	Regular Season					Playoffs				
	GP	G	A	PTS	PM	GP	G	A	PTS	PM
1974-75	59	4	15	19	172	9	1	3	4	21
1975-76	64	7	10	17	105	3	0	0	0	0
1977-78	55	1	9	10	103	-	-	-	-	-
1978-79	65	2	18	20	137	7	1	4	5	30
Pitt. Totals	243	14	52	66	517	19	2	7	9	51
NHL Totals	636	25	103	128	1292	45	4	10	14	181
WHA Totals	78	3	20	23	191	-	-	-	-	-

Selected in the 1973 Amateur Draft, 3rd choice, 27th overall

Signed as a free agent, September 20, 1974

Loaned to Colorado for the 1976-77 season with the trade of Simon Nolet and Michel Plasse for Denis Herron, September 1, 1976

Selected by Edmonton in the 1979 Expansion Draft, June 13, 1979

CAPUANO, DAVID ALAN (Dave)

Left Wing   Ht: 6-2 **Wt:** 190   **Shoots:** left
B: July 27, 1968, Warwick, Rhode Island

YR	Regular Season					Playoffs				
	GP	G	A	PTS	PM	GP	G	A	PTS	PM
1989-90	6	0	0	0	2	-	-	-	-	-
Pitt. Totals	6	0	0	0	2	-	-	-	-	-
NHL Totals	104	17	38	55	56	6	1	1	2	5

Selected in the 1986 Entry Draft, 2nd choice, 25th overall

Traded to Vancouver with Andrew McBain and Dan Quinn for Rod Buskas, Barry Pederson, and Tony Tanti, January 8, 1990

CAPUTI, LUCA

Left Wing   Ht: 6-3 **Wt:** 200   **Shoots:** left
B: October 1, 1988, Toronto, Ontario

YR	Regular Season					Playoffs				
	GP	G	A	PTS	PM	GP	G	A	PTS	PM
2008-09	5	1	0	1	4	-	-	-	-	-
2009-10	4	1	1	2	2	-	-	-	-	-
Pitt. Totals	9	2	1	3	6	-	-	-	-	-
NHL Totals	28	3	6	9	16	-	-	-	-	-

Selected in the 2007 Entry Draft, 5th choice, 111th overall

Traded to Toronto with Martin Skoula for Alexei Ponikarvosky, March 2, 2010

CARDWELL, STEPHEN MICHAEL (Steve)

Left Wing   Ht: 5-11 **Wt:** 190   **Shoots:** left
B: August 13, 1950, Toronto, Ontario

YR	Regular Season					Playoffs				
	GP	G	A	PTS	PM	GP	G	A	PTS	PM
1970-71	5	0	1	1	15	-	-	-	-	-
1971-72	28	7	8	15	18	4	0	0	0	2
1972-73	20	2	2	4	2	-	-	-	-	-
Pitt. Totals	53	9	11	20	35	4	0	0	0	2
NHL Totals	53	9	11	20	35	4	0	0	0	2
WHA Totals	152	32	36	68	227	15	0	1	1	34

Selected in the 1970 Amateur Draft, 5th choice, 63rd overall

Selected by Ottawa in the 1972 WHA General Player Draft, February 12, 1972

CARLYLE, RANDOLPH ROBERT (Randy)

Defense   Ht: 5-10 **Wt:** 200   **Shoots:** left
B: April 19, 1956, Sudbury, Ontario

YR	Regular Season					Playoffs				
	GP	G	A	PTS	PM	GP	G	A	PTS	PM
1978-79	70	13	34	47	78	7	0	0	0	12
1979-80	67	8	28	36	45	5	1	0	1	4
1980-81	76	16	67	83	136	5	4	5	9	9
1981-82	73	11	64	75	131	5	1	3	4	16
1982-83	61	15	41	56	110	-	-	-	-	-
1983-84	50	3	23	26	82	-	-	-	-	-
Pitt. Totals	397	66	257	323	582	22	6	8	14	41
NHL Totals	1055	148	499	647	1400	69	9	24	33	120

Acquired from Toronto with George Ferguson for Dave Burrows, June 14, 1978

Traded to Winnipeg for a 1st round choice in the 1984 Entry Draft and future considerations (Moe Mantha), March 5, 1984

Won the James Norris Memorial Trophy, 1980-81

First Team NHL All-Star, 1980-81

Prince of Wales Conference All-Star 1980-81, 1981-82

CARON, SEBASTIEN

Goaltender   Ht: 6-1 **Wt:** 170   **Catches:** left
B: June 25, 1980, Amqui, Quebec

YR	Regular Season					Playoffs				
	GP	MINS	GA	SH	AVE	GP	MINS	GA	SH	AVE
2002-03	24	1408	62	2	2.64	-	-	-	-	-
2003-04	40	2213	138	1	3.74	-	-	-	-	-
2005-06	26	1312	87	1	3.98	-	-	-	-	-
Pitt. Totals	90	4933	287	4	3.49	-	-	-	-	-
NHL Totals	92	5021	289	4	3.45	-	-	-	-	-

Selected in the 1999 Entry Draft, 4th choice, 86th overall

Signed as a free agent by Chicago, August 8, 2006

NHL All-Rookie Team 2002-03

CARR, EUGENE WILLIAM (Gene)

Center   **Ht:** 5-11   **Wt:** 185   **Shoots:** left
B: September 17, 1951, Nanaimo, British Columbia

YR	Regular Season					Playoffs				
	GP	G	A	PTS	PM	GP	G	A	PTS	PM
1977-78	70	17	37	54	76	-	-	-	-	-
Pitt. Totals	70	17	37	54	76	-	-	-	-	-
NHL Totals	465	79	136	215	365	35	5	8	13	66

Acquired from Los Angeles with Dave Schultz and a 4th round choice in the 1978 Amateur Draft for Syl Apps and Hartland Monahan, November 2, 1977

Signed as a free agent by Atlanta, June 6, 1978

CASSIDY, THOMAS E.J. (Tom)

Center   **Ht:** 5-11   **Wt:** 180   **Shoots:** left
B: March 15, 1952, Blind River, Ontario

YR	Regular Season					Playoffs				
	GP	G	A	PTS	PM	GP	G	A	PTS	PM
1977-78	26	3	4	7	15	-	-	-	-	-
Pitt. Totals	26	3	4	7	15	-	-	-	-	-
NHL Totals	26	3	4	7	15	-	-	-	-	-

Signed as a free agent, October 11, 1977

CAUFIELD, JAY

Right Wing   **Ht:** 6-4   **Wt:** 237   **Shoots:** right
B: July 17, 1960, Philadelphia, Pennsylvania

YR	Regular Season					Playoffs				
	GP	G	A	PTS	PM	GP	G	A	PTS	PM
1988-89	58	1	4	5	285	9	0	0	0	28
1989-90	37	1	2	3	123	-	-	-	-	-
1990-91	23	1	1	2	71	-	-	-	-	-
1991-92	50	0	0	0	175	5	0	0	0	2
1992-93	26	0	0	0	60	-	-	-	-	-
Pitt. Totals	194	3	7	10	714	14	0	0	0	30
NHL Totals	208	5	8	13	759	17	0	0	0	42

Claimed from Minnesota in the Waiver Draft, October 3, 1988

John Chabot, shown adjusting his equipment, was a playmaking center for the Pens in the mid-1980s.

CHABOT, JOHN DAVID

Center   **Ht:** 6-2   **Wt:** 200   **Shoots:** left
B: May 18, 1962, Summerside, Prince Edward Island

YR	Regular Season					Playoffs				
	GP	G	A	PTS	PM	GP	G	A	PTS	PM
1984-85	67	8	45	53	12	-	-	-	-	-
1985-86	77	14	31	45	6	-	-	-	-	-
1986-87	72	14	22	36	8	-	-	-	-	-
Pitt. Totals	216	36	98	134	26	-	-	-	-	-
NHL Totals	508	84	228	312	85	33	6	20	26	2

Acquired from Montreal for Ron Flockhart, November 9, 1984

Signed as a free agent by Detroit, June 25, 1987

The second overall pick in 1976, Blair Chapman never lived up to his advance billing.

CHARLESWORTH, TODD

Defense   Ht: 6-1 **Wt:** 190   **Shoots:** left
B: March 22, 1965, Calgary, Alberta

YR	Regular Season					Playoffs				
	GP	G	A	PTS	PM	GP	G	A	PTS	PM
1983-84	10	0	0	0	8	-	-	-	-	-
1984-85	67	1	8	9	31	-	-	-	-	-
1985-86	2	0	1	1	0	-	-	-	-	-
1986-87	1	0	0	0	0	-	-	-	-	-
1987-88	6	2	0	2	2	-	-	-	-	-
Pitt. Totals	86	3	9	12	41	-	-	-	-	-
NHL Totals	93	3	9	12	47	-	-	-	-	-

Selected in the 1983 Entry Draft, 2nd choice, 22nd overall

Signed as a free agent by Edmonton, June 21, 1989

CHEVRIER, ALAIN (Chevy)

Goaltender   Ht: 5-8 **Wt:** 180   **Catches:** left
B: April 23, 1961, Cornwall, Ontario

YR	Regular Season					Playoffs				
	GP	MINS	GA	SH	AVE	GP	MINS	GA	SH	AVE
1989-90	3	166	14	0	5.06	-	-	-	-	-
Pitt. Totals	3	166	14	0	5.06	-	-	-	-	-
NHL Totals	234	12202	845	2	4.16	16	1013	44	0	2.61

Acquired from Chicago for future considerations, March 6, 1990

Signed as a free agent by Detroit, July 5, 1990

CHIODO, ANDY

Goaltender   Ht: 5-11 **Wt:** 192   **Catches:** left
B: April 25, 1983, Toronto, Ontario

YR	Regular Season					Playoffs				
	GP	MINS	GA	SH	AVE	GP	MINS	GA	SH	AVE
2003-04	8	486	28	0	3.46	-	-	-	-	-
Pitt. Totals	8	486	28	0	3.46	-	-	-	-	-
NHL Totals	8	486	28	0	3.46	-	-	-	-	-

Selected in the 2003 Entry Draft, 7th choice, 199th overall

Signed as a free agent by HPK Hameenlinna (Finland), January 30, 2007

CHAPMAN, BLAIR DOUGLAS

Right Wing   Ht: 6-1 **Wt:** 190   **Shoots:** right
B: June 13, 1956, Lloydminster, Saskatchewan

YR	Regular Season					Playoffs				
	GP	G	A	PTS	PM	GP	G	A	PTS	PM
1976-77	80	14	23	37	16	3	1	1	2	7
1977-78	75	24	20	44	37	-	-	-	-	-
1978-79	71	10	8	18	18	7	1	0	1	2
1979-80	1	0	0	0	0	-	-	-	-	-
Pitt. Totals	227	48	51	99	71	10	2	1	3	9
NHL Totals	402	106	125	231	158	25	4	6	10	15

Selected in the 1976 Amateur Draft, 1st choice, 2nd overall

Traded to St. Louis for Bob Stewart, November 13, 1979

CHORNEY, MARC

Defense   **Ht:** 6-0 **Wt:** 200   **Shoots:** left
B: November 8, 1959, Sudbury, Ontario

	Regular Season					Playoffs				
YR	GP	G	A	PTS	PM	GP	G	A	PTS	PM
1980-81	8	1	6	7	14	2	0	1	1	2
1981-82	60	1	6	7	63	5	0	0	0	0
1982-83	67	3	5	8	66	-	-	-	-	-
1983-84	4	0	1	1	8	-	-	-	-	-
Pitt. Totals	139	5	18	23	151	7	0	1	1	2
NHL Totals	210	8	27	35	209	7	0	1	1	2

Selected in the 1979 Entry Draft, 5th choice, 115th overall

Traded to Los Angeles for a 6th round choice in the 1985 Entry Draft, October 15, 1983

CHORSKE, TOM

Left Wing   **Ht:** 6-1 **Wt:** 212   **Shoots:** right
B: September 18, 1966, Minneapolis, Minnesota

	Regular Season					Playoffs				
YR	GP	G	A	PTS	PM	GP	G	A	PTS	PM
1999-00	33	1	5	6	2	-	-	-	-	-
Pitt. Totals	33	1	5	6	2	-	-	-	-	-
NHL Totals	596	115	122	237	225	50	5	12	17	10

Signed as a free agent, September 2, 1999

CHRISTENSEN, ERIK

Center   **Ht:** 6-1 **Wt:** 210   **Shoots:** left
B: December 17, 1983, Edmonton, Alberta

	Regular Season					Playoffs				
YR	GP	G	A	PTS	PM	GP	G	A	PTS	PM
2005-06	33	6	7	13	34	-	-	-	-	-
2006-07	61	18	15	33	26	4	0	0	0	6
2007-08	49	9	11	20	28	-	-	-	-	-
Pitt. Totals	143	33	33	66	88	4	0	0	0	6
NHL Totals	275	50	74	124	136	12	0	2	2	6

Selected in the 2002 Entry Draft, 3rd choice, 69th overall

Traded to Atlanta with Colby Armstrong, Angelo Esposito, and a 1st round choice in the 2008 Entry Draft for Pascal Dupuis and Marian Hossa, February 26, 2008

CHRISTIAN, JEFF

Left Wing   **Ht:** 6-2 **Wt:** 210   **Shoots:** left
B: July 30, 1970, Burlington, Ontario

	Regular Season					Playoffs				
YR	GP	G	A	PTS	PM	GP	G	A	PTS	PM
1994-95	1	0	0	0	0	-	-	-	-	-
1995-96	3	0	0	0	2	-	-	-	-	-
1996-97	11	2	2	4	13	-	-	-	-	-
Pitt. Totals	15	2	2	4	15	-	-	-	-	-
NHL Totals	18	2	2	4	17	-	-	-	-	-

Signed as a free agent, August 2, 1994

Signed as a free agent by Phoenix, July 28, 1997

CHYCHRUN, JEFF

Defense   **Ht:** 6-4 **Wt:** 215   **Shoots:** right
B: May 3, 1966, LaSalle, Quebec

	Regular Season					Playoffs				
YR	GP	G	A	PTS	PM	GP	G	A	PTS	PM
1991-92	17	0	1	1	35	-	-	-	-	-
1992-93	1	0	0	0	2	-	-	-	-	-
Pitt. Totals	18	0	1	1	37	-	-	-	-	-
NHL Totals	262	3	22	25	744	19	0	2	2	65

Acquired from Los Angeles with Brian Benning and a 1st round choice in the 1992 Entry Draft for Paul Coffey, February 19, 1992

Traded to Los Angeles for Peter Ahola, November 6, 1992

CLACKSON, KIMBEL GERALD (Kim)

Defense   **Ht:** 5-11 **Wt:** 195   **Shoots:** right
B: February 13, 1955, Saskatoon, Saskatchewan

	Regular Season					Playoffs				
YR	GP	G	A	PTS	PM	GP	G	A	PTS	PM
1979-80	45	0	3	3	166	3	0	0	0	37
Pitt. Totals	45	0	3	3	166	3	0	0	0	37
NHL Totals	106	0	8	8	370	8	0	0	0	70
WHA Totals	271	6	39	45	932	33	0	7	7	138

Selected in the 1975 Amateur Draft, 5th choice, 85th overall

Claimed as a fill-in during the Expansion Draft, June 13, 1979

Sent to Quebec as compensation for Paul Baxter, August 7, 1980

COFFEY, PAUL DOUGLAS

Defense　**Ht:** 6-0　**Wt:** 205　**Shoots:** left
B: June 1, 1961, Weston, Ontario

YR	Regular Season					Playoffs				
	GP	G	A	PTS	PM	GP	G	A	PTS	PM
1987-88	46	15	52	67	93	-	-	-	-	-
1988-89	75	30	83	113	195	11	2	13	15	31
1989-90	**80**	29	74	103	95	-	-	-	-	-
1990-91	76	24	69	93	128	12	2	9	11	6
1991-92	54	10	54	64	62	-	-	-	-	-
Pitt. Totals	331	108	332	440	573	23	4	22	26	37
NHL Totals	1409	396	1135	1531	1802	194	59	137	196	264

Acquired from Edmonton with Dave Hunter and Wayne Van Dorp for Dave Hannan, Chris Joseph, Moe Mantha, and Craig Simpson, November 24, 1987

Traded to Los Angeles for Brian Benning, Jeff Chychrun, and a 1st round choice in the 1992 Entry Draft, February 19, 1992

First Team NHL All-Star 1988-89

Second Team NHL All-Star 1989-90

Prince of Wales Conference All-Star 1987-88, 1988-89, 1989-90, 1990-91, 1991-92

Penguins Hall of Fame, 2007

Hockey Hall of Fame (Player), 2004

CONKLIN, TY (Conks)

Goaltender　**Ht:** 6-0　**Wt:** 184　**Catches:** left
B: March 30, 1976, Anchorage, Alaska

YR	Regular Season					Playoffs				
	GP	MINS	GA	SH	AVE	GP	MINS	GA	SH	AVE
2007-08	33	1866	78	2	2.51	-	-	-	-	-
Pitt. Totals	33	1866	78	2	2.51	-	-	-	-	-
NHL Totals	175	9437	403	14	2.56	2	26	1	0	2.31

Signed as a free agent, July 19, 2007

Signed as a free agent by Detroit, July 1, 2008

CONNER, CHRIS

Right Wing　**Ht:** 5-8　**Wt:** 180　**Shoots:** left
B: December 23, 1983, Westland, Michigan

YR	Regular Season					Playoffs				
	GP	G	A	PTS	PM	GP	G	A	PTS	PM
2009-10	8	2	1	3	0	1	0	0	0	0
Pitt. Totals	8	2	1	3	0	1	0	0	0	0
NHL Totals	79	9	15	24	20	2	0	0	0	0

Signed as a free agent, July 5, 2009

COOKE, MATT (Cookie)

Left Wing　**Ht:** 5-11　**Wt:** 205　**Shoots:** left
B: September 7, 1978, Belleville, Ontario

YR	Regular Season					Playoffs				
	GP	G	A	PTS	PM	GP	G	A	PTS	PM
2008-09	76	13	18	31	101	**24**	1	6	7	22
2009-10	79	15	15	30	106	13	4	2	6	22
Pitt. Totals	155	28	33	61	207	37	5	8	13	44
NHL Totals	738	114	157	271	859	76	13	12	25	78

Signed as a free agent, July 6, 2008

CORBET, RENE

Left Wing　**Ht:** 6-0　**Wt:** 195　**Shoots:** left
B: June 25, 1973, Victoriaville, Quebec

YR	Regular Season					Playoffs				
	GP	G	A	PTS	PM	GP	G	A	PTS	PM
1999-00	4	1	0	1	0	7	1	1	2	9
2000-01	43	8	9	17	57	17	1	0	1	12
Pitt. Totals	47	9	9	18	57	24	2	1	3	21
NHL Totals	362	58	74	132	420	53	7	6	13	52

Acquired from Calgary with Tyler Moss for Brad Werenka, March 14, 2000

CORRIGAN, MICHAEL DOUGLAS (Mike)

Left Wing　**Ht:** 5-10　**Wt:** 175　**Shoots:** left
B: January 11, 1946, Ottawa, Ontario

YR	Regular Season					Playoffs				
	GP	G	A	PTS	PM	GP	G	A	PTS	PM
1976-77	73	14	27	41	36	2	0	0	0	0
1977-78	25	8	12	20	10	-	-	-	-	-
Pitt. Totals	98	22	39	61	46	2	0	0	0	0
NHL Totals	594	152	195	347	698	17	2	3	5	20

Acquired from Los Angeles for a 5th round choice in the 1977 Amateur Draft, October 18, 1976

COSSETTE, JACQUES

Right Wing **Ht:** 5-9 **Wt:** 185 **Shoots:** right
B: June 20, 1954, Rouyn, Quebec

YR	Regular Season					Playoffs				
	GP	G	A	PTS	PM	GP	G	A	PTS	PM
1975-76	7	0	2	2	9	-	-	-	-	-
1977-78	19	1	2	3	4	-	-	-	-	-
1978-79	38	7	2	9	16	3	0	1	1	4
Pitt. Totals	**64**	**8**	**6**	**14**	**29**	**3**	**0**	**1**	**1**	**4**
NHL Totals	**64**	**8**	**6**	**14**	**29**	**3**	**0**	**1**	**1**	**4**

Selected in the 1974 Amateur Draft, 2nd choice, 27th overall

CROSBY, SIDNEY (the Kid)

Center **Ht:** 5-11 **Wt:** 200 **Shoots:** left
B: August 7, 1987, Cole Harbour, Nova Scotia

YR	Regular Season					Playoffs				
	GP	G	A	PTS	PM	GP	G	A	PTS	PM
2005-06	81	39	63	102	110	-	-	-	-	-
2006-07	79	36	84	**120**	60	5	3	2	5	4
2007-08	53	24	48	72	39	20	6	**21**	**27**	12
2008-09	77	33	70	103	76	**24**	**15**	16	31	14
2009-10	81	**51**	58	109	71	13	6	13	19	6
Pitt. Totals	**371**	**183**	**323**	**506**	**356**	**62**	**30**	**52**	**82**	**36**
NHL Totals	**371**	**183**	**323**	**506**	**356**	**62**	**30**	**52**	**82**	**36**

Selected in the 2005 Entry Draft, 1st choice, 1st overall

Won the Lester B. Pearson Award 2006-07

Won the Art Ross Trophy 2006-07

Won the Hart Memorial Trophy 2006-07

Co-winner of the Maurice Richard Trophy (with Steven Stamkos) 2009–10

First Team NHL All-Star 2006-07

Second Team NHL All-Star 2009–10

Eastern Conference All-Star 2006-07, 2007-08, 2008-09, 2009-10

NHL All-Rookie Team 2005-06

CROSS, CORY

Defense **Ht:** 6-5 **Wt:** 225 **Shoots:** left
B: January 3, 1971, Lloydminster, Alberta

YR	Regular Season					Playoffs				
	GP	G	A	PTS	PM	GP	G	A	PTS	PM
2005-06	6	0	1	1	6	-	-	-	-	-
Pitt. Totals	**6**	**0**	**1**	**1**	**6**	**-**	**-**	**-**	**-**	**-**
NHL Totals	**659**	**34**	**97**	**131**	**684**	**47**	**2**	**4**	**6**	**62**

Acquired from Edmonton with Jani Rita for Dick Tarnstrom, January 26, 2006

Traded to Detroit for a 4th round choice in the 2007 Entry Draft, March 8, 2006

CROWDER, BRUCE

Right Wing **Ht:** 6-0 **Wt:** 180 **Shoots:** right
B: March 25, 1957, Essex, Ontario

YR	Regular Season					Playoffs				
	GP	G	A	PTS	PM	GP	G	A	PTS	PM
1984-85	26	4	7	11	23	-	-	-	-	-
Pitt. Totals	**26**	**4**	**7**	**11**	**23**	**-**	**-**	**-**	**-**	**-**
NHL Totals	**243**	**47**	**51**	**98**	**156**	**31**	**8**	**4**	**12**	**41**

Claimed from Boston in the Waiver Draft, October 9, 1984

CROZIER, GREG

Left Wing **Ht:** 6-3 **Wt:** 200 **Shoots:** left
B: July 6, 1976, Calgary, Alberta

YR	Regular Season					Playoffs				
	GP	G	A	PTS	PM	GP	G	A	PTS	PM
2000-01	1	0	0	0	0	-	-	-	-	-
Pitt. Totals	**1**	**0**	**0**	**0**	**0**	**-**	**-**	**-**	**-**	**-**
NHL Totals	**1**	**0**	**0**	**0**	**0**	**-**	**-**	**-**	**-**	**-**

Selected in the 1994 Entry Draft, 4th choice, 73rd overall

Signed as a free agent by Boston, August 8, 2001

Penguins (left to right) John Cullen, Mark Recchi, Chris Dahlquist, Gord Dineen, and Troy Loney gather after scoring a goal.

CULLEN, BARRY JOHN (John)

Center   Ht: 5-10 **Wt:** 182   **Shoots:** right
B: August 2, 1964, Puslinch, Ontario

	Regular Season					Playoffs				
YR	GP	G	A	PTS	PM	GP	G	A	PTS	PM
1988-89	79	12	37	49	112	11	3	6	9	28
1989-90	72	32	60	92	138	-	-	-	-	-
1990-91	65	31	63	94	83	-	-	-	-	-
1994-95	46	13	24	37	66	9	0	2	2	8
Pitt. Totals	262	88	184	272	399	20	3	8	11	36
NHL Totals	621	187	363	550	898	53	12	22	34	58

Signed as a free agent, June 21, 1988

Traded to Hartford with Jeff Parker and Zarley Zalapski for Ron Francis, Grant Jennings, and Ulf Samuelsson, March 4, 1991

Signed as a free agent, August 3, 1994

Signed as a free agent by Tampa Bay, September 11, 1995

Prince of Wales Conference All-Star 1990-91

CUNNEYWORTH, RANDOLPH WILLIAM (Randy)

Left Wing   Ht: 6-0 **Wt:** 198   **Shoots:** left
B: May 10, 1961, Etobicoke, Ontario

	Regular Season					Playoffs				
YR	GP	G	A	PTS	PM	GP	G	A	PTS	PM
1985-86	75	15	30	45	74	-	-	-	-	-
1986-87	79	26	27	53	142	-	-	-	-	-
1987-88	71	35	39	74	141	-	-	-	-	-
1988-89	70	25	19	44	156	11	3	5	8	26
Pitt. Totals	295	101	115	216	513	11	3	5	8	26
NHL Totals	866	189	225	414	1280	45	7	7	14	61

Acquired from Buffalo with Mike Moller for Pat Hughes, October 4, 1985

Traded to Winnipeg with Dave McLlwain and Rick Tabaracci for Randy Gilhen, Jim Kyte, and Andrew McBain, June 17, 1989

CURRY, JOHN

Goaltender   **Ht:** 5-11   **Wt:** 185   **Catches:** left
B: February 27, 1984, Shorewood, Minnesota

YR	GP	MINS	GA	SH	AVE	GP	MINS	GA	SH	AVE
		Regular Season					Playoffs			
2008-09	3	150	6	0	2.40	-	-	-	-	-
2009-10	1	24	5	0	12.50	-	-	-	-	-
Pitt. Totals	4	174	11	0	3.79	-	-	-	-	-
NHL Totals	4	174	11	0	3.79	-	-	-	-	-

Signed as a free agent, July 13, 2007

D

DAHLQUIST, CHRISTOPHER C. (Chris)

Defense   **Ht:** 6-1   **Wt:** 195   **Shoots:** left
B: December 14, 1962, Fridley, Minnesota

YR	GP	G	A	PTS	PM	GP	G	A	PTS	PM
		Regular Season					Playoffs			
1985-86	5	1	2	3	2	-	-	-	-	-
1986-87	19	0	1	1	20	-	-	-	-	-
1987-88	44	3	6	9	69	-	-	-	-	-
1988-89	43	1	5	6	42	2	0	0	0	0
1989-90	62	4	10	14	56	-	-	-	-	-
1990-91	22	1	2	3	30	-	-	-	-	-
Pitt. Totals	195	10	26	36	219	2	0	0	0	0
NHL Totals	532	19	71	90	488	39	4	7	11	30

Signed as a free agent, May 7, 1985

Traded to Minnesota with Jim Johnson for Larry Murphy and Peter Taglianetti, December 11, 1990

DAIGLE, ALEXANDRE

Center/Right Wing   **Ht:** 6-0   **Wt:** 195   **Shoots:** left
B: February 7, 1975, Montreal, Quebec

YR	GP	G	A	PTS	PM	GP	G	A	PTS	PM
		Regular Season					Playoffs			
2002-03	33	4	3	7	8	-	-	-	-	-
Pitt. Totals	33	4	3	7	8	-	-	-	-	-
NHL Totals	616	129	198	327	186	12	0	2	2	2

Signed as a free agent, August 13, 2002

Signed as a free agent by Minnesota, September 30, 2003

DAIGNEAULT, JEAN-JACQUES (J.J.)

Defense   **Ht:** 5-10   **Wt:** 192   **Shoots:** left
B: October 12, 1965, Montreal, Quebec

YR	GP	G	A	PTS	PM	GP	G	A	PTS	PM
		Regular Season					Playoffs			
1995-96	13	3	3	6	23	17	1	9	10	36
1996-97	53	3	14	17	36	-	-	-	-	-
Pitt. Totals	66	6	17	23	59	17	1	9	10	36
NHL Totals	899	53	197	250	687	99	5	26	31	100

Acquired from St. Louis for a 6th round choice in the 1996 Entry Draft, March 20, 1996

Traded to Anaheim for Garry Valk, February 21, 1997

DALEY, THOMAS JOSEPH (Joe)

Goaltender   **Ht:** 5-10   **Wt:** 170   **Catches:** left
B: February 20, 1943, Winnipeg, Manitoba

YR	GP	MINS	GA	SH	AVE	GP	MINS	GA	SH	AVE
		Regular Season					Playoffs			
1968-69	29	1615	87	2	3.23	-	-	-	-	-
1969-70	9	528	26	0	2.95	-	-	-	-	-
Pitt. Totals	38	2143	113	2	3.16	-	-	-	-	-
NHL Totals	105	5836	326	3	3.35	-	-	-	-	-
WHA Totals	308	17835	1002	12	3.37	49	2706	149	2	3.30

Selected from Detroit in the 1967 Expansion Draft, June 6, 1967

Claimed by Buffalo in the Intra-League Draft, June 9, 1970

DANIELS, JEFF

Left Wing   **Ht:** 6-1   **Wt:** 200   **Shoots:** left
B: June 24, 1968, Oshawa, Ontario

YR	GP	G	A	PTS	PM	GP	G	A	PTS	PM
		Regular Season					Playoffs			
1990-91	11	0	2	2	2	-	-	-	-	-
1991-92	2	0	0	0	0	-	-	-	-	-
1992-93	58	5	4	9	14	12	3	2	5	0
1993-94	63	3	5	8	20	-	-	-	-	-
Pitt. Totals	134	8	11	19	36	12	3	2	5	0
NHL Totals	425	17	26	43	83	41	3	5	8	2

Selected in the 1986 Entry Draft, 6th choice, 109th overall

Traded to Florida for Greg Hawgood, March 19, 1994

DAVIS, KIM

Center   **Ht:** 5-11   **Wt:** 170   **Shoots:** left
B: October 31, 1957, Flin Flon, Manitoba

	Regular Season					Playoffs				
YR	GP	G	A	PTS	PM	GP	G	A	PTS	PM
1977-78	1	0	0	0	0	-	-	-	-	-
1978-79	1	1	0	1	0	-	-	-	-	-
1979-80	24	3	7	10	43	4	0	0	0	0
1980-81	8	1	0	1	4	-	-	-	-	-
Pitt. Totals	34	5	7	12	47	4	0	0	0	0
NHL Totals	36	5	7	12	51	4	0	0	0	0

Selected in the 1977 Amateur Draft, 2nd choice, 48th overall

Traded to Toronto with Paul Marshall for Dave Burrows and Paul Gardner, November 18, 1980

DEA, WILLIAM FRASER (Billy)

Left Wing   **Ht:** 5-8   **Wt:** 175   **Shoots:** left
B: April 3, 1933, Edmonton, Alberta

	Regular Season					Playoffs				
YR	GP	G	A	PTS	PM	GP	G	A	PTS	PM
1967-68	73	16	12	28	6	-	-	-	-	-
1968-69	66	10	8	18	4	-	-	-	-	-
Pitt. Totals	139	26	20	46	10	-	-	-	-	-
NHL Totals	397	67	54	121	44	11	2	1	3	6

Selected from Chicago in the 1967 Expansion Draft, June 6, 1967

Traded to Detroit for Mike McMahon, October 28, 1969

DEBENEDET, NELSON

Left Wing   **Ht:** 6-1   **Wt:** 195   **Shoots:** left
B: December 31, 1947, Cordeno, Italy

	Regular Season					Playoffs				
YR	GP	G	A	PTS	PM	GP	G	A	PTS	PM
1974-75	31	6	3	9	11	-	-	-	-	-
Pitt. Totals	31	6	3	9	11	-	-	-	-	-
NHL Totals	46	10	4	14	13	-	-	-	-	-

Acquired from Detroit for Hank Nowak and a 3rd round choice in the 1974 Amateur Draft, May 27, 1974

DEFAZIO, DEAN

Left Wing   **Ht:** 5-11   **Wt:** 185   **Shoots:** left
B: April 16, 1963, Ottawa, Ontario

	Regular Season					Playoffs				
YR	GP	G	A	PTS	PM	GP	G	A	PTS	PM
1983-84	22	0	2	2	28	-	-	-	-	-
Pitt. Totals	22	0	2	2	28	-	-	-	-	-
NHL Totals	22	0	2	2	28	-	-	-	-	-

Selected in the 1981 Entry Draft, 8th choice, 175th overall

DELORME, GILBERT

Defense   **Ht:** 6-1   **Wt:** 199   **Shoots:** right
B: November 25, 1962, Boucherville, Quebec

	Regular Season					Playoffs				
YR	GP	G	A	PTS	PM	GP	G	A	PTS	PM
1989-90	54	3	7	10	44	-	-	-	-	-
Pitt. Totals	54	3	7	10	44	-	-	-	-	-
NHL Totals	541	31	92	123	520	56	1	9	10	56

Signed as a free agent, June 28, 1989

DEMARCO, ALBERT THOMAS, Jr. (Ab)

Defense   **Ht:** 6-0   **Wt:** 170   **Shoots:** right
B: February 27, 1949, Cleveland, Ohio

	Regular Season					Playoffs				
YR	GP	G	A	PTS	PM	GP	G	A	PTS	PM
1973-74	34	7	12	19	4	-	-	-	-	-
1974-75	8	2	1	3	4	-	-	-	-	-
Pitt. Totals	42	9	13	22	8	-	-	-	-	-
NHL Totals	344	44	80	124	75	25	1	2	3	17
WHA Totals	47	6	8	14	20	1	0	0	0	0

Acquired from St. Louis with Steve Durbano and Bob Kelly for Greg Polis, Bryan Watson, and a 2nd round choice in the 1974 Amateur Draft, January 17, 1974

Traded to Vancouver for Barry Wilkins, November 4, 1974

DEPALMA, LARRY

Left Wing   **Ht:** 6-0   **Wt:** 195   **Shoots:** left
B: October 27, 1965, Trenton, Michigan

	Regular Season					Playoffs				
YR	GP	G	A	PTS	PM	GP	G	A	PTS	PM
1993-94	7	1	0	1	5	1	0	0	0	0
Pitt. Totals	7	1	0	1	5	1	0	0	0	0
NHL Totals	148	21	20	41	408	3	0	0	0	6

Claimed on waivers from the NY Islanders, March 9, 1994

DEROUVILLE, PHILIPPE

Goaltender   **Ht:** 6-1   **Wt:** 185   **Catches:** left
B: August 7, 1974, Victoriaville, Quebec

YR	Regular Season					Playoffs				
	GP	MINS	GA	SH	AVE	GP	MINS	GA	SH	AVE
1994-95	1	60	3	0	3.00	-	-	-	-	-
1996-97	2	111	6	0	3.24	-	-	-	-	-
Pitt. Totals	**3**	**171**	**9**	**0**	**3.16**	**-**	**-**	**-**	**-**	**-**
NHL Totals	**3**	**171**	**9**	**0**	**3.16**	**-**	**-**	**-**	**-**	**-**

Selected in the 1992 Entry Draft, 5th choice, 115th overall

Signed as a free agent by Ayr Eagles (Britain), June 26, 2000

DILLABOUGH, ROBERT WELLINGTON (Bob)

Center   **Ht:** 5-10   **Wt:** 180   **Shoots:** left
B: April 27, 1941, Belleville, Ontario
D: March 27, 1997

YR	Regular Season					Playoffs				
	GP	G	A	PTS	PM	GP	G	A	PTS	PM
1967-68	47	7	12	19	18	-	-	-	-	-
1968-69	14	0	0	0	2	-	-	-	-	-
Pitt. Totals	**61**	**7**	**12**	**19**	**20**	**-**	**-**	**-**	**-**	**-**
NHL Totals	**283**	**32**	**54**	**86**	**76**	**17**	**3**	**0**	**3**	**0**
WHA Totals	**72**	**8**	**8**	**16**	**8**	**9**	**1**	**0**	**1**	**0**

Selected from Boston in the 1967 Expansion Draft, June 6, 1967

Traded to Oakland for Billy Harris, November 29, 1968

DINEEN, GORDON (Gord)

Defense   **Ht:** 6-0   **Wt:** 195   **Shoots:** right
B: September 21, 1962, Quebec City, Quebec

YR	Regular Season					Playoffs				
	GP	G	A	PTS	PM	GP	G	A	PTS	PM
1988-89	38	1	2	3	42	11	0	2	2	8
1989-90	69	1	8	9	125	-	-	-	-	-
1990-91	9	0	0	0	6	-	-	-	-	-
1991-92	1	0	0	0	0	-	-	-	-	-
Pitt. Totals	**117**	**2**	**10**	**12**	**173**	**11**	**0**	**2**	**2**	**8**
NHL Totals	**528**	**16**	**90**	**106**	**695**	**40**	**1**	**7**	**8**	**68**

Acquired from Minnesota with Scott Bjugstad for Steve Gotaas and Ville Siren, December 17, 1988

Signed as a free agent by Ottawa, August 31, 1992

DION, MICHEL

Goaltender   **Ht:** 5-10   **Wt:** 185   **Catches:** left
B: February 11, 1954, Granby, Quebec

YR	Regular Season					Playoffs				
	GP	MINS	GA	SH	AVE	GP	MINS	GA	SH	AVE
1981-82	62	3580	226	0	3.79	5	310	22	0	4.26
1982-83	49	2791	198	0	4.26	-	-	-	-	-
1983-84	30	1553	138	0	5.33	-	-	-	-	-
1984-85	10	553	43	0	4.67	-	-	-	-	-
Pitt. Totals	**151**	**8477**	**605**	**0**	**4.28**	**5**	**310**	**22**	**0**	**4.26**
NHL Totals	**227**	**12695**	**898**	**2**	**4.24**	**5**	**310**	**22**	**0**	**4.26**
WHA Totals	**149**	**8242**	**450**	**5**	**3.28**	**7**	**371**	**22**	**0**	**3.56**

Signed as a free agent, June 30, 1981

Prince of Wales Conference All-Star 1981-82

DOLLAS, BOBBY

Defense   **Ht:** 6-2   **Wt:** 212   **Shoots:** left
B: January 31, 1965, Montreal, Quebec

YR	Regular Season					Playoffs				
	GP	G	A	PTS	PM	GP	G	A	PTS	PM
1998-99	70	2	8	10	60	13	1	0	1	6
2000-01	5	0	0	0	4	-	-	-	-	-
Pitt. Totals	**75**	**2**	**8**	**10**	**64**	**13**	**1**	**0**	**1**	**6**
NHL Totals	**646**	**42**	**96**	**138**	**467**	**47**	**2**	**1**	**3**	**41**

Acquired from Edmonton with Tony Hrkac for Josef Beranek, June 16, 1998

Signed as a free agent by Ottawa, November 9, 1999

Acquired from San Jose with Johan Hedberg for Jeff Norton, March 12, 2001

Bobby Dollas (8) knocks a Devil to the ice.

DOME, ROBERT

Right Wing   Ht: 6-0 **Wt:** 210   **Shoots:** left
B: January 29, 1979, Skalica, Czechoslovakia

YR	Regular Season					Playoffs				
	GP	G	A	PTS	PM	GP	G	A	PTS	PM
1997-98	30	5	2	7	12	-	-	-	-	-
1999-00	22	2	5	7	0	-	-	-	-	-
Pitt. Totals	52	7	7	14	12	-	-	-	-	-
NHL Totals	53	7	7	14	12	-	-	-	-	-

Selected in the 1997 Entry Draft, 1st choice, 17th overall

Signed as a free agent by Calgary, July 17, 2002

DONOVAN, SHEAN

Right Wing   Ht: 6-3 **Wt:** 218   **Shoots:** right
B: January 22, 1975, Timmins, Ontario

YR	Regular Season					Playoffs				
	GP	G	A	PTS	PM	GP	G	A	PTS	PM
2001-02	13	2	1	3	4	-	-	-	-	-
2002-03	52	4	5	9	30	-	-	-	-	-
Pitt. Totals	65	6	6	12	34	-	-	-	-	-
NHL Totals	951	112	129	241	705	49	6	6	12	39

Claimed on waivers from Atlanta, March 15, 2002

Traded to Calgary for Micki DuPont and Mathias Johansson, March 11, 2003

DOPSON, ROBERT (Rob)

Goaltender   Ht: 6-0 **Wt:** 200   **Catches:** left
B: August 21, 1967, Smith Falls, Ontario

YR	Regular Season					Playoffs				
	GP	MINS	GA	SH	AVE	GP	MINS	GA	SH	AVE
1993-94	2	45	3	0	4.00	-	-	-	-	-
Pitt. Totals	2	45	3	0	4.00	-	-	-	-	-
NHL Totals	2	45	3	0	4.00	-	-	-	-	-

Signed as a free agent, July 6, 1991

DUBERMAN, JUSTIN

Right Wing   Ht: 6-1 **Wt:** 185   **Shoots:** right
B: March 23, 1970, New Haven, Connecticut

YR	Regular Season					Playoffs				
	GP	G	A	PTS	PM	GP	G	A	PTS	PM
1993-94	4	0	0	0	0	-	-	-	-	-
Pitt. Totals	4	0	0	0	0	-	-	-	-	-
NHL Totals	4	0	0	0	0	-	-	-	-	-

Signed as a free agent, November 2, 1992

DUGUAY, RONALD (Ron)

Center/Right Wing   Ht: 6-2 **Wt:** 200   **Shoots:** right
B: July 6, 1957, Sudbury, Ontario

YR	Regular Season					Playoffs				
	GP	G	A	PTS	PM	GP	G	A	PTS	PM
1985-86	13	6	7	13	6	-	-	-	-	-
1986-87	40	5	13	18	30	-	-	-	-	-
Pitt. Totals	53	11	20	31	36	-	-	-	-	-
NHL Totals	864	274	346	620	582	89	31	22	53	118

Acquired from Detroit for Doug Shedden, March 11, 1986

Traded to NY Rangers for Chris Kontos, January 21, 1987

DUPONT, MICKI

Defense   Ht: 5-10 **Wt:** 186   **Shoots:** right
B: April 15, 1980, Calgary, Alberta

YR	Regular Season					Playoffs				
	GP	G	A	PTS	PM	GP	G	A	PTS	PM
2006-07	3	0	1	1	4	-	-	-	-	-
Pitt. Totals	3	0	1	1	4	-	-	-	-	-
NHL Totals	23	1	3	4	12	-	-	-	-	-

Acquired from Calgary with Mathias Johansson for Shean Donovan, March 11, 2003

Signed as a free agent by Berlin (Germany), August 6, 2003

Signed as a free agent, June 15, 2006

Signed as a free agent by St. Louis, July 3, 2007

DUPUIS, PASCAL

Left Wing   Ht: 6-1 **Wt:** 205   **Shoots:** left
B: April 7, 1979, Laval, Quebec

YR	Regular Season					Playoffs				
	GP	G	A	PTS	PM	GP	G	A	PTS	PM
2007-08	16	2	10	12	8	20	2	5	7	18
2008-09	71	12	16	28	30	16	0	0	0	8
2009-10	81	18	20	38	16	13	2	6	8	4
Pitt. Totals	168	32	46	78	54	49	4	11	15	30
NHL Totals	587	113	127	240	244	69	9	17	26	42

Acquired from Atlanta with Marian Hossa for Colby Armstrong, Erik Christensen, Angelo Esposito, and a 1st round choice in the 2008 Entry Draft, February 26, 2008

DURBANO, HARRY STEVEN (Steve)

Defense   **Ht:** 6-1 **Wt:** 210   **Shoots:** left
B: December 12, 1951, Toronto, Ontario
D: November 16, 2002

YR	Regular Season					Playoffs				
	GP	G	A	PTS	PM	GP	G	A	PTS	PM
1973-74	33	4	14	18	138	-	-	-	-	-
1974-75	1	0	1	1	10	-	-	-	-	-
1975-76	32	0	8	8	161	-	-	-	-	-
Pitt. Totals	66	4	23	27	309	-	-	-	-	-
NHL Totals	220	13	60	73	1127	5	0	2	2	8
WHA Totals	45	6	4	10	284	4	0	2	2	16

Acquired from St. Louis with Ab DeMarco and Bob Kelly for Greg Polis, Bryan Watson, and a 2nd round choice in the 1974 Amateur Draft, January 17, 1974

Traded to Kansas City with Chuck Arnason for Ed Gilbert, Simon Nolet, and an exchange of 1st round choices in the 1976 Amateur Draft, January 9, 1976

DYKSTRA, STEVEN (Steve)

Defense   **Ht:** 6-2 **Wt:** 190   **Shoots:** left
B: December 1, 1962, Edmonton, Alberta

YR	Regular Season					Playoffs				
	GP	G	A	PTS	PM	GP	G	A	PTS	PM
1988-89	65	1	6	7	126	1	0	0	0	2
Pitt. Totals	65	1	6	7	126	1	0	0	0	2
NHL Totals	217	8	32	40	545	1	0	0	0	2

Claimed from Edmonton in the Waiver Draft, October 3, 1988

Signed as a free agent by Hartford, October 9, 1989

DZIEDZIC, JOE

Left Wing   **Ht:** 6-3 **Wt:** 227   **Shoots:** left
B: December 18, 1971, Minneapolis, Minnesota

YR	Regular Season					Playoffs				
	GP	G	A	PTS	PM	GP	G	A	PTS	PM
1995-96	69	5	5	10	68	16	1	2	3	19
1996-97	59	9	9	18	63	5	0	1	1	4
Pitt. Totals	128	14	14	28	131	21	1	3	4	23
NHL Totals	130	14	14	28	131	21	1	3	4	23

Selected in the 1990 Entry Draft, 2nd choice, 61st overall

Signed as a free agent by Phoenix, August 27, 1998

E

EASTWOOD, MIKE

Center   **Ht:** 6-3 **Wt:** 216   **Shoots:** right
B: July 1, 1967, Ottawa, Ontario

YR	Regular Season					Playoffs				
	GP	G	A	PTS	PM	GP	G	A	PTS	PM
2003-04	82	4	15	19	40	-	-	-	-	-
Pitt. Totals	82	4	15	19	40	-	-	-	-	-
NHL Totals	783	87	149	236	354	97	8	11	19	64

Signed as a free agent, July 31, 2003

EATON, MARK

Defense   **Ht:** 6-2 **Wt:** 204   **Shoots:** left
B: May 6, 1977, Wilmington, Delaware

YR	Regular Season					Playoffs				
	GP	G	A	PTS	PM	GP	G	A	PTS	PM
2006-07	35	0	3	3	16	5	0	0	0	0
2007-08	36	0	3	3	4	-	-	-	-	-
2008-09	68	4	5	9	36	24	4	3	7	10
2009-10	79	3	13	16	26	13	0	3	3	4
Pitt. Totals	218	7	24	31	82	42	4	6	10	14
NHL Totals	531	23	55	78	220	60	4	6	10	24

Signed as a free agent, July 3, 2006

Signed as a free agent by NY Islanders, July 2, 2010

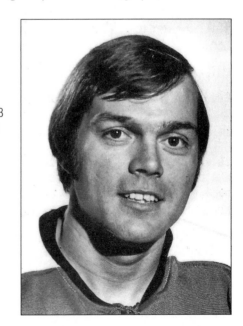

Darryl Edestrand's 15 goals in 1972–73 set a club record for defensemen.

EDESTRAND, DARRYL

Defense   Ht: 5-11 **Wt:** 180   **Shoots:** left
B: November 6, 1945, Strathroy, Ontario

YR	Regular Season					Playoffs				
	GP	G	A	PTS	PM	GP	G	A	PTS	PM
1971-72	77	10	23	33	52	4	0	2	2	0
1972-73	78	15	24	39	88	-	-	-	-	-
1973-74	3	0	0	0	0	-	-	-	-	-
Pitt. Totals	**158**	**25**	**47**	**72**	**140**	**4**	**0**	**2**	**2**	**0**
NHL Totals	**455**	**34**	**90**	**124**	**404**	**42**	**3**	**9**	**12**	**57**

Acquired from Philadelphia with Larry McKillop for Barry Ashbee, May 22, 1970

Traded to Boston for Nick Beverley, October 25, 1973

EDUR, THOMAS (Tom)

Defense   Ht: 6-1 **Wt:** 185   **Shoots:** right
B: November 18, 1954, Toronto, Ontario

YR	Regular Season					Playoffs				
	GP	G	A	PTS	PM	GP	G	A	PTS	PM
1977-78	58	5	38	43	18	-	-	-	-	-
Pitt. Totals	**58**	**5**	**38**	**43**	**18**	**-**	**-**	**-**	**-**	**-**
NHL Totals	**158**	**17**	**70**	**87**	**67**	**-**	**-**	**-**	**-**	**-**
WHA Totals	**217**	**17**	**79**	**96**	**116**	**13**	**3**	**4**	**7**	**0**

Acquired from Colorado for Dennis Owchar, December 2, 1977

Retired July 1978

Claimed in the 1979 Expansion Draft by Edmonton, June 13, 1979

EDWARDS, GARY WILLIAM

Goaltender   Ht: 5-9 **Wt:** 165   **Catches:** left
B: October 5, 1947, Toronto, Ontario

YR	Regular Season					Playoffs				
	GP	MINS	GA	SH	AVE	GP	MINS	GA	SH	AVE
1981-82	6	360	22	1	3.67	-	-	-	-	-
Pitt. Totals	**6**	**360**	**22**	**1**	**3.67**	**-**	**-**	**-**	**-**	**-**
NHL Totals	**286**	**16002**	**973**	**10**	**3.65**	**11**	**537**	**34**	**0**	**3.80**

Acquired from St. Louis for an 8th round choice in the 1984 Entry Draft, February 14, 1982

EDWARDS, MARVIN WAYNE (Marv)

Goaltender   Ht: 5-8 **Wt:** 155   **Catches:** left
B: August 15, 1935, St. Catharines, Ontario

YR	Regular Season					Playoffs				
	GP	MINS	GA	SH	AVE	GP	MINS	GA	SH	AVE
1968-69	1	60	3	0	3.00	-	-	-	-	-
Pitt. Totals	**1**	**60**	**3**	**0**	**3.00**	**-**	**-**	**-**	**-**	**-**
NHL Totals	**61**	**3467**	**218**	**2**	**3.77**	**-**	**-**	**-**	**-**	**-**

Signed as a free agent, September 1967

Claimed by Toronto in the Intra-League Draft, June 11, 1969

EDWARDS, ROY ALLEN

Goaltender   Ht: 5-8 **Wt:** 165   **Catches:** right
B: March 12, 1937, Seneca Township, Ontario
D: August 16, 1999

YR	Regular Season					Playoffs				
	GP	MINS	GA	SH	AVE	GP	MINS	GA	SH	AVE
1971-72	15	847	36	0	2.55	-	-	-	-	-
Pitt. Totals	**15**	**847**	**36**	**0**	**2.55**	**-**	**-**	**-**	**-**	**-**
NHL Totals	**236**	**13109**	**637**	**12**	**2.92**	**4**	**206**	**11**	**0**	**3.20**

Selected from Chicago in the 1967 Expansion Draft, June 6, 1967

Traded to Detroit for Hank Bassen, September 7, 1967

Claimed on waivers from Detroit, June 7, 1971

Traded to Detroit for cash, October 6, 1972

EKMAN, NILS

Left Wing   Ht: 6-0 **Wt:** 185   **Shoots:** left
B: March 11, 1976, Stockholm, Sweden

YR	Regular Season					Playoffs				
	GP	G	A	PTS	PM	GP	G	A	PTS	PM
2006-07	34	6	9	15	24	1	0	0	0	0
Pitt. Totals	**34**	**6**	**9**	**15**	**24**	**1**	**0**	**0**	**0**	**0**
NHL Totals	**264**	**60**	**91**	**151**	**188**	**28**	**2**	**5**	**7**	**16**

Acquired from San Jose with Patrick Ehelechner for a 2nd round choice in the 2007 Entry Draft, July 20, 2006

Signed as a free agent by Khimik Mytischi (Russia), August 12, 2007

ENDICOTT, SHANE

Center   **Ht:** 6-3   **Wt:** 214   **Shoots:** left
B: December 21, 1981, Saskatoon, Saskatchewan

YR	Regular Season					Playoffs				
	GP	G	A	PTS	PM	GP	G	A	PTS	PM
2001-02	4	0	1	1	4	-	-	-	-	-
2005-06	41	1	1	2	43	-	-	-	-	-
Pitt. Totals	45	1	2	3	47	-	-	-	-	-
NHL Totals	45	1	2	3	47	-	-	-	-	-

Selected in 2000 Entry Draft, 2nd choice, 52nd overall

Signed as a free agent by Nashville, July 17, 2006

ENGELLAND, DERYK

Defense   **Ht:** 6-2   **Wt:** 202   **Shoots:** right
B: April 3, 1982, Edmonton, Alberta

YR	Regular Season					Playoffs				
	GP	G	A	PTS	PM	GP	G	A	PTS	PM
2009-10	9	0	2	2	17	-	-	-	-	-
Pitt. Totals	9	0	2	2	17	-	-	-	-	-
NHL Totals	9	0	2	2	17	-	-	-	-	-

Signed as a free agent, July 16, 2007

ERICKSON, BRYAN (Butsy)

Right Wing   **Ht:** 5-9   **Wt:** 175   **Shoots:** right
B: March 7, 1960, Roseau, Minnesota

YR	Regular Season					Playoffs				
	GP	G	A	PTS	PM	GP	G	A	PTS	PM
1987-88	11	1	4	5	0	-	-	-	-	-
Pitt. Totals	11	1	4	5	0	-	-	-	-	-
NHL Totals	351	80	125	205	141	14	3	4	7	7

Acquired from Los Angeles for Chris Kontos and a 6th round choice in the 1988 Entry Draft, February 5, 1988

Signed as a free agent by Winnipeg, March 2, 1990

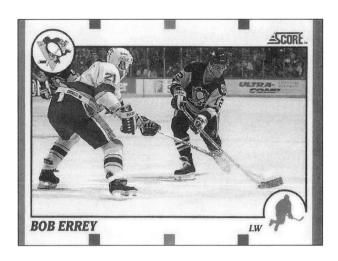

BOB ERREY   LW

ERREY, BOB

Left Wing   **Ht:** 5-10   **Wt:** 185   **Shoots:** left
B: September 21, 1964, Montreal, Quebec

YR	Regular Season					Playoffs				
	GP	G	A	PTS	PM	GP	G	A	PTS	PM
1983-84	65	9	13	22	29	-	-	-	-	-
1984-85	16	0	2	2	7	-	-	-	-	-
1985-86	37	11	6	17	8	-	-	-	-	-
1986-87	72	16	18	34	46	-	-	-	-	-
1987-88	17	3	6	9	18	-	-	-	-	-
1988-89	76	26	32	58	124	11	1	2	3	12
1989-90	78	20	19	39	109	-	-	-	-	-
1990-91	79	20	22	42	115	24	5	2	7	29
1991-92	78	19	16	35	119	14	3	0	3	10
1992-93	54	8	6	14	76	-	-	-	-	-
Pitt. Totals	572	132	140	272	651	49	9	4	13	51
NHL Totals	895	170	212	382	1005	99	13	16	29	109

Selected in the 1983 Entry Draft, 1st choice, 15th overall

Traded to Buffalo for Mike Ramsey, March 22, 1993

F

FALLOON, PAT

Right Wing   **Ht:** 5-11   **Wt:** 190   **Shoots:** right
B: September 22, 1972, Foxwarren, Manitoba

YR	Regular Season					Playoffs				
	GP	G	A	PTS	PM	GP	G	A	PTS	PM
1999-00	30	4	9	13	10	10	1	0	1	2
Pitt. Totals	30	4	9	13	10	10	1	0	1	2
NHL Totals	575	143	179	322	141	66	11	7	18	16

Claimed on waivers from Edmonton, February 4, 2000

Signed as a free agent by HC Davos (Switzerland), August 25, 2000

FATA, RICO

Right Wing   **Ht:** 6-0   **Wt:** 205   **Shoots:** left
B: February 12, 1980, Sault Ste. Marie, Ontario

YR	Regular Season					Playoffs				
	GP	G	A	PTS	PM	GP	G	A	PTS	PM
2002-03	27	5	8	13	10	-	-	-	-	-
2003-04	73	16	18	34	54	-	-	-	-	-
2005-06	20	0	0	0	10	-	-	-	-	-
Pitt. Totals	120	21	26	47	74	-	-	-	-	-
NHL Totals	230	27	36	63	104	-	-	-	-	-

Acquired from NY Rangers with Joel Bouchard, Richard Lintner, and Mikael Samuelsson for Alexei Kovalev, Dan LaCouture, Janne Laukkanen, and Mike Wilson, February 10, 2003

Claimed on waivers by Atlanta, January 31, 2006

FAUBERT, MARIO

Defense   **Ht:** 6-1   **Wt:** 175   **Shoots:** right
B: December 2, 1954, Valleyfield, Quebec

YR	Regular Season					Playoffs				
	GP	G	A	PTS	PM	GP	G	A	PTS	PM
1974-75	10	1	0	1	6	-	-	-	-	-
1975-76	21	1	8	9	10	-	-	-	-	-
1976-77	47	2	11	13	32	3	1	0	1	2
1977-78	18	0	6	6	11	-	-	-	-	-
1979-80	49	5	13	18	31	2	0	1	1	0
1980-81	72	8	44	52	118	5	1	1	2	4
1981-82	14	4	8	12	14	-	-	-	-	-
Pitt. Totals	231	21	90	111	222	10	2	2	4	6
NHL Totals	231	21	90	111	222	10	2	2	4	6

Selected in the 1974 Amateur Draft, 3rd choice, 62nd overall

FEDOTENKO, RUSLAN

Left Wing   **Ht:** 6-2   **Wt:** 195   **Shoots:** left
B: January 18, 1979, Kiev, USSR

YR	Regular Season					Playoffs				
	GP	G	A	PTS	PM	GP	G	A	PTS	PM
2008-09	65	16	23	39	44	24	7	7	14	4
2009-10	80	11	19	30	50	6	0	0	0	4
Pitt. Totals	145	27	42	69	94	30	7	7	14	8
NHL Totals	677	150	158	308	419	83	20	11	31	54

Signed as a free agent, July 3, 2008

Ruslan Fedotenko brought a scoring touch and Stanley Cup experience to the Pens in 2008.

FELTRIN, ANTHONY LOUIS (Tony)

Defense   **Ht:** 6-1   **Wt:** 184   **Shoots:** left
B: December 6, 1961, Ladysmith, British Columbia

YR	Regular Season					Playoffs				
	GP	G	A	PTS	PM	GP	G	A	PTS	PM
1980-81	2	0	0	0	0	-	-	-	-	-
1981-82	4	0	0	0	4	-	-	-	-	-
1982-83	32	3	3	6	40	-	-	-	-	-
Pitt. Totals	38	3	3	6	44	-	-	-	-	-
NHL Totals	48	3	3	6	65	-	-	-	-	-

Selected in the 1980 Entry Draft, 3rd choice, 72nd overall

Signed as a free agent by NY Rangers, October 8, 1985

FERENCE, ANDREW

Defense   **Ht:** 5-11 **Wt:** 189   **Shoots:** left
B: March 17, 1979, Edmonton, Alberta

YR	Regular Season					Playoffs				
	GP	G	A	PTS	PM	GP	G	A	PTS	PM
1999-00	30	2	4	6	20	-	-	-	-	-
2000-01	36	4	11	15	28	18	3	7	10	16
2001-02	75	4	7	11	73	-	-	-	-	-
2002-03	22	1	3	4	36	-	-	-	-	-
Pitt. Totals	163	11	25	36	157	18	3	7	10	16
NHL Totals	570	24	117	141	504	74	3	19	22	81

Selected in the 1997 Entry Draft, 8th choice, 208th overall

Traded to Calgary for a 3rd round choice in the 2004
Entry Draft, February 9, 2003

FERGUSON, GEORGE STEPHEN

Center/Right Wing   **Ht:** 6-0 **Wt:** 195   **Shoots:** right
B: August 22, 1952, Trenton, Ontario

YR	Regular Season					Playoffs				
	GP	G	A	PTS	PM	GP	G	A	PTS	PM
1978-79	80	21	29	50	37	7	2	1	3	0
1979-80	73	21	28	49	36	5	0	3	3	4
1980-81	79	25	18	43	42	5	2	6	8	9
1981-82	71	22	31	53	45	5	0	1	1	0
1982-83	7	0	0	0	2	-	-	-	-	-
Pitt. Totals	310	89	106	195	162	22	4	11	15	13
NHL Totals	797	160	238	398	431	86	14	23	37	44

Acquired from Toronto with Randy Carlyle for Dave
Burrows, June 14, 1978

Traded to Minnesota for Anders Hakansson, Ron
Meighan, and an exchange of 1st round choices in the 1983
Entry Draft, October 28, 1982

FERRARO, CHRIS

Center   **Ht:** 5-9 **Wt:** 175   **Shoots:** right
B: January 24, 1973, Port Jefferson, New York

YR	Regular Season					Playoffs				
	GP	G	A	PTS	PM	GP	G	A	PTS	PM
1997-98	46	3	4	7	43	-	-	-	-	-
Pitt. Totals	46	3	4	7	43	-	-	-	-	-
NHL Totals	74	7	9	16	57	-	-	-	-	-

Claimed on waivers from NY Rangers, October 1, 1997

Signed as a free agent by Edmonton, August 13, 1998

FERRARO, PETER

Left Wing   **Ht:** 5-10 **Wt:** 180   **Shoots:** right
B: January 24, 1973, Port Jefferson, New York

YR	Regular Season					Playoffs				
	GP	G	A	PTS	PM	GP	G	A	PTS	PM
1997-98	29	3	4	7	12	-	-	-	-	-
Pitt. Totals	29	3	4	7	12	-	-	-	-	-
NHL Totals	92	9	15	24	58	2	0	0	0	0

Claimed on waivers from NY Rangers, October 1, 1997

Claimed on waivers by NY Rangers, January 9, 1998

FILEWICH, JONATHAN

Right Wing   **Ht:** 6-2 **Wt:** 208   **Shoots:** right
B: October 2, 1984, Kelowna, British Columbia

YR	Regular Season					Playoffs				
	GP	G	A	PTS	PM	GP	G	A	PTS	PM
2007-08	5	0	0	0	0	-	-	-	-	-
Pitt. Totals	5	0	0	0	0	-	-	-	-	-
NHL Totals	5	0	0	0	0	-	-	-	-	-

Selected in the 2003 Entry Draft, 3rd choice, 70th overall

Traded to St. Louis for a conditional 6th round choice in
the 2010 Entry Draft, December 19, 2008

FITZGERALD, RUSTY

Center   **Ht:** 6-1 **Wt:** 210   **Shoots:** left
B: October 4, 1972, Minneapolis, Minnesota

YR	Regular Season					Playoffs				
	GP	G	A	PTS	PM	GP	G	A	PTS	PM
1994-95	4	1	0	1	0	5	0	0	0	4
1995-96	21	1	2	3	12	-	-	-	-	-
Pitt. Totals	25	2	2	4	12	5	0	0	0	4
NHL Totals	25	2	2	4	12	5	0	0	0	4

Selected in the 1991 Entry Draft, 2nd choice, 38th overall

Signed as a free agent by Iserlohn (Germany), June 16, 2001

FLESCH, JOHN PATRICK

Left Wing   **Ht:** 6-2 **Wt:** 200   **Shoots:** left
B: July 15, 1953, Sudbury, Ontario

YR	Regular Season					Playoffs				
	GP	G	A	PTS	PM	GP	G	A	PTS	PM
1977-78	29	7	5	12	19	-	-	-	-	-
Pitt. Totals	29	7	5	12	19	-	-	-	-	-
NHL Totals	124	18	23	41	117	-	-	-	-	-

Signed as a free agent, February 4, 1978

Signed as a free agent by Colorado, January 13, 1980

FLEURY, MARC-ANDRE (Flower)

Goaltender   **Ht:** 6-2 **Wt:** 180   **Catches:** left
B: November 28, 1984, Sorel, Quebec

YR	Regular Season					Playoffs				
	GP	MINS	GA	SH	AVE	GP	MINS	GA	SH	AVE
2003-04	21	1154	70	1	3.64	-	-	-	-	-
2005-06	50	2809	152	1	3.25	-	-	-	-	-
2006-07	67	3905	184	5	2.83	5	287	18	0	3.76
2007-08	35	1857	72	4	2.33	20	1251	41	3	1.97
2008-09	62	3641	162	4	2.67	24	1447	63	0	2.61
2009-10	67	3798	168	1	2.65	13	798	37	1	2.78
Pitt. Totals	302	17164	808	16	2.82	62	3783	159	4	2.52
NHL Totals	302	17164	808	16	2.82	62	3783	159	4	2.52

Selected in the 2003 Entry Draft, 1st choice, 1st overall

FLOCKHART, RONALD (Ron)

Center   **Ht:** 5-11 **Wt:** 190   **Shoots:** left
B: October 10, 1960, Smithers, British Columbia

YR	Regular Season					Playoffs				
	GP	G	A	PTS	PM	GP	G	A	PTS	PM
1983-84	68	27	18	45	40	-	-	-	-	-
1984-85	12	0	5	5	4	-	-	-	-	-
Pitt. Totals	80	27	23	50	44	-	-	-	-	-
NHL Totals	453	145	183	328	208	19	4	6	10	14

Acquired from Philadelphia with Andy Brickley, Mark Taylor, and 1st and 3rd round choices in the 1984 Entry Draft for Rich Sutter and 2nd and 3rd round choices in the 1984 Entry Draft, October 23, 1983

Traded to Montreal for John Chabot, November 9, 1984

Speedy Ron Flockhart was acquired from Philadelphia in 1983.

FOCHT, DAN

Defense   **Ht:** 6-6 **Wt:** 234   **Shoots:** left
B: December 31, 1977, Regina, Saskatchewan

YR	Regular Season					Playoffs				
	GP	G	A	PTS	PM	GP	G	A	PTS	PM
2002-03	12	0	3	3	19	-	-	-	-	-
2003-04	52	2	3	5	105	-	-	-	-	-
Pitt. Totals	64	2	6	8	124	-	-	-	-	-
NHL Totals	82	2	6	8	145	1	0	1	1	0

Acquired from Phoenix with Ramzi Abid and Guillaume Lefebvre for Jan Hrdina and Francois Leroux, March 11, 2003

Signed as a free agent by Florida, August 26, 2005

FOGARTY, BRYAN

Defense   **Ht:** 6-2 **Wt:** 206   **Shoots:** left
B: June 11, 1969, Brantford, Ontario
D: March 6, 2002

YR	Regular Season					Playoffs				
	GP	G	A	PTS	PM	GP	G	A	PTS	PM
1992-93	12	0	4	4	4	-	-	-	-	-
Pitt. Totals	12	0	4	4	4	-	-	-	-	-
NHL Totals	156	22	52	74	119	-	-	-	-	-

Acquired from Quebec for the rights to Scott Young, March 10, 1992

Signed as a free agent by Tampa Bay, September 28, 1993

FONTEYNE, VALERE RONALD (Val)

Left Wing **Ht:** 5-10 **Wt:** 160 **Shoots:** left
B: December 2, 1933, Wetaskiwin, Alberta

	Regular Season					Playoffs				
YR	GP	G	A	PTS	PM	GP	G	A	PTS	PM
1967-68	69	6	28	34	0	-	-	-	-	-
1968-69	74	12	17	29	2	-	-	-	-	-
1969-70	68	11	15	26	2	10	0	2	2	0
1970-71	70	4	9	13	0	-	-	-	-	-
1971-72	68	6	13	19	0	4	0	0	0	2
Pitt. Totals	349	39	82	121	4	14	0	2	2	2
NHL Totals	820	75	154	229	26	59	3	10	13	8
WHA Totals	149	16	45	61	4	5	1	0	1	0

Selected from Detroit in the 1967 Expansion Draft, June 6, 1967

Signed as a free agent by Edmonton (WHA), September 2, 1972

FORD, BRIAN

Goaltender **Ht:** 5-10 **Wt:** 170 **Catches:** left
B: September 22, 1961, Edmonton, Alberta

	Regular Season					Playoffs				
YR	GP	MINS	GA	SH	AVE	GP	MINS	GA	SH	AVE
1984-85	8	457	48	0	6.30	-	-	-	-	-
Pitt. Totals	8	457	48	0	6.30	-	-	-	-	-
NHL Totals	11	580	61	0	6.31	-	-	-	-	-

Acquired from Quebec for Tom Thornbury, December 6, 1984

FOSTER, COREY

Defense **Ht:** 6-3 **Wt:** 204 **Shoots:** left
B: October 27, 1969, Ottawa, Ontario

	Regular Season					Playoffs				
YR	GP	G	A	PTS	PM	GP	G	A	PTS	PM
1995-96	11	2	2	4	2	3	0	0	0	4
Pitt. Totals	11	2	2	4	2	3	0	0	0	4
NHL Totals	45	5	6	11	24	3	0	0	0	4

Signed as a free agent, August 7, 1995

Claimed by NY Islanders in the Waiver Draft, September 30, 1996

FOX, GREGORY BRENT (Greg)

Defense **Ht:** 6-2 **Wt:** 190 **Shoots:** left
B: August 12, 1953, Port McNeil, British Columbia

	Regular Season					Playoffs				
YR	GP	G	A	PTS	PM	GP	G	A	PTS	PM
1983-84	49	2	5	7	66	-	-	-	-	-
1984-85	26	2	5	7	26	-	-	-	-	-
Pitt. Totals	75	4	10	14	92	-	-	-	-	-
NHL Totals	494	14	92	106	637	44	1	9	10	67

Acquired from Chicago for Randy Boyd, December 6, 1983

FRANCIS, RONALD (Ron)

Center **Ht:** 6-2 **Wt:** 200 **Shoots:** left
B: March 1, 1963, Sault Ste. Marie, Ontario

	Regular Season					Playoffs				
YR	GP	G	A	PTS	PM	GP	G	A	PTS	PM
1990-91	14	2	9	11	21	24	7	10	17	24
1991-92	70	21	33	54	30	21	8	19	27	6
1992-93	84	24	76	100	68	12	6	11	17	19
1993-94	82	27	66	93	62	6	0	2	2	6
1994-95	44	11	48	59	18	12	6	13	19	4
1995-96	77	27	92	119	56	11	3	6	9	4
1996-97	81	27	63	90	20	5	1	2	3	2
1997-98	81	25	62	87	20	6	1	5	6	2
Pitt. Totals	533	164	449	613	295	97	32	68	100	67
NHL Totals	1731	549	1249	1798	979	171	46	97	143	95

Acquired from Hartford with Grant Jennings and Ulf Samuelsson for John Cullen, Jeff Parker, and Zarley Zalapski, March 4, 1991

Signed as a free agent by Carolina, July 13, 1998

Won the Frank J. Selke Memorial Trophy 1994-95

Won the Lady Byng Trophy 1994-95, 1997-98

Eastern Conference All-Star 1995-96

Hockey Hall of Fame (Player), 2007

FRAWLEY, WILLIAM DANIEL (Dan)

Right Wing   **Ht:** 6-1 **Wt:** 195   **Shoots:** right
B: June 2, 1962, Sturgeon Falls, Ontario

	Regular Season					Playoffs				
YR	GP	G	A	PTS	PM	GP	G	A	PTS	PM
1985-86	69	10	11	21	174	-	-	-	-	-
1986-87	78	14	14	28	218	-	-	-	-	-
1987-88	47	6	8	14	152	-	-	-	-	-
1988-89	46	3	4	7	66	-	-	-	-	-
Pitt. Totals	240	33	37	70	610	-	-	-	-	-
NHL Totals	273	37	40	77	674	1	0	0	0	0

Claimed from Chicago in the Waiver Draft, October 7, 1985

Signed as a free agent by Buffalo, September 1990

G

GALANOV, MAXIM

Defense   **Ht:** 6-1 **Wt:** 205   **Shoots:** left
B: March 13, 1974, Krasnoyarsk, USSR

	Regular Season					Playoffs				
YR	GP	G	A	PTS	PM	GP	G	A	PTS	PM
1998-99	51	4	3	7	14	1	0	0	0	0
Pitt. Totals	51	4	3	7	14	1	0	0	0	0
NHL Totals	122	8	12	20	44	1	0	0	0	0

Claimed from NY Rangers in the Waiver Draft, October 5, 1998

Claimed by Atlanta in the Expansion Draft, June 25, 1999

GANCHAR, PERRY

Right Wing   **Ht:** 5-9 **Wt:** 180   **Shoots:** right
B: October 28, 1963, Saskatoon, Saskatchewan

	Regular Season					Playoffs				
YR	GP	G	A	PTS	PM	GP	G	A	PTS	PM
1987-88	30	2	5	7	36	-	-	-	-	-
1988-89	3	0	0	0	0	-	-	-	-	-
Pitt. Totals	33	2	5	7	36	-	-	-	-	-
NHL Totals	42	3	7	10	36	7	3	1	4	0

Acquired from Montreal for future considerations, December 17, 1987

GARDNER, PAUL MALONE

Center   **Ht:** 6-0 **Wt:** 195   **Shoots:** left
B: March 5, 1956, Toronto, Ontario

	Regular Season					Playoffs				
YR	GP	G	A	PTS	PM	GP	G	A	PTS	PM
1980-81	62	34	40	74	59	5	1	0	1	8
1981-82	59	36	33	69	28	5	1	5	6	2
1982-83	70	28	27	55	12	-	-	-	-	-
1983-84	16	0	5	5	6	-	-	-	-	-
Pitt. Totals	207	98	105	203	105	10	2	5	7	10
NHL Totals	447	201	201	402	207	16	2	6	8	14

Acquired from Toronto with Dave Burrows for Kim Davis and Paul Marshall, November 18, 1980

Signed as a free agent by Washington, July 17, 1984

GARON, MATHIEU

Goaltender   **Ht:** 6-2 **Wt:** 207   **Catches:** right
B: January 9, 1978, Chandler, Quebec

	Regular Season					Playoffs				
YR	GP	MINS	GA	SH	AVE	GP	MINS	GA	SH	AVE
2008-09	4	206	10	0	2.91	1	24	0	0	0.00
Pitt. Totals	4	206	10	0	2.91	1	24	0	0	0.00
NHL Totals	239	13010	615	16	2.84	2	36	0	0	0.00

Acquired from Edmonton for Dany Sabourin, Ryan Stone, and a 4th round pick in the 2011 Entry Draft, January 17, 2009

Signed as a free agent by Columbus, July 1, 2009

GARNER, ROBERT WILLIAM (Rob)

Center   **Ht:** 5-11 **Wt:** 180   **Shoots:** left
B: August 17, 1958, Weston, Ontario

	Regular Season					Playoffs				
YR	GP	G	A	PTS	PM	GP	G	A	PTS	PM
1982-83	1	0	0	0	0	-	-	-	-	-
Pitt. Totals	1	0	0	0	0	-	-	-	-	-
NHL Totals	1	0	0	0	0	-	-	-	-	-

Selected in the 1978 Amateur Draft, 3rd choice, 75th overall

GATZOS, STEVE

Right Wing **Ht:** 5-11 **Wt:** 185 **Shoots:** right
B: June 22, 1961, Toronto, Ontario

YR	Regular Season					Playoffs				
	GP	G	A	PTS	PM	GP	G	A	PTS	PM
1981-82	16	6	8	14	14	1	0	0	0	0
1982-83	44	6	7	13	52	-	-	-	-	-
1983-84	23	3	3	6	15	-	-	-	-	-
1984-85	6	0	2	2	2	-	-	-	-	-
Pitt. Totals	**89**	**15**	**20**	**35**	**83**	**1**	**0**	**0**	**0**	**0**
NHL Totals	**89**	**15**	**20**	**35**	**83**	**1**	**0**	**0**	**0**	**0**

Selected in the 1981 Entry Draft, 1st choice, 28th overall

GEALE, ROBERT CHARLES (Bob)

Center **Ht:** 5-11 **Wt:** 175 **Shoots:** right
B: April 17, 1962, Edmonton, Alberta

YR	Regular Season					Playoffs				
	GP	G	A	PTS	PM	GP	G	A	PTS	PM
1984-85	1	0	0	0	2	-	-	-	-	-
Pitt. Totals	**1**	**0**	**0**	**0**	**2**	-	-	-	-	-
NHL Totals	**1**	**0**	**0**	**0**	**2**	-	-	-	-	-

Selected in the 1980 Entry Draft, 6th choice, 156th overall

GIFFIN, LEE

Right Wing **Ht:** 6-0 **Wt:** 188 **Shoots:** right
B: April 1, 1967, Chatham, Ontario

YR	Regular Season					Playoffs				
	GP	G	A	PTS	PM	GP	G	A	PTS	PM
1986-87	8	1	1	2	0	-	-	-	-	-
1987-88	19	0	2	2	9	-	-	-	-	-
Pitt. Totals	**27**	**1**	**3**	**4**	**9**	-	-	-	-	-
NHL Totals	**27**	**1**	**3**	**4**	**9**	-	-	-	-	-

Selected in the 1985 Entry Draft, 2nd choice, 23rd overall

Traded to NY Rangers for future considerations, September 14, 1989

GILBERT, EDWARD FERGUSON (Ed)

Center **Ht:** 6-0 **Wt:** 185 **Shoots:** left
B: March 12, 1952, Hamilton, Ontario

YR	Regular Season					Playoffs				
	GP	G	A	PTS	PM	GP	G	A	PTS	PM
1975-76	38	1	1	2	0	-	-	-	-	-
1976-77	7	0	0	0	0	-	-	-	-	-
Pitt. Totals	**45**	**1**	**1**	**2**	**0**	-	-	-	-	-
NHL Totals	**166**	**21**	**31**	**52**	**22**	-	-	-	-	-
WHA Totals	**29**	**3**	**3**	**6**	**6**	-	-	-	-	-

Acquired from Kansas City with Simon Nolet and an exchange of 1st round choices in the 1976 Amateur Draft for Chuck Arnason and Steve Durbano, January 9, 1976

Signed as a free agent by Cincinnati (WHA), October 1978

GILBERTSON, STANLEY FRANK (Stan)

Left Wing **Ht:** 6-0 **Wt:** 175 **Shoots:** left
B: October 9, 1944, Duluth, Minnesota

YR	Regular Season					Playoffs				
	GP	G	A	PTS	PM	GP	G	A	PTS	PM
1975-76	48	13	8	21	6	3	1	1	2	2
1976-77	67	6	9	15	13	-	-	-	-	-
Pitt. Totals	**115**	**19**	**17**	**36**	**19**	**3**	**1**	**1**	**2**	**2**
NHL Totals	**428**	**85**	**89**	**174**	**148**	**3**	**1**	**1**	**2**	**2**

Acquired from Washington for Harvey Bennett, December 16, 1975

GILHEN, RANDY

Center **Ht:** 6-0 **Wt:** 190 **Shoots:** left
B: June 13, 1963, Zweibrucken, West Germany

YR	Regular Season					Playoffs				
	GP	G	A	PTS	PM	GP	G	A	PTS	PM
1989-90	61	5	11	16	54	-	-	-	-	-
1990-91	72	15	10	25	51	16	1	0	1	14
Pitt. Totals	**133**	**20**	**21**	**41**	**105**	**16**	**1**	**0**	**1**	**14**
NHL Totals	**457**	**55**	**60**	**115**	**314**	**33**	**3**	**2**	**5**	**26**

Acquired from Winnipeg with Jim Kyte and Andrew McBain for Randy Cunneyworth, Dave McLlwain, and Rick Tabaracci, June 17, 1989

Selected by Minnesota in the 1991 Expansion Draft, May 30, 1991

GILL, HAL

Defense **Ht:** 6-7 **Wt:** 250 **Shoots:** left
B: April 6, 1975, Concord, Massachusetts

	Regular Season					Playoffs				
YR	GP	G	A	PTS	PM	GP	G	A	PTS	PM
2007-08	18	1	3	4	16	20	0	1	1	12
2008-09	62	2	8	10	53	**24**	0	2	2	6
Pitt. Totals	80	3	11	14	69	44	0	3	3	18
NHL Totals	919	33	129	162	868	98	0	6	6	66

Acquired from Toronto for a 2nd round choice in the 2008 Entry Draft and a 5th round choice in the 2009 Entry Draft, February 26, 2008

Signed as a free agent by Montreal, July 1, 2009

GLADNEY, ROBERT LAWRENCE (Bob)

Defense **Ht:** 5-11 **Wt:** 185 **Shoots:** left
B: August 27, 1957, Come-by-Chance, Newfoundland and Labrador

	Regular Season					Playoffs				
YR	GP	G	A	PTS	PM	GP	G	A	PTS	PM
1983-84	13	1	5	6	2	-	-	-	-	-
Pitt. Totals	13	1	5	6	2	-	-	-	-	-
NHL Totals	14	1	5	6	4	-	-	-	-	-

Signed as a free agent, September 12, 1983

GODARD, ERIC

Right Wing **Ht:** 6-4 **Wt:** 214 **Shoots:** right
B: March 7, 1980, Vernon, British Columbia

	Regular Season					Playoffs				
YR	GP	G	A	PTS	PM	GP	G	A	PTS	PM
2008-09	71	2	2	4	171	-	-	-	-	-
2009-10	45	1	2	3	76	-	-	-	-	-
Pitt. Totals	116	3	4	7	247	-	-	-	-	-
NHL Totals	316	6	9	15	728	7	0	1	1	6

Signed as a free agent, July 1, 2008

GOERTZ, DAVE

Defense **Ht:** 5-11 **Wt:** 210 **Shoots:** right
B: March 28, 1965, Edmonton, Alberta

	Regular Season					Playoffs				
YR	GP	G	A	PTS	PM	GP	G	A	PTS	PM
1987-88	2	0	0	0	2	-	-	-	-	-
Pitt. Totals	2	0	0	0	2	-	-	-	-	-
NHL Totals	2	0	0	0	2	-	-	-	-	-

Selected in the 1983 Entry Draft, 10th choice, 232nd overall

GOLIGOSKI, ALEX (Go Go)

Defense **Ht:** 5-11 **Wt:** 180 **Shoots:** left
B: July 30, 1985, Grand Rapids, Minnesota

	Regular Season					Playoffs				
YR	GP	G	A	PTS	PM	GP	G	A	PTS	PM
2007-08	3	0	2	2	2	-	-	-	-	-
2008-09	45	6	14	20	16	2	0	1	1	0
2009-10	69	8	29	37	22	13	2	7	9	2
Pitt. Totals	117	14	45	59	40	15	2	8	10	2
NHL Totals	117	14	45	59	40	15	2	8	10	2

Selected in the 2004 Entry Draft, 3rd choice, 61st overall

GONCHAR, SERGEI (Sarge)

Defense **Ht:** 6-2 **Wt:** 211 **Shoots:** left
B: April 13, 1974, Chelyabinsk, USSR

	Regular Season					Playoffs				
YR	GP	G	A	PTS	PM	GP	G	A	PTS	PM
2005-06	75	12	46	58	100	-	-	-	-	-
2006-07	82	13	54	67	72	5	1	3	4	2
2007-08	78	12	53	65	66	20	1	13	14	8
2008-09	25	6	13	19	26	22	3	11	14	12
2009-10	62	11	39	50	49	13	2	10	12	4
Pitt. Totals	322	54	205	259	313	60	7	37	44	26
NHL Totals	991	202	482	684	842	118	21	59	80	78

Signed as a free agent, August 3, 2005

Signed as a free agent by Ottawa, July 1, 2010

Eastern Conference All-Star 2007-08

GOTAAS, STEVE

Center **Ht:** 5-10 **Wt:** 180 **Shoots:** right
B: May 10, 1967, Camrose, Alberta

	Regular Season					Playoffs				
YR	GP	G	A	PTS	PM	GP	G	A	PTS	PM
1987-88	36	5	6	11	45	-	-	-	-	-
Pitt. Totals	36	5	6	11	45	-	-	-	-	-
NHL Totals	49	6	9	15	53	3	0	1	1	5

Selected in the 1985 Entry Draft, 4th choice, 86th overall

Traded to Minnesota with Ville Siren for Scott Bjugstad and Gord Dineen, December 17, 1988

GRAHAM, PATRICK THOMAS (Pat)

Left Wing   Ht: 6-1 **Wt:** 190   **Shoots:** left
B: May 25, 1961, Toronto, Ontario

YR	Regular Season					Playoffs				
	GP	G	A	PTS	PM	GP	G	A	PTS	PM
1981-82	42	6	8	14	55	4	0	0	0	2
1982-83	20	1	5	6	16	-	-	-	-	-
Pitt. Totals	62	7	13	20	71	4	0	0	0	2
NHL Totals	103	11	17	28	136	4	0	0	0	2

Selected in the 1980 Entry Draft, 5th choice, 114th overall

Traded to Toronto with Nick Ricci for Rocky Saganiuk and Vincent Tremblay, August 15, 1983

GRONMAN, TUOMAS

Defense   Ht: 6-3 **Wt:** 219   **Shoots:** left
B: March 22, 1974, Viitasaari, Finland

YR	Regular Season					Playoffs				
	GP	G	A	PTS	PM	GP	G	A	PTS	PM
1997-98	22	1	2	3	25	1	0	0	0	0
Pitt. Totals	22	1	2	3	25	1	0	0	0	0
NHL Totals	38	1	3	4	38	1	0	0	0	0

Acquired from Chicago for Greg Johnson, October 27, 1997

GRUHL, SCOTT KENNETH

Left Wing   Ht: 5-11 **Wt:** 185   **Shoots:** left
B: September 13, 1959, Port Colborne, Ontario

YR	Regular Season					Playoffs				
	GP	G	A	PTS	PM	GP	G	A	PTS	PM
1987-88	6	1	0	1	0	-	-	-	-	-
Pitt. Totals	6	1	0	1	0	-	-	-	-	-
NHL Totals	20	3	3	6	6	-	-	-	-	-

Signed as a free agent, December 14, 1987

GUENETTE, STEVE

Goaltender   Ht: 5-10 **Wt:** 175   **Catches:** left
B: November 13, 1965, Gloucester, Ontario

YR	Regular Season					Playoffs				
	GP	MINS	GA	SH	AVE	GP	MINS	GA	SH	AVE
1986-87	2	113	8	0	4.25	-	-	-	-	-
1987-88	19	1092	61	1	3.35	-	-	-	-	-
1988-89	11	574	41	0	4.29	-	-	-	-	-
Pitt. Totals	32	1779	110	1	3.71	-	-	-	-	-
NHL Totals	35	1958	122	1	3.74	-	-	-	-	-

Signed as a free agent, April 6, 1985

Traded to Calgary for a 6th round choice in the 1989 Entry Draft, January 9, 1989

GUENIN, NATE

Defense   Ht: 6-2 **Wt:** 210   **Shoots:** right
B: December 10, 1982, Sewickley, Pennsylvania

YR	Regular Season					Playoffs				
	GP	G	A	PTS	PM	GP	G	A	PTS	PM
2009-10	2	0	0	0	0	-	-	-	-	-
Pitt. Totals	2	0	0	0	0	-	-	-	-	-
NHL Totals	14	0	2	2	6	-	-	-	-	-

Signed as a free agent, July 3, 2009

Traded to St. Louis for Steve Wagner, February 11, 2010

GUERIN, BILL

Right Wing   Ht: 6-2 **Wt:** 220   **Shoots:** right
B: November 9, 1970, Worcester, Massachusetts

YR	Regular Season					Playoffs				
	GP	G	A	PTS	PM	GP	G	A	PTS	PM
2008-09	17	5	7	12	18	24	7	8	15	15
2009-10	78	21	24	45	75	11	4	5	9	2
Pitt. Totals	95	26	31	57	93	35	11	13	24	17
NHL Totals	1263	429	427	856	1660	140	39	35	74	162

Acquired from NY Islanders for a 3rd round choice in the 2009 Entry Draft, March 4, 2009

Bill Guerin (13) helped spark the Pens to a Stanley Cup in 2009.

H

HADFIELD, VICTOR EDWARD (Vic)

Left Wing   Ht: 6-0 **Wt:** 190   **Shoots:** left
B: October 4, 1940, Oakville, Ontario

	Regular Season					Playoffs				
YR	GP	G	A	PTS	PM	GP	G	A	PTS	PM
1974-75	78	31	42	73	72	9	4	2	6	0
1975-76	76	30	35	65	46	3	1	0	1	11
1976-77	9	0	2	2	0	-	-	-	-	-
Pitt. Totals	163	61	79	140	118	12	5	2	7	11
NHL Totals	1002	323	389	712	1154	73	27	21	48	117

Acquired from NY Rangers for Nick Beverley, May 27, 1974

HAKANSSON, ANDERS

Left Wing   Ht: 6-2 **Wt:** 190   **Shoots:** left
B: April 27, 1956, Munkfors, Sweden

	Regular Season					Playoffs				
YR	GP	G	A	PTS	PM	GP	G	A	PTS	PM
1982-83	62	9	12	21	26	-	-	-	-	-
Pitt. Totals	62	9	12	21	26	-	-	-	-	-
NHL Totals	330	52	46	98	141	6	0	0	0	2

Acquired from Minnesota with Ron Meighan for George Ferguson and an exchange of 1st round choices in the 1983 Entry Draft, October 28, 1982

Traded to Los Angeles for the rights to Kevin Stevens, September 9, 1983

HALL, ADAM

Right Wing   Ht: 6-3 **Wt:** 206   **Shoots:** right
B: August 14, 1980, Kalamazoo, Michigan

	Regular Season					Playoffs				
YR	GP	G	A	PTS	PM	GP	G	A	PTS	PM
2007-08	46	2	4	6	24	17	3	1	4	8
Pitt. Totals	46	2	4	6	24	17	3	1	4	8
NHL Totals	426	56	62	118	187	31	6	2	8	17

Signed as a free agent, October 1, 2007

Signed as a free agent by Tampa Bay, July 1, 2008

HAMILTON, JAMES (Jim)

Right Wing   Ht: 6-0 **Wt:** 180   **Shoots:** left
B: January 18, 1957, Barrie, Ontario

	Regular Season					Playoffs				
YR	GP	G	A	PTS	PM	GP	G	A	PTS	PM
1977-78	25	2	4	6	2	-	-	-	-	-
1978-79	2	0	0	0	0	5	3	0	3	0
1979-80	10	2	0	2	0	-	-	-	-	-
1980-81	20	1	6	7	18	1	0	0	0	0
1981-82	11	5	3	8	2	-	-	-	-	-
1982-83	5	0	2	2	2	-	-	-	-	-
1983-84	11	2	2	4	4	-	-	-	-	-
1984-85	11	2	1	3	0	-	-	-	-	-
Pitt. Totals	95	14	18	32	28	6	3	0	3	0
NHL Totals	95	14	18	32	28	6	3	0	3	0

Selected in the 1977 Amateur Draft, 1st choice, 30th overall

HANNAN, DAVID (Dave)

Center   Ht: 5-10 **Wt:** 180   **Shoots:** left
B: November 26, 1961, Sudbury, Ontario

	Regular Season					Playoffs				
YR	GP	G	A	PTS	PM	GP	G	A	PTS	PM
1981-82	1	0	0	0	0	-	-	-	-	-
1982-83	74	11	22	33	127	-	-	-	-	-
1983-84	24	2	3	5	33	-	-	-	-	-
1984-85	30	6	7	13	43	-	-	-	-	-
1985-86	75	17	18	35	91	-	-	-	-	-
1986-87	58	10	15	25	56	-	-	-	-	-
1987-88	21	4	3	7	23	-	-	-	-	-
1988-89	72	10	20	30	157	8	0	1	1	4
Pitt. Totals	355	60	88	148	530	8	0	1	1	4
NHL Totals	841	114	191	305	942	63	6	7	13	46

Selected in the 1981 Entry Draft, 9th choice, 196th overall

Traded to Edmonton with Chris Joseph, Moe Mantha, and Craig Simpson for Paul Coffey, Dave Hunter, and Wayne Van Dorp, November 24, 1987

Claimed from Edmonton in the Waiver Draft, October 3, 1988

Claimed by Toronto in the Waiver Draft, October 2, 1989

Checker Dave Hannan played in 355 games for the Pens in the 1980s.

Former Pittsburgh Hornet Billy Harris skated for the Pens during the 1968–69 season.

HARBARUK, MIKOLAJ NICKOLAS (Nick)

Right Wing   Ht: 6-0 **Wt:** 195   **Shoots:** right
B: August 16, 1943, Drohiczyn, Poland

YR	Regular Season					Playoffs				
	GP	G	A	PTS	PM	GP	G	A	PTS	PM
1969-70	74	5	17	22	56	10	3	0	3	20
1970-71	78	13	12	25	108	-	-	-	-	-
1971-72	78	12	17	29	46	4	0	1	1	0
1972-73	78	10	15	25	47	-	-	-	-	-
Pitt. Totals	308	40	61	101	257	14	3	1	4	20
NHL Totals	364	45	75	120	273	14	3	1	4	20
WHA Totals	181	45	44	89	80	13	3	1	4	10

Claimed from Vancouver (WHL) in the Inter-League Draft, June 10, 1969

Traded to St. Louis for Bob Johnson, October 4, 1973

HARRIS, WILLIAM EDWARD (Billy)

Center   Ht: 6-0 **Wt:** 155   **Shoots:** left
B: July 29, 1935, Toronto, Ontario
D: September 20, 2001

YR	Regular Season					Playoffs				
	GP	G	A	PTS	PM	GP	G	A	PTS	PM
1968-69	54	7	13	20	8	-	-	-	-	-
Pitt. Totals	54	7	13	20	8	-	-	-	-	-
NHL Totals	769	126	219	345	205	62	8	10	18	30

Acquired from Oakland for Bob Dillabough, November 29, 1968

HARRISON, PAUL DOUGLAS

Goaltender   Ht: 6-1 **Wt:** 196   **Catches:** left
B: February 11, 1955, Timmins, Ontario

YR	Regular Season					Playoffs				
	GP	MINS	GA	SH	AVE	GP	MINS	GA	SH	AVE
1981-82	13	700	64	0	5.49	-	-	-	-	-
Pitt. Totals	13	700	64	0	5.49	-	-	-	-	-
NHL Totals	109	5806	408	2	4.22	4	157	9	0	3.44

Acquired from Toronto for future considerations, September 11, 1981

Claimed on waivers by Buffalo, February 8, 1982

HATCHER, KEVIN

Defense   Ht: 6-3 **Wt:** 230   **Shoots:** right
B: September 9, 1966, Detroit, Michigan

YR	Regular Season					Playoffs				
	GP	G	A	PTS	PM	GP	G	A	PTS	PM
1996-97	80	15	39	54	103	5	1	1	2	4
1997-98	74	19	29	48	66	6	1	0	1	12
1998-99	66	11	27	38	24	13	2	3	5	4
Pitt. Totals	220	45	95	140	193	24	4	4	8	20
NHL Totals	1157	227	450	677	1392	118	22	37	59	252

Acquired from Dallas for Sergei Zubov, June 22, 1996

Traded to NY Rangers for Peter Popovic, September 30, 1999

Eastern Conference All-Star 1996-97

HAWGOOD, GREG

Defense   Ht: 5-10 **Wt:** 190   **Shoots:** left
B: August 10, 1968, Edmonton, Alberta

	Regular Season					Playoffs				
YR	GP	G	A	PTS	PM	GP	G	A	PTS	PM
1993-94	12	1	2	3	8	1	0	0	0	0
1994-95	21	1	4	5	25	-	-	-	-	-
Pitt. Totals	33	2	6	8	33	1	0	0	0	0
NHL Totals	474	60	164	224	426	42	2	8	10	37

Acquired from Florida for Jeff Daniels, March 19, 1994

Signed as a free agent by San Jose, September 25, 1996

HEDBERG, JOHAN (Moose)

Goaltender   Ht: 6-0 **Wt:** 185   **Catches:** left
B: May 5, 1973, Leksand, Sweden

	Regular Season					Playoffs				
YR	GP	MINS	GA	SH	AVE	GP	MINS	GA	SH	AVE
2000-01	9	545	24	0	2.64	18	1123	43	2	2.30
2001-02	66	3877	178	6	2.75	-	-	-	-	-
2002-03	41	2410	126	1	3.14	-	-	-	-	-
Pitt. Totals	116	6832	328	7	2.88	18	1123	43	2	2.30
NHL Totals	293	16342	799	14	2.93	22	1338	52	2	2.33

Acquired from San Jose with Bobby Dollas for Jeff Norton, March 12, 2001

Traded to Vancouver for a 2nd round pick in the 2004 Entry Draft, August 25, 2003

HEINS, SHAWN

Defense   Ht: 6-4 **Wt:** 210   **Shoots:** left
B: December 24, 1973, Eganville, Ontario

	Regular Season					Playoffs				
YR	GP	G	A	PTS	PM	GP	G	A	PTS	PM
2002-03	27	1	1	2	33	-	-	-	-	-
Pitt. Totals	27	1	1	2	33	-	-	-	-	-
NHL Totals	125	4	12	16	154	2	0	0	0	0

Acquired from San Jose for a 5th round choice in the 2003 Entry Draft, February 9, 2003

Signed as a free agent by Atlanta, September 10, 2003

Goaltenders Denis Herron (left) and Roberto Romano (right) take to the ice for a game-day skate.

HERRON, DENIS

Goaltender   Ht: 5-11 **Wt:** 165   **Catches:** left
B: June 18, 1952, Chambly, Quebec

	Regular Season					Playoffs				
YR	GP	MINS	GA	SH	AVE	GP	MINS	GA	SH	AVE
1972-73	18	967	55	2	3.41	-	-	-	-	-
1973-74	5	260	18	0	4.15	-	-	-	-	-
1974-75	3	108	11	0	6.11	-	-	-	-	-
1976-77	34	1920	94	1	2.94	3	180	11	0	3.67
1977-78	60	3534	210	0	3.57	-	-	-	-	-
1978-79	56	3208	180	0	3.37	7	421	24	0	3.42
1982-83	31	1707	151	1	5.31	-	-	-	-	-
1983-84	38	2028	138	1	4.08	-	-	-	-	-
1984-85	42	2193	170	1	4.65	-	-	-	-	-
1985-86	3	180	14	0	4.67	-	-	-	-	-
Pitt. Totals	290	16105	1041	6	3.88	10	601	35	0	3.49
NHL Totals	462	25608	1579	10	3.70	15	901	50	0	3.33

Selected in the 1972 Amateur Draft, 3rd choice, 40th overall

Traded to Kansas City with Jean-Guy Lagace for Michel Plasse, January 10, 1975

Signed as a free agent, August 7, 1976

Traded to Montreal with a 2nd round choice in the 1982 Entry Draft for Rob Holland and Pat Hughes, August 30, 1979

Acquired from Montreal for a 3rd round choice in the 1985 Entry Draft, September 15, 1982

HEXTALL, BRYAN LEE

Center   **Ht:** 5-11   **Wt:** 185   **Shoots:** left
B: May 23, 1941, Winnipeg, Manitoba

YR	GP	G	A	PTS	PM	GP	G	A	PTS	PM
	Regular Season					Playoffs				
1969-70	66	12	19	31	87	10	0	1	1	34
1970-71	76	16	32	48	133	-	-	-	-	-
1971-72	78	20	24	44	126	4	0	2	2	9
1972-73	78	21	33	54	113	-	-	-	-	-
1973-74	37	2	7	9	39	-	-	-	-	-
Pitt. Totals	335	71	115	186	498	14	0	3	3	43
NHL Totals	549	99	161	260	738	18	0	4	4	59

Acquired from Vancouver (WHL) for Paul Andrea, John Arbour, and the loan of Andy Bathgate for the 1969-70 season, May 20, 1969

Claimed on waivers by Atlanta, January 6, 1974

HICKE, WILLIAM LAWRENCE (Bill)

Right Wing   **Ht:** 5-8   **Wt:** 164   **Shoots:** left
B: March 31 1938, Regina, Saskatchewan
D: July 18, 2005

YR	GP	G	A	PTS	PM	GP	G	A	PTS	PM
	Regular Season					Playoffs				
1971-72	12	2	0	2	6	-	-	-	-	-
Pitt. Totals	12	2	0	2	6	-	-	-	-	-
NHL Totals	729	168	234	402	395	42	3	10	13	41
WHA Totals	73	14	24	38	20	-	-	-	-	-

Purchased from California, September 7, 1971

Sold to Detroit, November 22, 1971

HICKS, ALEX

Left Wing   **Ht:** 6-0   **Wt:** 190   **Shoots:** left
B: September 4, 1969, Calgary, Alberta

YR	GP	G	A	PTS	PM	GP	G	A	PTS	PM
	Regular Season					Playoffs				
1996-97	55	5	15	20	76	5	0	1	1	2
1997-98	58	7	13	20	54	6	0	0	0	2
Pitt. Totals	113	12	28	40	130	11	0	1	1	4
NHL Totals	258	25	54	79	247	15	0	2	2	8

Acquired from Anaheim with Fredrik Olausson for Shawn Antoski and Dmitri Mironov, November 19, 1996

Signed as a free agent by San Jose, October 1998

HICKS, WAYNE WILSON

Right Wing   **Ht:** 5-11   **Wt:** 185   **Shoots:** right
B: April 9, 1937, Aberdeen, Washington

YR	GP	G	A	PTS	PM	GP	G	A	PTS	PM
	Regular Season					Playoffs				
1967-68	15	4	7	11	2	-	-	-	-	-
Pitt. Totals	15	4	7	11	2	-	-	-	-	-
NHL Totals	115	13	23	36	22	2	0	1	1	2

Acquired from Philadelphia for Art Stratton, February 27, 1968

HILBERT, ANDY

Center/Left Wing   **Ht:** 5-11   **Wt:** 194   **Shoots:** left
B: February 6, 1981, Lansing, Michigan

YR	GP	G	A	PTS	PM	GP	G	A	PTS	PM
	Regular Season					Playoffs				
2005-06	19	7	11	18	16	-	-	-	-	-
Pitt. Totals	19	7	11	18	16	-	-	-	-	-
NHL Totals	307	42	62	104	132	10	1	0	1	2

Claimed on waivers from Chicago, March 9, 2006

Signed as a free agent by NY Islanders, July 4, 2006

HILLIER, RANDY GEORGE

Defense   **Ht:** 6-1   **Wt:** 192   **Shoots:** left
B: March 30, 1960, Toronto, Ontario

YR	GP	G	A	PTS	PM	GP	G	A	PTS	PM
	Regular Season					Playoffs				
1984-85	45	2	19	21	56	-	-	-	-	-
1985-86	28	0	3	3	53	-	-	-	-	-
1986-87	55	4	8	12	97	-	-	-	-	-
1987-88	55	1	12	13	144	-	-	-	-	-
1988-89	68	1	23	24	141	9	0	1	1	49
1989-90	61	3	12	15	71	-	-	-	-	-
1990-91	31	2	2	4	32	8	0	0	0	24
Pitt. Totals	343	13	79	92	594	17	0	1	1	73
NHL Totals	543	16	110	126	906	28	0	2	2	93

Acquired from Boston for a 4th round choice in the 1985 Entry Draft, October 15, 1984

Signed as a free agent by NY Islanders, June 30, 1991

HLUSHKO, TODD

Center   Ht: 5-11 **Wt:** 185   **Shoots:** left
B: February 7, 1970, Toronto, Ontario

YR	Regular Season					Playoffs				
	GP	G	A	PTS	PM	GP	G	A	PTS	PM
1998-99	-	-	-	-	-	2	0	0	0	0
Pitt. Totals	-	-	-	-	-	2	0	0	0	0
NHL Totals	79	8	13	21	84	3	0	0	0	2

Acquired from Calgary with German Titov for Dave Roche and Ken Wregget, June 17, 1998

HOGANSON, PAUL EDWARD

Goaltender   Ht: 5-11 **Wt:** 175   **Catches:** right
B: November 12, 1949, Toronto, Ontario

YR	Regular Season					Playoffs				
	GP	MINS	GA	SH	AVE	GP	MINS	GA	SH	AVE
1970-71	2	57	7	0	7.37	-	-	-	-	-
Pitt. Totals	2	57	7	0	7.37	-	-	-	-	-
NHL Totals	2	57	7	0	7.37	-	-	-	-	-
WHA Totals	143	7244	496	5	4.11	5	348	17	1	2.93

Selected in the 1969 Amateur Draft, 5th choice, 62nd overall

Selected by Los Angeles in the 1972 WHA General Player Draft, February 12, 1972

HOLLAND, ROBERT (Rob)

Goaltender   Ht: 6-1 **Wt:** 180   **Catches:** left
B: September 10, 1957, Montreal, Quebec

YR	Regular Season					Playoffs				
	GP	MINS	GA	SH	AVE	GP	MINS	GA	SH	AVE
1979-80	34	1974	126	1	3.83	-	-	-	-	-
1980-81	10	539	45	0	5.01	-	-	-	-	-
Pitt. Totals	44	2513	171	1	4.08	-	-	-	-	-
NHL Totals	44	2513	171	1	4.08	-	-	-	-	-

Acquired from Montreal with Pat Hughes for Denis Herron and a 2nd round choice in the 1982 Entry Draft, August 30, 1979

Traded to NY Islanders for future considerations, September 28, 1981

Paul Hoganson displays his form in a publicity shot.

HOLZINGER, BRIAN

Center   Ht: 5-11 **Wt:** 186   **Shoots:** right
B: October 10, 1972, Parma, Ohio

YR	Regular Season					Playoffs				
	GP	G	A	PTS	PM	GP	G	A	PTS	PM
2002-03	9	1	2	3	6	-	-	-	-	-
2003-04	61	6	15	21	38	-	-	-	-	-
Pitt. Totals	70	7	17	24	44	-	-	-	-	-
NHL Totals	547	93	145	238	339	52	11	18	29	61

Acquired from Tampa Bay for Marc Bergevin, March 11, 2003

Traded to Columbus for Lasse Pirjeta, March 9, 2004

HORTON, MILES GILBERT (Tim)

Defense   Ht: 5-10 **Wt:** 180   **Shoots:** right
B: January 12, 1930, Cochrane, Ontario
D: February 21, 1974

YR	Regular Season					Playoffs				
	GP	G	A	PTS	PM	GP	G	A	PTS	PM
1971-72	44	2	9	11	40	4	0	1	1	2
Pitt. Totals	44	2	9	11	40	4	0	1	1	2
NHL Totals	1446	115	403	518	1611	126	11	39	50	183

Claimed from NY Rangers in the Intra-League Draft, June 8, 1971

Claimed by Buffalo in the Intra-League Draft, June 5, 1972

Hockey Hall of Fame (Player), 1977

HOSSA, MARIAN

Right Wing   Ht: 6-1 **Wt:** 210   **Shoots:** left
B: January 12, 1979, Stara Lubovna, Czechoslovakia

YR	Regular Season					Playoffs				
	GP	G	A	PTS	PM	GP	G	A	PTS	PM
2007-08	12	3	7	10	6	20	12	14	26	12
Pitt. Totals	12	3	7	10	6	20	12	14	26	12
NHL Totals	832	363	407	770	476	120	34	57	91	71

Acquired from Atlanta with Pascal Dupuis for Colby Armstrong, Erik Christensen, Angelo Esposito, and a 1st round choice in the 2008 Entry Draft, February 26, 2008

Signed as a free agent by Detroit, July 2, 2008

HOTHAM, GREGORY (Greg)

Defense   Ht: 5-11 **Wt:** 183   **Shoots:** right
B: March 7, 1956, London, Ontario

YR	Regular Season					Playoffs				
	GP	G	A	PTS	PM	GP	G	A	PTS	PM
1981-82	25	4	6	10	16	5	0	3	3	6
1982-83	58	2	30	32	39	-	-	-	-	-
1983-84	76	5	25	30	59	-	-	-	-	-
1984-85	11	0	2	2	4	-	-	-	-	-
Pitt. Totals	170	11	63	74	118	5	0	3	3	6
NHL Totals	230	15	74	89	139	5	0	3	3	6

Acquired from Toronto for a 6th round choice in the 1982 Entry Draft, February 3, 1982

Signed as a free agent by Toronto, July 3, 1986

HRDINA, JAN

Center   Ht: 6-0 **Wt:** 205   **Shoots:** right
B: February 5, 1976, Hradec Kralove, Czechoslovakia

YR	Regular Season					Playoffs				
	GP	G	A	PTS	PM	GP	G	A	PTS	PM
1998-99	82	13	29	42	40	13	4	1	5	12
1999-00	70	13	33	46	43	9	4	8	12	2
2000-01	78	15	28	43	48	18	2	5	7	8
2001-02	79	24	33	57	50	-	-	-	-	-
2002-03	57	14	25	39	34	-	-	-	-	-
Pitt. Totals	366	79	148	227	215	40	10	14	24	22
NHL Totals	513	101	196	297	341	45	12	14	26	24

Selected in the 1995 Entry Draft, 4th choice, 128th overall

Traded to Phoenix with Francois Leroux for Ramzi Abid, Dan Focht, and Gulliame Lefebvre, March 11, 2003

HRDINA, JIRI (George)

Center   Ht: 6-0 **Wt:** 195   **Shoots:** left
B: January 5, 1958, Prague, Czechoslovakia

YR	Regular Season					Playoffs				
	GP	G	A	PTS	PM	GP	G	A	PTS	PM
1990-91	37	6	14	20	13	14	2	2	4	6
1991-92	56	3	13	16	16	21	0	2	2	16
Pitt. Totals	93	9	27	36	29	35	2	4	6	22
NHL Totals	250	45	85	130	92	46	2	5	7	24

Acquired from Calgary for Jim Kyte, December 13, 1990

HRYNEWICH, TIM

Left Wing   Ht: 5-11 **Wt:** 190   **Shoots:** left
B: October 2, 1963, Leamington, Ontario

YR	Regular Season					Playoffs				
	GP	G	A	PTS	PM	GP	G	A	PTS	PM
1982-83	30	2	3	5	48	-	-	-	-	-
1983-84	25	4	5	9	34	-	-	-	-	-
Pitt. Totals	55	6	8	14	82	-	-	-	-	-
NHL Totals	55	6	8	14	82	-	-	-	-	-

Selected in the 1982 Entry Draft, 2nd choice, 38th overall

Traded to Edmonton with Marty McSorley and future considerations for Gilles Meloche, September 11, 1985

HUDSON, ALEXANDER (Lex)

Defense   Ht: 6-3 **Wt:** 184   **Shoots:** left
B: December 31, 1955, Winnipeg, Manitoba

YR	Regular Season					Playoffs				
	GP	G	A	PTS	PM	GP	G	A	PTS	PM
1978-79	2	0	0	0	0	2	0	0	0	0
Pitt. Totals	2	0	0	0	0	2	0	0	0	0
NHL Totals	2	0	0	0	0	2	0	0	0	0

Selected in the 1975 Amateur Draft, 12th choice, 196th overall

HUDSON, MIKE

Center/Left Wing   Ht: 6-1 **Wt:** 205   **Shoots:** left
B: February 6, 1967, Guelph, Ontario

YR	Regular Season					Playoffs				
	GP	G	A	PTS	PM	GP	G	A	PTS	PM
1994-95	40	2	9	11	34	11	0	0	0	6
Pitt. Totals	40	2	9	11	34	11	0	0	0	6
NHL Totals	416	49	87	136	414	49	4	10	14	64

Claimed from NY Rangers in the Waiver Draft, January 18, 1995

Signed as a free agent by Toronto, September 22, 1995

HUGHES, PATRICK (Pat)

Right Wing   Ht: 6-1 **Wt:** 180   **Shoots:** right
B: March 25, 1955, Calgary, Alberta

YR	Regular Season					Playoffs				
	GP	G	A	PTS	PM	GP	G	A	PTS	PM
1979-80	76	18	14	32	78	5	0	0	0	21
1980-81	58	10	9	19	161	-	-	-	-	-
Pitt. Totals	134	28	23	51	239	5	0	0	0	21
NHL Totals	573	130	128	258	646	71	8	25	33	77

Acquired from Montreal with Rob Holland for Denis Herron and a 2nd round choice in the 1982 Entry Draft, August 30, 1979

Traded to Edmonton for Pat Price, March 10, 1981

Acquired from Edmonton for future considerations (Mike Moller), October 4, 1985

Traded to Buffalo for Randy Cunneyworth and Mike Moller, October 4, 1985

HUNTER, DAVID (Dave)

Left Wing   Ht: 5-11 **Wt:** 195   **Shoots:** left
B: January 1, 1958, Petrolia, Ontario

YR	Regular Season					Playoffs				
	GP	G	A	PTS	PM	GP	G	A	PTS	PM
1987-88	59	11	18	29	77	-	-	-	-	-
Pitt. Totals	59	11	18	29	77	-	-	-	-	-
NHL Totals	746	133	190	323	918	105	16	24	40	211
WHA Totals	72	7	25	32	134	13	2	3	5	42

Acquired from Edmonton with Paul Coffey and Wayne Van Dorp for Dave Hannan, Chris Joseph, Moe Mantha, and Craig Simpson, November 24, 1987

Rights transferred to Edmonton as compensation for claiming Dave Hannan in the Waiver Draft, October 3, 1988

HUSSEY, MATT

Center   Ht: 6-2 **Wt:** 212   **Shoots:** left
B: May 28, 1979, New Haven, Connecticut

YR	Regular Season					Playoffs				
	GP	G	A	PTS	PM	GP	G	A	PTS	PM
2003-04	3	2	1	3	0	-	-	-	-	-
2005-06	13	0	1	1	0	-	-	-	-	-
Pitt. Totals	16	2	2	4	0	-	-	-	-	-
NHL Totals	21	2	2	4	2	-	-	-	-	-

Selected in the 1998 Entry Draft, 10th choice, 254th overall

Signed as a free agent by Detroit, July 13, 2006

I

IGNATJEV, VICTOR

Defense   Ht: 6-4 **Wt:** 215   **Shoots:** left
B: April 26, 1970, Riga, USSR

YR	Regular Season					Playoffs				
	GP	G	A	PTS	PM	GP	G	A	PTS	PM
1998-99	11	0	1	1	6	1	0	0	0	2
Pitt. Totals	11	0	1	1	6	1	0	0	0	2
NHL Totals	11	0	1	1	6	1	0	0	0	2

Signed as a free agent, August 11, 1998

INGARFIELD, EARL THOMPSON

Center   Ht: 5-11 **Wt:** 185   **Shoots:** left
B: October 25, 1934, Lethbridge, Alberta

YR	Regular Season					Playoffs				
	GP	G	A	PTS	PM	GP	G	A	PTS	PM
1967-68	50	15	22	37	12	-	-	-	-	-
1968-69	40	8	15	23	4	-	-	-	-	-
Pitt. Totals	90	23	37	60	16	-	-	-	-	-
NHL Totals	746	179	226	405	239	21	9	8	17	10

Selected from NY Rangers in the 1967 Expansion Draft, June 6, 1967

Traded to Oakland with Dick Mattiussi and Gene Ubriaco for Tracy Pratt, George Swarbrick, and Bryan Watson, January 30, 1969

INNESS, GARY GEORGE

Goaltender   Ht: 6-0 **Wt:** 195   **Catches:** left
B: May 28, 1949, Toronto, Ontario

YR	Regular Season					Playoffs				
	GP	MINS	GA	SH	AVE	GP	MINS	GA	SH	AVE
1973-74	20	1032	56	0	3.26	-	-	-	-	-
1974-75	57	3122	161	2	3.09	9	540	24	0	2.67
1975-76	23	1212	82	0	4.06	-	-	-	-	-
Pitt. Totals	100	5366	299	2	3.34	9	540	24	0	2.67
NHL Totals	162	8710	494	2	3.40	9	540	24	0	2.67
WHA Totals	62	3459	251	0	4.35	-	-	-	-	-

Signed as a free agent, June 1973

Traded to Philadelphia with future considerations for Bob Taylor and Ed Van Impe, March 9, 1976

Owner of four college degrees, Gary Inness backstopped the Pens in the mid-1970s.

J

JACKMAN, RIC

Defense   Ht: 6-2 **Wt:** 214   **Shoots:** right
B: June 28, 1978, Toronto, Ontario

YR	Regular Season					Playoffs				
	GP	G	A	PTS	PM	GP	G	A	PTS	PM
2003-04	25	7	17	24	14	-	-	-	-	-
2005-06	49	6	22	28	46	-	-	-	-	-
Pitt. Totals	74	13	39	52	60	-	-	-	-	-
NHL Totals	231	19	58	77	166	7	1	1	2	2

Acquired from Toronto for Drake Berehowsky, February 11, 2004

Traded to Florida for Petr Taticek, March 9, 2006

JAGR, JAROMIR

Right Wing   Ht: 6-3 **Wt:** 240   **Shoots:** left
B: February 15, 1972, Kladno, Czechoslovakia

YR	Regular Season					Playoffs				
	GP	G	A	PTS	PM	GP	G	A	PTS	PM
1990-91	80	27	30	57	42	24	3	10	13	6
1991-92	70	32	37	69	34	21	11	13	24	6
1992-93	81	34	60	94	61	12	5	4	9	23
1993-94	80	32	67	99	61	6	2	4	6	16
1994-95	48	32	38	70	37	12	10	5	15	6
1995-96	82	62	87	149	96	18	11	12	23	18
1996-97	63	47	48	95	40	5	4	4	8	4
1997-98	77	35	67	102	64	6	4	5	9	2
1998-99	81	44	83	127	66	9	5	7	12	16
1999-00	63	42	54	96	50	11	8	8	16	6
2000-01	81	52	69	121	42	16	2	10	12	18
Pitt. Totals	806	439	640	1079	593	140	65	82	147	121
NHL Totals	1273	646	953	1599	907	169	77	104	181	149

Selected in the 1990 Entry Draft, 1st choice, 5th overall

Traded to Washington with Frantisek Kucera for Kris Beech, Ross Lupaschuk, Michal Sivek, and future considerations, July 11, 2001

Won the Hart Memorial Trophy 1998-99

Won the Art Ross Trophy 1994-95, 1997-98, 1998-99, 1999-00, 2000-01

Won the Lester B. Pearson Award 1998-99, 1999-00

First Team NHL All-Star 1994-95, 1995-96, 1997-98, 1998-99, 1999-00, 2000-01

Second Team NHL All-Star 1996-97

Prince of Wales Conference All-Star 1991-92, 1992-93

Eastern Conference All-Star 1993-94, 1995-96, 1996-97

World Team All-Star 1997-98, 1998-99, 1999-00, 2000-01

NHL All-Rookie Team 1990-91

JAKOPIN, JOHN

Defense   Ht: 6-5 **Wt:** 239   **Shoots:** right
B: May 16, 1975, Toronto, Ontario

YR	Regular Season					Playoffs				
	GP	G	A	PTS	PM	GP	G	A	PTS	PM
2001-02	19	0	4	4	42	-	-	-	-	-
Pitt. Totals	19	0	4	4	42	-	-	-	-	-
NHL Totals	113	1	6	7	145	-	-	-	-	-

Claimed on waivers from Florida, October 3, 2001

Signed as a free agent by San Jose, September 5, 2002

JAMES, CONNOR

Right Wing **Ht:** 5-10 **Wt:** 180 **Shoots:** right
B: August 25, 1982, Calgary, Alberta

	Regular Season					Playoffs				
YR	GP	G	A	PTS	PM	GP	G	A	PTS	PM
2007-08	13	1	0	1	2	-	-	-	-	-
2008-09	1	0	0	0	0	-	-	-	-	-
Pitt. Totals	14	1	0	1	2	-	-	-	-	-
NHL Totals	16	1	0	1	2	-	-	-	-	-

Signed as a free agent, August 9, 2006

Signed as a free agent by Augsburger (Germany), August 4, 2009

JAVANAINEN, ARTO

Right Wing **Ht:** 6-0 **Wt:** 185 **Shoots:** right
B: April 8, 1959, Pori, Finland

	Regular Season					Playoffs				
YR	GP	G	A	PTS	PM	GP	G	A	PTS	PM
1984-85	14	4	1	5	2	-	-	-	-	-
Pitt. Totals	14	4	1	5	2	-	-	-	-	-
NHL Totals	14	4	1	5	2	-	-	-	-	-

Selected in the 1984 Entry Draft, 5th choice, 85th overall

JEFFREY, DUSTIN

Center **Ht:** 6-1 **Wt:** 205 **Shoots:** left
B: February 27, 1988, Sarnia, Ontario

	Regular Season					Playoffs				
YR	GP	G	A	PTS	PM	GP	G	A	PTS	PM
2008-09	14	1	2	3	0	-	-	-	-	-
2009-10	1	0	0	0	0	-	-	-	-	-
Pitt. Totals	15	1	2	3	0	-	-	-	-	-
NHL Totals	15	1	2	3	0	-	-	-	-	-

Selected in the 2007 Entry Draft, 8th choice, 171st overall

JENNINGS, GRANT

Defense **Ht:** 6-3 **Wt:** 210 **Shoots:** left
B: May 5, 1965, Hudson Bay, Saskatchewan

	Regular Season					Playoffs				
YR	GP	G	A	PTS	PM	GP	G	A	PTS	PM
1990-91	13	1	3	4	26	13	1	1	2	16
1991-92	53	4	5	9	104	10	0	0	0	12
1992-93	58	0	5	5	65	12	0	0	0	8
1993-94	61	2	4	6	126	3	0	0	0	2
1994-95	25	0	4	4	36	-	-	-	-	-
Pitt. Totals	210	7	21	28	357	38	1	1	2	38
NHL Totals	389	14	43	57	804	54	2	1	3	68

Acquired from Hartford with Ron Francis and Ulf Samuelsson for John Cullen, Jeff Parker, and Zarley Zalapski, March 4, 1991

Traded to Toronto for Drake Berehowsky, April 7, 1995

JOHANSSON, ANDREAS

Center **Ht:** 6-0 **Wt:** 202 **Shoots:** left
B: May 19, 1973, Hofors, Sweden

	Regular Season					Playoffs				
YR	GP	G	A	PTS	PM	GP	G	A	PTS	PM
1996-97	27	2	7	9	20	-	-	-	-	-
1997-98	50	5	10	15	20	1	0	0	0	0
Pitt. Totals	77	7	17	24	40	1	0	0	0	0
NHL Totals	377	81	88	169	190	9	0	0	0	0

Acquired from NY Islanders with Darius Kasparaitis for Bryan Smolinski, November 17, 1996

Signed as a free agent by Ottawa, September 29, 1998

JOHANSSON, MATHIAS

Center **Ht:** 6-2 **Wt:** 185 **Shoots:** left
B: February 22, 1974, Oskarshamn, Sweden

	Regular Season					Playoffs				
YR	GP	G	A	PTS	PM	GP	G	A	PTS	PM
2002-03	12	1	5	6	4	-	-	-	-	-
Pitt. Totals	12	1	5	6	4	-	-	-	-	-
NHL Totals	58	5	10	15	16	-	-	-	-	-

Acquired from Calgary with Micki DuPont for Shean Donovan, March 11, 2003

Signed as a free agent by Farjestad (Sweden), August 7, 2003

JOHNSON, BRENT

Goaltender   Ht: 6-3 **Wt:** 199   **Catches:** left
B: March 12, 1977, Farmington, Michigan

YR	GP	MINS	GA	SH	AVE	GP	MINS	GA	SH	AVE
		Regular Season					**Playoffs**			
2009-10	23	1108	51	0	2.76	1	31	1	0	1.94
Pitt. Totals	**23**	**1108**	**51**	**0**	**2.76**	**1**	**31**	**1**	**0**	**1.94**
NHL Totals	**270**	**14870**	**655**	**13**	**2.64**	**13**	**683**	**21**	**3**	**1.84**

Signed as a free agent, July 21, 2009

JOHNSON, GREG

Center   Ht: 5-11 **Wt:** 200   **Shoots:** left
B: March 16, 1971, Thunder Bay, Ontario

YR	GP	G	A	PTS	PM	GP	G	A	PTS	PM
		Regular Season					**Playoffs**			
1996-97	32	7	9	16	14	5	1	0	1	2
1997-98	5	1	0	1	2	-	-	-	-	-
Pitt. Totals	**37**	**8**	**9**	**17**	**16**	**5**	**1**	**0**	**1**	**2**
NHL Totals	**785**	**145**	**224**	**369**	**345**	**37**	**7**	**6**	**13**	**14**

Acquired from Detroit for Tomas Sandstrom, January 27, 1997

Traded to Chicago for Tuomas Gronman, October 27, 1997

JOHNSON, JAMES ERIK (Jim)

Defense   Ht: 6-1 **Wt:** 190   **Shoots:** left
B: August 9, 1962, New Hope, Minnesota

YR	GP	G	A	PTS	PM	GP	G	A	PTS	PM
		Regular Season					**Playoffs**			
1985-86	80	3	26	29	115	-	-	-	-	-
1986-87	80	5	25	30	116	-	-	-	-	-
1987-88	55	1	12	13	87	-	-	-	-	-
1988-89	76	2	14	16	163	11	0	5	5	44
1989-90	75	3	13	16	154	-	-	-	-	-
1990-91	24	0	5	5	23	-	-	-	-	-
Pitt. Totals	**390**	**14**	**95**	**109**	**658**	**11**	**0**	**5**	**5**	**44**
NHL Totals	**829**	**29**	**166**	**195**	**1197**	**51**	**1**	**11**	**12**	**132**

Signed as a free agent, June 9, 1985

Traded to Minnesota with Chris Dahlquist for Larry Murphy and Peter Taglianetti, December 11, 1990

Aggressive Jim Johnson clears an opponent away from the net.

JOHNSON, MARK

Center   Ht: 5-9 **Wt:** 170   **Shoots:** left
B: September 22, 1957, Madison, Wisconsin

YR	GP	G	A	PTS	PM	GP	G	A	PTS	PM
		Regular Season					**Playoffs**			
1979-80	17	3	5	8	4	5	2	2	4	0
1980-81	73	10	23	33	50	5	2	1	3	6
1981-82	46	10	11	21	30	-	-	-	-	-
Pitt. Totals	**136**	**23**	**39**	**62**	**84**	**10**	**4**	**3**	**7**	**6**
NHL Totals	**669**	**203**	**305**	**508**	**260**	**37**	**16**	**12**	**28**	**10**

Selected in the 1977 Amateur Draft, 3rd choice, 66th overall

Traded to Minnesota for a 2nd round choice in the 1982 Entry Draft, March 2, 1982

The son of future coach Bob Johnson, U.S. Olympian Mark Johnson made his Penguins debut in 1980.

JOHNSON, NICK

Right Wing   Ht: 6-1 **Wt:** 202   **Shoots:** right
B: December 24, 1985, Calgary, Alberta

	Regular Season					Playoffs				
YR	GP	G	A	PTS	PM	GP	G	A	PTS	PM
2009-10	6	1	1	2	2	-	-	-	-	-
Pitt. Totals	6	1	1	2	2	-	-	-	-	-
NHL Totals	6	1	1	2	2	-	-	-	-	-

Selected in the 2004 Entry Draft, 4th choice, 67th overall

JOHNSON, ROBERT MARTIN (Bob)

Goaltender   Ht: 6-1 **Wt:** 185   **Catches:** left
B: November 12, 1948, Farmington, Michigan

	Regular Season					Playoffs				
YR	GP	MINS	GA	SH	AVE	GP	MINS	GA	SH	AVE
1974-75	12	476	40	0	5.04	-	-	-	-	-
Pitt. Totals	12	476	40	0	5.04	-	-	-	-	-
NHL Totals	24	1059	66	0	3.74	-	-	-	-	-
WHA Totals	42	2388	144	1	3.62	2	120	8	0	4.00

Acquired from St. Louis for Nick Harbaruk, October 4, 1973

Signed as a free agent by Denver (WHA), September 1975

JONATHAN, STANLEY CARL (Stan)

Left Wing   Ht: 5-8 **Wt:** 175   **Shoots:** left
B: September 5, 1955, Oshweken, Ontario

	Regular Season					Playoffs				
YR	GP	G	A	PTS	PM	GP	G	A	PTS	PM
1982-83	19	0	3	3	13	-	-	-	-	-
Pitt. Totals	19	0	3	3	13	-	-	-	-	-
NHL Totals	411	91	110	201	751	63	8	4	12	137

Acquired from Boston for cash, November 8, 1982

JONES, RONALD PERRY (Ron)

Defense   Ht: 6-1 **Wt:** 195   **Shoots:** left
B: April 11, 1951, Vermillion, Alberta

	Regular Season					Playoffs				
YR	GP	G	A	PTS	PM	GP	G	A	PTS	PM
1973-74	25	0	3	3	15	-	-	-	-	-
Pitt. Totals	25	0	3	3	15	-	-	-	-	-
NHL Totals	54	1	4	5	31	-	-	-	-	-

Claimed from Boston in the Intra-League Draft, June 12, 1973

Traded to Washington for Pete Laframboise, January 21, 1975

JONSSON, HANS

Defense   Ht: 6-1 **Wt:** 205   **Shoots:** left
B: August 2, 1973, Jarved, Sweden

	Regular Season					Playoffs				
YR	GP	G	A	PTS	PM	GP	G	A	PTS	PM
1999-00	68	3	11	14	12	11	0	1	1	6
2000-01	58	4	18	22	22	16	0	0	0	8
2001-02	53	2	5	7	22	-	-	-	-	-
2002-03	63	1	4	5	36	-	-	-	-	-
Pitt. Totals	242	10	38	48	92	27	0	1	1	14
NHL Totals	242	10	38	48	92	27	0	1	1	14

Selected in the 1993 Entry Draft, 11th choice, 286th overall

Signed as a free agent by Modo (Sweden), September 26, 2003

JOSEPH, ROBIN CHRISTOPHER (Chris)

Defense   Ht: 6-3 **Wt:** 212   **Shoots:** right
B: September 10, 1969, Burnaby, British Columbia

	Regular Season					Playoffs				
YR	GP	G	A	PTS	PM	GP	G	A	PTS	PM
1987-88	17	0	4	4	12	-	-	-	-	-
1994-95	33	5	10	15	46	10	1	1	2	12
1995-96	70	5	14	19	71	15	1	0	1	8
Pitt. Totals	120	10	28	38	129	25	2	1	3	20
NHL Totals	510	39	112	151	567	31	3	4	7	24

Selected in the 1987 Entry Draft, 1st choice, 5th overall

Traded to Edmonton with Dave Hannan, Moe Mantha, and Craig Simpson for Paul Coffey, Dave Hunter, and Wayne Van Dorp, November 24, 1987

Claimed from Tampa Bay in the Waiver Draft, January 18, 1995

Claimed by Vancouver in the Waiver Draft, September 30, 1996

K

KACHOWSKI, MARK EDWARD

Left Wing   **Ht:** 5-11   **Wt:** 200   **Shoots:** left
B: February 20, 1965, Edmonton, Alberta

	Regular Season					Playoffs				
YR	GP	G	A	PTS	PM	GP	G	A	PTS	PM
1987-88	38	5	3	8	126	-	-	-	-	-
1988-89	12	1	1	2	43	-	-	-	-	-
1989-90	14	0	1	1	40	-	-	-	-	-
Pitt. Totals	64	6	5	11	209	-	-	-	-	-
NHL Totals	64	6	5	11	209	-	-	-	-	-

Signed as a free agent, August 31, 1987

KANNEGIESSER, SHELDON BRUCE

Defense   **Ht:** 6-0   **Wt:** 198   **Shoots:** left
B: August 15, 1947, North Bay, Ontario

	Regular Season					Playoffs				
YR	GP	G	A	PTS	PM	GP	G	A	PTS	PM
1970-71	18	0	2	2	29	-	-	-	-	-
1971-72	54	2	4	6	47	-	-	-	-	-
1972-73	3	0	0	0	0	-	-	-	-	-
Pitt. Totals	75	2	6	8	76	-	-	-	-	-
NHL Totals	366	14	67	81	292	18	0	2	2	10

Acquired from NY Rangers with Syl Apps for Glen Sather, January 26, 1971

Traded to NY Rangers for future considerations (Steve Andrascik), March 2, 1973

KARABIN, LADISLAV

Left Wing   **Ht:** 6-1   **Wt:** 189   **Shoots:** left
B: February 16, 1970, Spisska Nova Ves, Czechoslovakia

	Regular Season					Playoffs				
YR	GP	G	A	PTS	PM	GP	G	A	PTS	PM
1993-94	9	0	0	0	2	-	-	-	-	-
Pitt. Totals	9	0	0	0	2	-	-	-	-	-
NHL Totals	9	0	0	0	2	-	-	-	-	-

Selected in the 1990 Entry Draft, 11th choice, 173rd overall

Signed as a free agent by Buffalo, September 20, 1995

KASPARAITIS, DARIUS

Defense   **Ht:** 5-11   **Wt:** 215   **Shoots:** left
B: October 16, 1972, Elektrenai, USSR

	Regular Season					Playoffs				
YR	GP	G	A	PTS	PM	GP	G	A	PTS	PM
1996-97	57	2	16	18	84	5	0	0	0	6
1997-98	81	4	8	12	127	5	0	0	0	8
1998-99	48	1	4	5	70	-	-	-	-	-
1999-00	73	3	12	15	146	11	1	1	2	10
2000-01	77	3	16	19	111	17	1	1	2	26
2001-02	69	2	12	14	123	-	-	-	-	-
Pitt. Totals	405	15	68	83	661	38	2	2	4	50
NHL Totals	863	27	136	163	1379	83	2	10	12	107

Acquired from NY Islanders with Andreas Johansson for Bryan Smolinski, November 17, 1996

Traded to Colorado for Rick Berry and Ville Nieminen, March 19, 2002

KEHOE, RICKY THOMAS (Rick)

Right Wing   **Ht:** 5-11   **Wt:** 180   **Shoots:** right
B: July 15, 1951, Windsor, Ontario

	Regular Season					Playoffs				
YR	GP	G	A	PTS	PM	GP	G	A	PTS	PM
1974-75	76	32	31	63	22	9	0	2	2	0
1975-76	71	29	47	76	6	3	0	0	0	0
1976-77	80	30	27	57	10	3	0	2	2	0
1977-78	70	29	21	50	10	-	-	-	-	-
1978-79	57	27	18	45	2	7	0	2	2	0
1979-80	79	30	30	60	4	5	2	5	7	0
1980-81	80	55	33	88	6	5	0	3	3	0
1981-82	71	33	52	85	8	5	2	3	5	2
1982-83	75	29	36	65	12	-	-	-	-	-
1983-84	57	18	27	45	8	-	-	-	-	-
1984-85	6	0	2	2	0	-	-	-	-	-
Pitt. Totals	722	312	324	636	88	37	4	17	21	2
NHL Totals	906	371	396	767	120	39	4	17	21	4

Acquired from Toronto for Blaine Stoughton and a 1st round choice in the 1977 Amateur Draft, September 13, 1974

Won the Lady Byng Trophy 1980-81

Prince of Wales Conference All-Star 1980-81, 1982-83

Penguins Hall of Fame, 1992

KELLY, JOHN ROBERT (Bob, Battleship)

Left Wing   Ht: 6-2 **Wt:** 195   **Shoots:** left
B: June 6, 1946, Fort William, Ontario

YR	Regular Season					Playoffs				
	GP	G	A	PTS	PM	GP	G	A	PTS	PM
1973-74	30	7	10	17	78	-	-	-	-	-
1974-75	69	27	24	51	120	9	5	3	8	17
1975-76	77	25	30	55	149	3	0	0	0	2
1976-77	74	10	21	31	115	3	1	0	1	4
Pitt. Totals	250	69	85	154	462	15	6	3	9	23
NHL Totals	425	87	109	196	687	23	6	3	9	40

Acquired from St Louis with Ab DeMarco and Steve Durbano for Greg Polis, Bryan Watson, and a 2nd round choice in the 1974 Amateur Draft, January 17, 1974

Signed as a free agent by Chicago, August 17, 1977

KENNEDY, TYLER

Right Wing   Ht: 5-11 **Wt:** 183   **Shoots:** right
B: July 15, 1986, Sault Ste. Marie, Ontario

YR	Regular Season					Playoffs				
	GP	G	A	PTS	PM	GP	G	A	PTS	PM
2007-08	55	10	9	19	35	20	0	4	4	13
2008-09	67	15	20	35	30	**24**	5	4	9	4
2009-10	64	13	12	25	31	10	0	0	0	2
Pitt. Totals	186	38	41	79	96	54	5	8	13	19
NHL Totals	186	38	41	79	96	54	5	8	13	19

Selected in the 2004 Entry Draft, 6th choice, 99th overall

Eastern Conference Young Star 2007-08

KESA, DAN

Right Wing   Ht: 6-1 **Wt:** 190   **Shoots:** right
B: November 23, 1971, Vancouver, British Columbia

YR	Regular Season					Playoffs				
	GP	G	A	PTS	PM	GP	G	A	PTS	PM
1998-99	67	2	8	10	27	13	1	0	1	0
Pitt. Totals	67	2	8	10	27	13	1	0	1	0
NHL Totals	139	8	22	30	66	13	1	0	1	0

Signed as a free agent, August 20, 1998

Signed as a free agent by Tampa Bay, September 6, 1999

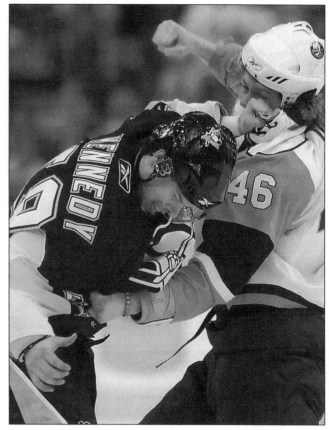

Scrappy Tyler Kennedy takes on an Islander.

KESSELL, RICHARD JOHN (Rick)

Center   Ht: 5-10 **Wt:** 175   **Shoots:** left
B: July 27, 1949, Toronto, Ontario

YR	Regular Season					Playoffs				
	GP	G	A	PTS	PM	GP	G	A	PTS	PM
1969-70	8	1	2	3	0	-	-	-	-	-
1970-71	6	0	2	2	2	-	-	-	-	-
1971-72	3	0	1	1	0	-	-	-	-	-
1972-73	67	1	13	14	0	-	-	-	-	-
Pitt. Totals	84	2	18	20	2	-	-	-	-	-
NHL Totals	135	4	24	28	6	-	-	-	-	-

Selected in the 1969 Amateur Draft, 1st choice, 15th overall

Claimed by Salt Lake City (WHL) in the Reverse Draft, June 13, 1973

KINDRACHUK, OREST

Center   **Ht:** 5-10 **Wt:** 175   **Shoots:** left
B: September 14, 1950, Nanton, Alberta

YR	Regular Season					Playoffs				
	GP	G	A	PTS	PM	GP	G	A	PTS	PM
1978-79	79	18	42	60	84	7	4	1	5	7
1979-80	52	17	29	46	63	-	-	-	-	-
1980-81	13	3	9	12	34	-	-	-	-	-
Pitt. Totals	144	38	80	118	181	7	4	1	5	7
NHL Totals	508	118	261	379	648	76	20	20	40	53

Acquired from Philadelphia with Tom Bladon and Ross Lonsberry for a 1st round choice in the 1978 Amateur Draft, June 14, 1978

Signed as a free agent by Washington, September 4, 1981

KLIMA, PETR

Right Wing   **Ht:** 6-0 **Wt:** 190   **Shoots:** right
B: December 23, 1964, Chomutov, Czechoslovakia

YR	Regular Season					Playoffs				
	GP	G	A	PTS	PM	GP	G	A	PTS	PM
1996-97	9	1	3	4	4	-	-	-	-	-
Pitt. Totals	9	1	3	4	4	-	-	-	-	-
NHL Totals	786	313	260	573	671	95	28	24	52	83

Acquired from Los Angeles for a conditional choice in the 1997 Entry Draft, October 25, 1996

Signed as a free agent by Edmonton, February 26, 1997

KOLTSOV, KONSTANTIN

Right Wing   **Ht:** 6-0 **Wt:** 206   **Shoots:** left
B: April 17, 1981, Minsk, USSR

YR	Regular Season					Playoffs				
	GP	G	A	PTS	PM	GP	G	A	PTS	PM
2002-03	2	0	0	0	0	-	-	-	-	-
2003-04	82	9	20	29	30	-	-	-	-	-
2005-06	60	3	6	9	20	-	-	-	-	-
Pitt. Totals	144	12	26	38	50	-	-	-	-	-
NHL Totals	144	12	26	38	50	-	-	-	-	-

Selected in the 1999 Entry Draft, 1st choice, 18th overall

Signed as a free agent by Ufa (Russia), August 17, 2006

Konstantin Koltsov was a first-round pick in 1999.

KONIK, GEORGE SAMUEL

Left Wing/Defense   **Ht:** 5-11 **Wt:** 190   **Shoots:** left
B: May 4, 1937, Flin Flon, Manitoba

YR	Regular Season					Playoffs				
	GP	G	A	PTS	PM	GP	G	A	PTS	PM
1967-68	52	7	8	15	26	-	-	-	-	-
Pitt. Totals	52	7	8	15	26	-	-	-	-	-
NHL Totals	52	7	8	15	26	-	-	-	-	-
WHA Totals	54	4	12	16	34	-	-	-	-	-

Acquired from NY Rangers with Paul Andrea, Frank Francis, and Dunc McCallum for Larry Jeffrey, June 6, 1967

Traded to Oakland for cash, July 4, 1968

KONTOS, CHRISTOPHER (Chris)

Left Wing/Center   **Ht:** 6-1 **Wt:** 195   **Shoots:** left
B: December 10, 1963, Toronto, Ontario

YR	Regular Season					Playoffs				
	GP	G	A	PTS	PM	GP	G	A	PTS	PM
1986-87	31	8	9	17	6	-	-	-	-	-
1987-88	36	1	7	8	12	-	-	-	-	-
Pitt. Totals	67	9	16	25	18	-	-	-	-	-
NHL Totals	230	54	69	123	103	20	11	0	11	12

Acquired from NY Rangers for Ron Duguay, January 21, 1987

Traded to Los Angeles with a 6th round choice in the 1988 Entry Draft for Bryan Erickson, February 5, 1988

KOSTOPOULOS, TOM

Right Wing   Ht: 6-0 **Wt:** 200   **Shoots:** right
B: January 24, 1979, Mississauga, Ontario

YR	Regular Season					Playoffs				
	GP	G	A	PTS	PM	GP	G	A	PTS	PM
2001-02	11	1	2	3	9	-	-	-	-	-
2002-03	8	0	1	1	0	-	-	-	-	-
2003-04	60	9	13	22	67	-	-	-	-	-
Pitt. Totals	79	10	16	26	76	-	-	-	-	-
NHL Totals	458	48	78	126	574	16	3	2	5	10

Selected in the 1999 Entry Draft, 9th choice, 204th overall

Signed as a free agent by Los Angeles, August 1, 2005

KOVALEV, ALEXEI (Kovy)

Right Wing   Ht: 6-1 **Wt:** 224   **Shoots:** left
B: February 24, 1973, Togliatti, USSR

YR	Regular Season					Playoffs				
	GP	G	A	PTS	PM	GP	G	A	PTS	PM
1998-99	63	20	26	46	37	10	5	7	12	14
1999-00	82	26	40	66	94	11	1	5	6	10
2000-01	79	44	51	95	96	18	5	5	10	16
2001-02	67	32	44	76	80	-	-	-	-	-
2002-03	54	27	37	64	50	-	-	-	-	-
Pitt. Totals	345	149	198	347	357	39	11	17	28	40
NHL Totals	1228	412	578	990	1254	116	44	54	98	104

Acquired from NY Rangers with Harry York for Petr Nedved, Sean Pronger, and Chris Tamer, November 25, 1998

Traded to NY Rangers with Dan LaCouture, Janne Laukkanen, and Mike Wilson for Joel Bouchard, Rico Fata, Richard Lintner, and Mikael Samuelsson, February 10, 2003

Eastern Conference All-Star 2000-01

World Team All-Star 2002-03

KRAFT, MILAN

Center   Ht: 6-4 **Wt:** 212   **Shoots:** right
B: January 17, 1980, Plzen, Czechoslovakia

YR	Regular Season					Playoffs				
	GP	G	A	PTS	PM	GP	G	A	PTS	PM
2000-01	42	7	7	14	8	8	0	0	0	2
2001-02	68	8	8	16	16	-	-	-	-	-
2002-03	31	7	5	12	10	-	-	-	-	-
2003-04	66	19	21	40	18	-	-	-	-	-
Pitt. Totals	207	41	41	82	52	8	0	0	0	2
NHL Totals	207	41	41	82	52	8	0	0	0	2

Selected in the 1998 Entry Draft, 1st choice, 23rd overall

Signed as a free agent by Plzen (Czech Republic), September 17, 2004

KUCERA, FRANTISEK

Defense   Ht: 6-2 **Wt:** 205   **Shoots:** right
B: February 3, 1968, Prague, Czechoslovakia

YR	Regular Season					Playoffs				
	GP	G	A	PTS	PM	GP	G	A	PTS	PM
2000-01	7	0	2	2	0	-	-	-	-	-
Pitt. Totals	7	0	2	2	0	-	-	-	-	-
NHL Totals	465	24	95	119	251	12	0	1	1	0

Acquired from Columbus for a 6th round choice in the 2001 Entry Draft, March 13, 2001

Traded to Washington with Jaromir Jagr for Kris Beech, Ross Lupaschuk, Michal Sivek, and future considerations, July 11, 2001

KUNITZ, CHRIS

Left Wing   Ht: 5-11 **Wt:** 195   **Shoots:** left
B: September 26, 1979, Regina, Saskatchewan

YR	Regular Season					Playoffs				
	GP	G	A	PTS	PM	GP	G	A	PTS	PM
2008-09	20	7	11	18	16	24	1	13	14	19
2009-10	50	13	19	32	39	13	4	7	11	8
Pitt. Totals	70	20	30	50	55	37	5	20	25	27
NHL Totals	385	101	141	242	354	72	9	32	41	62

Acquired from Anaheim with Eric Tangradi for Ryan Whitney, February 26, 2009

Tough guy Jim Kyte knocks an opponent to the ice.

KWIATKOWSKI, JOEL

Defense **Ht:** 6-2 **Wt:** 210 **Shoots:** left
B: March 22, 1977, Kindersley, Saskatchewan

	Regular Season					Playoffs				
YR	GP	G	A	PTS	PM	GP	G	A	PTS	PM
2006-07	1	0	0	0	0	-	-	-	-	-
Pitt. Totals	1	0	0	0	0	-	-	-	-	-
NHL Totals	282	16	29	45	245	6	0	0	0	2

Acquired from Florida for a 4th round choice in the 2007 Entry Draft, February 27, 2007

Signed as a free agent by Atlanta, August 30, 2007

KYTE, JAMES (Jim)

Defense **Ht:** 6-5 **Wt:** 210 **Shoots:** left
B: March 21, 1964, Ottawa, Ontario

	Regular Season					Playoffs				
YR	GP	G	A	PTS	PM	GP	G	A	PTS	PM
1989-90	56	3	1	4	125	-	-	-	-	-
1990-91	1	0	0	0	2	-	-	-	-	-
Pitt. Totals	57	3	1	4	127	-	-	-	-	-
NHL Totals	598	17	49	66	1342	42	0	6	6	94

Acquired from Winnipeg with Randy Gilhen and Andrew McBain for Randy Cunneyworth, Dave McLlwain, and Rick Tabaracci, June 17, 1989

Traded to Calgary for Jiri Hrdina, December 13, 1990

L

LABRE, YVON JULES

Defense **Ht:** 5-11 **Wt:** 190 **Shoots:** left
B: November 29, 1949, Sudbury, Ontario

	Regular Season					Playoffs				
YR	GP	G	A	PTS	PM	GP	G	A	PTS	PM
1970-71	21	1	1	2	19	-	-	-	-	-
1973-74	16	1	2	3	13	-	-	-	-	-
Pitt. Totals	37	2	3	5	32	-	-	-	-	-
NHL Totals	371	14	87	101	788	-	-	-	-	-

Selected in the 1969 Amateur Draft, 3rd choice, 38th overall

Selected by Washington in the 1974 Expansion Draft, June 12, 1974

LACOUTURE, DAN

Left Wing **Ht:** 6-2 **Wt:** 215 **Shoots:** left
B: April 18, 1977, Hyannis, Massachusetts

	Regular Season					Playoffs				
YR	GP	G	A	PTS	PM	GP	G	A	PTS	PM
2000-01	11	0	0	0	14	5	0	0	0	2
2001-02	82	6	11	17	71	-	-	-	-	-
2002-03	44	2	2	4	72	-	-	-	-	-
Pitt. Totals	137	8	13	21	157	5	0	0	0	2
NHL Totals	337	20	25	45	348	6	0	0	0	2

Acquired from Edmonton for Sven Butenschon, March 13, 2001

Traded to NY Rangers with Janne Laukkanen, Alexei Kovalev, and Mike Wilson for Joel Bouchard, Rico Fata, Richard Lintner, and Mikael Samuelsson, February 10, 2003

LAFRAMBOISE, PETER ALFRED (Pete)

Left Wing/Center **Ht:** 6-2 **Wt:** 185 **Shoots:** left
B: January 18, 1950, Ottawa, Ontario

	Regular Season					Playoffs				
YR	GP	G	A	PTS	PM	GP	G	A	PTS	PM
1974-75	35	5	13	18	8	9	1	0	1	0
Pitt. Totals	35	5	13	18	8	9	1	0	1	0
NHL Totals	227	33	55	88	70	9	1	0	1	0
WHA Totals	17	0	5	5	12	-	-	-	-	-

Acquired from Washington for Ron Jones, January 21, 1975

Signed as a free agent by Edmonton (WHA), May 1975

LAGACE, JEAN-GUY

Defense   Ht: 5-10 **Wt:** 185   **Shoots:** right
B: February 5, 1945, L'Abord-a-Plouffe, Quebec

YR	Regular Season					Playoffs				
	GP	G	A	PTS	PM	GP	G	A	PTS	PM
1968-69	17	0	1	1	14	-	-	-	-	-
1972-73	31	1	5	6	32	-	-	-	-	-
1973-74	31	2	6	8	34	-	-	-	-	-
1974-75	27	1	8	9	39	-	-	-	-	-
Pitt. Totals	**106**	**4**	**20**	**24**	**119**	-	-	-	-	-
NHL Totals	**197**	**9**	**39**	**48**	**251**	-	-	-	-	-
WHA Totals	**78**	**2**	**25**	**27**	**110**	-	-	-	-	-

Acquired from Montreal with cash for Larry Hillman, November 22, 1968

Claimed by Minnesota in the Intra-League Draft, June 9, 1970

Acquired from Buffalo for Terry Ball, January 24, 1971

Traded to Kansas City with Denis Herron for Michel Plasse, January 10, 1975

LALIME, PATRICK

Goaltender   Ht: 6-3 **Wt:** 189   **Catches:** left
B: July 7, 1974, St. Bonaventure, Quebec

YR	Regular Season					Playoffs				
	GP	MINS	GA	SH	AVE	GP	MINS	GA	SH	AVE
1996-97	39	2058	101	3	2.94	-	-	-	-	-
Pitt. Totals	**39**	**2058**	**101**	**3**	**2.94**	-	-	-	-	-
NHL Totals	**437**	**24876**	**1067**	**35**	**2.57**	**41**	**2549**	**75**	**5**	**1.77**

Selected in the 1993 Entry Draft, 6th choice, 156th overall

Traded to Anaheim for Sean Pronger, March 24, 1998

NHL All-Rookie Team 1996-97

LALONDE, RONALD LEO (Ron, Newsy)

Center   Ht: 5-10 **Wt:** 170   **Shoots:** left
B: October 30, 1952, Toronto, Ontario

YR	Regular Season					Playoffs				
	GP	G	A	PTS	PM	GP	G	A	PTS	PM
1972-73	9	0	0	0	2	-	-	-	-	-
1973-74	73	10	17	27	14	-	-	-	-	-
1974-75	24	0	3	3	0	-	-	-	-	-
Pitt. Totals	**106**	**10**	**20**	**30**	**16**	-	-	-	-	-
NHL Totals	**397**	**45**	**78**	**123**	**106**	-	-	-	-	-

Selected in the 1972 Amateur Draft, 4th choice, 56th overall

Traded to Washington for Lew Morrison, December 14, 1974

LAMOUREUX, MITCH

Center   Ht: 5-6 **Wt:** 175   **Shoots:** left
B: August 22, 1962, Ottawa, Ontario

YR	Regular Season					Playoffs				
	GP	G	A	PTS	PM	GP	G	A	PTS	PM
1983-84	8	1	1	2	6	-	-	-	-	-
1984-85	62	10	8	18	53	-	-	-	-	-
Pitt. Totals	**70**	**11**	**9**	**20**	**59**	-	-	-	-	-
NHL Totals	**73**	**11**	**9**	**20**	**59**	-	-	-	-	-

Selected in the 1981 Entry Draft, 7th choice, 154th overall

Signed as a free agent by Philadelphia, June 30, 1986

LANG, ROBERT

Center   Ht: 6-3 **Wt:** 216   **Shoots:** right
B: December 19, 1970, Teplice, Czechoslovakia

YR	Regular Season					Playoffs				
	GP	G	A	PTS	PM	GP	G	A	PTS	PM
1997-98	51	9	13	22	14	6	0	3	3	2
1998-99	72	21	23	44	24	12	0	2	2	0
1999-00	78	23	42	65	14	11	3	3	6	0
2000-01	82	32	48	80	28	16	4	4	8	4
2001-02	62	18	32	50	16	-	-	-	-	-
Pitt. Totals	**345**	**103**	**158**	**261**	**96**	**45**	**7**	**12**	**19**	**6**
NHL Totals	**989**	**261**	**442**	**703**	**422**	**91**	**18**	**28**	**46**	**24**

Signed as a free agent, September 2, 1997

Claimed by Boston in the 1997 Waiver Draft, September 28, 1997

Claimed on waivers from Boston, October 25, 1997

Signed as a free agent by Washington, July 1, 2002

Robert Lang (left) and Alexei Kovalev (right) provided scoring punch for the "Euro-Pens."

LANYON, EDWARD GEORGE (Ted)

Defense   **Ht:** 5-11 **Wt:** 175   **Shoots:** right
B: June 11, 1939, Winnipeg, Manitoba
D: May 21, 2008

	Regular Season					Playoffs				
YR	GP	G	A	PTS	PM	GP	G	A	PTS	PM
1967-68	5	0	0	0	4	-	-	-	-	-
Pitt. Totals	5	0	0	0	4	-	-	-	-	-
NHL Totals	5	0	0	0	4	-	-	-	-	-

Purchased from Cleveland (AHL), August 11, 1966

Loaned to Buffalo (AHL) for 1966-67 season, October 1966

LARAQUE, GEORGES

Right Wing   **Ht:** 6-3 **Wt:** 243   **Shoots:** right
B: December 7, 1976, Montreal, Quebec

	Regular Season					Playoffs				
YR	GP	G	A	PTS	PM	GP	G	A	PTS	PM
2006-07	17	0	2	2	18	2	0	0	0	0
2007-08	71	4	9	13	141	15	1	2	3	4
Pitt. Totals	88	4	11	15	159	17	1	2	3	4
NHL Totals	695	53	100	153	1126	57	4	8	12	72

Acquired from Phoenix for Daniel Carcillo and a 3rd round choice in the 2008 Entry Draft, February 27, 2007

Signed as a free agent by Montreal, July 3, 2008

Heavyweight Georges Laraque swaps punches with the Rangers' Colton Orr.

LAROUCHE, PIERRE

Center   **Ht:** 5-11 **Wt:** 175   **Shoots:** right
B: November 16, 1955, Taschereau, Quebec

	Regular Season					Playoffs				
YR	GP	G	A	PTS	PM	GP	G	A	PTS	PM
1974-75	79	31	37	68	52	9	2	5	7	2
1975-76	76	53	58	111	33	3	0	1	1	0
1976-77	65	29	34	63	14	3	0	3	3	0
1977-78	20	6	5	11	0	-	-	-	-	-
Pitt. Totals	240	119	134	253	99	15	2	9	11	2
NHL Totals	812	395	427	822	237	64	20	34	54	16

Selected in the 1974 Amateur Draft, 1st choice, 8th overall

Traded to Montreal with the rights to Peter Marsh for Peter Lee and Pete Mahovlich, November 29, 1977

Prince of Wales Conference All-Star 1975-76

LAUER, BRAD

Left Wing   **Ht:** 6-0 **Wt:** 195   **Shoots:** left
B: October 27, 1966, Humboldt, Saskatchewan

	Regular Season					Playoffs				
YR	GP	G	A	PTS	PM	GP	G	A	PTS	PM
1995-96	21	4	1	5	6	12	1	1	2	4
Pitt. Totals	21	4	1	5	6	12	1	1	2	4
NHL Totals	323	44	67	111	218	34	7	5	12	24

Signed as a free agent, August 10, 1995

Signed as a free agent by Sheffield (Britain), August 25, 2001

LAUKKANEN, JANNE

Defense   **Ht:** 6-0 **Wt:** 196   **Shoots:** left
B: March 19, 1970, Lahti, Finland

	Regular Season					Playoffs				
YR	GP	G	A	PTS	PM	GP	G	A	PTS	PM
1999-00	11	1	7	8	12	11	2	4	6	10
2000-01	50	3	17	20	34	18	2	2	4	14
2001-02	47	6	7	13	28	-	-	-	-	-
2002-03	17	1	6	7	8	-	-	-	-	-
Pitt. Totals	125	11	37	48	82	29	4	6	10	24
NHL Totals	407	22	99	121	335	59	7	9	16	46

Acquired from Ottawa with Ron Tugnutt for Tom Barrasso, March 14, 2000

Traded to NY Rangers with Dan LaCouture, Alexei Kovalev, and Mike Wilson for Joel Bouchard, Rico Fata, Richard Lintner, and Mikael Samuelsson, February 10, 2003

LAVALLEE, KEVIN A.

Left Wing   Ht: 5-8 **Wt:** 180   **Shoots:** left
B: September 16, 1961, Sudbury, Ontario

YR	Regular Season					Playoffs				
	GP	G	A	PTS	PM	GP	G	A	PTS	PM
1986-87	33	8	20	28	4	-	-	-	-	-
Pitt. Totals	33	8	20	28	4	-	-	-	-	-
NHL Totals	366	110	125	235	85	32	5	8	13	21

Signed as a free agent, September 13, 1986

LAXTON, GORDON (Gord)

Goaltender   Ht: 5-10 **Wt:** 195   **Catches:** left
B: March 16, 1955, Montreal, Quebec

YR	Regular Season						Playoffs				
	GP	MINS	GA	SH	AVE	GP	MINS	GA	SH	AVE	
1975-76	8	414	31	0	4.49	-	-	-	-	-	
1976-77	6	253	26	0	6.17	-	-	-	-	-	
1977-78	2	73	9	0	7.40	-	-	-	-	-	
1978-79	1	60	8	0	8.00	-	-	-	-	-	
Pitt. Totals	17	800	74	0	5.55	-	-	-	-	-	
NHL Totals	17	800	74	0	5.55	-	-	-	-	-	

Selected in the 1975 Amateur Draft, 1st choice, 13th overall

LEACH, STEPHEN (Steve)

Right Wing   Ht: 5-11 **Wt:** 197   **Shoots:** right
B: January 16, 1966, Cambridge, Massachusetts

YR	Regular Season					Playoffs				
	GP	G	A	PTS	PM	GP	G	A	PTS	PM
1999-00	56	2	3	5	24	-	-	-	-	-
Pitt. Totals	56	2	3	5	24	-	-	-	-	-
NHL Totals	702	130	153	283	978	92	15	11	26	87

Signed as a free agent, October 19, 1999

Signed as a free agent by Louisville (AHL), November 15, 2000

LEACH, WILLIAM (Jamie)

Right Wing   Ht: 6-1 **Wt:** 205   **Shoots:** right
B: August 25, 1969, Winnipeg, Manitoba

YR	Regular Season					Playoffs				
	GP	G	A	PTS	PM	GP	G	A	PTS	PM
1989-90	10	0	3	3	0	-	-	-	-	-
1990-91	7	2	0	2	0	-	-	-	-	-
1991-92	38	5	4	9	8	-	-	-	-	-
1992-93	5	0	0	0	2	-	-	-	-	-
Pitt. Totals	60	7	7	14	10	-	-	-	-	-
NHL Totals	81	11	9	20	12	-	-	-	-	-

Selected in the 1987 Entry Draft, 3rd choice, 47th overall

Claimed on waivers by Hartford, November 21, 1992

LEBEAU, PATRICK

Left Wing   Ht: 5-10 **Wt:** 172   **Shoots:** left
B: March 17, 1970, St. Jerome, Quebec

YR	Regular Season					Playoffs				
	GP	G	A	PTS	PM	GP	G	A	PTS	PM
1998-99	8	1	0	1	2	-	-	-	-	-
Pitt. Totals	8	1	0	1	2	-	-	-	-	-
NHL Totals	15	3	2	5	6	-	-	-	-	-

Signed as a free agent, October 18, 1998

Signed as a free agent by Frankfurt (Germany), November 21, 2002

LECAINE, WILLIAM JOSEPH (Bill)

Left Wing   Ht: 6-0 **Wt:** 172   **Shoots:** right
B: March 11, 1940, Moose Jaw, Saskatchewan

YR	Regular Season					Playoffs				
	GP	G	A	PTS	PM	GP	G	A	PTS	PM
1968-69	4	0	0	0	0	-	-	-	-	-
Pitt. Totals	4	0	0	0	0	-	-	-	-	-
NHL Totals	4	0	0	0	0	-	-	-	-	-

Signed as a free agent, August 1967

LECLAIR, JONATHAN CLARK (John)

Left Wing   Ht: 6-3 **Wt:** 226   **Shoots:** left
B: July 5, 1969, St. Albans, Vermont

YR	Regular Season					Playoffs				
	GP	G	A	PTS	PM	GP	G	A	PTS	PM
2005-06	73	22	29	51	61	-	-	-	-	-
2006-07	21	2	5	7	12	-	-	-	-	-
Pitt. Totals	94	24	34	58	73	-	-	-	-	-
NHL Totals	967	406	413	819	501	154	42	47	89	94

Signed as a free agent, August 15, 2005

LECUYER, DOUGLAS J. (Doug)

Left Wing   Ht: 5-9 **Wt:** 180   **Shoots:** left
B: March 10, 1958, Wainwright, Alberta

YR	Regular Season					Playoffs				
	GP	G	A	PTS	PM	GP	G	A	PTS	PM
1982-83	12	1	4	5	12	-	-	-	-	-
Pitt. Totals	12	1	4	5	12	-	-	-	-	-
NHL Totals	126	11	31	42	178	7	4	0	4	15

Claimed from Winnipeg in the Waiver Draft, October 4, 1982

LEE, PETER JOHN

Right Wing   **Ht:** 5-9 **Wt:** 180   **Shoots:** right
B: January 2, 1956, Ellesmere, United Kingdom

	Regular Season					Playoffs				
YR	GP	G	A	PTS	PM	GP	G	A	PTS	PM
1977-78	60	5	13	18	19	-	-	-	-	-
1978-79	80	32	26	58	24	7	0	3	3	0
1979-80	74	16	29	45	20	4	0	1	1	0
1980-81	80	30	34	64	86	5	0	4	4	4
1981-82	74	18	16	34	98	3	0	0	0	0
1982-83	63	13	13	26	10	-	-	-	-	-
Pitt. Totals	431	114	131	245	257	19	0	8	8	4
NHL Totals	431	114	131	245	257	19	0	8	8	4

Acquired from Montreal with Pete Mahovlich for Pierre Larouche and the rights to Peter Marsh, November 29, 1977

Signed to play in West Germany, August 15, 1983

LEFEBVRE, GUILLAUME

Left Wing   **Ht:** 6-1 **Wt:** 202   **Shoots:** left
B: May 7, 1981, Amos, Quebec

	Regular Season					Playoffs				
YR	GP	G	A	PTS	PM	GP	G	A	PTS	PM
2002-03	12	2	4	6	0	-	-	-	-	-
2005-06	9	0	0	0	9	-	-	-	-	-
Pitt. Totals	21	2	4	6	9	-	-	-	-	-
NHL Totals	39	2	4	6	13	-	-	-	-	-

Acquired from Phoenix with Ramzi Abid and Dan Focht for Jan Hrdina and Francois Leroux, March 11, 2003

Signed as a free agent by Boston, September 26, 2009

LEHTO, PETTERI

Defense   **Ht:** 6-0 **Wt:** 175   **Shoots:** left
B: March 23, 1961, Turku, Finland

	Regular Season					Playoffs				
YR	GP	G	A	PTS	PM	GP	G	A	PTS	PM
1984-85	6	0	0	0	4	-	-	-	-	-
Pitt. Totals	6	0	0	0	4	-	-	-	-	-
NHL Totals	6	0	0	0	4	-	-	-	-	-

Signed as a free agent, July 1984

Peter Lee (10) celebrates a goal with teammates Pat Price (2), Mark Johnson (9), and Paul Mulvey (26).

LEITER, ROBERT EDWARD (Bob)

Center   **Ht:** 5-9 **Wt:** 175   **Shoots:** left
B: March 22, 1941, Winnipeg, Manitoba

	Regular Season					Playoffs				
YR	GP	G	A	PTS	PM	GP	G	A	PTS	PM
1971-72	78	14	17	31	18	4	3	0	3	0
Pitt. Totals	78	14	17	31	18	4	3	0	3	0
NHL Totals	447	98	126	224	144	8	3	0	3	2
WHA Totals	51	17	17	34	8	3	2	0	2	0

Purchased from Boston, May 1971

Selected by Atlanta in the 1972 Expansion Draft, June 6, 1972

LEMIEUX, ALAIN

Center   **Ht:** 6-0 **Wt:** 185   **Shoots:** left
B: May 24, 1961, Montreal, Quebec

	Regular Season					Playoffs				
YR	GP	G	A	PTS	PM	GP	G	A	PTS	PM
1986-87	1	0	0	0	0	-	-	-	-	-
Pitt. Totals	1	0	0	0	0	-	-	-	-	-
NHL Totals	119	28	44	72	38	19	4	6	10	0

Signed as a free agent, December, 1986

LEMIEUX, MARIO

Center   Ht: 6-4 **Wt:** 230   **Shoots:** right
B: October 5, 1965, Montreal, Quebec

YR	GP	G	A	PTS	PM	GP	G	A	PTS	PM
		Regular Season					**Playoffs**			
1984-85	73	43	57	100	54	-	-	-	-	-
1985-86	79	48	93	141	43	-	-	-	-	-
1986-87	63	54	53	107	57	-	-	-	-	-
1987-88	77	**70**	98	**168**	92	-	-	-	-	-
1988-89	76	**85**	**114**	**199**	100	11	12	7	19	16
1989-90	59	45	78	123	78	-	-	-	-	-
1990-91	26	19	26	45	30	23	16	**28**	**44**	16
1991-92	64	44	87	**131**	94	15	**16**	18	**34**	2
1992-93	60	69	91	**160**	38	11	8	10	18	10
1993-94	22	17	20	37	32	6	4	3	7	2
1995-96	70	**69**	**92**	161	54	18	11	16	27	33
1996-97	76	50	**72**	122	65	5	3	3	6	4
2000-01	43	35	41	76	18	18	6	11	17	4
2001-02	24	6	25	31	14	-	-	-	-	-
2002-03	67	28	63	91	43	-	-	-	-	-
2003-04	10	1	8	9	6	-	-	-	-	-
2005-06	26	7	15	22	16	-	-	-	-	-
Pitt. Totals	**915**	**690**	**1033**	**1723**	**834**	**107**	**76**	**96**	**172**	**87**
NHL Totals	**915**	**690**	**1033**	**1723**	**834**	**107**	**76**	**96**	**172**	**87**

Selected in the 1984 Entry Draft, 1st choice, 1st overall

Won the Calder Memorial Trophy 1984-85

Won the Lester B. Pearson Award 1985-86, 1987-88, 1992-93, 1995-96

Won the Art Ross Trophy 1987-88, 1988-89, 1991-92, 1992-93, 1995-96, 1996-97

Won the Hart Memorial Trophy 1987-88, 1992-93, 1995-96

Won the Conn Smythe Trophy 1990-91, 1991-92

Won the Bill Masterton Trophy 1992-93

First Team NHL All-Star 1987-88, 1988-89, 1992-93, 1995-96, 1996-97

Second Team NHL All-Star 1985-86, 1986-87, 1991-92, 2000-01

Prince of Wales Conference All-Star 1984-85, 1985-86, 1987-88, 1988-89, 1989-90, 1991-92, 1992-93

Eastern Conference All-Star 1995-96, 1996-97, 2002-03

North America Team All-Star 2000-01, 2001-02

NHL All-Star 1986-87

NHL All-Rookie Team 1984-85

All-Star Game MVP 1985, 1988, 1990

Penguins Hall of Fame, 1997

Hockey Hall of Fame (Player), 1997

LEOPOLD, JORDAN

Defense   Ht: 6-1 **Wt:** 200   **Shoots:** left
B: August 3, 1980, Golden Valley, Minnesota

YR	GP	G	A	PTS	PM	GP	G	A	PTS	PM
		Regular Season					**Playoffs**			
2009-10	20	4	4	8	6	8	0	0	0	2
Pitt. Totals	**20**	**4**	**4**	**8**	**6**	**8**	**0**	**0**	**0**	**2**
NHL Totals	**436**	**40**	**95**	**135**	**190**	**54**	**0**	**15**	**15**	**20**

Acquired from Florida for a 2nd round pick in the 2010 Entry Draft, March 1, 2010

Signed as a free agent by Buffalo, July 1, 2010

LEROUX, FRANCOIS (Frankie)

Defense   Ht: 6-6 **Wt:** 247   **Shoots:** left
B: April 18, 1970, Ste-Adele, Quebec

YR	GP	G	A	PTS	PM	GP	G	A	PTS	PM
		Regular Season					**Playoffs**			
1994-95	40	0	2	2	114	12	0	2	2	14
1995-96	66	2	9	11	161	18	1	1	2	20
1996-97	59	0	3	3	81	3	0	0	0	0
Pitt. Totals	**165**	**2**	**14**	**16**	**356**	**33**	**1**	**3**	**4**	**34**
NHL Totals	**249**	**3**	**20**	**23**	**577**	**33**	**1**	**3**	**4**	**34**

Claimed from Ottawa in the Waiver Draft, January 18, 1995

Traded to Colorado for a 3rd round choice in the 1998 Entry Draft, September 28, 1997

Signed as a free agent, July 16, 2002

Traded to Phoenix with Jan Hrdina for Ramzi Abid, Dan Focht, and Guillaume Lefebvre, March 11, 2003

Towering Francois Leroux (18) bumps a Capital off the puck.

LETANG, KRISTOPHER (Tanger)

Defense   **Ht:** 6-0   **Wt:** 201   **Shoots:** right
B: April 24, 1987, Montreal, Quebec

YR	GP	G	A	PTS	PM	GP	G	A	PTS	PM
		Regular Season					**Playoffs**			
2006-07	7	2	0	2	4	-	-	-	-	-
2007-08	63	6	11	17	23	16	0	2	2	12
2008-09	74	10	23	33	24	23	4	9	13	26
2009-10	73	3	24	27	51	13	5	2	7	6
Pitt. Totals	217	21	58	79	102	52	9	13	22	44
NHL Totals	217	21	58	79	102	52	9	13	22	44

Selected in the 2005 Entry Draft, 3rd choice, 62nd overall
Eastern Conference Young Star 2007-08, 2008-09

LETESTU, MARK

Center   **Ht:** 5-11   **Wt:** 195   **Shoots:** right
B: February 4, 1985, Elk Point, Alberta

YR	GP	G	A	PTS	PM	GP	G	A	PTS	PM
		Regular Season					**Playoffs**			
2009-10	10	1	0	1	2	4	0	1	1	0
Pitt. Totals	10	1	0	1	2	4	0	1	1	0
NHL Totals	10	1	0	1	2	4	0	1	1	0

Signed as a free agent, March 22, 2007

LIBETT, LYNN NICHOLAS (Nick)

Left Wing   **Ht:** 6-1   **Wt:** 195   **Shoots:** left
B: December 9, 1945, Stratford, Ontario

YR	GP	G	A	PTS	PM	GP	G	A	PTS	PM
		Regular Season					**Playoffs**			
1979-80	78	14	12	26	14	5	1	1	2	0
1980-81	43	6	6	12	4	-	-	-	-	-
Pitt. Totals	121	20	18	38	18	5	1	1	2	0
NHL Totals	982	237	268	505	472	16	6	2	8	2

Acquired from Detroit for Pete Mahovlich, August 3, 1979

LINDSTROM, BO MORGAN WILLY (Willy)

Right Wing   **Ht:** 6-0   **Wt:** 180   **Shoots:** left
B: May 5, 1951, Grums, Sweden

YR	GP	G	A	PTS	PM	GP	G	A	PTS	PM
		Regular Season					**Playoffs**			
1985-86	71	14	17	31	30	-	-	-	-	-
1986-87	60	10	13	23	6	-	-	-	-	-
Pitt. Totals	131	24	30	54	36	-	-	-	-	-
NHL Totals	582	161	162	323	200	57	14	18	32	24
WHA Totals	316	123	138	261	133	51	26	22	48	50

Claimed from Edmonton in the Waiver Draft, October 7, 1985

LINTNER, RICHARD

Defense/Right Wing   **Ht:** 6-3   **Wt:** 212   **Shoots:** right
B: November 15, 1977, Trencin, Czechoslovakia

YR	GP	G	A	PTS	PM	GP	G	A	PTS	PM
		Regular Season					**Playoffs**			
2002-03	19	3	2	5	10	-	-	-	-	-
Pitt. Totals	19	3	2	5	10	-	-	-	-	-
NHL Totals	112	8	12	20	54	-	-	-	-	-

Acquired from NY Rangers with Joel Bouchard, Rico Fata, and Mikael Samuelsson for Alexei Kovalev, Dan LaCouture, Janne Laukkanen, and Mike Wilson, February 10, 2003

Signed as a free agent by Djurgarden (Sweden), August 20, 2003

LONEY, TROY

Left Wing   **Ht:** 6-3   **Wt:** 209   **Shoots:** left
B: September 21, 1963, Bow Island, Alberta

YR	GP	G	A	PTS	PM	GP	G	A	PTS	PM
		Regular Season					**Playoffs**			
1983-84	13	0	0	0	9	-	-	-	-	-
1984-85	46	10	8	18	59	-	-	-	-	-
1985-86	47	3	9	12	95	-	-	-	-	-
1986-87	23	8	7	15	22	-	-	-	-	-
1987-88	65	5	13	18	151	-	-	-	-	-
1988-89	69	10	6	16	165	11	1	3	4	24
1989-90	67	11	16	27	168	-	-	-	-	-
1990-91	44	7	9	16	85	24	2	2	4	41
1991-92	76	10	16	26	127	21	4	5	9	32
1992-93	82	5	16	21	99	10	1	4	5	0
Pitt. Totals	532	69	100	169	980	66	8	14	22	97
NHL Totals	624	87	110	197	1091	67	8	14	22	97

Selected in the 1982 Entry Draft, 3rd choice, 52nd overall

Selected by Anaheim in the 1993 Expansion Draft, June 24, 1993

LONSBERRY, DAVID ROSS (Ross)

Left Wing   **Ht:** 5-11   **Wt:** 195   **Shoots:** left
B: February 7, 1947, Humboldt, Saskatchewan

YR	GP	G	A	PTS	PM	GP	G	A	PTS	PM
		Regular Season					**Playoffs**			
1978-79	80	24	22	46	38	7	0	2	2	9
1979-80	76	15	18	33	36	5	2	1	3	2
1980-81	80	17	33	50	76	5	0	0	0	2
Pitt. Totals	236	56	73	129	150	17	2	3	5	13
NHL Totals	968	256	310	566	806	100	21	25	46	87

Acquired from Philadelphia with Tom Bladon and Orest Kindrachuk for a 1st round choice in the 1978 Amateur Draft, June 14, 1978

LOVEJOY, BEN

Defense   Ht: 6-2 **Wt:** 214   **Shoots:** right
B: February 20, 1984, Concord, New Hampshire

YR	Regular Season					Playoffs				
	GP	G	A	PTS	PM	GP	G	A	PTS	PM
2008-09	2	0	0	0	0	-	-	-	-	-
2009-10	12	0	3	3	2	-	-	-	-	-
Pitt. Totals	14	0	3	3	2	-	-	-	-	-
NHL Totals	14	0	3	3	2	-	-	-	-	-

Signed as a free agent, July 7, 2008

LOWE, DARREN

Right Wing   Ht: 5-10 **Wt:** 185   **Shoots:** right
B: October 13, 1960, Toronto, Ontario

YR	Regular Season					Playoffs				
	GP	G	A	PTS	PM	GP	G	A	PTS	PM
1983-84	8	1	2	3	0	-	-	-	-	-
Pitt. Totals	8	1	2	3	0	-	-	-	-	-
NHL Totals	8	1	2	3	0	-	-	-	-	-

Signed as a free agent, February 28, 1984

LUKOWICH, BERNARD JOSEPH (Bernie)

Right Wing   Ht: 6-0 **Wt:** 190   **Shoots:** right
B: March 18, 1952, North Battleford, Saskatchewan

YR	Regular Season					Playoffs				
	GP	G	A	PTS	PM	GP	G	A	PTS	PM
1973-74	53	9	10	19	32	-	-	-	-	-
Pitt. Totals	53	9	10	19	32	-	-	-	-	-
NHL Totals	79	13	15	28	34	2	0	0	0	0
WHA Totals	21	5	3	8	18	10	3	4	7	8

Selected in the 1972 Amateur Draft, 2nd choice, 30th overall

Traded to St. Louis for Bob Stumpf, January 20, 1975

LUNDBERG, BRIAN FREDERICK

Defense   Ht: 5-10 **Wt:** 190   **Shoots:** right
B: June 5, 1960, Burnaby, British Columbia

YR	Regular Season					Playoffs				
	GP	G	A	PTS	PM	GP	G	A	PTS	PM
1982-83	1	0	0	0	2	-	-	-	-	-
Pitt. Totals	1	0	0	0	2	-	-	-	-	-
NHL Totals	1	0	0	0	2	-	-	-	-	-

Selected in the 1980 Entry Draft, 7th choice, 177th overall

LUPASCHUK, ROSS

Defense   Ht: 6-1 **Wt:** 218   **Shoots:** right
B: January 19, 1981, Edmonton, Alberta

YR	Regular Season					Playoffs				
	GP	G	A	PTS	PM	GP	G	A	PTS	PM
2002-03	3	0	0	0	4	-	-	-	-	-
Pitt. Totals	3	0	0	0	4	-	-	-	-	-
NHL Totals	3	0	0	0	4	-	-	-	-	-

Acquired from Washington with Kris Beech, Michal Sivek, and future considerations for Jaromir Jagr and Frantisek Kucera, July 11, 2001

Signed as a free agent by Malmo (Sweden), July 30, 2006

LUPIEN, GILLES

Defense   Ht: 6-6 **Wt:** 210   **Shoots:** left
B: April 20, 1954, Lachute, Quebec

YR	Regular Season					Playoffs				
	GP	G	A	PTS	PM	GP	G	A	PTS	PM
1980-81	31	0	1	1	34	-	-	-	-	-
Pitt. Totals	31	0	1	1	34	-	-	-	-	-
NHL Totals	226	5	25	30	416	25	0	0	0	21

Acquired from Montreal for a 3rd round choice in the 1983 Entry Draft, September 26, 1980

Traded to Hartford for a 6th round choice in the 1981 Entry Draft, February 20, 1981

LYNCH, JOHN ALAN (Jack)

Defense   Ht: 6-2 **Wt:** 180   **Shoots:** right
B: May 28, 1952, Toronto, Ontario

YR	Regular Season					Playoffs				
	GP	G	A	PTS	PM	GP	G	A	PTS	PM
1972-73	47	1	18	19	40	-	-	-	-	-
1973-74	17	0	7	7	21	-	-	-	-	-
Pitt. Totals	64	1	25	26	61	-	-	-	-	-
NHL Totals	382	24	106	130	336	-	-	-	-	-

Selected in the 1972 Amateur Draft, 1st choice, 24th overall

Traded to Detroit with Jim Rutherford for Ron Stackhouse, January 17, 1974

Defenseman Jack Lynch was the Pens' top draft pick in 1972.

LYON, STEVEN (Steve)

Right Wing/Defense   **Ht:** 5-10 **Wt:** 169   **Shoots:** right
B: May 16, 1952, Toronto, Ontario

	Regular Season					Playoffs				
YR	GP	G	A	PTS	PM	GP	G	A	PTS	PM
1976-77	3	0	0	0	2	-	-	-	-	-
Pitt. Totals	3	0	0	0	2	-	-	-	-	-
NHL Totals	3	0	0	0	2	-	-	-	-	-

Signed as a free agent, November 1976

M

MacDONALD, LOWELL

Left Wing   **Ht:** 5-11 **Wt:** 185   **Shoots:** right
B: August 30, 1941, New Glasgow, Nova Scotia

	Regular Season					Playoffs				
YR	GP	G	A	PTS	PM	GP	G	A	PTS	PM
1970-71	10	0	1	1	0	-	-	-	-	-
1972-73	78	34	41	75	8	-	-	-	-	-
1973-74	78	43	39	82	14	-	-	-	-	-
1974-75	71	27	33	60	24	9	4	2	6	4
1975-76	69	30	43	73	12	3	1	0	1	0
1976-77	3	1	1	2	0	3	1	2	3	4
1977-78	19	5	8	13	2	-	-	-	-	-
Pitt. Totals	328	140	166	306	60	15	6	4	10	8
NHL Totals	506	180	210	390	92	30	11	11	22	12

Claimed from Los Angeles in the Intra-League Draft, June 9, 1970

Won the Bill Masterton Trophy 1972-73

West Division All-Star 1972-73, 1973-74

MACIVER, NORM

Defense   **Ht:** 5-11 **Wt:** 180   **Shoots:** left
B: September 8, 1964, Thunder Bay, Ontario

	Regular Season					Playoffs				
YR	GP	G	A	PTS	PM	GP	G	A	PTS	PM
1994-95	13	0	9	9	6	12	1	4	5	8
1995-96	32	2	21	23	32	-	-	-	-	-
Pitt. Totals	45	2	30	32	38	12	1	4	5	8
NHL Totals	500	55	230	285	350	56	3	11	14	32

Acquired from Ottawa with Troy Murray for Martin Straka, April 7, 1995

Traded to Winnipeg for Neil Wilkinson, December 28, 1995

MacLEISH, RICHARD GEORGE (Rick)

Left Wing   **Ht:** 5-11 **Wt:** 185   **Shoots:** left
B: January 3, 1950, Lindsay, Ontario

	Regular Season					Playoffs				
YR	GP	G	A	PTS	PM	GP	G	A	PTS	PM
1981-82	40	13	12	25	28	5	1	1	2	0
1982-83	6	0	5	5	2	-	-	-	-	-
Pitt. Totals	46	13	17	30	30	5	1	1	2	0
NHL Totals	846	349	410	759	434	114	54	53	107	38

Acquired from Hartford for Russ Anderson and an 8th round choice in the 1983 Entry Draft, December 29, 1981

Signed as a free agent by Philadelphia, October 6, 1983

MacNEIL, ALLSTER WENCES (Al)

Defense   **Ht:** 5-10 **Wt:** 183   **Shoots:** left
B: September 27, 1935, Sydney, Nova Scotia

	Regular Season					Playoffs				
YR	GP	G	A	PTS	PM	GP	G	A	PTS	PM
1967-68	74	2	10	12	58	-	-	-	-	-
Pitt. Totals	74	2	10	12	58	-	-	-	-	-
NHL Totals	524	17	75	92	617	37	0	4	4	67

Selected from NY Rangers in the 1967 Expansion Draft, June 6, 1967

Traded to Montreal for Wally Boyer, June 12, 1968

Pete Mahovlich (left) and Gregg Sheppard (right) check out their stats in *The World Almanac*.

MALKIN, EVGENI (Geno)

Center   Ht: 6-3 **Wt:** 195   **Shoots:** left
B: July 31, 1986, Magnitogorsk, USSR

YR	Regular Season					Playoffs				
	GP	G	A	PTS	PM	GP	G	A	PTS	PM
2006-07	78	33	52	85	80	5	0	4	4	8
2007-08	82	47	59	106	78	20	10	12	22	24
2008-09	82	35	**78**	**113**	80	**24**	14	**22**	**36**	51
2009-10	67	28	49	77	100	13	5	6	11	6
Pitt. Totals	309	143	238	381	338	62	29	44	73	89
NHL Totals	309	143	238	381	338	62	29	44	73	89

Selected in the 2004 Entry Draft, 1st choice, 2nd overall

Won the Calder Memorial Trophy 2006-07

Won the Art Ross Trophy 2008-09

Won the Conn Smythe Trophy 2008-09

NHL All-Rookie Team 2006-07

Eastern Conference Young Star 2006-07

Eastern Conference All-Star 2007-08, 2008-09

MAHOVLICH, PETER JOSEPH (Pete)

Center   Ht: 6-5 **Wt:** 210   **Shoots:** left
B: October 10, 1946, Timmins, Ontario

YR	Regular Season					Playoffs				
	GP	G	A	PTS	PM	GP	G	A	PTS	PM
1977-78	57	25	36	61	37	-	-	-	-	-
1978-79	60	14	39	53	39	2	0	1	1	0
Pitt. Totals	117	39	75	114	76	2	0	1	1	0
NHL Totals	884	288	485	773	916	88	30	42	72	134

Acquired from Montreal with Peter Lee for Pierre Larouche and the rights to Peter Marsh, November 29, 1977

Traded to Detroit for Nick Libett, August 3, 1979

MALONE, RYAN (Bugsy)

Left Wing   Ht: 6-4 **Wt:** 224   **Shoots:** left
B: December 1, 1979, Pittsburgh, Pennsylvania

YR	Regular Season					Playoffs				
	GP	G	A	PTS	PM	GP	G	A	PTS	PM
2003-04	81	22	21	43	64	-	-	-	-	-
2005-06	77	22	22	44	63	-	-	-	-	-
2006-07	64	16	15	31	71	5	0	0	0	0
2007-08	77	27	24	51	103	20	6	10	16	25
Pitt. Totals	299	87	82	169	301	25	6	10	16	25
NHL Totals	438	134	127	261	467	25	6	10	16	25

Selected in the 1999 Entry Draft, 5th choice, 115th overall

Rights traded to Tampa Bay with rights to Gary Roberts for a 3rd round choice in the 2009 Entry Draft, June 28, 2008

NHL All-Rookie Team 2003-04

MALONE, WILLIAM GREGORY (Greg)

Center **Ht:** 6-0 **Wt:** 190 **Shoots:** left
B: March 8, 1956, Fredericton, New Brunswick

YR	Regular Season					Playoffs				
	GP	G	A	PTS	PM	GP	G	A	PTS	PM
1976-77	66	18	19	37	43	3	1	1	2	2
1977-78	78	18	43	61	80	-	-	-	-	-
1978-79	80	35	30	65	52	7	0	1	1	10
1979-80	51	19	32	51	46	-	-	-	-	-
1980-81	62	21	29	50	68	5	2	3	5	16
1981-82	78	15	24	39	125	3	0	0	0	4
1982-83	80	17	44	61	82	-	-	-	-	-
Pitt. Totals	495	143	221	364	496	18	3	5	8	32
NHL Totals	704	191	310	501	661	20	3	5	8	32

Selected in the 1976 Amateur Draft, 2nd choice, 19th overall

Traded to Hartford for a 5th round choice in the 1985 Entry Draft, September 30, 1983

MANDERVILLE, KENT

Center **Ht:** 6-3 **Wt:** 200 **Shoots:** left
B: April 12, 1971, Edmonton, Alberta

YR	Regular Season					Playoffs				
	GP	G	A	PTS	PM	GP	G	A	PTS	PM
2001-02	4	1	0	1	4	-	-	-	-	-
2002-03	82	2	5	7	46	-	-	-	-	-
Pitt. Totals	86	3	5	8	50	-	-	-	-	-
NHL Totals	646	37	67	104	348	67	3	3	6	44

Acquired from Philadelphia for Billy Tibbetts, March 17, 2002

Signed as a free agent by Timra IK (Sweden), November 21, 2003

MANN, JAMES EDWARD (Jimmy, Bam Bam)

Right Wing **Ht:** 6-0 **Wt:** 205 **Shoots:** right
B: April 17, 1959, Montreal, Quebec

YR	Regular Season					Playoffs				
	GP	G	A	PTS	PM	GP	G	A	PTS	PM
1987-88	9	0	0	0	53	-	-	-	-	-
Pitt. Totals	9	0	0	0	53	-	-	-	-	-
NHL Totals	293	10	20	30	895	22	0	0	0	89

Signed as a free agent, June 16, 1987

Moe Mantha (20) and Roger Belanger (24) follow the puck.

MANTHA, MAURICE WILLIAM (Moe)

Defense **Ht:** 6-2 **Wt:** 210 **Shoots:** right
B: January 21, 1961, Lakewood, Ohio

YR	Regular Season					Playoffs				
	GP	G	A	PTS	PM	GP	G	A	PTS	PM
1984-85	71	11	40	51	54	-	-	-	-	-
1985-86	78	15	52	67	102	-	-	-	-	-
1986-87	62	9	31	40	44	-	-	-	-	-
1987-88	21	2	8	10	23	-	-	-	-	-
Pitt. Totals	232	37	131	168	223	-	-	-	-	-
NHL Totals	656	81	289	370	501	17	5	10	15	18

Acquired from Winnipeg to complete the transaction that sent Randy Carlyle to Winnipeg, May 1, 1984

Traded to Edmonton with Dave Hannan, Chris Joseph, and Craig Simpson for Paul Coffey, Dave Hunter, and Wayne Van Dorp, November 24, 1987

MARSHALL, PAUL A.

Left Wing   **Ht:** 6-2   **Wt:** 180   **Shoots:** left
B: September 7, 1960, Toronto, Ontario

YR	Regular Season					Playoffs				
	GP	G	A	PTS	PM	GP	G	A	PTS	PM
1979-80	46	9	12	21	9	1	0	0	0	0
1980-81	13	3	0	3	4	-	-	-	-	-
Pitt. Totals	59	12	12	24	13	1	0	0	0	0
NHL Totals	95	15	18	33	17	1	0	0	0	0

Selected in the 1979 Entry Draft, 1st choice, 31st overall

Traded to Toronto with Kim Davis for Dave Burrows and Paul Gardner, November 18, 1980

MATHIASEN, DWIGHT

Right Wing   **Ht:** 6-1   **Wt:** 190   **Shoots:** right
B: May 12, 1963, Brandon, Manitoba

YR	Regular Season					Playoffs				
	GP	G	A	PTS	PM	GP	G	A	PTS	PM
1985-86	4	1	0	1	2	-	-	-	-	-
1986-87	6	0	1	1	2	-	-	-	-	-
1987-88	23	0	6	6	14	-	-	-	-	-
Pitt. Totals	33	1	7	8	18	-	-	-	-	-
NHL Totals	33	1	7	8	18	-	-	-	-	-

Signed as a free agent, March 31, 1986

MATTIUSSI, RICHARD ARTHUR (Dick)

Defense   **Ht:** 5-10   **Wt:** 185   **Shoots:** left
B: May 1, 1938, Smooth Rock Falls, Ontario

YR	Regular Season					Playoffs				
	GP	G	A	PTS	PM	GP	G	A	PTS	PM
1967-68	32	0	2	2	18	-	-	-	-	-
1968-69	12	0	2	2	14	-	-	-	-	-
Pitt. Totals	44	0	4	4	32	-	-	-	-	-
NHL Totals	200	8	31	39	124	8	0	1	1	6

Purchased from Cleveland (AHL), August 11, 1966

Loaned to Cleveland (AHL) for the 1966-67 season for cash, October 1966

Traded to Oakland with Earl Ingarfield and Gene Ubriaco for Tracy Pratt, George Swarbrick, and Bryan Watson, January 30, 1969

MAXWELL, BRYAN CLIFFORD

Defense   **Ht:** 6-2   **Wt:** 200   **Shoots:** left
B: September 7, 1955, North Bay, Ontario

YR	Regular Season					Playoffs				
	GP	G	A	PTS	PM	GP	G	A	PTS	PM
1983-84	45	3	12	15	84	-	-	-	-	-
1984-85	44	0	8	8	57	-	-	-	-	-
Pitt. Totals	89	3	20	23	141	-	-	-	-	-
NHL Totals	331	18	77	95	745	15	1	1	2	86
WHA Totals	124	6	23	29	217	6	0	1	1	33

Claimed on waivers from Winnipeg, October 13, 1983

MAYER, PATRICK (Pat)

Defense   **Ht:** 6-3   **Wt:** 225   **Shoots:** left
B: July 24, 1961, Royal Oak, Michigan

YR	Regular Season					Playoffs				
	GP	G	A	PTS	PM	GP	G	A	PTS	PM
1987-88	1	0	0	0	4	-	-	-	-	-
Pitt. Totals	1	0	0	0	4	-	-	-	-	-
NHL Totals	1	0	0	0	4	-	-	-	-	-

Signed as a free agent, July 10, 1987

Traded to Los Angeles for Tim Tookey, March 7, 1989

McADAM, GARY (Wheels)

Left Wing   **Ht:** 5-11   **Wt:** 175   **Shoots:** left
B: December 31, 1955, Smith Falls, Ontario

YR	Regular Season					Playoffs				
	GP	G	A	PTS	PM	GP	G	A	PTS	PM
1978-79	28	5	9	14	2	7	2	1	3	0
1979-80	78	19	22	41	63	5	1	2	3	9
1980-81	34	3	9	12	30	-	-	-	-	-
Pitt. Totals	140	27	40	67	95	12	3	3	6	9
NHL Totals	534	96	132	228	243	30	6	5	11	16

Acquired from Buffalo for Dave Schultz, February 6, 1979

Traded to Detroit for Errol Thompson, January 8, 1981

McBAIN, ANDREW BURTON (Andy)

Right Wing   **Ht:** 6-1   **Wt:** 205   **Shoots:** right
B: January 18, 1965, Scarborough, Ontario

	Regular Season					Playoffs				
YR	GP	G	A	PTS	PM	GP	G	A	PTS	PM
1989-90	41	5	9	14	51	-	-	-	-	-
Pitt. Totals	41	5	9	14	51	-	-	-	-	-
NHL Totals	608	129	172	301	633	24	5	7	12	39

Acquired from Winnipeg with Randy Gilhen and Jim Kyte for Randy Cunneyworth, Dave McLlwain, and Rick Tabaracci, June 17, 1989

Traded to Vancouver with Dave Capuano and Dan Quinn for Rod Buskas, Barry Pederson, and Tony Tanti, January 8, 1990

McCALLUM, DUNCAN SELBY (Dunc)

Defense   **Ht:** 6-1   **Wt:** 193   **Shoots:** right
B: March 29, 1940, Flin Flon, Manitoba
D: March 31, 1983

	Regular Season					Playoffs				
YR	GP	G	A	PTS	PM	GP	G	A	PTS	PM
1967-68	32	0	2	2	36	-	-	-	-	-
1968-69	62	5	13	18	81	-	-	-	-	-
1969-70	14	0	0	0	16	10	1	2	3	12
1970-71	77	9	20	29	95	-	-	-	-	-
Pitt. Totals	185	14	35	49	228	10	1	2	3	12
NHL Totals	187	14	35	49	230	10	1	2	3	12
WHA Totals	100	9	30	39	136	10	2	3	5	6

Acquired from NY Rangers with Paul Andrea, Frank Francis, and George Konik for Larry Jeffrey, June 6, 1967

Claimed by Providence (AHL) in the Reverse Draft, June 12, 1969

Purchased from Providence (AHL), January 27, 1970

Selected by Dayton-Houston in the 1972 WHA General Player Draft, February 12, 1972

McCARTHY, KEVIN

Defense/Right Wing   **Ht:** 5-11   **Wt:** 195   **Shoots:** right
B: July 14, 1957, Winnipeg, Manitoba

	Regular Season					Playoffs				
YR	GP	G	A	PTS	PM	GP	G	A	PTS	PM
1983-84	31	4	16	20	52	-	-	-	-	-
1984-85	64	9	10	19	30	-	-	-	-	-
Pitt. Totals	95	13	26	39	82	-	-	-	-	-
NHL Totals	537	67	191	258	527	21	2	3	5	20

Acquired from Vancouver for a 3rd round choice in the 1984 Entry Draft, January 26, 1984

Signed as a free agent by Philadelphia, July 19, 1985

McCLELLAND, KEVIN WILLIAM

Right Wing   **Ht:** 6-2   **Wt:** 205   **Shoots:** right
B: July 4, 1962, Oshawa, Ontario

	Regular Season					Playoffs				
YR	GP	G	A	PTS	PM	GP	G	A	PTS	PM
1981-82	10	1	4	5	4	5	1	1	2	5
1982-83	38	5	4	9	73	-	-	-	-	-
1983-84	24	2	4	6	62	-	-	-	-	-
Pitt. Totals	72	8	12	20	139	5	1	1	2	5
NHL Totals	588	68	112	180	1672	98	11	18	29	281

Acquired from Hartford with Pat Boutette as compensation for Hartford's signing of Greg Millen, June 29, 1981

Traded to Edmonton with a 6th round choice in the 1984 Entry Draft for Tom Roulston, December 5, 1983

McCREARY, VERNON KEITH (Keith)

Left Wing   **Ht:** 5-10   **Wt:** 180   **Shoots:** left
B: June 19, 1940, Sundridge, Ontario
D: December 9, 2003

	Regular Season					Playoffs				
YR	GP	G	A	PTS	PM	GP	G	A	PTS	PM
1967-68	70	14	12	26	44	-	-	-	-	-
1968-69	70	25	23	48	42	-	-	-	-	-
1969-70	60	18	8	26	67	10	0	4	4	4
1970-71	59	21	12	33	24	-	-	-	-	-
1971-72	33	4	4	8	22	1	0	0	0	2
Pitt. Totals	292	82	59	141	199	11	0	4	4	6
NHL Totals	532	131	112	243	294	16	0	4	4	6

Selected from Montreal in the 1967 Expansion Draft, June 6, 1967

Selected by Atlanta in the 1972 Expansion Draft, June 6, 1972

McDONALD, ALVIN BRIAN (Ab)

Left Wing   **Ht:** 6-3 **Wt:** 192   **Shoots:** left
B: February 18, 1936, Winnipeg, Manitoba

YR	Regular Season					Playoffs				
	GP	G	A	PTS	PM	GP	G	A	PTS	PM
1967-68	74	22	21	43	38	-	-	-	-	-
Pitt. Totals	74	22	21	43	38	-	-	-	-	-
NHL Totals	762	182	248	430	200	84	21	29	50	42
WHA Totals	147	29	41	70	24	18	2	6	8	4

Selected from Detroit in the 1967 Expansion Draft, June 6, 1967

Traded to St. Louis for Lou Angotti, June 11, 1968

McDONNELL, JOSEPH PATRICK (Joe)

Defense   **Ht:** 6-2 **Wt:** 200   **Shoots:** right
B: May 11, 1961, Kitchener, Ontario

YR	Regular Season					Playoffs				
	GP	G	A	PTS	PM	GP	G	A	PTS	PM
1984-85	40	2	9	11	20	-	-	-	-	-
1985-86	3	0	0	0	2	-	-	-	-	-
Pitt. Totals	43	2	9	11	22	-	-	-	-	-
NHL Totals	50	2	10	12	34	-	-	-	-	-

Signed as a free agent, December 30, 1984

McDONOUGH, JAMES ALLISON (Al, the Mad Hatter)

Right Wing   **Ht:** 6-1 **Wt:** 175   **Shoots:** right
B: June 6, 1950, Hamilton, Ontario

YR	Regular Season					Playoffs				
	GP	G	A	PTS	PM	GP	G	A	PTS	PM
1971-72	37	7	11	18	8	4	0	1	1	0
1972-73	78	35	41	76	26	-	-	-	-	-
1973-74	37	14	22	36	12	-	-	-	-	-
Pitt. Totals	152	56	74	130	46	4	0	1	1	0
NHL Totals	237	73	88	161	73	8	0	1	1	2
WHA Totals	200	66	73	139	52	8	3	1	4	2

Acquired from Los Angeles for Bob Woytowich, January 11, 1972

Traded to Atlanta for Chuck Arnason and Bob Paradise, January 4, 1974

West Division All-Star 1973-74

Sean McEachern (left), Luc Robitaille (center), and Troy Murray (right) celebrate a goal.

McEACHERN, SHAWN

Right Wing   **Ht:** 5-11 **Wt:** 200   **Shoots:** left
B: February 28, 1969, Waltham, Massachusetts

YR	Regular Season					Playoffs				
	GP	G	A	PTS	PM	GP	G	A	PTS	PM
1991-92	15	0	4	4	0	19	2	7	9	4
1992-93	84	28	33	61	46	12	3	2	5	10
1993-94	27	12	9	21	10	6	1	0	1	2
1994-95	44	13	13	26	22	11	0	2	2	8
Pitt. Totals	170	53	59	112	78	48	6	11	17	24
NHL Totals	911	256	323	579	506	97	12	25	37	62

Selected in the 1987 Entry Draft, 6th choice, 110th overall

Traded to Los Angeles for Marty McSorley, August 27, 1993

Acquired from Los Angeles with Tomas Sandstrom for Marty McSorley and Jim Paek, February 16, 1994

Traded to Boston with Kevin Stevens for Glen Murray, Bryan Smolinski, and a 3rd round choice in the 1996 Entry Draft, August 2, 1995

McGEOUGH, JAMES (Jim)

Center   Ht: 5-8 **Wt:** 170   **Shoots:** left
B: April 13, 1963, Regina, Saskatchewan

YR	Regular Season					Playoffs				
	GP	G	A	PTS	PM	GP	G	A	PTS	PM
1984-85	14	0	4	4	4	-	-	-	-	-
1985-86	17	3	2	5	8	-	-	-	-	-
1986-87	11	1	4	5	8	-	-	-	-	-
Pitt. Totals	42	4	10	14	20	-	-	-	-	-
NHL Totals	57	7	10	17	32	-	-	-	-	-

Acquired from Washington for Mark Taylor, March 12, 1985

McKEE, JAY

Defense   Ht: 6-4 **Wt:** 203   **Shoots:** left
B: September 8, 1977, Kingston, Ontario

YR	Regular Season					Playoffs				
	GP	G	A	PTS	PM	GP	G	A	PTS	PM
2009-10	62	1	9	10	54	5	0	0	0	2
Pitt. Totals	62	1	9	10	54	5	0	0	0	2
NHL Totals	802	21	104	125	622	60	3	6	9	66

Signed as a free agent, July 10, 2009

McKENNA, STEVE

Left Wing   Ht: 6-8 **Wt:** 252   **Shoots:** left
B: August 21, 1973, Toronto, Ontario

YR	Regular Season					Playoffs				
	GP	G	A	PTS	PM	GP	G	A	PTS	PM
2000-01	34	0	0	0	100	-	-	-	-	-
2002-03	79	9	1	10	128	-	-	-	-	-
2003-04	49	1	2	3	85	-	-	-	-	-
Pitt. Totals	162	10	3	13	313	-	-	-	-	-
NHL Totals	373	18	14	32	824	3	0	1	1	8

Acquired from Minnesota for Roman Simicek, January 13, 2001

Signed as a free agent by NY Rangers, August 28, 2001

Signed as a free agent, July 12, 2002

Signed as a free agent by Nottingham (Britain), October 26, 2004

Big Steve McKenna provided muscle and a sense of humor in the early 2000s. He served as captain for one game.

McKENZIE, BRIAN STEWART

Left Wing   Ht: 5-10 **Wt:** 165   **Shoots:** left
B: March 16, 1951, St. Catharines, Ontario

YR	Regular Season					Playoffs				
	GP	G	A	PTS	PM	GP	G	A	PTS	PM
1971-72	6	1	1	2	4	-	-	-	-	-
Pitt. Totals	6	1	1	2	4	-	-	-	-	-
NHL Totals	6	1	1	2	4	-	-	-	-	-
WHA Totals	87	19	20	39	72	5	0	1	1	0

Selected in the 1971 Amateur Draft, 1st choice, 18th overall

Sold to Atlanta, October 1972

McKENZIE, JIM

Left Wing   Ht: 6-4 **Wt:** 230   **Shoots:** left
B: November 3, 1969, Gull Lake, Saskatchewan

YR	Regular Season					Playoffs				
	GP	G	A	PTS	PM	GP	G	A	PTS	PM
1993-94	11	0	0	0	16	3	0	0	0	0
1994-95	39	2	1	3	63	5	0	0	0	4
Pitt. Totals	50	2	1	3	79	8	0	0	0	4
NHL Totals	880	48	52	100	1739	51	0	0	0	38

Acquired from Dallas for Mike Needham, March 21, 1994

Signed as a free agent by NY Islanders, August 2, 1995

McLLWAIN, DAVID (Dave)

Center/Right Wing   **Ht:** 6-0   **Wt:** 185   **Shoots:** left
B: June 9, 1967, Seaforth, Ontario

	Regular Season					Playoffs				
YR	GP	G	A	PTS	PM	GP	G	A	PTS	PM
1987-88	66	11	8	19	40	-	-	-	-	-
1988-89	24	1	2	3	4	3	0	1	1	0
1995-96	18	2	4	6	4	6	0	0	0	0
Pitt. Totals	108	14	14	28	48	9	0	1	1	0
NHL Totals	501	100	107	207	292	20	0	2	2	2

Selected in the 1986 Entry Draft, 9th choice, 172nd overall

Traded to Winnipeg with Randy Cunneyworth and Rick Tabaracci for Randy Gilhen, Jim Kyte, and Andrew McBain, June 17, 1989

Acquired from Ottawa for an 8th round choice in the 1996 Entry Draft, March 1, 1996

Signed as a free agent by NY Islanders, July 29, 1996

McMAHON, MICHAEL WILLIAM (Mike)

Defense   **Ht:** 5-11   **Wt:** 180   **Shoots:** left
B: August 30, 1941, Quebec City, Quebec

	Regular Season					Playoffs				
YR	GP	G	A	PTS	PM	GP	G	A	PTS	PM
1969-70	12	1	3	4	19	-	-	-	-	-
Pitt. Totals	12	1	3	4	19	-	-	-	-	-
NHL Totals	224	15	68	83	171	14	3	7	10	4
WHA Totals	279	29	101	130	249	32	1	14	15	13

Acquired from Detroit for Billy Dea, October 28, 1969

Selected in the 1970 Expansion Draft by Buffalo, June 10, 1970

McMANAMA, ROBERT S. (Bob)

Center   **Ht:** 6-0   **Wt:** 180   **Shoots:** left
B: October 7, 1951, Belmont, Massachusetts

	Regular Season					Playoffs				
YR	GP	G	A	PTS	PM	GP	G	A	PTS	PM
1973-74	47	5	14	19	18	-	-	-	-	-
1974-75	40	5	9	14	6	8	0	1	1	6
1975-76	12	1	2	3	4	-	-	-	-	-
Pitt. Totals	99	11	25	36	28	8	0	1	1	6
NHL Totals	99	11	25	36	28	8	0	1	1	6
WHA Totals	37	3	10	13	28	12	4	3	7	4

Signed as a free agent, August 1973

Signed as a free agent by New England (WHA), December 1975

McSORLEY, MARTIN JAMES (Marty)

Defense   **Ht:** 6-1   **Wt:** 235   **Shoots:** right
B: May 18, 1963, Hamilton, Ontario

	Regular Season					Playoffs				
YR	GP	G	A	PTS	PM	GP	G	A	PTS	PM
1983-84	72	2	7	9	224	-	-	-	-	-
1984-85	15	0	0	0	15	-	-	-	-	-
1993-94	47	3	18	21	139	-	-	-	-	-
Pitt. Totals	134	5	25	30	378	-	-	-	-	-
NHL Totals	961	108	251	359	3381	115	10	19	29	374

Signed as a free agent, July 30, 1982

Traded to Edmonton with Tim Hrynewich and future considerations for Gilles Meloche, September 11, 1985

Acquired from Los Angeles for Shawn McEachern, August 27, 1993

Traded to Los Angeles with Jim Paek for Shawn McEachern and Tomas Sandstrom, February 16, 1994

MEEKER, MICHAEL THOMAS (Mike)

Right Wing   **Ht:** 5-11   **Wt:** 195   **Shoots:** right
B: February 23, 1958, Kingston, Ontario

	Regular Season					Playoffs				
YR	GP	G	A	PTS	PM	GP	G	A	PTS	PM
1978-79	4	0	0	0	5	-	-	-	-	-
Pitt. Totals	4	0	0	0	5	-	-	-	-	-
NHL Totals	4	0	0	0	5	-	-	-	-	-

Selected in the 1978 Amateur Draft, 1st choice, 25th overall

MEIGHAN, RON JAMES

Defense   **Ht:** 6-3   **Wt:** 195   **Shoots:** right
B: May 26, 1963, Montreal, Quebec

	Regular Season					Playoffs				
YR	GP	G	A	PTS	PM	GP	G	A	PTS	PM
1982-83	41	2	6	8	16	-	-	-	-	-
Pitt. Totals	41	2	6	8	16	-	-	-	-	-
NHL Totals	48	3	7	10	18	-	-	-	-	-

Acquired from Minnesota with Anders Hakansson for George Ferguson and an exchange of 1st round choices in the 1983 Entry Draft, October 28, 1982

MELICHAR, JOSEF

Defense   **Ht:** 6-2   **Wt:** 220   **Shoots:** left
B: January 20, 1979, Ceske Budejovice, Czechoslovakia

YR	Regular Season					Playoffs				
	GP	G	A	PTS	PM	GP	G	A	PTS	PM
2000-01	18	0	2	2	21	-	-	-	-	-
2001-02	60	0	3	3	68	-	-	-	-	-
2002-03	8	0	0	0	2	-	-	-	-	-
2003-04	82	3	5	8	62	-	-	-	-	-
2005-06	72	3	12	15	66					
2006-07	70	1	11	12	44	5	0	0	0	2
Pitt. Totals	310	7	33	40	263	5	0	0	0	2
NHL Totals	349	7	42	49	300	5	0	0	0	2

Selected in the 1997 Entry Draft, 3rd choice, 71st overall

Signed as a free agent by Linkopings (Sweden), October 3, 2007

MELOCHE, ERIC

Right Wing   **Ht:** 5-10   **Wt:** 202   **Shoots:** right
B: May 1, 1976, Montreal, Quebec

YR	Regular Season					Playoffs				
	GP	G	A	PTS	PM	GP	G	A	PTS	PM
2001-02	23	0	1	1	8	-	-	-	-	-
2002-03	13	5	1	6	4	-	-	-	-	-
2003-04	25	3	7	10	20	-	-	-	-	-
Pitt. Totals	61	8	9	17	32	-	-	-	-	-
NHL Totals	74	9	11	20	36	-	-	-	-	-

Selected in the 1996 Entry Draft, 7th choice, 186th overall

Signed as a free agent by Philadelphia, July 14, 2004

MELOCHE, GILLES

Goaltender   **Ht:** 5-9   **Wt:** 185   **Catches:** left
B: July 12, 1950, Montreal, Quebec

YR	Regular Season					Playoffs				
	GP	MINS	GA	SH	AVE	GP	MINS	GA	SH	AVE
1985-86	34	1989	119	0	3.59	-	-	-	-	-
1986-87	43	2343	134	0	3.43	-	-	-	-	-
1987-88	27	1394	95	0	4.09	-	-	-	-	-
Pitt. Totals	104	5726	348	0	3.65	-	-	-	-	-
NHL Totals	788	45401	2756	20	3.64	45	2464	143	2	3.48

Acquired from Edmonton for Tim Hrynewich, Marty McSorley, and future considerations, September 11, 1985

MICHAYLUK, DAVID (Dave)

Left Wing   **Ht:** 5-10   **Wt:** 189   **Shoots:** left
B: May 18, 1962, Wakaw, Saskatchewan

YR	Regular Season					Playoffs				
	GP	G	A	PTS	PM	GP	G	A	PTS	PM
1991-92	-	-	-	-	-	7	1	1	2	0
Pitt. Totals	-	-	-	-	-	7	1	1	2	0
NHL Totals	14	2	6	8	8	7	1	1	2	0

Signed as a free agent, May 24, 1989

MILLEN, GREG H.

Goaltender   **Ht:** 5-9   **Wt:** 175   **Catches:** right
B: June 25, 1957, Toronto, Ontario

YR	Regular Season					Playoffs				
	GP	MINS	GA	SH	AVE	GP	MINS	GA	SH	AVE
1978-79	28	1532	86	2	3.37	-	-	-	-	-
1979-80	44	2586	157	2	3.64	5	300	21	0	4.20
1980-81	63	3721	258	0	4.16	5	325	19	0	3.51
Pitt. Totals	135	7839	501	4	3.83	10	625	40	0	3.84
NHL Totals	604	35377	2281	17	3.87	59	3383	193	0	3.42

Selected in the 1977 Amateur Draft, 4th choice, 102nd overall

Signed as a free agent by Hartford, June 15, 1981

Greg Millen follows the puck into his catching glove.

MILLER, KEVIN

Center **Ht:** 5-11 **Wt:** 190 **Shoots:** right
B: September 2, 1965, Lansing, Michigan

YR	Regular Season					Playoffs				
	GP	G	A	PTS	PM	GP	G	A	PTS	PM
1995-96	13	6	5	11	4	18	3	2	5	8
Pitt. Totals	13	6	5	11	4	18	3	2	5	8
NHL Totals	620	150	185	335	429	61	7	10	17	49

Acquired from San Jose for a 5th round choice in the 1996 Entry Draft, March 20, 1996

Signed as a free agent by Chicago, July 18, 1996

MILLER, KIP

Left Wing/Center **Ht:** 5-10 **Wt:** 190 **Shoots:** left
B: June 11, 1969, Lansing, Michigan

YR	Regular Season					Playoffs				
	GP	G	A	PTS	PM	GP	G	A	PTS	PM
1998-99	77	19	23	42	22	13	2	7	9	19
1999-00	44	4	15	19	10	-	-	-	-	-
2000-01	33	3	8	11	6	-	-	-	-	-
Pitt. Totals	154	26	46	72	38	13	2	7	9	19
NHL Totals	449	74	165	239	105	25	6	11	17	23

Claimed from NY Islanders in the Waiver Draft, October 5, 1998

Traded to Anaheim for a 9th round choice in the 2000 Entry Draft, January 29, 2000

Signed as a free agent, September 24, 2000

Signed as a free agent by Grand Rapids (AHL), May 31, 2001

MINARD, CHRIS

Center **Ht:** 6-1 **Wt:** 190 **Shoots:** left
B: November 18, 1981, Thompson, Manitoba

YR	Regular Season					Playoffs				
	GP	G	A	PTS	PM	GP	G	A	PTS	PM
2007-08	15	1	1	2	10	-	-	-	-	-
2008-09	20	1	2	3	4	-	-	-	-	-
Pitt. Totals	35	2	3	5	14	-	-	-	-	-
NHL Totals	40	2	4	6	14	-	-	-	-	-

Signed as a free agent, July 12, 2007

Signed as a free agent by Edmonton, July 13, 2009

MIRONOV, DMITRI

Defense **Ht:** 6-4 **Wt:** 224 **Shoots:** right
B: December 25, 1965, Moscow, USSR

YR	Regular Season					Playoffs				
	GP	G	A	PTS	PM	GP	G	A	PTS	PM
1995-96	72	3	31	34	88	15	0	1	1	10
1996-97	15	1	5	6	24	-	-	-	-	-
Pitt. Totals	87	4	36	40	112	15	0	1	1	10
NHL Totals	556	54	206	260	568	75	10	26	36	48

Acquired from Toronto with a 2nd round choice in the 1996 Entry Draft for Larry Murphy, July 8, 1995

Traded to Anaheim with Shawn Antoski for Alex Hicks and Fredrik Olausson, November 19, 1996

MOKOSAK, CARL

Left Wing **Ht:** 6-1 **Wt:** 180 **Shoots:** left
B: September 22, 1962, Fort Saskatchewan, Alberta

YR	Regular Season					Playoffs				
	GP	G	A	PTS	PM	GP	G	A	PTS	PM
1986-87	3	0	0	0	4	-	-	-	-	-
Pitt. Totals	3	0	0	0	4	-	-	-	-	-
NHL Totals	83	11	15	26	170	1	0	0	0	0

Signed as a free agent, July 23, 1986

Signed as a free agent by Boston, October 4, 1988

MONAHAN, HARTLAND PATRICK

Right Wing **Ht:** 5-11 **Wt:** 197 **Shoots:** right
B: March 29, 1951, Montreal, Quebec

YR	Regular Season					Playoffs				
	GP	G	A	PTS	PM	GP	G	A	PTS	PM
1977-78	7	2	0	2	2	-	-	-	-	-
Pitt. Totals	7	2	0	2	2	-	-	-	-	-
NHL Totals	334	61	80	141	163	6	0	0	0	4

Acquired from Washington for a 1st round choice in the 1979 Entry Draft, October 17, 1977

Traded to Los Angeles with Syl Apps for Gene Carr, Dave Schultz, and a 4th round choice in the 1978 Amateur Draft, November 2, 1977

MOORE, DOMINIC

Center   **Ht:** 6-0 **Wt:** 190   **Shoots:** left
B: August 3, 1980, Sarnia, Ontario

YR	Regular Season					Playoffs				
	GP	G	A	PTS	PM	GP	G	A	PTS	PM
2006-07	59	6	9	15	46	-	-	-	-	-
Pitt. Totals	59	6	9	15	46	-	-	-	-	-
NHL Totals	374	45	83	128	243	23	4	1	5	8

Acquired from Nashville with Libor Pivko for a 3rd round choice in the 2007 Entry Draft, July 19, 2006

Traded to Minnesota for a 3rd round choice in the 2007 Entry Draft, February 27, 2007

MORAN, IAN

Defense/Center   **Ht:** 6-0 **Wt:** 206   **Shoots:** right
B: August 24, 1972, Cleveland, Ohio

YR	Regular Season					Playoffs				
	GP	G	A	PTS	PM	GP	G	A	PTS	PM
1994-95	-	-	-	-	-	8	0	0	0	0
1995-96	51	1	1	2	47	-	-	-	-	-
1996-97	36	4	5	9	22	5	1	2	3	4
1997-98	37	1	6	7	19	6	0	0	0	2
1998-99	62	4	5	9	37	13	0	2	2	8
1999-00	73	4	8	12	28	11	0	1	1	2
2000-01	40	3	4	7	28	18	0	1	1	4
2001-02	64	2	8	10	54	-	-	-	-	-
2002-03	70	0	7	7	46	-	-	-	-	-
Pitt. Totals	433	19	44	63	281	61	1	6	7	20
NHL Totals	489	21	50	71	321	66	1	7	8	24

Selected in the 1990 Entry Draft, 5th choice, 107th overall

Traded to Boston for a 4th round choice in the 2003 Entry Draft, March 11, 2003

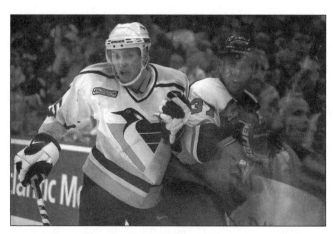

Aleksey Morozov rides Flyer Eric Desjardins into the boards.

MOROZOV, ALEKSEY

Right Wing   **Ht:** 6-1 **Wt:** 204   **Shoots:** left
B: February 16, 1977, Moscow, USSR

YR	Regular Season					Playoffs				
	GP	G	A	PTS	PM	GP	G	A	PTS	PM
1997-98	76	13	13	26	8	6	0	1	1	2
1998-99	67	9	10	19	14	10	1	1	2	0
1999-00	68	12	19	31	14	5	0	0	0	0
2000-01	66	5	14	19	6	18	3	3	6	6
2001-02	72	20	29	49	16	-	-	-	-	-
2002-03	27	9	16	25	16	-	-	-	-	-
2003-04	75	16	34	50	24	-	-	-	-	-
Pitt. Totals	451	84	135	219	98	39	4	5	9	8
NHL Totals	451	84	135	219	98	39	4	5	9	8

Selected in the 1995 Entry Draft, 1st choice, 24th overall

Signed as a free agent by Kazan (Russia), September 25, 2004

MORRISON, HENRY LEWIS (Lew)

Right Wing   **Ht:** 6-0 **Wt:** 185   **Shoots:** right
B: February 11, 1948, Gainsborough, Saskatchewan

YR	Regular Season					Playoffs				
	GP	G	A	PTS	PM	GP	G	A	PTS	PM
1974-75	52	7	5	12	4	9	0	0	0	0
1975-76	78	4	5	9	8	3	0	0	0	0
1976-77	76	2	1	3	0	1	0	0	0	0
1977-78	8	0	2	2	0	-	-	-	-	-
Pitt. Totals	214	13	13	26	12	13	0	0	0	0
NHL Totals	564	39	52	91	107	17	0	0	0	2

Acquired from Washington for Ron Lalonde, December 14, 1974

MORRISON, JAMES STUART HUNTER (Jim)

Defense   **Ht:** 5-10 **Wt:** 183   **Shoots:** left
B: October 11, 1931, Montreal, Quebec

YR	Regular Season					Playoffs				
	GP	G	A	PTS	PM	GP	G	A	PTS	PM
1969-70	59	5	15	20	40	8	0	3	3	10
1970-71	73	0	10	10	32	-	-	-	-	-
Pitt. Totals	132	5	25	30	72	8	0	3	3	10
NHL Totals	704	40	160	200	542	36	0	12	12	38

Acquired from Baltimore (AHL) for Bob Rivard and cash, October 1969

MULLEN, JOSEPH PATRICK (Joey)

Right Wing   Ht: 5-9 **Wt:** 180   **Shoots:** right
B: February 26, 1957, New York, New York

YR	Regular Season					Playoffs				
	GP	G	A	PTS	PM	GP	G	A	PTS	PM
1990-91	47	17	22	39	6	22	8	9	17	4
1991-92	77	42	45	87	30	9	3	1	4	4
1992-93	72	33	37	70	14	12	4	2	6	6
1993-94	84	38	32	70	41	6	1	0	1	2
1994-95	45	16	21	37	6	12	0	3	3	4
1996-97	54	7	15	22	4	1	0	0	0	0
Pitt. Totals	379	153	172	325	101	62	16	15	31	20
NHL Totals	1062	502	561	1063	241	143	60	46	106	42

Acquired from Calgary for a 2nd round choice in the 1990 Entry Draft, June 16, 1990

Signed as a free agent by Boston, September 13, 1995

Signed as a free agent, September 5, 1996

Eastern Conference All-Star 1993-94

Penguins Hall of Fame, 2000

Hockey Hall of Fame (Player), 2000

MULVENNA, GLENN

Center   Ht: 5-11 **Wt:** 187   **Shoots:** left
B: February 18, 1967, Calgary, Alberta

YR	Regular Season					Playoffs				
	GP	G	A	PTS	PM	GP	G	A	PTS	PM
1991-92	1	0	0	0	2	-	-	-	-	-
Pitt. Totals	1	0	0	0	2	-	-	-	-	-
NHL Totals	2	0	0	0	4	-	-	-	-	-

Signed as a free agent, December 3, 1987

Signed as a free agent by Philadelphia, July 11, 1992

MULVEY, PAUL JOSEPH

Left Wing   Ht: 6-4 **Wt:** 220   **Shoots:** left
B: September 27, 1958, Sudbury, Ontario

YR	Regular Season					Playoffs				
	GP	G	A	PTS	PM	GP	G	A	PTS	PM
1981-82	27	1	7	8	76	-	-	-	-	-
Pitt. Totals	27	1	7	8	76	-	-	-	-	-
NHL Totals	225	30	51	81	613	-	-	-	-	-

Acquired from Washington as compensation for Orest Kindrachuk, September 4, 1981

Claimed on waivers by Los Angeles, December 30, 1981

MUNI, CRAIG

Defense   Ht: 6-3 **Wt:** 208   **Shoots:** left
B: July 19, 1962, Toronto, Ontario

YR	Regular Season					Playoffs				
	GP	G	A	PTS	PM	GP	G	A	PTS	PM
1996-97	64	0	4	4	36	3	0	0	0	0
Pitt. Totals	64	0	4	4	36	3	0	0	0	0
NHL Totals	819	28	119	147	775	113	0	17	17	108

Acquired from Buffalo for cash, October 3, 1986

Traded to Edmonton to complete September 11, 1985, trade that sent Gilles Meloche to Pittsburgh for Tim Hrynewich and Marty McSorley, October 6, 1986

Signed as a free agent, October 2, 1996

Signed as a free agent by Dallas, October 2, 1997

MURLEY, MATT

Left Wing   Ht: 6-1 **Wt:** 206   **Shoots:** left
B: December 17, 1979, Troy, New York

YR	Regular Season					Playoffs				
	GP	G	A	PTS	PM	GP	G	A	PTS	PM
2003-04	18	1	1	2	14	-	-	-	-	-
2005-06	41	1	5	6	24	-	-	-	-	-
Pitt. Totals	59	2	6	8	38	-	-	-	-	-
NHL Totals	62	2	7	9	38	-	-	-	-	-

Selected in the 1999 Entry Draft, 2nd choice, 51st overall

Signed as a free agent by Colorado, July 12, 2006

MURPHY, LAWRENCE THOMAS (Larry)

Defense   Ht: 6-2 **Wt:** 210   **Shoots:** right
B: March 8, 1961, Scarborough, Ontario

YR	Regular Season					Playoffs				
	GP	G	A	PTS	PM	GP	G	A	PTS	PM
1990-91	44	5	23	28	30	23	5	18	23	44
1991-92	77	21	56	77	48	21	6	10	16	19
1992-93	83	22	63	85	73	12	2	11	13	10
1993-94	84	17	56	73	44	6	0	5	5	0
1994-95	48	13	25	38	18	12	2	13	15	0
Pitt. Totals	336	78	223	301	213	74	15	57	72	73
NHL Totals	1615	287	929	1216	1084	215	37	115	152	201

Acquired from Minnesota with Peter Taglianetti for Chris Dahlquist and Jim Johnson, December 11, 1990

Traded to Toronto for Dmitri Mironov and a 2nd round choice in the 1996 Entry Draft, July 8, 1995

Eastern Conference All-Star 1993-94

Second Team NHL All-Star 1992-93, 1994-95

Hockey Hall of Fame (Player), 2004

MURRAY, GLEN (Muzz)

Right Wing   **Ht:** 6-3   **Wt:** 218   **Shoots:** right
B: November 1, 1972, Halifax, Nova Scotia

YR	Regular Season					Playoffs				
	GP	G	A	PTS	PM	GP	G	A	PTS	PM
1995-96	69	14	15	29	57	18	2	6	8	10
1996-97	66	11	11	22	24	-	-	-	-	-
Pitt. Totals	135	25	26	51	81	18	2	6	8	10
NHL Totals	1009	337	314	651	679	94	20	22	42	66

Acquired from Boston with Bryan Smolinski and a 3rd round choice in the 1996 Entry Draft for Shawn McEachern and Kevin Stevens, August 2, 1995

Traded to Los Angeles for Ed Olczyk, March 18, 1997

MURRAY, TROY NORMAN

Center   **Ht:** 6-1   **Wt:** 195   **Shoots:** right
B: July 31, 1962, Calgary, Alberta

YR	Regular Season					Playoffs				
	GP	G	A	PTS	PM	GP	G	A	PTS	PM
1994-95	13	0	2	2	23	12	2	1	3	12
Pitt. Totals	13	0	2	2	23	12	2	1	3	12
NHL Totals	915	230	354	584	875	113	17	26	43	145

Acquired from Ottawa with Norm Maciver for Martin Straka, April 7, 1995

Signed as a free agent by Colorado, August 7, 1995

N

NASLUND, MARKUS

Left Wing   **Ht:** 6-0   **Wt:** 195   **Shoots:** left
B: July 30, 1973, Ornskoldsvik, Sweden

YR	Regular Season					Playoffs				
	GP	G	A	PTS	PM	GP	G	A	PTS	PM
1993-94	71	4	7	11	27	-	-	-	-	-
1994-95	14	2	2	4	2	-	-	-	-	-
1995-96	66	19	33	52	36	-	-	-	-	-
Pitt. Totals	151	25	42	67	65	-	-	-	-	-
NHL Totals	1117	395	474	869	736	52	14	22	36	56

Selected in the 1991 Entry Draft, 1st choice, 16th overall

Traded to Vancouver for Alek Stojanov, March 20, 1996

NASREDDINE, ALAIN

Defense   **Ht:** 6-1   **Wt:** 204   **Shoots:** left
B: July 10, 1975, Montreal, Quebec

YR	Regular Season					Playoffs				
	GP	G	A	PTS	PM	GP	G	A	PTS	PM
2005-06	6	0	0	0	8	-	-	-	-	-
2006-07	44	1	4	5	18	-	-	-	-	-
2007-08	6	0	0	0	4	-	-	-	-	-
Pitt. Totals	56	1	4	5	30	-	-	-	-	-
NHL Totals	74	1	4	5	84	-	-	-	-	-

Acquired from NY Islanders for Steve Webb, March 8, 2004

NEATON, PATRICK (Pat)

Defense   **Ht:** 6-0   **Wt:** 180   **Shoots:** left
B: May 21, 1971, Redford, Michigan

YR	Regular Season					Playoffs				
	GP	G	A	PTS	PM	GP	G	A	PTS	PM
1993-94	9	1	1	2	12	-	-	-	-	-
Pitt. Totals	9	1	1	2	12	-	-	-	-	-
NHL Totals	9	1	1	2	12	-	-	-	-	-

Selected in the 1990 Entry Draft, 9th choice, 145th overall

Signed as a free agent by Utah (IHL), August 10, 1999

NEDVED, PETR

Center   **Ht:** 6-3   **Wt:** 196   **Shoots:** left
B: December 9, 1971, Liberec, Czechoslovakia

YR	Regular Season					Playoffs				
	GP	G	A	PTS	PM	GP	G	A	PTS	PM
1995-96	80	45	54	99	68	18	10	10	20	16
1996-97	74	33	38	71	66	5	1	2	3	12
Pitt. Totals	154	78	92	170	134	23	11	12	23	28
NHL Totals	982	310	407	717	708	71	19	23	42	64

Acquired from NY Rangers with Sergei Zubov for Luc Robitaille and Ulf Samuelsson, August 31, 1995

Traded to NY Rangers with Sean Pronger and Chris Tamer for Alexei Kovalev and Harry York, November 25, 1998

NEEDHAM, MICHAEL (Mike)

Right Wing   **Ht:** 5-10   **Wt:** 185   **Shoots:** right
B: April 4, 1970, Calgary, Alberta

YR	Regular Season					Playoffs				
	GP	G	A	PTS	PM	GP	G	A	PTS	PM
1991-92	-	-	-	-	-	5	1	0	1	2
1992-93	56	8	5	13	14	9	1	0	1	2
1993-94	25	1	0	1	2	-	-	-	-	-
Pitt. Totals	**81**	**9**	**5**	**14**	**16**	**14**	**2**	**0**	**2**	**4**
NHL Totals	**86**	**9**	**5**	**14**	**16**	**14**	**2**	**0**	**2**	**4**

Selected in the 1989 Entry Draft, 7th choice, 126th overall

Traded to Dallas for Jim McKenzie, March 21, 1994

NELSON, TODD

Defense   **Ht:** 6-0   **Wt:** 201   **Shoots:** left
B: May 11, 1969, Prince Albert, Saskatchewan

YR	Regular Season					Playoffs				
	GP	G	A	PTS	PM	GP	G	A	PTS	PM
1991-92	1	0	0	0	0	-	-	-	-	-
Pitt. Totals	**1**	**0**	**0**	**0**	**0**	**-**	**-**	**-**	**-**	**-**
NHL Totals	**3**	**1**	**0**	**1**	**2**	**4**	**0**	**0**	**0**	**0**

Selected in the 1989 Entry Draft, 4th choice, 79th overall

Signed as a free agent by Washington, August 15, 1993

NEWTON, CAMERON CHARLES (Cam)

Goaltender   **Ht:** 5-11   **Wt:** 170   **Catches:** left
B: February 25, 1950, Peterborough, Ontario

YR	Regular Season					Playoffs				
	GP	MINS	GA	SH	AVE	GP	MINS	GA	SH	AVE
1970-71	5	281	16	0	3.42	-	-	-	-	-
1972-73	11	533	35	0	3.94	-	-	-	-	-
Pitt. Totals	**16**	**814**	**51**	**0**	**3.76**	**-**	**-**	**-**	**-**	**-**
NHL Totals	**16**	**814**	**51**	**0**	**3.76**	**-**	**-**	**-**	**-**	**-**
WHA Totals	**102**	**6106**	**352**	**2**	**3.46**	**11**	**546**	**40**	**0**	**4.40**

Selected in the 1970 Amateur Draft, 8th choice, 102th overall

Signed as a free agent by Chicago (WHA), May 18, 1973

NIEMINEN, VILLE

Left Wing   **Ht:** 5-11   **Wt:** 200   **Shoots:** left
B: April 6, 1977, Tampere, Finland

YR	Regular Season					Playoffs				
	GP	G	A	PTS	PM	GP	G	A	PTS	PM
2001-02	13	1	2	3	8	-	-	-	-	-
2002-03	75	9	12	21	93	-	-	-	-	-
Pitt. Totals	**88**	**10**	**14**	**24**	**101**	**-**	**-**	**-**	**-**	**-**
NHL Totals	**385**	**48**	**69**	**117**	**333**	**58**	**8**	**12**	**20**	**99**

Acquired from Colorado with Rick Berry for Darius Kasparaitis, March 19, 2002

Signed as a free agent by Chicago, July 29, 2003

NOLAN, THEODORE JOHN (Ted)

Center   **Ht:** 6-0   **Wt:** 185   **Shoots:** left
B: April 7, 1958, Sault Ste. Marie, Ontario

YR	Regular Season					Playoffs				
	GP	G	A	PTS	PM	GP	G	A	PTS	PM
1985-86	18	1	1	2	34	-	-	-	-	-
Pitt. Totals	**18**	**1**	**1**	**2**	**34**	**-**	**-**	**-**	**-**	**-**
NHL Totals	**78**	**6**	**16**	**22**	**105**	**-**	**-**	**-**	**-**	**-**

Purchased from Buffalo, September 16, 1985

NOLET, SIMON LAURENT

Right Wing   **Ht:** 5-9   **Wt:** 185   **Shoots:** right
B: November 23, 1941, St. Odilon, Quebec

YR	Regular Season					Playoffs				
	GP	G	A	PTS	PM	GP	G	A	PTS	PM
1975-76	39	9	8	17	2	3	0	0	0	0
Pitt. Totals	**39**	**9**	**8**	**17**	**2**	**3**	**0**	**0**	**0**	**0**
NHL Totals	**562**	**150**	**182**	**332**	**187**	**34**	**6**	**3**	**9**	**8**

Acquired from Kansas City with Ed Gilbert and exchange of 1st round choices in the 1976 Amateur Draft for Chuck Arnason and Steve Durbano, January 9, 1976

Traded to Colorado with Michel Plasse and loan of Colin Campbell for 1976-77 season as compensation for Denis Herron, August 7, 1976

NORDGREN, NIKLAS

Left Wing   **Ht:** 5-11 **Wt:** 185   **Shoots:** right
B: June 28, 1979, Ornskoldsvik, Sweden

	Regular Season					Playoffs				
YR	GP	G	A	PTS	PM	GP	G	A	PTS	PM
2005-06	15	0	0	0	4	-	-	-	-	-
Pitt. Totals	15	0	0	0	4	-	-	-	-	-
NHL Totals	58	4	2	6	34	-	-	-	-	-

Acquired from Carolina with Krys Kolanos and a 2nd round choice in the 2007 Entry Draft for Mark Recchi, March 9, 2006

Signed as a free agent by Rapperswil (Switzerland), May 10, 2006

NORIS, JOSEPH S. (Joe)

Center/Defense   **Ht:** 6-0 **Wt:** 185   **Shoots:** right
B: October 26, 1951, Denver, Colorado

	Regular Season					Playoffs				
YR	GP	G	A	PTS	PM	GP	G	A	PTS	PM
1971-72	35	2	5	7	20	-	-	-	-	-
Pitt. Totals	35	2	5	7	20	-	-	-	-	-
NHL Totals	55	2	5	7	22	-	-	-	-	-
WHA Totals	198	72	116	188	60	18	4	5	9	12

Selected in the 1971 Amateur Draft, 2nd choice, 32nd overall

Traded to St. Louis for Jim Shires, January 8, 1973

NORTON, JEFF

Defense   **Ht:** 6-2 **Wt:** 195   **Shoots:** left
B: November 25, 1965, Acton, Massachusetts

	Regular Season					Playoffs				
YR	GP	G	A	PTS	PM	GP	G	A	PTS	PM
2000-01	32	2	10	12	20	-	-	-	-	-
Pitt. Totals	32	2	10	12	20	-	-	-	-	-
NHL Totals	799	52	332	384	615	65	4	21	25	89

Signed as a free agent, November 14, 2000

Traded to San Jose for Bobby Dollas and Johan Hedberg, March 12, 2001

NOWAK, HENRY STANLEY (Hank)

Left Wing   **Ht:** 6-1 **Wt:** 195   **Shoots:** left
B: November 24, 1950, Oshawa, Ontario

	Regular Season					Playoffs				
YR	GP	G	A	PTS	PM	GP	G	A	PTS	PM
1973-74	13	0	0	0	11	-	-	-	-	-
Pitt. Totals	13	0	0	0	11	-	-	-	-	-
NHL Totals	180	26	29	55	161	13	1	0	1	8

Acquired from Hershey (AHL), May 22, 1973

Traded to Detroit with a 3rd round choice in the 1974 Amateur Draft for Nelson Debenedet, May 27, 1974

O

ODELEIN, LYLE

Defense   **Ht:** 6-0 **Wt:** 210   **Shoots:** right
B: July 21, 1968, Quill Lake, Saskatchewan

	Regular Season					Playoffs				
YR	GP	G	A	PTS	PM	GP	G	A	PTS	PM
2005-06	27	0	1	1	50	-	-	-	-	-
Pitt. Totals	27	0	1	1	50	-	-	-	-	-
NHL Totals	1056	50	202	252	2316	86	5	13	18	209

Signed as a free agent, September 2, 2005

OKSIUTA, ROMAN

Right Wing   **Ht:** 6-3 **Wt:** 230   **Shoots:** left
B: August 21, 1970, Murmansk, USSR

	Regular Season					Playoffs				
YR	GP	G	A	PTS	PM	GP	G	A	PTS	PM
1996-97	7	0	0	0	4	-	-	-	-	-
Pitt. Totals	7	0	0	0	4	-	-	-	-	-
NHL Totals	153	46	41	87	100	10	2	3	5	0

Acquired from Anaheim for Richard Park, March 18, 1997

OLAUSSON, FREDRIK

Defense   Ht: 6-2 **Wt:** 198   **Shoots:** right
B: October 5, 1966, Dadesjo, Sweden

YR	GP	G	A	PTS	PM	GP	G	A	PTS	PM

	Regular Season					Playoffs				
YR	GP	G	A	PTS	PM	GP	G	A	PTS	PM
1996-97	51	7	20	27	24	4	0	1	1	0
1997-98	76	6	27	33	42	6	0	3	3	2
Pitt. Totals	127	13	47	60	66	10	0	4	4	2
NHL Totals	1022	147	434	581	450	71	6	23	29	28

Acquired from Anaheim with Alex Hicks for Shawn Antoski and Dmitri Mironov, November 19, 1996

Signed as a free agent by Anaheim, August 28, 1998

OLCZYK, ED (Edzo)

Center   Ht: 6-1 **Wt:** 207   **Shoots:** left
B: August 16, 1966, Chicago, Illinois

	Regular Season					Playoffs				
YR	GP	G	A	PTS	PM	GP	G	A	PTS	PM
1996-97	12	4	7	11	6	5	1	0	1	12
1997-98	56	11	11	22	35	6	2	0	2	4
Pitt. Totals	68	15	18	33	41	11	3	0	3	16
NHL Totals	1031	342	452	794	874	57	19	15	34	57

Acquired from Los Angeles for Glen Murray, March 18, 1997

Signed as a free agent by Chicago, August 26, 1998

OLIWA, KRZYSZTOF (KO)

Left Wing   Ht: 6-5 **Wt:** 245   **Shoots:** left
B: April 12, 1973, Tychy, Poland

	Regular Season					Playoffs				
YR	GP	G	A	PTS	PM	GP	G	A	PTS	PM
2000-01	26	1	2	3	131	5	0	0	0	16
2001-02	57	0	2	2	150	-	-	-	-	-
Pitt. Totals	83	1	4	5	281	5	0	0	0	16
NHL Totals	410	17	28	45	1447	32	2	0	2	47

Acquired from Columbus for a 3rd round choice in the 2001 Entry Draft, January 14, 2001

Traded to NY Rangers for a 9th round choice in the 2003 Entry Draft, June 23, 2002

O'REGAN, THOMAS PATRICK (Tom)

Center   Ht: 5-10 **Wt:** 180   **Shoots:** left
B: December 29, 1961, Cambridge, Massachusetts

	Regular Season					Playoffs				
YR	GP	G	A	PTS	PM	GP	G	A	PTS	PM
1983-84	51	4	10	14	8	-	-	-	-	-
1984-85	1	0	0	0	0	-	-	-	-	-
1985-86	9	1	2	3	2	-	-	-	-	-
Pitt. Totals	61	5	12	17	10	-	-	-	-	-
NHL Totals	61	5	12	17	10	-	-	-	-	-

Signed as a free agent, September 4, 1983

Signed as a free agent by Detroit, September 29, 1986

ORPIK, BROOKS

Defense   Ht: 6-2 **Wt:** 219   **Shoots:** left
B: September 26, 1980, San Francisco, California

	Regular Season					Playoffs				
YR	GP	G	A	PTS	PM	GP	G	A	PTS	PM
2002-03	6	0	0	0	2	-	-	-	-	-
2003-04	79	1	9	10	127	-	-	-	-	-
2005-06	64	2	7	9	124	-	-	-	-	-
2006-07	70	0	6	6	82	5	0	0	0	8
2007-08	78	1	10	11	57	20	0	2	2	18
2008-09	79	2	17	19	73	24	0	4	4	22
2009-10	73	2	23	25	64	13	0	2	2	12
Pitt. Totals	449	8	72	80	529	62	0	8	8	60
NHL Totals	449	8	72	80	529	62	0	8	8	60

Selected in the 2000 Entry Draft, 1st choice, 18th overall

OUELLET, MICHEL

Right Wing   Ht: 6-1 **Wt:** 193   **Shoots:** right
B: March 5, 1982, Rimouski, Quebec

	Regular Season					Playoffs				
YR	GP	G	A	PTS	PM	GP	G	A	PTS	PM
2005-06	50	16	16	32	16	-	-	-	-	-
2006-07	73	19	29	48	30	5	0	2	2	6
Pitt. Totals	123	35	45	80	46	5	0	2	2	6
NHL Totals	190	52	64	116	58	5	0	2	2	6

Selected in the 2000 Entry Draft, 4th choice, 124th overall

Signed as a free agent by Tampa Bay, July 1, 2007

Bob Johnson (left) and Dennis Owchar (center) enjoy a break during a 1974 practice session.

OWCHAR, DENNIS (Owch)

Defense **Ht:** 5-11 **Wt:** 190 **Shoots:** right
B: March 28, 1953, Dryden, Ontario

	Regular Season					Playoffs				
YR	GP	G	A	PTS	PM	GP	G	A	PTS	PM
1974-75	46	6	11	17	67	6	0	1	1	4
1975-76	54	5	12	17	19	2	0	0	0	2
1976-77	46	5	18	23	37	-	-	-	-	-
1977-78	22	2	8	10	23	-	-	-	-	-
Pitt. Totals	168	18	49	67	146	8	0	1	1	6
NHL Totals	288	30	85	115	200	10	1	1	2	8

Selected in the 1973 Amateur Draft, 4th choice, 55th overall

Traded to Colorado for Tom Edur, December 2, 1977

P

PAEK, JIM

Defense **Ht:** 6-1 **Wt:** 195 **Shoots:** left
B: April 7, 1967, Seoul, Republic of Korea

	Regular Season					Playoffs				
YR	GP	G	A	PTS	PM	GP	G	A	PTS	PM
1990-91	3	0	0	0	9	8	1	0	1	2
1991-92	49	1	7	8	36	19	0	4	4	6
1992-93	77	3	15	18	64	-	-	-	-	-
1993-94	41	0	4	4	8	-	-	-	-	-
Pitt. Totals	170	4	26	30	117	27	1	4	5	8
NHL Totals	217	5	29	34	155	27	1	4	5	8

Selected in the 1985 Entry Draft, 9th choice, 170th overall

Traded to Los Angeles with Marty McSorley for Shawn McEachern and Tomas Sandstrom, February 16, 1994

PAIEMENT, WILFRED, JR. (Wilf)

Right Wing **Ht:** 6-1 **Wt:** 210 **Shoots:** right
B: October 16, 1955, Earlton, Ontario

	Regular Season					Playoffs				
YR	GP	G	A	PTS	PM	GP	G	A	PTS	PM
1987-88	23	2	6	8	39	-	-	-	-	-
Pitt. Totals	23	2	6	8	39	-	-	-	-	-
NHL Totals	946	356	458	814	1757	69	18	17	35	185

Signed as a free agent, September 10, 1987

PALFFY, ZIGMUND (Ziggy)

Right Wing **Ht:** 5-10 **Wt:** 183 **Shoots:** left
B: May 5, 1972, Skalica, Czechoslovakia

	Regular Season					Playoffs				
YR	GP	G	A	PTS	PM	GP	G	A	PTS	PM
2005-06	42	11	31	42	12	-	-	-	-	-
Pitt. Totals	42	11	31	42	12	-	-	-	-	-
NHL Totals	684	329	384	713	322	24	9	10	19	8

Signed as a free agent, August 6, 2005

Signed as a free agent by Skalica (Slovakia), July 19, 2007

Jim Paek was a steady defenseman on the Stanley Cup teams of the early 1990s.

PARADISE, ROBERT HARVEY (Bob)

Defense   Ht: 6-1 **Wt:** 205   **Shoots:** left
B: April 22, 1944, St. Paul, Minnesota

YR	Regular Season					Playoffs				
	GP	G	A	PTS	PM	GP	G	A	PTS	PM
1973-74	38	2	7	9	39	-	-	-	-	-
1974-75	78	3	15	18	109	6	0	1	1	17
1975-76	9	0	0	0	4	-	-	-	-	-
1977-78	64	2	10	12	53	-	-	-	-	-
1978-79	14	0	1	1	4	2	0	0	0	0
Pitt. Totals	**203**	**7**	**33**	**40**	**209**	**8**	**0**	**1**	**1**	**17**
NHL Totals	**368**	**8**	**54**	**62**	**393**	**12**	**0**	**1**	**1**	**19**

Acquired from Atlanta with Chuck Arnason for Al McDonough, January 4, 1974

Traded to Washington for a 2nd round choice in the 1976 Amateur Draft, November 26, 1975

Acquired from Washington for rights to Don Awrey, October 1, 1977

PARENT, RICH

Goaltender   Ht: 6-3 **Wt:** 195   **Catches:** left
B: January 12, 1973, Montreal, Quebec

YR	Regular Season					Playoffs				
	GP	MINS	GA	SH	AVE	GP	MINS	GA	SH	AVE
2000-01	7	332	17	0	3.07	-	-	-	-	-
Pitt. Totals	**7**	**332**	**17**	**0**	**3.07**	-	-	-	-	-
NHL Totals	**32**	**1561**	**82**	**1**	**3.15**	-	-	-	-	-

Signed as a free agent, September 20, 2000

Signed as a free agent by Iserlohn (Germany), July 12, 2001

PARK, RICHARD

Right Wing   Ht: 5-11 **Wt:** 190   **Shoots:** right
B: May 27, 1976, Seoul, Republic of Korea

YR	Regular Season					Playoffs				
	GP	G	A	PTS	PM	GP	G	A	PTS	PM
1994-95	1	0	1	1	2	3	0	0	0	2
1995-96	56	4	6	10	36	1	0	0	0	0
1996-97	1	0	0	0	0	-	-	-	-	-
Pitt. Totals	**58**	**4**	**7**	**11**	**38**	**4**	**0**	**0**	**0**	**2**
NHL Totals	**684**	**95**	**132**	**227**	**254**	**38**	**3**	**5**	**8**	**10**

Selected in the 1994 Entry Draft, 2nd choice, 50th overall

Traded to Anaheim for Roman Oksiuta, March 18, 1997

Rugged Bob Paradise clears future Pens coach Andre Savard away from the net.

PATTERSON, ED

Right Wing   Ht: 6-2 **Wt:** 213   **Shoots:** right
B: November 14, 1972, Delta, British Columbia

YR	Regular Season					Playoffs				
	GP	G	A	PTS	PM	GP	G	A	PTS	PM
1993-94	27	3	1	4	10	-	-	-	-	-
1995-96	35	0	2	2	38	-	-	-	-	-
1996-97	6	0	0	0	8	-	-	-	-	-
Pitt. Totals	**68**	**3**	**3**	**6**	**56**	-	-	-	-	-
NHL Totals	**68**	**3**	**3**	**6**	**56**	-	-	-	-	-

Selected in the 1991 Entry Draft, 7th choice, 148th overall

Signed as a free agent by Grand Rapids (IHL), September 14, 1999

PEARSON, GEORGE ALEXANDER MELVIN (Mel)

Left Wing   Ht: 5-10 **Wt:** 175   **Shoots:** left
B: April 29, 1938, Flin Flon, Manitoba
D: January 9, 1999

YR	Regular Season					Playoffs				
	GP	G	A	PTS	PM	GP	G	A	PTS	PM
1967-68	2	0	1	1	0	-	-	-	-	-
Pitt. Totals	**2**	**0**	**1**	**1**	**0**	-	-	-	-	-
NHL Totals	**38**	**2**	**6**	**8**	**25**	-	-	-	-	-
WHA Totals	**70**	**8**	**12**	**20**	**12**	**5**	**2**	**0**	**2**	**0**

Selected from Chicago in the 1967 Expansion Draft, June 6, 1967

Sold to Portland (WHL), August 1969

PECHURSKI, ALEXANDER

Goaltender   **Ht:** 6-0   **Wt:** 187   **Catches:** left
B: June 4, 1990, Magnitogorsk, USSR

	Regular Season					Playoffs				
YR	GP	MINS	GA	SH	AVE	GP	MINS	GA	SH	AVE
2009-10	1	36	1	0	1.67	-	-	-	-	-
Pitt. Totals	1	36	1	0	1.67	-	-	-	-	-
NHL Totals	1	36	1	0	1.67	-	-	-	-	-

Selected in the 2008 Entry Draft, 2nd choice, 150th overall

PEDERSON, BARRY ALAN

Center   **Ht:** 5-11   **Wt:** 185   **Shoots:** right
B: March 13, 1961, Big River, Saskatchewan

	Regular Season					Playoffs				
YR	GP	G	A	PTS	PM	GP	G	A	PTS	PM
1989-90	38	4	18	22	29	-	-	-	-	-
1990-91	46	6	8	14	21	-	-	-	-	-
Pitt. Totals	84	10	26	36	50	-	-	-	-	-
NHL Totals	701	238	416	654	472	34	22	30	52	25

Acquired from Vancouver with Rod Buskas and Tony Tanti for Dave Capuano, Andrew McBain, and Dan Quinn, January 8, 1990

Signed as a free agent by Hartford, September 5, 1991

PESONEN, JANNE

Left Wing   **Ht:** 5-11   **Wt:** 180   **Shoots:** left
B: May 11, 1982, Suomussalmi, Finland

	Regular Season					Playoffs				
YR	GP	G	A	PTS	PM	GP	G	A	PTS	PM
2008-09	7	0	0	0	0	-	-	-	-	-
Pitt. Totals	7	0	0	0	0	-	-	-	-	-
NHL Totals	7	0	0	0	0	-	-	-	-	-

Signed as a free agent, July 7, 2008

Signed as a free agent by Ak Bars Kazan (KHL), August 4, 2009

PETERSEN, TOBY

Center   **Ht:** 5-10   **Wt:** 197   **Shoots:** left
B: October 27, 1978, Minneapolis, Minnesota

	Regular Season					Playoffs				
YR	GP	G	A	PTS	PM	GP	G	A	PTS	PM
2000-01	12	2	6	8	4	-	-	-	-	-
2001-02	79	8	10	18	4	-	-	-	-	-
Pitt. Totals	91	10	16	26	8	-	-	-	-	-
NHL Totals	298	29	41	70	36	18	1	0	1	2

Selected in the 1998 Entry Draft, 9th choice, 244th overall

Signed as a free agent by Edmonton, July 30, 2004

PETROVICKY, RONALD

Right Wing   **Ht:** 5-11   **Wt:** 190   **Shoots:** right
B: February 15, 1977, Zilina, Czechoslovakia

	Regular Season					Playoffs				
YR	GP	G	A	PTS	PM	GP	G	A	PTS	PM
2006-07	31	3	3	6	28	3	0	0	0	2
Pitt. Totals	31	3	3	6	28	3	0	0	0	2
NHL Totals	342	41	51	92	429	3	0	0	0	2

Signed as a free agent, July 24, 2006

PIETRANGELO, FRANK

Goaltender   **Ht:** 5-10   **Wt:** 185   **Catches:** left
B: December 17, 1964, Niagara Falls, Ontario

	Regular Season					Playoffs				
YR	GP	MINS	GA	SH	AVE	GP	MINS	GA	SH	AVE
1987-88	21	1207	80	1	3.98	-	-	-	-	-
1988-89	15	669	45	0	4.04	-	-	-	-	-
1989-90	21	1066	77	0	4.33	-	-	-	-	-
1990-91	25	1311	86	0	3.94	5	288	15	1	3.12
1991-92	5	225	20	0	5.33	-	-	-	-	-
Pitt. Totals	87	4478	308	1	4.13	5	288	15	1	3.12
NHL Totals	141	7141	490	1	4.12	12	713	34	1	2.86

Selected in the 1983 Entry Draft, 4th choice, 64th overall

Traded to Hartford for 3rd and 7th round choices in the 1994 Entry Draft, March 10, 1992

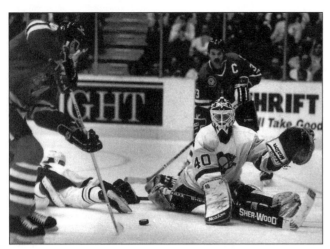

Frank Pietrangelo does a split as he prepares to gobble up a shot.

PIRJETA, LASSE

Center/Left Wing   Ht: 6-4 **Wt:** 225   **Shoots:** left
B: April 4, 1974, Haukipudas, Finland

YR	Regular Season					Playoffs				
	GP	G	A	PTS	PM	GP	G	A	PTS	PM
2003-04	13	6	6	12	0	-	-	-	-	-
2005-06	25	4	3	7	18	-	-	-	-	-
Pitt. Totals	38	10	9	19	18	-	-	-	-	-
NHL Totals	146	23	27	50	50	-	-	-	-	-

Acquired from Columbus for Brian Holzinger, March 9, 2004

Assigned to Kloten (Switzerland), January 20, 2006

PITTIS, DOMENIC

Center   Ht: 5-11 **Wt:** 190   **Shoots:** left
B: October 1, 1974, Calgary, Alberta

YR	Regular Season					Playoffs				
	GP	G	A	PTS	PM	GP	G	A	PTS	PM
1996-97	1	0	0	0	0	-	-	-	-	-
Pitt. Totals	1	0	0	0	0	-	-	-	-	-
NHL Totals	86	5	11	16	71	3	0	0	0	2

Selected in the 1993 Entry Draft, 2nd choice, 52nd overall

Signed as a free agent by Buffalo, August 10, 1998

PLASSE, MICHEL PIERRE

Goaltender   Ht: 5-11 **Wt:** 172   **Catches:** left
B: June 1, 1948, Montreal, Quebec
D: December 30, 2006

YR	Regular Season					Playoffs				
	GP	MINS	GA	SH	AVE	GP	MINS	GA	SH	AVE
1974-75	20	1094	73	0	4.00	-	-	-	-	-
1975-76	55	3096	178	2	3.45	3	180	8	1	2.67
Pitt. Totals	75	4190	251	2	3.59	3	180	8	1	2.67
NHL Totals	299	16760	1058	2	3.79	4	195	9	1	2.77

Acquired from Kansas City for Denis Herron and Jean-Guy Lagace, January 10, 1975

Sent to Colorado with Simon Nolet and the loan of Colin Campbell for the 1976-77 season for Denis Herron, August 7, 1976

POAPST, STEVE

Defense   Ht: 6-0 **Wt:** 199   **Shoots:** left
B: January 3, 1969, Cornwall, Ontario

YR	Regular Season					Playoffs				
	GP	G	A	PTS	PM	GP	G	A	PTS	PM
2005-06	21	0	4	4	10	-	-	-	-	-
Pitt. Totals	21	0	4	4	10	-	-	-	-	-
NHL Totals	307	8	28	36	173	11	0	0	0	0

Signed as a free agent, August 15, 2005

Traded to St. Louis for Eric Boguniecki, December 9, 2005

POLIS, GREGORY LINN (Greg)

Left Wing   Ht: 6-0 **Wt:** 195   **Shoots:** left
B: August 8, 1950, Westlock, Alberta

YR	Regular Season					Playoffs				
	GP	G	A	PTS	PM	GP	G	A	PTS	PM
1970-71	61	18	15	33	40	-	-	-	-	-
1971-72	76	30	19	49	38	4	0	2	2	0
1972-73	78	26	23	49	36	-	-	-	-	-
1973-74	41	14	13	27	32	-	-	-	-	-
Pitt. Totals	256	88	70	158	146	4	0	2	2	0
NHL Totals	615	174	169	343	391	7	0	2	2	6

Selected in the 1970 Amateur Draft, 1st choice, 7th overall

Traded to St. Louis with Bryan Watson and a 2nd round choice in the 1974 Amateur Draft for Ab DeMarco, Steve Durbano, and Bob Kelly, January 17, 1974

West Division All-Star 1970-71, 1971-72, 1972-73

All-Star Game MVP 1973

PONIKAROVSKY, ALEXEI (Poni)

Left Wing   Ht: 6-4 **Wt:** 220   **Shoots:** left
B: April 9, 1980, Kiev, USSR

	Regular Season					Playoffs				
YR	GP	G	A	PTS	PM	GP	G	A	PTS	PM
2009-10	16	2	7	9	17	11	1	4	5	4
Pitt. Totals	16	2	7	9	17	11	1	4	5	4
NHL Totals	493	116	150	266	335	34	2	7	9	16

Acquired from Toronto for Luca Caputi and Martin Skoula, March 2, 2010

Signed as a free agent by Los Angeles, July 27, 2010

POPOVIC, PETER

Defense   Ht: 6-6 **Wt:** 243   **Shoots:** left
B: February 10, 1968, Koping, Sweden

	Regular Season					Playoffs				
YR	GP	G	A	PTS	PM	GP	G	A	PTS	PM
1999-00	54	1	5	6	30	10	0	0	0	10
Pitt. Totals	54	1	5	6	30	10	0	0	0	10
NHL Totals	485	10	63	73	291	35	1	4	5	18

Acquired from NY Rangers for Kevin Hatcher, September 30, 1999

Signed as a free agent by Boston, July 2, 2000

PRATT, KELLY EDWARD

Right Wing   Ht: 5-9 **Wt:** 170   **Shoots:** right
B: February 8, 1953, High Prairie, Alberta

	Regular Season					Playoffs				
YR	GP	G	A	PTS	PM	GP	G	A	PTS	PM
1974-75	22	0	6	6	15	-	-	-	-	-
Pitt. Totals	22	0	6	6	15	-	-	-	-	-
NHL Totals	22	0	6	6	15	-	-	-	-	-
WHA Totals	46	4	6	10	50	-	-	-	-	-

Signed as a free agent, July 15, 1974

Sold to Hershey (AHL), August 28, 1975

PRATT, TRACY ARNOLD

Defense   Ht: 6-2 **Wt:** 195   **Shoots:** left
B: March 8, 1943, New York, New York

	Regular Season					Playoffs				
YR	GP	G	A	PTS	PM	GP	G	A	PTS	PM
1968-69	18	0	5	5	34	-	-	-	-	-
1969-70	65	5	7	12	124	10	0	1	1	51
Pitt. Totals	83	5	12	17	158	10	0	1	1	51
NHL Totals	580	17	97	114	1026	25	0	1	1	62

Acquired from Oakland with George Swarbrick and Bryan Watson for Earl Ingarfield, Dick Mattiussi, and Gene Ubriaco, January 30, 1969

Selected by Buffalo in the 1970 Expansion Draft, June 10, 1970

PRENTICE, DEAN SUTHERLAND

Left Wing   Ht: 5-11 **Wt:** 180   **Shoots:** left
B: October 5, 1932, Schumacher, Ontario

	Regular Season					Playoffs				
YR	GP	G	A	PTS	PM	GP	G	A	PTS	PM
1969-70	75	26	25	51	14	10	2	5	7	8
1970-71	69	21	17	38	18	-	-	-	-	-
Pitt. Totals	144	47	42	89	32	10	2	5	7	8
NHL Totals	1378	391	469	860	484	54	13	17	30	38

Claimed from Detroit in the Intra-League Draft, June 11, 1969

Sold to Minnesota, October 6, 1971

West Division All-Star 1969-70

PRICE, GARRY NOEL (Noel)

Defense   Ht: 6-0 **Wt:** 185   **Shoots:** left
B: December 9, 1935, Brockville, Ontario

	Regular Season					Playoffs				
YR	GP	G	A	PTS	PM	GP	G	A	PTS	PM
1967-68	70	6	27	33	48	-	-	-	-	-
1968-69	73	2	18	20	61	-	-	-	-	-
Pitt. Totals	143	8	45	53	109	-	-	-	-	-
NHL Totals	499	14	114	128	333	12	0	1	1	8

Selected from Montreal in the 1967 Expansion Draft, June 6, 1967

Claimed by Springfield (AHL) in the Reverse Draft, June 12, 1969

Known for his rugged play, Pat Price lugs the puck against the Whalers.

PRICE, SHAUN PATRICK (Pat)

Defense   Ht: 6-2 **Wt:** 200   **Shoots:** left
B: March 24, 1955, Nelson, British Columbia

YR	Regular Season					Playoffs				
	GP	G	A	PTS	PM	GP	G	A	PTS	PM
1980-81	13	0	10	10	33	5	1	1	2	21
1981-82	77	7	31	38	322	5	0	0	0	28
1982-83	38	1	11	12	104	-	-	-	-	-
Pitt. Totals	128	8	52	60	459	10	1	1	2	49
NHL Totals	726	43	218	261	1456	74	2	10	12	195
WHA Totals	68	5	29	34	15	-	-	-	-	-

Acquired from Edmonton for Pat Hughes, March 10, 1981

Claimed on waivers by Quebec, December 31, 1982

PRICE, THOMAS EDWARD (Tom)

Defense   Ht: 6-1 **Wt:** 190   **Shoots:** left
B: July 12, 1954, Toronto, Ontario

YR	Regular Season					Playoffs				
	GP	G	A	PTS	PM	GP	G	A	PTS	PM
1976-77	7	0	2	2	4	-	-	-	-	-
1977-78	10	0	0	0	0	-	-	-	-	-
1978-79	2	0	0	0	4	-	-	-	-	-
Pitt. Totals	19	0	2	2	8	-	-	-	-	-
NHL Totals	29	0	2	2	12	-	-	-	-	-

Signed as a free agent, February 28, 1977

PRIESTLAY, KEN

Center   Ht: 5-10 **Wt:** 190   **Shoots:** left
B: August 24, 1967, Richmond, British Columbia

YR	Regular Season					Playoffs				
	GP	G	A	PTS	PM	GP	G	A	PTS	PM
1990-91	2	0	1	1	0	-	-	-	-	-
1991-92	49	2	8	10	4	-	-	-	-	-
Pitt. Totals	51	2	9	11	4	-	-	-	-	-
NHL Totals	168	27	34	61	63	14	0	0	0	21

Acquired from Buffalo for Tony Tanti, March 5, 1991

PRIMEAU, WAYNE

Center   Ht: 6-4 **Wt:** 225   **Shoots:** left
B: June 4, 1976, Scarborough, Ontario

YR	Regular Season					Playoffs				
	GP	G	A	PTS	PM	GP	G	A	PTS	PM
2000-01	28	1	6	7	54	18	1	3	4	2
2001-02	33	3	7	10	18	-	-	-	-	-
2002-03	70	5	11	16	55	-	-	-	-	-
Pitt. Totals	131	9	24	33	127	18	1	3	4	2
NHL Totals	774	69	125	194	789	90	7	14	21	42

Acquired from Tampa Bay for Matthew Barnaby, February 1, 2001

Traded to San Jose for Matt Bradley, March 11, 2003

PRONGER, SEAN

Center   Ht: 6-3 **Wt:** 209   **Shoots:** left
B: November 30, 1972, Thunder Bay, Ontario

YR	Regular Season					Playoffs				
	GP	G	A	PTS	PM	GP	G	A	PTS	PM
1997-98	5	1	0	1	2	5	0	0	0	4
1998-99	2	0	0	0	0	-	-	-	-	-
Pitt. Totals	7	1	0	1	2	5	0	0	0	4
NHL Totals	260	23	36	59	159	14	0	2	2	8

Acquired from Anaheim for Patrick Lalime, March 24, 1998

Traded to NY Rangers with Petr Nedved and Chris Tamer for Alexei Kovalev and Harry York, November 25, 1998

PRONOVOST, JOSEPH JEAN DENIS (Jean)

Right Wing   **Ht:** 6-0 **Wt:** 185   **Shoots:** right
B: December 18, 1945, Shawinigan Falls, Quebec

	Regular Season					Playoffs				
YR	GP	G	A	PTS	PM	GP	G	A	PTS	PM
1968-69	76	16	25	41	41	-	-	-	-	-
1969-70	72	20	21	41	45	10	3	4	7	2
1970-71	78	21	24	45	35	-	-	-	-	-
1971-72	68	30	23	53	12	4	1	1	2	0
1972-73	66	21	22	43	16	-	-	-	-	-
1973-74	77	40	32	72	22	-	-	-	-	-
1974-75	78	43	32	75	37	9	3	3	6	6
1975-76	**80**	52	52	104	24	3	0	0	0	2
1976-77	79	33	31	64	24	3	2	1	3	2
1977-78	79	40	25	65	50	-	-	-	-	-
Pitt. Totals	**753**	**316**	**287**	**603**	**306**	**29**	**9**	**9**	**18**	**12**
NHL Totals	**998**	**391**	**383**	**774**	**413**	**35**	**11**	**9**	**20**	**14**

Acquired from Boston with John Arbour for a 1st round choice in the 1969 Amateur Draft and cash, May 21, 1968

Traded to Atlanta for Gregg Sheppard, September 6, 1978

Prince of Wales Conference All-Star 1974-75, 1975-76, 1976-77, 1977-78

Penguins Hall of Fame, 1992

PUSHOR, JAMIE

Defense   **Ht:** 6-3 **Wt:** 218   **Shoots:** right
B: February 11, 1973, Lethbridge, Alberta

	Regular Season					Playoffs				
YR	GP	G	A	PTS	PM	GP	G	A	PTS	PM
2001-02	15	0	2	2	30	-	-	-	-	-
2002-03	76	3	1	4	76	-	-	-	-	-
Pitt. Totals	**91**	**3**	**3**	**6**	**106**	**-**	**-**	**-**	**-**	**-**
NHL Totals	**521**	**14**	**46**	**60**	**648**	**14**	**0**	**1**	**1**	**16**

Acquired from Columbus for a 4th round draft choice in the 2003 Entry Draft, March 15, 2002

Signed by Syracuse (AHL) as a free agent, November 18, 2003

Q

QUINN, DAN

Center   **Ht:** 5-11 **Wt:** 182   **Shoots:** left
B: June 1, 1965, Ottawa, Ontario

	Regular Season					Playoffs				
YR	GP	G	A	PTS	PM	GP	G	A	PTS	PM
1986-87	64	28	43	71	40	-	-	-	-	-
1987-88	70	40	39	79	50	-	-	-	-	-
1988-89	79	34	60	94	102	11	6	3	9	10
1989-90	41	9	20	29	22	-	-	-	-	-
1996-97	16	0	3	3	10	-	-	-	-	-
Pitt. Totals	**270**	**111**	**165**	**276**	**224**	**11**	**6**	**3**	**9**	**10**
NHL Totals	**805**	**266**	**419**	**685**	**533**	**65**	**22**	**26**	**48**	**62**

Acquired from Calgary for Mike Bullard, November 12, 1986

Traded to Vancouver with Dave Capuano and Andrew McBain for Rod Buskas, Barry Pederson, and Tony Tanti, January 8, 1990

Signed as a free agent, July 17, 1996

Dan Quinn (10) and future Pen Alain Chevrier eye a fluttering puck.

R

RAMSEY, MICHAEL ALLAN (Mike)

Defense   Ht: 6-3 **Wt:** 195   **Shoots:** left
B: December 3, 1960, Minneapolis, Minnesota

YR	GP	G	A	PTS	PM	GP	G	A	PTS	PM
		Regular Season					Playoffs			
1992-93	12	1	2	3	8	12	0	6	6	4
1993-94	65	2	2	4	22	1	0	0	0	0
Pitt. Totals	77	3	4	7	30	13	0	6	6	4
NHL Totals	1070	79	266	345	1012	115	8	29	37	176

Acquired from Buffalo for Bob Errey, March 22, 1993

Signed as a free agent by Detroit, August 3, 1994

RECCHI, MARK

Right Wing   Ht: 5-10 **Wt:** 195   **Shoots:** left
B: February 1, 1968, Kamloops, British Columbia

YR	GP	G	A	PTS	PM	GP	G	A	PTS	PM
		Regular Season					Playoffs			
1988-89	15	1	1	2	0	-	-	-	-	-
1989-90	74	30	37	67	44	-	-	-	-	-
1990-91	78	40	73	113	48	24	10	24	34	33
1991-92	58	33	37	70	78	-	-	-	-	-
2005-06	63	24	33	57	56	-	-	-	-	-
2006-07	82	24	44	68	62	5	0	4	4	0
2007-08	19	2	6	8	12	-	-	-	-	-
Pitt. Totals	389	154	231	385	300	29	10	28	38	33
NHL Totals	1571	563	922	1485	998	164	56	77	133	85

Selected in the 1988 Entry Draft, 4th choice, 67th overall

Traded to Philadelphia with Brian Benning and a 1st round choice in the 1992 Entry Draft (acquired from LA) for Kjell Samuelsson, Rick Tocchet, Ken Wregget, and a 3rd round choice in the 1993 Entry Draft, February 19, 1992

Signed as a free agent, July 9, 2004

Traded to Carolina for Krys Kolanos, Niklas Nordgren, and a 2nd round choice in the 2007 Entry Draft, March 9, 2006

Signed as a free agent, July 25, 2006

Claimed on waivers by Atlanta, December 8, 2007

Prince of Wales Conference All-Star 1990-91

REDQUEST, GREG

Goaltender   Ht: 5-10 **Wt:** 190   **Catches:** left
B: July 30, 1956, Toronto, Ontario

YR	GP	MINS	GA	SH	AVE	GP	MINS	GA	SH	AVE
		Regular Season					Playoffs			
1977-78	1	13	3	0	13.85	-	-	-	-	-
Pitt. Totals	1	13	3	0	13.85	-	-	-	-	-
NHL Totals	1	13	3	0	13.85	-	-	-	-	-

Selected in the 1976 Amateur Draft, 5th choice, 65th overall

RICCI, JOSEPH NICK (Nick)

Goaltender   Ht: 5-10 **Wt:** 160   **Catches:** left
B: June 3, 1959, Niagara Falls, Ontario

YR	GP	MINS	GA	SH	AVE	GP	MINS	GA	SH	AVE
		Regular Season					Playoffs			
1979-80	4	240	14	0	3.50	-	-	-	-	-
1980-81	9	540	35	0	3.89	-	-	-	-	-
1981-82	3	160	14	0	5.25	-	-	-	-	-
1982-83	3	147	16	0	6.53	-	-	-	-	-
Pitt. Totals	19	1087	79	0	4.36	-	-	-	-	-
NHL Totals	19	1087	79	0	4.36	-	-	-	-	-

Selected in the 1979 Entry Draft, 4th choice, 94th overall

Traded to Toronto with Pat Graham for Rocky Saganiuk and Vincent Tremblay, August 15, 1983

RICHER, STEPHANE

Right Wing   Ht: 6-2 **Wt:** 215   **Shoots:** right
B: June 7, 1966, Ripon, Quebec

YR	GP	G	A	PTS	PM	GP	G	A	PTS	PM
		Regular Season					Playoffs			
2001-02	58	13	12	25	14	-	-	-	-	-
Pitt. Totals	58	13	12	25	14	-	-	-	-	-
NHL Totals	1054	421	398	819	614	134	53	45	98	61

Signed as a free agent, October 2, 2001

Traded to New Jersey for a 7th round choice in the 2003 Entry Draft, March 19, 2002

Pat Riggin scrambles to stop a shot.

RISSLING, GARY DANIEL (Pac Man)

Left Wing   **Ht:** 5-9 **Wt:** 175   **Shoots:** left
B: August 8, 1956, Saskatoon, Saskatchewan

YR	Regular Season					Playoffs				
	GP	G	A	PTS	PM	GP	G	A	PTS	PM
1980-81	25	1	0	1	143	5	0	1	1	4
1981-82	16	0	0	0	55	-	-	-	-	-
1982-83	40	5	4	9	128	-	-	-	-	-
1983-84	47	4	13	17	297	-	-	-	-	-
1984-85	56	10	9	19	209	-	-	-	-	-
Pitt. Totals	**184**	**20**	**26**	**46**	**832**	**5**	**0**	**1**	**1**	**4**
NHL Totals	**221**	**23**	**30**	**53**	**1008**	**5**	**0**	**1**	**1**	**4**

Acquired from Washington for a 5th round choice in the 1981 Entry Draft, January 2, 1981

RITA, JANI

Left Wing   **Ht:** 6-1 **Wt:** 206   **Shoots:** left
B: July 25, 1981, Helsinki, Finland

YR	Regular Season					Playoffs				
	GP	G	A	PTS	PM	GP	G	A	PTS	PM
2005-06	30	3	4	7	4	-	-	-	-	-
Pitt. Totals	**30**	**3**	**4**	**7**	**4**	**-**	**-**	**-**	**-**	**-**
NHL Totals	**66**	**9**	**5**	**14**	**10**	**-**	**-**	**-**	**-**	**-**

Acquired from Edmonton with Cory Cross for Dick Tarnstrom, January 26, 2006

RIGGIN, PATRICK MICHAEL (Pat)

Goaltender   **Ht:** 5-9 **Wt:** 170   **Catches:** right
B: May 26, 1959, Kincardine, Ontario

YR	Regular Season					Playoffs				
	GP	MINS	GA	SH	AVE	GP	MINS	GA	SH	AVE
1986-87	17	988	55	0	3.34	-	-	-	-	-
1987-88	22	1169	76	0	3.90	-	-	-	-	-
Pitt. Totals	**39**	**2157**	**131**	**0**	**3.64**	**-**	**-**	**-**	**-**	**-**
NHL Totals	**350**	**19872**	**1135**	**11**	**3.43**	**25**	**1336**	**72**	**0**	**3.23**
WHA Totals	**46**	**2511**	**158**	**1**	**3.78**	**-**	**-**	**-**	**-**	**-**

Acquired from Boston for Roberto Romano, February 6, 1987

Scrappy Gary Rissling mugs for the camera.

RIVARD, JOSEPH ROBERT (Bob)

Center/Left Wing   Ht: 5-8 **Wt:** 155   **Shoots:** left
B: August 1, 1939, Sherbrooke, Quebec

	Regular Season					Playoffs				
YR	GP	G	A	PTS	PM	GP	G	A	PTS	PM
1967-68	27	5	12	17	4	-	-	-	-	-
Pitt. Totals	27	5	12	17	4	-	-	-	-	-
NHL Totals	27	5	12	17	4	-	-	-	-	-

Selected from Montreal in the 1967 Expansion Draft, June 6, 1967

Traded to Baltimore (AHL) as compensation for Jim Morrison, November 1969

ROBERT, RENE PAUL

Right Wing   Ht: 5-10 **Wt:** 184   **Shoots:** right
B: December 31, 1948, Trois-Rivieres, Quebec

	Regular Season					Playoffs				
YR	GP	G	A	PTS	PM	GP	G	A	PTS	PM
1971-72	49	7	11	18	42	-	-	-	-	-
Pitt. Totals	49	7	11	18	42	-	-	-	-	-
NHL Totals	744	284	418	702	597	50	22	19	41	73

Claimed from Buffalo in the Intra-League Draft, June 8, 1971

Traded to Buffalo for Eddie Shack, March 4, 1972

ROBERTS, GARY

Left Wing   Ht: 6-2 **Wt:** 215   **Shoots:** left
B: May 23, 1966, North York, Ontario

	Regular Season					Playoffs				
YR	GP	G	A	PTS	PM	GP	G	A	PTS	PM
2006-07	19	7	6	13	26	5	2	2	4	2
2007-08	38	3	12	15	40	11	2	2	4	32
Pitt. Totals	57	10	18	28	66	16	4	4	8	34
NHL Totals	1224	438	472	910	2560	130	32	61	93	332

Acquired from Florida for Noah Welch, February 27, 2007

Rights traded to Tampa Bay with rights to Ryan Malone for a 3rd round choice in the 2009 Entry Draft, June 28, 2008

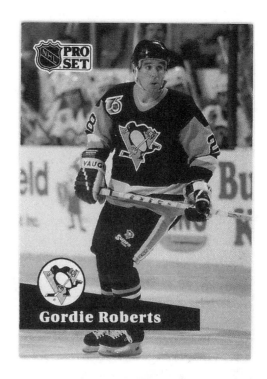

Gordie Roberts

ROBERTS, GORDON DOUGLAS (Gordie)

Defense   Ht: 6-1 **Wt:** 195   **Shoots:** left
B: October 2, 1957, Detroit, Michigan

	Regular Season					Playoffs				
YR	GP	G	A	PTS	PM	GP	G	A	PTS	PM
1990-91	61	3	12	15	70	**24**	1	2	3	63
1991-92	73	2	22	24	87	19	0	2	2	32
Pitt. Totals	134	5	34	39	157	43	1	4	5	95
NHL Totals	1097	61	359	420	1582	153	10	47	57	273
WHA Totals	311	42	144	186	502	46	4	20	24	79

Acquired from St. Louis for an 11th round choice in the 1992 Entry Draft, October 27, 1990

Signed as a free agent by Boston, July 23, 1992

ROBITAILLE, LUC

Left Wing   Ht: 6-1 **Wt:** 215   **Shoots:** left
B: February 17, 1966, Montreal, Quebec

	Regular Season					Playoffs				
YR	GP	G	A	PTS	PM	GP	G	A	PTS	PM
1994-95	46	23	19	42	37	12	7	4	11	26
Pitt. Totals	46	23	19	42	37	12	7	4	11	26
NHL Totals	1431	668	726	1394	1177	159	58	69	127	174

Acquired from Los Angeles for Rick Tocchet and a 2nd round choice in the 1995 Entry Draft, July 29, 1994

Traded to NY Rangers with Ulf Samuelsson for Petr Nedved and Sergei Zubov, August 31, 1995

Hockey Hall of Fame (Player), 2009

ROBITAILLE, RANDY

Center   **Ht:** 5-11 **Wt:** 200   **Shoots:** left
B: October 12, 1975, Ottawa, Ontario

YR	Regular Season					Playoffs				
	GP	G	A	PTS	PM	GP	G	A	PTS	PM
2001-02	40	10	20	30	16	-	-	-	-	-
2002-03	41	5	12	17	8	-	-	-	-	-
Pitt. Totals	81	15	32	47	24	-	-	-	-	-
NHL Totals	531	84	172	256	201	13	1	4	5	8

Claimed on waivers from Los Angeles, January 4, 2002

Traded to NY Islanders for a 5th round choice in the 2003 Entry Draft, March 9, 2003

ROCHE, DAVE

Left Wing   **Ht:** 6-4 **Wt:** 230   **Shoots:** left
B: June 13, 1975, Lindsay, Ontario

YR	Regular Season					Playoffs				
	GP	G	A	PTS	PM	GP	G	A	PTS	PM
1995-96	71	7	7	14	130	16	2	7	9	26
1996-97	61	5	5	10	155	-	-	-	-	-
Pitt. Totals	132	12	12	24	285	16	2	7	9	26
NHL Totals	171	15	15	30	334	16	2	7	9	26

Selected in the 1993 Entry Draft, 3rd choice, 62nd overall

Traded to Calgary with Ken Wregget for Todd Hlushko and German Titov, June 17, 1998

ROMANO, ROBERTO

Goaltender   **Ht:** 5-6 **Wt:** 170   **Catches:** left
B: October 10, 1962, Montreal, Quebec

YR	Regular Season					Playoffs				
	GP	MINS	GA	SH	AVE	GP	MINS	GA	SH	AVE
1982-83	3	155	18	0	6.97	-	-	-	-	-
1983-84	18	1020	78	1	4.59	-	-	-	-	-
1984-85	31	1629	120	1	4.42	-	-	-	-	-
1985-86	46	2684	159	2	3.55	-	-	-	-	-
1986-87	25	1438	87	0	3.63	-	-	-	-	-
1993-94	2	125	3	0	1.44	-	-	-	-	-
Pitt. Totals	125	7051	465	4	3.96	-	-	-	-	-
NHL Totals	126	7111	471	4	3.97	-	-	-	-	-

Signed as a free agent, December 6, 1982

Traded to Boston for Pat Riggin, February 6, 1987

Signed as a free agent, October 7, 1993

ROULSTON, THOMAS (Tom)

Center/Right Wing   **Ht:** 6-1 **Wt:** 184   **Shoots:** right
B: November 20, 1957, Winnipeg, Manitoba

YR	Regular Season					Playoffs				
	GP	G	A	PTS	PM	GP	G	A	PTS	PM
1983-84	53	11	17	28	8	-	-	-	-	-
1985-86	5	0	0	0	2	-	-	-	-	-
Pitt. Totals	58	11	17	28	10	-	-	-	-	-
NHL Totals	195	47	49	96	74	21	2	2	4	2

Acquired from Edmonton for Kevin McClelland and a 6th round choice in the 1984 Entry Draft, December 5, 1983

ROWE, MIKE

Defense   **Ht:** 6-1 **Wt:** 208   **Shoots:** left
B: March 8, 1965, Kingston, Ontario

YR	Regular Season					Playoffs				
	GP	G	A	PTS	PM	GP	G	A	PTS	PM
1984-85	6	0	0	0	7	-	-	-	-	-
1985-86	3	0	0	0	4	-	-	-	-	-
1986-87	2	0	0	0	0	-	-	-	-	-
Pitt. Totals	11	0	0	0	11	-	-	-	-	-
NHL Totals	11	0	0	0	11	-	-	-	-	-

Selected in the 1983 Entry Draft, 3rd choice, 59th overall

ROY, ANDRE

Right Wing   **Ht:** 6-4 **Wt:** 229   **Shoots:** left
B: February 8, 1975, Port Chester, New York

YR	Regular Season					Playoffs				
	GP	G	A	PTS	PM	GP	G	A	PTS	PM
2005-06	42	2	1	3	116	-	-	-	-	-
2006-07	5	0	0	0	12	-	-	-	-	-
Pitt. Totals	47	2	1	3	128	-	-	-	-	-
NHL Totals	515	35	33	68	1169	41	1	3	4	98

Signed as a free agent, August 4, 2005

Claimed on waivers by Tampa Bay, December 2, 2006

ROZSIVAL, MICHAL

Defense   **Ht:** 6-2 **Wt:** 210   **Shoots:** right
B: September 3, 1978, Vlasim, Czechoslovakia

YR	Regular Season					Playoffs				
	GP	G	A	PTS	PM	GP	G	A	PTS	PM
1999-00	75	4	17	21	48	2	0	0	0	4
2000-01	30	1	4	5	26	-	-	-	-	-
2001-02	79	9	20	29	47	-	-	-	-	-
2002-03	53	4	6	10	40	-	-	-	-	-
Pitt. Totals	237	18	47	65	161	2	0	0	0	4
NHL Totals	637	57	169	226	513	33	4	10	14	36

Selected in the 1996 Entry Draft, 5th choice, 105th overall

Signed as a free agent by NY Rangers, August 29, 2005

RUPP, DUANE EDWARD FRANKLIN

Defense   **Ht:** 6-1 **Wt:** 195   **Shoots:** left
B: March 29, 1938, MacNutt, Saskatchewan

YR	Regular Season					Playoffs				
	GP	G	A	PTS	PM	GP	G	A	PTS	PM
1968-69	30	3	10	13	24	-	-	-	-	-
1969-70	64	2	14	16	18	6	2	2	4	2
1970-71	59	5	28	33	34	-	-	-	-	-
1971-72	34	4	18	22	32	4	0	0	0	6
1972-73	78	7	13	20	62	-	-	-	-	-
Pitt. Totals	265	21	83	104	170	10	2	2	4	8
NHL Totals	374	24	93	117	220	10	2	2	4	8
WHA Totals	115	3	42	45	78	7	0	2	2	0

Acquired from Minnesota for Leo Boivin, January 24, 1969

Signed as a free agent with Vancouver (WHA), June 1974

RUPP, MIKE

Left Wing   **Ht:** 6-5 **Wt:** 230   **Shoots:** left
B: January 13, 1980, Cleveland, Ohio

YR	Regular Season					Playoffs				
	GP	G	A	PTS	PM	GP	G	A	PTS	PM
2009-10	81	13	6	19	120	11	0	0	0	8
Pitt. Totals	81	13	6	19	120	11	0	0	0	8
NHL Totals	416	40	32	72	532	36	1	5	6	31

Signed as a free agent, July 1, 2009

RUSKOWSKI, TERRY WALLACE (Rosco)

Left Wing/Center   **Ht:** 5-10 **Wt:** 178   **Shoots:** left
B: December 31, 1954, Prince Albert, Saskatchewan

YR	Regular Season					Playoffs				
	GP	G	A	PTS	PM	GP	G	A	PTS	PM
1985-86	73	26	37	63	162	-	-	-	-	-
1986-87	70	14	37	51	145	-	-	-	-	-
Pitt. Totals	143	40	74	114	307	-	-	-	-	-
NHL Totals	630	113	313	426	1354	21	1	6	7	86
WHA Totals	369	83	254	337	761	52	18	36	54	174

Signed as a free agent, October 3, 1985

Signed as a free agent with Minnesota, July 1987

RUTHERFORD, JAMES EARL (Jim)

Goaltender   **Ht:** 5-8 **Wt:** 168   **Catches:** left
B: February 17, 1949, Beeton, Ontario

YR	Regular Season					Playoffs				
	GP	MINS	GA	SH	AVE	GP	MINS	GA	SH	AVE
1971-72	40	2160	116	1	3.22	4	240	14	0	3.50
1972-73	49	2660	129	3	2.91	-	-	-	-	-
1973-74	26	1432	82	0	3.44	-	-	-	-	-
Pitt. Totals	115	6252	327	4	3.14	4	240	14	0	3.50
NHL Totals	457	25895	1576	14	3.65	8	440	28	0	3.82

Selected from Detroit in the Intra-League Draft, June 8, 1971

Traded to Detroit with Jack Lynch for Ron Stackhouse, January 17, 1974

RUUTU, JARKKO

Right Wing   **Ht:** 6-1 **Wt:** 200   **Shoots:** left
B: August 23, 1975, Vantaa, Finland

YR	Regular Season					Playoffs				
	GP	G	A	PTS	PM	GP	G	A	PTS	PM
2006-07	81	7	9	16	125	5	0	0	0	10
2007-08	71	6	10	16	138	20	2	1	3	26
Pitt. Totals	152	13	19	32	263	25	2	1	3	36
NHL Totals	579	55	75	130	981	55	5	5	10	102

Signed as a free agent, July 4, 2006

Signed as a free agent by Ottawa, July 2, 2008

S

SABOURIN, DANY (Sabu)

Goaltender   **Ht:** 6-4 **Wt:** 200   **Catches:** left
B: September 2, 1980, Val d'Or, Quebec

	Regular Season					Playoffs				
YR	GP	MINS	GA	SH	AVE	GP	MINS	GA	SH	AVE
2005-06	1	21	4	0	11.43	-	-	-	-	-
2007-08	24	1242	57	2	2.75	-	-	-	-	-
2008-09	19	989	47	0	2.85	-	-	-	-	-
Pitt. Totals	44	2252	108	2	2.88	-	-	-	-	-
NHL Totals	57	2901	139	2	2.87	2	14	1	0	4.29

Signed as a free agent, August 10, 2005

Claimed on waivers by Vancouver, October 4, 2006

Signed as a free agent, July 1, 2007

Traded to Edmonton with Ryan Stone and a 4th round pick in the 2011 Entry Draft for Mathieu Garon, January 17, 2009

SAGANIUK, ROCKY

Right Wing/Center   **Ht:** 5-8 **Wt:** 185   **Shoots:** right
B: October 15, 1957, Myrnan, Alberta

	Regular Season					Playoffs				
YR	GP	G	A	PTS	PM	GP	G	A	PTS	PM
1983-84	29	1	3	4	37	-	-	-	-	-
Pitt. Totals	29	1	3	4	37	-	-	-	-	-
NHL Totals	259	57	65	122	201	6	1	0	1	15

Acquired from Toronto with Vincent Tremblay for Pat Graham and Nick Ricci, August 15, 1983

Signed as a free agent by Toronto, August 21, 1984

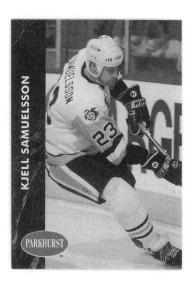

SAMUELSSON, KJELL

Defense   **Ht:** 6-6 **Wt:** 235   **Shoots:** right
B: October 18, 1958, Tingsryd, Sweden

	Regular Season					Playoffs				
YR	GP	G	A	PTS	PM	GP	G	A	PTS	PM
1991-92	20	1	2	3	34	15	0	3	3	12
1992-93	63	3	6	9	106	12	0	3	3	2
1993-94	59	5	8	13	118	6	0	0	0	26
1994-95	41	1	6	7	54	11	0	1	1	32
Pitt. Totals	183	10	22	32	312	44	0	7	7	72
NHL Totals	813	48	138	186	1225	123	4	20	24	178

Acquired from Philadelphia with Rick Tocchet, Ken Wregget, and a 3rd round choice in the 1993 Entry Draft for Brian Benning, Mark Recchi, and a 1st round choice in the 1992 Entry Draft (acquired from LA), February 19, 1992

Signed as a free agent by Philadelphia, August 31, 1995

SAMUELSSON, MIKAEL

Right Wing   **Ht:** 6-2 **Wt:** 213   **Shoots:** right
B: December 23, 1976, Mariefred, Sweden

	Regular Season					Playoffs				
YR	GP	G	A	PTS	PM	GP	G	A	PTS	PM
2002-03	22	2	0	2	8	-	-	-	-	-
Pitt. Totals	22	2	0	2	8	-	-	-	-	-
NHL Totals	540	116	145	261	308	81	21	29	50	50

Acquired from NY Rangers with Joel Bouchard, Rico Fata, and Richard Lintner for Alexei Kovalev, Dan LaCouture, Janne Laukkanen, and Mike Wilson, February 10, 2003

Traded to Florida with 1st and 2nd round choices in the 2003 Entry Draft for 1st and 3rd round choices in the 2003 Entry Draft, June 21, 2003

SAMUELSSON, ULF

Defense   Ht: 6-1 **Wt:** 205   **Shoots:** left
B: March 26, 1964, Fagersta, Sweden

	Regular Season					Playoffs				
YR	GP	G	A	PTS	PM	GP	G	A	PTS	PM
1990-91	14	1	4	5	37	20	3	2	5	34
1991-92	62	1	14	15	206	21	0	2	2	39
1992-93	77	3	26	29	249	12	1	5	6	24
1993-94	80	5	24	29	199	6	0	1	1	18
1994-95	44	1	15	16	113	7	0	2	2	8
Pitt. Totals	277	11	83	94	804	66	4	12	16	123
NHL Totals	1080	57	275	332	2453	132	7	27	34	272

Acquired from Hartford with Ron Francis and Grant Jennings for John Cullen, Jeff Parker, and Zarley Zalapski, March 4, 1991

Traded to NY Rangers with Luc Robitaille for Petr Nedved and Sergei Zubov, August 31, 1995

Penguins Hall of Fame, 2003

SANDERSON, DEREK MICHAEL (Turk)

Center   Ht: 6-0 **Wt:** 185   **Shoots:** left
B: June 16, 1946, Niagara Falls, Ontario

	Regular Season					Playoffs				
YR	GP	G	A	PTS	PM	GP	G	A	PTS	PM
1977-78	13	3	1	4	0	-	-	-	-	-
Pitt. Totals	13	3	1	4	0	-	-	-	-	-
NHL Totals	598	202	250	452	911	56	18	12	30	187
WHA Totals	8	3	3	6	69	-	-	-	-	-

Signed as a free agent, March 14, 1978

SANDSTROM, TOMAS

Right Wing   Ht: 6-2 **Wt:** 205   **Shoots:** left
B: September 4, 1964, Jakobstad, Finland

	Regular Season					Playoffs				
YR	GP	G	A	PTS	PM	GP	G	A	PTS	PM
1993-94	27	6	11	17	24	6	0	0	0	4
1994-95	47	21	23	44	42	12	3	3	6	16
1995-96	58	35	35	70	69	18	4	2	6	30
1996-97	40	9	15	24	33	-	-	-	-	-
Pitt. Totals	172	71	84	155	168	36	7	5	12	50
NHL Totals	983	394	462	856	1193	139	32	49	81	183

Acquired from Los Angeles with Shawn McEachern for Marty McSorley and Jim Paek, February 16, 1994

Traded to Detroit for Greg Johnson, January 27, 1997

SASSER, GRANT

Center   Ht: 5-10 **Wt:** 175   **Shoots:** right
B: February 13, 1964, Portland, Oregon

	Regular Season					Playoffs				
YR	GP	G	A	PTS	PM	GP	G	A	PTS	PM
1983-84	3	0	0	0	0	-	-	-	-	-
Pitt. Totals	3	0	0	0	0	-	-	-	-	-
NHL Totals	3	0	0	0	0	-	-	-	-	-

Selected in the 1982 Entry Draft, 4th choice, 94th overall

SATAN, MIROSLAV

Left Wing   Ht: 6-3 **Wt:** 191   **Shoots:** left
B: October 22, 1974, Topolcany, Czechoslovakia

	Regular Season					Playoffs				
YR	GP	G	A	PTS	PM	GP	G	A	PTS	PM
2008-09	65	17	19	36	36	17	1	5	6	11
Pitt. Totals	65	17	19	36	36	17	1	5	6	11
NHL Totals	1050	363	372	735	464	86	21	33	54	41

Signed as a free agent, July 3, 2008

Signed as a free agent by Boston, January 3, 2010

SATHER, GLEN CAMERON (Slats)

Left Wing   Ht: 5-11 **Wt:** 180   **Shoots:** left
B: September 2, 1943, High River, Alberta

	Regular Season					Playoffs				
YR	GP	G	A	PTS	PM	GP	G	A	PTS	PM
1969-70	76	12	14	26	114	10	0	2	2	17
1970-71	46	8	3	11	96	-	-	-	-	-
Pitt. Totals	122	20	17	37	210	10	0	2	2	17
NHL Totals	658	80	113	193	724	72	1	5	5	86
WHA Totals	81	19	34	53	77	5	1	1	2	2

Claimed from Boston in the Intra-League Draft, June 11, 1969

Traded to NY Rangers for Syl Apps and Sheldon Kannegiesser, January 26, 1971

Hockey Hall of Fame (Builder), 1997

SAVOIA, RYAN

Center   **Ht:** 6-1 **Wt:** 204   **Shoots:** right
B: May 6, 1973, Thorold, Ontario

YR	Regular Season					Playoffs				
	GP	G	A	PTS	PM	GP	G	A	PTS	PM
1998-99	3	0	0	0	0	-	-	-	-	-
Pitt. Totals	3	0	0	0	0	-	-	-	-	-
NHL Totals	3	0	0	0	0	-	-	-	-	-

Signed as a free agent, April 7, 1995

Signed as a free agent by HC Fribourg Gotteron (Switzerland), February 21, 2000

SCHINKEL, KENNETH CALVIN (Ken)

Right Wing   **Ht:** 5-10 **Wt:** 172   **Shoots:** right
B: November 27, 1932, Jansen, Saskatchewan

YR	Regular Season					Playoffs				
	GP	G	A	PTS	PM	GP	G	A	PTS	PM
1967-68	57	14	25	39	19	-	-	-	-	-
1968-69	76	18	34	52	18	-	-	-	-	-
1969-70	72	20	25	45	19	10	4	1	5	4
1970-71	50	15	19	34	6	-	-	-	-	-
1971-72	74	15	30	45	8	3	2	0	2	0
1972-73	42	11	10	21	16	-	-	-	-	-
Pitt. Totals	371	93	143	236	86	13	6	1	7	4
NHL Totals	636	127	198	325	163	19	7	2	9	4

Selected from NY Rangers in the 1967 Expansion Draft, June 6, 1967

NHL All-Star 1967-68

West Division All-Star 1968-69

SCHMIDT, NORM

Defense   **Ht:** 5-11 **Wt:** 190   **Shoots:** right
B: January 24, 1963, Sault Ste. Marie, Ontario

YR	Regular Season					Playoffs				
	GP	G	A	PTS	PM	GP	G	A	PTS	PM
1983-84	34	6	12	18	12	-	-	-	-	-
1985-86	66	15	14	29	57	-	-	-	-	-
1986-87	20	1	5	6	4	-	-	-	-	-
1987-88	5	1	2	3	0	-	-	-	-	-
Pitt. Totals	125	23	33	56	73	-	-	-	-	-
NHL Totals	125	23	33	56	73	-	-	-	-	-

Selected in the 1981 Entry Draft, 3rd choice, 70th overall

SCHOCK, RONALD LAWRENCE (Ron)

Center   **Ht:** 5-11 **Wt:** 180   **Shoots:** left
B: December 19, 1943, Chapleau, Ontario

YR	Regular Season					Playoffs				
	GP	G	A	PTS	PM	GP	G	A	PTS	PM
1969-70	**76**	8	21	29	40	10	1	6	7	7
1970-71	71	14	26	40	20	-	-	-	-	-
1971-72	77	17	29	46	22	4	1	0	1	6
1972-73	78	13	36	49	23	-	-	-	-	-
1973-74	77	14	29	43	22	-	-	-	-	-
1974-75	**80**	23	63	86	36	9	0	4	4	10
1975-76	**80**	18	44	62	28	3	0	1	1	0
1976-77	**80**	17	32	49	10	3	0	1	1	0
Pitt. Totals	619	124	280	404	201	29	2	12	14	23
NHL Totals	909	166	351	517	260	55	4	16	20	29

Acquired from St. Louis with Craig Cameron and a 2nd round choice in the 1971 Amateur Draft for Lou Angotti and a 1st round choice in the 1971 Amateur Draft, June 6, 1969

Traded to Buffalo for Brian Spencer, September 20, 1977

SCHOFIELD, DWIGHT HAMILTON

Defense   **Ht:** 6-3 **Wt:** 195   **Shoots:** left
B: March 25, 1956, Waltham, Massachusetts

YR	Regular Season					Playoffs				
	GP	G	A	PTS	PM	GP	G	A	PTS	PM
1986-87	25	1	6	7	59	-	-	-	-	-
Pitt. Totals	25	1	6	7	59	-	-	-	-	-
NHL Totals	211	8	22	30	631	9	0	0	0	55

Acquired from Washington for cash, October 8, 1986

Signed as a free agent by Winnipeg, July 1987

Pens (left to right) Dwight Schofield, Ville Siren, Randy Cunneyworth, and Dan Frawley gather to celebrate a goal.

Dave Schultz (center in white) hunts for a flying puck against the Cleveland Barons.

SCHULTZ, DAVID WILLIAM (Dave, the Hammer)

Left Wing   Ht: 6-1 **Wt:** 190   **Shoots:** left
B: October 14, 1949, Waldheim, Saskatchewan

YR	Regular Season					Playoffs				
	GP	G	A	PTS	PM	GP	G	A	PTS	PM
1977-78	66	9	25	34	378	-	-	-	-	-
1978-79	47	4	9	13	157	-	-	-	-	-
Pitt. Totals	113	13	34	47	535	-	-	-	-	-
NHL Totals	535	79	121	200	2294	73	8	12	20	412

Acquired from Los Angeles with Gene Carr and a 4th round choice in the 1978 Amateur Draft for Syl Apps and Hartland Monahan, November 2, 1977

Traded to Buffalo for Gary McAdam, February 6, 1979

SCHUTT, RODNEY (Rod)

Left Wing   Ht: 5-10 **Wt:** 185   **Shoots:** left
B: October 13, 1956, Bancroft, Ontario

YR	Regular Season					Playoffs				
	GP	G	A	PTS	PM	GP	G	A	PTS	PM
1978-79	74	24	21	45	33	7	2	0	2	4
1979-80	73	18	21	39	43	5	2	1	3	6
1980-81	80	25	35	60	55	5	3	3	6	16
1981-82	35	9	12	21	42	5	1	2	3	0
1982-83	5	0	0	0	0	-	-	-	-	-
1983-84	11	1	3	4	4	-	-	-	-	-
Pitt. Totals	278	77	92	169	177	22	8	6	14	26
NHL Totals	286	77	92	169	177	22	8	6	14	26

Acquired from Montreal for a 1st round choice in the 1981 Entry Draft, October 18, 1978

Signed as a free agent by Toronto, October 3, 1985

SCUDERI, ROB (Scuds)

Defense   Ht: 6-0 **Wt:** 218   **Shoots:** left
B: December 30, 1978, Syosset, New York

YR	Regular Season					Playoffs				
	GP	G	A	PTS	PM	GP	G	A	PTS	PM
2003-04	13	1	2	3	4	-	-	-	-	-
2005-06	57	0	4	4	36	-	-	-	-	-
2006-07	78	1	10	11	28	5	0	0	0	2
2007-08	71	0	5	5	26	20	0	3	3	2
2008-09	81	1	15	16	18	**24**	1	4	5	6
Pitt. Totals	300	3	36	39	112	49	1	7	8	10
NHL Totals	373	3	47	50	133	55	1	7	8	16

Selected in the 1998 Entry Draft, 5th choice, 134th overall

Signed as a free agent by Los Angeles, July 2, 2009

SEROWIK, JEFF

Defense   Ht: 6-1 **Wt:** 210   **Shoots:** right
B: January 10, 1967, Manchester, New Hampshire

YR	Regular Season					Playoffs				
	GP	G	A	PTS	PM	GP	G	A	PTS	PM
1998-99	26	0	6	6	16	-	-	-	-	-
Pitt. Totals	26	0	6	6	16	-	-	-	-	-
NHL Totals	28	0	6	6	16	-	-	-	-	-

Signed as a free agent, October 8, 1998

SHACK, EDWARD STEVEN PHILLIP (Eddie, the Entertainer)

Left Wing   Ht: 6-1 **Wt:** 200   **Shoots:** left
B: February 11, 1937, Sudbury, Ontario

YR	Regular Season					Playoffs				
	GP	G	A	PTS	PM	GP	G	A	PTS	PM
1971-72	18	5	9	14	12	4	0	1	1	15
1972-73	74	25	20	45	84	-	-	-	-	-
Pitt. Totals	92	30	29	59	96	4	0	1	1	15
NHL Totals	1047	239	226	465	1437	74	6	7	13	151

Acquired from Buffalo for Rene Robert, March 4, 1972

Purchased by Toronto, July 3, 1973

Doug Shedden (14) paced the Pens with 67 points in 1982–83.

SHEDDEN, DOUGLAS ARTHUR (Doug)

Right Wing   Ht: 6-0 **Wt:** 185   **Shoots:** right
B: April 29, 1961 Wallaceburg, Ontario

YR	Regular Season					Playoffs				
	GP	G	A	PTS	PM	GP	G	A	PTS	PM
1981-82	38	10	15	25	12	-	-	-	-	-
1982-83	80	24	43	67	54	-	-	-	-	-
1983-84	67	22	35	57	20	-	-	-	-	-
1984-85	80	35	32	67	30	-	-	-	-	-
1985-86	67	32	34	66	32	-	-	-	-	-
Pitt. Totals	332	123	159	282	148	-	-	-	-	-
NHL Totals	416	139	186	325	176	-	-	-	-	-

Selected in the 1980 Entry Draft, 4th choice, 93rd overall

Traded to Detroit for Ron Duguay, March 11, 1986

SHEPPARD, GREGORY WAYNE (Gregg)

Center   Ht: 5-8 **Wt:** 170   **Shoots:** left
B: April 23, 1949, North Battleford, Saskatchewan

YR	Regular Season					Playoffs				
	GP	G	A	PTS	PM	GP	G	A	PTS	PM
1978-79	60	15	22	37	9	7	1	2	3	0
1979-80	76	13	24	37	20	5	1	1	2	0
1980-81	47	11	17	28	49	5	2	4	6	2
1981-82	58	11	10	21	35	-	-	-	-	-
Pitt. Totals	241	50	73	123	113	17	4	7	11	2
NHL Totals	657	205	293	498	243	82	32	40	72	31

Acquired from Atlanta for Jean Pronovost, September 6, 1978

SHIRES, JAMES ARTHUR (Jim)

Left Wing   Ht: 6-0 **Wt:** 180   **Shoots:** left
B: November 15, 1945, Edmonton, Alberta

YR	Regular Season					Playoffs				
	GP	G	A	PTS	PM	GP	G	A	PTS	PM
1972-73	18	1	2	3	2	-	-	-	-	-
Pitt. Totals	18	1	2	3	2	-	-	-	-	-
NHL Totals	56	3	6	9	32	-	-	-	-	-

Acquired from St. Louis for Joe Noris, January 8, 1973

SIM, JONATHAN

Left Wing   Ht: 5-10 **Wt:** 195   **Shoots:** left
B: September 29, 1977, New Glasgow, Nova Scotia

YR	Regular Season					Playoffs				
	GP	G	A	PTS	PM	GP	G	A	PTS	PM
2003-04	15	2	3	5	6	-	-	-	-	-
Pitt. Totals	15	2	3	5	6	-	-	-	-	-
NHL Totals	435	74	61	135	292	15	1	0	1	6

Claimed from Los Angeles on waivers, March 4, 2004

Signed as a free agent by Phoenix, September 2, 2004

SIMICEK, ROMAN

Center   Ht: 6-1 **Wt:** 190   **Shoots:** left
B: November 4, 1971, Ostrava, Czechoslovakia

YR	Regular Season					Playoffs				
	GP	G	A	PTS	PM	GP	G	A	PTS	PM
2000-01	29	3	6	9	30	-	-	-	-	-
Pitt. Totals	29	3	6	9	30	-	-	-	-	-
NHL Totals	63	7	10	17	59	-	-	-	-	-

Selected in the 2000 Entry Draft, 9th choice, 273rd overall

Traded to Minnesota for Steve McKenna, January 13, 2001

SIMMER, CHARLES ROBERT (Charlie)

Left Wing   **Ht:** 6-3 **Wt:** 210   **Shoots:** left
B: March 20, 1954, Terrace Bay, Ontario

YR	Regular Season					Playoffs				
	GP	G	A	PTS	PM	GP	G	A	PTS	PM
1987-88	50	11	17	28	24	-	-	-	-	-
Pitt. Totals	50	11	17	28	24	-	-	-	-	-
NHL Totals	712	342	369	711	544	24	9	9	18	32

Claimed from Boston in the Waiver Draft, October 5, 1987

SIMPSON, CRAIG ANDREW

Center/Left Wing   **Ht:** 6-2 **Wt:** 195   **Shoots:** right
B: February 15, 1967, London, Ontario

YR	Regular Season					Playoffs				
	GP	G	A	PTS	PM	GP	G	A	PTS	PM
1985-86	76	11	17	28	49	-	-	-	-	-
1986-87	72	26	25	51	57	-	-	-	-	-
1987-88	21	13	13	26	34	-	-	-	-	-
Pitt. Totals	169	50	55	105	140	-	-	-	-	-
NHL Totals	634	247	250	497	659	67	36	32	68	56

Selected in the 1985 Entry Draft, 1st choice, 2nd overall

Traded to Edmonton with Dave Hannan, Chris Joseph, and Moe Mantha for Paul Coffey, Dave Hunter, and Wayne Van Dorp, November 24, 1967

SIMPSON, REID

Left Wing   **Ht:** 6-2 **Wt:** 216   **Shoots:** left
B: May 21, 1969, Flin Flon, Manitoba

YR	Regular Season					Playoffs				
	GP	G	A	PTS	PM	GP	G	A	PTS	PM
2003-04	2	0	0	0	17	-	-	-	-	-
Pitt. Totals	2	0	0	0	17	-	-	-	-	-
NHL Totals	301	18	18	36	838	10	0	0	0	31

Signed as a free agent, August 29, 2003

Signed as a free agent by Rockford (UHL), March 13, 2005

SIMPSON, ROBERT (Bobby)

Left Wing   **Ht:** 6-0 **Wt:** 190   **Shoots:** left
B: November 17, 1956, Caughnawaga, Quebec

YR	Regular Season					Playoffs				
	GP	G	A	PTS	PM	GP	G	A	PTS	PM
1981-82	26	9	9	18	4	2	0	0	0	0
1982-83	4	1	0	1	0	-	-	-	-	-
Pitt. Totals	30	10	9	19	4	2	0	0	0	0
NHL Totals	175	35	29	64	98	6	0	1	1	2

Signed as a free agent, October 1, 1981

SIREN, VILLE JUSSI

Defense   **Ht:** 6-2 **Wt:** 191   **Shoots:** left
B: February 11, 1964, Tampere, Finland

YR	Regular Season					Playoffs				
	GP	G	A	PTS	PM	GP	G	A	PTS	PM
1985-86	60	4	8	12	32	-	-	-	-	-
1986-87	69	5	17	22	50	-	-	-	-	-
1987-88	58	1	20	21	62	-	-	-	-	-
1988-89	12	1	0	1	14	-	-	-	-	-
Pitt. Totals	199	11	45	56	158	-	-	-	-	-
NHL Totals	290	14	68	82	276	7	0	0	0	6

Rights acquired from Hartford for Pat Boutette, November 16, 1984

Traded to Minnesota with Steve Gotaas for Scott Bjugstad and Gord Dineen, December 17, 1988

SIVEK, MICHAL

Center   **Ht:** 6-3 **Wt:** 213   **Shoots:** left
B: January 21, 1981, Nachod, Czechoslovakia

YR	Regular Season					Playoffs				
	GP	G	A	PTS	PM	GP	G	A	PTS	PM
2002-03	38	3	3	6	14	-	-	-	-	-
Pitt. Totals	38	3	3	6	14	-	-	-	-	-
NHL Totals	38	3	3	6	14	-	-	-	-	-

Acquired from Washington with Kris Beech, Ross Lupaschuk, and future considerations for Jaromir Jagr and Frantisek Kucera, July 11, 2001

Signed as a free agent by Sparta Praha (Czech Republic), May 19, 2004

SKOULA, MARTIN

Defense   Ht: 6-3 **Wt:** 226   **Shoots:** left
B: October 28, 1979, Litomerice, Czechoslovakia

YR	Regular Season					Playoffs				
	GP	G	A	PTS	PM	GP	G	A	PTS	PM
2009-10	33	3	5	8	6	-	-	-	-	-
Pitt. Totals	33	3	5	8	6	-	-	-	-	-
NHL Totals	776	44	152	196	328	83	1	13	14	22

Signed as a free agent, September 29, 2009

Traded to Toronto with Luca Caputi for Alexei Ponikarvosky, March 2, 2010

SKRBEK, PAVEL

Defense   Ht: 6-3 **Wt:** 217   **Shoots:** left
B: August 9, 1978, Kladno, Czechoslovakia

YR	Regular Season					Playoffs				
	GP	G	A	PTS	PM	GP	G	A	PTS	PM
1998-99	4	0	0	0	2	-	-	-	-	-
Pitt. Totals	4	0	0	0	2	-	-	-	-	-
NHL Totals	12	0	0	0	8	-	-	-	-	-

Selected in the 1996 Entry Draft, 2nd choice, 28th overall

Traded to Nashville for Bob Boughner, March 13, 2000

SKUDRA, PETER

Goaltender   Ht: 6-1 **Wt:** 189   **Catches:** left
B: April 24, 1973, Riga, USSR

YR	Regular Season					Playoffs				
	GP	MINS	GA	SH	AVE	GP	MINS	GA	SH	AVE
1997-98	17	851	26	0	1.83	-	-	-	-	-
1998-99	37	1914	89	3	2.79	-	-	-	-	-
1999-00	20	922	48	1	3.12	1	20	1	0	3.00
Pitt. Totals	74	3687	163	4	2.65	1	20	1	0	3.00
NHL Totals	146	7162	326	6	2.73	3	116	6	0	3.10

Signed as a free agent, September 25, 1997

Signed as a free agent by Boston, October 3, 2000

SLANEY, JOHN

Defense/Center   Ht: 6-0 **Wt:** 189   **Shoots:** left
B: February 7, 1972, St. John's, Newfoundland and Labrador

YR	Regular Season					Playoffs				
	GP	G	A	PTS	PM	GP	G	A	PTS	PM
1999-00	29	1	4	5	10	2	1	0	1	2
Pitt. Totals	29	1	4	5	10	2	1	0	1	2
NHL Totals	268	22	69	91	99	14	2	1	3	4

Signed as a free agent, September 30, 1999

Traded to Philadelphia for Kevin Stevens, January 14, 2001

The original No. 71—Jiri Slegr—celebrates a goal.

SLEGR, JIRI

Defense   Ht: 6-1 **Wt:** 210   **Shoots:** left
B: May 30, 1971, Jihlava, Czechoslovakia

YR	Regular Season					Playoffs				
	GP	G	A	PTS	PM	GP	G	A	PTS	PM
1997-98	73	5	12	17	109	6	0	4	4	2
1998-99	63	3	20	23	86	13	1	3	4	12
1999-00	74	11	20	31	82	10	2	3	5	19
2000-01	42	5	10	15	60	-	-	-	-	-
Pitt. Totals	252	24	62	86	337	29	3	10	13	33
NHL Totals	622	56	193	249	838	42	4	14	18	39

Acquired from Edmonton for a 3rd round choice in the 1998 Entry Draft, August 12, 1997

Traded to Atlanta for a 3rd round choice in the 2001 Entry Draft, January 14, 2001

SMITH, ALLAN ROBERT (Al)

Goaltender   Ht: 6-1 **Wt:** 200   **Catches:** left
B: November 10, 1945, Toronto, Ontario
D: August 7, 2002

		Regular Season					Playoffs			
YR	GP	MINS	GA	SH	AVE	GP	MINS	GA	SH	AVE
1969-70	46	2555	129	2	3.03	3	180	10	0	3.33
1970-71	46	2472	128	2	3.11	-	-	-	-	-
Pitt. Totals	92	5027	257	4	3.07	3	180	10	0	3.33
NHL Totals	233	12752	735	10	3.46	6	317	21	0	3.97
WHA Totals	260	15389	834	10	3.25	35	1947	124	1	3.82

Claimed from Toronto in the Intra-League Draft, June 11, 1969

Claimed by Detroit in the Intra-League Draft, June 8, 1971

SMITH, DOUGLAS ERIC (Doug)

Center   Ht: 5-11 **Wt:** 186   **Shoots:** right
B: May 17, 1963, Ottawa, Ontario

		Regular Season					Playoffs			
YR	GP	G	A	PTS	PM	GP	G	A	PTS	PM
1989-90	10	1	1	2	25	-	-	-	-	-
Pitt. Totals	10	1	1	2	25	-	-	-	-	-
NHL Totals	535	115	138	253	624	18	4	2	6	21

Acquired from Vancouver for cash, February 26, 1990

SMITH, NATHAN

Center   Ht: 6-2 **Wt:** 206   **Shoots:** left
B: February 9, 1982, Edmonton, Alberta

		Regular Season					Playoffs			
YR	GP	G	A	PTS	PM	GP	G	A	PTS	PM
2007-08	13	0	0	0	2	-	-	-	-	-
Pitt. Totals	13	0	0	0	2	-	-	-	-	-
NHL Totals	26	0	0	0	14	4	0	0	0	0

Signed as a free agent, July 12, 2007

Signed as a free agent by Colorado, July 14, 2008

SMOLINSKI, BRYAN (Smoke)

Center   Ht: 6-1 **Wt:** 203   **Shoots:** right
B: December 27, 1971, Toledo, Ohio

		Regular Season					Playoffs			
YR	GP	G	A	PTS	PM	GP	G	A	PTS	PM
1995-96	81	24	40	64	69	18	5	4	9	10
Pitt. Totals	81	24	40	64	69	18	5	4	9	10
NHL Totals	1056	274	377	651	606	123	23	29	52	60

Acquired from Boston with Glen Murray and a 3rd round choice in the 1996 Entry Draft for Shawn McEachern and Kevin Stevens, August 2, 1995

Traded to NY Islanders for Andreas Johansson and Darius Kasparaitis, November 17, 1996

SNELL, HAROLD EDWARD (Ted)

Right Wing   Ht: 5-9 **Wt:** 190   **Shoots:** right
B: May 28, 1946, Ottawa, Ontario

		Regular Season					Playoffs			
YR	GP	G	A	PTS	PM	GP	G	A	PTS	PM
1973-74	55	4	12	16	8	-	-	-	-	-
Pitt. Totals	55	4	12	16	8	-	-	-	-	-
NHL Totals	104	7	18	25	22	-	-	-	-	-

Signed as a free agent, October 1973

Selected by Kansas City in the 1974 Expansion Draft, June 12, 1974

SNELL, RONALD WAYNE (Ron)

Right Wing   Ht: 5-10 **Wt:** 158   **Shoots:** right
B: August 11, 1948, Regina, Saskatchewan

		Regular Season					Playoffs			
YR	GP	G	A	PTS	PM	GP	G	A	PTS	PM
1968-69	4	3	1	4	6	-	-	-	-	-
1969-70	3	0	1	1	0	-	-	-	-	-
Pitt. Totals	7	3	2	5	6	-	-	-	-	-
NHL Totals	7	3	2	5	6	-	-	-	-	-
WHA Totals	90	24	25	49	40	4	0	0	0	0

Selected in the 1968 Amateur Draft, 2nd choice, 14th overall

Sold to Hershey (AHL), June 1973

SNOW, GARTH

Goaltender   Ht: 6-3 **Wt:** 200   **Catches:** left
B: July 28, 1969, Wrentham, Massachusetts

YR	Regular Season					Playoffs				
	GP	MINS	GA	SH	AVE	GP	MINS	GA	SH	AVE
2000-01	35	2032	101	3	2.98	-	-	-	-	-
Pitt. Totals	35	2032	101	3	2.98	-	-	-	-	-
NHL Totals	368	19837	925	16	2.80	20	1040	48	1	2.77

Signed as a free agent, October 10, 2000

Signed as a free agent by NY Islanders, July 1, 2001

SONNENBERG, MARTIN

Left Wing   Ht: 6-0 **Wt:** 197   **Shoots:** left
B: January 23, 1978, Wetaskiwin, Alberta

YR	Regular Season					Playoffs				
	GP	G	A	PTS	PM	GP	G	A	PTS	PM
1998-99	44	1	1	2	19	7	0	0	0	0
1999-00	14	1	2	3	0	-	-	-	-	-
Pitt. Totals	58	2	3	5	19	7	0	0	0	0
NHL Totals	63	2	3	5	21	7	0	0	0	0

Signed as a free agent, October 9, 1998

Signed as a free agent by Calgary, July 9, 2002

SPEER, FRANCIS WILLIAM (Bill)

Defense   Ht: 5-11 **Wt:** 205   **Shoots:** left
B: March 20, 1942, Lindsay, Ontario
D: February 12, 1989

YR	Regular Season					Playoffs				
	GP	G	A	PTS	PM	GP	G	A	PTS	PM
1967-68	68	3	13	16	44	-	-	-	-	-
1968-69	34	1	4	5	27	-	-	-	-	-
Pitt. Totals	102	4	17	21	71	-	-	-	-	-
NHL Totals	130	5	20	25	79	8	1	0	1	4
WHA Totals	135	4	26	30	70	-	-	-	-	-

Purchased from Cleveland (AHL), August 11, 1966

Loaned to Buffalo (AHL) for the 1966-67 season, October 1966

Claimed by Boston in the Intra-League Draft, June 11, 1969

Brian "Spinner" Spencer (22) hooks up Don "Big Bird" Saleski in 1970s action.

SPENCER, BRIAN ROY (Spinner)

Left Wing   Ht: 5-11 **Wt:** 185   **Shoots:** left
B: September 3, 1949, Fort St. James, British Columbia
D: June 3, 1988

YR	Regular Season					Playoffs				
	GP	G	A	PTS	PM	GP	G	A	PTS	PM
1977-78	79	9	11	20	81	-	-	-	-	-
1978-79	7	0	0	0	0	-	-	-	-	-
Pitt. Totals	86	9	11	20	81	-	-	-	-	-
NHL Totals	553	80	143	223	634	37	1	5	6	29

Acquired from Buffalo for Ron Schock, September 20, 1977

Andre St. Laurent (34) swipes at the puck while the Islanders' Mike Bossy moves in.

ST. LAURENT, ANDRE

Center   Ht: 5-10 **Wt:** 180   **Shoots:** right
B: February 16, 1953, Rouyn, Quebec

	Regular Season					Playoffs				
YR	GP	G	A	PTS	PM	GP	G	A	PTS	PM
1981-82	18	8	5	13	4	5	2	1	3	8
1982-83	70	13	9	22	105	-	-	-	-	-
1983-84	8	2	0	2	21	-	-	-	-	-
Pitt. Totals	96	23	14	37	130	5	2	1	3	8
NHL Totals	644	129	187	316	749	59	8	12	20	48

Claimed on waivers from Los Angeles, February 23, 1982

Traded to Detroit for future considerations, October 24, 1983

STAAL, JORDAN

Center   Ht: 6-4 **Wt:** 220   **Shoots:** left
B: September 10, 1988, Thunder Bay, Ontario

	Regular Season					Playoffs				
YR	GP	G	A	PTS	PM	GP	G	A	PTS	PM
2006-07	81	29	13	42	24	5	3	0	3	2
2007-08	82	12	16	28	55	20	6	1	7	14
2008-09	82	22	27	49	37	24	4	5	9	8
2009-10	82	21	28	49	57	11	3	2	5	6
Pitt. Totals	327	84	84	168	173	60	16	8	24	30
NHL Totals	327	84	84	168	173	60	16	8	24	30

Selected in the 2006 Entry Draft, 1st choice, 2nd overall

Eastern Conference Young Star 2006-07

NHL All-Rookie Team 2006-07

STACKHOUSE, RONALD LORNE (Ron)

Defense   Ht: 6-3 **Wt:** 210   **Shoots:** right
B: August 26, 1949, Haliburton, Ontario

	Regular Season					Playoffs				
YR	GP	G	A	PTS	PM	GP	G	A	PTS	PM
1973-74	36	4	15	19	33	-	-	-	-	-
1974-75	72	15	45	60	52	9	2	6	8	10
1975-76	80	11	60	71	76	3	0	0	0	0
1976-77	80	7	34	41	72	3	2	1	3	0
1977-78	50	5	15	20	36	-	-	-	-	-
1978-79	75	10	33	43	54	7	0	0	0	4
1979-80	78	6	27	33	36	5	1	0	1	18
1980-81	74	6	29	35	86	4	0	1	1	6
1981-82	76	2	19	21	102	1	0	0	0	0
Pitt. Totals	621	66	277	343	547	32	5	8	13	38
NHL Totals	889	87	372	459	824	32	5	8	13	38

Acquired from Detroit for Jack Lynch and Jim Rutherford, January 17, 1974

Prince of Wales Conference All-Star 1979-80

STANTON, PAUL FREDRICK

Defense   Ht: 6-1 **Wt:** 195   **Shoots:** right
B: June 22, 1967, Boston, Massachusetts

	Regular Season					Playoffs				
YR	GP	G	A	PTS	PM	GP	G	A	PTS	PM
1990-91	75	5	18	23	40	22	1	2	3	24
1991-92	54	2	8	10	62	21	1	7	8	42
1992-93	77	4	12	16	97	1	0	1	1	0
Pitt. Totals	206	11	38	49	199	44	2	10	12	66
NHL Totals	295	14	49	63	262	44	2	10	12	66

Selected in the 1985 Entry Draft, 8th choice, 149th overall

Traded to Boston for a 3rd round choice in the 1994 Entry Draft, October 8, 1993

STAPLETON, MIKE (Whitey)

Center   Ht: 5-10 **Wt:** 183   **Shoots:** right
B: May 5, 1966, Sarnia, Ontario

YR	Regular Season					Playoffs				
	GP	G	A	PTS	PM	GP	G	A	PTS	PM
1992-93	78	4	9	13	10	4	0	0	0	0
1993-94	58	7	4	11	18	-	-	-	-	-
Pitt. Totals	136	11	13	24	28	4	0	0	0	0
NHL Totals	697	71	111	182	342	34	1	0	1	39

Signed as a free agent, September 30, 1992

Claimed on waivers by Edmonton, February 19, 1994

STEVENS, KEVIN MICHAEL (Artie)

Left Wing   Ht: 6-3 **Wt:** 230   **Shoots:** left
B: April 15, 1965, Brockton, Massachusetts

YR	Regular Season					Playoffs				
	GP	G	A	PTS	PM	GP	G	A	PTS	PM
1987-88	16	5	2	7	8	-	-	-	-	-
1988-89	24	12	3	15	19	11	3	7	10	16
1989-90	76	29	41	70	171	-	-	-	-	-
1990-91	80	40	46	86	133	**24**	17	16	33	53
1991-92	80	54	69	123	254	**21**	13	15	28	28
1992-93	72	55	56	111	177	12	5	11	16	22
1993-94	83	41	47	88	155	6	1	1	2	10
1994-95	27	15	12	27	51	12	4	7	11	21
2000-01	32	8	15	23	55	17	3	3	6	20
2001-02	32	1	4	5	25	-	-	-	-	-
Pitt. Totals	522	260	295	555	1048	103	46	60	106	170
NHL Totals	874	329	397	726	1470	103	46	60	106	170

Rights acquired from Los Angeles for Anders Hakansson, September 9, 1983

Traded to Boston with Shawn McEachern for Glen Murray, Bryan Smolinski, and a 3rd round choice in the 1996 Entry Draft, August 2, 1995

Acquired from Philadelphia for John Slaney, January 14, 2001

First Team NHL All-Star 1991-92

Second Team NHL All-Star 1990-91, 1992-93

Prince of Wales Conference All-Star 1990-91, 1991-92, 1992-93

STEWART, JOHN ALEXANDER

Left Wing   Ht: 6-0 **Wt:** 180   **Shoots:** left
B: May 16, 1950, Eriksdale, Manitoba

YR	Regular Season					Playoffs				
	GP	G	A	PTS	PM	GP	G	A	PTS	PM
1970-71	15	2	1	3	9	-	-	-	-	-
1971-72	25	2	8	10	23	-	-	-	-	-
Pitt. Totals	40	4	9	13	32	-	-	-	-	-
NHL Totals	258	58	60	118	158	4	0	0	0	10
WHA Totals	95	15	24	39	45	3	0	0	0	0

Selected in the 1970 Amateur Draft, 2nd choice, 21st overall

Selected by Atlanta in the 1972 Expansion Draft, June 6, 1972

STEWART, KARL

Left Wing   Ht: 5-11 **Wt:** 185   **Shoots:** left
B: June 30, 1983, Aurora, Ontario

YR	Regular Season					Playoffs				
	GP	G	A	PTS	PM	GP	G	A	PTS	PM
2006-07	3	0	0	0	2	-	-	-	-	-
Pitt. Totals	3	0	0	0	2	-	-	-	-	-
NHL Totals	69	2	4	6	68	-	-	-	-	-

Claimed on waivers from Anaheim, September 27, 2006

Claimed on waivers by Chicago, October 26, 2006

STEWART, ROBERT HAROLD (Bob)

Defense   Ht: 6-1 **Wt:** 206   **Shoots:** left
B: November 10, 1950, Charlottetown, Prince Edward Island

YR	Regular Season					Playoffs				
	GP	G	A	PTS	PM	GP	G	A	PTS	PM
1979-80	65	3	7	10	52	5	1	1	2	2
Pitt. Totals	65	3	7	10	52	5	1	1	2	2
NHL Totals	575	27	101	128	809	5	1	1	2	2

Acquired from St. Louis for Blair Chapman, November 13, 1979

STOJANOV, ALEK

Right Wing   Ht: 6-4 **Wt:** 225   **Shoots:** left
B: April 25, 1973, Windsor, Ontario

	Regular Season					Playoffs				
YR	GP	G	A	PTS	PM	GP	G	A	PTS	PM
1995-96	10	1	0	1	7	9	0	0	0	19
1996-97	35	1	4	5	79	-	-	-	-	-
Pitt. Totals	45	2	4	6	86	9	0	0	0	19
NHL Totals	107	2	5	7	222	14	0	0	0	21

Acquired from Vancouver for Markus Naslund, March 20, 1996

STONE, RYAN

Center   Ht: 6-2 **Wt:** 207   **Shoots:** left
B: March 20, 1985, Calgary, Alberta

	Regular Season					Playoffs				
YR	GP	G	A	PTS	PM	GP	G	A	PTS	PM
2007-08	6	0	1	1	5	-	-	-	-	-
2008-09	2	0	0	0	2	-	-	-	-	-
Pitt. Totals	8	0	1	1	7	-	-	-	-	-
NHL Totals	35	0	7	7	55	-	-	-	-	-

Selected in the 2003 Entry Draft, 2nd choice, 32nd overall

Traded to Edmonton with Dany Sabourin and a 4th round choice in the 2011 Entry Draft for Mathieu Garon, January 17, 2009

STOUGHTON, BLAINE

Right Wing   Ht: 5-11 **Wt:** 185   **Shoots:** right
B: March 13, 1953, Gilbert Plains, Manitoba

	Regular Season					Playoffs				
YR	GP	G	A	PTS	PM	GP	G	A	PTS	PM
1973-74	34	5	6	11	8	-	-	-	-	-
Pitt. Totals	34	5	6	11	8	-	-	-	-	-
NHL Totals	526	258	191	449	204	8	4	2	6	2
WHA Totals	219	89	90	179	121	11	4	6	10	6

Selected in the 1973 Amateur Draft, 1st choice, 7th overall

Traded to Toronto with a 1st round choice in the 1977 Amateur Draft for Rick Kehoe, September 13, 1974

STRAKA, MARTIN

Center/Left Wing   Ht: 5-9 **Wt:** 180   **Shoots:** left
B: September 3, 1972, Plzen, Czechoslovakia

	Regular Season					Playoffs				
YR	GP	G	A	PTS	PM	GP	G	A	PTS	PM
1992-93	42	3	13	16	29	11	2	1	3	2
1993-94	84	30	34	64	24	6	1	0	1	2
1994-95	31	4	12	16	16	-	-	-	-	-
1997-98	75	19	23	42	28	6	2	0	2	2
1998-99	80	35	48	83	26	13	6	9	15	6
1999-00	71	20	39	59	26	11	3	9	12	10
2000-01	82	27	68	95	38	18	5	8	13	8
2001-02	13	5	4	9	0	-	-	-	-	-
2002-03	60	18	28	46	12	-	-	-	-	-
2003-04	22	4	8	12	16	-	-	-	-	-
Pitt. Totals	560	165	277	442	215	65	19	27	46	30
NHL Totals	954	257	460	717	360	106	26	44	70	52

Selected in the 1992 Entry Draft, 1st choice, 19th overall

Traded to Ottawa for Norm Maciver and Troy Murray, April 7, 1995

Signed as a free agent, August 6, 1997

Traded to Los Angeles for Sergei Anshakov and Martin Strbak, November 30, 2003

World Team All-Star 1998-99

STRATTON, ARTHUR (Art)

Center/Left Wing   Ht: 5-11 **Wt:** 170   **Shoots:** left
B: October 8, 1935, Winnipeg, Manitoba

	Regular Season					Playoffs				
YR	GP	G	A	PTS	PM	GP	G	A	PTS	PM
1967-68	58	16	21	37	16	-	-	-	-	-
Pitt. Totals	58	16	21	37	16	-	-	-	-	-
NHL Totals	95	18	33	51	24	5	0	0	0	0

Selected from Chicago in the 1967 Expansion Draft, June 6, 1967

Traded to Philadelphia for Wayne Hicks, February 27, 1968

STRBAK, MARTIN

Defense   Ht: 6-3 **Wt:** 210   **Shoots:** left
B: January 15, 1975, Presov, Czechoslovakia

YR	Regular Season					Playoffs				
	GP	G	A	PTS	PM	GP	G	A	PTS	PM
2003-04	44	3	11	14	38	-	-	-	-	-
Pitt. Totals	44	3	11	14	38	-	-	-	-	-
NHL Totals	49	5	11	16	46	-	-	-	-	-

Acquired from Los Angeles with Sergei Anshakov for Martin Straka, November 30, 2003

Signed as a free agent by Kosice (Slovakia), October 2, 2004

STUMPF, ROBERT (Bob)

Defense/Right Wing   Ht: 6-1 **Wt:** 195   **Shoots:** right
B: April 25, 1953, Milo, Alberta

YR	Regular Season					Playoffs				
	GP	G	A	PTS	PM	GP	G	A	PTS	PM
1974-75	3	0	0	0	4	-	-	-	-	-
Pitt. Totals	3	0	0	0	4	-	-	-	-	-
NHL Totals	10	1	1	2	20	-	-	-	-	-

Acquired from St. Louis for Bernie Lukowich, January 20, 1975

SUROVY, TOMAS

Left Wing   Ht: 6-1 **Wt:** 205   **Shoots:** left
B: September 24, 1981, Banska Bystrica, Czechoslovakia

YR	Regular Season					Playoffs				
	GP	G	A	PTS	PM	GP	G	A	PTS	PM
2002-03	26	4	7	11	10	-	-	-	-	-
2003-04	47	11	12	23	16	-	-	-	-	-
2005-06	53	12	13	25	45	-	-	-	-	-
Pitt. Totals	126	27	32	59	71	-	-	-	-	-
NHL Totals	126	27	32	59	71	-	-	-	-	-

Selected in the 2001 Entry Draft, 5th choice, 120th overall

Signed as a free agent by Phoenix, July 13, 2007

SUTTER, RICHARD (Rich)

Right Wing   Ht: 5-11 **Wt:** 188   **Shoots:** right
B: December 2, 1963, Viking, Alberta

YR	Regular Season					Playoffs				
	GP	G	A	PTS	PM	GP	G	A	PTS	PM
1982-83	4	0	0	0	0	-	-	-	-	-
1983-84	5	0	0	0	0	-	-	-	-	-
Pitt. Totals	9	0	0	0	0	-	-	-	-	-
NHL Totals	874	149	166	315	1411	78	13	5	18	133

Selected in the 1982 Entry Draft, 1st choice, 10th overall

Traded to Philadelphia with 2nd and 3rd round choices in the 1984 Entry Draft for Andy Brickley, Ron Flockhart, Mark Taylor, and 1st and 3rd round choices in the 1984 Entry Draft, October 23, 1983

SWAIN, GARRY

Center   Ht: 5-8 **Wt:** 164   **Shoots:** left
B: September 11, 1947, Welland, Ontario

YR	Regular Season					Playoffs				
	GP	G	A	PTS	PM	GP	G	A	PTS	PM
1968-69	9	1	1	2	0	-	-	-	-	-
Pitt. Totals	9	1	1	2	0	-	-	-	-	-
NHL Totals	9	1	1	2	0	-	-	-	-	-
WHA Totals	171	22	33	55	70	25	3	5	8	56

Selected in the 1968 Amateur Draft, 1st choice, 4th overall

Selected by Calgary-Cleveland in the 1972 WHA General Player Draft, February 12, 1972

SWARBRICK, GEORGE RAYMOND

Right Wing   Ht: 5-10 **Wt:** 175   **Shoots:** right
B: February 16, 1942, Moose Jaw, Saskatchewan

YR	Regular Season					Playoffs				
	GP	G	A	PTS	PM	GP	G	A	PTS	PM
1968-69	19	1	6	7	28	-	-	-	-	-
1969-70	12	0	1	1	8	-	-	-	-	-
Pitt. Totals	31	1	7	8	36	-	-	-	-	-
NHL Totals	132	17	25	42	173	-	-	-	-	-

Acquired from Oakland with Tracy Pratt and Bryan Watson for Earl Ingarfield, Dick Mattiussi, and Gene Ubriaco, January 30, 1969

Traded to Philadelphia for Terry Ball, June 11, 1970

SYDOR, DARRYL

Defense   Ht: 6-1 **Wt:** 211   **Shoots:** left
B: May 13, 1972, Edmonton, Alberta

YR	GP	G	A	PTS	PM	GP	G	A	PTS	PM
	Regular Season					**Playoffs**				
2007-08	74	1	12	13	26	4	0	0	0	2
2008-09	8	1	1	2	2	-	-	-	-	-
Pitt. Totals	82	2	13	15	28	4	0	0	0	2
NHL Totals	1291	98	409	507	755	155	9	47	56	73

Signed as a free agent, July 2, 2007

Traded to Dallas for Philippe Boucher, November 16, 2008

SYKORA, PETR

Right Wing   Ht: 6-0 **Wt:** 190   **Shoots:** left
B: November 19, 1976, Plzen, Czechoslovakia

YR	GP	G	A	PTS	PM	GP	G	A	PTS	PM
	Regular Season					**Playoffs**				
2007-08	81	28	35	63	41	20	6	3	9	16
2008-09	76	25	21	46	36	7	0	1	1	0
Pitt. Totals	157	53	56	109	77	27	6	4	10	16
NHL Totals	935	302	375	677	415	115	32	37	69	56

Signed as a free agent, July 2, 2007

Signed as a free agent by Minnesota, September 17, 2009

Sniper Petr Sykora burns Ottawa's Martin Gerber during the 2008 playoffs.

T

TABARACCI, RICHARD STEPHEN (Rick)

Goaltender   Ht: 6-1 **Wt:** 190   **Catches:** left
B: January 2, 1969, Toronto, Ontario

YR	GP	MINS	GA	SH	AVE	GP	MINS	GA	SH	AVE
	Regular Season					**Playoffs**				
1988-89	1	33	4	0	7.27	-	-	-	-	-
Pitt. Totals	1	33	4	0	7.27	-	-	-	-	-
NHL Totals	286	15255	760	15	2.99	17	1025	53	0	3.10

Selected in the 1987 Entry Draft, 2nd choice, 26th overall

Traded to Winnipeg with Randy Cunneyworth and Dave McLlwain for Randy Gilhen, Jim Kyte, and Andrew McBain, June 17, 1989

TAFFE, JEFF

Center   Ht: 6-3 **Wt:** 207   **Shoots:** left
B: February 19, 1981, Hastings, Minnesota

YR	GP	G	A	PTS	PM	GP	G	A	PTS	PM
	Regular Season					**Playoffs**				
2007-08	45	5	7	12	8	-	-	-	-	-
2008-09	8	0	2	2	2	-	-	-	-	-
Pitt. Totals	53	5	9	14	10	-	-	-	-	-
NHL Totals	174	21	23	44	40	-	-	-	-	-

Signed as a free agent, July 13, 2007

Signed as a free agent by Florida, July 6, 2009

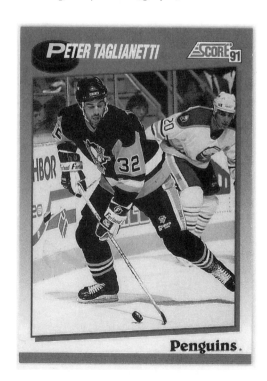

Pens (left to right) Max Talbot, Ryan Whitney, Brooks Orpik, and Ryan Malone model the team's new uniforms in 2007.

TAGLIANETTI, PETER ANTHONY

Defense   **Ht:** 6-2 **Wt:** 195   **Shoots:** left
B: August 15, 1963, Framingham, Massachusetts

YR	Regular Season					Playoffs				
	GP	G	A	PTS	PM	GP	G	A	PTS	PM
1990-91	39	3	8	11	93	19	0	3	3	49
1991-92	44	1	3	4	57	-	-	-	-	-
1992-93	11	1	4	5	34	11	1	2	3	16
1993-94	60	2	12	14	142	5	0	2	2	16
1994-95	13	0	1	1	12	4	0	0	0	2
Pitt. Totals	167	7	28	35	338	39	1	7	8	83
NHL Totals	451	18	74	92	1106	53	2	8	10	103

Acquired from Minnesota with Larry Murphy for Chris Dahlquist and Jim Johnson, December 11, 1990

Selected by Tampa Bay in the 1992 Expansion Draft, June 18, 1992

Acquired from Tampa Bay for a 3rd round choice in the 1993 Entry Draft, March 22, 1993

Signed as a free agent by Boston, August 9, 1995

TALBOT, MAXIME (Mad Max)

Center   **Ht:** 5-11 **Wt:** 190   **Shoots:** left
B: February 11, 1984, Lemoyne, Quebec

YR	Regular Season					Playoffs				
	GP	G	A	PTS	PM	GP	G	A	PTS	PM
2005-06	48	5	3	8	59	-	-	-	-	-
2006-07	75	13	11	24	53	5	0	1	1	7
2007-08	63	12	14	26	53	17	3	6	9	36
2008-09	75	12	10	22	63	24	8	5	13	19
2009-10	45	2	5	7	30	13	2	4	6	11
Pitt. Totals	306	44	43	87	258	59	13	16	29	73
NHL Totals	306	44	43	87	258	59	13	16	29	73

Selected in the 2002 Entry Draft, 9th choice, 234th overall

TALLON, MICHAEL DALE LEE (Dale)

Defense   **Ht:** 6-1 **Wt:** 195   **Shoots:** left
B: October 19, 1950, Noranda, Quebec

YR	Regular Season					Playoffs				
	GP	G	A	PTS	PM	GP	G	A	PTS	PM
1978-79	63	5	24	29	35	-	-	-	-	-
1979-80	32	5	9	14	18	4	0	0	0	4
Pitt. Totals	95	10	33	43	53	4	0	0	0	4
NHL Totals	642	98	238	336	568	33	2	10	12	45

Acquired from Chicago for a 2nd round choice in the 1980 Entry Draft, October 9, 1978

TAMER, CHRIS

Defense **Ht:** 6-2 **Wt:** 205 **Shoots:** left
B: November 17, 1970, Dearborn, Michigan

YR	Regular Season					Playoffs				
	GP	G	A	PTS	PM	GP	G	A	PTS	PM
1993-94	12	0	0	0	9	5	0	0	0	2
1994-95	36	2	0	2	82	4	0	0	0	18
1995-96	70	4	10	14	153	18	0	7	7	24
1996-97	45	2	4	6	131	4	0	0	0	4
1997-98	79	0	7	7	181	6	0	1	1	4
1998-99	11	0	0	0	32	-	-	-	-	-
Pitt. Totals	253	8	21	29	588	37	0	8	8	52
NHL Totals	644	21	64	85	1183	37	0	8	8	52

Selected in the 1990 Entry Draft, 3rd choice, 68th overall

Traded to NY Rangers with Petr Nedved and Sean Pronger for Alexei Kovalev and Harry York, November 25, 1998

TANGRADI, ERIC

Left Wing **Ht:** 6-4 **Wt:** 221 **Shoots:** left
B: February 10, 1989, Philadelphia, Pennsylvania

YR	Regular Season					Playoffs				
	GP	G	A	PTS	PM	GP	G	A	PTS	PM
2009-10	1	0	0	0	0	-	-	-	-	-
Pitt. Totals	1	0	0	0	0	-	-	-	-	-
NHL Totals	1	0	0	0	0	-	-	-	-	-

Acquired from Anaheim with Chris Kunitz for Ryan Whitney, February 26, 2009

TANTI, TONY

Right Wing **Ht:** 5-9 **Wt:** 180 **Shoots:** left
B: September 7, 1963, Toronto, Ontario

YR	Regular Season					Playoffs				
	GP	G	A	PTS	PM	GP	G	A	PTS	PM
1989-90	37	14	18	32	22	-	-	-	-	-
1990-91	46	6	12	18	44	-	-	-	-	-
Pitt. Totals	83	20	30	50	66	-	-	-	-	-
NHL Totals	697	287	273	560	661	30	3	12	15	27

Acquired from Vancouver with Rod Buskas and Barry Pederson for Dave Capuano, Andrew McBain, and Dan Quinn, January 8, 1990

Traded to Buffalo for Ken Priestlay, March 5, 1991

Dick Tarnstrom (32) was the team's MVP in 2003–04.

TARNSTROM, DICK

Defense **Ht:** 6-1 **Wt:** 205 **Shoots:** left
B: January 20, 1975, Sundbyberg, Sweden

YR	Regular Season					Playoffs				
	GP	G	A	PTS	PM	GP	G	A	PTS	PM
2002-03	61	7	34	41	50	-	-	-	-	-
2003-04	80	16	36	52	38	-	-	-	-	-
2005-06	33	5	5	10	52	-	-	-	-	-
Pitt. Totals	174	28	75	103	140	-	-	-	-	-
NHL Totals	306	35	105	140	254	17	0	2	2	12

Claimed on waivers from NY Islanders, August 6, 2002

Traded to Edmonton for Cory Cross and Jani Rita, January 26, 2006

TAYLOR, MARK

Center   **Ht:** 6-0 **Wt:** 190   **Shoots:** left
B: January 26, 1958, Vancouver, British Columbia

	Regular Season					Playoffs				
YR	GP	G	A	PTS	PM	GP	G	A	PTS	PM
1983-84	59	24	31	55	24	-	-	-	-	-
1984-85	47	7	10	17	19	-	-	-	-	-
Pitt. Totals	106	31	41	72	43	-	-	-	-	-
NHL Totals	209	42	68	110	73	6	0	0	0	0

Acquired from Philadelphia with Andy Brickley, Ron Flockhart, and 1st and 3rd round choices in the 1984 Entry Draft for Rich Sutter and 2nd and 3rd round choices in the 1984 Entry Draft, October 23, 1983

Traded to Washington for Jim McGeough, March 12, 1985

TAYLOR, ROBERT IAN (Bob)

Goaltender   **Ht:** 6-1 **Wt:** 180   **Catches:** left
B: January 24, 1945, Calgary, Alberta

	Regular Season					Playoffs				
YR	GP	MINS	GA	SH	AVE	GP	MINS	GA	SH	AVE
1975-76	2	78	7	0	5.38	-	-	-	-	-
Pitt. Totals	2	78	7	0	5.38	-	-	-	-	-
NHL Totals	46	2268	155	0	4.10	-	-	-	-	-

Acquired from Philadelphia with Ed Van Impe for Gary Inness and future considerations, March 9, 1976

TEBBUTT, GREGORY (Greg)

Defense   **Ht:** 6-3 **Wt:** 215   **Shoots:** left
B: May 11, 1957, North Vancouver, British Columbia

	Regular Season					Playoffs				
YR	GP	G	A	PTS	PM	GP	G	A	PTS	PM
1983-84	24	0	2	2	31	-	-	-	-	-
Pitt. Totals	24	0	2	2	31	-	-	-	-	-
NHL Totals	26	0	3	3	35	-	-	-	-	-
WHA Totals	38	2	5	7	83	-	-	-	-	-

Signed as a free agent, July 22, 1983

THIBAULT, JOCELYN

Goaltender   **Ht:** 5-11 **Wt:** 169   **Catches:** left
B: January 12, 1975, Montreal, Quebec

	Regular Season					Playoffs				
YR	GP	MINS	GA	SH	AVE	GP	MINS	GA	SH	AVE
2005-06	16	807	60	0	4.46	-	-	-	-	-
2006-07	22	1101	52	1	2.83	1	8	0	0	0.00
Pitt. Totals	38	1908	112	1	3.52	1	8	0	0	0.00
NHL Totals	586	32892	1508	39	2.75	18	848	50	0	3.54

Acquired from Chicago for a 4th round choice in the 2006 Entry Draft, August 10, 2005

Signed as a free agent by Buffalo, July 5, 2007

THOMAS, BILL

Right Wing   **Ht:** 6-1 **Wt:** 191   **Shoots:** right
B: June 20, 1983, Pittsburgh, Pennsylvania

	Regular Season					Playoffs				
YR	GP	G	A	PTS	PM	GP	G	A	PTS	PM
2008-09	16	2	1	3	2	-	-	-	-	-
Pitt. Totals	16	2	1	3	2	-	-	-	-	-
NHL Totals	56	11	9	20	12	-	-	-	-	-

Signed as a free agent, July 15, 2008

Signed as a free agent by HC Lugano (Switzerland), January 20, 2010

THOMPSON, LORAN ERROL (Errol)

Left Wing   **Ht:** 5-9 **Wt:** 185   **Shoots:** left
B: May 28, 1950, Summerside, Prince Edward Island

	Regular Season					Playoffs				
YR	GP	G	A	PTS	PM	GP	G	A	PTS	PM
1980-81	34	6	8	14	12	-	-	-	-	-
Pitt. Totals	34	6	8	14	12	-	-	-	-	-
NHL Totals	599	208	185	393	184	34	7	5	12	11

Acquired from Detroit for Gary McAdam, January 8, 1981

THORBURN, CHRIS

Center/Right Wing   **Ht:** 6-3 **Wt:** 225   **Shoots:** right
B: June 3, 1983, Sault Ste. Marie, Ontario

	Regular Season					Playoffs				
YR	GP	G	A	PTS	PM	GP	G	A	PTS	PM
2006-07	39	3	2	5	69	-	-	-	-	-
Pitt. Totals	39	3	2	5	69	-	-	-	-	-
NHL Totals	272	19	33	52	361	-	-	-	-	-

Claimed on waivers from Buffalo, October 3, 2006

Traded to Atlanta for a 3rd round choice in the 2007 Entry Draft, June 22, 2007

THORNBURY, TOM

Defense   Ht: 5-11 **Wt:** 175   **Shoots:** right
B: March 17, 1963, Lindsay, Ontario

YR	Regular Season					Playoffs				
	GP	G	A	PTS	PM	GP	G	A	PTS	PM
1983-84	14	1	8	9	16	-	-	-	-	-
Pitt. Totals	14	1	8	9	16	-	-	-	-	-
NHL Totals	14	1	8	9	16	-	-	-	-	-

Selected in the 1981 Entry Draft, 2nd choice, 49th overall

Traded to Quebec for Brian Ford, December 6, 1984

TIBBETTS, BILLY

Right Wing   Ht: 6-2 **Wt:** 215   **Shoots:** right
B: October 14, 1974, Boston, Massachusetts

YR	Regular Season					Playoffs				
	GP	G	A	PTS	PM	GP	G	A	PTS	PM
2000-01	29	1	2	3	79	-	-	-	-	-
2001-02	33	1	5	6	109	-	-	-	-	-
Pitt. Totals	62	2	7	9	188	-	-	-	-	-
NHL Totals	82	2	8	10	269	-	-	-	-	-

Signed as a free agent, April 10, 2000

Traded to Philadelphia for Kent Manderville, March 17, 2002

TIPPETT, DAVID G. (Dave)

Center/Left Wing   Ht: 5-10 **Wt:** 180   **Shoots:** left
B: August 25, 1961, Moosomin, Saskatchewan

YR	Regular Season					Playoffs				
	GP	G	A	PTS	PM	GP	G	A	PTS	PM
1992-93	74	6	19	25	56	12	1	4	5	14
Pitt. Totals	74	6	19	25	56	12	1	4	5	14
NHL Totals	721	93	169	262	317	62	6	16	22	34

Signed as a free agent, August 25, 1992

Signed as a free agent by Philadelphia, August 30, 1993

TITOV, GERMAN

Left Wing   Ht: 6-1 **Wt:** 203   **Shoots:** left
B: October 16, 1965, Moscow, USSR

YR	Regular Season					Playoffs				
	GP	G	A	PTS	PM	GP	G	A	PTS	PM
1998-99	72	11	45	56	34	11	3	5	8	4
1999-00	63	17	25	42	34	-	-	-	-	-
Pitt. Totals	135	28	70	98	68	11	3	5	8	4
NHL Totals	624	157	220	377	311	34	11	12	23	18

Acquired from Calgary with Todd Hlushko for Dave Roche and Ken Wregget, June 17, 1998

Traded to Edmonton for Josef Beranek, March 14, 2000

TOCCHET, RICK

Right Wing   Ht: 6-0 **Wt:** 210   **Shoots:** right
B: April 9, 1964, Scarborough, Ontario

YR	Regular Season					Playoffs				
	GP	G	A	PTS	PM	GP	G	A	PTS	PM
1991-92	19	14	16	30	49	14	6	13	19	24
1992-93	80	48	61	109	252	12	7	6	13	24
1993-94	51	14	26	40	134	6	2	3	5	20
Pitt. Totals	150	76	103	179	435	32	15	22	37	68
NHL Totals	1144	440	512	952	2972	145	52	60	112	471

Acquired from Philadelphia with Kjell Samuelsson, Ken Wregget, and a 3rd round choice in the 1993 Entry Draft for Brian Benning, Mark Recchi, and a 1st round choice in the 1992 Entry Draft (acquired from LA), February 19, 1992

Traded to Los Angeles with a 2nd round choice in the 1995 Entry Draft for Luc Robitaille, July 29, 1994

Prince of Wales Conference All-Star 1992-93

TOMS, JEFF

Center   Ht: 6-5 **Wt:** 200   **Shoots:** left
B: June 4, 1974, Swift Current, Saskatchewan

YR	Regular Season					Playoffs				
	GP	G	A	PTS	PM	GP	G	A	PTS	PM
2001-02	14	2	1	3	4	-	-	-	-	-
Pitt. Totals	14	2	1	3	4	-	-	-	-	-
NHL Totals	236	22	33	55	59	1	0	0	0	0

Claimed on waivers from NY Rangers, March 16, 2002

Signed as a free agent by Florida, July 11, 2002

TOOKEY, TIMOTHY RAYMOND (Tim)

Center   **Ht:** 5-11 **Wt:** 185   **Shoots:** left
B: August 29, 1960, Edmonton, Alberta

YR	Regular Season					Playoffs				
	GP	G	A	PTS	PM	GP	G	A	PTS	PM
1983-84	8	0	2	2	2	-	-	-	-	-
Pitt. Totals	8	0	2	2	2	-	-	-	-	-
NHL Totals	106	22	36	58	71	10	1	3	4	2

Signed as a free agent, September 12, 1983

Signed as a free agent by Philadelphia, July 11, 1985

Acquired from Los Angeles for Pat Mayer, March 7, 1989

Signed as a free agent by Philadelphia, June 30, 1989

TREBIL, DANIEL

Defense   **Ht:** 6-3 **Wt:** 210   **Shoots:** right
B: April 10, 1974, Bloomington, Minnesota

YR	Regular Season					Playoffs				
	GP	G	A	PTS	PM	GP	G	A	PTS	PM
1999-00	3	1	0	1	0	-	-	-	-	-
2000-01	16	0	0	0	7	-	-	-	-	-
Pitt. Totals	19	1	0	1	7	-	-	-	-	-
NHL Totals	85	4	4	8	32	10	0	1	1	8

Acquired from Anaheim for a 5th round choice in the 2000 Entry Draft, March 14, 2000

Signed as a free agent by NY Islanders, July 31, 2000

Acquired from NY Islanders for a 9th round choice in the 2001 Entry Draft, November 14, 2000

Traded to St. Louis for Marc Bergevin, December 28, 2000

TREMBLAY, VINCENT

Goaltender   **Ht:** 6-1 **Wt:** 180   **Catches:** left
B: October 21, 1959, Quebec City, Quebec

YR	Regular Season					Playoffs				
	GP	MINS	GA	SH	AVE	GP	MINS	GA	SH	AVE
1983-84	4	240	24	0	6.00	-	-	-	-	-
Pitt. Totals	4	240	24	0	6.00	-	-	-	-	-
NHL Totals	58	2785	223	1	4.80	-	-	-	-	-

Acquired from Toronto with Rocky Saganiuk for Pat Graham and Nick Ricci, August 15, 1983

Signed as a free agent by Buffalo, March 7, 1985

TROTTIER, BRYAN JOHN

Center   **Ht:** 5-11 **Wt:** 195   **Shoots:** left
B: July 17, 1956, Val Marie, Saskatchewan

YR	Regular Season					Playoffs				
	GP	G	A	PTS	PM	GP	G	A	PTS	PM
1990-91	52	9	19	28	24	23	3	4	7	49
1991-92	63	11	18	29	54	21	4	3	7	8
1993-94	41	4	11	15	36	2	0	0	0	0
Pitt. Totals	156	24	48	72	114	46	7	7	14	57
NHL Totals	1279	524	901	1425	912	221	71	113	184	277

Signed as a free agent, July 20, 1990

Signed as a free agent, June 22, 1993

Prince of Wales Conference All-Star 1991-92

Hockey Hall of Fame (Player), 1997

TUGNUTT, RON

Goaltender   **Ht:** 5-11 **Wt:** 160   **Catches:** left
B: October 22, 1967, Scarborough, Ontario

YR	Regular Season					Playoffs				
	GP	MINS	GA	SH	AVE	GP	MINS	GA	SH	AVE
1999-00	7	374	15	0	2.41	11	746	22	2	1.77
Pitt. Totals	7	374	15	0	2.41	11	746	22	2	1.77
NHL Totals	537	29486	1497	26	3.05	25	1482	56	3	2.27

Acquired from Ottawa with Janne Laukkanen for Tom Barrasso, March 14, 2000

Signed as a free agent by Columbus, July 4, 2000

Ron Tugnutt was spectacular during his brief tour with the Pens in 2000.

TURNBULL, IAN WAYNE

Defense **Ht:** 6-0 **Wt:** 200 **Shoots:** left
B: December 22, 1953, Montreal, Quebec

YR	Regular Season					Playoffs				
	GP	G	A	PTS	PM	GP	G	A	PTS	PM
1982-83	6	0	0	0	4	-	-	-	-	-
Pitt. Totals	6	0	0	0	4	-	-	-	-	-
NHL Totals	628	123	317	440	736	55	13	32	45	94

Signed as a free agent, October 4, 1982

U

UBRIACO, EUGENE STEPHEN (Gene)

Left Wing/Center **Ht:** 5-8 **Wt:** 157 **Shoots:** left
B: December 26, 1937, Sault Ste. Marie, Ontario

YR	Regular Season					Playoffs				
	GP	G	A	PTS	PM	GP	G	A	PTS	PM
1967-68	65	18	15	33	16	-	-	-	-	-
1968-69	49	15	11	26	14	-	-	-	-	-
Pitt. Totals	114	33	26	59	30	-	-	-	-	-
NHL Totals	177	39	35	74	50	11	2	0	2	4

Acquired from Hershey (AHL) for Jeannot Gilbert, October 11, 1967

Traded to Oakland with Earl Ingarfield and Dick Mattiussi for Tracy Pratt, George Swarbrick, and Bryan Watson, January 30, 1969

V

VALK, GARRY

Right Wing **Ht:** 6-1 **Wt:** 200 **Shoots:** left
B: November 27, 1967, Edmonton, Alberta

YR	Regular Season					Playoffs				
	GP	G	A	PTS	PM	GP	G	A	PTS	PM
1996-97	17	3	4	7	25	-	-	-	-	-
1997-98	39	2	1	3	33	-	-	-	-	-
Pitt. Totals	56	5	5	10	58	-	-	-	-	-
NHL Totals	777	100	156	256	747	61	6	7	13	79

Acquired from Anaheim for J.J. Daigneault, February 21, 1997

Signed as a free agent by Toronto, October 8, 1998

VANDENBUSSCHE, RYAN

Right Wing **Ht:** 6-0 **Wt:** 200 **Shoots:** right
B: February 28, 1973, Simcoe, Ontario

YR	Regular Season					Playoffs				
	GP	G	A	PTS	PM	GP	G	A	PTS	PM
2005-06	20	1	0	1	42	-	-	-	-	-
Pitt. Totals	20	1	0	1	42	-	-	-	-	-
NHL Totals	310	10	10	20	702	1	0	0	0	0

Signed as a free agent, July 12, 2004

Signed as a free agent by Jokerit Helsinki (Finland), September 26, 2006

VAN DORP, WAYNE

Left Wing **Ht:** 6-4 **Wt:** 225 **Shoots:** left
B: May 19, 1961, Vancouver, British Columbia

YR	Regular Season					Playoffs				
	GP	G	A	PTS	PM	GP	G	A	PTS	PM
1987-88	25	1	3	4	75	-	-	-	-	-
Pitt. Totals	25	1	3	4	75	-	-	-	-	-
NHL Totals	125	12	12	24	565	27	0	1	1	42

Acquired from Edmonton with Paul Coffey and Dave Hunter for Dave Hannan, Chris Joseph, Moe Mantha, and Craig Simpson, November 24, 1987

Traded to Buffalo for future considerations, September 30, 1988

VAN IMPE, EDWARD CHARLES (Ed)

Defense **Ht:** 5-10 **Wt:** 205 **Shoots:** left
B: May 27, 1940, Saskatoon, Saskatchewan

YR	Regular Season					Playoffs				
	GP	G	A	PTS	PM	GP	G	A	PTS	PM
1975-76	12	0	5	5	16	3	0	1	1	2
1976-77	10	0	3	3	6	-	-	-	-	-
Pitt. Totals	22	0	8	8	22	3	0	1	1	2
NHL Totals	700	27	126	153	1025	66	1	12	13	131

Acquired from Philadelphia with Bob Taylor for Gary Inness and cash, March 9, 1976

VUJTEK, VLADIMIR

Left Wing   **Ht:** 6-2   **Wt:** 200   **Shoots:** left
B: February 17, 1972, Ostrava, Czechoslovakia

	Regular Season					Playoffs				
YR	GP	G	A	PTS	PM	GP	G	A	PTS	PM
2002-03	5	0	1	1	0	-	-	-	-	-
Pitt. Totals	5	0	1	1	0	-	-	-	-	-
NHL Totals	110	7	30	37	38	-	-	-	-	-

Signed as a free agent, July 15, 2002

Signed as a free agent by HC Vitkovice (Czech Republic), November 15, 2002

W

WALLACE, TIM

Right Wing   **Ht:** 6-1   **Wt:** 207   **Shoots:** right
B: August 6, 1984, Anchorage, Alaska

	Regular Season					Playoffs				
YR	GP	G	A	PTS	PM	GP	G	A	PTS	PM
2008-09	16	0	2	2	7	-	-	-	-	-
2009-10	1	0	0	0	0	-	-	-	-	-
Pitt. Totals	17	0	2	2	7	-	-	-	-	-
NHL Totals	17	0	2	2	7	-	-	-	-	-

Signed as a free agent, May 29, 2007

WATSON, BRYAN JOSEPH (Bugsy)

Defense   **Ht:** 5-9   **Wt:** 175   **Shoots:** right
B: November 14, 1942, Bancroft, Ontario

	Regular Season					Playoffs				
YR	GP	G	A	PTS	PM	GP	G	A	PTS	PM
1968-69	18	0	4	4	35	-	-	-	-	-
1969-70	61	1	9	10	189	10	0	0	0	17
1970-71	43	2	6	8	119	-	-	-	-	-
1971-72	75	3	17	20	**212**	4	0	0	0	21
1972-73	69	1	17	18	179	-	-	-	-	-
1973-74	38	1	4	5	137	-	-	-	-	-
Pitt. Totals	304	8	57	65	871	14	0	0	0	38
NHL Totals	878	17	135	152	2212	32	2	0	2	70
WHA Totals	21	0	2	2	56	3	0	1	1	2

Acquired from Oakland with Tracy Pratt and George Swarbrick for Earl Ingarfield, Dick Mattiussi, and Gene Ubriaco, January 30, 1969

Traded to St. Louis with Greg Polis and a 2nd round choice in the 1974 Amateur Draft for Ab DeMarco, Steve Durbano, and Bob Kelly, January 17, 1974

WEBB, STEVE

Right Wing   **Ht:** 6-0   **Wt:** 211   **Shoots:** right
B: April 30, 1975, Peterborough, Ontario

	Regular Season					Playoffs				
YR	GP	G	A	PTS	PM	GP	G	A	PTS	PM
2003-04	5	0	0	0	2	-	-	-	-	-
Pitt. Totals	5	0	0	0	2	-	-	-	-	-
NHL Totals	321	5	13	18	532	14	0	0	0	28

Acquired on waivers from Philadelphia, October 22, 2003

Traded to NY Islanders for Alain Nasreddine, March 8, 2004

WEIR, WALLY

Defense   **Ht:** 6-2   **Wt:** 200   **Shoots:** right
B: June 3, 1954, Verdun, Quebec

	Regular Season					Playoffs				
YR	GP	G	A	PTS	PM	GP	G	A	PTS	PM
1984-85	14	0	3	3	34	-	-	-	-	-
Pitt. Totals	14	0	3	3	34	-	-	-	-	-
NHL Totals	320	21	45	66	625	23	0	1	1	96
WHA Totals	150	5	24	29	410	32	2	8	10	67

Acquired on waivers from Hartford, March 1, 1985

WELCH, NOAH

Defense   **Ht:** 6-4   **Wt:** 218   **Shoots:** left
B: August 26, 1982, Brighton, Massachusetts

	Regular Season					Playoffs				
YR	GP	G	A	PTS	PM	GP	G	A	PTS	PM
2005-06	5	1	3	4	2	-	-	-	-	-
2006-07	22	1	1	2	22	-	-	-	-	-
Pitt. Totals	27	2	4	6	24	-	-	-	-	-
NHL Totals	73	4	5	9	58	-	-	-	-	-

Selected in the 2001 Entry Draft, 2nd choice, 54th overall

Traded to Florida for Gary Roberts, February 27, 2007

WELLS, CHRIS

Center   Ht: 6-6 **Wt:** 223   **Shoots:** left
B: November 12, 1975, Calgary, Alberta

YR	Regular Season					Playoffs				
	GP	G	A	PTS	PM	GP	G	A	PTS	PM
1995-96	54	2	2	4	59	-	-	-	-	-
Pitt. Totals	54	2	2	4	59	-	-	-	-	-
NHL Totals	195	9	20	29	193	3	0	0	0	0

Selected in the 1994 Entry Draft, 1st choice, 24th overall

Traded to Florida for Stu Barnes and Jason Woolley, November 19, 1996

WERENKA, BRAD

Defense   Ht: 6-1 **Wt:** 221   **Shoots:** left
B: February 12, 1969, Two Hills, Alberta

YR	Regular Season					Playoffs				
	GP	G	A	PTS	PM	GP	G	A	PTS	PM
1997-98	71	3	15	18	46	6	1	0	1	8
1998-99	81	6	18	24	93	13	1	1	2	6
1999-00	61	3	8	11	69	-	-	-	-	-
Pitt. Totals	213	12	41	53	208	19	2	1	3	14
NHL Totals	320	19	61	80	299	19	2	1	3	14

Signed as a free agent July 31, 1997

Traded to Calgary for Rene Corbet and Tyler Moss, March 14, 2000

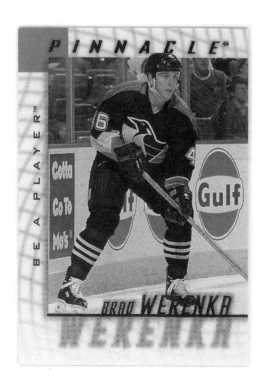

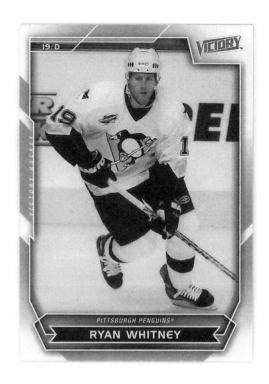

WHITNEY, RYAN

Defense   Ht: 6-4 **Wt:** 219   **Shoots:** left
B: February 19, 1983, Boston, Massachusetts

YR	Regular Season					Playoffs				
	GP	G	A	PTS	PM	GP	G	A	PTS	PM
2005-06	68	6	32	38	85	-	-	-	-	-
2006-07	81	14	45	59	77	5	1	1	2	6
2007-08	76	12	28	40	45	20	1	5	6	25
2008-09	28	2	11	13	16	-	-	-	-	-
Pitt. Totals	253	34	116	150	223	25	2	6	8	31
NHL Totals	354	41	158	199	305	38	3	11	14	40

Selected in the 2002 Entry Draft, 1st choice, 5th overall

Traded to Anaheim for Chris Kunitz and Eric Tangradi, February 26, 2009

Eastern Conference Young Star 2006-07

WILEY, JAMES THOMAS (Jim)

Center   Ht: 6-2 **Wt:** 200   **Shoots:** left
B: April 28, 1950, Sault Ste. Marie, Ontario

YR	Regular Season					Playoffs				
	GP	G	A	PTS	PM	GP	G	A	PTS	PM
1972-73	4	0	1	1	0	-	-	-	-	-
1973-74	22	0	3	3	2	-	-	-	-	-
Pitt. Totals	26	0	4	4	2	-	-	-	-	-
NHL Totals	63	4	10	14	8	-	-	-	-	-

Signed as a free agent, June 25, 1972

Claimed by Vancouver in the Intra-League Draft, June 10, 1974

WILKINS, BARRY JAMES

Defense   Ht: 6-0 **Wt:** 190   **Shoots:** left
B: February 28, 1947, Toronto, Ontario

YR	GP	G	A	PTS	PM	GP	G	A	PTS	PM
	Regular Season					**Playoffs**				
1974-75	59	5	29	34	97	3	0	0	0	0
1975-76	75	0	27	27	106	3	0	1	1	4
Pitt. Totals	**134**	**5**	**56**	**61**	**203**	**6**	**0**	**1**	**1**	**4**
NHL Totals	**418**	**27**	**125**	**152**	**663**	**6**	**0**	**1**	**1**	**4**
WHA Totals	**130**	**6**	**45**	**51**	**154**	**4**	**0**	**1**	**1**	**2**

Acquired from Vancouver for Ab DeMarco, November 4, 1974

Signed as a free agent by Edmonton (WHA), September 2, 1976

WILKINSON, NEIL

Defense   Ht: 6-3 **Wt:** 194   **Shoots:** right
B: August 15, 1967, Selkirk, Manitoba

YR	GP	G	A	PTS	PM	GP	G	A	PTS	PM
	Regular Season					**Playoffs**				
1995-96	41	2	10	12	87	15	0	1	1	14
1996-97	23	0	0	0	36	5	0	0	0	4
1997-98	34	2	4	6	24	-	-	-	-	-
1998-99	24	0	0	0	22	-	-	-	-	-
Pitt. Totals	**122**	**4**	**14**	**18**	**169**	**20**	**0**	**1**	**1**	**18**
NHL Totals	**460**	**16**	**67**	**83**	**813**	**53**	**3**	**6**	**9**	**41**

Acquired from Winnipeg for Norm Maciver, December 28, 1995

WILSON, DUNCAN SHEPHERD (Dunc)

Goaltender   Ht: 5-11 **Wt:** 175   **Catches:** left
B: March 22, 1948, Toronto, Ontario

YR	GP	MINS	GA	SH	AVE	GP	MINS	GA	SH	AVE
	Regular Season					**Playoffs**				
1976-77	45	2627	129	5	2.95	-	-	-	-	-
1977-78	21	1180	95	0	4.83	-	-	-	-	-
Pitt. Totals	**66**	**3807**	**224**	**5**	**3.53**	**-**	**-**	**-**	**-**	**-**
NHL Totals	**287**	**15851**	**988**	**8**	**3.74**	**-**	**-**	**-**	**-**	**-**

Acquired from NY Rangers for a 4th round choice in the 1978 Amateur Draft, October 8, 1976

Purchased by Vancouver, November 17, 1978

WILSON, LANDON

Right Wing   Ht: 6-3 **Wt:** 226   **Shoots:** right
B: March 13, 1975, St. Louis, Missouri

YR	GP	G	A	PTS	PM	GP	G	A	PTS	PM
	Regular Season					**Playoffs**				
2003-04	19	5	1	6	31	-	-	-	-	-
Pitt. Totals	**19**	**5**	**1**	**6**	**31**	**-**	**-**	**-**	**-**	**-**
NHL Totals	**375**	**53**	**66**	**119**	**352**	**13**	**1**	**1**	**2**	**20**

Acquired from Phoenix for future considerations, February 22, 2004

Signed as a free agent by Espoo (Finland), June 23, 2004

WILSON, MIKE

Defense   Ht: 6-6 **Wt:** 229   **Shoots:** left
B: February 26, 1975, Brampton, Ontario

YR	GP	G	A	PTS	PM	GP	G	A	PTS	PM
	Regular Season					**Playoffs**				
2001-02	21	1	1	2	17	-	-	-	-	-
Pitt. Totals	**21**	**1**	**1**	**2**	**17**	**-**	**-**	**-**	**-**	**-**
NHL Totals	**336**	**16**	**41**	**57**	**264**	**29**	**0**	**2**	**2**	**15**

Signed as a free agent, July 5, 2001

Traded to NY Rangers with Dan LaCouture, Alexei Kovalev, and Janne Laukkanen for Joel Bouchard, Rico Fata, Richard Lintner, and Mikael Samuelsson, February 10, 2003

WILSON, MITCH

Center   Ht: 5-8 **Wt:** 190   **Shoots:** right
B: February 15, 1962, Kelowna, British Columbia

YR	GP	G	A	PTS	PM	GP	G	A	PTS	PM
	Regular Season					**Playoffs**				
1986-87	17	2	1	3	83	-	-	-	-	-
Pitt. Totals	**17**	**2**	**1**	**3**	**83**	**-**	**-**	**-**	**-**	**-**
NHL Totals	**26**	**2**	**3**	**5**	**104**	**-**	**-**	**-**	**-**	**-**

Signed as a free agent, July 24, 1986

WOLF, BENNETT MARTIN

Defense   **Ht:** 6-3 **Wt:** 205   **Shoots:** right
B: October 23, 1959, Kitchener, Ontario

YR	Regular Season					Playoffs				
	GP	G	A	PTS	PM	GP	G	A	PTS	PM
1980-81	24	0	1	1	94	-	-	-	-	-
1981-82	1	0	0	0	2	-	-	-	-	-
1982-83	5	0	0	0	37	-	-	-	-	-
Pitt. Totals	30	0	1	1	133	-	-	-	-	-
NHL Totals	30	0	1	1	133	-	-	-	-	-

Selected in the 1979 Entry Draft, 2nd choice, 52nd overall

WOOLLEY, JASON

Defense   **Ht:** 6-0 **Wt:** 203   **Shoots:** left
B: July 27, 1969, Toronto, Ontario

YR	Regular Season					Playoffs				
	GP	G	A	PTS	PM	GP	G	A	PTS	PM
1996-97	57	6	30	36	28	5	0	3	3	0
Pitt. Totals	57	6	30	36	28	5	0	3	3	0
NHL Totals	718	68	246	314	430	79	11	36	47	44

Acquired from Florida with Stu Barnes for Chris Wells, November 19, 1996

Traded to Buffalo for a 5th round choice in the 1998 Entry Draft, September 24, 1997

WOYTOWICH, ROBERT IVAN (Bob)

Defense   **Ht:** 6-0 **Wt:** 185   **Shoots:** right
B: August 18, 1941, Winnipeg, Manitoba
D: July 30, 1988

YR	Regular Season					Playoffs				
	GP	G	A	PTS	PM	GP	G	A	PTS	PM
1968-69	71	9	20	29	62	-	-	-	-	-
1969-70	68	8	25	33	49	10	1	2	3	2
1970-71	78	4	22	26	30	-	-	-	-	-
1971-72	31	1	4	5	8	-	-	-	-	-
Pitt. Totals	248	22	71	93	149	10	1	2	3	2
NHL Totals	503	32	126	158	352	24	1	3	4	20
WHA Totals	242	9	51	60	140	18	1	1	2	4

Acquired from Minnesota for a 1st round choice in the 1972 Amateur Draft, October 1, 1968

Traded to Los Angeles for Al McDonough, January 11, 1972

West Division All-Star 1969-70

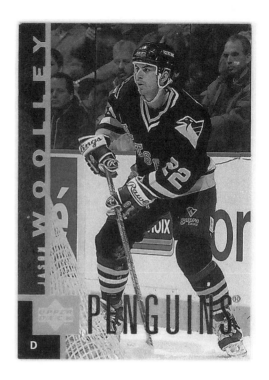

WREGGET, KENNETH (Ken)

Goaltender   **Ht:** 6-1 **Wt:** 201   **Catches:** left
B: March 25, 1964, Brandon, Manitoba

YR	Regular Season					Playoffs				
	GP	MINS	GA	SH	AVE	GP	MINS	GA	SH	AVE
1991-92	9	448	31	0	4.15	1	40	4	0	6.00
1992-93	25	1368	78	0	3.42	-	-	-	-	-
1993-94	42	2456	138	1	3.37	-	-	-	-	-
1994-95	38	2208	118	0	3.21	11	661	33	1	3.00
1995-96	37	2132	115	3	3.24	9	599	23	0	2.30
1996-97	46	2514	136	2	3.25	5	297	18	0	3.64
1997-98	15	611	28	0	2.75	-	-	-	-	-
Pitt. Totals	212	11737	644	6	3.29	26	1597	78	1	2.93
NHL Totals	575	31663	1917	9	3.63	56	3341	160	3	2.87

Acquired from Philadelphia with Kjell Samuelsson, Rick Tocchet, and a conditional 3rd round choice in the 1993 Entry Draft for Brian Benning, Mark Recchi, and a 1st round choice in the 1992 Entry Draft (acquired from LA), February 19, 1992

Traded to Calgary with Dave Roche for Todd Hlushko and German Titov, June 17, 1998

Agitator Tyler Wright tries to plaster New Jersey's Ken Daneyko into the boards with a flying check.

Y

YORK, HARRY

Center   **Ht:** 6-2   **Wt:** 215   **Shoots:** left
B: April 16, 1974, Ponoka, Alberta

	Regular Season					Playoffs				
YR	GP	G	A	PTS	PM	GP	G	A	PTS	PM
1998-99	2	0	0	0	0	-	-	-	-	-
Pitt. Totals	2	0	0	0	0	-	-	-	-	-
NHL Totals	244	29	46	75	99	5	0	0	0	2

Acquired from NY Rangers with Alexei Kovalev for Petr Nedved, Sean Pronger, and Chris Tamer, November 25, 1998

Claimed on waivers by Vancouver, December 7, 1998

YOUNG, SCOTT ALLEN

Right Wing   **Ht:** 6-1   **Wt:** 200   **Shoots:** right
B: October 1, 1967, Clinton, Massachusetts

	Regular Season					Playoffs				
YR	GP	G	A	PTS	PM	GP	G	A	PTS	PM
1990-91	43	11	16	27	33	17	1	6	7	2
Pitt. Totals	43	11	16	27	33	17	1	6	7	2
NHL Totals	1181	342	415	757	448	141	44	43	87	64

Acquired from Hartford for Rob Brown, December 21, 1990

Traded to Quebec for Bryan Fogarty, March 10, 1992

YOUNG, WARREN HOWARD

Left Wing   **Ht:** 6-3   **Wt:** 195   **Shoots:** left
B: January 11, 1956, Toronto, Ontario

	Regular Season					Playoffs				
YR	GP	G	A	PTS	PM	GP	G	A	PTS	PM
1983-84	15	1	7	8	19	-	-	-	-	-
1984-85	80	40	32	72	174	-	-	-	-	-
1986-87	50	8	13	21	103	-	-	-	-	-
1987-88	7	0	0	0	15	-	-	-	-	-
Pitt. Totals	152	49	52	101	311	-	-	-	-	-
NHL Totals	236	72	77	149	472	-	-	-	-	-

Signed as a free agent, August 12, 1983

Signed as a free agent by Detroit, July 10, 1985

Acquired from Detroit for cash, October 8, 1986

NHL All-Rookie Team 1984-85

WRIGHT, TYLER

Center   **Ht:** 6-0   **Wt:** 190   **Shoots:** right
B: April 6, 1973, Kamsack, Saskatchewan

	Regular Season					Playoffs				
YR	GP	G	A	PTS	PM	GP	G	A	PTS	PM
1996-97	45	2	2	4	70	-	-	-	-	-
1997-98	82	3	4	7	112	6	0	1	1	4
1998-99	61	0	0	0	90	13	0	0	0	19
1999-00	50	12	10	22	45	11	3	1	4	17
Pitt. Totals	238	17	16	33	317	30	3	2	5	40
NHL Totals	613	79	70	149	854	30	3	2	5	40

Acquired from Edmonton for a 7th round choice in the 1996 Entry Draft, June 22, 1996

Claimed by Columbus in the 2000 Expansion Draft, June 23, 2000

YOUNG, WENDELL

Goaltender   **Ht:** 5-9   **Wt:** 181   **Shoots:** Left
B: August 1, 1963, Halifax, Nova Scotia

	Regular Season					Playoffs				
YR	GP	MINS	GA	SH	AVE	GP	MINS	GA	SH	AVE
1988-89	22	1150	92	0	4.80	1	39	1	0	1.54
1989-90	43	2318	181	1	4.17	-	-	-	-	-
1990-91	18	773	52	0	4.04	-	-	-	-	-
1991-92	18	838	53	0	3.79	-	-	-	-	-
1994-95	10	497	27	0	3.26	-	-	-	-	-
Pitt. Totals	111	5576	385	1	4.14	1	39	1	0	1.54
NHL Totals	187	9410	618	2	3.94	2	99	6	0	3.64

Acquired from Philadelphia with a 7th round choice in the 1990 Entry Draft for a 3rd round choice in the 1990 Entry Draft, September 1, 1988

Selected by Tampa Bay in 1992 Expansion Draft, June 18, 1992

Acquired from Tampa Bay for future considerations, February 16, 1995

Z

ZAINE, RODNEY CARL (Rod)

Center   **Ht:** 5-10   **Wt:** 180   **Shoots:** left
B: May 18, 1946, Ottawa, Ontario

	Regular Season					Playoffs				
YR	GP	G	A	PTS	PM	GP	G	A	PTS	PM
1970-71	37	8	5	13	21	-	-	-	-	-
Pitt. Totals	37	8	5	13	21	-	-	-	-	-
NHL Totals	61	10	6	16	25	-	-	-	-	-
WHA Totals	219	11	33	44	58	18	2	1	3	2

Purchased from Baltimore (AHL), July 1970

Claimed by Buffalo in the Intra-League Draft, June 8, 1971

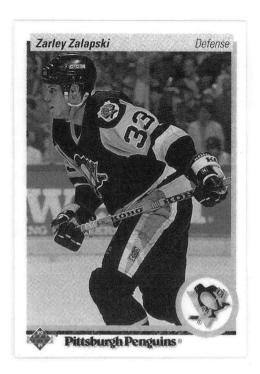

Zarley Zalapski   Defense

Pittsburgh Penguins®

ZALAPSKI, ZARLEY

Defense   **Ht:** 6-1   **Wt:** 215   **Shoots:** left
B: April 22, 1968, Edmonton, Alberta

	Regular Season					Playoffs				
YR	GP	G	A	PTS	PM	GP	G	A	PTS	PM
1987-88	15	3	8	11	7	-	-	-	-	-
1988-89	58	12	33	45	57	11	1	8	9	13
1989-90	51	6	25	31	37	-	-	-	-	-
1990-91	66	12	36	48	59	-	-	-	-	-
Pitt. Totals	190	33	102	135	160	11	1	8	9	13
NHL Totals	637	99	285	384	684	48	4	23	27	47

Selected in the 1986 Entry Draft, 1st choice, 4th overall

Traded to Hartford with John Cullen and Jeff Parker for Ron Francis, Grant Jennings, and Ulf Samuelsson, March 4, 1991

NHL All-Rookie Team 1988-89

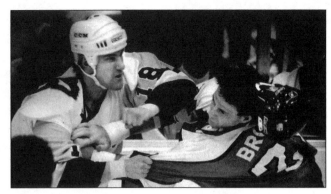

Enforcer Richard Zemlak (18) sends Dave Brown's helmet flying with a left.

ZEMLAK, RICHARD ANDREW

Right Wing   Ht: 6-2 **Wt:** 190   **Shoots:** right
B: March 3, 1963, Wynard, Saskatchewan

YR	Regular Season					Playoffs				
	GP	G	A	PTS	PM	GP	G	A	PTS	PM
1988-89	31	0	0	0	135	1	0	0	0	10
1989-90	19	1	5	6	43	-	-	-	-	-
Pitt. Totals	50	1	5	6	178	1	0	0	0	10
NHL Totals	132	2	12	14	587	1	0	0	0	10

Acquired from Minnesota for the rights to Rob Gaudreau, November 1, 1988

Signed as a free agent by Calgary, November 8, 1990

ZIGOMANIS, MIKE

Center   Ht: 6-1 **Wt:** 200   **Shoots:** right
B: January 17, 1981, Toronto, Ontario

YR	Regular Season					Playoffs				
	GP	G	A	PTS	PM	GP	G	A	PTS	PM
2008-09	22	2	4	6	27	-	-	-	-	-
Pitt. Totals	22	2	4	6	27	-	-	-	-	-
NHL Totals	189	21	18	39	85	-	-	-	-	-

Acquired from Phoenix for future considerations, October 9, 2008

Signed as a free agent by Djurgardens (Sweden), November 10, 2009

ZUBOV, SERGEI

Defense   Ht: 6-1 **Wt:** 198   **Shoots:** right
B: July 22, 1970, Moscow, USSR

YR	Regular Season					Playoffs				
	GP	G	A	PTS	PM	GP	G	A	PTS	PM
1995-96	64	11	55	66	22	18	1	14	15	26
Pitt. Totals	64	11	55	66	22	18	1	14	15	26
NHL Totals	1068	152	619	771	337	164	24	93	117	62

Acquired from NY Rangers with Petr Nedved for Luc Robitaille and Ulf Samuelsson, August 31, 1995

Traded to Dallas for Kevin Hatcher, June 22, 1996

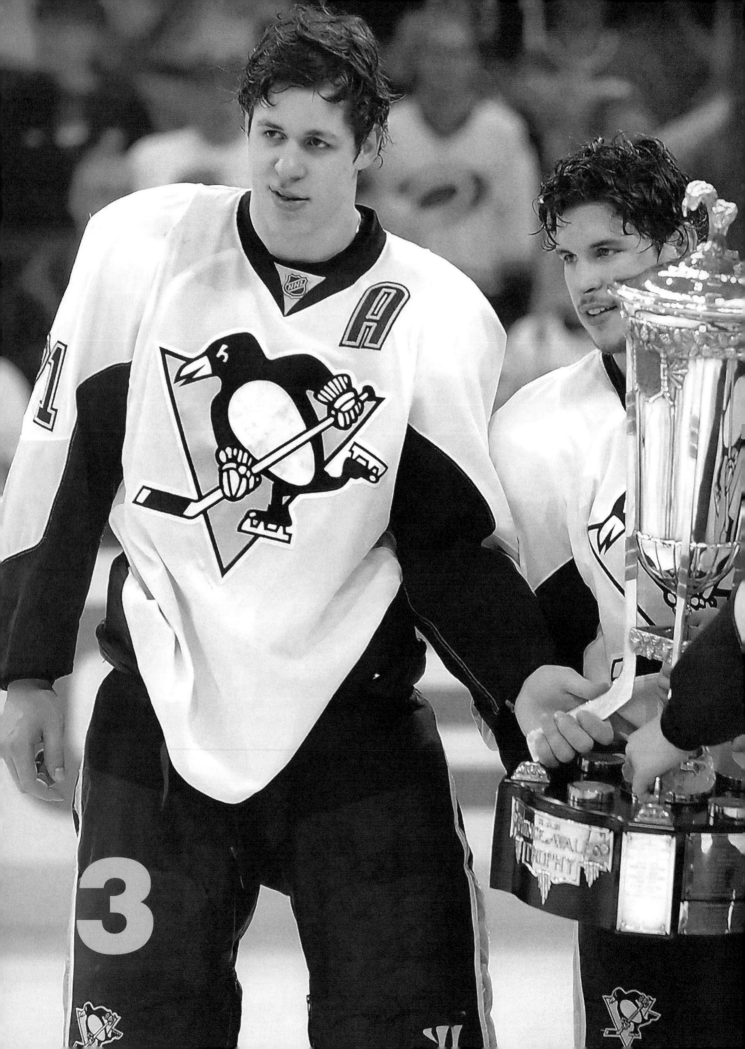

Player Profiles

Over the course of the Penguins' 43-year history, some of the game's greatest and brightest stars have graced the ice surface of the Mellon Arena. In particular, the list of players who passed through the Steel City during the decade of the 1990s could fill the pages of a *Who's Who in Hockey*.

To honor the greatest of them all—Penguins owner Mario Lemieux—we compiled biographies on 66 of the greatest players ever to wear the black and gold (and blue and white). Paring the list of Penguins players past and present down to the "Select 66" was no easy task. So many players served the team with distinction and honor through the years and are deserving of recognition.

There is a natural inclination to favor players of the recent era over players who skated for the team in the past. However, a conscious effort was made to represent players from each era in Penguins history. With that goal in mind, the chapter is divided into four main sections: The Captains, The All-Stars, The Role Players, and The Goalies. A special Honorable Mention section is included at the end for players who didn't make the final cut.

Thirteen players are represented in The Captains section. Some of the team's all-time greats have worn the "C," such as Mario Lemieux, Jaromir Jagr, and Sidney Crosby. However, muckers and grinders have served as captains too, including Dan Frawley and Terry Ruskowski. The Captains section does not include Paul Coffey, John Cullen, and Randy Hillier, who served as fill-in captains. Each was awarded the "C" on an interim basis during Mario Lemieux's absence in 1990 due to a herniated disc. They are profiled elsewhere in the chapter.

The All-Stars was the easiest and most objective section to compile. In order to qualify, a player had to be selected to play in an NHL All-Star Game or named to a postseason NHL All-Star Team. Twenty-seven Penguins (not including captains) past and present were named to an All-Star team, including luminaries such as Pierre Larouche, Evgeni Malkin, and Kevin Stevens. Al McDonough was voted to the 1973–74 West Division squad while still with the Penguins, but actually skated in the All-Star Game as a member of the Atlanta Flames. He is included in this section. Players who were voted to the NHL All-Rookie Team or who skated in the NHL Young Stars Game are not featured.

While Pittsburgh has never been regarded as a breeding ground for puck-stoppers, six players are featured in The Goalies section, including popular netminders Les Binkley and Marc-Andre Fleury.

The Role Players provides a catch-all category for players who didn't grab headlines or scoring titles, but were no less important to the fabric of the team. This was by far the most difficult and subjective section to compile. Some of the 20 players featured in this section were on the cusp of stardom, such as Michel Briere and Greg Malone. Others, including hard-hitting defenseman Darius Kasparaitis and tough guy Jay Caufield, filled an important niche or role.

Evgeni Malkin, Sidney Crosby, and Sergei Gonchar show off the Prince of Wales Trophy in 2009.

The Captains

Bullard, Mike

Penguins: 1980–86　**Birthplace:** Ottawa, Ontario
Center　B: March 10, 1961
Shoots: left　**Ht.** 6-0　**Wt.** 195
Captain: 1984–86　**Nickname:** The Bullet

YR	Regular Season					Playoffs				
	GP	G	A	PTS	PM	GP	G	A	PTS	PM
1980–81	15	1	2	3	19	4	3	3	6	0
1981–82	75	36	27	63	91	5	1	1	2	4
1982–83	57	22	22	44	60	-	-	-	-	-
1983–84	76	51	41	92	57	-	-	-	-	-
1984–85	68	32	31	63	75	-	-	-	-	-
1985–86	77	41	42	83	69	-	-	-	-	-
1986–87	14	2	10	12	17	-	-	-	-	-
NHL	**727**	**329**	**345**	**674**	**703**	**40**	**11**	**18**	**29**	**44**

Seen here ragging the puck, Mike Bullard scored 51 goals in 1983–84.

As a rink rat growing up in Ottawa, Ontario, Mike Bullard displayed a scorer's touch from an early age. Although not especially big or fast, he was excellent at ragging the puck and drove to the net with a bulldog determination.

The Penguins had hoped to land Kitchener's speedy defenseman, Paul Coffey, with their first pick in the 1980 Entry Draft. However, the Edmonton Oilers beat them to the punch. Fortunately, Bullard was still available, so the Pens grabbed the Brantford Alexanders scoring ace with the ninth overall pick.

Bullard made a strong first impression during the 1981 Stanley Cup Playoffs. Following a huge year with Brantford (107 points in 42 games), he was called up by the Penguins for the stretch run. After seeing little ice time during a 15-game cameo, the 19-year-old center didn't expect to see much action in the postseason.

Prior to Game 2, coach Eddie Johnston called the rookie into his office. Much to his surprise, Bullard was informed that he'd be centering a line for Gregg Sheppard and George Ferguson.

Admittedly nervous, Bullard promptly went out and scored a big goal to spark the team to a 6–4 victory over St. Louis. It was the first of many he would score with the Penguins.

Displaying excellent hand-eye coordination and a nose for the net, he enjoyed an outstanding rookie season in 1981–82. Bullard tied veteran Paul Gardner for the team lead in scoring with 36 goals, smashing the club's previous record for first-year players set by Pierre Larouche.

In the playoffs that spring, he scored a huge goal to give the Penguins the lead in a Game 5 showdown against the Islanders. Following a New York rally that sent the game into overtime, Bullard rang a shot off the pipe. Had the puck gone in, it would've ended the Islanders' two-year reign as Cup champions. Ironically, it was the last playoff game Bullard ever played for the Pens.

Following the near-miss against the Islanders, the Penguins became a bad team—one of the worst in NHL history. Despite the dismal circumstances, Bullard did his best. In 1982–83 he overcame a bout with mononucleosis to score 22 goals in 57 games. The next season he became the fourth 50-goal scorer in Penguins history—a truly remarkable feat given how bad the team was.

Although he replaced Randy Carlyle as team captain, Bullard would soon share the spotlight with another big-time scorer—phenom Mario Lemieux. Unaccustomed to playing second-fiddle, the 23-year-old Bullard struggled to adjust, dipping to 32 goals in 1984–85 while logging a horrendous plus/minus rating of minus 43. In January he was arrested for drunk driving—hardly the type of behavior the team needed from its captain.

Bullard did his best to clean up his act. He rebounded with a strong 41-goal season in 1985–86. However, a slow start the following year prompted a trade to Calgary for Dan Quinn.

The move out west was like a breath of fresh air. Skating on a strong, veteran team for the first time in his career, Bullard flourished. With the 800-pound gorilla of having to carry a team removed from his back, "the Bullet" struck for 48 goals and a career-best 103 points.

Despite an early playoff exit, he appeared set for a long and productive run in Alberta. However, Bullard became an unfortunate victim of his own success. The Flames used him as the centerpiece of a package to acquire Doug Gilmour from St. Louis. Stung by the deal, he floundered through 20 games with the Blues before being shipped to Philadelphia.

Once again surrounded by a strong team, Bullard scored at close to a point-per-game clip for the Flyers. On April 29, 1989, he exacted a measure of revenge on the Penguins, scoring the back-breaking goal in Game 7 of the Patrick Division Finals to vanquish his old team.

Although he enjoyed a solid season for the Flyers in 1989–90, Bullard opted to play in Switzerland the next year. Skating for HC Ambri-Piotta, he piled up 69 points in 36 games.

Bullard returned to the NHL to play for Toronto in 1991–92. However, he had slowed a bit during his time overseas. Following a disappointing 14-goal campaign with the Leafs, he returned to Europe, where he starred in Germany for 10 seasons.

Carlyle, Randy

Penguins: 1978–84   **Birthplace:** Sudbury, Ontario
Defense   B: April 19, 1956
Shoots: left   **Ht.** 5-10 **Wt.** 200
Captain: 1981–84   **Nickname:** Kitty

Randy Carlyle won the Norris Trophy in 1981.

	Regular Season					Playoffs				
YR	GP	G	A	PTS	PM	GP	G	A	PTS	PM
1978–79	70	13	34	47	78	7	0	0	0	12
1979–80	67	8	28	36	45	5	1	0	1	4
1980–81	76	16	67	83	136	5	4	5	9	9
1981–82	73	11	64	75	131	5	1	3	4	16
1982–83	61	15	41	56	110	-	-	-	-	-
1983–84	50	3	23	26	82	-	-	-	-	-
NHL	1055	148	499	647	1400	69	9	24	33	120

Over the course of five-plus years with the Penguins, Randy Carlyle appeared in 397 games and racked up the impressive totals of 66 goals, 257 assists, and 323 points. He also appeared in two NHL All-Star Games and was named an NHL First Team All-Star in 1981. Those achievements alone would be more than enough to place him among the team's all-time greats. However, in 1980–81 he accomplished something that no Penguins defenseman managed to do before or since. He won the Norris Trophy.

The Toronto Maple Leafs expected good things from Carlyle when they selected him with their second pick in the 1976 Entry Draft. The husky young defenseman had displayed decent offensive ability during his junior hockey career with the Sudbury Wolves, along with a taste for physical play. However, the Maple Leafs boasted a trio of top-flight offensive rearguards, including Jim McKenny, Borje

Salming, and Ian Turnbull. Consigned to a stay-at-home role, Carlyle rarely got a chance to shine during his two seasons with the Leafs.

Seeking an established defenseman to help his team reach the next level, Toronto general manager Jim Gregory traded Carlyle and versatile forward George Ferguson to the Penguins on June 14, 1978, for All-Star Dave Burrows. While the Penguins were pleased with the return, they could not have imagined what was in store.

Given a free hand to join the rush by Pens coach Johnny Wilson, Carlyle began to flash his latent offensive skills. Although a choppy skater, he possessed outstanding vision and excelled at leading the breakout. "Kitty" scored 13 goals his first season in the Steel City, along with a healthy 47 points.

Following a down year in 1979–80, Wilson was replaced behind the bench by Eddie Johnston. A former Boston mainstay, Johnston brought with him the secrets of the Bruins' imposing power play.

A superb puckhandler and playmaker, Carlyle was ideally suited to serve as the quarterback. With the tousle-haired defender directing traffic from the point and dangerous scorers Paul Gardner and Rick Kehoe serving as the triggermen, the Pens exploded for 92 power-play goals in 1980–81.

Almost overnight, Carlyle blossomed into a scoring sensation, tallying 16 goals and 83 points—tops among NHL defensemen. Although his offensive performance outstripped his defensive play (minus 16), he became the first player from a 1967 expansion team to win the Norris Trophy.

Now serving as the Penguins' captain, Carlyle nearly repeated his Norris Trophy performance in 1981–82. Once again spearheading the team's deadly power play (99 goals), he registered 11 goals and 64 assists to lead the Pens to a playoff berth. Unfortunately, Carlyle was victimized by a bad bounce late in Game 5, and the Penguins fell to the Islanders in overtime.

Although Randy continued to post big numbers in 1982–83 (15 goals, 56 points), the team fell on hard times. The following season he was involved in one of the most controversial trades in NHL history. With the Penguins on a fast track to oblivion, general manager Eddie Johnston traded the high-scoring defender to Winnipeg on March 5, 1984, for a first-round pick and future considerations.

Shorn of their best defenseman, the Pens stumbled to a miserable 2–11 finish, nudging out the equally awful New Jersey Devils for the right to draft Mario Lemieux.

As for Carlyle, he continued his strong production for the Jets, averaging 15 goals and 50 points per year over the next four seasons. Although advancing age and weight problems began to take their toll in the late 1980s, Carlyle played on through the 1992–93 season before retiring.

Following his playing career, the former Pens captain entered the coaching ranks. In 2007 he led the Anaheim Ducks to a Stanley Cup title.

Crosby, Sidney

Penguins: 2005– **Birthplace:** Cole Harbour, Nova Scotia
Center B: August 7, 1987
Shoots: left **Ht.** 5-11 **Wt.** 200
Captain: 2007–
Nicknames: Sid the Kid, The Wizard of Cros

	Regular Season					Playoffs				
YR	GP	G	A	PTS	PM	GP	G	A	PTS	PM
2005–06	81	39	63	102	110	-	-	-	-	-
2006–07	79	36	84	120	60	5	3	2	5	4
2007–08	53	24	48	72	39	20	6	21	27	12
2008–09	77	33	70	103	76	24	15	16	31	14
2009-10	81	51	58	109	71	13	6	13	19	6
NHL	371	183	323	506	356	62	30	52	82	36

Perhaps no player embodies the Penguins' hopes for future Stanley Cup glory more than their captain and most gifted player, Sidney Crosby. During his brief career, he has captured every major award while establishing himself as the poster boy for the "New NHL."

Like his onetime landlord, Penguins owner Mario Lemieux, Crosby seemed destined for greatness at an early age. As a toddler, he showed an instinct for the game by shooting toy pucks off the dryer in his family's home in Cole Harbour, Nova Scotia. Noting that the appliance was taking quite a beating, his father John—a former draft pick of the Montreal Canadiens—began to teach his son how to skate.

The youngster quickly blossomed. At the age of 13, he piled up a staggering 182 points while leading his local Bantam team, the Cole Harbour Red Wings, to a second-place finish in the Air Canada Cup tournament. Two years later Sid enrolled at the prestigious Shattuck St. Mary's Boarding School and sparked the Sabres to the U.S. National Championship.

Already a celebrity in his native Canada, he joined the moribund Rimouski Oceanic in 2003–04. Crosby made a clean sweep of the Quebec Major Junior Hockey League's major awards, including Top Rookie, Top Scorer, and Player of the Year, while leading the Oceanic to a stunning 51-point improvement. The following season he upped the ante, racking up 168 points while propelling Rimouski to the Memorial Cup finals.

By the time the 2005 NHL Entry Draft rolled around there was little doubt that the precocious 17-year-old would be the first pick. The only question was which team would be fortunate enough to select him. Emerging from the strike-marred 2004–05 season, the NHL decided to institute a lottery. Every team would have a chance to win the coveted No. 1 pick. On July 22 the lottery balls were dropped, and the one adorned with a skating penguin logo entered the tube.

For the Penguins, who had plummeted from the status of perennial contenders to bottom feeders, the gates of heaven had opened.

"Getting Sidney Crosby was the happiest day of my life," former Penguins GM Craig Patrick said.

Scouts were universal in their praise, hailing the youngster as a hybrid of Mario and "the Great One" himself, Wayne Gretzky. In his typically modest fashion, "Sid the Kid" downplayed the hype.

"I'm not trying to be the next Wayne Gretzky or Mario Lemieux," he said. "I am putting pressure on myself to do my best and perform to my potential. That's all I can do."

It soon became apparent that Crosby was, indeed, a special player. While the Penguins continued to sag, the 18-year-old took off like a rocket, capturing Rookie of the Month honors for October. Following Mario's retirement in December of 2005, Sid was named as an alternate captain.

The appointment raised eyebrows among hockey's old guard.

"An 18-year-old kid says he's going to give us ideas," analyst Don Cherry sniffed. "What, from the Quebec League, he's going to give them ideas? Come on. That's ridiculous."

Sid received a rude welcome on the ice as well. During his first visit to Philadelphia, referees Paul Devorski and Ian Walsh turned a blind eye as he absorbed a vicious high stick from Derian Hatcher. With his mouth bloodied and his front teeth chipped, Crosby played the rest of the game with a controlled fury. Gathering in a pass from Lyle Odelein, he drilled the puck past Antero Niittymaki to spark a Penguins rally.

As the season progressed, Sid's unique style began to crystallize. A terrific skater and a brilliant passer, another exemplary element of his game began to emerge—grit. Blessed with powerful legs and incredible balance, the 5'11", 200-pounder worked the corners and high-traffic areas with the tenacity of a sled dog. Displaying remarkable passion, he never took a shift off.

"He's got it all," Buffalo coach Lindy Ruff said. "He's a tremendous skater, a tremendous stickhandler. He's good in every area. I don't think the kid has any holes. He's got everything."

Aided by the strong play of fellow rookie Colby Armstrong, Crosby finished his rookie campaign with a rush to register 102 points, breaking Mario's club record for first-year players. He placed second in the tightly contested Calder Trophy voting to Washington supernova Alexander Ovechkin.

The next season Sid truly was a sight to behold. Displaying uncommon focus and maturity, the 19-year-old wonder rolled up a league-leading 120 points to easily outpace his Russian rival. He became the youngest scoring champion in NHL history and the youngest ever to garner the league's three major awards—the Hart Trophy (MVP), the Art Ross Trophy (Scoring), and the Lester B. Pearson Award (NHL Players Association MVP).

Following Crosby's lead, the Penguins registered a staggering 47-point improvement and burst into prominence as the most exciting young team in all of hockey. Poised for postseason success, they were overwhelmed by battle-hardened Ottawa in the opening round of the playoffs. But once more Sid showed his mettle. Playing on a broken foot, he paced the team in scoring while providing inspiration and leadership for his teammates.

The Penguins brass took note. On May 31, 2007, they officially appointed Crosby as team captain, making him the youngest player to serve as captain in league history. This time there were no cries of derision.

"Sidney has done so much for this franchise in his first two seasons, made so much history, that you have to keep reminding yourself that he is only 19 years old," general manager Ray Shero said. "It is obvious to all of us—coaches, players, management, staff—that he has grown into the acknowledged leader of the Pittsburgh Penguins. It is only appropriate that he wears the 'C' as team captain."

Taking his new role to heart, Crosby zoomed to the top of the NHL scoring race in 2007–08. However, adversity struck on January 18 when Sid suffered a high-ankle sprain—a nagging injury that often took months to fully heal.

He returned to the lineup for the stretch run flanked by a new set of linemates. While Crosby was recuperating, Shero acquired All-Star sniper Marian Hossa and speedy checker Pascal Dupuis from Atlanta.

Following a brief adjustment period, the trio began to click during the postseason. Although hampered by

The Savior II: superstar Sidney Crosby won the Art Ross and Hart Trophies in 2006–07.

lingering effects of his injury, Crosby led the team to convincing victories over the Senators, Rangers, and Flyers to set up a Stanley Cup Finals matchup with Detroit.

His new linemates were clearly impressed.

"Everyone knows what he can do on the ice," Dupuis said. "What brings him to another level is he's so driven. That's his main quality. He wants to win so bad."

That drive was on display for everyone to see during the finals. After the Penguins were whitewashed by the Red Wings in Games 1 and 2, Crosby made it his personal mission to lift the team to victory. "The Wizard of Cros" scored two huge goals in Game 3 to get the Pens untracked.

True to form, Crosby tied Conn Smythe Trophy winner Henrik Zetterberg for the playoff lead in points, while turning Hossa—a perennial postseason flop—into a scoring machine. Despite Sid's superb individual effort, the Penguins succumbed to their powerful adversary in six grueling games.

Crestfallen, Crosby tried to put things in perspective.

"That was a huge year for us," he said. "We gained a lot of experience pretty quickly. Hopefully, we'll get another chance and it will have a different outcome."

The 2008–09 season would prove to be the most challenging of Crosby's young career. Hossa defected to Detroit during the off-season, leaving Sid without a true scoring winger. Ray Shero attempted to plug the gap with veteran free agent Miroslav Satan, but the experiment failed miserably. By midseason, Crosby—skating with third liners Dupuis and Tyler Kennedy—was clearly struggling.

Faced with a mountain of adversity, the Pens' 21-year-old captain responded the only way he knew how—by giving 110 percent every single shift. Buoyed by the acquisition of wingers Chris Kunitz and Bill Guerin at the trade deadline, Sid promptly caught fire, tallying 31 points during his final 21 games. Not coincidentally, the Pens went on a scorching 18–3–4 tear to nail down fourth place in the Eastern Conference.

Once more, Crosby rose to the occasion during the caldron of the Stanley Cup Playoffs. His character forged to a diamond-hard edge, he scored eight goals to key a come-from-behind triumph over archrival Alexander Ovechkin and the Washington Capitals.

Dan Bylsma marveled at Sid's performance.

"He works tirelessly," the Penguins coach said. "He really enjoys the competition, putting it out there, laying it on the line. He was focused. He knew the opportunity he had. He did a big job on the big stage."

Despite being held to three points during a hotly contested rematch with the Red Wings in the Stanley Cup Finals, his leadership and poise were never more evident. Back checking with the diligence of a coal miner, Crosby helped to shut down Detroit's big guns while leading his team to a Stanley Cup.

Although he tallied 103 points during the regular season and paced all playoff scorers with 15 goals, Crosby was shut out at the postseason awards banquet. It mattered little. The highest honor of all—having his name engraved on the Stanley Cup—was his.

"It's everything you dream of," Sid said. "It's an amazing feeling."

Not content to rest on his laurels, Crosby worked tirelessly over the summer to improve his game. In an effort to gain more velocity on his shot he experimented with a new composite stick.

"I want it to work," he said. "It's something that takes time—going from wood to one-piece—but I'm giving it a chance, and we'll see what happens."

Armed with the new stick, Sid enjoyed a sensational season in 2009–10. The Pens' 22-year-old captain struck for a career-best 51 goals to earn a share of the Maurice Richard Trophy. The Hart Trophy finalist narrowly missed out on his second scoring title, finishing two points behind Vancouver's Henrik Sedin.

Although Crosby was unable to lead the Penguins to a second straight Stanley Cup, he enjoyed a moment in the sun while competing for Team Canada in the XXI Winter Olympics. In his typically dramatic fashion, Sid the Kid scored the game-winning goal in overtime to clinch the gold medal for his country.

"That's Sid for you," Olympic teammate Ryan Getzlaf said. "There's a reason he's the best player in the world. He always shows up in those big moments and scores those big goals."

Francis, Ron

Penguins: 1991–98   **Birthplace:** Sault Ste. Marie, Ontario
Center   B: March 1, 1963
Shoots: left   **Ht.** 6-2 **Wt.** 200
Captain: 1994–95, 1997–98   **Nickname:** Ronnie Franchise

| | Regular Season | | | | | Playoffs | | | | |
YR	GP	G	A	PTS	PM	GP	G	A	PTS	PM
1990–91	14	2	9	11	21	24	7	10	17	24
1991–92	70	21	33	54	30	21	8	19	27	6
1992–93	84	24	76	100	68	12	6	11	17	19
1993–94	82	27	66	93	62	6	0	2	2	6
1994–95	44	11	48	59	18	12	6	13	19	4
1995–96	77	27	92	119	56	11	3	6	9	4
1996–97	81	27	63	90	20	5	1	2	3	2
1997–98	81	25	62	87	20	6	1	5	6	2
NHL	**1731**	**549**	**1249**	**1798**	**979**	**171**	**46**	**97**	**143**	**95**

It's only fitting that Ron Francis was inducted into the Hockey Hall of Fame in 2007. His numbers alone are staggering—1,731 games, 549 goals, 1,249 assists (second all-time), and 1,798 points (fourth all-time). But statistics tell only part of the story. They say nothing of the leadership, heart, and desire he displayed over the course of an exemplary 23-year career that enabled him to coax every ounce of ability from his 6'2", 200-pound frame.

Francis' character was forged to a large degree by his upbringing. He grew up in Sault Ste. Marie, Ontario—a gritty steel town not unlike Pittsburgh of a generation ago. The youngster learned the value of discipline and hard work from his father, who worked in the mills for 41 years.

Honing his skills on backyard rinks and local organized teams, Francis gradually progressed through the youth hockey ranks. At the age of 16 he piled up 149 points in 45 games for the Sault Ste. Marie Legion of the Northern Ontario Hockey Association. Less than two years later he was in the National Hockey League. Not only was he skating a regular shift for the Hartford Whalers, but he was averaging better than a point per game to boot.

Francis became an instant folk hero with the fans in Hartford, who admired him for his diligent two-way play. The Whalers management saw him as a player to build a team around. He became "Ronnie Franchise."

The hardworking center didn't disappoint. Over the next eight seasons he never scored fewer than 24 goals, while reaching the 30-goal plateau three times. He registered 80 points or better five times, including 101 points in 1989–90. He manned the power play, killed penalties, won key faceoffs, and back checked with authority. In short, he was a model citizen.

It isn't entirely clear what caused things to sour in Hartford. Perhaps it was the Whalers' lack of playoff success, which by no means could be attributed to Francis. By the middle of the 1990–91 season, however, Francis had clearly run afoul of coach Rick Ley and owner Richard Gordon.

Ron Francis was one of the finest two-way centers in the history of the game.

Still, it was a shock when Whalers general manager Eddie Johnston traded the team's long-time captain to the Penguins along with Grant Jennings and Ulf Samuelsson for John Cullen, Jeff Parker, and Zarley Zalapski.

Although opinion was sharply divided among the experts on which team got the better of the deal, it was a major coup for Pittsburgh. The rugged, abrasive Samuelsson was the backline thumper the Penguins had always lacked. Although essentially a depth defenseman, Jennings also played with an edge.

Without question the plum in the deal was Francis. He was a rare find—a top-line center who was capable of filling a second-line-center role behind Mario Lemieux. In addition, the 28-year-old Francis brought a defensive conscience to a team that was sorely in need of one.

The Penguins responded with a 9–3–2 stretch run to nail down the Patrick Division crown. Teaming with burly Kevin Stevens and old pro Joe Mullen on a solid second line, Francis provided superb two-way play and helped propel the Penguins to their first Stanley Cup.

Following a difficult 1991–92 season that brought more changes, the veteran center once again proved his worth in the Patrick Division Finals. Mario was gone—out for the series with a broken hand. The Rangers held a 2–1 series lead and were up by two goals in Game 4. To make matters worse, they were working on a five-minute power play.

With hopes of a second Cup all but dashed, Francis rose to the occasion with a superhuman effort. Playing on a banged-up knee, he stepped over the boards to quell the potent New York power play. When the penalty expired, he burst toward the Rangers' blue line and fooled goalie Mike Richter with a knuckling slap shot from long range. Inspired, the Penguins promptly chased Richter with another goal and pushed the Rangers to overtime.

Early in the extra frame Francis delivered again. Larry Murphy stripped the puck from Mark Messier and fired it toward the Rangers' goal. Francis, who was planted in the slot with his back to the net, deflected the puck between his own legs and past goalie John Vanbiesbrouck.

Thanks to Francis, the Pens had snatched victory from the jaws of defeat. They would not lose another game during their incredible run to a second Stanley Cup.

Firmly entrenched as one of the most beloved and popular players on the team, Francis remained at the very core of the Penguins' success for six more seasons. In 1994–95 he stepped up to assume the captaincy when Lemieux sat out a year due to the lingering effects of radiation treatments. The hardworking center was rewarded for his unselfish play with the Lady Byng and Selke Trophies.

He enjoyed a career year in 1995–96, piling up 119 points and a league-leading 92 assists to help lead the Penguins to the conference finals. When Mario entered his first retirement in 1997, Francis once again was awarded the "C."

Sadly, Francis and the Penguins parted ways during the summer of 1998. It was not due to a lack of respect—general manager Craig Patrick simply couldn't afford to sign him to a new deal. Although he was now 35 years old, Francis enjoyed a wonderful second career with the Carolina Hurricanes. Displaying his trademark consistency, he averaged nearly 22 goals and 65 points during five full seasons in Carolina. In 2001–02 he led the 'Canes to the Stanley Cup Finals.

The Hall of Famer currently serves the Hurricanes as an associate head coach and director of player personnel.

Frawley, Dan

Penguins: 1985–89   **Birthplace:** Sturgeon Falls, Ontario
Right wing   **B:** June 2, 1962
Shoots: right   **Ht.** 6-1   **Wt.** 195
Captain: 1987

Dan Frawley after one of his many battles.

	Regular Season					Playoffs				
YR	GP	G	A	PTS	PM	GP	G	A	PTS	PM
1985–86	69	10	11	21	174	-	-	-	-	-
1986–87	78	14	14	28	218	-	-	-	-	-
1987–88	47	6	8	14	152	-	-	-	-	-
1988–89	46	3	4	7	66	-	-	-	-	-
NHL	**273**	**37**	**40**	**77**	**674**	**1**	**0**	**0**	**0**	**0**

When the Chicago Black Hawks selected Dan Frawley with the 204th pick in the 1980 Entry Draft, they weren't expecting the next Bobby Hull. But the Black Hawks liked his pluck and determination. They hoped he might someday become a useful grinder.

The young winger exceeded expectations during his first two seasons as a pro, scoring 52 goals for the Springfield Indians of the American Hockey League. Frawley's spirited play earned him a promotion to the Hawks in 1983–84, where he saw mostly spot duty.

Penguins general manager Eddie Johnston, who was the Black Hawks coach when Frawley was drafted, took note. Seeking to reinforce his young club with an underpinning of grit and enthusiasm, he plucked Frawley from Chicago in the 1985 Waiver Draft.

The hustling winger made an immediate impression. Flinging his body into the corners with reckless abandon, Frawley earned a spot with the Penguins in 1985–86. Under the guidance of veteran coach Bob Berry, he developed into a decent role player with some offensive upside, scoring 11 goals.

Frawley enjoyed his best NHL season in 1986–87. Playing mostly on the third and fourth lines, he notched 14 goals while piling up 218 penalty minutes. Although by no means a great fighter, the fearless winger took on all comers and dropped the mitts a team-high 21 times.

Few players have accomplished more with less. A poor skater, Frawley literally hauled himself up and down the ice. His stick was constantly churning in an odd rowing motion as if he was holding an oar and paddling his way around the ice. But he never failed to give 100 percent.

It came as no surprise when Frawley was named the Penguins' captain in 1987—an honor usually reserved for more gifted players. It was a clear indication of how much admiration and respect his teammates had for the hardworking winger.

His reign as team captain was brief. When he was knocked out of the lineup by an early season knee injury, he graciously ceded the "C" to a big fellow who wore No. 66.

After scoring three goals as a part-timer in 1988–89, Frawley was released by the Penguins in 1990. He signed on as a minor league free agent with Rochester, where he became a mainstay. Frawley retired after three solid seasons with the Americans in 1993. Following a two-year absence, he returned to the ice and helped lead the Amerks to a Calder Cup title in 1996.

Ingarfield, Earl

Penguins: 1967–69   **Birthplace:** Lethbridge, Alberta
Center   **B:** October 25, 1934
Shoots: left   **Ht.** 5-11   **Wt.** 185
Captain: 1968–69

	Regular Season					Playoffs				
YR	GP	G	A	PTS	PM	GP	G	A	PTS	PM
1967–68	50	15	22	37	12	-	-	-	-	-
1968–69	40	8	15	23	4	-	-	-	-	-
NHL	**746**	**179**	**226**	**405**	**239**	**21**	**9**	**8**	**17**	**10**

During a strong junior career with his hometown Lethbridge Native Sons, Earl Ingarfield established himself as a good team player and a top scorer. After leading the Western Canadian Junior Hockey League in goals two years running, the hardworking center started his pro career in the New York Rangers organization.

Earl Ingarfield, the Pens'
second captain.

Following a three-year apprenticeship in the minors, Ingarfield earned a spot with the Rangers in 1958. A fringe player at first, he gradually worked his way into a more prominent role. Skating on the Rangers' top line with fellow future Penguins Andy Bathgate and Dean Prentice, the speedy center enjoyed a banner year in 1961–62. He notched 26 goals and 57 points to win the team's Player's Player Award.

For the next five seasons Ingarfield provided the Blueshirts with solid two-way hockey. In 1967, however, he was placed on the team's unprotected list for the upcoming Expansion Draft. Mindful of making his team strong down the middle, Penguins general manager Jack Riley chose the veteran center as his first position player.

Reunited with Bathgate, his old Rangers linemate, Ingarfield helped the team to a good start.

"Earl knows that a wing has to have the puck as he busts over the blue line," said an appreciative Bathgate. "He knows that a center must be around the net after making his passes. He just knows what to do."

In late October, however, the durable center suffered a knee injury—the first significant injury of his career. Although he returned to the lineup around the holidays to post 37 points in 50 games, the Penguins missed the playoffs.

When team captain Ab McDonald was traded over the summer, the highly respected Ingarfield was named as his successor. Although it was by no means a reflection of his leadership, the Pens stumbled to a miserable 10–32–7 start. In an effort to right the Pens' sinking ship, Jack Riley peddled the 35-year-old center to Oakland along with Dick Mattiussi and Gene Ubriaco for Tracy Pratt, George Swarbrick, and Bryan Watson.

Proving he still had something left, Ingarfield became one of the Seals' top players. During the next season and a half he tallied 29 goals and 69 points in 80 games to lead Oakland to its only playoff berths—including a 1970 quarterfinals matchup against the Penguins.

Following his retirement in 1972, Ingarfield briefly coached the Regina Pats and the fledgling New York Islanders. He moved into scouting and played a key role in bringing Bryan Trottier to Long Island. In the mid-1970s he purchased the Lethbridge Broncos and served as the team's coach and assistant general manager before returning to the Islanders as a scout in 1982.

Jagr, Jaromir

Penguins: 1990–01   **Birthplace:** Kladno, Czechoslovakia
Right wing   **B:** February 15, 1972
Shoots: left   **Ht.** 6-3   **Wt.** 240
Captain: 1998–01   **Nickname:** Jags

YR	Regular Season GP	G	A	PTS	PM	Playoffs GP	G	A	PTS	PM
1990–91	80	27	30	57	42	24	3	10	13	6
1991–92	70	32	37	69	34	21	11	13	24	6
1992–93	81	34	60	94	61	12	5	4	9	23
1993–94	80	32	67	99	61	6	2	4	6	16
1994–95	48	32	38	70	37	12	10	5	15	6
1995–96	82	62	87	149	96	18	11	12	23	18
1996–97	63	47	48	95	40	5	4	4	8	4
1997–98	77	35	67	102	64	6	4	5	9	2
1998–99	81	44	83	127	66	9	5	7	12	16
1999–00	63	42	54	96	50	11	8	8	16	6
2000–01	81	52	69	121	42	16	2	10	12	18
NHL	**1273**	**646**	**953**	**1599**	**907**	**169**	**77**	**104**	**181**	**149**

Perhaps no athlete in the annals of Pittsburgh sports is more vilified than Jaromir Jagr. That's saying a lot considering the less-than-cordial reception that greeted ex-Pirates slugger Barry Bonds when he came to town. But the treatment Bonds received paled in comparison to the bitter and unrelenting chorus of boos that rained down on Jagr when he visited the Mellon Arena.

It wasn't always so. Once upon a time, "Jags" was the darling of Pittsburgh hockey fans—the heir apparent to succeed Mario Lemieux as the king on the Penguins' throne.

He was thrust onto hockey's center stage as a gangly 18-year-old with enormous potential. A member of the illustrious draft class of 1990, the Czech Republic native was picked fifth overall by the Penguins behind luminaries such as Owen Nolan, countryman Petr Nedved, Keith Primeau, and Mike Ricci, and just ahead of Darryl Sydor and Derian Hatcher. Although all would make an impact, Jagr's star by far shone the brightest.

His career nearly ended before it began. After a quick start to his rookie season Jagr grew terribly despondent and homesick.

"Most people have friends but no money," he said. "I have the opposite. I don't have a chance to talk to my real friends, the ones I've had since I was five years old. Sometimes I wish I could bring Czechoslovakia to America. Then I would be the happiest guy in the world."

The great Jaromir Jagr turns to follow the play. "Jags" won five NHL scoring titles as a member of the Pens.

With Jagr's frame of mind worsening with each passing day, Penguins GM Craig Patrick acquired Jiri Hrdina, a former captain of the Czech national team, to provide companionship and mentoring.

The move worked like a charm. Hrdina and Jagr quickly became inseparable, and the youngster's play began to improve. Surrounded by a talented veteran team, he did not have the added pressure of playing the savior as Mario had, which helped him to relax even more.

His extraordinary gifts soon bubbled to the surface. In Game 2 of the 1991 Patrick Division Semifinals he scored a spectacular goal against the Devils. Controlling the puck with one hand on his stick, he shed the persistent checking of rugged John MacLean, glided through the slot, and waited out goaltender Chris Terreri before snapping home the game winner.

Comparisons to Lemieux were inevitable. As a local scribe was quick to point out, the name Jaromir was an anagram for "Mario Jr." Certainly there were striking similarities. Both were strong, powerful skaters with a flair for the dramatic. It was obvious that Jagr idolized Lemieux and tried to emulate him.

"Every student needs a teacher, and Mario was my teacher," he said.

He also had one glaring flaw. Jagr shot almost exclusively from the backhand, a tendency that severely limited his goal-scoring potential. To his credit the youngster worked long hours with onetime Pens sniper Rick Kehoe to develop a lethal wrist shot.

His game now complete, Jagr was electrifying during the Pens' march to their second Stanley Cup in 1992. With Mario out of action, the 20-year-old wonder stepped forward in style, notching the winning goal in three straight games. All told, the brilliant young winger scored 11 goals and 24 points in 21 postseason games.

The fans loved his exuberance, the way he would remove a glove and shake his fist after scoring an important goal. Signs reading "Zivio Jagr" ("Cheers Jagr") hung from the balconies at the Civic Arena like championship banners. With his long, flowing locks and boyish good looks, he achieved the type of status usually reserved for rock stars. Every young woman in Pittsburgh wanted to date him. A local radio station, WDVE, held a 21st birthday party for the popular young superstar at a local night club. When he revealed that he enjoyed Kit Kat candy bars, he received thousands of the treats in the mail.

"I eat them all," he said with a huge grin.

As Jagr began to mature physically he shed the coltishness of youth and added yet another element to his game—power. Blessed with huge legs, he would eventually tip the scales at a well-proportioned 245 pounds, which made him virtually impossible to stop.

When Mario was forced to sit out the 1994–95 season, Jagr truly emerged as a world-class player. Skating on a line with crafty setup man Ron Francis, he came into his own and captured his first scoring title. He would win the Art Ross Trophy four more times and add the Hart Trophy to his burgeoning collection of silverware. It seemed the city of Pittsburgh, and indeed the entire hockey world, was his oyster.

If Jagr was a prince in waiting, he bore the crown uneasily. Although quick with a smile or a joke, beneath the surface he was a deeply sensitive young man given to periods of brooding and introspection. He did not fit the mold of a classic leader in the way of a Lemieux or a Francis. When the former retired and the latter departed through free agency, the Penguins became Jagr's team. Craig Patrick added several fellow Czechs to the mix to help, including Martin Straka, Robert Lang, and Jiri Slegr. Try as he might, Jagr was unable to lead the "Euro-Pens" to another Cup.

By the late 1990s the joy and passion that had been a hallmark of Jagr's play began to seep from his game. There were very public squabbles with coaches Kevin Constantine and Ivan Hlinka over what were politely termed philosophical differences, and the infamous quote about "dying alive" during a rare scoring slump. More alarming were the persistent rumors of an off-ice gambling problem. Perhaps all the fame and honors and adulation had come too easily and too quickly.

By the spring of 2001 it all came to a head. Negotiations that were set to begin on a new contract never took place.

"This could be my last year in Pittsburgh," Jagr said glumly. "If they want to trade me, they're going to do it."

Bound by financial constraints and weary of Jagr's declining attitude, Craig Patrick was actively seeking a trade. In July he found a taker in the Washington Capitals. The return for arguably the greatest hockey player in the world was less than earth-shattering, setting off a firestorm of criticism.

The day Jagr packed his suitcase and left town was the day the final curtain came crashing down on the Penguins' glory years. We're left to wonder what might have been had the Jagr saga turned out differently. Perhaps that's why he is so reviled in Pittsburgh, as if the fans somehow saw him as the architect of the team's demise. They had taken him to their hearts and made him their favorite son, and he had betrayed them. Anakin Skywalker had become Darth Vader.

One fact is clear. Jagr was an awesome talent. In 2006–07 he became only the second player in NHL history to score at least 30 goals in 15 straight seasons, a testament to his supreme skill and durability.

Kindrachuk, Orest

Penguins: 1978–81   **Birthplace:** Nanton, Alberta
Center   B: September 14, 1950
Shoots: left   **Ht.** 5-10 **Wt.** 175
Captain: 1978–81   **Nicknames:** Chuckles, Little O, Russ

		Regular Season						Playoffs		
YR	GP	G	A	PTS	PM	GP	G	A	PTS	PM
1978–79	79	18	42	60	84	7	4	1	5	7
1979–80	52	17	29	46	63	-	-	-	-	-
1980–81	13	3	9	12	34	-	-	-	-	-
NHL	508	118	261	379	648	76	20	20	40	53

A thinking man's hockey player, Orest Kindrachuk was always preparing for the future. In the midst of a promising junior career with the Saskatoon Blades, he stepped away from hockey for a season to attend the University of Saskatchewan. The Nanton, Alberta, native had decided to become an optometrist.

"I felt at the time that I really wanted to be a doctor and the odds of making the NHL were slim because there were a lot less teams than there are today," Kindrachuk recalled.

After a year of college, he choose to resume his hockey career. Skating as an overage junior, he enjoyed a monster season for Saskatoon, racking up 149 points. His fine play earned him an invitation to the Philadelphia Flyers' training camp.

Following a two-year apprenticeship in the minors, Kindrachuk made the Flyers in 1973–74. Skating on the checking line with rugged wingers Don "Big Bird" Saleski and Dave "the Hammer" Schultz, the scrappy little center proved to be an important cog on the Flyers' Stanley Cup–winning teams.

Although not a fast skater, Kindrachuk was tenacious and fearless. Equally adept in an offensive or defensive role, he manned the power play and killed penalties—a crucial job on the rough and tumble "Broad Street Bullies."

Pens captain Orest Kindrachuk is upended by the Caps' Dennis Hextall.

"He was the kind of player you wanted out there in the tough situations because he had both brains and guts," Flyers coach Fred Shero said.

In 1975–76 Kindrachuk enjoyed a career year, tallying 26 goals and 75 points while playing mostly on the third line. However, a chronic back injury soon slowed him down. Although he remained a very effective player—he was a plus 35 in 1977–78—his production dipped over the next two seasons.

Meanwhile, the Penguins desperately needed an infusion of new blood. Seeking to bolster the team with players who knew how to win, Pittsburgh general manager Baz Bastien acquired Kindrachuk, Tom Bladon, and Ross Lonsberry from the Flyers for a first-round draft pick. The feisty forward was immediately named captain of the Penguins, replacing the departed Jean Pronovost.

"To be named captain for an NHL team is something I really feel good about," Kindrachuk said. "That was quite an honor."

The feeling was mutual. Pittsburgh fans quickly took a shine to the hardworking center, hanging a banner that proclaimed, "Our captain is O.K."

Proving he was more than up to the task, he enjoyed an excellent first season in the Steel City. Centering a line for Lonsberry and crafty Rick Kehoe, he paced the Pens in assists (42) and finished second in points (60). Always a strong playoff performer, Kindrachuk scored a team-high four goals to lead the Penguins to the second round.

His winning attitude was rubbing off on his teammates. The Pens achieved new heights in 1979–80, briefly bumping aside the powerful Montreal Canadiens to take over first place in the Norris Division. Unfortunately, following a strong first half (46 points in 52 games), Kindrachuk's back miseries flared up with a vengeance. With their captain sidelined, the Penguins slogged to a miserable finish.

Submitting to regular treatments from a chiropractor friend back home, Kindrachuk tried to bounce back in 1980–81. Typically, he scored at a point-per-game clip. However, the disc problem forced him from the lineup after just 13 games.

Fearing that his career was over, the Penguins reluctantly released Kindrachuk over the off-season. He appeared in four games with Washington, but the pain was too great. The gritty competitor was forced to retire.

Lemieux, Mario

Penguins: 1984–94, 1995–1997, 2000–06
Birthplace: Montreal, Quebec
Center   B: October 5, 1965
Shoots: right   **Ht.** 6-4 **Wt.** 230
Captain: 1987–94, 1995–1997, 2001–06
Nicknames: Ace, Super Mario

	Regular Season					Playoffs				
YR	GP	G	A	PTS	PM	GP	G	A	PTS	PM
1984–85	73	43	57	100	54	-	-	-	-	-
1985–86	79	48	93	141	43	-	-	-	-	-
1986–87	63	54	53	107	57	-	-	-	-	-
1987–88	77	70	98	168	92	-	-	-	-	-
1988–89	76	85	114	199	100	11	12	7	19	16
1989–90	59	45	78	123	78	-	-	-	-	-
1990–91	26	19	26	45	30	23	16	28	44	16
1991–92	64	44	87	131	94	15	16	18	34	2
1992–93	60	69	91	160	38	11	8	10	18	10
1993–94	22	17	20	37	32	6	4	3	7	2
1995–96	70	69	92	161	54	18	11	16	27	33
1996–97	76	50	72	122	65	5	3	3	6	4
2000–01	43	35	41	76	18	18	6	11	17	4
2001–02	24	6	25	31	14	-	-	-	-	-
2002–03	67	28	63	91	43	-	-	-	-	-
2003–04	10	1	8	9	6	-	-	-	-	-
2005–06	26	7	15	22	16	-	-	-	-	-
NHL	915	690	1033	1723	834	107	76	96	172	87

January 24, 2006, was a sad day for hockey fans the world over. At 2:00 PM, arguably the greatest player ever to lace on a pair of skates strode bravely to the podium at the Igloo Club in the Mellon Arena. With misty eyes, the tall, darkly handsome 40-year-old with the regal bearing announced that he was retiring from the game he loved.

"The time is right because I can no longer play the game at the level I'm accustomed to," he said. "I think the best decision is to turn the game over to the younger guys. It's a young man's game now. Winning two Stanley Cups allows me to leave in peace."

Close your eyes and the images come flooding back: big No. 66 in black and gold eluding Bruins great Raymond Bourque to score on his first shot on goal; taking a picture-perfect pass from Wayne Gretzky in the 1987 Canada Cup and firing the series winner past Soviet goalie Sergei Mylnikov; dragging the Nordiques' Marc Fortier halfway down the ice to deposit the puck in the net; and splitting Minnesota's defense like a knife going through hot butter in the 1991 Stanley Cup Finals to score perhaps the most brilliant goal ever witnessed.

Blessed with an exquisite blend of size, reach, touch, quickness, power, and deception, Mario was a magician on the ice. He transformed seemingly routine plays into treasure-trove goals through his marvelous sleight of hand. For all his incredible gifts, his vision was perhaps his greatest quality of all. Lemieux saw the game at ice level the way most of us do gazing down from a great seat at the arena. It was as if he had a hidden camera in his mind that allowed him to exploit the smallest of openings—openings that were invisible to other players.

"What he can do, I couldn't do," offered Bobby Orr, who was widely regarded as the finest player in the history of the game. "He can do more things than any other player I've ever seen."

Yet Mario's storied career was much more than the highlight-reel goals or the supreme talent that allowed him to roll up an astronomical 690 goals and 1033 assists in only 915 games. The numbers have long since earned him his rightful place in the Hockey Hall of Fame. Rather, his story is one of remarkable courage and grace under the most trying and difficult of circumstances.

In the spring of 1984, Mario Lemieux was arguably the most sought-after player ever to come out of the Canadian junior ranks. As an 18-year-old with the Laval Voison, he had obliterated the major junior hockey scoring records with an astounding 282 points. Like a Triple Crown race run in reverse, the Penguins and the New Jersey Devils plummeted neck-and-neck through the standings for the right to draft the young phenom. In an era before the draft lottery, Penguins general manager Eddie Johnston resorted to all sorts of chicanery to ensure his team would finish dead last.

From the start, Mario faced daunting adversity. Few players have ever carried heavier expectations. He was expected to be the savior for a moribund team that barely had a pulse, let alone a bevy of NHL-quality players to help him. It was an enormous responsibility for a shy, quiet young man who was still in his teens.

Lemieux also stared down a firestorm of criticism in his early years, for he dared to dethrone the world's greatest and most popular player, Wayne Gretzky. While Gretzky was a media darling, Mario—still trying to learn English—was an introvert by nature. The fact that he was French Canadian only served to heighten the prejudice against him.

But Lemieux persevered. In his fourth season he captured the first of his six scoring titles and, more importantly, the Hart Trophy as the league's Most Valuable Player.

In 1988–89 Mario came of age. Although Gretzky had posted slightly higher scoring totals, it's doubtful that any player ever enjoyed a better year. Plain and simply, Lemieux was unstoppable. He was quite literally a threat to score every time his skates touched the ice. With no legal means to defend against his extraordinary talents, opponents took to fouling him and the old-guard NHL referees allowed it.

"I remember seeing Mario carry three guys on his back from the blue line for 60 feet and still score," Nashville general manager David Poile recalled. "He was magnificent to watch."

Unfortunately, the abuse he was absorbing began to take its toll. The following season, Mario experienced back problems that would plague him for the rest of his career. We may never truly know just how great Lemieux could've been because the injury struck just as he was reaching the very peak of his abilities.

"You wonder what kind of career he would have had," said Bill Torrey, architect of the great Islanders dynasty. "Guys had no idea how to defend him. I don't know of anyone who has frozen players like Mario. He could beat you with his stick handling, with his shot, or just by holding on to the puck. Defensemen would drop down thinking he was going to shoot. Goalies would commit before he did. On breakaways, he was the best I've ever seen."

Showing enormous character, Mario overcame his back problems to lead the Penguins to consecutive Stanley Cups in 1991 and 1992, at long last silencing his critics. Yet it was the adversity he would face the following season that would elevate him to the status of a champion for the ages.

With Mario leading the way, the two-time defending champions bolted from the starting blocks in 1992–93 at a scorching pace. His balky back a thing of the past, the big center was on target to shatter Gretzky's single-season scoring mark of 215 points. But on January 13 came news that stunned the sports world to its core. Lemieux had been diagnosed with Hodgkin's disease.

While the prognosis for recovery was good, no one knew when—or if—Mario would be able to return. At the very least, he seemed finished for the season. But Lemieux responded well to his radiation treatments. Displaying recuperative abilities bordering on the superhuman, he made his

Mario Lemieux saved the Pens from extinction in 1984. His scoring rate of 1.88 points per game ranks second all time.

triumphant return against the Flyers in the Spectrum on March 2—less than two months after learning of his illness.

Infamous as among the most hostile fans in all of sports, the Flyers faithful stood in unison and gave Mario a warm, heartfelt ovation. Missing a patch of hair and wearing a protective collar to protect his singed neck, Lemieux remarkably notched a goal and an assist.

It was then that he issued a staggering proclamation. He intended to surpass Buffalo's Pat LaFontaine in the scoring race.

"I felt that the scoring title was mine to lose," Mario would recall. "Even when I was sick, when I was going through the treatments, I always thought about coming back and winning the scoring title."

At the time, Lemieux trailed the Sabres' gifted center by a dozen points—with only 19 games to play. Even his most ardent supporters gave Mario little or no chance. After all, he was barely a month removed from energy-sapping radiation treatments.

Mario would astonish the hockey world once more with perhaps the greatest athletic achievement of all time. Playing like a man possessed, he tallied *51 points* over a 16-game stretch—an astounding average of 3.19 points per game. Not only did he catch LaFontaine, he buried his rival by 12 points to capture his fourth Art Ross Trophy. During that span, the equally hot Penguins established an NHL record with 17 consecutive victories.

Two more dramatic comebacks followed. After missing the entire 1994–95 campaign to rest and recuperate from Hodgkin's disease he returned with a vengeance to capture two more scoring titles and lead his team to the conference finals. In December of 2000, after missing three and a half years due to a premature retirement, the 35-year-old wonder stepped back into the spotlight to showcase his exceptional abilities one last time.

As with all athletes, Lemieux's body began to give way to age in his final seasons. Yet even at considerably less than 100 percent he remained a formidable player, helping to lead his native Canada to a gold medal in the 2002 Olympics despite an ailing hip. Mario was able to play long enough to hand the baton of leadership to the Penguins' next great superstar, Sidney Crosby.

On April 2, 2008, Mario was chosen as the "Best Athlete in Pittsburgh Sports History" at the *Pittsburgh Post-Gazette* Dapper Dan awards banquet over luminaries such as Roberto Clemente and Honus Wagner. It was a fitting honor for a man who provided so many special moments of on-ice artistry for a generation of hockey fans.

McDonald, Ab

Penguins: 1967–68   **Birthplace:** Winnipeg, Manitoba
Left wing   B: February 18, 1936
Shoots: left   **Ht.** 6-3 **Wt.** 192
Captain: 1967–68

YR	Regular Season					Playoffs				
	GP	G	A	PTS	PM	GP	G	A	PTS	PM
1967–68	74	22	21	43	38	-	-	-	-	-
NHL	762	182	248	430	200	84	21	29	50	42
WHA	147	29	41	70	24	18	2	6	8	4

Few players enjoyed a more successful start to their NHL career than the Penguins' first captain, Ab McDonald. Following two strong seasons with the Rochester Americans, the big left wing was called up by the Montreal Canadiens for the 1958 playoffs. Although he played just two games for the powerful Habs, the 22-year-old got to sip champagne from Lord Stanley's coveted Cup.

It was more of the same in 1958–59. After a solid rookie season, he once more got to hoist the most prized trophy in all of sport. Two years, two Stanley Cups. Not a bad way to start a career.

The Cup seemed to follow McDonald wherever he went. In 1960 the Canadiens traded him to Chicago as part of a blockbuster nine-player deal. Skating on the original "Scooter Line" with Stan Mikita and Ken Wharram, he potted 17 goals and helped the Black Hawks to their first Stanley Cup in 33 years.

The team's first captain, Ab McDonald led the Penguin with 22 goals in 1967–68.

"I guess we got our nickname because we moved the puck around so well and that we were all over the ice when we played," McDonald said. "We scored a lot of points during the time we were together."

Firmly entrenched as the second-line left wing behind the great Bobby Hull, McDonald blossomed in the Windy City. In 1961–62 he scored 22 goals to lead the Black Hawks back to the Stanley Cup Finals. Ab enjoyed an outstanding postseason, tallying six goals and 12 points. He followed up with his finest season, notching 20 goals and 61 points in 1962–63.

A trade to Boston in 1964 derailed the big winger's career. Ab endured a dismal year in the Hub City, scoring only nine goals. He soon moved on to Detroit, where he split time between the Red Wings and the Pittsburgh Hornets. In 1967 he won another championship, sparking "the Wasps" to a Calder Cup triumph.

It was a no-brainer when Penguins general manager Jack Riley plucked McDonald from the Red Wings in the Expansion Draft that summer. Thanks to his experience and playoff success, the 6'3" winger was ideally suited to serve as the team's first captain.

Skating on a line with fellow Winnipeg native Andy Bathgate, McDonald had a strong year for the Pens. While Bathgate paced all West Division scorers with 59 points, Ab topped the team with 22 goals.

Unfortunately, the Penguins missed the playoffs by a scant two points. Concerned over the team's lack of depth down the middle, Riley peddled McDonald to the St. Louis Blues on June 11, 1968, for center Lou Angotti.

The trade would backfire mightily. Although a gritty, capable performer, Angotti clashed with equally feisty Pens coach Red Sullivan. Ironically, he too was traded to the Blues following the season for future team captain Ron Schock.

Meanwhile, on the banks of the Mississippi, McDonald enjoyed two fine seasons with St. Louis. Twice topping the

20-goal mark, he became a fixture on the Blues' deadly power play while earning West Division All-Star Team honors. The Blues made it to the Stanley Cup Finals in each of his seasons with St. Louis.

McDonald finally hit a downturn in 1970. He moved on to the World Hockey Association in 1972 and played for his hometown Winnipeg Jets for two seasons before retiring.

Pronovost, Jean

Penguins: 1968–78   **Birthplace:** Shawinigan Falls, Quebec
Right wing   **B:** December 18, 1945
Shoots: right   **Ht.** 6-0 **Wt.** 185
Captain: 1977–78   **Nickname:** Prony

	Regular Season					Playoffs				
YR	GP	G	A	PTS	PM	GP	G	A	PTS	PM
1968–69	76	16	25	41	41	-	-	-	-	-
1969–70	72	20	21	41	45	10	3	4	7	2
1970–71	78	21	24	45	35	-	-	-	-	-
1971–72	68	30	23	53	12	4	1	1	2	0
1972–73	66	21	22	43	16	-	-	-	-	-
1973–74	77	40	32	72	22	-	-	-	-	-
1974–75	78	43	32	75	37	9	3	3	6	6
1975–76	80	52	52	104	24	3	0	0	0	2
1976–77	79	33	31	64	24	3	2	1	3	2
1977–78	79	40	25	65	50	-	-	-	-	-
NHL	**998**	**391**	**383**	**774**	**413**	**35**	**11**	**9**	**20**	**14**

The 11th of 12 children, Jean Pronovost grew up idolizing his big brother Marcel. He has vivid memories of watching his older sibling skate for Detroit during the Stanley Cup Playoffs on a neighbor's TV. Hoping to emulate Marcel, he took to the ice every day after school with other local kids.

Jean soon gained the attention of the Boston Bruins. Skating for the Bruins' Junior A team, the Niagara Falls Flyers, he developed into a strong two-way player who paid equal attention to his offensive and defensive chores. At 19, he scored 30 goals in 54 games and helped the Flyers capture the Memorial Cup championship.

Following his junior career, the Bruins assigned Pronovost to the Oklahoma City Blazers of the Central Professional Hockey League. In his first year with the Blazers, the team won the CPHL title. The next year he reinforced his reputation as a player with a bright future, notching 25 goals in 49 games.

The Bruins, however, were stocked with established right wingers Ken Hodge, John McKenzie, and Tommy Williams. There was no room for a rookie, even one as promising as Pronovost. The Pittsburgh Penguins, on the other hand, were in desperate need of young talent. Immediately following the 1967–68 season, general manager Jack Riley acquired the raw-boned winger for a first-round draft pick.

Pittsburgh was not an easy place to begin a career, especially for a French-speaking youth who was still learning the nuances of English. But "Prony" proved to be one of the few

The Century Line

Throughout hockey history there have been many storied line combinations. The powerhouse Red Wings of the early 1950s boasted the "Production Line" of Gordie Howe, Sid Abel, and Ted Lindsay. Later in the decade Montreal rode the stellar play of "Rocket" Richard and his "Punch Line" mates to Stanley Cup glory.

It would take the Penguins several years to construct a great line of their own. Each member was cast off from another team.

The first to join the fold was 23-year-old right wing Jean Pronovost. Acquired from the talent-rich Bruins in May of 1968, "Prony" was a solid performer through the team's early years.

Next on the scene was the oft-injured Lowell MacDonald. Picked up from the Kings in June of 1970, he'd once starred for the Pittsburgh Hornets. However, MacDonald had a history of knee problems.

The third and final piece of the puzzle arrived the following January in the form of center Syl Apps Jr. Aside from the fact that he bore the same name as his Hall of Fame father, there was little to suggest that Apps was a star in the making. Opting to attend Queen's University rather than play junior hockey, he'd taken the long road to the NHL. In half a season with the Rangers he had tallied one measly goal.

From the moment they were united by coach Ken Schinkel the trio made sweet music. Initially dubbed "the MAP Line"—a play on the first letters of their last names—they had a wonderful chemistry.

Taking full advantage of the Civic Arena's 207' x 92' ice surface, they employed an up-tempo style that featured plenty of puck movement and skating.

With the skilled, graceful Apps setting the table and MacDonald and Pronovost shredding opposing goaltenders, the line accumulated more than 100 goals during the 1973–74 campaign to earn a dynamic new nickname—"the Century Line."

bright spots of an otherwise dismal season, scoring 16 goals to win the team's Rookie of the Year award.

In 1969–70 he was joined by a second French Canadian—a 20-year-old rookie center named Michel Briere. Like Pronovost, the youngster hailed from the province of Quebec. The two bonded instantly, on and off the ice.

Skating together on the speedy "Jet Line," the duo flourished. Pronovost scored 20 goals and paced the club's regulars in plus/minus rating, while Briere topped the team with

Jean Pronovost, shown providing tips to a young fan, was one of the Pens' all-time greats.

They would quickly become one of the most prolific combinations in team history. In 1971–72—their first full season together—Pronovost established a new team high with 30 goals, while Apps set club records for assists and points.

After being separated for a season, they were reunited during the 1973–74 campaign along with a new left winger, Lowell MacDonald. The trio blended together like smooth Irish whiskey. While Apps piled up 61 assists and 85 points, Prony struck for 40 goals and MacDonald 43.

For the next two seasons "the Century Line" was among the most lethal units in the league. In 1974–75 they tallied 94 goals, including a team-high 43 by Pronovost. The following season they were virtually unstoppable. While Prony enjoyed a career year (52 goals and 104 points), Apps struck for 32 goals and MacDonald potted 30 for an astounding total of 114 goals.

Unfortunately, MacDonald's ravaged left knee gave out in 1976. Apps was traded early in the 1977–78 season, leaving Prony as the last man standing. Now serving as the Penguins' captain, he managed to net 40 goals for a bad team.

By the fall of 1978 he'd had enough. Frustrated with the organization's inability to ice a competitive team, he requested a trade. At first, general manager Baz Bastien tried to keep him. But Pronovost refused to budge. On September 6, 1978, he got his wish, moving to Atlanta for center Gregg Sheppard.

He enjoyed two good seasons with the Flames before being traded to Washington. Skating on the "Roaring Twenties Line" with Bob "Hound" Kelly and Dennis Maruk, Prony registered his 12th consecutive 20-plus goal season. Following a slow start in 1981–82, however, he was sent to Hershey of the American Hockey League, where he finished his pro career.

To honor his outstanding achievements, Pronovost was inducted into the Penguins Hall of Fame in 1992. He remains the third-best goal scorer in team history—behind a couple of guys named Lemieux and Jagr.

Ruskowski, Terry

Penguins: 1985–87   **Birthplace:** Prince Albert, Saskatchewan
Left wing   B: December 31, 1954
Shoots: left   **Ht.** 5-10   **Wt.** 178
Captain: 1986–87   **Nickname:** Rosco

		Regular Season						Playoffs		
YR	GP	G	A	PTS	PM	GP	G	A	PTS	PM
1985–86	73	26	37	63	162	-	-	-	-	-
1986–87	70	14	37	51	145	-	-	-	-	-
NHL	**630**	**113**	**313**	**426**	**1354**	**21**	**1**	**6**	**7**	**86**
WHA	**369**	**83**	**254**	**337**	**761**	**52**	**18**	**36**	**54**	**174**

During the summer of 1985, Penguins general manager Eddie Johnston had a huge hole to fill. Forty-goal scorer Warren Young had signed a lucrative deal with Detroit,

32 assists. They continued their hot hand in the playoffs, combining for eight of the Penguins' 23 goals.

Tragically, Briere was critically injured in a car accident just two weeks after the team was eliminated from postseason play. While his dear friend lay in a coma at a Montreal hospital, Pronovost kept a constant vigil at his bedside. Prony prayed that Briere would recover, but he never did. He passed away on April 13, 1971.

Grief-stricken, Pronovost channeled his energies into becoming the best hockey player he could be. Fortunately, help had arrived in January in the form of a new linemate—Syl Apps.

"It was funny how we clicked so quickly, right from the first game," Pronovost recalled in Jim O'Brien's book, *Penguin Profiles.* "I didn't even know who Syl Apps was—I mean, I knew him as a player for the New York Rangers, and that was it—when we were put together on the same line. We just played well together. We 'read' each other well."

leaving the Pens without a left wing—and a protector—for prized young superstar Mario Lemieux.

Mining the free-agent market, Johnston turned up a gem. Former Black Hawks captain Terry Ruskowski had been cut loose by the Los Angeles Kings. Johnston was familiar with "Rosco," having coached him in the Windy City. The two quickly agreed to terms.

A 5'10", 178-pound package of pure dynamite, Ruskowski had carved out a reputation as a battler while skating for the Swift Current Broncos junior team.

"You had to decide on a style," Terry recalled. "You can't kid yourself because that's when the pros are watching. I realized my only chance was to forecheck the best I could and hustle like crazy."

Following an outstanding junior career with the Broncos, Chicago took Ruskowski in the fourth round of the 1974 Amateur Draft. It was clear, however, the Black Hawks intended to send him to the minors for seasoning. The Houston Aeros of the World Hockey Association came knocking, offering more money to boot. Ruskowski decided to sign with Houston.

There was another huge bonus to playing with the Aeros. Ruskowski got to skate alongside "Mr. Hockey" himself, Gordie Howe. Learning the tricks of the old-school trade from his legendary linemate, the gritty little center quickly became one of the WHA's toughest and most dynamic players. His linemate, Rich Preston, insisted Rosco never lost a fight. Although he was not a fast skater or a particularly good shooter, he developed into a terrific playmaker, averaging nearly 70 points per season. Along the way he played on two Avco Cup champions.

In 1979 the faltering WHA merged with the NHL. Ruskowski's WHA team, the Winnipeg Jets, desperately wanted to keep him. However, entry restrictions placed on the new clubs made it impossible.

"I'm not only giving up probably the best player in our league, I'm giving up the heart of our hockey club," Jets general manager John Ferguson lamented.

The Black Hawks welcomed Rosco back with open arms. Skating on the "RPM" line with Preston and Grant Mulvey, the 25-year-old enjoyed an outstanding first season in the NHL, tallying 55 assists and 70 points to go with 252 minutes in the sin bin.

Following three seasons with Chicago, Ruskowski was traded to the Kings in 1982. Filling more of a checking role, he dipped to seven goals in 1983–84 before bouncing back to pot 16 the next season.

The spike in production convinced Eddie Johnston to sign Ruskowski and try him with Mario Lemieux. The move worked like a charm. Although hardly a big-time scorer, Rosco enjoyed the finest season of his career, piling up a career-high 26 goals.

True to form, he kept the would-be Mario muggers at bay. In January of 1986 he schooled the Flyers tough young

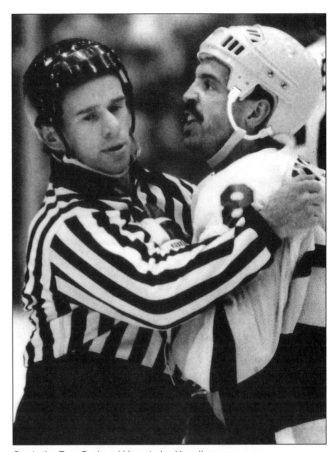
Combative Terry Ruskowski is restrained by a linesman.

winger, Rick Tocchet, to earn a unanimous decision. As a reward for his gritty, team-first play, Ruskowski was named captain.

Unfortunately, 1985–86 would prove to be his high-water mark with the Pens. Although he was skating with one of the greatest setup men the game had ever seen, Ruskowski struggled to produce. He still posted decent numbers—14 goals and 51 points—but it was not enough. The Penguins released the tough little winger over the summer.

Ruskowski hooked on with the Minnesota North Stars. At age 33, however, the wear and tear of more than a decade of battling in the trenches had taken its toll. He retired early in the 1988–89 season.

Schock, Ron

Penguins: 1969–77   **Birthplace:** Chapleau, Ontario
Center   **B:** December 19, 1943
Shoots: left   **Ht.** 5-11 **Wt.** 180
Captain: 1973–77   **Nickname:** Schocker

	Regular Season					Playoffs				
YR	GP	G	A	PTS	PM	GP	G	A	PTS	PM
1969–70	76	8	21	29	40	10	1	6	7	7
1970–71	71	14	26	40	20	-	-	-	-	-
1971–72	77	17	29	46	22	4	1	0	1	6
1972–73	78	13	36	49	23	-	-	-	-	-
1973–74	77	14	29	43	22	-	-	-	-	-
1974–75	80	23	63	86	36	9	0	4	4	10
1975–76	80	18	44	62	28	3	0	1	1	0
1976–77	80	17	32	49	10	3	0	1	1	0
NHL	**909**	**166**	**351**	**517**	**260**	**55**	**4**	**16**	**20**	**29**

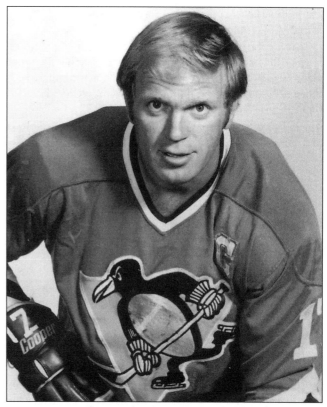

A diligent two-way center, Ron Schock paced the Pens with 86 points in 1974–75.

As a member of the Boston Bruins, Ron Schock took great pride in the fact that he made it to the National Hockey League in the pre-expansion era.

"I knew I was lucky to be with the Bruins, let alone being in the NHL," he said. "I think any of us who made it at that time just wanted to be wanted by someone."

The Chapleau, Ontario, native played several seasons for the Bruins, serving mostly as a penalty killer and fringe player. In 1967, however, he was claimed by the St. Louis Blues in the Expansion Draft. After skating for two seasons with the Blues—and playing in two Stanley Cup Finals—he was dealt to the Penguins on June 6, 1969.

A heart-and-soul player, Schock took the news of the trade hard. Already regarded as somewhat of a hockey Siberia, Pittsburgh was one of the two cities (New York being the other) where he *didn't* want to play. But the Penguins were beginning to improve, and Schock soon adjusted to his new surroundings while filling an important two-way role.

He was certainly one of the team's most noticeable players. Sporting a thick mop of blonde hair and muttonchop sideburns, Schock was a nonstop scrambler who hustled every second he was on the ice.

"I was a contributor," he recalled in Jim O'Brien's book, *Penguin Profiles*. "I gave the best effort that I had, both away and at home. Sometimes it was better than other times. It was the best I had that night."

The Penguins brass took note. The team had been without a captain since Earl Ingarfield was traded in 1969. They felt the likeable, unselfish, and steady veteran would be the perfect man to wear the "C." In 1973 he officially was named the third captain in team history, a role he would fill with distinction.

Although he averaged 44 points per season over a four-year span, Schock was regarded as primarily a defensive player. That perception would change—dramatically—with the arrival of Vic Hadfield and Rick Kehoe in the summer of 1974. Slotted between the newcomers, "Schocker" enjoyed

the finest season of his career, exploding for career highs in goals (23), assists (63), and points (86). Not coincidentally, the Penguins responded with the first winning season in franchise history.

"I think, as a team during that season, we were never beaten," he said. "Some games we were behind by two or three goals, but we never thought we were going to lose. We were never out of the game."

Unfortunately, the Penguins ran into a team with a similar mind-set in the playoffs—the New York Islanders. Down 3–0, the Islanders rallied to win four straight.

As team captain, Schock did his best to rally the troops. Determined to lead by example, he had another strong season in 1975–76, tallying 18 goals and 62 points. But the Penguins fell in a Preliminary Round matchup to Toronto.

Following another early playoff exit in 1977, new general manager Baz Bastien decided it was time to break up the old gang. On September 20, 1977, he sent Schock to Buffalo for aggressive winger Brian Spencer.

The trade seemed to take the heart out of the former Pens captain. Seeing mostly spot duty with the Sabres, he scored just four goals in 40 games. After spending two seasons in the minors, he retired in 1980.

He currently ranks sixth on the Pens' all-time list in games played (619), 10th in assists (280), and 11th in points (404).

The All-Stars

Apps, Syl

Penguins: 1971–77   **Birthplace:** Toronto, Ontario
Center   B: August 1, 1947
Shoots: right   **Ht.** 6-0 **Wt.** 185

YR	Regular Season					Playoffs				
	GP	G	A	PTS	PM	GP	G	A	PTS	PM
1970–71	31	9	16	25	21	-	-	-	-	-
1971–72	72	15	44	59	78	4	1	0	1	2
1972–73	77	29	56	85	18	-	-	-	-	-
1973–74	75	24	61	85	37	-	-	-	-	-
1974–75	79	24	55	79	43	9	2	3	5	9
1975–76	80	32	67	99	24	3	0	1	1	0
1976–77	72	18	43	61	20	3	1	0	1	12
1977–78	9	0	7	7	0	-	-	-	-	-
NHL	**727**	**183**	**423**	**606**	**311**	**23**	**5**	**5**	**10**	**23**

Son of a famous father, Syl Apps was the Pens' first superstar. He was the MVP of the 1975 NHL All-Star Game.

When Syl Apps first skated out onto the Civic Arena ice on January 27, 1971, it was hardly to a hero's welcome. The day before, Penguins general manager Red Kelly had sent Glen Sather to the New York Rangers for Apps and young defenseman Sheldon Kannegiesser. A player of modest ability but enormous spunk and charisma, "Slats" had been wildly popular in Pittsburgh. The huge banner that hung directly across from the Penguins' bench said it all—"Why Slats?"

Apps would soon provide the answer. Gathering in a lead pass from Jean Pronovost, he hurtled into the Toronto zone on a breakaway, deked Hall of Fame goalie Jacques Plante to the ice, and ripped the puck into the net. The 23-year-old center also collected an assist on a power-play goal by Greg Polis for a two-point night. Not a bad way to make an entrance.

Although Apps had tallied just three points prior to his Steel City debut, there was no questioning his ability. An early scouting report summed up his play in glowing terms. "Apps Jr. is a splendid skater, a good puckhandler and play-maker, just like his father."

The father happened to be Syl Apps Sr., a Hall of Fame center who established himself as one of the game's greatest players while starring for Toronto in the 1930s and '40s.

"Young Syl's dad was a great guy and a great player," said Kelly, who played against him on numerous occasions. "He went so fast I looked like a post on the ice by comparison. His son shows similar qualities. He's strong and he hits and he has a good fake. This is something that has to be born in a hockey player. It comes from breeding. Young Syl has the breeding and I've always said that bloodlines are a wonderful thing."

Slotted between Polis and Pronovost on a promising young line, Apps finished the 1970–71 campaign with nine goals and 16 assists in 31 games for the Pens. The next season was even better. While his wingers established a new club scoring mark with 30 goals apiece, Syl set new team records with 44 assists and 59 points.

The following season Kelly took a bit of a gamble. Hoping to come up with two strong scoring lines, he broke up the "PAP Line" and assigned a new set of wingers to Apps—Lowell MacDonald and Al McDonough. Both were unknown quantities; MacDonald was a former 20-goal scorer who was trying to bounce back from knee surgery; McDonough was talented but green.

The trio meshed beautifully. McDonough struck for a club-record 35 goals, including three hat tricks, while MacDonald culminated an amazing comeback by scoring 34 goals and garnering the Masterton Trophy. The silky-smooth Apps enjoyed one of his finest seasons, collecting 29 goals, 56 assists, and 85 points.

McDonough was traded to Atlanta midway through the 1973–74 season. Pronovost rejoined the line, which quickly emerged as one of the most lethal combinations in the league.

With Apps setting the table and his opportunistic wingers finding the net with stunning frequency, the trio struck for a whopping 107 goals to earn the nickname, "the Century Line."

"Prony knew if he could get to a certain spot, I'd look for him," Apps recalled for Jim O'Brien in *Penguin Profiles*. "And he'd look for me the same way. Lowell was something, considering he couldn't see 20 feet in front of him, yet he could find the corner of the nets with his shot."

Realizing he had a bona fide superstar on his hands, Penguins owner Tad Potter signed Apps to a record contract for $125,000 per year. The darkly handsome center proved to be worth every penny. Over the next two seasons he rolled up 178 points, including a career-high 99 in 1975–76.

Unfortunately, knee injuries to Apps and MacDonald signaled the end of "the Century Line," and with it, the club's brief stab at respectability. After he dipped to 61 points in 1976–77, Syl was traded to Los Angeles, where he played for three seasons before finishing out his career.

The Apps' family legacy was carried on by Syl's children. His son, Syl III, starred at Princeton in the late 1990s and played several years of pro hockey. Daughter Gillian made headlines when she led the Canadian Women's team to a gold medal at the 2006 and 2010 Winter Olympics.

Barrasso, Tom

Penguins: 1988–00   **Birthplace:** Boston, Massachusetts
Goaltender   B: March 31, 1965
Catches: right   **Ht.** 6-3   **Wt.** 210
Nicknames: Tomcat, Tommy B

YR	GP	MINS	GA	SH	AVE	GP	MINS	GA	SH	AVE
		Regular Season					Playoffs			
1988–89	44	2406	162	0	4.04	11	631	40	0	3.80
1989–90	24	1294	101	0	4.68	-	-	-	-	-
1990–91	48	2754	165	1	3.59	20	1175	51	1	2.60
1991–92	57	3329	196	1	3.53	21	1233	58	1	2.82
1992–93	63	3702	186	4	3.01	12	722	35	2	2.91
1993–94	44	2482	139	2	3.36	6	356	17	0	2.87
1994–95	2	125	8	0	3.84	2	80	8	0	6.00
1995–96	49	2799	160	2	3.43	10	558	26	1	2.80
1996–97	5	270	26	0	5.78	-	-	-	-	-
1997–98	63	3542	122	7	2.07	6	376	17	0	2.71
1998–99	43	2306	98	4	2.55	13	787	35	1	2.67
1999–00	18	870	46	1	3.17	-	-	-	-	-
NHL	777	44180	2385	38	3.24	119	6953	349	6	3.01

It's often said that in baseball pitching is the key to victory. The hockey equivalent is goaltending. For a two-year stretch in the early '90s, nobody stopped the puck better than Thomas Patrick Barrasso. Next to Mario Lemieux, he was arguably the most important cog in the Pens' championship machine.

A year before Mario captured hockey's spotlight, Barrasso burst upon the scene as an 18-year-old wonder with the

Tom Barrasso draws a bead on the puck. He was the first American-born goalie in NHL history to record 300 victories.

Buffalo Sabres. Fresh out of Acton-Boxborough High School in Boston, the youngster set the NHL on its ear by capturing the Calder and Vezina Trophies.

Experts marveled at his ability to dominate at such a callow age. Goaltenders usually took years to develop, but Barrasso indeed was a rare breed. Large for a goalie at 6'3" and 210 pounds, he possessed the cat-like quickness of his smaller contemporaries, which allowed him to cover the net with relative ease. Renowned for his great glove hand, he also was an exceptional puckhandler.

After three strong seasons, Barrasso's play slipped noticeably during the 1986–87 campaign. By the fall of 1988 he had lost his starting job to Darren Puppa. Desperate for a starting goalie to backstop his high-octane but porous team, Penguins GM Tony Esposito acquired Barrasso for talented young defenseman Doug Bodger and first-round draft pick Darrin Shannon.

Although an improvement over the Pens' goaltender-by-committee approach, Barrasso did not shine right away. He posted an unsightly 4.04 goals-against average—nearly a goal and a half higher than his rookie average.

The worst was yet to come. In the fall of 1989 Barrasso's young daughter Ashley was stricken with cancer. The 24-year-old goalie was granted an extended leave of absence to care for her. On the rare occasions when he suited up, he played like a man whose mind was understandably elsewhere.

By the time training camp opened the following year, Barrasso was no longer mentioned in discussions of elite goalies. In fact, he wasn't even at the top of the Penguins' depth chart. During the early going, new coach Bob Johnson alternated him with Wendell Young and Frank Pietrangelo.

Remarkably, Barrasso's confidence never wavered. Suddenly, he ran off a six-game winning streak to grab the goaltending reins—reins he would not relinquish except due to injury for the next decade. The Penguins' net was his.

Still, questions lingered about Barrasso's ability to perform at crunch time. Even during his best days in Buffalo he had struggled mightily in postseason play. Yet Barrasso seized the opportunity to showcase his abilities. Displaying marvelous consistency and coolness under fire, he led all playoff goaltenders with a 2.60 goals-against average and helped pave the way to the Pens' first Stanley Cup.

The young goalie was even better in the 1992 playoffs. With Lemieux out of action with a broken hand, Barrasso took charge, winning 11 straight games during the march to the Cup. While Mario returned to garner the Conn Smythe Trophy, many felt that Barrasso was the true MVP.

"Tom Barrasso was magnificent," play-by-play announcer Mike Lange said.

With a pair of Stanley Cups under his belt Barrasso finally began to receive some well-deserved recognition. However, his moment in the sun was short-lived. In the seventh game of the 1993 Patrick Division Finals he surrendered a goal to the Islanders' David Volek to bring an abrupt end to the Penguins' championship run. While he was hardly to blame—the Islanders had streamed into the Pittsburgh zone on a three-on-one break—doubts about his ability to perform in the clutch resurfaced.

In temperament and personality Barrasso was similar to the man who brought him to the NHL, Scotty Bowman. Intelligent and well-spoken, he was supremely confident in his abilities. He also displayed a degree of churlishness when things weren't going well—a by-product of his intense nature.

A model citizen during the Cup years, Barrasso's razor-edge temperament soon bubbled to the surface. Never one to back down from a challenge, he was involved in a scrap with some unruly patrons at a Pittsburgh watering hole shortly after an embarrassing first-round playoff loss to the Capitals in 1994. Eschewing a warm-and-fuzzy approach, he was especially tough on young goaltenders Patrick Lalime and Jean-Sebastien Aubin.

Yet more than one former teammate insisted that Barrasso's rep as a bad actor was overblown.

"I'll go to war with Tom Barrasso any day," Phil Bourque declared. It was the ultimate compliment for the ultimate competitor.

Intensely proud, Barrasso made a remarkable comeback from wrist surgery during the 1997–98 campaign. However, by the spring of 2000 his play was slipping. Craig Patrick dealt the winningest goalie in franchise history to Ottawa for journeyman Ron Tugnutt.

Barrasso would play two more seasons before hanging up his skates, becoming the first American-born goalie to record more than 300 victories. In June of 2003, Patrick quietly signed him as a free agent so he could retire as a Penguin. It was a fitting end to the career of a man who had been instrumental in leading the team to two Stanley Cups.

Brown, Rob

Penguins: 1987–90, 1997–00 **Birthplace:** Kingston, Ontario
Right wing **B:** April 10, 1968
Shoots: left **Ht.** 5-10 **Wt.** 177
Nickname: Brownie

	Regular Season					Playoffs				
YR	GP	G	A	PTS	PM	GP	G	A	PTS	PM
1987–88	51	24	20	44	56	-	-	-	-	-
1988–89	68	49	66	115	118	11	5	3	8	22
1989–90	80	33	47	80	102	-	-	-	-	-
1990–91	25	6	10	16	31	-	-	-	-	-
1997–98	82	15	25	40	59	6	1	0	1	4
1998–99	58	13	11	24	16	13	2	5	7	8
1999–00	50	10	13	23	10	11	1	2	3	0
NHL	**543**	**190**	**248**	**438**	**599**	**54**	**12**	**14**	**26**	**45**

Rob Brown was born to score goals. It came as naturally to him as breathing. And he scored lots of them—a whopping 616 over the course of a junior, minor league, and NHL career that spanned 20 years.

Perhaps it came too easily to him. A happy-go-lucky kid who never took himself or his talent too seriously, Brown didn't have to work very hard to excel—at least not during his formative years. It was a trait that would come back to haunt him.

Rob Brown turns as the Flyers' Ron Hextall clears the puck. Hardly a fan, Hextall called the high-scoring winger a "goal suck."

Skating for the Kamloops Blazers under future NHL coach Ken Hitchcock, the youngster set the Western Hockey League on its ear. As a 17-year-old sniper, he piled up 173 points. The following season he upped that total to an astronomical 212 points to win the Canadian Major Junior Player of the Year Award.

Despite his burgeoning talent, Brown did have some flaws. Neither big nor fast, he didn't care much for the nuances of defensive play. But he could flat-out score.

Seeking to add punch to his emerging young team, Penguins general manager Eddie Johnston selected Brown with his fourth pick in the 1986 Entry Draft. Following his final season at Kamloops, the high-scoring rookie earned a spot with the Penguins in 1987–88. A natural center, Brown was soon converted to right wing and slotted next to another former junior scoring champion, Mario Lemieux.

The two players instantly clicked. Thanks to his keen sense of anticipation, Brown was able to read and react to Lemieux and vice versa. Blending together like peas and carrots, the dynamic duo enjoyed monster seasons in 1988–89. While Mario rolled up a career-high 199 points, "Brownie" exploded for 49 goals and 115 points. His brilliant scoring earned him a spot on the Prince of Wales All-Star Team.

Still, respect came grudgingly for Brown. Many experts believed he was just riding Mario's coattails. The charge seemed to gain some validity the following season. With Lemieux missing a large chunk of time due to a back injury, Brown's production dipped to 33 goals and 80 points.

In the summer of 1990 the Penguins hired legendary coach "Badger Bob" Johnson to lead them to the promised land. Johnson's system required speed and two-way play from his forwards, attributes that were not on Brown's resume. Following a slow start, Penguins general manager Craig Patrick dealt him to the Whalers for swift-skating Scott Young.

Brown played well in Hartford. In 86 games with the Whalers he tallied 34 goals and 73 points. However, on January 24, 1992, he was traded again—this time to the Blackhawks for defenseman Steve Konroyd.

Although Chicago was seeking a sniper to bolster its defense-first team, it was not a match made in heaven. Blackhawks coach "Iron" Mike Keenan demanded accountability and back checking from his players. Brown provided neither.

He saw action against his old Penguins teammates in the 1992 Stanley Cup Finals, but the Hawks cut him loose following a dismal 1992–93 campaign.

After washing out in the Windy City, Brown entered phase two of his career. For the next four seasons he held the distinction of being the best player—certainly the best scorer—in the minor leagues. Starring for Kalamazoo, Phoenix, and the Chicago Wolves, he rolled up an incredible 522 points during that span to capture three International Hockey League scoring titles.

It appeared the high-scoring winger was destined to finish out his career as the top player outside of the NHL. However, opportunity came knocking when Craig Patrick invited him to the Penguins' training camp in 1997. Determined to seize what might be his last chance to make it back to the big show, Brown hired a trainer and whipped himself into top shape.

Showing a ton of heart and desire, Brown earned a spot on the Pens, albeit in a brand-new role. Remarkably, he was cast in a *defensive* role on the checking line. Even more remarkably, he excelled, providing the team with solid two-way play. While no longer a big-time scorer, he still possessed terrific offensive instincts and that magic wand of a stick. During a three-year run in the Steel City he scored 38 goals, including 17 on the power play.

When Herb Brooks took over as the Penguins' coach in December of 1999, the handwriting was on the wall. Although not for a lack of effort, Brown was not Brooks' kind of player. Neither was he coach-in-waiting Ivan Hlinka's kind of player. The 1999–00 season would be Brown's last in Pittsburgh.

Brown returned to the Chicago Wolves, where he played for three more seasons. In 2002 he tied an American Hockey League playoff record with 26 assists to help lead the Wolves to the Calder Cup. He retired following the 2002–03 season.

Burrows, Dave

Penguins: 1971–78, 1980–81   **Birthplace:** Toronto, Ontario
Defense   B: January 11, 1949
Shoots: left   **Ht.** 6-1   **Wt.** 190
Nickname: Bone Rack

	Regular Season					Playoffs				
YR	GP	G	A	PTS	PM	GP	G	A	PTS	PM
1971–72	77	2	10	12	48	4	0	0	0	4
1972–73	78	3	24	27	42	-	-	-	-	-
1973–74	71	3	14	17	30	-	-	-	-	-
1974–75	78	2	15	17	49	9	1	1	2	12
1975–76	80	7	22	29	51	3	0	0	0	0
1976–77	69	3	6	9	29	3	0	2	2	0
1977–78	67	4	15	19	24	-	-	-	-	-
1980–81	53	0	2	2	28	1	0	0	0	0
NHL	**724**	**29**	**135**	**164**	**373**	**29**	**1**	**5**	**6**	**25**

Playing in an era when offensive-minded defenseman such as Bobby Orr, Brad Park, and Denis Potvin were revolutionizing the game, Dave Burrows was a throwback to earlier times. Caring little about his point totals, he focused his energy on protecting his goaltender and preventing goals. Few have done it better.

The foundation of Burrows' game was his skating. Blessed with outstanding speed and agility, he could skate backward faster than many players of his day could skate forward, which allowed him to keep the play in front of him at all times.

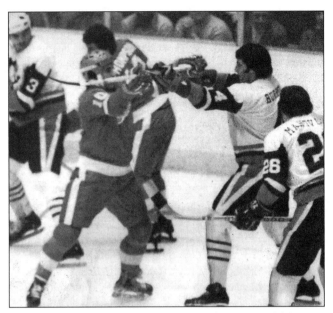
One of the league's best defensemen in the 1970s, Dave Burrows (4) fences with Detroit's Dale McCourt (10).

"I took a lot of pride in being able to move laterally and backward with great ease," he said. "It took a lot of practice, but it was something I enjoyed doing."

A born-again Christian, Burrows played the game hard but clean. Using his skating ability and 6'1" frame to fullest advantage, he excelled at angling the puck-carrier away from the net and into the boards. He also was an outstanding shot blocker who selflessly gave up his body time and time again to prevent scoring chances. His teammates teased him about his legs, which were perpetually bruised. Burrows didn't seem to mind.

"I knew I wasn't an offensive threat; I wasn't a goal scorer," he recalled in Jim O'Brien's book, *Penguin Profiles*. "I always got a thrill out of breaking up a two-on-one break. I was a stay-at-home defenseman. I was happy with that role. You have to use the ability God gives you."

As a youngster growing up in Toronto, Burrows idolized the Maples Leafs' great defenseman Tim Horton. Although he dreamed of one day skating for his hometown Leafs, Chicago beat Toronto to the punch and signed the sturdy defenseman following two solid seasons of Junior A hockey.

Ironically, when the Penguins claimed Burrows from Chicago in the 1971 Intra-League Draft, they picked up Horton from the Rangers as well. Needless to say, it was a delight for the 22-year-old Burrows to play on the same team as his idol.

"The biggest thrill of my career was playing defense with Tim when we were together in Pittsburgh," he said. "He helped me out with a lot of little things in my game. He's a man I'll never forget, I owe him a lot."

Despite his less-than-gaudy point totals, Burrows quickly earned the respect of his peers for his sound positioning and rock-solid defensive play. In 1973–74 he was named to the West Division All-Star Team. Playing in Chicago, he helped his team earn a 6–4 victory over the powerful East Division squad. However, he sustained a dislocated shoulder, an injury that would trouble him for the rest of his career.

Still, Burrows remained the Penguins' top defenseman for the next four seasons. In 1975–76 he enjoyed the finest season of his career, topping a talented Pens squad with a plus/minus rating of plus 27. He flashed a little offense as well, registering career highs in goals (seven) and points (29).

In June of 1978 the Penguins traded the ultrareliable defenseman to Toronto for Randy Carlyle and George Ferguson. It should've been the realization of a boyhood dream, but Burrows missed playing in Pittsburgh. Fortunately, the Penguins reacquired him in November of 1980, enabling him to finish his career in the Steel City.

The bedrock defender is currently seventh on the Penguins' all-time list of games played (573), second among defenseman to his former teammate Ron Stackhouse.

Coffey, Paul

Penguins: 1987–92   **Birthplace:** Weston, Ontario
Defense   B: June 1, 1961
Shoots: left   **Ht.** 6-0 **Wt.** 205
Nickname: Coff

	Regular Season					Playoffs				
YR	GP	G	A	PTS	PM	GP	G	A	PTS	PM
1987–88	46	15	52	67	93	-	-	-	-	-
1988–89	75	30	83	113	195	11	2	13	15	31
1989–90	80	29	74	103	95	-	-	-	-	-
1990–91	76	24	69	93	128	12	2	9	11	6
1991–92	54	10	54	64	62	-	-	-	-	-
NHL	1409	396	1135	1531	1802	194	59	137	196	264

Prior to Paul Coffey's arrival in the Steel City, the Penguins were (not so) loveable losers—a mediocre bunch that was perpetually consigned to the infernal regions of the NHL standings. Following his arrival, the team embarked on a glorious run that included 11 consecutive playoff berths and two Stanley Cup championships.

The acquisition of Coffey from the Edmonton Oilers in the fall of 1987 was a major turning point in franchise history. While Mario Lemieux served as the fulcrum for the Penguins' championship machine, Coffey was the lever that sprang it to life.

If the Penguins had had their way, Coffey would've been a member of the team long before Mario. The club planned to select the speedy Kitchener rearguard with its first pick in the 1979 Amateur Draft. However, Edmonton Oilers general manager Glen Sather, seeking a puck-rushing defender to team with his young superstar—Wayne Gretzky—beat the luckless Pens to the punch.

He proved to be just the right tonic for the dynamic young Oilers. After taking a year to adjust to the rigors of the pro

Paul Coffey speeds away from the Flyers' Keith Acton.

game, Coffey developed into a superb offensive defense-man—the likes of which hadn't been seen since the days of Bobby Orr.

Like Orr, the cornerstone of Coffey's game was skating. Wedging his feet into skates that were several sizes too small, he could accelerate to warp speed in a matter of strides. Then he simply glided through the neutral zone past would-be checkers. Thanks to the sturdy play of his defense partner, Charlie Huddy, Coffey was given the green light to join the rush virtually every time he stepped onto the ice.

With Coffey quarterbacking the power play and wreaking havoc in the attacking zone, the Oilers captured three Stanley Cups in four seasons to establish a new dynasty. Along the way, "Coff" broke Orr's record for most goals in a season by a defenseman (48). During the 1985 playoffs he tallied 37 points—an incredible total for a forward let alone a blue-liner.

In 1987, however, Coffey became embroiled in a contract dispute with Sather. Desperate to hold the line on his burgeoning payroll, the Oilers' combative general manager refused to budge. The talented defenseman sat out the first two months of the season while Sather entertained trade offers.

Meanwhile, in Pittsburgh, Eddie Johnston was desperately looking for ways to upgrade his struggling young club. A particular bone of contention was the absence of a star-quality player to team with Lemieux. Johnston approached owner Edward J. DeBartolo Sr. about making a bid for Coffey. DeBartolo gave his blessing.

On September 24, 1987, the Penguins general manager proudly announced that he'd acquired Coffey as part of a blockbuster seven-player trade. He'd parted with a considerable chunk of talent, including promising youngsters Craig Simpson and Chris Joseph and veterans Moe Mantha and Dave Hannan. But the return was well worth the price.

"A player of Paul Coffey's caliber comes along probably every 15, 20 years," Johnston said. "We're looking at a world-class player. They put him in the category of Orr. There's not too many guys like that who come around."

Coffey's arrival marked an immediate upturn in the team's fortunes. In an instant the hockey buzz in the Steel City grew to a fever pitch. Fans turned out in droves to see the swift-skating marvel team up with Lemieux.

They were in for a rare treat. With his skates barely skimming the ice, Coffey literally flew around the rink. His blazing speed and skilled puck handling forced opposing checkers to back off at every turn. Soon he was springing No. 66 loose with his patented home-run passes. Even without an accomplished set of wingers Mario caught fire and nailed down his first scoring title.

During the next three seasons Coffey flashed his Norris Trophy form. In 1988–89, the quicksilver defenseman tallied 30 goals and 113 points to help lead the Pens to their first playoff berth in seven years. The following year he rolled up 103 points while filling the leadership void when Mario was struck down with back miseries.

In 1990–91 Coffey and the Penguins hit pay dirt. Once again putting up big-time numbers (24 goals and 69 assists), the 29-year-old defenseman helped the team capture its first division title. Although injuries limited him to a dozen games in the postseason, he returned in the Finals to reinvigorate the power play and lead the Pens to their first Stanley Cup.

If there was a chink in Coffey's armor, it was his less-than-stellar defensive play. It was a flaw that didn't escape the critical eye of the Penguins' new coach, Scotty Bowman. Although Coffey was named to the Wales Conference All-Star Team for the fifth straight year, it did little to sway Bowman's opinion. On February 15, 1992, the speedy blue-liner was dealt to the Kings in a big three-team trade that netted the Penguins Kjell Samuelsson, Rick Tocchet, and Ken Wregget.

Coffey would play eight-plus seasons after leaving Pittsburgh. Remarkably, he was reunited with Bowman in Detroit, where he won his fourth Norris Trophy in 1995. However, following a trade to Hartford on the eve of the 1996 season he became a nomad, playing for five different teams during his final five seasons. Although he racked up more frequent-flyer miles than points during that period, he retired as the NHL's all-time leading scorer among defensemen and a sure-fire Hall of Famer.

Cullen, John

Penguins: 1988–90, 1994–95   **Birthplace:** Puslinch, Ontario
Center   B: August 2, 1964
Shoots: right   **Ht.** 5-10 **Wt.** 182
Nickname: Cully

	Regular Season					Playoffs				
YR	GP	G	A	PTS	PM	GP	G	A	PTS	PM
1988–89	79	12	37	49	112	11	3	6	9	28
1989–90	72	32	60	92	138	-	-	-	-	-
1990–91	65	31	63	94	83	-	-	-	-	-
1994–95	46	13	24	37	66	9	0	2	2	8
NHL	**621**	**187**	**363**	**550**	**898**	**53**	**12**	**22**	**34**	**58**

Growing up in the tiny township of Puslinch, Ontario, it was only natural for John Cullen to dream of one day playing in the National Hockey League. His father Barry had skated for five seasons with Toronto and Detroit in the 1950s alongside his uncle Brian. Another uncle, Ray, made it to the NHL as well.

Following a strong season with the Cambridge Winterhawks at the Junior B level, Cullen enrolled at Boston University. It was altogether fitting that he chose to play for the Terriers; the abrasive little center displayed terrier-like instincts as he battled his way up and down the ice.

Although he enjoyed an outstanding collegiate career, his output dipped during his senior year. Noting his lack of size and breakaway speed, the Buffalo Sabres elected not to sign him.

Undaunted, the gritty center joined Flint of the International Hockey League for the 1987–88 season. He enjoyed a huge year with the Spirits, racking up an astonishing 48 goals and 157 points to make a clean sweep of the circuit's major awards.

Cullen's fine play drew the attention of Penguins general manager Tony Esposito, who brought him to Pittsburgh. Skating mostly on the checking line, "Cully" still managed to flash his offensive skills, notching 12 goals and 37 assists.

Promoted to second-line duty in 1989–90 behind the great Mario Lemieux, he prospered. Blessed with marvelous hand-eye coordination and outstanding vision, he used a remarkably short stick to set up his linemates with crisp, tape-to-tape passes. The feisty forward struck for 32 goals and 92 points, the third-highest total on the team.

With Mario sidelined through the first half of the 1990–91 season, Cullen assumed the role of first-line center. Meshing beautifully with fellow young guns Mark Recchi and Kevin Stevens, he zoomed to the top of the NHL scoring race to secure a berth on the Wales Conference All-Star Team. However, on March 4, 1991, Pens general manager Craig Patrick sent him to Hartford as part of a huge blockbuster deal.

Although stunned by the trade, Cullen did his best for the Whalers. Scoring at his now customary point-per-game pace, he finished the season with a whopping 110 points. Unfortunately, the bloom soon came off the rose. In 1992–93 Cullen dipped to a still-impressive 77 points. It was a good total to be sure but not good enough to meet the high expectations of the Whalers management and fans.

When he stumbled to a slow start the following season, the peppery little center was traded again—this time to Toronto. The Maple Leafs were coached by Pat Burns, who preached a defense-first style of play. Cullen did his best to become a better all-around player, but checking was never his strong suit.

During the summer of 1994 he rejoined the Penguins, who were seeking additional firepower in the wake of Lemieux's one-year sabbatical. Thrilled to be back in black and gold, Cullen struck for 12 goals in his first 25 games to help the Penguins to a blistering start. Following a leg injury that forced him to miss two games, however, he fell into a miserable slump, easily the longest and most protracted of his career. He scored only one goal over his final 30 games to end his second go-round with the Pens.

Over the off-season, Cullen hooked on with Tampa Bay. Offered a chance at redemption, the veteran center tallied 105 points during his two seasons with the Lightning.

Gritty John Cullen blossomed into a big-time scorer for the Pens.

However, Cullen would face by far the biggest challenge of his life in 1997. Diagnosed with non-Hodgkin's lymphoma, he underwent grueling radiation treatments and painful bone-marrow transplants.

Thankfully, he survived the ordeal and made a full recovery. Remarkably, Cullen returned to the ice to skate in four games for the Lightning in 1998–99—an incredible achievement for a man who was given a 50 percent chance to live. Following a typically productive six-game stint with the Cleveland Lumberjacks (nine points), he retired.

"I don't think I'm a hero," he said modestly. "I'm a guy who got cancer. All along, I expected to beat this. I consider myself as someone who people can look up to when they are battling cancer and see me, and I can give them hope."

Michel Dion kicks out a shot by the Islanders' Bryan Trottier. The acrobatic goalie earned All-Star honors in 1981–82.

Dion, Michel

Penguins: 1981–85   **Birthplace:** Granby, Quebec
Goaltender   **B:** February 11, 1954
Catches: left   **Ht.** 5-10 **Wt.** 185

		Regular Season					Playoffs			
YR	GP	MINS	GA	SH	AVE	GP	MINS	GA	SH	AVE
1981–82	62	3580	226	0	3.79	5	310	22	0	4.26
1982–83	49	2791	198	0	4.26	-	-	-	-	-
1983–84	30	1553	138	0	5.33	-	-	-	-	-
1984–85	10	553	43	0	4.67	-	-	-	-	-
NHL	227	12695	898	2	4.24	5	310	22	0	4.26
WHA	149	8242	450	5	3.28	7	371	22	0	3.56

A talented multisport athlete, Michel Dion was proficient enough at baseball to play 22 games with the Montreal Expos organization in 1972. However, the 18-year-old catcher struggled at the plate, batting .182 in 44 at-bats. He soon swapped his catcher's mask for a goalie mask.

His flirtation with baseball slowed his development on the ice. Dion played two seasons of junior hockey with Montreal in the Quebec Major Junior Hockey League, where he served primarily as a backup. Fortunately, the World Hockey Association was hungry for young talent. Dion joined the Indianapolis Racers in 1975–76.

Sharing the goaltending duties with former Penguin Andy Brown, Dion enjoyed a terrific rookie season. Posting a league-best 2.74 goals-against average and a sterling .910 save percentage, he was awarded the Ben Hatskin Trophy—the WHA's version of the Vezina Trophy.

Following three solid seasons in the WHA, Dion made his NHL debut with the Quebec Nordiques in 1979–80. After a decent first year, he faltered badly in 1980–81.

Seeking a goaltender to replace the departed Greg Millen, the Penguins gambled on Dion. Before they signed him, however, they sent him to an eye doctor, who told him he needed contact lenses.

"The doctor said I had no depth perception," Dion said. "Last year I noticed more screen shots and blue-line shots were going in. I just didn't realize it was because I needed contacts."

His vision problems corrected thanks to the new lenses, Dion enjoyed a brilliant start to his Penguins career. He quickly became a darling of the Civic Arena faithful with his spectacular, acrobatic style. Organist Vince Lascheid broke into a rendition of "Michelle My Belle" whenever Dion made one of his electrifying saves.

By midseason the Penguins were battling the New York Islanders for Patrick Division supremacy. One of the big reasons was the extraordinary play of Dion, who earned a spot on the Wales Conference All-Star Team. He appeared in 62 games and tied a club record with 25 wins while posting a respectable 3.79 goals-against average.

That spring the Penguins met the Islanders in the opening round of the playoffs. After being strafed for 15 goals in Games 1 and 2, Dion held New York to just three goals in the next two contests as his team rallied to tie the series. Twenty minutes away from a stunning upset in Game 5, the Penguins couldn't keep the determined Islanders at bay. John Tonelli struck for the series winner in overtime to overcome a heroic 42-save effort by Dion.

Following the Cinderella 1981–82 season, the wheels fell off the Penguins' wagon. Dion played reasonably well behind a porous team, recording a 4.26 goals-against average while splitting time with Denis Herron. However, by 1983–84 the wear and tear began to show. His average ballooned to an unsightly 5.33 goals per game with a weak .853 save percentage. The next season Dion was consigned to Baltimore, where he finished his career.

After his retirement Michel turned to another of his passions—golf. In 1991 he became a Certified Master Teacher with the U.S. Golf Teachers Federation.

Gonchar, Sergei

Penguins: 2005–10   **Birthplace:** Chelyabinsk, USSR
Defense   B: April 13, 1974
Shoots: left   **Ht.** 6-2 **Wt.** 211
Nickname: Sarge

YR	Regular Season					Playoffs				
	GP	G	A	PTS	PM	GP	G	A	PTS	PM
2005–06	75	12	46	58	100	-	-	-	-	-
2006–07	82	13	54	67	72	5	1	3	4	2
2007–08	78	12	53	65	66	20	1	13	14	8
2008–09	25	6	13	19	26	22	3	11	14	12
2009-10	62	11	39	50	49	13	2	10	12	4
NHL	**991**	**202**	**482**	**684**	**842**	**118**	**21**	**59**	**80**	**78**

When one watches Sergei Gonchar quarterback the power play with the style and elegance of a master Russian pianist, it's hard to imagine that in his formative years with Dynamo Moscow he was rarely involved in the offense. Remarkably, the 6'2", 211-pounder played the role of a stay-at-home bruiser, piling up 70 penalty minutes in 31 games as an 18-year-old defenseman.

Upon joining the Washington Capitals in 1995, he was encouraged to develop the offensive side of his game. Noting how well the big Russian handled the puck and how effortlessly he glided along the ice, Caps coach Ron Wilson began to use him on the power play.

Gonchar's latent offensive skills were soon in full bloom. Using his deadly accurate wrist shot and outstanding mobility to full advantage, he averaged 17 goals per year for the Caps from 1995 through 2003. During that span he established himself as one of the finest defensemen in the league, twice earning NHL Second Team All-Star honors.

Although the Caps were a talent-laden club, boasting the likes of explosive scorer Peter Bondra and former Penguins stars Jaromir Jagr and Robert Lang, their skill level rarely translated into playoff success. Forced to clean house, general manager George McPhee peddled Gonchar to the Bruins in March of 2004.

Following the lockout year of 2004–05, the smooth-skating Russian signed a lucrative five-year, $25 million deal with the Penguins. With Gonchar and fellow big-name free agents John LeClair and Ziggy Palffy joining Mario Lemieux and super rookie Sidney Crosby, the Pens were expected to compete for the Atlantic Division title. However, the team failed to mesh. Gonchar in particular got off to a dreadful start, prompting a network color analyst to ask, "Who's the impostor wearing No. 55?"

In the midst of a lost season, Michel Therrien took over the Penguins' helm and installed a system similar to the one Gonchar had played in Washington. Almost overnight, the star defender returned to pre-lockout form.

Determined to show the Penguins they had made a wise investment, "Sarge" whipped himself into top shape over the off-season. A notoriously slow starter, he jumped out of the starting blocks in 2006–07 at a sizzling pace to lead the resurgent Pens to their first playoff berth in six years.

Extremely popular with his teammates, he proved to be a wonderful leader and mentor. When Evgeni Malkin defected from Russia prior to the season, Gonchar moved the young phenom into his Sewickley home and took him under his wing. Malkin responded with a fine 33-goal season to capture the Calder Trophy.

By the 2007–08 campaign, the Penguins were ready to contend for the Stanley Cup. Gonchar played a prominent role. Enjoying a season worthy of Norris Trophy consideration, he tallied 12 goals and 65 points—second among NHL defenseman—while once again keying the Pens' deadly power play.

He earned further distinction that spring, not to mention the undying respect of his teammates. During the early stages of a do-or-die Game 5 versus Detroit in the Stanley Cup Finals, Gonchar injured his back. Although he could barely skate, he returned to the ice for a power play in the third overtime and promptly set up the game winner by Petr Sykora.

"I was just trying to help the team any way I could," he said.

Although the Penguins succumbed to the Red Wings in six games, they appeared to be ready to challenge for the Cup again in 2008–09. However, Sarge suffered a dislocated shoulder during the preseason and the team floundered

Few players have manned the point as elegantly as Sergei Gonchar.

in his absence. After missing 56 games, he returned to the lineup. With Gonchar piling up 19 points in 25 games, the Penguins went 18–4–4 to nail down second place in the Atlantic Division.

Once again, Sarge displayed his mettle in the postseason. In Game 4 of the Eastern Conference Semifinals, he absorbed a brutal knee-on-knee check from countryman Alexander Ovechkin. Expected to be out for the remainder of the playoffs, he returned after missing just two games. His winning goal in Game 3 of the Finals was a turning point, as the Penguins vanquished the Red Wings to capture the Stanley Cup.

The ultrasmooth defenseman was at his puck-moving best in 2009–10. Despite missing 20 games due to various ailments Gonchar enjoyed another banner year, notching 11 goals and 39 assists to pace the Penguins' defense.

Hatcher, Kevin

Penguins: 1996–99   **Birthplace:** Detroit, Michigan
Defense   B: September 9, 1966
Shoots: right   **Ht.** 6-3 **Wt.** 230

	Regular Season					Playoffs				
YR	GP	G	A	PTS	PM	GP	G	A	PTS	PM
1996–97	80	15	39	54	103	5	1	1	2	4
1997–98	74	19	29	48	66	6	1	0	1	12
1998–99	66	11	27	38	24	13	2	3	5	4
NHL	1157	227	450	677	1392	118	22	37	59	252

When hockey experts discuss the merits of Kevin Hatcher, it's often with a tinge of disappointment. Had Hatcher applied himself more consistently, he could have been one of the game's all-time greats. As it stands, he was a very good defenseman over the course of his 17-year NHL career who never quite measured up to the sum of his abilities.

Growing up in the Motor City, Hatcher first drew the attention of scouts as a 16-year-old. Skating for Detroit Compuware, the big defenseman piled up 75 points in 75 games. The following season he graduated to the North Bay Centennials of the Ontario Hockey League. Enamored of Hatcher's imposing size and blistering shot, the Washington Capitals took him with their first pick in the 1984 Entry Draft.

By the time he was 19, Hatcher was skating a regular shift in the NHL. He joined a defensive corps that was packed with gifted performers, including rising stars Larry Murphy and Scott Stevens and former Norris Trophy winner Rod Langway.

With Langway teaching him the finer points of the game, Hatcher began to blossom. In 1987–88 he scored 14 goals to begin a remarkable run of 12 straight seasons of double-figure goal production.

Hatcher hit his peak in the early 1990s. As a 24-year-old he paced the Capitals in goals (24), assists (50), and points

(74) while making his second of three straight NHL All-Star Game appearances. He enjoyed a career year in 1992–93, tallying an astonishing 34 goals and 79 points.

In his prime Hatcher was, at times, a dominant player. A powerful straight-ahead skater thanks to his long stride, he excelled at joining the rush and working the give-and-go. Possessing a cannon of a shot, he needed no encouragement to shoot (329 shots on goal in 1992–93). Standing 6'3" and tipping the scales at 230 pounds, he wasn't shy about throwing his weight around. Having trained at the famous Kronk Gym, Hatcher was a very capable fighter when riled.

The big blue-liner had his weaknesses, too. Like most big men, he lacked lateral mobility and could get caught out of position when trying to make a hit. Prone to turning the puck over, he was plagued by fits of inconsistency—especially in his own end.

Following 10 strong years in Washington, the Caps sent Hatcher to Dallas in a blockbuster trade just prior to the start of the strike-shortened 1995 season. With Kevin joining his younger brother Derian, the Stars had visions of a two-headed monster on defense.

What they got was something less. The aggressiveness slowly began to seep from Hatcher's play. Worse yet, his presence seemed to take the edge off Derian's game as well.

Meanwhile, the Penguins were disenchanted with their own star defenseman, Sergei Zubov. Although wondrously skilled, "Zubie" tended to overpass the puck on the power play, a trait that frustrated his teammates—in particular Mario Lemieux. On June 22, 1996, the teams swapped the high-profile stars.

Big Kevin Hatcher battles future Pen Petr Sykora for a loose puck.

Hatcher performed well for the Pens. During his first season with the club he racked up 15 goals and 54 points to earn a spot on the Eastern Conference All-Star Team. In 1997–98, he pounded home 19 goals—including a whopping 13 on the power play.

However, just as he had in Dallas, Hatcher showed little interest in playing a physical game. He became more one-dimensional, hammering off shots from the point but doing little else to distinguish himself.

Following the 1998–99 campaign, the Penguins peddled the big defenseman to the Rangers for journeyman Peter Popovic. Hatcher played one year for the Blueshirts and one for Carolina before retiring in 2001.

Kehoe, Rick

Penguins: 1974–84   **Birthplace:** Windsor, Ontario
Right wing   B: July 15, 1951
Shoots: right   **Ht.** 5-11   **Wt.** 180
Nickname: Chico

Rick Kehoe (left) bumps Blues defender Rod Seiling off the puck. "Chico" topped the 20-goal mark in nine straight seasons.

YR	Regular Season					Playoffs				
	GP	G	A	PTS	PM	GP	G	A	PTS	PM
1974–75	76	32	31	63	22	9	0	2	2	0
1975–76	71	29	47	76	6	3	0	0	0	0
1976–77	80	30	27	57	10	3	0	2	2	0
1977–78	70	29	21	50	10	-	-	-	-	-
1978–79	57	27	18	45	2	7	0	2	2	0
1979–80	79	30	30	60	4	5	2	5	7	0
1980–81	80	55	33	88	6	5	0	3	3	0
1981–82	71	33	52	85	8	5	2	3	5	2
1982–83	75	29	36	65	12	-	-	-	-	-
1983–84	57	18	27	45	8	-	-	-	-	-
1984–85	6	0	2	2	0	-	-	-	-	-
NHL	**906**	**371**	**396**	**767**	**120**	**39**	**4**	**17**	**21**	**4**

Rick Kehoe was a wonderfully consistent goal-scorer through perhaps the most trying period in Penguins history. Enduring a nearly endless succession of rebuilding programs with a calm stoicism, he never scored fewer than 27 goals during a remarkable nine-season run, including four years of 30-plus goals and a career-best 55 tallies in 1980–81.

His given name was Rick, but everyone called him "Chico" for his likeness to the late *Chico and the Man* TV star, Freddie Prinze. Indeed, with his swarthy complexion and signature mustache he resembled a bandito on the ice for the way he picked goaltenders' pockets.

Pens general manager Jack Button acquired Kehoe from Toronto in the summer of 1974 for Blaine Stoughton, a gifted but underachieving first-round pick. Playing on a line with veterans Ron Schock and Vic Hadfield, Chico made an immediate splash by pumping in 32 goals. In the playoffs, however, the speedy winger failed to find the net. It was a bugaboo that would haunt him throughout his otherwise distinguished career.

Kehoe rolled along until the 1980–81 campaign, when Eddie Johnston took over as coach. A power-play wizard, EJ opened up the attack and Chico responded with a breakout year.

"I was pretty consistent around the 30-goal mark until '80–81, when I was fortunate enough to have a big year," he recalled. "It just seems that some years the puck goes in more than other years."

He was being modest. With talented defenseman Randy Carlyle manning the point and newly acquired Paul Gardner setting the table, Kehoe became the triggerman on a power-play unit that was the scourge of the league. At the postseason awards banquet he received the Lady Byng Trophy for his stellar and gentlemanly play.

Racking up 33 goals and a team-high 85 points, Kehoe had yet another strong season in 1981–82. In the playoffs the Pens squared off against the powerhouse New York Islanders in a best-of-five series. Trailing the two-time defending Stanley Cup champs 2–0, the gritty Penguins managed to force Game 3 into overtime.

The stage was set for Chico's long-awaited moment of postseason glory. Just 4:14 into the extra frame he snapped off his laser of a wrist shot. The puck bounded through a tangle of players and past Billy Smith.

With the monkey finally off his back, Kehoe struck again in Game 4 as the inspired Penguins knotted the series. They fought valiantly before succumbing to the Islanders in a pulsating deciding game.

The veteran winger hung up his skates in 1984 as the team's all-time leading scorer, but not before he got a chance to play alongside the man who would eventually surpass him—Mario Lemieux. In many ways Kehoe served as the bridge between the Pens' early playoff teams and their Stanley Cup champions.

Three years later he began his second career when he rejoined the team as an assistant coach. In perhaps his greatest contribution, Kehoe helped budding superstar Jaromir Jagr develop his lethal wrist shot.

Following a brief stint as a scout, Chico returned to the bench as an assistant under Herb Brooks. In the fall of 2001 he assumed the coaching reins from Ivan Hlinka and guided the team for nearly two full seasons. After being replaced by Ed Olczyk, he returned to his role as pro scout. He presently serves as a professional scout for the New York Rangers.

Alexei Kovalev bowls over New Jersey's Scott Stevens in pursuit of the puck.

Kovalev, Alexei

Penguins: 1998–03   **Birthplace:** Togliatti, USSR
Right wing   **B:** February 24, 1973
Shoots: left   **Ht.** 6-1   **Wt.** 224
Nickname: Kovy

YR	Regular Season					Playoffs				
	GP	G	A	PTS	PM	GP	G	A	PTS	PM
1998–99	63	20	26	46	37	10	5	7	12	14
1999–00	82	26	40	66	94	11	1	5	6	10
2000–01	79	44	51	95	96	18	5	5	10	16
2001–02	67	32	44	76	80	-	-	-	-	-
2002–03	54	27	37	64	50	-	-	-	-	-
NHL	**1228**	**412**	**578**	**990**	**1254**	**116**	**44**	**54**	**98**	**104**

In the fall of 1998, Penguins general manager Craig Patrick was faced with a dilemma. He felt his team needed more scoring punch to remain competitive, especially since free agent Ron Francis had departed for Carolina over the summer. However, he was operating under tight financial constraints that severely restricted his trade options.

Fortunately, Patrick had an ace in the hole. The Pens still held the rights to talented but enigmatic Petr Nedved, who had not played in over a year due to a contract squabble. Nedved's previous team, the Rangers, desperately wanted him back. On November 25, 1998, Patrick peddled the problem child to New York as part of a five-player trade for Alexei Kovalev.

There were few players as gifted as Kovalev. When asked about the 25-year-old winger, Jaromir Jagr offered, "He's probably one of the five most talented guys I've ever seen."

"Kovy" had all the tools: a powerful skating stride; the ability to effortlessly shift gears; and an overpowering shot honed from practicing with lead-filled pucks as a youth. Standing 6'1" and tipping the scales at a solid 224 pounds, he possessed incredible strength. He could shrug off even the largest and most persistent defenders.

While Kovalev displayed moments of breathtaking brilliance, there were far too many nights when the player didn't measure up to the sum of his prodigious skills.

"Until Alex understands that the object of hockey is to put the puck in the net, he'll continue to have problems," Rangers general manager Neil Smith warned.

Craig Patrick was far more charitable.

"He's just a real good, solid hockey player," Patrick said. "He has great one-on-one skills. He's got great speed. He's got a great shot. We think in our environment he's going to be very, very productive."

Patrick's instincts proved to be spot on. Sprung from the glare of the Manhattan spotlights, Kovalev developed into a dominant offensive force. Following a solid 20-goal campaign in his first year with the Penguins, he rolled up 26 goals and 66 points in 1999–00.

The 27-year-old winger put it all together in 2000–01. Using his lethal wrist shot to fullest advantage, he emerged as perhaps the most dangerous player in all of hockey. Skating on a line with fellow stars Robert Lang and Martin Straka, he exploded for a career-best 44 goals and 95 points to earn a spot on the Eastern Conference All-Star Team.

Kovy continued to perform well over the next two seasons, racking up 59 goals in 121 games. However, the Penguins were once again in dire financial straits. Knowing full well he wouldn't be able to sign the unrestricted free agent to a new contract, Patrick shipped the big Russian back to the Rangers on February 10, 2003.

Unfortunately for Kovalev, his second tour of duty with the Blueshirts went no better than his first. In the spring of 2004 the Rangers sent him north of the border to play for the fabled Montreal Canadiens.

The silky-smooth winger returned to All-Star form with the Habs, averaging 25 goals and 65 points per year during his four seasons wearing *les bleu, blanc, et rouge*. However, he endured a love-hate relationship with the hard-core Montreal fans, who adored him during his hot streaks and despised him during his frequent cold snaps.

Seeking a change of scenery, Kovalev signed a free-agent deal with the Ottawa Senators during the summer of 2009. Still a potent shooter, he scored a hat trick on December 12 to reach 400 career goals. Not too shabby for a player who many regarded as an underachiever.

The Penguins' second great French Canadian center, Pierre Larouche. "Lucky Pierre" scored 53 goals in 1975–76.

Larouche, Pierre

Penguins: 1974–77   **Birthplace:** Taschereau, Quebec
Center   B: November 16, 1955
Shoots: right   **Ht.** 5-11 **Wt.** 175
Nicknames: Lucky Pierre, The King

	Regular Season					Playoffs				
YR	GP	G	A	PTS	PM	GP	G	A	PTS	PM
1974–75	79	31	37	68	52	9	2	5	7	2
1975–76	76	53	58	111	33	3	0	1	1	0
1976–77	65	29	34	63	14	3	0	3	3	0
1977–78	20	6	5	11	0	-	-	-	-	-
NHL	812	395	427	822	237	64	20	34	54	16

In the summer of 1974 the Penguins struck gold in the Amateur Draft. With the eighth overall pick they snagged gifted 19-year-old center Pierre Larouche. Although undersized, he had rolled up an incredible 251 points with Sorel in the high-flying Quebec League.

Despite his gaudy numbers, the Pens weren't sure Larouche was ready for the rigors of NHL competition. Any lingering doubts were quickly erased during training camp. Placed on the third line between rugged Battleship Kelly and hard-shooting Chuck Arnason, the cocksure rookie immediately made his mark. Not only was he scoring at a point-per-game clip, but he had turned his linemates into offensive threats as well. The trio produced a whopping 84 goals—nearly as many as the team's potent first and second lines.

He was scoring off the ice as well. Aptly nicknamed "Lucky Pierre" by announcer Mike Lange, he quickly became the darling of Penguins fans, especially those of the fairer sex. He became so popular that the team sponsored a "Date with Pierre" contest.

The underlying reason for Pierre's unprecedented popularity went deeper than his boyish good looks and charm. In the wake of Michel Briere's tragic death only a few short years earlier, he was like a healing balm for the Steel City's hockey fans.

Although he led all rookie scorers with 68 points, Larouche finished a close second to Atlanta's Eric Vail in the race for the Calder Trophy. Lucky Pierre left little doubt about who the real superstar was during his sophomore season. At the callow age of 20, he exploded for a remarkable 53 goals and 58 assists to place fifth in the NHL scoring race.

The crafty young center with the magic touch had barely scratched the surface of his potential. However, by the 1976–77 season the Penguins were an aging team in transition. With top scorers Vic Hadfield and Lowell MacDonald shelved due to injuries, coach Ken Schinkel was determined to tighten the reins.

Never a bastion of back checking or self-discipline, Larouche chafed under the new restrictions. He enjoyed partying into the wee hours and regarded curfew as a rule that was meant to be broken. After serving a team-mandated suspension, Lucky Pierre's production slipped below his rookie-season totals.

His attitude deteriorated even more rapidly. During the off-season he made it clear he wanted out of Pittsburgh. General manager Baz Bastien obliged, engineering a deal with Cleveland that would have netted the Pens two solid pros. Unwilling to play for the Barons, Larouche did an about-face and invoked a no-trade clause in his contract.

Amid the turmoil, the 1977–78 Pens nosedived to an ugly start. Larouche was barely on pace for a 40-point season, a travesty considering his supreme talents. At wits' end, Bastien finally found a taker for his bad boy, packing him off to Montreal for soon-to-be-over-the-hill Pete Mahovlich and green prospect Peter Lee. While the return was decidedly less than expected for a player of Larouche's caliber, it was a case of addition by subtraction. He had single-handedly shredded any pretense of team unity.

Following a slow start with the Canadiens, Larouche potted 50 goals in 1979–80 to become the first player in NHL history to score 50 goals for two different teams. However, the Habs eventually grew tired of his shortcomings and peddled him to the Whalers, who in turn traded him to the Rangers. While he remained a dangerous scorer to the end, he never fulfilled the promise of his thrilling second season in Pittsburgh.

Shorn of yet another potential superstar, the Penguins wallowed in mediocrity for over a decade before another French Canadian center would lift the team onto his broad shoulders and carry it to Stanley Cup glory.

MacDonald, Lowell

Penguins: 1970, 1972–1978
Birthplace: New Glasgow, Nova Scotia
Left wing   B: August 30, 1941
Shoots: right   **Ht.** 5-11   **Wt.** 185

	Regular Season					Playoffs				
YR	GP	G	A	PTS	PM	GP	G	A	PTS	PM
1970–71	10	0	1	1	0	-	-	-	-	-
1972–73	78	34	41	75	8	-	-	-	-	-
1973–74	78	43	39	82	14	-	-	-	-	-
1974–75	71	27	33	60	24	9	4	2	6	4
1975–76	69	30	43	73	12	3	1	0	1	0
1976–77	3	1	1	2	0	3	1	2	3	4
1977–78	19	5	8	13	2	-	-	-	-	-
NHL	**506**	**180**	**210**	**390**	**92**	**30**	**11**	**11**	**22**	**12**

When Lowell MacDonald was awarded the Masterton Trophy in 1973, it was a case of quiet vindication for a player who had scaled some huge hurdles in order to pursue his hockey dreams. Indeed, the trophy seemed to have been created with MacDonald in mind. Few players in the history of the game have displayed more perseverance and dedication on the road to stardom.

Following a promising junior career that culminated in a Memorial Cup triumph for his Hamilton Red Wings, MacDonald began his pro career with Detroit. Although undeniably talented, the youngster had a difficult time cracking the Red Wings' experienced lineup. He enjoyed greater success with the team's AHL affiliate, the Pittsburgh Hornets. In three seasons with the minor league club, Lowell scored 77 goals, including 31 during the 1963–64 campaign.

After a trade to Toronto in 1965, the Nova Scotia native toiled for two seasons with Tulsa in the Central Hockey League. MacDonald finally became a full-time player in the NHL in 1967 when he was drafted by Los Angeles. He enjoyed a terrific first season with the Kings, notching 21 goals. Although his production dipped the following year, MacDonald had established himself as a solid big-league performer.

There was, however, a downside to playing in Los Angeles. MacDonald hated flying.

"I had a major fear of flying; I was in really bad shape," he confessed. "My two years in Los Angeles really took its toll. We flew over 100,000 miles a year."

Preparing to leave training camp in 1969, MacDonald narrowly missed boarding a plane that was hijacked to Cuba. It was the last straw. At 28 years of age, Lowell decided to retire rather than endure the agony of flying.

Taking a year off to earn his bachelor's degree from St. Mary's University in Halifax, MacDonald played a handful of home games for the Kings' minor league affiliate in Springfield, Massachusetts.

The following summer, MacDonald was contacted by Penguins general manager Red Kelly, his former Kings coach, about playing for the Penguins.

"He called me," MacDonald said. "He said they flew only 30,000 to 35,000 miles a year in Pittsburgh. I said I'd come if he wanted me. So Pittsburgh picked me up from Los Angeles in the 1970 Intra-League Draft."

Classy Lowell MacDonald was a member of "the Century Line."

Unfortunately, MacDonald injured his troublesome left knee in training camp. After skating a shift here and there, he submitted to season-ending surgery. The operation was performed by the Penguins' team physician, Dr. Charles Stone. MacDonald would credit Stone with saving his career.

For two years MacDonald stayed away from the game. He began to think his career was over until his wife Joyce encouraged him to give hockey one more try. Whipping himself into peak condition, he won a spot on the Penguins roster in 1972.

Acting on a hunch, Kelly placed the 31-year-old veteran on a line with rising stars Syl Apps and Al McDonough. Playing the off wing, MacDonald responded with a huge season. He racked up 34 goals and 41 assists while leading the team with a sparkling plus/minus rating of plus 37.

Those who doubted whether MacDonald could repeat his success were in for a surprise. In 1973–74 he enjoyed the finest season of his career. Skating on the explosive "Century Line" with Apps and Jean Pronovost, he tallied a club-record 43 goals and 82 points while garnering his second straight West Division All-Star berth.

"Syl and Prony and I just clicked," he recalled for Jim O'Brien in *Penguin Profiles*. "We roamed all over the place. It was more dangerous running into Prony and Apps than it was those guys like [Dave] Schultz on the Flyers. But we had a chemistry where we just knew where the other guys were going to be."

Due in part to a more balanced attack, Lowell slipped to 27 goals in 1974–75. He returned to 30-goal form the following season.

Unfortunately, the injury bugaboo resurfaced late in MacDonald's career. After sitting out virtually all of the 1976–77 season following his seventh knee surgery, the classy old pro was limited to 19 games in 1977–78. At 37 years of age, MacDonald decided it was time to hang up his skates.

Lowell retired as the third-leading goal scorer in team history, behind his linemates Apps and Pronovost. It was a remarkable achievement given his relatively brief career. Entering 2010–11, he still ranks 17th on the Pens' all-time list of goal scorers.

Malkin, Evgeni

Penguins: 2006–   **Birthplace:** Magnitogorsk, USSR
Center   B: July 31, 1986
Shoots: left   **Ht.** 6-3 **Wt.** 195
Nickname: Geno

	Regular Season					Playoffs				
YR	GP	G	A	PTS	PM	GP	G	A	PTS	PM
2006–07	78	33	52	85	80	5	0	4	4	8
2007–08	82	47	59	106	78	20	10	12	22	24
2008–09	82	35	78	113	80	24	14	22	36	51
2009-10	67	28	49	77	100	13	5	6	11	6
NHL	**309**	**143**	**238**	**381**	**338**	**62**	**29**	**44**	**73**	**89**

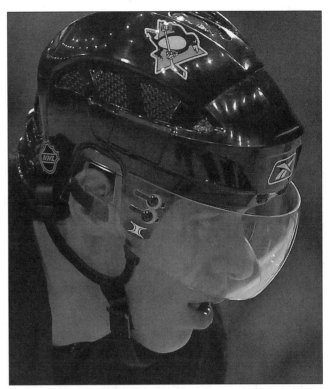

The mercurial Russian Evgeni Malkin. "Geno" won the Conn Smythe and Art Ross Trophies in 2009 while leading the Pens to a Cup.

It seemed only natural that Evgeni Vladimirovich Malkin would one day play for the Pittsburgh Penguins. After all, he was born and raised in Magnitogorsk—Russia's version of "the Steel City."

Malkin's father Vladimir, himself a former defenseman, enrolled his son in the local hockey program. It soon became apparent that he had a prodigy on his hands. From an early age the tall, rangy youngster displayed an offensive flair that foretold of bigger things to come.

By the 2003–04 season Malkin was skating for Metallurg Magnitogorsk in the fast Russian Superleague. That spring the budding 17-year-old star led Russia to a gold medal in the World Under 18 Junior Championships.

His strong two-way play quickly drew the attention of NHL scouts. Penguins general manager Craig Patrick selected Malkin with the second pick at the 2004 Entry Draft—one slot behind his more heralded countryman, Alexander Ovechkin. While the sleek and powerful Ovechkin may have been the more glamorous choice, many scouts believed that Malkin was the better all-around player.

Following two strong seasons with Magnitogorsk, Malkin expressed his desire to play for Pittsburgh. However, Metallurg club officials weren't willing to release their prized phenom. Following a negotiating session that harkened back to the days of the iron-fisted Soviet regime, the team announced that it had signed Malkin for another year.

The situation escalated in August of 2006 when Malkin bolted from the club's training camp in Helsinki. Upon his arrival in the United States, he made it clear that he was pressured into signing with Magnitogorsk. Invoking a provision in Russian labor law that allowed him to cancel the agreement with two weeks notice, the big center arrived in Pittsburgh on September 5 and signed a contract with the Penguins.

Malkin's NHL debut was delayed when he suffered a dislocated shoulder during a training-camp collision with John LeClair. When he finally hit the ice on October 18 against New Jersey, he gave a tantalizing preview of what was in store. Bursting into the slot, he faked future Hall of Famer Martin Brodeur out of position and whipped a backhander past the stunned goalie.

The 20-year-old promptly exploded, scoring at least one goal in each of his first six games—a pace unmatched by a rookie in 90 years. Maintaining his torrid early season pace, "Geno" piled up 85 points to easily capture the Calder Trophy.

Occasionally he shared the ice with fellow supernova Sidney Crosby. Hockey fans were in for a rare treat. With Sid setting the table for Malkin's crackling wrist shot, the Penguins' power play became the scourge of the league.

The dynamic duo also engaged in a little friendly one-upmanship, constantly pushing themselves to outdo the other.

"The competition is great," Malkin said with a smile. "Competing against Sid is great."

Malkin came of age during the 2007–08 campaign. When Crosby went down with a high-ankle sprain on January 18, the responsibility for pacing the attack fell on the quiet Russian's shoulders.

"Right now, since we lost our leader and our captain, I'm going to try my best and raise my game," Malkin said. "I'm going to try to do a little more."

A little more, indeed. Skating on the powerful "Steel City Line" with wingers Ryan Malone and Petr Sykora, Geno rolled up 48 points during Crosby's 29-game absence while dispelling concerns about his readiness to lead the team. Following a dazzling two-goal performance against Los Angeles, Kings coach Marc Crawford sang his praises.

"By far, Malkin was the best player on the ice," Crawford said. "He was the difference-maker. He wanted to put on a show, and he did."

Continuing his superb play down the homestretch, Geno tallied a team-high 47 goals and 106 points to place second in the NHL scoring race behind Ovechkin.

Unfortunately, the magic dust wore off during the post-season. Following a strong performance through the first three rounds of the playoffs, Geno faded during the Pens' loss to Detroit in the Stanley Cup Finals. Although it was later revealed that he was suffering from the flu, questions surfaced about his ability to produce at crunch time.

The criticism only strengthened the big center's resolve. Entering his third season, he was a more confident, mature

player. Skating as if he had something to prove, Geno captured his first Art Ross Trophy on the strength of a 113-point season.

His English was vastly improved as well. Prior to 2008–09, teammate Sergei Gonchar or Penguins staffer George Birman always served as translators during interviews. Suddenly, Geno began speaking to the press on his own, which endeared him even more to his adoring fans.

Malkin continued to shine during the opening round of the 2009 playoffs, tallying nine points to help the Penguins down Philadelphia. The victory over the Flyers set up what proved to be an epic matchup with the Washington Capitals and his arch-nemesis Ovechkin in the Eastern Conference Semifinals.

Rarely have two players with such opposite personalities been so closely linked. In 2004 the twin sensations became the first Russians ever to be selected first and second in the National Hockey League Entry Draft. Four years later they became the first Russian duo to finish first and second in the NHL scoring race.

As always, Malkin played best man to Ovechkin's bride-groom. While his bold and brash countryman was constantly grabbing the headlines, Geno seemed content to go about his business with a quiet excellence.

A feud was festering between the two as well. In August of 2007 Ovechkin punched Malkin's Russian agent, Gennady Ushakov, at a Moscow night club. On the ice, the rambunctious Capital rarely missed an opportunity to deliver a big hit on his former Olympic team linemate, often in borderline fashion.

Although they appeared to settle their differences at the 2009 NHL All-Star Game, Malkin was no less determined to emerge from his rival's shadow.

"Yes, I want to," he said. "I try. I want to try to be better [than Ovechkin]. Maybe this year I'll be better."

Unfortunately for the Penguins, it was Ovechkin who held the upper hand during the first two games of the series. He scored four goals and fired off an astounding 21 shots, far outdistancing Malkin's eight shots and two assists. Worse yet, Geno drew a tripping penalty that led to Ovechkin's game winner in the second contest.

It was a pivotal moment for the Penguins and Malkin—the kind that can make or break a champion. With his team's Stanley Cup hopes hanging in the balance, Geno stepped forward with arguably the finest performance of his career in Game 3. No one—not Ovechkin nor Penguins teammate Sidney Crosby—would match Malkin on this night. Playing both ends of the ice with a singular brilliance, he dominated the action, unleashing a game-high nine shots and scoring the Penguins' second goal.

"He was at a different level," Penguins coach Dan Bylsma said. "Another level."

Geno's game remained at another level for the remainder of the playoffs. He torched All-Star goalie Cam Ward for six goals during the Pens' four-game sweep of Carolina in the Eastern Conference Finals, including an electrifying tally in Game 2 that was instantly dubbed "the Geno."

Saving his best for last, Malkin paced all Penguins scorers with eight points against Detroit to lead his team to Stanley Cup glory. In addition to elevating his own play, he helped turn lunch-pail winger Max Talbot into a scoring threat. For his supreme effort he was awarded the Conn Smythe Trophy as the MVP of the playoffs.

"I think he answered the bell," Crosby said. "I'm thinking he's pretty happy and people realize how great a player he is. This isn't an easy time of year. You've got to find ways to battle through and he did that all playoffs long."

Although the accolades were most welcome, what mattered most of all to the modest Russian was winning the Stanley Cup.

"I saw Geno crying, he's from Russia," Talbot said. "This is how important and huge it is for him."

"Big day in my life," Malkin said. "My friends are happy, I'm happy. I think about it a lot, especially these last [two] weeks. It's my dream. Me and Sid, just like that."

Unfortunately, Geno endured a subpar season in 2009–10. Hampered by shoulder and foot injuries, his production dipped to a career-low 77 points.

Still, the big center remained as popular as ever with the Steel City faithful. On March 25, 2010, he received the prestigious Dapper Dan Sportsman of the Year Award from the *Pittsburgh Post-Gazette*.

McDonough, Al

Penguins: 1972–74   **Birthplace:** Hamilton, Ontario
Right wing   B: June 6, 1950
Shoots: right   **Ht.** 6-1   **Wt.** 175
Nickname: The Mad Hatter

YR	Regular Season					Playoffs				
	GP	G	A	PTS	PM	GP	G	A	PTS	PM
1971–72	37	7	11	18	8	4	0	1	1	0
1972–73	78	35	41	76	26	-	-	-	-	-
1973–74	37	14	22	36	12	-	-	-	-	-
NHL	**237**	**73**	**88**	**161**	**73**	**8**	**0**	**1**	**1**	**2**
WHA	**200**	**66**	**73**	**139**	**52**	**8**	**3**	**1**	**4**	**2**

During his three seasons with the St. Catharines Black Hawks of the Ontario Hockey Association, Al McDonough established himself as a skilled and resourceful goal scorer. For a brief time, he would enjoy similar success in the National Hockey League.

Following a strong 33-goal season with Springfield of the American Hockey League, McDonough earned a promotion to the Los Angeles Kings in 1971–72. Remarkably, the Kings gave up on the rookie after only 35 games, sending him to the Penguins for veteran defenseman Bob Woytowich.

Upon his arrival in Pittsburgh, the tall, slender right wing showed promise as a scorer. In 37 games he notched a respectable 18 points, including seven goals. One thing was certain—McDonough wasn't afraid to shoot the puck. He fired off 113 shots during his half season with the Pens.

Penguins coach Red Kelly liked what he saw. The following season he moved McDonough to the top line with Syl Apps and Lowell MacDonald. Meshing beautifully with his new linemates, McDonough responded with a breakout year, striking for a club-record 35 goals. During a piping-hot 20-game stretch from October 11, 1972, through November 22, 1972, he scored three hat tricks to earn the nickname "Mad Hatter."

"I guess three has to be my favorite number," he told Dan Donovan of the *Pittsburgh Press*. "I can't get past it."

Coming off his big season, the 23-year-old winger appeared to have a bright future in the Steel City. But the Penguins bottomed out through the early stages of the 1973–74 campaign. Among the team's myriad problems was a lack of aggression and desire. Although McDonough still was productive—14 goals and a team-high 36 points through 37 games—his sometimes lackadaisical approach cast him in a poor light. On January 4, 1974, he was traded to Atlanta for Chuck Arnason and tough defenseman Bob Paradise. Ironically, he had just been named to the West Division All-Star Team.

McDonough was never the same player following the trade. Although he managed 10 goals in 35 games with the

Nicknamed "the Mad Hatter," Al McDonough struck for three hat tricks during a 20-game stretch in 1972.

Flames, he was viewed as an underachiever. He jumped to the Cleveland Crusaders of the World Hockey Association in 1974–75 and scored 34 goals. However, his output gradually tailed off during three seasons in the WHA. Following a cup of coffee with the Detroit Red Wings in 1977–78, McDonough retired from the game at the age of 27.

Mullen, Joe

Penguins: 1990–95, 1996–97
Birthplace: New York, New York
Right wing   B: February 26, 1957
Shoots: right   **Ht.** 5-9 **Wt.** 180
Nickname: Slippery Rock Joe

	Regular Season					Playoffs				
YR	GP	G	A	PTS	PM	GP	G	A	PTS	PM
1990–91	47	17	22	39	6	22	8	9	17	4
1991–92	77	42	45	87	30	9	3	1	4	4
1992–93	72	33	37	70	14	12	4	2	6	6
1993–94	84	38	32	70	41	6	1	0	1	2
1994–95	45	16	21	37	6	12	0	3	3	4
1996–97	54	7	15	22	4	1	0	0	0	0
NHL	1062	502	561	1063	241	143	60	46	106	42

As goal scorers go, Joe Mullen wasn't especially pretty to watch. He didn't fly down the wing with the grace and élan of a Guy Lafleur, firing tracer bullets past terrified goalies. On the contrary, he scored most of his goals while twisting and driving through traffic, often releasing the puck from awkward angles as he was tumbling to the ice. But my, was he effective.

Mullen learned his trade playing roller hockey on the playgrounds and streets of the tough Hell's Kitchen section of Manhattan, which accounted for his less-than-smooth skating style. When he finally got the opportunity to play on ice, he proved to be a dynamo. Starring for the New York Westsiders of the New York Junior Hockey League, he piled up an astronomical 110 goals and 182 points in only 40 games.

Joe Mullen recoils from a collision with the Devils' Ken Daneyko. Despite numerous injuries, Mullen topped the 30-goal mark three times for the Pens.

Following a distinguished collegiate career at Boston College, Mullen signed as a free agent with the St. Louis Blues in the summer of 1979. The Blues assigned him to Salt Lake of the Central Hockey League, where he served a two-and-a-half-year apprenticeship with the Golden Eagles. Proving he was way too good for the minor leagues, he struck for 120 goals and 237 points in 182 games to earn a promotion to the Blues.

He instantly became a dominant performer at the big-league level. Although an ordinary skater at best, he made up for his lack of speed with hustle and a keen understanding of the game, which enabled him to always be properly positioned on the ice. During his four-plus seasons in St. Louis he averaged well over a point per game while twice reaching the 40-goal mark. Remarkably, the Blues peddled him to Calgary midway through 1985–86 season for the less-than-inspired package of Eddy Beers, Charles Bourgeois, and Gino Cavallini.

Skating for former Team USA coach Bob Johnson, Mullen flourished in Calgary. One of the premier snipers in all of hockey, he scored 40 goals in three straight seasons, including a monster 51-goal campaign in 1988–89. That spring he struck for 16 goals in the postseason to lead the Flames to the Stanley Cup. His sterling, gentlemanly play earned him the Lady Byng Trophy and First Team All-Star honors.

When Bob Johnson took over the coaching reins in Pittsburgh in the summer of 1990, he prodded general manager Craig Patrick to inquire about Mullen. Much to Patrick's surprise and delight, the Flames were willing to part with the high-scoring winger for a second-round draft choice.

With Mullen and fellow future Hall of Famer Bryan Trottier on hand to provide veteran leadership, the Penguins suddenly had the look of a contender. After a solid first half, however, Mullen was forced to undergo surgery to remove a herniated disc from his neck.

Many feared it was the end of the line for the 33-year-old winger. But Mullen, displaying his trademark bulldog tenacity, beat the odds. Wearing a horse collar for protection, he returned to action in the playoffs and scored eight goals—including two in Game 6 of the Finals—to help spark the Penguins to their first-ever Stanley Cup.

He was at his best during the adversity-strewn 1991–92 campaign. Seeing regular ice time alongside the great Mario Lemieux, he erupted for back-to-back four-goal games in late December. The hardworking winger finished the season with 42 goals—third-best on a talent-laden team.

Unfortunately, Mullen suffered another severe injury. In Game 2 of the Patrick Division Semifinals, he absorbed a crushing hit from Rangers tough guy Kris King, resulting in a strained knee ligament. A week later he grudgingly submitted to season-ending surgery.

Again, there were doubts about whether Mullen could bounce back. Again, the gritty winger defied the odds, returning to score 33 goals in 1992–93 and 38 the next year to earn a spot on the Eastern Conference All-Star Team.

Following the lockout season of 1994–95, the Penguins allowed Mullen to leave via free agency. He signed a one-year deal with the Bruins. Unfortunately, age seemed to creep up on the veteran winger as he tumbled to his lowest output as a pro.

At 39 years of age, it appeared he had finally reached the end of the line. But the Penguins missed his reliable two-way play and his penchant for scoring clutch goals. Returning to the Steel City for one last hurrah, the man Mike Lange dubbed "Slippery Rock Joe" potted his 500th career goal on March 14, 1997.

Murphy, Larry

Penguins: 1990–95 **Birthplace:** Scarborough, Ontario
Defense B: March 8, 1961
Shoots: right **Ht.** 6-2 **Wt.** 210
Nickname: Murph

	Regular Season					Playoffs				
YR	GP	G	A	PTS	PM	GP	G	A	PTS	PM
1990–91	44	5	23	28	30	23	5	18	23	44
1991–92	77	21	56	77	48	21	6	10	16	19
1992–93	83	22	63	85	73	12	2	11	13	10
1993–94	84	17	56	73	44	6	0	5	5	0
1994–95	48	13	25	38	18	12	2	13	15	0
NHL	1615	287	929	1216	1084	215	37	115	152	201

Perhaps no defenseman in the history of the game went about his business more quietly—or with greater efficiency—than Larry Murphy. He was the ultimate thinking man's defenseman, relying on intelligence, creativity, and superb positioning to control the tempo of a game. Few have done it better.

Following a brilliant 89-point campaign as an 18-year-old with the Peterborough Petes, Murphy was selected fourth overall by the Los Angeles Kings in the 1980 Entry Draft. He enjoyed one of the finest rookie seasons ever produced by a rearguard, piling up the astonishing totals of 16 goals and 76 points—a record for first-year defensemen. Remarkably, the Scarborough, Ontario, native finished second to Quebec center Peter Stastny—his senior by five years—in the voting for the Calder Trophy. It was not the last time in his career Murphy's accomplishments would be overlooked.

The youngster continued to provide superb two-way defensive play for the Kings over the next two seasons. However, in October of 1983 he was sent to the Washington Capitals for veterans Brian Engblom and Ken Houston.

It proved to be an excellent trade—for the Capitals. Joining forces with veteran Rod Langway and fellow young defensive stars Kevin Hatcher and Scott Stevens, Murphy became a more consistent player in his own end while providing his customary offensive production. Powered by their "big four," the previously woeful Capitals developed into one of the top teams in the league.

Following an outstanding season in 1986–87 (23 goals and 58 assists) that earned him Second NHL All-Star Team honors, "Murph" played in the thrilling Canada Cup series.

Calm, cool, and collected, Larry Murphy leads a Penguins rush.

He participated in one of the most memorable plays in hockey history, serving as the decoy on a three-on-one break with Wayne Gretzky and Mario Lemieux that resulted in Mario's spectacular series winner.

Curiously, Murphy's play took a dip that fall. Suddenly unable to find the net, he scored only one even-strength goal in 1987–88. Disenchanted with their erstwhile All-Star, the Capitals' boo-birds were quick to pounce. By the spring of 1989 the situation had become untenable, forcing general manager David Poile to peddle Murphy to the Minnesota North Stars.

It was a second trade—to the Penguins in December of 1990—that would restore Murphy's sagging reputation and revive his career. Given a badly needed boost of confidence and the freedom to play his game by coach Bob Johnson, Murph flourished in the Steel City. Teaming with hard-rock Ulf Samuelsson to form an exquisitely balanced tandem, he scored 23 points in the postseason to help pace the Pens to a Stanley Cup victory over his former club, the North Stars.

During the next two seasons Murphy was at the top of his game, averaging nearly 22 goals and 81 points per year. While he would never win a fastest skater competition, he possessed outstanding agility and lateral mobility. On the power play, he was a master at gobbling up wayward clearing attempts and turning them into scoring opportunities.

Defensively, he was cool and poised under fire. He always seemed to make the right read and the proper play.

"Murph was a smart and studious player," said his admiring coach, Scotty Bowman. "It was his understanding of what he could do that made him special."

After helping the Bowman-led Penguins to the Stanley Cup in 1992, Murphy gave the Penguins two more terrific seasons. In the summer of 1995, however, general manager Craig Patrick shipped him off to Toronto for Dmitri Mironov. The trade that brought Murph to Pittsburgh was one of the best in team history; the deal that sent him to the Leafs was among the worst.

Stung by the trade, the veteran defender languished in Toronto. In March of 1997 the Red Wings acquired him for future considerations. Once again, Murphy turned out to be the bargain of the century. Paired with Norris Trophy winner Nicklas Lidstrom, he won back-to-back Stanley Cups in the Motor City.

Polis, Greg

Penguins: 1970–74   **Birthplace:** Westlock, Alberta
Left wing   B: August 8, 1950
Shoots: left   **Ht.** 6-0 **Wt.** 195
Nickname: Porky

	Regular Season					Playoffs				
YR	GP	G	A	PTS	PM	GP	G	A	PTS	PM
1970–71	61	18	15	33	40	-	-	-	-	-
1971–72	76	30	19	49	38	4	0	2	2	0
1972–73	78	26	23	49	36	-	-	-	-	-
1973–74	41	14	13	27	32	-	-	-	-	-
NHL	**615**	**174**	**169**	**343**	**391**	**7**	**0**	**2**	**2**	**6**

When the Penguins chose Greg Polis with the seventh overall pick in the 1970 Amateur Draft, they believed they had a can't-miss prospect on their hands. Skating for the Estevan Bruins, the husky left wing finished second in scoring in the Western Canadian Junior Hockey League two years running.

Indeed, Polis possessed all the tools to become a great one. The Alberta farm boy could skate like the wind, thanks to the hours he spent as a youth on local ponds. He also was a terrific puckhandler, a result of playing keep-away with his black Labrador retriever.

Sure enough, the 20-year-old Polis made the Penguins straight out of junior. The rookie was one of the few bright spots in an otherwise dreary season. Although he missed 17 games due to injury, he scored a respectable 18 goals and was named to the West Division All-Star Team.

Skating with fellow rising stars Syl Apps and Jean Pronovost, Polis enjoyed his best NHL season in 1971–72. Serving as the line's corner man, the husky left wing established a new club record with 30 goals, tying him for the team lead with Pronovost. His strong play earned him a spot on the All-Star team for the second year in a row.

Polis appeared to be set for a long and successful run with the Penguins. However, in 1972–73 coach Red Kelly moved him off the Apps line in favor of veteran Lowell MacDonald. Although Polis managed to score 26 goals, he registered a team-worst plus/minus rating of minus 32.

Still, he achieved a moment of glory at the 1973 All-Star Game. Playing before a packed house at New York's Madison Square Garden, Polis scored two goals and was named the game's Most Valuable Player.

The following season would be his last in the Steel City. In January of 1974, Polis was traded to St. Louis with another mainstay, Bryan Watson, for Ab DeMarco and tough guys Steve Durbano and Battleship Kelly. Ironically, he moved on to the Rangers the following summer as a replacement for Vic Hadfield, who joined the Penguins.

While Polis scored 26 goals skating on the top line with Blueshirts legends Jean Ratelle and Rob Gilbert, he never truly achieved his full potential. Slowed by knee injuries, he finished his NHL career with Washington.

A former first-round pick, Greg Polis earned All-Star Game MVP honors in 1973.

Veteran Dean Prentice paced the Pens' attack in 1969–70 with 26 goals.

Prentice, Dean

Penguins: 1969–71   **Birthplace:** Schumacher, Ontario
Left wing   **B:** October 5, 1932
Shoots: left   **Ht.** 5-11 **Wt.** 180

	Regular Season					Playoffs				
YR	GP	G	A	PTS	PM	GP	G	A	PTS	PM
1969–70	75	26	25	51	14	10	2	5	7	8
1970–71	69	21	17	38	18	-	-	-	-	-
NHL	1378	391	469	860	484	54	13	17	30	38

Dean Prentice grew up in the small mining town of Shumacher, Ontario, where the local residents dug for gold and played hockey in their spare time. Likewise, it was no stretch to say that Penguins general manager Jack Riley hit the mother lode when he claimed Prentice from Detroit in the 1969 Intra-League Draft.

Regarded as one of the most underrated players of his era, the quiet, unassuming left wing broke into the NHL with the New York Rangers in 1952. After struggling through his first two seasons, Prentice hit his stride while skating on a line with Larry Popein and another future Penguin, Andy Bathgate.

While the flashy Bathgate grabbed the headlines, Prentice became a model of consistency. An outstanding all-around player, he worked the corners, back checked with diligence, killed penalties, and manned the power play. Over the next eight seasons Prentice averaged 20 goals per year for the Blueshirts and played in three NHL All-Star Games. He enjoyed his finest season in 1959–60, garnering Second Team NHL All-Star honors while notching a career-best 32 goals.

Following a trade to the Bruins in 1963, the hardworking winger continued his steady brand of play. He spent four seasons in Boston before moving on to Detroit.

Like a fine wine, Prentice improved with age. He sparkled during his first season in Pittsburgh, notching a team-high 26 goals and 51 points while leading the Pens to their first-ever playoff berth. His superb play earned him a spot on the West Division All-Star Team.

The following season he was reunited with Bathgate, his old Rangers linemate. Although the greybeard wingers combined to pot 36 goals—including a team-leading 21 by Prentice—the Penguins endured a miserable season and missed the playoffs.

Convinced he was nearing the end of the line, Red Kelly sold Prentice to Minnesota on the eve of the 1971–72 season. But the old pro still had some hockey left in him. Skating for the North Stars' "Over the Hill Gang," he struck for 46 goals over the next two seasons—including 26 at the ripe old age of 40. The grizzled veteran finally hung up his skates in 1974 with 391 goals and 860 points to his credit.

Recchi, Mark

Penguins: 1988–92, 2005–06, 2006–07
Birthplace: Kamloops, British Columbia
Right wing   **B:** February 1, 1968
Shoots: left   **Ht.** 5-10 **Wt.** 195
Nicknames: Recchs, the Recchin' Ball

	Regular Season					Playoffs				
YR	GP	G	A	PTS	PM	GP	G	A	PTS	PM
1988–89	15	1	1	2	0	-	-	-	-	-
1989–90	74	30	37	67	44	-	-	-	-	-
1990–91	78	40	73	113	48	24	10	24	34	33
1991–92	58	33	37	70	78	-	-	-	-	-
2005–06	63	24	33	57	56	-	-	-	-	-
2006–07	82	24	44	68	62	5	0	4	4	0
2007–08	19	2	6	8	12	-	-	-	-	-
NHL	1571	563	922	1485	998	164	56	77	133	85

As a youth playing hockey in his hometown of Kamloops, British Columbia, Mark Recchi heard an all-too-familiar refrain. He was too small to excel in such a rugged sport.

"I heard it a lot," he recalled in the Penguins' highlight video, *One from the Heart*. "I even remember everyone that said it, too. It always seemed to get back to me, which people said it."

Fortunately, the callous evaluation only served to fuel his competitive fire. Determined to prove the so-called experts wrong, Recchi enjoyed a productive junior hockey career, capped off by a sensational 154-point season with Kamloops in 1987–88.

"I wanted to prove I could play no matter what size I was," he said, "and that sometimes the heart is bigger than how tall you are."

Duly impressed, the Penguins selected Recchi—generously listed at 5'10" and 195 pounds—with their fourth pick in the 1988 Entry Draft. The hardworking youngster exploded for 50 goals in his first pro season at Muskegon. Earning a promotion to the Penguins in 1989–90, he enjoyed a wonderful rookie season, potting 30 goals.

Playing on "the Option Line" with fellow young stars and free-agents-to-be John Cullen and Kevin Stevens, Recchi burst into prominence in 1990–91. With supernova Mario Lemieux missing a huge chunk of the season, the 22-year-old right wing paced the team in points (113) while tying Stevens for the goal-scoring lead (40). His outstanding play earned him a spot on the Wales Conference All-Star Team.

In the playoffs, the gritty little winger shone like a diamond. Targeted for abuse by big defensemen like Washington's Kevin Hatcher, Recchi shook off the rough treatment and scored 10 goals to help lead the Penguins to a Stanley Cup.

Dubbed "the Recchin' Ball" by play-by-play announcer Mike Lange, he displayed a curious skating style. At times he appeared to be running on his blades as he dashed along the ice. However, Recchi was a dangerous scorer—especially off the rush—catching goalies off-balance with his lightning-quick release and hard, accurate shot.

Recchi rushed to a fine start in 1991–92, piling up 70 points in 58 games. The Penguins, however, were struggling to keep pace in the playoff chase. In February of 1992, general manager Craig Patrick pulled off a blockbuster three-way trade, sending Recchi to Philadelphia as the centerpiece of the deal for Rick Tocchet, Kjell Samuelsson, and Ken Wregget.

News of the trade devastated the youngster. Extremely loyal to his club, he was the type of player who bled black and gold. It seemed inconceivable that he was now a member of the hated Flyers.

His close friend Stevens was equally dejected.

"We definitely needed some help somewhere, but I don't know if this is the way we should've gone about it," he said.

Recchi responded the only way he knew how. Digging deep into his enormous reservoir of character, he enjoyed a monster 53-goal, 123-point season with Philadelphia in 1992–93. Skating for the Flyers, the Canadiens, and then the Flyers again, he averaged more than 26 goals and 72 points per season during an 11-year span while appearing in five NHL All-Star Games. In 2000, Kamloops chose Recchi

Mark Recchi flattens Buffalo's Alexander Mogilny in pursuit of the puck. "The Recchin' Ball" served three tours of duty with the Pens.

as its male athlete of the 20th century and renamed a street "Mark Recchi Way" in his honor.

Seeking a veteran leader for his improving young team, Craig Patrick righted an old wrong by signing Recchi to a free-agent deal during the summer of 2004. The move was lauded in the Steel City, where the Recchin' Ball remained a revered and popular player.

Showing he still had plenty of juice left in his legs, the 37-year-old Recchi averaged nearly a point per game. Taking note, the Carolina Hurricanes came knocking on Patrick's door in March of 2006. With Recchi's blessing, the Pens' general manager traded him to Carolina, where he at long last won his elusive second Stanley Cup.

The deal turned out to be little more than a lend-lease agreement. Recchi returned to Pittsburgh for his third tour of duty in 2006–07. Playing like a kid half his age, he flung himself into the corners and battled for loose pucks while setting a sterling example for his youthful teammates.

On January 26, 2007, the grizzled old pro notched his 500th goal against the Dallas Stars, a fitting achievement for a player who epitomized heart and soul throughout his career. He went on to score 24 goals and 68 points while leading the Pens to their first playoff berth in six years.

Recchi hoped to finish his career in Pittsburgh. Sadly, it didn't work out. Following a slow start to the 2007–08 campaign, he was unceremoniously placed on waivers and claimed by Atlanta. Determined to prove he was still a top-six forward, Recchi scored 40 points in 53 games for the Thrashers.

Splitting time with Tampa Bay and Boston the following season, he tallied 23 goals and 61 points—including 10 goals during his 18 games with the Bruins. It was a remarkable achievement for a 40-year-old.

Entering the 2010–11 season, Recchi ranked 13th in points (1,485) and 22nd in goals (563) in the NHL record book. Not bad for a player who was too small to make it in the NHL.

Schinkel, Ken

Penguins: 1967–73   **Birthplace:** Jansen, Saskatchewan
Right wing   B: November 27, 1932
Shoots: right   **Ht.** 5-10 **Wt.** 172
Nicknames: Schink

| | | Regular Season | | | | | Playoffs | | | |
YR	GP	G	A	PTS	PM	GP	G	A	PTS	PM
1967–68	57	14	25	39	19	-	-	-	-	-
1968–69	76	18	34	52	18	-	-	-	-	-
1969–70	72	20	25	45	19	10	4	1	5	4
1970–71	50	15	19	34	6	-	-	-	-	-
1971–72	74	15	30	45	8	3	2	0	2	0
1972–73	42	11	10	21	16	-	-	-	-	-
NHL	636	127	198	325	163	19	7	2	9	4

Like many hockey players of the Original Six era, Ken Schinkel's path to the National Hockey League was a test of patience and endurance.

A late bloomer, Schinkel played one season of junior hockey for St. Catharines as a 20-year-old winger. In the days before the Entry Draft, the Jansen, Saskatchewan, native was left to fend for himself. Determined to continue his career, he signed a contract to play for Springfield (Massachusetts) in 1953.

The Indians were owned by legendary Hall of Famer Eddie Shore. As a player, Shore had earned a reputation for being a tough, fearless competitor. As an owner, he was regarded as a penny-pinching miser who often made life miserable for his own players.

Since Springfield was not affiliated with an NHL team, Schinkel had no choice but to persevere. He toiled for five long years with the Indians while honing his skills. In 1958–59 Schinkel enjoyed a breakout season, leading the American Hockey League with 43 goals to attract the attention of the New York Rangers. A short time later the Rangers acquired the hardworking right wing for future considerations.

Schinkel earned a spot on the Rangers in 1959–60 and was cast in the role of a defensive forward. The 27-year-old rookie displayed a scoring touch as well, potting 13 goals for the Blueshirts in 69 games.

For the next three seasons "Schink" plied his trade on the checking line, shadowing the opposition's top scorers and killing penalties. By the mid-1960s, however, the Rangers had begun a youth movement. Viewed as excess baggage, Schinkel was shipped to the minors.

Recast in an offensive role, the veteran forward soon rediscovered his scoring touch. Skating for the Baltimore Clippers in the AHL, he averaged 27 goals and nearly 65 points per year from 1963 through 1967.

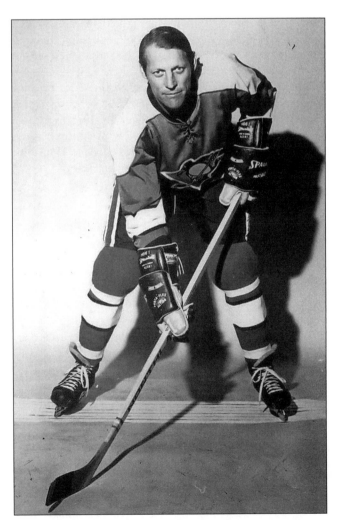

Two-time All-Star Ken Schinkel was the Pens' leading scorer in 1968–69.

When the NHL expanded to a dozen teams in 1967, it afforded many old pros a new lease on life. At 35 years of age, however, Schinkel was considered ancient even by expansion-team standards. Fortunately, Penguins general manager Jack Riley remembered the greybeard winger from his days as an AHL executive. He plucked Schinkel from the Rangers in the Expansion Draft.

In hindsight, it seemed that Schinkel was destined to play for Pittsburgh. Thanks to his flattop haircut, he bore an uncanny resemblance to Steel City football legend Johnny Unitas. Schinkel made an immediate impression. In the team's sixth game, coach Red Sullivan assigned him the daunting task of shadowing Chicago great Bobby Hull. The crafty old pro not only shut down "the Golden Jet," but he scored a hat trick to pace a 4–2 Penguins victory.

Following a decent first season, Schinkel became one of the Penguins' top players. In 1968–69 he led the club in scoring with 52 points and was named to the West Division All-Star Team. The following season he notched a career-high 20 goals. In the playoffs, the steady veteran finished second behind young star Michel Briere with four goals in 10 games.

Over the next two seasons he continued to perform at a high level, averaging 40 points per year despite missing 32 games due to injury. Skating on the tongue-twisting "Schink-Schock-Shack" line, he helped spark the Pens to their second playoff berth in 1971–72.

Remarkably, the 40-year-old opened the 1972–73 campaign by scoring at his customary pace. At the behest of Jack Riley, he hung up his skates in January of 1973 to assume the coaching duties from Red Kelly. Schinkel retired as the Pens' all-time leading scorer—a distinction he held until Jean Pronovost surpassed him the following year.

Stackhouse, Ron

Penguins: 1974–82   **Birthplace:** Haliburton, Ontario
Defense   B: August 26, 1949
Shoots: right   **Ht.** 6-3 **Wt.** 210

	Regular Season					Playoffs				
YR	GP	G	A	PTS	PM	GP	G	A	PTS	PM
1973–74	36	4	15	19	33	-	-	-	-	-
1974–75	72	15	45	60	52	9	2	6	8	10
1975–76	80	11	60	71	76	3	0	0	0	0
1976–77	80	7	34	41	72	3	2	1	3	0
1977–78	50	5	15	20	36	-	-	-	-	-
1978–79	75	10	33	43	54	7	0	0	0	4
1979–80	78	6	27	33	36	5	1	0	1	18
1980–81	74	6	29	35	86	4	0	1	1	6
1981–82	76	2	19	21	102	1	0	0	0	0
NHL	889	87	372	459	824	32	5	8	13	38

Following a dreadful start to the 1973–74 season, Penguins owner Tad Potter replaced longtime general manager Jack Riley with director of player personnel Jack Button. Seeking

Ron Stackhouse (left) battles the Flames' Willi Plett for position in 1970s action.

to reshape the team's character, Button promptly sent Jack Lynch and popular goalie Jim Rutherford to Detroit for defenseman Ron Stackhouse.

The trade came as a shock to Stackhouse, who thought he'd found a home in the Motor City. After a slow start to his career, the former California draft pick had shown steady improvement during his two-plus seasons with the Red Wings. A decent skater for a big man, he had developed into a good shot-blocker and an offensive threat thanks to his low, hard shot.

Following his arrival in Pittsburgh, Stackhouse performed solidly while adjusting to his new team. Determined to prove his worth, he enjoyed a breakout season in 1974–75. Serving as the quarterback for the Pens' deadly power play, he set new club records for goals (15), assists (45), and points (60) by a defenseman. He tied an NHL record for defensemen on March 8, 1975, by racking up six assists during an 8–2 demolition of the defending Stanley Cup champion Flyers.

The following year the Haliburton, Ontario, native was even better. He broke his own club records with 60 assists and 71 points to go with a strong plus/minus rating of plus 19. On April 3, 1976, he fired off an incredible 14 shots during a game against Washington.

In 1977–78, Stackhouse suffered a separated shoulder and endured a subpar season. Although he was supplanted by Randy Carlyle as the team's top offensive defenseman, he bounced back to score 10 goals in 1978–79. The following season he made his first and only appearance in an NHL All-Star Game.

Sadly for Stackhouse, he never was fully appreciated in Pittsburgh. Standing 6'3" and weighing 210 pounds, he was a huge player for his day. Because of his stature, the Civic Arena faithful expected him to be a banger. Stackhouse was far from timid—he used his size effectively whenever necessary—but he did not possess a mean streak. Perhaps no player in the history of the franchise endured more catcalls and verbal abuse.

"Maybe it was because of my style, or rather my lack of style," Stackhouse said.

Ironically, Stackhouse did play a more physical brand of hockey in the latter stages of his career. Early in the 1981–82 season, he stunned his teammates by chasing down and challenging Quebec's pugnacious Dale Hunter. He finished the campaign with 102 penalty minutes—the only time in his 12-year NHL career that he eclipsed the century mark.

Following the season, the big defenseman called it quits. While he had undeniably slowed a step, Stackhouse was only 33 years old and likely had a few more seasons left in him. However, the rough treatment he'd received from the Steel City fans no doubt hastened his departure from the game.

He retired as the all-time leading scorer among Penguins defensemen with 66 goals, 277 assists, and 343 points. To this day, Hall of Famers Paul Coffey and Larry Murphy are the only black-and-gold defenders to score more goals; only Coffey has topped his point total. None have shown more perseverance.

Stevens, Kevin

Penguins: 1987–95, 2001–02
Birthplace: Brockton, Massachusetts
Left wing   B: April 15, 1965
Shoots: left   **Ht.** 6-3 **Wt.** 230
Nickname: Artie

The "A-Train" Kevin Stevens joins the rush. The best Penguins power forward ever, Stevens scored 190 goals over a four-year span.

	Regular Season					Playoffs				
YR	GP	G	A	PTS	PM	GP	G	A	PTS	PM
1987–88	16	5	2	7	8	-	-	-	-	-
1988–89	24	12	3	15	19	11	3	7	10	16
1989–90	76	29	41	70	171	-	-	-	-	-
1990–91	80	40	46	86	133	24	17	16	33	53
1991–92	80	54	69	123	254	21	13	15	28	28
1992–93	72	55	56	111	177	12	5	11	16	22
1993–94	83	41	47	88	155	6	1	1	2	10
1994–95	27	15	12	27	51	12	4	7	11	21
2000–01	32	8	15	23	55	17	3	3	6	20
2001–02	32	1	4	5	25	-	-	-	-	-
NHL	**874**	**329**	**397**	**726**	**1470**	**103**	**46**	**60**	**106**	**170**

It's fair to say that no Penguins superstar ever came on the scene with less fanfare—or made more noise once he arrived—than Kevin Stevens. Just months after being

drafted fresh out of high school by Los Angeles, general manager Eddie Johnston acquired his rights from the Kings for Anders Hakansson.

The trade barely caused a ripple. Stevens quickly disappeared from the radar screen while the Pens struggled to build a team around Mario Lemieux. Having grown up within shouting distance of the fabled Boston Garden, he fulfilled a dream by skating for his hometown Boston College Eagles.

For Eddie Johnston, the temptation to rush Stevens to the NHL must have been great. He had tried an endless succession of wingers on Mario's port side. With few exceptions all had failed. But Johnston wisely let the husky 6'3", 230-pounder develop at his own pace.

EJ's patience was soon rewarded. After showing steady improvement through his first three years at Boston College, Stevens exploded for 35 goals as a senior. His stellar play earned him a berth on the 1988 U.S. National and Olympic teams and a late-season cameo with the Pens.

Playing on a line with Mario and fellow up-and-comer Mark Recchi, he scored a team-leading 40 goals in 1990–91 and burst into prominence as one of the top power forwards in all of hockey.

It was in the playoffs that Stevens' star shone the brightest. During the 1991 Patrick Division Finals against Washington he scored three straight game-winning goals. When the Pens fell behind the Bruins 2–0 in the Wales Conference Finals, he guaranteed a victory and backed up his pledge by scoring the all-important first goal in Game 3. Arguably the Pens' most valuable player, he went on to lead all playoff scorers with 17 goals.

In his prime, Stevens was a sight to behold. Blessed with decent speed, an accurate shot, and an unquenchable thirst to win, he became virtually unstoppable. It must have scared the daylights out of opposing goalies to see this freight train of a winger barreling in on them with his dark eyes gleaming and the puck cradled on his stick. Undeniably the best left wing in hockey, he scored a whopping 109 goals over the next two seasons while helping to lead the Pens to a second Cup.

"Kevin's probably the purest power forward in the league," Rick Tocchet said. "He reminds me of a big running back in the NFL who just wears you down."

Few players were more popular or beloved. Affectionately nicknamed "Artie" after his dad, he was an irrepressible and boisterous presence and a true leader. During Penguins games you could hear him above the din, bellowing for the puck.

A tragic incident during Game 7 of the 1993 Patrick Division Finals would have a far-reaching effect on his career. Playing with his typical gusto, Stevens collided with Islanders defenseman Rich Pilon while chasing down a loose puck. Pilon's protective shield caught Artie full-force, knocking him unconscious. He dropped to the ice face-first with a sickening thud. His nose and forehead were shattered as if someone had struck a pane of glass with a hammer. As he was carted off the ice on a stretcher the Penguins' hopes of a third Stanley Cup went with him.

"Losing him hurt us quite a bit," Larry Murphy said. "We had a lot of scoring chances and he has a tremendous touch. He's a key guy for us."

Remarkably, Stevens recovered from his injuries to score 41 goals the following season, but he was never quite the same. Even during the good times Stevens was somewhat of an Othello—powerful and confident on the outside but sensitive and filled with self-doubt on the inside. Those doubts seemed to magnify later in his career.

As part of a retooling process, Stevens was dealt to Boston during the summer of 1995. What should have been a triumphant homecoming went sour as the big winger struggled to find himself. Halfway through the season he was traded again, this time to the Kings for old friend Rick Tocchet.

Artie was to enjoy one more season in the sun. In January of 2001 Craig Patrick acquired him from Philadelphia and placed him on a line with Mario Lemieux, who had recently come out of retirement. The old magic returned as Stevens began to score once more. He helped to lead the Pens to the Conference Finals.

It proved to be his swan song. He retired midway through the following season as the highest-scoring left wing in team history. Today he serves as a scout in the Pens' front office, scouring the northeastern United States for talent.

Straka, Martin

Penguins: 1992–95, 1997–03
Birthplace: Plzen, Czechoslovakia
Center/Left wing   B: September 3, 1972
Shoots: left   **Ht.** 5-9 **Wt.** 180

	Regular Season					Playoffs				
YR	GP	G	A	PTS	PM	GP	G	A	PTS	PM
1992–93	42	3	13	16	29	11	2	1	3	2
1993–94	84	30	34	64	24	6	1	0	1	2
1994–95	31	4	12	16	16	-	-	-	-	-
1997–98	75	19	23	42	28	6	2	0	2	2
1998–99	80	35	48	83	26	13	6	9	15	6
1999–00	71	20	39	59	26	11	3	9	12	10
2000–01	82	27	68	95	38	18	5	8	13	8
2001–02	13	5	4	9	0	-	-	-	-	-
2002–03	60	18	28	46	12	-	-	-	-	-
2003–04	22	4	8	12	16	-	-	-	-	-
NHL	**954**	**257**	**460**	**717**	**360**	**106**	**26**	**44**	**70**	**52**

When Martin Straka arrived in Pittsburgh in the fall of 1992, he seemed almost overwhelmed by his new surroundings. Bearing a striking resemblance to Radar O'Reilly, Gary Burghoff's character from *M*A*S*H*, he spoke little English.

Speedy Martin Straka fights through a check from former Pen Kevin Hatcher.

Fortunately, the Penguins had another player from the Czech Republic on hand to ease Straka's transition—Jaromir Jagr. The 20-year-old rookie stuck to his older teammate like glue. Soon they became inseparable.

A talented player in his own right, Straka was the Pens' first-round draft pick in 1992, courtesy of a strong 55-point season with HC Skoda Plzen in the fast Czech League. However, cracking the Pens' talent-laden lineup was no easy task. Seeing mostly spot duty, "Marty" scored just three goals in his first season.

Injuries to key players in 1993–94 opened the door. Pressed into service, Straka gave a tantalizing glimpse of what he could do. Playing in all 84 of his team's games, he exploded for 30 goals while leading the club with a sparkling plus/minus rating of plus 24.

Following his big year, the little center's career took a strange detour. With his output hovering near his rookie-season totals, the Penguins traded him to Ottawa on April 7, 1995, for veterans Norm Maciver and Troy Murray.

In 1995–96 he endured a season that would have overwhelmed a seasoned veteran, let alone a 23-year-old from the Czech Republic who was still learning English. Dealt from Ottawa to the New York Islanders on January 23, 1996, he skated for two months on Long Island before being claimed on waivers by the Florida Panthers.

As fate would have it, the Panthers met the Penguins in the Conference Finals that spring. Despite being relegated to part-time play, Straka scored two goals against his former team—including a huge goal late in Game 6 that turned the tide of the series.

Penguins general manager Craig Patrick took note. When the Panthers released Straka in 1997, Patrick plucked the speedy little center from the scrap heap and signed him to a free-agent contract.

One couldn't help but notice the difference in Straka. The difficult times had hardened his resolve and forged his character. His personality seemed transformed as well. No longer shy and retiring, he'd become more outgoing and assertive.

The changes were evident on the ice, too. Following a solid 19-goal campaign, Straka burst forth like a supernova in 1998–99 to tally 35 goals and 83 points. Hockey's answer to the Energizer Bunny, he emerged as a nonstop player who did everything at warp speed.

Following a typically brilliant effort against the Devils in the 1999 playoffs, Pens coach Kevin Constantine sang his praises.

"He made a toe save like Terry Sawchuk, escaped a tackle like Barry Sanders, hurdled like Edwin Moses, and tapped [the puck] in like Jack Nicklaus," Constantine said. "[It was the] second-best individual effort I've seen from a player all year."

During the next two seasons, Straka continued to perform at a high level. Blessed with tremendous speed and agility, he also possessed great hands and terrific playmaking skills. Unselfish to the core, he meshed beautifully with Jagr, his more heralded countryman. Although he often played in

No. 68's considerable shadow, the good-natured center didn't seem to mind. He was appreciated by the people who mattered the most—his teammates, coaches, and fans.

In 2000–01 Straka enjoyed the finest season of his career. Skating on a line with Alexei Kovalev and Robert Lang, he rolled up 95 points and helped power the Penguins to the Conference Finals.

Unfortunately, Marty suffered a broken leg early in the 2001–02 campaign. After missing virtually the entire season, he rebounded to score 18 goals the next year. However, when the cash-strapped Penguins dealt him to Los Angeles in November of 2003, his career appeared to be on the wane.

Following the lockout year of 2004–05, the 33-year-old forward signed on with the Rangers, joining his old friend Jagr once more. Ideally suited to the new, speed-oriented NHL, Straka enjoyed two terrific years with the Blueshirts. He retired from the NHL following the 2007–08 season with 257 goals, 460 assists, and 717 points to his credit.

Tocchet, Rick

Penguins: 1992–94   **Birthplace:** Scarborough, Ontario
Right wing   B: April 9, 1964
Shoots: right   **Ht.** 6-0 **Wt.** 210
Nicknames: Dicky, Toc

YR	Regular Season					Playoffs				
	GP	G	A	PTS	PM	GP	G	A	PTS	PM
1991–92	19	14	16	30	49	14	6	13	19	24
1992–93	80	48	61	109	252	12	7	6	13	24
1993–94	51	14	26	40	134	6	2	3	5	20
NHL	1144	440	512	952	2972	145	52	60	112	471

In February of 1992, barely nine months after their first Stanley Cup, the Penguins found themselves in danger of slipping from playoff contention. Beloved coach Bob Johnson had passed away. After a decent first half the team was struggling to find its rhythm.

It was not for a lack of talent. The Pens' lineup fairly glittered with crown jewels. But something was missing.

General manager Craig Patrick was not averse to making big trades. He'd pulled off a blockbuster the previous spring that brought in Ron Francis and Ulf Samuelsson—a trade that led directly to a Cup victory. It seemed inconceivable that he could swing another deal that would have the same impact.

Yet once again Patrick defied the odds. On February 18, he engineered a huge three-team trade with Los Angeles and Philadelphia that in many ways was more shocking than the big swap the previous spring. Gone were two of the team's most gifted and popular players, Mark Recchi and Paul Coffey. Arriving from Philly were Kjell Samuelsson, Ken Wregget, and Rick Tocchet.

Blessed with a Pterodactyl-like wing span, the 6'6", 235-pound Samuelsson was a terrific stay-at-home defenseman

Wearing a "spaceman's" helmet to protect his fractured jaw, rugged Rick Tocchet celebrates a goal.

who promised to bolster the Pens' leaky defensive corps. Wregget was considered by many to be the best backup goalie in the league. But without question the key player in the deal was Tocchet.

He was unlike any player who had ever donned a Penguins uniform. Tocchet entered the league as a fighter, and an especially ferocious one at that. But he also had a burning desire to prove himself as a hockey player. Although a plodding skater at best, he possessed a goal-scorer's touch and vastly underrated hockey sense that made up for his lack of speed. Befitting his rugged nature, he wasn't the least bit shy about venturing into traffic to make plays.

"Rick is a self-made player who's had to work for everything he's accomplished," said Mike Keenan, his coach with the Flyers. "He's a tireless worker who enjoys playing under pressure."

Initially, the Penguins were disheartened by the trade. Kevin Stevens must've had an especially difficult time gazing across the ice and seeing the rough-hewn Tocchet skating in place of his best buddy Recchi.

The turning point came in a mid-March showdown with the rugged Blackhawks. Chicago had grabbed an early

two-goal lead. To make matters worse, Tocchet was struck on the jaw by an errant shot, forcing him from the game. Employing their grinding, defensive style to perfection, the Blackhawks soon forged a 3–1 third-period lead.

Then Tocchet put his heart on his sleeve for all his teammates to see. With blood stains spattered on the front of his uniform, he gamely returned to the ice wearing a face shield to protect his injured jaw. A player of lesser fortitude would have avoided the scrums, but not the gutsy winger. Refusing to compromise his smashmouth style, he plowed headlong into a goal-mouth scramble and stuffed the puck past Chicago goaltender Dominik Hasek.

Minutes later Tocchet again planted himself in harm's way and scored the game-tying goal on a deflection. It was a display of raw courage rarely seen. Suitably inspired, the Pens took charge and won the game. Afterward it was revealed that Tocchet had played with a fractured jaw.

"I know the type of person he is," said Pens trainer Skip Thayer. "He's a rare commodity. He's a tough kid, a competitor. His jaw had to be hurting him, no doubt about it. But he was able to go out there and keep a positive attitude."

From that moment on "Toc" became a treasured member of the team. Not coincidentally, the Pens began to resemble Stanley Cup champions again. Along the way there were many more examples of his legendary toughness, including fights with Kris King and Kevin Hatcher while his broken jaw was still on the mend, and an early return from a separated shoulder during the Patrick Division Finals when the club desperately needed his fire and physical presence. Tocchet contributed mightily on the score sheet as well, tallying six goals and 19 points in just 14 playoff games.

"Rick delivered when we needed it most," Scotty Bowman said. "He's versatile enough to beat you in a lot of ways: with his shot, with his savvy, and with his body."

The tough winger was never better than during the record-breaking 1992–93 campaign, when he racked up 48 goals and 109 points along with a team-leading 252 penalty minutes. In a crucial late-season showdown against Montreal when the Pens were on the verge of tying the Islanders' record 15-game winning streak, he scored a hat trick to key a huge victory.

Extremely popular with teammates and fans who loved his hard-nosed style, it appeared that Tocchet would have a long and eventful stay in Pittsburgh. Sadly it was not to be. He hurt his back while lifting weights during the summer of 1993, an injury that seriously curtailed his physical play and scoring if not his indomitable will. After the season Craig Patrick had a chance to acquire Luc Robitaille, one of the premier left wings in all of hockey. The price was Tocchet.

Tocchet never again tasted the statistical success he'd achieved with the Penguins. But he remained a valuable and productive warrior to the end, plying his trade in the trenches for eight more seasons.

Trottier, Bryan
Penguins: 1990–92, 1993–94
Birthplace: Val Marie, Saskatchewan
Center   B: July 17, 1956
Shoots: left   **Ht.** 5-11 **Wt.** 195
Nickname: Trots

YR	Regular Season					Playoffs				
	GP	G	A	PTS	PM	GP	G	A	PTS	PM
1990–91	52	9	19	28	24	23	3	4	7	49
1991–92	63	11	18	29	54	21	4	3	7	8
1993–94	41	4	11	15	36	2	0	0	0	0
NHL	1279	524	901	1425	912	221	71	113	184	277

Old pro Bryan Trottier (19) shakes free from Washington's Peter Bondra.

There was no denying Bryan Trottier had slowed a step when he signed a free-agent deal with the Penguins on July 20, 1990. His once lofty production had tailed off dramatically during his final two seasons with the New York Islanders. But the native of Val Marie, Saskatchewan, still believed he had some good hockey in him.

"I kept telling myself I had something left," he recalled in Jim O'Brien's book, *Penguin Profiles*.

One of the best two-way centers in the history of the game, Trottier had enjoyed an outstanding 15-year run with the Islanders. In addition to winning four Stanley Cups, he'd captured virtually every major award the game had to offer, including the Art Ross, Hart, Conn Smythe, and Calder Trophies.

Penguins general manager Craig Patrick wasn't expecting big numbers from the future Hall of Famer. He was seeking a veteran leader for his young team, someone to be the voice of experience on the ice and in the locker room. It was a role the 34-year-old Trottier was perfectly suited to fill.

Thanks to his savvy, work ethic, and attention to detail on defense, Trottier became an effective checking center for the Penguins. Skating with fellow members of the lunch-pail gang, including Phil Bourque, Bob Errey, and Troy Loney, "Trots" played 52 games for the Pens in 1990–91 and scored 28 points. In the playoffs, he served as a stabilizing influence during the team's march to the Stanley Cup.

His leadership was never more evident than during the difficult 1991–92 season. Following the tragic death of the team's beloved coach, Bob Johnson, the Penguins looked to their veterans for support. Trottier was there to provide it, along with his characteristically sturdy defensive play.

In honor of his outstanding on-ice achievements, Trots was named to the Wales Conference All-Star Team as a special Commissioner's selection. Old No. 19 didn't disappoint, notching a goal early in the third period.

Remarkably, Trottier could still provide offense when called upon. With Mario Lemieux sidelined for six games in February with back problems, interim coach Scotty Bowman slotted the veteran center on the top line between Mark Recchi and Kevin Stevens. Trots promptly went on

a tear, piling up 11 points in a half-dozen games. Fueled in part by Trottier's drive and desire, the Pens went on to capture their second Stanley Cup that spring.

Suffering from chronic back problems of his own, Bryan retired over the off-season to take a front office position with the Islanders. However, he quickly grew bored. When the Penguins offered to bring him back as a player/assistant coach in the summer of 1993, he jumped at the chance.

Displaying his typical fun-loving attitude and zest for the game, Trots played 41 games for the Penguins in 1993–94 before hanging up his skates for good. He remained with the team as an assistant coach through the 1996–97 season.

Woytowich, Bob

Penguins: 1968–72   **Birthplace:** Winnipeg, Manitoba
Defense   B: August 18, 1941
Shoots: right   **D:** July 30, 1988
Nickname: Woyto   **Ht.** 6-0   **Wt.** 185

	Regular Season					Playoffs				
YR	GP	G	A	PTS	PM	GP	G	A	PTS	PM
1968–69	71	9	20	29	62	-	-	-	-	-
1969–70	68	8	25	33	49	10	1	2	3	2
1970–71	78	4	22	26	30	-	-	-	-	-
1971–72	31	1	4	5	8	-	-	-	-	-
NHL	503	32	126	158	352	24	1	3	4	20
WHA	242	9	51	60	140	18	1	1	2	4

On the eve of the 1968–69 season, Penguins general manager Jack Riley was seeking an experienced rearguard to stabilize the team's defense. A few months earlier he'd traded veteran Al MacNeil to the Canadiens, creating a large hole in his defensive corps. He rectified the problem by dealing a first-round pick in the 1972 Amateur Draft to Minnesota for Bob Woytowich.

It was a steep price to pay, but Woytowich proved to be well worth it. He was a rare commodity—an experienced NHL defenseman who had established himself in the pre-expansion days. Although not especially gifted, "Woyto" was a smart, heady defender who excelled at reading the play. Adept at making a good first pass, he became a solid contributor on the power play.

Serving as the Pens' top defenseman, Woytowich paced the team's blue-liners with nine goals and 29 points in 1968–69. The following season he enjoyed a career year, tallying 33 points to help lead the Penguins to their first-ever playoff berth. His fine play earned him a spot on the West Division All-Star Team.

Woytowich was extremely popular in Pittsburgh, and not just for his steady play. Born of Polish descent, he naturally became a favorite of the team's contingent of Polish fans. He also became a celebrity of sorts, appearing in a local TV commercial for Harmony Milk.

Following three solid seasons in Pittsburgh, Woytowich's play tailed off noticeably. On January 11, 1972, Riley shipped the veteran rearguard off to Los Angeles for promising young winger Al McDonough.

One of a growing number of older players who extended their pro careers in the World Hockey Association, Woytowich

Steady Bob Woytowich earned All-Star recognition in 1969–70.

skated three seasons for Winnipeg and Indianapolis before retiring in 1978.

Tragically, he didn't get to enjoy his retirement for long. On July 30, 1988, Woytowich suffered a heart attack while driving near his hometown of Winnipeg. The former All-Star died in the resulting car accident. He was one month away from celebrating his 47th birthday.

The Role Players

Bourque, Phil
Penguins: 1983–84, 1985–92
Birthplace: Chelmsford, Massachusetts
Left wing/Defense   B: June 8, 1962
Shoots: left   **Ht.** 6-1 **Wt.** 196
Nicknames: Bourquie, Bubba

| | Regular Season | | | | | Playoffs | | | | |
YR	GP	G	A	PTS	PM	GP	G	A	PTS	PM
1983–84	5	0	1	1	12	-	-	-	-	-
1985–86	4	0	0	0	2	-	-	-	-	-
1986–87	22	2	3	5	32	-	-	-	-	-
1987–88	21	4	12	16	20	-	-	-	-	-
1988–89	80	17	26	43	97	11	4	1	5	66
1989–90	76	22	17	39	108	-	-	-	-	-
1990–91	78	20	14	34	106	24	6	7	13	16
1991–92	58	10	16	26	58	21	3	4	7	25
NHL	**477**	**88**	**111**	**199**	**516**	**56**	**13**	**12**	**25**	**107**

Philippe Richard Bourque grew up near Boston, which was the hockey home of his more famous namesake Ray. Hoping to emulate the Bruins' All-Star defenseman, Phil joined the Kingston Canadians of the Ontario Hockey Association as an 18-year-old.

Junior hockey represented a step up in competition for the young American. However, Bourque soon adapted. Flashing good offensive skill, he tallied 51 points in his second year with Kingston. Although he was bypassed in the Entry Draft, the Penguins liked his grit and speed and signed him as a free agent on October 4, 1982.

After spending a year with the Baltimore Skipjacks of the American Hockey League, "Bourquie" earned a spot with the Penguins in the fall of 1983. However, the 21-year-old defenseman was quickly returned to Baltimore following a brief trial with the Pens.

Over the next few seasons the Massachusetts native gradually developed his game. Hoping to make the Penguins as a tough guy in 1986–87, Bourque switched to left wing and bulked up to 220 pounds. However, the added size impeded his skating. The following season he slimmed back down to his natural playing weight of 196 pounds.

Switching back to defense, he enjoyed a banner year with Muskegon of the International Hockey League. Rolling up 52 points in 52 games, he captured the Governor's Trophy as the league's top defenseman. During a 21-game trial with the Penguins he performed brilliantly to earn a permanent spot on the team.

Seeking to take advantage of Bourque's natural speed and aggressiveness, Penguins coach Gene Ubriaco converted him back to left wing during training camp. The move worked like a charm. Sporting his trademark mullet and beard, Bourque scored 17 goals in 1988–89 and helped spark the team to its first playoff berth in seven years.

Skilled enough to play on the top two lines yet gritty enough to fill a defensive role, he became a versatile and valuable player. In each of the next two seasons he reached the 20-goal mark. Bourque filled an important two-way role during the team's march to the 1991 Stanley Cup, chasing down loose pucks and mucking in the corners while scoring six big goals.

During a victory celebration at Point State Park in Pittsburgh, the colorful winger hoisted the Cup and proclaimed to an adoring audience, "What do you say we take this thing to the river and party all summer!"

Days later he earned lasting fame when he took Lord Stanley's chalice for a dip in Mario Lemieux's swimming pool. While Bourque resurfaced, the waterlogged Cup remained firmly anchored to the bottom of the pool.

Unfortunately for the fun-loving winger, the good times would soon come to an end. Injuries and a strained relationship with interim coach Scotty Bowman combined to curtail his effectiveness in 1991–92. Still, he remained a clutch playoff performer. Providing offense when his team needed it the most, Bourque scored two game-tying goals in the pivotal series against the Capitals. His power-play goal in Game 1 of the Finals sparked a Pens rally and helped pave the way to a second Stanley Cup.

Following the 1992 Cup victory, Bourque signed a big free-agent deal with the archrival New York Rangers. However, his career soon fizzled out. After a miserable season and change with the Rangers, he was dealt to the

Scrappy Phil Bourque fights through a check.

lowly Ottawa Senators in 1994. Over the summer he narrowly escaped death, surviving a 40-foot fall down a cliff near Lake Powell in Arizona.

Older and wiser, "the Old Two-Niner" currently serves as the color analyst for Penguins' radio broadcasts.

Briere, Michel

Penguins: 1969–70 **Birthplace:** Malartic, Quebec
Center **B:** October 21, 1949
Shoots: left **D:** April 13, 1971
Ht: 5-10 **Wt:** 165

YR	Regular Season					Playoffs				
	GP	G	A	PTS	PM	GP	G	A	PTS	PM
1969–70	76	12	32	44	20	10	5	3	8	17
NHL	**76**	**12**	**32**	**44**	**20**	**10**	**5**	**3**	**8**	**17**

His was a tragic legacy of promise cut short—of a shooting star that burned brightly across the night sky only to plummet to earth. He would play only one season for the Penguins, and yet during that all-too-brief time he left an indelible imprint that placed him among the team's all-time greats.

In stark contrast to Mario Lemieux, Michel Edouard Briere did not arrive in the Steel City to the blaring of trumpets. After heeding the persistent pleas of scout Dick Coss, general manager Jack Riley selected the will o' the wisp center in the third round of the 1969 Amateur Draft. Twenty-five players were picked ahead of him.

Briere was not without pedigree. He had led the Quebec Major Junior Hockey League in scoring two years running while piling up an impressive 320 points.

"He skated easily," wrote newspaper columnist Roy McHugh. "He skimmed across the ice like a water bug, not with great speed but with a phantom elusiveness, deftly avoiding bodychecks, probing and questing for the puck. His shot was quick rather than powerful, coming invariably when the goaltender least expected it, preceded as likely as not by a feint, a dip of the shoulder."

It was clear that Briere believed in himself, too. When Riley offered him a $4,000 signing bonus, the rookie demanded an additional $1,000.

"I asked him why," Riley recalled. "It's really not that much extra money," Briere responded, "because I'll be playing for the Penguins for the next 20 years."

Like the team, Briere started the 1969–70 campaign slowly. However, he showed enough potential to earn a more prominent role. Soon coach Red Kelly slotted him between speedy wingers Val Fonteyne and Jean Pronovost on the "Jet Line."

Shifty and clever, Briere began to produce and the team began to win. As the season wore on it became apparent that the 20-year-old rookie was something special. In an era when few players made the jump from junior hockey to the NHL, Briere flourished. He led the club in assists and finishing third in scoring.

Also-rans in their first two seasons, the Penguins finished in second place in the West Division and captured a playoff spot. They quickly disposed of the Oakland Seals in the quarterfinals round to set up a semifinal series against their bitter rivals, the St. Louis Blues.

Considered the Pens' brightest star, Briere was immediately targeted for abuse. Time and time again bashers Noel Picard and Bob Plager came at the slender rookie with elbows high.

Briere made the brawny St. Louis defenders look foolish. Using his quickness and wits to his fullest advantage, he left them grasping at air, as if they were trying to hit a ghost. With the Blues' defensemen lumbering in his vapor trail, he had an extraordinary series, racking up four goals.

Red Kelly remembered one in particular. "Michel was going over the blue line and he put a shift on the defenseman, who took the fake and started going to his right," the coach recalled. "Jacques Plante went for the fake, too. Even though Michel just crossed the blue line, he shot the puck into the open side of the net. That's how elusive he was on the ice."

The Penguins succumbed to the deeper, more talented Blues in six hotly contested games. But the hockey world that had virtually ignored Briere in the draft was now effusive in its praise. Indeed, his future seemed as boundless as the summer sky.

However, fate can be unkind at times if not downright cruel. On the evening of May 15, 1970, it dealt a crushing blow. Briere was driving with two friends on Highway 117 near his hometown of Malartic, Quebec, on his way to make preparations for his wedding that summer. It was a rainy night, and the road was as slick as the Civic Arena ice he had mastered so beautifully. His 1970 Mercury Cougar failed to negotiate a turn and skidded off the road.

His companions suffered multiple fractures but survived. Briere wasn't so lucky. When emergency crews arrived on the scene they found him lying unconscious some distance from the car. Unlike his friends, there wasn't a mark on him. But Briere had suffered a far worse injury. He sustained brain damage while being thrown from the car.

Compounding the horrific ordeal, the ambulance transporting Briere to the hospital struck a pedestrian, 18-year-old Raymond Perreault, killing him instantly. The unfortunate soul was a friend of Briere's.

For the next two months Briere lay in a coma before showing signs of consciousness. While it was painfully evident that he would never play hockey again, there was hope that he would survive.

However, the damage to Briere's brain was severe and it began to swell. Several surgeries failed to relieve the pressure. On April 13, 1971, his young life slipped away.

Even now, nearly four decades later, the tragedy is almost impossible to comprehend. The countless goals he never scored; the laughs he never shared with teammates; the fiancé he never wed; the unborn son he never knew.

Perhaps the finest tribute to the fallen star came from his teammates.

"He was one of the greatest competitors I ever played with," Ken Schinkel said. "He would never take defeat. He really wanted to win and he would try to do it by himself if he had to. He would have been a star in the league for a long time."

"He had a great attitude," Ron Schock added. "I sat beside him in the dressing room. He was a real, nice young kid. I liked him very much."

Caufield, Jay

Penguins: 1988–93   **Birthplace:** Philadelphia, Pennsylvania
Right wing   B: July 17, 1960
Shoots: right   **Ht.** 6-4 **Wt.** 237
Nickname: Jaybird

	Regular Season					Playoffs				
YR	GP	G	A	PTS	PM	GP	G	A	PTS	PM
1988–89	58	1	4	5	285	9	0	0	0	28
1989–90	37	1	2	3	123	-	-	-	-	-
1990–91	23	1	1	2	71	-	-	-	-	-
1991–92	50	0	0	0	175	5	0	0	0	2
1992–93	26	0	0	0	60	-	-	-	-	-
NHL	**208**	**5**	**8**	**13**	**759**	**17**	**0**	**0**	**0**	**42**

Through the years, the Penguins have employed their share of tough guys. Rambunctious Bryan Watson served as the team's protector through the early years. Heavyweights such as Steve Durbano, Battleship Kelly, and Bob Paradise earned plenty of respect in the mid-1970s. Russ Anderson, Colin Campbell, and penalty kings Paul Baxter and Dave "the Hammer" Schultz plied their trade while wearing Penguins colors.

Perhaps no tough guy was more important to the team than Jay Caufield. During an era when opposing teams painted a bulls-eye on Penguins stars like Mario Lemieux and Paul Coffey, Caufield was always ready to answer the bell.

In retrospect, his career as a pro hockey player—modest as it was—stands as a remarkable achievement. Although the Philadelphia native enjoyed hockey and played a season of Junior B with the Milton Flyers, his first love was football. A linebacker at the University of North Dakota, his collegiate hockey career consisted of one game.

Still, toughness was at a premium in the NHL. Impressed with Caufield's size and strength, then-Rangers general manager Craig Patrick signed the 6'4", 237-pounder to a contract. After splitting time between Toledo and New Haven in 1985–86, Caufield earned a 13-game cameo with the Rangers in 1986–87. Utterly fearless, he fought Philadelphia's imposing lefty Dave Brown three times.

Although they loved his eagerness and team-first attitude, the Rangers decided the 26-year-old Caufield was too raw. They shipped him off to Minnesota, who in turn sent him to their Kalamazoo farm club. Skating for the K-Wings, Caufield piled up 273 penalty minutes in 1987–88.

Meanwhile, the Penguins were in the market for a tough guy. Noting how his resident enforcer, Wayne Van Dorp, stood idly by while Montreal's Steve Martinson roughed up Mario Lemieux during a preseason contest, general manager Tony Esposito claimed Caufield in the Waiver Draft.

Big Jay quickly made an impression. During the 1988–89 campaign he engaged some of the toughest customers in the league, including Brown, Jeff Chychrun, and Mick Vukota. Although he wasn't an especially good fighter due to balance problems, he earned the respect and admiration of his teammates.

His willingness to tangle with anyone, at any time, was never more evident than during a showdown with the Rangers on St. Patrick's Day in 1991. The Blueshirts had just acquired Joey Kocur, perhaps the most fearsome fighter in all of hockey. From the opening draw their strategy was clear—they intended to run the Penguins right out of Madison Square Garden.

Thirty-three seconds into the game Kocur slammed a gloved fist into Ulf Samuelsson's face. When the bruising winger buzzed the Penguins' net on his next shift, Caufield was waiting. Showing total disregard for "Joey KO's" sledgehammer right, he battled the pugnacious Ranger to a draw. Inspired by "Jaybird's" courageous display, the Pens bounced the Rangers 4–2 to grab first place in the Patrick Division.

A poor skater who possessed limited skills, Caufield worked hard to develop his game. He often stayed on the ice after practice, toiling long hours to improve his puck handling and shot. In an effort to better his balance, he would grab a goal cage and swing it around the ice, mimicking the movements of a fight.

The extra work paid dividends in 1991–92, when the big winger saw increased ice time under interim coach Scotty

Jay Caufield squares off with the Blues' Tony Twist.

Bowman. However, the acquisition of Rick Tocchet—who combined toughness and skill—signaled the beginning of the end. Caufield was released by the Penguins after playing in only 26 games during the 1992–93 season.

Always in peak physical condition, Jay became a personal trainer following his hockey career. He helped whip his old teammate, Mario Lemieux, into shape for his spectacular comeback in 2000. Today Jay serves as an analyst on *FSN Live: Penguins Post Game*.

Errey, Bob

Penguins: 1983–93   **Birthplace:** Montreal, Quebec
Left wing   B: September 21, 1964
Shoots: left   **Ht.** 5-10 **Wt.** 185
Nicknames: Bibs, Bibster

	Regular Season					Playoffs				
YR	GP	G	A	PTS	PM	GP	G	A	PTS	PM
1983–84	65	9	13	22	29	-	-	-	-	-
1984–85	16	0	2	2	7	-	-	-	-	-
1985–86	37	11	6	17	8	-	-	-	-	-
1986–87	72	16	18	34	46	-	-	-	-	-
1987–88	17	3	6	9	18	-	-	-	-	-
1988–89	76	26	32	58	124	11	1	2	3	12
1989–90	78	20	19	39	109	-	-	-	-	-
1990–91	79	20	22	42	115	24	5	2	7	29
1991–92	78	19	16	35	119	14	3	0	3	10
1992–93	54	8	6	14	76	-	-	-	-	-
NHL	**895**	**170**	**212**	**382**	**1005**	**99**	**13**	**16**	**29**	**109**

As a youngster playing for Peterborough of the Ontario Hockey League, Bob Errey displayed lots of promise. Skating alongside another up-and-comer named Steve Yzerman, the speedy left wing scored 53 goals and 100 points for the Petes in 1982–83.

Taken 15th overall in the 1983 Entry Draft by the Penguins, Errey made the parent club that fall. Big things were expected of the rookie. However, with no one approaching the skilled Yzerman to set him up, the 19-year-old winger struggled to produce.

Knowing full-well he'd rushed Errey to the NHL, Pens general manager Eddie Johnston sent the youngster to the minors for seasoning. However, during a 16-game trial with the big club in 1984–85, Errey looked lost, tallying a paltry two assists.

Faced with the realization he might never make it as a goal scorer, Errey worked hard to transform himself. Blessed with tremendous speed and desire, he developed into a gritty all-around player who was capable of filling a checking role. By the time he rejoined the Penguins during the 1985–86 season, Errey had totally remade his game.

Seeking a two-way performer for his top line, coach Gene Ubriaco slotted Errey next to Hart Trophy winner Mario Lemieux and high-scoring Rob Brown. With the scrappy left wing serving as the line's defensive conscience, the trio

exploded for 160 goals in 1988–89—including a career-best 26 by Errey.

"The Bibster" reached the 20-goal mark in each of the next two seasons while helping the Penguins to a Stanley Cup victory in 1991. During the 1992 Prince of Wales Conference Semifinals he enjoyed perhaps his finest hour. With the Penguins down 3–1 to Washington and facing almost certain elimination, coach Scotty Bowman handed Errey the daunting task of shadowing feisty Dino Ciccarelli.

It was like being asked to check the Tasmanian Devil. Not only was Ciccarelli a one-man wrecking crew—he'd scored four goals in Game 4—but he was a nasty player to boot. Undeterred, Errey dove into his assignment with unbridled enthusiasm. In Game 5 he held the Capitals' winger without a shot on goal while scoring two huge goals of his own. With Ciccarelli completely neutralized, the Pens rallied to beat the Caps in seven games.

Sadly, Errey was traded to Buffalo in March of 1993 for Mike Ramsey. He moved to San Jose the following season, where he served as the Sharks' captain for two years. The plucky little winger also played for the Red Wings, Stars, and Rangers before retiring in 1999.

Following an aborted comeback attempt with the Penguins in 2001, Errey joined the FSN Pittsburgh broadcast team. He currently serves as a color commentator for his partner, Paul Steigerwald.

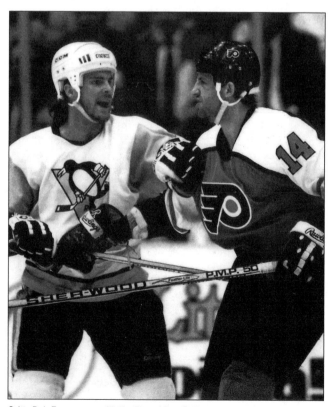

Gritty Bob Errey spars with the Flyers' Ron Sutter.

Ferguson, George
Penguins: 1978–82   **Birthplace:** Trenton, Ontario
Right wing/Center   **B:** August 22, 1952
Shoots: right   **Ht.** 6-0 **Wt.** 195
Nicknames: Chief, Fergie, the Fergie Flyer

	Regular Season					Playoffs				
YR	GP	G	A	PTS	PM	GP	G	A	PTS	PM
1978–79	80	21	29	50	37	7	2	1	3	0
1979–80	73	21	28	49	36	5	0	3	3	4
1980–81	79	25	18	43	42	5	2	6	8	9
1981–82	71	22	31	53	45	5	0	1	1	0
1982–83	7	0	0	0	2	-	-	-	-	-
NHL	797	160	238	398	431	86	14	23	37	44

George Ferguson was a versatile and valuable performer who typified the Penguins teams of the late 1970s and early 1980s. While not a star, he was an excellent two-way player who exhibited a team-first attitude and a penchant for scoring big goals.

Following a 92-point season with the Toronto Marlboros of the Ontario Hockey Association, Ferguson was taken with the 11th overall pick by the Maple Leafs in the 1972 Entry Draft.

A new league, the World Hockey Association, had pirated away a number of the Leafs' veteran players, which opened the door for Ferguson. He enjoyed a decent rookie season, but spent most of the following year skating for Oklahoma City in the Central Hockey League. Scoring 49 points in 35 games, he proved to be too good for the minor leagues.

Ferguson returned to Toronto in 1974–75. Slotted between promising scorers Lanny McDonald and Errol Thompson, he developed into a solid if unspectacular two-way center. However, Ferguson's scoring totals gradually decreased over the next few seasons—especially after the arrival of defensive-minded coach Roger Neilson.

In the summer of 1978 he got a new lease on life. Seeking to overhaul his shopworn team, Penguins general manager Baz Bastien traded All-Star defenseman Dave Burrows to the Leafs for Ferguson and Randy Carlyle.

Freed from the restrictions placed on him by Neilson, Ferguson flourished in Pittsburgh. Equally adept in an offensive or defensive role, he skated on the power play and became one of the Penguins' top penalty killers. Taking advantage of "Fergie's" adaptability, Penguins coach Johnny Wilson used him at right wing and center. The speedy forward responded with a fine 21-goal, 50-point season.

Always a clutch playoff performer, Ferguson scored the tying and winning goals in Game 3 of the Preliminary Round series to lead the Pens past Buffalo.

A model of consistency, Ferguson tallied 68 goals and 145 points over the next three seasons while helping the Penguins to a playoff berth each year. He was especially brilliant in the opening-round series against St. Louis in 1981, notching two goals and six assists in five games.

George Ferguson battles through a check by the Islanders' Ken Morrow.

After four solid seasons in Pittsburgh, Ferguson got off to a slow start in 1982–83. With the team sagging as well, Bastien shipped the popular winger to Minnesota for Anders Hakansson, Ron Meighan, and an exchange of first-round choices in the upcoming Entry Draft. The deal became more noteworthy as the Penguins plummeted to the bottom of the standings: Bastien had unwittingly traded away the first overall pick.

Fergie failed to regain his scoring touch in Minnesota. However, he remained a valuable role player to the end and helped the North Stars reach the Campbell Conference Finals in 1984.

Fonteyne, Val
Penguins: 1967–72   **Birthplace:** Wetaskiwin, Alberta
Left wing   **B:** December 2, 1933
Shoots: left   **Ht.** 5-10 **Wt.** 160

	Regular Season					Playoffs				
YR	GP	G	A	PTS	PM	GP	G	A	PTS	PM
1967–68	69	6	28	34	0	-	-	-	-	-
1968–69	74	12	17	29	2	-	-	-	-	-
1969–70	68	11	15	26	2	10	0	2	2	0
1970–71	70	4	9	13	0	-	-	-	-	-
1971–72	68	6	13	19	0	4	0	0	0	2
NHL	820	75	154	229	26	59	3	10	13	8
WHA	149	16	45	61	4	5	1	0	1	0

If the National Hockey League ever decided to hand out lifetime achievement awards, Val Fonteyne would win the career version of the Lady Byng Trophy hands down. Over

Val Fonteyne was a crackerjack checker for the Pens' early teams.

Jean Pronovost, Val notched 11 goals while serving as the unit's defensive conscience. Sparked by the Jet Line's strong play, the Penguins earned a second-place finish and a post-season berth.

With the Pens constantly adding younger players to the mix, Fonteyne was gradually reduced to the role of penalty-killing specialist. As his ice time and production dwindled, he seemed to be a forgotten man.

However, in the spring of 1972 he was resurrected for one final flourish. Acting on a hunch, coach Red Kelly pulled young gun Greg Polis off the top line and replaced him with the 39-year-old Fonteyne. The move worked like a charm. Meshing beautifully with Pronovost and Syl Apps, the unselfish old pro helped lead the team to the playoffs.

Fittingly, he finished his NHL career by skating 158 consecutive games without a penalty.

Hextall, Bryan

Penguins: 1969–74   **Birthplace:** Winnipeg, Manitoba
Center   B: May 23, 1941
Shoots: left   **Ht.** 5-11   **Wt.** 185
Nickname: Hexy

	Regular Season					Playoffs				
YR	GP	G	A	PTS	PM	GP	G	A	PTS	PM
1969–70	66	12	19	31	87	10	0	1	1	34
1970–71	76	16	32	48	133	-	-	-	-	-
1971–72	78	20	24	44	126	4	0	2	2	9
1972–73	78	21	33	54	113	-	-	-	-	-
1973–74	37	2	7	9	39	-	-	-	-	-
NHL	**549**	**99**	**161**	**260**	**738**	**18**	**0**	**4**	**4**	**59**

the course of a 13-year NHL career that spanned some 820 games, the wispy native of Wetaskiwin, Alberta, drew only 13 minor penalties.

Given the paucity of penalties and his 160-pound frame, one would think Fonteyne was a perimeter player who avoided contact at all costs. However, nothing could be further from the truth. On the contrary, he was a diligent, hardworking performer who dug in the corners and did the dirty work in the trenches.

While not a scorer—at least not at the NHL level—Fonteyne was a valuable role player for the Rangers and the Red Wings in the pre-expansion era. In 1961, his exceptional penalty killing helped propel Detroit to the Stanley Cup Finals.

After splitting time between the Red Wings and the Pittsburgh Hornets in 1966–67, Fonteyne was selected by the Penguins in the 1967 Expansion Draft. He instantly became one of the team's most popular and likeable players while notching six goals and a career-high 34 points. The following season he set another personal best with 12 goals.

In 1969–70, Fonteyne was finally afforded an opportunity to play in a more offensive role. Skating on the speedy "Jet Line" with promising youngsters Michel Briere and

Unlike most Canadian youths of his day, Bryan Hextall Jr. did not learn to skate on a frozen pond or lake. The son of New York Rangers forward Bryan Hextall Sr., the Manitoba-born youngster took his first tentative strides on the manicured ice of Madison Square Garden.

It was an auspicious beginning for the son of a legend. Acknowledged as the finest right wing of his era, Bryan Sr. had carved out a Hall of Fame career as a clean but tough player who specialized in scoring goals. He left some very large footprints for his son to follow.

As a young player, Bryan Jr. displayed the same blend of toughness and scoring ability as his dad. Following three strong seasons with the Brandon Wheat Kings, Hextall was on the fast track to the NHL. However, he fizzled during a 21-game trial with the Rangers in 1962–63 and was soon returned to the minors for seasoning. Little did he realize it would take seven long years to return to the NHL.

Immediately following the 1968–69 season, the Penguins acquired his services from Vancouver of the Western Hockey League for Paul Andrea, John Arbour, and the loan of Andy Bathgate. If Hextall was daunted by the fact that the Pens gave up three players to get him, it didn't show. He

Rugged Bryan Hextall led the club in points, assists, and penalty minutes in 1970–71.

for the rough stuff. Following a dismal start to the 1973–74 campaign (two goals in 37 games), the Pens placed him on waivers. He hooked on with Atlanta, where he served as a fourth-line grinder.

Hextall drifted from the Flames to the Red Wings and finally to the North Stars, where he finished his career in 1975–76. As a special treat, Bryan finally got to play alongside his younger brother Dennis.

A decade later, the family name would resurface through Bryan's son. Displaying the same combative nature as his dad, Ron Hextall won the Conn Smythe and Vezina Trophies in 1987 as a member of the Flyers.

Hillier, Randy

Penguins: 1984–91   **Birthplace:** Toronto, Ontario
Defense   B: March 30, 1960
Shoots: left   **Ht.** 6-1 **Wt.** 192

YR	Regular Season					Playoffs				
	GP	G	A	PTS	PM	GP	G	A	PTS	PM
1984–85	45	2	19	21	56	-	-	-	-	-
1985–86	28	0	3	3	53	-	-	-	-	-
1986–87	55	4	8	12	97	-	-	-	-	-
1987–88	55	1	12	13	144	-	-	-	-	-
1988–89	68	1	23	24	141	9	0	1	1	49
1989–90	61	3	12	15	71	-	-	-	-	-
1990–91	31	2	2	4	32	8	0	0	0	24
NHL	**543**	**16**	**110**	**126**	**906**	**28**	**0**	**2**	**2**	**93**

Over the course of a workmanlike 11-year NHL career, Randy Hillier suffered a laundry list of injuries that would have kept a hospital staff fully employed. He missed time due to torn and strained knee ligaments, a separated shoulder, a neck injury, broken bones, torn muscles, bone chips, assorted bruises, lacerations, and charley horses, to name a few. Like badges of honor, the gritty defenseman bore them all. It was the price he paid for a pro hockey career.

After playing youth hockey in his native Toronto, Hillier joined the Sudbury Wolves of the Ontario Hockey League in 1977. He showed steady improvement during three seasons with the Wolves. In 1979–80 he flashed an offensive upside, tallying 65 points in 60 games to earn All-Star honors. His surprising production drew the attention of the Bruins, who selected him with their fifth pick in the Entry Draft.

Following his junior career, Hillier spent a season with the Springfield Indians of the American Hockey League before gradually working his way into the Bruins' lineup. It was quickly apparent, however, that the youngster's offensive instincts did not translate to the NHL. Randy would have to carve out a career as a defensive defenseman.

Not that he seemed to mind. Indeed, the 190-pounder was most at home in his own end of the rink, banging bodies and steering opposing attackers away from the net.

Seeking to upgrade his defensive corps, Penguins general manager Eddie Johnston acquired Hillier from the Bruins

immediately established himself as a tough customer who possessed an underrated scoring touch.

Over the next three years, "Hexy" showed steady improvement. Although hardly a star, in 1970–71 he paced the Pens in assists (32), points (48), and penalty minutes (133). The following season he reached the 20-goal mark for the first time. In 1972–73 he enjoyed his best year, tallying 21 goals and 54 points to go with 113 minutes in the slammer. Along the way, the hard-nosed center earned plenty of respect throughout the league for his rugged play and willingness to drop the mitts to defend a teammate.

Unfortunately, Hextall's career took a sudden and inexorable downward turn. On the heels of his finest season as pro, his skills seemed to fade overnight, along with his taste

Randy Hillier (left) angles an opponent into the boards.

Kasparaitis, Darius

Penguins: 1996–02   **Birthplace:** Elektrenai, USSR
Defense   B: October 16, 1972
Shoots: left   **Ht.** 5-11   **Wt.** 215
Nickname: Kaspar

YR	Regular Season					Playoffs				
	GP	G	A	PTS	PM	GP	G	A	PTS	PM
1996–97	57	2	16	18	84	5	0	0	0	6
1997–98	81	4	8	12	127	5	0	0	0	8
1998–99	48	1	4	5	70	-	-	-	-	-
1999–00	73	3	12	15	146	11	1	1	2	10
2000–01	77	3	16	19	111	17	1	1	2	26
2001–02	69	2	12	14	123	-	-	-	-	-
NHL	**863**	**27**	**136**	**163**	**1379**	**83**	**2**	**10**	**12**	**107**

in 1984 for a fourth-round pick. It was an exciting time in Pittsburgh—his arrival coincided with Mario Lemieux's.

Hillier performed well during his first year in the Steel City, notching 21 points in 45 games. However, his rugged style of play already had begun to take its toll. After missing more than 30 games in 1984–85, he was limited to 28 games the next season.

The pattern would repeat itself throughout his career. Hillier would return to the lineup and play well, as he did in 1986–87 when he led the team's defenders with a plus/minus rating of plus 12. Then another injury would force him from the lineup for an extended stretch.

Despite the setbacks, Hillier began to emerge as a leader on an improving young team. His teammates admired him for his sturdy, stay-at-home play and his willingness to drop the gloves to stand up for the team.

After being nominated for the Masterton Trophy in 1988, Hillier enjoyed the two best seasons of his career. Comparatively injury-free by his standards, he scored 24 points in 1988–89 and helped the Penguins secure their first playoff berth in seven years. The next season he topped the team with a plus/minus rating of plus 11. In recognition of his contributions, Randy was honored with the team's Player's Player Award.

By the 1990–91 campaign the Penguins had turned the corner. Reduced to the role of a part-timer, Hillier performed capably when called upon. When a rash of injuries threatened to derail the team's march to the Stanley Cup, Randy stepped forward to provide his customary, no-frills brand of defense. Although he didn't see action in the Finals, his name was engraved on the Cup.

Hillier played one more season in the NHL, splitting time with the New York Islanders and the Buffalo Sabres. He retired in 1993 after skating for Klagenfurter AC in Austria.

Darius Kasparaitis made quite a first impression on the Penguins. During the ill-fated 1993 Patrick Division Finals, the trash-talking, hip-checking Islanders defender harassed the great Mario Lemieux and his teammates to the point of distraction.

"Guys from Pittsburgh hate me," he said. "They said in the paper I play like [a] little dog."

It was an opinion that would be shared by virtually every player in the National Hockey League—everyone expect his teammates, that is. Over the course of his 14-year NHL career, "Kaspar" made more enemies than Simon Legree.

A longshot to make it in the pro ranks, Kasparaitis hailed from Elektrenai, Lithuania. Known more for producing basketball players, the country hadn't placed a single hockey player on any Soviet major league team until the 16-year-old

Wrecking-ball defenseman Darius Kasparaitis zeroes in on a target.

Kasparaitis made his debut with the Moscow Dynamo in 1988.

An excellent skater, the youngster soon made a splash on the international scene. In 1992 he helped lead the Unified Russian Team to a gold medal at the Winter Olympics in Albertville, France. Later that year he was named the best defenseman at the World Junior Championships, which gained the attention of NHL scouts. The Islanders took him with the fifth overall pick in the Entry Draft that summer.

After earning a spot on the Islanders, the brash young defenseman became an immediate "hit." Blessed with a low center of gravity and powerful legs, Kasparaitis sent many a foe cartwheeling to the ice with his patented hip checks. His body-banging style quickly drew the attention of rival enforcers, not to mention the league office, which soon outlawed his "low-bridge" hits for fear of injury.

Undeterred, Kaspar continued to employ his aggressive, hard-hitting game. However, early in the 1994–95 season he suffered a serious knee injury that threatened to derail his budding career. Many opponents felt it was fair retribution for the damage *he* had inflicted. The 22-year-old blue-liner endured months of grueling rehab and once again emerged as a top-notch defensive defenseman.

Remembering the rough treatment he'd received during the 1993 playoffs, Mario Lemieux encouraged Pens general manager Craig Patrick to trade for Kasparaitis in 1996. Upon his arrival in the Steel City, his teammates were surprised to learn that the spirited defenseman was not the second coming of Attila the Hun. On the contrary, he was bright, friendly, and fun loving. He quickly became one of the most popular players on the team.

During his six-year run with the Penguins, Kaspar enjoyed many memorable moments. On March 7, 1998, he crushed the Flyers' mammoth star, Eric Lindros, with a devastating bodycheck, cementing his place as a folk hero in Pittsburgh. During Game 7 of a hotly contested playoff series against Buffalo in 2001, he struck for an overtime goal to send the Penguins to the Conference Finals. The sight of Kaspar belly-flopping to the ice in celebration while his teammates piled on is one of the most enduring images in franchise history. Few can forget the courage he displayed during the 1998–99 season, when he played 48 games with partially torn ligaments in his knee.

Sadly, finances forced the Pens to trade the colorful soon-to-be free agent to Colorado in 2002 for Rick Berry and Ville Nieminen. Kaspar moved back to New York the following season—this time with the Rangers—where he finished his NHL career in 2007.

Loney, Troy

Penguins: 1983–93   **Birthplace:** Bow Island, Alberta
Left wing   B: September 21, 1963
Shoots: left   **Ht.** 6-3   **Wt.** 209
Nickname: Big Red

| YR | Regular Season | | | | | Playoffs | | | | |
	GP	G	A	PTS	PM	GP	G	A	PTS	PM
1983–84	13	0	0	0	9	-	-	-	-	-
1984–85	46	10	8	18	59	-	-	-	-	-
1985–86	47	3	9	12	95	-	-	-	-	-
1986–87	23	8	7	15	22	-	-	-	-	-
1987–88	65	5	13	18	151	-	-	-	-	-
1988–89	69	10	6	16	165	11	1	3	4	24
1989–90	67	11	16	27	168	-	-	-	-	-
1990–91	44	7	9	16	85	24	2	2	4	41
1991–92	76	10	16	26	127	21	4	5	9	32
1992–93	82	5	16	21	99	10	1	4	5	0
NHL	624	87	110	197	1091	67	8	14	22	97

Troy Loney—a.k.a. "Big Red"—was an invaluable role player on the Pens' Cup-winning teams of the early 1990s.

Historically a small team up front, the Penguins broke with tradition when they selected Troy Loney with their third pick in the 1983 Entry Draft. The husky 6'3", 209-pound left wing had shown steady improvement over three junior seasons with the Lethbridge Broncos, while displaying a willingness to battle.

Initially, the Penguins hoped the big redhead would develop into a power forward along the lines of Philadelphia's bruising Paul Holmgren. While it didn't quite turn out that way, the club was no less pleased with the results.

Following an 18-goal season with Baltimore in 1983–84, Loney split time between the Skipjacks and the Penguins during his early years as a pro. In 1986–87 the slimmed-down winger appeared to emerge as an offensive threat, potting eight goals in just 23 games with the Pens. However, the following year his output dipped to five goals and his role began to crystallize.

While "Big Red" lacked the foot speed to be a consistent scoring threat, he developed into a solid grinder. Defensively reliable and strong in the corners, he grew into a smart, resourceful player who relied on hard work to get the job done. Not averse to dropping the gloves, he also became a protector on an emerging young team.

Beginning in 1988–89 Loney hit his stride, reaching double figures in goal production during three of the next four seasons. Although prone to long scoreless stretches, he occasionally heated up thanks to his surprisingly soft hands. Colorful play-by-play announcer Mike Lange dubbed each of these infrequent binges "the Loney Watch."

During the cauldron of the Stanley Cup Playoffs, Loney provided the team with an underpinning of grit along with some excellent penalty killing. He enjoyed his moment in the sun during Game 5 of the Stanley Cup Finals in 1991. With the Penguins nursing a one-goal lead late in a tight game, Loney rambled to the net and muscled the puck past Minnesota goalie Jon Casey to seal a victory. A year later, he scored a crucial game-tying goal in the pivotal fourth game of the Rangers series.

Along with fellow muckers Phil Bourque and Bob Errey, Loney supplied much of the heart and soul for the Penguins' two Cup winners. The last of the trio to leave the Steel City, Big Red was claimed by Anaheim in the 1993 Expansion Draft. He served as the team's first captain and struck for a career-high 13 goals before finishing his career with the Islanders and Rangers.

Malone, Greg

Penguins: 1976–83   **Birthplace:** Fredericton, New Brunswick
Center   B: March 8, 1956
Shoots: left   **Ht.** 6-0   **Wt.** 190
Nickname: Bugsy

YR	Regular Season					Playoffs				
	GP	G	A	PTS	PM	GP	G	A	PTS	PM
1976–77	66	18	19	37	43	3	1	1	2	2
1977–78	78	18	43	61	80	-	-	-	-	-
1978–79	80	35	30	65	52	7	0	1	1	10
1979–80	51	19	32	51	46	-	-	-	-	-
1980–81	62	21	29	50	68	5	2	3	5	16
1981–82	78	15	24	39	125	3	0	0	0	4
1982–83	80	17	44	61	82	-	-	-	-	-
NHL	**704**	**191**	**310**	**501**	**661**	**20**	**3**	**5**	**8**	**32**

As a youngster growing up in the small town of Chatham, New Brunswick, Greg Malone had two options. He could work in the local pulp mill like his dad Bill, or he could play hockey. Fortunately for Penguins fans, he chose the latter.

After starring for the Fredericton Black Kats as a 16-year-old forward, Malone joined the Oshawa Generals of the

A solid contributor in the 1970s and '80s, Greg Malone turns to follow the play.

Ontario Hockey League. While he developed into a solid two-way player for the Generals—scoring 73 goals during his final two seasons of junior hockey—he was hardly a star.

But Penguins general manager Baz Bastien saw something in the rugged, hardworking center. Looking to infuse his veteran team with new blood, he grabbed Malone with the 19th overall pick in the 1976 Amateur Draft.

Malone rewarded him by securing a spot on the 1976–77 Penguins squad. Centering "the Kid Line" for Wayne Bianchin and fellow rookie Blair Chapman, he scored a respectable 18 goals. He also earned the admiration of his teammates for his sterling attitude and willingness to do the dirty work in the corners.

Showing steady improvement during his sophomore season, "Bugsy" tallied 61 points while developing into a good playmaker. However, Penguins coach Johnny Wilson noticed Malone was reluctant to shoot. During a team meeting he encouraged the young center to abandon his pass-first philosophy.

Malone got the message. Taking his coach's words to heart, he exploded for a career-best 35 goals in 1978–79 to lead the Pens to a playoff berth. No one was more appreciative of his efforts than Wilson.

"Malone really works his tail off," the veteran skipper said. "He's a strong, tough kid who'll go into the corners and get the puck for you. And he's got a heck of a shot. He's a hard guy to knock off the puck. He does the very most with the talent he's got."

The *Pittsburgh Press* sportswriter Dan Donovan also was a big fan. "When Greg Malone gets up a head of steam," Donovan wrote, "he is a locomotive on the rampage, impossible to stop."

Indeed, Malone appeared to be on the verge of stardom. On November 28, 1979, he tied a club record with a dazzling six-assist performance against Quebec. With the 23-year-old center scoring at a point-per-game clip, the Penguins challenged for the Norris Division lead.

However, during a mid-February tilt with Toronto he was struck down by a blind-side hit. Suffering torn ligaments and a ripped tendon in his right knee, Bugsy was finished for the season.

Although he remained a very good player for the Pens—averaging 50 points per year over the next three seasons—he was never quite the same. In September of 1983 general manager Eddie Johnston traded him to Hartford for a fifth-round pick. The deal turned out to be a bargain for the Whalers as Malone enjoyed two solid seasons. In 1984–85 he tallied 22 goals and 61 points—his best post-surgery output.

The following season the Whalers shipped him to Quebec. With his career winding down, he spent a half-season with his hometown Fredericton Express in 1986–87 before retiring.

Malone, Ryan

Penguins: 2003–08 **Birthplace:** Pittsburgh, Pennsylvania
Left wing/Center B: December 1, 1979
Shoots: left **Ht.** 6-4 **Wt.** 224
Nickname: Bugsy

YR	Regular Season					Playoffs				
	GP	G	A	PTS	PM	GP	G	A	PTS	PM
2003–04	81	22	21	43	64	-	-	-	-	-
2005–06	77	22	22	44	63	-	-	-	-	-
2006–07	64	16	15	31	71	5	0	0	0	0
2007–08	77	27	24	51	103	20	6	10	16	25
NHL	**438**	**134**	**127**	**261**	**467**	**25**	**6**	**10**	**16**	**25**

The eldest son of former Pittsburgh player and head scout Greg Malone, Ryan Malone played two years of high school hockey in suburban Upper St. Clair and dreamed of one day skating for his hometown Penguins.

In 1997 the tall, rangy center was sent off to Fairbault, Minnesota, to play for fabled Shattuck-St. Mary's Boarding School. He moved on to the Omaha Lancers of the fast United States Hockey League during his senior year of high school, where he drew the attention of NHL scouts—including his dad. That summer, the elder Malone selected his

Big Ryan Malone slams through a check in pursuit of the puck.

son with the Penguins' fourth-round pick in the 1999 Entry Draft.

Displaying genuine promise, Ryan enrolled at St. Cloud State. After two decent years with the Huskies, he exploded for 40 goals and 85 points during his junior and senior seasons to earn a cameo with the Wilkes-Barre Scranton Penguins.

Following in his father's footsteps, Malone cracked the Penguins' opening-day lineup in 2003–04, becoming the first Pittsburgh-born player ever to skate for the club. Although the "X-Generation Pens" were a woeful team, Malone enjoyed a fine rookie campaign. He scored a team-leading 22 goals to earn a spot on the NHL's All-Rookie Team.

After playing in Europe during the lockout season, the big forward returned to the Pens in 2005–06. Playing left wing and center, the 6'4", 224-pounder equaled his first-year output of 22 goals. His game, however, was plagued by inconsistency. On some nights he was the best player on the ice. On other nights he was barely noticeable.

The trend continued in 2006–07, when Malone dipped to 16 goals. He often ran afoul of Penguins coach Michel Therrien, who benched the big winger in a crucial game during the 2007 Stanley Cup Playoffs.

Taking Therrien's criticism to heart, a different Ryan Malone emerged in 2008–09. Displaying a new level of focus and intensity, he drove to the net with authority and dropped the mitts when necessary to defend a teammate, while developing into a top-flight penalty killer. Duly impressed by Malone's transformation, Therrien named him as an alternate captain.

Suddenly one of the league's premier power forwards, Malone established new career highs with 27 goals and 51 points. He continued his gritty, determined play during the team's march to the Stanley Cup Finals. Already playing with a broken nose, he absorbed a Hal Gill slap shot to the face in the early stages of Game 5. In an extraordinary display of courage, he packed cotton balls into his nostrils and returned to skate a regular shift during the Pens' marathon triple-overtime victory.

Following his postseason heroics, Malone became an unrestricted free agent. In a different era, the Penguins no doubt would have made a strong bid to keep the budding winger. Due to salary-cap restrictions, however, Pens general manager Ray Shero was unable to extend a competitive offer. On June 28, 2008, he traded negotiating rights to the big left winger to Tampa Bay for a third-round draft choice. A short time later, Malone signed a lucrative seven-year deal worth $31.5 million with the Lightning.

"Bugsy" picked up right where he'd left off in Pittsburgh. Playing on a poor team, he banged home 26 goals in 2008–09 while leading the NHL in shooting percentage. In 2009–10 he earned a spot on the U.S. Olympic team.

Moran, Ian

Penguins: 1995–03   **Birthplace:** Cleveland, Ohio
Defense/Center   **B:** August 24, 1972
Shoots: right   **Ht.** 6-0 **Wt.** 206

	Regular Season					Playoffs				
YR	GP	G	A	PTS	PM	GP	G	A	PTS	PM
1994–95	-	-	-	-	-	8	0	0	0	0
1995–96	51	1	1	2	47	-	-	-	-	-
1996–97	36	4	5	9	22	5	1	2	3	4
1997–98	37	1	6	7	19	6	0	0	0	2
1998–99	62	4	5	9	37	13	0	2	2	8
1999–00	73	4	8	12	28	11	0	1	1	2
2000–01	40	3	4	7	28	18	0	1	1	4
2001–02	64	2	8	10	54	-	-	-	-	-
2002–03	70	0	7	7	46	-	-	-	-	-
NHL	**489**	**21**	**50**	**71**	**321**	**66**	**1**	**7**	**8**	**24**

Of all the players who have donned a Penguins uniform, none has defined the term "role player" quite like Ian Moran. During his eight-plus seasons in Pittsburgh, Moran served as the quintessential spare in the Pens' trunk in case one of the team's tires sprang a leak.

Ironically, when the Penguins selected Moran with their fifth choice in the 1990 Entry Draft, he was projected to be a star. Fresh off a sterling 46-point season (in 23 games) with Belmont Hill High School, he had the makings of a top-flight offensive defenseman. Quick and mobile, the Cleveland native excelled at making a good first pass and was particularly effective at jump-starting the transition game.

Following two years at Boston College, Moran spent part of the 1993–94 season with Team USA before turning pro with his hometown Cleveland Lumberjacks. During his minor league apprenticeship he continued to post solid numbers, tallying 56 points in 97 games.

The quintessential role player, Ian Moran (24) stops a New Jersey Devil in his tracks.

Ian got his first taste of big-league action when he was called up by the Penguins during the 1995 Eastern Conference Quarterfinals. Thrust into action due to injuries, he performed well.

During the summer of 1995, general manager Craig Patrick shook up the Penguins' defense when he traded veterans Larry Murphy and Ulf Samuelsson and released Kjell Samuelsson. The moves opened the door for the 23-year-old Moran to make his entrance.

It quickly became apparent that Ian's offensive skills did not translate to the NHL. Hampered by a weak shot, the rookie registered just two points in 51 games, despite playing on a prolific team that boasted three 100-point scorers. He was, however, a better than adequate defenseman who displayed a surprisingly feisty edge.

Moran split time between the Penguins and Cleveland in 1996–97. The following summer he was granted a reprieve of sorts when Kevin Constantine became the Pens' coach. A disciple of systematic hockey, Constantine preferred players with speed who were reliable in their own zone. Moran was a perfect fit.

Under the new coach, Ian developed into a jack of all trades. Equally at home on the blue line or skating on a checking line, he split time between forward and defense. Although his production remained marginal at best, he was a versatile and valuable performer during the Constantine era, killing penalties and shadowing opponents' top scorers.

When Ivan Hlinka assumed the coaching reins in 2000–01, he returned Moran to the role of full-time defenseman. While Ian never developed the offensive side of his game at the pro level, he was one of the Penguins' steadiest and most reliable defenders over the next few seasons.

Moran's tour with the Penguins ended on March 11, 2003, when he was traded to Boston for a fourth-round draft pick. The stocky defender played parts of three injury-plagued seasons in the Hub before moving on to Anaheim in 2006. He signed as a free agent with New Jersey during the summer of 2007. Ian failed to make the team and was sent to Lowell, where he finished out his career.

Orpik, Brooks

Penguins: 2002–   **Birthplace:** San Francisco, California
Defense   **B:** September 26, 1980
Shoots: left   **Ht.** 6-2   **Wt.** 219

	Regular Season					Playoffs				
YR	GP	G	A	PTS	PM	GP	G	A	PTS	PM
2002–03	6	0	0	0	2	-	-	-	-	-
2003–04	79	1	9	10	127	-	-	-	-	-
2005–06	64	2	7	9	124					
2006–07	70	0	6	6	82	5	0	0	0	8
2007–08	78	1	10	11	57	20	0	2	2	18
2008–09	79	2	17	19	73	24	0	4	4	22
2009-10	73	2	23	25	64	13	0	2	2	12
NHL	**449**	**8**	**72**	**80**	**529**	**62**	**0**	**8**	**8**	**60**

Brooks Orpik provides bruising, stay-at-home defense.

During the latter stages of the 1990s the Penguins used their top draft picks almost exclusively on European skill players such as Aleksey Morozov, Robert Dome, Milan Kraft, and Konstantin Koltsov. With the exception of Morozov, who was marginally productive, all were busts.

Noting their lack of success, the Pens did an about-face in 2000 and selected Brooks Orpik with their first pick. The polar opposite of his high-flying predecessors, there was nothing subtle about Orpik's game. A proverbial bulldozer in a construction yard, he took the shortest distance to the puck and arrived ill-humored.

Named after former Penguins coach and USA hockey legend Herb Brooks, Orpik was born in San Francisco but spent his formative years in Buffalo. After skating for two seasons with Thayer Academy in Massachusetts he enrolled at Boston College. The burly 6'2", 219-pounder quickly established himself as one of the most dynamic hitters in collegiate hockey.

After helping the Eagles capture the NCAA championship in 2001, Orpik joined the Wilkes-Barre Scranton Penguins. Despite his impressive credentials at Boston College, the rugged defenseman developed slowly. Displaying little of his customary aggression, he seemed at times to be feeling his way along.

The Penguins had little time to wait on a late bloomer. Desperate for defensive help, they promoted the former

No. 1 pick in 2003. In what amounted to on-the-job training, Orpik endured a difficult rookie season, logging a plus/minus rating of minus 36.

With the arrival of coach Michel Therrien in 2005, the youthful Penguins began to improve. Clearly benefiting from Therrien's structured system, Orpik's game solidified. As his confidence grew, he reemerged as a physical force on the blue line and a leader in the locker room.

Mirroring the team's stunning metamorphosis into a Stanley Cup contender, Orpik placed fifth in the NHL (second among defensemen) with 239 hits in 2007–08. In the playoffs that spring he was a one-man wrecking crew, leading all postseason performers with 102 hits and 61 blocked shots. During Game 3 of the Stanley Cup Finals versus Detroit, he single-handedly sealed a Pens victory by delivering four bone-crushing hits during an even-strength shift.

"That shift was just amazing," teammate Max Talbot said. "When you're on the bench, it gives us a lot of energy. You just want to go out there and do the same thing."

Despite his newfound success, the outspoken Orpik had—at best—a strained relationship with Michel Therrien. The unrestricted free agent was eager to test the open market in the summer of 2008—until he was deluged with pleas from his teammates to re-sign with the Penguins. Spurning more lucrative offers from clubs including the Rangers, the rugged blue-liner agreed to stay put and signed a six-year, $22.5 million deal.

His team-first attitude was soon rewarded. With Orpik serving as the defensive bulwark, the Pens rebounded from a slow start to earn a playoff berth. Skating with his trademark wide-eyed intensity, the 29-year-old Orpik finished second in the league with 309 hits while tallying a career-high 19 points.

Reunited with his partner Sergei Gonchar, Orpik enjoyed a terrific postseason. He set the tone early in Game 1 of the Finals with a jarring hit on Detroit sniper Marian Hossa. Ever mindful of Orpik's looming presence, the former Penguins winger failed to find the net, while Pittsburgh captured the Stanley Cup. Brooks finished the playoffs with a whopping 112 hits and 51 blocked shots.

After hoisting Lord Stanley's chalice, Orpik said, "This is why I stayed, to play in games like this. I knew we had a team that would win games like this."

The rugged rearguard emerged as an All-Star-caliber performer in 2009–10. Shaking off the effects of a nagging abdominal injury that required off-season surgery, he ranked sixth in the league with 255 hits while establishing a new career high with 25 points. His rock-rib play earned him a spot on the 2010 U.S. Olympic team.

Samuelsson, Ulf

Penguins: 1991–95　**Birthplace:** Fagersta, Sweden
Defense　**B:** March 26, 1964
Shoots: left　**Ht.** 6-1　**Wt.** 205
Nickname: Robocop

YR	Regular Season					Playoffs				
	GP	G	A	PTS	PM	GP	G	A	PTS	PM
1990–91	14	1	4	5	37	20	3	2	5	34
1991–92	62	1	14	15	206	21	0	2	2	39
1992–93	77	3	26	29	249	12	1	5	6	24
1993–94	80	5	24	29	199	6	0	1	1	18
1994–95	44	1	15	16	113	7	0	2	2	8
NHL	**1080**	**57**	**275**	**332**	**2453**	**132**	**7**	**27**	**34**	**272**

On a team not noted for employing physical defensemen, Ulf Samuelsson stands as a glaring exception to the rule. In many ways he was a dinosaur—a throwback to an earlier time when rugged rearguards like "Bashin'" Bill Barilko, Bobby Baun, and Leo Boivin put the fear of God into opposing forwards with their brutally efficient physical play.

There was nothing subtle about Samuelsson's game. Although hardly a heavyweight, the Swedish-born defender employed an edgy, in-your-face style that delighted his teammates and infuriated opponents.

The slot was Ulfie's turf. Opposing forwards who had the nerve to venture in were treated like trespassers. He used every weapon in his considerable arsenal—bodychecks, cross checks, slashes, elbows, rabbit punches, and the occasional face wash—to make sure they didn't linger.

Ulf spent his formative years playing in his native Sweden, where he starred as a teenager for Leksands of the Swedish Elite League. He inherited his fiery, ultracompetitive nature

Ulf Samuelsson applies a face wash to Minnesota's Brian Propp during the 1991 Stanley Cup Finals.

from his dad Bo, who was a budding pro soccer player before rheumatism shortened his career.

Attracted by the youngster's spirited, physical brand of defense, the Hartford Whalers made him their fourth choice in the 1982 Entry Draft. Two years later he was in the NHL, banging bodies and making enemies at a rapid rate.

"No, I didn't like him," future teammate Rick Tocchet said. "In fact, like most people who don't know him, I hated him."

For nearly six seasons he patrolled the Whalers' blue line. Occasionally he flashed an offensive upside—notching eight goals and 41 points in 1987–88 and a career-high nine goals the following season. But his bread and butter remained his relentless physical play.

By 1990–91 the Whalers were in turmoil. Despite a string of solid seasons, they couldn't get past the first round of the playoffs. Armed with a mandate to shake his team up—or else—Whalers general manager Eddie Johnston sent Samuelsson, Ron Francis, and Grant Jennings to the Penguins in a blockbuster six-player trade.

Rejuvenated by the change of scenery, Ulf belted any opponent who had the temerity to cross his path. He quickly became a favorite of the Mellon Arena faithful, who loved his straight-on, take-no-prisoners style. Not by coincidence, the Pens churned through the homestretch to win their first division crown.

Samuelsson cemented his physical reputation against the Bruins during the bitterly fought 1991 Wales Conference Finals. He went head-to-head with Cam Neely, an old foe from his days as a Whaler. A 6'1", 210-pound slab of granite, Neely was considered far and away the top power forward in the league—equally adept at delivering pulverizing body checks as he was at scoring goals.

"Cam Neely was a big, strong winger and he was very difficult to play against," the late Bob Johnson recalled in the highlight video, *One From the Heart.* "A lot of players couldn't handle him—he just physically overpowered them. Ulf accepted the challenge. He's the toughest guy I've ever been around."

Samuelsson and Neely hammered away at each other through three emotionally charged contests. Like a pit bull terrier, Ulfie kept coming after the imposing Bruin.

The turning point of the series came late in Game 3. With the Penguins protecting a two-goal lead in a must-win game, Samuelsson lined up Neely once more. At the last second the Boston strongman took evasive action, but the tough defenseman instinctively stuck out a knee to block his path. Neely went down in a heap.

Out for blood in Game 4, the revenge-minded Bruins came at him with a bare-knuckled fury. Ulfie never wavered. Like a spent bullet, Boston faded while the Pens went on to capture their first Stanley Cup.

Over the next four seasons, the rugged Swede was at his head-knocking best. He played some of the finest hockey of his career during the Penguins' march to a second Cup in

1992. The following season he logged a sterling plus/minus rating of plus 36 while helping to lead the team to a stunning 56-win season and the President's Trophy.

One of the most treasured members of the team, Penguins fans hoped Ulfie would finish his career in Pittsburgh. Sadly, it was not to be. During the summer of 1995 he was traded to the Rangers with Luc Robitaille, ending his four-plus year run in Pittsburgh. He departed as one of the most popular players in team history.

Perhaps the Samuelsson saga will have one more chapter. In June of 2009, the Penguins selected Ulf's son Philip with their second pick in the Entry Draft. The 6'3", 200-pounder reportedly plays with a mean streak—just like his dad.

Scuderi, Rob

Penguins: 2004–09   **Birthplace:** Syosset, New York
Defense   B: December 30, 1978
Shoots: left   **Ht.** 6-0   **Wt.** 218
Nickname: Scuds, the Piece

	Regular Season					Playoffs				
YR	GP	G	A	PTS	PM	GP	G	A	PTS	PM
2003–04	13	1	2	3	4	-	-	-	-	-
2005–06	57	0	4	4	36	-	-	-	-	-
2006–07	78	1	10	11	28	5	0	0	0	2
2007–08	71	0	5	5	26	20	0	3	3	2
2008–09	81	1	15	16	18	24	1	4	5	6
NHL	373	3	47	50	133	55	1	7	8	16

If one was to look up the term "stay-at-home defenseman" in a hockey dictionary, chances are good there will be a photo of Rob Scuderi next to the description. Indeed, no player of the present era better defines the attributes of a shot-blocking, poke-checking, positionally sound defender than "Scuds."

The native of Syosset, New York, played high school hockey at St. Anthony's in South Huntington. Following a solid freshman season at Boston College, Scuderi was selected by the Penguins with their fifth pick in the 1998 Entry Draft. Opting to finish college and earn his degree, the steady rearguard helped the Eagles win an NCAA championship his senior year.

After serving a three-year apprenticeship with Wilkes-Barre Scranton, Scuderi was called up by the Penguins late in the 2003–04 season. When he arrived, the hapless "X-Generation" Pens were capping off a dismal year. Perhaps not by coincidence, the Pens went a surprising 8–3–2 during his 13-game cameo.

Scuderi returned to Wilkes-Barre during the lockout season of 2004–05. He secured full-time work with the Penguins the following year. One thing was clear—Scuds wasn't the second coming of Bobby Orr. However, he had the makings of a reliable, versatile defenseman who could play the left or right side with equal ability.

Rob Scuderi defined the term "shutdown defenseman" during his four-plus seasons with the team.

As the Penguins turned the corner in 2006–07, Scuderi became an increasingly valuable performer. Thanks to his "educated" stick, he developed into an outstanding penalty killer. Using a move not taught at hockey schools, he would drop to a knee and lay his stick flat on the ice to block shots or sweep the puck from harm's way.

Although his solid play went largely unnoticed, Penguins coach Michel Therrien was most appreciative.

"You always know what you're going to get from Rob, game in and game out," Therrien said. "He very rarely has a bad game. He's very consistent."

Scuderi continued to emerge as one of the league's top defensive defensemen in 2007–08. Anchoring the Pens' blue-line corps, he blocked 110 shots while helping the team to the Stanley Cup Finals. The following season he was even better, blocking a club-best 164 shots while teaming with mammoth Hal Gill to form a shutdown pairing.

Saving his best work for the playoffs, Scuderi enjoyed his moment in the sun during a Finals rematch with Detroit. In the waning seconds of a must-win Game 6, Red Wings power forward Johan Franzen was planted in the slot with the puck cradled on his blade. Realizing Marc-Andre Fleury was hopelessly out of position, Scuderi dropped to his knees

amid furious traffic and stopped three rapid-fire shots—one with his stick and two with his left skate—to preserve a 2–1 Penguins victory. Two nights later the Pens vanquished the Red Wings to win the Stanley Cup.

Following the glorious Cup victory, Scuderi grudgingly hit the open market as an unrestricted free agent. The Kings made him an offer he couldn't refuse—$13.6 million over four years.

"I've never been through the frenzy that is free agency," he said. "I held out pretty long, hoping we could figure something out. I'm really sad to leave, but, of the choices I had, I was pretty confident with my choice."

"We really wanted him back," Pens general manager Ray Shero said. "But at the same time, I don't know if I can be any happier for a guy and his wife and his family."

Playing his typically solid game in 2009–10, Scuderi helped lead the Kings to their first playoff berth in seven years, while serving as a mentor for promising young defensemen Drew Doughty and Jack Johnson.

Staal, Jordan

Penguins: 2006–   **Birthplace:** Thunder Bay, Ontario
Center/Left wing   **B:** September 10, 1988
Shoots: left   **Ht.** 6-4   **Wt.** 220
Nickname: Gronk

	Regular Season					Playoffs				
YR	GP	G	A	PTS	PM	GP	G	A	PTS	PM
2006–07	81	29	13	42	24	5	3	0	3	2
2007–08	82	12	16	28	55	20	6	1	7	14
2008–09	82	22	27	49	37	24	4	5	9	8
2009-10	82	21	28	49	57	11	3	2	5	6
NHL	327	84	84	168	173	60	16	8	24	30

Growing up on his father's sod farm near Thunder Bay, Ontario, Jordan Staal enjoyed an idyllic childhood straight out of a Norman Rockwell painting. During the summer months, the tow-headed youth built up his physique toiling on the farm. Every winter, his dad Henry would build an ice skating rink in the back yard so Jordan and his brothers Eric, Marc, and Jared could play hockey.

Following in big brother Eric's footsteps, Jordan played junior hockey for the Peterborough Petes of the Ontario Hockey League. The tall, rangy center tallied 68 points in his second year while helping the Petes capture the OHL championship. His strong two-way play quickly drew the attention of scouts. At the 2006 Entry Draft he was taken second overall by the Penguins.

When he arrived at the Penguins' training camp that fall, no one truly expected the 18-year-old Staal to make the team. However, as the team began exhibition play, he continued to make an impression. Remarkably well schooled and responsible for such a young player, he surprised everyone by earning a spot in the opening-day lineup.

Jordan Staal (left) scored 29 goals as a rookie in 2006–07.

Coach Michel Therrien used him primarily in a defensive role through the early going. However, an injury to Nils Ekman and the retirement of John LeClair created an opening at left wing. Acting on a hunch, Therrien moved Staal to the port side—with stunning results. The kid began to score goals in bunches. Not by coincidence, the Penguins began to heat up.

Nicknamed "Gronk" by fun-loving teammate Colby Armstrong, Jordan finished his rookie season with 29 goals. It was a remarkable achievement given that Staal was playing an unfamiliar position and didn't see regular ice time until midseason.

Staal set a slew of NHL records during his magical first year. He was the youngest player in league history to score a hat trick; the youngest to score on a penalty shot; and the youngest to score two shorthanded goals in one game. His league-leading seven shorthanded goals were the most ever by a rookie. He was the third-youngest player—behind only Ted Lindsay and teammate Sidney Crosby—to score 20 goals.

Jordan had set the bar high—perhaps too high. Suffering a case of the sophomore jinx, his production and overall play tumbled in 2007–08. Shots that found their way into the net during his rookie season were now missing the mark. His output dropped to 12 goals and 16 assists. Fortunately, the Penguins never lost sight of the fact that he was only 19 years old.

Still, it seemed Jordan might duplicate Eric's feat of winning a Stanley Cup in his second season. The Penguins

sliced through the competition in the Eastern Conference like a hot knife going through butter. However, they ran into a brick wall in the Finals in the form of the Detroit Red Wings. Jordan acquitted himself well in postseason play, scoring six goals.

Entering the 2008–09 campaign, Therrien once again tried Staal at left wing with fellow wonder boy Evgeni Malkin. This time, however, the combination didn't work. Jordan was returned to his natural position of center. He clicked with feisty wingers Matt Cooke and Tyler Kennedy. The trio soon emerged as a rock-solid third line.

Buoyed by the presence of his new linemates, Staal closed with a rush to tally 22 goals and 27 assists—excellent totals for a third-line center.

Once more, the Penguins toppled their Eastern Conference opponents to set up a Stanley Cup Finals rematch with Detroit. The Pens dropped the first two games to their powerful foe, and trailed 2–1 in the second period of Game 3. Worse yet, Brooks Orpik was serving a minor penalty.

The stage was set for Staal's coming of age. Gathering in a lead pass from Max Talbot, the big center bulled his way past Brian Rafalski and wristed the puck into the net. The play was the turning point of the series. Given a new boost of confidence, the Penguins beat the Red Wings 4–2 and won three of the next four games to capture the Stanley Cup.

Staal took his game to new heights in 2009–10. Now regarded as one of the finest two-way players in the league, the durable center tallied 49 points while running his iron-man streak to 302 games. The 21-year-old Staal was nominated for the Frank J. Selke Trophy for his superb defensive work.

Talbot, Max

Penguins: 2005–   **Birthplace:** Lemoyne, Quebec
Center/Right wing   **B:** February 11, 1984
Shoots: left   **Ht.** 5-11 **Wt.** 190
Nicknames: Mad Max, Superstar

YR	Regular Season					Playoffs				
	GP	G	A	PTS	PM	GP	G	A	PTS	PM
2005–06	48	5	3	8	59	-	-	-	-	-
2006–07	75	13	11	24	53	5	0	1	1	7
2007–08	63	12	14	26	53	17	3	6	9	36
2008–09	75	12	10	22	63	24	8	5	13	19
2009-10	45	2	5	7	30	13	2	4	6	11
NHL	**306**	**44**	**43**	**87**	**258**	**59**	**13**	**16**	**29**	**73**

Through the years the Penguins have enjoyed tremendous success drafting centers of French Canadian descent. First came the late Michel Briere, then Pierre Larouche, and last but certainly not least, a big fellow who wore No. 66. So it was no great surprise when they selected peppery Hull Olympiques center Max Talbot in the eighth round of the 2002 Entry Draft.

"Mad Max" Talbot scored two goals in Game 7 of the 2009 Finals to secure the Stanley Cup.

"Max really stepped up," teammate Tyler Kennedy said. "He showed a ton of guts."

Playing his gritty, hell-for-leather style, Talbot came up even bigger during the Stanley Cup Finals against Detroit. He scored a team-high four goals during the series, including two huge goals during a winner-take-all seventh game to lead the Pens to a third Cup.

Weeks later it was revealed that he'd skated for much of the season with a dislocated shoulder, which made his feats all the more remarkable.

"He played hurt this year, even though it didn't look like it in Game 7," Talbot's agent Pat Brisson said. "It shows how much character he has. That shoulder was popping in and out."

The 2009–10 campaign would prove to be a difficult one for the Pens' playoff hero. Struggling to overcome the effects of off-season shoulder surgery, Talbot scored only two goals in 45 games. Typically, Mad Max regained his mojo in time for the playoffs. Displaying his customary grit, he notched the winning goal in Game 4 of the Eastern Conference Quarterfinals.

Watson, Bryan

Penguins: 1969–1974   **Birthplace:** Bancroft, Ontario
Defense   B: November 14, 1942
Shoots: right   **Ht.** 5-9 **Wt.** 175
Nickname: Bugsy, Superpest

	Regular Season					Playoffs				
YR	GP	G	A	PTS	PM	GP	G	A	PTS	PM
1968–69	18	0	4	4	35	-	-	-	-	-
1969–70	61	1	9	10	189	10	0	0	0	17
1970–71	43	2	6	8	119	-	-	-	-	-
1971–72	75	3	17	20	212	4	0	0	0	21
1972–73	69	1	17	18	179	-	-	-	-	-
1973–74	38	1	4	5	137	-	-	-	-	-
NHL	**878**	**17**	**135**	**152**	**2212**	**32**	**2**	**0**	**2**	**70**
WHA	**21**	**0**	**2**	**2**	**56**	**3**	**0**	**1**	**1**	**2**

Bryan Joseph Watson was a rambunctious little defenseman whose heart was several times bigger than his undersized body. Serving as the Penguins' first "policeman," he earned a reputation for being one of the toughest players in the game.

"I felt it when Bryan came to say hello in the corners," said Pens teammate Ken Schinkel, who played against Watson on many occasions. "You always knew you got hit when 'Bugsy' got to you."

Watson came by his colorful nickname honestly. As a callow 23-year-old utility player with the Detroit Red Wings, he was assigned the awesome task of shadowing Chicago's legendary Bobby Hull in the 1966 Stanley Cup Semifinals.

It was like David versus Goliath on ice. Watson weighed 175 pounds soaking wet. The powerful Hull was a

Unlike his predecessors, Talbot was not projected to be a star. Although he tallied 202 points during his final two seasons with the Olympiques, he was neither big nor especially fast. But he possessed a ton of intangibles, including a winning attitude, underrated skills, and the heart of a lion.

Nicknamed "Mad Max" by his teammates for his colorful and irrepressible personality, he soon became a media darling. In 2007 he starred in a kitschy local TV commercial for A & L Motors with teammates Colby Armstrong, Sergei Gonchar, and Evgeni Malkin. Talbot stole the show, proclaiming, "I am the superstar." The new nickname stuck.

While nobody was confusing Talbot with Malkin or Sidney Crosby, he developed into a solid role player who had a penchant for producing in clutch situations. During Game 5 of the 2008 Stanley Cup Finals, he banged home the dramatic tying goal with 34 seconds remaining to propel his team to a triple-overtime victory over Detroit.

"Superstar" was even better during the 2009 Cup run. With the opening-round series against Philadelphia hanging in the balance, he turned the tide by taking on Flyers tough guy Daniel Carcillo.

golden-haired Adonis who possessed the body and strength of a blacksmith.

Undaunted, Watson resorted to tactics both legal and illegal—including a liberal dose of stick work—to hold "the Golden Jet" in check. Indeed, he stuck so close to Hull that he was labeled "the Boy on Bobby's Back."

Hull was less flattering. When asked about his tormentor after the Black Hawks had been vanquished, the normally gracious Hull steamed, "Boy, does that guy bug me!" From then on Watson was known as "Bugsy."

When he arrived in Pittsburgh in January 1969 as part of a big six-player trade with Oakland, the Pens were mired in the West Division cellar and hopelessly out of playoff contention. They were reasonably skilled by expansion team standards, but sadly lacking in character and grit.

That all changed from the moment Watson first stepped onto the Civic Arena ice. Suddenly opponents who tried to take liberties with his less combative teammates found themselves nose-to-nose with the little roughneck. Not coincidentally, the Pens rallied sharply and played nearly .500 hockey down the homestretch.

Management took note. By the start of the 1969–70 season the Penguins had added several rugged performers to the mix, including abrasive winger Glen "Slats" Sather. It was a good thing, too, because the bad blood that had been boiling between the Pens and the division-leading St. Louis Blues erupted into an on-ice version of the Hatfields and the McCoys. The teams clashed in the Stanley Cup Playoffs, where Watson and Sather nearly drove the Blues crazy with their acid-tongued barbs and antics.

"They were constantly chirping at us from the bench," recalled Bob Plager, one of the Blues' rough-and-tumble Plager brothers. "But when Barclay or I would challenge them to go a round, they'd just laugh at us and say, 'See you next shift.'"

Watson's confrontational style made him wildly popular in Pittsburgh. Although far from physically imposing and average with his dukes at best, he was nonetheless a very effective on-ice cop.

"Pound for pound, he was the toughest and most hard-nosed player ever," said the late John Ferguson, a former Montreal teammate and NHL heavyweight champ.

However, the rules of engagement abruptly changed in 1972 when the Philadelphia Flyers assembled a gang of two-fisted brawlers known as "the Broad Street Bullies." In an effort to protect its core of budding young stars, the Pens dealt Watson and Greg Polis to the hated Blues in January of 1974 for tough guys Steve Durbano and Bob "Battleship" Kelly. The torch had been passed.

Watson had a brief stay with the Blues—where he was reunited with Sather, his old partner in crime—before returning to Detroit. He quickly became a card-carrying member of one of the toughest teams of that era, skating alongside bruising Dan Maloney and feisty Dennis Polonich. After departing from the Motor City, Bugsy joined the Washington Capitals before finishing his pro career with the Cincinnati Stingers of the World Hockey Association in 1979.

Colorful to the end, Watson told a story of how he had a rare breakaway opportunity with the Capitals one night. Chugging in all alone on the opposing goaltender, he made his move, cut loose a shot…and missed the net by 30 feet.

When he returned to the bench, his exasperated coach, Tommy McVie, demanded an explanation. Ever the cut-up, Watson quipped, "Coach, I just couldn't get my stick out of cross check."

The Penguins' first policeman, Bryan Watson. "Bugsy" led the NHL with 212 penalty minutes in 1971–72.

Young, Warren

Penguins: 1983–85, 1986–88   **Birthplace:** Toronto, Ontario
Left wing   **B:** January 11, 1956
Shoots: left   **Ht.** 6-3   **Wt.** 195
Nicknames: Scorin' Warren, Warren Old

| | Regular Season | | | | | Playoffs | | | | |
YR	GP	G	A	PTS	PM	GP	G	A	PTS	PM
1983–84	15	1	7	8	19	-	-	-	-	-
1984–85	80	40	32	72	174	-	-	-	-	-
1986–87	50	8	13	21	103	-	-	-	-	-
1987–88	7	0	0	0	15	-	-	-	-	-
NHL	**236**	**72**	**77**	**149**	**472**	**-**	**-**	**-**	**-**	**-**

The rags to riches (to rags again) tale of Warren Young is truly one of the most remarkable stories in the history of the National Hockey League.

By all accounts a late bloomer, Young played one season of Junior B hockey before attending Michigan Tech. Following a solid freshman year, the tall, rangy left wing was selected by the California Golden Seals in the fourth round of the 1976 Amateur Draft. He enjoyed his best collegiate season as a sophomore, racking up 19 goals and 26 assists in just 37 games. However, Young's production mysteriously declined during his final two seasons with the Huskies and he was assigned to Baltimore of the Eastern Hockey League.

Although the rough-and-tumble EHL was no picnic, Young scored 53 goals with the Clippers to earn a promotion

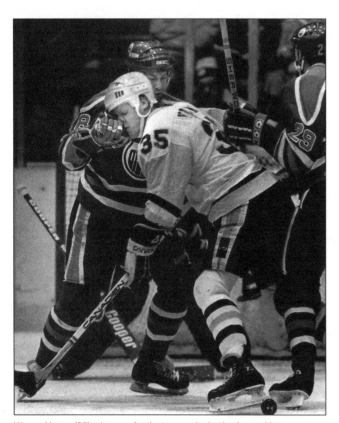

Warren Young (35) takes one for the team as he battles for position.

to Oklahoma City of the Central Hockey League. Over the next three seasons he continued to put up decent numbers while adding a physical edge to his game.

Desperate for anything resembling big-league talent, Penguins general manager Eddie Johnston signed Young to a free-agent deal during the summer of 1983. When the big winger was called up by the Pens for a late-season cameo, he made the most of the opportunity. During a meaningless game versus the Rangers, Young stepped up to challenge tough guy Steve Richmond, who was bullying his smaller teammates.

"Warren stood up to Richmond," Johnston recalled. "Fought him. Beat him pretty good."

Young had made an impression. When training camp broke in the fall of 1984, he was on the Penguins' roster. Not only had he made the team, but he found himself skating alongside prized rookie Mario Lemieux.

The pair quickly developed a wonderful chemistry. Although Young was a step slow, he read the play very well and used his good size to the fullest advantage. Standing 6'3" and weighing 195 pounds, he was a fearless and capable fighter, which afforded him and his gifted linemate extra time and space to make plays.

Aided by Lemieux's picture-perfect setups, the 28-year-old rookie found the net with stunning regularity. By season's end, he had scored 40 goals—a remarkable achievement for a player who was previously regarded as a career minor leaguer. Young's outstanding play earned him a spot on the NHL's All-Rookie Team and folk hero status in Pittsburgh.

With his contract up for renewal, "Scorin' Warren" was surprised when Eddie Johnston encouraged him to field offers from other clubs. Although he preferred to remain a Penguin, Detroit made Young an offer he couldn't refuse—$1 million over four years.

He did his best to live up to the big contract. However, the Red Wings were a terrible team—even worse than the Penguins. With little help, Young's output dipped to 22 goals and 46 points. Respectable totals for sure, but not enough to justify the money he was making.

Seeking to unload his fat contract, the Red Wings sold Young back to the Penguins on the eve of the 1986–87 season. He was thrilled to return to Pittsburgh, but this was one fairy tale that would not have a happy ending. In his second go-round with the Pens, the big winger struggled to rediscover his scoring touch. He finished the season with eight goals in 50 games—hardly the stuff of legend.

Following a brief seven-game stint with the club in 1987–88, Young was shipped to the Muskegon Lumberjacks, where he finished his career. Although he endured an inglorious end, Young's sudden rise to stardom remains one of the true feel-good stories in the team's long and colorful history.

The Goalies

Binkley, Les

Penguins: 1967–72   **Birthplace:** Owen Sound, Ontario
Goaltender   B: June 6, 1934
Catches: right   **Ht.** 6-0 **Wt.** 175
Nickname: Bink

| | | Regular Season | | | | | Playoffs | | | |
YR	GP	MINS	GA	SH	AVE	GP	MINS	GA	SH	AVE
1967–68	54	3141	151	6	2.88	-	-	-	-	-
1968–69	50	2885	158	0	3.29	-	-	-	-	-
1969–70	27	1477	79	3	3.21	7	428	15	0	2.10
1970–71	34	1870	89	2	2.86	-	-	-	-	-
1971–72	31	1673	98	0	3.51	-	-	-	-	-
NHL	**196**	**11046**	**575**	**11**	**3.12**	**7**	**428**	**15**	**0**	**2.10**
WHA	**81**	**4228**	**262**	**1**	**3.72**	**10**	**464**	**40**	**0**	**5.17**

Les Binkley provided the Pens with solid goaltending during the early 1970s.

After watching Penguins goalie Les Binkley shut down the Flyers with a typically strong performance, Hugh Brown of the *Philadelphia Evening Bulletin* made an astute observation.

"Binkley looks somewhat like he sounds, meaning he could pass for a near-sighted, narrow-chested bird watcher," Brown wrote.

Binkley was, indeed, near-sighted, and narrow-chested to boot. Instead of watching birds flutter about in the summer breeze, however, the maskless goalie earned his keep by tracking down 100 mile-per-hour slap shots—a decidedly tougher way to make a living.

Back in the pre-expansion days of the Original Six, Binkley toiled in the minor leagues for 13 long seasons, stopping pucks in remote hockey outposts such as Charlotte, Toledo, and Ft. Wayne. It was a trial that would've discouraged a lesser man. But Binkley never gave up on his dream.

"I always hoped I would make it [to the NHL] someday," he said.

Binkley got his first big break in 1960. Cleveland Barons general manager Jim Heady offered him a job as a spare goalie—and a trainer. Although "Bink" knew nothing about training, the Barons played in the American Hockey League—the top minor pro circuit. He jumped at the chance.

The following year he took over as the team's starting goalie. Over the next five seasons, he established himself as one of the premier puck-stoppers in the AHL, earning All-Star honors while capturing the Dudley "Red" Garrett Memorial Award (rookie of the year) and the Harry "Hap" Holmes Memorial Award (top goalie).

Still, a call up to the "big show" never came.

"You have to remember that those were the years of the old six-team NHL," he said. "There were only six goalies playing in the NHL and most of them were pretty solid. Four of those guys—Bower, Hall, Plante, and Sawchuk—played in the NHL during my duration in the minors."

It wasn't until the NHL expanded to 12 teams in 1967 that Binkley got his chance to shine. Signed as a free agent by Penguins general manager Jack Riley, the 33-year-old goalie was expected to serve as a backup to veteran Hank Bassen, who had seen action with Chicago and Detroit. But Bink quickly established himself as the No. 1 goalie.

He was sensational during the club's inaugural season. Appearing in 54 games, he recorded a sterling 2.88 goals-against average and six shutouts while winning 20 games for a non-playoff team.

Penguins coach Red Sullivan was a big fan.

"I know of only one man who had the edge on Binkley," Sullivan said, "and that was Johnny Bower of Toronto. There were one or two others who were Bink's equal. There are several who get more publicity. But there is no one outside of Bower who has more ability as a goaltender than Binkley."

The Penguins struggled mightily during the early years, missing the playoffs three out of their first five seasons. However, Binkley remained a veritable Rock of Gibraltar in goal, winning 58 games while posting a solid 3.12 goals-against average.

With young Jim Rutherford set to take over the Penguins' netminding duties in 1972, Binkley jumped to the World

Hockey Association. In 1973–74, at the age of 39, he registered a .901 save percentage for the Toronto Toros—an extraordinary number in those days.

Following his playing days, Binkley returned to the Penguins organization in 1988. He was a member of the scouting staff when the Pens won two Stanley Cups in the early 1990s.

Fleury, Marc-Andre

Penguins: 2003–   **Birthplace:** Sorel, Quebec
Goaltender   **B:** November 28, 1984
Catches: left   **Ht.** 6-2 **Wt.** 180
Nickname: Flower

		Regular Season					Playoffs			
YR	GP	MINS	GA	SH	AVE	GP	MINS	GA	SH	AVE
2003–04	21	1154	70	1	3.64	-	-	-	-	-
2005–06	50	2809	152	1	3.25	-	-	-	-	-
2006–07	67	3905	184	5	2.83	5	287	18	0	3.76
2007–08	35	1857	72	4	2.33	20	1251	41	3	1.97
2008–09	62	3641	162	4	2.67	24	1447	63	0	2.61
2009-10	67	3798	168	1	2.65	13	798	37	1	2.78
NHL	**302**	**17164**	**808**	**16**	**2.82**	**62**	**3783**	**159**	**4**	**2.52**

When Penguins general manager Craig Patrick traded up on draft day in 2003 to select Marc-Andre Fleury with the first overall pick, it was clear that great things were expected of him.

"We were looking to build a championship team from goal on out," said Pens goaltending coach Gilles Meloche. "Not too many goalies like Marc-Andre come along."

The willowy netminder made quite a first impression. On October 10, 2003, the 18-year-old Fleury turned in a dazzling 46-save performance during a 3–0 loss to the Kings. In his next start, the precocious youngster earned his first victory, topping the powerhouse Red Wings. "The Flower" easily won Rookie of the Month honors for the month of October.

However, things soon began to sour. Playing behind a woeful defensive corps, he tried to win games single-handedly, which hurt his performance. Seeking to avoid incentives in Fleury's contract, the cash-strapped Penguins loaned him to Team Canada for the 2004 World Junior Championships. By season's end he was toiling for Cape Breton, his junior team.

Undaunted, the unflappable goalie with the ready smile worked long hours with Meloche to improve his fundamentals while learning to rely less on his extraordinary reflexes.

The hard work paid off handsomely during the 2006–07 season. His positioning and rebound control dramatically improved, Fleury helped to lead the surprising Penguins to a stunning 47-point improvement and a berth in the Stanley Cup Playoffs.

The following season would prove to be the most challenging of his young career. After an uneven start, Fleury

Marc-Andre Fleury sprawls to gobble up a loose puck. "The Flower" backstopped the Pens to a Stanley Cup in 2009.

suffered a high-ankle sprain on December 8. During his three-month absence, veteran Ty Conklin turned in a superb performance, prompting coach Michel Therrien to assert that Fleury would have to earn the starting job upon his return.

The youngster proved that he was up to the task. Displaying an intensity that belied his easygoing nature, Fleury outshone Conklin to snatch the goaltending reins.

In the Stanley Cup Playoffs, he came of age. Posting a sparkling 1.97 goals-against average and three shutouts, he led the Penguins to within two wins of the Stanley Cup. His efforts were rewarded with a brand-new, seven-year, $35 million contract.

He proved to be worth every penny. With "the Flower" in top form, the Penguins tore through the stretch run in 2008–09 to capture second place in the Atlantic Division.

Again, Fleury was magnificent in the postseason. His supernatural toe save on Jeff Carter in Game 2 of the opening round robbed the Flyers of a certain victory. During a winner-take-all Game 7 versus the Capitals he thwarted Alexander Ovechkin on an early breakaway attempt to key a Penguins win.

Saving his best for last, he held the mighty Red Wings to a paltry two goals in Games 6 and 7 of the Stanley Cup Finals. In the closing seconds of the series finale he made a spectacular save on Nicklas Lidstrom to seal the Pens' Stanley Cup triumph.

The Flower once again carried the load for the Penguins in 2009–10. He appeared in 67 games—tying his own club record—and registered 37 wins, the third-highest single-season total in team history. Fleury's strong play earned him a spot on the Canadian Olympic team.

Hedberg, Johan

Penguins: 2001–03 **Birthplace:** Leksand, Sweden
Goaltender **B:** May 5, 1973
Catches: left **Ht.** 6-0 **Wt.** 185
Nicknames: Moose, Yo-Yo

		Regular Season					Playoffs			
YR	GP	MINS	GA	SH	AVE	GP	MINS	GA	SH	AVE
2000–01	9	545	24	0	2.64	18	1123	43	2	2.30
2001–02	66	3877	178	6	2.75	-	-	-	-	-
2002–03	41	2410	126	1	3.14	-	-	-	-	-
NHL	293	16342	799	14	2.93	22	1338	52	2	2.33

Following a brilliant career in the World Hockey Association with the Winnipeg Jets, Swedish hockey legend Anders Hedberg was welcomed to the National Hockey League with open arms. For his kid brother Johan, the road to the NHL was much more arduous.

Selected by the Philadelphia Flyers in the ninth round of the 1994 Entry Draft, Johan Hedberg served a five-year apprenticeship with Leksands of the Swedish Elite League. The 24-year-old goalie made his North American debut in 1997 to little fanfare. Splitting time between the Detroit Vipers and the Manitoba Moose of the International Hockey League, he performed ably.

Ultracompetitive Johan Hedberg voices his opinion.

The following summer the Flyers traded the youngster to the San Jose Sharks. Determined to make it to the NHL, he reported to the Kentucky Thoroughblades in the fall of 1999. Hedberg had an excellent season, posting a razor-sharp .917 save percentage. However, he was outshone by his more heralded partner, Miikka Kiprusoff.

The competition for playing time was stiff. The Sharks had stockpiled a quartet of good young goalies, including Hedberg, Kiprusoff, Evgeni Nabokov, and Vesa Toskala. With Toskala set to take over the reins in Kentucky, Hedberg was assigned to Manitoba. Toiling in relative anonymity, the 27-year-old put up solid numbers for the Moose.

His fortunes were about to take a dramatic turn for the better. Buoyed by the return of Mario Lemieux, the Pittsburgh Penguins hoped to make a run at the Stanley Cup. However, they lacked a top-flight goaltender to lead the way. Unbeknown to Hedberg, Penguins assistant general manager Eddie Johnston had scouted the plucky goalie and liked what he saw. On March 12, 2001, the Pens acquired Hedberg from the Sharks for Jeff Norton.

Dubbed "Moose" for the cartoon image of a moose on his mask, the unassuming Hedberg quickly became a darling of the Mellon Arena faithful. He also proved to be quite a find. Posting a sterling 7–1–1 record, he backstopped his new team to a third-place finish in the Atlantic Division.

Hedberg was brilliant through the first two rounds of the playoffs. Outplaying his more established counterparts Olaf Kolzig and Dominik Hasek, he led the Penguins past the Capitals and Sabres to a berth in the Conference Finals. Although the Pens were vanquished by the Devils in five games, it did nothing to detract from the rookie's stunning achievements.

In his first full season in 2001–02, Hedberg was a tower of strength. Appearing in a then-team-record 66 games, he registered 25 wins, a 2.75 goals-against average, and six shutouts—the second-highest total in club history.

Unfortunately, the cash-strapped Penguins were in the midst of a precipitous decline. Suffering through an injury-plagued 2002–03 campaign, Hedberg's play slipped a bit. After just two short seasons in Pittsburgh, the Penguins released him.

Although his time as a starter was over, Moose served as an effective backup for Vancouver and Dallas. In the summer of 2006 he signed a free-agent deal with the Atlanta Thrashers. Thanks to his superb conditioning, determination, and unselfish nature, Hedberg provided strong relief work for the Thrashers.

On April 10, 2010, the veteran goalie turned in a sparkling 33-save performance to blank the Penguins 1–0. The loss knocked his former team out of first place in the Atlantic Division.

Herron, Denis

Penguins: 1972–75, 1976–79, 1982–86
Birthplace: Chambly, Quebec
Goaltender   B: June 18, 1952
Catches: left   **Ht.** 5-11 **Wt.** 165

		Regular Season						Playoffs			
YR	GP	MINS	GA	SH	AVE	GP	MINS	GA	SH	AVE
1972–73	18	967	55	2	3.41	-	-	-	-	-
1973–74	5	260	18	0	4.15	-	-	-	-	-
1974–75	3	108	11	0	6.11	-	-	-	-	-
1976–77	34	1920	94	1	2.94	3	180	11	0	3.67
1977–78	60	3534	210	0	3.57	-	-	-	-	-
1978–79	56	3208	180	0	3.37	7	421	24	0	3.42
1982–83	31	1707	151	1	5.31	-	-	-	-	-
1983–84	38	2028	138	1	4.08	-	-	-	-	-
1984–85	42	2193	170	1	4.65	-	-	-	-	-
1985–86	3	180	14	0	4.67	-	-	-	-	-
NHL	**462**	**25608**	**1579**	**10**	**3.70**	**15**	**901**	**50**	**0**	**3.33**

When 20-year-old goalie Denis Herron earned a spot on the 1972 Penguins, he made National Hockey League history. The rail-thin rookie was the first goalie to make the jump directly from junior hockey to the NHL.

Herron played well enough to challenge Jim Rutherford, another good young netminder, for the starting job. Sharing the goaltending duties with his more seasoned partner, Herron posted a solid 3.41 goals-against average and two shutouts. However, the Pens decided he needed some seasoning, so they sent him to Hershey midway through the season.

His size, or lack of it, was a major concern. Worried that the 165-pounder would wear down over the course of a full season, Penguins trainers made sure Herron drank his share of milkshakes.

Denis Herron makes a big save. The undersized goalie served three tours of duty with the Pens.

Rutherford was dealt to Detroit in January of 1974, paving the way for Herron to assume the starting job. However, Gary Inness took over between the pipes. Surprisingly, the Penguins soon gave up on their prized prospect. On January 10, 1975, general manager Jack Button traded him to Kansas City for veteran puck-stopper Michel Plasse.

Playing for a weak Scouts team, Herron established himself as a bona fide starter. Dispelling the notion that he couldn't carry a heavy workload, he appeared in 64 games in 1975–76.

The following summer Herron returned to the Steel City as a free agent. Although he suffered a broken arm in the 1976–77 season opener, he returned to register 15 wins and a sparkling 2.94 goals-against average.

For the next two seasons Herron was a bulwark between the pipes. He appeared in 116 games and backstopped the Pens to the Stanley Cup Quarterfinals in 1979.

The Montreal Canadiens were looking for a goaltender to replace their legendary ace, Ken Dryden, who had retired during the summer. They set their sights on Herron. With promising youngster Greg Millen waiting in the wings, the Pens sent Herron to the Habs for Pat Hughes and backup Rob Holland.

With the addition of Herron, the Canadiens had a quartet of goalies—including Michel Larocque, Richard Sevigny, and Rick Wamsley—vying for the starting job. While the ex-Penguin performed well—sharing the Vezina Trophy in 1981 and leading the league with a 2.64 goals-against average the following year—he failed to emerge as the full-time starter.

Seeking to pare down their glut of goalies, Montreal shipped Herron back to Pittsburgh on September 15, 1982, for a third-round draft choice. With Denis and All-Star incumbent Michel Dion guarding the net, the Pens boasted what appeared to be one of the better goaltending tandems in the league.

However, Herron's third tour of duty with the club would prove to be his most difficult. Unaccustomed to tending goal in a shooting gallery following his "easy" years in Montreal, his goals-against average more than doubled to a whopping 5.31. Nonplussed, the veteran netminder soon regained his form and wrestled the starting job from Dion. Backstopping one of the worst teams in NHL history—the hapless 1983–84 "Boys of Winter"—he managed a respectable 4.08 goals-against mark.

By his final season in 1985–86, Herron had slipped to third on the depth chart behind youngster Roberto Romano and veteran Gilles Meloche. He appeared in just three regular-season games. However, he enjoyed one final moment in the spotlight. On January 4, 1986, Herron was given the starting nod when the Pens squared off against Dynamo Moscow in a Super Series exhibition match. Playing before a sellout crowd at the Civic Arena, the 34-year-old goalie stood on his head to earn a 3–3 tie for the Penguins.

Rutherford, Jim

Penguins: 1971–74   **Birthplace:** Beeton, Ontario
Goaltender   **B:** February 17, 1949
Catches: left   **Ht.** 5-8 **Wt.** 168
Nicknames: Roach, Rut

| | | Regular Season | | | | | Playoffs | | | |
YR	GP	MINS	GA	SH	AVE	GP	MINS	GA	SH	AVE
1971–72	40	2160	116	1	3.22	4	240	14	0	3.50
1972–73	49	2660	129	3	2.91	-	-	-	-	-
1973–74	26	1432	82	0	3.44	-	-	-	-	-
NHL	**457**	**25895**	**1576**	**14**	**3.65**	**8**	**440**	**28**	**0**	**3.82**

As a youngster growing up in Beeton, Ontario, Jim Rutherford was all too aware of his limitations. Standing just 5'8" and tipping the scales at a meager 160 pounds, he did not have the size to fill the net like larger goalies. Nor did he possess the cat-like quickness of a Jacques Plante. Instead, he relied on solid positioning, a decent glove hand, and plain old-fashioned guts and determination.

Those qualities served him well during his junior hockey career with Hamilton. After filling a backup role in 1967–68, Rutherford blossomed into an OHA First Team All-Star in his final season. Duly impressed, the Detroit Red Wings made the diminutive netminder the 10th overall pick at the 1969 Amateur Draft.

After cutting his professional hockey teeth with Ft. Worth of the Central Hockey League, Rutherford made the big club in 1970–71. Unfortunately, his arrival coincided with a Red Wings collapse. Struggling to meet expectations, the youngster endured a so-so rookie campaign.

Seeking an experienced goalie, Detroit plucked combative veteran Al Smith off the Penguins' roster during the 1971 Intra-League Draft. The Pens promptly snapped up the 22-year-old Rutherford.

He proved to be a terrific acquisition. Pushing aside veterans Les Binkley and Roy Edwards to claim the starting job, Rutherford paced the Pens in appearances (40), wins (17), and goals-against average (3.22). He compiled a winning record—no small feat on a team that finished 12 games under the break-even mark.

Although the Penguins were swept aside in four straight games by Chicago in the playoffs, the spunky goalie enjoyed an outstanding series.

In 1972–73 Rutherford had the best season of his career. Playing in 49 games, he recorded a sparking 2.91 goals-against average and tied Binkley's club record with 20 wins. For good measure, he also posted three shutouts.

Rutherford continued to do a solid job during the first half of 1973–74. However, the Penguins nosedived and were badly in need of an overhaul. With 21-year-old Denis Herron and Gary Inness waiting in the wings, general manager Jack Button shipped Rutherford back to the Red Wings for giant defenseman Ron Stackhouse.

Shown here guarding the Red Wings' net, Jim Rutherford provided the Pens with solid goaltending in the early 1970s.

He performed admirably in the Motor City, beating back the challenges of veterans Ed Giacomin and Ron Low to hang on to the Red Wings' starting job for four seasons. In February of 1976 he registered three straight shutouts to tie a club record established by Hall of Famer Glenn Hall. Rutherford was finally supplanted in 1978 by high-profile free agent Rogie Vachon.

Following his playing career, Jim served as a manager for Compuware Sports Corporation. In 1994 he was appointed general manager of the lowly Hartford Whalers. Displaying the same bulldog determination he exhibited as a goalie, Rutherford slowly built the Whalers/Hurricanes into a Stanley Cup champion.

Wregget, Ken

Penguins: 1992–98   **Birthplace:** Brandon, Manitoba
Goaltender   B: March 25, 1964
Catches: left   **Ht.** 6-1 **Wt.** 201
Nicknames: Mikey, Wreggs

		Regular Season						Playoffs		
YR	GP	MINS	GA	SH	AVE	GP	MINS	GA	SH	AVE
1991–92	9	448	31	0	4.15	1	40	4	0	6.00
1992–93	25	1368	78	0	3.42	-	-	-	-	-
1993–94	42	2456	138	1	3.37	-	-	-	-	-
1994–95	38	2208	118	0	3.21	11	661	33	1	3.00
1995–96	37	2132	115	3	3.24	9	599	23	0	2.30
1996–97	46	2514	136	2	3.25	5	297	18	0	3.64
1997–98	15	611	28	0	2.75	-	-	-	-	-
NHL	575	31663	1917	9	3.63	56	3341	160	3	2.87

Supersub Ken Wregget dives to smother a loose puck.

The Penguins were more than a little familiar with goaltender Ken Wregget prior to his arrival in the Steel City. Filling in for an injured Ron Hextall, Wregget stoned the Pens in Game 7 of the 1989 Patrick Division Finals to lead the Flyers to an upset victory.

Fast-forward to February of 1992. Hoping to pull his team out of a tailspin, Penguins general manager Craig Patrick engineered a huge five-player trade with Philadelphia. Among the three players he received was Wregget.

Initially, the 27-year-old goalie appeared to be little more than a throw-in. The Pens were well-stocked in goal, boasting Stanley Cup winner Tom Barrasso and capable backups Frank Pietrangelo and Wendell Young.

Wregget soon changed that perception. After providing solid support for Barrasso through 1993, he stepped into a more prominent role in 1993–94. Splitting time with his more heralded partner, Wregget posted a solid 3.37 goals-against average and 21 wins.

He was even better during the strike-shortened 1994–95 campaign. Thrust into the starting job due to Barrasso's hand injury, Wregget responded with 25 victories to lead all NHL goalies.

Stylistically, he wasn't the prettiest netminder to watch. A cross between a standup goalie and a flopper, Wregget was best described as a scrambler. He had a curious habit of turning off-angle toward the post on face-offs—much like a batter in baseball with an extreme open stance. But he was very effective.

In 1995–96, Barrasso and Wregget once again served as goalies 1 and 1A. While Barrasso shouldered most of the load, Wregget logged 20 wins and topped the team with a 3.24 goals-against average and three shutouts.

At his best in big games, Wregget enjoyed his moment of glory that spring during the Eastern Conference Quarterfinals. Entering the pivotal fourth game, the Penguins trailed Washington 2–1. When Barrasso went down with back spasms early in the contest, coach Eddie Johnston summoned Wregget from the bench. Although he

hadn't played in nearly two weeks he turned in a brilliant performance, stopping 53 of 54 shots (including 42 in overtime) to lead the Penguins to a marathon quadruple-overtime triumph over the Capitals. He went on to win six out of eight starts before yielding to Barrasso in the Conference Finals.

Following another injury-plagued season, Barrasso finally returned to full health in 1997–98, pushing the popular Wregget into a reduced role. The following summer the Penguins traded him to Calgary for forward German Titov. As he had done in Pittsburgh, the veteran goalie provided solid relief work for the Flames before moving on to Detroit. Wregget finished his career with the Manitoba Moose before retiring in 2001.

He ranks third on the Penguins' all-time list behind Barrasso and Marc-Andre Fleury in regular-season wins (104) and playoff wins (13). Not bad for a "backup" goalie.

66 Plus 21 Makes 87

In honor of Penguins captain Sidney Crosby, we've included brief biographies on 21 players who didn't quite make the "Select 66," bringing the total number of featured players to 87. Some, such as Vic Hadfield, Pete Mahovlich, and Luc Robitaille, were All-Star performers for other NHL teams. Others were very good players who enjoyed long and distinguished careers. All are deserving of recognition.

Randy Cunneyworth trades punches with the Devils' Claude Loiselle (19).

Bodger, Doug

Penguins: 1984–88   **Birthplace:** Chemainus, British Columbia
Defense   **B:** June 18, 1966
Shoots: left   **Ht.** 6-2 **Wt.** 210

TOTALS	Regular Season					Playoffs				
	GP	G	A	PTS	PM	GP	G	A	PTS	PM
Penguins	299	35	132	167	292	-	-	-	-	-
NHL	**1071**	**106**	**422**	**528**	**1007**	**47**	**6**	**18**	**24**	**25**

Selected in the same draft class as Mario Lemieux, Doug Bodger earned full-time work with the Penguins as an 18-year-old blue-liner. Possessing good offensive skills, the smart, heady rearguard averaged 40 points per year during four-plus seasons with the Pens. Traded for Tom Barrasso in 1988, Bodger never played a game in the minor leagues during his 16-year pro career.

Boutette, Pat

Penguins: 1981–84   **Birthplace:** Windsor, Ontario
Left wing   **B:** March 1, 1952
Shoots: left   **Ht.** 5-8 **Wt.** 175
Nickname: Booter

TOTALS	Regular Season					Playoffs				
	GP	G	A	PTS	PM	GP	G	A	PTS	PM
Penguins	247	65	109	174	548	5	3	1	4	8
NHL	**756**	**171**	**282**	**453**	**1354**	**46**	**10**	**14**	**24**	**109**

A feisty little forward, Pat Boutette came to Pittsburgh from Hartford as compensation for Greg Millen. Skating on a line with top scorers Paul Gardner and Rick Kehoe, he piled up 23 goals and 74 points in 1981–82 while providing a welcome physical presence. One of the last Penguins to play without a helmet, "Booter" was traded back to the Whalers in 1984 for Ville Siren.

Cunneyworth, Randy

Penguins: 1985–89   **Birthplace:** Etobicoke, Ontario
Left wing/Right wing   **B:** May 10, 1961
Shoots: left   **Ht.** 6-0 **Wt.** 198

TOTALS	Regular Season					Playoffs				
	GP	G	A	PTS	PM	GP	G	A	PTS	PM
Penguins	295	101	115	216	513	11	3	5	8	26
NHL	**866**	**189**	**225**	**414**	**1280**	**45**	**7**	**7**	**14**	**61**

Tough and wiry, Randy Cunneyworth played left wing with the intensity of a pit bull terrier. Acquired from Buffalo in 1985 for Pat Hughes, he averaged 25 goals per year during his four seasons with the Pens, including a career-best 35 in 1987–88. Cunneyworth was traded to Winnipeg in 1989 with Dave McLlwain and Rick Tabaracci for Randy Gilhen, Jim Kyte, and Andrew McBain.

Gardner, Paul

Penguins: 1980–84   **Birthplace:** Toronto, Ontario
Center   **B:** March 5, 1956
Shoots: left   **Ht.** 6-0 **Wt.** 195

TOTALS	Regular Season					Playoffs				
	GP	G	A	PTS	PM	GP	G	A	PTS	PM
Penguins	207	98	105	203	105	10	2	5	7	10
NHL	**447**	**201**	**201**	**402**	**207**	**16**	**2**	**6**	**8**	**14**

The son of Hockey Hall of Famer Cal Gardner, Paul Gardner was an established NHL scorer when he arrived in Pittsburgh in 1980. A slow skater, Gardner compensated by planting himself in the slot and scoring on rebounds and deflections. On December 13, 1980, he became the first Penguin ever to score four goals in one game. After averaging nearly 33 goals per year over three seasons, Gardner fell off a ladder and sustained two broken heels. The injuries effectively ended his NHL career.

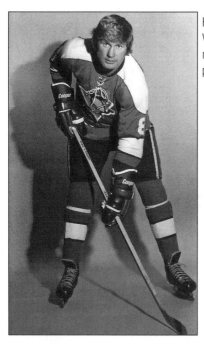

Former Rangers captain Vic Hadfield twice reached the 30-goal plateau for the Pens.

Hadfield, Vic

Penguins: 1974–77   **Birthplace:** Oakville, Ontario
Left wing   B: October 4, 1940
Shoots: left   **Ht.** 6-0 **Wt.** 190

TOTALS	Regular Season					Playoffs				
	GP	G	A	PTS	PM	GP	G	A	PTS	PM
Penguins	163	61	79	140	118	12	5	2	7	11
NHL	**1002**	**323**	**389**	**712**	**1154**	**73**	**27**	**21**	**48**	**117**

In one of the team's best trades ever, Vic Hadfield was acquired from the Rangers in the summer of 1974 for Nick Beverley. A former Rangers captain and 50-goal scorer, the veteran left wing reached the 30-goal mark twice for the Pens while playing a key role on the power play. Knee injuries forced Vic to retire in 1977.

Kelly, Bob

Penguins: 1974–77   **Birthplace:** Fort William, Ontario
Left wing   B: June 6, 1946
Shoots: left   **Ht.** 6-2 **Wt.** 195
Nickname: Battleship

TOTALS	Regular Season					Playoffs				
	GP	G	A	PTS	PM	GP	G	A	PTS	PM
Penguins	250	69	85	154	462	15	6	3	9	23
NHL	**425**	**87**	**109**	**196**	**687**	**23**	**6**	**3**	**9**	**40**

Bob Kelly arrived in a big trade from St. Louis in January 1974 with Steve Durbano and Ab DeMarco. One of the league's toughest and most respected fighters, "Battleship" also possessed a deft scoring touch. During his three and a half seasons in Pittsburgh, the rangy left wing served as an effective deterrent while notching 69 goals. He signed as a free agent with Chicago in 1977.

Lang, Robert

Penguins: 1997–02   **Birthplace:** Teplice, Czechoslovakia
Center   B: December 19, 1970
Shoots: right   **Ht.** 6-3 **Wt.** 216
Nickname: Langer

TOTALS	Regular Season					Playoffs				
	GP	G	A	PTS	PM	GP	G	A	PTS	PM
Penguins	345	103	158	261	96	45	7	12	19	6
NHL	**989**	**261**	**442**	**703**	**422**	**91**	**18**	**28**	**46**	**24**

Following a disappointing start to his NHL career, Robert Lang joined the Penguins in 1997. The big center fulfilled his promise in Pittsburgh, averaging more than 50 points per year with the Pens. Lang enjoyed his finest season in 2000–01, notching 32 goals and 80 points while skating on a line with Alexei Kovalev and Martin Straka. He signed a free-agent deal with Washington in 2002.

Lee, Peter

Penguins: 1977–83   **Birthplace:** Ellesmere, United Kingdom
Right wing   B: January 2, 1956
Shoots: right   **Ht.** 5-9 **Wt.** 180

TOTALS	Regular Season					Playoffs				
	GP	G	A	PTS	PM	GP	G	A	PTS	PM
Penguins	431	114	131	245	257	19	0	8	8	4
NHL	**431**	**114**	**131**	**245**	**257**	**19**	**0**	**8**	**8**	**4**

Peter Lee arrived with Pete Mahovlich from Montreal in 1977 in the big trade for Pierre Larouche. A streaky scorer, the speedy little winger twice reached the 30-goal mark for the Pens, sandwiched around lesser seasons of 16 and 18 goals. After leaving Pittsburgh, Lee starred for a dozen years in Germany.

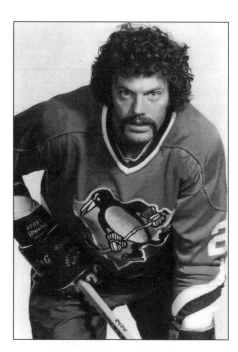

Bob "Battleship" Kelly was one of the most feared fighters in hockey.

Big Pete Mahovlich joins the rush.

Mahovlich, Pete

Penguins: 1977–79   **Birthplace:** Timmins, Ontario
Center   B: October 10, 1946
Shoots: left   **Ht.** 6-5   **Wt.** 210
Nickname: Little M

	Regular Season					Playoffs				
TOTALS	GP	G	A	PTS	PM	GP	G	A	PTS	PM
Penguins	117	39	75	114	76	2	0	1	1	0
NHL	884	288	485	773	916	88	30	42	72	134

The younger brother of Hall of Famer Frank "Big M" Mahovlich, Pete was acquired from Montreal in 1977 for Pierre Larouche. A former Pittsburgh Hornet, the tall, rangy center enjoyed an outstanding first season with the Pens, tallying 25 goals and 61 points in only 57 games. Although Mahovlich suffered through an injury-plagued 1978–79 campaign, he still managed a respectable 53 points in 60 games. Following the season he was traded to Detroit for Nick Libett.

McCreary, Keith

Penguins: 1967–72   **B:** June 19, 1940
Left wing   D: December 9, 2003
Shoots: left   **Ht.** 5-10   **Wt.** 180
Birthplace: Sundridge, Ontario

	Regular Season					Playoffs				
YR	GP	G	A	PTS	PM	GP	G	A	PTS	PM
Penguins	292	82	59	141	199	11	0	4	4	6
NHL	532	131	112	243	294	16	0	4	4	6

An original Penguin, Keith McCreary was plucked from the Montreal Canadiens in the 1967 Expansion Draft. After a solid first season with the Pens, McCreary paced the club with 25 goals in 1968–69. Although he never wore the "C," the scrappy, hardworking left wing emerged as one of the team's early leaders. McCreary was claimed by Atlanta in the 1972 Expansion Draft, where he served as the Flames' first captain.

McEachern, Shawn

Penguins: 1992–95   **Birthplace:** Waltham, Massachusetts
Right wing/Center   B: February 28, 1969
Shoots: left   **Ht.** 5-11   **Wt.** 200

	Regular Season					Playoffs				
TOTALS	GP	G	A	PTS	PM	GP	G	A	PTS	PM
Penguins	170	53	59	112	78	48	6	11	17	24
NHL	911	256	323	579	506	97	12	25	37	62

Drafted out of Matignon High School in Massachusetts, Shawn McEachern first made an impact with the Penguins during the 1992 Stanley Cup Playoffs. The following year, the speedy winger enjoyed a fine rookie season, piling up 28 goals and 61 points. McEachern scored 53 goals during two tours of duty with the team before being traded to Boston in 1995.

Nedved, Petr

Penguins: 1995–97   **Birthplace:** Liberec, Czechoslovakia
Right wing/Center   B: December 9, 1971
Shoots: left   **Ht.** 6-3   **Wt.** 196

	Regular Season					Playoffs				
TOTALS	GP	G	A	PTS	PM	GP	G	A	PTS	PM
Penguins	154	78	92	170	134	23	11	12	23	28
NHL	982	310	407	717	708	71	19	23	42	64

Gifted but enigmatic, Petr Nedved was a question mark when he arrived in Pittsburgh during the summer of 1995. The speedy winger quickly dispelled any concerns about his ability, notching career highs of 45 goals and 99 points in 1995–96. However, after striking for 33 goals the following season, he entered into a protracted contract dispute that lasted more than a year. He was traded to the Rangers in November of 1998 for Alexei Kovalev.

Quinn, Dan

Penguins: 1986–90, 1996   **Birthplace:** Ottawa, Ontario
Center   B: June 1, 1965
Shoots: left   **Ht.** 5-11   **Wt.** 182

TOTALS	Regular Season					Playoffs				
	GP	G	A	PTS	PM	GP	G	A	PTS	PM
Penguins	270	111	165	276	224	11	6	3	9	10
NHL	**805**	**266**	**419**	**685**	**533**	**65**	**22**	**26**	**48**	**62**

Dan Quinn arrived in the Steel City in 1985 following a big trade with Calgary for Mike Bullard. A power-play wizard, the slender center averaged more than 30 goals and nearly 80 points per year during his three and a half seasons in Pittsburgh. A close friend of Mario Lemieux, Quinn returned in 1996 to finish his career with the Penguins.

Robitaille, Luc

Penguins: 1994–95   **Birthplace:** Montreal, Quebec
Left wing   B: February 17, 1966
Shoots: left   **Ht.** 6-1   **Wt.** 215
Nickname: Lucky

TOTALS	Regular Season					Playoffs				
	GP	G	A	PTS	PM	GP	G	A	PTS	PM
Penguins	46	23	19	42	37	12	7	4	11	26
NHL	**1431**	**668**	**726**	**1394**	**1177**	**159**	**58**	**69**	**127**	**174**

"Lucky Luc" arrived in 1994 via a trade with Los Angeles for Rick Tocchet. Skating for the club during the lockout-shortened 1994–95 season, Robitaille finished second to Jaromir Jagr with 23 goals. The future Hall of Famer was dealt to the Rangers over the off-season, robbing him of a chance to play alongside Mario Lemieux.

Rupp, Duane

Penguins: 1969–73   **Birthplace:** MacNutt, Saskatchewan
Defense   B: March 29, 1938
Shoots: left   **Ht.** 6-1   **Wt.** 195

TOTALS	Regular Season					Playoffs				
	GP	G	A	PTS	PM	GP	G	A	PTS	PM
Penguins	265	21	83	104	170	10	2	2	4	8
NHL	**374**	**24**	**93**	**117**	**220**	**10**	**2**	**2**	**4**	**8**
WHA	**115**	**3**	**42**	**45**	**78**	**7**	**0**	**2**	**2**	**0**

Sporting a bristling Fu Manchu mustache, Duane Rupp patrolled the Penguins' blue line for four-plus seasons in the early 1970s. Big for his day at 6'1" and 195 pounds, Rupp played a steady, stay-at-home brand of defense. Under coach Red Kelly, he gradually developed his offensive skills, tying the club record for points by a defenseman in 1970–71. While a member of the team, he opened Rupp's Sporting Goods in suburban Pittsburgh.

Samuelsson, Kjell

Penguins: 1992–95   **Birthplace:** Tingsryd, Sweden
Defense   B: October 18, 1958
Shoots: right   **Ht.** 6-6   **Wt.** 235
Nicknames: Sammy

TOTALS	Regular Season					Playoffs				
	GP	G	A	PTS	PM	GP	G	A	PTS	PM
Penguins	183	10	22	32	312	44	0	7	7	72
NHL	**813**	**48**	**138**	**186**	**1225**	**123**	**4**	**20**	**24**	**178**

Kjell Samuelsson made his Pittsburgh debut following a big three-team trade in February of 1992. Blessed with a gigantic wingspan, the hulking defenseman made life miserable for opposing forwards with his smothering style of play. For three-plus seasons the ex-Flyer anchored the Pens' defense before returning to Philadelphia.

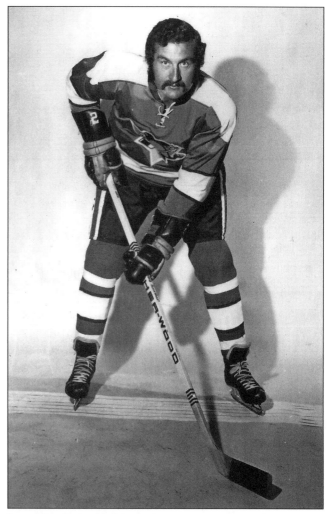

Duane Rupp displays his defensive form.

Sandstrom, Tomas

Penguins: 1994–97 **Birthplace:** Jakobstad, Finland
Right wing **B:** September 4, 1964
Shoots: left **Ht.** 6-2 **Wt.** 205
Nickname: Tommie Gun

TOTALS	Regular Season					Playoffs				
	GP	G	A	PTS	PM	GP	G	A	PTS	PM
Penguins	172	71	84	155	168	36	7	5	12	50
NHL	983	394	462	856	1193	139	32	49	81	183

Acquired from the Kings in 1994 for Marty McSorley, Tomas Sandstrom gave the Penguins two strong seasons. In 1994–95 the abrasive winger tallied 21 goals and 44 points—third-best on the team. The following year he overcame a rash of injuries to score 35 goals in only 58 games. When his production declined in 1996–97, he was traded to Detroit for Greg Johnson.

Shedden, Doug

Penguins: 1981–86 **Birthplace:** Wallaceburg, Ontario
Right wing **B:** April 29, 1961
Shoots: right **Ht.** 6-0 **Wt.** 185

TOTALS	Regular Season					Playoffs				
	GP	G	A	PTS	PM	GP	G	A	PTS	PM
Penguins	332	123	159	282	148	-	-	-	-	-
NHL	416	139	186	325	176	-	-	-	-	-

Doug Shedden was an underrated scorer during his four and a half seasons with the Penguins. In 1982–83, at the age of 21, the hard-shooting right wing paced the Pens with 67 points. After topping the 30-goal mark for two straight seasons, the Wallaceburg, Ontario, native was traded to Detroit for Ron Duguay in March of 1986.

Whitney, Ryan

Penguins: 2005–09 **Birthplace:** Boston, Massachusetts
Defense **B:** February 19, 1983
Shoots: left **Ht.** 6-4 **Wt.** 219
Nickname: Whits

TOTALS	Regular Season					Playoffs				
	GP	G	A	PTS	PM	GP	G	A	PTS	PM
Penguins	253	34	116	150	223	25	2	6	8	31
NHL	354	41	158	199	305	38	3	11	14	40

Chosen by the Penguins with the fifth overall pick in the 2002 Entry Draft, Ryan Whitney had all the tools. Big, strong, and mobile, he possessed a terrific shot and good playmaking skills. The product of Boston University enjoyed an outstanding season in 2006–07, rolling up 14 goals and 59 points. Due in part to a congenital foot problem, Whitney regressed over the next two seasons. He was traded to Anaheim in February of 2009 for Chris Kunitz and Eric Tangradi.

Zalapski, Zarley

Penguins: 1988–91 **Birthplace:** Edmonton, Alberta
Defense **B:** April 22, 1968
Shoots: left **Ht.** 6-1 **Wt.** 215
Nicknames: Double Z, ZZ Top

TOTALS	Regular Season					Playoffs				
	GP	G	A	PTS	PM	GP	G	A	PTS	PM
Penguins	190	33	102	135	160	11	1	8	9	13
NHL	637	99	285	384	684	48	4	23	27	47

A "can't-miss" prospect, Zarley Zalapski was taken fourth overall by the Pens in the 1986 Entry Draft. Named after PGA pro golfer Kermit Zarley, he was blessed with tremendous speed and agility. The offensive-minded rearguard tallied 33 goals and 135 points in nearly three full seasons with the club. In March of 1990, "ZZ Top" was dealt to Hartford along with John Cullen as part of "the Trade."

Zubov, Sergei

Penguins: 1995–96 **Birthplace:** Moscow, USSR
Defense **B:** July 22, 1970
Shoots: right **Ht.** 6-1 **Wt.** 198
Nickname: Zubie

TOTALS	Regular Season					Playoffs				
	GP	G	A	PTS	PM	GP	G	A	PTS	PM
Penguins	64	11	55	66	22	18	1	14	15	26
NHL	1068	152	619	771	337	164	24	93	117	62

Sergei Zubov was acquired from the Rangers in the summer of 1995 in the trade that sent Luc Robitaille and Ulf Samuelsson to New York. Flashing his supreme offensive skills, the smooth-skating defenseman tallied 11 goals and 55 assists for the Pens in 1995–96. Following the season, "Zubie" was traded to Dallas for Kevin Hatcher.

Michel Therrien barks out instructions. The fiery skipper guided the team to 135 wins—the second-highest total of any Penguins coach.

The Coaches and General Managers

During the Penguins' long and storied history, 26 men have served as coaches and general managers. The men who guided the team's fortunes include some of the greatest minds in hockey history. Hall of Famers such as Scotty Bowman, Bob Johnson, and Craig Patrick all played pivotal roles in building a championship organization.

The Penguins' first management team consisted of general manager Jack Riley and coach Red Sullivan. An experienced hockey man, Riley had served as the GM of the Rochester Americans and later as the president of the American Hockey League. A former Rangers captain and coach, the fiery Sullivan was highly regarded.

Although a favorite of Riley's, "Sully" would last only two seasons. He was replaced in 1969 by another redhead—iconic Hall of Famer Red Kelly. Under the popular and jovial Irishman, the Pens earned two playoff berths. For a time Kelly served as the club's general manager, bumping Riley to club president.

Next in line was the team's career scoring leader, Ken Schinkel, who hung up his skates when Kelly was dismissed in January of 1973. While "Schink" had no previous coaching experience, he served two moderately successful terms behind the bench.

The team enjoyed its greatest early success under the tandem of Jack Button and Marc Boileau. Wholly capable, Button quickly built the team into a contender through a series of savvy trades. Nicknamed "Popeye" for his feisty nature, Boileau supplied a spark from the bench. However, a crushing playoff loss to the Islanders in 1975 signaled the end for the popular duo.

Following a brief transition period under Wren Blair, Baz Bastien assumed the GM reins in 1976. During the Bastien era, the Penguins specialized in quick-fix trades and heartbreaking postseason defeats under coaches Johnny Wilson and Eddie Johnston.

Johnston stepped forward to take over the GM duties after Bastien's tragic death in 1983.

Determined to break with the team's tradition of dealing draft choices for veterans, he shrugged off a series of tempting offers in favor of selecting Mario Lemieux. The move was widely hailed for saving the franchise.

Under EJ's watchful eye, the team slowly began to improve. In 1987, however, he chose Pierre Creamer to replace Bob Berry at the Pens' helm. Although a capable hockey man, Creamer struggled with English. The team missed the playoffs for the sixth straight season, sealing Johnston and Creamer's fate.

After a short run under Tony Esposito and Gene Ubriaco, the Penguins entered their golden age when the DeBartolo family hired Craig Patrick in 1989. Patrick immediately brought stability and a winning attitude to the Penguins' front office. Trading brilliantly, he quickly built the Penguins into Stanley Cup champions.

Patrick presided over the team's fortunes for 17 years, making him the longest-tenured general manager in club history. During the 1990s, he hired skillfully—bringing highly regarded coaches such as Johnson, Bowman, Kevin Constantine, and Herb Brooks to the Steel City.

However, the funk that hit the team in the new millennium adversely affected Patrick. His choice of Czech coaching legend Ivan Hlinka proved to be a disaster. Rick Kehoe was an able hockey man better suited to scouting. While popular and likeable, Ed Olczyk was a virtual novice when he assumed the reins in 2003.

In the summer of 2006 president and CEO Ken Sawyer replaced Patrick with bright young executive Ray Shero. Under Shero's stewardship, the Penguins blossomed into a Cup contender. When the club stumbled in 2008–09 he moved boldly, replacing holdover coach Michel Therrien with Dan Bylsma. Although unproven, the 38-year-old Bylsma proved to be the right tonic, leading the team to Stanley Cup glory.

Coach Profiles

1967–69

Sullivan, George "Red"

Record: 47–79–24 (.393)
Birthplace: Peterborough, Ontario
B: December 24, 1929

	Regular Season						Playoffs			
	G	W	L	T	PTS	PCT	G	W	L	PCT
1967–68	74	27	34	13	67	.453	-	-	-	-
1968–69	76	20	45	11	51	.336	-	-	-	-
Penguins	**150**	**47**	**79**	**24**	**118**	**.393**	-	-	-	-
NHL	**364**	**107**	**198**	**59**	**273**	**.375**	-	-	-	-

During his playing career, Red Sullivan earned a reputation as a fiery competitor who would do anything to help his team win. Regarded by some as a dirty player, the peppery center had a nasty habit of charging into goalies. Montreal star Jacques Plante was a favorite target.

It was only a matter of time before Sullivan got his comeuppance. As a member of the Rangers he ran over Plante once too often. Habs defenseman Doug Harvey speared him in the stomach, rupturing the little redhead's spleen. Near death, he received last rites from a Catholic priest.

Miraculously, Sullivan recovered from his injuries to skate four more seasons with the Blueshirts. He served as team captain until a nine-goal season in 1960–61 convinced him that his playing career was on the wane.

Rangers general manager Muzz Patrick loved Sullivan. Impressed with his leadership skills and winning attitude, he encouraged Red to try his hand at coaching. After serving a brief apprenticeship in the minors, Sullivan was called to New York to assume the coaching reins from Patrick in 1962–63.

It was not an easy transition. Retired for only two seasons, the 33-year-old Sullivan was coaching players he had recently skated with. The senior member of the team happened to be Doug Harvey—the same Doug Harvey who had nearly killed him six years earlier.

The Rangers enjoyed little success during Sullivan's tenure. An aging team in transition, they limped to a pair of fifth-place finishes in a six-team league. When the team got off to a slow start in 1965–66, Red was replaced by Emile Francis.

Sullivan re-entered the coaching ranks in 1966 when Jack Riley offered him the Penguins job. Since "Sully" had skated with or against many of the players who would be available in the Expansion Draft, his input was highly valued.

Not coincidentally, eight former Rangers—including ex-teammates Andy Bathgate, Earl Ingarfield, and Ken Schinkel—made the inaugural Penguins squad. The team even borrowed from the Rangers' uniform style, choosing to display "Pittsburgh" in diagonal block letters across the front of the jersey instead of its skating penguin logo.

A veteran club that boasted two future Hall of Famers, the 1967–68 Penguins were expected to compete for the West Division crown. Following a decent start, however, they fell out of the pack and spent most of the season in fifth place. A four-game winning streak to close the campaign brought the Pens to the brink of a playoff spot, but it was not enough. They missed the postseason by a mere two points.

Losing never sat well with the ultracompetitive Sullivan. More often than not, he would vent his frustrations at the team's star players. When Riley traded the team's captain and leading goal scorer, Ab McDonald, to St. Louis during the off-season for Lou Angotti, he applauded the move. However, when Sullivan tried to shift Angotti to right wing, the former Flyers captain angrily stalked out of training camp. Similar in makeup and temperament, the two butted heads all season long.

Relations between Sullivan and scoring leader Andy Bathgate were strained as well. The star winger quit the team before the first puck was dropped in 1968–69, setting the tone for a truly miserable season.

While the team engaged in a season-long struggle to stay out of the cellar, Penguins fans voiced their displeasure. "Sully Must Go" signs adorned the Civic Arena like championship banners. Despite another late push the Pens finished tied for fifth, some 25 games under the break-even mark. Sullivan's fate was sealed.

Still highly regarded by Riley, he agreed to stay on as a scout. In a backhanded way, Sullivan had found his true calling. An outstanding judge of talent, the well-liked Irishman served as a bird dog for several NHL teams over the next 25 years before retiring at the end of the 1992–93 season.

On the night of April 8, 2010, the 80-year-old Sullivan made a triumphant return to the Steel City to help the team celebrate the final regular-season game at the Mellon Arena. Taking part in the pregame ceremony, Sully was introduced to an adoring throng along with his old friend and former boss, Jack Riley.

1969–73

Kelly, Leonard "Red"

Record: 90–132–52 (.423)
Birthplace: Simcoe, Ontario
B: July 9, 1927

	Regular Season						Playoffs			
	G	W	L	T	PTS	PCT	G	W	L	PCT
1969–70	76	26	38	12	64	.421	-	-	-	-
1970–71	78	21	37	20	62	.397	10	6	4	.600
1971–72	78	26	38	14	66	.423	4	0	4	.000
1972–73	42	17	19	6	40	.476	-	-	-	-
Penguins	**274**	**90**	**132**	**52**	**232**	**.423**	**14**	**6**	**8**	**.429**
NHL	**742**	**278**	**330**	**134**	**690**	**.465**	**62**	**24**	**38**	**.387**

Over the course of his Hall of Fame playing career, Red Kelly established himself as one of the finest players in the history of the game. A defenseman by trade, he helped the Red Wings win four Stanley Cups in the 1950s, in the process earning a Norris Trophy, three Lady Byng Trophies, and First-Team All-Star honors five years in a row.

Following a controversial trade to Toronto in 1960, he was converted to center by Punch Imlach. Thanks to his excellent playmaking skills and strong defensive foundation, he became one of the best two-way centers in the business, garnering a fourth Lady Byng Trophy. Skating beside fellow Hall of Famer Frank Mahovlich, he led the Leafs to four Stanley Cups. The gentleman hockey player also served two terms in the Canadian Parliament.

After winning his eighth Stanley Cup with the Leafs in 1967, Red had nothing left to prove on the ice. Seeking a new challenge, the 40-year-old Kelly negotiated a deal to become the first coach of the expansion Los Angeles Kings.

Nothing much was expected of the Kings, who were considered to be the weakest of the expansion teams. Although he had never coached on a professional level, Kelly surprised everyone by guiding the club to a strong second-place finish in the West Division. The team slipped to fourth the following year, but made it to the Stanley Cup Semifinals before bowing to St. Louis.

Concerned over the way the Kings were being managed, Kelly left Los Angeles in the summer of 1969 to assume the coaching reins in Pittsburgh. The sad-sack Penguins had missed the playoffs in each of their first two seasons. Once again Kelly fooled the experts, piloting an undermanned but spirited club to a second-place finish and a berth in the semis. Although the "Pesky Pens" fell to the Blues in a hotly contested six-game set, Kelly's achievements earned him Coach of the Year honors.

Penguins owner Donald Parsons immediately rewarded Red with a promotion to the dual role of coach and general manager. Although he did a good job as GM—adding talented young players such as Syl Apps, Dave Burrows, and

Can I Get a Witness?

Entering their first-ever playoff game on April 8, 1970, Red Kelly's Penguins were slight favorites to beat their West Division rivals, the Oakland Seals.

Determined to get a jump on the Seals before their hometown fans, the Pens drew first blood on a goal by Jean Pronovost. However, Oakland soon knotted the score. The game morphed into a tight defensive struggle, with neither team giving an inch.

In the waning moments of the third period, light-scoring Nick Harbaruk took advantage of heavy traffic around Oakland goalie Gary Smith to pot the game winner. The Seals cried foul, claiming one of Kelly's players was in the crease when the puck went in. They insisted the game films would prove their point.

Normally a paragon of diplomacy, the Penguins' coach quashed Oakland's hopes for a reprieve.

"We don't lend out our game films," Kelly wryly noted.

Greg Polis—the extra responsibilities seemed to affect his coaching. The Penguins tumbled to a sixth-place finish in 1970–71.

When the team staggered to a poor start the next season, it was clear something had to be done. Seeking to ease Red's workload, new owner Tad Potter handed the general manager duties back to Jack Riley. The move worked like a charm. Free to concentrate on coaching, Kelly led the resurgent Pens to a 14–9–5 finish during the final two months of the season to qualify for postseason play.

Creative and resourceful, Kelly was exceedingly popular among his players. Lowell MacDonald, who also played for Red in Los Angeles, was a big fan. "I never met a classier individual than Red Kelly," he recalled for Jim O'Brien in *Penguin Profiles*. "People said he was too easy, but when you look back only one thing counts—the decency of a human being."

Unfortunately, popularity wasn't translating into wins—at least not enough to suit Riley. With the Pens mired in a 2–7–3 slide that threatened to remove them from playoff contention, he fired Kelly on January 10, 1973.

The genial Irishman would have the last laugh. The next season he returned to Toronto to take over the Maple Leafs. Outfoxing the man who replaced him, Ken Schinkel, he guided the Leafs to first-round playoff victories over the Penguins in 1976 and 1977.

1973–74; 1976–77

Schinkel, Ken

Record: 83–92–28 (.478)
Birthplace: Jansen, Saskatchewan
B: November 27, 1932

	Regular Season						Playoffs			
	G	W	L	T	PTS	PCT	G	W	L	PCT
1972–73	36	15	18	3	33	.458	-	-	-	-
1973–74	50	14	31	5	33	.330	-	-	-	-
1975–76	37	20	10	7	47	.635	3	1	2	.333
1976–77	80	34	33	13	81	.506	3	1	2	.333
Penguins	**203**	**83**	**92**	**28**	**194**	**.478**	**6**	**2**	**4**	**.333**
NHL	**203**	**83**	**92**	**28**	**194**	**.478**	**6**	**2**	**4**	**.333**

Ken Schinkel addresses the team at training camp.

Through the Penguins' early years, Ken Schinkel was a strong, consistent presence. A leader both on and off the ice, the two-time West Division All-Star served for a time as the team's assistant captain.

It was precisely those qualities that led to a premature end to his playing career. In 1972–73 the 40-year-old "Schink" was enjoying a typically solid season. But on January 13, 1973, he was asked to retire in order to assume the coaching duties from Red Kelly.

The fact that Schinkel was highly respected and well liked by his former teammates helped ease the transition. They performed about as well for him as they had under Kelly, going 15–18–3 down the homestretch.

With a full off-season to prepare, Schinkel felt confident he could guide the team to a playoff spot. However, the 1973–74 Penguins sputtered out of the starting gate. Despite his best attempts to motivate the team, Schinkel couldn't coax a solid effort from his players. The Pens responded to a couple of big trades in January by winning three games in a row. However, when the club slipped into a five-game tailspin, general manager Jack Button replaced Schinkel with Marc Boileau.

Despite his failure to produce a winner, the Penguins' brass thought highly of Schinkel. He stayed with the organization as a scout through the next two seasons. However, by January of 1976 the club was once again in dire straits. With the season rapidly slipping away, Schinkel was summoned from the front office to replace Boileau.

His calm, low-key approach was a welcome change from his predecessor's frenetic style. In a complete reversal of form, the Penguins bolted through the final 37 games at a 20–10–7 clip, including an 11-game unbeaten streak. Although they were upset by Toronto in the opening round of the playoffs, Schinkel's job was secure.

He did some of his finest work the following season. From the drop of the first puck, the Penguins were plagued by injuries to key players. Facing his stiffest challenge, Schinkel transformed the formerly freewheeling Pens into a strong defensive team. He also earned the players' respect for standing up to talented but temperamental superstar Pierre Larouche. The team responded with a record of 34–33–13, a highly respectable mark given the rash of injuries.

Although Schinkel had done a solid job during his second stint behind the Penguins' bench, he found the rigors of coaching too stressful. He resigned in the summer of 1977 and moved back into the front office. Schink served the team in various capacities over the next dozen years, including scouting director and assistant general manager. One of his biggest thrills occurred in 1984 when the team drafted Mario Lemieux.

"For me, he's one of the top one or two players that ever played in the league as far as talent, and that's saying a lot when you talk about the Gordie Howes, Rocket Richards, and Wayne Gretzkys," Schinkel said.

In 1989 he followed Eddie Johnston to Hartford, where he served as the Whalers' assistant general manager for several seasons. After retiring, Schinkel moved to Bonita Springs, Florida. He remained active, coaching local hockey teams and doing radio color commentary for the Florida Everblades of the East Coast Hockey League.

1974–76

Boileau, Marc

Record: 66–61–24 (.517)
Birthplace: Pointe Claire, Quebec
B: September 3, 1932
D: December 27, 2000

	Regular Season						Playoffs			
	G	W	L	T	PTS	PCT	G	W	L	PCT
1973–74	28	14	10	4	32	.571	-	-	-	-
1974–75	80	37	28	15	89	.556	9	5	4	.556
1975–76	43	15	23	5	35	.407	-	-	-	-
Penguins	151	66	61	24	156	.517	9	5	4	.556
NHL	151	66	61	24	156	.517	9	5	4	.556
WHA	140	74	61	5	153	.546	17	12	5	.706

Fiery Marc Boileau piloted the Pens to their first winning season in 1974–75.

As a promising young center for the St. Jerome Eagles of the Quebec Junior Hockey League, Marc Boileau was greatly admired by his teammates for his work ethic and desire. The gritty teenager hoped to one day follow in the footsteps of his father Rene, who had played for the New York Americans in the 1920s.

Following a long, eight-year apprenticeship in hockey outposts such as Fort Wayne, Indianapolis, and Seattle, Boileau realized his dream in 1961–62 when he made the Detroit Red Wings. Nicknamed "Popeye" for his fiercely competitive nature, the 29-year-old rookie tallied 11 points in 54 games while filling a defensive role.

Boileau had waited an eternity for a chance to play in the NHL. By contrast, his rise to big-league coach was positively meteoric. Less than three years after he accepted his first coaching job, Boileau was promoted by Penguins general manager Jack Button in February of 1974 to breathe life into his moribund team.

The fiery skipper did just that. Prior to his arrival, the Pens were 14–31–5. Following his arrival they went 14–10–4.

To honor the new coach, Civic Arena organist Vince Lascheid broke into a rendition of "Popeye the Sailor" after each Penguins victory. During the 1974–75 campaign the refrain was musical spinach to Boileau's ears. Blessed with a supercharged lineup that featured nine 20-goal scorers, he led the club to an impressive record of 37–28–15 (the best in the team's eight-year history).

Paced by "the Century Line" of Syl Apps, Lowell MacDonald, and Jean Pronovost, the Penguins had the look of a legitimate Cup contender. After sweeping St. Louis in two games, they cruised to three straight victories over the callow New York Islanders. A berth in the Stanley Cup semifinals seemed imminent. Then the unthinkable occurred. The Pens lost four in a row to blow the series. Worse yet, the team was forced into receivership.

Assuming he was out of a job, Boileau began to seek employment elsewhere. However, the Penguins were purchased by a new group of owners, who moved quickly to retain his services.

Still loaded with firepower, the team was largely unchanged from the previous year. During an interview with *Sports Illustrated*, Boileau made it clear he expected more from his squad.

"What we need is one guy to kick fannies in our dressing room," he said. "Why is it that we lose to the Flyers in Philadelphia by scores of 4–0, 6–0, and 9–0 but beat them in Pittsburgh by scores of 6–1 and 8–2? Character! We don't have enough character yet."

The chemistry between the coach and his players quickly dissolved. As the Pens sank deeper in the standings, Boileau's famous temper was often on display. Following a dismal 4–1 loss to the Flyers on January 15, 1976, he was replaced by the man he had succeeded—Ken Schinkel.

Undaunted by his failure with the Penguins, Boileau quickly restored his reputation. The next season he guided the Quebec Nordiques to the WHA's Avco Cup. At the final WHA All-Star Game in 1978 he led the Nordiques to a thrilling 5–4 victory over a team of all-stars. As feisty as ever, Boileau was reported to have engaged in a scuffle with Winnipeg coach Bobby Kromm during a meeting intended, ironically, to explore ways of curbing league violence.

Boileau and the Nordiques parted ways in 1979. With the demise of the WHA, he returned to his roots and coached for several seasons in the IHL and WHL.

On December 27, 2000, the old coach went out for a skate with his children. He planned to watch Mario Lemieux's triumphant comeback on television that night, but he never made it home. His heart finally gave out.

1977–80

Wilson, Johnny

Record: 91–105–44 (.471)
Birthplace: Kincardine, Ontario
B: June 14, 1929

	Regular Season						Playoffs			
	G	W	L	T	PTS	PCT	G	W	L	PCT
1977–78	80	25	37	18	68	.425	-	-	-	-
1978–79	80	36	31	13	85	.531	7	2	5	.286
1979–80	80	30	37	13	73	.456	5	2	3	.400
Penguins	**240**	**91**	**105**	**44**	**226**	**.471**	**12**	**4**	**8**	**.333**
NHL	**517**	**187**	**241**	**89**	**463**	**.448**	**12**	**4**	**8**	**.333**
WHA	**158**	**56**	**93**	**9**	**121**	**.383**	**3**	**0**	**3**	**.000**

Growing up in the wintry mining community of Rouyn-Noranda, Quebec, young Johnny Wilson learned the value of hard work and consistency. They were qualities that would serve him well during the course of a professional playing and coaching career that spanned 34 years.

A key member of Detroit's great Stanley Cup teams of the 1950s, the rugged youngster served as a grinding, no-frills left wing on a team laden with stars. While he possessed an underrated scoring touch, twice topping the 20-goal mark, he was greatly valued for his steady, two-way play. The NHL's original iron man, the tough, durable winger set a league record (since broken) by skating in 580 consecutive games.

Following a long apprenticeship, Wilson returned to the Motor City in 1971 to assume the Red Wings' coaching job. Although he led Detroit to a winning record over the next two seasons, he was axed by unpopular general manager Ned Harkness in the summer of 1973—a move that drew tons of criticism from the Red Wings faithful.

Over the next few seasons Wilson became somewhat of a vagabond, serving a series of one-year assignments in the WHA before returning to the NHL in 1976–77 with the Colorado Rockies. Wilson finally got an opportunity to establish some roots when his friend, Baz Bastien, brought him to Pittsburgh in 1977.

When Wilson arrived in the Steel City, the team was undergoing a massive rebuilding program. High-profile stars such as Syl Apps, Pierre Larouche, and Ron Schock were shipped out in favor of scrappy newcomers Gene Carr, Pete Mahovlich, Dave Schultz, and Brian Spencer.

No fan of fancy hockey, the changes suited Wilson just fine. He preferred his teams to play a simple, straightforward game, much as he had during his playing days. Unfortunately, the Penguins had parted with a little too much talent. Wilson's first team finished a distant fourth with an uninspired record of 25–37–18.

The Penguins fared much better in 1978–79. Reinforced by a host of battle-hardened veterans, the club took second place in the Norris Division while posting the second-best record in team history to date. Although the plucky Pens were bounced out in the Stanley Cup quarterfinals, Wilson appeared to have found a home in Pittsburgh.

However, the fortunes of an NHL coach can turn on a dime, and Wilson was no exception. He guided the team through a solid first half in 1979–80, but seemed at a loss when the club nosedived to a lackluster 14–26–2 mark over the last 42 games.

"You guys have been playing since you were five years old," he told his charges, "so go out there and play."

In fairness to Wilson, the Penguins lost key players Orest Kindrachuk and Greg Malone, which contributed greatly to the team's poor showing. But the injuries exposed Wilson as an old-school coach who lacked creativity and imagination. Following the season the former iron man was replaced by Eddie Johnston.

His failure to produce a winner in Pittsburgh signaled the end of Wilson's NHL coaching career. The next season he was in Springfield, where he guided the Indians to a sub-.500 record. It proved to be his swan song.

Former NHL iron man Johnny Wilson directs a practice session.

1980–83; 1993–97

Johnston, Eddie

Record: 232–224–60 (.508)
Birthplace: Montreal, Quebec
B: November 24, 1935

	Regular Season						Playoffs			
	G	W	L	T	PTS	PCT	G	W	L	PCT
1980–81	80	30	37	13	73	.456	5	2	3	.400
1981–82	80	31	36	13	75	.469	5	2	3	.400
1982–83	80	18	53	9	45	.281	-	-	-	-
1993–94	84	44	27	13	101	.601	6	2	4	.333
1994–95	48	29	16	3	61	.635	12	5	7	.417
1995–96	82	49	29	4	102	.622	18	11	7	.611
1996–97	62	31	26	5	67	.540	-	-	-	-
Penguins	**516**	**232**	**224**	**60**	**524**	**.508**	**46**	**22**	**24**	**.478**
NHL	**596**	**266**	**251**	**79**	**611**	**.513**	**53**	**25**	**28**	**.472**

Eddie Johnston served two terms as coach. During his second stint at the helm "EJ" posted a .600 winning percentage.

During an NHL career that spanned 16 seasons, Eddie Johnston seemed to have more lives than a cat. One of the last goalies to play without a mask, he once suffered three broken noses over a 10-day stretch. On Halloween night in 1968 he was struck in the temple by an errant shot during pregame warm-ups. It nearly killed him. Two months later he returned to action, backstopping Boston to a 2–2 tie with the North Stars.

"EJ" displayed a similar resilience after moving into management. He was replaced three times during his coaching career and twice as a general manager. But he always found another job—often with the same team.

"I've been so blessed," he said.

Johnston certainly paid his dues. As an anglophile growing up in Montreal's rugged West End, he boxed against neighborhood toughs and convicts. Fortunately, he showed enough promise as a goaltender to give up pugilism. After toiling in the minors for several seasons, he received his break in 1962 when the Bruins claimed him from Chicago in the Intra-League Draft.

The 27-year-old Johnston quickly established himself. In 1963–64 he played in every minute of every Bruins game—the last NHL goalie to do so. In the early 1970s he won two Stanley Cups while sharing the netminding chores with Gerry Cheevers.

After hanging up his skates in 1978, EJ stepped into coaching. In his first year at the helm of an NHL team he guided the Black Hawks to the Smythe Division title. He was let go, however, following a dispute with Chicago GM Bob Pulford.

In the market for a bright young coach, the Penguins immediately hired Johnston. It was the start of a long and memorable 23-year relationship between EJ and the organization.

Although the Pens of the early 1980s were a less-than-imposing bunch, Johnston kept the team competitive during his first go-round as coach. The key to the club's modest success was the power play, which Johnston had learned one night at a Boston bar from former Celtics star Tommy Heinsohn. Using the basketball pick play, the Pens struck for a whopping 272 power-play goals over a three-year span.

Following Baz Bastien's untimely death in 1983, Johnston assumed the role of general manager. In his first season on the job he earned lasting fame—and a permanent place in the hearts of Steel City fans—by ensuring the Pens would be in a position to draft Mario Lemieux.

"Drafting Mario, we wouldn't have a franchise here if we'd taken somebody else," he said.

EJ did a solid job during his five years as the team's GM. He drafted brilliantly, adding promising young players Doug Bodger, Craig Simpson, and Zarley Zalapski to the fold. But the DeBartolo family, weary of missing the playoffs, decided to go in a different direction in 1988. They hired Tony Esposito, a contemporary of Johnston's, while EJ was demoted to assistant general manager. Following the 1988–89 season he left Pittsburgh to take over as the Hartford Whalers' general manager.

Johnston made a triumphant return to Pittsburgh in the summer of 1993, when the Penguins brought him back as a replacement for Scotty Bowman. Finally given a chance to coach a competitive team, he led the Penguins to a .600 winning percentage over three-plus seasons and a berth in the 1996 Eastern Conference Finals.

After being bumped upstairs to the post of assistant general manager in March of 1997, Johnston continued to serve the team in a variety of capacities. In 1999 he stepped behind the bench one last time as an assistant to coach Herb Brooks. Following the season he returned to the front office as a special advisor, a post he held through the team's Stanley Cup triumph in 2009.

The sight of the grandfatherly Johnston hoisting the Cup was truly one of the most heartwarming moments in team history. It also provided a perfect ending to a career that spanned more than 50 years.

"What a way for me to go out," he said. "It's time. They have such a great hockey staff in place now."

1983–84

Angotti, Lou

Record: 16–58–6 (.238)
Birthplace: Toronto, Ontario
B: January 16, 1938

	Regular Season						Playoffs			
	G	W	L	T	PTS	PCT	G	W	L	PCT
1983–84	80	16	58	6	38	.238	-	-	-	-
Penguins	**80**	**16**	**58**	**6**	**38**	**.238**	-	-	-	-
NHL	**112**	**22**	**78**	**12**	**56**	**.250**	-	-	-	-

Leadership roles were nothing new to Lou Angotti. A feisty checking center who carved out a 13-year pro career, he had served as the first team captain of the Philadelphia Flyers. Immediately following his playing career, he coached the St. Louis Blues for parts of two seasons. Prior to his promotion to Pittsburgh in 1983, he'd served as the bench boss for the Penguins' AHL affiliates in Erie and Baltimore.

Nothing, however, could have prepared him for the trial he was about to endure. The 1983–84 Penguins were terrible—easily one the worst non-expansion teams of all time. Opening the season with only a handful of legitimate big-league players, "the Boys of Winter" were essentially a minor league club competing in the National Hockey League.

Whether the Penguins were constructed that way on purpose by general manager Eddie Johnston in order to draft Laval phenom Mario Lemieux was a topic of hot debate. But the team's deplorable play clearly took a toll on Angotti.

Prior to a late-season contest with equally putrid New Jersey, Devils president Bob Butera twanged the wrong nerve.

"I'm not being accusatory," Butera said, "but I think the Penguins' talent is better than they've shown."

Lou Angotti presided over the dreadful 1983–84 "Boys of Winter." The Pens finished dead last—and earned the right to draft Mario Lemieux.

Following a brawl-filled 6–5 Devils victory, a clearly frustrated Angotti erupted in response.

"Bob Butera's got no [expletive] class," he fumed. "What he said about our team is a disgrace. We do everything we can to win every game we can."

The Penguins survived the season (barely) and selected Lemieux with the first overall pick of the 1984 Entry Draft. The same could not be said for Angotti, who was clearly burned out following the ordeal. Although he became a member of the Pens' scouting staff, he never coached again.

Years later Angotti admitted what had long been suspected—the Penguins had, indeed, tanked the season to get Lemieux. In a 2004 interview with Chuck Finder of the *Pittsburgh Post-Gazette*, he said the plan was hatched during a midseason lunch meeting with Johnston.

"If Pittsburgh hadn't gotten Mario Lemieux that year, I think the franchise would've folded," he said. "We didn't actually try to throw games. But, you know, we went in there with the understanding…we weren't going to be upset if we lost."

1984–87

Berry, Bob

Record: 88–127–25 (.419)
Birthplace: Montreal, Quebec
B: November 29, 1943

	Regular Season						Playoffs			
	G	W	L	T	PTS	PCT	G	W	L	PCT
1984–85	80	24	51	5	53	.331	-	-	-	-
1985–86	80	34	38	8	76	.475	-	-	-	-
1986–87	80	30	38	12	72	.450	-	-	-	-
Penguins	**240**	**88**	**127**	**25**	**201**	**.419**	-	-	-	-
NHL	**860**	**384**	**355**	**121**	**889**	**.517**	**33**	**11**	**22**	**.333**

Following an outstanding collegiate career at Sir George Williams College, Bob Berry enjoyed a solid seven-year NHL career with the Los Angeles Kings. A smart, creative left wing, he topped the 20-goal mark five times, including a career-best 36 in 1972–73.

Highly respected for his leadership on and off the ice, Berry was a natural to join the coaching ranks. Although he had no previous coaching experience, Kings general manager George Maguire hired the 35-year-old Berry to guide the Kings upon his retirement as a player in 1978.

Receiving what amounted to a serious dose of on-the-job training, Berry proved to be more than capable of handling the coaching duties. In his third season behind the bench the Kings registered a 99-point season to finish a strong second in the Norris Division.

Viewed as one of the brightest young coaches in hockey, Berry was tapped to lead the most storied franchise in the

Bob Berry instructs his troops at a practice session. The Penguins improved under Berry, but not enough to make the playoffs.

NHL in 1981—the Montreal Canadiens. For the Montreal native, coaching the legendary Habs was the realization of a boyhood dream.

Only three years removed from their dynastic run of four straight Stanley Cups, expectations for the club were exceedingly high. All went according to form during the regular season, when the powerhouse Canadiens reeled off a 109-point season. In the opening round of the playoffs, however, they dropped a shocking five-game set to their bitter rivals, the Nordiques, in "the Battle of Quebec."

It was all downhill for Berry after that. As the Canadiens gradually dissolved into a mediocre team, the young coach took the heat. Amid a firestorm of criticism from the unforgiving Montreal press and fans, he was dismissed in February of 1984.

Fortunately for Berry, redemption arrived shortly after the season. Penguins general manager Eddie Johnston was seeking an experienced coach for his young team. Berry fit the bill perfectly.

Noting that the Penguins had leaked for an astronomical 390 goals, he announced, "We want to improve our defensive effort right away."

Thanks in large part to Berry's attention to detail, the Penguins did improve their defense—not to mention their overall play—during his three seasons in Pittsburgh. After registering 53 points during a difficult first year, they jumped to 76 points in 1985–86 while paring their goals against to a more palatable 305.

Unfortunately, Berry's Penguins also were prone to catastrophic late-season collapses. The 1984–85 team earned a respectable 38 points in the first half, followed by a pathetic 15 in the second half. In 1985–86 the Pens were virtually assured of a playoff berth until they blew a tire, winning just three of their final 16 games. The next year the team set a

club record with seven straight victories to open the season. They limped home eight games below the .500 mark. Johnston had little choice but to fire the veteran coach.

Experienced and knowledgeable, Berry wasn't out of work for long. In 1988 he joined the St. Louis Blues as an assistant coach. Eleven games into the 1992–93 campaign he replaced Bob Plager as the head man and guided the Blues to winning records and playoff berths in each of the next two seasons.

He continued to serve the Blues as an associate coach under Mike Keenan from 1994 through 1996 before joining the San Jose Sharks as an assistant in the late 1990s.

1987–88

Creamer, Pierre

Record: 36–35–9 (.506)
Birthplace: Chomedy, Quebec
B: July 6, 1944

	Regular Season						Playoffs			
	G	W	L	T	PTS	PCT	G	W	L	PCT
1987–88	80	36	35	9	81	.506	-	-	-	-
Penguins	**80**	**36**	**35**	**9**	**81**	**.506**	-	-	-	-
NHL	**80**	**36**	**35**	**9**	**81**	**.506**	-	-	-	-

After the Penguins missed the Stanley Cup Playoffs for the fifth year in a row in 1986–87, general manager Eddie Johnston dismissed veteran coach Bob Berry. As he searched for a replacement, the name of Pierre Creamer popped up on his radar screen.

Pierre Creamer follows the action from behind the Penguins' bench. Although he led the team to a winning record, Creamer was dismissed after one season.

The 43-year-old native of Chomedy, Quebec, was seen as a rising star among coaches. After leading Verdun to the Quebec Major Junior Hockey League title in 1983, Creamer was hired by Montreal to coach their top farm club in Sherbrooke. During three seasons at the helm, he guided the team to an American Hockey League championship and a second appearance in the Calder Cup Finals.

Armed with a glowing endorsement from Montreal general manager Serge Savard, Johnston named Creamer to be the Penguins' ninth head coach on June 4, 1987.

"Our target is the playoffs, no doubt on that," Creamer said.

However, as training camp opened that fall, it was apparent that Creamer was a less-than-ideal choice. Having never coached outside La Belle Province, he struggled mightily with the subtleties of English. Creamer's difficulty with the language, coupled with his awkward appearance and mannerisms, set him up as a target of ridicule among the players. Behind his back, they referred to him as "Fred Flintstone."

Following a sluggish start, the Penguins received a considerable boost when Eddie Johnston acquired former Norris Trophy winner Paul Coffey from Edmonton. A banner reading, "We've Got Coffey And Creamer And Now We Want The Cup," hung from a Civic Arena balcony.

Creamer was astute enough to make sure the All-Star defenseman shared the ice with Mario Lemieux at every opportunity. He also shifted Rob Brown, a slow-skating but offensively gifted center, to the right wing slot beside Mario. No. 66 responded by scoring 70 goals.

Unfortunately, a late-season incident sealed Creamer's reputation as a bungler. Believing a tie would keep the Penguins' flickering playoff hopes alive, he refused to pull goalie Steve Guenette during the late stages of a 6–6 overtime game with Washington. With the players in near revolt on the bench, he was informed on the headset by Johnston that the Penguins, indeed, needed a win. Creamer finally gave Guenette the signal to come off the ice, and Lemieux promptly potted the game winner.

Due in large part to the sterling play of Coffey and Lemieux—who won the Hart and Art Ross Trophies—the Penguins actually improved under Creamer, posting their first winning season in nine years. Alas, it was not enough to secure a playoff spot—or to save the embattled coach's job. On June 14, 1988, he was fired by the team's new general manager, Tony Esposito.

The tumultuous season in the Steel City affixed a permanent stain to Creamer's record and ended any chance he had for future employment in the NHL. In 1989–90 he assumed the coaching reins of the struggling Laval Titan from Paulin Bordeleau and led the team to a playoff berth. It was the last time, however, that he would coach a team at the professional or major junior level. A genuinely kindhearted man, he deserved a better fate.

Following his coaching career Creamer became actively involved with the Canadian Cancer Society. Starting in 1990, he and his brother-in-law, Hall of Famer Mike Bossy, sponsored the Bossy-Creamer Open, a popular fund-raising golf tournament.

1988–89

Ubriaco, Gene

Record: 50–47–9 (.514)
Birthplace: Sault Ste. Marie, Ontario
B: December 26, 1937

	Regular Season						Playoffs			
	G	W	L	T	PTS	PCT	G	W	L	PCT
1988–89	80	40	33	7	87	.544	11	7	4	.636
1989–90	26	10	14	2	22	.423	-	-	-	-
Penguins	**106**	**50**	**47**	**9**	**109**	**.514**	**11**	**7**	**4**	**.636**
NHL	**106**	**50**	**47**	**9**	**109**	**.514**	**11**	**7**	**4**	**.636**

As an undersized left wing during the pre-expansion era, Gene Ubriaco was an outstanding minor league scorer who never quite made the grade in the NHL. Ironically, his coaching career would follow a similar path.

Following a 12-year pro career that included a 114-game stint with the Penguins, the Sault Ste. Marie native joined the coaching ranks. Working his way up from the low minor leagues, "Ubie" was hired to coach Minnesota's top farm club, the South Stars, in 1981. It was the beginning of a four-year run that saw his teams average 43 wins per season. During that span he earned consecutive Coach of the Year honors.

Now a member of the Penguins organization, Ubriaco received his big break in 1988 when he was hired by new general manager and hometown acquaintance Tony Esposito to take over the Pens. Although he had no big-league coaching experience, the 50-year-old Ubriaco was confident he could improve the team's fortunes.

Ubriaco's brief tenure was a mixed bag. On the plus side, he had good instincts for line combinations and displayed a keen eye for undervalued talent. John Cullen blossomed into a big-time scorer on his watch. Likewise, he gave fringe players Phil Bourque, Bob Errey, and Troy Loney expanded roles. Ubriaco had the good sense to place the defensive-minded Errey on a line with big-time scorers Mario Lemieux and Rob Brown. The trio blossomed into the most dangerous combination in the league.

However, Ubriaco had a minor league mentality that rubbed the players the wrong way. He insisted on giving them nicknames, which they hated. Hardly a great tactician, he seemed at a loss when it came to teaching the finer points of the game. His basic philosophy—turn 'em loose and let 'em play—was reflected in the team's uneven performance. The Penguins scored 347 goals. They gave up 349.

He tried hard to be a players' coach. The gregarious skipper could often be seen with an arm draped around a player's shoulder, offering words of encouragement. Despite his best efforts, rumors circulated that the team had tuned him out.

Gene Ubriaco (background) agonizes over a missed opportunity.

Still, the Penguins reached some milestones during his first year. On February 2, 1989, they snapped a horrendous 42-game winless streak in Philadelphia with a 5–3 victory over the Flyers. After flirting with first place for much of the season, the Pens finished second in the Patrick Division to qualify for postseason play for the first time in seven years. Following a sweep of the Rangers, they gave a good showing in a competitive seven-game set against the battle-hardened Flyers.

Unfortunately, the strained relations between Ubriaco and the team quickly deteriorated the next season. With the Penguins floundering four games below the .500 mark and in near revolt, he was fired along with Esposito on December 5, 1989. Bitter over his treatment, he lashed out at stars Lemieux and Paul Coffey, whom he accused of deserting him.

"It was almost impossible to coach Lemieux," he said. "It was like trying to teach a shark table manners."

After being dismissed by the Penguins, Ubriaco returned to minor league coaching. He enjoyed a great deal of success during two seasons with the Atlanta Knights of the International Hockey League before joining the Chicago Wolves in 1994. Following two decent seasons behind the bench he was promoted to the dual post of director of hockey operations and assistant general manager. In 2009 he was named the team's senior advisor.

1989–90; 1997

Patrick, Craig

Record: 29–36–9 (.453)
Birthplace: Detroit, Michigan
B: May 20, 1946

| | Regular Season | | | | | | Playoffs | | | |
	G	W	L	T	PTS	PCT	G	W	L	PCT
1989–90	54	22	26	6	50	.463	-	-	-	-
1996–97	20	7	10	3	17	.425	5	1	4	.200
Penguins	**74**	**29**	**36**	**9**	**67**	**.453**	**5**	**1**	**4**	**.200**
NHL	**169**	**66**	**81**	**22**	**154**	**.456**	**22**	**8**	**14**	**.364**

During the 17 years he presided over the Penguins' fortunes, Craig Patrick earned his stripes as a Hall of Fame general manager. However, on two separate occasions he served as the team's coach.

Upon his arrival in December of 1989, Patrick immediately contacted USA hockey legend Bob Johnson about the Penguins' coaching job. "Badger Bob" agreed to take over the Pens' helm. Due to prior commitments, however, he would not be available until the summer of 1990.

No stranger to running a bench, Patrick had coached the Rangers during his first season in New York. He also had served as Herb Brooks' top assistant on the 1980 "Miracle on Ice" team. He decided to assume the Penguins' coaching duties for the remainder of the 1989–90 season.

Patrick's stint behind the bench gave him a bird's-eye view of the team's strengths and weaknesses. Convinced that his club lacked leadership, he acquired established pros Joe Mullen and Bryan Trottier following the season—moves that helped the team win two Stanley Cups.

Seven years later he returned to the Penguins' bench. Once again he gained valuable insight into the club's psyche. Noting how the team lacked focus and intensity, he hired bright young coach Kevin Constantine to provide structure and discipline.

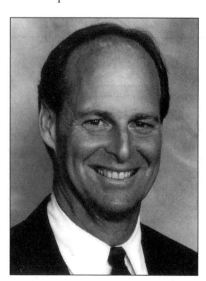

Known primarily for his stellar work as general manager, Craig Patrick coached the Pens for parts of two seasons.

1990–91

Johnson, Bob

Record: 41–33–6 (.550)
Birthplace: Minneapolis, Minnesota
B: March 4, 1931
D: November 26, 1991

| | Regular Season | | | | | | Playoffs | | | |
	G	W	L	T	PTS	PCT	G	W	L	PCT
1990–91	80	41	33	6	88	.550	24	16	8	.667
Penguins	**80**	**41**	**33**	**6**	**88**	**.550**	**24**	**16**	**8**	**.667**
NHL	**480**	**234**	**188**	**58**	**526**	**.548**	**76**	**41**	**35**	**.539**

Perhaps no individual left as indelible an imprint on Penguins hockey as the late Bob Johnson. His tenure was brief—tragically cut short by the brain tumor that would prematurely end his life. But during his stay he had a profound influence on those he touched.

Born on March 4, 1931, in Minneapolis, Minnesota, Johnson took to the ice like a duck to water. By age 13 he was already coaching—honing his teaching skills with a local midget team. A pretty fair player in his own right, Johnson was a star forward for the University of North Dakota and the University of Minnesota, where he led the Golden Gophers to two conference championships.

At the callow age of 25, Johnson was hired to coach Warroad High School. Earning a reputation as an excellent teacher and communicator, he quickly moved up the coaching ladder. In 1966 he became the coach of the University of Wisconsin. Under his steady hand, the Badgers became a powerhouse, capturing three national titles during his 15-year reign. It was there that he was given his enduring nickname—"Badger Bob."

During this period he helped put college hockey on the map. The NHL was dominated by players who had come up through the Canadian junior hockey leagues. Thanks in no small part to Johnson's success with the U.S. National teams, American colleges were soon acknowledged as a viable alternative to player development.

In 1982 Johnson made his grand entrance into the NHL when he took over as coach of the talented but underachieving Calgary Flames. With a lineup seasoned with American-born stars Joey Mullen, Joel Otto, and Gary Suter, he led the Flames to the Stanley Cup Finals in 1986.

Following a disappointing 1986–87 campaign, Johnson left the Flames to become executive director of USA Hockey. It appeared to be a match made in heaven. But in December of 1989 old friend Craig Patrick asked if he would be willing to coach the Penguins.

Although Johnson was unable to accept the offer at that time due to prior commitments, he agreed to take over the helm at the start of the 1990–91 season.

Upon his arrival in Pittsburgh, Badger Bob dove into his new assignment with his typical unbridled enthusiasm.

"Badger Bob" Johnson in a reflective moment. The beloved coach led the Penguins to their first Stanley Cup before succumbing to cancer.

"He created an atmosphere where you wanted to play for him and you wanted to win for him," Phil Bourque recalled. "And he taught us to play defense, something I never thought any coach could do."

By the sheer force of his personality, Johnson began to transform the Penguins from a group of talented individuals into champions. He became a surrogate father to many of the players, who found his positive, upbeat personality irrepressible.

"He approached every day with an enthusiasm that I've never seen in anyone except little children," Tom Barrasso noted. "He was able to translate his enthusiasm for life and hockey to the people around him."

The Pens had their tough times under Johnson, including a disastrous road trip in early March that left the club in peril of slipping out of playoff contention. Through it all the buoyant Badger remained the same—optimistic and wholly confident in his team's abilities.

The rest, as they say, is history. In rapid succession, the underdog Penguins gunned down the Devils, Capitals, Bruins, and North Stars—each in comeback fashion—to capture their first Stanley Cup.

A wave of adulation swept over Johnson and his players. Hopes were high for a second Cup victory the following season. While the Pens would go on to achieve this remarkable feat, they would accomplish it without their beloved mentor. For in the summer of 1991, he fell gravely ill—stricken with cancer.

After surgery and a courageous battle, Badger Bob passed away on November 26, 1991. To honor their fallen coach, one of his favorite sayings—"It's a Great Day for Hockey"—was emblazoned on the Civic Arena ice. It served as a constant reminder for all to be the best they could be each and every day.

Bob Johnson was inducted into the Hockey Hall of Fame in 1992.

1991–93

Bowman, Scotty

Record: 95–53–16 (.628)
Birthplace: Montreal, Quebec
B: September 18, 1933

	Regular Season							Playoffs			
	G	W	L	T	OL	PTS	PCT	G	W	L	PCT
1991–92	80	39	32	9	-	87	.544	21	16	5	.762
1992–93	84	56	21	7	-	119	.708	12	7	5	.583
Penguins	**164**	**95**	**53**	**16**	**-**	**206**	**.628**	**33**	**23**	**10**	**.697**
NHL	**2141**	**1244**	**573**	**314**	**10**	**2812**	**.657**	**353**	**223**	**130**	**.632**

Scotty Bowman was a rare breed. In terms of relations with his players, he was decidedly old-school. He felt a team performed at its best when it was on edge. To that end, he constantly challenged his players in an effort to keep them motivated.

"He was the captain of the first team I played for," Eddie Johnston recalled. "I was 16 or 17. He terrorized me."

In terms of strategy, however, he was an innovator. There may never have been a finer "in game" coach than Bowman. Rarely caught off guard by an opponent's tactics, he always seemed to be 10 steps ahead.

No one could argue with the results. Starting in 1968, Bowman-led teams appeared in the Stanley Cup Finals *eight times* during a 12-year span. His Montreal teams of the 1970s—among the greatest of all time—posted an extraordinary winning percentage of .734 over seven seasons and won five Cups.

In 1979–80 Bowman took over the helm of the Buffalo Sabres, serving as both coach and general manager. It was the one and only time during his storied career that success eluded him. By the end of his seven-year term the Sabres had dissolved into a losing team.

As incredible as it seemed, it would be several seasons before Bowman was given another opportunity to coach. He served as an analyst on CBC's *Hockey Night in Canada* until Penguins general manager Craig Patrick brought him to Pittsburgh in 1990. The hiring took on added significance the following summer when coach Bob Johnson was stricken with a brain tumor. In the wake of the tragedy, Patrick asked Bowman to step behind the Pens' bench.

Grasping the delicate nature of the situation, the veteran coach went easy on the players through the early going. However, as the Pens began to stumble in January, Bowman turned up the heat. He was especially critical of All-Star defenseman Paul Coffey—one of the team's most established and popular players.

The Penguins had a long history of rebelling against coaches. During a western road trip in March of 1992 their frustration boiled over. With Bowman spending an extra night at home in Buffalo, Patrick held a meeting with the

Intensely competitive hockey legend Scotty Bowman assumed the coaching duties from an ailing Bob Johnson and led the team to a Stanley Cup.

players. Many complained bitterly of Bowman's hard-line tactics. The Pens' GM listened, but urged the team to give Scotty a chance.

Following the meeting the tension seemed to ease. In the postseason, Bowman masterfully guided the Penguins to comeback victories over the Capitals and Rangers. With the coach and team in perfect sync, the Pens proceeded to sweep Boston and Chicago to win their second Stanley Cup.

In 1992–93 Bowman continued to push the right buttons. Despite losing Mario Lemieux to Hodgkin's disease for a third of the season, the Penguins soared to a 56-win campaign to capture the President's Trophy. However, the Pens lost their edge and fell to an inspired Islanders squad to end their hopes of a three-peat.

Unhappy with the way Patrick had insulated him from the players—electing to have assistants Rick Paterson and Barry Smith run the team's practices—Bowman entertained offers from other teams. When Patrick pressed him for a commitment, he balked. The Red Wings welcomed the Hall of Fame coach with open arms.

It was the start of a luminous second career for Bowman. Nearly matching his stunning achievements in Montreal, he guided Detroit to three Stanley Cups over a nine-year span before retiring in 2002 as the winningest coach in NHL history.

Still active in his seventies, Bowman moved to Chicago in 2008. Working alongside his son, Stan, he serves as the team's senior advisor of hockey operations.

1997–99

Constantine, Kevin

Record: 86–64–35–4 (.558)
Birthplace: International Falls, Minnesota
B: December 27, 1958

	Regular Season							Playoffs			
	G	W	L	T	OL	PTS	PCT	G	W	L	PCT
1997–98	82	40	24	18	-	98	.598	6	2	4	.333
1998–99	82	38	30	14	-	90	.549	13	6	7	.462
1999–00	25	8	10	3	4	23	.460	-	-	-	-
Penguins	**189**	**86**	**64**	**35**	**4**	**211**	**.558**	**19**	**8**	**11**	**.421**
NHL	**377**	**161**	**150**	**61**	**5**	**388**	**.515**	**50**	**21**	**29**	**.420**

Possessing a keen knowledge of the game, Kevin Constantine specialized in bringing order from chaos. An outstanding administrator and teacher, he developed a highly structured system of hockey that produced favorable results.

Born in International Falls, Minnesota, Constantine was a goaltender during his youth. He displayed enough promise to be selected by Montreal in the ninth round of the 1978 Entry Draft. However, after serving primarily as a backup at Rensselaer Polytechnic Institute, he decided to abandon his playing career in favor of coaching.

Following a successful start to his career at the amateur level, Constantine was named head coach of San Jose's top affiliate, the Kansas City Blades, in 1991. During his first season at the helm he led the Blades to an IHL-best 56 wins and the Turner Cup championship. Two years later he was tapped to replace George Kingston in San Jose.

Constantine's achievements in San Jose were truly remarkable. Under Kingston, the toothless Sharks had won a grand total of 28 games over two dismal seasons. In 1993–94, Constantine guided essentially the same collection of players to 33 victories, good for a jaw-dropping 58-point improvement. The Sharks pulled off a stunning upset in the opening round of the playoffs, knocking off Scotty Bowman's powerful Detroit Red Wings.

Regarded as the NHL's brightest young coach, Constantine enjoyed similar success the following season. However, in 1995–96 the Sharks—weary of Constantine's ultrademanding approach—staged a mutiny. With only three wins in 25 games, he was fired.

Although the bloom appeared to be off the rose, Constantine was granted a reprieve in 1997 when he was hired to coach the Penguins. In many ways, it was a perfect match. Stripped of many of their high-priced stars, the Pens were stocked primarily with players of ordinary pedigree. It was precisely the type of team that responded best to Constantine's systematic, disciplined style.

Following a now-familiar pattern, the Penguins performed well during Constantine's first two seasons. In 1997–98 they won 40 games and captured the Northeast Division title. The next year the club fought through

Kevin Constantine provided discipline and structure during his two-plus seasons as coach.

impending bankruptcy to earn a third-place finish in the tough Atlantic Division. Constantine cemented his reputation as a giant-killer, guiding the Pens to an opening-round upset over New Jersey. In the process, he became the first coach in NHL history to lead two eighth-seeded teams to first-round victories.

Once again, however, a Constantine-led team suffered burnout in his third season. Weary of the endless succession of meetings and video sessions, the Penguins stumbled through 25 games before general manager Craig Patrick made a coaching change.

"Some players were kind of not having fun anymore," Darius Kasparaitis confessed.

Never one to focus on the past, Constantine turned his considerable energies to founding a brand-new amateur team—the Pittsburgh Forge. Under Constantine's direction, the Forge posted an impressive 80–24–8 record during their two seasons in the North American Hockey League. However, on January 28, 2002, he was called back to the NHL to take over the coaching reins at New Jersey. A .500 team prior to Constantine's arrival, the Devils went 20–8–3 under their new coach. Unfortunately, an early playoff exit led to his dismissal.

In 2003 Constantine joined the Everett Silvertips of the Western Hockey League. During his four seasons at the Silvertips' helm, he led the team to a WHL Finals appearance while averaging 40 wins per year.

Following his successful run with the Silvertips, Constantine returned to the pro ranks in 2007–08 with the Houston Aeros of the American Hockey League. He was replaced during the summer of 2010 by former Pens assistant Mike Yeo.

First and foremost a teacher, Kevin created "Kevin Constantine's Total Hockey," an interactive instructional series designed to help young players learn the game.

1999–00

Brooks, Herb

Record: 29–21–5–2 (.570)
Birthplace: St. Paul, Minnesota
B: August 5, 1937
D: August 11, 2003

	Regular Season							Playoffs			
	G	W	L	T	OL	PTS	PCT	G	W	L	PCT
1999–00	57	29	21	5	2	65	.570	11	6	5	.545
Penguins	**57**	**29**	**21**	**5**	**2**	**65**	**.570**	**11**	**6**	**5**	**.545**
NHL	**506**	**219**	**219**	**66**	**2**	**506**	**.500**	**40**	**19**	**21**	**.475**

At age 62, Herb Brooks had settled quite comfortably into his post-coaching career. The United States hockey legend was serving as a scout for the Pittsburgh Penguins, which afforded him the opportunity to spend more time at home with his family.

However, in December of 1999 he received a phone call from Penguins general manager Craig Patrick. The team was badly underperforming under incumbent coach Kevin Constantine and needed a spark. Patrick asked his old friend and mentor to take over the coaching duties. Brooks agreed.

Under Constantine, the Penguins played a rigid, defensive system that served to stymie some of the team's star players like Jaromir Jagr and Alexei Kovalev. Brooks preferred a swirling, creative style that blended the best attributes of the North American and European games. A master motivator, he was famous for Brooks-isms such as "The legs feed the wolf" and "Hard work beats talent when talent doesn't work hard."

The Penguins flourished under the crafty old coach, going 10–3–1 in his first 13 games. An incident in Colorado on January 13, 2000, cemented his popularity with the players. In the late stages of a 4–3 loss to the Avalanche, Matthew Barnaby was knocked unconscious courtesy of a borderline hit by Aleksie Gusarov. When Avs play-by-play announcer John Kelly suggested Barnaby was faking it, Brooks went ballistic.

"Did you make that call on Barnaby?" Brooks shouted. "You say he has a tendency to embellish? What the hell kind of call was that?"

The tirade earned him a two-game suspension—and the undying admiration and respect of his team.

"It's just ridiculous," Barnaby said of Brooks' suspension. "He gets suspended indefinitely for standing up for one of his players."

With the team firmly united behind their coach, the Penguins finished in third place in the Atlantic Division. In the Stanley Cup Playoffs that spring, they stunned the heavily favored Capitals before bowing to the powerful Flyers in six games.

Despite the presence of coach-in-waiting Ivan Hlinka, Patrick would have undoubtedly welcomed Brooks back for

The mastermind of Team USA's "Miracle on Ice" triumph, Herb Brooks guided the Pens to a playoff berth in 2000.

another season. However, the mastermind of the "Miracle on Ice" elected to return to his role as scout.

In 2002 he came out of retirement one last time to lead the United States team to a silver medal at the Winter Olympics in Salt Lake City. Always in demand, he was courted by New York Rangers general manager Glen Sather. Brooks decided to remain with the Penguins, who named him as their director of player development.

Sadly, his life came to a tragic and untimely end on August 11, 2003, when he was killed in a car accident near Forest Lake, Minnesota. He was posthumously inducted into the Hockey Hall of Fame in 2006.

Although his time at the Penguins' helm was brief, Brooks made a lasting impression on his players.

"It was awesome," Ron Tugnutt recalled in an interview with the *Pittsburgh Post-Gazette*. "My oldest son, he goes, 'You played for Herb Brooks, Dad?' because he watched [the film *Miracle*] over and over again. He was a special man. He was totally different than everyone else. I really enjoyed playing for him."

2000–01

Hlinka, Ivan

Record: 42–32–9–3 (.558)
Birthplace: Most, Czechoslovakia
B: January 26, 1950
D: August 16, 2004

	Regular Season							Playoffs			
	G	W	L	T	OL	PTS	PCT	G	W	L	PCT
2000–01	82	42	28	9	3	96	.585	18	9	9	.500
2001–02	4	0	4	0	0	0	.000	-	-	-	-
Penguins	86	42	32	9	3	96	.558	18	9	9	.500
NHL	86	42	32	9	3	96	.558	18	9	9	.500

During an international career as a player and coach that spanned nearly 40 seasons, Ivan Hlinka established himself as a trailblazer. A star in his native Czechoslovakia, he became one of the first Czech-born players to skate in the National Hockey League. Years later he was the second European ever to be named head coach of an NHL team.

Hlinka began his career at the age of 16, skating with the Litvinov club of the Czech Extraliga. Standing 6'2" and weighing 220 pounds, the burly center quickly developed into a top-notch scorer. Blessed with excellent playmaking skills and a rapier-like wrist shot, he soon became known as Czechoslovakia's version of Boston great Phil Esposito.

Following a standout career with Litvinov, as well as with the Czech National and Olympic teams, Hlinka joined the Vancouver Canucks for the 1981–82 season. Proving that his international achievements were no fluke, he scored 23 goals and 60 points as an NHL "rookie." His sterling play helped propel the Canucks to a berth in the Stanley Cup Finals.

In 1983 Hlinka returned to Europe, where he starred for two seasons with EV Zug of the Swiss Nationalliga. After finishing his playing career with Litvinov in 1986–87, he became the team's coach. In the 1990s he assumed the helm of the Czech National Team. Hlinka's clubs became a consistent power on the international circuit, winning a slew of bronze medals.

The veteran Czech skipper enjoyed his finest hour at the 1998 Nagano Olympics. Guiding a team stocked with Penguins stars such as Jaromir Jagr, Jiri Slegr, and Martin Straka, he led the Czech team to a stunning gold-medal triumph. He reinforced his reputation the following year by capturing a second gold medal at the World Championships.

Seeking an experienced coach who could connect with Jagr and the team's other Czech stars, Penguins general manager Craig Patrick brought Hlinka to Pittsburgh in February of 2000. After serving a three-month apprenticeship as associate coach to another hockey legend, Herb Brooks, he was formally promoted to head coach in June of 2000.

Despite his proven track record in his native Czech Republic, the appointment was somewhat of a gamble. Although he had played in North America and was a fixture on the international scene, Hlinka spoke only halting English.

Still, the Penguins performed well under the grey-haired coach. They posted a solid 42–28–12 record and made it all the way to the Conference Finals before bowing to New Jersey. Of course, it didn't hurt that Mario Lemieux made a stirring comeback in midseason.

Fully aware that Jagr had played his last game in Pittsburgh, Patrick urged Hlinka to enroll in an English class over the summer. The proud old coach failed to comply, opting to listen to language tapes instead. Upon his arrival at the Penguins' 2001 training camp, it was apparent his command of English had not improved.

Stung by what amounted to insubordination, Patrick relieved Hlinka of the coaching duties only four games into the 2001–02 campaign.

Bitter over his dismissal, Hlinka filed a federal lawsuit against the team for breech of contract. After settling with the Penguins in May of 2002, he was reappointed coach of the Czech National Team. In the summer of 2004 he was

Ivan Hlinka addresses the press. The Czech coaching legend guided the Pens to the Conference Finals in 2001.

preparing to lead the team in the World Cup tournament. Sadly, he would not live to lead his team into action. Almost a year to the day after Brooks perished in a car accident, Hlinka met with a similar tragic fate. On August 16, 2004, he was driving near Karlovy Vary in the Czech Republic when he was involved in a head-on collision with a truck. The driver of the truck claimed he had swerved into Hlinka's lane to avoid hitting an animal. Regardless of the cause, the hockey world had lost one of its finest and most beloved coaches.

2001–03

Kehoe, Rick

Record: 55–81–14–10 (.419)
Birthplace: Windsor, Ontario
B: July, 15, 1951

	Regular Season							Playoffs			
	G	W	L	T	OL	PTS	PCT	G	W	L	PCT
2001–02	78	28	37	8	5	69	.442	-	-	-	-
2002–03	82	27	44	6	5	65	.396	-	-	-	-
Penguins	**160**	**55**	**81**	**14**	**10**	**134**	**.419**	-	-	-	-
NHL	**160**	**55**	**81**	**14**	**10**	**134**	**.419**	-	-	-	-

A quick glance at the Penguins' record book tells you all you need to know about Rick Kehoe the player. The numbers tell the story of a marvelously consistent scorer who racked up nine straight 20-goal seasons on the way to a Penguins total of 312—the fourth-highest mark in franchise history. Along the way, he played in two NHL All-Star Games and was awarded the Lady Byng Trophy.

Long-time assistant Rick Kehoe took over the Pens' helm in 2001.

As a scout and assistant coach, Kehoe approached his job with the same quiet consistency. He officially joined the Penguins' staff in 1986 and served the team effectively in a dual role for the next 15 years. In perhaps his most significant achievement, he worked long hours with Jaromir Jagr to help the youngster develop his lethal wrist shot.

Never one to seek the spotlight, Kehoe seemed content to wear an assistant's hat. However, in the fall of 2001 relations between general manager Craig Patrick and coach Ivan Hlinka had deteriorated to the point of no return. When Patrick dismissed the veteran Czech skipper four games into the season, Kehoe was promoted to head coach.

The move surprised Penguins watchers, who fully expected Herb Brooks or venerable Eddie Johnston to take over the reins, not the mild-mannered Kehoe. However, the veteran assistant seized the opportunity and made a strong impression.

"He's a competitor, an intense, high-energy guy," Patrick said.

"He's definitely tough," Kevin Stevens added. "He can be as tough as anyone."

It was a difficult time to make a coaching debut. Kehoe's appointment coincided with a significant downturn in the team's fortunes. Jagr had been traded to Washington over the summer. The team's remaining stars—Mario Lemieux, Alexei Kovalev, Robert Lang, and Martin Straka—each missed significant time due to injuries. The Pens tumbled below the .500 mark and missed the playoffs for the first time in a dozen years.

"It's always a disappointment," Kehoe said of missing the playoffs. "We've had a run for a long time, starting in 1990–91. It's hard. It's something we're not used to happening in the organization and it's hard to swallow."

Competitive and proud, Kehoe worked diligently over the summer to prepare for the 2002–03 season. His efforts paid off handsomely as the surprising Penguins jumped

to an 11–5–6 start. However, injuries to Aleksey Morozov and Dick Tarnstrom contributed to a dismal 10-game slide in December. In early February, Kovalev was dealt to the Rangers, sealing the Pens' fate—and Kehoe's. He was fired shortly after the season ended.

During the next three seasons, Kehoe once again served as a scout. When Michel Therrien was summoned from Wilkes-Barre to replace Ed Olczyk in December of 2005, Kehoe stepped behind the Baby Pens' bench for three games.

His long tenure with the Penguins finally came to an end during the summer of 2006 when Ray Shero took over as general manager. Highly regarded throughout the league, Kehoe promptly joined the staff of the New York Rangers as a professional scout.

2003–05

Olczyk, Ed

Record: 31–64–8–10 (.354)
Birthplace: Chicago, Illinois
B: August 16, 1966

	Regular Season							Playoffs			
	G	W	L	T	OL	PTS	PCT	G	W	L	PCT
2003–04	82	23	47	8	4	58	.354	-	-	-	-
2005–06	31	8	17	-	6	22	.355	-	-	-	-
Penguins	113	31	64	8	10	80	.354	-	-	-	-
NHL	113	31	64	8	10	80	.354	-	-	-	-

The year 1984 will forever be etched in hockey lore as the year the Penguins drafted Mario Lemieux. While no one will ever second-guess the Pens for taking "Le Magnifique" with the first overall pick, a youngster from the Windy City had pro scouts salivating as well.

Coming off a fine season with Team USA, 18-year-old Ed Olczyk made headlines of his own. Blessed with outstanding playmaking skills and a quick release, the speedy center was the first Chicago native ever to be drafted in the opening round by the Black Hawks.

Big things were expected of the third overall pick. Although he didn't quite put up Mario-type numbers, he went on to enjoy an outstanding NHL career. Skating for seven teams over the course of 16 seasons, he played in 1,031 games and tallied 794 points, including 342 goals.

As his career was winding down, "Edzo" skated for a season and change with the Penguins. During his stay he was one of the team's most popular players. Bright, handsome, and personable, he seemed a natural to make the transition to the broadcast booth.

Immediately following his playing days, FSN Pittsburgh hired the Chicagoan in 2000 to serve as the TV color analyst for legendary play-by-play announcer Mike Lange. Taking to his new assignment with his typical unbridled enthusiasm,

Ed Olczyk addresses the media. He guided the "X Generation" Pens for 113 games spanning two seasons.

Olczyk added a fresh perspective to the Penguins' broadcasts.

During his three seasons in the broadcast booth, the Pens fell into a sudden and precipitous decline. When general manager Craig Patrick began to search for a new coach in the summer of 2003 to replace Rick Kehoe, Olczyk threw his hat into the ring. Amazingly, Edzo landed the job, even though his only previous coaching experience was with a youth hockey team.

Guiding the "X Generation" Penguins would be no easy task. The team featured an aging and ailing Mario Lemieux, 18-year-old goaltending phenom Marc-Andre Fleury, and little else in the way of established big-league talent.

Following a wobbly start, the wheels fell off the wagon. Resembling the flightless waterfowl for which they were named, the undermanned Pens waddled, slipped, and belly-flopped to an 18-game winless streak—one shy of the league record for futility.

It was a trial that would've broken even the most experienced of coaches, let alone a green one. Yet somehow the energetic, upbeat Olczyk kept himself and the team together. Remarkably, the team followed its epic cold spell with a dazzling 12–5–3 sprint to the finish line. The team's stunning turnaround earned the rookie coach praise and a new level of respect.

Heading into the post-lockout season of 2005–06, expectations were high. Thanks to the new collective bargaining agreement and an extremely lucky bounce at the draft lottery, Patrick had added big-name free agents Sergei Gonchar, John LeClair, Ziggy Palffy, and super rookie Sidney Crosby. Most experts picked the club to end its three-year playoff drought.

Unfortunately, Olczyk's top assistant, Lorne Molleken, had resigned to become coach and general manager of the Saskatoon Blades. Shorn of his right-hand man, Edzo's inexperience at running a professional bench began to show. The Penguins appeared to be in total disarray at times, falling before their adversaries like a set of perfectly positioned dominos. Desperate to find a solution for the team's tepid start, Olczyk shifted Crosby to left wing. A short time later Edzo was relieved of the coaching duties.

A class act, Olczyk bore his dismissal with grace and dignity. He returned to the broadcast booth, joining Pat Foley on Chicago Blackhawks television broadcasts. Always in demand, the popular announcer also serves as the lead game analyst for *NHL on NBC* and as a studio and color analyst for *NHL on Versus*.

2005–09

Therrien, Michel

Record: 135–105–32 (.555)
Birthplace: Montreal, Quebec
B: November 4, 1963

	Regular Season							Playoffs			
	G	W	L	T	OL	PTS	PCT	G	W	L	PCT
2005–06	51	14	29	-	8	36	.353	-	-	-	-
2006–07	82	47	24	-	11	105	.640	5	1	4	.200
2007–08	82	47	27	-	8	102	.622	20	14	6	.700
2008–09	57	27	25	-	5	59	.518	-	-	-	-
Penguins	**272**	**135**	**105**	**-**	**32**	**302**	**.555**	**25**	**15**	**10**	**.600**
NHL	**462**	**212**	**182**	**23**	**45**	**492**	**.532**	**37**	**21**	**16**	**.568**

If Dan Bylsma provided the finishing touches to the Penguins' 2009 Stanley Cup champions, it was Michel Therrien who poured the foundation. During his five-plus seasons with the organization, he taught the younger players the basic fundamentals that are essential to a winning team.

Therrien joined the Penguins in 2003, when he was hired by general manager Craig Patrick to coach the team's Wilkes-Barre Scranton affiliate. One thing was evident right away: the former Montreal Canadiens bench boss was not a warm-and-fuzzy type.

"I was not there to be a popular guy," Therrien told Ron Cook of the *Pittsburgh Post-Gazette.* "I was there to bring guys along and make them better players. You don't become champions with no structure, no commitment, and no discipline."

An excellent teacher, Michel Therrien offers some pointers during a practice session.

Those qualities were in short supply prior to Therrien's arrival. For years the Penguins had been regarded as a country club organization. The hard-driving coach changed the culture almost single-handedly.

After guiding the Baby Pens to a scorching 21–1–3 start in 2005–06, Therrien was summoned to take over the coaching duties in Pittsburgh. Despite the presence of phenom Sidney Crosby and a host of high-priced veterans, the Penguins had dissolved into a dissolute team totally lacking in effort and discipline.

It took only two games for Therrien to assert his authority. Ten minutes into a sorry showing against Buffalo, he called a timeout and ripped into his charges with an expletive-laced tirade. The Penguins got the message. Although they dropped a 4–3 decision to the Sabres, they skated hard for the rest of the game.

The turnaround under Therrien was imperceptible at first as the losses continued to mount. However, as the season turned into the homestretch, the Penguins began to grasp his defense-first system. Clearly improved, they went a respectable 8–9–2 during the final 19 games.

Penguins president and CEO Ken Sawyer was impressed. When he hired new general manager Ray Shero during the summer of 2006, it was with the stipulation that Therrien be retained.

The no-nonsense coach responded to the vote of confidence by turning the Pens into a Stanley Cup contender. In 2006–07, the team won 47 games to register a stunning 47-point improvement. The next year they were even better, rolling through the Eastern Conference before being halted in the Finals by the battle-hardened Red Wings.

Thanks to Therrien's fine work behind the bench, Shero rewarded him with a new three-year contract.

"Michel has done a tremendous job with our team over the past two and a half seasons, developing our young players while leading us to division and conference championships and the Stanley Cup Finals," Shero said.

Despite a series of free-agent defections that had robbed the team of scoring punch and grit, the veteran coach kept the Pens on track through the first two months of the 2008–09 season. However, one loss would prove to be too much to overcome. Sergei Gonchar, the team's offensive catalyst from the blue line, had suffered a dislocated shoulder during the exhibition season. Without "Sarge" manning the point, the once potent power play evaporated.

As the team skidded in December, Therrien began to shuffle his forward lines at a frenetic pace. The line juggling only worsened the team's problems. The Pens staggered through a 28-game stretch with a horrible record of 10–16–2. Following a dismal 6–2 loss to Toronto on Valentine's Day, Shero replaced Therrien with Dan Bylsma.

It was a sad day for the Penguins and for Therrien, who deserved so much credit for shaping the team into a contender. However, the Pens were slipping from playoff contention. Worse yet, his message was falling on deaf ears.

Still a Penguin at heart, the classy former coach watched nearly every minute of the team's march to the Stanley Cup.

"I am so proud of those guys," he said.

2009–

Bylsma, Dan

Record: 65–31–11 (.659)
Birthplace: Grand Haven, Michigan
B: September 19, 1970

	Regular Season							Playoffs			
	G	W	L	T	OL	PTS	PCT	G	W	L	PCT
2008-09	25	18	3	-	4	40	.800	24	16	8	.667
2009-10	82	47	28	-	7	101	.616	13	7	6	.538
Penguins	**107**	**65**	**31**	**-**	**11**	**141**	**.659**	**37**	**23**	**14**	**.622**
NHL	**107**	**65**	**31**	**-**	**11**	**141**	**.659**	**37**	**23**	**14**	**.622**

It took Dan Bylsma just a few short months to accomplish what most coaches never achieve in a lifetime. Displaying the poise, acumen, and presence of a man far beyond his years, he won a Stanley Cup in his first season behind an NHL bench.

While Bylsma's comet-like rise to Stanley Cup champion seemed to happen overnight, he most certainly had paid his dues as a player. The graduate of Bowling Green came up the hard way, mucking his way through the ECHL, AHL, and IHL before making it to the National Hockey League. Short on talent but long on grit and determination, he carved out a nine-year career in the NHL thanks to his dogged defensive play and never-say-die attitude.

His efforts were rewarded in 2003, when he played in the Stanley Cup Finals for Anaheim. Early in Game 7 Bylsma

One of the game's brightest young coaches, Dan Bylsma led the Pens to a Cup in 2009.

had a golden opportunity to break a scoreless tie, but he failed to beat New Jersey goalie Martin Brodeur. The Devils went on to capture the Stanley Cup.

"The *USA Today* the following morning had a picture of me and Marty Brodeur with the puck in the air," he recalled. "That was my chance when it was 0–0, and I do remember it very vividly."

It was as close as Bylsma would come to winning a Cup as a player. After finishing out his career with the AHL's Cincinnati Mighty Ducks in 2003–04, he entered the coaching ranks as an assistant. In the summer of 2008 Penguins general manager Ray Shero offered him the head coaching job at Wilkes-Barre Scranton.

The co-author of four sports-related books, the bright young skipper led the Baby Pens to a fine 35–16–3 mark in 54 games. Then, on February 15, he received the call that would alter his destiny. Shero had decided to make a coaching change. He wanted Bylsma to take over the Penguins' helm on an interim basis.

Less than 24 hours later he was at the Nassau County Coliseum, preparing the team to face the Islanders. Although he barely had time for introductions, the Pens played well in a losing effort.

Believing the best defense is a good offense, Bylsma immediately switched from Michel Therrien's trap-oriented system to an aggressive, up-tempo game. The change in philosophy was heartily endorsed by his players.

"It's a lot like the way I played it when we won the Cup [in Tampa Bay]," Ruslan Fedotenko said. "When [Bylsma] took over, it took a couple of games for us to adjust to it, but now we're doing it really well. You play in their zone, make them take long shifts, tire them out. We're not hesitating."

The new style suited the Penguins to a T. Just as important, they seemed to enjoy playing for their new coach. During a crucial road game versus the Blackhawks in late February, the camera panned to Bylsma, who was engaged in a lively conversation with winger Pascal Dupuis. It was the sort of banter that rarely took place under Therrien.

In a turnaround that bordered on the miraculous, the Penguins ripped through the homestretch at an incendiary 18–3–4 clip. The club earned 40 points—the second-highest total for any rookie coach in his first 25 games.

However, success during the regular season is one thing. Success in the postseason, when the intensity level and pressure are ratcheted to a fever pitch, is something entirely different. It remained to be seen how the unflappable 38-year-old coach would fare during the cauldron of the Stanley Cup Playoffs.

Bylsma passed his test with flying colors. In rapid-fire succession, the piping-hot Pens disposed of the Flyers, Capitals, Hurricanes, and Red Wings to capture the team's third Stanley Cup.

For the first-year coach, it was quite a ride.

"I can't believe that's me in the picture in the paper," he said. "That's me holding the Stanley Cup. I don't wake up and see myself as the coach of the Pittsburgh Penguins. It's surreal. It's a little bit out of body."

Perhaps 75-year-old Eddie Johnston, who knows a thing or two about coaching, summed up Bylsma's achievements best.

"In the annals of hockey history, I don't think anyone ever came in and did the job that Dan has done," EJ said. "In February, we were dead in the water. We were trying to just get in the playoffs. He had a great first meeting, emphasized the change of attitude. He said we'd have more fun, get more involved in the offense. Everyone jumped into it, the way he coached."

The 2009–10 season would prove to be a bit more problematic. Following a meteoric 12–3 start, the Pens fell back to earth. Although the team failed in its quest for a second straight Stanley Cup, Bylsma remained popular with his players.

"He's real energetic, real outgoing, easy to talk to, and he's got a drive to win," Jordan Staal said. "He doesn't shove the system down your throat, but he puts it out there. He's a great coach."

General Manager Profiles

1967–70; 1972–74

Riley, Jack

Birthplace: Toronto, Ontario
B: June 14, 1919

Jack Riley, the Penguins' first general manager, remembers the good old days like they were yesterday. In particular, he recalls the bedsheet banners that adorned the Civic Arena like championship bunting. One read, "RILEY AND RUPP AND NO STANLEY CUP." Another was more to the point—"SULLY MUST GO, AND RILEY, TOO."

"They must have run out of paint on that one," he chuckled, "because it started out with red letters and finished up with green letters."

Riley was no stranger to tough times. As a youth growing up in Toronto during the teeth of the Great Depression, he was fortunate to play hockey on the same team as Stafford Smythe, the son of Maple Leafs owner Conn Smythe. Riley's team occasionally practiced in Maple Leafs Gardens.

The youngster showed promise as a playmaking forward. However, after serving a tour of duty as a lieutenant in the Canadian Army during World War II, his career was sabotaged with the introduction of the center red line, which placed a premium on speed. The change consigned him to a career in the low minor leagues.

As his playing days drew to a close, Riley began to work his way into management. In 1959 he was named general manager of the Rochester Americans. Under Riley's watch, the Amerks enjoyed five competitive seasons before he moved on to serve as president of the American Hockey League.

With the first wave of NHL expansion, Penguins owner Senator Jack McGregor sought an experienced executive to guide his fledgling team. He found his man in Riley.

Undaunted by the challenge of building a hockey team from scratch, Riley and his staff worked wonders at the 1967 Expansion Draft. The Penguins' first lineup featured two future Hall of Famers—Andy Bathgate and Leo Boivin—and solid pros such as Earl Ingarfield, Ab McDonald, and Ken Schinkel.

"We were the first expansion team to beat one of the old clubs," he said proudly. "We beat the Chicago Black Hawks here [in Pittsburgh] on a Saturday night."

Good things were expected of that inaugural team. However, the organization was totally devoid of a farm system due to tight finances—an all-too-familiar refrain that would be repeated many times over during the coming years. When injuries struck, Riley and his coach, Red Sullivan, had no one to plug the holes.

Jack Riley was the Pens' first general manager. Hired in 1966, he built the team from scratch.

Riley's tenure was interrupted following the team's first playoff appearance in 1970. Owner Donald Parsons promoted Red Kelly to the dual role of coach and general manager. Kelly insisted that his former boss be retained, so Riley assumed the post of club president.

On January 29, 1972, Riley reassumed the GM duties. By the 1973–74 season he had a talented nucleus in place. The Pens boasted a bevy of fine young stars, including All-Star-caliber performers Syl Apps, Dave Burrows, Greg Polis, and Jean Pronovost. However, Riley was unable to lead the club over the hump to contender status. In January of 1974 he was replaced by his long-time assistant, Jack Button.

Through the years Riley remained loyal to the Penguins. Following his resignation he worked in the team's scouting department. In the early 1990s he returned to the Civic Arena to serve as a goal judge.

Spry and active at 90 years of age, Jack still attends Penguins games and team functions. In December of 2009 he received a special token of appreciation for his years of service: the Penguins awarded him a Stanley Cup ring.

1970–72

Kelly, Leonard "Red"

Birthplace: Simcoe, Ontario
B: July 9, 1927

Following the Penguins' rousing performance against St. Louis in the 1970 Stanley Cup Semifinals, Red Kelly was the toast of the town. The popular and affable Irishman was seen as the catalyst who would lead the team to future success.

As a reward for Kelly's fine work behind the bench, owner Donald Parsons promoted the redhead to the dual role of coach and general manager. It was a challenging job to be sure, but one that Red seemed wholly capable of handling.

Kelly, indeed, performed well during his brief tenure as general manager. On January 26, 1971, he engineered one of the best trades in club history, sending journeyman Glen Sather to the Rangers for Sheldon Kannegiesser and talented young center Syl Apps. He convinced veteran left wing Lowell MacDonald, who would enjoy a stellar career with the Pens, to end his premature retirement. Displaying a sharp eye for young talent, he traded for Al McDonough and picked up future stars Dave Burrows and Rene Robert in the Intra-League Draft.

Unfortunately, wearing two hats seemed to detract from Kelly's coaching. During his stint as general manager and skipper the team lost nearly twice as many games as it won. New owners Tad Potter and Peter Block did not have deep enough pockets to subsidize a loser. In January of 1972, Kelly agreed to relinquish the GM duties to Jack Riley. Reenergized, he promptly led the Penguins to their second playoff berth.

In addition to his coaching duties, Red Kelly served as the Penguins' general manager for nearly two seasons.

1974–75

Button, Jack

B: 1940
D: August 1, 1996

If one were to compile a list of the Penguins' most underrated executives, Jack Button's name would appear at the top. His term as general manager was brief—barely a season and a half. During that time he presided over the team's first winning season while posting a .543 winning percentage—second only to Ray Shero.

Button got his start in management at an early age. In his mid-twenties he served as the publicity director for the American Hockey League, working closely with league president Jack Riley.

When Riley became the general manager of the Penguins in 1966, he brought Button along as his assistant. In the summer of 1968 the hardworking junior executive was picked to serve as the general manager for the Penguins' new farm team, the Amarillo Wranglers. Although the Wranglers lasted just one season, Button gained valuable on-the-job training.

The 29-year-old Button returned to Pittsburgh the following season to become the Penguins' director of player personnel. He served in that capacity until January of 1974, when owner Tad Potter promoted him to general manager to replace Riley.

"I am just asking for everyone's cooperation and understanding," he said at a press conference. "I don't expect to have your confidence now, but I expect to earn it."

A talented but underachieving team, the Penguins were badly in need of a shakeup. Button saw that they got it. During his first week on the job, the Pens made two huge trades. On January 17 they sent mainstays Greg Polis and Bryan "Bugsy" Watson to St. Louis for puck-moving defenseman Ab DeMarco and tough guys Steve Durbano and Bob "Battleship" Kelly. Later that day Button shipped starting goalie Jim Rutherford and Jack Lynch to Detroit for giant defenseman Ron Stackhouse. The Pens caught fire and finished the season on a 14–10–4 run.

His finest trades were yet to come. In the summer of 1974 he acquired former Rangers captain and 50-goal man Vic Hadfield for journeyman defender Nick Beverley. Next he pried scoring winger Rick Kehoe from Toronto for talented but unproven Blaine Stoughton. He added a third scorer, junior hockey sensation Pierre Larouche, in the Amateur Draft.

Thanks to Button, the Penguins suddenly had a big-league feel. Not content to rest on his laurels, he continued to tweak the team as the season progressed. He acquired a rugged defenseman (Barry Wilkins), a proven penalty killer

The Puck Stops Here

After assuming the general manager post from Jack Riley in January of 1974, Jack Button wasted little time building the Pens into a contender. In rapid succession he acquired puck-moving defenseman Ron Stackhouse and tough guys Steve Durbano and Bob "Battleship" Kelly. Over the summer he bolstered the team even further by adding scorers Vic Hadfield, Rick Kehoe, and Pierre Larouche to a talented core.

The only weakness was in goal. Entering the 1974–75 campaign Button planned to use second-year men Gary Inness and Bob Johnson between the pipes. The duo boasted a mere 32 games of NHL experience.

"I'm not worried about my goaltending," Button told *Sports Illustrated*.

"No, he's scared to death," cracked a rival GM.

(Lew Morrison), a solid backup goalie (Michel Plasse), and extra scoring depth (Pete Laframboise).

The Penguins responded with the finest season in their brief history. With newcomers Hadfield, Kehoe, and Larouche each topping the 30-goal mark, they posted a 37–28–15 record to earn their third Stanley Cup playoff berth. Especially tough at the Civic Arena, the team reeled off a 20-game unbeaten streak on home ice.

There was, however, a price for the team's newfound success. The Pens needed to make it to the semifinals in order for owner Tad Potter to pay off his debts. They fell one victory short, losing their second-round series to the New York Islanders in inglorious fashion.

The Penguins were purchased over the summer by a group headed by investment broker Al Savill. One of the principals was Wren Blair, the former general manager of the Minnesota North Stars. It was clear he intended to run the team. Although Button had done much during his brief tenure to transform the team's losing culture, he was out of a job.

"It was obvious from the start that if Blair's group got the Penguins, there would be no room for me," he said.

Impressed by his work in the Steel City, the NHL immediately hired Button to serve as the first director of the newly formed Central Scouting service. In 1979 Button moved on to the Washington Capitals, where he served as a scout and later as the team's director of player personnel. Blessed with a keen eye for talent, he was credited with discovering a bevy of talented young stars, including Peter Bondra, Jim Carey, Michal Pivonka, and Sergei Gonchar.

Tragically, Button was diagnosed with leukemia in April of 1995. After receiving bone marrow transplants, he battled the illness bravely. He passed away on August 1, 1996.

"It's a huge loss for the organization and a huge loss for me personally," Capitals general manager David Poile said.

During the 1996–97 season the Capitals wore a special memorial patch on their uniforms with the initials "JB" and the image of a bulldog. In his honor, they created the Jack Button Award, which is given each year to the Capitals' top prospect.

Jack's legacy lives on through his sons. Craig, a former executive with Dallas and Calgary, currently serves as a scout for Toronto. Tod is the director of scouting for the Flames.

1975–77

Blair, Wren

Birthplace: Lindsay, Ontario
B: October 2, 1925

While serving as a scout for Boston in the 1960s, Wren "Bird" Blair made one of the most important finds in hockey history. On his recommendation, the Bruins signed a 14-year-old defenseman from Parry Sound, Ontario, who displayed uncommon offensive skills. The youngster's name was Bobby Orr.

Nicknamed "DOBO" (Discoverer of Bobby Orr) by then-Bruins president Weston Adams, Blair was well-established in hockey circles. An outstanding amateur coach, he guided the Whitby Dunlops to the world championship in Oslo in 1958. Blair was instrumental in the rebirth of the storied Oshawa Generals franchise in the early 1960s. When the NHL expanded to 12 teams in 1967, he was hired to lead the Minnesota North Stars.

Feisty and competitive, Blair realized the quickest way to build a contending team was with players from the established clubs. Over the next several seasons he pried plums

Wren Blair helped rescue the Pens from receivership in 1975.

such as Barry Gibbs, Danny Grant, and Danny O'Shea loose from Boston and Montreal.

He also possessed a keen eye for veteran talent. With a lineup packed with grizzled veterans such as Doug Mohns, Murray Oliver, and Dean Prentice, the North Stars soon became known as the "Over the Hill Gang."

Beginning in 1971, the team enjoyed two strong seasons under Blair's watch. However, the wheels fell off the wagon during the 1973–74 campaign as the aging North Stars sagged to a seventh-place finish. Blair and the team parted ways following the season.

Seeking a new challenge, Blair came to Pittsburgh in July of 1975 as part of the ownership group that purchased the Penguins out of receivership. He immediately set himself up as the club's new president and general manager, bumping aside capable incumbent Jack Button.

Despite the difficult circumstances, Blair inherited a very talented team. Possessing a balanced blend of skill and grit, the Pens boasted three strong forward lines and top-notch performers Dave Burrows and Ron Stackhouse on defense.

Predictably, the team got older in a hurry. Following the formula he used in Minnesota, Blair exchanged twentysomethings Chuck Arnason, Harvey Bennett, Steve Durbano, and Gary Inness for greybeards Stan Gilbertson, Simon Nolet, Bob Taylor, and Ed Van Impe.

While the Pens were still an undeniably talented bunch, the trades stripped away a huge chunk of the team's muscle. They were bounced from the playoffs in the opening round by a less-skilled but infinitely tougher Toronto squad.

To Blair's credit, he directed one of the team's finest amateur drafts that summer. His first four picks—Blair Chapman, Greg Malone, Peter Marsh, and Morris Lukowich—enjoyed good to outstanding pro careers. Unfortunately, Blair was unable to sign Marsh and Lukowich (who blossomed into a star in the WHA).

By the 1976–77 season a fading Blair had begun to remove himself from the team's operations. In December he handed the general manager reins over to his assistant, Baz Bastien. Following the season, he stepped down as the club president.

1977–83

Bastien, Aldege "Baz"

Birthplace: Timmins, Ontario
B: August 29, 1919
D: March 15, 1983

It seemed written in the stars that Aldege "Baz" Bastien would one day serve as the Penguins' general manager. Three decades earlier he'd been a promising young goalie for the Pittsburgh Hornets, until he was struck in the right eye by a puck during training camp. The damage was so severe the eye needed to be removed.

Unfazed by the abrupt end to his playing career, the plucky Bastien assumed the Hornets' coaching duties that very same year. The following season the 31-year-old was named general manager. In 1953 he returned to the team's bench, guiding "the Wasps" to a fourth-place finish.

When the Hornets resumed operations in 1961 upon completion of the Civic Arena, Bastien was a key member of the organization. He was appointed general manager for the second time, a role he would fill until the team ceased operations in 1967. In a storybook ending, Bastien coached the Hornets to a Calder Cup in their final year of existence.

The next year Baz began a long apprenticeship in the NHL, serving as assistant general manager to another former Hornet, Sid Abel, in Detroit. When Abel took over the expansion Kansas City Scouts in 1974, Bastien once

Baz

In a tragic postscript to the disappointing 1982–83 season, Pens general manager Baz Bastien died on March 15, 1983, from injuries sustained in an automobile accident. He was driving home from a sportswriters' dinner held that evening.

"Everyone was having such a great time," assistant coach Mike Corrigan said. "That's the first time all year I've seen Baz have a good time. It was the first time I'd seen him open up, talking with everybody, shaking everyone's hand. Then, bang, it was like someone shot a bullet through you."

"It was almost like he knew something was going to happen," Michel Dion added. "He opened up to me. He never opened up to me in two years."

For Eddie Johnston, Bastien's untimely death was a particularly bitter pill to swallow. The two had had their share of run-ins, leading to what was at best a tense working relationship.

But Bastien surprised the Penguins' coach by approaching him at the banquet in a conciliatory tone. "Let's pull together," he said. "We've got to pull together."

"We left our conversation saying we're going to work together, the two of us, to get this [franchise] turned around," Johnston said. "We said 'Great,' shook hands, and away he went."

Perhaps Greg Malone, who was honored at the dinner that evening, paid the most fitting tribute to the Pens' late GM.

"At first, he'd give you that tough image to make the younger guys scared of him," Malone said. "But once you'd get past that tough image, he'd give you anything you wanted. He had a heart of gold."

again served as his aide. During the Scouts' first season, he convinced his boss to trade for Denis Herron, the Penguins' promising goalie. Herron quickly emerged as a star for a bad team.

In 1976, Bastien's odyssey came full circle when he returned to Pittsburgh as Wren Blair's handpicked successor. The move was well-received among Steel City fans, who felt he had been unjustly passed over by the club a decade earlier.

"You can't imagine how happy I am to come back to the city where I played my hockey," he said. "I always loved Pittsburgh. And I go back to the days when if you wore a white shirt, at noon you had to change it."

Although he was thrilled to be back in Pittsburgh, he faced a daunting task. Following a respectable three-year run in the mid-1970s, the aging Penguins were beginning to fade. The team had virtually no farm system. Worse yet, the club's marginal finances did not afford Bastien the luxury of building through the draft.

Adept at plugging short-term gaps from his years as a minor league executive, Bastien used the only collateral at his disposal. He traded draft choices—lots of them—to acquire players from other teams. Over the course of his six-plus seasons as general manager, he dealt four first-round picks, as well as second- and third-round choices.

The moves worked for a time. Fueled largely by Bastien-acquired talent, the Pens finished a solid second in the Norris Division in 1978–79. The club's strong showing earned the veteran GM Executive of the Year honors. However, the improvement was largely a case of smoke and mirrors.

"The problem was, every year you went into training camp and there was never a young star to hang your hat on," Paul Steigerwald recalled. "We always traded our draft picks."

Following three fair-to-middling seasons, the practice of robbing Peter to pay Paul finally caught up to Bastien and the Penguins in 1982–83. Bereft of young talent, the team spiraled to a last-place finish in the Patrick Division.

Sadly, Bastien would not live to preside over a revival. While driving home from a hockey writers' dinner in his honor, he died from injuries sustained in an automobile accident on March 15, 1983.

The following season two awards were created to honor Bastien's legacy. The American Hockey League established the Aldege "Baz" Bastien Award, which is given each year to the best goaltender in the league. The Pittsburgh chapter of the Professional Hockey Writers Association created the Aldege "Baz" Bastien Memorial Good Guy Award, which is bestowed upon the Penguin judged to be most cooperative with the media.

1983–88

Johnston, Eddie

Birthplace: Montreal, Quebec
B: November 24, 1935

Eddie Johnston will forever hold a special place in the hearts of Penguins fans for drafting Mario Lemieux. It took an enormous amount of perseverance, not to mention a bit of skullduggery, for the first-year general manager to ensure the Penguins would be in a position to draft the Laval Titan phenom.

While the Pens didn't exactly tank games—at least by nobody's admission—Johnston made sure they didn't stray too far from the prescribed course. When promising young goalie Roberto Romano had the temerity to win consecutive games, he was sent to the minors in favor of Vincent Tremblay.

"We want to see what [Tremblay] can do," Johnston said.

Four games and 24 goals against later he had his answer—not to mention the top pick in the Entry Draft. On June 9, 1984, Lemieux became a Penguin.

"There was no way I was going to trade [the pick]," EJ told Ron Cook of the *Pittsburgh Post-Gazette*. "We were getting a guy who comes along once in a lifetime. Mellon Arena would be a parking lot now if not for Mario. There would be no hockey in Pittsburgh."

Three years later, Johnston worked his magic a second time. In a blockbuster seven-player trade with Edmonton, he acquired Norris Trophy defenseman Paul Coffey to team with Lemieux. Thanks to EJ, the building blocks for a future Stanley Cup champion were in place.

Unfortunately, he would not share in the triumph. After being demoted to assistant general manager in 1988, he departed to take the GM position in Hartford. While serving

Eddie Johnston served as the team's general manager for five seasons. He drafted Mario Lemieux and traded for Paul Coffey.

with the Whalers, he unintentionally provided the Penguins with the final pieces to their Stanley Cup puzzle by trading Ron Francis and Ulf Samuelsson to the Steel City for John Cullen and Zarley Zalapski.

"That was such a great trade for the Penguins that they probably should've given me a small ring or something," he chuckled.

The Penguins went one better. In the summer of 1993 they brought him back as a replacement for Scotty Bowman. He would remain in the organization through 2009, when he got to sip champagne from the Stanley Cup.

1988–89

Esposito, Tony

Birthplace: Sault Ste. Marie, Ontario
B: April 23, 1943

Twenty years ahead of his time, Tony Esposito helped revolutionize the sport of hockey. During an era when standup goalies like Bernie Parent dominated the game, Esposito introduced the butterfly style, with great results.

The younger brother of Boston Bruins great Phil Esposito, "Tony O" won 423 games while posting a sparkling 2.92 goals-against average and 76 shutouts, the ninth-highest total of all time. He won three Vezina Trophies and earned NHL First Team All-Star honors three times. In September of 1972 he participated in the Summit Series against the Soviets and posted the lowest goals-against average in the tournament.

Confident and self-assured, Tony served as president of the NHL Players' Association from February of 1981 until October of 1984, succeeding his brother Phil. A popular figure on the banquet circuit, he cultivated a friendship with the DeBartolo family. Soon he was serving as an unofficial advisor for Edward Jr., who had taken a more active role in the Penguins' operations.

When Pens general manager Eddie Johnston tried to swing a deal for Edmonton goalie Andy Moog in March of 1988, DeBartolo stepped in to block the trade. He was rumored to have consulted with Esposito before nixing the deal. Less than two weeks after the Pens played their final game of the 1987–88 season, Esposito was named director of hockey operations, bumping Johnston to the post of assistant general manager. The move was met with skepticism.

"[Esposito] has no background in the job at all," Boston general manager Harry Sinden said. "He hasn't coached, he hasn't done any managing work with a team."

Nonplussed, Esposito insisted he was the right man for the job.

"I know the game," he said. "We're going to have a first-class organization here. You'll see."

For one year, at least, he proved to be true to his word. In the fourth round of the Entry Draft he turned up a gem

Tony Esposito's tenure as general manager was brief, but he helped lay the foundation for a Stanley Cup winner.

in right wing Mark Recchi. Showing a sharp eye for undervalued talent, Esposito signed minor league sensation John Cullen to a free-agent deal. Early in the 1988–89 season he sent talented defenseman Doug Bodger and first-round pick Darrin Shannon to Buffalo for goalie Tom Barrasso.

Much improved, the Penguins made the playoffs for the first time in seven years. In the Stanley Cup Playoffs they swept Phil's team, the Rangers, before dropping a tough seven-game set to the Flyers in the Patrick Division Finals.

Over the summer Esposito moved boldly to fill what he perceived to be the team's biggest needs—a scoring winger and a tough, stay-at-home defender. In a big six-player swap, he sent Randy Cunneyworth and youngsters Dave McLlwain and Rick Tabaracci to Winnipeg for Randy Gilhen, Jim Kyte, and Andrew McBain.

The Penguins appeared to be loaded for the upcoming campaign. However, Esposito soon shot himself in the foot. Famously xenophobic, he refused to sign European players. During contract negotiations with Mario Lemieux, he attempted to lowball the Penguins superstar. Relations between the two became strained to the breaking point, forcing Edward DeBartolo Jr. to step in and smooth things over.

With the tone set, the Penguins lurched through the first two months of the 1989–90 season. As the team floundered, Esposito and his coach, Gene Ubriaco, came under heavy fire. Presented with an opportunity to hire bright young executive Craig Patrick, Edward Jr. handed the ill-fated pair their walking papers on December 5, 1989.

As always, Tony O landed on his feet. In 1991 he joined Phil in Tampa Bay. The Hall of Famer served as the team's chief scout until 1998, when he and his brother were dismissed. He remains a popular speaker on the banquet circuit.

1989–06

Patrick, Craig

Birthplace: Detroit, Michigan
B: May 20, 1946

It's safe to say that no one aside from Mario Lemieux has had a greater hand in turning the Penguins into a winning organization than Craig Patrick. Prior to his arrival in 1989, the Pens perpetually had a minor league feel about them—accompanied by minor league results. Patrick immediately breathed new life into the franchise while instilling a much-needed air of professionalism.

During the preceding 22 years, the Penguins' goal was always to make the playoffs. Patrick willed the team to aim higher.

Perhaps no general manager in the history of the sport did better work than Patrick during his first full season in the Pens' front office. During the summer of 1990 he hired well-respected hockey men Bob Johnson and Scotty Bowman to assist him. For an organization that had been fed a steady diet of Pierre Creamers, Tony Espositos, and Gene Ubriacos, it was heady stuff.

Noting that his talented young team lacked leadership, Patrick acquired seasoned veterans and Stanley Cup winners Joe Mullen and Bryan Trottier for a pittance. At the Entry Draft he selected a gangly, mullet-topped kid from the Czech Republic named Jaromir Jagr. Over the course of the season, he traded for future Hall of Famers Ron Francis and Larry Murphy, as well as established pros Gordie Roberts, Ulf Samuelsson, and Peter Taglianetti. In little more than 18 months he transformed the team from perennial also-rans into Stanley Cup champions.

Craig Patrick built the Pens into a Stanley Cup champion in the early 1990s.

The following season Patrick faced even bigger challenges. In the wake of Bob Johnson's tragic and untimely death, he convinced Bowman to take over the coaching reins. With the club sagging at the two-thirds pole, he displayed the brass of a riverboat gambler by trading popular stars Paul Coffey and Mark Recchi for Kjell Samuelsson, Rick Tocchet, and Ken Wregget. Infused with sorely needed grit and fire, the Pens heated up and rolled to a second straight Stanley Cup.

During the next nine years, Patrick kept the Penguins on the short list of Cup contenders. He continued to display a flair for the big trade, adding an endless succession of stars such as Alexei Kovalev, Petr Nedved, Luc Robitaille, Tomas Sandstrom, and Sergei Zubov to the fold. When the team was rocked by bankruptcy in the late 1990s, he did some of his finest work. Showing a sharp eye for undervalued talent, he acquired solid performers Robert Lang, Jiri Slegr, and Martin Straka.

As the Penguins entered the new millennium, however, some of the luster began to fade from Patrick's reputation. A string of poor drafts, combined with the club's ever-tightening finances, caused the Pens to falter. In the summer of 2001 he traded Jagr to Washington for three prospects who never panned out, further weakening a struggling team.

Under heavy criticism for the Jagr deal and a series of questionable coaching hires, Patrick quietly began to rebuild through the draft. Top picks Colby Armstrong, Brooks Orpik, and Ryan Whitney would soon have an impact. In 2003 he boldly traded up to snatch prized goaltending phenom Marc-Andre Fleury. After selecting Russian prodigy Evgeni Malkin in 2004, he earned the right to choose Sidney Crosby at the 2005 draft lottery. Teeming with good young talent, the Penguins were poised for a comeback—one that would ultimately lead to a third Stanley Cup.

Patrick had hoped to preside over the team's resurgence. Sadly, it was not to be. After 17 years of service, the Hall of Fame general manager was let go in the summer of 2006. Still in demand, he has been contacted by several NHL teams, including Phoenix, Tampa Bay, and Toronto.

2006–

Shero, Ray

Birthplace: St. Paul, Minnesota
B: July 28, 1962

For Penguins general manager Rejean "Ray" Shero, hoisting the Stanley Cup has become a family tradition. His late father, Fred Shero, coached Philadelphia's infamous "Broad Street Bullies" to back-to-back Cups in the mid-1970s.

Growing up in a hockey family, it was only natural for young Ray to follow in his dad's footsteps. A promising left wing in his own right, he enrolled at St. Laurence University.

Although he missed his entire sophomore season due to a severe knee injury, he was selected in the 11th round of the 1982 Entry Draft by the Kings. Following the injury, Shero enjoyed three solid seasons with the Saints while serving as the team's captain, but he was never quite the same.

Armed with a double major in economics and sociology, Shero joined the Sports Consulting Group in 1986. Serving as a senior partner and player agent, he became a resourceful and proficient contract negotiator—a skill set that would serve him well on his next assignment.

"He's a passionate guy, and I mean that in a positive way," agent Steve Bartlett noted. "He's competitive, and he fights hard for his position."

On June 1, 1993, Shero was hired by the Ottawa Senators to the post of assistant general manager. Working alongside fellow St. Lawrence grad Randy Sexton, he helped lay the foundation for a powerful team. During Shero's tenure, the Senators drafted future stars such as Daniel Alfredsson, Marian Hossa, and Chris Phillips.

Seeking a new challenge, Shero moved to another expansion team, the Nashville Predators, in 1998. Once again filling the role of assistant general manager, he helped build the Predators into a contender.

Considered one of the brightest young executives in hockey, it was only a matter of time before Shero was picked to run a team of his own. In the summer of 2006, the Pittsburgh Penguins came knocking. Seeking a replacement for Hall of Famer Craig Patrick, Pens president Ken Sawyer hired Shero as his team's executive vice president and general manager on May 25, 2006. The move earned a ringing endorsement from Shero's former boss, David Poile.

"Ray was an extension of what I was doing," the Nashville GM said. "[The Penguins] are going to be very happy with him."

Inheriting a team with a talented young core that included superstar Sidney Crosby, Shero immediately set about the task of filling in the missing pieces. He inked veteran free agents Mark Eaton, Mark Recchi, and the abrasive Jarkko Ruutu to deals. Blessed with a keen eye for talent, he plucked 18-year-old center Jordan Staal from Peterborough in the Entry Draft. At the trade deadline, he added veteran leadership and toughness by acquiring power forward Gary Roberts and enforcer Georges Laraque. The Penguins responded with a stunning 47-point improvement to grab their first playoff berth since 2001.

Never one to rest on his laurels, Shero continued to improve the club in 2007–08. He added sniper Petr Sykora to the mix and signed undervalued goalie Ty Conklin, who proved to be worth his weight in gold. With the team humming toward another 100-point season, he pulled off the biggest deals at the trade deadline, acquiring All-Star winger Marian Hossa and behemoth defender Hal Gill. That spring, the Pens made it all the way to the Stanley Cup Finals before dropping a six-game set to Detroit.

Shero would soon face his stiffest test. A host of key players, including veterans Hossa, Roberts, and Ruutu and

One of the top young executives in hockey, Ray Shero molded a Stanley Cup champion.

rising stars Ryan Malone and Brooks Orpik, were eligible for free agency. In addition, new deals needed to be negotiated for Evgeni Malkin, Marc-Andre Fleury, and Staal. It was a challenge that would've given even the most experienced of GMs an ulcer.

A consummate professional, Shero navigated the negotiating minefield with skill and poise. Focusing his attention on the team's young core, he signed Fleury, Malkin, Orpik, and Staal to long-term deals. When the biggest fish of all—Hossa—wriggled off the hook, Shero plugged the dike with experienced free agents Ruslan Fedotenko and Miroslav Satan.

His problems, however, were only beginning. After a decent start, the Penguins hit the skids midway through the 2008–09 campaign. With the team slipping from playoff contention, Shero moved boldly. He replaced established coach Michel Therrien with unproven Dan Bylsma and acquired scoring wingers Bill Guerin and Chris Kunitz. Rejuvenated, the Pens tore through the homestretch at an 18–3–4 clip to qualify for postseason play. In the playoffs they beat back the challenge of the defending champion Red Wings to capture the Stanley Cup.

"Our role players did such a great job," Shero said during the victory celebration. "Win or lose, I was so proud of this team."

When asked how his dad would've felt about his accomplishment, Shero smiled and said, "I think he'd be proud."

The bright young GM did some of his finest work over the summer of 2009. Moving decisively to fill in the missing pieces, he signed battle-tested free agents Jay McKee and Mike Rupp, and imported veteran Brent Johnson to provide backup support for Marc-Andre Fleury. The Penguins responded with another strong season, finishing second in the Atlantic Division with a record of 47–28–7.

5

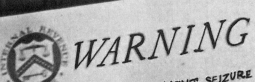

WARNING
UNITED STATES GOVERNMENT SEIZURE

The Owners

The Pittsburgh Penguins were willed into existence in the spring of 1965 by two men who shared a passion for big-league hockey. Upon learning of the National Hockey League's plan to add six teams, Pennsylvania senator Jack McGregor and attorney Peter Block began rounding up investors on behalf of a Pittsburgh entry.

Two years later McGregor handed over a check for $2 million to the board of governors, and the Penguins were officially members of the NHL.

Backed by a 20-man syndicate that included the most prominent names in Pittsburgh business society, the Pens appeared to be on firm financial footing. However, lagging attendance and the owners' failed entry in the National Professional Soccer League quickly drained the coffers. At the end of the team's inaugural season, ownership was transferred to a group headed by Donald Parsons.

Eager to build a winner, Parsons spared no expense. He invested in a farm team—the ill-fated Amarillo Wranglers—and paid players performance bonuses. Unfortunately, he underestimated the cost of running a professional hockey club. On December 1, 1970, he was forced to turn control of the team over to the league.

Five months later the Penguins were purchased by Pittsburgh businessmen Tad Potter, Peter Block, Peter Burchfield, and Elmore Keener. Perhaps no group of owners—with the possible exception of the Lemieux Group—cared more about bringing a winning team to the Steel City.

Imbued with a sense of civic pride and a sincere love for the sport, Potter's group attempted to turn the franchise into a first-class organization. They worked hand in hand with Civic Arena manager Charles Strong to expand the Igloo's seating capacity. Players and coaches were rewarded with handsome contracts.

Unfortunately, Potter and his associates may have cared too much. Dreadfully overextended, they were forced into receivership following a catastrophic playoff loss to the New York Islanders in 1975.

The next group of owners—Al Savill, Otto Frenzel, and Wren Blair—saved hockey in Pittsburgh but lacked the resources to run a successful franchise. There was, however, a silver lining. Savill was connected to Edward J. DeBartolo Sr., one of the wealthiest men in America. Savill convinced his friend to assume control of the financially troubled club.

A reluctant owner at first, DeBartolo grew to love his team. He absorbed enormous losses, particularly through the early years of his reign, but doggedly stayed the course. His perseverance was rewarded with a Stanley Cup in 1991.

Having reached the pinnacle of the sport, DeBartolo sold the Penguins in the fall of 1991 to Howard Baldwin and his partners, Morris Belzberg and Thomas Ruta. Under the entrepreneurial Baldwin, the Pens won a second Stanley Cup. However, his penchant for approving lavish contracts while failing to increase revenues forced him to seek additional backing.

In 1997 he welcomed hard-nosed Bostonian Roger Marino to the fold. Baldwin and Marino mixed as well as oil and water. They waged a pitched battle for control, plunging the team deeper into debt. On October 13, 1998, they filed for bankruptcy.

The Penguins' financial collapse was a blessing in disguise. The team's largest creditor—Mario Lemieux—assembled a group of investors. In September of 1999 the league transferred ownership of the team to the Lemieux Group LP, which included wealthy Californian Ron Burkle.

Mario turned out to be a savvy owner. Under his stewardship, the team pared its expenses in anticipation of the new collective bargaining agreement. In 2007 he used his considerable clout to broker a deal for a badly needed new arena. Even more remarkably, the Penguins are consistently turning a profit for the first time in their 43-year history.

ancial problems plagued the Penguins from the start. On June 12, 5, the Internal Revenue Service padlocked the team's offices for ure to pay withholding taxes.

February 1966–March 1968

Senator Jack McGregor and Peter Block

The Penguins were birthed into existence on a spring day in 1965 by a pair of former law school classmates. While driving along the Pennsylvania Turnpike to Harrisburg, Pennsylvania, Senator Jack McGregor and attorney Peter Block engaged in a lively conversation about the National Hockey League's plan to expand to 12 teams.

An avid hockey fan, Block told McGregor he believed Pittsburgh was ready for a professional team. The city had faithfully supported the minor league Hornets for nearly 30 years. It was time to step up in class.

A plan was soon hatched to secure an entry for Pittsburgh. McGregor would approach city and civic leaders about using big-league hockey as a tool for urban renewal. Meanwhile, Block would gather information about the NHL's bidding process.

Flush with civic pride following the city's first Renaissance, local leaders wholeheartedly endorsed the idea of bringing the NHL to Pittsburgh. McGregor quickly lined up a list of 20 investors to back the team, including H. J. Heinz III, Richard M. Scaife (heir to the Mellon fortune), and industrialist Henry Hillman. Pittsburgh Steelers owner Art Rooney Sr. proved to be an invaluable ally, helping to secure support from the NHL owners for the Steel City entry. On February 8, 1966, McGregor's group was officially awarded a franchise.

Although the investors included the crème de la crème of Pittsburgh business society, in hindsight it was clear there would be problems. Prior to cutting a check to the NHL for

The founder of the Penguins, Pennsylvania senator Jack McGregor.

the $2 million entry fee, they asked McGregor to leave the funds in an account for as long as possible in order to collect the maximum amount of interest.

In addition to the entry fee, the owners had to pony up $750,000 for startup costs, which included the expansion of the Civic Arena's capacity from 10,732 to a league-mandated minimum of 12,500. They also were required to pay a settlement to Detroit Red Wings owner Bruce Norris for displacing the Hornets.

However, the kicker was an ill-fated entry into professional soccer. A true sportsman, Block believed soccer was the up-and-coming sport in North America. He convinced the Penguins' owners to back an entry in the National Professional Soccer League, the Pittsburgh Phantoms.

Unfortunately, Block was 30 years ahead of his time. The Phantoms fell flat while playing before mostly empty seats. The excursion cost Penguins investors another $700,000 before the first puck was dropped.

Nor was the fledgling hockey team an easy sell. The Hornets had won the Calder Cup in 1967. Gone but not forgotten, they remained near and dear in the hearts of Steel City fans. The upstart Penguins would have to prove themselves worthy.

Although the team was blessed with two future Hall of Famers and a cast of solid pros, they stumbled on the ice—and at the gate. The Pens averaged around 7,400 fans per game during their inaugural season. Not shabby by expansion-team standards, but not enough to fill the team's depleted coffers.

"You knew it was shaky because [the Penguins] had so many investors," said publicity director Joe Gordon. "You had a lot of guys who didn't have a lot of cash lying around."

Toward the end of the season there were signs that all was not well in the front office.

"The original 20 owners just didn't have the staying power," Jack Riley said. "When I saw they couldn't pay to put in lines for the soccer games at Forbes Field I knew we were in trouble. They wanted out in a hurry, and they headed south as soon as the bills started stacking up on their desks. They weren't bad guys; they just didn't have much hockey know-how or enough money."

McGregor reluctantly was forced to seek additional backing. He quickly found an interested party in Detroit bank executive Donald Parsons. Reassured that Parsons intended to keep the team in Pittsburgh, McGregor announced on March 21, 1968, that a substantial portion of the club's stock had been sold to the Michigan banker and his group.

"There are no plans to move the National Hockey League franchise out of Pittsburgh," McGregor told the press corps. "Nor are any changes contemplated for the club, its management, or staff."

Under the terms of the agreement, the original investors were given 30 days to decide if they wanted to sell or continue to hold a stake in the club. McGregor stayed on as president, while Parsons assumed the role of chairman and governor.

March 1968–April 1971

Donald Parsons

The sale of 80 percent of the Penguins' stock to a group of nine Michigan businessmen headed by Detroit bank executive Donald H. Parsons caused a sharp divide among the original investors. While John Heinz and the Mellons wholeheartedly endorsed the deal, it was vigorously opposed by another faction led by Henry Hillman. However, the sale gained immediate approval from the NHL Board of Governors, who were anxious to shore up the team's sagging finances.

On the surface, Parsons appeared to have the financial wherewithal to make a go of things. A 1952 graduate of Yale University, he served as the board chairman for the Bank of Commonwealth in Detroit. His group included Thomas Wagner, chairman of the Peoples Bank of Port Huron and Monroe Bank and Trust, and George Kilborne, chairman of the Coopersville State Bank and president of Creative Capital of Michigan, Inc.

Parsons pledged to work hand in hand with Jack McGregor and the Penguins' existing investors in order to build a strong team. He also planned to take an active role in the team's operations, replacing McGregor on the board of governors.

"It is our joint aim to bring an NHL championship to Pittsburgh," he said upon completion of the deal.

A free spender, Parsons sank plenty of money into the club. Recognizing the need for a farm system to develop young talent, he backed McGregor's plan to create the Amarillo Wranglers of the Central Hockey League. While it was a sound idea, the Wranglers went belly up due to poor attendance.

Entering the 1969–70 season, he guaranteed each player a $400 bonus if the team finished in third place or higher, which it did. When Michel Briere was critically injured in a car accident, Parsons promised to provide a lifetime of financial security for the family of the Penguins' fallen star.

Parson's lavishness and generosity soon outstripped his means. Although attendance at the Civic Arena was on the rise following the team's rousing showing in the 1970 Stanley Cup Playoffs, it was still well below capacity. In the fall of 1970 the well ran dry.

"I really don't know all the ramifications," Jack Riley recalled in Joe Starkey's book, *Tales from the Pittsburgh Penguins*. "But I know this: when we went to the draft the first year Parsons was here, he picked me up in his private plane. The next year we had to send him a plane ticket to Montreal, because the league was going to run the team."

Unable to pay his debts, Parsons turned control of the Penguins over to the National Hockey League on December 1, 1970. The league ran the club for the rest of the season while Parsons searched for a buyer.

"Henry Hillman, as usual, turned out to be right," McGregor later recalled. "Parsons, while a good guy, was not financially strong enough to be a long-term player."

Donald Parsons poses for a photo with general manager Jack Riley (left) and coach Red Kelly (right).

April 1971–June 1975

Tad Potter, Peter Block, Peter Burchfield III, and Elmore Keener Jr.

April 21, 1971, was a day of celebration for Penguins fans. After fielding offers from four groups—one of which included famous singer Andy Williams—NHL president Clarence Campbell announced the club had been purchased by a group of local investors for $7 million.

"We reviewed four very attractive offers," Campbell said, "and I tell you that the Pittsburgh hockey club, which has had tremendous growth this past season and greatly increased fan support by the fans, is in good hands. We are pleased that the ownership is made up 100 percent by Pittsburgh residents."

Heading the group was Thayer R. "Tad" Potter, a marketing executive for the Peoples Natural Gas Company and a grandson of famous Pittsburgh industrialist W. F. Rockwell. He was joined by former Penguins owner Peter H. Block, Elmore L. Keener Jr. (a partner with the investment firm of Arthurs-Lestrange & Short), and A. H. "Peter" Burchfield III (vice president of the Joseph Horne Company).

The sale almost didn't take place. Potter was preparing to take his wife Jeannie on a skiing vacation in Colorado when word leaked out that the Pens were about to be sold to an out-of-town contingent.

"I apologized to her, told her we'd have to cancel the trip, and then went to work with my associates here to get the franchise for Pittsburgh," he said.

A former "Hockey Hound," Pittsburgh businessman Tad Potter and his partners purchased the Penguins on April 21, 1971.

At a news conference two days later, Potter shared his ambitions for the team with a packed audience of newsmen at the Civic Arena's Igloo Club.

"We want to expand our player development program in the minor leagues," he said. "We don't intend to be giving away draft choices and must develop our own players."

Potter assumed the dual role of governor and chairman, while Keener (president), Block (alternate governor), and Burchfield (treasurer) filled other key positions. He also gave the Pens' management team of Red Kelly and Jack Riley a full vote of confidence.

"I want it understood that there is no such thing as a one-man show," he said. "We have to respect the judgment of Jack Riley and Red Kelly. We know that they are two of the best executives in hockey."

Potter and his group—named the Pittsburgh Penguin Partners—worked hard to turn the franchise into a first-class organization. During the summer of 1973 they added more than 500 new seats to the Civic Arena, with 3,000 more planned for the 1975–76 season. He certainly didn't skimp when it came to his players. Potter awarded the team's All-Star center, Syl Apps, a contract worth $125,000 per year (one-third of the payroll for the original Penguins club). Each player received a car, courtesy of the team.

Despite the red-carpet treatment, the players didn't always respond. During the difficult 1973–74 season Potter glumly noted, "I got the feeling the players think the energy crisis means them, so they're only giving 85 percent."

Determined to bring winning hockey to Pittsburgh, he made sweeping changes. He replaced Riley on January 13 with energetic Jack Button. The owner and his new general manager agreed the team was badly in need of a shake-up.

"We were hardly an entertaining team," Button recalled. "We had [Dave] Burrows on defense and the line of Apps, [Jean] Pronovost, and [Lowell] MacDonald. That was all."

With Potter's help, Button engineered a huge five-player deal with St. Louis that changed the face and nature of the team. Two of the club's most popular players, winger Greg Polis and disturber Bryan "Bugsy" Watson, were sent to the Blues for Ab DeMarco and tough guys Steve Durbano and Bob "Battleship" Kelly. Suddenly, the Penguins had nasty teams like the Blues and the Flyers looking over their shoulders.

Although the team was losing $1 million per year, Potter courageously pulled out all stops in the summer of 1974. He allowed Button to trade for veteran scorer Vic Hadfield and his $200,000 salary. More high-priced talent soon joined the fold, including sniper Rick Kehoe and flashy rookie Pierre Larouche.

Through it all, Potter never said a peep about the team's financial woes.

"My wife and his wife Jeannie became good friends," said Pens captain Ron Schock. "We never talked business. I

Dave Burrows (left) and Syl Apps (right) show off a "Save the Pens" bumper sticker. Although the campaign boosted ticket sales, the team went into receivership in June of 1975.

never had a problem with monies, and I was always treated extremely well. That was Tad's way of doing things. A lot of the problems in the office didn't leak down to the clubhouse."

Word finally got out in January of 1975 that the Penguin Partners were skating on thin ice. The city and fans quickly rallied around the team. Mayor Pete Flaherty called a breakfast meeting of civic leaders and launched a "Save the Penguins" campaign. Flaherty's wife Nancy spent several weeks on the phone, imploring local business leaders to purchase blocks of seats. The team's average attendance jumped by more than 25 percent during the final two and a half months of the season.

The Penguins entered the postseason knowing they needed to make it into the third round of the playoffs for the franchise to remain solvent. When the team swept past St. Louis and raced to a 3–0 lead over the New York Islanders in the quarterfinals, it appeared that Potter and his associates might receive their miracle.

Then the unthinkable occurred. The Pens became only the second team in NHL history to drop four straight games and lose a playoff series.

Potter and his partners were left holding the bag. With time running out, he made a furious attempt to round up a local buyer. Sadly, none was forthcoming.

"I don't understand it," he said. "The club's going well, they're adding 3,000 seats to the building, and still nothing has happened here. The three groups I'm talking to now are from Philadelphia, Seattle, and New York. Who knows what they'll do if they buy control?"

Potter never got an opportunity to find out. On Thursday, June 12, 1975, the I.R.S. padlocked the team's offices for failure to pay $532,000 in withholding taxes. Equibank filed six writs of execution in order to attach the team's bank accounts in an attempt to recover $5 million in unpaid loans. In addition, Potter had borrowed $600,000 from his fellow NHL owners.

Out of options, he and his associates voluntarily went into receivership—effectively filing for bankruptcy. The move protected them from creditors until they could come up with a plan to put the team back on a sound financial course. U.S. District Court Judge Hubert Teitelbaum gave Potter until July 31 to file a schedule of the team's assets and liabilities, and until September 30 to develop a schedule for paying off creditors.

Button was appointed receiver, which meant that he was in charge of the club's day-to-day operations. Although he had done so much to bring a winning hockey team to Pittsburgh, Potter's reign was effectively at an end.

"Even though they drew more fans than the Steelers," wrote *Pittsburgh Press* sports editor Pat Livingston, "the Penguins collapsed because Tad Potter, imbued with the dream of building a winner, irresponsibly made promises to players which he couldn't cover. No team can pay more in salaries than it takes in."

Others were far more charitable in their assessment of the situation.

"You had to know there were problems," Schock said. "We'd get about 11,000 for our games on some Saturday nights, and we'd get about 3,500 on Tuesdays and Wednesdays. You could hardly open the building for that kind of crowd. They tried, I know they tried."

July 1975–April 1978

Al Savill, Otto Frenzel, and Wren Blair

Following the collapse of the Penguin Partners in June of 1975, the Penguins' future in the Steel City looked bleak. Acting as the team's court-appointed receiver, general manager Jack Button worked feverishly to find new investors. Remarkably, within one month he lined up a set of buyers.

Heading the group of prospective owners was Columbus, Ohio, investment broker Al Savill, who owned the minor league Columbus Owls. He was joined by Otto "Nick" Frenzel, chairman of the board of Merchants Bank of Indianapolis, and former Minnesota North Stars general manager Wren Blair.

For Savill, saving financially troubled hockey teams had become somewhat of a specialty. In 1973 he purchased the woeful Columbus Golden Seals of the International Hockey League from famed Oakland A's owner Charles O. Finley. He renamed the club the Owls and oversaw a gradual transformation from cellar dweller to playoff contender, earning him acclaim as the savior of Columbus hockey

Although the new owners hardly had deep pockets, the NHL was anxious to solve "the Penguins problem." On July 11, 1975, the league approved the sale of the team for the bargain-basement price of $3.8 million—considerably less than the two previous owners had paid. Savill served as chairman and governor, while Frenzel assumed control of the team's finances. Blair filled the dual role of president and

general manager and managed the Pens' hockey operations.

It was clear from the start the new owners intended to run a tight ship. Noting the club had lost $1.7 million the previous season, Savill said, "We will do everything in moderation."

Accordingly, Blair slashed the Pens' training camp roster from 62 players to 25.

"We pretty well know who we will invite to camp," Blair said. "Right now we are talking about only 25 players, but we may change our minds and invite 30. That doesn't mean that a player doing well in Hershey won't be invited to move up. We will keep a close watch on the Hershey camp."

He also served notice to the players that they wouldn't receive the special perks they'd enjoyed under the Potter regime.

"There seemed to be a carte blanche policy of cars for every player here," he said. "We won't have that. If the players have some silly extras that are not part of the standard contract, we will try to get out of that, too."

That included paying league fines incurred for fighting and other infractions. When enforcer Bob "Battleship" Kelly learned of the club's new stance, he was irate.

"They told me they weren't going to pay my fines from last season, and that browned me off," Kelly said. "So I told them I wouldn't fight anymore."

Despite the occasional clash over policy, the new owners had inherited a talented team. Blessed with three potent scoring lines, most experts—including former GM Jack Button—placed the club on a short list of Stanley Cup contenders.

"I will be interested to see if they can keep going what we started," he said.

The Penguins bolted from the starting gate with four straight victories, outscoring their opponents by the whopping margin of 25–12. However, they were drubbed by the powerful Canadiens 7–1 in their first big test. The club soon hit the skids.

An early savior, Columbus investment broker Al Savill bought the Penguins on July 11, 1975, and kept the team in Pittsburgh.

It didn't take long for Blair to break up the old gang. In a series of trades, he swapped popular defenseman and team leader Bob Paradise, along with youngsters Chuck Arnason, Harvey Bennett, Steve Durbano, and Gary Inness, for veterans Stan Gilbertson, Simon Nolet, Bob Taylor, and Ed Van Impe. While the Penguins rebounded to make the playoffs, they morphed into an aging team almost overnight.

The owners' lack of resources was having a telling effect. Operating without a farm system, the Pens were forced to make desperation trades to plug short-term gaps. When injuries shortened the bench, Savill used Steve Lyon, one of his minor league players at Columbus, as a fill in.

Fan support at the Civic Arena was on the wane as well. After peaking at an average of 11,455 in 1975–76, attendance dropped by more than 1,000 patrons per game.

"It's disturbing," Savill said. "I think it shows we haven't done a good job of marketing our product."

By the spring of 1977 the three-man syndicate was showing signs of coming apart. Having already relinquished the general manager duties to Baz Bastien, Blair wanted out. Savill turned to his close friend, Edward J. DeBartolo Sr. The shopping-mall magnate agreed to buy out Blair—who owned 20 percent of the team—as well as a portion of Savill and Frenzel's share.

"This is a viable franchise," Savill said upon completion of the sale. "And it's even better with Ed's money and experience as part of it. He's my good friend and one of the best businessmen in the world."

Savill scoffed at the notion that DeBartolo would soon be running the team.

"I've known Eddie for 10 or 12 years, and more on a personal level than business-wise," he said. "I don't think he's ever seen a hockey game in his life."

One year later Savill and Frenzel—faced with mounting debts and declining fan support—sold their remaining shares to DeBartolo.

April 1978–November 1991

Edward J. DeBartolo Sr.

The ownership of Edward J. DeBartolo Sr. did not begin or end in extreme financial duress. That fact alone makes his tenure at the top of the Penguins organization fairly remarkable.

Unlike previous owners, DeBartolo never intended to own a hockey team. He knew little about the sport and cared even less about it. However, he was friends with Al Savill, who owned a share of the Penguins. The Columbus investment broker and his partner, Otto Frenzel, were seeking a new investor to replace Wren Blair. In February of 1977 Savill convinced DeBartolo, who had amassed a fortune through his construction company, the Edward J. DeBartolo Corporation, to purchase a one-third interest in the team. It marked the beginning of 14 years of stable ownership.

By April 5, 1978, the Youngstown, Ohio, native had assumed complete control of the team. Initially he kept his

Construction magnate Edward J. DeBartolo Sr. provided the Penguins with stable ownership. Despite enormous losses, he stayed the course for 14 years and won a Stanley Cup.

distance, preferring to let his son, Edward Jr., and aides Vince Bartimo and Paul Martha run the club. But like any prudent investor, "Mr. D" soon began to take a more active role.

The Penguins were not a good hockey team when DeBartolo arrived on the scene. After a few modestly successful seasons, the club collapsed in the early 1980s. As the team's performance worsened, attendance plummeted to an average of fewer than 7,000 fans per game. The team was hemorrhaging millions of dollars. Rumors were swirling that the Penguins would relocate to Hamilton or Saskatoon following the 1983–84 season.

"You'd walk into the arena for a game and there would be 3,800 people in the place, and most of them were booing, and some of them had bags on their heads," Paul Steigerwald recalled in Tom McMillan's book, *The Penguins: Cellar to Summit.* "Hockey in Pittsburgh had reached the bottom, the absolute pits of professional sports. It was torture. You had to cry to keep from laughing."

One man who wasn't laughing was the boss. An intense, driven man, DeBartolo would phone the Penguins' offices from his headquarters in Youngstown each morning, demanding explanations.

"I remember a lot of days when no one wanted to be the first one in the office because no one wanted to have to answer the phone," said Tom Rooney, the team's vice president of advertising. "Especially after some horrible loss on the road."

Although he brought badly needed stability and accountability to the organization, DeBartolo was not an especially popular owner during the early years. Viewed as an outsider by the clannish Steel City fans, he came under fire for the team's performance and his penchant for raising ticket prices. Sick of all the losing and criticism, DeBartolo seriously considered putting the team up for sale. Fortunately, Penguins vice president Paul Martha—a former Pitt and Steelers football standout—had strong connections in the city.

"I went to the mayor and other civic and county leaders and we got things done that enabled Mr. DeBartolo to remain here," he said.

After purchasing control of the Civic Arena, DeBartolo decided to tough it out. In 1984 the Penguins' on-ice fortunes took a dramatic turn for the better when the club drafted Laval Titan phenom Mario Lemieux. With "Super Mario" serving as the star attraction, the team's attendance soared. However, it would take several seasons—and countless millions in losses—before the Penguins developed into a competitive team.

Through it all, DeBartolo persevered. In 1991 his willingness to see the team through the lean years was finally rewarded. With Lemieux leading the way, the Penguins won the Stanley Cup. By his own estimation, it had cost DeBartolo some $25 million for the honor of hoisting Lord Stanley's chalice.

His moment in the sun was remarkably brief. The shopping center industry—DeBartolo's bread and butter—had taken a downturn in the late 1980s. With his core business suffering and the costs of operating a hockey team continuing to spiral upward, DeBartolo decided it was time to pull out. In October of 1991 he sold the Penguins to a group headed by Howard Baldwin for $31 million. A noted philanthropist, he promptly donated $33 million to his alma mater, Notre Dame, for construction of the DeBartolo Quadrangle, which was dedicated in 1992.

DeBartolo passed away three short years later at the age of 85. In his honor the Penguins created the Edward J. DeBartolo Community Service Award, which is given each year to the player who is most involved in community and charity projects. His legacy in Pittsburgh will never be forgotten.

"I don't think anyone should underestimate what DeBartolo and his family meant to hockey in Pittsburgh," Rooney said. "There's no question that Mario Lemieux was the savior of the franchise, but Mr. D had to keep it alive just to let him be the savior. He took a tremendous financial beating all those years. And if it wasn't for his hard-headedness…hey, Mario might have been saving the *Saskatchewan* Penguins. Think of that."

November 1991–September 1999

Howard Baldwin, Morris Belzberg, Thomas Ruta, and Roger Marino

Howard Baldwin burst onto the hockey scene in 1971 with the formation of the World Hockey Association. At 28 years of age, he became a founder and partner of the Boston Whalers, making him one of the youngest owners in sports history.

Bright and energetic, Baldwin was a driving force behind the WHA's early popularity and growth. In 1976 he was

Roger Marino addresses the media. The abrasive Bostonian joined the Penguins' ownership group in 1997.

named league president. Three years later he helped broker the successful merger of the WHA and the National Hockey League. Baldwin continued to serve as the Whalers' managing general partner until 1988, when he sold the team to Richard Gordon.

Following his long tenure with the Whalers, Baldwin and his partner, Morris Belzberg, petitioned the NHL for a San Francisco Bay–area franchise. However, Minnesota owners George and Gordon Gund had the inside track on the soon-to-be San Jose Sharks. Undeterred, Baldwin and Belzberg purchased the North Stars from the Gunds in 1990 for $38.1 million. Norm Green, a late addition to the group, owned 51 percent of the team, while the Baldwin-Belzberg combination held 49 percent.

The new ownership group quickly dissolved. Green bought out Baldwin following a dispute over finances. In October of 1990, Belzberg sold his share of the team to Green as well.

Baldwin and Belzberg would shortly get another opportunity to own an NHL team. Following years of heavy losses, Penguins owner Edward J. DeBartolo Sr. put the team up for sale in the summer of 1991. With Belzberg and Thomas Ruta serving as backers, Baldwin made a bid to purchase the Steel City club.

On October 17, 1991, Baldwin and his associates purchased the Penguins for $31 million. The deal was largely bankrolled by the wealthy Belzberg, the former chairman of the Budget Rent A Car Corporation.

Unfortunately, they were unable to maintain control of the lease to the Civic Arena, which was sold to Philadelphia-based SMG for $24 million. SMG was owned in part by Spectacor, an entertainment company run by Ed Snider, the patriarch of the Flyers. It was a bad omen.

Nor did the sale receive instant acclaim in Pittsburgh. Saddled for years with an unfavorable public image, DeBartolo's patience and persistence—not to mention a Stanley Cup victory in 1991—had turned him into a folk hero. Rumors swirled that Baldwin and his associates intended to pare the team's payroll by selling off some high-priced stars. Alarmed by the accusations, it took the NHL Board of Governors over a month to approve the sale.

Predictably, Baldwin was not welcomed with open arms. At a meet-and-greet press conference, venerable Steel City sportswriter Beano Cook challenged the new Penguins owner, betting him $1,000 that he wouldn't last five years in Pittsburgh. Baldwin accepted—and later collected on the wager.

"If I had said eight years, I would have won it," Cook recalled.

Still, the early years of Baldwin's reign were among the most successful in franchise history. In 1992 the Penguins repeated as Stanley Cup champions. The following season the team enjoyed its finest year ever, winning 56 games and capturing the President's Trophy. Stocked with some of the brightest stars in hockey, the club was perennially on a short list of Cup contenders. Average attendance hovered near sellout levels—including a high of 16,714 in 1993–94.

Betraying no hint of financial distress, Baldwin rewarded his players with lavish contracts. In the fall of 1992 he called a press conference at the Westin William Penn to announce that he'd signed superstar Mario Lemieux to a six-year deal worth $42 million. At the time it was the richest contract ever awarded to an NHL player.

The Penguins' financial fortunes began an inexorable downward spiral during the 1994–95 season. Hoping to break the players' union and slash salaries, the NHL owners called for a lockout. Baldwin, who'd been experiencing financial success despite high operating costs, was one of four owners who voted against the lockout. He and his faction were overruled, and the league shut down for half a season.

The owners' hardball tactics failed miserably. When the league resumed operations in January of 1995, player salaries were at the same high level. Worse yet, the teams had lost countless millions in revenue.

No team was hit harder than the Penguins. Never blessed with deep pockets, Baldwin estimated that he lost nearly $25 million during the three-month lockout. Scrambling to recoup his losses, he struck up a television deal with Fox

Thomas Ruta, Morris Belzberg, and Howard Baldwin purchased the Penguins in 1991.

Sports Pittsburgh that earned him a sizeable chunk of cash. In the process, however, he surrendered the rights to key revenue generators, including arena advertising and marketing rights.

Seeking to reduce his short-term debt, Baldwin worked to defer payments on Lemieux's contract. Over the course of the next few seasons Mario agreed to several restructurings, usually accompanied by additional concessions of more money. The Penguins' captain also negotiated a provision that allowed him to receive the full value of his contract, even if he retired prematurely. Following the 1996–97 season, Mario did just that.

Baldwin suffered another crippling blow in the spring of 1997. Belzberg, his long-time backer, decided to sell his interest in the team. However, Baldwin appeared to make lemonade from lemons, convincing wealthy Bostonian Roger Marino to ante up $40 million for a 50 percent stake in the team.

First and foremost a businessman, Marino had amassed a $300 million fortune through his data storage company, EMC. Although he knew next to nothing about hockey, he was astute enough to understand when an organization was on shaky ground. Upon examining the books, he was aghast at the voodoo nature of the club's economics. He found the lease with SMG particularly galling. Under the terms of the agreement, SMG was making $4 million per year in profits—money Marino felt rightfully should've been going to the team.

"Even Dracula leaves his victims half alive after sucking the blood out of them, so he can come back and suck the next day," he said. "These people don't have that concept down."

Although he and Baldwin each owned an equal share of the Penguins, there was little doubt about who was running the show. Lively and abrasive, the 60-year-old Marino wasn't going to play second banana to anyone—including his partner.

He immediately began ruffling feathers. After meeting with the cantankerous owner, Pittsburgh mayor Tom Murphy was clearly flustered by Marino's off-color antics.

"The first time I met him he was flailing away at everybody," Murphy said. "I was bewildered by his approach."

Marino's strong-arm tactics didn't make him popular, but they were effective for a time. In the summer of 1998 the Penguins secured $12.9 million in public funding for upgrades to the Civic Arena, in exchange for a promise to keep the team in Pittsburgh through 2007. Marino wrung concessions from SMG as well, including kickbacks of $1 million per year and an agreement to let the club keep the 1997 profits from new club seats and lounges.

While Marino took charge, Baldwin seemed to distance himself from the team, staying in California to work on his movie production business. They appeared together in January of 1998 to announce the signing of Jaromir Jagr to a $48 million contract. However, it was clear the two were on less-than-cordial terms. Locked in a titanic power struggle, each threatened to buy the other out.

Nonplussed, Marino continued to operate as if he was the sole owner. Taking dead aim at what he considered to be sacred cows, he announced plans to pull out of the television agreement with Fox Sports Pittsburgh and start Marino Sports Television. Fox Sports took him to court to ensure they could continue to televise Penguins games.

In late June, SMG sued the team for failure to pay a $545,000 installment on a $1 million promissory note. However, Marino's most onerous move took place earlier in the year, when he defaulted on a scheduled payment to Mario Lemieux. Although Baldwin had missed a similar payment, the former Penguins superstar filed a suit against Marino in Allegheny County Common Pleas Court on June 28, 1998.

"We had no choice," Lemieux said. "I didn't want to bring the Penguins to court. It's a team that I played 13 years for and had a great relationship with until Marino came in. Now it has become a personal issue with myself and Marino."

Marino's true intentions in the matter remain unclear. Most likely, he was trying to force Lemieux out of retirement or to accept a reduced settlement. However, his shabby treatment of the local deity was a fatal mistake. In the court of public opinion, he was public enemy No. 1.

Remarkably, Marino responded by plunging the team even deeper into controversy. Despite Baldwin's vigorous protests, in July of 1998 he announced his intention to declare bankruptcy. The NHL, in the process of negotiating a $600 million television deal with the Walt Disney Company, threatened to seize control of the Penguins if Marino followed through with his plan.

Unperturbed, the Pens' owner visited Kansas City, where he was given a guided tour of the Kemper Arena. City and county leaders joined with SMG to file a lawsuit to prevent Marino from talking to other cities.

Stung by the mountain of bad press percolating out of the Steel City, the NHL was compelled to take a closer look at the Penguins' tenuous finances. Duly alarmed, the league reversed itself and allowed Marino to file for bankruptcy. With no other options, Baldwin reluctantly agreed. On October 13, 1998, the Penguins became the second team in NHL history to file for bankruptcy under Chapter 11.

Given until June of 1999 to come up with a reorganization plan, Marino and Baldwin decided to bury the hatchet and end their very public feud.

"The past few weeks, we've been working together again, and it's been a lot of fun," Baldwin said. "It's great. We get to roll up our sleeves and make this thing go again."

However, another player had entered the picture. Struck by the reality that he was unlikely to receive much, if any, of the $33 million he was owed, Lemieux began to organize his own group of investors. In September of 1999, the NHL accepted Mario's proposal. The tumultuous Marino-Baldwin era was over.

September 1999–

Lemieux Group LP

Perhaps no man has done more for Pittsburgh hockey than Mario Lemieux. As a player of unparalleled abilities, he was widely acclaimed as the savior of the Penguins. However, Mario's contributions as an owner may outstrip his accomplishments on the ice.

The seeds of Lemieux's ownership were planted in 1992 when he agreed to a then-record contract of $42 million. As the Penguins gradually ran into financial difficulty over the next few years, owner Howard Baldwin asked Mario if he would be willing to defer payments on his contract. Lemieux agreed.

Prior to his first retirement in 1997, the team missed a payment of $2 million that was scheduled for January 1, 1997. Mario, who enjoyed a good relationship with Baldwin, understood the precarious nature of the team's finances and did not press the issue.

However, his relationship with his old team quickly soured when Roger Marino purchased a 50 percent interest in the spring of 1997. A mover and a shaker, Marino had a penchant for rubbing everyone the wrong way, including the former Penguins superstar.

On January 1, 1998, the team skipped another $2 million payment. Worse yet, Marino made it clear this was no oversight. He said the expense of paying the retired superstar was financially hurting the team.

Lemieux's agent, Tom Reich, was incensed. He referred to Marino as "a poor man's Wayne Huizenga" who "thinks he can come in here and intimidate and force 'haircuts' on people he owes money to."

Marino, who fed off conflict like a shark dining on a school of mackerel, shot back, "I smacked his boy in the face although that was not my intention."

While the Penguins' co-owner clearly felt justified in his actions, he had made enemies with the wrong man. When pushed, Lemieux displayed a stubbornness that bordered on obstinacy. There was no way he would lie down and allow Marino to default on his contract.

On June 25, 1998, Lemieux filed a suit against Marino in Allegheny County Common Pleas Court, contending the team owed him more than $33 million. It was the first in a rapid-fire series of lawsuits that would, in part, lead the Penguins to file for bankruptcy a few months later.

As the team's largest creditor, Lemieux was appointed to serve as a co-chairman on a seven-member board of creditors. The group was asked to develop a plan for the team to pay its creditors from the assets that remained. It appeared the Penguins might have to fold in order to sufficiently cover its debts. Under that bleak scenario, everyone—the city, the team's loyal fans, the players, and Mario—would lose.

Lemieux quickly came to the realization that the best solution was for him to assume ownership. He spent the better part of the 1998–99 season rounding up investors, including wealthy Californian Ron Burkle, who would enable him to pay off the other creditors and gain a controlling interest in the team. The former Penguins superstar also met with state and city leaders, as well as NHL commissioner Gary Bettman, to gain support for his plan.

Marino was hard at work on a restructuring plan of his own. However, support for the abrasive Bostonian was nonexistent. Pittsburgh mayor Tom Murphy delivered the death blow, stating that he would help Lemieux secure a new arena, but not Marino.

On September 1 1999, the NHL officially accepted Lemieux's proposal. After a final ruling by Bankruptcy Court Judge Bernard Markovitz, ownership of the Penguins was officially transferred to the Lemieux Group LP two days later. To help finance the deal, Mario had forgiven $12.5 million of the deferred salary that was owed him. With the remaining $20 million, he purchased a 22 percent stake in the team.

The tensions that hung over the club like an impenetrable fog immediately lifted. Unlike Marino, who had an almost pathological need for the spotlight, Lemieux's relaxed manner had a calming, soothing effect.

"You don't see him much [around the team]," FSN announcer and former teammate Bob Errey said. "But I think he likes being on the outside a little bit. He doesn't want to be a vocal guy, much like when he played."

After becoming the first former NHL player to own a majority interest in his former team, Mario had an even bigger surprise in store. In December of 2000, he announced his comeback as a player.

"We were struggling," explained Jaromir Jagr, "and [general manager] Craig Patrick told me 'Mario wants to talk to you.' I had nobody to play with. I told Mario, 'We need a centerman.' He told me, 'I might have one for you.' I said, 'Who is it?' And he said, 'He's pretty good.'"

Lemieux's comeback was the stuff of legend. Thirty-three seconds into his first game he assisted on a goal by Jagr. He piled up 76 points in 43 games while leading the Penguins to the conference finals. Mario went on to play four more seasons before hanging up his skates for good.

While Mario savored his return to the ice, he took his ownership duties seriously. Knowing full-well the Penguins needed a new arena to remain viable, he approved the purchase of a tract of land directly adjacent to the Mellon Arena in November of 2000. Popular and well-connected, he began to lobby city and county officials for funding.

Determined to make the organization financially viable, he instructed Craig Patrick to eschew big-ticket free agents in favor of building through the draft. Predictably, the team's performance and attendance took a tumble. Following the dismal 2003–04 season when the Penguins averaged a league-low 11,877 fans per game, Lemieux was poised to sell a majority interest in the team to a golfing buddy, William "Boots" DelBiaggio.

Mario Lemieux rescued the team from bankruptcy in September of 1999. Nearly a decade later he hoisted his third Stanley Cup.

A stroke of good fortune changed his mind. The Penguins hit the mother lode at the 2005 draft lottery when they earned the right to select phenom Sidney Crosby. Widely regarded as the finest prospect to enter the NHL since Lemieux himself, the 18-year-old Crosby accepted an offer to live as a guest in Mario's Sewickley home.

Thanks to Crosby's presence and a new collective bargaining agreement that featured a much-needed salary cap, a rejuvenated Lemieux pulled back his offer to DelBiaggio. With the Penguins poised to thrive in the "New NHL," Mario recognized it was time to push for a new arena.

"When Mario and his group acquired the team [in 1999], they also were given a written promise that by June of 2002—three years hence—there would be a financial plan in place [for a new arena]," said Penguins president and CEO Ken Sawyer. "We have invested over $11 million so far in this project. That's an enormous sum for an operation our size, but we view a new arena as absolutely essential to our long-term viability."

Unfortunately, the city's limited resources were maxed out following the construction of two other sports facilities, PNC Park and Heinz Field. Forced to look elsewhere for funding, the Lemieux Group struck an innovative deal with the Isle of Capri, a Biloxi, Mississippi, casino developer that was bidding on a state-granted slots license in Pittsburgh. Under the terms of the agreement, the Isle of Capri would pledge $290 million toward the construction of a new arena as part of its proposed casino complex.

Although the arrangement with the Isle of Capri required no public funding, government officials were lukewarm. They cautioned that the Isle of Capri plan could not be endorsed unless the developer was awarded the slots license by the Pennsylvania Gaming Control Board. Instead, they gave lip service to the notion that a new arena would be built with a combination of state, local, and team funding. However, no real progress was made.

By January of 2006 Lemieux was fed up. Weary of empty promises, he put the team up for sale with the stipulation that the new owner be bound by the Isle of Capri plan.

On the eve of the 2006–07 season, Canadian business magnate Jim Balsillie agreed to purchase the Penguins for $175 million. However, when pressed for a commitment to keep the club in Pittsburgh, Balsillie reneged on his offer. On December 20, 2006, the Pennsylvania Gaming Control Board awarded the slots license to Majestic Star.

With the Isle of Capri deal dead in the water, a frustrated Lemieux shifted into high gear. He pulled the team off the market and began to entertain offers from other cities, most notably Kansas City. Alarmed that Mario was, indeed, serious about moving the team, state and local officials finally got down to business. Following an intense round of bargaining sessions, a deal for a new arena was reached on March 12, 2007.

"We've been through a lot the last few years," Mario told the Versus network the following night. "And to have the

Silent Partner

He rarely seeks the spotlight. Yet without him, it's unlikely the Pittsburgh Penguins would exist today.

The life of Penguins owner Ronald Wayne Burkle reads like a true Horatio Alger success story. Born in Pamona, California, on November 12, 1952, he started working as a box boy at age 13 for Stater Brothers grocery—a store managed by his father. Burkle attended California State Polytechnic University, but chose to drop out before earning a degree.

After leaving school, he returned to the grocery and worked his way into management. However, when Burkle tried to purchase the company, he was let go.

The setback didn't deter him. In 1986 Burkle founded Yucaipa Companies, an investment firm that specializes in buying and selling regional groceries. Possessing a keen eye for undervalued companies, the bright and driven Burkle soon amassed a fortune through his savvy business deals.

His wealth enabled him to play the role of white knight. In 1999, Burkle doled out $20 million in cash to help Mario Lemieux purchase the Penguins out of bankruptcy.

"I think at the time his biggest intent was helping Mario," said John Brabender, a spokesman for Mario during the bankruptcy proceedings.

"If he sees an undervalued asset, he writes a check," said long-time associate Lloyd Greif. "If he sees an ability…to fix things that are broken, all the better."

A true silent partner, Burkle prefers to let Lemieux serve as the face of the franchise. However, when the Penguins were negotiating with government officials for a new arena in 2007, Burkle took a lead role.

"He's a hard bargainer," Pennsylvania governor Ed Rendell said. "He's very intense. He's very passionate about everything he does. In the end, he's a good business person."

team that we have and a new arena, it's going to be very exciting in the coming years. Our goal is to win a Stanley Cup."

He wouldn't have long to wait. On Friday, June 12, 2009, the Penguins defeated the Detroit Red Wings 2–1 in a thrilling Game 7 at Joe Louis Arena to capture the team's third Stanley Cup.

Addressing a huge throng at a victory celebration in downtown Pittsburgh three days later, Lemieux smiled and said, "The Stanley Cup is finally back where it belongs."

6

The Hall of Famers

Located in Toronto, Ontario, Canada, the Hockey Hall of Fame is dedicated to the history of ice hockey. Serving as both a hall of fame and a museum, the magnificent stone building at the corner of Yonge and Front streets features exhibits, memorabilia, and multimedia presentations honoring the individuals and teams who brought special distinction to the game. The Hockey Hall of Fame also serves as a home for National Hockey League trophies, including the Stanley Cup.

Since its inception in 1943, a total of 247 players, 101 builders, and 15 on-ice officials have been inducted into the Hockey Hall of Fame. The inductees include 17 former Penguins players, coaches, and executives.

Among the honored Penguins players, Andy Bathgate, Leo Boivin, Tim Horton, Luc Robitaille, and Bryan Trottier spent a small portion of their careers with Pittsburgh. Selected in the 1967 Expansion Draft, Bathgate and Boivin were original Penguins. Two of the greatest players of their day, both were nearing the end of the line when they arrived in Pittsburgh. Horton and Robitaille each played one abbreviated season for the club—the former due to an ankle injury and the latter due to the lockout in 1994–95. The popular Trottier tasted the most success, winning a pair of Stanley Cups.

Paul Coffey, Ron Francis, Joe Mullen, and Larry Murphy skated four or more seasons for the club. Each was a gifted performer who played an integral role on the Stanley Cup–winning teams of the early 1990s.

It seems altogether fitting that the incomparable Mario Lemieux is the lone member of the Hall of Fame to spend his entire career in Pittsburgh. If not for Mario's Herculean efforts—both as a player and an owner—there would be no NHL team in Pittsburgh today. Presently, he is the only Penguins draft pick to be honored.

Among the builders, general manager Craig Patrick had the most profound influence. The architect of two Stanley Cup winners, he led the Pens to 11 consecutive playoff berths during his 17-year tenure. Coaching legends Scotty Bowman, Herb Brooks, and Bob Johnson spent at least part of one season behind the Pens' bench. Bowman and Johnson each guided the team to a Stanley Cup.

While not regarded as full inductees, two members of the Steel City media have been honored by the Hockey Hall of Fame. Colorful play-by-play announcer Mike Lange, who was awarded the Foster Hewitt Memorial Award for broadcasters, is still going strong after more than 30 years of calling Penguins games. *Pittsburgh Post-Gazette* sportswriter Dave Molinari received the Elmer Ferguson Memorial Award for his insightful, witty, and accurate reporting during the course of a 27-year career.

In addition to the present group of honorees, several former Penguins merit serious consideration. Five-time Art Ross Trophy winner Jaromir Jagr is a virtual lock for future induction. Tom Barrasso, who recorded more wins than any other American-born goalie, is a strong candidate as well. With a career that spanned more than 1,500 games as a player, coach, and general manager, popular Eddie Johnston could be a sentimental choice with the veterans' committee. A push was made for Dave Burrows, a defensive stalwart during the 1970s. However, he appears to lack the offensive numbers to gain entrance.

Tony Esposito and Leonard "Red" Kelly are included in this section of the book. Each was inducted into the Hall of Fame as a player. Kelly served as a coach and general manager with the Pens from 1969 through 1973. Esposito was the team's general manager for a season and a half in the late 1980s.

Likewise, this chapter features a bio on Glen Sather, who was inducted as a builder in 1997. Sather played in 122 games for the Penguins from 1969 through January of 1971.

Mario Lemieux was inducted into the Hockey Hall of Fame in 1997, shortly after his first retirement.

Bathgate, Andrew James

Right Wing
Penguins: 1967–68, 1970–71
NHL: 1952–71
WHA: 1974–75
Inducted into Hockey Hall of Fame: 1978 (Player)
Birthplace: Winnipeg, Manitoba
B: August 28, 1932
Shoots: right

	Regular Season					Playoffs				
	GP	G	A	PTS	PM	GP	G	A	PTS	PM
Pittsburgh	150	35	68	103	89	-	-	-	-	-
NHL	**1069**	**349**	**624**	**973**	**624**	**54**	**21**	**14**	**35**	**76**
WHA	**11**	**1**	**6**	**7**	**2**	**-**	**-**	**-**	**-**	**-**

During an NHL career that spanned almost 20 seasons, Andy Bathgate established himself as one of the game's most dynamic stars. Blessed with good size, he was a strong, athletic skater who handled the puck with skill and creativity. Possessing a hard, accurate shot, he was one of the first players to employ the slap shot. It was a Bathgate blast that convinced Hall of Fame goalie Jacques Plante to don a mask.

From the start Bathgate had to overcome enormous adversity. He suffered a severe knee injury during his first shift in junior hockey—an injury that required a steel plate be inserted into his left knee. For the rest of his career he wore heavy knee braces, which made his accomplishments all the more astonishing.

Bathgate hit his stride while playing for the Rangers. In 1958–59 he scored 40 goals and was awarded the Hart Trophy. Three years later he tied Chicago great Bobby Hull for the scoring title. Following a trade to Toronto in 1964, he helped the Leafs win the Stanley Cup.

Andrew James
Bathgate

Although Bathgate was for the most part a clean player who preferred to stick to hockey, he was the wrong guy to mess with. Having grown up in a tough section of Winnipeg that produced quite a few boxers, Andy knew how to handle himself.

By 1967 Bathgate's star was waning. But the Penguins, convinced that he had a couple of good years left, plucked him from the Red Wings in the 17th round of the Expansion Draft. Their judgment proved to be spot on. The veteran winger notched 20 goals and led all West Division players with 59 points.

However, Bathgate had grown weary of life on the road. Wishing to spend more time with his family, he arranged for the Penguins to loan him to Vancouver of the Western League. He starred for the Canucks for two seasons before making a surprise return to the Pens in 1970–71. Although 38 years old and playing on aching knees, Andy was still good enough to tally 44 points.

Remarkably, he played 11 games for the Vancouver Blazers in the WHA at age 42—and scored seven points—before retiring for good.

Boivin, Leo Joseph

Defense
Penguins: 1967–69
NHL: 1951–70
Inducted into Hockey Hall of Fame: 1986 (Player)
Birthplace: Prescott, Ontario
B: August 2, 1932
Shoots: left

	Regular Season					Playoffs				
	GP	G	A	PTS	PM	GP	G	A	PTS	PM
Pittsburgh	114	14	26	40	100	-	-	-	-	-
NHL	**1150**	**72**	**250**	**322**	**1192**	**54**	**3**	**10**	**13**	**59**

Over the course of an NHL career that spanned 1,150 games, Leo Boivin established himself as one of the game's most fearsome open-ice hitters. No less an authority than fellow Hall of Famer Tim Horton considered him the toughest defenseman in the league to beat one on one.

Boivin's career nearly ended before it began. Homesick, he walked out of the Maple Leafs' training camp in 1951. But Conn Smythe, Toronto's legendary owner, knew a hockey player when he saw one—especially one who hit as hard as Boivin. He convinced the youngster to give hockey another try.

Following two seasons with Toronto, Smythe sent Boivin to one of the league's have-nots, the lowly Boston Bruins. What was intended to be a short-term "loan" quickly became a permanent fix. Boivin was so popular in Boston that Bruins owner Walter Brown pleaded with Smythe to let him stay.

Leo Joseph Boivin

Squat and powerful, the 5'7", 190-pounder had a low center of gravity—perfect for hitting. His arsenal included the shoulder check and the hip check, often thrown with devastating results. Although he rarely put a stick, elbow, or knee into his checks, he was one of the most feared men in the league. Doug Mohns likened being hit by "the Fireplug" to colliding with a freight train.

Eager to add some mustard to their blue-line corps, the Penguins claimed Boivin in the 1967 Expansion Draft. However, his stay with the Pens was relatively brief. Midway through his second season Jack Riley traded him to Minnesota for Duane Rupp. Leo played with the North Stars through the 1969–70 campaign before hanging up his skates.

Bowman, William Scott

Coach
Penguins: 1991–93
NHL: 1967–87, 1991–02
Inducted into Hockey Hall of Fame: 1991 (Builder)
Birthplace: Montreal, Quebec
B: September 18, 1933

	Regular Season							Playoffs			
	G	W	L	T	OL	PTS	PCT	G	W	L	PCT
Pittsburgh	164	95	53	16	-	206	.628	33	23	10	.697
NHL	**2141**	**1244**	**573**	**314**	**10**	**2812**	**.657**	**353**	**223**	**130**	**.632**

During his 30 seasons as an NHL coach, William Scott Bowman won nine Stanley Cups and set a standard of excellence unmatched in the history of the game. An old-school coach who preferred to keep his players on edge, Bowman would never win a popularity contest. However, he was a master motivator who knew precisely which buttons to push to get the most out of his teams. Possessing a keen hockey

mind, he was a brilliant strategist who excelled at making adjustments during the course of a game.

Bowman served his coaching apprenticeship in the Montreal system, where he studied the methods of the legendary Toe Blake. In 1967–68 he joined the St. Louis Blues as an assistant coach, but soon took over the helm when the club staggered to a poor start. The Blues began an immediate turnaround and made it all the way to the Stanley Cup Finals, where they faced off against the Canadiens and his old mentor, Blake. Although the Habs swept the upstart Blues in four straight games, it was a remarkable achievement for the rookie coach.

Prodded by their iron-willed coach, the Blues easily became the class of the expansion teams. They returned to the Stanley Cup Finals in each of the next two seasons, but were eliminated in four-game sets by the Canadiens and Bruins.

Bowman left St. Louis in 1971 following a dispute with the Blues' maverick owner, Sid Salomon Jr. He was immediately hired to coach the most storied franchise in the NHL, the Canadiens. During his eight-year reign the Habs *averaged* 52 wins a season and captured five Stanley Cups. His 1976–77 juggernaut—arguably the greatest team of all time—won an astounding 60 games.

Seeking a new challenge, Bowman left Montreal in 1979 to become coach and general manager of the Buffalo Sabres. The success that had become almost second nature would elude him on the Niagara frontier. Following a strong first season, the Sabres grew progressively worse. When the team failed to qualify for the playoffs for two consecutive seasons he was unceremoniously fired in 1987.

William Scott Bowman

Bowman worked as an analyst on CBC's *Hockey Night in Canada* until the summer of 1990, when he was hired to serve as the director of player personnel for the Pittsburgh Penguins. On his recommendation the club acquired veteran defenseman Gordie Roberts for an 11th-round draft pick. A steadying influence on two Stanley Cup winners, Roberts proved to be well worth the price.

Basking in the afterglow of the team's first Cup victory, Bowman seemed content to remain in the front office. However, tragedy would soon alter the course of his career. In the summer of 1991, coach Bob Johnson was diagnosed with a malignant brain tumor. General manager Craig Patrick asked Bowman to step behind the bench and reluctantly he agreed.

The players were in for a culture shock. Gruff and abrasive, Bowman was a far cry from the fatherly, upbeat Johnson. Relations between the coach and team deteriorated until the players were in full revolt. Following a closed-door meeting with Patrick, tensions eased and the club began to respond to the legendary coach. The result was a second Stanley Cup.

In 1992–93 Bowman guided the Penguins to a stunning 56-win season and the President's Trophy. However, the Pens were upset by the Islanders in the second round of the playoffs. With the strain between the coach and the team still palpable, Bowman decided to look for greener pastures. Within a month he was hired to coach the Red Wings.

In many ways it was a rebirth for Bowman. His work in Detroit would rival his accomplishments in Montreal. In nine seasons as the Red Wings' bench boss he won three more Stanley Cups. He retired from the coaching ranks in 2002 with 1,244 career wins and an extraordinary .657 winning percentage—marks that likely will never be equaled.

Brooks, Herbert Paul, Jr.

Coach
Penguins: 1999–00
NHL: 1981–85, 1987–88, 1992–93, 1999–00
Inducted into Hockey Hall of Fame: 2006 (Builder)
Birthplace: St. Paul, Minnesota
B: August 5, 1937
D: August 11, 2003

	Regular Season							Playoffs			
	G	W	L	T	OL	PTS	PCT	G	W	L	PCT
Pittsburgh	57	29	21	5	2	65	.570	11	6	5	.545
NHL	**506**	**219**	**219**	**66**	**2**	**506**	**.500**	**40**	**19**	**21**	**.475**

Herb Brooks will forever be remembered as the architect of Team USA's "Miracle on Ice" triumph at the 1980 Winter Olympic Games. However, his influence on the game goes far deeper than any singular accomplishment. During a collegiate, international, and professional coaching career that spanned nearly three decades, he earned a reputation for

Herbert Paul Brooks Jr.

being one of the sport's most brilliant teachers, innovators, and motivators.

As a youth growing up in St. Paul, Minnesota, Brooks played hockey and dreamed of one day making it as a pro. After starring for St. Paul Johnson High School, Herb was a standout at the University of Minnesota.

In 1960 he appeared to earn a spot on the United States Olympic team. However, a week before the games began Brooks received the crushing news that he'd been cut from the squad. Relegated to the role of spectator, he watched as his former teammates captured the gold medal.

The personal setback galvanized him. After playing on the 1964 and 1968 USA Olympic teams, Brooks entered the coaching ranks in 1972 with his alma mater, Minnesota. During his seven years at the helm Herb led the Golden Gophers to three NCAA titles.

In the summer of 1979 Brooks was named general manager and head coach of Team USA for the 1980 Winter Olympics. Determined to defeat the powerhouse Soviet team that had dominated international hockey, Herb devised a hybrid system that combined aspects of the Soviet's highly effective weaving style with the NHL's more traditional game. The result was a stunning gold-medal victory, perhaps the greatest achievement in the history of sports.

Considered the brightest young coach in hockey, Brooks was hired in 1981 by Craig Patrick, his former Olympic team assistant, to lead the New York Rangers. Working on hockey's biggest stage, Herb immediately installed the swirling, creative style of play that had revolutionized the game. His Rangers squads included several players from the 1980 gold-medal team, including Mark Pavelich, Rob McClanahan, Bill Baker, and Dave Silk.

Brooks became the fastest coach in Rangers history to win 100 games. However, playoff success eluded him. When the Blueshirts stumbled during his fourth season, Patrick made the painful decision to fire his former mentor.

Following his dismissal, Brooks returned to the college ranks to coach St. Cloud State. In 1987 he was hired by former Olympic team associate Lou Nanne to coach the Minnesota North Stars. What should have been a triumphant homecoming for Brooks nearly ruined his career. Following a dismal 19-win season in Bloomington he was relieved of his duties.

It appeared the luster of his spectacular Olympic triumph had finally worn off. Brooks didn't land another head coaching job until 1991, when he was hired by the Utica Devils of the American Hockey League. His performance earned him a promotion to the New Jersey Devils, but he was let go after just one season.

Herb joined the Pittsburgh Penguins as a head scout in 1995, where he was reunited with his old friend Craig Patrick. When the team floundered at the start of the 1999–2000 season, Patrick asked the coaching legend to step behind the bench. The Penguins responded to Brooks' inspirational style with a strong second half and a solid showing in the Stanley Cup Playoffs.

Although Herb chose to return to scouting following the season, his success with the Pens sparked a renewed interest in coaching. In February of 2002 he led Team USA to a silver medal at the XIX Winter Olympic Games. That summer Brooks was courted by Rangers general manager Glen Sather but he declined the offer, preferring to spend time with his family in Minnesota.

Tragically, on the afternoon of August 11, 2003, Herb was killed while driving home from a golf tournament fundraiser. It's believed that the 66-year-old Brooks fell asleep at the wheel. He left behind a legacy of unparalleled innovation and achievement.

Coffey, Paul Douglas

Defense
Penguins: 1987–92
NHL: 1980–01
Inducted into Hockey Hall of Fame: 2004 (Player)
Inducted into Penguins Hall of Fame: 2007
Birthplace: Weston, Ontario
B: June 1, 1961
Shoots: left

| | Regular Season | | | | | Playoffs | | | | |
	GP	G	A	PTS	PM	GP	G	A	PTS	PM
Pittsburgh	331	108	332	440	573	23	4	22	26	37
NHL	**1409**	**396**	**1135**	**1531**	**1802**	**194**	**59**	**137**	**196**	**264**

On the day of the 1980 Entry Draft the Penguins hoped to select speedy Kitchener defenseman Paul Coffey with their first choice. Having played with the incomparable Bobby Orr, Pens coach Eddie Johnston knew full well what a

Paul Douglas Coffey

puck-rushing defender could do for a team. Unfortunately, the Edmonton Oilers wrecked the Penguins' plans by snagging Coffey with the sixth overall pick.

The Pens' misfortune was Coffey's good fortune. He arrived in Edmonton just as general manager Glen Sather was assembling arguably the finest collection of skill players in the history of the game. The Oilers' lineup was packed with future stars such as Mark Messier, Jari Kurri, and Glenn Anderson, not to mention a skinny kid from Brantford, Ontario, named Gretzky.

After taking a year to get acclimated, Coffey exploded with an 89-point season in 1981–82. The following year he topped the 100-point mark while helping the Oilers win their first of five Stanley Cups. He was supernatural during the 1985 postseason, rolling up *37 points*—a record for defensemen that will most likely never be broken. In 1985–86 he scored 48 goals to eclipse Orr's single-season standard for a defenseman.

In many ways Coffey was a throwback to the early days of the sport when teams played with seven players a side. The extra man—called a "rover"—played a hybrid position of forward and defense. This described Coffey's game to a T. Using his supreme offensive skills to the fullest measure, he often joined the attack as a fourth forward. Yet he was fast enough to cover his own zone on defense.

In 1987 Coffey became embroiled in a contract dispute with Sather. While he sat out the first two months of the season, Penguins general manager Eddie

Johnston—desperate to find a superstar to team with Mario Lemieux—approached the Oilers about a trade. On November 24, 1987, a deal was finally struck and "Coff" headed east to Pittsburgh.

The trade marked an audible turning point in Penguins hockey. With the quicksilver defenseman springing Lemieux loose with his picture-perfect passes, Mario captured the first of his six scoring titles.

Over the next three seasons Coffey amassed an amazing 309 points while Pens general manager Craig Patrick assembled a Stanley Cup–caliber team. Although he suffered a broken jaw early in the 1991 playoffs, Coffey returned in the finals to spark the Penguins to their first Cup.

The next season Coffey suddenly found himself in hot water. Never a textbook defender, his lapses displeased Penguins coach Scotty Bowman. Almost as an insult, Bowman used the speedy blue-liner at forward. In February of 1992 the Pens sent the future Hall of Famer to Los Angeles as part of a huge three-team deal that brought Rick Tocchet to Pittsburgh.

Much to Coffey's credit, he took Bowman's criticism to heart. Instead of pouting over the treatment he'd received, he concentrated on improving his defensive play. In January of 1993 the Kings traded him to the Red Wings—*Scotty Bowman's* Red Wings. His game now complete, Coffey served as the defensive anchor for the President's Trophy–winning Wings. In 1994–95 he captured his third Norris Trophy while leading Detroit in scoring.

Coffey became somewhat of a gypsy during his final seasons, playing for five different teams. He often served as a rental player for clubs hoping to make a playoff run. Still, his legacy as one of the sport's true greats remained intact. He retired in 2001 as the all-time points leader among defensemen (since surpassed by Raymond Bourque).

Esposito, Anthony James

General Manager
Penguins: 1988–89
NHL: 1968–98
Inducted into Hockey Hall of Fame: 1988 (Player)
Birthplace: Sault Ste. Marie, Ontario
B: April 23, 1943

	Regular Season						Playoffs			
	G	W	L	T	PTS	PCT	G	W	L	PCT
Pittsburgh	106	50	47	9	109	.514	11	7	4	.636
NHL	**106**	**50**	**47**	**9**	**109**	**.514**	**11**	**7**	**4**	**.636**

One half of the most famous brother combination in hockey history, Tony Esposito was the kid brother of Boston's great goal scorer, Phil Esposito. As youngsters growing up in Sault Ste. Marie, Phil would practice shooting against Tony for hours on end. The basic training would serve Tony well in the years ahead.

Anthony James Esposito

A late bloomer, he opted to attend Michigan Tech rather than play junior hockey. It was a curious choice for a Canadian youth, but it proved to be a wise one. Esposito turned in three solid seasons with the Huskies. He soon drew the attention of Montreal's famed general manager Sam Pollock, who signed the young netminder to a free-agent deal.

Buried on the depth chart behind veteran Gump Worsley and fellow up-and-comer Rogie Vachon, Esposito played only 13 games during his first season. Although he displayed flashes of brilliance, the Habs exposed him in the Intra-League Draft. He was promptly snapped up by the Black Hawks.

In 1969–70 Esposito took the league by storm. Still technically a rookie, the 26-year-old goalie posted a sterling 2.17 goals-against average and a league-leading 15 shutouts to earn the Calder Trophy. He became the first rookie goalie since Frank Brimsek to win the Vezina Trophy.

One of the first goalies to employ the butterfly style, Esposito confounded the shooters of his day. Offering a tantalizing glimpse of the five hole, he lured them in like so many moths to a flame. Then he would snap his legs shut when they tried to exploit the opening. Blessed with a cat-quick glove hand, he also was a proficient poke-checker.

"Tony O" continued to dominate for the next several seasons. He added two more Vezinas to his burgeoning trophy case, as well as NHL First Team All-Star honors in 1971–72. Although the Black Hawks were a strong, veteran team, success in the postseason was more elusive. When the

Hawks met his old team, the Canadiens, in the 1973 Finals, Esposito gave a surprisingly weak performance.

Displaying plenty of resilience, he bounced back to enjoy a Hall of Fame career. By the time he hung up his pads in 1984, he had amassed 423 wins (seventh all-time) and 76 shutouts (ninth all-time).

A popular figure on the banquet circuit, the outgoing Esposito struck up a friendship with the DeBartolo family, who owned the Penguins. He obviously made an impression. Although he had no previous management experience, they appointed him director of hockey operations in the summer of 1988.

During Esposito's first year at the helm the Penguins earned a playoff berth, something they hadn't done since 1982. He also acquired talented young goalie Tom Barrasso, who would serve as a cornerstone for the team's future Stanley Cup champions. However, Esposito soon ran afoul of the DeBartolos and was dismissed in December of 1989.

Francis, Ronald

Center
Penguins: 1991–98
NHL: 1981–04
Inducted into Hockey Hall of Fame: 2007 (Player)
Birthplace: Sault Ste. Marie, Ontario
B: March 1, 1963
Shoots: left

	Regular Season					Playoffs				
	GP	G	A	PTS	PM	GP	G	A	PTS	PM
Pittsburgh	533	164	449	613	295	97	32	68	100	67
NHL	**1731**	**549**	**1249**	**1798**	**979**	**171**	**46**	**97**	**143**	**95**

Although in hindsight it's hard to imagine, Ron Francis was not the player the Hartford Whalers were hoping to select with the fourth overall pick in the 1981 Entry Draft. Whalers general manager Emile "the Cat" Francis had his eyes on Bobby Carpenter, the speedy scoring sensation from St. John's High School in nearby Shrewsbury, Massachusetts. However, when the Capitals traded up to snag Carpenter, the Whalers had to "settle" for Francis.

It would prove to be an incredible stroke of good fortune. Carpenter scored 53 goals in 1984–85 and totaled 728 points for his career, but he never lived up to his advance billing as "The Can't Miss Kid." Meanwhile, Francis would tally 1,798 points during an exemplary NHL career that spanned 23 seasons.

From the moment he first skated onto an NHL rink, Francis was a complete player. As a 19-year-old rookie with the Whalers, he scored 25 goals and 68 points in just 59 games.

Over the next eight seasons he averaged 85 points per year for Hartford, including 101 points in 1989–90. Displaying the remarkable consistency that would be a hallmark of his career, he never scored fewer than 23 goals or 75 points in a season during that span.

Success in the postseason was harder to achieve. Although it was by no means a reflection of Francis' play, the Whalers failed to advance past the first round of the playoffs in four straight seasons. As team captain, Francis began to take some heat.

Midway through the 1990–91 season he was stripped of the captaincy by coach Rick Ley. Under intense pressure from owner Richard Gordon to move Francis or suffer the consequences, general manager Eddie Johnston sent the star center to Pittsburgh as part of a whopping six-player trade.

Hartford's loss was the Penguins' gain. Francis immediately established himself in Pittsburgh with his diligent two-way play. Filling the vital role of second-line center behind Mario Lemieux, he helped propel the Penguins to their first Stanley Cup.

Perhaps no player in the history of the sport has read the game as well as Francis. An ordinary skater at best, he possessed an uncanny knack for arriving at the right place at the right time. Unselfish with the puck, he was an outstanding playmaker. Francis also displayed a penchant for scoring big goals and winning key face-offs. Combined with his superb defensive play, tireless work ethic, and sterling leadership, he was one of the most complete players the sport has ever seen.

His value was never more evident than during the 1992 Patrick Division Finals. With Lemieux sidelined with a broken hand, Francis brought the Pens back from the brink, scoring two huge goals in Game 4 to turn the tide of the series. In Game 4 of the Finals he notched the game winner to clinch the Penguins' second straight Stanley Cup.

Ronald Francis

Francis would remain a valuable member of the Penguins for six more seasons. Twice during that span he led the league in assists, while capturing the Selke and Lady Byng trophies in 1994–95. The following season he registered a career-best 119 points.

His contract with the Penguins expired in 1998. Unable to come to terms with Francis, general manager Craig Patrick reluctantly allowed him to become a free agent. His old club, which had relocated to Carolina, desperately wanted him back. With an opportunity to right an old wrong, owner Peter Karmanos signed the 35-year-old veteran to a long-term deal.

Francis played five-plus seasons for Carolina and led the team to the Stanley Cup Finals in 2002. In the spring of 2004 the Hurricanes traded their all-time points leader to Toronto for a final chance at the Cup. The quiet superstar officially retired following the lockout season as the fourth-highest scorer in NHL history.

Miles Gilbert Horton

Horton, Miles Gilbert

Defense
Penguins: 1971–72
NHL: 1949–74
Inducted into Hockey Hall of Fame: 1977 (Player)
Birthplace: Cochrane, Ontario
B: January 12, 1930
D: February 21, 1974
Shoots: right

	Regular Season					Playoffs				
	GP	G	A	PTS	PM	GP	G	A	PTS	PM
Pittsburgh	44	2	9	11	40	4	0	1	1	2
NHL	1446	115	403	518	1611	126	11	39	50	183

Long before Bobby Orr revolutionized the game, another young defenseman had NHL scouts raving about his potential. In the late 1940s Miles Gilbert "Tim" Horton caused an unbelievable stir while skating for St. Michael's College in the Ontario League. Blessed with a body hewn from granite, he could skate, pass, shoot, and hit with the best of them. Many experts felt Horton would develop into the greatest defenseman of all time.

For a time Horton struggled to meet those early expectations. Instead of bursting on the scene like a comet, he developed slowly. The turning point came in 1958 when Toronto coach Billy Reay paired him with Allan Stanley. With the rock-solid Stanley handling the defensive chores, Horton was free to carry the puck and join the attack.

Horton's physical strength was legendary. Many regarded him as pound for pound the strongest player ever—certainly the strongest of his day. While he wasn't a rabble-rouser, he was no shrinking violet either. Far from a classic puncher,

he preferred wrestling tactics. More often than not he would wrap an opponent in a vice-like bear hug and slam him to the ice.

Following a string of four Stanley Cups the Leafs began to decline in the late 1960s. Although Horton was still at the top of his game, Toronto traded the All-Star defenseman to the Rangers in the spring of 1970. Having started a successful string of donut shops that bore his name, Horton seriously considered retiring until the Rangers doubled his salary.

In 1971 Penguins general manager Red Kelly, an old friend and teammate on Toronto's great Cup teams, claimed Horton in the Intra-League Draft to anchor his young defensive corps. It was a homecoming of sorts for Horton, who had served his minor league apprenticeship with the Pittsburgh Hornets.

With the 41-year-old Horton serving as an on-ice coach, the Penguins jumped to a 5–1 start. However, Horton suffered a broken ankle in the sixth game of the year and the team lost its early momentum. The following summer he was claimed by Buffalo, reuniting him with his former Leafs coach Punch Imlach.

Early in the morning of February 21, 1974, Horton's life came to a tragic and untimely end. For reasons unknown he was speeding from Toronto to his home in Buffalo following a game. Police who were called to the chase clocked Horton's sports car at speeds of over 100 miles per hour. The pursuit ended when Horton crashed just outside of St. Catharines, Ontario.

In a sendoff befitting a future Hall of Famer, the veteran defender was named the number No. 3 star in his final game.

Johnson, Robert

Coach
Penguins: 1990–91
NHL: 1982–87, 1990–91
Inducted into Hockey Hall of Fame: 1992 (Builder)
Inducted into Penguins Hall of Fame: 1992
Birthplace: Minneapolis, Minnesota
B: March 4, 1931
D: November 26, 1991

| | Regular Season | | | | | | Playoffs | | | |
	G	W	L	T	PTS	PCT	G	W	L	PCT
Pittsburgh	80	41	33	6	88	.550	24	16	8	.667
NHL	**480**	**234**	**188**	**58**	**526**	**.548**	**76**	**41**	**35**	**.539**

There is perhaps no coach in the history of the game who was more beloved than Bob Johnson. He approached each and every game with an unbridled enthusiasm that set him apart from other coaches. His positive, upbeat attitude served as an inspiration for everyone who played for him.

The son of Swedish immigrants, Johnson was born in Minneapolis, Minnesota, on March 4, 1931. As a youngster he played hockey in the City Park Board League. A natural leader, he took on his first coaching assignment at age 13 when he guided a local midget team.

After starring for Minneapolis Central High School, Johnson played for the University of North Dakota before transferring to Minnesota. It was there that he skated for legendary coach John Mariucci.

A talented forward, Johnson paced the Golden Gophers in scoring and led them to two conference championships. Had he played in a later era, Johnson might have gone on to a career in the National Hockey League. In his day, however, the doors were decidedly closed to American-born players.

Following a tour of duty in Korea as a medic, Johnson began his coaching career at Warroad High School. He moved on to Roosevelt High School in Minneapolis and led the team to four city titles in six seasons. After serving as head coach at Colorado College he accepted the coaching position at the University of Wisconsin in 1966.

It was with the Badgers that he gained lasting fame. During his 15 seasons at the helm, Wisconsin won three national titles. He also would receive his enduring nickname—"Badger Bob."

Johnson made his long-awaited entry into the NHL in 1982 when he was hired to coach the Calgary Flames. Although the Flames had the misfortune of playing in the same division as the powerhouse Edmonton Oilers, Badger Bob led them to the Stanley Cup Finals in 1986, where they were vanquished by Montreal.

In 1987 Johnson left Calgary to become the executive director of USA Hockey. A wonderful administrator, the position seemed to suit him well. But when Pittsburgh general manager Craig Patrick approached him in 1990 with an offer to coach the Penguins, Badger Bob couldn't resist returning to his first love.

Guiding the Penguins would be no easy task. An exceptionally talented team, they were a prickly bunch that had a history of overthrowing coaches. Never one to back down from a challenge, Johnson dove into his new assignment with his typical high energy and zeal. With his infectious personality, he gradually won the players over while teaching them the value of good defensive play.

In the playoffs, he masterfully guided the Pens past the Devils, Capitals, Bruins, and North Stars—each in come-from-behind fashion—to capture the Stanley Cup. He became only the second American-born coach in modern NHL history to win a Cup.

Sadly, tragedy would soon follow his greatest triumph. Johnson had suffered from headaches during the Pens' Cup run, but he shrugged them off as a natural reaction to playoff stress. However, he began to experience slurred speech while preparing Team USA for the upcoming Canada Cup Tournament. During a six-game road trip in August of 1991 his condition worsened dramatically and he was hospitalized.

Tests revealed two brain tumors. Doctors immediately performed an operation to remove one of the tumors, but the second had to be treated with radiation. Following a courageous battle, Johnson passed away at his home in Colorado Springs on November 26, 1991.

To honor their fallen coach, the Penguins emblazoned his favorite saying, "It's a Great Day for Hockey," onto the Civic Arena ice.

Badger Bob was inducted posthumously into the Hockey Hall of Fame in 1992.

Robert Johnson

Kelly, Leonard Patrick

Coach/General Manager
Penguins: 1969–73
NHL: 1947–77
Inducted into Hockey Hall of Fame: 1969 (Player)
Birthplace: Simcoe, Ontario
B: July 9, 1927

| | Regular Season | | | | | | Playoffs | | | |
	G	W	L	T	PTS	PCT	G	W	L	PCT
Pittsburgh	274	90	132	52	232	.423	14	6	8	.429
NHL	**742**	**278**	**330**	**134**	**690**	**.465**	**62**	**24**	**38**	**.387**

Perhaps no player in the history of the NHL enjoyed a more remarkable career than Leonard Patrick "Red" Kelly. The redhead proved to be one of the game's most accomplished and versatile players during a legendary career that spanned 20 years.

As a youngster Kelly drew the attention of NHL scouts while skating for St. Michael's College in the Ontario League. Having grown up a Toronto fan it seemed a given that the smooth-skating defenseman would play for the Maple Leafs. However, a Toronto scout claimed that Red would never play more than 20 games in the NHL. Stung by the assessment, Kelly signed with the Detroit Red Wings.

It soon became apparent that the scout had missed the mark. Playing on a team that boasted future Hall of Famers such as Gordie Howe and "Terrible" Ted Lindsay, Kelly developed into one of the top defensemen in the league. An excellent puck carrier, the skilled and mobile rearguard was a key to the Red Wings' deadly transition game.

Leonard Patrick Kelly

During his stay in the Motor City the Red Wings won four Stanley Cups. Kelly was named to the postseason All-Star team eight straight seasons, including six First Team selections. Although he had been a champion boxer at St. Michael's, he played a clean brand of hockey—a style that earned him four Lady Byng Trophies. In 1953–54 he was the first defenseman to receive the James Norris Memorial Trophy.

By the late 1950s, however, a rift had developed between Kelly and the Detroit high command. On February 4, 1960, the Wings shocked the hockey world by trading their star defender to the Rangers for Eddie Shack. Kelly refused to report to New York and immediately announced his retirement.

Toronto coach Punch Imlach desperately wanted Kelly. He talked the perennial All-Star out of retiring and acquired his services for Marc Reaume. It would prove to be one of the most lopsided deals in league history.

Imlach had a surprise in store. He wanted to take advantage of Red's skating and puck-handling abilities by using him at center. Kelly, who occasionally played left wing for Detroit, agreed to give it a try.

He proved to be a natural at his new position. In his first full season with the Leafs, Kelly tallied 70 points while helping linemate Frank Mahovlich to a 40-goal season. Red reached the 20-goal mark three times with Toronto and blossomed into one of the best two-way centers in the game. He won four more Stanley Cups with the Leafs before retiring after the 1966–67 season.

Kelly, who would later serve as coach and general manager of the Penguins, was inducted into the Hockey Hall of Fame as a player in 1969.

Lange, Mike

Announcer
Penguins/NHL: 1974–75, 1976–present
Foster Hewitt Memorial Award: 2001
Inducted into Penguins Hall of Fame: 2001
Birthplace: Sacramento, California
B: March 3, 1948

"It's a *hockey night* in Pittsburgh." For more than 30 seasons, play-by-play announcer Mike Lange has welcomed Penguins fans to broadcasts with this simple but eloquent greeting. He became *the* voice of the Penguins, much as the late Bob Prince was the voice of the Pittsburgh Pirates.

Born in Sacramento, California, Lange started doing radio play-by-play for the Phoenix Roadrunners of the old Western Hockey League. He got his break in 1974 when the Penguins hired him to replace Joe Starkey.

His arrival coincided with the team's first winning season. Lange's dramatic and colorful style added an extra level of

Mike Lange

excitement to the broadcasts. He punctuated each Penguins goal with his signature call, "Heeeeeee shoots and scores!"

Concerned about the team's financial woes, Lange and the Penguins briefly parted ways in 1975. After a one-year absence he returned to the broadcast booth and has been a fixture ever since.

Encouraged by Prince, who did the team's TV play-by-play in 1977–78, Lange began to expand on his repertoire of colorful catchphrases. Distinctive expressions such as "You'd have to be here to believe it," "Scratch my back with a hacksaw," and "He beat him like a rented mule" became as much a part of Penguins hockey lore as Mario Lemieux's highlight-reel goals.

Lange began doing simulcasts for TV and radio in 1979. He was at the microphone for every game during the team's phoenixlike rise from the ashes of the early 1980s through the glory of the Stanley Cup years. Through it all he continued to hone his unique style, leaving an indelible imprint on the game.

In 2001 Lange received the Hockey Hall of Fame's Foster Hewitt Memorial Award, given each year to a member of the radio and television industry who has made outstanding contributions to their profession and to the game of hockey. He was inducted into the Penguins Hall of Fame the same year. They were fitting tributes to the man who helped make hockey such a popular sport in Pittsburgh.

Sadly, in the summer of 2006 Lange was relieved of his TV play-by-play duties by Fox Sports Net. The dismissal set off a firestorm of criticism, the likes of which hadn't been seen since Prince was fired by KDKA some 30 years earlier.

The Penguins immediately hired the legendary broadcaster to do play-by-play on the radio. The colorful announcer had come full circle.

Lemieux, Mario

Center
Penguins/NHL: 1984–94, 1995–1997, 2000–06
Inducted into Hockey Hall of Fame: 1997 (Player)
Inducted into Penguins Hall of Fame: 1999
Birthplace: Montreal, Quebec
B: October 5, 1965
Shoots: right

	Regular Season					Playoffs				
	GP	G	A	PTS	PM	GP	G	A	PTS	PM
Pittsburgh	915	690	1033	1723	834	107	76	96	172	87
NHL	**915**	**690**	**1033**	**1723**	**834**	**107**	**76**	**96**	**172**	**87**

Ask any hockey historian where Mario Lemieux stands among the game's greatest stars, and most will agree that he ranks among the top four players of all time, alongside fellow luminaries Wayne Gretzky, Bobby Orr, and Gordie Howe. Ask a Pittsburgh Penguins fan the same question, and you'll get a different answer. Lemieux—as his surname suggests in French—was *the best*.

Mario was destined for greatness from an early age. When he was three years old he attended a hockey clinic in his hometown of Montreal with other toddlers. During a breakaway drill he skated in on the goaltender, instinctively dipped a shoulder, and shot the puck into the net. The adult instructors looked at each other in slack-jawed awe. No one had ever seen a three-year-old deke a goalie.

By the time Lemieux entered the junior hockey ranks with Laval, NHL scouts were already projecting him to be a first overall pick. Anticipating the lowly Whalers would be in a position to draft the 16-year-old wonder, the Canadiens traded Pierre Larouche to Hartford for the Whalers' 1984 first round pick—*in December of 1981.*

Mario's play only served to heighten the expectations. In his final season with Laval he scored an astronomical 133 goals and 282 points while capturing the Canadian Major Junior Player of the Year honors. As if to put an exclamation point on his junior career, he tallied six goals and 12 points in his final game.

Much to the chagrin of the Canadiens, Hartford was not the worst team in the NHL that season. The "honor" went to the pitiful Pittsburgh Penguins, winners of just 16 games. Like a flock of buzzards, opposing general managers descended on Penguins GM Eddie Johnston with an astounding array of proposals. The Quebec Nordiques reportedly offered their All-Star forward line of Peter, Anton, and Marian Stastny for the Pens' top pick. Minnesota countered by offering every pick they had in the 1984 Draft. The Canadiens also made a big push.

Wisely, Johnston refused to bite. He was rewarded during Lemieux's very first practice with the team. As Mario put on a show, owner Edward DeBartolo Sr. turned to EJ and said, "Thank God you didn't trade that pick."

Mario Lemieux

Lemieux made his much-anticipated debut on Thursday, October 11, 1984, at the Boston Garden. On his very first shift he stole the puck from All-Star Raymond Bourque, sped in on goalie Pete Peeters, and backhanded the puck into the net. The 19-year-old sensation went on to score 43 goals and 100 points, making him only the third rookie in league history to reach the century mark in points. He easily captured the Calder Trophy.

Mario showed steady improvement over the next two seasons. However, in 1987 his game took a quantum leap forward. Prior to the season he was selected to play for Team Canada in the Canada Cup Tournament. Skating on a line with Gretzky, Mario exploded for 11 goals, including the game winner in the series finale against the Soviets.

It was clear that Lemieux was ready to take hockey's center stage. However, the Penguins were still rebuilding. The team lacked a set of scoring wingers who were capable of converting Mario's picture-perfect passes. In November of 1987 Eddie Johnston made a bold move to correct the problem by acquiring All-Star defenseman Paul Coffey from Edmonton. With Coffey igniting the transition game, Mario rolled up 70 goals and 168 points to nail down his first scoring title. He collected his first Hart Trophy, as well as his second Lester B. Pearson Award.

By 1988–89 Lemieux had blossomed into the most dominant player in the game. Confronted by an almost perfect blend of size, speed, power, and deception, opponents had no idea how to stop him. Many resorted to fouling the big center, clinging to him like leeches. Even that didn't work. Mario enjoyed an extraordinary season, striking for 85 goals, 114 assists, and 199 points to outdistance his closest rival, Gretzky, by a whopping 31 points.

However, the abuse he was absorbing would soon take a toll. In February of 1990, while in the midst of a stunning 46-game point scoring streak, he was forced to remove himself from the lineup due to excruciating back pain. An examination revealed a herniated disc.

The following summer he submitted to surgery to repair the damage. His recovery appeared to progress as planned until he was struck down by searing pain during a preseason road trip. Doctors discovered an infection around the surgically repaired disc. The only treatment was rest.

Barely able to walk much less skate, Mario feared that his career might be over. Mercifully, the infection cleared and he rejoined the Penguins in time for the 1990–91 stretch run. Skating relatively free of pain, he turned the playoffs into a personal showcase for his wondrous abilities. He tallied 44 points while leading the Pens to their first Stanley Cup. He would duplicate his Conn Smythe Trophy performance the following season, overcoming a broken hand to propel the team to a second straight Cup.

In 1992–93 Lemieux bolted from the starting gate like a thoroughbred race horse. With his back fully healed, he was ready to dominate like never before. However, after piling up 101 points in just 38 games, Mario received some crushing news: he had contracted Hodgkin's disease. Once more fate had cruelly risen up to strike him down just as he reached the very pinnacle of his abilities.

Following surgery to remove an infected lymph node, Mario underwent a series of radiation treatments. Fortunately, the prognosis was good, and the big center was given the green light to return to the ice.

What followed was one of the most remarkable achievements in sports history. Barely one month removed from radiation treatments, Mario returned to action with a vengeance. Over a 16-game stretch, he scored an astounding 51 points—an average of better than *three points per game*. He locked up his fourth Art Ross Trophy and second Hart Trophy despite missing 24 games.

Unfortunately, No. 66 would soon suffer from a crippling case of anemia caused by the lingering effects of the radiation. He missed most of the 1993–94 season and all of the strike-shortened 1994–95 campaign while attempting to recuperate. Many experts doubted whether Lemieux could overcome such a setback. Yet once more he defied the odds by capturing two more scoring titles.

In 1997 the wear and tear finally caught up to him. Following the playoffs, Mario announced his retirement from the game. For two years he devoted himself to his family while enjoying an occasional round of golf. However, in the fall of 1999 he made a surprising bid to purchase the Penguins out of bankruptcy. The league accepted Mario's offer, and suddenly he was an owner.

He had one more great surprise in store. On the night of December 27, 2000, Lemieux stepped back onto the Mellon Arena ice following a three-and-a-half-year absence. He stole the show, assisting on a goal just 33 seconds into the game and collecting three points for the evening. Mario went on to score 35 goals and 76 points in just 43 games while leading the Pens to the Conference Finals.

In the twilight of his career "Le Magnifique" finally began to show signs of mortality. Chronic back and hip injuries had stripped much of the quickness and deception from his game. Despite his physical limitations, he still was good enough to average over a point per game during his final four seasons.

Suffering from the effects of atrial fibrillation, he announced his retirement on January 24, 2006. Over the course of his remarkable career he had tallied 690 goals, 1,033 assists, and 1,723 points. His career scoring average of 1.88 points per game ranks second to only Wayne Gretzky's 1.92 points per game.

Molinari, Dave

Journalist
Pittsburgh Press/Pittsburgh Post-Gazette: 1983–present
Elmer Ferguson Memorial Award: 2009
Birthplace: Glassport, Pennsylvania
B: October 2, 1955

Talk about a tough way to begin a career. When Dave Molinari started covering the Penguins as a beat writer for the *Pittsburgh Press* in 1983, the team was limping through the worst season in franchise history.

Covering the lowly "Boys of Winter" would be a test for a veteran journalist, let alone a rookie. But Molinari quickly established himself as a skilled writer who told the team's story with a compelling blend of humor, sarcasm, and truth.

Born in Glassport, Pennsylvania, Molinari attended Elizabeth Forward High School and Pennsylvania State University. Upon graduating from Penn State in 1977 with a degree in journalism he returned to the Pittsburgh area and started writing for the *McKeesport Daily News*. He joined the *Pittsburgh Press* in 1980 and was assigned to the Penguins three years later. When the newspaper folded in the early 1990s, he went to work for the *Pittsburgh Post-Gazette*.

During his 27 years as a writer Molinari documented the careers of the Penguins' greatest stars, including Mario Lemieux, Jaromir Jagr, Sidney Crosby, and Evgeni Malkin. In 1993 he penned a popular book, *Best in the Game*, that chronicled the team's dramatic rise to Stanley Cup champions.

In 2009 Molinari received the Hockey Hall of Fame's esteemed Elmer Ferguson Memorial Award, bestowed each year to the member of the hockey writing profession whose words have brought honor to journalism and to the game of hockey.

Mullen, Joseph Patrick

Right Wing
Penguins: 1990–95, 1996–97
NHL: 1981–97
Inducted into Hockey Hall of Fame: 2000 (Player)
Inducted into Penguins Hall of Fame: 2000
Birthplace: New York, New York
B: February 26, 1957
Shoots: right

	Regular Season					Playoffs				
	GP	G	A	PTS	PM	GP	G	A	PTS	PM
Pittsburgh	379	153	172	325	101	62	16	15	31	20
NHL	**1062**	**502**	**561**	**1063**	**241**	**143**	**60**	**46**	**106**	**42**

As a kid growing up in the tough Hell's Kitchen section of New York City, Joe Mullen played roller hockey with his younger brother Brian and dreamed of one day making it to the NHL. The family's apartment was a half-block away from the old Madison Square Garden where his dad, Tom Mullen, worked on the maintenance staff. In the days before the Zamboni, Tom was one of the men who skated the barrels of resurfacing water around the rink between periods.

Although the West Side of Manhattan was hardly known as a hockey hotbed, Mullen pursued his dreams with bulldog tenacity. He played roller hockey every day after school. When he was 10 years old, Rangers general manager Emile Francis started the Metropolitan Junior Hockey League, which gave Joe a chance to play on ice.

In 1974–75 he dominated the league, scoring 110 goals in just 40 games. His outstanding play earned him a partial scholarship to Boston College. In four seasons with the Eagles, Mullen piled up another 110 goals and drew the attention of pro scouts. The St. Louis Blues signed him as a free agent in August of 1979.

Initially there were some concerns about his small stature and his skating. He had a choppy stride, a byproduct of his roller hockey days. But Mullen possessed great balance and surprising strength, along with a nose for the net. After tearing up the Central League for two and a half seasons, he was called up by the Blues in 1981.

Joseph Patrick Mellen

Mullen immediately established himself as a big-time scorer. In 1983–84 he banged home 41 goals—the first of six consecutive 40-plus goal seasons. However, on February 1, 1986, the Blues sent him to Calgary as part of a big six-player deal.

The hardworking winger hit his stride with the Flames. He enjoyed a career year in 1988–89, scoring 51 goals and registering a league-high plus 51 while leading the Flames to a Stanley Cup.

Following an "off year" by Mullen's standards (36 goals) the Calgary brass felt his best days were behind him. In the summer of 1990 they peddled the 33-year-old Mullen to Pittsburgh for a second-round draft pick. The trade would reap significant dividends—for the Penguins.

Although he suffered a serious neck injury during the 1990–91 campaign, the resilient old pro returned following surgery to pot eight goals in the playoffs, including two in the Pens' Cup-winning game. The following season he racked up 42 goals while becoming the first player in team history to score four goals in back-to-back games. Over the next two seasons the ageless wonder knocked in 71 goals, as well as a respectable 16 during the strike-shortened 1994–95 season.

Father Time finally caught up with Mullen in 1995. He signed a free-agent deal with Boston, but endured a largely forgettable season in Beantown. In 1996 he returned to the Penguins for what proved to be his last hurrah.

Mullen went out with a bang. On the night of March 14, 1997, he beat fellow Hall of Famer Patrick Roy for his 500th career goal. He currently ranks fifth on the list of highest-scoring American-born players in NHL history.

Murphy, Lawrence Thomas

Defense
Penguins: 1990–95
NHL: 1980–01
Inducted into Hockey Hall of Fame: 2004 (Player)
Birthplace: Scarborough, Ontario
B: March 8, 1961
Shoots: right

	Regular Season					Playoffs				
	GP	G	A	PTS	PM	GP	G	A	PTS	PM
Pittsburgh	336	78	223	301	213	74	15	57	72	73
NHL	**1615**	**287**	**929**	**1216**	**1084**	**215**	**37**	**115**	**152**	**201**

It's hard to imagine that a Hall of Fame defenseman—especially one who would play in 1,615 NHL games and score 1,216 points—could be considered undervalued or underrated. But that was precisely the case with Lawrence Thomas Murphy.

Perhaps it was due to his style of play, which was a triumph of substance over flash. Murphy didn't fly around the ice at warp speed like a Bobby Orr or a Paul Coffey. Yet

Lawrence Thomas Murphy

he controlled the flow of a game like no other with a subtle shift in speed or an artful pass. He didn't throw booming checks or pound opponents into submission in the manner of a Scott Stevens. Instead, he relied on superb positioning and the brilliant use of his stick. In short, Murphy was a thinking man's defenseman.

Remarkably, he became a defenseman almost by default. As a youth growing up in Scarborough, Ontario, he played both forward and defense. However, the team he wanted to play for had only one opening—on the blue line. Murphy accepted his role and played defense from that day on.

Following a promising junior career at Peterborough—where his team won the Memorial Cup—Murphy earned a spot with the Los Angeles Kings. The 19-year-old enjoyed an outstanding rookie season, scoring 16 goals and 76 points. He lost out in the Calder Trophy voting to a player five years his senior—Quebec's Peter Stastny.

In a grievous error in judgment, the Kings traded the young defender to Washington in 1983 for veterans Brian Engblom and Ken Houston. However, after a string of highly productive seasons, Murphy's play slipped a bit in the late 1980s. Unforgiving fans at the Capital Centre made a loud "whooping" noise whenever he stepped onto the ice—perhaps to mimic the sound of a goal siren—which eroded his confidence even further.

In March of 1989 the Caps sent him to the North Stars as part of a four-player trade. Murphy spent an uneventful season and change in Minnesota before being dealt again—this time to Pittsburgh.

The move revived his career. Penguins coach Bob Johnson had the good sense to let Murph be Murph. His confidence restored, the veteran rearguard rewarded the Pens with some of the finest defensive play ever seen on Civic Arena ice.

Murphy was an absolute master on the power play. His keen sense of anticipation, coupled with his good lateral mobility, allowed him to keep more pucks alive in the attacking zone than perhaps any point man in the history of the game.

With Murphy setting the tempo the Penguins won back-to-back Stanley Cups in 1991 and 1992. In 1992–93 he had the finest season of his career, rolling up 22 goals and 85 points to go with a sterling plus/minus rating of plus 45. He was rewarded with a berth on the Second All-Star Team.

Seeking to pare down their payroll, the Penguins traded Murphy to Toronto in the summer of 1995. What should have been a glorious homecoming turned sour as Murph struggled in front of the critical Maple Leafs fans. He was virtually on the scrap heap when Detroit acquired his services in the spring of 1997 for future considerations.

Rejuvenated by the change of scenery, Murphy won two more Stanley Cups with the Wings before retiring in 2001.

Patrick, Craig

General Manager/Coach
Penguins: 1989–06
NHL: 1981–85, 1989–06
Inducted into Hockey Hall of Fame: 2001 (Builder)
Inducted into Penguins Hall of Fame: 2001
Birthplace: Detroit, Michigan
B: May 20, 1946

| | **Regular Season** | | | | | | | **Playoffs** | | | |
	G	W	L	T	OL/SL	PTS	PCT	G	W	L	PCT
Pittsburgh	1250	575	511	127	37	1314	.526	146	81	65	.555
NHL	**1650**	**753**	**684**	**176**	**37**	**1719**	**.521**	**189**	**101**	**88**	**.534**

A descendant of hockey's royal family, Craig Patrick was destined to make his mark in the sport. His grandfather Lester Patrick—the legendary "Silver Fox"—helped form the Pacific Coast Hockey Association and later gained fame as the first coach and general manager of the Rangers. His father, Lynn Patrick, was a Hall of Fame left wing who starred for the Rangers' 1940 Stanley Cup champions. For good measure his great-uncle, Frank, also was inducted into the Hall of Fame.

It was only natural that young Craig would pursue a career in hockey. A right wing of some promise, he earned a scholarship to the University of Denver and helped lead the team to national championships in 1968 and 1969. He

signed as a free agent with the California Golden Seals in 1971 and scored 20 goals in his first full season. It proved to be the high point of an NHL career that spanned 401 games.

In 1979 he retired as a player and was immediately contacted by Herb Brooks to serve as the assistant coach and assistant general manager for the 1980 USA Olympic team. Following the team's scintillating gold-medal performance, Patrick was named assistant general manager of the Rangers. He was promoted to the post of general manager in June of 1981.

Patrick's first move was to hire his friend and mentor, Brooks, to serve as the Rangers' coach. Although the duo enjoyed a successful run on Broadway, they weren't able to bring home a Stanley Cup. Sadly, Patrick fired Brooks in 1985. A year later he, too, left the Rangers to serve as the athletic director for his alma mater, the University of Denver.

In December of 1989, Patrick was approached by the DeBartolo family with an offer to join the Penguins. He became the team's general manager, a move that would change the course of his career and bring him lasting acclaim.

Displaying the skill and acumen of a master craftsman, Patrick quickly built a Stanley Cup team in Pittsburgh. He hired great leaders (Bob Johnson and Scotty Bowman). His trades, which netted stars such as Ron Francis, Joe Mullen, Larry Murphy, and Rick Tocchet, were uniformly brilliant. He displayed a Midas touch at the draft table as well, selecting budding superstars Jaromir Jagr and Markus Naslund.

Craig Patrick

Following the Penguins' Cup years in the early 1990s, Patrick kept the team competitive for over a decade. Reinforced by his savvy trades and free-agent acquisitions, the Pens made it to the Conference Finals in 1996 and again in 2001.

Like all general managers, Patrick engineered some clunkers as well. The deal that sent Naslund to Vancouver for Alek Stojanov is widely regarded as one of the worst of all time. He also oversaw a series of poor drafts in the 1990s that resulted in a string of first-round busts.

It was his trade of Jagr in the summer of 2001 that ultimately proved to be his undoing. Operating under tight financial constraints, he was unable to secure equal value in return for the game's reigning superstar. The trade ended the Pens' glorious run of 11 consecutive playoff seasons and sealed Patrick's fate.

Although his days were numbered, the veteran general manager stockpiled an incredible collection of young talent in the early 2000s. Under his watch promising first-round picks Evgeni Malkin, Marc-Andre Fleury, and Ryan Whitney joined the fold. Plums such as Ryan Malone, Alex Goligoski, and Kris Letang were gleaned in later rounds. Patrick struck gold at the 2005 Entry Draft when he selected phenom Sidney Crosby with the first overall pick.

Thanks to his astute draft-day decisions, the Penguins were suddenly a team with a bright future. However, Patrick would not preside over the resurgence. After 17 years of service he was relieved of his duties on April 20, 2006, by club president Ken Sawyer.

Stung by the dismissal, Patrick avoided hockey-related functions for a time. But on April 2, 2008, he accepted an invitation to join Mario Lemieux in the owner's box. He watched with pride as the team he helped build defeated the Flyers to clinch the Eastern Conference crown.

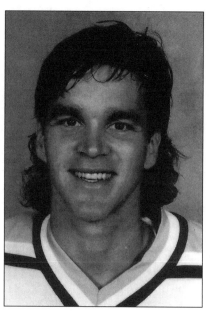

Luc Robitaille

Robitaille, Luc

Left Wing
Penguins: 1994–95
NHL: 1986–06
Inducted into Hockey Hall of Fame: 2009 (Player)
Birthplace: Montreal, Quebec
B: February 17, 1966
Shoots: left

	Regular Season					Playoffs				
	GP	G	A	PTS	PM	GP	G	A	PTS	PM
Pittsburgh	46	23	19	42	37	12	7	4	11	26
NHL	1431	668	726	1394	1177	159	58	69	127	174

Although he racked up some astonishing numbers during his three seasons in the Quebec League, no one dreamed that Luc Robitaille would one day be inducted into the Hockey Hall of Fame. Despite his gaudy numbers, most scouts thought he would be lucky to make it in the NHL. He was too slow, they said.

Robitaille had played one moderately productive season with the Hull Olympiques when he became eligible for the 1984 Entry Draft. Round after round passed without a taker. Finally, the Los Angeles Kings selected Luc in the ninth round with the 171st pick. He proved to be the greatest steal in the history of the draft.

Rather than rush him to the NHL, the Kings wisely let the 18-year-old Robitaille finish out his junior career. He showed dramatic improvement, piling up 149 points in 1984–85 before exploding for 191 points during his final season with Hull.

It soon became apparent that Robitaille was no plow horse. What he lacked in pure speed he more than made up for in guile and determination. And the kid could flat-out score. As a rookie in 1986–87 he lit the lamp 45 times to win the Calder Trophy. He was even better the following season, notching 53 goals and 111 points while earning the left wing slot on the First All-Star Team.

On August 9, 1988, Kings owner Bruce McNall swung an epic deal with Edmonton that brought "the Great One," Wayne Gretzky, to L.A. With perhaps the greatest playmaker in the history of the game setting the table, Robitaille went on a goal-scoring rampage. Over the next six seasons, "Lucky Luc" struck for 294 goals, including a career-best 63 in 1992–93.

By the summer of 1994, however, the Kings were slipping. In a shocking trade that was heavily influenced by Gretzky, Los Angeles peddled Robitaille to the Penguins for the rugged Rick Tocchet.

Although surprised by the trade, the upbeat winger embraced his new home. During the lockout-marred 1994–95 campaign he scored 23 goals in 46 games—a 40-goal pace for a full season.

With Mario Lemieux returning from a one-year hiatus, it appeared Luc would once more serve as the trigger man for an all-time great—a role he was born to play. But in a second stunning trade, the Penguins sent Robitaille and Ulf Samuelsson to the Rangers for Petr Nedved and Sergei Zubov.

Luc's career finally hit a speed bump on Broadway. He endured two largely forgettable seasons before moving back to L.A., where he quickly regained his scoring touch. In 2001 he signed as a free agent with Detroit and helped lead the Wings to a Stanley Cup.

Following a final stint with the Kings he hung up his skates in 2006. The kid who was too slow retired as the highest-scoring left wing in NHL history.

Sather, Glen Cameron

Left Wing
Penguins: 1969–70
NHL: 1966–76
WHA: 1976–77
Inducted into Hockey Hall of Fame: 1997 (Builder)
Birthplace: High River, Alberta
B: September 2, 1943
Shoots: left

	Regular Season					Playoffs				
	GP	G	A	PTS	PM	GP	G	A	PTS	PM
Pittsburgh	122	20	17	37	210	10	0	2	2	17
NHL	**658**	**80**	**113**	**193**	**724**	**72**	**1**	**5**	**6**	**86**
WHA	**81**	**19**	**34**	**53**	**77**	**5**	**1**	**1**	**2**	**2**

Mention the name Glen Sather to a present-day Penguins fan and you're sure to draw a negative response. After all, "Slats" serves as general manager for the New York Rangers, one of the Pens' most bitter Atlantic Division rivals. However, in the late 1960s and early 1970s, Sather was among the most popular players to don the Penguins' powder blue and white.

A decade before he built the Edmonton Oilers into a Stanley Cup dynasty—a feat that earned him induction into the Hockey Hall of Fame in 1997—Sather served as a feisty left wing for several NHL clubs. Short on talent but long on spunk, he earned a reputation for his fiercely competitive play. A skilled and resourceful agitator, the Alberta native excelled at needling opponents to throw them off their game.

Among his favorite targets were the St. Louis Blues' rough-and-tumble Plager brothers, Barclay and Bob. After joining the Penguins in the fall of 1969, Sather and fellow disturber Bryan "Bugsy" Watson engaged the Blues' toughies in some memorable battles. On the night of January 31, 1970, Slats and Barclay Plager were the chief combatants in a bench-clearing brawl that catapulted the previously punchless Pens to a playoff berth. Two months later Sather and his teammates locked horns with the Blues in a thrilling semifinals matchup, a series that earned the club hundreds of new fans.

In Memory

For nearly 40 years, John Barbero served as the public address announcer for Penguins home games at the Civic (later Mellon) Arena. Known for his professionalism and silky-smooth delivery, he had a special way of announcing goals—especially Mario Lemieux's. He would draw Mario's last name out in an elongated "Lemieuuuuux," which heightened the sense of joy and celebration for Steel City fans.

A schoolteacher by trade, Barbero broke into broadcasting as a disc jockey for radio station WESA. The Penguins took note and hired him as their PA announcer in 1972. He remained a fixture at the Arena through the 2009 playoffs, working Game 6 of the Stanley Cup Finals. A short time later, the retired principal of the Central Greene School District took a medical leave to receive treatments for a brain tumor.

"He wanted to do [Penguins games] as long as he could," said his son Brady. "He really wanted to be able to announce games in that new arena [Consol Energy Center]. He loved the Penguins."

Sadly, it wasn't to be. On July 26, 2010, Barbero passed away at the age of 65.

"John was one of a kind, a true professional, and he will always be remembered as a member of the Penguins family," Lemieux said. "He will be missed."

The blond-haired winger quickly became a darling of the Civic Arena faithful, who loved his aggressive style. He occasionally contributed on the score sheet as well, potting 20 goals in 122 games with the Penguins. However, his greatest contribution may have occurred when he departed from the Steel City. On January 26, 1971, Pittsburgh peddled Slats to the Rangers for defenseman Sheldon Kannegiesser and promising young center Syl Apps. Although the deal was wildly unpopular at the time, Apps would emerge as the Pens' first star.

Sather continued to ply his trade for several seasons, including stops with the Rangers, Blues, Canadiens, and North Stars, before finishing his career in 1976–77 with the Edmonton Oilers in the World Hockey Association. During the final 18 games of the season he handled the dual role of player-coach. He retired over the summer to concentrate on coaching full time.

It was a major stroke of good fortune. Stocked with future Hall of Famers Glenn Anderson, Wayne Gretzky, and Mark Messier, the Oilers were evolving into a powerhouse. Sather would play a lead role in the transformation. After assuming the general manager duties in 1980, he drafted budding superstars Paul Coffey, Grant Fuhr, and Jari Kurri. To make sure his skill players had plenty of room to maneuver, Sather pried tough guys Kevin McClelland and Marty McSorley loose from the Penguins. The Oilers went on to capture five

Stanley Cups during his reign, earning him a reputation as one of the finest executives in NHL history.

Already a member of the Hockey Hall of Fame, Sather left Edmonton in 2000 to fill the GM post with the Rangers. Operating on hockey's biggest stage, he elevated the Blueshirts from also-rans to contender status through a series of high-profile moves. In 2004 he brought former Penguins great Jaromir Jagr to Broadway to serve as the centerpiece for his improving team. Jagr rewarded him with three strong seasons.

Although Sather is frequently under fire for his lavish spending, he remains one of the most colorful, controversial, and high-profile executives in hockey.

Trottier, Bryan John

Center
Penguins: 1990–92, 1993–94
NHL: 1975–94
Inducted into Hockey Hall of Fame: 1997 (Player)
Birthplace: Val Marie, Saskatchewan
B: July 17, 1956
Shoots: left

Bryan John Trottier

	Regular Season					Playoffs				
	GP	G	A	PTS	PM	GP	G	A	PTS	PM
Pittsburgh	156	24	48	72	114	46	7	7	14	57
NHL	**1279**	**524**	**901**	**1425**	**912**	**221**	**71**	**113**	**184**	**277**

During a storied NHL career that spanned nearly 20 seasons, Bryan John Trottier established himself as one of the finest all-around centers in the history of the game. The two-time First Team All-Star captured just about every major team and individual award the sport had to offer.

Following a strong season with the Swift Current Broncos, the New York Islanders selected the native of Val Marie, Saskatchewan, with their second pick in the 1974 Amateur Draft. Although scouts admired his diligent two-way play, few thought he had the makings of a superstar. He would soon prove them wrong.

Trottier burst onto the scene in 1975–76 as a 19-year-old rookie with the Islanders. In only his second NHL game he scored a hat trick and tallied five points. He went on to establish a new NHL rookie record with 95 points, easily winning the Calder Trophy.

His arrival coincided with the Islanders' rapid ascent. Skating on a line with bruising Clark Gillies and rookie sniper Mike Bossy, he exploded for 123 points in 1977–78—including a league-high 77 assists. The following season he was even better. "Trots" piled up 134 points to capture the Art Ross and Hart Memorial trophies.

In 1979–80 the Islanders began their incredible run of four straight Stanley Cups. Trottier was at the very core of the dynasty, averaging 106 points per year and winning the Conn Smythe Trophy as the top playoff performer in 1980.

In his prime Trottier was a terrific all-around player. He wasn't particularly fast, nor did he possess an overpowering shot. However, he was an exceptionally smart hockey player who made up for his shortcomings with superb playmaking, outstanding vision, and a nose for the net. Surprisingly physical for a top scorer, he put his solid 195-pound frame to good use by routinely dishing out teeth-rattling checks.

Although the Islanders' championship streak had ended by the mid-1980s, Trottier remained a potent offensive player. Following the 1987–88 season, however, his production tailed off dramatically. Convinced the 34-year-old Trots had reached the end of the line, the Islanders released him in the summer of 1990.

While Trottier's skills had undeniably eroded, he still had some hockey left. Penguins general manager Craig Patrick, seeking a veteran leader for his up-and-coming young team, signed Trottier to a two-year deal.

Settling into a defensive role, he checked the opponents' top scorers, mucked in the corners, and took key face-offs. A steady yet fun-loving presence in the locker room, Trots was an integral piece of the Penguins' Stanley Cup teams. He retired in 1992 to take a front office position with the Islanders, but soon grew restless. When the Penguins invited him back a year later to fill the dual role of player and assistant coach, he jumped at the chance.

Trottier finally hung up his skates for good following the 1993–94 season. He presently ranks 15th on the all-time list of NHL scorers.

Penguins Hall of Famers

The Penguins Hall of Fame was established in 1992 to honor the achievements of the team's greatest players, coaches, executives, and staff members.

Honorees include some of the brightest stars ever to don a Penguins uniform, such as Syl Apps, Les Binkley, Dave Burrows, Rick Kehoe, Jean Pronovost, and Ulf Samuelsson. Several members of the Penguins Hall of Fame, including Paul Coffey, Bob Johnson, Mike Lange, Mario Lemieux, Joe Mullen, and Craig Patrick, also are inductees in the Hockey Hall of Fame.

Owner Edward J. DeBartolo Sr. and Jack Riley, the team's first general manager, are honored in the builders section alongside Johnson and Patrick. The Penguins Hall of Fame also recognizes the important contributions of former executive assistant Elaine Heufelder, longtime support staff members Anthony "A.T." Caggiano and Frank Scuilli, and Mellon Arena organist Vince Lascheid.

Apps, Sylvanus Marshall

Center
Penguins: 1971–77
NHL: 1971–80
Inducted into Penguins Hall of Fame: 1994
Birthplace: Toronto, Ontario
B: August 1, 1947
Shoots: right

	Regular Season					Playoffs				
	GP	G	A	PTS	PM	GP	G	A	PTS	PM
Pittsburgh	495	151	349	500	241	19	4	4	8	23
NHL	**727**	**183**	**423**	**606**	**311**	**23**	**5**	**5**	**10**	**23**

Sylvanus Marshall Apps

Sylvanus Marshall Apps grew up as the son of perhaps the most famous and revered man in all of Canada. His father, Charles Joseph Sylvanus (Syl) Apps, was a Hall of Fame center for the Toronto Maple Leafs in the 1930s and 1940s. Beyond his legendary achievements on the ice, the senior Apps served in the Ontario provincial parliament. He was regarded as a man of impeccable character and integrity. For young Syl, they were some large shoes to fill.

Fortunately, the acorn didn't fall far from the tree. A fine man in his own right, Apps also inherited his dad's athleticism. After attending Princeton University as a freshman, he enrolled at Queens University and played hockey for Kingston in the Ontario Senior League. The New York Rangers liked what they saw and signed him to a contract.

Following a strong season in Omaha, Apps earned a spot with the Rangers in 1970–71. Relegated to fourth-line duty, he scored just one goal in 31 games. In January of 1971 he was traded to the Penguins for disturber Glen "Slats" Sather.

Apps hardly received a hero's welcome. The Penguins were in the midst of a miserable season. To make matters worse, Sather had been extremely popular with the Civic Arena faithful. A large banner hung directly across from the team's bench read "Why Slats?"

The youngster quickly silenced the critics. In his first game as a Penguin he scored a spectacular breakaway goal against Toronto's Jacques Plante. It was a promise of things to come.

Centering the Pens' top line in 1971–72, Apps established new club records for assists (44) and points (59). He enjoyed a breakout season the following year, shattering his own records with 56 assists and 85 points. As his skills developed, Apps emerged as a leader on an improving young team.

In 1973–74 Pens coach Ken Schinkel placed the high-scoring center on a line with wingers Lowell MacDonald and Jean Pronovost. Dubbed "the Century Line" because they topped 100 goals, the trio became one of the most lethal combinations in the league.

Although playing in Pittsburgh didn't always afford Apps the recognition he deserved, he enjoyed a moment in the sun at the 1975 NHL All-Star Game. He scored two goals to lead the Wales Conference to a resounding 7–1 victory and was named the game's MVP. It was a proud moment for the Apps family—young Syl was the first son of an All-Star Game participant to play in the game himself.

Apps had his finest season in 1975–76, rolling up 32 goals, 67 assists, and 99 points. However, in the playoffs he suffered a knee injury. Although he played in 72 games the following season, he was never quite the same.

In October of 1977 the Penguins traded "Sly Syl" to Los Angeles, where he finished his career. Apps departed as the Pens' all-time assist leader—a distinction he would hold until Mario Lemieux surpassed him.

Binkley, Leslie John

Goalie
Penguins: 1967–72
NHL: 1967–72
WHA: 1972–76
Inducted into Penguins Hall of Fame: 2003
Birthplace: Owen Sound, Ontario
B: June 6, 1934
Catches: right

Leslie John Binkley

	Regular Season					Playoffs				
	GP	MINS	GA	SH	AVE	GP	MINS	GA	SH	AVE
Pittsburgh	196	11046	575	11	3.12	7	428	15	0	2.10
NHL	**196**	**11046**	**575**	**11**	**3.12**	**7**	**428**	**15**	**0**	**2.10**
WHA	**81**	**4228**	**262**	**1**	**3.72**	**10**	**464**	**40**	**0**	**5.17**

For Penguins goalie Les Binkley, the road to the NHL was longer than most. He toiled in the minor leagues for a dozen years, stopping pucks for teams such as the Charlotte Clippers, Toledo Mercurys, and San Diego Gulls before finally making it to the big show.

In 1960 Binkley got his first big break. The Cleveland Barons of the American Hockey League invited him to their training camp to fill the dual role of practice goalie and *trainer*. Determined to work his way up from the low minor leagues, the 26-year-old Binkley jumped at the chance, even though he knew nothing about the training business. He took some correspondence courses and soon became "the fastest scissors in the league."

The following season he took over as Cleveland's starting goalie. Over the next five years he helped lead the Barons to the Calder Cup while winning the Harry Holmes Memorial Award as the AHL's top goaltender.

Although Binkley possessed exceptionally quick reflexes, he had one major flaw. He was nearsighted, a condition that required him to wear contact lenses when he played. In the days of the Original Six, when only a dozen goalies found regular work in the NHL, managers were loath to gamble on a nearsighted netminder.

"Bink" received his second big break when the NHL added six new teams. He met with Penguins general manager Jack Riley in the fall of 1966 to discuss a deal. Signing a contract scrawled on a paper napkin, he became "the Original Penguin."

Binkley lived up to the honor. After beating out veteran Hank Bassen for the starting job in 1967–68, he played in 54 games and posted a 2.88 goals-against average with six

shutouts. More than 40 years later it remains one of the finest seasons ever recorded by a Penguins goalie.

He continued to shine through the team's difficult early years. In the 1970 Stanley Cup Playoffs Binkley posted a sterling 2.10 goals-against average and won five of seven games before he was felled by a knee injury. The following season he registered a .500 record for a team that finished 16 games below the break-even mark.

By 1972 the Penguins were grooming young Jim Rutherford as their goaltender of the future, so Binkley moved to the World Hockey Association. He played three-plus seasons for Ottawa and Toronto before retiring at the ripe old age of 41.

Burrows, David James

Defense
Penguins: 1971–77, 1980–81
NHL: 1971–81
Inducted into Penguins Hall of Fame: 1996
Birthplace: Toronto, Ontario
B: January 11, 1949
Shoots: left

	Regular Season					Playoffs				
	GP	G	A	PTS	PM	GP	G	A	PTS	PM
Pittsburgh	573	24	108	132	301	20	1	3	4	16
NHL	**724**	**29**	**135**	**164**	**373**	**29**	**1**	**5**	**6**	**25**

There's an old adage that says never judge a book by its cover. The same is true of Dave Burrows. While his statistics were ordinary, his play was nothing less than extraordinary.

Long before the Penguins were hoisting Stanley Cups, Burrows made his mark as a textbook defender for the team in the 1970s. One of the club's first true stars, he gave Penguins fans a reason to cheer with his steady if unspectacular play.

David James Burrows

Caggiano, Anthony

Locker Room Assistant
Penguins: 1967–00
Inducted into Penguins Hall of Fame: 2001
D: May 16, 2000

As a youngster growing up in Toronto he idolized Tim Horton, the Maple Leafs' great defenseman. Burrows studied his hero and would try to mimic his moves on the ice.

Skating for St. Catharines in the Ontario League, he soon developed into a top-notch prospect. Following two strong seasons in the minors Burrows was acquired by Penguins general manager Red Kelly from the talent-rich Black Hawks in the Intra-League Draft.

It just so happened that Kelly also picked up Horton from the Rangers. The future Hall of Famer immediately took Burrows under his wing and taught him the tricks of the trade. The youngster proved to be a quick study. By his third season he had developed into the Pens' best defenseman while earning a spot on the West Division All-Star Team.

In his prime Burrows was truly a marvel to watch. A smooth, effortless skater, he was almost impossible to beat one on one. Blessed with a tall, angular build, he was especially adept at forcing opponents wide of the net and off the puck.

Burrows enjoyed his finest season with the Penguins in 1975–76. He registered career highs with seven goals, 22 assists, and 29 points, while leading the club with a sparkling plus 27 rating. However a dislocated shoulder would hamper him for the remainder of his career.

As part of a rebuilding program, Baz Bastien shipped the popular defenseman to Toronto in 1978 for Randy Carlyle and George Ferguson. Following two solid seasons with the Leafs, Burrows returned to the Penguins in 1980 for his final season. Although still a capable defender at age 32, Burrows decided to retire when he found his desire for the game was waning.

During his 33 years of service as a locker room assistant, Anthony Caggiano never missed a game. Nicknamed "A.T." and "Uncle Sunny" for his cheery disposition, the World War II veteran was often the first person to arrive at the Civic Arena in the morning and the last to leave.

Encouraged to work for the Penguins by his wife Julia, Caggiano became an indispensable part of the Penguins' behind-the-scenes staff. He took care of the players' needs and prepped the visitors' locker room.

The kindly Uncle Sunny often brought home hockey sticks and pucks for the neighborhood kids in Swisshelm Park. In 1992 he gave them a special treat when he put the Stanley Cup on display on his front lawn.

"You've never seen so many kids, so many people, young and old, so happy," said his nephew, Mark Checchio. "To this day they still talk about that party. They'll be talking about it forever."

Anthony also worked as a baker for Nabisco for 46 years. He often put in a full day at the bakery before heading over to the Arena.

"He loved to work," Checchio said. "He was very devoted to everything he did."

Following Anthony's death in May of 2000, the Penguins Booster Club renamed their annual award the "A.T. Caggiano Memorial Award" in his honor.

Anthony Caggiano

Le Magnifique

Throughout his career, Mario received the highest of praise from his fellow players, who marveled at his abilities.

Former NHL defender and hockey analyst Brian Engblom gave perhaps the most eloquent description of what it was like to compete against big No. 66.

"The toughest one-on-one player I ever faced was Mario Lemieux," Engblom said. "He was pure magic. At 6'4" and around 215 pounds, he could do things to you with his stick-handling ability like no one else before or since…not even Gretzky. Mario needed no help, either. Just the two of you straight-up. Try and stop him. Deceptive speed, fluid motion, magic hands, and perfect depth perception, he could put moves on you that left you feeling violated!

"He was too big and strong to be intimidated physically, too fast for you to get a half step on him, too smart to allow himself to be boxed into a small space, and way too good at stick handling to allow you to risk trying to steal the puck from him. To this day, I have no answer as to how to stop Mario when he's on his game."

DeBartolo, Edward John, Sr.

Owner
Penguins: 1977–91
Inducted into Penguins Hall of Fame: 1996
Birthplace: Youngstown, Ohio
B: May 17, 1909
D: December 19, 1994

There's an old axiom in sports—championship teams start at the top. This may explain, at least in part, why the Penguins struggled so mightily through their early years.

Edward John DeBartolo Sr.

The first ownership group, a 21-man consortium led by Pennsylvania senator Jack McGregor, was tapped out by the end of the team's inaugural season. The club's second owner, Detroit bank executive Donald Parsons, fared little better. He was forced to relinquish control of the team to the NHL in the middle of his second season. In 1971 the Pens were purchased by a local group spearheaded by Thayer "Tad" Potter. He and his associates entered into receivership following the team's playoff collapse in 1975.

The next group of owners to arrive on the scene included investment broker Al Savill. Although he and his partners, Otto Frenzel and Wren Blair, bought the team at the bargain-basement price of $3.8 million, they soon ran into financial difficulties as well.

Fortunately, Savill was friends with one of the wealthiest men in America—Edward J. DeBartolo Sr. In the middle of the 1976–77 season, he talked the Youngstown construction magnate into purchasing a one-third interest in the team. A year later DeBartolo became the sole owner.

By his own admission, Edward knew nothing about hockey. What he lacked in firsthand knowledge of the sport he more than made up for with patience, determination, and business acumen.

Edward J. DeBartolo Sr. was a true American success story. His mother and father emigrated from Italy and settled in Youngstown, Ohio. After his father died, his mother married Michael DeBartolo. An industrious man in his own right, Michael was a builder and paving contractor. As a teenager, young Edward transcribed paving contracts for his stepfather, who did not write in English.

After graduating from Notre Dame with a degree in civil engineering, DeBartolo served in the U.S. Army Corps of Engineers during World War II. Following the war he and his wife, Marie, formed the Edward J. DeBartolo Corporation.

It was a master stroke of good fortune. As Americans moved to the suburbs following the war there was a demand for stores and shopping plazas. The DeBartolo Corporation became one of the first contractors in the country to build shopping centers in suburban communities. By 1971 his company ranked 47th in the nation among construction contractors. In 1983 Edward was included on *Forbes*' list of richest Americans.

For the Penguins, DeBartolo's presence in the front office was a godsend. Freed from financial worries, the team's management could finally concentrate on building a competitive hockey team.

The transformation from ugly ducklings to champions didn't happen overnight. On the contrary, the team suffered through a string of lean years that would've sunk a lesser man. But DeBartolo persevered while continuing to provide the steady, stable ownership that was so vital to the club's success. Along the way he became an avid hockey fan.

In 1991 his patience was at long last rewarded with a Stanley Cup. During the victory celebration that followed, the 82-year-old owner proclaimed it to be "perhaps the proudest moment of my life." It was richly deserved.

Heufelder, Elaine

Executive Assistant
Penguins: 1967–03
Inducted into Penguins Hall of Fame: 1996

Through the years there were many changes to the Penguins front office staff. Ownership groups came and went. The one constant was executive assistant Elaine Heufelder.

Elaine joined the team in 1967 and served as an assistant to Charles Strong, the Civic Arena's first building manager. Over the next 35 years she worked for Paul Martha, Edward J. DeBartolo Sr., Roger Marino, and Mario Lemieux. During her career, Elaine worked tirelessly to ensure that the building and the team's front office operated smoothly and efficiently.

Inducted into the Penguins Hall of Fame in 1996, Elaine retired following the 2002–03 season.

Kehoe, Ricky Thomas

Right Wing
Penguins: 1974–85
NHL: 1971–85
Inducted into Penguins Hall of Fame: 1992
Birthplace: Windsor, Ontario
B: July 15, 1951
Shoots: right

| | Regular Season | | | | | Playoffs | | | | |
	GP	G	A	PTS	PM	GP	G	A	PTS	PM
Pittsburgh	722	312	324	636	88	37	4	17	21	2
NHL	**906**	**371**	**396**	**767**	**120**	**39**	**4**	**17**	**21**	**4**

When the Penguins acquired Rick Kehoe from Toronto in the summer of 1974, the speedy winger was already an accomplished goal scorer. Playing on a line with rising star Darryl Sittler, Kehoe racked up 33 goals in 1972–73—his first full season in the NHL. However, new Leafs coach Red Kelly pulled him off the top line the following year and his goal production plummeted.

Kehoe arrived in Pittsburgh at just the right time. General manager Jack Button had added former 50-goal scorer Vic Hadfield and flashy center Pierre Larouche to a talented core that included the likes of Syl Apps, Lowell MacDonald, and Jean Pronovost. Suddenly, the Penguins were an offensive powerhouse.

Skating on a line with Hadfield and veteran center Ron Schock, Kehoe struck for 32 goals his first year in Pittsburgh.

Ricky Thomas Kehoe

It was the start of a remarkable run of nine seasons in which he scored at least 27 goals each year.

Over the next five seasons Kehoe was marvelously consistent. He hovered around the 30-goal mark despite an ongoing rebuilding program that resulted in a revolving door of linemates.

In the fall of 1980 former Bruins great Eddie Johnston took over the Pens' helm. Using a system he'd learned from Boston Celtics Hall of Famer Tommy Heinsohn, he opened up the attack. Kehoe responded with a career season, exploding for a club-record 55 goals. The sharp-shooting winger's stellar play earned him the Lady Byng Trophy and a spot on the Wales Conference All-Star Team.

Kehoe's production tailed off slightly in 1981–82, although he still tallied 33 goals and a team-high 85 points. He shook off an old bugaboo of underachieving in the playoffs by scoring two huge goals during a five-game series against the Islanders, including a game winner in overtime.

Things went from bad to worse for the Penguins the following season. Still, Kehoe once again led all the team's scorers with 29 goals. He was chugging along toward a 10th straight 20-goal season when he was felled by a neck injury in February of 1984.

Playing with numbness in his right arm and risking permanent damage, the 33-year-old sniper retired early in the following season. "Ramblin' Rick" finished his career as the Pens' all-time leading point-getter (636) and second-leading goal-scorer (312).

After hanging up his skates Kehoe began a second career with the Penguins. He served the team for more than 20 years as a scout, assistant coach, and head coach, winning two Stanley Cups.

Lascheid, Vincent Charles, Jr.

Organist
Penguins: 1970–03
Inducted into Penguins Hall of Fame: 2003
Birthplace: Cleveland, Ohio
B: December 26, 1923
D: March 19, 2009

For 33 years Vince Lascheid played the organ during Penguins games with a wonderful blend of skill and humor. In the days before teams played recorded music, his lilting tunes filled the Civic Arena with a carnival-like atmosphere of excitement and anticipation.

An accomplished musician, Vince played piano in the 1940s with some of the leading big bands of the day, including the Glenn Miller Band and Tex Benecke's group. In 1956 he opened a record store, Vince Lascheid Music, in suburban Pittsburgh. He began his gig with the Penguins in 1970.

To stir the crowd he would play a little ditty while the fans chanted "Let's Go Pens." One of his more colorful renditions

Vincent Charles Lascheid Jr.

was "Anchors Aweigh," which he played whenever Pens tough guy Bob "Battleship" Kelly stepped onto the ice. The Beatles' "Michelle My Belle" was for goalie Michel Dion. When officials made a bad call, he piped up with "Three Blind Mice"—until the league politely asked him to stop.

Vince retired in 2003 and was immediately inducted into the Penguins Hall of Fame.

Pronovost, Joseph Jean Denis

Right Wing
Penguins: 1968–78
NHL: 1968–82
Inducted into Penguins Hall of Fame: 1992
Birthplace: Shawinigan Falls, Quebec
B: December 18, 1945
Shoots: right

	Regular Season					Playoffs				
	GP	G	A	PTS	PM	GP	G	A	PTS	PM
Pittsburgh	753	316	287	603	306	29	9	9	18	12
NHL	**998**	**391**	**383**	**774**	**413**	**35**	**11**	**9**	**20**	**14**

As a young boy growing up in Shawinigan Falls, Quebec, Jean Pronovost idolized his big brother, Marcel. The older Pronovost had carved out a career as a Hall of Fame

Joseph Jean Denis Pronovost

A model of consistency, Pronovost led the club in scoring for the next two seasons—including another 40-goal campaign in 1977–78. But the Penguins were a team in decline. Weary of the constant management changes and personnel moves, he surprised general manager Baz Bastien in the fall of 1978 by requesting a trade. Bastien did his best to accommodate the four-time All-Star, sending him to Atlanta for Gregg Sheppard.

Although Pronovost had two good years with the Flames before finishing his career in Washington, he would later regret the trade. After 10 years in a Penguins uniform, Pittsburgh was his hockey home.

He retired as the Pens' all-time leader in goals (316) and points (603). Former teammate Rick Kehoe eventually topped his point total. His goal-scoring mark stood for over a decade until it was broken by another French Canadian—a big center who wore No. 66.

Riley, Jack

General Manager
Penguins: 1967–74
Inducted into Penguins Hall of Fame: 1999
Birthplace: Toronto, Ontario
B: June 14, 1919

| | Regular Season | | | | | | Playoffs | | | |
	G	W	L	T	PTS	PCT	G	W	L	PCT
Pittsburgh	375	130	190	55	315	.420	14	6	8	.429
NHL	**375**	**130**	**190**	**55**	**315**	**.420**	**14**	**6**	**8**	**.429**

Like any kid who grew up in Toronto, Jack Riley dreamed of one day playing for the hometown Maple Leafs. Using the cut-down sticks of Leafs greats such as Charlie Conacher and King Clancy, he played center and right wing for the Toronto Lions, a local Junior A team. At times the club practiced at the hallowed Maple Leaf Gardens.

Unfortunately, it was as close as Riley would come to fulfilling his dream. A slick passer but an average skater, he spent the majority of his playing career in the low minor leagues with teams like the Baltimore Clippers, the Philadelphia Falcons, and the Washington Lions.

After hanging up his skates in 1950 Riley moved into coaching. Showing a keen aptitude for the game, the energetic Irishman quickly moved up the ladder. In 1959 he became general manager of the American Hockey League's Rochester Americans. After five years with the Amerks he was named president of the AHL in 1964. Riley served as the league's executive officer until May of 1966, when he was hired by Pennsylvania senator Jack McGregor to become the first general manager of the Penguins.

Building a competitive team in Pittsburgh would be no easy task. In the days before the Amateur Draft became a

defenseman that spanned nearly 20 years. Jean hoped to follow in his brother's footsteps.

After a successful junior career with Niagara Falls, Pronovost was signed by Boston. Having learned the value of strong defensive play from Marcel, the speedy youngster developed into a solid two-way player. The Penguins took note. Shortly after the 1967–68 season they acquired him from the Bruins for a first-round draft pick.

It was not an easy transition. Pronovost was the only French Canadian on the Penguins roster. In many ways Pittsburgh was like a foreign land. But the rookie played well enough to notch 16 goals.

The following season the Penguins added another player from Quebec, a will-o'-the-wisp center named Michel Briere. The two became fast friends and linemates. With his buddy feeding him the puck, "Prony" reached the 20-goal mark as a sophomore.

However, tragedy struck over the summer when Briere was critically injured in a car accident. Pronovost was a frequent visitor at his friend's bedside until Briere passed away a year later. Briere's death was a terrible blow to Pronovost, but the born-again Christian persevered thanks to his strong faith in God. Picking up the mantle for his fallen friend, Pronovost soon emerged as one of the Penguins' brightest young stars.

In 1971–72 he scored 30 goals to establish a new single-season club record. Two years later Prony came into his own when he was placed on a line with Syl Apps and Lowell MacDonald. The hardworking right wing exploded for 40 goals—the first of three straight 40-plus goal seasons.

The highlight of his career came on Wednesday evening, March 24, 1976. Playing before a hometown throng at the Civic Arena, Prony beat Boston goalie Gilles Gilbert to become the first player in team history to score 50 goals.

Jack Riley

With the club still struggling to meet expectations, Riley was replaced in January of 1974 by his assistant, Jack Button. He remained with the Penguins as a scout through the 1974–75 season.

After leaving the Penguins, Riley stayed active in hockey. From 1975 through January of 1977 he served as commissioner of the Southern Hockey League, overseeing teams such as the colorful Macon Whoopees. In 1979 he began a four-year stint as commissioner of the International Hockey League. After retiring in 1983 he continued to serve as a consultant for the IHL and the East Coast Hockey League. In his honor, the ECHL named its original championship trophy the Jack Riley Cup.

Riley also served as a goal judge at the Civic Arena, but retired in 1993–94 so he could enjoy the games. Still spry at age 90, the popular former general manager remains a fixture on the Pittsburgh hockey scene.

Samuelsson, Ulf

Defense
Penguins: 1991–95
NHL: 1984–00
Inducted into Penguins Hall of Fame: 2003
Birthplace: Fagersta, Sweden
B: March 26, 1964
Shoots: left

	Regular Season					Playoffs				
	GP	G	A	PTS	PM	GP	G	A	PTS	PM
Pittsburgh	277	11	83	94	804	66	4	12	16	123
NHL	**1080**	**57**	**275**	**332**	**2453**	**132**	**7**	**27**	**34**	**272**

Prior to the arrival of Ulf Samuelsson, foreign-born players were regarded somewhat dismissively by their North American brethren. They were considered "soft" by old-school hockey standards. Although players such as Toronto's great Swedish defenseman Borje Salming displayed an abundance of heart and character, the negative perception didn't change until Samuelsson began plying his trade on NHL rinks.

Looking to add some grit to their back line, the Hartford Whalers selected the 18-year-old defenseman with their fourth pick in the 1982 Entry Draft. Following three strong seasons with Leksand in the fast Swedish Elite League, Samuelsson joined the Whalers midway through the 1984–85 season.

Although hardly a heavyweight at 6'1" and 195 pounds, he immediately established himself as one of the league's toughest and nastiest players. In March of 1985 he inadvertently clipped Montreal forward Pierre Mondou with a high stick to the eye, ending his career. Although the hit was accidental, it cemented Ulf's reputation as one of the dirtiest players in the game.

viable means of adding talent, Riley had to scrounge for players. He struck pay dirt with his first signing—a near-sighted goalie named Les Binkley who became one of the team's early stars.

Working primarily through the Expansion Draft, Riley assembled what most experts felt was a strong, veteran team. However, the Pens fell short in their inaugural season, missing the playoffs by two points.

The following year the team collapsed, forcing Riley to rebuild. Through a series of savvy trades and waiver pickups he added solid players such as Bryan Hextall, Dean Prentice, and Jean Pronovost, one of the team's all-time greats. In the 1969 Amateur Draft he selected bright young star Michel Briere.

The Penguins responded with a second-place finish and their first-ever playoff berth. In the 1970 playoffs the club came within two wins of reaching the Stanley Cup Finals. The team's strong showing earned Riley a promotion to club president.

However, by the middle of the 1971–72 season the Penguins were floundering once more. Riley reassumed the general manager duties from Red Kelly and engineered a series of moves that helped propel the team back to the playoffs.

Although the Pens' defenseman was vilified for the hit, he shrugged it off as one of those things that happen in the heat of battle. Neely was never a factor for the remainder of the series as the Penguins went on to capture their first Stanley Cup.

Samuelsson followed up with another strong season in 1991–92. In the Stanley Cup Finals against Chicago he played nearly flawless defense while adding a new level of discipline to his game.

It appeared Samuelsson would serve as the Pens' defensive stalwart for years to come. However, in 1995 Craig Patrick sent him to the Rangers as part of a four-player trade. Following a four-year tour on Broadway, New York sent the hard-hitting defenseman to Detroit at the 1999 trade deadline. Ulf played one more season with the Flyers before retiring in 2000 as the all-time leader in penalty minutes among foreign-born players.

Sciulli, Francis John, Sr.

Locker Room Assistant
Penguins: 1967–07
Inducted into Penguins Hall of Fame: 2007
Birthplace: Pittsburgh, Pennsylvania
B: July 23, 1925
D: August 18, 2007

Frank Sciulli was a fixture on the Pittsburgh sports scene nearly all of his life. As a youngster growing up in the Oakland section of the city, he served as a batboy for the Pittsburgh Pirates. Later he became a locker room attendant and cultivated friendships with some of the game's all-time greats, including Pirates outfielder Paul Waner.

Genial and low-key, Sciulli began serving as a locker room assistant for the Pittsburgh Hornets in 1964. When big-league hockey returned to Pittsburgh in 1967, Frank filled the same role for the Penguins. He also served as a locker room attendant for the Pittsburgh Steelers.

For four decades he looked after the players' needs. He did laundry, organized equipment, poured Gatorade, served up towels, and did any odd job asked of him. Some days, he might inflate footballs in the afternoon and arrange hockey sticks in the evening.

Frank was inducted into the Penguins Hall of Fame in 2007.

Ulf Samuelsson

There was no denying Samuelsson's penchant for borderline play. A fierce competitor, he used every weapon at his disposal to discourage opposing forwards from venturing too close to the net. However, he also developed into a solid defenseman. Over the next five seasons he anchored Hartford's defense while averaging nearly 30 points and 170 penalty minutes per season.

By 1990–91 the Whalers were a fading team that was badly in need of an overhaul. Weary of playing for a mediocre club, Samuelsson was considering a return to his native Sweden. Meanwhile, the Penguins were in desperate need of a tough, stay-at-home defender to bolster their blue-line corps. In March of 1991, the two teams swung a blockbuster six-player deal. Suddenly Samuelsson was a Penguin.

The move revitalized the rugged Swede. Hitting anything that moved, Ulf became an instant folk hero in Pittsburgh. Penguins color man Paul Steigerwald immediately dubbed him "Jack Lambert on skates."

Samuelsson earned lasting notoriety during the Wales Conference Finals in 1991, which pitted him against the Bruins' great forward, Cam Neely. His competitive fires stoked to a fever pitch, the rugged defender thumped the Boston strongman every time he touched the puck. Late in Game 3, Ulf jolted Neely with a jarring knee-to-knee hit. The big winger crumpled to the ice.

The Stanley Cup Playoffs

Since joining the National Hockey League in 1967, the Pittsburgh Penguins have enjoyed a rich and storied history in Stanley Cup Playoffs competition. Led by some of the game's brightest stars, including Mario Lemieux, Jaromir Jagr, and Sidney Crosby, the Penguins have won three Stanley Cups—more than any other 1967 expansion team.

The Pens endured their share of heartbreak as well. An epic collapse against the New York Islanders in 1975 sent the team spiraling into financial distress and mediocrity. A disappointing loss to the Islanders in the 1993 Patrick Division Finals derailed a dynasty in the making.

Pittsburgh's playoff history is sharply divided into two distinct eras—P.M. (pre Mario) and A.M. (after Mario). Prior to the arrival of No. 66, the Penguins tasted little postseason success, winning only three playoff matchups. Following his arrival the team became a juggernaut, capturing four Prince of Wales Trophies and three Stanley Cups.

The Penguins were the last of the 1967 expansion teams to make the playoffs, earning a postseason berth in their third year. Following a sweep of the Oakland Seals the Pens took on their archrival, the St. Louis Blues. The "Pesky Pens" came within two wins of reaching the Stanley Cup Finals before bowing out in a hotly contested six-game set.

Buoyed by a change in ownership, the decade of the 1970s ushered in a brief era of respectability. An improving young team qualified for the playoffs in 1972. Sparked by the addition of big-time scorers Vic Hadfield, Rick Kehoe, and Pierre Larouche, the 1974–75 Pens posted the first winning season in franchise history. However, they blew a 3–0 series lead over the Islanders to earn an ignominious place in NHL history.

In 1982 a gritty but undermanned Penguins club nearly dethroned the two-time defending Stanley Cup champion Islanders. Following its near miss, the team waddled through two dismal seasons to "earn" the first pick in the 1984 Entry Draft. General manager Eddie Johnston wisely selected Lemieux, and the team began its storybook rags-to-riches ascent.

After missing the playoffs for six straight seasons, the Lemieux-led Penguins earned a postseason berth in 1989. The following season Craig Patrick took over as general manager and the team entered its first Golden Age. Paced by Mario and fellow stars Tom Barrasso, Ron Francis, Jaromir Jagr, Larry Murphy, and Kevin Stevens, the Penguins won back-to-back Stanley Cups in 1991 and 1992. Along the way they established an NHL playoff record with 14 straight postseason victories.

The Pens remained a perennial Cup contender for the rest of the decade, reaching the Eastern Conference Finals in 1996. Lemieux's health problems and premature retirement, coupled with ever-looming financial problems, kept the team a step away.

Entering the new millennium, Lemieux purchased the team out of bankruptcy and ended his three-and-a-half-year retirement. Sparked by Mario's return, the Pens made it to the Conference Finals in 2001. However, financial constraints forced Craig Patrick to trade superstars Jaromir Jagr and Alexei Kovalev. The club fell on hard times, ending a run of 11 consecutive playoff berths.

During the dry spell, Patrick restocked the team with bright young stars Sidney Crosby, Evgeni Malkin, and Marc-Andre Fleury. The poster team for the new NHL, the Penguins re-emerged as a league power. In 2007–08 they captured first place in the Atlantic Division and rolled through the competition before losing to the tough Detroit Red Wings in the Stanley Cup Finals.

Following an up-and-down regular season, the Penguins returned to the Finals in 2009. Paced by the brilliant play of Crosby, Malkin, and Fleury, they toppled Detroit in the rematch to win their third Stanley Cup.

Drumming up support for the 1975 playoffs (left to right): owner Tad Potter, Mayor Pete Flaherty, Chamber of Commerce member Justin Horon, and head coach Marc Boileau.

1970

After watching his team muddle through two dismal seasons, Penguins general manager Jack Riley made wholesale changes over the summer of 1969. Using every means at his disposal, he culled a quartet of solid players from the Intra-League Draft, including shot-blocking defenseman Bob Blackburn, scoring winger Dean Prentice, goalie Al Smith, and agitator Glen "Slats" Sather. He improved the team down the middle, a traditional weak spot, by trading for centers Bryan Hextall and Ron Schock.

However, Riley's best addition came through the Amateur Draft. In the third round he selected a will-o'-the wisp center from Shawinigan in the Quebec League named Michel Briere. Although undersized, the high-scoring rookie quickly established himself as one of the team's best players.

Despite the infusion of new blood, the Penguins struggled through the first half of the season. The turning point came on January 31, when the Pens beat the division-leading St. Louis Blues in a brawl-filled contest at the Civic Arena. Buoyed by the big win, the "Pesky Pens" went on a 10–5 run to finish second in the West Division and qualify for the Stanley Cup Playoffs.

Penguins vs. Seals, Quarterfinals

The Penguins opened their first-ever playoff series against a fellow expansion team, the Oakland Seals. The Seals had slipped to fourth place following a strong season in 1968–69, but they were not to be taken lightly.

Oakland's best players included ex-Pen Earl Ingarfield, former Pittsburgh Hornets star Ted Hampson, and hot-tempered Carol Vadnais, who played both forward and defense. Hulking Gary Smith played 65 games during the regular season and was a tower of strength in goal.

Playing before a modest crowd of 8,051 spectators at the Civic Arena, the Penguins got on the scoreboard quickly. The Seals drew even on a goal by veteran winger Gerry Ehman. The game remained deadlocked until midway through the final period, when defensive-minded winger Nick Harbaruk scored to give the Pens' their first postseason victory.

"It was the sixth-best goal I ever scored," Harbaruk said. "I saw the whole side of the net open. I would've kicked myself if I missed it."

Oakland struck first in Game 2 on a goal by former Hornet Gary Jarrett. The lead held up until the 11-minute mark of the second period, when Harbaruk and Wally Boyer scored just 34 seconds apart. The Pens continued to get offense from unexpected sources when defenseman Dunc McCallum beat Smith in the third period to put the finishing touches on a crisp 3–1 victory.

Unhappy with his team's performance, Oakland coach Fred Glover dressed Neil Nicholson, Howie Menard, and tough Tony Featherstone for Game 3. The Seals responded

St. Louis villain Barclay Plager smiles for the camera.

with their best period of the series. Ingarfield staked Oakland to an early lead with a shorthanded goal, while Smith stopped Dean Prentice and Jean Pronovost on good scoring chances.

But the Seals' intensity waned in the second period and the Penguins quickly took advantage. Harbaruk, who had tallied only five goals during the regular season, notched his third goal of the series. Ken Schinkel soon followed with his first goal of the playoffs. The Pens went up 3–1 when McCallum dug the puck loose from a scrum and fed Pronovost, who beat Smith through a screen. Hampson closed the gap early in the third period, but Schinkel notched the Pens' first playoff hat trick to put the game out of reach.

Facing elimination in Game 4, the Seals gave their best effort of the series. Vadnais scored twice to stake the Seals to one-goal leads. But each time the Penguins rallied to tie. The Seals in particular seemed to be feeling the effects of their fourth game in five nights.

"They seemed to get a little tired," Sather said. "It was just a matter of time before we beat 'em."

The Pens prevailed at 8:28 of overtime when rookie Michel Briere slipped his first goal of the series past Smith.

"I saw the goalie with his legs spread and that's why I slid it on the ice," Briere said. "I hope I score a bigger goal than this."

Series Summary
Beat Oakland 4–0

Game	Date	City	Result	Winning Goal	Winning Goalie
1	April 8	Pittsburgh	Pittsburgh 2–1	Nick Harbaruk	Les Binkley
2	April 9	Pittsburgh	Pittsburgh 3–1	Wally Boyer	Les Binkley
3	April 11	Oakland	Pittsburgh 5–2	Jean Pronovost	Les Binkley
4	April 12	Oakland	Pittsburgh 3–2 (OT)	Michel Briere	Les Binkley

Penguins vs. Blues, Semifinals

The Penguins' sweep of the Seals set up a matchup against the West Division champion St. Louis Blues. Easily the best of the expansion teams, the Blues possessed a powerful offense led by Red Berenson, Phil Goyette, and ex-Pen Ab McDonald, and a power play that ranked second in the league. On the blue line, St. Louis boasted a robust defensive corps featuring the notorious Plager brothers, Barclay and Bob. They were backed by Hall of Fame goaltenders Glenn Hall and Jacques Plante.

It took all of 19 seconds for the bitter rivals to renew hostilities. Noel Picard, a boisterous 210-pound defenseman, squirted gasoline on the smoldering embers when he mugged Pronovost in the St. Louis zone. Bryan Watson flew at Picard and Bob Plager pounced on Bugsy. Soon gloves and sticks littered the ice.

Although the Penguins were holding their own in the fisticuffs, St. Louis tallied three goals in a six-minute span of the second period to put the game out of reach. To set the tone for the next contest, Picard jumped Briere at the end of the game to spark yet another brawl that featured Tracy Pratt and Bob Plager in the main event. All told, the two teams accounted for 149 minutes in penalties.

"They think they're going to kick the hell out of us, but they're not," declared a defiant Jack Riley.

"When it comes to the rough stuff, our guys are just a little better than St. Louis is," Pratt added.

In an effort to neutralize the Blues' intimidating defensive tandem of Picard and Bob Plager, Pens coach Red Kelly started Game 2 with a makeshift forward line that featured two of his biggest and toughest players—Pratt and McCallum—alongside Bryan Hextall.

The move was intended to be a show of strength. Kelly gave the two defensemen strict orders to exit the ice at the earliest opportunity. Pratt heeded his coach's plea. However, the lead-footed McCallum chose to linger and the Blues promptly scored on an odd-man break. St. Louis rolled up a three-goal first-period advantage en route to a convincing 4–1 win.

"McCallum was supposed to get the hell off the ice," Kelly lamented.

With the series shifting to Pittsburgh for Game 3, Penguins fans turned out in droves to witness the battle. To ensure that his team was properly motivated, Kelly entered the dressing room just before game time and emptied a brown paper bag containing the winning playoff share of $7,250 onto the floor.

Suitably inspired, the Pens dominated the action from the opening face-off. Playing with a newfound confidence, they held the high-powered Blues in check and rolled to a 3–2 victory.

The team's euphoria was short-lived. Binkley, who was absolutely sensational in goal, had suffered a knee injury. Al Smith—barely recovered from a case of the measles—would replace him for Game 4. Blues coach Scotty Bowman also made a goaltending change, inserting 29-year-old rookie Ernie Wakely in place of Jacques Plante.

A record throng of 12,962 jammed the Civic Arena to see if the Penguins could even the series. They were treated to another superb effort by their hometown heroes.

Seven minutes into the contest Briere dropped the puck off to Pronovost, who set up Duane Rupp for a 20-foot backhander. Andre Boudrias knotted the score for the Blues in the second period, but the Jet Line soon struck again. Briere faked a pass to Pronovost at the St. Louis line, deked Bob Plager to the ice, and slid the puck between Wakely's legs.

Desperate for a tying goal, Bowman pulled his goalie for an extra attacker. Playing with energy and fervor, the Pens promptly launched four shots at the empty St. Louis net. They triumphed 2–1 to knot the series at two games apiece.

The Penguins were riding an incredible wave of emotion. What had seemed unthinkable—a berth in the Stanley Cup Finals—was now within their grasp.

Stoked to a fever pitch, they opened Game 5 hitting anything that moved. However, the strategy backfired when Sather, Hextall, and Watson drew penalties in rapid succession.

The Penguins gamely killed off the first two power plays, but Frank St. Marseille cashed in on the third to give St. Louis the lead. The Blues romped to an easy 5–0 win.

With their backs against the wall, the Penguins came out smoking in Game 6. Playing before another near-capacity crowd at the Civic Arena they grabbed the lead on goals by Rupp and Schock. Red Berenson scored in the second period to pull the Blues within one going into the final frame.

In the wildest finish of the series St. Louis tied the game at 5:26, only to watch Briere pot his fifth goal of the playoffs less than a minute later. The Pens had barely finished celebrating when the Blues' Tim Ecclestone evened the score again. The defenses stiffened until the 14-minute mark, when Larry Keenan fired the game winner past Al Smith to break the hearts of the Penguins and their fans.

"You feel bad about losing," Red Kelly said, "but you never feel bad when you've given everything you have and that's what this team did. This club has more heart than any club in the world."

Even Scotty Bowman, who had taken verbal pot shots at several of the Penguins during the heat of battle, praised them for their effort.

"I think it will be a while before Pittsburgh is down again," he said. "They play the game the right way. They don't score a lot of goals, but they make it tough for you to score."

Series Summary
Lost to St. Louis 4–2

Game	Date	City	Result	Winning Goal	Winning Goalie
1	April 19	St. Louis	St. Louis 3–1	Phil Goyette	Glenn Hall
2	April 21	St. Louis	St. Louis 4–1	Larry Keenan	Jacques Plante
3	April 23	Pittsburgh	Pittsburgh 3–2	Michel Briere	Les Binkley
4	April 26	Pittsburgh	Pittsburgh 2–1	Michel Briere	Al Smith
5	April 28	St. Louis	St. Louis 5–0	Frank St. Marseille	Jacques Plante
6	April 30	Pittsburgh	St. Louis 4–3	Larry Keenan	Glenn Hall

1972

1972 will forever be etched in Steel City lore as the year of the "Immaculate Reception." Eight months earlier, however, the Penguins enjoyed their own slice of divine intervention.

Despite a strong 5–1–5 stretch run, the Pens trailed Philadelphia on the final night of the regular season by two points in the race for the fourth and final playoff spot in the West Division. Needing a win over their bitter rival, St. Louis, coupled with a Flyers loss, the Pens bombed the Blues 6–2.

"I told my guys Buffalo was ahead 2–1 after two periods," Pens coach Red Kelly said. "I wasn't taking any chances."

In reality, the Flyers were in the process of closing out a 2–2 tie with Buffalo, which would've clinched a postseason berth for Philly. In his book, *Score!*, the Flyers' late announcer Gene Hart vividly recalled the game.

"I did a lot of counting down on the air that day, counting down to the playoffs, from 10 minutes, eight minutes, six, five, four, three, two, one minute to go to the playoffs…then I was counting down the seconds, and I remember looking at the clock with eight, seven seconds left, and I was thinking, *Here come the playoffs!* when I saw former Flyer Gerry Meehan skate down the left side and let go a 60-footer which sailed over Doug Favell's left shoulder and into the net. I recall saying, 'Shot, score, Gerry Meehan. And that just does it for the Flyers. Three-two Buffalo with four seconds left.'"

The Penguins were understandably elated…and not the least bit surprised by their stroke of good fortune.

"I really figured Buffalo was going to win," Bryan Hextall said. "Buffalo was sitting there waiting for Philadelphia. They didn't play Saturday night, and the Flyers had played five times in eight days."

Jean Pronovost swoops in for a shot against the Black Hawks.

Penguins vs. Black Hawks, Quarterfinals

Thanks to the miracle finish, the Penguins suddenly found themselves in the playoffs. Their "reward" was an opening-round matchup against the powerful Chicago Black Hawks. Paced by 50-goal scorer Bobby Hull, Chicago had breezed through the West Division en route to an outstanding record of 46–17–15, including a 5–0–1 mark against the Pens. Loaded with marquee players like Hull, Stan Mikita, and Vezina Trophy winner Tony Esposito, the Black Hawks seemed a sure bet to win.

Although hopelessly outmanned, the Penguins were determined to carry the play to their star-studded adversary. They broke on top early in Game 1 on a goal by Bob Leiter, but Chicago battled back to even the score.

The game remained deadlocked until the final period, when sharpshooter Jim Pappin and former Hornet Pit Martin scored to put the game out of reach. Although he came out on the losing end, Penguins goalie Jim Rutherford stopped 35 shots in a stellar performance.

Taking a page from the Penguins' playbook, Chicago came out smoking in Game 2 and grabbed a quick two-goal lead. Midway through the second period Jean Pronovost scored a shorthanded tally on a pretty feed from Darryl Edestrand to cut the Black Hawks' lead to one. Although veteran Chico Maki restored Chicago's two-goal margin in the third period, the determined Penguins rebounded again on a power-play goal by Leiter while the Hawks were two men short. The Pens peppered Esposito in a desperate attempt to tie the score, but the All-Star netminder stood firm.

Still upbeat, the Penguins looked forward to Games 3 and 4 in Pittsburgh.

"We know we can play with them," Jean Pronovost said. "We can go home and win two. We've been down before."

Coach Red Kelly agreed. "The home ice and home crowd will help us," he said.

Black Hawks coach Billy Reay stirred up a bit of controversy for Game 3 by naming Gary Smith as his starting goaltender. On the surface Reay appeared to be taking a gamble. But Smith, widely regarded as the best backup goaltender in the league, had beaten the Penguins on four occasions during the regular season. Not to be outdone, Pens coach Red Kelly benched one of his top players, Ken Schinkel, in favor of Keith McCreary, who had been out since January with a knee injury.

Neither team scored in the first period, as both clubs seemed to feel the effects of their third game in four nights. Chicago got on the board early in the second frame when Bobby Hull drew the attention of three Penguins defenders and slipped the puck to Christian Bordeleau, who snapped it past Rutherford from the left-wing circle.

With 15 seconds left in the period the Pens had a golden opportunity to tie the game. Greg Polis deflected an Eddie Shack blast through Smith's pads, and the puck dropped to the ice just inches from the goal line. Defenseman Doug

Jarrett coolly swept the rubber from harm's way before the Penguins could poke it home.

The Pens had several chances to even the score in the final period, but youngster Al McDonough misfired on a breakaway, while Smith stopped Nick Harbaruk and Steve Cardwell from point-blank range. Chicago finally put the game out of reach when McDonough inadvertently steered a shot by Mikita into his own net.

A healthy crowd of 12,415 turned out at the Civic Arena to see if their team could stave off elimination in Game 4. They were treated to the most exciting game of the series.

The Black Hawks rolled to another early lead, but the Penguins refused to quit. Determined to put up a fight, they exploded for four goals in the second period to grab a two-goal edge.

Incredibly, the Penguins had the mighty Black Hawks on the run. However, Chicago came roaring back in the third period to retake the lead. The situation looked grim until Leiter struck for a miracle goal with two minutes remaining to send the game into overtime.

The end came all too suddenly. Martin won the face-off to begin overtime and dumped the puck into the Penguins' zone. As Rutherford sprawled to smother it, the puck glanced off of Tim Horton's skate and into the net.

"It wasn't very complicated," Horton said after the game. "The puck hit my skate and went in."

Although they lost in four straight games, the Pens battled hard. Rutherford in particular had made an impression. "Young Jim Rutherford, the kid, really played well," Red Kelly said. "He stood pretty tall in the old nets."

Series Summary
Lost to Chicago 4–0

Game	Date	City	Result	Winning Goal	Winning Goalie
1	April 5	Chicago	Chicago 3–1	Jim Pappin	Tony Esposito
2	April 6	Chicago	Chicago 3–2	Wayne Maki	Tony Esposito
3	April 8	Pittsburgh	Chicago 2–0	Christian Bordeleau	Gary Smith
4	April 9	Pittsburgh	Chicago 6–5 (OT)	Pit Martin	Gerry Desjardins

1975

After scuffling through their first six seasons, the Penguins began to turn the corner midway through the 1973–74 season. Following a dismal start, new general manager Jack Button reshaped the team by acquiring tough guys Steve Durbano and Bob "Battleship" Kelly from St. Louis and hulking defenseman Ron Stackhouse from Detroit. The Pens responded with a 14–10–4 finish.

Button continued to upgrade the team during the summer of 1974, adding scorers Vic Hadfield, Rick Kehoe, and Pierre Larouche to a talented nucleus that included established stars such as Syl Apps, Dave Burrows, Lowell MacDonald, and Jean Pronovost.

Despite a rocky 11–16–6 start to the 1974–75 season, the Pens were clearly improved. Buoyed by a 20-game unbeaten streak at the Civic Arena, which included an 8–2 thrashing of the defending Stanley Cup champion Flyers, the club caught fire in the second half to register the first winning season in franchise history.

Leading the way was veteran center Ron Schock, who enjoyed a career year with 86 points. Pronovost paced the goal scorers, lighting the lamp 43 times, while Kehoe (32), Hadfield (31), and Larouche (31) each topped the 30-goal plateau.

Penguins vs. Blues, Preliminary Round

Boasting three potent lines, the Penguins had the look of a contender when they opened the playoffs against archenemy St. Louis in a best-of-three Preliminary Round series. Adding fuel to the fire were rumors that the volcanic Durbano—who missed virtually the entire season with a wrist injury—was ready to suit up against his former teammates.

Although the Penguins appeared to be the stronger team, the visiting Blues got off to a quick start in Game 1. Claude Larose and Wayne Merrick beat Pens goalie Gary Inness to stake St. Louis to a two-goal edge. With their big goalie, John Davidson, in top form it looked as though the Blues would carry the lead into the second intermission. But 15 seconds before the buzzer Larouche won a face-off deep in the St. Louis zone and skated to the sideboards with the puck. When the Blues dutifully gave chase, the crafty young center flipped the puck to Battleship Kelly, who rifled it past Davidson.

Garry Unger responded quickly for the Blues in the opening minute of the third period, but the momentum had swung to the Penguins. Chuck Arnason scored a pair of goals six minutes apart to even the score. Later in the period Vic Hadfield set up Larouche for the game winner. Afterward, St. Louis coach Garry Young was furious with his team for letting the game slip away.

The Blues took the initiative again in Game 2, as veterans Red Berenson and Bill Collins struck for a pair of first-period goals. Displaying remarkable resilience, the Pens soon evened the score on tallies by Pronovost and Stackhouse. Hard-shooting Larry Sacharuk put St. Louis up by one midway through the second period, but Apps knotted the score again on the power play.

The Penguins next goal came from an unexpected source. Harvard grad Bob McManama was killing a penalty early in the third period when he intercepted an errant pass and took off toward the St. Louis zone. Just as the young center was hit by Barclay Plager, he dished a pass to rookie defenseman Colin Campbell, who streaked in and slipped the puck beneath Blues goalie Eddie Johnston. Hadfield scored late in the period to clinch the game and the series for Pittsburgh.

Series Summary
Beat St. Louis 2–0

Game	Date	City	Result	Winning Goal	Winning Goalie
1	April 8	Pittsburgh	Pittsburgh 4–3	Pierre Larouche	Gary Inness
2	April 10	St. Louis	Pittsburgh 5–3	Colin Campbell	Gary Inness

Jean Pronovost is stopped by the Islanders' Glenn Resch, while Ed Westfall (18) and Dave Lewis (25) look on.

Penguins vs. Islanders, Quarterfinals

The Penguins' sweep of the Blues set up a matchup with the surprising New York Islanders. Under the watchful eye of bespectacled coach Al Arbour, the Islanders had made the playoffs in only their third year of existence. Featuring a curious blend of veterans, castoffs, and rising young stars such as Denis Potvin, the Islanders had melded into a spirited team that played a tight checking game. They would prove to be a most formidable opponent.

Starting quickly in Game 1 before their hometown fans, the Pens raced to a three-goal first-period lead. It appeared they would coast to an easy victory, but the visitors from Long Island staged a furious rally to make a game of it. The Pens held on to win 5–4 but suffered a severe blow when Barry Wilkins—one of their top defensemen—went down with a separated shoulder.

His replacement, Dennis Owchar, set the tone for Game 2 with a crushing open-ice check on Bob Bourne. Suitably inspired, the Penguins swarmed all over the Islanders. Paced by Lowell MacDonald's two-goal night, they dominated the game from start to finish and rolled to a 3–1 victory.

But misfortune struck again when Bob Paradise sustained a shoulder injury, leaving the club with only four healthy defensemen. With nowhere else to turn, Button recalled inexperienced Larry Bignell from Hershey to plug the hole.

The series shifted to the Nassau County Coliseum for Game 3, where the Penguins prevailed in a wild and wooly affair. Jean Pronovost and Battleship Kelly staked Pittsburgh to a 2–0 lead. Kelly made it a three-goal margin early in the second frame when he outmuscled Potvin to bang home a rebound.

However, the gritty Islanders weren't finished. Veteran Ed Westfall scored to set up a wide-open third period in which the teams exchanged six goals. Although New York controlled the play in the final 20 minutes, the Pens were at their sharpshooting best, beating Billy Smith on three of six shots.

Overcome with joy, the Penguins celebrated into the wee hours at a Long Island night spot, convinced that the series was theirs for the taking. The revelry would prove to be incredibly premature.

In an effort to shake things up, Islanders coach Al Arbour replaced the beleaguered Smith with Glenn "Chico" Resch. Little did he realize that this seemingly insignificant move would have a dramatic effect on the outcome of the series.

The Islanders finally scored the opening goal in Game 4, which allowed them to settle into their close-checking style. Kelly, who had become the Pens' most dangerous weapon, slipped a backhander past Resch to even the score.

It was all the offense he and his mates could muster. Clark Gillies and Jean-Paul Parise scored in the third period to put the final touches on a crisp 3–1 Islanders victory.

Despite their failure to finish New York off, the Penguins still were a confident bunch. After all, the series was returning to the friendly confines of the Civic Arena, where they were virtually unbeatable. The plan was simple: take control early and force the less-skilled Islanders to play a more wide-open game.

Unfortunately, the Islanders quickly piled up a two-goal lead. Although Hadfield scored midway through the second period to cut New York's lead in half, Westfall responded with a power-play goal. Jude Drouin drove home an empty netter to seal the Pens' fate.

Suddenly, things didn't appear so rosy. The Penguins' snipers were having more luck clanking shots off the goal posts than finding the back of the net. It was as if Resch had made a deal with the devil and had grafted the iron to his body.

"They're like a disease that you can't get rid of," Kelly grumbled following the loss.

"We're not out of it yet," Ron Schock added. "We still have a 3–2 lead in games. We knew it wasn't going to be an easy series. Now we are finding out how hard it is."

Although clearly annoyed that the plucky Islanders were still lingering, the Penguins liked their chances, especially with Paradise returning to action for Game 6.

Once more the Islanders grabbed the early lead, but Larouche struck back quickly. Just as the Pens appeared to be gathering momentum, Garry Howatt scored a crucial goal to give the Islanders a lead they would never relinquish. Again the Penguins attacked with everything they had. Again Resch stopped them cold. To make matters worse, Hadfield—a key member of the power play—suffered two broken ribs. He would play only a single shift in the series finale.

Game 7 was a dramatic affair played before a sellout crowd of 13,404 at the Civic Arena. Tempers flared as the teams battled for control. A pair of genuine heavyweights, Paradise and Gillies, slugged it out five minutes into the contest. Kelly and Dave Lewis soon followed suit, but the rest of the game was played hard and clean.

The game remained scoreless through two periods as Gary Inness and his counterpart Resch put on a goaltending clinic. The Penguins had two big scoring opportunities in the final frame. True to form, a deflection by Pronovost bounced harmlessly off a goal post. Resch then smothered a good chance by Larouche from in close.

"I had the net," a disconsolate Pierre would recall. "I have Resch beat."

Finally, with less than six minutes remaining, Bert Marshall lugged the puck into the Penguins' zone while J.P. Parise veered toward the net. Using Parise as a decoy, Marshall slipped the puck to Westfall, who beat Inness with a high backhander.

Stunned by the turn of events, the Pens failed to muster a shot on goal in the final minutes of play. The Islanders became the first team in 33 years to rally from a 3–0 deficit and win a playoff series.

In the hush of the losing locker room, Marc Boileau stared into his half-empty can of beer and struggled to explain what went wrong. "We got overconfident...definitely," he said. "All they did was work for seven games."

Years later author and Penguins vice present of communications Tom McMillan interviewed owner Tad Potter for his book, *The Pittsburgh Penguins: Cellar to Summit*.

"We dinged crossbars, we hit pipes, we had guys in alone with Resch flat on his back," Potter recalled. "Didn't matter. It was like a greater power was saying something like, 'You aren't supposed to win.'...The next series against the Flyers, if there'd been one, would've bailed us out of our financial hole. Ownership would have stabilized. We were an organization which at that point was a couple of players away from being a real contender."

Instead, on June 13, 1975, the IRS placed a lien on the club for $532,000 and padlocked the team offices. The following day Equibank sued the team for $5 million in unpaid loans. Potter and Peter Block had no choice but to enter into receivership.

Series Summary
Lost to New York Islanders 4–3

Game	Date	City	Result	Winning Goal	Winning Goalie
1	April 13	Pittsburgh	Pittsburgh 5–4	Dave Burrows	Gary Inness
2	April 15	Pittsburgh	Pittsburgh 3–1	Lowell MacDonald	Gary Inness
3	April 17	New York	Pittsburgh 6–4	Syl Apps	Gary Inness
4	April 20	New York	NY Islanders 3–1	Clark Gillies	Glenn Resch
5	April 22	Pittsburgh	NY Islanders 4–2	Ed Westfall	Glenn Resch
6	April 24	New York	NY Islanders 4–1	Garry Howatt	Glenn Resch
7	April 26	Pittsburgh	NY Islanders 1–0	Ed Westfall	Glenn Resch

1976

The summer of 1975 was a turbulent one for the Penguins. Following the crushing playoff loss to the Islanders, owner Tad Potter and his partners were forced to enter into receivership. Although the Pens were purchased within a month by a new ownership group headed by investment broker Al Savill, the club's financial instability seemed to permeate into the deepest levels of the organization.

There was no denying the 1975–76 Penguins were an extremely talented bunch. Whiz kid Pierre Larouche and Jean Pronovost each cracked the 50-goal barrier, while Syl Apps, Vic Hadfield, and Lowell MacDonald reached the 30-goal mark.

However, the Pens also were wildly inconsistent. Sandwiched around a pair of four-game winning streaks was a dismal 7–23–5 stretch that cost coach Marc Boileau his job.

At wits end, general manager Wren Blair turned the reins over to Ken Schinkel, who had previously coached the team for parts of two seasons. The bipolar Penguins responded by going 20–10–7 under Schinkel to nail down third place in the Norris Division and a postseason berth.

Penguins vs. Maple Leafs, Preliminary Round

By the time the playoffs rolled around the Penguins had regained much of their old swagger. Even the usually mild-mannered Schinkel was upbeat. Prior to his team's Preliminary Round matchup with Toronto, he sounded off to the local press.

"I know we can win the home game," he boasted, "and I think we can win one of two games in Toronto."

But the Maple Leafs were a rugged team with a battle plan—hit the Pens at every turn and see if they had the guts to hit back. In Game 1 they executed their plan with brutal precision.

With Lanny McDonald and Brian Glennie leading the assault, Toronto belted the Penguins all over the Maple Leaf Gardens ice. While the stunned visitors tried to regroup, the Leafs raced to a three-goal lead. The Pens mounted a modest comeback when Stan Gilbertson scored early in the third period, but Toronto quickly quelled the uprising.

"We outworked and outhustled them as a team," Leafs goalie Wayne Thomas said. "We hit them the whole game, and that's how we stopped them."

"Pittsburgh usually makes the pretty play," Darryl Sittler added. "So we had to check them closely to take that away from them. If we don't, they have the passers and shooters to blow us out."

To their credit, the Penguins responded with some fire of their own in Game 2. With the venue shifting to Pittsburgh, Schinkel had the last line change. He matched his checking

Defensive stalwart Dave Burrows drops to the ice to block a shot by Toronto's Darryl Sittler (27).

unit of Vic Hadfield, Ron Schock, and Gilbertson against the high-scoring Sittler line.

The 35-year-old Hadfield set the tone by swapping punches with Sittler just moments after the opening face-off. Inspired by their old warrior, the Penguins carried the physical play to Toronto for the rest of the evening.

"We had to show Toronto right off the bat we weren't going to lie down for them," Hadfield said. "We did what we have been preaching all season—taking the body along the boards."

Another old-timer, Lowell MacDonald, put the Pens on the board with a power-play goal. The score remained 1–0 until Toronto's Errol Thompson inadvertently tipped a pass into his own net in the final minute of play. Despite the low score, the Penguins pressured the Leafs throughout the game, unleashing 49 shots at Thomas.

"We played a helluva game as a team," goalie Michel Plasse said. "We simply deserved to win."

Following the Pens' rousing effort in Game 2, the finale figured to be an all-out war. Once again Toronto came out aggressively on home ice. However, their intimidation tactics seemed to backfire when pugnacious Dave "Tiger" Williams drew a five-minute major for high sticking Pens defenseman Barry Wilkins.

Handed a golden opportunity to take control, the Penguins muffed their chance. Shortly after the penalty expired Glennie slammed into Syl Apps. As the star center hobbled off the ice with strained knee ligaments, the Pens' flickering playoff hopes went with him. Toronto cruised to an easy 4–0 victory to take the series.

"Killing that penalty was the key to the game," Toronto coach Red Kelly said. "After that, we took charge of everything."

Series Summary
Lost to Toronto 2–1

Game	Date	City	Result	Winning Goal	Winning Goalie
1	April 6	Toronto	Toronto 4–1	Lanny McDonald	Wayne Thomas
2	April 8	Pittsburgh	Pittsburgh 2–0	Lowell MacDonald	Michel Plasse
3	April 9	Toronto	Toronto 4–0	Jim McKenny	Wayne Thomas

1977

The 1976–77 campaign would prove to be a transition year for the Penguins. Older players such as Vic Hadfield, Lowell MacDonald, and Ed Van Impe were phased out due to age or injury. Youngsters such as Russ Anderson and the "Kid Line" of Wayne Bianchin, Blair Chapman, and Greg Malone were promoted to fill their slots.

While the fresh faces added a sorely needed infusion of new blood, they couldn't match the output of the old pros. The team's production plummeted by nearly 100 goals, forcing coach Ken Schinkel to install a tight checking system.

There were other worries as well. Following two outstanding seasons, the team's brightest young star, Pierre Larouche, seemed to regress. With the full support of new general manager Baz Bastien, Schinkel suspended "Lucky Pierre" for two games in November for his bad attitude and poor work habits.

Although no longer an offensive powerhouse the Pens were much improved defensively, thanks to the goaltending tandem of veteran Dunc Wilson and 24-year-old Denis Herron. The result was another third-place finish and a third consecutive playoff berth.

Penguins vs. Maple Leafs, Preliminary Round
Once again, the Penguins were pitted against the Maple Leafs in the opening round of the playoffs. This time, however, they held the home-ice advantage.

Determined to avenge their dismal showing of the previous year, the Pens swarmed the Toronto defense from the opening face-off. Battleship Kelly struck for an early goal to stake his team to a 1–0 lead. But the Penguins stopped hitting after Anderson was ejected from the game for being the third man in an altercation.

As the Penguins' aggressiveness waned, Toronto pounded three straight goals past goalie Denis Herron to snatch a 3–1 lead. Late in the third period Mario Faubert beat Leafs netminder Wayne Thomas to pare the lead in half, but the Pens would get no closer.

"We should have run away with the game in the first period," Jean Pronovost said, "but we didn't. We had enough good scoring chances, but we didn't get the puck in the net."

Prior to Game 2, Toronto tough guy Dave "Tiger" Williams provided the Penguins with some extra motivation.

"Them guys is done like dinner," he boasted to a TV reporter.

Hoping to make Williams eat his words, the visiting Penguins rebounded with a solid effort. Grabbing a quick 3–0 lead, it appeared they would breeze to an easy victory. However, the Leafs battled back to even the score in the third period.

It took a great bit of teamwork by the "Kid Line" to save the day. Bianchin started the play with a crisp pass off the sideboards to Chapman, who was racing in full stride toward the Toronto net. Instead of shooting, Chapman slipped the puck to his linemate Malone, who fired it past Thomas to restore the Pens' lead.

"I saw Wayne with the puck and I yelled at him," Chapman said. "He passed it to me and I was going to shoot when I saw Greg come in all alone in front of the net, so I slid it over to him. I knew it was going in. He had lots of room."

Undaunted, the Maple Leafs continued to apply pressure. Toronto coach Red Kelly turned up the heat by pulling Thomas for an extra attacker with less than a minute to go. But Pierre Larouche won a critical face-off deep in the Penguins' zone and passed the puck to Ron Stackhouse, who coolly banked it off the sideboards and into the empty net.

Wayne Bianchin chases down a loose puck in the Toronto zone. Future Pen Randy Carlyle applies the hook.

"Everybody wanted to win," Pronovost said. "We knew if we just hung tough, we would be all right, even if we would have to win it in overtime."

Convinced that a goaltending change was in order, Kelly replaced Thomas with young Mike Palmateer for Game 3. Playing before a throng of 15,934 at the Civic Arena—the largest crowd to witness a playoff game—the Leafs snatched the lead on a power-play goal by Swedish defenseman Borje Salming. Minutes later, with Tiger Williams wreaking havoc in the crease, Ian Turnbull beat Herron with a blast from the point.

Enraged, the little goalie flailed away at his tormentor, much to the surprise of the league's penalty king. Fortunately, Syl Apps came to Herron's rescue before Williams could launch a counterassault. However, his heroics earned him a game misconduct penalty.

With the high-scoring Apps removed from the deciding game for the second year in a row, Toronto showed no mercy. Paced by a Lanny McDonald hat trick, they crushed the Penguins 5–2.

Series Summary
Lost to Toronto 2–1

Game	Date	City	Result	Winning Goal	Winning Goalie
1	April 5	Pittsburgh	Toronto 4–2	Dave Williams	Wayne Thomas
2	April 7	Toronto	Pittsburgh 6–4	Greg Malone	Denis Herron
3	April 9	Pittsburgh	Toronto 5–2	Lanny McDonald	Mike Palmateer

1979

After the Penguins missed the playoffs in 1977–78, general manager Baz Bastien had his hands full. The team was badly in need of a full-scale overhaul. Yet the farm system, pared to the bone by owner Al Savill's shoestring budget, was bare.

Undaunted, Bastien did his best to parlay the Pens' few expendable assets into big-league talent. The team's first-round pick in the Entry Draft netted three solid pros from Philadelphia—Tom Bladon, Orest Kindrachuk, and Ross Lonsberry. Defensive stalwart Dave Burrows was dealt to Toronto in exchange for versatile forward George Ferguson and promising young defenseman Randy Carlyle. Center Gregg Sheppard arrived from Atlanta for the club's all-time leading scorer, Jean Pronovost. Dale Tallon and Rod Schutt were acquired for draft picks.

Rejuvenated by the trades, the Pens jelled in December, rolling through the month at a 9–2–4 clip. After a so-so midseason stretch, the team caught fire again in March and registered a 10-game unbeaten streak. Paced by 30-goal seasons from youngsters Peter Lee and Greg Malone, the Penguins finished in second place for the first time since the 1969–70 season to qualify for postseason play.

Penguins vs. Sabres, Preliminary Round
The Penguins squared off against the Buffalo Sabres in a best-of-three Preliminary Round series to open the 1979 playoffs.

The Sabres, who had reached the Stanley Cup Finals just four years earlier, were still loaded with top-drawer talent. Paced by the flashy "French Connection Line" of Gilbert Perreault, Rick Martin, and former Penguin Rene Robert, Buffalo also featured the imposing "Muscle Beach" defensive tandem of Jerry "King Kong" Korab and Jim Schoenfeld.

Entering the series with a burgeoning injury list that included Pete Mahovlich, Russ Anderson, and Wayne Bianchin, the Pens appeared to be no match for their powerful adversary.

It came as no surprise when the host Sabres grabbed a 2–1 lead in the series opener. To add injury to insult, the monstrous Korab smashed Gregg Sheppard into the boards, sending the veteran center to the hospital with an injured cheekbone.

Then the unthinkable occurred. Outmanned and outplayed, the pesky Penguins stunned the Sabres with a third-period rally. Blair Chapman, playing with an elbow that was badly swollen from a severe cut, ignited the comeback with a goal just five minutes into the final period. Ex-Sabre Gary "Wheels" McAdam staked the Penguins to a lead at 13:54. They held on thanks to the superb goaltending of Denis Herron, who kicked out 28 shots despite a nagging shoulder injury.

"That's the sign of a good team," Randy Carlyle said. "We have a lot of injuries. But you forget them. You forget the injuries and just play hockey."

With the series shifting to the friendly confines of the Civic Arena, the Penguins appeared to be in good shape. The X-rays on Sheppard's injured cheek were negative, and Chapman would dress despite his banged-up elbow. In an extra stroke of good fortune, Buffalo's starting goaltender, Don Edwards, was down with the flu.

Game 2 began fast and furious, as Ross Lonsberry slugged it out with Danny Gare moments after the opening draw. After battling the Sabres on even terms, however, Rick Dudley beat Herron with just eight seconds remaining in the opening period.

As the Penguins sagged, Buffalo pounced. Jacques Richard scored early in the second stanza to give the Sabres a two-goal edge. Colin Campbell struck late in the period to draw the Penguins to within one, but it was as close as they got. With backup goalie Bob Sauve turning in a fine performance, the Sabres evened the series.

In the rubber match Perreault and Pens rookie Jim Hamilton set an NHL record for the fastest two goals by two teams—exchanging a pair of goals within five seconds. Craig Ramsay connected late in the first period to give Buffalo the lead, but the gritty Penguins continued to battle back. The speedy Hamilton notched his second goal of the game, only to watch the Sabres retake the lead.

Buffalo completely dominated play in the final frame, outshooting the Pens by the dizzying margin of 18–3. However, George Ferguson scored the only goal of the period to send the game into overtime. The extra stanza had barely begun when the "Fergie Flyer" swooped into the Sabres' end and drilled a 15-footer past Sauve to give the Penguins their first series victory in four years.

"On the winning goal, I noticed the left side of the rink was open," Ferguson said. "So I just took off and when I thought I could score I let it fly."

Series Summary
Beat Buffalo 2–1

Game	Date	City	Result	Winning Goal	Winning Goalie
1	April 10	Buffalo	Pittsburgh 4–3	Orest Kindrachuk	Denis Herron
2	April 12	Pittsburgh	Buffalo 3–1	Jacques Richard	Bob Sauve
3	April 14	Buffalo	Pittsburgh 4–3 (OT)	George Ferguson	Denis Herron

Penguins vs. Bruins, Quarterfinals

The Penguins' reward was a date with the Boston Bruins. Although their determined showing against Buffalo gave them cause for hope, Boston was a deep and powerful team.

With Russ Anderson on the shelf, scrappy Colin Campbell was left alone to defend his teammates against a Bruins lineup that was chock-full of rugged performers. In Game 1 the Bruins executed their physical, forechecking style to perfection and pounded the Penguins into submission 6–2.

"They're a difficult playoff team, and we realized they'd give us problems here," Sheppard noted. "The rink is geared to their style of play. It's small, which helps their physical game."

To their credit, the Pens regrouped for Game 2. They drew first blood on a marker by Hamilton, their new scoring sensation. Unfortunately, the goal only served to awaken a sleeping giant. Within minutes the Bruins had taken the lead on tallies by Jean Ratelle and Dwight Foster. When hulking Peter McNab slipped the puck past Denis Herron at 14:15 of the second period, the Bruins appeared to be well on their way to victory. However, the Pens responded with a goal of their own just 37 seconds later, as Orest Kindrachuk beat Gerry Cheevers.

The Penguins gamely turned up the pressure in an attempt to score the tying goal, but Bob Miller cashed in midway through the final period to put the game out of reach. Kindrachuk knocked in his second goal of the contest with six seconds left to make the final score a respectable 4–3.

"You need to get a few breaks if you're going to win in the playoffs," Kindrachuk said. "But it's a little frustrating to play as well as we did and come away without a win."

With the series moving to Pittsburgh for Game 3, the Pens got a huge emotional lift when Anderson and Pete Mahovlich returned to the lineup.

"Big Pete" immediately made his presence felt, setting up McAdam for the first goal of the game. But the Bruins were relentless. McNab knotted the score late in the opening period. Slick winger Rick Middleton notched a power-play goal to give Boston a commanding 3–0 series lead.

Pete Mahovlich drives to the Bruins' net for a scoring chance.

Game 4 followed an all-too-familiar pattern. Rod Schutt blasted a 45-foot slap shot past Cheevers to stake the Pens to another early lead, but the Bruins struck back on goals by Bobby Schmautz and Ratelle. Following a scoreless second period, Boston pulled away in the final frame on goals by Ratelle and Don Marcotte.

The Penguins' listless power play was a major reason for their demise. After failing to score on 14 opportunities against Buffalo, they converted on only two of 15 chances against the Bruins.

"When you're playing a team like Boston, you have to score on the power play," Kindrachuk said.

Series Summary
Lost to Boston 4–0

Game	Date	City	Result	Winning Goal	Winning Goalie
1	April 16	Boston	Boston 6–2	Mike Milbury	Gerry Cheevers
2	April 18	Boston	Boston 4–3	Bob Miller	Gerry Cheevers
3	April 21	Pittsburgh	Boston 2–1	Rick Middleton	Gerry Cheevers
4	April 22	Pittsburgh	Boston 4–1	Jean Ratelle	Gerry Cheevers

1980

As the decade of the 1980s dawned, Penguins fans were hoping for better days to come. Featuring promising youngsters Randy Carlyle, Peter Lee, and Greg Malone, along with a solid cast of veterans, the 1979–80 squad seemed ready to provide them.

Although hardly a powerhouse, the team performed remarkably well through the first half of the season. On January 3, the Pens toppled the mighty New York Islanders to gain sole possession of first place in the Norris Division. It marked the first time in franchise history that the club had attained such lofty heights.

The team also changed its colors during the season. Switching from their traditional columbia blue, navy blue, and white to black and gold, the Pens hoped to better identify with the winning traditions established by the Steel City's other pro sports teams, the Pirates and the Steelers.

Unaccustomed to success, the new-look Penguins promptly did an about-face. Riddled by injuries to key players Malone and Orest Kindrachuk, they slogged through the second half of the season with a dismal record of 14–26–2. The poster child for the team's erratic play was speedy winger Gary McAdam. By the end of December, "Wheels" had piled up an impressive 18 goals. He scored only one more the rest of the way.

Penguins vs. Bruins, Preliminary Round

In the Stanley Cup Playoffs the Penguins met Boston again, this time in a best-of-five Preliminary Round series. The Bruins were tougher and more talented than ever, led by stars Jean Ratelle, Rick Middleton, and Gary Cheevers, and armed with bruisers Terry O'Reilly, Stan Jonathan, and John Wensink.

Bucking the odds, the Penguins stunned the heavily favored Bruins in the series opener before a sparse crowd of 9,725 at the Boston Garden. With McAdam and Olympic hero Mark Johnson pacing the attack they grabbed a 3–0 lead through two periods of play. Although Boston nicked young Greg Millen for a pair of goals in the final period, ex-Bruin Gregg Sheppard scored into an empty net to put his former teammates away.

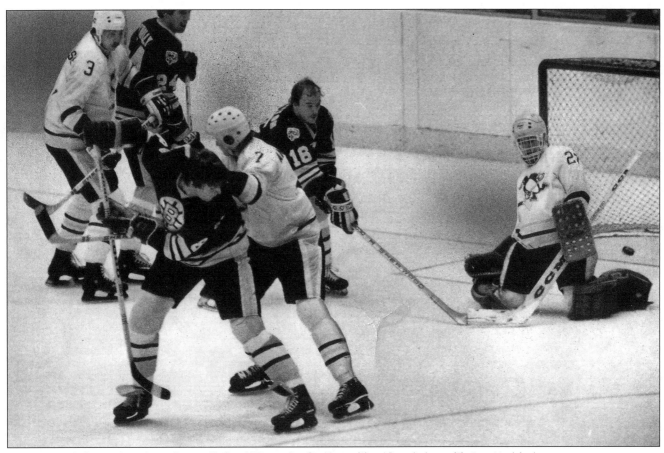

Rick Middleton (16) swats the puck past Pens goalie Greg Millen, as Ron Stackhouse (3) and Russ Anderson (7) attempt to defend.

"It's always nice to come into a series as the underdog," Pens coach Johnny Wilson said. "We came into this place loose and prepared to play. And now we've put some pressure on them."

The second game was a far different story. From the opening draw the Bruins applied ceaseless pressure to the Penguins' defense while piling up a whopping 42–17 advantage in shots. Millen wilted under the barrage of rubber and the Bruins rolled to a decisive 4–1 victory.

"They just took the game away from us that second period," Millen said. "You can't ever let Boston take control like that without it hurting you."

A less-than-capacity crowd turned out at the Civic Arena for Game 3. Those in attendance witnessed the Penguins' best effort since midseason. Sparked by two goals from Ross Lonsberry and another brilliant performance by Millen, they methodically dismantled the Bruins 4–1.

As incredible as it seemed, the up-and-down Penguins were poised to pull off one of the greatest upsets in Stanley Cup history. But the "Big Bad Bruins" had other ideas. They overwhelmed the Pens from the opening face-off in Game 4, pumping five first-period goals past Millen. The Bruins tacked on two more tallies in the second period to carry a resounding 7–0 lead into the final frame.

The flaccid Penguins finally showed some life by scoring three third-period goals, but the outcome had long since been decided. They would now have to beat the Bruins in the unfriendly confines of the Boston Garden to win the series.

Like sharks at a feeding frenzy, the Bruins ripped through their hapless foe and grabbed a commanding 4–0 lead. With the contest in the bag, the Bruins concentrated on extracting a pound of flesh. In a game attempt to uphold his team's honor, gritty Kim Clackson took on several of Boston's most rugged players. It was no use. The Penguins were crushed 6–2.

Series Summary
Lost to Boston 3–2

Game	Date	City	Result	Winning Goal	Winning Goalie
1	April 8	Boston	Pittsburgh 4–2	Mark Johnson	Greg Millen
2	April 10	Boston	Boston 4–1	Don Marcotte	Gerry Cheevers
3	April 12	Pittsburgh	Pittsburgh 4–1	Ross Lonsberry	Greg Millen
4	April 13	Pittsburgh	Boston 8–3	Peter McNab	Gerry Cheevers
5	April 15	Boston	Boston 6–2	Dwight Foster	Gerry Cheevers

1981

In many ways, the 1980–81 Penguins and the previous year's version were opposite sides of the same coin. Each team finished in third place in the Norris Division with an identical record of 30–37–13. However, their paths to mediocrity were achieved in dramatically different fashions.

The 1980–81 Penguins started slowly…and got progressively worse. Decimated by injuries to key players Russ Anderson, Paul Baxter, Orest Kindrachuk, and Gregg Sheppard, the team lacked the depth to plug the gaps. By mid-January the Pens had tumbled into the Norris Division cellar.

Fortunately, general manager Baz Bastien responded with some of his finest trades. He peddled fringe players Kim Davis and Paul Marshall to Toronto for ex-Pen Dave Burrows and perennial 30-goal man Paul Gardner. Gary McAdam was sent to Detroit for established scorer Errol Thompson. In March Bastien bolstered the team's defense by acquiring combative Pat Price from Edmonton for struggling winger Pat Hughes.

Ironically, it was another contest with the Islanders—this one a 6–3 loss—that proved to be the turning point. Deeply frustrated by their poor showing, the Pens suddenly caught fire and registered a 17–14–6 mark to finish the season on a high note.

Penguins vs. Blues, Preliminary Round

The Penguins opened the playoffs against their old nemesis, the St. Louis Blues, in a best-of-five series. Led by a crack group of forwards that included All-Star center Bernie Federko, 50-goal man Wayne Babych, and tough Brian Sutter, the resurgent Blues also boasted a marvelous young goaltender in All-Star Mike Liut.

No stranger to stopping pucks, Pens coach Eddie Johnston caused a mild stir when he claimed to have discovered a flaw in Liut's style. He appeared to be blowing smoke until Greg Malone struck for the fastest goal in Penguins playoff history just 15 seconds after the opening draw. However, Liut quickly regained his composure and the Blues rolled to a 4–2 victory. While outclassed, the Penguins got strong performances from goalie Greg Millen and the line of Peter Lee, Greg Malone, and Rod Schutt.

Johnston made several adjustments for Game 2. He split up Rick Kehoe and slumping Paul Gardner so the St. Louis checkers couldn't key on one line. Veteran Dave Burrows was benched in favor of rookie center Mike Bullard. The Pens' coach also instructed his forwards to dump the puck into the St. Louis zone and force the Blues' defensemen—their foe's weak underbelly—to handle the puck.

The Blues continued to control the tempo as Joe Micheletti scored an early power-play goal. But Johnston made another key move to start the second period. He placed the speedy Bullard between Gregg Sheppard and George Ferguson, and

Blues winger Mike Zuke goes top shelf on Penguins goalie Greg Millen.

the Penguins promptly exploded for six goals in 21 minutes. The Blues mounted a mild third-period rally but the Pens held on for a 6–4 victory.

Afterward, a gracious Liut handed the game puck to Bullard. "He said he thought I earned it," the Pens' rookie said.

A frenzied crowd of 14,646 packed the Civic Arena for Game 3. With emotions stoked to a fever pitch, referee Bob Myers took control and ushered five Blues and two Penguins to the penalty box before the contest was five minutes old.

Neither team was able to gain a clear-cut advantage until Bernie Federko struck late in the second period to give the Blues a 4–3 lead. Sheppard tapped in a pretty feed from Carlyle early in the final frame to draw the Pens even. However, Federko sealed a Blues victory with his second goal of the night.

Although attendance at the Civic Arena dropped to 12,042 for Game 4, the crowd was no less boisterous. The Pens spotted the Blues two early goals before Bullard ignited a comeback with a spectacular power-play goal. Mark Johnson tied the game with his second tally in two nights.

Midway through the second period the Pens grabbed the lead on a shorthanded goal by Carlyle, who picked off a clearing pass and beat Liut with a 35-foot slap shot. Mike Zuke responded with a power-play goal to knot the score again. But Bullard buried a goal-mouth pass from Ferguson and the Penguins never looked back.

"We came out flat in the first period, but we didn't get our heads down," Carlyle said. "We just said, 'Let's get it together.'"

"There was no tomorrow if we lost," added Johnston. "Either we win or play golf the next day…and I don't want to play golf this early."

Acting on a hunch, Johnston shuffled the deck one more time. Choosing to dress only five defensemen, he sat Ron Stackhouse and inserted Jim Hamilton—the hero of the 1979 playoffs. Little did he realize that his club was about to play one of the longest games in team history.

Gardner finally got off the schneid with his first goal of the series to stake the Pens to an early lead. However, the Blues sandwiched a pair of second-period goals around a tally by Ferguson to even the score. Rick Lapointe beat Millen early in the third period, but the gritty Penguins rallied to force the game into overtime.

The momentum continued to swing back and forth, as first the Blues and then the Penguins dominated the action. While both teams had their chances, Millen and Liut were nothing short of spectacular.

Then, five minutes into the second overtime, Blues winger Mike Zuke sped into the Penguins' zone. Mark Johnson quickly pinned Zuke against the boards, but somehow the puck squirted past Johnson and Randy Carlyle and onto the stick of Mike Crombeen, who was waiting patiently in the slot. Crombeen made no mistake and whipped the puck past Millen to give St. Louis the game and the series.

"I was just very, very proud of them," Johnston said afterward. "I have never seen a series like that—never mind a game like that. When you get into overtime it's just a guts thing. You push yourself. You do it with determination and intestinal fortitude. Both teams had that tonight, although I really felt in my heart we should have won."

"This game will stick in my mind for a long, long time because of the heart everybody showed," Malone said. "I'm including their guys, too."

Series Summary
Lost to St. Louis 3–2

Game	Date	City	Result	Winning Goal	Winning Goalie
1	April 8	St. Louis	St. Louis 4–2	Jorgen Pettersson	Mike Liut
2	April 9	St. Louis	Pittsburgh 6–4	Rod Schutt	Greg Millen
3	April 11	Pittsburgh	St. Louis 5–4	Bernie Federko	Mike Liut
4	April 12	Pittsburgh	Pittsburgh 6–3	Mike Bullard	Greg Millen
5	April 14	St. Louis	St. Louis 4–3 (2 OT)	Mike Crombeen	Mike Liut

1982

For the championship-starved hockey fans of Pittsburgh, 1981–82 would prove to be a heartbreaking season. Buoyed by the Penguins' strong showing against St. Louis the previous spring, hopes were high over the off-season, especially when general manager Baz Bastien parlayed free agent Greg Millen into feisty 80-point scorer Pat Boutette and promising junior player Kevin McClelland. He also added some toughness and character to the mix by acquiring giant winger Paul Mulvey and acrobatic goalie Michel Dion.

Backed by the spectacular play of Dion and the big-time scoring of Paul Gardner, Rick Kehoe, and Mike Bullard, the Penguins got off to a fast start. Following a 9–1–2 hot streak, the likes of which had rarely been seen in the Steel City, the Pens were nipping at the heels of the division-leading New York Islanders.

When the team began to cool off in mid-December, Bastien made more changes. He traded Russ Anderson to Hartford for veteran Rick MacLeish and sent rookie winger Doug Shedden—who had performed well—to the minors. Bastien then waived Mulvey and dealt versatile Mark Johnson to Minnesota for a draft pick. The Pens never fully recovered and trundled to a fourth-place finish in the Patrick Division.

Penguins vs. Islanders, Patrick Division Semifinals

As fate—or misfortune—would have it, the Penguins drew the defending Stanley Cup champion Islanders in the best-of-five opening round of the playoffs. The tone was set in a fight-filled regular-season finale in Pittsburgh, which the Pens won 7–2.

A snow storm delayed the team's arrival on Long Island until the day of the opening game. With the brusque treatment they received the week before still fresh in their minds, the powerhouse Islanders showed no mercy and routed their foes 8–1.

Braced for another offensive barrage in Game 2, the Pens offered only token resistance as the Islanders rolled to another blowout win.

Bruised and battered, the Penguins limped back to Pittsburgh, where they hoped to regroup on home ice. Instead, they received a tongue-lashing from owner Edward DeBartolo Sr.

Rugged Paul Baxter rifles off a shot against the Islanders.

"No one is more upset and disappointed with the play of the Pittsburgh Penguins than me," he said. "I am not attending Saturday night's playoff game and I empathize with you fans who have decided not to come to the Civic Arena tomorrow night."

DeBartolo backed up his words by offering the Pens faithful a full refund for their tickets. Fortunately, only 200 fans accepted his offer, while 14,310 turned out to watch a decidedly different team in action.

The Islanders broke on top late in the first period on a goal by defenseman Mike McEwen. However, coach Eddie Johnston made a key adjustment by matching his checking unit of Rod Schutt, Andre St. Laurent, and rugged rookie Kevin McClelland against the potent Bryan Trottier line.

With the Islanders' attack finally neutralized, the Penguins began to take control. Pat Boutette notched his third goal of the series to send the game into overtime. Four minutes into the extra period, Rick Kehoe snapped a bad-angle shot through a maze of players to lift his team to a dramatic win.

Buoyed by their solid effort in Game 3, the Pens dug down even deeper in Game 4. Islanders coach Al Arbour added fuel to the fire by starting backup goaltender Rollie Melanson in place of incumbent Billy Smith.

In a surprise move of his own, Johnston used only four defensemen. The plan worked to perfection as the Penguins shut down the Islanders' imposing offense again. Clark Gillies spotted the New Yorkers an early lead, but the Pens rallied to earn a 5–2 victory.

The momentum had shifted. Now it was the mighty Islanders who were back on their heels. In the fifth and deciding game the two teams battled through a scoreless first period before a sellout crowd at the Nassau County Coliseum. Although the Islanders had the better scoring chances, Michel Dion was a veritable fortress in goal.

When New York finally scored midway through the second period, the partisan crowd breathed a collective sigh of relief. But McClelland ignited a rally just 43 seconds later when he tipped in a Greg Hotham blast from the point.

The Islanders were stunned by the sudden turn of events. Before they could regroup Mike Bullard and Randy Carlyle struck for a pair of beautiful goals to stake Pittsburgh to a 3–1 lead. Only 20 minutes stood between the Penguins and arguably the greatest playoff upset of all time.

Watching their dreams of a third straight Stanley Cup evaporate before their eyes, the Islanders unleashed a furious offensive assault at Dion. Playing the game of his life, the spirited goalie held firm until 14:33, when McEwen struck for a power-play goal.

Then, with two minutes remaining, Gord Lane dumped the puck into the corner and Carlyle skated over to retrieve it. In a play eerily reminiscent of the Blues' overtime winner the previous year, the puck skipped by the young defenseman to John Tonelli, who quickly rifled it past Dion. Although

shocked, the Penguins held the swarming Islanders at bay and forced the game into overtime.

The Pens grimly dug in for one last stand. Bullard almost scored the game winner early in overtime, but his shot rang off a goal post. At the six-minute mark the ever-present Tonelli beat Dion again to bring the final curtain down on the Penguins' Cinderella story.

As the dejected goalie knelt in front of the net, Billy Smith—who usually avoided any fraternization with opposing players—skated the length of the ice to console his adversary. Dion had made 42 saves in a gritty, heroic effort.

"A lot of people counted us out, including our owner," Carlyle declared. "But we showed people we weren't about to be kicked when we were down…that we're a proud hockey club."

Once more the team had fought valiantly against a much stronger opponent, only to come up short. Little did anyone realize it would be seven long years before the Penguins would appear in another playoff game.

Series Summary
Lost to New York Islanders 3–2

Game	Date	City	Result	Winning Goal	Winning Goalie
1	April 7	New York	NY Islanders 8–1	Clark Gillies	Billy Smith
2	April 8	New York	NY Islanders 7–2	Butch Goring	Billy Smith
3	April 10	Pittsburgh	Pittsburgh 2–1 (OT)	Rick Kehoe	Michel Dion
4	April 11	Pittsburgh	Pittsburgh 5–2	Rick Kehoe	Michel Dion
5	April 13	New York	NY Islanders 4–3 (OT)	John Tonelli	Billy Smith

1989

Following a prolonged dry spell that spanned six miserable seasons, the Penguins finally had accumulated enough talent to challenge for a playoff spot in 1988–89. Quality players such as world-class defenseman Paul Coffey and high-scoring forwards Rob Brown, John Cullen, Randy Cunneyworth, and Dan Quinn joined forces with phenom Mario Lemieux to form a strong nucleus. Two-way performers Phil Bourque, Bob Errey, and Troy Loney filled important checking roles while providing extra offensive punch. Tom Barrasso arrived in a trade to solidify the goaltending.

Despite their less-than-stellar defensive play, the Penguins challenged for first place in the Patrick Division throughout much of the season. Although a cold spell in February and March prevented the team from claiming its first division crown, the team finished a solid second to qualify for the Stanley Cup Playoffs.

Paced by Lemieux's incredible 85-goal, 199-point campaign, the free-wheeling Pens struck for 347 goals. True to form, they also leaked for a whopping 349 goals against.

Penguins vs. Rangers, Patrick Division Semifinals

In their first playoff series in seven years the Penguins squared off against their mortal enemies, the New York Rangers. While no one could predict how the callow young Pens would respond to the pressure of postseason play, they would not lack for motivation. Triggered by a high-sticking incident involving Lemieux and Rangers defenseman David Shaw, there was enough bad blood between the bitter rivals to fill an oil tanker.

Like the Penguins, the Rangers had hovered around first place until the final month of the season. When they faltered in the homestretch, general manager Phil Esposito abruptly fired popular coach Michel Bergeron and stepped behind the bench. By the time the postseason began, New York was clearly a demoralized club.

The Penguins took full advantage. In the first playoff game hosted at the Civic Arena since 1982 they rode a pair of power-play goals by Coffey to a 3–1 victory. Although he was held without a goal, Mario Lemieux was especially pleased with his team's defensive play.

"We made up our mind we have to take care of our defense if we want to have a chance to win some hockey games," Lemieux said. "Everybody does it in the playoffs and we're no exception."

Showing surprising poise for a team with little collective playoff experience, the Pens dominated Game 2. Striking for four first-period goals, they powered their way to a convincing 7–4 triumph.

With the series shifting to Madison Square Garden for Game 3, the Rangers made a last-ditch effort to climb back into the series. They charged out of the starting gate and piled up an early 7–1 advantage in shots. But Pens goalie Tom Barrasso was razor-sharp, and the Rangers' attack soon ran out of steam.

As the Rangers faded, the Penguins' super-charged offense shifted into high gear. Sparked by Mario's power-play goal at 7:29 of the first period, the Pens methodically forged a 4–1 lead. Although a marker by Rangers winger John Ogrodnick cut the margin to two early in the third period, Quinn scored his second goal of the game to restore the Pens' three-goal edge. The star of the game was Barrasso, who turned aside 43 shots in a stellar performance.

"In the playoffs, if you're going to go far, you need strong goaltending," John Cullen said. "And Tommy is playing up to his potential."

Pittsburgh jumped on New York in Game 4, snatching a 3–0 lead on a pair of goals by Bourque and one by Lemieux. The Rangers pelted Barrasso with 49 shots, including 21 in the final period, but the young goalie stood his ground. The Penguins won 4–3 to earn their first playoff sweep in a best-of-seven series since 1970.

"We just really took it to them, right from the opening face-off," Bourque said. "We set the pace and we never really let up."

Series Summary
Beat New York Rangers 4–0

Game	Date	City	Result	Winning Goal	Winning Goalie
1	April 5	Pittsburgh	Pittsburgh 3–1	Paul Coffey	Tom Barrasso
2	April 6	Pittsburgh	Pittsburgh 7–4	Randy Cunneyworth	Tom Barrasso
3	April 8	New York	Pittsburgh 5–3	Dan Quinn	Tom Barrasso
4	April 9	New York	Pittsburgh 4–3	Rob Brown	Tom Barrasso

Penguins vs. Flyers, Patrick Division Finals

The Penguins' stirring performance against the Rangers set up a Patrick Division Finals showdown against Philadelphia. Although the Flyers had slipped a bit since their glory years, they still boasted stars like 48-goal scorer Tim Kerr and defenseman Mark Howe. Backstopping this battle-tested team was hot-tempered goalie Ron Hextall, the son of former Penguin Bryan Hextall.

Philadelphia took control from the outset of Game 1 and raced to a 3–1 lead. However, this was a decidedly different Penguins team than the ones the Flyers had dominated in the past.

"We were still up," Rob Brown explained. "We knew we hadn't played our best hockey and we knew we could score. It was a matter of 'keep coming, keep coming.'"

Showing plenty of grit, the Pens rallied to tie the score on a pair of goals by Dan Quinn and John Cullen just 33 seconds apart. Brown struck midway through the third period on a beautiful setup from Kevin Stevens. The Penguins hung on to win 4–3.

After displaying nearly flawless form through their early postseason run, the Pens served up a clunker in Game 2. After grabbing the lead on a power-play goal by Quinn, they were relegated to the role of spectators as the Flyers roared back to take command on a hat trick by Kerr. To make matters worse, Barrasso complained of blurred vision and was replaced by backup Wendell Young. Philly rolled to an easy 4–2 win.

The series shifted to the Penguins' den of horrors, the Spectrum, for Game 3. Fortunately, Barrasso had recovered from his vision problems and was ready for action.

"The other night he was seeing double," Pens coach Gene Ubriaco said. "Tonight he was seeing manhole covers."

It was the most exciting game of the series. The Penguins grabbed the lead on power-play goals by Lemieux and Quinn, only to watch the Flyers even the score in the second period. Later in the contest Jock Callander and the Flyers' Dave Poulin exchanged goals. The score remained deadlocked through the end of regulation.

The momentum was firmly with the Flyers, who had dominated play since the opening period. But 12 minutes

Mario Lemieux beats the Flyers' Ron Hextall during a record-setting five-goal game.

into overtime Brown blew around Mark Howe with an uncharacteristic burst of speed and fed the puck to Bourque, who snapped the game winner past Hextall.

Losing a tough game in overtime would have broken the spirit of many teams. But the Flyers were a tough, resilient bunch. After spotting the Pens an early lead in Game 4, they roared back to take control thanks to a two-goal effort by Kerr.

"We've got to pay closer attention to him the rest of the series," Penguins defenseman Rod Buskas said.

Late in the third period the Pens received a huge scare when Lemieux and Cunneyworth collided while chasing down Terry Carkner at center ice. A dazed No. 66 was forced to leave the game with a neck injury. With Mario finished for the evening, the Penguins fell with a thud 4–1.

There were serious concerns about Lemieux's condition prior to Game 5. He soon laid them to rest with one of the most dynamic performances in Stanley Cup history. Hextall stopped Mario's first shot, but the next three found the mark as the big center registered a hat trick before the game was seven minutes old. By the end of the first period the Pens had piled up a 6–1 lead.

The onslaught continued in the second period. When Robbie Brown scored yet another goal and launched into his famous windmill celebration, Hextall became unglued. Shaking his big goaltender's blade, he chased after the plucky winger, who ran for his life. Flyers coach Paul Holmgren

immediately pulled the frazzled goalie, to the delight of the "Hex-Towel" waving throng.

Philly never quit. Unfazed by the Penguins' dazzling display, the Flyers closed to within two goals before Lemieux finished out the scoring in a wild 10–7 victory. Mario enjoyed a spectacular night, tying the records for most goals (five) and points (eight) in a postseason game.

"I've never seen a performance like Mario had tonight," Holmgren said afterward.

"He just elevated his game to the point where he just showed everyone else how much better than us he can be," Barrasso said.

Unfortunately, another slow start by the Penguins in Game 6 would prove costly. The ever-dangerous Kerr, who had set up permanent residence in front of Barrasso, banged home a pair of goals to open the scoring. Cunneyworth countered with two goals of his own, but the Flyers were relentless. The Pens registered just three shots in the final period en route to a dismal 6–2 defeat.

For the second time in franchise history the Penguins were playing a seventh and deciding game. Despite their poor performance in Game 6 they appeared to have the advantage. The contest was slated for the friendly confines of the Civic Arena. Mario, with his sore neck fully recovered, was in top form.

From the Flyers' locker room came more good news: Hextall had suffered a knee injury. Ken Wregget—fresh off a bout with mononucleosis—would start in goal. Like a pack of hungry wolves, the Pens were poised to devour their prey.

The hunters soon became the hunted. Brown had a chance for a quick goal, but the sharpshooting winger pushed the puck wide of an open net. While Wregget turned aside shot after shot, Brian Propp scored late in the first period to give Philadelphia the edge.

Lemieux cashed in on the power play early in the second period, but Philly reclaimed the lead on a shorthanded tally by Dave Poulin. Former teammate Mike Bullard sealed the Pens' fate with a crushing third-period goal.

Series Summary
Lost to Philadelphia 4–3

Game	Date	City	Result	Winning Goal	Winning Goalie
1	April 17	Pittsburgh	Pittsburgh 4–3	Rob Brown	Tom Barrasso
2	April 19	Pittsburgh	Philadelphia 4–2	Tim Kerr	Ron Hextall
3	April 21	Philadelphia	Pittsburgh 4–3 (OT)	Phil Bourque	Tom Barrasso
4	April 23	Philadelphia	Philadelphia 4–1	Tim Kerr	Ron Hextall
5	April 25	Pittsburgh	Pittsburgh 10–7	Rob Brown	Tom Barrasso
6	April 27	Philadelphia	Philadelphia 6–2	Derrick Smith	Ron Hextall
7	April 29	Pittsburgh	Philadelphia 4–1	Dave Poulin	Ken Wregget

1991

After the Penguins failed to qualify for the postseason in 1989–90, general manager Craig Patrick was a man on a mission. Determined to build a team that could compete for the Stanley Cup, he set about the task of adding the missing pieces with a single-minded purpose.

In June of 1990 Patrick hired hockey legends "Badger Bob" Johnson and Scotty Bowman to fill the posts of coach and director of player personnel. He acquired perennial All-Stars Joe Mullen and Bryan Trottier to provide leadership and scoring punch for his up-and-coming young club. Suddenly, the Pens had a big-league feel.

Patrick continued to reshape the team as the season progressed. He added a host of accomplished veterans with proven track records, including Jiri Hrdina, Larry Murphy, Gordie Roberts, and Peter Taglianetti. On March 4, he swung a blockbuster of epic proportions, dealing John Cullen, Jeff Parker, and Zarley Zalapski to Hartford for Ron Francis, Grant Jennings, and Ulf Samuelsson.

Galvanized by "the Trade," the Pens went on a 9–3–2 roll to nail down the Patrick Division crown—the first division title in the team's 24-year history.

Penguins vs. Devils, Patrick Division Semifinals

The hockey buzz in Pittsburgh was at a fever pitch as the Penguins opened the playoffs against fourth-place New Jersey. A talented but underachieving bunch that had failed to jell during the regular season, the Devils didn't catch fire until owner John McMullen replaced John Cunniff with old pro Tommy McVie. While far from a brilliant strategist, the little coach with the foghorn voice had a knack for squeezing the most out of a team.

Playing before a packed house at the Civic Arena, the Pens grabbed the lead midway through the second period on a power-play goal by Mario Lemieux. After that it was all New Jersey. The Penguins' defense broke down early in the final frame and the Devils rolled to a 3–1 victory. It was the club's worst performance since a disastrous West Coast road trip a month earlier.

The Devils picked up right where they left off in Game 2. Dominating their more talented adversary through 60 minutes of play, they pushed the Penguins into overtime.

At the six-minute mark rookie Jaromir Jagr stepped forward with a flourish. No. 68 gathered up a pass from Phil Bourque and flew into the Devils' zone. As he swooped down the right side he drew the attention of John MacLean, a sturdy checker.

With MacLean draped all over him, Jagr swerved sharply toward the New Jersey net, stick handling with one hand while fending off the Devils winger with the other. He pried himself loose and glided through the crease, waiting for goalie Chris Terreri to make a move. After what seemed like an eternity, Terreri sprawled to the ice. The 19-year-old rookie calmly flipped the puck into the open net.

The youngster's astounding goal had earned the Pens a victory, but they had been badly outplayed.

"We're not getting the puck into their end and we're not taking the body," a frustrated Bob Errey said. "That's what they're doing, but not what we're doing. We have to take the body."

Still, the Penguins had the momentum. Buoyed by the return of Joe Mullen, they eclipsed the Devils in Game 3 to grab the series lead.

But McVie had a few tricks up his sleeve. A tough guy during his playing days in the old Western Hockey League, he urged his charges to hit the Penguins hard and often. New Jersey opened Game 4 in a frenzy. Leading the hit parade was Slava Fetisov, who smashed Lemieux to the ice with a thunderous check.

"That's what I like to call old-time hockey," McVie gloated. "It's old-time hockey when guys make hits like that."

As the Penguins reeled from the jackhammer assault, the Devils quickly took charge. To add injury to insult Fetisov struck again in the third period—this time clipping Paul Coffey in the left eye with his stick. The Soviet defenseman was ejected from the game, but the damage was done. Coffey was hospitalized with a scratched cornea. The Penguins fell 4–1.

Determined to minimize the distraction of losing his star defenseman, Bob Johnson did his best to keep the team on course. "It's a best-of-three series now," he said. "Forget about the first four games. It's best-of-three."

The Devils toned down their bullying tactics in Game 5, but the results were the same. Backed by Terreri's stingy goaltending, New Jersey smothered the Penguins with tenacious checking and cruised to a 4–2 victory. As if the Pens hadn't swallowed enough misfortune, Barrasso suffered a shoulder injury. He would miss the crucial sixth game.

With the series returning to the hostile surroundings of the Brendan Byrne Arena, the Penguins appeared to be finished. The Devils had throttled their potent offense and shut down their vaunted power play. Feisty Laurie Boschman had done a superb job of shadowing Lemieux, who looked terribly lethargic. Frank Pietrangelo, who had appeared in only three games in the second half of the season, would start in goal. Indeed, the only question was not whether New Jersey would win, but by how much.

Once again the Devils took command early thanks to a fluke goal by MacLean. However, Kevin Stevens would not be denied. Playing with a broken nose, big "Artie" battled his way through heavy traffic and struck twice to give the Penguins a precarious one-goal lead.

It was then that an unlikely hero stepped forward to literally save the day. Fifteen minutes into the first period Peter Stastny found himself all alone in front of the Penguins' net with the puck cradled on his blade. A deadly accurate shooter, the New Jersey sniper rarely missed a scoring opportunity from point-blank range. He confidently whipped the puck toward the wide-open net and waited for the red light to signal the game-tying goal.

From out of nowhere Frank Pietrangelo's gloved left hand flashed like a phantom. Straining every fiber and sinew in his body to its limit, he reached across the goal crease at the last possible moment to snatch the puck out of midair.

Stastny and his teammates were stunned. They could not believe the puck hadn't gone in. Yet there was Pietrangelo, flipping the vulcanized rubber to a linesman as casually as if he were picking berries on a Sunday afternoon.

"That was probably the turning point of the playoffs for us," Mario would later recall.

Deflated by "the Save" and their miserable luck, the Devils' attack finally lost its steam. The Penguins had succeeded in forcing a seventh and deciding game in Pittsburgh.

What figured to be a barn burner turned out to be anticlimactic as the inspired Penguins ran roughshod over the Devils. Leading the way was Jiri Hrdina, who snapped an 18-game scoring drought with a pair of goals. Pietrangelo snuffed out the Devils' few scoring chances en route to a 4–0 victory. The team had passed its first test.

Series Summary
Beat New Jersey 4–3

Game	Date	City	Result	Winning Goal	Winning Goalie
1	April 3	Pittsburgh	New Jersey 3–1	Peter Stastny	Chris Terreri
2	April 5	Pittsburgh	Pittsburgh 5–4 (OT)	Jaromir Jagr	Tom Barrasso
3	April 7	New Jersey	Pittsburgh 4–3	Mark Recchi	Tom Barrasso
4	April 9	New Jersey	New Jersey 4–1	Claude Lemieux	Chris Terreri
5	April 11	Pittsburgh	New Jersey 4–2	Peter Stastny	Chris Terreri
6	April 13	New Jersey	Pittsburgh 4–3	Ron Francis	Frank Pietrangelo
7	April 15	Pittsburgh	Pittsburgh 4–0	Jiri Hrdina	Frank Pietrangelo

First Fan

In the wake of their Stanley Cup triumph in 1991, the Penguins became the first NHL team ever to visit the White House.

Dressed in their Sunday best, the players toured the Executive Mansion and rubbed elbows with prominent government officials, including President George H.W. Bush.

With his teammates beaming their approval, Mario Lemieux presented the commander-in-chief with an autographed jersey during a special ceremony.

As he turned to accept the gift, President Bush gave Mario a quizzical look.

"And you are…?" he asked.

Penguins vs. Capitals, Patrick Division Finals

Next on the Pens' dance card were the Washington Capitals, who had dumped the heavily favored Rangers in a first-round matchup. An up-and-down team during the regular season, the Caps had finished strong. They were peaking at precisely the right time.

Game 1 mirrored the opener of the New Jersey series. The Penguins carried a one-goal advantage into the final frame, but Washington gradually took control of the neutral zone with persistent forechecking. Indeed, the entire third period seemed to be played in the Pittsburgh zone. The Caps rallied to capture a 4–2 victory.

Game 2 would prove to be the most entertaining of the series. Powered by a pair of goals by Mark Recchi and one each from Bourque, Mullen, and Stevens, the Pens carried a two-goal lead into the final period.

Sensing a change was in order, Capitals coach Terry Murray replaced beleaguered goalie Don Beaupre with veteran Mike Liut. Washington immediately settled down. With Gordie Roberts off for hooking, Dino Ciccarelli barged into the slot and snapped the puck past Pietrangelo. Minutes later the feisty Ciccarelli scored again to tie the game.

The worst was yet to come. Just past the midway point of the period Paul Stanton inadvertently steered the puck past Pietrangelo to hand the Capitals the lead.

On the brink of a two-game deficit, the Penguins responded like champions. More angry than flustered, they mounted a withering counterattack. With a delayed penalty called against Tim Bergland they stormed the Caps' net.

Sensing an opportunity, Bob Johnson immediately motioned Pietrangelo to the bench. Unsung Randy Gilhen hopped over the boards and pounded home a backhander to send the game into overtime.

Midway through the extra frame Francis lugged the puck into the Capitals' zone and laid a perfect pass onto the stick of Stevens. The burly winger beat Liut with a tracer bullet from the left hash mark.

Once again, the Penguins had snatched victory from the jaws of defeat. But once more, the victory had come with a heavy price. Coffey sustained a fractured jaw courtesy of a well-placed Dale Hunter elbow. Samuelsson had suffered a broken hand. Both would miss the remainder of the series.

Still, the team's hopes received a considerable boost when Barrasso was given the green light to play. While Pietrangelo had done an admirable job in relief, the defensive corps was in shambles and the team needed every possible edge.

Another more critical development turned in the Penguins' favor. Mario Lemieux had finally shaken off the lethargy that had gripped him like a vice since the opening of the playoffs. Skating freely and fluidly at last, big No. 66 began to assert himself as only he could, spelling doom for the opposition. The playoffs would become a personal showcase for his wondrous abilities.

Powered by Lemieux and the strong goaltending of Barrasso, the Penguins outgunned the Capitals in the next three contests.

Series Summary
Beat Washington 4–1

Game	Date	City	Result	Winning Goal	Winning Goalie
1	April 17	Pittsburgh	Washington 4–2	Al Iafrate	Don Beaupre
2	April 19	Pittsburgh	Pittsburgh 7–6 (OT)	Kevin Stevens	Frank Pietrangelo
3	April 21	Washington	Pittsburgh 3–1	Kevin Stevens	Tom Barrasso
4	April 23	Washington	Pittsburgh 3–1	Kevin Stevens	Tom Barrasso
5	April 25	Pittsburgh	Pittsburgh 4–1	Ron Francis	Tom Barrasso

Penguins vs. Bruins, Wales Conference Finals

While the Pens convalesced, Boston wrestled a hotly contested seven-game set from the Canadiens. The Bruins weren't a particularly deep team. Indeed, their only stars were Ray Bourque, Andy Moog, and Cam Neely, a battering ram of a forward. Under the guidance of former Bruins stalwart Mike Milbury, they relied on relentless forechecking to wear down their opponents.

Thanks to their long layoff the Penguins appeared to be the fresher team. They grabbed the lead in Game 1 on a pretty goal by Mullen, but soon suffered another attack of first-game jitters. Taking full advantage, the Bruins coasted to an easy 6–3 victory.

Game 2 turned out to be the most tightly contested of the series. Playing from behind for most of the game, the Pens

wrenched the lead from the Bruins on a third-period goal by Lemieux.

They promptly fell into a defensive shell, a move that proved costly. With Taglianetti and Roberts in the penalty box the Bruins scored a power-play goal to send the game into overtime. Eight minutes into the extra stanza Vladimir Ruzicka capped off the Bruins' comeback by banging home a rebound. Boston now held an imposing 2–0 series lead.

Although clearly on the ropes, the Penguins weren't ready to throw in the towel. From the gloom of the losing locker room Kevin Stevens issued a stunning proclamation.

"I guarantee we'll win the series," he said.

Determined to back up his words with deeds, Stevens got the team off and running in Game 3 with his 10th goal of the playoffs. Playing before an amped-up crowd at the Civic Arena, the Pens dominated the action until Ray Bourque scored a huge goal that threatened to change the complexion of the game.

Lemieux made sure that Boston's revival was fleeting. Mario gathered up a loose puck and flicked a long, routine shot toward the Boston goal. Moog easily swatted the puck aside, but he pushed it right to the stick of Grant Jennings, who had ventured deep into the Bruins' zone. The rugged defenseman calmly flipped a backhander past the startled goalie to restore the Pens' two-goal edge.

Moments later, Samuelsson delivered the coup de grace when he caught Cam Neely with a jarring check at the Bruins' blue line. The big winger crumpled to the ice in pain, ending any hopes for a Boston comeback.

Mike Milbury was livid. He believed Samuelsson was gunning for Neely's tender knees. He railed at Bob Johnson for the Penguins' perceived dirty tactics.

"For all of Bob Johnson's seven-point plan...there must have been somewhere in that seven-point plan where you make sure you take as many cheap shots as you can against the other team's key players," he steamed. "So the professor of hockey, as he often projects himself, is also subtly a professor of goonism. And we can't take it any longer."

Itching to deliver some frontier justice, Milbury inserted hatchet men Lyndon Byers and Nevin Markwart, along with bruising defenseman Allan Pedersen.

True to their coach's word, the Bruins came out hitting in Game 4. Undaunted, the Penguins shrugged off their foe's body-bending tactics and grabbed the lead.

Trailing by a pair late in the game, the Bruins abandoned all thoughts of winning and concentrated on extracting a pound of flesh. Chris Nilan slashed Lemieux and picked a fight with Recchi, while Byers engaged Stevens in a brief skirmish. Tempers flared again at the final buzzer when Pedersen and Markwart tussled with Taglianetti and Jennings.

Milbury's decision to use a hammer-and-tongs approach was the tactical blunder of the series. Not only had Boston's intimidation tactics failed miserably, but they succeeded in awakening a sleeping giant. Playing with remarkable poise and determination, the Pens rolled over the Bruins in Games 5 and 6 to close out the series.

Series Summary
Beat Boston 4–2

Game	Date	City	Result	Winning Goal	Winning Goalie
1	May 1	Boston	Boston 6–3	Cam Neely	Andy Moog
2	May 3	Boston	Boston 5–4 (OT)	Vladimir Ruzicka	Andy Moog
3	May 5	Pittsburgh	Pittsburgh 4–1	Ron Francis	Tom Barrasso
4	May 7	Pittsburgh	Pittsburgh 4–1	Ron Francis	Tom Barrasso
5	May 9	Boston	Pittsburgh 7–2	Bryan Trottier	Tom Barrasso
6	May 11	Pittsburgh	Pittsburgh 5–3	Mark Recchi	Tom Barrasso

Penguins vs. North Stars, Stanley Cup Finals

Stanley Cup fever was sweeping through Pittsburgh like wildfire. The "City of Champions" hadn't been so crazy about a team since the 1960 Pirates, when the Benny Benack tune "Beat 'em Bucs" blared on every radio. From downtown office buildings to suburban malls, it seemed the entire city was awash in a sea of black and gold.

If the Penguins were unlikely candidates to capture Lord Stanley's coveted silverware, the Minnesota North Stars were even more of a long shot.

Few teams had overcome more adversity than the Campbell Conference champs. The North Stars had started the season as virtual orphans in their own hometown. Alienated by the club's previous owners, the Gunds, the hockey-mad fans of the Twin Cities avoided North Stars games like the plague. The fact that the woebegone "No Stars" stumbled out of the starting gate didn't help matters. By mid-January they were battling fellow weak

sisters Toronto and Quebec for the right to draft phenom Eric Lindros.

Then, almost overnight, the team began to improve. Buoyed by the emergence of a tough, young defensive corps and the steady play of veterans Bobby Smith, Neal Broten, and Brian Bellows, they clawed their way to the final playoff berth in the Norris Division.

What followed was one of the most improbable runs in Stanley Cup history. The North Stars stunned the league's top two teams, Chicago and St. Louis. Then they disposed of the defending Stanley Cup champion Oilers to reach the Finals. Along the way they won back their fans with gritty, emotionally charged play.

On the night of May 15 a sellout crowd of 16,164 jammed the Civic Arena to cheer their heroes on. However, the North Stars soon stole the show. Broten and Penguin-killer Ulf Dalhen staked Minnesota to a quick lead. Showing total disregard for Pittsburgh's vaunted power play, the North Stars banged the Penguins all over the ice. Although Lemieux struck for a shorthanded goal in the second period, Minnesota disposed of the Pens with stunning ease.

Bob Johnson made some surprising adjustments. Having seen enough of his team's punchless power play he dressed Paul Coffey, who was still on the mend from a broken jaw. Badger Bob shuffled the defensive corps as well, benching Jennings in favor of rookie Jim Paek.

The Penguins gave a much stronger effort in Game 2. Although Coffey was restricted to power-play duty, his presence forced the North Stars' penalty killers to skate with less abandon. Playing with a knife-blade edge, Samuelsson torpedoed Brian Bellows with a booming check at center ice.

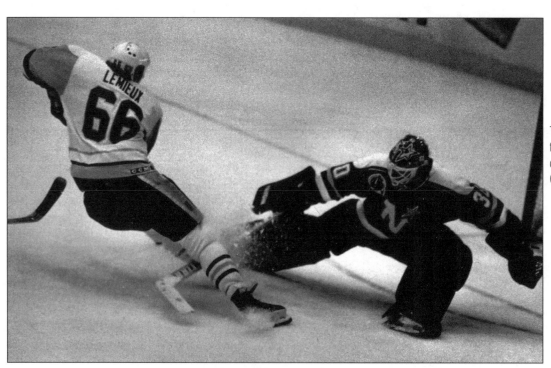

The Goal. Mario Lemieux turns Jon Casey inside out during the 1991 Stanley Cup Finals.

The stage was set for one of the most spectacular goals in Stanley Cup history, one that would simply and eloquently become known as "the Goal." The play began innocently enough as Lemieux gathered in a short pass from Phil Bourque deep in the Penguins' end. Gaining speed with each stride, Mario flashed through the neutral zone and caught the young defensive tandem of Shawn Chambers and Neil Wilkinson by surprise.

Still accelerating as he crossed the blue line, Lemieux sliced past Wilkinson and slipped the puck between Chambers' legs, turning the young defenseman into spaghetti. Skating at warp speed, he bore down on Jon Casey, who had moved out to the top of the crease. Mario was practically on top of the little goalie when he swerved sharply to his left and swept the puck into the net.

Even the most veteran observers were stunned by Mario's awesome display. The goal left the North Stars completely deflated. Moments later Stevens banged home his second tally of the night to clinch a 4–1 victory.

With the North Stars back on their heels, the series moved to Bloomington for Game 3. Minnesota received a huge break when Lemieux was scratched just before the opening face-off because of back spasms. Sensing an opportunity, the North Stars played an inspired game. They came away with a relatively easy 3–1 victory and an ill-fated dose of overconfidence.

Convinced that the Stanley Cup was theirs for the taking, Twin Cities dignitaries began plotting out a victory parade route. Several North Stars spoke of plans to visit the White House after they had secured the Cup. *Sports Illustrated* magazine hit the newsstands with a one-sided article that trumpeted Minnesota's Cinderella story.

In the Pittsburgh locker room the Penguins did a slow burn. To a man they had risen to meet every challenge placed in front of them. The true character of this proud team would be on display—the character of a champion. Leading the way was No. 66.

Any doubts about the team's resolve were immediately put to rest. Stevens, Francis, and Lemieux pumped the fastest three goals ever scored in the Stanley Cup Finals past a suddenly vulnerable Casey. Dave Gagner struck for a big goal late in the first period to revive the staggering North Stars, but Trottier answered midway through the second period.

The Penguins seemed poised to turn the game into a rout. However, a series of skirmishes left them shorthanded by two men. Soon they began to unravel. The Pens went to the locker room clinging to a precarious 4–3 lead.

Like an experienced corner man soothing a battered boxer, Bob Johnson calmed his charges during the intermission. But the Penguins couldn't stay out of the penalty box. When Troy Loney clipped Mark Tinordi with a high stick, referee Andy van Hellemond issued a five-minute major and a game misconduct. It seemed the game—and the Stanley Cup—were being handed to the North Stars on a silver platter.

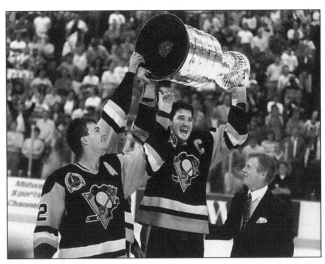
"Super Mario" hoists the Stanley Cup.

With their backs to the wall the Penguins showed their enormous collective heart. Led by Lemieux and Gilhen, the penalty killers forced turnover after turnover as the harried North Stars struggled to control the puck.

Finally, after Minnesota had failed to register a shot on goal in nearly four minutes of power-play time, Casey dumped Bourque behind his net to draw an interference penalty. North Stars coach Bob Gainey promptly pulled his goalie in favor of an extra attacker, but the ubiquitous Bourque scored an empty netter to even the series. Remarkably, the Penguins did not allow a shot on goal in the final seven minutes of play.

Without a doubt the supernatural penalty-killing effort turned the tide. With the momentum now firmly on their side, the Penguins throttled the North Stars right from the opening draw in Game 5. Lemieux ignited the team with his 15th tally of the playoffs. The Pens ran off three more goals in rapid-fire succession to chase Casey from the Minnesota net.

In the face of Pittsburgh's overwhelming firepower the North Stars were reduced to thuggery. Tough guy Basil McRae slammed into Barrasso, aggravating the netminder's already tender groin. Barrasso gamely finished the period, but he could not continue. Once again, backup Frank Pietrangelo was thrust into action at a critical juncture.

The second period was played on even terms as Gagner and Francis exchanged goals. But in the final stanza the North Stars mounted one last charge. Dahlen and Gagner took advantage of heavy traffic around Pietrangelo to score on rebounds. Minnesota closed the gap to 5–4.

It was the North Stars' final moment of glory. With less than two minutes remaining Loney scored the backbreaker from a goal-mouth scramble to salt the game away.

The Penguins' fantastic journey was one game away from completion. The North Stars planned to test Barrasso's balky groin and grab an early Game 6 lead so they could dictate play, but their hopes were dashed when Broten drew an interference penalty. Samuelsson scored on the power play and the Pens proceeded to pour it on.

The North Stars surged at Barrasso in a frantic effort to tie the game, but they were destiny's darlings no more. Once again it was Lemieux who scored the critical goal, beating Casey on yet another shorthanded breakaway.

Less than a minute later, Stevens lured the hapless netminder out of his cage and pushed a beautiful cross-ice pass to Mullen, who drilled the puck into an open net. The rout was on.

In desperation Gainey pulled Casey in favor of Brian Hayward. The backup goalie was given the same rude treatment as his partner. Twenty-one minutes and four goals later he, too, was driven from the Minnesota net.

Murphy added a power-play goal to run the score to 8–0, and the Pens went about the business of preserving the shutout for Barrasso.

As the final seconds ticked off the clock, Phil Bourque turned to Mark Recchi on the Penguins bench.

"Recchs, we won the Stanley Cup!" he yelled.

In the corner of the jubilant locker room stood a frail-looking older man clad in a dark suit. Caught up in the revelry of the moment, most of the players seemed not to notice him, with the exception of Tom Barrasso. The Cup-winning goalie approached the gentleman.

"Glad to bring it home to you," he said, extending a hand. The man was Edward DeBartolo Sr.

Following the Cup finale Lemieux was awarded the Conn Smythe Trophy as the MVP of the playoffs. After a slow start he rebounded to play magnificently. Mario scored at least one point in each of his final 18 playoff games, and he tallied no less than one goal in each of his last 10. His 44 points were the second-highest total ever recorded in post-season competition.

The vanquished North Stars were certainly impressed. "When somebody that big and that good wants to win that badly, there isn't much you can do," Dave Gagner said.

"We were hoping that Mario would be just regular," Bob Gainey added, "but he wasn't."

Yet as Lemieux was quick to point out, the Cup win was truly a team effort. "I could very easily share this [Conn Smythe Trophy] with Kevin Stevens, Mark Recchi, or Tom Barrasso," he said.

Bob Johnson was fond of saying that it took 28 men to bring the Stanley Cup to Pittsburgh. It would take even more for the Penguins to repeat as champions. As the players basked in the afterglow of victory, they could not foresee the troubles that lay just ahead.

Series Summary
Beat Minnesota 4–2 (Won Stanley Cup)

Game	Date	City	Result	Winning Goal	Winning Goalie
1	May 15	Pittsburgh	Minnesota 5–4	Bobby Smith	Jon Casey
2	May 17	Pittsburgh	Pittsburgh 4–1	Kevin Stevens	Tom Barrasso
3	May 19	Minnesota	Minnesota 3–1	Bobby Smith	Jon Casey
4	May 21	Minnesota	Pittsburgh 5–3	Bryan Trottier	Tom Barrasso
5	May 23	Pittsburgh	Pittsburgh 6–4	Ron Francis	Frank Pietrangelo
6	May 25	Minnesota	Pittsburgh 8–0	Ulf Samuelsson	Tom Barrasso

1992

The 1991–92 season would prove to be one of great trial and travail. Ultimately, it would serve to forge the team's character—the character of a true champion.

Immediately following the Penguins' Stanley Cup triumph in 1991, the club was plagued by misfortune. Owner Edward J. DeBartolo Sr., who had endured so many difficult seasons with a quiet stoicism and resolve, put the team up for sale. Key free agents Ron Francis, Mark Recchi, and Kevin Stevens entered into long and protracted contract negotiations with no end in sight.

However, these were minor distractions compared to the tragedy that was soon to follow. On the evening of August 23, 1991, the Pens' beloved coach, Bob Johnson, underwent emergency surgery to remove a malignant brain tumor. Badger Bob would pass away just three short months later.

With Scotty Bowman at the helm on an interim basis, the Penguins lurched through an up-and-down campaign. The team didn't regain its focus until February 19, 1992, when Craig Patrick pulled the trigger on another blockbuster trade. In a three-way deal with Los Angeles and Philadelphia, he acquired Kjell Samuelsson, Rick Tocchet, and Ken Wregget for Paul Coffey and Mark Recchi.

Following a brief adjustment period, the team once again caught fire in the homestretch, going 12–5–1 to sew up third place in the Patrick Division and a chance to defend their Stanley Cup title.

Cup Quotes

"It's a great thrill to reach the top of the mountain. A dream come true for all of our players."
—Bob Johnson

"This is the best thing that ever happened to me. This puts a blanket over all those [bad] years."
—Phil Bourque

"I never would have expected this in a million years. It's unbelievable."
—Troy Loney

"Don't ever wake me up."
—Jim Paek

Penguins vs. Capitals, Patrick Division Semifinals

The Penguins opened the playoffs on Easter Sunday in a matinee matchup against Washington at the Capital Centre. Unfortunately, they would open the series without Mario Lemieux, who was on the mend from a separated shoulder.

After a scoreless opening period the Capitals gradually took control. With the game well in hand they sent a message by turning up the physical play. Dale Hunter jumped Murphy along the boards, while Kevin Hatcher took a whack at Francis. Playing with a fractured jaw, Tocchet displayed his tremendous heart by stepping up to challenge the imposing Hatcher. After absorbing a couple of blows from the big defenseman, the fearless winger countered with several stinging lefts.

Despite the series-opening loss, the Penguins received a huge lift when Lemieux was given the green light to play. Buoyed by the presence of big No. 66, they stormed out of the starting gate in Game 2. Mario quickly set up a pair of power-play goals by Murphy and Stevens. Just when it appeared that the Pens would run the Capitals out of the building, someone threw an invisible switch.

The tide abruptly turned when Dmitri Khristich cashed in on a power play to cut the Penguins' lead in half. A short time later, Peter Bondra turned Gordie Roberts inside out and beat Barrasso with a blistering shot.

For the rest of the game the Penguins appeared to be skating in quicksand, while the Capitals attacked in an ever-increasing blur of speed and precision. Mercifully, Lemieux emerged from the 6–2 pasting unscathed. With his club hopelessly outclassed, Bowman wisely rested Mario in the final period.

The Pens received another jolt prior to Game 3 when Tocchet was scratched from the lineup with a badly bruised shoulder. Once again, Bowman was forced to juggle his line combinations. He teamed Lemieux with Bourque and Jagr, while reuniting the Stevens-Francis-Mullen trio that had played so well the previous spring. On the blue line he replaced the struggling Roberts with youngster Jim Paek.

When Washington struck for a quick shorthanded tally, the Penguins appeared to be in deep trouble. But as he had done so often throughout his career, Lemieux stepped forward with a virtuoso performance. In arguably his finest playoff game ever, Mario collected three goals and three assists as the Penguins triumphed.

"If we would've lost tonight it would've been almost impossible to come back and win four straight against a good team like the Capitals," Lemieux said. "That was a key game for us. We've just got to take one game at a time."

The stage was set for one of the Penguins' patented comebacks in Game 4. However, the Capitals swarmed the Pittsburgh net from the opening face-off and charged to a three-goal lead.

Sensing a shakeup was in order, Bowman replaced the beleaguered Barrasso with backup Ken Wregget. The shuffle had little effect. When the Pens tried to open up their offense Washington buried Wregget beneath an avalanche of pucks. Keyed by Dino Ciccarelli's four-goal performance, the Caps routed the Penguins again.

With the series returning to Landover for Game 5, the Capitals were on the verge of bouncing the Penguins from postseason play. They had humiliated the defending champs twice. With the notable exception of Game 3 they had completely neutralized Pittsburgh's vaunted attack.

Adding to the Pens' woes, Tocchet had reinjured his tender shoulder. Big Kjell Samuelsson was suffering from a badly jammed wrist. They appeared to be easy pickings for the powerhouse Capitals.

A ray of hope shone through the gloom of the Pittsburgh locker room. Realizing they would never beat the quick-striking Caps in a wide-open game, Lemieux and Francis suggested the team switch to a more defensive style known as the "one-four delay"—later to gain fame as the neutral-zone trap.

Under the one-four delay, a lone forechecker would harass the puck carrier while the rest of the team waited to disrupt the Washington attack in the neutral zone. Ideally, this would frustrate the Capitals, who by this time believed that they could score at will, while opening up some chances on the counterattack.

"We knew if we could play that type of game and wait for our chances, we had the better team and we knew we could win," Mario said.

At first Scotty Bowman was reluctant to make the switch, insisting that the Pens simply needed better execution. But the players were determined to use the new system, and the veteran coach relented.

The normally stoic Bowman also made an impassioned plea for the players to give their all. "Don't go out like this," he urged. "Don't just let the Washington Capitals sweep you under the carpet."

Employing the one-four delay to perfection, the Penguins surprised their overconfident foe in Game 5. With Bob Errey shadowing the dangerous Ciccarelli, they held the Capitals in check and coasted to a 5–2 victory.

The team had scaled a huge hurdle, but there was still more work to be done. Another strong effort would be needed to force a seventh game. A sage bit of advice from an unexpected source would prove invaluable. Prior to Game 6, Mark Recchi phoned his friend Kevin Stevens and told the slumping winger to shoot the puck high on Beaupre.

Following his buddy's tip to the letter, Stevens struck for a pair of quick goals in Game 6. The momentum appeared to be firmly in the Pens' favor, but they soon frittered away the lead.

Down 4–2 in a must-win game, the Penguins were in dire straits. Remarkably, the team's fighting spirit remained intact. They calmly waited for an opportunity to strike back. The opening presented itself midway through the second period when Mullen beat Beaupre on a breakaway. Moments

Larry Murphy and Tom Barrasso slam the door on feisty Dino Ciccarelli.

later, Bourque blasted a 40-footer between the little goalie's pads to knot the score again.

Now it was the Capitals who were rattled. When Hatcher foolishly presented the Penguins with another power play, No. 66 went to work.

Jagr started the play by lugging the puck into Washington's zone. When the Capitals' penalty killers swarmed to challenge him, the young winger flipped a diagonal pass to Lemieux, who took the puck on his backhand and fought through a check by Mike Ridley.

While Beaupre sprawled to the ice in anticipation, Mario drifted past the net. He appeared to be in way too deep to score. But with a flash of his marvelous hands he turned the puck over to his forehand and tucked it inside the goal post.

In the final period the Penguins tightened their defense and shut down the Capitals' attack. Frustrated by his inability to stop the Pens' snipers, Beaupre took a big swipe at Lemieux with his goaltender's blade. Mario kept his composure and responded with a power-play goal to put the Capitals away. The Penguins were very much alive.

The seventh and deciding game was played before a sellout crowd of 17,783 at the Cap Centre, including some 5,000 Penguins faithful who made the trek to Landover to cheer their heroes on.

Washington coach Terry Murray had resisted the urge to make changes. However, with the series on the line he made a concerted effort to keep Ciccarelli away from Errey, who had checked the scrappy winger to a standstill. In response to the way the Penguins were standing his team up at the blue line, Murray instructed the Capitals to play a more conservative dump-and-chase game.

The teams started slowly, like a pair of prize fighters probing for a weakness. The Caps got the first power-play opportunity, but their best chance missed by a fraction of an inch when Ridley rifled a shot off a goal post. The puck

ricocheted out to Murphy, who sent Francis and Lemieux scurrying away on a two-on-one break.

Using Mario as a decoy, Francis carried the puck down the middle of the ice and drove a hard slap shot at Beaupre. The acrobatic goalie made the save, but he kicked the puck right to Lemieux, who fired a laser beam into the net.

Although the Capitals rallied to tie the score, the Penguins never wavered. Jagr struck for a power-play goal and Mullen zipped in an empty netter to complete the improbable comeback.

"To make it to a seventh game and win tells you a lot about our team," a proud Scotty Bowman offered.

"There's just so much emotion on this team right now, that it's an unbelievable feeling," Kevin Stevens said. "The guys are buzzing. This is what this team is all about."

Series Summary
Beat Washington 4–3

Game	Date	City	Result	Winning Goal	Winning Goalie
1	April 19	Washington	Washington 3–1	John Druce	Don Beaupre
2	April 21	Washington	Washington 6–2	Michal Pivonka	Don Beaupre
3	April 23	Pittsburgh	Pittsburgh 6–4	Mario Lemieux	Tom Barrasso
4	April 25	Pittsburgh	Washington 7–2	Dmitri Khristich	Don Beaupre
5	April 27	Washington	Pittsburgh 5–2	Larry Murphy	Tom Barrasso
6	April 29	Pittsburgh	Pittsburgh 6–4	Mario Lemieux	Tom Barrasso
7	May 1	Washington	Pittsburgh 3–1	Jaromir Jagr	Tom Barrasso

Penguins vs. Rangers, Patrick Division Finals

The Penguins had little time to celebrate. The Patrick Division Finals were scheduled to begin two nights later in Madison Square Garden against their bitter rivals, the Rangers. At first glance New York appeared to be a good matchup for the Pens. But the Blueshirts were loaded with talent. The Rangers had run away with the Patrick Division title. For good measure, they had captured the President's Trophy.

Drained from playing emotional seventh games, the teams came out flat in the series opener. The Rangers tested Barrasso often through the early going, but most of their chances were from long range. In his typical workman-like fashion, Troy Loney scored from the slot to give the Penguins the lead. Murphy beat goalie John Vanbiesbrouck with a rising wrist shot to make it 2–0.

As the Penguins settled into the one-four delay and shut down the Rangers' attack, the frustrated New Yorkers tried to pick up the physical play. Rugged Kris King tussled with Barrasso, only to be leveled by Kevin Stevens. When King tried to return the favor Stevens flattened him again.

While buoyed by the impressive victory, the Pens knew they hadn't seen the Rangers at their best—or toughest. New York coach Roger Neilson admitted the Rangers were caught off guard by the Penguins' disciplined, defensive style. Disappointed in his team's play, he guaranteed a more physical contest in Game 2.

True to Neilson's word the Rangers came out hitting. Undaunted, Stevens beat Mike Richter with a bullet from the left hash mark. The Pens were threatening to score again when Joe Cirella was called for elbowing.

What followed drastically changed the complexion of the series. Francis won the face-off to begin the power play and drew the puck back to Lemieux at the left point. As the Pens' captain gathered in the pass, Rangers penalty killer Adam Graves skated toward him with bad intentions.

"When I saw Adam coming I knew he wasn't kidding around," Mario recalled.

Wielding his stick like a baseball bat, Graves swung for the fences and caught Lemieux with a wicked two-handed slash across the left wrist. The big center crumpled to the ice in pain to the jeers of the Madison Square Garden crowd. After what seemed like an eternity, Mario picked himself up and skated to the bench.

It was the shot heard 'round the hockey world and seen by all—except referee Dan Marouelli. Instead of banishing Graves from the game he issued only a minor penalty, giving the Rangers the green light to continue their barbaric play. Moments later King laid out Joey Mullen with a vicious check, tearing up the veteran winger's knee. In the span of a few minutes the Pens had been stripped of their second- and third-leading goal scorers.

Clearly stunned by the Rangers' ferocity, the Penguins stubbornly held on until the closing minutes, when Jeff Beukeboom beat Barrasso with a long-range slap shot to knot the score at 2–2. The Rangers continued to apply the pressure until King swept the game winner past Barrasso.

Afterward, the Penguins' worst fears were realized. Lemieux had a broken bone in his left hand. Supervisor of officials Dave Newell sent a videotape of the slashing incident to the league office for review. There was speculation that Neilson, who had a well-known affinity for back-alley tactics, had placed a bounty on Mario. It was later revealed that he'd encouraged his charges to "take Lemieux out of the game."

Bowman urged his players to forget about revenge and concentrate on winning the series. "Putting the puck in the net is the worst aggression to another team," he said. "We want to put more pucks in the net."

Phil Bourque echoed the veteran coach's sentiments. "I think the best revenge would be just to beat them in the series," he said.

In Game 3 the Penguins treated the capacity crowd at the Civic Arena to one of their most spirited efforts of the playoffs. The Rangers sprinted to a quick two-goal lead, but the Penguins battled back. Late in the third period Stevens barreled over the New York blue line and beat Mike Richter with a booming slap shot to send the game into overtime.

Both teams went for the quick kill. Francis had a golden opportunity to seal a Penguins victory, but Richter robbed him with a brilliant save. Paul Broten scooped up the rebound and bolted up the ice. He fired the puck off the end boards and onto the waiting stick of King, who was stationed beside the net. The hustling winger pulled the trigger and beat Barrasso for the game winner.

Prior to Game 4 the league office made a ruling on the Graves-Lemieux incident. The Penguins were stunned to learn that the Rangers' winger had been suspended for a mere four playoff games.

Angered by the league's leniency, the Pens' already raw emotions were stoked to a boiling point. Yet the riveting intensity that had marked their performance in Game 3 was lacking. Taking full advantage, the Rangers struck for a pair of quick goals. The visitors from Broadway threatened to turn the game into a rout, but rookie Mike Needham scored a huge goal to keep his team in the game.

The Pens soon found themselves in another hole. Forty-six seconds into the final period Mark Messier roared down the ice like a runaway freight train and ripped a bullet beneath Barrasso's pads to restore the Rangers' two-goal edge. Moments later Gordie Roberts drew a major penalty. Just 15 minutes stood between the Rangers and a commanding 3–1 series lead.

Although crippled by the loss of Bob Errey to a shoulder injury, the Penguins' penalty-killing unit turned the tide. Thanks to the extraordinary efforts of Francis and Loney, they kept the Rangers' power play bottled up. When the penalty expired Francis immediately went on the attack. He wheeled toward the Rangers' blue line and fooled Richter with a knuckling long-range shot to cut the New York lead to 4–3.

The Rangers were stunned by the Pens' tenacity. Before they could regroup, Jagr set up Loney for the game-tying goal.

Roger Neilson had seen enough. Shuffling his goaltenders once more, he pulled the shell-shocked Richter in favor of Vanbiesbrouck. The surging Penguins immediately put "Beezer" to the test, but he made several key saves to force yet another overtime.

Once again, both teams went for the early kill. Barely two minutes into the extra frame, Jagr slipped through the Rangers' defense and forced Beukeboom to execute a takedown.

As the big defenseman watched helplessly from the penalty box, Murphy made a heady play. He stripped the puck from Messier and pushed it to Francis, who was stationed in front of the net. With his back to the goal, the veteran center steered the puck between his own legs and past the startled Vanbiesbrouck. Pandemonium broke out as Francis was mobbed by his joyous teammates.

"Ronnie had a big night and a great series against those guys," Kevin Stevens recalled. "The Rangers were the team we really wanted to beat. Everybody was talking about how they were going to mop up everybody, and to beat them gave us new life."

That new life was severely tested. Although clearly stung by their gut-wrenching loss in Game 4, the Rangers came at the Penguins with guns ablaze in Game 5. However, the momentum had irretrievably shifted. Riding their big-play offense and the spectacular goaltending of Barrasso, the Pens nipped the Blueshirts in Game 5 and buried them in Game 6 to take the series.

"I said before the series when you play the champions, you can't just beat them, you have to knock them out," a disconsolate Messier said. "We felt we had them in the fourth game leading 4–2 with 10 minutes to go. We let them get off the ropes and let them get back up and I think that came back to haunt us."

Series Summary
Beat New York Rangers 4–2

Game	Date	City	Result	Winning Goal	Winning Goalie
1	May 3	New York	Pittsburgh 4–2	Kevin Stevens	Tom Barrasso
2	May 5	New York	NY Rangers 4–2	Kris King	Mike Richter
3	May 7	Pittsburgh	NY Rangers 6–5 (OT)	Kris King	Mike Richter
4	May 9	Pittsburgh	Pittsburgh 5–4 (OT)	Ron Francis	Tom Barrasso
5	May 11	New York	Pittsburgh 3–2	Jaromir Jagr	Tom Barrasso
6	May 13	Pittsburgh	Pittsburgh 5–1	Jaromir Jagr	Tom Barrasso

Penguins vs. Bruins, Wales Conference Finals

After a well-deserved day off, the Penguins began to prepare for a return match with their Wales Conference Finals opponent, the Bruins. Like the Pens, Boston had foundered through much of the regular season until GM Mike Milbury made a huge trade in January, sending Craig Janney and Stephane Quintal to St. Louis in exchange for playmaking center Adam Oates. Following a strong stretch run, the Bruins nipped Buffalo and swept aside Montreal to reach the Conference Finals.

Itching to avenge their playoff defeat at the hands of the Penguins the previous spring, the Bruins dominated the series opener. Taking advantage of some uncharacteristically sloppy play by their hosts, they carried a 3–2 lead into the final frame.

With less than eight minutes remaining the Penguins' dormant offense finally sprang to life. Boston native Shawn McEachern scooped up a Rick Tocchet rebound and zipped it past goalie Andy Moog to send the game into overtime.

The stage was set for 20-year-old whiz kid Jaromir Jagr. In a play reminiscent of Lemieux's sparking goal in the 1991 Cup Finals, Jagr gathered in a short pass from Kjell Samuelsson and turned on the afterburners. After tying rookie defenseman Matt Hervey into knots with a series of fakes, he beat Moog for his fourth game winner of the playoffs.

Leading up to Game 2, much of the media attention focused on the status of wounded superstars Ray Bourque and Mario Lemieux. Bourque, Boston's superb puck-rushing defenseman, had suffered a broken finger during the Adams Division Finals. The Bruins received a huge lift when he pronounced himself ready to play.

The Pens didn't appear to be as fortunate with Lemieux. Although he had been skating with the team and his hand was healing well, he appeared to be several games away from returning. But Mario knew all too well that the Bruins would be an inspired team with Bourque in the lineup. He boldly announced that he, too, would return to action.

Initially, Scotty Bowman planned to use him exclusively on the power play. However, after a couple of shifts it was obvious the big center was ready for regular duty. Showing few ill effects from his injury, he notched two goals and an assist to key a 5–2 Pens triumph.

"This was a one-sided series from the time Mario stepped on the ice," Oates glumly noted.

With the series shifting to the fabled Boston Garden for Game 3, the Penguins braced themselves for a tough battle. But Kevin Stevens stole the show. Shaking off his own nagging injuries, the big winger exploded for four goals. The Pens routed the Bruins 5–1 to grab a commanding 3–0 series lead.

The Bruins were in a complete state of shock. Unable to cope with the Penguins' awesome firepower, they resorted to bullying tactics in Game 4 in an effort to turn the tide.

At the earliest opportunity, Boston coach Rick Bowness dispatched feisty winger Brent Hughes to work over Jagr, who had turned the Bruins' zone into his personal playground. However, after taking a few ineffective runs at his target, Hughes suddenly found himself nose to nose with Tocchet. The Boston bad boy sagged to the ice under a hail of punches.

Having failed miserably at intimidation, the Bruins were ripe for the knockout blow. Lemieux soon delivered it while killing a penalty.

After picking off a wayward pass, Mario set sail for the Bruins' end. At the red line he encountered Ray Bourque, who was backpedaling furiously in an effort to gain position. With stunning precision Mario threaded the puck between the future Hall of Famer's legs and raced toward the Bruins' goal, where he beat the beleaguered Moog with ease.

"There wasn't a guy on the bench who wasn't picked up two feet when he scored that goal," Ron Francis said.

It was the final nail in the Bruins' coffin. The Penguins were advancing to the Stanley Cup Finals for the second straight season.

Series Summary
Beat Boston 4–0

Game	Date	City	Result	Winning Goal	Winning Goalie
1	May 17	Pittsburgh	Pittsburgh 4–3 (OT)	Jaromir Jagr	Tom Barrasso
2	May 19	Pittsburgh	Pittsburgh 5–2	Rick Tocchet	Tom Barrasso
3	May 21	Boston	Pittsburgh 5–1	Kevin Stevens	Tom Barrasso
4	May 23	Boston	Pittsburgh 5–1	Mario Lemieux	Tom Barrasso

Penguins vs. Blackhawks, Stanley Cup Finals

While the Penguins were making short work of Boston, the Chicago Blackhawks completed a similar demolition of the Oilers. One thing was certain—neither team had backed its way into the Stanley Cup Finals. While the Pens had won seven in a row, the piping-hot Blackhawks had swept Detroit and Edmonton en route to a playoff-record 11 consecutive victories.

A formidable opponent, the Blackhawks had evolved into a bruising defensive team under the tutelage of former Bowman assistant "Iron" Mike Keenan. Chicago's stars included 53-goal scorer Jeremy Roenick, veteran winger Steve Larmer, and the nasty defensive tandem of Steve Smith and Chris Chelios.

Between the pipes the Blackhawks boasted the finest young goalie in the league in Ed Belfour. Like Tom Barrasso, "Eddie the Eagle" had captured the Calder and Vezina Trophies as a rookie.

Unfazed, the Pens came out flying. Displaying remarkable speed and skill, Lemieux, Jagr, and Stevens swooped around the Chicago net like giant birds of prey.

However, after killing off an early penalty to Mike Hudson, the visitors began to flex their muscles. Chelios and Smith belted Lemieux every time he touched the puck. As the normally stout-hearted Penguins ran for cover, the Blackhawks piled up a 4–1 lead.

It seemed as though Chicago had the game in the bag. But the Penguins adjusted to the Hawks' hard-hitting style. By the middle of the second period they were matching their foe check for check.

"We're not the most aggressive team in the world," Rick Tocchet recalled, "but we do play aggressively when we have to."

The tough winger ignited the Pens' comeback when he beat Belfour with a perfectly timed deflection.

Moments later Lemieux and Stevens wove their way through traffic on a two-man foray into Chicago ice. With Stevens running interference, Lemieux veered off to the right side of the Blackhawks' zone. In an amazing display of skill, he banked the puck off of Belfour's right leg and into the net.

The goal proved to be the turning point. Revitalized, the Penguins pressed the attack in the third period. Barrasso held Chicago at bay with several key saves, keeping his team within striking distance.

Still, the defending champs trailed until scarcely five minutes remained. It took a gem of a goal by Jaromir Jagr to even the score.

The young winger started the play by gathering up a loose puck high in the Chicago zone. He eluded Dirk Graham, only to be confronted by Brent Sutter. Displaying a presence of mind far beyond his years, Jagr played cat-and-mouse with the veteran center, dangling the puck like a carrot on his stick until Sutter lurched forward in pursuit. He darted past Sutter and skated toward the left side of the

Chicago net, where Frantisek Kucera stepped up to challenge. The Penguins' boy wonder coolly sidestepped the Hawks defender and slipped past his partner, Igor Kravchuk, who was entangled with Shawn McEachern. Mesmerized, Belfour barely twitched a muscle while Jagr slid the game-tying goal between his legs.

The Civic Arena crowd went wild with glee. "That was probably the greatest goal I've ever seen," a smiling Lemieux said afterward.

The best was yet to come. After the Pens weathered a penalty to Murphy, Mario was dumped to the ice by Smith in the final minute of play to draw a hooking call. Seventeen seconds remained on the clock—enough time to mount one last attack.

Lemieux decided to gamble. Mario knew if Francis won the face-off he would try to move the puck to Murphy at the right point. As soon as the puck was dropped No. 66 broke toward the net.

"Actually, I gambled maybe a little too much on that play," he recalled in the highlight video *Against the Odds*. "If the puck gets by Larry Murphy they have a two on none and they have a good chance to score."

The play unfolded precisely as the big center had anticipated. Francis won the draw and pushed the puck back to Murphy, who immediately fired a shot on the Chicago goal. Belfour kicked the puck aside. As if drawn by an invisible magnet, the rebound came directly to Lemieux, who was racing in from the left-wing circle. Broken hand and all, Mario snapped a beautiful shot over the Hawks goalie to cap the Pens' incredible comeback.

Everyone was awed by Mario's amazing exploits—with one notable exception.

"I can't respect Mario for diving," Mike Keenan fumed. "The world's best player is embarrassing himself and embarrassing the game."

Keenan vowed that the Hawks would be even more physical in Game 2. Following their coach's game plan to the

Jaromir Jagr emerged as a world-class player during the 1992 playoffs. Here he chases down Chicago's Jocelyn Lemieux.

The Pens are No. 1.

letter, big Mike Peluso rattled Jagr with a couple of big hits, while rugged Bryan Marchment flattened Tocchet at center ice with a terrific check.

The Penguins were unperturbed.

"That was my kind of game," Tocchet said. "A lot of talking and pushing at the face-offs. They had guys out there trying to stir things up, but we weren't going to lose control and get into fights. Our team isn't going to be intimidated by anyone."

Shaking off Chicago's body-banging tactics, the Pens snatched a 3–1 lead on a pair of second-period tallies by Lemieux. In the final frame they gave the defensive-minded Hawks a clinic on protecting a lead. Keenan virtually conceded defeat by keeping his best players—Roenick, Chelios, and Smith—tethered to the bench.

A change in venue offered the Blackhawks a ray of hope. Games 3 and 4 would be played within the unfriendly confines of Chicago Stadium, perhaps the most intimidating arena in all of hockey. Aided by the fanatical Blackhawks fans and a Barton organ that could equal the decibel level of 25 brass bands, the 62-year-old structure was one of the noisiest buildings in the league. Chicago Stadium also featured a tiny ice surface that was 15 feet shorter than a regulation

NHL rink—ideal for the Hawks' punishing style of play.

True to form, the rabid Blackhawks fans were stoked to a frenzy by the end of the national anthem. Suitably inspired, the Hawks unleashed a flurry of shots to open the game. Tom Barrasso stood his ground, and soon the momentum shifted to the black-and-gold-clad visitors.

Late in the first period the Penguins broke through on a rather innocent-looking play. Shawn McEachern won a face-off in the Blackhawks' zone and drew the puck back to Jim Paek at the point. Known more for his steady defensive play than his offense, Paek uncorked a drive that pinballed off Tocchet and Stevens before finding the back of the Chicago net.

It was all the offense Pittsburgh would need. Backed by Barrasso's sparkling 27-save performance, the Pens prevailed 1–0.

The Blackhawks were in dire straits. Only two teams at that time—the 1942 Red Wings and the 1975 Islanders—had rallied from a 3–0 deficit to win a playoff series.

If Game 3 was a defensive masterpiece, Game 4 was an ode to fire-wagon hockey. The die was cast 90 seconds into the contest when Jagr wheeled off the sideboards and beat Belfour with a sizzling wrist shot. Five minutes later, Dirk

Graham popped the puck past Barrasso for the first of his three first-period goals.

Although the Blackhawks were holding their own, a shootout clearly favored the talent-laden Penguins. Desperate to find an edge, Keenan brazenly pulled Belfour in favor of backup Dominik Hasek.

The switch worked for a time. Lemieux had two breakaway chances, but the master of the one-on-one failed to solve the unorthodox Hasek. When Mario sent Stevens steaming in on yet another breakaway, the young Czech goalie surprised the burly winger by skating 50 feet out of his net to knock the puck off of his blade.

As brilliantly as Hasek played, the Penguins would not be denied. Five minutes into the final frame Murphy scored a beautiful goal from the slot. Chicago responded with a furious attack, but Francis broke into the Blackhawks' zone and blew the puck past a fading Hasek to extend the Pens' lead to 6–4.

The goal clearly took the starch out of Chicago. In one memorable sequence Lemieux and Jagr played keep-away with the puck, reducing the bewildered Hawks to an on-ice version of the Keystone Kops chasing after Buster Keaton and Harold Lloyd.

In desperation the Blackhawks swarmed the Penguins net in the closing minutes, but Barrasso slammed the door. As the final seconds ticked off the game clock he thrust his arms into the air while the Pens mobbed each other in the corner of the ice.

For the second year in a row they had captured hockey's Holy Grail, erasing any doubts about whether they were a team worthy of the Stanley Cup.

"When you win once, people wonder," Stevens said. "When you win twice, it's no fluke."

The Penguins had been accused of beating inferior teams on the way to their first Cup. No one could make such a claim this time around. They had overcome a plethora of adversity to capture their second consecutive Cup in thoroughly impressive fashion—beating the top two regular-season finishers and sweeping Boston and Chicago.

Along the way they tied the Blackhawks' mark of 11 straight playoff victories while establishing a record for most consecutive wins to close out the playoffs. They were, indeed, a team worthy of being called champions.

Once again, Mario led the way. He overcame a separated shoulder and a broken hand to lead all playoff scorers with 16 goals and 34 points, including a record-tying five game-winning goals. For the second straight year he was awarded the Conn Smythe Trophy.

The Pens got an opportunity to revel in their triumph on June 4, when 40,000 fans jammed Three Rivers Stadium for a victory celebration. In perhaps the most lighthearted moment of the day, Bryan Trottier took the Stanley Cup for several slides on the rain-slicked tarpaulin to the delight of the huge throng.

It also provided the team with a final opportunity to pay homage to Bob Johnson. "The coach of the Pittsburgh Penguins will always be Bob Johnson," Scotty Bowman graciously said. "Thanks to his vision, all of this today is possible."

Around the NHL there was talk of a new dynasty.

Series Summary
Beat Chicago 4–0 (Won Stanley Cup)

Game	Date	City	Result	Winning Goal	Winning Goalie
1	May 26	Pittsburgh	Pittsburgh 5–4	Mario Lemieux	Tom Barrasso
2	May 28	Pittsburgh	Pittsburgh 3–1	Mario Lemieux	Tom Barrasso
3	May 30	Chicago	Pittsburgh 1–0	Kevin Stevens	Tom Barrasso
4	June 1	Chicago	Pittsburgh 6–5	Ron Francis	Tom Barrasso

A joyous Scotty Bowman.

1993

The Penguins followed up their second straight Stanley Cup triumph with a season for the ages. Paced by Mario Lemieux's piping-hot start, the Pens ripped through the first half of the 1992–93 campaign at a scorching 28–10–4 clip.

Then came the announcement that stunned the sports world: Mario had contracted Hodgkin's disease. Following a battery of tests, the big center underwent surgery to remove an infected lymph node. A short time later he began a series of radiation treatments.

Fortunately, the Penguins were a deep, strong team. Boasting an elite group of forwards, including Ron Francis, Jaromir Jagr, Kevin Stevens, and Rick Tocchet, and a solid defense anchored by Larry Murphy and the Samuelssons, the club barely missed a beat.

Remarkably, Mario returned to the lineup for the stretch run. He went on an incredible tear, rolling up 51 points over a 16-game stretch to bury Pat LaFontaine in the scoring race. Not coincidentally, the team finished the season on a 17–0–1 run to capture the President's Trophy.

Penguins vs. Devils, Patrick Division Semifinals

The Penguins opened the playoffs against the New Jersey Devils before a sellout crowd at the Civic Arena. The game was aired on ABC—the first NHL playoff contest televised by a major network in 13 years. The Pens did their best to put on a good show.

True to form, the Devils planned to employ a physical style. However, their strategy backfired when Dave Barr drew a high-sticking penalty just seconds into the contest. Tocchet jammed the puck past goalie Chris Terreri on the ensuing power play and the Penguins were off to the races.

Moments later, Jaromir Jagr undressed Scott Niedermayer at the New Jersey blue line and dished off a beautiful pass to Mario Lemieux, who fired the puck past Terreri.

Try as they might, the Devils were no match for the talent-laden Penguins. Lemieux, Ron Francis, and Dave Tippett scored second-period goals, and Jagr added an insurance tally as the Pens coasted to an easy 6–3 victory.

Game 2 was a virtual replay of the series opener. Sparked by a four-goal second-period outburst, the Penguins spanked the undermanned Devils 7–0 to snatch a 2–0 series lead.

The Penguins were playing nearly perfect hockey. Every facet of their game, from the goaltending to the defense to the power play, was operating at maximum efficiency. It seemed inconceivable that any club could stand up to this juggernaut. Little did anyone realize that this magnificent team—arguably the best in franchise history—had peaked too soon.

Desperate to find an edge, Devils coach Herb Brooks turned to his backup goalie, Craig Billington, in Game 3. For 40 minutes the move worked like a charm as "the Biller"

limited the high-powered Penguins to a lone goal.

In the final period, however, the flood gates opened. The Pens pounded three goals past the beleaguered backup to capture their 14th consecutive playoff victory—an NHL record that stands to this day.

New Jersey managed to avoid a sweep in Game 4 thanks to a strong performance by Terreri. But the Penguins rode a two-goal effort from role player Jeff Daniels in Game 5 to close out the series.

Series Summary
Beat New Jersey 4–1

Game	Date	City	Result	Winning Goal	Winning Goalie
1	April 18	Pittsburgh	Pittsburgh 6–3	Ron Francis	Tom Barrasso
2	April 20	Pittsburgh	Pittsburgh 7–0	Shawn McEachern	Tom Barrasso
3	April 22	New Jersey	Pittsburgh 4–3	Larry Murphy	Tom Barrasso
4	April 25	New Jersey	New Jersey 4–1	Tommy Albelin	Chris Terreri
5	April 26	Pittsburgh	Pittsburgh 5–3	Jeff Daniels	Tom Barrasso

Penguins vs. Islanders, Patrick Division Finals

The stage was set for a Patrick Division Finals matchup with the New York Islanders. On paper it looked like another easy series. New York's best player, Pierre Turgeon, was sidelined with a shoulder injury. Although the Islanders still boasted a bevy of talented players, including 30-goal men Benoit Hogue, Derek King, and Steve Thomas, they appeared to be no more than a speed bump on the road to a third Stanley Cup.

Yet the brash young Islanders clearly intended to give the Penguins a run for their money. From the opening draw they employed an aggressive, up-tempo style that confused the defending champs. With unheralded Glenn Healy matching Tom Barrasso save for save, the teams split the first four games.

The Penguins seemed genuinely stunned by the Islanders' grit. To make matters worse, Mario's back clenched up during the series opener, forcing him to miss Game 2. After giving traction a try he submitted to cortisone injections in a last-ditch effort to relieve the pain.

In stark contrast to their loose and confident adversaries, the Pens appeared brittle and tense prior to Game 5. However, when referee Kerry Fraser dropped the puck they blitzed their foe with a ferocious offensive assault. With a revitalized Lemieux leading the way, they piled up a three-goal lead in 90 seconds and breezed to an impressive 6–3 victory.

Having clawed their way to a 3–2 advantage, the Penguins appeared to be on the verge of closing out the series. But a worrisome trend had developed—one that would prove costly to the defending champions.

The energetic Islanders were consistently beating them to the loose pucks. The trades that had brought in so many accomplished veterans also had robbed the team of a precious commodity—speed. Burners such as Bourque, Coffey, and Errey were long gone. The club's pronounced lack of mobility was particularly evident on defense, where only bit player Paul Stanton had the wheels to elude the fleet Islanders' forecheckers. It was the Achilles' heel of the mighty Penguins and it would prove to be their downfall.

The Islanders weren't going down without a fight. Any thoughts of an easy victory vanished when Brad Dalgarno scored just 25 seconds into Game 6. For the next several minutes New York swarmed all over the bewildered Penguins, setting a physical tone that would carry through for the rest of the evening.

Having weathered the Islanders' early storm, the Pens began to find their rhythm. Following an exchange of first-period tallies, Mario blew a blistering shot past Healy early in the second frame to knot the score at 2–2.

The Pens seemed poised to finish off the pesky Islanders, but the tide abruptly turned when Ron Francis was issued a match penalty for high sticking.

Forced to play without their top defensive center and face-off man, the Penguins sagged while the Islanders poured it on. Uwe Krupp potted an empty-net goal to cap off an impressive 7–5 triumph. The gritty Islanders had extended their mighty foe to a seventh game.

The irony was impossible to ignore. Eleven years earlier a scrappy but outgunned Penguins squad had squared off against the two-time Stanley Cup champion Islanders. Led by the superb goaltending of Michel Dion, the underdog Penguins came within minutes of ending the Islanders' championship run. Now the roles were reversed.

Game 7 opened with a bang. Determined to diffuse the Islanders' body-bending tactics, Kevin Stevens skirmished with Dalgarno right from the opening draw. Moments later Stevens found Rich Pilon in his crosshairs and hurled his big frame into the rugged defenseman. The booming check sent Pilon flying off his skates, but it was Stevens who got the worst of the collision. Pilon's protective shield caught him flush in the face. Knocked unconscious, the burly winger struck the ice facefirst with a sickening thud.

A hush fell over the crowd as Stevens lay motionless. After several minutes the big winger came to his senses, but he was in no condition to continue. He had suffered a host of gruesome facial injuries. The sight of "Artie" being wheeled off the ice on a stretcher sickened his teammates and the Pens faithful.

Although badly shaken, the Penguins responded like champions. Francis sent Lemieux steaming in on a short-handed breakaway, but Mario rang the puck off a goal post. Murphy, Lemieux, and Tocchet teamed up on a crisp tic-tac-toe passing play, but Healy made an equally brilliant pad save. At the 13-minute mark Lemieux unleashed a beautiful spinning shot, only to be denied again by the acrobatic goalie.

The rest of the period followed the same pattern. The Penguins fired shot after shot at Healy, only to come up

empty. Despite outshooting the Islanders 19–7, they had nothing to show for their efforts.

Undaunted, the Pens continued to turn up the heat in the second frame. Lemieux had another shorthanded opportunity, but once again he was repelled by Healy. They finally broke through at 7:59, when Ulf Samuelsson gathered in a pass from Mario and launched a hard slap shot that found the mark.

The tough defenseman would soon turn from hero to goat. Moments later Benoit Hogue picked off his outlet pass and set up Steve Thomas for the Islanders' first goal.

Again, the Penguins had dominated play, limiting New York to just four shots during the period. Again, they had nothing to show for it.

Thanks to Healy's spectacular goaltending, the Islanders had survived the onslaught. In the final period they returned with some fire of their own. Six minutes into the frame they grabbed a 2–1 lead on a pretty play by David Volek and scrappy Ray Ferraro. The Islanders increased their lead moments later when Hogue fired a routine slap shot that deflected off of Murphy's stick and past Barrasso.

Meanwhile, at the other end of the ice Healy continued to make save after save as the Penguins desperately pressed for a goal. With less than five minutes remaining their hopes

Jaromir Jagr and Shawn McEachern revel after beating Islanders goalie Glenn Healy. Their moment of glory was brief—New York dethroned the defending Cup champs.

seemed to vanish for good when Lemieux was ushered to the penalty box with Krupp.

Remarkably, the team's great fighting spirit surfaced one more time. At 16:38, Murphy gained possession of the puck behind the Islanders' goal and fed it to Francis, who whacked a knuckler past Healy.

Then, with exactly one minute remaining on the clock and an empty net yawning behind him, Murphy took a pass from Joey Mullen and ripped off a quick shot. The puck bounded crazily off Francis to Tocchet, who deflected it home. The Civic Arena crowd exploded in a loud roar as the team celebrated one of the most spectacular comebacks in Stanley Cup history.

Hell-bent on putting New York away, the Penguins went full-throttle in overtime. Lemieux had a great chance to pot the game winner. For all his wondrous ability he was unable to work the puck through the Islanders' defense to a wide-open net.

Undeterred, the Pens continued to press the attack. At the four-minute mark Mario scooped up a loose puck and got it to Francis, who was streaking toward the Islanders' zone. The veteran center cut loose a wicked slap shot, but Healy made a spectacular glove save to blunt what would be the Penguins' final scoring chance.

Moments later, with Ulf Samuelsson pinching to keep an offensive flurry alive, the Islanders gained possession of the puck and burst into the Penguins' end on a three-on-one. Volek took a pass from Ferraro in full stride and blasted the puck over Barrasso's shoulder. In the blink of an eye, Pittsburgh's two-year reign as Stanley Cup champions was over.

In the days that followed the heartbreaking loss many sought to blame Scotty Bowman for his inability to lead the team to victory. But the Islanders had outhustled and outhit the Penguins and they deserved to win. The Pens had won the Stanley Cup as a team, defended it as a team, and lost it as a team.

"We put ourselves in a position where anything could happen and the worst did," Barrasso said.

Years later, Ron Francis still felt the sting. "You never know when or even if you're going to get back [to the Finals]," he said. "Look at our '93 team. That was our best team and we didn't win the Cup. You just never know."

Series Summary
Lost to New York Islanders 4–3

Game	Date	City	Result	Winning Goal	Winning Goalie
1	May 2	Pittsburgh	NY Islanders 3–2	Benoit Hogue	Glenn Healy
2	May 4	Pittsburgh	Pittsburgh 3–0	Joe Mullen	Tom Barrasso
3	May 6	New York	Pittsburgh 3–1	Jaromir Jagr	Tom Barrasso
4	May 8	New York	NY Islanders 6–5	Derek King	Glenn Healy
5	May 10	Pittsburgh	Pittsburgh 6–3	Mario Lemieux	Tom Barrasso
6	May 12	New York	NY Islanders 7–5	Steve Thomas	Glenn Healy
7	May 14	Pittsburgh	NY Islanders 4–3 (OT)	David Volek	Glenn Healy

1994

Entering the 1993–94 season, most experts felt that Lord Stanley's Cup would be returning to Pittsburgh. The team's early playoff exit in 1993 was considered a fluke—a temporary interruption in what was sure to be hockey's newest dynasty. After all, the Pens were still loaded with top-flight players such as Mario Lemieux, Ron Francis, Jaromir Jagr, Joe Mullen, Larry Murphy, and Kevin Stevens. Although Scotty Bowman had departed the Steel City to join the Red Wings, many believed new/old coach Eddie Johnston would be a better fit for the players and the organization.

However, it was quickly apparent that this Penguins team would not dominate the league like its predecessor. Plagued by bouts of anemia and lower back problems, Mario was once again forced from the lineup for an extended stretch. Beset by back miseries of his own, Rick Tocchet dipped from a career-best 48 goals to 14. Kevin Stevens struggled to keep pace after extensive off-season facial surgery.

Once again, Craig Patrick pulled off a big trade to right the team's fortunes. In February he dealt off-season acquisition Marty McSorley and steady defender Jim Paek to Los Angeles for sniper Tomas Sandstrom and ex-Pen Shawn McEachern. The team responded with a 16–9–2 run to close out the season. During the final week, however, they were blown out by New Jersey and Montreal in a pair of lopsided losses by a combined score of 16–3.

Penguins vs. Capitals, Eastern Conference Quarterfinals

Despite their erratic play during the regular season, the Penguins were heavy favorites to defeat the Washington Capitals in the opening round of the playoffs. The Caps had finished a distant third in the Atlantic Division, some 24 points behind the New York Rangers.

But the Capitals would be no easy mark. In many ways they resembled the Islanders team that had ended the Penguins' dreams of a third Stanley Cup. Although they lacked a game breaker like Mario Lemieux, the Caps' lineup featured a core of talented forwards including Dmitri Khristich, Peter Bondra, and newcomer Joey Juneau. More significantly, Washington boasted a battalion of aggressive role players led by Dale Hunter and backed up by feisty Keith Jones and gritty Steve Konowalchuk. They were precisely the type of team that gave the Penguins fits.

In Game 1 the Capitals established the aggressive forecheck that they would employ throughout the series. Still, the Penguins forged a 2–1 lead on goals by Lemieux and Joe Mullen. But the Pens fell asleep in the second period and the Capitals made them pay, pounding three goals past Tom Barrasso. Washington staved off a mild Penguins rally to prevail 5–3.

Shortly before the start of Game 2, Capitals coach Jim Schoenfeld dropped a bombshell when he announced that rookie Byron Dafoe would start in goal instead of veteran Don Beaupre. While most observers questioned the switch, it was a savvy move. The Penguins had a long history of breaking goalies over the course of a series, and Beaupre was no exception. By starting Dafoe, Schoenfeld gave the Pens a different look.

The move appeared to backfire when the Penguins struck for two quick goals. However, after a strong opening period, they wilted like month-old lettuce. Khristich cashed in on the power play early in the second frame, and the Capitals washed over their foe in waves. Fortunately, Barrasso was razor-sharp and the Pens pulled out a 2–1 nail-biter.

If the Penguins didn't deserve to win Game 2, the opposite was true about Game 3. From the opening face-off they played with the purpose and fire befitting a champion. For the better part of the evening, they outworked, outskated, and outhit the Capitals.

Twice during the second period Pittsburgh killed off five-on-three power plays. But when the Pens' power play swung into action with seven minutes left in the period, light-scoring Caps defenseman Joe Reekie tallied a shorthanded goal.

The Penguins grimly stepped up the attack in the final period, but goalie Don Beaupre was up to the task. The outcome was in doubt until the final minute of play, when the ubiquitous Reekie potted an empty netter.

In desperate need of a victory, the Pens were determined to seize control in Game 4. While coach Eddie Johnston shuffled his lines in an effort to find a winning combination, the team ramped up the physical play. To make sure Washington got the message, Peter Taglianetti smashed Randy Burridge to the ice with a thunderous bodycheck.

Undeterred, the underdog Caps continued to exploit the Pens' weaknesses with surgical precision. Powered by goals from their big three of Khristich, Bondra, and Juneau, the Capitals thumped the sagging Penguins 4–1.

Fighting for their playoff lives, the Penguins finally delivered a winning effort in Game 5, thanks to the clutch scoring of big guns Jaromir Jagr, Kevin Stevens, and Shawn McEachern. However, it was painfully clear that the team had run out of gas. Veterans Ron Francis, Joe Mullen, and Larry Murphy were worn out from overuse. Stevens, who was unable to train properly over the summer, could barely skate. The Pens proved to be easy prey for the hustling Capitals, who took them to the woodshed in Game 6 to close out the series.

The stunning defeat ended any talk of a dynasty. It seemed the great spirit and determination that carried the team to a pair of Stanley Cups had been extinguished.

"Where'd our hunger go?" Craig Patrick lamented.

Perhaps Marty McSorley, who was dealt to Los Angeles in February, summed it up best.

"I thought I fell into a gold mine…because I thought there would be a team that would really die to get back into the Stanley Cup Finals," he said. "But I'm not sure the fire was there like I expected."

Series Summary
Lost to Washington 4–2

Game	Date	City	Result	Winning Goal	Winning Goalie
1	April 17	Pittsburgh	Washington 5–3	Joey Juneau	Don Beaupre
2	April 19	Pittsburgh	Pittsburgh 2–1	Rick Tocchet	Tom Barrasso
3	April 21	Washington	Washington 2–0	Joe Reekie	Don Beaupre
4	April 23	Washington	Washington 4–1	Peter Bondra	Don Beaupre
5	April 25	Pittsburgh	Pittsburgh 3–2	Jaromir Jagr	Tom Barrasso
6	April 27	Washington	Washington 6–3	Calle Johansson	Don Beaupre

Jaromir Jagr exults after scoring against Capitals goalie Byron Dafoe.

1995

Due to a prolonged impasse over the new collective bargaining agreement, the 1994–95 season was pared to 48 games per team—the shortest in the NHL since 1941–42. The abbreviated slate seemed ideally suited to the veteran Penguins, who featured nine players in their thirties.

Prior to the lockout, general manager Craig Patrick had not been idle. In the wake of his team's shocking first-round loss to Washington the previous season, he made a series of moves to bolster the team's attack. In July he swung another big trade with Los Angeles, shipping popular Rick Tocchet and a draft pick to the Kings for sniper Luc Robitaille. Patrick also re-signed high-scoring Tomas Sandstrom and inked gritty former Pen John Cullen to a contract.

The deals for additional firepower took on added significance when Mario Lemieux announced that he would sit out the season in an effort to recover from the anemia that had dogged him since his radiation treatments.

Looking every bit like a Stanley Cup contender, the remodeled Penguins bolted from the starting gate with seven consecutive wins. Following a pair of victories over the equally hot Quebec Nordiques in late February, the Pens were perched atop the Eastern Conference with a sizzling record of 14–3–2.

However, injuries soon took a toll. With Cullen (leg), Chris Joseph (shoulder), and Kevin Stevens (ankle) sidelined for extended stretches, the team's performance began to slip. Although the Pens hung on to finish second in the conference, there was ample cause for concern. During the final week of the regular season they dropped three straight games, including a 7–2 shellacking at the hands of the Capitals, their first-round playoff opponent.

Penguins vs. Capitals, Eastern Conference Quarterfinals

In many ways, the Capitals and Penguins of 1994–95 were hockey's version of the tortoise and the hare. While the jackrabbit Pens sprung from the lockout at a torrid pace, the defensive-minded Caps literally crawled out of the starting gate. By late February the Penguins had claimed first place in the conference. In the nation's capital, the local sextet had posted a miserable 3–10–5 mark to challenge the woebegone Ottawa Senators for the cellar.

Desperate to find a spark, the Capitals promoted promising young goalie Jim Carey from the Portland Pirates. With "the Mask" guarding the net, Washington's fortunes turned on a dime. While the Pens closed out the regular season at a pedestrian 15–13–1 clip, the Caps—suddenly one of the hottest teams in the league—finished on a 19–8–3 tear.

The teams stayed true to form in the series opener. Anxious to avenge their humiliating playoff defeat of the previous spring, the Penguins jumped to a quick 3–0 lead in Game 1 on goals by Len Barrie, Kevin Stevens, and Tomas Sandstrom. However, gifted young defenseman Sergei Gonchar struck early in the second period to ignite a Washington comeback. The Caps pounded four more goals past a beleaguered Ken Wregget to down the Pens 5–4.

Never one to stand pat, coach Eddie Johnston changed his line combinations for Game 2. Larry Murphy drove the puck past Carey from the high slot to stake the Penguins to another early lead. But the aggressive Capitals soon imposed their will. Thanks to goals by Sylvain Cote, Peter Bondra, and Keith Jones, they snatched a 3–1 lead heading into the first intermission.

After watching his team stumble through a dismal second period with only four shots on goal, Johnston juggled his lines again. This time he hit on a winner. Paced by two goals from Luc Robitaille and a sparkling four-assist performance by captain Ron Francis, the Pens rallied to dump the Caps 5–3.

In an effort to shore up his team's porous defense, Johnston resurrected the one-four delay for Game 3. Unfortunately, the change in strategy backfired on a grand scale. With the Penguins back on their heels, the Capitals rolled to a pair of resounding 6–2 victories.

Down 3–1 and facing elimination, the Pens appeared to be doomed. Aside from shuffling his lines and encouraging his charges to crash the net, Eddie Johnston seemed powerless to come up with any tactical solutions to aid his floundering club.

The situation worsened when the opportunistic Caps pounced to a quick two-goal lead in Game 5. Yet somehow the Penguins found a way to respond. While killing off a penalty to Rusty Fitzgerald, old pro Ron Francis spotted an opening and fed Jagr with a perfect lead pass. His long locks flying in the breeze, No. 68 streaked into the Capitals' zone and whipped a backhander past Carey.

It was as if a thunderbolt had struck the Pittsburgh bench. Energized by the sudden turn of events, the Pens battled Washington to a 5–5 standoff in regulation play.

Still displaying plenty of hop, the Capitals appeared to have the advantage in overtime. However, the Penguins would not be denied. The difference maker was the unlikeliest of heroes—Francois Leroux.

Although the towering defenseman had established himself as a fan favorite with his bone-crushing hits, he was hardly an offensive threat. Yet "Frankie" astonished everyone—including his own teammates—by lugging the puck deep into the attacking zone.

"I never, never, never dare to do that," he confided.

With the bewildered Caps frozen in place, Leroux dished a backhand pass to Robitaille, who directed the puck past Carey. As the Capitals skated dejectedly off the ice, the Penguins joyously mobbed Leroux and Robitaille.

"For a minute there, the way he beat the guy to the corner, I thought he was Mario," Robitaille quipped.

"It was funny on the bench," Jagr added. "The players screamed at him, 'Stay back. Don't go there. Just dump it.'

All of a sudden he beats this guy, passes, [Robitaille] scores the goal, and he's a big hero."

The dramatic overtime victory turned the tide of the series. Rejuvenated, the Penguins flashed their awesome firepower in Game 6. Paced by two-goal efforts from Jagr, Robitaille, and Sandstrom, the Pens crushed the Capitals 7–1 to set up a winner-take-all Game 7.

More importantly, the Penguins had broken the spirit of the Caps and their young goalie, Carey, who was yanked on two separate occasions in Game 6. They cruised to an easy 3–0 victory in the deciding game to seal their remarkable comeback.

Series Summary
Beat Washington 4–3

Game	Date	City	Result	Winning Goal	Winning Goalie
1	May 6	Pittsburgh	Washington 5–4	Sergei Gonchar	Olaf Kolzig
2	May 8	Pittsburgh	Pittsburgh 5–3	Kevin Stevens	Ken Wregget
3	May 10	Washington	Washington 6–2	Peter Bondra	Jim Carey
4	May 12	Washington	Washington 6–2	Rob Pearson	Jim Carey
5	May 14	Pittsburgh	Pittsburgh 6–5 (OT)	Luc Robitaille	Ken Wregget
6	May 16	Washington	Pittsburgh 7–1	Jaromir Jagr	Ken Wregget
7	May 18	Pittsburgh	Pittsburgh 3–0	Norm Maciver	Ken Wregget

Penguins vs. Devils, Eastern Conference Semifinals

For the second time in four years the Penguins clawed their way back from the brink to defeat Washington in an opening-round series. However, they had little time to celebrate. As the vanquished Capitals left town, the New Jersey Devils arrived for the next series.

An up-and-coming team, the Devils were on the cusp of greatness. Featuring a marvelous blend of established pros such as John MacLean, Stephane Richer, and Scott Stevens and rising young stars Martin Brodeur, Bill Guerin, and Scott Niedermayer, they had pushed the eventual Stanley Cup champion Rangers to a seventh game in the 1994 Conference Finals before succumbing.

It was a hobbled Penguins team that greeted the Devils. As the quarterfinal series slipped away, the Capitals seemed intent on extracting a pound of flesh. While Ulf Samuelsson was nursing badly bruised ribs, Kjell Samuelsson had his mouth and chin rearranged to the tune of 60 stitches, courtesy of a vicious high stick from Michal Pivonka. Rugged Chris Tamer was out as well with a fractured ankle. The Pens plugged the gaps with green youngsters Drake Berehowsky, Ian Moran, and old warhorse Peter Taglianetti.

Unlike the Caps series, which was played at a fast and furious pace, Game 1 unfolded slowly. Richer opened the scoring at 11:39 of the first period to stake the visitors to an early lead. The Pens knotted the score midway through the second period when Francis gathered in a crisp cross-ice feed from Norm Maciver and drove the puck past Brodeur from the right face-off circle.

The Pens mob Francois Leroux after he sets up the Game 5 winner against the Caps.

As the game clock ticked down to the final minute of play, the contest appeared to be headed to overtime. However, Larry Murphy sprung Robitaille loose with a beautiful pass. "Lucky Luc" sliced in front of the net and flipped a backhander past Brodeur for his second game-winning goal of the postseason.

"I was a little lucky to be there," Robitaille said. "I tried to roof it, and the goalie brought his glove up and knocked it in. Sometimes you need a little luck."

Buoyed by their last-minute victory, the Pens came out aggressively in Game 2. On the opening shift, Leroux lumbered down the slot and fired a sizzling shot that rang off the right goal post. Unfortunately, Frankie's near miss set the tone for his snake-bitten teammates. Sharpshooters Francis and Robitaille each banged shots off the pipes. Troy Murray flubbed a pass from Joe Mullen and failed to muster a shot on a rare two-on-none break.

The Devils were having just as much trouble lighting the lamp. With Wregget stranded far from his cage, Valeri Zelepukin somehow missed a wide-open net. However, Claude Lemieux finally found the range at 7:39 of the third period to give New Jersey a 2–1 lead.

With the Devils employing the neutral-zone trap to perfection, the Pens had little chance for a comeback. However, with just over a minute remaining, Jagr struck for a goal that seemed to epitomize a strange night of hockey.

Following an extended shift, No. 68 was skating to the bench when he found the puck on his stick. On a night when even the most prolific scorers couldn't buy a goal, Jagr flipped a harmless backhander to the net that deflected off Tommy Albelin's skate and past Brodeur.

Eschewing their good fortune, the Penguins promptly handed the game back to the Devils. On the ensuing rush, Scott Stevens churned over the blue line and ripped off a shot that Wregget stopped but failed to control. As the Pens' defense parted like the Red Sea during the Exodus, Stevens gathered in the rebound and buried the puck behind Wregget.

"That shouldn't happen," a frustrated Kevin Stevens said. "We shouldn't give up a goal, especially when we play 59 minutes of pretty tight hockey."

The Penguins never recovered from their Game 2 meltdown. Following a dismal 5–1 loss in Game 3, they were systematically swept aside in five games.

New Jersey would go on to capture its first Stanley Cup. For the fading former champions, the future was filled with question marks.

Series Summary
Lost to New Jersey 4–1

Game	Date	City	Result	Winning Goal	Winning Goalie
1	May 20	Pittsburgh	Pittsburgh 3–2	Luc Robitaille	Ken Wregget
2	May 22	Pittsburgh	New Jersey 4–2	Scott Stevens	Martin Brodeur
3	May 24	New Jersey	New Jersey 5–1	Bobby Holik	Martin Brodeur
4	May 26	New Jersey	New Jersey 2–1 (OT)	Neal Broten	Martin Brodeur
5	May 28	Pittsburgh	New Jersey 4–1	Claude Lemieux	Martin Brodeur

1996

Following the disappointing playoff loss to the Devils in 1995, general manager Craig Patrick decided it was time for a fresh start. Old pros John Cullen, Joe Mullen, and Kjell Samuelsson were released over the summer. Seeking to pare his burgeoning payroll while adding new blood, Patrick swung three major trades. He sent future Hall of Famer Larry Murphy to Toronto for Dmitri Mironov. Boston natives Shawn McEachern and Kevin Stevens went to the Bruins in exchange for Glen Murray and Bryan Smolinski. In perhaps the most shocking deal of all, Luc Robitaille and Ulf Samuelsson were peddled to the Rangers for Petr Nedved and Sergei Zubov.

However, the most important addition was not a new face but an old one. After a one-year absence, a hale and hardy Mario Lemieux returned to the Penguins' lineup with fire in his eyes. Playing as if he'd never missed a game, No. 66 piled up 69 goals and 161 points.

The team responded remarkably well to the changes. While Mario captured his fifth scoring title, Ron Francis (119 points), Jaromir Jagr (62 goals), and Nedved (45 goals) enjoyed banner years. The Penguins rolled to a 102-point season—the third-highest total in franchise history—to win the Northeast Division crown.

Unfortunately, Craig Patrick went to the well once too often. In what is universally hailed as one of the worst hockey trades of all time, he dealt promising young winger Markus Naslund to Vancouver for Alek Stojanov.

Penguins vs. Capitals, Eastern Conference Quarterfinals

For the fourth time in five years the Penguins opened the playoffs against Washington. Normally a nettlesome foe, the Capitals entered the series with a burgeoning injury list that included key role players Keith Jones and Steve Konowalchuk and top defensemen Calle Johansson and Joe

The dynamic duo—Ron Francis and Jaromir Jagr—celebrate a goal.

Pens assistant Bryan Trottier and Capitals coach Jim Schoenfeld go nose to nose.

Reekie. The Caps appeared to be no match for their power-ful hosts, who had won 32 of 41 regular-season games at the Civic Arena.

Determined to get the jump on the hobbled Capitals, the Penguins picked up right where they'd left off the previous spring. By the three-minute mark of the opening period, Petr Nedved had beaten Caps goalie Jim Carey twice from the left hash mark. Following second-period tallies by Ron Francis and Tomas Sandstrom, Washington coach Jim Schoenfeld pulled Carey in favor of Olaf Kolzig.

It was as if someone had thrown an invisible switch. After playing almost perfect hockey for 30 minutes, the Pens fell into complete disarray. Holding an impromptu clinic on the finer points of blowing a lead, they leaked for five straight goals en route to a disgraceful 6–4 loss.

"We made a lot of dumb mistakes," coach Eddie Johnston said. "And they outworked us."

Mortified by his team's tepid performance, Johnston cracked the whip and drove the Penguins through their most

grueling practice of the season. The boot-camp session had the desired effect. Displaying much more fire and intensity in Game 2, the Pens snatched another two-goal first-period lead.

Once again, they were unable to make it stand up. Unheralded Pat Peake banged in two goals from the doorstep to knot the score. Although Jaromir Jagr briefly restored the Pens' one-goal edge early in the third period, the Caps tacked on three more goals to grab a 2–0 series lead.

With the Penguins one loss away from almost certain elimination, Johnston shuffled his lineup. He benched Dave McLlwain in favor of husky Joe Dziedzic and gave rugged Dave Roche a more prominent role. Johnston also granted a reprieve to veteran defender Neil Wilkinson, who was glued to the bench in Game 2.

In the Capitals' camp, Schoenfeld made one big change. He replaced Kolzig, who'd done a superb job in relief, with his ace Jim Carey.

The temptation to go with Carey was understandable. A tower of strength during the regular season, he posted a sparkling 2.26 goals-against average and nine shutouts to capture the Vezina Trophy. Once again, however, the Penguins made Schoenfeld pay dearly for his decision.

While the Capitals made a concerted effort to rally around their goalie, he was clearly struggling. Sensing Carey's vulnerability, the Pens strafed the shaky netminder for four goals, including a pair by Glen Murray, to take a commanding 4–0 lead into the third period. Although the Caps dominated the shot total 17–1 over the final 20 minutes, they could only nick Tom Barrasso for a single goal.

The Pens finally proved they could play a full 60 minutes of playoff-style hockey. Little did they realize that more—much more—would be required to win the pivotal fourth game.

Sparked by Mario Lemieux, who enjoyed a break-out four-assist performance in Game 3, the Pens opened Game 4 with confidence. However, Kolzig was back in the Washington net, and he was razor-sharp to boot. Inspired by the rangy goalie's superb play, the Capitals snatched a quick 2–0 lead.

Meanwhile, the Penguins received what appeared to be an ill-timed dose of misfortune when Barrasso was forced from the game with back spasms. Ken Wregget, who hadn't played since a dismal 6–2 loss to the Islanders on April 10, was thrust into the spotlight. Widely regarded as the best backup goalie in the league, Wregget had a penchant for coming up big in playoff competition. This game would prove to be no exception.

However, adversity soon struck again. Following a Jaromir Jagr goal that pared the Capitals' lead in half, Lemieux became embroiled in a fight with Todd Krygier. Although the feisty Caps winger had instigated the skirmish with a punch to the head, Mario drew a five-minute major and a game misconduct.

Faced with the daunting task of playing without their captain and leader, the Penguins rose to the occasion. Ron Francis and Sergei Zubov led an inspired penalty-killing effort. When Michal Pivonka drew a needless roughing penalty at 6:17 the Pens made him pay. With seconds remaining on the man advantage, Nedved wristed the puck past Kolzig from the right-wing circle to send the game into overtime.

The Pens had enjoyed the better of the play since the midway point of the game. But in overtime, the well-conditioned Caps dominated the action. At 13:17, Stefan Ustorf uncorked a scorching wrist shot from point-blank range, but Wregget made a spectacular glove save to rob his adversary of a sure goal.

Late in the second overtime, referee Dan Marouelli invoked an obscure rule to award the Caps a penalty shot. Joey Juneau bore down on Wregget at breakneck speed, but the bad ice hampered his stickhandling. His shot trickled harmlessly into the Pens' goalie.

The game soon lurched into a third overtime period, and then a fourth. The Capitals threw everything but the proverbial kitchen sink at Wregget, but the veteran netminder stood firm. Finally, with less than a minute remaining in the fourth overtime, Nedved launched a routine shot from the left face-off circle that slithered through a maze of players and past Kolzig. The Penguins had won the third-longest game in NHL history to date.

Frustrated by the marathon loss and another imminent collapse, Washington was out for blood in Game 5. During the late stages of a 4–1 Pens triumph, Craig Berube and Dale Hunter chased down and pummeled peacenik defenseman Sergei Zubov.

On the next shift, Pens tough guy Alek Stojanov pounced on big Mark Tinordi, and the tension spilled over to the benches. His frustration boiling into rage, Schoenfeld raced to the Plexiglas partition separating the benches and screamed at Eddie Johnston. He was quickly confronted by assistant coach Bryan Trottier.

"I was very upset with what I thought was Eddie's obvious attack on Mark Tinordi," a calmer Schoenfeld said in the aftermath.

"You think Berube was in there to score goals?" Johnston steamed in response. "If he's going to go after our top guy, he's going to have to answer the bell with his top guys."

Braced for another physical encounter in Game 6, the Pens clobbered the clearly spent Capitals 7–3. In the waning moments Johnston was struck on the head by an errant shot, opening up a 10-stitch gash. Bloodied but unbowed, the plucky old coach refused to leave the bench.

"I'll take one on the head every night if we win," he said.

Series Summary
Beat Washington 4–2

Game	Date	City	Result	Winning Goal	Winning Goalie
1	April 17	Pittsburgh	Washington 6–4	Sergei Gonchar	Olaf Kolzig
2	April 19	Pittsburgh	Washington 5–3	Peter Bondra	Olaf Kolzig
3	April 22	Washington	Pittsburgh 4–1	Glen Murray	Tom Barrasso
4	April 24	Washington	Pittsburgh 3–2 (4 OT)	Petr Nedved	Ken Wregget
5	April 26	Pittsburgh	Pittsburgh 4–1	Francois Leroux	Ken Wregget
6	April 28	Washington	Pittsburgh 3–2	Ron Francis	Ken Wregget

Penguins vs. Rangers, Eastern Conference Semifinals

The Penguins' triumph over the Capitals earned them a matchup with another hated foe from the old Patrick Division, the New York Rangers. Loaded with stars such as Mark Messier, Brian Leetch, and Mike Richter, the Rangers were a tough, veteran team. Following a strong second-place finish in the Atlantic Division, they easily defeated the Montreal Canadiens in the opening round to advance to the semifinals.

There were few rivalries more bitter than the Penguins and the Rangers. The seeds were sown a decade earlier following a high-sticking incident between then-Rangers defenseman David Shaw and Pens superstar Mario Lemieux. Adam Graves' infamous slash on Mario and the Rangers' subsequent ouster in the 1992 playoffs only served to intensify the bad blood.

Yet the mortal enemies also shared a strong connection. Penguins general manager Craig Patrick had served in the same capacity with the Rangers. The teams had cross-pollinated the previous summer, with Luc Robitaille and Ulf Samuelsson joining the Blueshirts while Petr Nedved and Sergei Zubov donned the black and gold. The Rangers were coached by former Pens defenseman Colin "Soupy" Campbell.

Campbell wasted little time in fanning the flames. During a radio interview prior to the series, he openly questioned the Penguins' machismo, calling them "soft" and "crybabies."

The Pens did their best to avoid a war of words. When informed of Campbell's caustic comments, Jaromir Jagr laughed and said, "He's probably talking about me."

Despite the hype, the teams took some time to get untracked in Game 1. Following a scoreless opening frame, the contest heated up in the second period. Jagr opened the scoring when he beat Richter with a wicked snap shot from the right-wing circle. Suitably inspired, the Pens carried the play to the Rangers for the next several minutes. However, rookie Niklas Sundstrom soon evened the score from a goal-mouth scramble. The Pens quickly recovered, as Jagr notched his second goal of the period.

The visitors weren't going down without a fight. Feisty Pat Verbeek scored on a wraparound, and Messier tipped in a Leetch blast from the point to give the Rangers their first lead of the night. Showing plenty of mettle, the Penguins bounced right back. Husky Dave Roche beat Richter with a nifty backhander to even the score. With the game clock winding down, Jagr slipped around Bruce Driver and head-manned the puck to Lemieux, who tapped it past Richter for the game winner.

With the momentum firmly in their favor, the Pens had a golden opportunity to put the Rangers in a hole in Game 2. Inexplicably, they came out flat. While the Penguins appeared to be out for a leisurely Sunday afternoon skate, the Rangers turned on the jets. Powered by goals from big guns Alexei Kovalev, Messier, and Robitaille, the Blueshirts walloped the punchless Pens 6–3 to even the series.

"You can't play 10 or 12 minutes of a hockey game," Eddie Johnston lamented. "Our intensity level was not there, and it should be. There's no excuse for that."

Dismayed by his team's lack of effort, Johnston made sweeping changes. Glen Murray and late-season acquisition Kevin Miller weren't meshing with Lemieux, so the veteran coach teamed his superstar center with Jagr and Tomas Sandstrom. The second line featured Francis centering for Nedved and Murray, while Miller joined Smolinski and Stojanov on the third unit.

EJ's deck-shuffling tactics worked to perfection. Campbell's strategy was based on shadowing Jagr with Ulf Samuelsson, while Messier and Leetch went head-to-head with Lemieux. By moving Jagr to Mario's line, Johnston forced Campbell to choose between shadowing Jagr with Leetch, a much smaller man, or splitting up his top two offensive players to maintain the Samuelsson-Jagr matchup.

Much to Messier's chagrin, his coach chose the second option. Playing without his favorite setup man, the Rangers' captain endured a subpar series the rest of the way.

While the bewildered Campbell struggled to match lines, the Penguins dominated the opening period of Game 3. Following a quick tally by Sandstrom, Mario scored twice to propel the Pens to a 3–0 lead.

Once again the Penguins had grave difficulty protecting a lead. Led by Messier, who plastered Joe Dziedzic into the boards, the host Rangers took a more physical approach to begin the second period. Within minutes they stuck for a pair of rapid-fire goals by tough guy Shane Churla and Sundstrom to close the gap.

Fortunately for the Pens, Ken Wregget was at the top of his game. Displaying extraordinary coolness under fire, he blunted every Rangers thrust to preserve a 3–2 victory.

After the game, New York's frustration boiled over. Campbell openly accused the Penguins of diving to draw penalties.

"Nedved, one whack and he goes down like he'll be out a couple of games," Campbell fumed. "Leroux dives like he's in tremendous pain every time he gets checked. He died when Churla hit him [today], he died when Churla hit him the game before that, he's died several times during the playoffs."

The Rangers stubbornly stuck with their physical game plan in Game 4. Leading the way was Messier, who whacked any Penguin who had the temerity to cross his path. While the Blueshirts persisted in their attempts at intimidation, the Pens' stars made better use of their sticks. Jagr, Nedved, Murray, and Lemieux each scored to pace a crisp 4–1 victory.

Down 3–1, the Rangers had played their last card. Playing before a packed house at the Civic Arena, Lemieux and Jagr each scored a hat trick as the Penguins thrashed the Rangers 7–3 to advance to the Conference Finals. All told, the dynamic duo accounted for a whopping 15 of the team's 21 goals during the series.

Unfortunately, the Penguins had suffered a crippling blow. Old pro Ron Francis, so vital to the team's success, would miss the remainder of the playoffs with a broken foot.

Series Summary
Beat New York Rangers 4–1

Game	Date	City	Result	Winning Goal	Winning Goalie
1	May 3	Pittsburgh	Pittsburgh 4–3	Mario Lemieux	Ken Wregget
2	May 5	Pittsburgh	NY Rangers 6–3	Mark Messier	Mike Richter
3	May 7	New York	Pittsburgh 3–2	Tomas Sandstrom	Ken Wregget
4	May 9	New York	Pittsburgh 4–1	Petr Nedved	Ken Wregget
5	May 11	Pittsburgh	Pittsburgh 7–3	Jaromir Jagr	Ken Wregget

Penguins vs. Panthers, Eastern Conference Finals

Everyone in the hockey world anticipated a Penguins-Flyers matchup in the Eastern Conference Finals—with the notable exception of the Florida Panthers. Backed by veteran goalie John Vanbiesbrouck, the gritty Panthers pulled off a shocking upset by whipping Eric Lindros and the powerful Flyers in six games.

Privately, the Penguins felt they had dodged a bullet. Although the Panthers possessed a handful of capable scorers, including Ray Sheppard and Scott Mellanby, they were largely a collection of greenhorn youngsters and grizzled veterans cast off from other teams. However, Florida would prove to be a more-than-worthy adversary. The Panthers' stock in trade was the neutral-zone trap, and they employed it better than any team in the league.

The series opened on May 18 before a sellout crowd at the Civic Arena. Despite Florida's reputation for stingy defensive play, the Penguins had a surprising number of good

Tom Barrasso gives up a goal during the 1996 Eastern Conference Finals.

scoring chances. Lemieux nearly struck for the opening goal a minute into the contest, but Vanbiesbrouck made a big save.

The Panthers soon regained their composure. With their checkers sticking to the Penguins like glue, they coasted to an easy 5–1 victory.

Never one to stand pat, Eddie Johnston pulled a shocker by starting Tom Barrasso in Game 2. Had it not been for the sterling play of Wregget the Penguins would've long since traded in their hockey sticks for golf clubs.

But Johnston had sound reasons for making the switch. He believed Barrasso's superior puck-handling skills would diffuse the Panthers' relentless forecheck, while serving to jump-start the Pens' sagging transition game.

Johnston's judgment proved to be spot-on. Backed by Barrasso's 30-save performance and timely scoring from Sergei Zubov, Jaromir Jagr, and Mario Lemieux, the Pens won 3–2 to even the series.

"Barrasso made the big saves when he had to," Johnston said.

Following their strong effort, the Penguins felt good about their chances. However, Games 3 and 4 would be contested in the unfriendly confines of the Miami Arena. The Florida fans had developed a highly unusual ritual of tossing plastic rats onto the ice when the Panthers scored—a craze that started when Mellanby one-timed a real rat to its death before the season opener. It was estimated that as many as 800 fake rodents were flung to the ice to celebrate each Panthers goal.

To counteract the effects of the vermin-crazed crowd the Penguins wore their third uniform—affectionately known as the "third bird." The team was undefeated in 11 games wearing the lucky uniforms, including five road playoff victories.

Unfortunately, the magical powers soon wore off. After grabbing a 2–1 lead on goals by Bryan Smolinski and Nedved, the Pens were little more than disinterested spectators. The hustling Panthers pounded Barrasso with 61 shots to turn a nail-biter into a 5–2 rout.

The Panthers continued their onslaught in Game 4. They strafed the Pens net through the early going and hammered the visitors with hard bodychecks.

Somehow, the Penguins refused to fold. After weathering the early storm, they gradually regained control. Early in the third period Brad Lauer punched a Nedved rebound past Vanbiesbrouck to knot the score at 1–1. Then big No. 66 took over. In a play that was vintage Lemieux, he used his speed to drive three Florida defenders back on their net. Cutting across the slot, Mario unleashed a soft wrist shot that popped off Vanbiesbrouck and onto the waiting stick of Smolinski, who fired the puck home.

"We knew that we couldn't lose this game," Tomas Sandstrom said. "That it was going to be tough to be down 3–1 against those guys."

Brimming with confidence following their big win, the Penguins gave by far their best performance of the series in Game 5. Noting that the Panthers' forwards were skating deep into their own zone to help with the defensive chores, Johnston instructed his players to move the puck out to the blue line. The plan worked to perfection. With plenty of room to make plays, Pens defensemen J.J. Daigneault and Sergei Zubov keyed a crisp 3–0 victory.

Although Lemieux struggled to solve Vanbiesbrouck, his defensive work was never more brilliant. Displaying an acumen boarding on the clairvoyant, Mario intercepted passes with stunning frequency. It was as if he had suddenly become a trusted member of the Florida team and the puck was going to him by design.

The comeback was nearly complete. A lone victory separated the Penguins from a return to the Stanley Cup Finals. However, the team that opened Game 6 was a decidedly different bunch than the one that had performed so effectively in Game 5. Almost by reflex they fell back and allowed Florida to carry the play. The upstart Panthers prevailed 4–3 to force a seventh game.

Intent on gaining a physical edge in the series finale, Eddie Johnston gave musclemen Joe Dziedzic, Dave Roche, and Alek Stojanov plenty of ice time in the early going.

Meanwhile, the Panthers continued to employ their smothering, defense-first style. Their diligence was soon rewarded. Veteran Mike Hough took a pass from Robert Svehla on a two-on-one break and drove the puck past Barrasso.

Midway through the second period the momentum began to shift when Barrasso made a sensational save to thwart a breakaway attempt by Bill Lindsay. Old-school referee Don Koharski—whose hands-off approach favored the clutch-and-grab Panthers—banished the Panthers' Gord Murphy to the penalty box. Nedved ended the Pens' scoring drought when he blew the game-tying goal by Vanbiesbrouck.

The revival was fleeting. With 14 minutes remaining, Tom Fitzgerald gained the Pens' blue line and cut loose an ordinary slap shot before chasing off for a line change.

While Fitzgerald's shot may have been ordinary, the results were anything but. The puck glanced off the stick of defenseman Neil Wilkinson and fluttered under Barrasso's blocker pad.

The Penguins rallied around their goalie, but the hockey gods had decided on the Panthers. They tacked on a late insurance goal to dash the Pens' Stanley Cup hopes.

"There was just no room out there," a dejected Lemieux observed. "I said after the last game that's the best team defense I've ever played against. If you beat one guy, there were two more guys in your face."

Series Summary
Lost to Florida 4–3

Game	Date	City	Result	Winning Goal	Winning Goalie
1	May 18	Pittsburgh	Florida 5–1	Tom Fitzgerald	J. Vanbiesbrouck
2	May 20	Pittsburgh	Pittsburgh 3–2	Mario Lemieux	Tom Barrasso
3	May 24	Miami	Florida 5–2	Stu Barnes	J. Vanbiesbrouck
4	May 26	Miami	Pittsburgh 2–1	Bryan Smolinski	Tom Barrasso
5	May 28	Pittsburgh	Pittsburgh 3–0	J.J. Daigneault	Tom Barrasso
6	May 30	Miami	Florida 4–3	Rob Niedermayer	J. Vanbiesbrouck
7	June 1	Pittsburgh	Florida 3–1	Tom Fitzgerald	J. Vanbiesbrouck

1997

The 1996–97 Penguins were a huge team—by far the biggest and heaviest in franchise history. Operating under the premise that size mattered, the club opened the season with no fewer than 11 players who tipped the scales at 220 pounds or more, including Shawn Antoski, Stefan Bergkvist, Joe Dziedzic, Kevin Hatcher, Jaromir Jagr, Mario Lemieux, Francois Leroux, Dmitri Mironov, Glen Murray, Dave Roche, and Alek Stojanov.

But bigger wasn't necessarily better. After the lead-footed Pens plodded to a ghastly 2–9 start, general manager Craig Patrick retooled his heavyweight squad. A trio of savvy trades with Anaheim, Florida, and the New York Islanders added comparative lightweights Stu Barnes, Alex Hicks, Andreas Johansson, Darius Kasparaitis, Fredrik Olausson, and Jason Woolley to the mix, along with a key missing ingredient—speed.

The recast Penguins promptly went on a 28–9–5 tear to vault back into the playoff picture. During the hot streak, rookie goalie Patrick Lalime set an NHL record by starting his career with a 16-game unbeaten streak.

Heading into the final two months of the regular season, the Pens appeared to be in good shape. But a dreadful 8–18–3 finish cast a shadow over the team's midseason performance.

Penguins vs. Flyers, Eastern Conference Quarterfinals

The Penguins matchup with the Flyers in the 1997 Eastern Conference Quarterfinals was a definitive case of two teams heading in opposite directions.

Just one short year after reaching the Conference Finals, the Penguins were in a state of flux. The team had sputtered through a wildly inconsistent regular season, leading to the dismissal of long-time coach Eddie Johnston. Fewer than half of the players remained from the squad that had come within a victory of reaching the Stanley Cup Finals. To make matters worse, rumors swirled that the team's iconic star, Mario Lemieux, planned to retire following the playoffs.

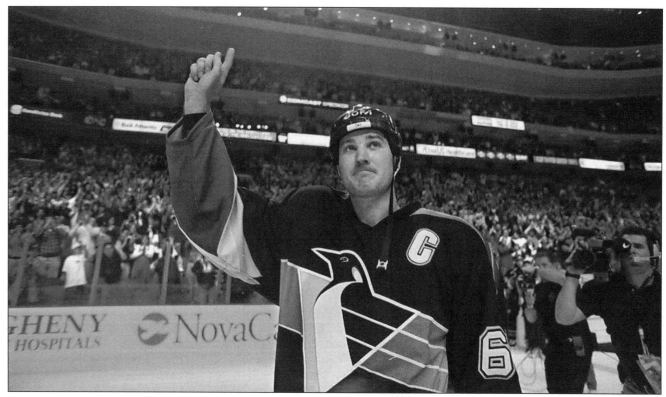

Mario Lemieux leaves the ice after his final game. "Super Mario" would make a triumphant return in 2000.

The Flyers, on the other hand, were a team on the rise. Powered by bruising young star Eric Lindros and his "Legion of Doom" linemates, John LeClair and Mikael Renberg, Philly had rolled to a 103-point season.

Pittsburgh fans who were hoping for a miracle playoff run to cap Mario's career were in for a huge letdown. In the series opener, the hungry young Flyers dominated every phase of the game and squashed the listless Penguins 5–1.

Determined to atone for their poor performance, the Pens rebounded with a strong effort in Game 2. Lemieux struck for the opening goal midway through the first period. Thanks to the solid work of goalie Ken Wregget, the lead stood until the three-minute mark of the final period, when Joel Otto knotted the score for the Flyers.

Jaromir Jagr responded with a tally just over a minute later to provide the Pens with a glimmer of hope. But the Flyers immediately tied the score on a goal by LeClair at 5:52. Eight minutes later grinder Trent Klatt swatted the game winner past a fading Wregget.

The Penguins tried to regroup before their hometown faithful in Game 3. Taking advantage of Philly's overly aggressive play, Jagr staked his team to an early lead with a pair of power-play goals. Undaunted, the hard-charging Flyers hammered home three second-period goals to pound the Pens into submission.

Down 3–0, the Penguins were all but finished. Remarkably, they dug down deep and produced a gem of an effort to stave off elimination. Hoping to shake things up, coach Craig Patrick sent his checking line of Joe Dziedzic, Alex Hicks, and Ian Moran over the boards to open Game 4. The light-scoring Moran surprised everyone, including himself, by beating Flyers goalie Garth Snow a minute into the contest.

A scant 36 seconds later Shjon Podein evened the score. However, on this evening the Pens would not be denied. Knowing that Mario was, in all likelihood, playing his final game at the Civic Arena, they pressed the Flyers with a furious attack. Just past the 13-minute mark, Ed Olczyk blew the puck past Snow for a shorthanded goal. Five minutes later, Petr Nedved struck for a second shorthanded tally.

The stage was set for the grand finale. With barely a minute left to play and the crowd chanting "Mario, Mario," No. 66 scooped up a loose puck and raced toward the Flyers' net.

"I got a lucky bounce at the blue line," Mario said afterward. "I went in all alone and got my favorite move, which is to come across and try to open [Snow] up. Which he did. I went five hole."

The red light flashed and the Civic Arena faithful exploded with emotion. As he had done so many times throughout his storied career, Mario had served up one last bit of magic.

Fittingly, he was named the No. 1 star. When his name was announced Lemieux returned to the ice for an extended skate. He waved and blew kisses and cried while the fans showered him with a thunderous outpouring of love and appreciation.

For all intents the series ended that night. Emotionally drained, the Penguins somehow managed to grab a 2–1 lead midway through the first period of Game 5, thanks to Mario's third goal of the series. But Rod Brind'Amour struck for two shorthanded goals while killing a penalty to Petr Svoboda. The Penguins were finished.

During the traditional post-series handshake a weary Mario draped an arm around the massive Lindros and offered him encouragement.

"It's your time," he whispered. "Go out and win the Cup."

The torch had been passed to a new generation. Staying true to his word, Mario retired following the series.

Series Summary
Lost to Philadelphia 4–1

Game	Date	City	Result	Winning Goal	Winning Goalie
1	April 17	Philadelphia	Philadelphia 5–1	John LeClair	Garth Snow
2	April 19	Philadelphia	Philadelphia 3–2	Trent Klatt	Garth Snow
3	April 21	Pittsburgh	Philadelphia 5–3	John LeClair	Garth Snow
4	April 23	Pittsburgh	Pittsburgh 4–1	Ed Olczyk	Ken Wregget
5	April 26	Philadelphia	Philadelphia 6–3	John LeClair	Garth Snow

1998

The 1997–98 season marked the beginning of a new era in Penguins hockey. For the past decade the Pens had been one of the NHL's most explosive offensive clubs. However, the team's reigning superstar, Mario Lemieux, had hung up his skates following the 1997 playoffs.

Faced with an ever-shrinking pool of elite talent and serious budget constraints, general manager Craig Patrick embraced a totally new philosophy in order to keep the team competitive. Seeking to emulate the success of tight-checking teams like New Jersey, he hired defensive-minded coach Kevin Constantine, who had worked wonders for the undermanned San Jose Sharks.

Patrick also did some of his finest work over the off-season. Mining the marketplace for undervalued talent, he acquired defenseman Jiri Slegr for a third-round pick and signed free agents Rob Brown, Robert Lang, and Martin Straka to bargain-basement contacts.

Despite the dearth of marquee players, the team adapted well to Constantine's highly structured system. The result was a solid first-place finish in the Northeast Division.

Remarkably, the heretofore freewheeling Pens allowed the fourth-fewest number of goals in the league.

Penguins vs. Canadiens, Eastern Conference Quarterfinals

The Penguins seemed set for a long playoff run. Following a worrisome 1–5–4 slide down the stretch, they righted the ship with three straight wins to enter the postseason on a hot streak. However, there was a fly in the ointment. The club relied heavily—perhaps too heavily—on the trio of Jaromir Jagr, Ron Francis, and Stu Barnes to generate offense.

By contrast, their first-round playoff opponent, the Montreal Canadiens, featured a balanced attack spearheaded by former Penguin Mark Recchi and 20-goal men Shayne Corson, Martin Rucinsky, and Brian Savage. Montreal also possessed a big, mobile defensive corps that combined toughness and skill. The Habs would prove to be a formidable opponent.

Montreal's rookie coach, Alain Vigneault, made a surprising goaltender shuffle, starting veteran Andy Moog in place of Jocelyn Thibault in Game 1. The move worked like a charm. With the 38-year-old Moog turning aside 33 shots, the Canadiens nipped the Pens in the series opener on Benoit Brunet's overtime goal.

Although stunned by the series-opening loss, the Penguins rebounded with a strong effort in Game 2. The turning point occurred midway through the second period when the Habs'

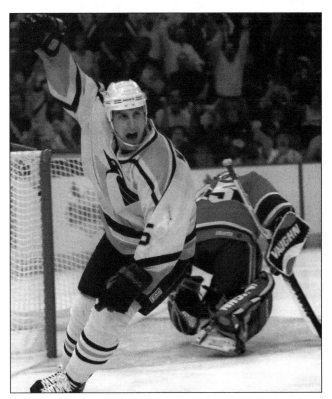
Brad Werenka celebrates a goal against Andy Moog.

enigmatic defenseman, Vladimir Malakhov, inadvertently shot the puck into his own net to hand the Pens a 2–1 lead.

Sensing a shift in the momentum, Constantine dispatched his checking line of Robbie Brown, Alex Hicks, and Sean Pronger to turn up the heat. With the Civic Arena crowd chanting "Rob-bie, Rob-bie," Brown hurled his 185-pound frame at everyone wearing *les bleu, blanc, et rouge*. Although bloodied in a collision with Vincent Damphousse, "Brownie" had given his team a badly needed shot of adrenalin.

"It's a new role for me," the former 49-goal scorer said afterward. "It's just nice the fans appreciate the hard work."

Suitably inspired, the Penguins tacked on a pair of third-period goals to dump the Habs 4–1.

Games 3 and 4 were played in Montreal's sparkling new arena, the Molson Centre. Skating before a hockey-mad crowd of more than 21,000, the Canadiens came out hitting. Shrugging off the persistent attention of hulking defenseman Peter Popovic, Jaromir Jagr struck for his first goal of the series to stake his team to an early lead. However, the home-standing Canadiens gradually took control. Limiting the Pens to only 22 shots, they coasted to a 3–1 win.

The Penguins' dormant offense sprang to life in Game 4. Fueled by power-play goals from Brown, Jagr, and Kevin Hatcher and shorthanded tallies by Ed Olczyk and Martin Straka, they shelled Montreal 6–3 to even the series at 2–2.

With the venue shifting back to Pittsburgh, the Penguins appeared to be in the driver's seat. They had finally cracked Moog, who was yanked from the net in Game 4 after allowing five goals on nine shots. Physical defenseman Stephane Quintal and scoring winger Brian Savage would sit out Game 5 due to injuries. The peppery Brunet was hobbled as well.

However, it was the banged-up Canadiens who pressed the attack from the opening draw. Patrice Brisebois beat Tom Barrasso midway through the game to break a score-less tie, followed in rapid succession by tallies from Corson and Recchi. The Pens fought back to make a game of it on goals by Straka and Jagr. But with one minute to play, Damphousse scored to salt the game away.

Playing with their backs to the wall was nothing new for the Penguins. However, this time they weren't able to respond. Making good use of his Pterodactyl-like wing-span, Popovic engulfed Jagr every time he touched the puck in Game 6. Once again, Moog outdueled Barrasso. The Canadiens closed out the series with a strong 3–0 victory.

Series Summary

Lost to Montreal 4–2

Game	Date	City	Result	Winning Goal	Winning Goalie
1	April 23	Pittsburgh	Montreal 3–2 (OT)	Benoit Brunet	Andy Moog
2	April 25	Pittsburgh	Pittsburgh 4–1	Stu Barnes	Tom Barrasso
3	April 27	Montreal	Montreal 3–1	Shayne Corson	Andy Moog
4	April 29	Montreal	Pittsburgh 6–3	Ed Olczyk	Tom Barrasso
5	May 1	Pittsburgh	Montreal 5–2	Mark Recchi	Andy Moog
6	May 3	Montreal	Montreal 3–0	Mark Recchi	Andy Moog

1999

The summer of 1998 would prove to be an especially trying time for the Penguins. Ron Francis, one of the most respected and beloved players ever to wear the black and gold, departed through free agency, stripping the team of one of its few remaining stars. Petr Nedved entered the second year of his prolonged holdout, with no hope for a resolution in sight.

On the eve of the season came the third, most devastating blow. With debts exceeding $100 million, owners Howard Baldwin and Roger Marino filed for bankruptcy under Chapter 11. The NHL considered shutting down the Penguins for a season in order for Baldwin and Marino to get the team's finances under control.

Faced with a mountain of adversity, the players had every reason to fold up the tent. Yet they responded by pulling together. On November 25, Craig Patrick boosted the team's morale—and its playoff aspirations—by dealing Nedved to the Rangers for supremely gifted winger Alexei Kovalev.

The Pens responded with a strong surge through the dog days of January and February, including winning streaks of six and 10 games. Paced by strong performances from scoring champ Jaromir Jagr and emerging stars Kovalev, Robert Lang, and Martin Straka, the Penguins placed third in the tough Atlantic Division.

Penguins vs. Devils, Eastern Conference Quarterfinals

By virtue of their eighth-place finish in the conference, the Penguins were pitted against the powerful New Jersey Devils in the opening-round series.

It was truly a David vs. Goliath matchup—one that Constantine clearly relished. Indeed, the defending Stanley Cup champions seemed to hold all the high cards. While New Jersey lacked a game breaker, coach Robbie Ftorek had four solid lines at his disposal, including flashy Petr Sykora and rugged centers Jason Arnott and Bobby Holik.

On defense the Devils combined the speed and artistry of Scott Niedermayer with the old-school, body-banging approach of Scott Stevens and Ken Daneyko. Martin Brodeur was widely acclaimed as the best goaltender east of Colorado great Patrick Roy.

In Game 1, everything went according to form. The Devils clogged the neutral zone, muscled the smaller Penguins around, and produced a solid 3–1 victory on home ice.

However, there was a loose thread. Under Ftorek, the Devils employed a more wide-open style that at times left their slow-footed defense exposed. Utilizing his team's greatest asset—speed—Constantine devised a plan to exploit the Devils' weakness.

Unfortunately, the Penguins would have to battle back without their best player. Jaromir Jagr had suffered a groin injury and would miss the next four games.

Minus their captain and scoring leader, the Pens turned in a gem of an effort. Executing Constantine's swift-skating, close-checking system to a T, they stunned the heavily favored Devils 4–1. Just as the Penguins coach had envisioned, his speedy forwards outmaneuvered and frustrated New Jersey's lumbering blue-liners while forcing them into turnovers.

Watching from the press box, Jagr had nothing but praise for his teammates.

"They played excellent," he said. "Everybody did whatever the coach told them to do."

Playing before a packed house at the Civic Arena, the Pens once again got the jump on New Jersey in Game 3. At 5:52 of the opening frame, Martin Straka rifled a slap shot past Brodeur from the high slot. However, the Devils soon regained their composure. Sergei Brylin evened the score with a power-play goal at 12:51. The hulking Arnott struck late in the second period to give the visitors their first lead since Game 2.

Entering the final period, the Penguins faced an uphill climb. The Devils were virtually unbeatable—37-3-4—when they held a lead after two periods. But the Pens shocked their powerful adversary by scoring a pair of quick goals to retake the lead.

Ian Moran gathered up the puck from the opening draw and sent a "Murphy flip" high in the air toward the Devils' zone. German Titov corralled the loose puck as it tumbled to the ice and fired off a quick shot. Brodeur made the initial save, but the puck bounded out to Straka, who beat the All-Star goalie with a 10-footer.

Twenty-seven seconds later Alexei Kovalev gathered in a pass from Jan Hrdina and blew a wicked shot past Brodeur. Straka applied the finishing stroke in the final minute of play

The "Energizer Bunny," Martin Straka, finishes off the Devils.

Planet of the Apes

Like all athletes, hockey players will go to great lengths to gain a psychological edge over an adversary. This is especially true during the pressure-packed Stanley Cup Playoffs when the intensity level is high and tempers boil over.

A particularly brutal exchange took place between Penguins agitator Matthew Barnaby and Devils defenseman Lyle Odelein during the spring of 1999.

Barnaby fired the opening salvo when he claimed Odelein bore more than a passing resemblance to a simian character from the movie *Planet of the Apes*.

"Look at him," Barnaby chuckled. "Seriously. He looks like Cornelius."

Hardly at a loss for words, Odelein offered up a stinging retort.

"I don't know what he's yapping about," the rugged rearguard snapped. "He should take a look at his wife. She's god-awful to look at."

As gunslingers used to say in the Wild West, "Them's fightin' words." Antagonists in one of hockey's most famous feuds, Barnaby and Odelein dropped the mitts with each other nine times during their respective careers.

when he stripped the puck from Niedermayer and backhanded the puck into an empty net for his first playoff hat trick.

Incredibly, the Penguins had the mighty Devils on the run. However, during the warm-ups prior to Game 4, agitator Matthew Barnaby foolishly provided fodder for New Jersey when he engaged several players in some not-so-friendly banter and tussling.

Barnaby's ill-conceived antics awakened a sleeping giant. Their competitive fires stoked to a white-hot edge, the Devils outshot the Pens 39–18 and rolled to a convincing 4–2 victory to even the series.

Game 5 featured more of the same. Paced by a two-goal effort from rugged Randy McKay and the brilliant goaltending of Brodeur, New Jersey bested the Pens 4–3 to reclaim the series lead.

Suddenly, the Pens were the ones in dire straits. With his team facing a do-or-die Game 6, Jagr decided to suit up, balky groin and all. The sight of No. 68 skating out for the pregame warm-ups electrified his teammates and the Civic Arena faithful.

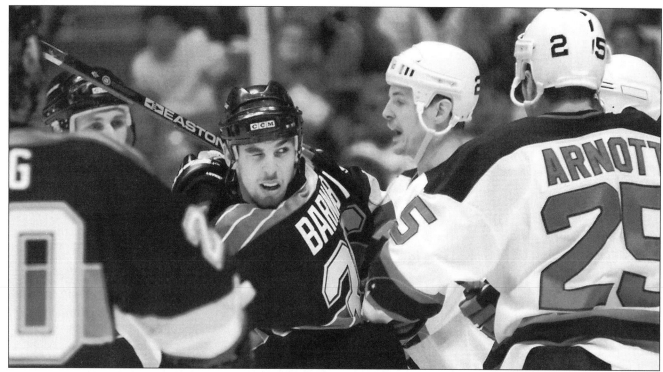

The eye of the storm—Pens agitator Matthew Barnaby.

"The energy he brought to the team—the energy he brought to the entire night—we were able to feed off that," Rob Brown said. "It was just an incredible feeling."

Although his skating clearly was impeded—Jagr estimated he played at "about 60 percent"—he was good enough to provide some late-game heroics. With his team trailing by a goal late in the third period, the NHL scoring champ stuffed a Titov pass behind Brodeur to send the game into overtime.

Nine minutes into the extra frame, "Jags" struck again. The big winger swatted a cross-ice feed from Straka past Brodeur to preserve the Pens' playoff hopes.

"I'm so excited," Jagr said afterward. "But I don't want to get overexcited. We still have a long way to go."

Indeed, the Penguins still had to beat New Jersey in the unfriendly confines of the Continental Airlines Arena to take the series. With their playoff lives on the line, the Devils made a concerted effort to take Jagr out of the game. Midway through the first period, the rough-hewn Daneyko hammered the Pens' winger with a brutal check. Clearly hobbled, Jagr only saw about 10 minutes of ice time the rest of the way. Much to his credit, he picked up two huge assists.

Inspired by their teammate's courageous effort, the Penguins picked up the slack. Barrasso served up some magic from the Stanley Cup years and outdueled Brodeur, who yielded an unsightly four goals on only 13 shots. Titov, Kovalev, and Hrdina scored to stake the Pens to a 3–2

third-period lead. Once again Straka supplied the knock-out punch, scoring with six minutes remaining to seal the victory and earn the Devils' respect.

"I didn't know [Straka] was this good," Brad Bombardir said. "You know, this is a guy who's gone through quite a few teams, and you wonder how that happened. He's real quick, especially in the neutral zone. He seems to have a lot of confidence in himself."

Series Summary
Beat New Jersey 4–3

Game	Date	City	Result	Winning Goal	Winning Goalie
1	April 22	New Jersey	New Jersey 3–1	Petr Sykora	Martin Brodeur
2	April 24	New Jersey	Pittsburgh 4–1	Greg Andrusak	Tom Barrasso
3	April 25	Pittsburgh	Pittsburgh 4–2	Alexei Kovalev	Tom Barrasso
4	April 27	Pittsburgh	New Jersey 4–2	Sergei Brylin	Martin Brodeur
5	April 30	New Jersey	New Jersey 4–3	Randy McKay	Martin Brodeur
6	May 2	Pittsburgh	Pittsburgh 3–2 (OT)	Jaromir Jagr	Tom Barrasso
7	May 4	New Jersey	Pittsburgh 4–2	Jan Hrdina	Tom Barrasso

Penguins vs. Maple Leafs, Eastern Conference Semifinals

Fresh off their pulsating conquest of New Jersey, the Penguins prepared to meet the equally tough Toronto Maple Leafs in an Eastern Conference Semifinals tilt. It was the first time the teams had hooked up in postseason play since 1977.

In many ways, the Maple Leafs resembled the Devils. Led by noted "Penguin killer" Mats Sundin, former Islanders thorns Derek King and Steve Thomas, and 37-goal scorer Sergei Berezin, Toronto featured a deep and balanced attack. They, too, boasted a top-flight goalie in Curtis Joseph. Unlike New Jersey, however, the Leafs possessed a mobile, puck-moving defense spearheaded by Bryan Berard, Sylvain Cote, and Dmitry Yushkevich.

The upstart Penguins stole Game 1 before a packed house at the Air Canada Centre. Bit player Dan Kesa, getting a rare opportunity to skate on the power play, beat Joseph with a bullet from the left hash mark midway through the first period.

"I had a lot of time," Kesa explained. "I just teed it up. I saw [Joseph] was down so I tried to go high. I just shot as hard as I could."

Backed by Barrasso's rock-solid goaltending, the Pens made the lead stand up until German Titov popped in an empty netter in the final minute of play.

The Maple Leafs evened the series in Game 2 thanks to some strong production from an unexpected source. Toronto coach Pat Quinn made a surprise move when he inserted Lonny Bohonos, a 25-year-old career minor leaguer, into the left-wing slot beside Sundin.

"I didn't even know I was playing until after the pregame warm-ups," Bohonos said. "And then I went out there and found out I was playing with Mats. It's just unbelievable."

The speedy winger scored the opening goal and picked up two assists to earn the game's No. 3 star. Sundin had a monster game as well, notching two goals and two assists.

"Sundin's a great player," noted Pens defenseman Kevin Hatcher. "There certainly was some pressure on him this evening to put some points up, and he had a big night. We can't be giving him three- and four-point nights and expect to win."

Game 3 was a classic playoff dogfight. Following a scoreless first period at the Mellon Arena, the teams erupted for five second-period goals, including three within a span of 39 seconds.

Down by a goal entering the final frame, the Pens once again displayed some moxie. Working with a man advantage, Jagr one-timed a feed from Rob Brown past a startled Joseph at 9:03 to knot the score. Less than two minutes later, Jiri Slegr ripped his first goal of the postseason past Joseph to cap a hard-earned 4–3 victory.

Heroes included Tom Barrasso, who made 29 saves in a sparkling performance, and Brown, who collected three assists to earn the game's No. 2 star.

Poised to take control of the series, the Penguins jumped out to an early lead in Game 4 on a goal by Jagr. But once again Bohonos wrecked their plans. Early in the second period the unheralded winger set up Sundin for the tying goal. At 5:28 of the third he beat Barrasso to give the Leafs the lead. Although Brad Werenka knotted the score minutes later, Toronto prevailed on an overtime tally by Berezin.

With the series now up for grabs, the Leafs decided it was time for some old-time hockey. Harkening back to original owner Conn Smythe's famous mantra—"If you can't beat 'em in the alley, you can't beat 'em on the ice"—the Leafs dominated the Penguins physically. Like bulls in a china shop, they set picks, worked the boards with a vengeance, and knocked the Pens on their collective wallets. The result was a crisp 4–1 victory.

Down but not out, Pittsburgh rebounded with a strong effort to start Game 6. Brown scored the opening goal on the power play at 5:04. Alexei Kovalev padded the Pens' lead with his first tally of the series at 14:06.

However, the Leafs would not be denied. Once again, it was their role players who paved the way to victory. Bohonos and grinder Garry Valk, a former Pen, struck for a pair of bang-bang goals to open the second frame. Early in overtime, Valk slammed home a Berezin rebound to send the Penguins packing.

"They were better, more lucky in crucial situations," a glum Jagr said.

Still, coach Kevin Constantine was justifiably proud of his troops. Making a reference to the team's disastrous financial situation, he said, "They refused to ever latch on to a real, legitimate excuse because they wanted to win a Stanley Cup. Bad."

Series Summary
Lost to Toronto 4–2

Game	Date	City	Result	Winning Goal	Winning Goalie
1	May 7	Toronto	Pittsburgh 2–0	Dan Kesa	Tom Barrasso
2	May 9	Toronto	Toronto 4–2	Mats Sundin	Curtis Joseph
3	May 11	Pittsburgh	Pittsburgh 4–3	Jiri Slegr	Tom Barrasso
4	May 13	Pittsburgh	Toronto 3–2 (OT)	Sergei Berezin	Curtis Joseph
5	May 15	Toronto	Toronto 4–1	Mike Johnson	Curtis Joseph
6	May 17	Pittsburgh	Toronto 4–3 (OT)	Garry Valk	Curtis Joseph

2000

The 1999–2000 campaign would prove to be one of the most trying and yet rewarding seasons of the decade. In September, Mario Lemieux purchased the team out of bankruptcy, ending the parsimonious reign of unpopular owner Roger Marino. Fresh from a solid showing in the playoffs the previous spring, the Penguins appeared to be set to challenge for the Atlantic Division title.

While not as talent laden as the Stanley Cup champions of the early 1990s, the Pens still were a dangerous club. Along with three-time Art Ross Trophy winner Jaromir Jagr, the team boasted accomplished players such as Alexei Kovalev, Robert Lang, and Martin Straka.

However, it was apparent from the drop of the first puck that all was not well. Over the first two months of the season the Pens grew progressively stale and lifeless. In particular, the team's top players had grave difficulty conforming to coach Kevin Constantine's rigid system.

With the club teetering on the verge of collapse, general manager Craig Patrick replaced Constantine with his old friend and mentor Herb Brooks. The architect of Team USA's stunning gold-medal triumph in the 1980 Olympics, Brooks immediately removed the restraining bolts and gave his players more leeway.

Bolstered by trade-deadline acquisitions Bob Boughner, Rene Corbet, Janne Laukkanen, and Ron Tugnutt, the team responded with a strong second half to earn its 10th consecutive playoff berth.

Penguins vs. Capitals, Eastern Conference Quarterfinals

For the fifth time in nine seasons the Penguins opened the Stanley Cup Playoffs against the Washington Capitals. The Pens had been prohibitive favorites in prior matchups between the bitter rivals. However, this time around the Caps appeared to hold a decided edge. Led by behemoth power forward Chris Simon and fellow stars Peter Bondra, Sergei Gonchar, and Adam Oates, Washington had rolled up 102 points—14 more than the Pens—and cruised to the Southeast Division crown. They seemed a cinch to win the series.

It came as an absolute shock when the Penguins steamrolled the Capitals 7–0 in the series opener. They were so superior in all aspects of the game that the home-standing Caps resembled a team of rash minor leaguers.

"They're a good, solid team," Matthew Barnaby said afterward. "We had all guns going, and things were working for us. And pucks were going in the net."

Shaking off their deplorable performance in the opener, the Caps responded with a strong effort in Game 2. Employing their close-checking style to perfection, they snatched the lead on a power-play goal by the sharpshooting Bondra.

Thanks to the stellar play of goalie Ron Tugnutt, who turned aside 37 shots, the Penguins hung tough. Midway through the second period they evened the score on a goal by Jan Hrdina. Following a scoreless third, the game went into overtime.

Five minutes into the extra frame, Jaromir Jagr gathered up the puck just above the Caps' right-wing circle and cocked his stick to shoot. Following the action from the Penguins' net some 200 feet away, Tugnutt recalled thinking, "Why is he shooting from there?"

Why, indeed. The puck jumped off of Jagr's blade and found the tiniest of openings over goalie Olaf Kolzig's left shoulder on the short side for the game winner.

The complexion changed only slightly in Game 3. Determined to claw their way back into the series, the Caps once again drew first blood on a goal by Simon. But it was a night for the Penguins' unsung heroes to shine. Fourth-line winger Pat Falloon scored his only goal of the playoffs to stake his team to a second-period lead. The quiet, unassuming Hrdina potted two goals and assisted on Jiri Slegr's third-period tally to key a 4–3 Pens triumph.

Washington managed to stave off an embarrassing sweep by dumping the Penguins in Game 4. However, cagey Herb Brooks had prepared his charges beautifully. Sparked by the sensational play of Jagr, Hrdina, and Tugnutt, the Pens finished off the Caps with a thrilling 2–1 victory in Game 5.

Tugnutt, in particular, played brilliantly. The unheralded netminder stopped 152 of 160 shots to earn the praise of his teammates.

"He made some great saves," Barnaby said. "Definitely some I didn't know he could make under pressure. He definitely proved he can do it."

Series Summary
Beat Washington 4–1

Game	Date	City	Result	Winning Goal	Winning Goalie
1	April 13	Washington	Pittsburgh 7–0	Janne Laukkanen	Ron Tugnutt
2	April 15	Pittsburgh	Pittsburgh 2–1 (OT)	Jaromir Jagr	Ron Tugnutt
3	April 17	Pittsburgh	Pittsburgh 4–3	Jiri Slegr	Ron Tugnutt
4	April 19	Washington	Washington 3–2	Jeff Halpern	Olaf Kolzig
5	April 21	Washington	Pittsburgh 2–1	Jaromir Jagr	Ron Tugnutt

Penguins vs. Flyers, Eastern Conference Semifinals

Having disposed of Washington with relative ease, the Penguins were faced with an even more formidable adversary—the Atlantic Division champion Flyers. As always, Philly was armed and dangerous. Leading their attack were ex-Pen Mark Recchi and bruising 40-goal man John LeClair. Physically, the Flyers were far superior, bristling with bangers such as Rick Tocchet, Keith Primeau, and Luke Richardson.

But once more, the plucky Penguins got the jump on a heavily favored opponent. With Tugnutt literally standing on his head they swept the first two games in Philadelphia by scores of 2–0 and 4–1.

"It's phenomenal," Bob Boughner said. "It's almost like he knows he's going to do that before he gets out on the ice."

"It's not just me," Tugnutt said modestly. "We're playing well as a team. We really are."

Exasperated by the Pens' shocking dominance, Flyers coach Craig Ramsay dispatched a hit squad of Craig Berube, Daymond Langkow, Richardson, and Tocchet late in Game 2 to square off against Barnaby, Boughner, Tyler Wright, and Rene Corbet. On the ensuing face-off, Tocchet ignored the puck and jumped Wright to spark a wild four-on-four brawl. The lone noncombatants—Janne Laukkanen and Andy Delmore—had ringside seats as the Flyers dominated the fisticuffs.

Although the red-hot Penguins were hardly intimidated, the donnybrook seemed to throw them off their game while serving to inspire the down-but-not-out Flyers. A sage, if simple, bit of advice from Ramsay also helped. Prior to Game 3 he told his charges, "Hit the net. Miss Tugnutt."

Bob Boughner and Ron Tugnutt battle the Flyers' John LeClair for position in second-round action.

Following their coach's instructions to the letter the Flyers outshot the Pens 44–18 and turned in a dominant performance. They jumped to a two-goal first-period lead on tallies by Keith Jones and defenseman Andy Delmore, who would play a key role in the series.

Although badly outplayed, the Penguins responded in the second period. Jaromir Jagr cashed in on the opening shift, and Martin Straka knotted the score at 10:23. LeClair and Jagr exchanged goals in the third period to send the game into overtime. At the 11-minute mark of the extra frame, Delmore beat Tugnutt a second time to seal a victory for Philly.

Game 4 would prove to be the turning point. Following a hotly contested 60 minutes of action, the game was tied 1–1. Locked in a titanic death struggle, the teams lurched through a first overtime, then a second, then a third, then a fourth.

As his stars ran out of gas, Herb Brooks turned to his fourth line of Rob Brown, Pat Falloon, and Ian Moran. While the energetic trio produced a number of good scoring chances, they couldn't beat Flyers goalie Brian Boucher.

Finally, after 152 minutes of hockey, Keith Primeau ended the game with a great individual effort. The big center swooped down the right side of the Penguins' zone and made a sudden stop-start move to freeze defenseman Darius Kasparaitis. Switching the puck from his backhand to his forehand, he fired a wicked shot high inside the right post to beat Tugnutt.

"We gave our best," Kasparaitis said. "We competed so hard. This is hockey; somebody has to lose. Unfortunately, it was our team."

"We feel good about ourselves," Tugnutt said, trying to remain upbeat. "The series is still up for grabs."

The Flyers knew better.

"After a big game like that, it's not easy," Langkow said. "I think the momentum's going to carry over to Game 5."

The Philly forward proved to be prescient. Twenty-three seconds into Game 5, he beat Tugnutt to stake the Flyers to the lead. Delmore followed up with the first of his three goals and the Flyers never looked back. Sparked by Delmore's hat trick and a five-point night from Mark Recchi, Philly chased an exhausted Tugnutt and pounded the Penguins 6–3.

Ron Tugnutt makes another key save. The unheralded goalie posted a stunning 1.77 goals-against average during the 2000 playoffs.

Despite the unfortunate turn of events, the Pens still had some fight left. Forty-eight seconds into Game 6, Boughner laid out Primeau with a crushing shoulder check. The sight of their teammate being carted off the ice on a stretcher only strengthened the Flyers' resolve. Recchi and LeClair provided the offense as Philly closed out the hard-fought series with a 2–1 victory.

Afterward, an emotional Herb Brooks struggled to sum up his feelings.

"I really liked our hockey club," he said. "In my heart of hearts, I felt like we could've gone a long way."

The Flyers were duly impressed with their in-state rivals.

"That's a good hockey team over there," Eric Desjardins said. "A lot of great players."

"They worked hard," Recchi added. "We had to earn it."

Series Summary
Lost to Philadelphia 4–2

Game	Date	City	Result	Winning Goal	Winning Goalie
1	April 27	Philadelphia	Pittsburgh 2–0	Jaromir Jagr	Ron Tugnutt
2	April 29	Philadelphia	Pittsburgh 4–1	Jaromir Jagr	Ron Tugnutt
3	May 2	Pittsburgh	Philadelphia 4–3 (OT)	Andy Delmore	Brian Boucher
4	May 4	Pittsburgh	Philadelphia 2–1 (5 OT)	Keith Primeau	Brian Boucher
5	May 7	Philadelphia	Philadelphia 6–3	Mark Recchi	Brian Boucher
6	May 9	Pittsburgh	Philadelphia 2–1	John LeClair	Brian Boucher

2001

Despite the heart-wrenching loss to the Flyers the previous spring, the Penguins had the look of a contender. However, two huge question marks hovered over the team as it prepared to start the new season.

The first was in goal. Ron Tugnutt, the hero of the 2000 playoffs, had signed a lucrative free-agent deal with the expansion Columbus Blue Jackets. He would be replaced between the pipes by the tandem of veteran Garth Snow and talented but erratic youngster Jean-Sebastien Aubin.

The second was behind the bench. Herb Brooks, who'd done a wonderful job of leading the team to a strong finish in 1999–00, was replaced by Ivan Hlinka. While the Czech coaching legend possessed a keen hockey mind, he did not speak fluent English. It remained to be seen whether he was capable of guiding an NHL team.

Fortunately, there was a huge surprise in store for the Penguins and their fans. In mid-December, owner Mario Lemieux announced that he would resume his playing career following a three-and-a-half-year absence. On the evening of December 27, arguably the greatest player in the history of the game made his triumphant return. Thirty-three seconds into his first shift Mario set up Jaromir Jagr for the game's opening goal to the thunderous applause of the Mellon Arena faithful.

Mario's return was no nostalgia trip. Displaying remarkably little rust from his prolonged layoff, he scored an astonishing 35 goals and 76 points in 43 games. Inspired by their boss' play, the Penguins powered through a solid second half to place third in the Atlantic Division.

Penguins vs. Capitals, Eastern Conference Quarterfinals

In what had become a seemingly annual rite of spring, the Penguins faced off against Washington in the opening round of the playoffs. Once again, the Capitals had captured the Southeast Division title, courtesy of a solid 96-point campaign.

While the Caps did not possess the firepower of the Pens, they still featured a bevy of top-flight players, including NHL assist leader Adam Oates, 45-goal scorer Peter Bondra, and puck-moving defenseman Sergei Gonchar. Typically, Washington's lineup was sprinkled with gritty, two-way performers such as Jeff Halpern and Steve Konowalchuk.

From the opening face-off, it was clear Caps coach Ron Wilson planned to shadow Mario Lemieux with one of his checkers. The strategy worked to perfection in Game 1. With Halpern sticking to Mario like glue, the Caps limited the Pens to just 16 shots en route to a 1–0 victory.

"Every second they put someone against him," lamented Pens coach Ivan Hlinka.

Noting the Capitals' slavish dedication to team defense, Pens veteran defenseman Marc Bergevin exhorted his teammates for a similar commitment in Game 2. The result was a defensive masterpiece.

Kevin Stevens opened the scoring with a power-play goal at 7:13 of the first period—his first postseason tally since 1995. "Artie" had a little help from his friend, Mario Lemieux, who banked the puck off the big winger.

"It hit me in the hands, I think," Stevens recalled. "I really don't know…. The best thing about that was I didn't have to shoot it."

The Caps knotted the score two minutes later on a power-play marker by Bondra, courtesy of an ill-timed charging penalty by the Pens' big enforcer, Krzysztof Oliwa. But Lemieux struck late in the period off a pretty feed by Jaromir Jagr, and the Pens never looked back. Taking a page from their opponent, they shut down the Capitals' attack for the final 40 minutes to even the series.

"I had my doubts that we could play like this as a team," Bergevin said. "We played a flawless game."

With the series shifting to Mellon Arena for Game 3, the Penguins continued to carry the play to their foe. Once again Stevens opened the scoring, this time with an unassisted goal. Alexei Kovalev and Jan Hrdina tacked on a pair of third-period tallies, and the Pens whitewashed the Caps 3–0 to grab the series lead.

The No. 1 star of the game was the Pens' 27-year-old rookie netminder, Johan Hedberg. "Moose" stopped 34 shots to earn the praise of his teammates.

"He's just coming up with huge saves," defenseman Bob Boughner said. "It's playoff hockey, and he's just coming up huge."

Heading into Game 4, the Penguins appeared to be firmly in control. However, the gritty Capitals responded with an inspired effort to even the series at 2–2. Taking advantage of the Pens' sloppy, undisciplined play, the Caps pounded three power-play goals past the previously unbeatable Hedberg. Although the home team responded with two power-play markers of their own to send the game into overtime, Washington prevailed on Halpern's game winner.

The game left a sour taste in Ivan Hlinka's mouth.

"Games like that you have to play with discipline, concentrate on the game," he said.

The series was now up for grabs. With the venue shifting back to the MCI Center for Game 5, the Penguins needed to regain their focus in a hurry. Fortunately they turned in another superb defensive effort.

Light-scoring Pens defenseman Andrew Ference drew first blood at 6:35, followed in rapid succession by a Lemieux tally 30 seconds later. It was all the offense the Penguins would need. Once again Hedberg was at the top of his game, turning aside 21 of 22 shots to seal the victory.

Determined to put the Capitals away in Game 6, the Pens once again got the jump on their foe. At 7:21 of the opening frame, Mario eluded defenseman Calle Johansson and tossed a backhander past goalie Olaf Kolzig. Robert Lang

scored for his first goal of the playoffs two minutes later to stake the Pens to a two-goal lead.

However, the Capitals weren't through. Brendan Witt struck at the 14-minute mark of the second period to pare the Pens' lead in half. Jeff Halpern knotted the score with a power-play goal at 17:28.

It appeared the teams would skate into the intermission with the score tied 2–2. However, the overly aggressive Capitals drew a pair of penalties in the closing minutes of the period to hand the Pens a five-on-three power play. With one tick left on the scoreboard clock, Kovalev hammered a slap shot past Kolzig from the top of the left face-off circle.

Despite their misfortune, the Caps still weren't finished. With less than three minutes remaining in the game, Johansson beat Hedberg to send the game into overtime.

The Mellon Arena faithful were treated to a delicious finish. Following 13 minutes of riveting back-and-forth action, Martin Straka stole the puck from Gonchar and broke in alone on Kolzig.

"The guys told me…he was going down on every shot, and he's a big guy, so you should try to go up high if you have a chance," Straka recalled.

The rites of spring. Mario Lemieux celebrates a goal against the Caps.

Heeding his teammates' advice, the little center snapped the puck over Kolzig's right shoulder to clinch the series for the Pens.

Series Summary
Beat Washington 4–2

Game	Date	City	Result	Winning Goal	Winning Goalie
1	April 12	Washington	Washington 1–0	Peter Bondra	Olaf Kolzig
2	April 14	Washington	Pittsburgh 2–1	Mario Lemieux	Johan Hedberg
3	April 16	Pittsburgh	Pittsburgh 3–0	Kevin Stevens	Johan Hedberg
4	April 18	Pittsburgh	Washington 4–3 (OT)	Jeff Halpern	Olaf Kolzig
5	April 21	Washington	Pittsburgh 2–1	Mario Lemieux	Johan Hedberg
6	April 23	Pittsburgh	Pittsburgh 4–3 (OT)	Martin Straka	Johan Hedberg

Penguins vs. Sabres, Eastern Conference Semifinals

The Penguins' scintillating conquest of the Capitals set up an Eastern Conference Semifinals matchup with the Buffalo Sabres. It marked the second time the teams had squared off in postseason play. Twenty-two years earlier the Pens had vanquished the Sabres in a best-of-three Preliminary Round series.

Buffalo would prove to be a most worthy opponent. Armed with game-breakers Donald Audette and Miroslav Satan, the Sabres had finished a strong second in the Northeast Division. Buffalo's strength was its depth. Coach Lindy Ruff could roll out four solid lines. Virtually every player at his disposal was a scoring threat. Backstopping this tough, speedy team was Jennings Trophy winner Dominik Hasek.

Much of the Sabres' preseries preparation was devoted to studying video of Johan Hedberg—with good reason. The rookie goalie was brilliant against the Capitals, stopping 151 of 161 shots to post a stunning 93.8 save percentage.

"We showed where we think we can go on him," Ruff said. "There are probably six or seven minutes [on video] of what his tendencies are."

It didn't help. In the series opener Hedberg gave another flawless performance, turning aside 25 shots to backstop the Penguins to a 3–0 victory. Two nights later he stoned the Sabres again, stopping 21 of 22 shots to propel his team to a two-game sweep in Buffalo.

Thanks to their rookie sensation, the Penguins appeared to be in complete command as the series shifted to Pittsburgh for Game 3. But the hustling Sabres were determined to fight back.

Following another game-opening goal by Stevens, Buffalo took charge. Curtis Brown knotted the score for the Sabres midway through the second period. Ex-Pen Jason Woolley scored the go-ahead goal at 9:51 of the third. Woolley earned the game's No. 1 star as the Sabres prevailed 4–1.

The Penguins were hardly pleased with their effort.

"We didn't deserve [to win]," Ference said. "And everybody knows it."

The Pens received a boost when Jaromir Jagr, who missed the previous two contests with a shoulder injury, returned to the lineup for Game 4. However, Jagr's presence was nullified by the performance of another former Pen, Stu Barnes. The peppery little center struck for two goals and an assist as the Sabres stuffed the Penguins 5–2.

Once again, the home team served up a stinker of an effort, launching only 17 shots on Hasek.

"We blew a great chance to take command of the series," Bob Boughner lamented. "We can't seem to put 60 [good minutes] together now."

To make matters worse, the Sabres appeared to solve the Hedberg riddle.

"One thing we noticed about Hedberg is that he squares up to the shooter extremely well," Lindy Ruff explained. "If we were going to score we had to put him in situations where he had to scramble."

Determined to regain control in Game 5, the Penguins pounced to a two-goal lead on tallies by Jagr and Aleksey Morozov. But the Pens seemed to wear down as the game progressed while the Sabres gathered momentum. Chris Gratton scored on the power play midway through the second period. The ubiquitous Brown struck for a shorthanded goal at 11:16 of the final period to send the game into overtime. Eight minutes into the extra frame, Barnes burned his former team again to put the Sabres up 3–2.

The Penguins seemed to have few answers for the Sabres' sudden dominance. Hlinka's stubborn insistence on using only three lines had left his team vulnerable to Buffalo's superior speed and depth. Following a shaky start to the series, Hasek had the Sabres' net sealed off tighter than a

Andrew Ference leaps into Mario's arms after scoring the winning goal in Game 2 against Buffalo.

maximum-security prison. Another disappointing playoff exit appeared imminent.

Fighting for their playoff lives before a packed house at the Mellon Arena, the Penguins trailed the Sabres 2–1 late in Game 6. With 93 seconds remaining on the game clock, Hlinka pulled Hedberg for an extra attacker. During the ensuing sequence Kovalev fired off a shot that hit Curtis Brown's stick and popped high into the air. As if guided by providence the "Immaculate Deflection" landed in the slot—directly in front of Mario Lemieux. Wasting no time, Mario jammed the puck past Hasek to stave off elimination.

Midway through the overtime period Martin Straka directed a nifty pass from Kovalev past a shaken Hasek. The Pens were very much alive.

They had one more hill to climb—a climactic seventh-game showdown in Buffalo. Once again the Sabres forged a 2–1 third-period lead, only to watch the Penguins rally on a late goal by Robert Lang to force overtime.

Thirteen minutes into the extra stanza an unlikely hero stepped forward with a flourish. Darius Kasparaitis—known more for his crunching checks than for his offense—gathered in a perfect pass from Lang and rifled a crackling shot past Hasek. Overcome with joy, "Kaspar" flung himself to the ice in a headlong slide as his delirious teammates piled on.

"I was going to pass it," the rugged defender gushed, "but I said, 'I've got to shoot the puck.' I shot the puck, and I saw it going in. I still can't believe I scored a goal."

Neither could Kevin Stevens. "I haven't seen Kaspar score a goal in practice, never mind in a game," he quipped.

But score he did. The Pens were on their way to the Eastern Conference Finals for the first time since 1996.

Series Summary
Beat Buffalo 4–3

Game	Date	City	Result	Winning Goal	Winning Goalie
1	April 26	Buffalo	Pittsburgh 3–0	Mario Lemieux	Johan Hedberg
2	April 28	Buffalo	Pittsburgh 3–1	Andrew Ference	Johan Hedberg
3	April 30	Pittsburgh	Buffalo 4–1	Jason Woolley	Dominik Hasek
4	May 2	Pittsburgh	Buffalo 5–2	Stu Barnes	Dominik Hasek
5	May 5	Buffalo	Buffalo 3–2 (OT)	Stu Barnes	Dominik Hasek
6	May 8	Pittsburgh	Pittsburgh 3–2 (OT)	Martin Straka	Johan Hedberg
7	May 10	Buffalo	Pittsburgh 3–2 (OT)	Darius Kasparaitis	Johan Hedberg

Penguins vs. Devils, Eastern Conference Finals

Following their electrifying triumph over the Sabres, the Penguins had less than 48 hours to prepare for an all-too-familiar and formidable foe—the New Jersey Devils. Under the guidance of coach Larry Robinson, the Devils had cruised to a 111-point season while easily capturing first place in the Atlantic Division.

Remarkably, the Pens had fared well against New Jersey during the regular season, compiling a 3–1–1 record against

A happy Darius Kasparaitis shows off a souvenir, courtesy of his series-winning goal against the Sabres.

the division champs. They also boasted a secret weapon of sorts. Although somewhat of an underachiever, Russian right wing Aleksey Morozov turned into a latter-day version of Rocket Richard whenever he faced New Jersey.

Mighty mite Martin Straka opened the scoring in Game 1 with a nifty power-play goal. However, it soon was apparent that the Penguins didn't have their legs. Drained from their rousing victory over the Sabres, the Pens fell to the Devils 3–1.

"Obviously it was a very emotional series against Buffalo," Lemieux said afterward. "To win in overtime and not get much rest in the last day or so, I think it showed in the third period."

Coach Ivan Hlinka immediately juggled his lines. He reunited the Kovalev-Lang-Straka trio that had torn up the league during the regular season. Morozov and Josef Beranek joined Lemieux, while slumping Jaromir Jagr moved alongside Czech-mates Jan Hrdina and Milan Kraft. Rene Corbet, Wayne Primeau, and Kevin Stevens filled out the fourth line.

The Pens responded with a strong effort in Game 2. The turning point came midway through the second period. While killing a penalty with his team down 2–0, Mario picked off an errant pass and fed the puck to Morozov. "The Devil Killer" swooped to the net and jammed the puck past Martin Brodeur.

In rapid-fire succession, Corbet and Kovalev beat the All-Star goalie to stake the Penguins to the lead. Lang applied the finishing touch five minutes into the final frame to seal a 4–2 victory.

With the series shifting to the friendly confines of the Mellon Arena for games 3 and 4, the Pens appeared to be in good shape. But the Devils had other ideas. Playing with their trademark machine-like precision, they dominated the next three contests to take the series.

Mario Lemieux was clearly impressed.

"That's the perfect model to compete for the Stanley Cup," he said. "They play four lines and are committed to a great system."

For the Penguins, the playoff loss to the Devils marked the end of an era. Although no one realized it at the time, the team's two greatest stars—Lemieux and Jagr—had each played their final playoff game in the black and gold.

Series Summary
Lost to New Jersey 4–1

Game	Date	City	Result	Winning Goal	Winning Goalie
1	May 12	New Jersey	New Jersey 3–1	Petr Sykora	Martin Brodeur
2	May 15	New Jersey	Pittsburgh 4–2	Rene Corbet	Johan Hedberg
3	May 17	Pittsburgh	New Jersey 3–0	Brian Rafalski	Martin Brodeur
4	May 19	Pittsburgh	New Jersey 5–0	Patrik Elias	Martin Brodeur
5	May 22	New Jersey	New Jersey 4–2	Jason Arnott	Martin Brodeur

2007

After missing the postseason four years in a row, the Penguins were finally ready to contend for a playoff spot in 2006–07… and then some. Bolstered by the addition of rookie centers Evgeni Malkin and 18-year-old Jordan Staal to a talented young core that featured former first-round picks Colby Armstrong, Sidney Crosby, Marc-Andre Fleury, Brooks Orpik, and Ryan Whitney, the Pens were the surprise team of the NHL.

Young gun Jordan Staal and grizzled veteran Gary Roberts celebrate. Staal scored three goals in a losing effort against Ottawa.

Following a so-so first half, the club caught fire in January and reeled off a 16-game unbeaten streak to vault into the thick of the playoff race. At the trade deadline, first-year general manager Ray Shero added some leadership and muscle to the mix when he acquired rugged 40-year-old winger Gary Roberts and NHL heavyweight champ Georges Laraque.

Paced by the sterling play of Crosby, who captured the Art Ross and Hart Trophies, and strong seasons from Malkin, Staal, and veteran Sergei Gonchar, the Cinderella Pens registered a stunning 47-point improvement en route to a second-place finish in the Atlantic Division.

Penguins vs. Senators, Eastern Conference Quarterfinals

The Penguins opened their first playoff series in six years against the Ottawa Senators. Although the Senators had matched the Pens' impressive point total, it looked like a favorable matchup for Pittsburgh. The Pens had won three out of the four regular-season meetings between the clubs and appeared to enjoy a psychological edge.

However, the Senators were no pushover. Boasting the likes of Daniel Alfredsson, Dany Heatley, and Jason Spezza, they were a deep and powerful team. In the series opener they schooled their callow opponent in the finer points of playoff hockey. Taking dead aim at the Pens' weak underbelly—an undermanned defense—the battle-hardened Senators pressured them into a series of costly mistakes. After piling up a five-goal lead, they coasted to an easy 6–3 victory.

The Penguins were clearly in awe.

"That's the quickest team I've faced since I turned pro," Brooks Orpik said.

"They came out and played their best game," Mark Recchi added. "And we didn't play a very good game."

Determined to avenge their poor showing in the series opener, the Pens responded with some fire of their own in Game 2. They grabbed the lead on a goal by Ryan Whitney while matching the physical Senators check for check.

But once more Ottawa seized control. Dominating the Penguins on the shot clock, they rallied to take a 2–1 lead after two periods.

The Penguins were desperately in need of a spark. And in the final period, 40-year-old Gary Roberts stepped forward to deliver it. Playing his customary take-no-prisoners style, he barged into the slot and banged the puck past Senators goalie Ray Emery to knot the score. Inspired by their old warrior—who registered a game-high seven hits—the Penguins snatched the lead on goals by Jordan Staal and Sidney Crosby and staved off a late Ottawa surge to win the game.

With the series shifting to the friendly confines of the Mellon Arena, the Penguins appeared to have the momentum. An early goal by Roberts stoked the sellout crowd to a frenzy in Game 3. For the first time in the series the

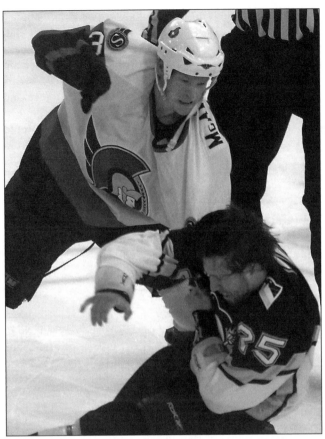

"Mad Max" Talbot swaps punches with the Senators' Dean McAmmond.

Senators were sagging on the ropes, awaiting the knockout punch.

However, the Pens failed to convert on two power plays. When Dean McAmmond punched the puck past Marc-Andre Fleury just before the first-period buzzer, the air went out of the Mellon Arena. As the Penguins stumbled, the opportunistic Senators struck for three second-period goals and rolled to a 4–2 win.

Fighting for their playoff lives, the Pens dug down deep and gave a superb effort in Game 4. Applying relentless pressure, they forced the Senators into a defensive mode. Midway through the second period, with Roberts wreaking havoc in the crease, Staal found an opening and beat Emery to knot the score.

Try as they might, the Pens couldn't manufacture the go-ahead goal. With 10 minutes left to play, Anton Volchenkov blew the puck past Fleury from the slot and the Senators prevailed. Backed by Emery's razor-sharp play, Ottawa closed out the series with a 3–0 shutout in Game 5.

Despite the disappointment of an early playoff exit, the Penguins learned some valuable lessons.

"You have to stay focused, you have to be consistent," said Crosby, who scored three goals while playing with a broken foot. "Unfortunately, we learned that the hard way."

Justifiably proud of the progress his young team had made, coach Michel Therrien put things in perspective.

"There's nothing to be ashamed of," he said. "You look at the big picture, it's a huge step."

Series Summary
Lost to Ottawa 4–1

Game	Date	City	Result	Winning Goal	Winning Goalie
1	April 11	Ottawa	Ottawa 6–3	Chris Neil	Ray Emery
2	April 14	Ottawa	Pittsburgh 4–3	Sidney Crosby	Marc-Andre Fleury
3	April 15	Pittsburgh	Ottawa 4–2	Daniel Alfredsson	Ray Emery
4	April 17	Pittsburgh	Ottawa 2–1	Anton Volchenkov	Ray Emery
5	April 19	Ottawa	Ottawa 3–0	Dany Heatley	Ray Emery

2008

Over the summer general manager Ray Shero concentrated on reinforcing his talented young team with a veteran presence. He inked greybeards Mark Recchi and Gary Roberts to new deals and signed free agents Darryl Sydor and Petr Sykora to two-year pacts.

With the newcomers in tow, a heightened sense of anticipation surrounded the Penguins as they opened the 2007–08 campaign. Much to everyone's surprise, however, the team flopped out of the starting gate. Languishing three games below the break-even mark, the Pens traveled to Ottawa on November 22 to take on the piping-hot Senators. Down by two goals, they rallied to beat their bitter rival on Jarkko Ruutu's shootout goal.

Despite injuries to key performers Sidney Crosby and Marc-Andre Fleury, the Pens soon regained their rhythm. Paced by the extraordinary play of Evgeni Malkin and unheralded backup goalie Ty Conklin, they zoomed into playoff contention.

Sensing his young team was ready to challenge for the Cup, Shero swung a blockbuster deal with Atlanta at the trade deadline. In exchange for popular winger Colby Armstrong, shootout specialist Erik Christensen, youngster Angelo Esposito, and a first-round pick, he acquired checking forward Pascal Dupuis and All-Star sniper Marian Hossa. In addition, he picked up behemoth defender Hal Gill from Toronto.

Although Hossa suffered a knee injury in his first game with the club, the Pens barely missed a beat. They finished the season with a sparkling record of 47–27–8 to capture the Atlantic Division crown.

Penguins vs. Senators, Eastern Conference Quarterfinals

For the second year in a row the Penguins squared off against Ottawa in the opening round of the playoffs. Although the Senators had staggered into the postseason with a burgeoning list of injuries, the Pens weren't taking their opponent lightly.

"They have a lot of character," Brooks Orpik said. "We have a lot of respect for that whole team. It's going to be a long series."

Determined to get the jump on their foe, the Pens came out flying before a packed house at the Mellon Arena. Orpik immediately set the tone with a crushing hit on Dany Heatley. Then Michel Therrien made a surprise move by sending out his fourth line of Gary Roberts, Max Talbot, and Georges Laraque.

Playing with his trademark snarl, Roberts outmuscled defenseman Wade Redden behind the Ottawa net. The puck squirted free to Talbot, who quickly dished it to Laraque. The Pens' enforcer found Roberts in the slot with a picture-perfect pass, and the tough old pro turned and spun a back-hander past goalie Martin Gerber.

The Penguins never let up. Applying constant pressure to Ottawa's overmatched defense, they cruised to an impressive 4–0 victory.

"It's a good feeling for us, for sure," said Roberts, who scored two goals. "Last year, I think we were in shock after Game 1 in Ottawa, they came out so hard and battled us real hard. But that feeling, I don't think it's left in this dressing room."

"Scary Gary" had clearly gotten into the Senators' heads. While Ottawa focused their attention on engaging Roberts, his Penguins teammates pounced to a 3–0 lead in Game 2. The Pens appeared to have the game well in hand. But the down-but-not-out Senators rallied for three goals of their own to knot the score.

As the clock ticked down to the final minute of play, the game appeared to be headed to overtime. However, Martin Lapointe drew a foolish penalty for high sticking to hand the Pens a power play. Ryan Malone wheeled from behind the net and tucked the puck inside the far post for the game winner.

The last-minute loss drained the life out of Ottawa. Displaying remarkable poise and intensity, the Pens dumped the Senators in Games 3 and 4 to sweep the series.

Series Summary
Beat Ottawa 4–0

Game	Date	City	Result	Winning Goal	Winning Goalie
1	April 9	Pittsburgh	Pittsburgh 4–0	Gary Roberts	Marc-Andre Fleury
2	April 11	Pittsburgh	Pittsburgh 5–3	Ryan Malone	Marc-Andre Fleury
3	April 14	Ottawa	Pittsburgh 4–1	Sidney Crosby	Marc-Andre Fleury
4	April 16	Ottawa	Pittsburgh 3–1	Jarkko Ruutu	Marc-Andre Fleury

Penguins vs. Rangers, Eastern Conference Semifinals

The stunning sweep of Ottawa set up an Eastern Conference Semifinals clash with the New York Rangers. Lead by former Penguins Jaromir Jagr and Martin Straka and backed by the

Evgeni Malkin powers past Brian Lee in first-round action.

superb goaltending of Henrik Lundqvist, the Rangers were one of the Pens' toughest foes during the regular season, winning five of eight meetings.

Continuing their surprising dominance, the Rangers raced to a 3–0 lead in the series opener. Following their third goal, agitator Sean Avery celebrated as if he'd just won the Stanley Cup.

Infuriated by Avery's antics, the Penguins immediately responded. Jarkko Ruutu drove to the Rangers' net and scored on a deflection. Fourteen seconds later Pascal Dupuis pounded a hard shot past Lundqvist off a beautiful feed from Crosby.

Trailing 3–2 entering the final period, the Pens struck again on a pair of rapid-fire goals by Marian Hossa and Petr Sykora. Although reeling from the Penguins' offensive assault, the Rangers knotted the score midway through the period.

The stage was set for a thrilling finish. With Straka serving an interference penalty, Crosby ripped off a slap shot from the sideboards. The puck glanced off Malkin, who was camped in the slot, and into the Rangers' net.

Afterward, in a lighthearted moment, the big Russian gave his take on the game-winning goal.

"His [Crosby's] slap shot is, uhh, not that good," Geno said through an interpreter. "That shot he just put everything in it, all the motion, all the power and he shot that puck hard."

Sparked by the dramatic comeback, the Pens downed the Rangers in Games 2 and 3 to seize control of the series.

However, New York came up with a big effort in Game 4. Paced by a two-goal effort from Jagr and Lundqvist's flawless goaltending, the Rangers prevailed to force a fifth game in Pittsburgh.

Determined to put New York away, the Penguins weathered an early Rangers storm to grab a 2–0 lead. Clearly deflated, the Blueshirts failed to register a shot on goal over the final 15 minutes of the second period.

It appeared that the Penguins had the game—and the series—in the bag. But New York mounted one last charge, knotting the score early in the third period on goals by rookie Lauri Korpikoski and Nigel Dawes 82 seconds apart.

The Penguins refused to panic.

"It was the exact opposite," Brooks Orpik said. "We weathered [New York's surge] pretty well, and just kept doing what we were doing."

Their diligence soon paid off. Seven minutes into overtime, Crosby found Hossa with a pretty pass. The veteran winger drilled the series winner past Lundqvist to touch off a wild victory celebration.

"I don't think I've ever scored a playoff goal in overtime," Hossa said. "So this was big, yeah. Sid was driving hard to the net, and I don't know what happened but the puck just came to me. It was a lucky one."

Series Summary
Beat New York Rangers 4–1

Game	Date	City	Result	Winning Goal	Winning Goalie
1	April 25	Pittsburgh	Pittsburgh 5–4	Evgeni Malkin	Marc-Andre Fleury
2	April 27	Pittsburgh	Pittsburgh 2–0	Jordan Staal	Marc-Andre Fleury
3	April 29	New York	Pittsburgh 5–3	Evgeni Malkin	Marc-Andre Fleury
4	May 1	New York	NY Rangers 3–0	Jaromir Jagr	Henrik Lundqvist
5	May 4	Pittsburgh	Pittsburgh 3–2 (OT)	Marian Hossa	Marc-Andre Fleury

Penguins vs. Flyers, Eastern Conference Finals

The Penguins' reward was an Eastern Conference Finals tilt with the Flyers. Following a dismal 2006–07 campaign, Philadelphia had rebounded under the leadership of general manager Paul Holmgren and Coach of the Year candidate John Stevens to improve by 39 points.

Adding fuel to the fire was the notion that the Pens had purposely lost their regular-season finale in Philly to avoid facing their bitter in-state rivals in the opening round of the playoffs.

"It's almost like they threw the game," Flyers tough guy Riley Cote said.

"Maybe they're scared of us, I don't know," center Jeff Carter added.

Clearly miffed at the inference, the normally tight-lipped Penguins responded.

"People can say what they want," Gary Roberts said. "Is anybody in the NHL going to think you can purposely go out and try to lose a hockey game? I've never done it and I know we never did."

"We'll see what happens in the series," Georges Laraque added. "Then we'll talk."

The war of words spilled onto the ice in Game 1. Orpik leveled Pittsburgh native R.J. Umberger with a huge check, setting the tone for a very physical battle. In all, the two teams combined for a whopping 69 hits.

While the Penguins struggled to find their rhythm, Philly's Mike Richards staked his team to a quick 2–1 lead. However, the Pens' wonder boys soon found the range. Crosby knotted the score on a pretty deflection. Late in the opening frame Malkin drove a blistering shot past goalie Martin Biron from the right hash mark.

Early in the second period Malkin struck again. Shaking off the effects of a thunderous check by Richards, he scored on a shorthanded breakaway to provide some cushion. The Pens choked off the Flyers' attack and emerged with a hard-fought 4–2 victory.

Backed by the sensational goaltending of Fleury, the Penguins rolled to a 3–0 series lead. But the stubborn Flyers weren't going down without a fight. Striking for three first-period goals, they eclipsed the Penguins in Game 4 to send the series back to Pittsburgh.

For the first time during their remarkable postseason run, the Pens were playing a pivotal game. A loss in Game 5 would breathe new life into the Flyers and send the series back to Philly.

The Penguins quickly dispelled any concerns about their readiness. Playing before a raucous sellout crowd at the Mellon Arena, they treated their hometown fans to a special performance. Once again the "Sid and Geno Show" paced the attack.

Crosby opened the scoring barely two minutes into the game by banking a shot/pass off Ryan Malone's skate and past a shaky Biron. Moments later, Malkin snatched up a loose puck beside the Flyers' net and tucked it inside the right goal post.

Any hopes for a Flyers comeback were extinguished midway through the second period. Following a sloppy clearing attempt, Richards scooped up the puck and steamed toward the Penguins' net. In his inimitable hustling style, Crosby stole the puck from the Flyers' star and sped into the Philly zone. He laid a beautiful drop pass onto the stick of Hossa, who blew a wicked shot past Biron.

The Penguins proceeded to pour it on. Malone and Staal struck for second-period goals. Pascal Dupuis capped off the scoring early in the final frame to vanquish the Flyers 6–0. For the first time in 16 years, the Penguins were headed to the Stanley Cup Finals.

With all due respect to Hossa, who tallied eight points against the Flyers, the star of the game and indeed, the series, was Crosby. Shaking off the lingering effects of his high-ankle sprain, the "Wizard of Cros" was superb. He scored two key goals and added five assists while providing sterling leadership.

"Sid has so much pride," Roberts said. "He has so much passion for the game. It's unbelievable."

Series Summary
Beat Philadelphia 4–1

Game	Date	City	Result	Winning Goal	Winning Goalie
1	May 9	Pittsburgh	Pittsburgh 4–2	Evgeni Malkin	Marc-Andre Fleury
2	May 11	Pittsburgh	Pittsburgh 4–2	Max Talbot	Marc-Andre Fleury
3	May 13	Philadelphia	Pittsburgh 4–1	Marian Hossa	Marc-Andre Fleury
4	May 15	Philadelphia	Philadelphia 4–2	Jeff Carter	Martin Biron
5	May 18	Pittsburgh	Pittsburgh 6–0	Ryan Malone	Marc-Andre Fleury

Penguins vs. Red Wings, Stanley Cup Finals

Capturing a third Stanley Cup would be no easy feat. Standing between the Penguins and Lord Stanley's coveted chalice was a formidable foe—the Detroit Red Wings. Runaway President's Trophy winners, the Western Conference champs enjoyed an equally impressive march to the Finals, dispatching Nashville, Colorado, and Dallas with ease. A tough, veteran team with plenty of playoff experience, the Red Wings boasted their own stable of high-profile stars, including Henrik Zetterberg, Pavel Datsyuk, and perennial Norris Trophy winner Nicklas Lidstrom.

Hoping to get the jump on their more seasoned adversary, the brash young Penguins fell flat in Game 1. Marc-Andre Fleury took a pratfall as he led the team onto the ice from the visitors' runway. While the young goalie suffered nothing more than a bruised ego, it was an omen of things to come.

Understandably nervous, the Penguins appeared to be tight in the early going. Playing the role of obliging hosts, Detroit handed the Pens four straight power plays. Despite good chances by Crosby and Hossa, the Penguins couldn't beat Chris Osgood, who was razor sharp.

Utilizing their tremendous team speed to full advantage, the Red Wings began to dominate their inexperienced opponent. Midway through the second period, ex-Pen Mikael Samuelsson swooped around the Penguins' net and tucked the puck inside the far post for the all-important first goal.

The ubiquitous Swede struck again early in the third period, capitalizing on a puck-handling gaffe by Fleury. Shutting down every Penguins thrust, Detroit tacked on a pair of late goals to complete an impressive 4–0 shutout.

Adversity had arrived on the Penguins' doorstep with a pronounced thud. For the first time in the postseason their character would be put to the test.

"We'll bounce back," Max Talbot said. "We've been through a lot. This team knows how to bounce back after a bad game."

Coach Michel Therrien immediately went to work. Shuffling his line combinations, he moved Malone to the top unit alongside Crosby and Hossa. The energetic Talbot joined Malkin and Sykora on the slumping "Steel City Line." Dupuis shifted to the checking line with Staal and feisty Tyler Kennedy. Gary Roberts—recovered from a bout with pneumonia—was grafted onto the fourth unit with Adam Hall and Ruutu.

The changes had little effect. Skating as if they were navigating a minefield, the Penguins failed to register a shot during the first 12 minutes of play in Game 2. While they tiptoed around the ice, the opportunistic Red Wings struck for a pair of quick goals.

Shaken from their slumber, the Penguins finally began to apply some pressure in the second period. However, a highlight-reel goal by Valtteri Filppula early in the final frame dashed any hopes of a comeback. Playing air-tight defense, the Red Wings slammed the door and whitewashed the Pens again.

The Penguins were in shock. Their goalless skein had reached 135 minutes and counting—unthinkable for a team that boasted so much firepower. But the Red Wings' swarming defense had completely neutralized their vaunted attack.

"Because of their experience and skill level, they play a real smart game in their own end," Roberts said. "They just don't give you much room. It's not fun. You feel like you're chasing the puck all night, chasing the puck all over the ice. You use so much energy trying to find the puck that by the time you get it, you're exhausted."

A change in venue offered a ray of hope. Games 3 and 4 would be played in the friendly confines of the Mellon Arena, where the Penguins had won eight straight postseason contests and 16 in a row overall. Indeed, the partisan crowd would serve as a sixth attacker throughout the evening.

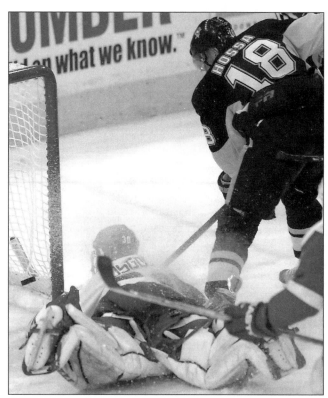
Acquired at the 2008 trade deadline, Slovakian sniper Marian Hossa flips the puck over Detroit's Chris Osgood.

Therrien made one more tweak to the lineup, inserting veteran Darryl Sydor in place of rookie Kris Letang. The move worked like a charm. Sydor, who had played for Cup winners in Dallas and Tampa Bay, would have a calming, stabilizing effect on the defense.

Inspired by their howling hometown crowd, the Penguins jumped out of the starting gate. Following a big save by Osgood, however, the Red Wings once more seized control. With their blitzkrieg attack in high gear, they peppered Fleury with nine straight shots. Displaying remarkable poise and command, the young netminder stood his ground.

The Pens finally broke through late in the opening period. Detroit defenseman Brad Stuart misfired on a clearing pass. Crosby pounced on the loose puck and fed it to Hossa. The ultrasmooth Slovakian quickly dished the puck back to Sid, who gunned it between Osgood's pads. As the red light flashed, Crosby pumped his fists in celebration.

"You could just see his intensity and his passion," Ryan Whitney said. "You don't see him fist-pumping like that very often. He knew what this game meant to us."

With the monkey finally off their backs, the Penguins began to assert themselves. Early in the second period Crosby struck again, finishing off a tic-tac-toe passing play from Hossa and Malone to stake the Pens to a two-goal lead.

Buoyed by Sid's big night, the Penguins choked off the Red Wings' lethal attack and emerged with a hard-fought 3–2 victory. To a man, the Penguins credited their captain for leading the way.

"There's no doubt that you're looking for your best player to bring an A-game," Michel Therrien said. "Certainly, Sid did that tonight."

"I love the guy," Talbot added. "I'm older than him and I look up to him. What a true leader. The rest of us have no choice but to follow."

The Penguins hoped to even the series with another strong effort in Game 4. Playing before another amped-up crowd at the Mellon Arena, they struck for an early power-play goal by Hossa to grab the lead.

Moments later the sharpshooting winger nearly beat Osgood again, but his rising backhander bounced off the crossbar.

The Red Wings quickly countered. Just seconds after a penalty to Dupuis had expired, Nicklas Lidstrom snapped a low shot through a tangle of bodies to knot the score.

Try as they might, the Penguins couldn't get a leg up on their determined foe. Early in the third period they failed to clear the puck from their own end and Detroit made them pay, as Jiri Hudler drove the puck home for the go-ahead goal.

Still, the Pens had one last chance to even the score when Kirk Maltby and Andreas Lilja handed them a two-man advantage. Their best opportunity came late on the five-on-three when the puck squirted through to Crosby, who was camped beside the Red Wings' net. Just as Sid was about to shoot, Zetterberg made a brilliant defensive play to chop

Rugged Ryan Malone is knocked to the ice by Red Wing Brad Stuart. The Pittsburgh native played in the Finals with a badly broken nose.

down on No. 87's stick. The puck trickled harmlessly into Osgood's pads.

Tightening their force-field defense, the Red Wings smothered the Pens' attack and took a commanding 3–1 series lead.

The Penguins' situation was grim. One loss away from elimination, they appeared to have few answers for the mighty Red Wings. Indeed, Detroit had been so dominant in all phases of the game that they resembled the great Soviet National teams of the 1970s and '80s.

"We have to keep our chins up," Hossa said. "They have to win one more game, and we have to make it really tough on them."

Down but not out, the Penguins responded with their best period of the series to open Game 5. Eight minutes in, Dupuis won a battle along the boards and fed the puck to Crosby, who quickly moved it to Hossa. The veteran winger made no mistake and whipped the puck past Osgood for his 11th goal of the playoffs.

Late in the period, the Pens struck again. Adam Hall bounced off a check by Johan Franzen and charged to the front of the Detroit net, only to have the puck stripped away by Niklas Kronwall. However, when the Red Wings' defender tried to clear the puck from harm's way, it deflected off Hall's skate and over Osgood's shoulder.

Skating with a two-goal lead, the Penguins appeared to be in the driver's seat. But the Red Wings were far from

Wait 'til next year. A glum group of Penguins await the post-series handshake after losing Game 6 to Detroit.

finished. Early in the second period, Darren Helm scored on a deflection to cut the Pens' lead in half

In the final frame the Wings unleashed a wicked onslaught at Fleury. Pavel Datsyuk knotted the score with a power-play goal at 6:43. Minutes later, slick defenseman Brian Rafalski drilled the puck past the beleaguered goalie from the right hash mark to stake the Wings to the lead.

Awash in a sea of bright-red jerseys, the Penguins struggled to mount a counterattack. It was as if an unseen hand had tilted the ice surface toward the Pittsburgh zone. To make matters worse, star defenseman Sergei Gonchar was forced to the locker room with a back injury, while Ryan Malone—already playing with a broken nose—absorbed a Hal Gill shot to the face.

As the game clock ticked down to the final minute, Michel Therrien pulled Fleury for an extra attacker. Talbot hopped over the boards and flew into action. Setting up shop beside the Detroit net, the hustling winger gathered in a pretty pass from Hossa and wrapped the puck around the goal post. No goal. He took another whack at the rubber. This time the red light flashed. "Mad Max" had tied the game with 34.3 seconds to play.

The Red Wings were stunned. The Stanley Cup had literally been in their grasp, only to be snatched away. Yet it

hardly affected their play. Moving the puck with their trademark speed and precision, they overwhelmed the Penguins in the first overtime period, outshooting their foe by the lopsided margin of 13–2. But Fleury was magnificent.

By the third overtime, the Penguins appeared to be on their last legs. However, at the nine-minute mark Lady Luck finally smiled, albeit painfully. While battling for the puck, Rob Scuderi took a stick to the mouth to draw a four-minute penalty.

With the series hanging in the balance, Gonchar courageously shook off his injury and returned to the ice to quarterback the power play.

"I was trying to help the team any way I could," he said.

"Sarge" did just that. The hobbled blue-liner passed the puck to Petr Sykora, who uncorked a drive that was kicked aside by Osgood. Malkin scooped up the rebound and fed it back to Sykora. This time the Czech winger found the mark, rifling the puck past the Detroit goalie for the game winner.

It was a gritty, heroic effort by the Pens—one that signified the team's coming of age. Marc-Andre Fleury played the game of his life, stopping 55 of 58 shots. In Gonchar's absence, Ryan Whitney logged a mind-blowing 50 minutes of ice time. Malone skated the last half of the game with cotton packed in his nose to staunch the bleeding. Indeed,

Shades of "the Babe"

During the 1932 World Series, famed Yankees slugger Babe Ruth made headlines the world over when he pointed toward the center-field bleachers and blasted the next pitch into the seats.

Fast-forward to Game 5 of the 2008 Stanley Cup Finals. The Penguins were locked in a titanic overtime struggle with the Red Wings for their playoff lives. That's when slumping winger Petr Sykora issued a staggering proclamation.

"I think I've got one, guys," he said.

Color announcer Pierre McGuire, who was stationed between the benches, said Sykora pointed to himself as if to say, "I'm scoring the game winner."

"When a guy like that steps out and says, 'I've got one, guys,' you look at him and you hope he's saying the truth," Max Talbot said.

No false prophet, Sykora proceeded to back up his words with deeds. At 9:57 of the third overtime, he snapped the winning goal past Chris Osgood—just as he'd predicted.

Osgood's glove. As the puck dropped to the ice, Hossa raced in and poked it behind the Detroit goalie, only to watch the rubber slide harmlessly through the crease. Had the puck crossed the goal line it would not have counted—the final buzzer had sounded. But the never-say-die Penguins battled until the last millisecond.

In the hush of the losing locker room, the players were understandably heartbroken, none more so than Sidney Crosby.

"This feeling, it's not a good feeling at all," the Pens' captain said, his voice cracking with emotion. "It's not something I want to experience [again]."

"I'm almost speechless right now," Michel Therrien said. "When you're that close, it is really tough. We got beat by a quality team. They were tough to play against. The hockey gods were not on our side tonight. It hurts. You could feel the pain. But I'm proud of our guys. They grew up really quickly in the last two years."

Although clearly disappointed at the near miss, owner Mario Lemieux chose to look at the bright side.

"This is certainly a big step," Mario said. "It's always disappointing not to win in the Finals, but we feel that we'll be back and we'll be much better next time."

Series Summary
Lost to Detroit 4–2

Game	Date	City	Result	Winning Goal	Winning Goalie
1	May 24	Detroit	Detroit 4–0	Mikael Samuelsson	Chris Osgood
2	May 26	Detroit	Detroit 3–0	Brad Stuart	Chris Osgood
3	May 28	Pittsburgh	Pittsburgh 3–2	Adam Hall	Marc-Andre Fleury
4	May 31	Pittsburgh	Detroit 2–1	Jiri Hudler	Chris Osgood
5	June 2	Detroit	Pittsburgh 4–3 (3 OT)	Petr Sykora	Marc-Andre Fleury
6	June 4	Pittsburgh	Detroit 3–2	Henrik Zetterberg	Chris Osgood

2009

Following their march to the Stanley Cup Finals in 2008, the Penguins entered the 2008–09 season with high expectations. However, a series of defections over the summer weakened the club dramatically and threatened to derail its dreams of a Stanley Cup.

Emerging power forward Ryan Malone signed a free-agent deal with Tampa Bay, as did old pro Gary Roberts and checking center Adam Hall. Abrasive winger Jarkko Ruutu jumped to Ottawa, while burly enforcer Georges Laraque joined the Canadiens. But by far the most stunning—and damaging—loss was high-scoring forward Marian Hossa, who spurned a lucrative long-term offer from the Penguins to sign with Detroit.

General manager Ray Shero did his best to plug the gaps, inking veterans Ruslan Fedotenko and Miroslav Satan to one-year deals. However, the Pens clearly weren't the same team. After a decent start, they stumbled through December and January at a dismal 10–16–2 pace.

the entire team battled through the adversity with the heart of a lion.

"We've got guys who would go through a brick wall for each other," Malone said.

In the "City of Champions," the Penguins' gallant performance sparked renewed hope. However, the determined Red Wings immediately gained the upper hand in Game 6, striking for a pair of first-period goals by Rafalski and Filppula.

Shaking off the effects of the flu and a rib injury that had hampered him throughout the series, Malkin ended his long scoring drought with a power-play tally at 15:26 of the second period. But Zetterberg countered with a fluke goal early in the final frame to give the Wings a commanding 3–1 lead.

Backed into a corner, the Pens were unable to mount a sustained attack until the final minutes of play, when they served up one last bit of magic. With Hudler serving a hooking minor and Fleury pulled for an extra attacker, Gonchar skated to center point and snapped a low, hard shot toward the Detroit goal. Fighting his way through heavy traffic, Hossa tipped the puck as it sailed by, deflecting it past Osgood.

The Pens nearly scored another miracle goal in the closing seconds—one that would've sent the game to overtime. Playing with true desperation, Crosby streaked into the Detroit zone and launched a backhander that skipped off of

Following a disastrous 6–2 loss to Toronto on Valentine's Day, Shero dismissed embattled coach Michel Therrien and promoted Dan Bylsma from Wilkes-Barre.

The Pens immediately responded to the energetic Bylsma, who favored an up-tempo, puck-possession game. Bolstered by the acquisitions of aggressive wingers Bill Guerin and Chris Kunitz, the Pens went on an incredible 18–3–4 tear to snatch second place in the Atlantic Division and earn a playoff berth.

Penguins vs. Flyers, Eastern Conference Quarterfinals

The Penguins drew their bitter rivals, the Flyers, in the Eastern Conference Quarterfinals. Beating Philadelphia would be no easy task. Armed with 46-goal scorer Jeff Carter and 30-goal men Mike Richards, Simon Gagne, and Scott Hartnell, Philly possessed more than enough firepower to battle the Pens on even terms.

The Penguins were up to the challenge. Playing with threshing-machine precision, they ripped through their foe in the series opener en route to an impressive 4–1 victory.

Game 2 was a different story. Displaying considerably more hop, the Flyers carried a 2–1 lead into the final period. With eight minutes remaining, Carter had a golden opportunity to put the game on ice when he flicked the puck toward a yawning Penguins net. However at the last possible second Fleury stretched across the crease to kick the puck aside.

"I happened to see that save looking up on the Jumbotron," Bylsma said. "It looked like a for-sure goal. Somehow, he got his skate or his pad out there to stop it."

Moments later Letang struck on the power play to send the game into overtime. The swashbuckling Flyers had displayed uncommon discipline for most of the game, but late in the extra frame they drew two penalties to hand the Penguins a five-on-three advantage. Bill Guerin promptly snapped the puck home to secure the victory.

If the Flyers were discouraged by the series-opening losses, it wasn't evident in Game 3. Playing before a packed house at the Wachovia Center, they set a physical tone that carried through the rest of the evening. When Chris Kunitz responded with a thundering hit on Kimmo Timonen, the lid blew off. Hartnell chased down Kunitz to deliver some frontier justice. Moments later the teams engaged in a wild five-on-five scrum.

While the Penguins were hardly intimidated, the donnybrook seemed to interrupt their flow. As the Pens faded, Philly pumped six shots past Fleury to score a resounding victory.

"We maybe lost our focus a little bit, doing some of the little things that had made us successful," Matt Cooke said.

Thanks to a heroic effort by Fleury in Game 4, the Pens split the next two contests. However, the momentum had firmly shifted to the team wearing the orange and black. When the Flyers raced to a 3–0 second-period lead in Game

Rob Scuderi puts the hip into Flyer Darroll Powe.

6 before a howling mob at the Wachovia Center, the series seemed to be slipping through the Penguins' fingers.

It was gut-check time and Max Talbot responded. Immediately following the Flyers' third goal, "Mad Max" challenged reigning NHL penalty king and former Penguins draft pick Daniel Carcillo to a fight. In a spirited go, the rough-and-tumble Carcillo quickly gained the upper hand and pounded an overmatched Talbot to the ice with a volley of hard rights.

While Max clearly lost the fight, he won the war. Fourteen seconds after the battle ex-Flyer Ruslan Fedotenko snaked the puck past Martin Biron from a goal-mouth scramble. Two minutes later Mark Eaton bunted his second goal of the series into the Flyers' net. And in the closing minutes of the period, Crosby scored another baseball-style goal, swatting the puck out of midair and over Biron's shoulder.

Completely stunned, the Flyers watched helplessly as the Pens snatched the lead on a tally by Gonchar early in third period. Crosby supplied the icing on the cake when he tucked in an empty netter in the final minute of play.

The victory was particularly sweet for the Penguins' captain, who was the target of verbal abuse from the Flyers' raucous fans throughout the series.

"It felt good," Sid said. "They were playing well and the crowd was into it, so to hear a little silence [at the end] was gratifying."

"They tested us," Bylsma added. "That's something we needed to have happen. We've been tested. And we've responded."

Series Summary
Beat Philadelphia 4–2

Game	Date	City	Result	Winning Goal	Winning Goalie
1	April 15	Pittsburgh	Pittsburgh 4–1	Tyler Kennedy	Marc-Andre Fleury
2	April 17	Pittsburgh	Pittsburgh 3–2 (OT)	Bill Guerin	Marc-Andre Fleury
3	April 19	Philadelphia	Philadelphia 6–3	Simon Gagne	Martin Biron
4	April 21	Philadelphia	Pittsburgh 3–1	Tyler Kennedy	Marc-Andre Fleury
5	April 23	Pittsburgh	Philadelphia 3–0	Arron Asham	Martin Biron
6	April 25	Philadelphia	Pittsburgh 5–3	Sergei Gonchar	Marc-Andre Fleury

Penguins vs. Capitals, Eastern Conference Semifinals

The Pens' rousing victory over the Flyers set up an Eastern Conference Semifinals series with another old rival, the Washington Capitals. Paced by supernova winger Alexander Ovechkin and Semyon Varlamov, a 21-year-old rookie goalie, the second-seeded Caps had rallied from a 3–1 deficit to down the Rangers in their opening-round series.

With Crosby and Malkin going head to head against Ovechkin and fellow Russian Alexander Semin, it was the marquee matchup the NHL and its fans had only dreamed about. The teams would not disappoint.

Sid vs. Ovy

From the day Sidney Crosby first skated onto the Mellon Arena ice, a compelling rivalry began to emerge between the Penguins' wonder boy and Washington superstar Alexander Ovechkin. It was only a matter of time before a healthy dose of dislike began to percolate between the former No. 1 picks.

Ironically, the first shot in the simmering feud was fired by Ovechkin's teammate, fellow Russian Alexander Semin. When asked to comment on Crosby during an October 2008 interview with Dmitry Chesnokov of *Sovetsky Sport* newspaper, he offered some unflattering observations.

"What's so special about Crosby?" Semin asked. "I don't see anything special there. Yes, he does skate well, has a good head, good pass. But there's nothing else. Even if you compare him to Patrick Kane from Chicago…Kane is a much more interesting player."

The bad blood intensified following a 5–2 Penguins loss to the Capitals in February of 2009, when Crosby took exception to Ovechkin's wild goal-celebration antics.

"Some people like it, some people don't," he said. "Personally, I don't like it."

Archrivals Alexander Ovechkin and Sidney Crosby were All-Star linemates in 2007.

"He is a good player," Ovechkin responded. "But he talks too much."

The feud came to a head during the hotly contested Eastern Conference Semifinals, when the two antagonists squared off mano a mano. Fortunately, they let their sticks do the talking.

To the delight of hockey fans everywhere, both stars were at the top of their game. Each scored eight goals during the series while doing his utmost to help his team win. In the end, it was Crosby's star that shone the brightest. He struck for two huge goals in Game 7 to lead his team to victory.

And what about Semin, the man who squirted lighter fluid on the smoldering embers? Following a largely ineffective series (six assists and a minus six) the chagrined Capital paid his respects.

"The way Crosby played in this series, they should build a monument to him," he said.

Sergei Gonchar absorbs a knee-to-knee hit from countryman Alexander Ovechkin. "Sarge" missed two games before returning to action.

Playing before a packed house at the Verizon Center, the hungry young Caps got the jump on the Penguins. Riding the hot goaltending of Varlamov, they rallied from an early deficit to capture the series opener, thanks to Tomas Fleischmann's game winner.

Game 2 proved to be the "Sid and Ovy Show." Playing with an intensity that mirrored their simmering rivalry, each netted a hat trick while attempting to outdo the other. However, the third spoke in the wheel—Evgeni Malkin— was noticeably absent. Playing his second straight lackluster game, Malkin drew a tripping penalty in the third period that led to Ovechkin's game-winning goal.

Down 2–0 in the series, the Penguins had dug themselves a deep hole. The hole quickly became a trench when Ovechkin parlayed a bad bounce off the end boards into his fifth goal of the series a minute into Game 3.

The Penguins refused to buckle. Turning up the heat, they outshot the Capitals by a staggering 15–4 margin in the second period. Their hard work paid dividends when Fedotenko gathered in his own blocked pass and ripped the puck past Varlamov.

Then, late in the final frame, Semin drew a hooking penalty to hand the Pens a power play. As the Mellon Arena faithful chanted "Geno, Geno," Malkin made an electric move to cut into the high slot. With Guerin providing a perfect screen, he fired home the go-ahead goal.

Although Nicklas Backstrom knotted the score with a

power-play goal in the closing minutes, Kris Letang struck for the game winner at 11:23 of overtime. The Penguins had broken the Caps' stranglehold.

Leading the way was Malkin, who was a force all night long while launching a game-high nine shots.

"He has a lot of pride, and a lot of character, and we saw it tonight," Bill Guerin said. "He wanted to get involved in this series, and I think he did tonight."

The Penguins' scintillating victory in Game 3 had turned the tide. Although Gonchar suffered a knee injury courtesy of a borderline hit by Ovechkin, Pittsburgh evened the series in Game 4 and snatched the lead in Game 5 on Malkin's overtime winner.

The Capitals refused to quit. Weathering an early offensive barrage, they eclipsed the Pens in Game 6 to force a winner-take-all seventh game.

History was not on the Penguins' side. The team had never won a Game 7 after losing a Game 6. To make matters worse, the deciding contest would be played in the unfriendly confines of the Verizon Center.

At least one player was unconcerned.

"It's a challenge, but if any group of guys is capable of doing it, it's the guys in our locker room," Crosby said. "We really believe in the way we're playing. If we do that again, it'll work out."

Sid proved to be prescient. Three minutes into the game, Fleury stopped Ovechkin cold on a breakaway with a stunning glove save. After that, it was all Penguins. By the 2:12 mark of the second period, Crosby, Craig Adams, Guerin, and Letang had pounded pucks past the previously unbeatable Varlamov. Staal and Crosby tacked on insurance goals as the Pens coasted to a resounding 6–2 victory.

With all due respect to Ovechkin, who was superb in a losing cause (eight goals and six assists in the seven games), the star of the series was Crosby. He scored eight huge goals and added five assists while earning the respect of friends and foes alike, including former critic Don Cherry.

"He's the best all-around player in the NHL," Cherry said. "I like Ovechkin. He's exciting. The wild bull of the Pampas. And he was everybody's darling. But I said before this series that Crosby wins draws now, he hits, he blocks shots, he plays down low, he's dropped the gloves twice. He's a complete player."

Series Summary
Beat Washington 4–3

Game	Date	City	Result	Winning Goal	Winning Goalie
1	May 2	Washington	Washington 3–2	Tomas Fleischmann	Semyon Varlamov
2	May 4	Washington	Washington 4–3	Alexander Ovechkin	Semyon Varlamov
3	May 6	Pittsburgh	Pittsburgh 3–2 (OT)	Kris Letang	Marc-Andre Fleury
4	May 8	Pittsburgh	Pittsburgh 5–3	Sidney Crosby	Marc-Andre Fleury
5	May 9	Washington	Pittsburgh 4–3 (OT)	Evgeni Malkin	Marc-Andre Fleury
6	May 11	Pittsburgh	Washington 5–4 (OT)	David Steckel	Semyon Varlamov
7	May 13	Washington	Pittsburgh 6–2	Bill Guerin	Marc-Andre Fleury

Penguins vs. Hurricanes, Eastern Conference Finals

The Penguins squared off against a brand-new adversary in the Eastern Conference Finals—the Carolina Hurricanes. In many ways, it was like facing a mirror image. The league's hottest team during the second half of the season, the "Cardiac Canes" employed the same swift-skating, up-tempo style as the Pens.

Unlike the Penguins, their lineup featured few marquee players. Aside from 40-goal man Eric Staal and All-Star goalie Cam Ward, a former Conn Smythe Trophy winner, the plucky Hurricanes were largely constructed of castoffs from other teams.

Game 1 would, indeed, be a night for unsung heroes—the ones sporting the Penguins' black and gold. Midway through the opening period, Matt Cooke sprung Miroslav Satan loose on a breakaway. The much-maligned winger made a quick move to his backhand and swept the puck behind a stunned Ward.

Then, as the Pens clung to a precarious 2–1 third-period lead, Philippe Boucher stepped into the limelight. Serving as an insurance policy in case Gonchar's balky right knee gave out, the veteran defender gathered in a pretty pass from Crosby and snapped the game winner past Ward.

Hoping to build on their stirring victory, the Pens opened Game 2 brimming with passion and intensity. Less than two minutes into the contest, Crosby punched home a beautiful

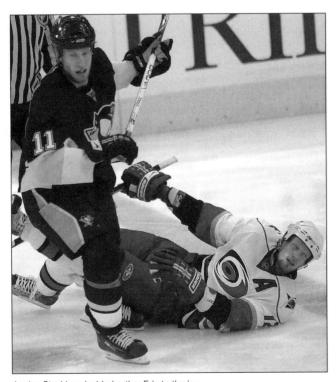

Jordan Staal knocks big brother Eric to the ice.

More Borscht, Please

During the 2008–09 season, Natalia and Vladimir Malkin made several trips to Pittsburgh from their home in Magnitogorsk, Russia, to visit their famous son and attend some Penguins games.

For Evgeni, who loves his parents dearly, there was an added bonus—his mom's home cooking.

After scoring a hat trick in Game 2 of the Eastern Conference Finals, he revealed the secret of his success to a *Toronto Sun* reporter.

"Every time before a game, I get great cooking," he said. "Great Russian food."

When Natalia revealed that her son's favorite dish was red borscht, her recipe was promptly published in the *Pittsburgh Post-Gazette*.

"I haven't had his mom's food, but I've been begging to go over to his house now because he's always talking about how good his mom's cooking is," Brooks Orpik said.

goal-mouth pass from Kunitz. At 8:15 Malkin joined the scoring parade on a sizzling wrist shot.

However, the hustling Hurricanes were determined to put up a fight. They pumped three first-period goals past a somnambulant Fleury, who played as if he was still groggy from his pregame nap.

Once more "Mad Max" Talbot stepped forward with a big play when his team needed it the most. Early in the second stanza, he gathered in a lead pass from Malkin and beat Ward cleanly to the stick-hand side. Rejuvenated, the Pens grabbed the lead in the waning seconds of the period on a blue-collar goal by Kunitz—his first of the playoffs.

Although Carolina knotted the score early in the third period, Canes scrapper Ray LaRose committed a cardinal sin by engaging Malkin in a shoving match.

His competitive fire now stoked, the big Russian rammed home the go-ahead goal at the 8:50 mark. Four minutes later he applied the coup de grace with a stunning goal destined to go down in Penguins' lore as "the Geno."

Working a set play, Malkin won a face-off deep in the Carolina end and snapped the puck to the end boards. As Hurricanes defenseman Dennis Seidenberg chased after him in hot pursuit, Geno regained the puck and quickly circled behind the cage. With his back to the net, he suddenly wheeled and whipped a seeing-eye backhander that sailed over Ward's shoulder.

"He told me what he was going to do and he did it," an astonished Talbot said.

"An amazing display of skill," Crosby added.

Or, as Versus hockey analyst Brian Engblom succinctly put it, "The Geno is out of the bottle."

Try as they might, the Hurricanes were no match for the Penguins. With Malkin and Crosby scoring at will, the Pens steamrollered Carolina in Games 3 and 4 to sweep the series.

Understandably, most of the post-series comments focused on the combined brilliance of the Penguins' dynamic duo.

"They're unbelievable," Craig Adams said. "To me, they're 1 and 1A, and I don't know which one is which. Just so competitive, so talented. They just want to play in these big games and score the goals, and they're doing it."

Series Summary
Beat Carolina 4–0

Game	Date	City	Result	Winning Goal	Winning Goalie
1	May 18	Pittsburgh	Pittsburgh 3–2	Philippe Boucher	Marc-Andre Fleury
2	May 21	Pittsburgh	Pittsburgh 7–4	Evgeni Malkin	Marc-Andre Fleury
3	May 23	Carolina	Pittsburgh 6–2	Evgeni Malkin	Marc-Andre Fleury
4	May 26	Carolina	Pittsburgh 4–1	Max Talbot	Marc-Andre Fleury

Penguins vs. Red Wings, Stanley Cup Finals

While the Penguins completed their sweep of Carolina, a powerful old foe was running the table in the Western Conference. In a rematch of the 2008 Finals, the Pens would once again battle the Detroit Red Wings for the right to claim Lord Stanley's Cup.

Surprisingly, the Penguins were itching for a return engagement.

"I was so happy when they defeated Chicago [in the Western Conference Finals] because I really wanted to play them," Max Talbot later recalled. "And I remember just cheering for Detroit for one game."

Beating the defending champions would be no easy task. As potent as ever, the Red Wings boasted the likes of former-Pen Marian Hossa and perennial All-Stars Pavel Datsyuk, Henrik Zetterberg, and Nicklas Lidstrom. They would present a most formidable obstacle to the Penguins' quest for the Cup.

With Datsyuk shelved with a foot injury and the 39-year-old Lidstrom hobbled as well, the hale and hardy Penguins appeared to have an edge. However, it was the Red Wings who controlled the action from the opening draw. Storming the Pens' net before a sellout throng at Joe Louis Arena, they snatched the lead midway through the first period on a fluke goal by Brad Stuart.

The Penguins refused to buckle. Brooks Orpik rocked Hossa with a huge hit in the neutral zone, and the team began to find its rhythm. At 18:37 Malkin picked off a clearing attempt by Stuart and fired the puck on goal. Chris Osgood made the save, but he couldn't control the rebound.

Marc-Andre Fleury was superb throughout the 2009 playoffs. His last-second save on Detroit's Nicklas Lidstrom sealed the Pens' Cup victory.

As the puck trickled away from his pads, Fedotenko cruised in and swept the puck home.

Given new life, the Penguins carried the play to the Red Wings during the second period. However, they failed to capitalize on two power plays and several glorious scoring chances, including a breakaway attempt by Malkin.

In the final minute of the period, Johan Franzen slipped the puck past a sprawling Fleury to stake the Wings to a 2–1 lead. Rookie Justin Abdelkader tacked on an insurance goal early in the third period, and Detroit choked off the Pens' attack to capture Game 1.

"The bounces just didn't go our way," Rob Scuderi said. "They scored a couple of weird goals. But if we keep playing like this, we're pretty confident about our chances."

Unfortunately for Pittsburgh, Game 2 proved to be a virtual replay of the series opener. Malkin struck for an early power-play goal, but the Red Wings rallied to grab a 2–1 lead. Early in the final frame the ubiquitous Abdelkader skirted past Scuderi and Gill and snapped a rolling puck over Fleury's shoulder.

The Penguins' worst nightmares had come true. They trailed the mighty Red Wings 2–0.

With the series shifting to the Mellon Arena for Game 3, the Penguins desperately needed a win. Indeed, only one team—the 1971 Canadiens—had rallied to win the Cup after losing the first two games on the road.

Determined to wrench control, the Penguins swarmed the Red Wings from the opening draw. Five minutes into the contest Talbot snapped the puck past Osgood from the slot to draw first blood.

It took Detroit less than two minutes to respond. Zetterberg lashed the puck past Fleury at 6:19, and Franzen followed suit midway through the period to hand the Wings yet another lead.

A holding penalty to Detroit winger Dan Cleary opened the door. Exploiting the Wings' Achilles' heel—a less-than-stellar penalty-killing unit—Letang gathered in a pretty cross-ice feed from Malkin and ripped the puck through Osgood's five-hole to knot the score.

Heading into the second period, the Penguins appeared to have the momentum. However, it was the Red Wings who seized control. Shifting their puck-possession game into high gear, they overwhelmed their beleaguered foe while holding the Pens to a paltry four shots on goal.

Fortunately, Marc-Andre Fleury was up to the challenge. Under heavy fire for allowing soft goals during the first two games, he was magnificent, turning aside 14 shots to keep his team in the game.

The tide began to turn early in the third period when Orpik crushed super pest Darren Helm with a thunderous shoulder check. Suddenly, the Penguins were flying all over the ice. Applying relentless pressure to Detroit's defense, they forced Jonathan Ericsson to take an interference penalty.

The Penguins pounced. With Bill Guerin providing traffic in front of the Red Wings' net, Sergei Gonchar skated into the slot and unleashed a bullet that sailed over Osgood's glove. Talbot added an empty netter in the final minute of play to clinch a crucial 4–2 victory.

"I don't want to say it was a must-win," said Talbot, one of the Penguins' heroes. "But I think everyone knows we needed to win."

"We needed big performances from our special teams and our goaltender, and we certainly got them," Bylsma added. "When you can get two power-play goals in a key game like this...it was a great thing to have."

Playing before a packed house, the Pens jumped to another quick start in Game 4. With Kronwall serving a tripping penalty, Malkin struck on the power play to stake the Penguins to an early lead.

However, the Red Wings weathered the Pens' early blitz and soon responded with some fire of their own. Outshooting their host by a whopping 19–11 margin, they cashed in late in the opening frame on a giveaway by the normally redoubtable Rob Scuderi. Defenseman Brad Stuart beat Fleury through a screen just 46 seconds into the second period. Suddenly, the Wings were up by a goal.

Detroit's swift burst knocked the Penguins back on their heels. When Malkin and Orpik drew back-to-back penalties, the table was set for the kill shot.

In danger of falling behind 3–1 in the series, the Penguins desperately needed a big play. With their Cup chances hanging in the balance, 20-year-old Jordan Staal stepped forward to provide it.

Relatively silent through the first three rounds of the playoffs, Staal had quietly stepped up his game against the Red Wings—especially on the penalty kill. Now he was ready to take center stage. Gathering in a lead pass from Talbot, the rangy center sped around Brian Rafalski and pumped a sizzling wrist shot past Osgood.

The shorthanded goal ignited the Penguins.

"Jordan's goal was huge," Crosby said. "They had a little bit of momentum at that point. They had two power plays right in a row and it was three minutes into the power plays before he scored. That was a huge momentum shift. We bounced back right away after that."

Two minutes later Crosby converted a pretty feed from Malkin into the go-ahead goal. The Pens then added an insurance tally on a beautiful tic-tac-toe passing play. Kunitz stole the puck from Zetterberg and slid a cross-ice pass to Crosby. Sid promptly fed the puck to Tyler Kennedy, who was streaking toward the net from his off-wing. With Osgood hopelessly out of position, "the Little Tiger" ripped the rubber into a wide-open net.

Backed by Fleury's razor-sharp goaltending, the Pens slammed the door in the final period to even the series at 2–2.

"It's a race to four [wins] now," winger Pascal Dupuis said.

"We're going back into their building, and they're going to battle," Talbot added. "It won't be easy from now until the end."

The plucky winger was eerily prophetic. Sparked by the return of star center Pavel Datsyuk, the battle-hardened Red Wings torched the Pens with a four-goal second-period onslaught to chase Fleury from the net. Thoroughly outclassed, the Penguins fell 5–0.

As the Penguins dragged themselves off the ice, a familiar figure stood near the entrance to the locker room. Sporting a scruffy playoff beard, Mario Lemieux offered words of encouragement to his players.

"Walking off the ice after Game 5 he was there outside our locker room," Jordan Staal said. "He still had a calm look on his face...a positive look. He was shaking his head and he's like, 'It's all right, boys, shake this one off. It's just one game.'"

"To have Mario around after that game when you're frustrated and disappointed and thinking you just let the series get away...it boosts you," Dan Bylsma said. "You puff up and you're ready to go and you want to lay it on the line."

With a rare two-day rest between games, the Pens worked to shake off any lingering effects of their lopsided loss. While Bylsma prepared his charges for the upcoming battle, he pooh-poohed the notion that the club needed more production from its stars.

"We don't need one person to go out and be the difference-maker," he said. "We need our team to play better. We need to play the way we know how to play, the way we've shown we can play."

Speedy Tyler Kennedy scores the game winner against Chris Osgood in Game 6.

Taking their coach's words to heart, the Penguins displayed plenty of jump during a spirited opening period in Game 6. While they failed to convert on two power-play opportunities, they held a decided edge in territorial play.

Indeed, the Penguins' young legs had begun to take a toll on the veteran Wings. Although a superbly conditioned team, Detroit featured 10 regulars who were at least 30 years of age, including six who were over 35. Suddenly, the Western Conference champions found themselves a step behind their supercharged adversaries.

As the Red Wings wilted, the Penguins stepped up their attack. Early in the second period, Staal and Cooke stripped the puck from Valtteri Filppula and flew into the Detroit zone on a two-on-one break. Staal's initial shot bounced off of Chris Osgood's chest, but the big center calmly scooped up the rebound and tucked it inside the right goal post.

Brimming with confidence, the Pens struck for a soft goal early in the final period that proved to be the game winner. Ruslan Fedotenko won a battle for a loose puck and shoveled it to Talbot, who in turn relayed it to Kennedy. The scrappy winger circled out from behind the net and jammed the puck past Osgood.

Meanwhile, at the other end of the ice, Fleury atoned for his poor performance in Game 5 with a series of sparkling saves. Following a Kris Draper goal that cut the Pens' lead in half, he stopped Dan Cleary cold on a breakaway attempt with less than two minutes remaining.

"He was unbelievable for us," Crosby said.

"The Flower" also received a little help from his teammates. In the waning seconds Rob Scuderi stepped into the crease to thwart a final thrust by Johan Franzen. The Penguins prevailed 2–1 to push the mighty Wings to a seventh and deciding game back in Detroit.

"We've given ourselves a chance to go up there," Talbot said. "One hundred and eleven games down for the season, and it comes down to one."

"Now it's anyone's game," Crosby added. "We have to battle and find a way to pull it off."

The Penguins were facing a daunting task. No club had won a Game 7 of a Stanley Cup Finals on the road since Montreal turned the trick against Chicago in 1971.

Despite their poor play at Joe Louis Arena, one man believed his team could do it. The morning of the series finale, Mario Lemieux sent a special text message to each player.

"This is a chance of a lifetime to realize your childhood dream to win a Stanley Cup," he wrote. "Play without fear and you will be successful! See you at center ice."

Mario's message galvanized the team. Following an early flurry by Detroit, the Penguins settled into their speed game while matching the potent Red Wings shot for shot.

Lightning struck early in the second period—Penguins lightning. Malkin, whose superb defensive work had helped key the crucial victory in Game 6, deflected a clearing attempt by Brad Stuart. Talbot corralled the loose rubber at the right hash mark and snapped a low shot between Osgood's pads.

Incredibly, "Mad Max" struck again midway through the period. Gathering in a chip pass from Chris Kunitz, the winger raced into the Detroit end and ripped the puck over Osgood's shoulder.

Unfortunately, the Pens soon swallowed a heaping spoonful of adversity. While chasing down a loose puck in the neutral zone, Crosby was smashed into the sideboards by the hulking Franzen. Sid came away from the collision hobbling on a banged-up left knee. He would skate only one shift in the final period.

"We tried to make it so I couldn't feel it anymore," Sid said, "but it just didn't work."

In Pittsburgh, an entire city held its collective breath. The Red Wings were down 2–0, but hardly out. How would the Penguins be able to keep the defending champs at bay without their heart-and-soul leader?

The answer was provided by No. 29. Thrust onto center stage in the biggest game of his career, Marc-Andre Fleury responded with a magnificent performance. His positioning flawless, his rebound control superb, Fleury repelled every shot the Red Wings threw his way.

Although Detroit finally broke through on a Jonathan Ericsson rocket with six minutes to play, Fleury's confidence never wavered. He made a pair of brilliant saves in the closing seconds, including a spectacular lunging stop on sharpshooting Nicklas Lidstrom.

"I saw the shot coming in, and I just tried to do everything I could to get over there," Fleury said.

As the puck skipped harmlessly to the corner, his teammates poured into the crease and mobbed the victorious goalie. At long last Lord Stanley had returned to the 'Burgh!

Although they were serenaded by a chorus of boos from the downtrodden Detroit faithful, the Penguins celebrated

The Piece

When Rob Scuderi joined the Penguins in the spring of 2004, few thought he had the makings of an impact player. While the Syosset, New York, native gradually developed into an ultrareliable defenseman, he wasn't exactly a household name.

Fast-forward to the 2009 Stanley Cup Finals. Unaccustomed to the media attention usually reserved for his more heralded teammates, the modest Scuderi tried to explain to a reporter that he was just a piece of his team's puzzle.

"But it was a misquote and it came out that I was 'the piece,'" Scuderi said.

Following a typical shutdown performance by the unsung defender in Game 4, his fun-loving teammates pounced.

"He's unbelievable with blocking and getting in front of pucks, and he does a great job of battling," Jordan Staal said. "Scuds, he's 'the Piece.'"

While Scuderi's teammates may have teased him, no one doubted his importance to the team.

"What he does you can't put a value on," coach Dan Bylsma said.

Unsung hero Max Talbot celebrates his second goal of the night to clinch the Cup.

like little kids. Perhaps the most heartwarming moment occurred when 73-year-old Eddie Johnston—still serving the team as a senior advisor—hoisted the Cup.

As the grandfatherly Johnston handed the chalice to Mario, the booing suddenly melted away and cheers began to resonate around Joe Louis Arena. It was a touching display of respect and admiration for arguably the greatest player ever to lace on a pair of skates.

After watching his boss lift the Cup, Sidney Crosby said, "It's great, he's done so much. He's at the top and this starts at the top. Mario, Ray Shero, all the people that add to this."

In a typical display of class, Crosby also paid homage to former coach Michel Therrien.

"He had us when we were young," Sid said. "He had a lot to do with this [victory]."

There was no shortage of heroes to share the spotlight with Sid, who became the youngest captain ever to lead his team to a Cup. Evgeni Malkin capped off his coming-of-age postseason by capturing the Conn Smythe Trophy.

"He told us before the playoffs that he was going to lead us to the Stanley Cup," Bill Guerin said. "He's an amazing competitor, an amazing player."

Marc-Andre Fleury may have drawn criticism from the hometown fans, but he drew only praise from his appreciative teammates.

The Penguins win the Cup…and go wild.

"It's only fitting that he made that save with a second left to clinch it for us," Mark Eaton said. "You can't say enough about the way he's played, and what he did for us."

Dan Bylsma became only the second coach in NHL history to take over a team in midseason and lead it to a championship.

"Where we've come since last year at this time, since the start of the season, since February 15, wherever you want to pick up the storyline, it's an amazing thing to have accomplished and earned," he said.

Cup Quotes II

"When I took over the team in 1999, this was my goal. To lift the Cup again."

—Mario Lemieux

"I can't believe that's me in the picture in the paper. That's me holding the Stanley Cup."

—Dan Bylsma

"It's an amazing feeling. I never experienced anything like it in my life."

—Sergei Gonchar

"I don't know if it's sunk in yet. It doesn't get any better than this."

—Mark Eaton

"This is why I came back."

—Brooks Orpik

Last, but far from least, was Max Talbot, who racked up eight goals during the playoffs, including a team-high four during the Finals.

"It's the biggest day of my life," a joyous Max said. "I'm not really thinking I'm a hero. I scored two goals, but everybody on this team is a hero. I wasn't trying to do anything special. I just wanted to win the Cup."

With the team's talented young core of Crosby, Malkin, Fleury, and Staal secured, there was much reason for optimism.

"This team is set up for a great future," Guerin said. "These guys are all in their early twenties."

"We could have clubs for the next eight or nine years like this," Eddie Johnston added.

Series Summary
Beat Detroit 4–3 (Won Stanley Cup)

Game	Date	City	Result	Winning Goal	Winning Goalie
1	May 30	Detroit	Detroit 3–1	Johan Franzen	Chris Osgood
2	May 31	Detroit	Detroit 3–1	Valtteri Filppula	Chris Osgood
3	June 2	Pittsburgh	Pittsburgh 4–2	Sergei Gonchar	Marc-Andre Fleury
4	June 4	Pittsburgh	Pittsburgh 4–2	Sidney Crosby	Marc-Andre Fleury
5	June 6	Detroit	Detroit 5–0	Dan Cleary	Chris Osgood
6	June 9	Pittsburgh	Pittsburgh 2–1	Tyler Kennedy	Marc-Andre Fleury
7	June 12	Detroit	Pittsburgh 2–1	Max Talbot	Marc-Andre Fleury

2010

In many ways the 2009–10 Penguins were an amalgam of two teams from an earlier era. During a sizzling 12–3 start they invoked memories of arguably the greatest team in franchise history—the President's Trophy–winning 1992–93 club. However, as the campaign wore on they more closely resembled the 1993–94 squad that stumbled through an uneven regular season before falling to the Capitals in the opening round of the playoffs.

A lack of high-end scoring on the wings and an inability to play shutdown defense were the main culprits. The Pens' dreadful record against the other top teams in the Eastern Conference also had a telling effect. They registered a woeful 0–8–2 mark against fellow heavyweights New Jersey and Washington.

Still, the Penguins remained in contention for the Atlantic Division title until the final week of the season, when a 1–0 loss to the Atlanta Thrashers consigned them to second place. The defeat set up an opening-round tilt with an old foe from the Northeast Division—the Ottawa Senators.

Penguins vs. Senators, Eastern Conference Quarterfinals

As the Penguins entered the 2010 Stanley Cup Playoffs, many experts wondered if the team had lost its edge. However, the players were confident they could find the elusive "on" switch to their game. Despite an up-and-down regular season, they showed some life down the homestretch.

Shaking off a foot injury, Evgeni Malkin scored four goals in his final four games. Team MVP Sidney Crosby closed with a rush to earn a share of the Maurice Richard Trophy. Goalie Marc-Andre Fleury was rounding into playoff form.

The Pens' first-round opponent would provide a test. Following a slow start, the Ottawa Senators were one of the league's hottest teams in the second half. In addition to top-drawer talents like Daniel Alfredsson and Jason Spezza, they boasted enviable depth and rugged role players such as Chris Neil and ex-Pen Jarkko Ruutu. On defense Ottawa featured the shutdown pair of Chris Phillips and Anton Volchenkov.

"Both teams know each other pretty well from our history in the playoffs," Crosby said. "They've got depth. They've had solid goaltending for the last little while, too."

The Penguins opened their defense of the Cup in high gear. Barely three minutes into Game 1 Malkin gathered in a pass from Sergei Gonchar at the right face-off dot and ripped the puck past Brian Elliot for a power-play goal. Unfortunately, a shaky Fleury—who arrived at the Arena just moments before the opening face-off—was unable to hold down the fort. Fueled by soft goals from Chris Kelly and Ruutu, Ottawa survived a late rally to snatch the series opener 5–4.

Fortunately the Penguins had a history of rebounding after series-opening losses at the Igloo. However, the Senators struck just 18 seconds into the first shift of Game 2. The contest had scarcely begun and the Pens were down by a goal.

The defending Cup champs refused to buckle. Leading the way was none other than Sidney Crosby. Displaying his

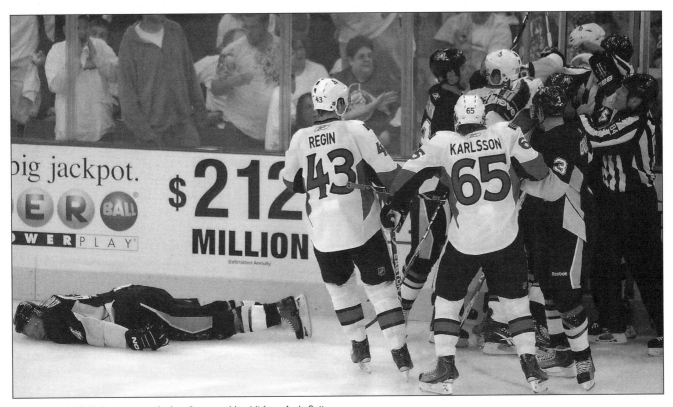

Jordan Leopold (left) lies prone on the ice after a crushing hit from Andy Sutton.

trademark grit and determination, the Pens' captain crashed the net and swatted home a Chris Kunitz rebound at 8:45 to tie the score.

Playing with the purpose and fire that was missing in Game 1, the Pens battled the Senators on even terms through two periods of play. The score remained deadlocked at 1–1 entering the final frame.

The stage was set for a dramatic finish. As the game clock ticked down to five minutes, Crosby outworked the Senators' defense and scrambled out to the right face-off circle. From his knees he found Kris Letang with a picture-perfect pass at the right point. The speedy defenseman ripped the puck past Elliot for the game winner.

"We battled through that one," Jordan Staal said. "We knew it would be a really tough road if we didn't show up tonight."

Having regained their focus, the Pens gave another strong showing in Game 3. Alexei Ponikarovsky silenced the capacity crowd at Scotiabank Place by snapping the puck between Brian Elliot's pads a minute into the contest.

Following a power-play goal by Mike Fisher at 1:53 of the second period, the Penguins' big guns took over. Malkin pounced on a loose puck beside the Senators' net at 5:57 to restore the Pens' lead. In the final minute of the frame Crosby eluded hulking Andy Sutton down low and drilled the puck past Elliot from a sharp angle.

"I just tried to take it across the net, and was able to hold onto it for a little bit and find an opening," Crosby explained afterward.

Veteran Bill Guerin applied the icing on the cake early in the final period when he flagged down a lead pass from Kunitz and beat Elliot on a breakaway. Fleury made a spectacular sprawling save on a deflection attempt to seal an impressive 4–2 victory.

Brooks Orpik (44) pokes the puck away from Ottawa's Matt Cullen.

Paced by a brilliant four-point effort by Crosby, the Penguins thumped Ottawa 7–4 in Game 4 to grab a commanding 3–1 series lead. With the teams returning to Pittsburgh for Game 5, the Pens hoped to close out the series on home ice.

But vanquishing the Senators would prove to be a prickly proposition. Ottawa coach Cory Clouston gave the starting nod in goal to Pascal Leclaire, who had replaced the beleaguered Elliot midway through Game 4. Taking full advantage of a tepid start by their hosts, the Senators forged a quick 2–0 lead.

Facing an uphill climb, the Pens finally showed signs of life. With Phillips serving a hooking minor, Letang scooped up a loose puck in the left face-off circle and shoveled it past Leclaire.

The Pens dominated second-period action, outshooting their foes by a whopping 19–5 margin. They evened the score at 18:34 on a disputed goal by Kunitz, who chipped in a Crosby rebound from the right side of the cage. Midway through the final frame the Pens completed their comeback when Sid swept the puck past Leclaire.

It took the Senators all of 83 seconds to counter. Peter Regin gathered in a feed from Spezza and drove a blistering slap shot past Fleury for his third goal of the series. The clubs battled through a scoreless 10 minutes to send the game into overtime.

Hoping for a quick finish, the Pens buzzed the Ottawa net. However, the defending champs were in for a long night. With Leclaire standing tall between the pipes, the hard-charging Senators pushed the game through two extra frames. At 7:06 of the third overtime former Penguin farmhand Matt Carkner unleashed a shot that deflected off Matt Cooke and past Fleury. Thanks in large part to the Pens' sluggish start, Ottawa was very much alive.

"Obviously, it's disappointing," Letang said afterward. "We battled back, but the main point was that we didn't show up in the first."

The Penguins once again found themselves behind the eight ball early in Game 6. Matt Cullen struck for the Senators five minutes into the opening frame. By the middle of the second period Ottawa had cruised to a 3–0 lead.

In Game 6 of the 2009 Eastern Conference Quarterfinals the Penguins had rallied from a similar deficit on the road to defeat the Flyers. It seemed inconceivable that they could mount a similar comeback against the Senators.

Yet that's precisely what they did. Barely a minute after Ottawa's third goal, Cooke punched the puck past Leclaire from a goal-mouth scramble.

"That was big for us," defenseman Alex Goligoski said. "Really, from there on, we took the play to them."

The Pens dodged a bullet at 16:19 when Fisher barged into the crease and appeared to knock the clincher past a sprawling Fleury. But after a lengthy review it was ruled that the net had come off its moorings before the puck crossed the line.

Granted a reprieve, the Pens dominated the third period while piling up an 18–4 advantage in shots. On a night when the dynamic duo of Crosby and Malkin was held to a lone assist, the support players continued to shine. Guerin pulled the Pens to within one with a power-play tally at 7:03. Five minutes later the scrappy Cooke popped the puck past Leclaire from the edge of the crease to send the game into overtime.

Midway through the extra frame the Pens struck for the game winner on a great bit of teamwork. Venturing deep into the Senators' zone, Mark Eaton nudged the puck to Jordan Staal along the end boards. Staal, whose unit was uncharacteristically outplayed by Ottawa's third line, outmuscled a defender and slipped a pass to Pascal Dupuis. The hustling winger beat Leclaire with a bullet from below the left hash mark to vanquish the Senators.

"I didn't know it was in until everybody started jumping on me," Dupuis said. "It's an unbelievable feeling."

Series Summary
Beat Ottawa 4–2

Game	Date	City	Result	Winning Goal	Winning Goalie
1	April 14	Pittsburgh	Ottawa 5–4	Jarkko Ruutu	Brian Elliot
2	April 16	Pittsburgh	Pittsburgh 2–1	Kris Letang	Marc-Andre Fleury
3	April 18	Ottawa	Pittsburgh 4–2	Sidney Crosby	Marc-Andre Fleury
4	April 20	Ottawa	Pittsburgh 7–4	Max Talbot	Marc-Andre Fleury
5	April 22	Pittsburgh	Ottawa 4–3 (3 OT)	Matt Carkner	Pascal Leclaire
6	April 24	Ottawa	Pittsburgh 4–3 (OT)	Pascal Dupuis	Marc-Andre Fleury

Penguins vs. Canadiens, Eastern Conference Semifinals

While the Penguins were polishing off Ottawa, the other top seeds in the Eastern Conference fell like dominos. The Flyers dumped Atlantic Division champ New Jersey in five games while Boston disposed of Buffalo in six. In the most shocking upset of all, eighth-seeded Montreal stormed back from a 3–1 deficit to vanquish powerhouse Washington. In one fell swoop the Pens' most difficult foes had been eliminated.

Although the defending Cup champs were now the beast of the East, they weren't taking their second-round opponent—the Canadiens—lightly. While Montreal couldn't match the Pens in terms of talent, coach Jacques Martin had installed a lane-clogging defense spearheaded by ex-Penguins stalwart Hal Gill. The Habs boasted a red-hot goalie to boot: unheralded Jaroslav Halak had stopped an incredible 131 of 134 shots during the final three games against the Capitals.

The Canadiens struck for the series-opening goal, thanks to a long shot by rookie P.K. Subban. However, the magic dust quickly wore off. In rapid succession the Penguins pounded three power-play goals past Halak to snatch a 3–1 second-period lead. Paced by four power-play goals, they cruised to a 6–3 win.

Unfortunately, the victory had come with a heavy price. Jordan Staal, a key cog in the Pens' machine, had suffered a severed tendon in his right foot after colliding with Subban.

Dapper Dan

On March 25, 2010, Evgeni Malkin received the prestigious Dapper Dan Sportsman of the Year Award from the *Pittsburgh Post-Gazette*.

At a banquet that evening, Geno gave his acceptance speech in English. He humbly thanked his parents, teammates, and the fans for their support.

"It's truly an honor to be sportsman of the year in the city of champions," he said.

While giving special recognition to his road roommates, Brooks Orpik and Max Talbot, for helping him with his English, the big Russian flashed his sense of humor.

"They told me not to use any of the words Max taught me," he joked.

He also poked fun at Sidney Crosby. After thanking Sergei Gonchar for allowing him to stay at his home, he said, "The spare room at Mario's house was already taken."

"He's a big part of our team," Crosby said. "It's not something that's easy to deal with, but that's what you face. There's no use feeling sorry for ourselves. There's nothing you can do. It's out of our control."

Although surgery would hasten Staal's return, the big center missed the next two games. Reaching into his bag of spare parts, Pens coach Dan Bylsma plugged the gap with Max Talbot. The hero of the 2009 playoffs wasted little time in making an impact. Four minutes into Game 2 he teamed up with Pascal Dupuis and Matt Cooke on a beautiful tic-tac-toe passing play to stake the Penguins to an early lead.

Suitably inspired, the Pens threatened to blow the Canadiens out of Mellon Arena. But Halak, who leaked for five goals on 20 shots before being pulled in Game 1, held his ground. Following an ill-timed interference penalty to Ruslan Fedotenko, the Pens' early surge petered out. On the ensuing power play Brian Gionta popped the puck past Fleury from the slot to even the score.

The game remained deadlocked until midway through the second period, when Montreal cashed in on another power play. Subban stripped the puck from a Pens defender and shoveled it toward Mike Cammalleri. The speedy winger bunted the rubber over Fleury's glove for the go-ahead goal. Cammalleri supplied the icing on the cake in the third period with a breakaway goal.

It was a disappointing loss for the Pens, who played well enough to win. But they were hardly surprised by Montreal's gritty, determined effort.

"We expected them to play this way," Bylsma said. "We expected games like this, where their goaltender plays well, and their defense plays like it did."

Jaroslav Halak and Roman Hamrlik (44) team up to stop the Pens' Pascal Dupuis.

"I don't think we played poorly at all," Bill Guerin added, while tipping his hat to the Canadiens. "I thought Montreal played exceptional defense."

The Penguins had controlled the play through the first two games of the series. But Game 3 was a different story. Skating before a packed house at the Bell Centre, the Canadiens dominated the first period while holding the skittish Pens to a paltry three shots.

"They came out hard," Sergei Gonchar said afterward. "We didn't respond very well."

Fortunately for the Penguins, Marc-Andre Fleury was razor sharp. Under fire from the Steel City media for his unsightly .890 save percentage, he stoned the host Habs while his teammates regrouped.

"That's the best I've seen him play in a long time," Brooks Orpik said. "His rebound control was pretty good, and he was playing the puck pretty well, too, which is big for us."

The Penguins gradually seized control, outshooting the Canadiens 22–11 over the final two periods. Early in the final frame they broke through against Halak, who turned in another dazzling effort. Working on the power play, Gonchar found Malkin in the right face-off circle with a pretty cross-ice pass. With Crosby creating traffic in front, Geno ripped off a sizzling shot that sailed between Halak and the goal post. Dupuis notched an empty netter in the closing seconds to seal a Pens victory.

Determined to make a series of it, Montreal struck first in Game 4. Tom Pyatt drilled the puck between Fleury's pads from the left face-off circle at 2:34 to stake the Canadiens to an early lead. Displayed plenty of resilience, the Pens knotted the score 53 seconds later on a pretty goal by Max Talbot. At 5:18 they snatched the lead on a power-play tally by Chris Kunitz.

Buoyed by the return of Jordan Staal, the Penguins piled up a 26–9 advantage in shots through 40 minutes of play. In the third period, however, they gave a clinic on blowing a lead. Two minutes into the final frame Maxim Lapierre outmuscled Alex Goligoski behind the net and scored on a wraparound. Ninety-three seconds later Gionta tossed the puck into the slot and watched as it glanced off Kris Letang's skate and into the net.

"They got a good bounce, but we turned over the puck inside the blue line in a tie game," a glum Opik noted.

Try as they might the Penguins could not push the equalizer past Halak, who made 33 saves in a sterling performance. Although they had dominated the territorial play, the Pens were struggling to crack Montreal's trap-style box defense. To make matters worse, slippery forwards Cammalleri and Gionta were springing loose with alarming regularity. While stay-at-home defenders Orpik and Mark Eaton were doing their best, the team obviously missed the shutdown play of departed free agents Gill and Rob Scuderi.

With the venue shifting to Pittsburgh for the pivotal fifth game, Dan Bylsma shook up his troops. In an effort to add some mustard he reinserted bangers Mike Rupp and Bill Guerin—who missed two games with an undisclosed injury—while sitting out snake-bitten Ukrainians Fedotenko and Ponikarvosky.

The shuffle worked like a charm. From the opening face-off the Pens played with an aggression and fire that carried through for the rest of the evening. Drawing a bead on their foe's stubborn defense, Rupp and Craig Adams pounded the Habs' blue-liners with hard bodychecks.

"When you're a fourth-line guy, you want to do anything you can to bring energy to your team," said Adams, who leveled Josh Gorges with a huge hit.

Guerin made his presence felt late in the opening period. With the Pens working on a power play, the veteran winger provided a perfect screen while Letang drove a hard slap shot past Halak.

The grinders chipped in midway through the second period. Rupp dug the puck out of a scrum and shoveled it to rookie Mark Letestu, who started an around-the-horn passing play to Gonchar. With Rupp planted firmly in front of Halak, "Sarge" beat the Slovakian netminder with a blistering drive from the right point.

Meanwhile, at the other end of ice, Fleury atoned for a marginal performance in Game 4 with a sparkling 32-save effort. The Pens held the Canadiens off the scoreboard until the final minute of play and emerged with a hard-fought 2–1 victory.

Now holding a 3–2 edge in the series, the Penguins were determined to finish off the nettlesome Habs in Game 6.

"We don't want to go to a one-game series against these guys," Rupp said. "They're a good team, and they're playing really well against us."

"We want to go in with a do-or-die mind-set, for sure," Matt Cooke added.

The defending champs immediately fell behind. Barely a minute into the opening period Letang turned the puck over in the neutral zone. The opportunistic Cammalleri pounced to give Montreal a quick 1–0 lead.

Much their credit, the Pens battled back. At 7:22 Crosby swatted home his first goal of the series to knot the score. Early in the second period Letang atoned for his early gaffe by blasting the puck past Halak on the power play.

The Penguins finally appeared to be in the driver's seat. However, their hard-earned lead would be short lived. Once again Cammalleri provided the spark, beating Fleury with a backhander at 10:45 for his sixth goal of the series. Moments later, with the huge throng at the Bell Centre roaring its approval, Jaroslav Spacek ripped a slap shot past the Pens' goalie to restore the Canadiens' lead.

Midway through the final frame, Lapierre once again victimized Goligoski to provide some insurance. Bill Guerin tipped home a Gonchar rocket at 18:36, but it was too little,

Super Duper

During the course of his eight-year NHL career, Pascal Dupuis earned a reputation for solid penalty killing and defensive play. While he possessed blazing speed and a hard slap shot, he never scored more than 20 goals in a season.

After spending four-plus seasons with the Minnesota Wild, Dupuis became somewhat of a vagabond. In 2006–07 he was traded twice—first to the Rangers and then to Atlanta. The following season he joined the Penguins in the Marian Hossa deal.

Although Dupuis often skated on a line with superstar Sidney Crosby, his offensive output was pedestrian at best. Possessing what writer Michael Farber described as "flinty hands," Dupuis totaled a dozen goals in 2008–09. Due to lackluster production, he was a frequent scratch during the Pens' march to the Stanley Cup.

Over the off-season coach Dan Bylsma spoke with Dupuis. He asked the speedy winger to improve his conditioning and for a commitment to do the dirty work in the corners.

Dupuis followed his coach's instructions to the letter. Rededicating himself to training, he rode the exercise bike every day during the summer. When he arrived in training camp, he was sleeker—and even faster.

His dedication paid off handsomely. After beginning the season on the fourth line, Dupuis gradually earned more ice time. His game transformed, he crashed and banged along the boards while displaying vastly improved hands. By the stretch run "Duper" had reclaimed his spot on the top line beside Crosby. Arguably the team's most improved player, the 30-year-old winger potted 18 goals—the second-best total of his career.

too late. The Canadiens had succeeded in forcing a deciding Game 7 in Pittsburgh.

"It's obviously not what we were looking for," Guerin said afterward. "[But] it's been a hard-fought series since Game 1."

The odds—and the hockey gods—did not favor the Penguins. For all of their success, they owned a less-than-inspiring 2–4 record in seventh games at the Mellon Arena. Worse yet, the series bore an uneasy resemblance to the 1993 Patrick Division Finals, when the Pens had the Islanders on the ropes but failed to deliver the knockout punch.

No less an authority than Montreal legend Jean Beliveau, who scored the first goal at the Igloo, liked the Habs' chances.

Sidney Crosby struggles to escape the grasp of Montreal's Scott Gomez.

"I don't think Pittsburgh wanted a seventh game," the Hall of Famer noted. "I played quite a few, and the stress is something very special. It's not handled the same by each player, and I believe the Canadiens have put the pressure back on the Penguins."

Still, the Pens remained upbeat.

"When you play the best-of-seven, usually the best team wins," Orpik said. "So, I think we're pretty confident going into it."

In Game 7 the best team was Montreal. Clearly frustrated by the Canadiens' rope-a-dope tactics, Sidney Crosby drew a boarding penalty just 10 seconds after the opening draw. Twenty-two seconds later Brian Gionta beat Fleury with a shot that trickled inside the right goal post. By the five-minute mark of the second period the Habs had piled up a 4–0 lead.

"The Penguins have fallen asleep," play-by-play announcer Paul Steigerwald lamented.

With Fleury leaking goals like a crumbling dam, Bylsma pulled his harried starter in favor of backup Brent Johnson.

The Pens finally showed signs of life, popping a pair of markers past Halak before the second intermission.

Hoping for some late-game heroics, the overflow Mellon Arena crowd cheered the Pens with a rousing ovation during a TV timeout. Determined to go out on their collective shield, the home team responded by peppering Halak with 18 shots in the final period. Once more the unflappable goalie stood his ground. The upstart Canadiens had done what few outside of La Belle Province thought they could do. They dethroned the defending champs.

"It's definitely disappointing," Crosby said afterward. "Game 7, anything can happen and, unfortunately, we weren't at our best."

Brooks Orpik was more magnanimous.

"They beat Washington, now they beat us," the rugged defenseman said. "I think it's time to give this team some credit for what they've done, rather than picking apart why we didn't do what we were supposed to do."

Although understandably downcast, the Penguins gathered together following the traditional postgame handshake and raised their sticks in a touching salute to the fans. In a send-off befitting a team that had provided so many thrilling memories, the Steel City partisans rose in unison and gave the players another heartfelt ovation.

It also was a poignant way to bid farewell to the Mellon Arena. After 42 seasons, the grand old girl was closing her doors forever. Beginning in 2010 the Penguins will showcase their extraordinary skills in the brand-new 18,087-seat Consol Energy Center.

Despite the disappointing loss to the Canadiens the future was, indeed, bright. With the team's talented core securely in place, the Pens figure to be a contender for Lord Stanley's coveted Cup for years to come.

To borrow from the late Bob Johnson's favorite saying, "It's a great day for Penguins hockey."

Series Summary
Lost to Montreal 4–3

Game	Date	City	Result	Winning Goal	Winning Goalie
1	April 30	Pittsburgh	Pittsburgh 6–3	Craig Adams	Marc-Andre Fleury
2	May 2	Pittsburgh	Montreal 3–1	Mike Cammalleri	Jaroslav Halak
3	May 4	Montreal	Pittsburgh 2–0	Evgeni Malkin	Marc-Andre Fleury
4	May 6	Montreal	Montreal 3–2	Brian Gionta	Jaroslav Halak
5	May 8	Pittsburgh	Pittsburgh 2–1	Sergei Gonchar	Marc-Andre Fleury
6	May 10	Montreal	Montreal 4–3	Maxim Lapierre	Jaroslav Halak
7	May 12	Pittsburgh	Montreal 5–2	Mike Cammalleri	Jaroslav Halak

Year-by-Year Playoff Scoring and Goaltending Statistics

1970

	GP	G	A	PTS	PM
Michel Briere	10	5	3	8	17
Jean Pronovost	10	3	4	7	2
Dean Prentice	10	2	5	7	8
Ron Schock	10	1	6	7	7
Ken Schinkel	10	4	1	5	4
Duane Rupp	6	2	2	4	2
Keith McCreary	10	0	4	4	4
Nick Harbaruk	10	3	0	3	20
Wally Boyer	10	1	2	3	0
Dunc McCallum	10	1	2	3	12
Bob Woytowich	10	1	2	3	2
Jim Morrison	8	0	3	3	10
Val Fonteyne	10	0	2	2	0
Glen Sather	10	0	2	2	17
Bryan Hextall	10	0	1	1	34
Tracy Pratt	10	0	1	1	51
Al Smith	3	0	0	0	0
Bob Blackburn	6	0	0	0	4
Les Binkley	7	0	0	0	0
Bryan Watson	10	0	0	0	17

	GP	MINS	GA	SH	AVG	W	L
Les Binkley	7	428	15	0	2.10	5	2
Al Smith	3	180	10	0	3.33	1	2
	10	608	25	0	2.47	6	4

1972

	GP	G	A	PTS	PM
Bob Leiter	4	3	0	3	0
Ken Schinkel	3	2	0	2	0
Jean Pronovost	4	1	1	2	0
Darryl Edestrand	4	0	2	2	0
Bryan Hextall	4	0	2	2	9
Greg Polis	4	0	2	2	0
Syl Apps	4	1	0	1	2
Ron Schock	4	1	0	1	6
Tim Horton	4	0	1	1	2
Nick Harbaruk	4	0	1	1	0
Al McDonough	4	0	1	1	0
Eddie Shack	4	0	1	1	15
Keith McCreary	1	0	0	0	2
Dave Burrows	4	0	0	0	4
Steve Cardwell	4	0	0	0	2
Val Fonteyne	4	0	0	0	2
Duane Rupp	4	0	0	0	6
Jim Rutherford	4	0	0	0	0
Bryan Watson	4	0	0	0	21

	GP	MINS	GA	SH	AVG	W	L
Jim Rutherford	4	240	14	0	3.50	0	4
	4	240	14	0	3.50	0	4

1975

	GP	G	A	PTS	PM
Bob Kelly	9	5	3	8	17
Ron Stackhouse	9	2	6	8	10
Pierre Larouche	9	2	5	7	2
Vic Hadfield	9	4	2	6	0
Lowell MacDonald	9	4	2	6	4
Jean Pronovost	9	3	3	6	6
Chuck Arnason	9	2	4	6	4
Syl Apps	9	2	3	5	9
Colin Campbell	9	1	3	4	21
Ron Schock	9	0	4	4	10
Dave Burrows	9	1	1	2	12
Rick Kehoe	9	0	2	2	0
Pete Laframboise	9	1	0	1	0
Dennis Owchar	6	0	1	1	4
Bob Paradise	6	0	1	1	17
Bob McManama	8	0	1	1	6
Larry Bignell	3	0	0	0	2
Barry Wilkins	3	0	0	0	0
Gary Inness	9	0	0	0	2
Lew Morrison	9	0	0	0	0

	GP	MINS	GA	SH	AVG	W	L
Gary Inness	9	540	24	0	2.67	5	4
	9	540	27	0	3.00	5	4

1976

	GP	G	A	PTS	PM
Stan Gilbertson	3	1	1	2	2
Vic Hadfield	3	1	0	1	11
Lowell MacDonald	3	1	0	1	0
Syl Apps	3	0	1	1	0
Pierre Larouche	3	0	1	1	0
Ron Schock	3	0	1	1	0
Ed Van Impe	3	0	1	1	2
Barry Wilkins	3	0	1	1	4
Dennis Owchar	2	0	0	0	2
Dave Burrows	3	0	0	0	0
Colin Campbell	3	0	0	0	0
Rick Kehoe	3	0	0	0	0
Bob Kelly	3	0	0	0	2
Lew Morrison	3	0	0	0	0
Simon Nolet	3	0	0	0	0
Michel Plasse	3	0	0	0	0
Jean Pronovost	3	0	0	0	2
Ron Stackhouse	3	0	0	0	0

	GP	MINS	GA	SH	AVG	W	L
Michel Plasse	3	180	8	1	2.67	1	2
	3	180	8	1	2.67	1	2

1977

	GP	G	A	PTS	PM
Jean Pronovost	3	2	1	3	2
Ron Stackhouse	3	2	1	3	0
Lowell MacDonald	3	1	2	3	4
Pierre Larouche	3	0	3	3	0
Blair Chapman	3	1	1	2	7
Greg Malone	3	1	1	2	2
Dave Burrows	3	0	2	2	0
Rick Kehoe	3	0	2	2	0
Syl Apps	3	1	0	1	12
Mario Faubert	3	1	0	1	2
Bob Kelly	3	1	0	1	4
Russ Anderson	3	0	1	1	14
Don Awrey	3	0	1	1	0
Wayne Bianchin	3	0	1	1	6
Ron Schock	3	0	1	1	0
Lew Morrison	1	0	0	0	0
Mike Corrigan	2	0	0	0	0
Denis Herron	3	0	0	0	5

	GP	MINS	GA	SH	AVG	W	L
Denis Herron	3	180	11	0	3.67	1	2
	3	180	13	0	4.33	1	2

1979

	GP	G	A	PTS	PM
Orest Kindrachuk	7	4	1	5	7
Colin Campbell	7	1	4	5	30
Tom Bladon	7	0	4	4	2
Jim Hamilton	5	3	0	3	0
George Ferguson	7	2	1	3	0
Gary McAdam	7	2	1	3	0
Gregg Sheppard	7	1	2	3	0
Peter Lee	7	0	3	3	0
Rod Schutt	7	2	0	2	4
Rick Kehoe	7	0	2	2	0
Ross Lonsberry	7	0	2	2	9
Blair Chapman	7	1	0	1	2
Pete Mahovlich	2	0	1	1	0
Jacques Cossette	3	0	1	1	4
Greg Malone	7	0	1	1	10
Bob Paradise	2	0	0	0	0
Russ Anderson	2	0	0	0	0
Lex Hudson	2	0	0	0	0
Randy Carlyle	7	0	0	0	12
Denis Herron	7	0	0	0	0
Ron Stackhouse	7	0	0	0	4

	GP	MINS	GA	SH	AVG	W	L
Denis Herron	7	421	24	0	3.42	2	5
	7	421	25	0	3.56	2	5

1980

	GP	G	A	PTS	PM
Rick Kehoe	5	2	5	7	0
Mark Johnson	5	2	2	4	0

	GP	G	A	PTS	PM
Ross Lonsberry	5	2	1	3	2
Rod Schutt	5	2	1	3	6
Gary McAdam	5	1	2	3	9
George Ferguson	5	0	3	3	4
Nick Libett	5	1	1	2	0
Gregg Sheppard	5	1	1	2	0
Bob Stewart	5	1	1	2	2
Russ Anderson	5	0	2	2	14
Randy Carlyle	5	1	0	1	4
Ron Stackhouse	5	1	0	1	18
Tom Bladon	1	0	1	1	0
Mario Faubert	2	0	1	1	0
Peter Lee	4	0	1	1	0
Paul Marshall	1	0	0	0	0
Kim Clackson	3	0	0	0	37
Kim Davis	4	0	0	0	0
Dale Tallon	4	0	0	0	4
Pat Hughes	5	0	0	0	21
Greg Millen	5	0	0	0	0

	GP	MINS	GA	SH	AVG	W	L
Greg Millen	5	300	21	0	4.20	2	3
	5	300	21	0	4.20	2	3

1981

	GP	G	A	PTS	PM
Randy Carlyle	5	4	5	9	9
George Ferguson	5	2	6	8	9
Mike Bullard	4	3	3	6	0
Rod Schutt	5	3	3	6	16
Gregg Sheppard	5	2	4	6	2
Greg Malone	5	2	3	5	16
Peter Lee	5	0	4	4	4
Mark Johnson	5	2	1	3	6
Rick Kehoe	5	0	3	3	0
Mario Faubert	5	1	1	2	4
Pat Price	5	1	1	2	21
Paul Gardner	5	1	0	1	8
Marc Chorney	2	0	1	1	2
Ron Stackhouse	4	0	1	1	6
Paul Baxter	5	0	1	1	28
Gary Rissling	5	0	1	1	4
Dave Burrows	1	0	0	0	0
Jim Hamilton	1	0	0	0	0
Ross Lonsberry	5	0	0	0	2
Greg Millen	5	0	0	0	0

	GP	MINS	GA	SH	AVG	W	L
Greg Millen	5	325	19	0	3.51	2	3
	5	325	20	0	3.69	2	3

1982

	GP	G	A	PTS	PM
Paul Gardner	5	1	5	6	2
Rick Kehoe	5	2	3	5	2
Pat Boutette	5	3	1	4	8
Randy Carlyle	5	1	3	4	16
Andre St. Laurent	5	2	1	3	8
Rod Schutt	5	1	2	3	0

	GP	G	A	PTS	PM	
Greg Hotham	5	0	3	3	6	
Mike Bullard	5	1	1	2	4	
Rick MacLeish	5	1	1	2	0	
Kevin McClelland	5	1	1	2	5	
George Ferguson	5	0	1	1	0	
Steve Gatzos	1	0	0	0	0	
Ron Stackhouse	1	0	0	0	0	
Bobby Simpson	2	0	0	0	0	
Randy Boyd	3	0	0	0	11	
Peter Lee	3	0	0	0	0	
Greg Malone	3	0	0	0	4	
Pat Graham	4	0	0	0	2	
Paul Baxter	5	0	0	0	14	
Marc Chorney	5	0	0	0	0	
Michel Dion	5	0	0	0	0	
Pat Price	5	0	0	0	28	

	GP	MINS	GA	SH	AVG	W	L
Michel Dion	5	310	22	0	4.26	2	3
	5	310	22	0	4.26	2	3

1989

	GP	G	A	PTS	PM	+/-
Mario Lemieux	11	12	7	19	16	- 1
Paul Coffey	11	2	13	15	31	- 7
Kevin Stevens	11	3	7	10	16	- 1
Dan Quinn	11	6	3	9	10	- 6
John Cullen	11	3	6	9	28	4
Zarley Zalapski	11	1	8	9	13	- 2
Rob Brown	11	5	3	8	22	- 2
Randy Cunneyworth	11	3	5	8	26	- 1
John Callander	10	2	5	7	10	6
Phil Bourque	11	4	1	5	66	2
Jim Johnson	11	0	5	5	44	7
Troy Loney	11	1	3	4	24	3
Bob Errey	11	1	2	3	12	1
Gord Dineen	11	0	2	2	8	8
Dave McLlwain	3	0	1	1	0	0
Dave Hannan	8	0	1	1	4	0
Randy Hillier	9	0	1	1	49	- 1
Tom Barrasso	11	0	1	1	8	0
Richard Zemlak	1	0	0	0	10	0
Steve Dykstra	1	0	0	0	2	0
Wendell Young	1	0	0	0	0	0
Chris Dahlquist	2	0	0	0	0	0
Jay Caufield	9	0	0	0	28	- 2
Rod Buskas	10	0	0	0	23	- 1

	GP	MINS	GA	SH	AVG	W	L
Wendell Young	1	39	1	0	1.54	0	0
Tom Barrasso	11	631	40	0	3.80	7	4
	11	672	42	0	3.75	7	4

1991

	GP	G	A	PTS	PM	+/-
Mario Lemieux	23	16	28	44	16	14
Mark Recchi	24	10	24	34	33	6
Kevin Stevens	24	17	16	33	53	14

	GP	G	A	PTS	PM	+/-
Larry Murphy	23	5	18	23	44	17
Joe Mullen	22	8	9	17	4	17
Ron Francis	24	7	10	17	24	13
Phil Bourque	24	6	7	13	16	6
Jaromir Jagr	24	3	10	13	6	2
Paul Coffey	12	2	9	11	6	- 1
Bob Errey	24	5	2	7	29	5
Bryan Trottier	23	3	4	7	49	- 1
Scott Young	17	1	6	7	2	1
Ulf Samuelsson	20	3	2	5	34	7
Jiri Hrdina	14	2	2	4	6	1
Troy Loney	24	2	2	4	41	- 3
Paul Stanton	22	1	2	3	24	6
Gordie Roberts	24	1	2	3	63	13
Peter Taglianetti	19	0	3	3	49	7
Grant Jennings	13	1	1	2	16	3
Jim Paek	8	1	0	1	2	2
Randy Gilhen	16	1	0	1	14	- 4
Frank Pietrangelo	5	0	1	1	2	0
Tom Barrasso	20	0	1	1	2	0
Randy Hillier	8	0	0	0	24	1

	GP	MINS	GA	SH	AVG	W	L
Tom Barrasso	20	1175	51	1	2.60	12	7
Frank Pietrangelo	5	288	15	1	3.12	4	1
	24	1465	68	2	2.78	16	8

1992

	GP	G	A	PTS	PM	+/-
Mario Lemieux	15	16	18	34	2	6
Kevin Stevens	21	13	15	28	28	2
Ron Francis	21	8	19	27	6	8
Jaromir Jagr	21	11	13	24	6	4
Rick Tocchet	14	6	13	19	24	0
Larry Murphy	21	6	10	16	19	- 4
Troy Loney	21	4	5	9	32	1
Shawn McEachern	19	2	7	9	4	6
Paul Stanton	21	1	7	8	42	6
Bryan Trottier	21	4	3	7	8	0
Phil Bourque	21	3	4	7	25	- 1
Joe Mullen	9	3	1	4	4	- 4
John Callander	12	1	3	4	2	0
Jim Paek	19	0	4	4	6	10
Bob Errey	14	3	0	3	10	0
Kjell Samuelsson	15	0	3	3	12	6
Dave Michayluk	7	1	1	2	0	1
Gordie Roberts	19	0	2	2	32	- 1
Tom Barrasso	21	0	2	2	4	0
Jiri Hrdina	21	0	2	2	16	- 6
Ulf Samuelsson	21	0	2	2	39	7
Mike Needham	5	1	0	1	2	0
Ken Wregget	1	0	0	0	0	0
Jay Caufield	5	0	0	0	2	0
Grant Jennings	10	0	0	0	12	- 9

	GP	MINS	GA	SH	AVG	W	L
Tom Barrasso	21	1233	58	1	2.82	16	5
Ken Wregget	1	40	4	0	6.00	0	0
	21	1274	63	1	2.97	16	5

1993

	GP	G	A	PTS	PM	+/-
Mario Lemieux	11	8	10	18	10	2
Ron Francis	12	6	11	17	19	5
Kevin Stevens	12	5	11	16	22	2
Rick Tocchet	12	7	6	13	24	2
Larry Murphy	12	2	11	13	10	2
Jaromir Jagr	12	5	4	9	23	3
Joe Mullen	12	4	2	6	6	4
Ulf Samuelsson	12	1	5	6	24	5
Mike Ramsey	12	0	6	6	4	10
Jeff Daniels	12	3	2	5	0	1
Shawn McEachern	12	3	2	5	10	0
Troy Loney	10	1	4	5	0	3
Dave Tippett	12	1	4	5	14	- 3
Martin Straka	11	2	1	3	2	2
Peter Taglianetti	11	1	2	3	16	2
Tom Barrasso	12	0	3	3	4	0
Kjell Samuelsson	12	0	3	3	2	4
Mike Needham	9	1	0	1	2	1
Paul Stanton	1	0	1	1	0	0
Mike Stapleton	4	0	0	0	0	1
Grant Jennings	12	0	0	0	8	1

	GP	MINS	GA	SH	AVG	W	L
Tom Barrasso	12	722	35	2	2.91	7	5
	12	725	37	2	3.06	7	5

1994

	GP	G	A	PTS	PM	+/-
Mario Lemieux	6	4	3	7	2	- 4
Jaromir Jagr	6	2	4	6	16	- 3
Rick Tocchet	6	2	3	5	20	- 2
Larry Murphy	6	0	5	5	0	- 6
Kevin Stevens	6	1	1	2	10	- 5
Peter Taglianetti	5	0	2	2	16	2
Ron Francis	6	0	2	2	6	- 2
Shawn McEachern	6	1	0	1	2	- 2
Joe Mullen	6	1	0	1	2	- 1
Martin Straka	6	1	0	1	2	- 3
Greg Brown	6	0	1	1	4	- 2
Ulf Samuelsson	6	0	1	1	18	- 3
Larry DePalma	1	0	0	0	0	0
Greg Hawgood	1	0	0	0	0	0
Mike Ramsey	1	0	0	0	0	0
Bryan Trottier	2	0	0	0	0	0
Grant Jennings	3	0	0	0	2	- 1
Jim McKenzie	3	0	0	0	0	0
Chris Tamer	5	0	0	0	2	1
Tom Barrasso	6	0	0	0	4	0
Doug Brown	6	0	0	0	2	0
Kjell Samuelsson	6	0	0	0	26	0
Tomas Sandstrom	6	0	0	0	4	- 4

	GP	MINS	GA	SH	AVG	W	L
Tom Barrasso	6	356	17	0	2.87	2	4
	6	360	20	0	3.33	2	4

1995

	GP	G	A	PTS	PM	+/-
Ron Francis	12	6	13	19	4	3
Jaromir Jagr	12	10	5	15	6	3
Larry Murphy	12	2	13	15	0	3
Luc Robitaille	12	7	4	11	26	5
Kevin Stevens	12	4	7	11	21	- 5
Tomas Sandstrom	12	3	3	6	16	- 5
Norm Maciver	12	1	4	5	8	- 4
Troy Murray	12	2	1	3	12	- 1
Joe Mullen	12	0	3	3	4	- 5
Chris Joseph	10	1	1	2	12	- 4
Ulf Samuelsson	7	0	2	2	8	2
John Cullen	9	0	2	2	8	- 4
Shawn McEachern	11	0	2	2	8	- 2
Francois Leroux	12	0	2	2	14	0
Len Barrie	4	1	0	1	8	- 6
Kjell Samuelsson	11	0	1	1	32	- 4
Drake Berehowsky	1	0	0	0	0	- 1
Tom Barrasso	2	0	0	0	2	0
Richard Park	3	0	0	0	2	- 1
Peter Taglianetti	4	0	0	0	2	- 3
Chris Tamer	4	0	0	0	18	- 4
Rusty Fitzgerald	5	0	0	0	4	- 1
Jim McKenzie	5	0	0	0	4	0
Ian Moran	8	0	0	0	0	0
Mike Hudson	11	0	0	0	6	- 3
Ken Wregget	11	0	0	0	7	0

	GP	MINS	GA	SH	AVG	W	L
Ken Wregget	11	661	33	1	3.00	5	6
Tom Barrasso	2	80	8	0	6.00	0	1
	12	743	43	1	3.47	5	7

1996

	GP	G	A	PTS	PM	+/-
Mario Lemieux	18	11	16	27	33	3
Jaromir Jagr	18	11	12	23	18	7
Petr Nedved	18	10	10	20	16	3
Sergei Zubov	18	1	14	15	26	9
J.J. Daigneault	17	1	9	10	36	4
Bryan Smolinski	18	5	4	9	10	- 4
Ron Francis	11	3	6	9	4	3
Dave Roche	16	2	7	9	26	1
Glen Murray	18	2	6	8	10	2
Chris Tamer	18	0	7	7	24	0
Tomas Sandstrom	18	4	2	6	30	- 6
Kevin Miller	18	3	2	5	8	- 6
Joe Dziedzic	16	1	2	3	19	1
Brad Lauer	12	1	1	2	4	0

	GP	G	A	PTS	PM	+/-
Francois Leroux	18	1	1	2	20	2
Chris Joseph	15	1	0	1	8	1
Ken Wregget	9	0	1	1	0	0
Dmitri Mironov	15	0	1	1	10	- 6
Neil Wilkinson	15	0	1	1	14	- 2
Richard Park	1	0	0	0	0	0
Corey Foster	3	0	0	0	4	- 2
Stefan Bergkvist	4	0	0	0	2	- 1
Dave McLlwain	6	0	0	0	0	0
Alek Stojanov	9	0	0	0	19	0
Tom Barrasso	10	0	0	0	8	0

	GP	MINS	GA	SH	AVG	W	L
Ken Wregget	9	599	23	0	2.30	7	2
Tom Barrasso	10	558	26	1	2.80	4	5
	18	1159	52	1	2.69	11	7

	GP	G	A	PTS	PM	+/-
Kevin Hatcher	6	1	0	1	12	1
Brad Werenka	6	1	0	1	8	- 3
Aleksey Morozov	6	0	1	1	2	- 3
Chris Tamer	6	0	1	1	4	- 1
Tyler Wright	6	0	1	1	4	0
Tuomas Gronman	1	0	0	0	0	0
Andreas Johansson	1	0	0	0	0	0
Darius Kasparaitis	5	0	0	0	8	- 2
Sean Pronger	5	0	0	0	4	- 1
Tom Barrasso	6	0	0	0	2	0
Alex Hicks	6	0	0	0	2	- 5
Ian Moran	6	0	0	0	2	- 1

	GP	MINS	GA	SH	AVG	W	L
Tom Barrasso	6	376	17	0	2.71	2	4
	6	379	18	0	2.85	2	4

1997

	GP	G	A	PTS	PM	+/-
Jaromir Jagr	5	4	4	8	4	- 4
Mario Lemieux	5	3	3	6	4	- 4
Ron Francis	5	1	2	3	2	- 7
Ian Moran	5	1	2	3	4	1
Petr Nedved	5	1	2	3	12	- 2
Jason Woolley	5	0	3	3	0	- 1
Kevin Hatcher	5	1	1	2	4	- 5
Greg Johnson	5	1	0	1	2	- 1
Ed Olczyk	5	1	0	1	12	- 2
Fredrik Olausson	4	0	1	1	0	- 1
Stu Barnes	5	0	1	1	0	0
Joe Dziedzic	5	0	1	1	4	- 1
Alex Hicks	5	0	1	1	2	- 1
Joey Mullen	1	0	0	0	0	0
Francois Leroux	3	0	0	0	0	0
Craig Muni	3	0	0	0	0	0
Chris Tamer	4	0	0	0	4	- 1
Josef Beranek	5	0	0	0	2	- 4
Darius Kasparaitis	5	0	0	0	6	- 4
Neil Wilkinson	5	0	0	0	4	- 2
Ken Wregget	5	0	0	0	2	0

	GP	MINS	GA	SH	AVG	W	L
Ken Wregget	5	297	18	0	3.64	1	4
	5	300	20	0	4.00	1	4

1998

	GP	G	A	PTS	PM	+/-
Jaromir Jagr	6	4	5	9	2	5
Stu Barnes	6	3	3	6	2	2
Ron Francis	6	1	5	6	2	5
Jiri Slegr	6	0	4	4	2	3
Robert Lang	6	0	3	3	2	- 4
Fredrik Olausson	6	0	3	3	2	0
Ed Olczyk	6	2	0	2	4	- 3
Martin Straka	6	2	0	2	2	- 3
Rob Brown	6	1	0	1	4	- 4

1999

	GP	G	A	PTS	PM	+/-
Martin Straka	13	6	9	15	6	0
Jaromir Jagr	9	5	7	12	16	1
Alexei Kovalev	10	5	7	12	14	0
Kip Miller	13	2	7	9	19	- 1
German Titov	11	3	5	8	4	4
Rob Brown	13	2	5	7	8	- 2
Jan Hrdina	13	4	1	5	12	- 1
Kevin Hatcher	13	2	3	5	4	1
Jiri Slegr	13	1	3	4	12	1
Aleksey Morozov	10	1	1	2	0	1
Brad Werenka	13	1	1	2	6	0
Robert Lang	12	0	2	2	0	- 3
Ian Moran	13	0	2	2	8	- 3
Greg Andrusak	12	1	0	1	6	- 1
Bobby Dollas	13	1	0	1	6	- 4
Dan Kesa	13	1	0	1	0	- 2
Maxim Galanov	1	0	0	0	0	0
Victor Ignatjev	1	0	0	0	2	0
Todd Hlushko	2	0	0	0	0	0
Brian Bonin	3	0	0	0	0	- 1
Martin Sonnenberg	7	0	0	0	0	- 2
Matthew Barnaby	13	0	0	0	35	- 2
Tom Barrasso	13	0	0	0	4	0
Tyler Wright	13	0	0	0	19	- 2

	GP	MINS	GA	SH	AVG	W	L
Tom Barrasso	13	787	35	1	2.67	6	7
	13	793	36	1	2.72	6	7

2000

	GP	G	A	PTS	PM	+/-
Jaromir Jagr	11	8	8	16	6	5
Jan Hrdina	9	4	8	12	2	9
Martin Straka	11	3	9	12	10	5
Robert Lang	11	3	3	6	0	- 1
Janne Laukkanen	11	2	4	6	10	6
Alexei Kovalev	11	1	5	6	10	- 1

	GP	G	A	PTS	PM	+/-
Jiri Slegr	10	2	3	5	19	5
Tyler Wright	11	3	1	4	17	0
Rob Brown	11	1	2	3	0	1
Josef Beranek	11	0	3	3	4	2
Rene Corbet	7	1	1	2	9	-2
Darius Kasparaitis	11	1	1	2	10	-3
Matthew Barnaby	11	0	2	2	29	-1
Bob Boughner	11	0	2	2	15	6
John Slaney	2	1	0	1	2	0
Pat Falloon	10	1	0	1	2	0
Hans Jonsson	11	0	1	1	6	2
Ian Moran	11	0	1	1	2	0
Peter Skudra	1	0	0	0	0	0
Michal Rozsival	2	0	0	0	4	0
Aleksey Morozov	5	0	0	0	0	-1
Peter Popovic	10	0	0	0	10	-2
Ron Tugnutt	11	0	0	0	2	0

	GP	MINS	GA	SH	AVG	W	L
Ron Tugnutt	11	746	22	2	1.77	6	5
Peter Skudra	1	20	1	0	3.00	0	0
	11	769	23	2	1.79	6	5

2001

	GP	G	A	PTS	PM	+/-
Mario Lemieux	18	6	11	17	4	4
Martin Straka	18	5	8	13	8	-1
Jaromir Jagr	16	2	10	12	18	4
Alexei Kovalev	18	5	5	10	16	-2
Andrew Ference	18	3	7	10	16	0
Robert Lang	16	4	4	8	4	2
Jan Hrdina	18	2	5	7	8	-4
Kevin Stevens	17	3	3	6	20	-4
Aleksey Morozov	18	3	3	6	6	0
Janne Laukkanen	18	2	2	4	14	6
Wayne Primeau	18	1	3	4	2	-2
Darius Kasparaitis	17	1	1	2	26	-5
Josef Beranek	13	0	2	2	2	1
Rene Corbet	17	1	0	1	12	-5
Marc Bergevin	12	0	1	1	2	2
Bob Boughner	18	0	1	1	22	5
Ian Moran	18	0	1	1	4	-3
Jean-Sebastien Aubin	1	0	0	0	0	0
Dan LaCouture	5	0	0	0	2	0
Krzysztof Oliwa	5	0	0	0	16	0
Milan Kraft	8	0	0	0	2	-4
Hans Jonsson	16	0	0	0	8	-2
Johan Hedberg	18	0	0	0	0	0

	GP	MINS	GA	SH	AVG	W	L
Jean-Sebastien Aubin	1	1	0	0	0.00	0	0
Johan Hedberg	18	1123	43	2	2.30	9	9
	18	1130	44	2	2.34	9	9

2007

	GP	G	A	PTS	PM	+/-
Sidney Crosby	5	3	2	5	4	0
Gary Roberts	5	2	2	4	2	0
Sergei Gonchar	5	1	3	4	2	-3
Evgeni Malkin	5	0	4	4	8	-1
Mark Recchi	5	0	4	4	0	-3
Jordan Staal	5	3	0	3	2	-1
Ryan Whitney	5	1	1	2	6	-4
Michel Ouellet	5	0	2	2	6	-1
Colby Armstrong	5	0	1	1	11	-2
Maxime Talbot	5	0	1	1	7	-2
Nils Ekman	1	0	0	0	0	0
Jocelyn Thibault	1	0	0	0	0	0
Georges Laraque	2	0	0	0	0	-1
Ronald Petrovicky	3	0	0	0	2	0
Erik Christensen	4	0	0	0	6	-1
Mark Eaton	5	0	0	0	0	-1
Marc-Andre Fleury	5	0	0	0	0	0
Ryan Malone	5	0	0	0	0	-4
Josef Melichar	5	0	0	0	2	-1
Brooks Orpik	5	0	0	0	8	-2
Jarkko Ruutu	5	0	0	0	10	-1
Rob Scuderi	5	0	0	0	2	-1

	GP	MINS	GA	SH	AVG	W	L
Jocelyn Thibault	1	8	0	0	0.00	0	0
Marc-Andre Fleury	5	287	18	0	3.76	1	4
	5	300	18	0	3.60	1	4

2008

	GP	G	A	PTS	PM	+/-
Sidney Crosby	20	6	21	27	12	7
Marian Hossa	20	12	14	26	12	8
Evgeni Malkin	20	10	12	22	24	3
Ryan Malone	20	6	10	16	25	4
Sergei Gonchar	20	1	13	14	8	4
Petr Sykora	20	6	3	9	16	2
Maxime Talbot	17	3	6	9	36	4
Jordan Staal	20	6	1	7	14	-4
Pascal Dupuis	20	2	5	7	18	5
Ryan Whitney	20	1	5	6	25	8
Adam Hall	17	3	1	4	8	-1
Gary Roberts	11	2	2	4	32	-4
Tyler Kennedy	20	0	4	4	13	0
Jarkko Ruutu	20	2	1	3	26	-1
Georges Laraque	15	1	2	3	4	-1
Rob Scuderi	20	0	3	3	2	5
Kris Letang	16	0	2	2	12	5
Brooks Orpik	20	0	2	2	18	-3
Hal Gill	20	0	1	1	12	2
Darryl Sydor	4	0	0	0	2	1
Marc-Andre Fleury	20	0	0	0	2	0

	GP	MINS	GA	SH	AVG	W	L
Marc-Andre Fleury	20	1251	41	3	1.97	14	6
	20	1257	43	3	2.05	14	6

2009

	GP	G	A	PTS	PM	+/-
Evgeni Malkin	24	14	22	36	51	3
Sidney Crosby	24	15	16	31	14	9
Bill Guerin	24	7	8	15	15	8
Ruslan Fedotenko	24	7	7	14	4	9
Sergei Gonchar	22	3	11	14	12	3
Chris Kunitz	24	1	13	14	19	3
Maxime Talbot	24	8	5	13	19	8
Kris Letang	23	4	9	13	26	1
Tyler Kennedy	24	5	4	9	4	- 1
Jordan Staal	24	4	5	9	8	- 5
Mark Eaton	24	4	3	7	10	4
Matt Cooke	24	1	6	7	22	- 2
Miroslav Satan	17	1	5	6	11	1
Craig Adams	24	3	2	5	16	- 1
Rob Scuderi	24	1	4	5	6	5
Philippe Boucher	9	1	3	4	4	- 2
Brooks Orpik	24	0	4	4	22	- 1
Hal Gill	24	0	2	2	6	8
Alex Goligoski	2	0	1	1	0	- 1
Petr Sykora	7	0	1	1	0	- 3
Mathieu Garon	1	0	0	0	0	0
Pascal Dupuis	16	0	0	0	8	- 5
Marc-Andre Fleury	24	0	0	0	2	0

	GP	MINS	GA	SH	AVG	W	L
Mathieu Garon	1	24	0	0	0.00	0	0
Marc-Andre Fleury	24	1447	63	0	2.61	16	8
	24	1480	64	0	2.59	16	8

2010

	GP	G	A	PTS	PM	+/-
Sidney Crosby	13	6	13	19	6	6
Sergei Gonchar	13	2	10	12	4	4
Evgeni Malkin	13	5	6	11	6	0
Chris Kunitz	13	4	7	11	8	3
Bill Guerin	11	4	5	9	2	3
Alex Goligoski	13	2	7	9	2	4
Pascal Dupuis	13	2	6	8	4	5
Kristopher Letang	13	5	2	7	6	- 5
Matt Cooke	13	4	2	6	22	- 4
Maxime Talbot	13	2	4	6	11	1
Jordan Staal	11	3	2	5	6	- 4
Alexei Ponikarovsky	11	1	4	5	4	0
Craig Adams	13	2	1	3	15	2
Mark Eaton	13	0	3	3	4	- 4
Brooks Orpik	13	0	2	2	12	3
Mark Letestu	4	0	1	1	0	0
Chris Conner	1	0	0	0	0	0
Brent Johnson	1	0	0	0	0	0
Jay McKee	5	0	0	0	2	2
Ruslan Fedotenko	6	0	0	0	4	- 3
Jordan Leopold	8	0	0	0	2	- 2

	GP	G	A	PTS	PM	+/-
Tyler Kennedy	10	0	0	0	2	- 6
Mike Rupp	11	0	0	0	8	0
Marc-Andre Fleury	13	0	0	0	2	0

	GP	MINS	GA	SH	AVG	W	L
Brent Johnson	1	31	1	0	1.94	0	0
Marc-Andre Fleury	13	798	37	1	2.78	7	6
	13	837	38	1	2.72	7	6

Penguins Stanley Cup Playoffs Fast Facts

Stanley Cup Playoffs
Appearances: 24 (1970, 1972, 1975–1977, 1979–1982, 1989, 1991–2001, 2007–2010)

Stanley Cup Playoff Series
Total: 50
Wins: 28
Losses: 22

Stanley Cup Playoff Games
Total: 270
Wins: 147
Losses: 123
Winning Percentage: .544

Stanley Cup Finals
Appearances: 4 (1991, 1992, 2008, 2009)
Series Wins: 3 (1991, 1992, 2009)
Series Losses: 1 (2008)

Wales Conference Finals
Appearances: 2 (1991, 1992)
Series Wins: 2 (1991, 1992)

Eastern Conference Finals
Appearances: 4 (1996, 2001, 2008, 2009)
Series Wins: 2 (2008, 2009)
Series Losses: 2 (1996, 2001)

8

Phil Bourque (29) and Jaromir Jagr
celebrate a big goal against the Capitals in
the 1992 Stanley Cup Playoffs.

The Greatest Games

Over the course of their 43-year history the Penguins have played hundreds of big games. For this chapter, we've selected 25 of the most memorable. While it is by no means an all-encompassing list, we attempted to select the games that were the most notable or had the greatest impact. Of course, the fans have the final say in any such list.

Several of the Penguins' biggest games were played during the early 1990s. The 8–0 pasting of the Minnesota North Stars in Game 6 of the 1991 Stanley Cup Finals ranks as perhaps the greatest game in franchise history. Following a close second is the Penguins' second Cup winner, a thrilling 6–5 victory over the Blackhawks in 1992. Of course, the team would never have reached the Finals if not for a tremendous comeback against Washington in the opening round of the playoffs.

Game 7 of the team's Stanley Cup–winning effort in 2009 is included, as well as the pulsating triple-overtime victory over Detroit the previous spring. For sheer spectacle and drama, few games can match the Penguins' "Ice Bowl" triumph over the Sabres in the 2008 Winter Classic.

Any list of greatest games must include the Pens' record-setting five-goal outburst against the St. Louis Blues in 1972. Likewise, no list would be complete without the team's epic 5–3 triumph over the Flyers in the Spectrum in February of 1989—a victory that snapped a mind-boggling 42-game winless streak in the "City of Brotherly Shove."

It's only natural that Mario Lemieux's finest games are well represented. Few can forget his electric debut in 1984; his five-goal efforts against the Devils and Flyers during the 1988–89 season; or his magical comeback following more than three years of retirement on December 27, 2000.

During their roller-coaster ride from the depths of the standings to Stanley Cup champions, the Penguins have endured more than their share of disappointments, too. We've included six of the most heartbreaking losses in franchise history. Ironically, three of them involved the New York Islanders.

The Pens earned an ignominious place in the NHL record books during the 1975 playoffs when they blew a 3–0 series lead and lost four straight to the Islanders. The stunning collapse forced the franchise into receivership and permanently derailed a promising young team.

In 1982, an undermanned but gritty Penguins squad had a chance to dethrone the two-time defending Cup champions. The Islanders rallied from a 3–1 third-period deficit in the fifth and deciding game to oust the Cinderella Pens. Eleven years later a scrappy New York team beat the Penguins in a dramatic overtime thriller to end the team's hopes of a three-peat.

We also included a section on the team's greatest brawls. Hockey is unique among the major pro sports because it tolerates fighting. Over the years teams such as Philadelphia's "Broad Street Bullies," Boston's "Big, Bad Bruins" and the St. Louis Blues, to name a few, have employed roughhouse play as a weapon to bludgeon opponents into submission. Traditionally a skill-oriented team, the Penguins often found themselves on the receiving end of the intimidation tactics. Occasionally, however, they fought back, producing some spectacular and noteworthy brawls.

Penguins Score Five Goals in Two Minutes
November 22, 1972

In the early 1970s, the Penguins and the St. Louis Blues were antagonists in one of the NHL's fiercest feuds. Contests between the teams invariably featured a liberal dose of brawling and rough play. Pens toughies Bryan "Bugsy" Watson and Bryan Hextall and the Blues' equally rugged Plager brothers, Barclay and Bob, were usually at the center of the mayhem.

A near-capacity crowd of more than 12,400 fans jammed the Civic Arena on a mid-November night in 1972 to watch the bitter rivals go at it. They were treated to fireworks of a different kind.

The archenemies stayed true to form during a nasty first period. Penguins winger Greg Polis engaged Mike Murphy in the obligatory fisticuffs, while feisty Blues center Garry Unger piled up 22 minutes in penalties. Thanks to some aggressive skating and forechecking, the Pens snatched a 3–1 lead.

Heading into the second period, the home team appeared to have the game well in hand. However, the Blues took advantage of sloppy defensive play to poke two pucks past Pens goalie Jim Rutherford. When St. Louis center Fran Huck scored barely a minute into the final frame, it appeared the game was slipping away.

Al McDonough immediately knotted the score for the Pens with his second goal of the evening. The game remained deadlocked until the nine-minute mark, when Hextall and Jean Pronovost set up Polis for the go-ahead goal.

That's when things really heated up. In rapid-fire succession, the Penguins hammered five goals past Blues netminder Wayne Stephenson is just over two minutes. Hextall tipped in a blast from the point for a power-play tally at 12:00. Eighteen seconds later, Pronovost beat the beleaguered goalie again. After a brief respite, McDonough lit the lamp at 13:40, followed in short order by Ken Schinkel (13:49) and Ron Schock (14:07).

The sudden outburst set two NHL records: the fastest five goals ever by one team (2:07), and the fastest seven goals ever by one team (12:13).

Penguins 10 • Blues 4

SCORING BY PERIODS

St. Louis	1	2	1	4
Pittsburgh	3	0	7	10

FIRST PERIOD

SCORING—1. Pittsburgh, Apps 9 (Lynch, McDonough) 3:59; 2. Pittsburgh, Watson 1 (Edestrand, Kessell) 11:40; 3. St. Louis, Roberto 3 (Murphy) 13:50; 4. Pittsburgh, McDonough 9 (Apps) 14:31.

PENALTIES—Unger, StL, minor-misconduct (slashing) 3:59; Shack, Pit (hooking) 6:15; Watson, Pit (high-sticking) 7:57; Murphy, StL (elbowing) 11:00; Harbaruk, Pit (high-sticking) 11:00; Murphy, StL, minor-major (high-sticking and fighting) 14:07; Polis, Pit, minor-major (high-sticking and fighting) 14:07; Unger, StL (game misconduct) 14:07; K. O'Shea, StL (high-sticking) 16:00; Burrows, Pit (high-sticking) 16:00; Dupont, StL (holding) 17:17.

SECOND PERIOD

SCORING—5. St. Louis, Roberto 4 (Huck, Thomson) 1:58; 6. St. Louis, D. O'Shea 3 (Evans) 7:36.

PENALTIES—Barclay Plager, StL (cross-checking) 5:39; Hextall, Pit, major (high-sticking) 10:49; Murphy, StL (hooking) 16:57.

THIRD PERIOD

SCORING—7. St. Louis, Huck 1 (Roberto, Murphy) 1:22; 8. Pittsburgh, McDonough 10 (Apps) 1:56; 9. Pittsburgh, Polis (Pronovost, Hextall) 9:05; 10. Pittsburgh, Hextall 9 (Lynch, Polis) 12:00 (pp); 11. Pittsburgh, Pronovost 5 (Polis) 12:18; 12. Pittsburgh, McDonough 11 (Apps) 13:40; 13. Pittsburgh, Schinkel 10 (Burrows, Shack) 13:49; 14. Pittsburgh, Schock (Schinkel, Lynch) 14:07.

PENALTY—D. O'Shea, StL (slashing) 11:47.

SHOTS ON GOAL

St. Louis 13-15-14—42; Pittsburgh 10-9-15—34

GOALIES

St. Louis, Stephenson (34 shots—24 saves); Pittsburgh, Rutherford (42 shots—38 saves).

ATTENDANCE—12,486

Mario Lemieux Makes His Debut, Scores on His First Shot
October 11, 1984

Mario Lemieux entered the National Hockey League in the fall of 1984 as the most ballyhooed rookie since Wayne Gretzky—and with good reason. While skating for the Laval Voisin of the Quebec League, the 18-year-old Lemieux had amassed a staggering total of 282 points to shatter the junior hockey scoring records. Experts and fans alike were anxious to see if the Penguins' No. 1 pick could duplicate his mind-boggling success on a professional level.

Lemieux's first test would come against one of the league's best and toughest teams, the Boston Bruins. The Bruins' lineup featured All-Star defenseman Ray Bourque and goalie Pete Peeters, who once registered a 27-game unbeaten streak as a member of the Flyers.

It didn't take long for the big fellow to make his mark. Barely a minute into the game, Lemieux stripped the puck from Bourque and sped in alone on Peeters. After freezing the veteran netminder with a supernatural move, Mario flipped the puck into an open net. First shift, first shot, first goal.

The Bruins were clearly impressed—especially his two victims.

"I tried to pass the puck between his stick and his skate," Bourque explained. "It hit his skate and he was just gone. I think he's going to be a big help to that club."

"When this guy gets it going, he'll be awesome," Peeters added. "He's going to flower after 30, 35 games, after he feels his way around the league."

Lemieux added a second-period assist on a goal by fellow rookie Warren Young to give him a two-point night. Not a bad showing in the unfriendly confines of the Boston Garden. Despite Mario's best efforts, however, the Penguins fell to the Bruins 4–3.

"All things considered, I'm happy," Lemieux said afterward in a hushed tone. "But it would have been better if we would have won the game."

Bruins 4 • Penguins 3

SCORING BY PERIODS

Pittsburgh	2	1	0	3
Boston	0	2	2	4

FIRST PERIOD

SCORING—1. Pittsburgh, Lemieux 1 (unassisted) 2:59; 2. Pittsburgh, Young 1 (Flockhart, Babych) 13:53.

PENALTIES—K. Crowder, Bos, minor-major (high-sticking and fighting) 0:25; Buskas, Pit, minor-major (high-sticking and fighting) 0:25; O'Connell, Bos (high-sticking) 2:30; Boutette, Pit (slashing) 2:30; Milbury, Bos (cross-checking) 3:47; Boutette, Pit (hooking) 5:01.

SECOND PERIOD
SCORING—3. Boston, Fergus 1 (Byers, Markwart) 8:13; 4. Pittsburgh, Young 2 (Lemieux, Kehoe) 18:09; 5. Boston, Linseman 1 (O'Reilly, Bourque) 18:56 (pp).
PENALTIES—Buskas, Pit (interference) 10:22; Linseman, Bos (holding) 10:57; Hannan, Pit (broken stick) 14:14; McCarthy, Pit (hooking) 18:34; Maxwell, Pit (roughing) 19:36; Markwart, Bos (roughing) 19:36.

THIRD PERIOD
SCORING—6. Boston, O'Connell 1 (Silk, Middleton) 0:38; 7. Boston, Bourque 1 (Middleton, Silk) 14:28.
PENALTIES—Kostynski, Bos (hooking) 9:34; Bullard, Pit (roughing) 10:59; Young, Pit, major (fighting) 16:38; Byers, Bos, major (fighting) 16:38.

SHOTS ON GOAL
Pittsburgh 12-5-8—25; Boston 12-14-10—36

GOALIES
Pittsburgh, Herron (36 shots—32 saves); Boston, Peeters (25 shots—22 saves).

ATTENDANCE—14,451

Lemieux Scores Five Goals in Five Different Ways

December 31, 1988

From the moment he first stepped onto NHL ice, Mario Lemieux served notice that he was a once-in-a-generation player. He scored on his very first shot on goal, undressing All-Star Ray Bourque in the process. In only his second season Lemieux was honored with the Lester B. Pearson Award, given to the league's outstanding performer by the NHL Players Association. After emerging as a true superstar in the 1987 Canada Cup tournament, he captured the Hart and Art Ross Trophies.

By the 1988–89 season, Penguins fans had grown accustomed to Mario's amazing exploits. However, nothing could have prepared them for the treat that was in store on New Year's Eve.

The New Jersey Devils were in town—the same Devils who had almost earned the right to draft Lemieux in 1984. Spurred on by their bright young coach, Jim Schoenfeld, the Devils were at the top of their game. They outplayed the home-standing Penguins. They outshot their hosts by the whopping margin of 35–19. They lost the game 8–6. The reason was Lemieux.

In a supernatural performance that has never been equaled before or since, Mario scored five goals in five different ways. His big night began rather innocently. After the Devils grabbed a 1–0 lead, Lemieux was credited with an even-strength goal when his centering pass deflected in off Craig Wolanin's skate.

The Penguins' captain soon heated up. While killing a penalty, he beat Bob Sauve on a slap shot from the left face-off dot. Three minutes later he struck for a power-play goal.

The onslaught continued in the second period. Referee Dan Marouelli awarded Lemieux a penalty shot after replacement goalie Chris Terreri threw his stick at the puck. Employing his favorite move, Mario beat Terreri through the five hole. No. 66 capped off his extraordinary evening with an empty netter.

"I think we all just saw Mario's gift, a little late for Christmas, to me and the fans," coach Gene Ubriaco said. "I'm not going to say 'Awesome,' I've said that too many times."

"Some of the things he did out there were amazing," added linemate Rob Brown. "They're going to have videotapes of tonight's game for kids to buy and watch, because it was just amazing."

Penguins 8 • Devils 6

SCORING BY PERIODS

New Jersey	2	3	1	6
Pittsburgh	3	4	1	8

FIRST PERIOD
SCORING—1. New Jersey, Korn 8 (Muller, Kurvers) 3:39; 2. Pittsburgh, Lemieux 39 (R. Brown) 4:17; 3. Pittsburgh, Lemieux 40 (Hillier) 7:50 (sh); 4. New Jersey, Muller 12 (Verbeek, Korn) 9:46 (pp); 5. Pittsburgh, Lemieux 41 (Coffey, Dineen) 10:59 (pp).
PENALTIES—Loiselle, NJ (roughing) 0:13; Cullen, Pit (slashing) 0:13; Bourque, Pit (holding) 6:29; Broten, NJ (high-sticking) 8:05; Errey, Pit (high-sticking) 8:05; Johnson, Pit (hooking) 9:40; Muller, NJ (hooking) 10:38; NJ bench, served by Verbeek (too many men on ice) 10:38; Quinn, Pit (hooking) 17:00; Rooney, NJ, minor-major-game misconduct (roughing and cross-checking) 17:31; Loney, Pit (roughing) 17:31.

SECOND PERIOD
SCORING—6. Pittsburgh, R. Brown 27 (Quinn, Lemieux) 0:39 (pp); 7. New Jersey, Albelin 4 (D. Brown, Carlsson) 5:14; 8. Pittsburgh, Quinn 18 (Lemieux, R. Brown) 7:39 (pp); 9. New Jersey, Muller 13 (Cichocki, Albelin) 8:27; 10. Pittsburgh, Lemieux 42 (penalty shot) 11:14; 11. New Jersey, Kurvers 11 (Muller, Korn) 11:43; 12. Pittsburgh, Bourque 13 (Lemieux, R. Brown) 16:35 (pp).
PENALTIES—Cichocki, NJ (holding) 6:21; Korn, NJ (hooking) 9:10; Quinn, Pit (hooking) 9:30; Hillier, Pit (roughing) 12:23; Anderson, NJ (high-sticking) 14:57; Cunneyworth, Pit (high-sticking) 18:41; Hannan, Pit (holding) 19:56.

THIRD PERIOD
SCORING—13. New Jersey, Carlsson 2 (Muller, Anderson) 16:24; 14. Pittsburgh, Lemieux 43 (Caufield) 19:59 (en).
PENALTIES—Hannan, Pit (hooking) 5:43; Bourque, Pit (interference) 9:14; Broten, NJ (roughing) 10:37; Lemieux, Pit (roughing) 10:37; Hannan, Pit (misconduct) 13:46.

SHOTS ON GOAL
New Jersey 11-10-14—35; Pittsburgh 8-6-5—19

GOALIES
New Jersey, Sauve (10 shots—5 saves), Terreri (7:39 second, 8 shots—6 saves); Pittsburgh, Barrasso (35 shots—29 saves).

ATTENDANCE—16,025

Penguins Snap 42-Game Winless Streak at the Spectrum
February 2, 1989

When the Penguins visited Philadelphia during the 1970s and '80s, talk invariably turned to "the Streak." As incredible as it seemed, the Pens had not won a game in the Spectrum since January 20, 1974, when they beat the Flyers 5–3. Since that fateful day, the Penguins had gone *42 games* without a win in the "City of Brotherly Shove."

Marc Boileau was the coach of the Penguins when the Streak began on February 7, 1974. Over the next 15 years it took on a life of its own. No fewer than seven Steel City coaches—Boileau, Ken Schinkel, Johnny Wilson, Eddie Johnston, Lou Angotti, Bob Berry, and Pierre Creamer—failed to win in Philly. Worse yet, the team rarely came close. The 42-game skein included only *three* ties. The rest were Philadelphia wins.

"I graduated from high school, graduated from college, got a job, got married, got divorced, moved to San Diego, moved back to Pittsburgh, and the Penguins still hadn't beaten the Flyers in Philadelphia," Penguins vice president Tom McMillan said.

The Streak reflected the disparity between the clubs. Winners of consecutive Stanley Cups in the mid 1970s, the Flyers were a perennial powerhouse who played a bruising, take-no-prisoners style. By contrast, the Penguins were mediocre at best.

By 1988–89, however, the roles were beginning to reverse. With superstars Mario Lemieux and Paul Coffey leading the way, the resurgent Pens would soon equal Philly's feat of back-to-back Stanley Cups. Meanwhile, the Flyers were on the verge of a Penguins-esque streak of missing the postseason five years in a row.

Still, the Streak was very much alive when the Pens rolled into Philadelphia to challenge the Flyers on February 2, 1989. In an effort to disrupt the bad karma, Penguins coach Gene Ubriaco gave goalie Wendell Young—a former Flyer—the starting nod.

Midway through the opening frame, rookie center John Cullen staked the Pens to an early lead. Phil Bourque padded the advantage at 18:19, but Ron Sutter struck for the Flyers in the final minute of the period.

The Penguins proceeded to shake off any lingering juju. Bob Errey and Rob Brown scored in the second period.

Dan Quinn supplied the frosting on the cake in the final frame. The Flyers mounted a mild rally, but Young stood tall, kicking aside 39 shots. The final score was 5–3—ironically the same score as the last Penguins victory in Philly all those years ago. The Streak was finally over.

"It's a great thing for the organization," Pens winger Troy Loney said. "Especially the guys who have been around here four or five years and put up with this."

His teammate Bourque summed it up best.

"We're not the fire hydrant anymore," he said. "We're the bigger dog."

Penguins 5 • Flyers 3

SCORING BY PERIODS
Pittsburgh	2	2	1	5
Philadelphia	1	0	2	3

FIRST PERIOD
SCORING—1. Pittsburgh, Cullen 10 (R. Brown, Lemieux) 10:45; 2. Pittsburgh, Bourque 15 (Cullen) 18:19; 3. Philadelphia, Sutter 18 (Samuelsson, Tocchet) 19:03.
PENALTIES—Howe, Phi (interference) 8:56; Tocchet, Phi (cross-checking) 13:15; Bjugstad, Pit (cross-checking) 15:20.

SECOND PERIOD
SCORING—4. Pittsburgh, Errey 19 (Lemieux) 7:10 (sh); 5. Pittsburgh, R. Brown 38 (Loney) 9:53.
PENALTIES—Johnson, Pit (hooking) 5:35; D. Brown, Phi, major (fighting) 9:07; Caufield, Pit, major (fighting) 9:07; Berube, Phi (charging) 13:46; Berube, Phi (roughing) 15:51; Cullen, Pit (roughing) 15:51; Samuelsson, Phi (unsportsmanlike conduct) 15:51; Coffey, Pit (holding) 17:49; Carkner, Phi (hooking) 18:07; Propp, Phi (misconduct) 18:07.

THIRD PERIOD
SCORING—6. Philadelphia, Bullard 18 (Carkner, Samuelsson) 1:09; 7. Pittsburgh, Quinn 26 (Hannan) 6:36; 8. Philadelphia, Eklund 11 (Sutter, Tocchet) 7:56.
PENALTIES—Johnson, Pit (hooking) 8:20; Murphy, Phi (tripping) 9:34; Johnson, Pit, major (fighting) 14:12; Tocchet, Phi, major (fighting) 14:12; Dykstra, Pit (roughing) 14:12; Sutter, Phi (roughing) 14:12; Frawley, Pit, minor-misconduct (roughing) 14:12; Berube, Phi, minor-misconduct (roughing) 14:12.

SHOTS ON GOAL
Pittsburgh 7-15-9—31; Philadelphia 12-14-16—42

GOALIES
Pittsburgh, Young (42 shots—39 saves); Philadelphia, Hextall (31 shots—26 saves).

ATTENDANCE—17,423

Zarley Zalapski (33) and Wendell Young team up to thwart the Flyers.

Lemieux Scores Five Goals to Tie Playoff Mark

April 25, 1989

In 1988–89 the Penguins were a team on the rise. After missing the playoffs for six straight seasons, they qualified for postseason play thanks to a strong second-place finish in the Patrick Division. Powered by Art Ross Trophy winner Mario Lemieux, the improving Pens were a team to be reckoned with.

After sweeping aside the Rangers in four straight, the Penguins met their archenemies—the Flyers—in the Patrick Division Finals. Although Philly had slipped a bit, they were still a tough, veteran team. The Pens soon found themselves locked in mortal combat with their more experienced rival.

By his lofty standards, Lemieux had been comparatively quiet. After collecting a goal in each of the first three games of the series, he was held off the score sheet in Game 4. Worse yet, he'd collided with teammate Randy Cunneyworth late in the contest. The Penguins' captain retired to the locker room after suffering what trainer Skip Thayer described as "a whiplash type injury."

Heading into Game 5, there was tremendous concern over Mario's condition. With the series tied at 2–2, the Pens could ill afford to have their superstar on the sideline. The Civic Arena faithful exploded with a loud roar when No. 66 took to the ice for the warm-ups prior to Game 6.

Shaking off the lingering effects of his injury, Lemieux appeared to be in his usual top form.

"The first shift, he had extra jump in him and you knew he was going to have a good game," said linemate Rob Brown.

Philadelphia goalie Ron Hextall stopped Lemieux's first shot. It would be the highlight of the evening for the former Conn Smythe and Vezina Trophy winner. On the next rush Mario streaked up the ice and beat Hextall on a breakaway. The wail from the goal siren had barely faded when "Le Magnifique" scored again at 3:45. Three minutes later Mario banged the puck past the flustered netminder to record a natural hat trick. He'd potted three goals on three shots, all within a span of 4:40.

"With a great player like Mario, it's only a matter of time," Paul Coffey said.

Incredibly, Lemieux wasn't finished. At 17:09 he struck for his fourth goal of the opening period—a power-play tally that gave the Pens a 5–1 lead. Desperate to shield his All-Star goalie from further embarrassment, Flyers coach Paul Holmgren soon pulled Hextall in favor of Ken Wregget.

Mario was content to play the role of setup man in the second period, dishing out three assists. When the Flyers closed the gap with a furious third-period rally, Lemieux sealed the victory with an empty-net goal. The big fellow had collected five goals and three assists in arguably the greatest postseason performance of all time.

Penguins 10 • Flyers 7

SCORING BY PERIODS
Philadelphia   1   2   4   7
Pittsburgh   6   3   1   10

FIRST PERIOD
SCORING—1. Pittsburgh, Lemieux 7 (Coffey, Stevens) 2:15; 2. Pittsburgh, Lemieux 8 (Errey, Coffey) 3:45; 3. Pittsburgh, Lemieux 9 (Cullen) 6:55 (pp); 4. Pittsburgh, Errey 1 (R. Brown, Johnson) 7:07; 5. Philadelphia, Bullard 2 (Kerr, Samuelsson) 11:45; 6. Pittsburgh, Lemieux 10 (Quinn) 17:09 (pp); 7. Pittsburgh, Loney 1 (Johnson, Hannan) 17:44.
PENALTIES—Secord, Phi (high-sticking) 0:10; Cullen, Pit (holding) 4:36; Howe, Phi (slashing) 5:39; Buskas, Pit (holding) 12:37; Kerr, Phi (holding) 16:47; Pit bench, served by Callander (too many men on ice) 19:19.
SECOND PERIOD

SCORING—8. Philadelphia, Eklund 2 (Kerr) 0:06 (pp); 9. Pittsburgh, Stevens 3 (Coffey, Lemieux) 1:43; 10. Philadelphia, Propp 10 (Sutter, Chychrun) 9:07; 11. Pittsburgh, R. Brown 4 (Lemieux, Zalapski) 10:35; 12. Pittsburgh, R. Brown 5 (Lemieux, Coffey) 12:55 (pp).
PENALTIES—Wells, Phi (slashing) 11:53; Hextall, Phi, served by Poulin (misconduct) 12:55; Dobbin, Phi, major-match penalty, served by Berube (fighting and attempt to injure) 17:03; Cullen, Pit, major (fighting) 17:03; Pit bench, served by R. Brown (too many men on ice) 18:17.

THIRD PERIOD
SCORING—13. Philadelphia, Smith 1 (Carkner, Howe) 0:48 (sh); 14. Philadelphia, Kerr 11 (Secord, Acton) 10:21; 15. Philadelphia, Eklund 3 (Propp, Murphy) 13:02 (pp); 16. Philadelphia, Kerr 12 (Secord) 17:23; 17. Pittsburgh, Lemieux 11 (Errey) 19:23 (en).
PENALTIES—Berube, Phi (roughing) 2:27; Johnson, Pit (roughing) 2:27; Dykstra, Pit (hooking) 7:34; Johnson, Pit (hooking) 12:43; Mellanby, Phi, major (fighting) 19:44; Chychrun, Phi (slashing) 19:44; Carkner, Phi, double

Mario Lemieux pumps the puck past a helpless Ron Hextall during his record-tying performance.

minor (charging and elbowing) 19:44; Johnson, Pit, major (fighting) 19:44; Wells, Phi, major-misconduct (fighting) 19:51; Acton, Phi, double-minor (roughing and slashing) 19:51; Wregget, Phi, double minor-misconduct (roughing and leaving the crease) 19:51; Murphy, Phi, major (fighting) 19:51; Buskas, Pit, major-misconduct (fighting) 19:51; Zalapski, Pit, major (fighting) 19:51; R. Brown, Pit (slashing) 19:51.

SHOTS ON GOAL
Philadelphia 9-15-21—45; Pittsburgh 18-10-7—35

GOALIES
Philadelphia, Hextall (17 shots—11 saves), Wregget (17:44 first, 1 shot—1 save), Hextall (0:00 second, 9 shots—6 saves), Wregget (12:35 second, 7 shots—7 saves), Hextall (19:51 third, 0 shots—0 saves); Pittsburgh, Barrasso (45 shots—38 saves).

ATTENDANCE—16,025

Penguins Bomb Minnesota, Win the 1991 Stanley Cup
May 25, 1991

On the morning of May 25, 1991, the Penguins found themselves on the cusp of realizing their boyhood dreams. After 24 years of unmitigated futility, the Stanley Cup—the most prized trophy in all of hockey—was within their grasp.

Standing in the way was a fellow member of the expansion class of 1967, the Minnesota North Stars. Although not nearly as talented as the Penguins, the North Stars had proven to be a tough and worthy adversary. They battled the Pens on even terms through five hard-fought games. Game 6 figured to be no exception.

An aggressive bunch, the North Stars decided to test Pens goalie Tom Barrasso, who'd been knocked out of the latter stages of Game 5 with a groin injury. Immediately after the opening face-off, Neal Broten made a beeline for Barrasso. However, the veteran forward drew an interference penalty, which opened the door for the Pens' potent power play.

At the two-minute mark, the unlikely duo of Bryan Trottier and Peter Taglianetti set up an even more unlikely recipient—Ulf Samuelsson—for a power-play goal. The score remained 1–0 until Mario Lemieux chased down a loose puck and beat Jon Casey on a shorthanded breakaway at 12:19. Less than a minute later, veteran Joe Mullen scooped up a cross-ice pass from Kevin Stevens and rifled the puck past Casey.

Realizing the Penguins had Casey's number, North Stars coach Bob Gainey pulled his starter in favor of Brian Hayward to begin the second period. The move worked for a time. Hayward held the Pens off the scoreboard for 13 minutes. Despite the 3–0 deficit, Minnesota had begun to find its rhythm.

Unfortunately for the North Stars, it was the calm before the storm. Mucker Bob Errey deflected a Jaromir Jagr pass behind Hayward at 13:15. Moments later, Ron Francis scurried up the ice to score the back-breaker on a breakaway. The North Stars' discipline quickly dissolved, as Dave Gagner drew a roughing penalty. Mullen made them pay, notching his second power-play goal of the night.

Trailing by six goals going into the final period, Minnesota was clearly demoralized. However, there would be no letup in the Penguins' onslaught. With dreams of a Stanley Cup dancing in their heads, Lemieux set up light-scoring defenseman Jim Paek at 1:19 on a two-on-one break. Former North Star Larry Murphy applied the final stroke with a power-play tally at 13:45. Following their eighth goal, the Pens settled into a defensive mode to preserve the shutout for Barrasso—and the Cup.

"There are guys who play for 10 or 15 years in the league and never get a chance to participate in the Finals," said Lemieux from the euphoric Pens locker room. "The feeling is unbelievable."

"I've coached at every level of the game, but I never thought I'd put on a Stanley Cup ring," coach Bob Johnson said. "This is an unbelievable night."

Penguins 8 • North Stars 0

SCORING BY PERIODS
Pittsburgh	3	3	2	8
Minnesota	0	0	0	0

FIRST PERIOD
SCORING—1. Pittsburgh, Samuelsson 3 (Taglianetti, Trottier) 2:00 (pp); 2. Pittsburgh, Lemieux 16 (Murphy) 12:19 (sh); 3. Pittsburgh, Mullen 7 (Stevens, Taglianetti) 13:16 (pp).
PENALTIES—Broten, Min (interference) 0:09; Johnson, Min (high-sticking) 6:20; Stevens, Pit (holding) 10:25; Roberts, Pit (roughing) 10:59; Modano, Min (interference) 11:17; Roberts, Pit (interference) 13:58; Taglianetti, Pit (tripping) 17:35.

SECOND PERIOD
SCORING—4. Pittsburgh, Errey 5 (Jagr, Lemieux) 13:15; 5. Pittsburgh, Francis 7 (Mullen) 14:28; 6. Pittsburgh, Mullen 8 (Stevens, Samuelsson) 18:44.
PENALTIES—Samuelsson, Pit (roughing) 8:03; Recchi, Pit (roughing) 8:03; Churla, Min (roughing) 8:03; McRae, Min (misconduct) 8:03; Tinordi, Min double minor (roughing) 8:03; Gagner, Min (roughing) 15:18.

THIRD PERIOD
SCORING—7. Pittsburgh, Paek 1 (Lemieux) 1:19; 8. Pittsburgh, Murphy 5 (Lemieux) 13:45 (pp).
PENALTIES—McRae, Min (slashing) 12:27; Stevens, Pit (slashing) 13:03; Gavin, Min (slashing) 13:03.

SHOTS ON GOAL
Pittsburgh 11-9-8—28; Minnesota 16-7-16—39

GOALIES
Pittsburgh, Barrasso (39 shots—39 saves); Minnesota, Casey (11 shots—8 saves), Hayward (0:00 second, 11 shots—7 saves); Casey (1:19 third, 6 shots—5 saves).

ATTENDANCE—15,378

Penguins Complete Comeback, Beat Capitals in Game 7
May 1, 1992

In the spring of 1992 the Penguins opened their defense of the Stanley Cup against their division rivals, the Washington Capitals. Although the Pens had finished the regular season on a roll, beating Washington would be no easy task. Owners of the second-best record in the league, the Caps had taken five out of seven regular-season meetings between the clubs.

Paced by offensive-minded defensemen Kevin Hatcher and Al Iafrate, the Capitals dominated the Pens through the early going. Worse yet, Washington was beating the defending champs at their own game. Following a dismal 7–2 loss at the Civic Arena in Game 4, the Penguins wisely changed tactics.

"Game 5 in Washington we called a meeting," Mario Lemieux recalled. "We came up with trying to go with the one-four delay to try to contain their defensemen."

The plan worked to perfection. The Pens surprised the Capitals by taking Games 5 and 6. However, another victory was needed to complete the comeback.

Game 7 opened cautiously. Neither club wanted to make a crucial mistake that would hand their adversary an advantage. At 13:43, however, Troy Loney opened the door for the Caps when he drew an interference penalty. Washington's Mike Ridley broke free and cut loose a shot that clanged off a goal post. The puck ricocheted to Larry Murphy, who hit Ron Francis in stride with a beautiful lead pass. Using Mario Lemieux as a decoy, Francis steamed down the middle of the ice and ripped off a hard shot. Goalie Don Beaupre made a sprawling save but kicked the puck directly to Lemieux. Mario

Bob Errey takes flight during the Pens' Game 7 victory over the Caps.

snapped the puck into the upper right corner of the net.

Washington soon knotted the score. In the opening minute of the second period, Iafrate froze Murphy and Tom Barrasso with a series of fakes before launching a rocket into the Pens' net.

The Penguins refused to panic. Playing their newly disciplined game, they calmly waited for an opportunity to press the attack. Late in the period, Todd Krygier was whistled off for interference. Working the power play to perfection, Lemieux found Jaromir Jagr with a pretty pass in the slot. Jagr deftly moved the puck to his backhand and flipped a shot over Beaupre.

Try as they might, the Capitals failed to respond. In the final minute of play Joe Mullen tossed in an empty netter to seal the Penguins' comeback. They became only the 11th team in Stanley Cup history to rally from a 3–1 deficit to win a series.

"That seventh game was a game they never wanted played in that series," Barrasso said afterward. "We knew we had to play seven games in order to have a chance. I think that really gave us a very big psychological edge, because we had faced elimination the previous two nights. To face it again didn't seem like much of a challenge."

Penguins 3 • Capitals 1

SCORING BY PERIODS
Pittsburgh   1   1   1   3
Washington   0   1   0   1

FIRST PERIOD
SCORING—1. Pittsburgh, Lemieux 7 (Francis, Murphy) 14:01 (sh).
PENALTY—Loney, Pit (interference) 13:43.

SECOND PERIOD
SCORING—2. Washington, Iafrate 4 (Ridley) 0:24; 3. Pittsburgh, Jagr 3 (Lemieux, Francis) 9:40 (pp).
PENALTY—Krygier, Was (interference) 7:41.

THIRD PERIOD
SCORING—4. Pittsburgh, Mullen 3 (Francis) 19:27 (en).
PENALTY—U. Samuelsson, Pit (holding) 7:52.

SHOTS ON GOAL
Pittsburgh 7-8-6—21; Washington 6-5-8—19

GOALIES
Pittsburgh, Barrasso (19 shots—18 saves); Washington, Beaupre (20 shots—18 saves).

ATTENDANCE—17,783

Penguins Sweep Chicago, Capture the 1992 Stanley Cup

June 1, 1992

Entering their 1992 Stanley Cup Finals matchup with the Penguins, the Chicago Blackhawks were brimming with confidence. A tough, veteran team, Chicago had rolled to an NHL-record 11 straight postseason victories. Paced by 50-goal man Jeremy Roenick and superb young goalie Ed Belfour, the high-flying Blackhawks were poised to bring the Stanley Cup back to the Windy City.

The Penguins, however, were a team of enormous fiber and character. During the season, they'd weathered the tragic death of coach Bob Johnson, the trade of Paul Coffey and Mark Recchi, and postseason injuries to stars Mario Lemieux and Joe Mullen without flinching.

"We stay on an even keel and do what it takes to win," said power forward Kevin Stevens.

The tone was set in the series opener. Led by their All-Star defensive tandem of Chris Chelios and Steve Smith, the Blackhawks snatched a 4–1 lead and banged Lemieux and the other Penguins stars around without mercy. But the Pens weathered the storm and rallied to beat the Hawks on Mario's last-minute goal. In Games 2 and 3, the Steel City sextet prevailed in tight, defensive struggles.

Throwing caution to the wind, Chicago coach "Iron" Mike Keenan decided to remove the restraining bolts for Game 4. Playing before a frenzied throng at Chicago Stadium, Blackhawks captain Dirk Graham responded with a first-period hat trick. However, the Penguins countered with three goals of their own, including one each by big guns Jaromir Jagr, Stevens, and Lemieux.

The second period featured furious end-to-end action. Rugged Rick Tocchet staked the Pens to a 4–3 lead with his sixth goal of the playoffs. Lemieux and Stevens sprung loose for numerous breakaway opportunities. They were repeatedly denied by unheralded Dominik Hasek, who had replaced Belfour between the pipes. Thanks to Hasek's brilliant play, the Hawks knotted the score late in the period on a tally by Roenick.

However, the folly of engaging the talent-laden Penguins in a shootout soon took its toll. Five minutes into the final frame, Mario separated Chelios from the puck with a crisp check. Tocchet pounced on the rubber and fed it to Larry Murphy, who fired a beautiful shot into the upper-right corner of the net. Moments later, Ron Francis steamed into the Chicago zone. Using linemate Shawn McEachern as a decoy, he blew the puck past a fading Hasek.

Although Roenick scored his second goal of the game with nine minutes remaining, the outcome was never in doubt. Settling into their one-four delay, the Pens set up a protective cocoon around Tom Barrasso. The veteran goalie stopped a final shot by Chelios in the closing seconds and thrust his hands into the air. The Penguins had won their second straight Stanley Cup.

Penguins 6 • Blackhawks 5

SCORING BY PERIODS
Pittsburgh   3   1   2   6
Chicago   3   1   1   5

FIRST PERIOD
SCORING—1. Pittsburgh, Jagr 11 (Loney) 1:37; 2. Chicago, Graham 5 (Matteau, Chelios) 6:21; 3. Pittsburgh, Stevens 13 (M. Lemieux, Tocchet) 6:33; 4. Chicago, Graham 6 (Chelios) 6:51; 5. Pittsburgh, M. Lemieux 16 (Murphy, Stevens) 10:13 (pp); 6. Chicago, Graham 7 (Noonan, J. Lemieux) 16:18.
PENALTIES—U. Samuelsson, Pit (interference) 7:28; Stanton, Pit (misconduct) 7:28; Gilbert, Chi (misconduct) 7:28; Chelios, Chi (elbowing) 8:17; Roberts, Pit (roughing) 12:44.

SECOND PERIOD
SCORING—7. Pittsburgh, Tocchet 6 (M. Lemieux, Stevens) 0:58; 8. Chicago, Roenick 11 (Noonan, Gilbert) 15:40.
PENALTIES—Stanton, Pit (hooking) 2:21; Tocchet, Pit (holding) 5:41.

THIRD PERIOD
SCORING—9. Pittsburgh, Murphy 6 (Tocchet) 4:51; 10. Pittsburgh, Francis 8 (McEachern, Paek) 7:59; 11. Chicago, Roenick 12 (Grimson, Buskas) 11:18.
PENALTIES—None.

SHOTS ON GOAL
Pittsburgh 12-9-8—29; Chicago 8-14-7—29

GOALIES
Pittsburgh, Barrasso (29 shots—24 saves); Chicago, Belfour (4 shots—2 saves), Hasek (13:24 first, 25 shots—21 saves).

ATTENDANCE—18,472

Penguins Win 16th Straight, Set NHL Record
April 9, 1993

The 1992–93 campaign proved to be a veritable roller coaster of dizzying heights and equally devastating lows. After finishing the 1992 playoffs with an NHL-record 11 straight victories, the Penguins cruised to a stunning 11–1–2 start. By the new year they were well ahead of the competition. Their achievements impressed everyone, including team captain Mario Lemieux.

"This is the best team I ever played with," Lemieux said. "We have three lines that can score a lot of goals, a lot of guys who can put the puck in the net…. It's pretty tough to find, guys who score 30, 40, 50 goals, which we have on every line."

Mario was enjoying perhaps the finest season of his career. He was on pace to eclipse Wayne Gretzky's record of 215 points. Then the unthinkable occurred. On January 13, 1993, the Penguins announced Lemieux had contracted Hodgkin's disease. While the prognosis for recovery was

favorable, the big center would be out of action for at least four to six weeks—perhaps even longer.

The battle-hardened Penguins were used to adversity. They had overcome obstacles that rivaled the 10 plagues of Egypt during their march to the 1992 Cup. However, playing without big No. 66 soon took its toll. During Mario's absence, the Pens struggled to maintain a .500 pace.

Fortunately, Lemieux responded well to his treatments. In early March, with the club in the midst of a dismal 2–5–1 slide, he pronounced himself fit to play.

After losing two games with their captain in the lineup, the Penguins began to find their rhythm. Soon they were building a winning streak that would reach epic proportions. On March 25 they trimmed New Jersey for their eighth win in a row, establishing a new franchise record. Two weeks later they tied the Islanders' mark of 15 consecutive wins with a thrilling overtime victory over Montreal.

On April 9 the Penguins visited their bitter rivals, the Rangers, with a chance to make NHL history. The Blueshirts, who had slipped from playoff contention, were eager to play the role of spoilers.

For half a game the Rangers traded goals with their powerful adversary. Adam Graves, John McIntyre, and Tony Amonte connected for New York, while Lemieux, Joe Mullen, and Larry Murphy countered for the Pens.

As he had done so many times in his fabled career, Mario eventually took over. After striking for a power-play goal at 8:09 of the second period, Lemieux applied the coup de grace with a stunning shorthanded tally.

"That was a big turning point for us," Mullen said. "It gave us a lot of momentum, especially when Mario scored."

Like a shark smelling blood, the Penguins moved in for the kill. Lemieux and Mullen each scored a pair of third-period goals, sandwiched around a tally by Jaromir Jagr. The Madison Square Garden fans—among the most boorish in all of hockey—gave Mario a standing ovation following his fifth goal.

The Penguins had earned their place in the NHL record books. The following night they beat the Rangers again to run their streak to 17 games before settling for a tie in the season finale against the Devils.

Penguins 10 • Rangers 4

SCORING BY PERIODS
Pittsburgh   2   3   5   10
NY Rangers   2   1   1   4

FIRST PERIOD
SCORING—1. Pittsburgh, Mullen 30 (unassisted) 11:02 (sh); 2. NY Rangers, Graves 35 (unassisted) 15:25; 3. Pittsburgh, Murphy 22 (Stevens, Tocchet) 16:24; 4. NY Rangers, McIntyre 3 (Erixon, Wells) 16:41.
PENALTIES—Jennings, Pit (slashing) 5:34; Jennings, Pit (tripping) 9:46; K. Samuelsson, Pit (slashing) 11:42; Tikkanen, NYR (hooking) 12:34; Wells, NYR (holding stick) 19:05.

SECOND PERIOD
SCORING—5. Pittsburgh, Lemieux 63 (U. Samuelsson) 4:43; 6. NY Rangers, Amonte 32 (Tikkanen, Cirella) 6:01; 7. Pittsburgh, Lemieux 64 (Francis, Tocchet) 8:09 (pp); 8. Pittsburgh, Lemieux 65 (Barrasso) 16:05 (sh).
PENALTIES—Kovalev, NYR (holding) 6:15; McEachern, Pit (holding) 10:05; Taglianetti, Pit, major-game misconduct (high-sticking) 11:31; Beukeboom, NYR double minor (slashing and roughing) 19:27.

THIRD PERIOD
SCORING—9. Pittsburgh, Mullen 31 (Jagr, U. Samuelsson) 1:52 (pp); 10. Pittsburgh, Lemieux 66 (Tocchet, Stevens) 4:14; 11. Pittsburgh, Jagr 34 (Barrasso) 8:14; 12. Pittsburgh, Mullen 32 (Francis) 9:21; 13. Pittsburgh, Lemieux 67 (Stevens, Jennings) 11:15; 14. NY Rangers, Kovalev 20 (unassisted) 18:40.
PENALTY—Jennings, Pit (elbowing) 16:38.

SHOTS ON GOAL
Pittsburgh 17-8-15—40; NY Rangers 9-5-11—25

GOALIES
Pittsburgh, Barrasso (25 shots—21 saves); NY Rangers, Hirsch (25 shots—20 saves), Richter (0:00 third, 15 shots—10 saves).

ATTENDANCE—18,200

Penguins Beat Capitals in Quadruple-Overtime Marathon
April 24, 1996

Following disappointing playoff exits in each of the previous three seasons, the 1995–96 Penguins were poised for a run at the Stanley Cup. Pacing the attack was a revitalized Mario Lemieux, who returned after sitting out the 1994–95 campaign to score 161 points. Jaromir Jagr (62 goals), Ron Francis (119 points), and newcomer Petr Nedved (47 goals) enjoyed huge years as well.

The Pens drew the Washington Capitals as their first-round playoff opponent. Playing the Capitals had become a rite of spring—the teams had met in four of the previous five postseasons. While the Penguins had won three of those matchups, Washington always proved to be a prickly foe.

This time around was no exception. Playing their physical, close-checking game to perfection, the Caps stunned the heavily favored Penguins by sweeping the first two games in Pittsburgh. Thanks to the strong goaltending of Tom Barrasso, the Pens bounced back to take Game 3. However, they would need a victory in Game 4 to keep their Cup hopes alive.

The Penguins swarmed the Capitals' net from the opening face-off, launching 16 first-period shots on Olaf Kolzig. However, they failed to convert on three power-play opportunities. When the Caps finally got an opportunity with the man advantage, they made it count. Michal

Pivonka whipped a shot past Barrasso from the right circle to stake his team to a lead.

Down 1–0, the Pens received a jolt between periods. Barrasso was suffering from back spasms and could not continue. Ken Wregget, who had not seen game action for two weeks, was thrust between the pipes.

While the rusty Wregget tried to get his bearings, explosive Peter Bondra struck for another Washington goal. It appeared the Penguins would go to the second intermission down by a pair. Then, at 18:42, Jagr chased down a lead pass from Francis and beat Kolzig for a shorthanded tally.

The momentum appeared to have shifted. However, in the closing seconds of the period Todd Krygier drilled Lemieux with a punch to the side of the head. Enraged, Mario chased down the plucky Caps center and pummeled him to the ice. Referee Dan Marouelli issued a fighting major and a game misconduct to the Penguins' captain.

With a major penalty to kill, the Pens rose to the occasion and held the Caps off the scoreboard. At the eight-minute mark Nedved snapped a blur of a wrist shot over Kolzig's glove to knot the score and force overtime.

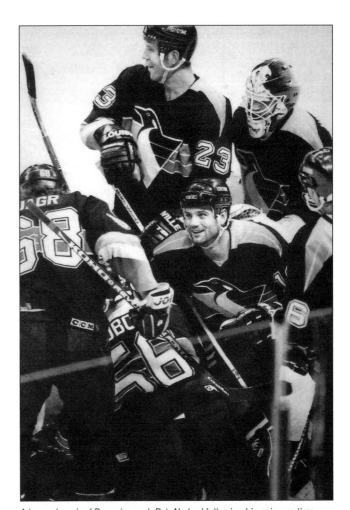
A happy bunch of Penguins mob Petr Nedved following his epic overtime winner.

The Pens had dominated play during regulation, out-shooting Washington by a 2-to-1 margin. However, the home-standing Caps quickly took control in overtime. They poured into the Penguins' zone, peppering Wregget with shot after shot. The veteran goalie was more than up to the challenge. He stopped 37 shots through three overtimes, including a penalty shot by crafty Joey Juneau.

Demoralized by the super sub's brilliant play, the Caps finally began to fade. With 45 seconds remaining in the fourth overtime, Nedved struck for his second goal of the night at 2:16 AM. Thanks to the heroics of Wregget and Nedved, the Pens had won the third-longest game in NHL history.

Penguins 3 • Capitals 2

SCORING BY PERIODS
Pittsburgh 0 1 1 0 0 0 1   3
Washington 1 1 0 0 0 0 0   2

FIRST PERIOD
SCORING—1. Washington, Pivonka 3 (Hunter, Gonchar) 13:50 (pp).
PENALTIES— Charron, Was (tripping) 1:07; Bondra, Was (slashing) 4:22; Gonchar, Was (hooking) 10:17; Joseph, Pit (holding stick) 12:42.

SECOND PERIOD
SCORING—2. Washington, Bondra 3 (Juneau, Brunette) 7:36 (pp); 3. Pittsburgh, Jagr 1 (Francis) 18:42 (sh).
PENALTIES—Hunter, Was (tripping) 1:25; Wilkinson, Pit (hooking) 6:13; Kelly Miller, Was (hooking) 9:30; Zubov, Pit (tripping) 13:26; Sandstrom, Pit (roughing) 17:21; Lemieux, Pit, double minor-major-game misconduct (slashing, instigator and fighting) 19:24; Peake, Was, minor-game misconduct (roughing) 19:24; Krygier, Was (roughing) 19:24.

THIRD PERIOD
SCORING—4. Pittsburgh, Nedved 5 (Daigneault, Zubov) 8:00 (pp).
PENALTIES—Pivonka, Was (roughing) 6:17; Sandstrom, Pit (roughing) 8:31; Johnson, Was (roughing) 8:31; Krygier, Was (interference) 11:11.

FIRST OVERTIME
SCORING—None.
PENALTIES—Jagr, Pit (hooking) 4:50; Nelson, Was (hooking) 10:39.

SECOND OVERTIME
SCORING—None.
PENALTIES—Bondra, Was (roughing) 4:33; Tamer, Pit (roughing) 4:33.

THIRD OVERTIME
SCORING—None.
PENALTIES—Joseph, Pit (slashing) 3:24; Cote, Was (tripping) 4:36; Dziedzic, Pit (slashing) 19:17.

FOURTH OVERTIME
SCORING—5. Pittsburgh, Nedved 6 (Zubov, Jagr) 19:15 (pp).
PENALTY—Johnson, Was (hooking) 17:21.

SHOTS ON GOAL
Pittsburgh 16-7-19-3-4-5-11—65; Washington 9-7-5-14-12-11-5—63

GOALIES
Pittsburgh, Barrasso (9 shots—8 saves), Wregget (0:00 second, 54 shots—53 saves); Washington, Kolzig (65 shots—62 saves).

ATTENDANCE—18,130

Lemieux Returns, Scores Three Points
December 27, 2000

By the fall of 2000, Mario Lemieux was firmly established in his new role as Penguins owner. The team's front office staff had grown accustomed to seeing the big fellow in the office, sporting a suit and tie. He seemed perfectly content in retirement.

There was, however, a loose thread. His young son Austin had never seen him play.

"He's only four years old," Lemieux said. "Of course we watch tapes here from the Stanley Cup years, but I don't think he realized how many years I played."

Inspired by the thought of playing for his son, Mario contacted former teammate Jay Caufield in November of 2000 and asked the fitness guru to whip him into shape. Working in secret, they began a series of grueling training sessions. Soon Mario had honed his 6'4" frame to a rock-solid 238 pounds.

On December 11, Mario officially announced that he was making a comeback. It was a great relief to Penguins insiders, who found it nearly impossible to keep hockey's most closely guarded secret.

But first he broke the news to Austin.

"Daddy is coming back to play with Jagr," he told him.

Two days after Christmas, Lemieux made his triumphant return against the Toronto Maple Leafs. When he stepped onto the Mellon Arena ice for the pregame warm-ups, he was showered with one of the longest and loudest ovations of his storied career.

It took Mario all of 33 seconds to make an impact. On his first shift in a competitive game in three and a half years, he set up Jagr with a nifty pass from behind the net. The roar from the crowd was so loud it nearly blew the retractable dome off the Mellon Arena.

The 35-year-old marvel was just getting warmed up. Midway through the second period he gathered in a pass from Jagr in the left face-off circle and snapped the puck past Toronto goalie Curtis Joseph for career goal No. 614. At 14:23 he scooped up a loose puck and fed a blind backhand pass to Jan Hrdina, who beat Joseph from the left circle.

"What was disappointing was that after two periods, he had three times as many points as me, and he's been out for three and a half years," defenseman Ian Moran joked.

Remarkably, Mario didn't earn the game's No. 1 star. That honor went to Austin's favorite player, Jagr, who collected two goals and two assists in a 5–0 Pens victory. But by all accounts Lemieux's return was a rousing success.

"That was unbelievable to come back and play like that," Martin Straka said. "He could have had seven or eight points, easy. That was an awesome show."

"I think that with a lot of hard work and dedication, I feel like I could still be the best in the world," Mario said. "I'm still only 35 years old…. I have a fresh start physically and mentally, and I feel that I can achieve my goal to be the best again."

Penguins 5 • Maple Leafs 0

SCORING BY PERIODS
Toronto   0   0   0   0
Pittsburgh   2   3   0   5

FIRST PERIOD
SCORING—1. Pittsburgh, Jagr 20 (Hrdina, Lemieux) 0:33; 2. Pittsburgh, Kovalev 19 (Straka, Laukkanen) 10:19 (pp).
PENALTIES—Valk, Tor, double minor (high-sticking) 6:26; Domi, Tor (roughing) 12:05; Jonsson, Pit (interference) 17:34.

SECOND PERIOD
SCORING—3. Pittsburgh, Lemieux 1 (Jagr, Kasparaitis) 10:33; 4. Pittsburgh, Hrdina 9 (Lemieux, Jagr) 14:23; 5. Pittsburgh, Jagr 21 (unassisted) 19:57 (sh).
PENALTIES—Jonsson, Pit (tripping) 4:25; Pit bench, served by Petersen (too many men on ice) 19:10.

THIRD PERIOD
SCORING—None.
PENALTIES—Slegr, Pit (roughing) 1:57; Domi, Tor, major (fighting) 4:49; Slegr, Pit, major (fighting) 4:49; Snow, Pit, served by Petersen (delay of game) 12:31.

SHOTS ON GOAL
Toronto 5-12-23—40; Pittsburgh 13-12-6—31

GOALIES
Toronto, Joseph (31 shots—26 saves); Pittsburgh, Snow (40 shots—40 saves).

ATTENDANCE—17,148

Penguins Top Buffalo in the Ice Bowl
January 1, 2008

The Penguins made history on New Year's Day 2008 when they participated in the NHL's first Winter Classic. It was the second NHL regular-season game ever to be contested outdoors. In 2003 more than 57,000 fans had flocked to Commonwealth Stadium in Edmonton to watch the Oilers take on the Canadiens in the Heritage Classic.

An elated Sidney Crosby celebrates after clinching "the Ice Bowl" with a shootout goal.

Two days before Christmas, work crews began the arduous task of constructing an NHL rink at Buffalo's Ralph Wilson Stadium.

"We tarped the field and removed the goal posts and spent the next few hours just doing a site survey, getting our points that we start to level the field with since there's a nine-inch crown in that football field," said Don Renzulli, the NHL's Senior Vice President of Events and Entertainment. "We started with that and slowly started leveling that field off with about 3,000 sheets of plywood and Styrofoam. Then, we started the rink and the ice process."

The Pens' creative department was hard at work, too. They planned to unveil a new third jersey for the event, featuring the logo and powder blue color scheme worn by the team in the late 1960s.

By game time, more than 71,000 fans had packed Ralph Wilson Stadium to watch the Penguins and Sabres do battle. They were greeted by 30-degree temperatures and a healthy dose of wind, sleet, and snow. Millions of additional viewers tuned in on NBC, making "the Ice Bowl" the highest-rated regular-season hockey game in more than a decade.

The Penguins wasted little time in lighting the lamp. On the opening shift, Colby Armstrong gathered in a Sidney Crosby rebound and whipped the puck past Ryan Miller.

"It just popped right to me," Armstrong said.

That goal stood up until 1:25 of the second period, when the Sabres evened the score on a rocket of a shot by Brian Campbell. Due to the less-than-ideal conditions, the game evolved into a defensive struggle.

"You couldn't stickhandle," Campbell said. "You had to push the puck along later in the period. You had to change your game a lot."

The contest was frequently interrupted to allow for repairs to the ice. Midway through each period, action was halted while the Zambonis performed their magic. The teams also switched ends so neither club would gain an advantage due to the elements or ice conditions.

With Miller and his Penguins counterpart, Ty Conklin, making save after save, the score remained knotted at 1–1 after 60 minutes of play. Armstrong nearly wore the goat horns when he drew a hooking penalty as time expired to hand Buffalo a 4-on-3 advantage in overtime. Fortunately for the popular winger, his teammates bailed him out and forced a shootout.

"I had a lot of time to sit there [in the penalty box] and think about it while they were scrapping on the ice," he said. "It wasn't the most fun place to be. It's cold and lonely, for sure."

The stage was set for a dramatic finish. With the shootout knotted at 1–1, Sidney Crosby stickhandled through the driving snow and snapped the puck between Miller's pads to set off a wild victory celebration.

"It couldn't have worked out any better for [NBC]," Pens defenseman Ryan Whitney said. "They got the snowfall, they got Sidney to end the game. That's just what they wanted."

Penguins 2 • Sabres 1

SCORING BY PERIODS
Pittsburgh   1   0   0   0   2
Buffalo   0   1   0   0   1

FIRST PERIOD
SCORING—1. Pittsburgh, Armstrong 6 (Crosby) 0:21.
PENALTIES—Connolly, Buf (hooking) 4:22; Afinogenov, Buf (hooking) 7:16; Vanek, Buf (hooking) 12:17; Armstrong, Pit (goaltender interference) 13:02.

SECOND PERIOD
SCORING—2. Buffalo, Campbell 4 (Connolly, Paille) 1:25.
PENALTIES—None.

THIRD PERIOD
SCORING—None.
PENALTY—Armstrong, Pit (hooking) 20:00.

OVERTIME
SCORING—None.
PENALTIES—None.

SHOOTOUT
SCORING—Pittsburgh 2 (Christensen NG, Letang G, Crosby G); Buffalo 1 (Kotalik G, Connolly NG, Afinogenov NG).

SHOTS ON GOAL
Pittsburgh 11-2-12-0—25; Buffalo 9-14-7-7—37

GOALIES
Pittsburgh, Conklin (37 shots—36 saves); Buffalo, Miller (25 shots—24 saves).

ATTENDANCE—71,217

Penguins Beat Detroit in Triple-Overtime Thriller
June 2, 2008

Paced by brilliant young superstars Sidney Crosby and Evgeni Malkin, the 2007–08 Penguins seemed poised to bring the Stanley Cup back to Pittsburgh. After capturing the Atlantic Division crown on the strength of a 102-point season, the Pens made short work of their Eastern Conference foes to win the Prince of Wales Trophy.

However, their Stanley Cup Finals opponent, the battle-tested Detroit Red Wings, were proving to be a brick wall. The Red Wings dominated the first four games of the series to take a commanding 3–1 lead.

Determined to claw their way back, the Penguins responded with a strong opening period in Game 5. Just past the eight-minute mark Marian Hossa, acquired in a trade-deadline blockbuster, whipped his 11th goal of the postseason by Chris Osgood. At 14:41 Adam Hall was credited with a goal when a Niklas Kronwall clearing attempt deflected in off his skate.

Playing before their hometown fans at the Joe Louis Arena, the Red Wings soon mounted a withering comeback. Early in the second period, Darren Helm struck for the Motor City sextet to slice the Pens' lead in half. In the final frame, Pavel Datsyuk and Brian Rafalski beat a beleaguered Marc-Andre Fleury to give Detroit a 3–2 advantage.

Things didn't look good for the Penguins, who were badly outplayed by the Red Wings over the final two periods. As the game clock ticked down under a minute to play, coach Michel Therrien pulled Fleury in favor of an extra attacker. Acting on a hunch, he sent grinder Max Talbot over the boards.

The hustling winger made a beeline for the Detroit net. Setting up shop beside the cage, he gathered in a pass from Hossa and slung the puck around the goal post. Osgood stopped his first attempt, but Talbot took another poke at the puck. This time the rubber eluded the Detroit netminder. Thanks to Talbot's persistence, the Penguins had tied the game with 34.3 seconds left to play.

The Red Wings were hardly fazed by the last-minute heroics. During the first overtime they poured over the Penguins in waves, outshooting their foe by a whopping 13–2 margin. But Fleury, who stopped 55 shots in a virtuoso performance, saved the day with his spectacular goaltending.

"That was the game of his life," Ryan Whitney said afterward.

Buoyed by Fleury's brilliance, the Pens skated on even terms with the Wings through a second overtime. However, it would take another superhuman effort for the Penguins to emerge with a victory.

At 9:21 of the third overtime, Jiri Hudler drew a double minor for high-sticking Rob Scuderi. With the game on the line, Sergei Gonchar, who suffered a back injury early in the third period, gamely returned to the ice to quarterback the power play.

"His back was killing him," Brooks Orpik said. "They asked him if he could push through it if we got a power play. He said he'd try. That was just a gutsy effort by him."

Manning his customary spot on the point, Gonchar fed the puck to Petr Sykora, who ripped off a shot. The rebound caromed to Malkin, who passed the puck back to Sykora. This time the Czech sniper found the range, beating Osgood with a blistering drive to give his team a hard-earned 4–3 victory.

"We just didn't want our season to end," Scuderi explained.

Penguins 4 • Red Wings 3

SCORING BY PERIODS
Pittsburgh 2 0 1 0 0 1 4
Detroit   0 1 2 0 0 0 3

FIRST PERIOD
SCORING—1. Pittsburgh, Hossa 11 (Crosby, Dupuis) 8:37; 2. Pittsburgh, Hall 3 (unassisted) 14:41.
PENALTIES—Orpik, Pit (hooking) 2:06; Pit bench, served by Kennedy (too many men on ice) 4:15; Datsyuk, Det (tripping) 5:24; Maltby, Det (roughing) 10:50; Talbot, Pit (roughing) 10:50.

SECOND PERIOD
SCORING—3. Detroit, Helm 2 (Maltby) 2:54.
PENALTIES—Maltby, Det (interference) 5:48; Crosby, Pit (high-sticking) 10:18.

THIRD PERIOD
SCORING—4. Detroit, Datsyuk 10 (Zetterberg, Rafalski) 6:43 (pp); 5. Detroit, Rafalski 3 (Franzen, Zetterberg) 9:23; 6. Pittsburgh, Talbot 3 (Hossa, Crosby) 19:25.
PENALTY—Kennedy, Pit (hooking) 6:21.

FIRST OVERTIME
SCORING—None.
PENALTY—Zetterberg, Det (goalie interference) 17:25.

SECOND OVERTIME
SCORING—None.
PENALTIES—Cleary, Det (goalie interference) 3:41; Sykora, Pit (hooking) 17:44.

THIRD OVERTIME
SCORING—7. Pittsburgh, Sykora 6 (Malkin, Gonchar) 9:52 (pp).
PENALTY—Hudler, Det, double minor (high-sticking) 9:21.

SHOTS ON GOAL
Pittsburgh 7-7-4-2-8-4—32; Detroit 8-12-14-13-7-4—58

GOALIES
Pittsburgh, Fleury (58 shots—55 saves); Detroit, Osgood (32 shots—28 saves).

ATTENDANCE—20,066

Penguins Topple Detroit, Win 2009 Stanley Cup
June 12, 2009

The 2008–09 season would prove to be one of the most challenging—and rewarding—in franchise history. After bowing to Detroit in the 2008 Stanley Cup Finals, the Penguins suffered a string of devastating defections. Several key players, including Ryan Malone, Gary Roberts, and Jarkko Ruutu, signed with other teams. The biggest free agent of them all, Marian Hossa, spurned a lucrative long-term offer to sign a one-year deal with the Red Wings.

"When I compared the two teams, I felt like I had a better chance to win the Cup in Detroit," he explained.

Hossa's defection set the tone for the season. The Penguins jumped to a quick start but struggled mightily though January and February. The extended cold snap cost coach Michel Therrien his job. General manager Ray Shero named Dan Bylsma, a bright but relatively unproven coach, as Therrien's successor.

Playing Bylsma's up-tempo style, the Penguins responded with a dazzling stretch run to nail down a playoff berth. They continued their hot streak through the first three rounds of the playoffs, ousting the Flyers, Capitals, and Hurricanes to earn a return match with Detroit in the Finals.

The defending Cup champions once again proved to be a difficult foe. When the Red Wings took Games 1 and 2 by identical 3–1 scores, they appeared set to repeat their triumph of the previous spring.

This time, however, the Penguins refused to fold. Displaying a remarkable resilience, they took three of the next four games to set up a winner-take-all Game 7 in Detroit.

Prior to the contest, owner Mario Lemieux sent a text message to each of his players.

"This is a chance of a lifetime to realize your childhood dream to win a Stanley Cup," he wrote. "Play without fear and you will be successful! See you at center ice."

Following an early salvo by the Red Wings, the inspired Penguins began to seize control. Early in the second period Evgeni Malkin harassed Detroit blue-liner Brad Stuart into a turnover. The puck squirted loose to Max Talbot, who snapped a low wrist shot between Chris Osgood's pads.

Ten minutes later the ubiquitous Talbot struck again. Gathering in a pass from Chris Kunitz, he sped into the Detroit zone and ripped the puck over Osgood's shoulder. Thanks to the supreme efforts of "Mad Max," the Penguins were up by two.

"I wasn't trying to do anything special," he recalled. "I just wanted to win the Cup."

Detroit wasn't going down without a fight. Aided by a knee injury to Sidney Crosby that kept the Pens' captain tethered to the bench, the Red Wings outshot the Penguins 8–1 in the final period. At 13:53 defenseman Jonathan Ericsson beat Marc-Andre Fleury with a blast from the point.

Tightening their defenses, the Pens held Detroit at bay until the final minute. As time was ticking off the clock,

Fleury made a huge save on Wings captain Nicklas Lidstrom to preserve a 2–1 victory. After a 17-year hiatus, Lord Stanley's coveted Cup was returning to the Steel City.

"It's everything you dream of," Crosby said during the postgame celebration. "It's an amazing feeling."

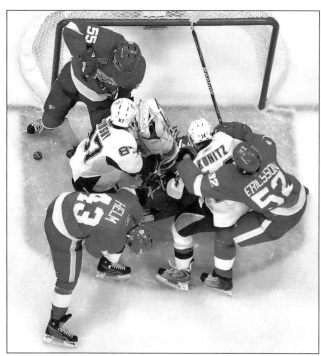

Sidney Crosby and Chris Kunitz buzz the Red Wings' net in Game 7 of the 2009 Stanley Cup Finals.

Penguins 2 • Red Wings 1

SCORING BY PERIODS
Pittsburgh   0   2   0   2
Detroit   0   0   1   1

FIRST PERIOD
SCORING—None.
PENALTY—Stuart, Det (slashing) 11:24.

SECOND PERIOD
SCORING—1. Pittsburgh, Talbot 7 (Malkin) 1:13; 2. Pittsburgh, Talbot 8 (Kunitz, Scuderi) 10:07.
PENALTIES—Staal, Pit (hooking) 1:59; Holmstrom, Det (holding) 1:59; Gill, Pit (holding) 6:16.

THIRD PERIOD
SCORING—3. Detroit, Ericsson 4 (Lidstrom, Hudler) 13:53.
PENALTY—Eaton, Pit (tripping) 2:36.

SHOTS ON GOAL
Pittsburgh 10-7-1—18; Detroit 6-11-7—24

GOALIES
Pittsburgh, Fleury (24 shots—23 saves); Detroit, Osgood (18 shots—16 saves).

ATTENDANCE—20,066

The Heartbreaks

Penguins Drop Fourth Straight to Islanders
April 26, 1975

In the spring of 1975 the Penguins were a team of immense promise. Blessed with nine 20-goal scorers—the most of any club in franchise history—they had finished a strong third in the Norris Division. Featuring a near-perfect blend of youth, experience, toughness, and skill, they were expected to make their mark in the postseason.

All went according to form through the early stages of the Stanley Cup Playoffs. Following a two-game sweep of archrival St. Louis in the Preliminary Round, the Penguins rolled to three straight victories over the New York Islanders. Overjoyed by the team's success, owner Tad Potter threw a party for his players following a rousing 6–4 victory in Game 3.

The streaking Penguins finally hit a speed bump in Game 4, dropping a 3–1 decision to the Islanders at the Nassau County Coliseum. Still, there seemed little cause for alarm. While the Islanders were a solid team that featured rising stars such as Denis Potvin and Clark Gillies, they were no match for the Penguins on paper.

Hockey games, however, are contested on the ice. In Games 5 and 6 the Islanders employed their tight-checking, hardworking style to perfection. With unsung goalie Glenn "Chico" Resch doing his best Georges Vezina imitation, New York held the high-powered Pens in check to force a seventh game.

Playing before a sellout crowd of 13,404 at the Civic Arena, the Penguins were determined to break the Islanders' stranglehold. Tough guys Bob Paradise and Bob "Battleship" Kelly sent a message by scoring decisions over Gillies and Dave Lewis. Skating with a purpose for the first time since Game 3, the home team peppered Resch with 14 first-period shots. The little Islanders goalie was up to the task.

Jean Pronovost (in white) deflects the puck off a goal post in Game 7 action.

"Resch repeatedly made the big saves," New York coach Al Arbour said.

Undaunted, the Penguins continued to dominate in the second period. They outshot the Islanders 11–6 while earning a decided advantage in territorial play. Once again, however, they failed to solve Resch.

The Islanders began to skate on even terms with their hosts in the third period. Still, the Pens enjoyed their two best scoring chances of the night. Jean Pronovost thought he had a sure goal when he tipped a Syl Apps shot past Resch, but the puck bounced harmlessly off a goal post. Moments later super rookie Pierre Larouche glided in on a breakaway and deked Resch out of position. However, he missed a wide-open net and went crashing into the boards.

"Potvin tripped me," he said. "I had the net open to me."

Two minutes later Bert Marshall, a former Pittsburgh Hornet, lugged the puck over the blue line. As the Penguins swarmed to greet him, they left veteran Ed Westfall unattended in front of goalie Gary Inness.

"All the Penguins went towards Bert so I yelled to him," Westfall said. "I held the puck for a second when I got it. [Inness] was leaning a little toward J. P. Parise coming in on his right side. So I put it up high and tried to get the puck in the eight inches he left open near the post."

Westfall's shot found the mark. Demoralized by the sudden turn of events, the Penguins failed to register a shot during the final five minutes. They became the first team in 33 years to lose four straight playoff games after taking a three-game series lead.

"All [the Islanders] did was work for seven games," Pens coach Marc Boileau lamented.

Islanders 1 • Penguins 0

SCORING BY PERIODS
NY Islanders   0   0   1   1
Pittsburgh   0   0   0   0

FIRST PERIOD
SCORING—None.
PENALTIES—Gillies, NYI, major (fighting) 2:44; Paradise, Pit, major (fighting) 2:44; Burrows, Pit (tripping) 3:48; Lewis, NYI (hooking) 6:06; Westfall, NYI (elbowing) 7:27; Owchar, Pit (elbowing) 11:17; Lewis, NYI, major (fighting) 17:25; Kelly, Pit, major (fighting) 17:25; St. Laurent, NYI (high-sticking) 18:07; Campbell, Pit (high-sticking) 18:07; Hart, NYI (boarding) 20:00; MacDonald, Pit (slashing) 20:00.

SECOND PERIOD
SCORING—None.
PENALTIES—Pronovost, Pit (holding) 1:11; J. Potvin, NYI (tripping) 3:11; Arnason, Pit (tripping) 15:36.

THIRD PERIOD
SCORING—1. NY Islanders, Westfall 4 (Marshall) 14:42.
PENALTY—Howatt, NYI (hooking) 5:48.

SHOTS ON GOAL
NY Islanders 5-6-7—18; Pittsburgh 14-11-5—30

GOALIES
NY Islanders, Resch (30 shots—30 saves); Pittsburgh, Inness (18 shots—17 saves).

ATTENDANCE—13,404

Penguins Drop Game 5 to St. Louis
April 14, 1981

Although the Penguins finished a distant third in the Norris Division in 1980–81, there was reason to believe the team might do some damage in the playoffs. Following a dreadful first half, the Pens played better than .500 hockey over the final 37 games. Thanks to fiery coach Eddie Johnston, the club boasted one of the top power-play units in the league, striking for 92 man-advantage goals. Newcomers Paul Gardner, Paul Baxter, and Pat Price added some badly needed scoring and aggression to the mix.

The Pens' opening-round playoff opponent was an old rival from the early 1970s—the St. Louis Blues. Under the guidance of former star Red Berenson, the resurgent Blues had rolled up 107 points to capture the Smythe Division crown. A powerful offensive club, St. Louis boasted five 30-goal scorers, including Wayne Babych, Bernie Federko, and Jorgen Pettersson.

Remarkably, the Penguins proved to be an even match for their high-flying foe. After dropping the series opener 4–2, they took two of the next three contests. All-Star defenseman Randy Carlyle was enjoying a sensational series, as was third-year goalie Greg Millen.

The fifth and deciding game was played before a standing-room-only crowd of 18,150 at the Checkerdome. The Penguins drew first blood, as Gardner deflected a Rick Kehoe slap shot past Mike Liut. Typifying the back-and-forth nature of the series, the Blues knotted the score on second-period goals by Brian Sutter and Federko, sandwiched around a tally by George Ferguson.

St. Louis grabbed the lead early in the final period on a goal by Rick LaPointe. But once more the pesky Pens battled back. At 10:36 Greg Malone gathered in a pass from Rod Schutt and beat Liut to tie the game at 3–3. Following nine minutes of thrilling end-to-end action, the game went to overtime.

The Blues opened the extra stanza firing on all cylinders, but Greg Millen was up to the task, making a series of highlight-reel saves.

"I don't think I've ever seen any goaltender play as well as Millen played in my five years in the NHL," Carlyle said later.

Inspired by their little goalie, the Penguins suddenly sprang to life. They fired the last seven shots of the period at Liut, who likewise was in top form. At the 15-minute mark the Blues' netminder stopped Gardner's jam attempt from the slot to snuff out the Pens' best scoring chance.

Five minutes into the second overtime Blues winger Mike Zuke scooped up the puck and flew into the Penguins' end. Mark Johnson quickly pinned Zuke against the boards. However, he couldn't prevent a bounce pass that hopped past Carlyle and onto the stick of Mike Crombeen, who was camped in the slot. Crombeen whipped the game winner into the upper left corner of the net.

Afterward, the vanquished Penguins struggled to come to terms with their emotions.

"It's almost a shock to your system to play so well and fall short," Baxter said. "You just can't comprehend what happened. It's almost agonizing to fall so short, though not for a lack of effort. I've never seen a group of guys give so much of themselves as we did tonight. A game like this builds character. Guys grow from these kind of games."

Blues 4 • Penguins 3

SCORING BY PERIODS

Pittsburgh	1	1	1	0	0	3
St. Louis	0	2	1	0	1	4

FIRST PERIOD
SCORING—1. Pittsburgh, Gardner 1 (Kehoe, Carlyle) 7:48 (pp). PENALTIES—Carlyle, Pit, major (fighting) 1:00; Schutt, Pit (misconduct) 1:00; Pit bench (failure to clear area of a fight) 1:00; Sutter, StL, major (fighting) 1:00; StL bench (failure to clear area of a fight) 1:00; Baxter, Pit (tripping) 1:28; Maxwell, StL, double minor (high-sticking and cross-checking) 4:37; Faubert, Pit (slashing) 6:04; Hart, StL (slashing) 6:04; Schutt, Pit (cross-checking) 15:44.

SECOND PERIOD
SCORING—2. St. Louis, Sutter 2 (Federko, Currie) 11:17; 3. Pittsburgh, Ferguson 2 (Johnson, Sheppard) 15:06; 4. St. Louis, Federko 4 (Sutter, Currie) 16:06 (pp). PENALTIES—Patey, StL (tripping) 0:57; Johnson, Pit (hooking) 15:53.

THIRD PERIOD
SCORING—5. St. Louis, LaPointe 1 (Chapman, Patey) 3:34; 6. Pittsburgh, Malone 2 (Schutt, Baxter) 10:36. PENALTIES—Price, Pit (high-sticking) 3:44; Patey, StL (high-sticking) 9:29; Price, Pit (high-sticking) 9:29; LaPointe, StL (roughing) 18:58; Sheppard, Pit (roughing) 18:58.

FIRST OVERTIME
SCORING—None. PENALTIES—Baxter, Pit (roughing) 9:56; Patey, StL (roughing) 9:56.

SECOND OVERTIME
SCORING—7. St. Louis, Crombeen 2 (Zuke, LaPointe) 5:16. PENALTIES—None.

SHOTS ON GOAL
Pittsburgh 10-13-10-13-5—51; St. Louis 17-12-9-13-1—52

GOALIES
Pittsburgh, Millen (52 shots—48 saves); St. Louis, Liut (51 shots—48 saves).

ATTENDANCE—18,150

Penguins Fall to Islanders in Overtime
April 13, 1982

Following an up-and-down regular season, the Penguins squared off against the powerhouse New York Islanders in the opening round of the 1982 playoffs. The Islanders had won back-to-back Stanley Cups, and their dynasty was in full bloom. Worse yet, the pesky Pens had drawn their ire during a rugged regular-season finale. The Islanders were out for blood.

Predictably, the defending Cup champions thrashed the Penguins by a combined score of 15–3 in Games 1 and 2. Dismayed by his club's shabby performance, owner Edward J. DeBartolo Sr. offered Penguins fans a full refund for their tickets prior to Game 3.

Stung by their owner's offer, the undermanned Penguins pulled together. They staved off elimination with a thrilling 2–1 victory, thanks to Rick Kehoe's game winner in overtime. In Game 4 they stunned the Islanders 5–2 to set up a deciding fifth game in Uniondale.

The Islanders came out smoking. They outshot the Penguins 13–4 in the first period and dominated the action. But Penguins goalie Michel Dion stopped them cold.

"All year he's been outstanding," Pens coach Eddie Johnston said. "Tonight he was phenomenal."

Bob Nystrom finally nicked Dion for a goal at 10:18 of the second period. However, the Penguins continued to employ the dump-and-chase game that had frustrated the Islanders throughout the series. It soon paid dividends. Less than a minute later, they knotted the score when rugged rookie Kevin McClelland deflected a Greg Hotham blast over Billy Smith's left arm.

Before the Islanders could respond, the Pens struck for two more goals. Mike Bullard blew around defenseman Mike McEwen and flipped a backhander past Smith at 16:10. Then, as the period was winding down, Paul Gardner stripped the puck from Ken Morrow and fed Randy Carlyle, who pounded home a 35-foot slap shot. The Penguins went to the dressing room holding a 3–1 lead.

With their dreams of another Stanley Cup slipping through their fingers, the Islanders turned up the heat in the third period. They pounded Dion with salvo after salvo, but again the acrobatic goalie held firm. However, a hooking penalty to Carlyle at 12:56 opened the door. Seconds before the penalty expired McEwen rapped in a Mike Bossy rebound.

Galvanized by the goal, the Islanders continued to carry the play. As the clock ticked down under three minutes they struck again on a fluke goal. Ex-Penguin farmhand Gord Lane dumped the puck into the corner. As Carlyle skated over to retrieve it, the puck hopped over his stick to John Tonelli, who rifled it into a wide-open net.

The Pens had one last chance for redemption. Early in overtime Bullard broke in on Smith, but the feisty goalie made a spectacular save. The Islanders counterattacked and Tonelli beat Dion for the game winner.

"I was feeling really high because I thought we had it in our back pockets," Johnston said afterward. "We were two goals ahead with six minutes to go, then they got a questionable penalty and a lucky bounce. A great club capitalizes on those breaks and, let's face it, they're a great hockey club."

The Islanders had nothing but praise for the plucky Penguins—especially Dion.

"They should stop everything and give him the Conn Smythe right now," Billy Smith said. "I've watched him this whole series and I've never seen anything like him. He's incredible."

Islanders 4 • Penguins 3

SCORING BY PERIODS

Pittsburgh	0	3	0	0	3
NY Islanders	0	1	2	1	4

FIRST PERIOD
SCORING—None.
PENALTIES—Baxter, Pit (holding) 5:27; Trottier, NYI (holding) 5:46; Gillies, NYI (tripping) 8:48; Trottier, NYI (tripping) 11:58; Baxter, Pit (interference) 14:20; Kehoe, Pit (hooking) 17:36.

SECOND PERIOD
SCORING—1. NY Islanders, Nystrom 1 (Bourne, McEwen) 10:18; 2. Pittsburgh, McClelland 1 (Hotham, Schutt) 11:01; 3. Pittsburgh, Bullard 1 (MacLeish, Hotham) 16:10; 3. Pittsburgh, Carlyle 1 (Gardner) 18:31.
PENALTIES—Pit bench, served by Simpson (too many men on ice) 1:34; Bullard, Pit (tripping) 5:25; Carlyle, Pit (interference) 6:02; Gillies, NYI (high-sticking) 6:02.

THIRD PERIOD
SCORING—5. NY Islanders, McEwen 2 (Bossy) 14:33 (pp); 6. NY Islanders, Tonelli 2 (Lane, Morrow) 17:39.
PENALTIES—Nystrom, NYI (charging) 7:31; Carlyle, Pit (hooking) 12:56.

FIRST OVERTIME
SCORING—7. NY Islanders, Tonelli 3 (Nystrom, Bourne) 6:19.
PENALTIES—None.

SHOTS ON GOAL
Pittsburgh 4-7-7-3—21; NY Islanders 13-12-18-3—46

GOALIES
Pittsburgh, Dion (46 shots—42 saves); NY Islanders, Smith (21 shots—18 saves).

ATTENDANCE—15,230

Penguins Lose to Islanders, Miss Chance at Three-Peat

May 14, 1993

The 1992–93 Penguins were arguably the finest team in franchise history. They boasted no fewer than four 100-point scorers—Mario Lemieux, Kevin Stevens, Rick Tocchet, and Ron Francis. The club was so deep up front that gifted Jaromir Jagr often skated on the *third* line.

Following Lemieux's return from Hodgkin's disease treatments in March, the Pens went on a record-setting 17–0–1 tear. Racking up a staggering 119 points, they easily captured the President's Trophy. A third straight Stanley Cup was a virtual lock.

Opinions were hardly swayed during the team's opening-round series against New Jersey. Usually one of the Penguins' tougher opponents, the Devils succumbed in a relatively easy five-game set.

On deck were the New York Islanders. Although they possessed some firepower in 30-goal men Benoit Hogue, Derek King, and Steve Thomas, they were largely a nondescript team that relied more on elbow grease than pure talent. The team's lone superstar, Pierre Turgeon, would miss most of the series with a shoulder separation.

Nobody expected New York to offer much of a challenge—except perhaps the Islanders themselves. Displaying the tenacity of a junkyard dog, they pushed the mighty Pens to a seventh and deciding game.

Determined to exert their superiority, the Penguins opened the game in a combative mood. At the five-minute mark Stevens launched his 230-pound frame into Rich Pilon. As he delivered the check his forehead connected flush with Pilon's visor. Momentarily knocked unconscious, Stevens fell to the ice facefirst, landing full force with a sickening thud.

The big power forward suffered a host of ghastly injuries, including a broken nose, a severe cut above his right eye, and a concussion. Play was halted while the trainers lifted Stevens onto a stretcher and carted him off the ice.

No strangers to adversity, the Penguins responded by swarming the Islanders' net. They peppered New York goalie Glenn Healy with 19 first-period shots, including a breakaway chance by Lemieux. But Healy stood firm.

The second period was a virtual replay of the first. The Penguins finally broke through at 7:59 when Ulf Samuelsson beat Healy with a hard slap shot. Late in the period, however, the rugged defender made an errant clearing pass that the Islanders converted into a goal.

With the momentum firmly in their favor, the visitors beat Tom Barrasso twice early in the third period to grab a 3–1 lead. The Penguins' dimming hopes seemed to vanish for good at 15:35 when a frustrated Lemieux was ushered to the penalty box with Uwe Krupp. But in a remarkable display of character, Francis and Tocchet struck in the final four minutes to even the score and send the game into overtime.

Their spirits renewed, the Penguins went for the quick kill. Lemieux and Francis each had an opportunity to put

the plucky Islanders away. Once again, however, Healy slammed the door. Five minutes into the extra period, Ray Ferraro and David Volek broke into the Penguins' zone on an odd-man break. Taking a picture-perfect pass in full stride, Volek blasted the puck over Barrasso's shoulder. David had slain the mighty Goliath.

Islanders 4 • Penguins 3

SCORING BY PERIODS

NY Islanders	0	1	2	1	4
Pittsburgh	0	1	2	0	3

FIRST PERIOD
SCORING—None.
PENALTIES—Dalgarno, NYI (roughing) 0:08; Stevens, Pit (holding) 0:08; Tocchet, Pit (interference) 5:25; Vaske, NYI (interference) 7:45; Kasparaitis, NYI (cross-checking) 9:56; J. Mullen, Pit (high-sticking) 9:56; Thomas, NYI (charging) 18:00.

SECOND PERIOD
SCORING—1. Pittsburgh, U. Samuelsson 1 (Lemieux, K. Samuelsson) 7:59; 2. NY Islanders, Thomas 6 (Hogue) 18:28.
PENALTIES—Tippett, Pit (holding stick) 2:32; Malakhov, NYI (interference) 5:46.

THIRD PERIOD
SCORING—3. NY Islanders, Volek 1 (Ferraro, Fitzgerald) 6:10; 4. NY Islanders, Hogue 4 (Malakhov, Healy) 9:09; 5. Pittsburgh, Francis 6 (Murphy) 16:13; 6. Pittsburgh, Tocchet 7 (Francis, Murphy) 19:00.
PENALTIES—Pilon, NYI (unsportsmanlike conduct) 7:50; Tocchet, Pit (unsportsmanlike conduct) 7:50; Krupp, NYI (slashing) 15:35; Lemieux, Pit (slashing) 15:35.

FIRST OVERTIME
SCORING—7. NY Islanders, Volek 2 (Ferraro, Vaske) 5:16.
PENALTIES—None.

SHOTS ON GOAL
NY Islanders 7-4-6-3—20; Pittsburgh 19-7-16-3—45

GOALIES
NY Islanders, Healy (45 shots—42 saves); Pittsburgh, Barrasso (20 shots—16 saves).

ATTENDANCE—16,164

Penguins Drop Quintuple-Overtime Marathon to Philadelphia

May 4, 2000

After spending nearly a decade on a short list of Stanley Cup contenders, the Penguins entered the 2000 postseason in the unfamiliar role of underdogs. The club had nosedived

Nemesis

During an NHL career that spanned more than 1,000 games, Tom Fitzgerald carved out a reputation as a solid defensive forward. But the Penguins could be excused for believing that the Melrose, Massachusetts, native was the second coming of Attila the Hun. The unspectacular winger almost single-handedly derailed the Pens' Stanley Cup express train on two separate occasions.

In the spring of 1993 the Penguins—fresh off a five-game demolition of New Jersey—were looking to defend their Stanley Cup championship. They held a 2–1 series lead against the plucky Islanders, who were proving to be a determined foe.

With the score knotted at 1–1 late in the second period of Game 4, the Penguins' power play sprang into action. Normally this spelled doom for the opposition. As the final seconds of the period ticked off the clock, however, the Islanders stole the puck and sped into the Pittsburgh zone on a three-on-one break. Tom

Barrasso made a brilliant save, and the redoubtable Joe Mullen corralled the rebound and lofted it toward center ice.

In an incredible display of hand-eye coordination, Fitzgerald timed Mullen's clearing attempt perfectly. He batted the puck out of midair and rifled it past Barrasso before the startled goalie could react.

Fitzgerald wasn't finished. In the opening moments of the final period he burned the Penguins with a second shorthanded tally on the same penalty. Buoyed by the gritty winger's spectacular effort, the Islanders won Game 4 and turned the series around.

That alone would qualify Fitzgerald as one of the all-time Penguin villains. Three years later he drove another stake through the team's heart, scoring the series-winning goal for Florida in the hotly contested Wales Conference Finals.

Ironically, Fitzgerald joined the Pens' staff in 2008. The team responded by winning a third Stanley Cup—a prize that Fitzgerald had helped snatch from its grasp 16 years earlier.

early under demanding coach Kevin Constantine before rebounding to earn a playoff spot under USA hockey legend Herb Brooks.

Despite their less-than-inspired record, the Pens had jelled into a quick, resourceful team. Scoring champion Jaromir Jagr paced an underrated attack that included the likes of Alexei Kovalev, Robert Lang, and Martin Straka. At the trade deadline Craig Patrick imported dependable defenders Bob Boughner and Janne Laukkanen along with goalie Ron Tugnutt. They proved to be just the right tonic.

In the opening round of the playoffs the Pens dispatched the heavily favored Capitals with shocking ease. Even more remarkably, they swept the first two games of their Eastern Conference Semifinal series with the powerful Flyers—in Philadelphia, no less. Although the Flyers bounced back to win Game 3 in Pittsburgh, it did little to undermine the Pens' burgeoning confidence.

The Penguins got the jump on Philly in Game 4, as Kovalev struck at 2:22 of the opening frame. It was all the offense either side could muster for the next 40 minutes. The unheralded Tugnutt, who was proving to be a marvel, stopped the Flyers dead in their tracks. While not as active as his counterpart, Philadelphia's Brian Boucher made key saves when called upon.

A slashing penalty to Straka early in third period opened the door. Four seconds into the power play, John LeClair rambled to the net and snapped the puck past Tugnutt. Once again the defenses stiffened, forcing the game to overtime.

With the goaltenders serving up goose eggs, the teams churned through a first overtime. A second overtime came and went. Then a third and a fourth. As the game rolled into a fifth overtime with no end in sight, the players teetered on the brink of exhaustion…and delirium.

"You can't even describe how it felt," Darius Kasparaitis said. "You don't even think what you're doing…. When you're tired, it's tough to think. You make mistakes. Things happen."

Something, indeed, happened at 12:01 of the fifth overtime. Big Keith Primeau made a sharp skate stop to elude the onrushing Kasparaitis. Then he pulled the puck back to his forehand and beat Tugnutt with a missile that clanged off the crossbar and into the net.

The plucky little goalie was hardly at fault. Over the course of 152 minutes he'd stopped an astounding 70 of 72 shots to earn the No. 1 star in a losing cause.

"He was great," Herb Brooks said.

Despite the deflating loss, the Penguins remained surprisingly upbeat.

"Our psyche is fine," said Matthew Barnaby, who drank six Gatorades and ate nine slices of pizza to maintain his energy during the marathon loss. "I mean, I think I could speak for all of us and say, 'Let's get back at it tomorrow.'"

Then he grinned and added, "Maybe I'll resist saying that since I'm so tired. But I will say, 'Let's go at it again Sunday.' We'll see what happens then."

Flyers 2 • Penguins 1

SCORING BY PERIODS

Philadelphia	0	0	1	0	0	0	0	1	2
Pittsburgh	1	0	0	0	0	0	0	0	1

FIRST PERIOD
SCORING—1. Pittsburgh, Kovalev 1 (Lang) 2:22.
PENALTIES— Kasparaitis, Pit (high-sticking) 4:09; Langkow, Phi (slashing) 9:23; LeClair, Phi (obstruction-holding) 15:20.

SECOND PERIOD
SCORING—None.
PENALTIES—Popovic, Pit (interference) 4:11; Rozsival, Pit (hooking) 19:38.

THIRD PERIOD
SCORING—2. Philadelphia, LeClair 5 (Desjardins, Langkow) 4:47 (pp).
PENALTY—Straka, Pit (slashing) 4:43.

FIRST OVERTIME
SCORING—None.
PENALTIES—Manderville, Phi (roughing) 6:38; Rozsival, Pit (roughing) 6:38.

SECOND OVERTIME
SCORING—None.
PENALTIES—None.

THIRD OVERTIME
SCORING—None.
PENALTIES—Langkow, Phi (high-sticking) 0:25; Phi bench, served by Tocchet (too many men on ice) 10:22; Kasparaitis, Pit (holding) 13:21.

FOURTH OVERTIME
SCORING—None.
PENALTIES—None.

FIFTH OVERTIME
SCORING—3. Philadelphia, Primeau 1 (McGillis, Richardson) 12:01.
PENALTIES—None.

SHOTS ON GOAL
Philadelphia 9-12-8-8-7-13-10-5—72; Pittsburgh 6-8-5-6-7-9-9-8—58

GOALIES
Philadelphia, Boucher (58 shots—57 saves); Pittsburgh, Tugnutt (72 shots—70 saves).

ATTENDANCE—17,148

Penguins Lose to Detroit in 2008 Stanley Cup Finals

June 4, 2008

The Penguins entered the 2008 Stanley Cup Finals on a roll. After nailing down first place in the Atlantic Division, they marched through the Senators, Rangers, and Flyers in rapid-fire succession to claim Eastern Conference supremacy.

However, a tough, battle-hardened foe awaited them. The Detroit Red Wings had won the Cup as recently as 2002. In stark contrast to the callow Penguins, no fewer than 10 of their players had earned Cup rings.

The edge in experience quickly became apparent. Playing coach Mike Babcock's blitzkrieg-style, puck-possession game, the Red Wings dominated the Pens through the early stages of the series. Carrying a 3–1 lead into Game 5, Detroit came within 34 seconds of claiming the Cup. But a late goal in regulation by Max Talbot, followed by Petr Sykora's overtime winner, saved the day for the Penguins.

A capacity crowd turned out at the Mellon Arena for Game 6, hopeful that their heroes could stave off elimination and force a Game 7. They were in for a letdown.

Try as they might, the Penguins couldn't wrestle control from the high-flying Wings. Early in the first period veteran Darryl Sydor drew an interference penalty. Detroit immediately cashed in, as Brian Rafalski banked in a shot off of Hal Gill's leg.

Three minutes later the visitors handed the Penguins a golden opportunity. Dallas Drake drew a charging penalty at 8:28, followed in short order by a roughing call to Kris Draper. But the Pens were unable to beat stingy Chris Osgood, who enjoyed a superb series.

Midway through the second period Valtteri Fippula struck for a soft goal—one of the few allowed by Pens netminder Marc-Andre Fleury. However, at 15:26 Evgeni Malkin revived his team's sagging hopes when he blew the puck past Osgood on the power play.

The game was up for grabs until 7:36 of the final period, when Henrik Zetterberg was credited with a fluke goal. Following a Red Wings salvo, the puck sat motionless in the crease behind Fleury. Having lost sight of the rubber, the young goalie instinctively fell backward in an attempt to cover it. The puck squirted off his backside and across the goal line.

The untimely tally took the starch out of the Penguins. They mustered only one third-period shot until 18:13, when Jiri Hudler was whistled off for hooking. Sensing it was his club's final gasp, Pens coach Michel Therrien pulled Fleury for an extra attacker. In his typically poised fashion, Sergei Gonchar skated to center point and ripped off a low, hard shot. Marian Hossa jabbed at the puck as it sailed by, deflecting it past Osgood.

Down 3–2 with over a minute to play, the Pens seemed poised for an electric comeback. However, they failed to mount an attack until the closing seconds, when Sidney Crosby flew into the slot and ripped off a backhander. The puck deflected off Osgood's glove and into the crease. It hung there for a tantalizing millisecond before Hossa raced in to give it a nudge. The disk slid harmlessly along the goal line as the buzzer sounded. Even had it crossed the line it would not have counted.

The Penguins were understandably dismayed.

"It's such an empty feeling right now," said defenseman Ryan Whitney. "It's something we're going to have to think about in the summer. This is what makes you a better player. You don't want to feel this way again."

Red Wings 3 • Penguins 2

SCORING BY PERIODS
Detroit   1   1   1   3
Pittsburgh   0   1   1   2

FIRST PERIOD
SCORING—1. Detroit, Rafalski 4 (Zetterberg, Datsyuk) 5:03 (pp).
PENALTIES—Sydor, Pit (interference) 4:17; Drake, Det (charging) 8:28;
Draper, Det (roughing) 8:55; Hall, Pit (high-sticking) 11:15.

SECOND PERIOD
SCORING—2. Detroit, Filppula 5 (Samuelsson, Kronwall) 8:07; 3.
Pittsburgh, Malkin 10 (Crosby, Hossa) 15:26 (pp).
PENALTIES—Lilja, Det (slashing) 2:06; Datsyuk, Det (interference) 14:22;
Roberts, Pit (high-sticking) 16:13; Franzen, Det (roughing) 17:58; Orpik, Pit
(roughing) 17:58.

THIRD PERIOD
SCORING—4. Detroit, Zetterberg 13 (Datsyuk, Kronwall) 7:36; 5. Pittsburgh,
Hossa 12 (Gonchar, Malkin) 18:33 (pp).
PENALTY—Hudler, Det (hooking) 18:13.

SHOTS ON GOAL
Detroit 9-9-12—30; Pittsburgh 8-8-6—22

GOALIES
Detroit, Osgood (22 shots—20 saves); Pittsburgh, Fleury (30 shots—27
saves).

ATTENDANCE—17,132

Dejected Evgeni Malkin takes a knee following the Pens' crushing loss to the
Red Wings.

The Brawls

Penguins vs. St. Louis
January 31, 1970

During the early years, the St. Louis Blues and the Penguins
represented the extreme north and south poles of the 1967
expansion teams. Led by brilliant young coach Scotty
Bowman, the Blues made it to the Stanley Cup Finals in
each of their first two seasons. The Penguins, on the other
hand, had missed the playoffs two years running while going
from bad to worse.

When the Blues visited the Civic Arena on January 31,
1970, to take on the Pens, it seemed little had changed. St.
Louis held first place in the West Division by a wide margin.
In their first year under coach Red Kelly, the Penguins were
stumbling along with a dismal record of 13–24–8.

There were, however, some signs of life. In an effort to
make the Pens more competitive, general manager Jack
Riley had added a slew of hard-nosed performers. Boasting
toughies such as Bryan Hextall, Tracy Pratt, Glen "Slats"

Sather, and Bryan "Bugsy" Watson, the Penguins were a
difficult foe. You might beat them, but—as St. Louis would
soon learn—you would pay a price.

The Blues were hardly comprised of choir boys. Their
defense was anchored by the notorious Plager brothers,
Barclay and Bob. During the 1967–68 campaign "Barc the
Spark" had wiped out Pens defenseman Dunc McCallum
with a brutal check. Bob, the larger of the siblings, was
reputed to punch (and skate) like Sonny Liston.

The first period was fairly uneventful. Pens winger Ken
Schinkel and the Blues' Jim Roberts each drew a hooking
minor. St. Louis grabbed the lead on a goal by Tim
Ecclestone.

Early in the second period the action heated up. Bugsy
Watson and Barclay Plager—two players cut from the same
cloth—attempted to skewer each other with their sticks. At
the 16:30 mark, Plager spotted Watson and skated straight
for the spunky Pens defender. Before he could reach his
target, Sather intercepted him.

In an instant the combatants shed their sticks and gloves and began firing punches. Players from both sides quickly joined the skirmish, triggering a full-scale brawl. The action drifted from in front of the Pittsburgh bench to the St. Louis bench. Noticing that his teammates were suddenly in a precarious spot, Penguins goalie Al Smith left his crease to join the fray. Bob Plager hopped over the boards to help his brother. The Penguins bench emptied en masse.

While the 9,679 partisans roared their approval, the fights tilted in favor of the home team. At the eye of the storm, Barclay Plager engaged in three separate fights—two with Sather and one with Hextall. He received a broken nose for his pugilistic efforts. After 10 minutes of nonstop mayhem, order was finally restored.

Inspired, the pumped-up Penguins swarmed the Blues in the third period, outshooting their beleaguered foe by a margin of 11–3. Keith McCreary and Wally Boyer scored to cap a 2–1 victory.

The brawl marked an early turning point in franchise history. Patsies no more, the "Pesky Pens" played .500 hockey over the final two months of the season. In April they clashed with the Blues again in an epic semifinals series that featured another record-setting fracas.

Penguins 2 • Blues 1

SCORING BY PERIODS
St. Louis   1   0   0   1
Pittsburgh   0   0   2   2

FIRST PERIOD
SCORING—1. St. Louis, Ecclestone 8 (St. Marseille) 8:53.
PENALTIES—Schinkel, Pit (hooking) 4:03; Roberts, StL (hooking) 9:05.

SECOND PERIOD
SCORING—None.
PENALTIES—Barclay Plager, StL (spearing) 2:50; Watson, Pit (spearing) 2:50; Talbot, StL (interference) 15:17; Barclay Plager, StL, double major-misconduct (fighting) 16:30; Bob Plager, StL (roughing) 16:30; Sather, Pit, double major-misconduct (fighting) 16:30; Hextall, Pit, major (fighting) 16:30; Pratt, Pit (roughing) 16:30.

THIRD PERIOD
SCORING—2. Pittsburgh, K. McCreary 13 (Pronovost) 8:50; 3. Pittsburgh, Boyer 7 (Fonteyne, Morrison) 11:40.
PENALTY—B. McCreary, StL (tripping) 2:16.

SHOTS ON GOAL
St. Louis 12-13-3—28; Pittsburgh 8-9-11—28

GOALIES
St. Louis, Wakely (28 shots—26 saves); Pittsburgh, Smith (28 shots—27 saves).

ATTENDANCE—9,679

Penguins vs. Edmonton
January 19, 1980

When the Edmonton Oilers visited the Civic Arena on January 19, 1980, for a Saturday night game, none of the 12,896 fans in attendance were expecting fireworks. After all, it was the first-ever meeting between the Penguins and the Oilers, who joined the league from the World Hockey Association. It would be a memorable one.

Bad blood began to flow as soon as the first puck was dropped. Pens captain Orest Kindrachuk and Edmonton's big Cam Connor whacked each other with their sticks, while Russ Anderson decked the Oilers' husky 19-year-old, Mark Messier, with one punch.

Early in the second period Anderson and Messier clashed again at center ice. Just as they were ready to engage, the Oilers' Dave Lumley intervened. Following a brief exchange between Lumley and Anderson, Messier grabbed the Pens' defenseman from behind and yanked him to the ice.

Six minutes later Edmonton's young star, Wayne Gretzky, skated behind the Pittsburgh net, where he collided with rugged Kim Clackson. "The Great One" hit the deck as if he'd been shot. While Gretzky lay prone on the ice, the Edmonton trainer was escorted onto the ice by several of his teammates, one of whom happened to be noted pugilist Dave Semenko.

The Oilers' enforcer headed straight for Clackson. A former WHA penalty king, the fierce Penguins defenseman didn't need an engraved invitation to fight. They dropped their mitts and went at it, with the burly Semenko getting the better of the exchange. As the battle intensified, Kindrachuk motioned to the Penguins bench for help. Players from both sides poured onto the ice, fueling the donnybrook.

By this time officials managed to usher the original antagonists to the sin bin. However, the parties continued to jaw at one another. Finally, with the beleaguered linesmen occupied with breaking up other bouts, Semenko and Clackson left the penalty box for round two.

As the other fights slowly petered out from exhaustion, the officials once again turned their attention to Clackson and Semenko. They succeeded in prying them apart...but only briefly. The Oiler made a gesture that enraged Clackson, and the tough little Penguin literally dragged the linesmen back to where Semenko was standing to engage him a third time.

Again the officials separated the combatants. Clackson was ushered off the ice with the help of a security guard. The situation finally seemed to be under control. Moments later, however, the plucky Penguin returned to the bench to gather his equipment, drawing the ire of Oilers coach Glen Sather.

"Clackson deliberately tried to injure Gretzky with his stick," Sather said afterward. "A goof like that shouldn't be in hockey. That stuff went out with the dark ages."

His anger boiling over, Sather flung a water bottle at the Pens bench. Clackson fired it back and scored a direct hit, knocking "Slats" off balance.

Russ Anderson slugs it out with the Oilers' Mark Messier.

Now it was the fans' turn. They showered the Edmonton bench with beer. In a scene straight from the movie *Slap Shot*, the Oilers threatened to seek retribution by charging into the stands. Fortunately, the security staff intervened and the unruly situation was finally diffused.

Play had been halted for nearly an hour. Eight players, including chief brawlers Clackson and Semenko, were tossed from the game. The clubs combined for a staggering total of 257 minutes in penalties.

Oh yes, a hockey game was played. The Oilers beat the Penguins 5–2.

Oilers 5 • Penguins 2

SCORING BY PERIODS

Edmonton	1	3	1	5
Pittsburgh	1	1	0	2

FIRST PERIOD
SCORING—1. Edmonton, MacDonald 26 (Gretzky) 7:38; 2. Pittsburgh, Malone 12 (Lee, Faubert) 14:53.
PENALTIES—Connor, Edm (slashing) 2:11; Messier, Edm, major (fighting) 2:11; Anderson, Pit, major (fighting) 2:11; Kindrachuk, Pit (slashing) 2:11; Callighen, Edm (tripping) 5:02; Kindrachuk, Pit (slashing) 6:17; Kindrachuk, Pit (hooking) 11:45; Lowe, Edm (elbowing) 14:05.

SECOND PERIOD
SCORING—3. Edmonton, MacDonald 27 (Gretzky, Callighen) 6:28; 4. Edmonton, Gretzky 24 (Siltanen, Hicks) 11:24 (pp); 5. Pittsburgh, Malone 13 (Carlyle, Faubert) 12:15; 6. Edmonton, MacDonald 28 (Chipperfield) 18:47.
PENALTIES—Lumley, Edm, minor-major (roughing and fighting) 1:21; Anderson, Pit, double minor-major (slashing, unsportsmanlike conduct and fighting) 1:21; Clackson, Pit, double minor-major-double game misconduct (high-sticking, leaving penalty box and fighting) 7:33; Anderson, Pit, minor-major-double game misconduct (leaving penalty box and fighting) 7:33; Kindrachuk, Pit, double minor-major-double game misconduct (fighting) 7:33; Hughes, Pit, major-game misconduct (fighting) 7:33; Millen, Pit (leaving the crease) 7:33; Semenko, Edm, double major-game misconduct (fighting) 7:33; Lumley, Edm, minor-major-double game misconduct (leaving penalty box and fighting) 7:33; Connor, Edm, major-game misconduct (fighting) 7:33; Messier, Edm, major-double game misconduct (fighting) 7:33; Mio, Edm (leaving the crease) 7:33; Fogolin, Edm (hooking) 11:58; Carlyle, Pit, minor-major (roughing and fighting) 13:34; Callighen, Edm, minor-major (roughing and fighting) 13:34; Malone, Pit, major (fighting) 17:13; Campbell, Edm, major (fighting) 17:13.

THIRD PERIOD
SCORING—7. Edmonton, Gretzky 25 (MacDonald, Price) 6:17.
PENALTY—Schmautz, Edm (hooking) 16:21.

SHOTS ON GOAL
Edmonton 13-13-9—35; Pittsburgh 10-5-9—24

GOALIES
Edmonton, Mio (24 shots—22 saves); Pittsburgh, Millen (35 shots—30 saves).

ATTENDANCE—12,896

Penguins vs. Philadelphia
October 29, 1981

For years the Penguins played the role of patsies for their in-state rivals, the Philadelphia Flyers. The "Broad Street Bullies" weren't just better. They were infinitely bigger, rougher, and meaner. Attending a Pens-Flyers game was like watching a flock of lambs being led to slaughter.

That changed in the fall of 1981. Choosing to fight fire with fire, Penguins general manager Baz Bastien built a team that could rival the Flyers in terms of toughness, if not talent. He imported giant winger Paul Mulvey from Washington. As compensation for free-agent goalie Greg Millen, he acquired hard-nosed players Pat Boutette and Kevin McClelland from Hartford. They joined forces with incumbents Russ Anderson, Paul Baxter, Pat Price, and Gary Rissling to give the Penguins a decidedly physical edge.

Eager to earn their spurs, the new-look Pens put their willingness to battle on display in an showdown with the Flyers at the Spectrum early in the season. Eight seconds into the contest, Rissling and his dance partner, menacing Glen Cochrane, were ushered to the penalty box. Minutes later Philly's Brian Propp incited a near riot when he speared Anderson.

A melee immediately erupted. Anderson and Baxter tried desperately to get at Propp, who had taken refuge behind his teammates. Frustrated in his attempts to reach the chippy forward, Baxter coldcocked the nearest Flyer, Behn Wilson. Surprised by the punch, Wilson crumbled to the ice.

Flyers agitator Ken Linseman immediately moved in and taunted Baxter. Anderson, who was still fuming over Propp's attempt at amateur surgery, promptly decked "the Rat" with a roundhouse right.

A giant pileup ensued, with players from both sides grabbing a man. Price left the penalty box to pin Propp to the ice. Meanwhile, Wilson had regained his feet with the help of a linesman. As his head cleared, the Flyers' tough guy pursued Baxter to center ice. The two locked up again, with Baxter landing a volley of quick lefts before Wilson gained the advantage with a stream of uppercuts.

The battle royale continued throughout the evening. Along with countless skirmishes, there were two more main events. Price swapped punches with mammoth Tim Kerr during the second period. Late in the game Baxter and Wilson hooked up for round three. The Penguins lost 6–4 but gained a huge moral victory by standing up to the Flyers.

Following the game, a blistering war of words ensued between Philly coach Pat Quinn and Pens skipper Eddie Johnston.

"Their game plan was obvious from the start and we got surprised by it," Quinn remarked. "But we laid down the ground rules for next time. [Johnston's] tactic wasn't to intimidate us, but to take some of our better players off the ice."

"That's his IQ," Johnston retorted. "Dummies like him we don't need in this game. What do you think his team's been doing all these years? Does he think they've got class players, finesse players? Cochrane and guys like that? You tell me who's trying to intimidate who."

Flyers 6 • Penguins 4

SCORING BY PERIODS

Pittsburgh	2	0	2	4
Philadelphia	3	1	2	6

FIRST PERIOD

SCORING—1. Pittsburgh, Ferguson 2 (Price, Baxter) 8:40; 2. Philadelphia, Propp 7 (Linseman, Bridgman) 9:13; 3. Philadelphia, Bridgman 3 (Linseman, Propp) 11:17 (pp); 4. Philadelphia, Sinisalo 4 (Clarke, Leach) 12:43; 5. Pittsburgh, Johnson 4 (Mulvey, Stackhouse) 18:47 (pp).
PENALTIES—Rissling, Pit (roughing) 0:08; Cochrane, Phi (roughing) 0:08; Rissling, Pit (charging) 4:04; Cochrane, Phi 6:46; Rissling, Pit (misconduct) 6:46; Kerr, Phi (misconduct) 6:46; Price, Pit (tripping) 9:44; Baxter, Pit, major-double misconduct (fighting) 11:17; Anderson, Pit, minor-major-misconduct (roughing and fighting) 11:17; Price, Pit (misconduct) 11:17; Ferguson, Pit (misconduct) 11:17; Malone, Pit (misconduct) 11:17; Propp, Phi, minor-major-misconduct (roughing and fighting) 11:17; Wilson, Phi, major-double misconduct (fighting) 11:17; Bridgman, Phi (misconduct) 11:17; Barber, Phi (misconduct) 11:17; Linseman, Phi (misconduct) 11:17; Cochrane, Phi (interference) 14:05; Carson, Phi (hooking) 17:09.

SECOND PERIOD

SCORING—6. Philadelphia, Bridgman 4 (Linseman, Bathe) 18:56.
PENALTIES—Boutette, Pit (slashing) 1:44; Cochrane, Phi (slashing) 1:44; Rissling, Pit (hooking) 5:00; Barber, Phi (tripping) 5:26; Price, Pit, major (fighting) 5:50; Kerr, Phi, major (fighting) 5:50; Rissling, Pit (holding) 7:18; Bridgman, Phi (hooking) 19:07; Dailey, Phi (unsportsmanlike conduct) 19:07.

THIRD PERIOD

SCORING—7. Pittsburgh, Boutette 4 (Kehoe, Faubert) 0:49 (pp); 8. Pittsburgh, Ferguson 3 (Carlyle, Malone) 13:51; 9. Philadelphia, Bridgman 5 (Linseman, Propp) 15:38 (pp); 10. Philadelphia, Clarke 3 (Bathe) 19:32 (en).
PENALTIES—Boutette, Pit (high-sticking) 7:01; Linseman, Phi (high-sticking) 7:01; Price, Pit (tripping) 15:01; Cochrane, Phi (high-sticking) 17:47; Wilson, Phi, major (fighting) 17:47; Baxter, Pit, major (fighting) 17:47; Boutette, Pit (high-sticking) 17:47.

SHOTS ON GOAL
Pittsburgh 6-8-7—21; Philadelphia 18-10-14—42

GOALIES
Pittsburgh, Dion (41 shots—36 saves); Philadelphia, St. Croix (21 shots—17 saves).

ATTENDANCE—17,077

Put 'Em Up

As a general rule hockey fights aren't a whole lot of fun. There's lots of pushing and shoving, not to mention the odd haymaker whistling toward your noggin. Yet it was just such a melee that produced perhaps the most comical moment in Penguins history.

One night during a hotly contested game, Bob Errey found himself in the middle of a wild scrum along with the St. Louis Blues' Sergio Momesso, a tough customer who outweighed the gritty Pens winger by 40 pounds.

Nonplussed, "the Bibster" reached a gloved hand through the tangle of bodies, grabbed Momesso's prominent nose between his thumb and index finger, and gave it a good pinch.

From his perch in the broadcast booth Mike Lange roared with laughter. He joked that the big winger "looked like a V-8 engine."

Flabbergasted, Momesso retreated from the pileup. Under normal circumstances, he would've mopped up the ice with Errey. But he was so shocked, he didn't know how to respond.

Scrappy Bob Errey wasn't afraid to take on larger foes.

Penguins vs. New York Rangers
October 30, 1988

In the fall of 1988 the Penguins and Rangers each got off to a fast start. By the time they hooked up for their first meeting at Madison Square Garden on October 30, the clubs were challenging for first place in the rugged Patrick Division.

Unfortunately, the game would not be a classic—at least not in hockey terms. The Penguins had skated to a pulsating 5–4 victory over the Canadiens in Montreal the night before and were suffering from jet lag. The Rangers, meanwhile, were fresh as daisies. After piling up a whopping 6–1 first-period lead, they carried an 8–2 advantage into the final frame.

Lopsided losses were nothing new to the Penguins, but this was a different kind of team. Stocked with tough, combative players, the club was not about to lie down.

"They got frustrated after the second period and when I feel like I saw their starting lineup for the third, they were going for this," Rangers coach Michel Bergeron said afterward.

"This" turned out to be a brawl-filled period the likes of which had rarely been seen in the annals of hockey history. The mayhem began just five seconds in when scrappy John Cullen took a poke at Rangers superstar Marcel Dionne. Immediately gloves and sticks hit the ice. Looking to make a statement, Penguins Mark Kachowski and Troy Loney tangled with James Patrick and Chris Nilan. The bouts were mere preliminaries to the main event that would shortly follow.

The volatile situation exploded three minutes later. New York's David Shaw took Pens captain and scoring leader Mario Lemieux hard into the boards. Momentarily shaken, Lemieux skated back in Shaw's direction, only to be clubbed in the head by the Rangers' defender. Mario went down in a heap.

While trainer Skip Thayer rushed onto the ice to attend to Lemieux, Dan Quinn moved in and attempted to spear Shaw with his stick blade. Incensed, the larger Shaw wrenched Quinn's stick from his grasp and pounded him to the ice.

The linesmen quickly broke up the fight, but getting Shaw off the ice was another matter. The runway to the Rangers' dressing room was located between the benches. When the officials attempted to escort Shaw to the runway, a host of angry Penguins—including Rod Buskas, Steve Dykstra, and Randy Cunneyworth—swarmed to the end of the bench. With sticks waving, they tried to break down a Plexiglas partition to get at the embattled Ranger. After several failed attempts, Shaw was finally led down the runway with the help of security personnel.

The contest degenerated into a pier-six brawl. At 15:29 Buskas and Bob Errey traded punches with peace-loving Rangers Brian Leetch and Ulf Dahlen. Two minutes later all hell broke loose, as Randy Hillier, Jim Johnson, Cunneyworth, and Loney battled Blueshirts Ron Greschner, Kelly Kisio, Michel Petit, and Nilan in four-on-four action. Thanks to a match penalty and eight game misconducts doled out by referee Andy van Hellemond, the teams barely had enough players to finish out the game.

Afterward, Bergeron was livid. He accused Penguins coach Gene Ubriaco of losing control of his team.

"I've coached in this league for nine years," he said, "and it's the first time I've seen a team so frustrated. I control my team and I really believe he didn't control his team. Even at the end of the game, I saw Dykstra slashing Marcel Dionne for nothing. It was bad."

Dykstra was hardly penitent.

"Next time we play New York, he's dead," he said, referring to Shaw. "And if he doesn't have the [courage] to dress, I'll get him in the stands."

Rangers 9 • Penguins 2

SCORING BY PERIODS
Pittsburgh	1	1	0	2
NY Rangers	6	2	1	9

FIRST PERIOD
SCORING—1. NY Rangers, Shaw 1 (Kisio, Dahlen) 0:25; 2. NY Rangers, Leetch 4 (Kisio, Maloney) 4:39; 3. NY Rangers, Sandstrom 2 (Leetch, Kisio) 6:00; 4. NY Rangers, Granato 3 (Dionne, Greschner) 8:56; 5. Pittsburgh, Quinn 6 (Coffey, Lemieux) 11:30 (pp); 6. NY Rangers, Kisio 3 (Leetch, Sandstrom) 15:14 (pp); 7. NY Rangers, Granato 4 (Petit) 19:57 (sh). PENALTIES—Johnson, Pit (tripping) 0:45; Kisio, NYR (tripping) 2:28; Frawley, Pit (elbowing) 6:12; DeBlois, NYR (roughing) 10:47; Hillier, Pit (holding) 14:48; Johnson, Pit (roughing) 14:57; Shaw, NYR (cross-checking) 18:47.

SECOND PERIOD
SCORING—8. NY Rangers, Granato 5 (Nilan, Dionne) 1:26; 9. NY Rangers, Granato 6 (Nilan) 7:11; 10. Pittsburgh, Siren 1 (Callander, Hillier) 17:04. PENALTIES—Errey, Pit (high-sticking) 14:18; Cunneyworth, Pit (slashing) 16:08; Dahlen, NYR (slashing) 16:08.

THIRD PERIOD
SCORING—11. NY Rangers, Leetch 5 (unassisted) 15:39 (pp). PENALTIES—Cullen, Pit, double minor-misconduct (roughing) 0:05; Loney, Pit, major (fighting) 0:05; Dionne, NYR (roughing) 0:05; Nilan, NYR, major (fighting) 0:05; Kachowski, Pit, minor-major (instigator and fighting) 3:00; Patrick, NYR, double minor (elbowing and roughing) 3:00; Vanbiesbrouck, NYR, served by Lawton (leaving the crease) 3:00; Lemieux, Pit (cross-checking) 3:41; Quinn, Pit, major-game misconduct (spearing) 3:41; Shaw, NYR, major-match penalty (slashing) 3:41; Hillier, Pit (roughing) 6:24; Petit, NYR (roughing) 6:24; Sandstrom, NYR (misconduct) 6:24; Mullen, NYR (slashing) 13:20; Brown, Pit (roughing) 14:22; Siren, Pit (hooking) 15:11; Pietrangelo, Pit, served by Siren (leaving the crease) 15:39; Buskas, Pit, major (fighting) 15:39; Errey, Pit, double major-misconduct-game misconduct (cross-checking and fighting) 15:39; Leetch, NYR, major (fighting) 15:39; Dahlen, NYR, double minor-major (instigator, wearing a visor and fighting) 15:39; Mullen, NYR, (game misconduct) 15:39; Loney, Pit, major-game misconduct (fighting) 17:36; Hillier, Pit, major (fighting) 17:36; Cunneyworth, Pit, major-game misconduct (fighting) 17:36; Johnson, Pit, major-game misconduct (fighting) 17:36; Nilan, NYR, major-misconduct-game misconduct (fighting) 17:36; Petit, NYR, major (fighting) 17:36; Kisio, NYR, major (fighting) 17:36; Greschner, NYR, major-game misconduct (fighting) 17:36; Brown, Pit (misconduct) 19:04.

SHOTS ON GOAL
Pittsburgh 10-11-6—27; NY Rangers 19-16-12—47

GOALIES
Pittsburgh, Guenette (12 shots—8 saves), Pietrangelo (8:56 first, 35 shots—30 saves); NY Rangers, Vanbiesbrouck (27 shots—25 saves).

ATTENDANCE—17,319

Penguins vs. Philadelphia
December 11, 2007

After sweeping the season series with Philadelphia the previous year, the Penguins were finding the going considerably tougher in 2007–08. The Flyers had rebounded under bright young coach John Stevens to challenge for Atlantic Division supremacy.

In the first meeting between the cross-state rivals, the Flyers had dispatched the home-standing Pens with relative ease. The Penguins hoped to return the favor when they visited the Wachovia Center on December 11, 2007.

Typically, sparks began to fly shortly after the opening face-off. Twenty seconds into the contest Ryan Malone and the Flyers' Jason Smith engaged in a spirited slugging match. The stage was set for a rugged affair that featured four scraps in all.

After spotting Philly an early two-goal lead, the Pens came roaring back to knot the score on tallies by Ryan Whitney and Petr Sykora. In the second period, however, the Flyers struck for three unanswered goals against Dany Sabourin to take control of the game.

Three minutes into the third period the lid blew off. Seeking to make a statement, Penguins heavyweight Georges Laraque challenged Flyers tough guy Ben Eager to a go. Eager declined…or so it seemed. Seconds later, while Laraque was digging for a loose puck along the boards, the husky Flyer barreled in and hammered big Georges with a forearm to the jaw. Remarkably, Laraque shook off the blow and slammed his antagonist to the ice.

Officials quickly intervened. It seemed—momentarily—that cooler heads would prevail. As Eager skated to the bench, however, he was challenged by the Pens' 42-year-old winger, Gary Roberts. Eager accepted and began pumping lefts at the tough old pro. An experienced gunslinger, Roberts weathered the early salvo while getting a firm grip on Eager's jersey. Then he took over. Firing his own left with stunning speed and fury, he pummeled a man 18 years his junior.

Even Sidney Crosby got involved. When Martin Biron skated behind his net to corral a loose puck, the Pens' captain swooped in and delivered a not-so-subtle slew foot, knocking the Flyers' goalie to the ice. An angry Biron quickly scrambled to his feet and shook his stick at Crosby, who skated away wearing an innocent expression. Moments later Laraque crashed into Biron with a skate-first slide that would've made a base stealer like Rickey Henderson proud.

Although the Penguins were feeling their oats, the Flyers were hardly intimidated. They dominated play in the third period, tacking on three more goals to score a resounding 8–2 victory. With the game in the bag, Philly gained a measure of revenge. During a scrum at 13:49 Jeff Carter decisioned Whitney, while Scott Hartnell bested scrappy but outgunned Colby Armstrong.

Evgeni Malkin and Ryan Malone take on the Flyers.

The bad blood was evident following the game. When Eager passed Penguins coach Michel Therrien in the corridor outside the Pens' locker room, he said, "You're a joke." Therrien's response was unprintable.

"Everyone knows there's [a rivalry] here," said Crosby, who was serenaded by catcalls throughout the afternoon. "But it seems like it's escalated each game."

Flyers 8 • Penguins 2

SCORING BY PERIODS
Pittsburgh   2   0   0   2
Philadelphia   2   3   3   8

FIRST PERIOD
SCORING—1. Philadelphia, Lupul 7 (Umberger, Richards) 1:11; 2. Philadelphia, Lupul 8 (Coburn, Richards) 3:44; 3. Pittsburgh, Whitney 6 (Gonchar, Crosby) 12:39 (pp); 4. Pittsburgh, Sykora 11 (Malkin, Crosby) 4:28 (pp).
PENALTIES—Smith, Phi, major (fighting) 0:20; Malone, Pit, major (fighting) 0:20; Potulny, Phi (slashing) 12:13; Carter, Phi (interference) 13:46; Sykora, Pit (roughing) 18:51.

SECOND PERIOD
SCORING—5. Philadelphia, Umberger 4 (Lupul, Richards) 8:10; 6. Philadelphia, Umberger 5 (Lupul, Smith) 10:10; 7. Philadelphia, Knuble 9 (Lupul, Timonen) 19:50 (pp).

PENALTIES—Roberts, Pit (high-sticking) 2:24; Gonchar, Pit (roughing) 3:33; Kukkonen, Phi (holding) 14:10; Christensen, Pit (roughing) 14:10; Jones, Phi (hooking) 14:52; Letang, Pit, double minor (unsportsmanlike conduct and roughing) 19:02.

THIRD PERIOD
SCORING—8. Philadelphia, Lupul 9 (Knuble, Briere) 4:07 (pp); 9. Philadelphia, Coburn 2 (Umberger, Jones) 6:09 (pp); 10. Philadelphia, Umberger 6 (Potulny) 17:48 (pp).
PENALTIES—Laraque, Pit, double minor (roughing) 3:02; Roberts, Pit, major (fighting) 3:02; Eager, Phi, major (fighting) 3:02; Gonchar, Pit (delay of game) 6:01; Armstrong, Pit (roughing) 7:19; Laraque, Pit (cross-checking) 9:50; Orpik, Pit (slashing) 12:20; Whitney, Pit, major-misconduct (fighting) 13:49; Armstrong, Pit, major-game misconduct (fighting) 13:49; Carter, Phi, major-misconduct (fighting) 13:49; Hartnell, Phi, major-game misconduct (fighting) 13:49; Laraque, Pit, minor-misconduct (interference) 16:47; Malkin, Pit (misconduct) 16:47; Torpeko, Phi (misconduct) 16:47; Ruutu, Pit, minor-misconduct (roughing) 19:00.

SHOTS ON GOAL
Pittsburgh 12-8-2—22; Philadelphia 11-14-15—40

GOALIES
Pittsburgh, Sabourin (25 shots—20 saves), Conklin (0:00 third, 15 shots—12 saves); Philadelphia, Biron (22 shots—20 saves).

ATTENDANCE—19,409

9

The Arenas

Since entering the National Hockey League in 1967, the Penguins have played exclusively at the Mellon (formerly Civic) Arena, which is located in Pittsburgh's Lower Hill section. This includes some 1,667 regular-season games and another 135 postseason contests.

Initially conceived as a home for Pittsburgh's Civic Light Opera, the Arena was willed into existence by department store magnate Edgar J. Kaufmann and city councilman Abraham Wolk. Hailed as an architectural wonder when it was completed in 1961, it was the first major sports stadium to feature a retractable dome. The Arena gained notoriety as the largest domed structure in the world until it was surpassed by the Houston Astrodome.

In more than 40 years of serving as the home of the Penguins, the Arena played host to thousands of sporting events, including the 1990 NHL All-Star Game and four Stanley Cup Finals. Hanging proudly from beneath her glittering dome are three Stanley Cup championship banners.

However, the story of Pittsburgh hockey reaches far beyond the Penguins and the Mellon Arena. In the 1890s, the Steel City was home to one of the first artificial ice surfaces in North America. The indoor rink at the Schenley Park Casino in Oakland quickly became a popular destination for the general public and the region's earliest hockey teams. Players throughout the United States and Canada flocked to Pittsburgh to skate on the Casino's ice during the summer months. Sadly, the building called "the finest of its kind in the world" by the *New York Times* burned to the ground after operating for only 19 months.

Following the fire that destroyed the Casino, another Oakland arena—the Duquesne Gardens—became the hub of Pittsburgh hockey. Originally a streetcar barn, the Gardens was transformed into a state-of-the-art facility in 1896 that used the latest in ice-making and refrigeration technology. Renowned the world over for the quality of its ice surface, the Gardens was home to one of the earliest professional leagues—the Western Pennsylvania Hockey League. In 1925, big-league hockey came to town when the Pittsburgh Pirates joined the NHL. After the Pirates departed, the Gardens served as the home rink for the American Hockey League's Pittsburgh Hornets for 20 seasons.

A third old-time ice palace—the Winter Garden—was installed at the Main Hall of the Pittsburgh Exposition in 1916. Featuring the largest ice surface of any of Pittsburgh's indoor arenas, the Winter Garden hosted hockey games from 1916 through 1920, including some of the first women's league contests. The legendary Hobey Baker played his final hockey game at the Winter Garden before enlisting in the army during World War I.

In the fall of 2010 the Penguins moved into the brand-new Consol Energy Center. Seating 18,087 for hockey, the multipurpose facility is one of the most technologically advanced buildings in the country. Designed by Populous—the firm that created the designs for PNC Park and Heinz Field—the Consol Energy Center will attempt to become the NHL's first Leadership in Energy and Environmental Design (LEED) certified arena.

Mellon Arena
1961–2010

If the stainless steel walls of the Mellon Arena could talk, they would have countless stories to tell. The world's first major indoor sports arena with a retractable roof hosted thousands of events over the years, from hockey games and boxing matches to rock concerts and circuses.

Ironically, the multipurpose venue was originally designed for a more refined form of entertainment. In 1946 Pittsburgh's Civic Light Opera debuted with a performance of Victor Herbert's classic *Naughty Marietta* at Pitt Stadium. The CLO quickly became a popular diversion among the city's cultural elite. The intent of the musical theater company was to offer outdoor performances "under the stars." However, the Steel City's unpredictable weather forced a series of cancellations.

Two years earlier, department store magnate Edgar J. Kaufmann Sr. and city councilman Abraham Wolk had proposed an idea for a new memorial amphitheater—intended to be the largest in the world.

"What will you do if it rains?" a reporter asked Wolk.

"I had to think fast," Wolk recalled in an interview with the *Pittsburgh Press* in 1961. "I just put my arms over my head, moved around a little, and said that we are going to have a moveable roof."

Fortunately, his good friend Kaufmann was no stranger to innovative design. A patron of the arts, he had commissioned famed architect Frank Lloyd Wright to build a weekend home for his family in 1934, far from the hubbub of the city. The result was Fallingwater, a true architectural masterpiece.

On February 4, 1949, Kaufmann and the city each pledged $500,000 toward the construction of the new amphitheater. A year later architects James A. Mitchell and Dalhen K. Ritchey presented plans for the new facility. Designed to seat 10,500 people, the most striking feature was a retractable roof. Suspended from a cantilevered steel arm and consisting of two fabric-covered plastic "bat wings" that resembled giant Oriental fans, the roof could be opened or closed, depending on the weather.

The Mellon Arena glitters like a crown jewel beneath the Steel City skyline.

A melting pot of diverse ethnic backgrounds, the Lower Hill was a vibrant, bustling neighborhood. Frank Bolden, a writer for the *Pittsburgh Courier*, boasted that Wylie Avenue was the only street in the country that began at a church (St. John's AME Zion) and ended at a jail (Allegheny County Jail). Home to some 1,600 families, the Lower Hill served as a cultural hub for the city's African American community. Although its housing was generally considered to be substandard and dilapidated, many of the residents were lower middle-class. But progress was the watchword of the day, and the Lower Hill stood in its path.

In March of 1953 the City of Pittsburgh and Allegheny County formed the Public Auditorium Authority to plan the construction of the new arena and assist in purchasing the land. Two years later the plan was approved by the federal government and $17.4 million in loans and grants were released to help fund the project.

Demolition of 1,300 homes and businesses began on May 31, 1956. It was a gloomy day for residents of the Lower Hill. "People went all directions settling wherever they could find a place," a woman recalled.

Construction of the new arena began on April 25, 1958. Originally named the Civic Auditorium, it soon was changed to the Civic Arena.

The design had been altered somewhat in the years since the initial plans were conceived. According to an early architect's model, the seats were designed to face the stage area in a style similar to an amphitheater. This gave way to a single-tiered bowl that encircled a central playing surface to better accommodate hockey and other sporting events. A bank of seats on the west side of the Arena tilted back to create a stage for the CLO.

The Civic Arena's most striking feature—the retractable roof—came under heavy fire from critics due to the added cost. But Kaufmann persevered.

"We should be very reluctant to surrender the idea of a removable roof," he said. "It will be heralded the length and breadth of the world. [It] will stand as the symbol of an era here."

The fabric-covered wings from the original design were deemed impractical. Instead, the new arena would feature a retractable stainless steel dome, 417 feet in diameter and 109 feet tall. The dome gave the building its signature appearance and led to its enduring nickname—"the Igloo."

Comprised of eight 300-ton leaf-like roof sections, the dome was truly an architectural marvel. Powered by five

Kaufmann had his design. What he did not have, however, was a location. Initially he had hoped to build the facility on the edge of the Robert King estate near Highland Park. However, the proposed site met with stiff resistance from King and other residents and had to be abandoned. The Allegheny Conference and Pittsburgh Regional Planning Association suggested a second site—Schenley Park. That, too, fell through.

A powerful ally soon joined forces with Kaufmann. Pittsburgh mayor David L. Lawrence was a man with a vision. He was determined to transform Pittsburgh from the grimy "Smoky City" of iron and steel into a true cosmopolitan center. With the full support of leading businessmen such as Kaufmann and Richard King Mellon, he spearheaded an ambitious plan for renewal and growth that quickly became known as the "Renaissance."

Lawrence, too, saw the need for a home for the CLO, as well as an updated facility for the Pittsburgh Hornets hockey team, which was playing in the antiquated Duquesne Gardens. Eager to give the city's rundown Point district a makeover, he suggested a plan for building a new multipurpose arena near the site of the old Winter Garden, one of Pittsburgh's first indoor ice skating facilities.

However, in 1951 the Urban Redevelopment Authority revealed a plan to redevelop a 95-acre site in the Lower Hill District. Under the terms of the proposal, the area would include a multipurpose arena, a 935-family apartment complex, a motel, an art museum, and a parking garage. Mayor Lawrence and the other civic leaders quickly endorsed the new location.

motors apiece, six of the sections could be retracted to slide under the two fixed sections with the touch of a button, opening the dome in just over two minutes. In a remarkable feat of engineering, the roof had no interior supports; instead, the moveable sections were supported from above by a giant 260-foot cantilever arm.

Due to the innovative roof design, the Arena took 40 months to build at a cost of $21.7 million. When it was finished the Civic Arena was the largest domed structure in the world—a distinction it would hold until the Houston Astrodome was completed in 1965.

Sadly, the man who was instrumental in bringing the new facility to Pittsburgh never got to see it. Edgar J. Kaufmann passed away in 1955, shortly before the construction had begun. True to his word, the arena he had helped birth earned accolades the world over and became an iconic symbol of Pittsburgh's Renaissance.

"The great steel dome has a meaning that goes beyond Pittsburgh," *Fortune* magazine wrote. "If one of the drabbest and dirtiest cities has been able to remake itself in shining pride, any city in the [United States] should be able to follow its example."

By the fall of 1961 the sparkling new arena was finally ready for business. With local dignitaries such as Mayor Joseph Barr in attendance, the Civic Arena played host to the Ice Capades on September 19, 1961.

To celebrate the grand opening, two sections of the dome were opened. However, concerns that the 74-degree temperature outside would melt the ice forced building officials to close the roof after just 22 minutes.

Hockey made its long-awaited debut at the Civic Arena on October 14, 1961, in a match between the Pittsburgh Hornets and the Buffalo Bisons. The Hornets, who had been mothballed for five years following the demolition of

The Civic Arena officially opened for business on September 18, 1961. Performing the honors at the ribbon-cutting ceremony are (left to right): David J. McDonald, president of the United Steel Workers; Governor David L. Lawrence; County Commissioner William D. McClelland; William B. McFall, chairman of the Auditorium Authority; and Mayor Joseph M. Barr.

the rickety Duquesne Gardens, dropped a tight 2–1 decision to the Bisons before 9,317 fans. The Hornets' lone goal was tallied by rookie defenseman Paul Jackson.

It would be a long year for Jackson and his teammates. Essentially an expansion team, the Hornets won only 10 games. Ironically, several members of the dreadful 1961–62 squad, including Roy Edwards, Nick Harbaruk, Dick Mattiussi, and Gene Ubriaco, would later play for the Pittsburgh Penguins. Goalie Gerry Cheevers went on to enjoy a Hall of Fame career with Boston.

The new arena was well-suited for hockey and other sporting events, but it turned out to be a less than ideal home for the CLO. A laundry list of conditions placed restrictions on opening the roof, which meant that many of the CLO's performances were held totally indoors. While the Arena's stainless steel construction made for an eye-catching space-age design, the acoustics were poor and it lacked the intimacy needed for musical theater. Following a performance of *How Now, Dow Jones* on July 26, 1969, the CLO abandoned the Civic Arena and moved to Heinz Hall. The stage was promptly converted into the West Igloo Club lounge.

Meanwhile, the improving Hornets continued to be a solid draw, averaging about 5,000 fans per game. In 1966–67 they treated Steel City hockey fans to a wonderful season. A strong, balanced team that boasted seven 20-goal scorers,

The Igloo shortly after its grand opening.

The Penguins raise the banner for their first Stanley Cup.

the Hornets captured first place in the West Division of the American Hockey League. On April 30, 1967, they completed a four-game sweep of two-time defending champion Rochester on a Billy Harris goal 26 seconds into overtime to capture the Calder Cup. It remains the only time a local professional hockey team has won a championship on their home ice.

It would be the Hornets' final game. Big-league hockey was coming to Pittsburgh the very next year in the form of a brand-new team, the Penguins. Under a mandate by the National Hockey League to increase seating capacity, the Civic Arena underwent its first major facelift. New sections were added to increase the capacity from 10,732 to 12,580.

Another new tenant would arrive in 1967 thanks to the birth of the American Basketball Association. Led by flashy superstar and league MVP Connie Hawkins, the Pittsburgh Pipers captured the first ABA championship, beating the New Orleans Buccaneers in Game 7 of the finals before a throng of 11,457 at the Civic Arena.

Unfortunately, the Pipers' success on the court didn't translate at the box office. After averaging about 3,200 fans per game during their inaugural season, the franchise moved to Minnesota in 1968. Following an injury-plagued year in Minneapolis, the Pipers returned to Pittsburgh for the 1969–70 season. However, Hawkins had bolted to the NBA's Phoenix Suns, stripping the team of its star player and major gate attraction. After changing its name to the Condors, the team played before mostly empty seats before folding in June of 1972.

The Penguins fared somewhat better. On the night of October 11, 1967, they faced off against the Montreal Canadiens before a healthy crowd of 9,307 fans. Penguins general manager Jack Riley had purposely asked league officials to schedule the powerful Canadiens for his team's home opener.

"I wanted an attraction," explained Riley, "and I thought we might sneak up on them. I figured they might not take us too seriously right out of the gate."

His instincts proved to be spot-on. Andy Bathgate struck for the first goal in franchise history when he beat Montreal goalie Rogie Vachon at 7:06 of the third period. The Pens lost 2–1 in a tight defensive struggle, but battled hard and gave a good showing.

Still, it would take several years for the Penguins to gain a firm foothold in the Pittsburgh market. More than one critic blamed the Arena's antiseptic ambience for the lack of fan support.

"The fan who pays $5 to $7 for a ticket there doesn't get his money's worth," said an official from another NHL club. "He sees the game okay, but it's so quiet in there he doesn't feel it. He doesn't get the excitement you get in places like St. Louis and Philadelphia and Minnesota. Or even in Oakland. Why, 5,000 people in Oakland's arena sound like 10,000 when they get worked up. In Pittsburgh 5,000 people sound like 2,000."

No fewer than 13 professional sports teams would eventually grace the Civic Arena's playing surface. In addition to the Penguins, Hornets, Pipers, and Condors, teams such as the Rens and Xplosion (basketball), the Gladiators (arena football), the Phantoms (roller hockey), the Bulls and CrossFire (box lacrosse), the Stingers and Spirit (indoor soccer), and Triangles (indoor tennis) called the Arena home. However, none would achieve the enduring success of the Penguins.

The Dapper Dan Roundball Classic, America's first high school All-Star game, was held annually at the Civic Arena from 1965 through 1992. The World Figure Skating Championships took center stage in 1983. On January 21, 1990, the Arena hosted the 41st NHL All-Star Game, and Penguins fans were treated to Stanley Cup Finals action in 1991, 1992, 2008, and 2009.

While sports were undeniably the building's lifeblood, it also became a popular venue for performers and recording artists. On September 14, 1964, Britain's pop sensation, The Beatles, belted out their tunes before a screaming mob of teenagers. In July of 1971, a standing-room-only crowd of

13,000 packed the Arena to witness a performance of the Andrew Lloyd Webber smash *Jesus Christ Superstar.*

The "King" of rock 'n' roll, Elvis Presley, played before packed houses on July 25 and 26, 1973, and again on New Year's Eve 1976, shortly before his death. In his honor The Fans of Elvis Presley dedicated a plaque that was placed near Section B16. It reads "A legendary performer who earned the love and respect of millions. His presence will always be missed."

Driven by the demand for more seats, the Civic Arena underwent two more major expansions during its lifetime. In the summer of 1975 E-level "end zone" balconies were constructed at the north and south ends, increasing capacity to 16,402. In 1993 F-level balconies, luxury skyboxes, and privately catered club seats swelled the capacity by an additional 1,000 seats.

"If I was a fan, I'd want to sit in one of the balconies," current Penguins coach Dan Bylsma said. "There's not a lot of buildings that have overhanging balconies. It's unique."

Sadly, attempts to modernize the aging facility also resulted in the demise of its most unique feature—the ability to open the roof. The installation of a new JumboTron scoreboard in 1995 prohibited more than two sections of the roof from being retracted.

In December 1999 the Arena changed its name for a third time. The Penguins entered into a 10-year naming rights agreement with Mellon Financial Corporation for $18 million, and the grand old building was rechristened Mellon Arena (soon to become known as "the Mellon").

As the city entered the new millennium, talk of a new arena began to gather momentum. The Penguins purchased a tract of land adjacent to the Arena with the clear intent of building a new facility. Concerned about the Arena's future, two of the city's preservation groups—Pittsburgh History and Landmarks Federation and Preservation Pittsburgh—nominated the building as a City Designated Historic (Structure) Landmark.

Under the terms of the designation, changes to the exterior or demolition would require the approval of the Historic Review Commission. The Arena met several of the criteria for designation, such as being an example of a significant type of architecture and playing an important role in the city's history. However, the nomination was voted down 4–3 by the sharply divided Commission on August 7, 2002, leaving it vulnerable to the wrecking ball.

"This one was a no-brainer," said commission chairman John DeSantis, who cast his vote with the losing side. "The Arena is one of the best buildings this community produced during the 20th century."

Preservation Pittsburgh vice president Rob Pfaffmann insisted that the Mellon Arena could be revitalized for $100 million—far less than the cost of a new arena. But his pleas fell on deaf ears.

By the middle of the decade the grand old girl was clearly on her last legs. During a Penguins–Maple Leafs contest on March 19, 2006, the power went out on two separate occasions. An electrical fire was reported near Gate C, causing emergency crews to be summoned. A year later the Mellon Arena's fate was sealed when the Penguins reached an agreement with state and local officials for a new multipurpose facility.

Still, the Arena had one last bit of oomph left. In 2008 and 2009 it once more played host to the Stanley Cup Finals. In a final shining moment, a third Stanley Cup banner was raised to the stainless steel dome on October 2, 2009.

The Igloo closed its doors for good on May 12, 2010, following a disappointing 5–2 Penguins loss to Montreal in the Eastern Conference Semifinals. Perhaps it was poetic justice—the Pens had lost their first Arena home game to the Canadiens 42 years earlier. Jordan Staal scored the final goal for the black and gold at 16:30 of the second period.

The Penguins moved into their dazzling new facility, Consol Energy Center, for the 2010-11 season. Inevitably, something is lost when something is gained. Despite its cramped quarters and lack of amenities, more than a few people confess they'll miss the old Arena.

"I'm a little disappointed that we didn't build another Igloo because it's so distinguishable," play-by-play announcer

The Civic Arena offered a spectacular view of the Pittsburgh cityscape in 1986.

The Penguins held a special service in memory of coach Bob Johnson on November 27, 1991.

Mike Lange lamented. "It's an eye opener for the players walking up from the city. Kids are in awe if it snows and they've never seen the Arena."

"I remember coming here with my dad when I was younger, coming here for Stanley Cup playoff games," former Penguins defenseman and Pittsburgh native Nate Guenin said. "Just walking around here, you see a different setup than other arenas, the way the ramps are set up. It's still got the same old smell from back in the day. It'll be sad to see it go."

"We have a beautiful new building and I can't wait to get into it," Dan Bylsma said. "But when the dome is not here, it'll be an odd feeling driving to this part of the city and not seeing it.

"There will definitely be something that's missed because of the dome. It's certainly a unique building, and a lot of the unique buildings are going by the wayside, so it's sad to see that."

The shuttering of the Mellon Arena marked the end of an era in Pittsburgh—an era that began decades ago with lofty ideals and a vision for a better way of life for the city and its residents.

Mellon Arena Fast Facts

Former names—Civic Auditorium, Civic Arena
Location—66 Mario Lemieux Place, Pittsburgh, Pennsylvania
Broke ground—March 12, 1957
Opened—September 18, 1961
Owner—Sports and Exhibition Authority of Pittsburgh and Allegheny County
Ice surface dimensions—205 feet x 85 feet (original) / 200 feet x 85 feet (shortened)
Construction cost—$22 million (US)
Architect—Mitchell and Ritchey
Capacity—Ice hockey: 16,940
    Hockey (standing room): 17,132
    Basketball: 17,537
    Concert: End Stage 12,800, Center Stage 18,039
Teams—Pittsburgh Penguins, NHL (1967–2010)
    Pittsburgh Rens, ABL (1961–1963)
    Pittsburgh Hornets, AHL (1961–1967)
    Pittsburgh Pipers, ABA (1967–1968, 1969–1970)
    Pittsburgh Condors, ABA (1970–1972)
    Pittsburgh Triangles, WTT (1974–1976)
    Pittsburgh Spirit, MISL (1978–1980, 1981–1986)
    Pittsburgh Gladiators, AFL (1987–1990)
    Pittsburgh Bulls, MILL (1990–1993)
    Pittsburgh Phantoms, RHI (1994)
    Pittsburgh Stingers, CISL (1994–1995)
    Pittsburgh Piranhas, CBA (1994–1995)
    Pittsburgh CrosseFire, NLL (2000)
    Pittsburgh Xplosion, CBA (2005–2008)
Firsts—First major sports stadium with a retractable roof

A Night to Remember

On the evening of April 8, 2010, an overflow crowd of 17,132 jammed the Mellon Arena to celebrate the final regular-season game ever to be played at the Igloo.

The fans stood and cheered as more than 50 former players, coaches, and club executives were introduced by announcers Mike Lange and Paul Steigerwald. Following the ceremony, the alumni gathered at center ice with the current Penguins for a team photo.

"It's a real honor to be a part of it," said Andy Bathgate, who scored the first goal in franchise history during the Pens' home opener at the Arena in 1967.

"There's a feeling you get when you walk in here," Rob Brown said. "You know good things happened here."

Naturally, the loudest ovation was reserved for Brown's former linemate, Mario Lemieux, who donned his iconic No. 66 jersey for the first time since his retirement.

"I always think of it as Mario's place," Pens captain Sidney Crosby said. "You look at what he's done in the city and so many nights here, I think it's safe to say that this is his place."

In a send-off befitting the grand old arena, the Penguins bombed the Islanders 7–3. Crosby made sure it would be a night to remember. In his typical dramatic fashion, he tallied four points to become the third-youngest player in NHL history to score 500 points.

Alumni in Attendance

Syl Apps	John Cullen	Mario Lemieux	Frank Pietrangelo	Peter Taglianetti
Andy Bathgate	Bob Errey	Francois Leroux	Greg Polis	Bryan Trottier
Bob Berry	Mario Faubert	Troy Loney	Jean Pronovost	Gene Ubriaco
Les Binkley	George Ferguson	Lowell MacDonald	Jack Riley	Bryan Watson
Phil Bourque	Dave Hannan	Greg Malone	Gary Rissling	Ken Wregget
Rob Brown	Randy Hillier	Gilles Meloche	Gary Roberts	Warren Young
Mike Bullard	Mark Johnson	Larry Murphy	Duane Rupp	Wendell Young
Dave Burrows	Eddie Johnston	Ed Olczyk	Ken Schinkel	
Jay Caufield	Mark Kachowski	Dennis Owchar	Ron Schock	
Kim Clackson	Rick Kehoe	Bob Paradise	Ron Stackhouse	
Paul Coffey	Pierre Larouche	Craig Patrick	Red Sullivan	

Mario Lemieux waves to the crowd before the Penguins' final regular-season game at Mellon Arena.

Other Arenas

Schenley Park Casino
1895–1896

In the late 19ᵗʰ century, Pittsburgh was booming. Boasting a population of nearly 250,000 residents, the city had begun an eastward sprawl into the heavily wooded area of Oakland, which bordered on Schenley Park. Already one of the more affluent neighborhoods in the city, Oakland would soon grow into a cultural center following the completion of the Carnegie Library and Museum in 1895.

Seeking to capitalize on the area's potential for growth, an idea was proposed to build a facility that would serve as a recreational and social gathering place for "people of stature and the common man." According to the original plans, the multipurpose building would feature luxury boxes and a grand theater. It would be operated by the Schenley Park Amusement Company.

Although it was a magnificent concept in scope and endeavor, funding for the proposal was nonexistent until James Conant, an ice hockey enthusiast who would serve as building manager, suggested the new building feature an indoor ice skating rink. Upon learning that it was indeed possible to construct an artificial ice surface, the project quickly gained momentum. Investors provided $400,000 to help finance the complex—named the Schenley Park Casino—and construction was completed by the spring of 1895.

Located at the entrance to Schenley Park, the Casino was a magnificent structure. Constructed of limestone and brick, the roofline featured a series of wooden corbels and copper cornices. Above the large, arched entryway rested a grand patio—an ideal viewing space for parade reviews and political rallies. At night, the Casino glittered like a crown jewel, thanks to more than 1,500 incandescent, arc, and white calcium lights.

Exquisitely appointed, the interior featured oak panels on the main floor and a tasteful buff and cream stucco ceiling. Oil paintings and tapestries adorned the walls of 20 dressing rooms, which were owned by politicians and wealthy business tycoons. A theater opened onto the main floor, serviced by a well-appointed café at the south end of the building.

The first floor featured more than 40 large windows—each 18-feet tall—that filled the Casino with natural light. Initially, heat from the sunlight threatened to wreak havoc with the ice. A series of large interior window coverings were installed on the eastern side of the facility to minimize the problem.

The artificial ice surface truly was a marvel. Measuring 225 feet by 70 feet, it rested on a main floor that sat below the viewing area in an elliptical bowl. Constructed of a concrete and marble chip aggregate, the floor was specially designed to hold water. A series of looping chiller pipes that carried ammonia gas from a nearby ice-making room served to freeze the concrete floor and the one-inch-thick ice surface above.

"The body of ice has a remarkable smoothness and the excellence of its surroundings is unsurpassed anywhere in the world," boasted an article in the *Pittsburgh Press*.

Pittsburghers agreed. During the grand opening on May 29, 1895, they flocked to the Casino to try out the city's newest attraction. More than 2,800 tickets were sold for the afternoon skating session, which lasted from 1:00 PM to 4:30 PM.

"The skating rink was the scene of great gliding," noted the *Pittsburgh Commercial Gazette*. "Between 500 and 600 lovers of the sport continually circled the arena. Many ambitious skaters tasted the humiliation of doing some of their fancy feats in getting up off the ice instead of cutting figures on the ice, to the great amusement of the spectators."

The Casino was open to the public on weekdays. For an admission fee of 5¢, patrons could rent a pair of steel skate blades and cruise around the ice during public skating sessions. On the weekends, the ice surface was reserved for hockey exhibitions and private parties.

As the Casino's fame spread, it attracted the attention of hockey players throughout the United States and Canada. Hockey clubs from across North America would soon travel to challenge the Pittsburgh Keystones, which was comprised of players from Carnegie Tech and Western University (later the University of Pittsburgh).

A natural promoter, James Conant saw an opportunity. Convinced the city would fall in love with the speed, grace, and athleticism of the sport, he began to organize hockey exhibitions on Friday evenings following the public skating session. Thanks to its large balcony the Casino provided a bird's-eye view of the ice surface 20 feet below. In December of 1895, the *Pittsburg Press* mentioned a "friendly hockey match" that drew some 10,000 spectators. While the attendance figure seems heavily inflated, the sport had clearly taken hold in the Steel City.

Sadly, the Casino would not survive to play a part in hockey's growing popularity. Early in the morning of December 17, 1896, a pipe carrying the ammonia gas began to leak. Although no one can be certain, it's believed that the gas mixed with grease to set off an explosion. By the time firefighters arrived on the scene, the blaze was already out of control. A second, deadlier explosion of the main ammonia storage tank razed the rear of the building. Heat from the conflagration grew so intense it melted the glass at the nearby Phipps Conservancy.

Overwhelmed by a cauldron of flames, flying debris, dense smoke, and deadly ammonia fumes, the firefighters were forced to withdraw. Within an hour the Casino had burned to the ground.

Ironically, Conant would meet a similar ill-timed fate. On March 14, 1906, the 43-year-old "Father of Pittsburgh Hockey" was found dead in his room at the Navarra Hotel in New York City. Although the official cause of his death was listed as "heart attack," foul play was suspected.

Schenley Park Casino Fast Facts

Location—Schenley Park, Pittsburgh, Pennsylvania
Broke ground—1893
Opened—May 29, 1895
Destroyed by fire—December 17, 1896
Owner—The Schenley Park Amusement Company
Ice surface dimensions—225 feet x 70 feet
Construction cost—$540,000 (US)
Operator—James Conant
Capacity—Ice hockey: 1,200
    Theater: 3,500
Teams—Pittsburgh Keystones
    Various Local Teams
Firsts—First artificial ice surface in North America
    First building in Pittsburgh where organized hockey was
    played

Duquesne Gardens
1899–1956

The fire that destroyed the Schenley Park Casino in 1896 was truly a devastating event for Pittsburgh. Not only did the loss of the Casino leave the city without an indoor skating rink and multipurpose venue, but it was a blow to the city's civic pride as well.

Fortunately, the city fathers were quick to react. A year earlier railroad magnate and political heavyweight Christopher Magee had purchased a large red-brick structure on North Craig Street in Oakland. Formerly the Duquesne Traction Company, it was built in 1890 to serve as a trolley barn.

Hastened by the loss of the Casino, Magee sank $500,000 into the purchase and renovation of the building, including the installation of a movie theater and a state-of-the-art ice skating rank. He rechristened the building the Duquesne Gardens in 1896. "The Gardens" (or "the Arena" as it was popularly known) opened its doors for public skating on January 23, 1899. The following evening the Gardens hosted its first hockey game, a match between the Pittsburgh

Athletic Club and Western University (later the University of Pittsburgh). Program covers trumpeted the Gardens as "The Largest and Most Beautiful Skating Palace in the World."

Much like its predecessor, the Gardens was renowned for the quality—and size—of its artificial ice. Featuring a 250-foot-long ice surface (later shortened to 200 feet to meet NHL standards), it was constructed using the most up-to-date refrigeration technology of its day.

"Lester Patrick, Craig's grandfather, started a league on the Pacific Coast early in the 20th century," hockey writer Stan Fischler said. "To learn how to get proper ice refrigeration, he came to Pittsburgh to see how it was done. It's ironic that the Canadians came to the States for that."

With a brand-new arena, hockey flourished in Pittsburgh in the early 20th century. Nearly a dozen amateur, college, and professional teams played their home games at the Gardens—including the Fort Pitt Hornets, the Pittsburgh Athletic Club, and the Pittsburgh Pro HC. One of the earliest professional leagues—the Western Pennsylvania Hockey League—was formed in Pittsburgh. Players and teams from Canada flocked to the city, often performing before sellout crowds.

"Pittsburgh is hockey crazy," the manager of a Canadian team told the *Toronto Globe*, according to a story in *Total Hockey*. "Over 10,000 turned out for three games there. The general admission being 35 cents and 75 cents for a box seat…the Pittsburgh rink is a dream. What a marvelous place it is."

Despite its popularity, the Gardens briefly lost its preeminent place among the city's hockey palaces. In 1916 several teams moved to a newer venue, the Winter Garden, which was located at the Pittsburgh Exposition near the Point. During this period, the Oakland arena continued to host hockey games as well as a variety of other events, including circuses, rodeos, and boxing matches. When the Exposition ceased operations in the spring of 1920, the Gardens once more became the undisputed center of Steel City hockey.

In 1915, players from several local clubs joined forces to form the Pittsburgh Yellow Jackets. Playing in the United States Amateur Hockey Association, the Yellow Jackets quickly became a powerhouse, capturing the USAHA title in 1924 and again in 1925.

Duquesne Gardens prior to demolition in March 1956.

The Gardens' fabled marquee.

Encouraged by the Yellow Jackets' success, James Callahan and William Dwyer purchased the club in 1925. Renamed the Pirates, the team would compete in a relatively new professional circuit—the National Hockey League.

Big-league hockey made its debut at the Gardens on December 2, 1925. Packing the place to the rafters, 8,200 fans (some 2,600 over the official seating capacity) watched as the Pirates lost to the New York Americans 2–1 in overtime.

Although it still boasted one of the finest artificial ice surfaces in the world, the Gardens had become antiquated by the late 1920s. Compared to newer arenas such as New York's Madison Square Garden (which seated more than 18,000 people), the Gardens seemed a quaint relic of an earlier time. With no room to expand the single-tiered seating area and thus increase revenues, the Pirates limped along until 1930, when the franchise moved to Philadelphia.

Immediately there was a public outcry to build a new arena. However, the country had plunged headlong into the Great Depression and funds simply weren't available. Pittsburgh would have to make do with the Gardens.

During the early 1930s, the recast Yellow Jackets and the Pittsburgh Shamrocks played their home games at the Gardens. Then, in 1936, local theater owner and founder of the Ice Capades, John Harris, purchased the Detroit Olympics of the International-American Hockey League and moved them to Pittsburgh. He renamed the team the Hornets.

The arrival of the Hornets sparked a second golden age for the Gardens. Although the arena gradually fell into disrepair (eventually it was condemned), it remained the Hornets' home for 20 years. During that span the team captured two Calder Cups.

The Hornets played their final game at the Gardens on March 31, 1956, dropping a 6–4 decision to the Cleveland Barons. Situated on prime real estate, the old car barn didn't have long to live. The wrecking ball arrived on August 13, 1956. Within months the new Plaza Park Apartments and a Stouffer's Restaurant stood on the former site of the arena.

A piece of the Gardens still remains. Two 11-feet-wide sections of red-brick wall were preserved during construction of the restaurant. Running along North Craig Street, they had once served as the back wall to the visitor's dressing room.

Duquesne Gardens Fast Facts

Former name—The Duquesne Traction Company
Location—110 North Craig Street, Pittsburgh,
    Pennsylvania
Broke ground—1886
Built—1890 (trolley barn), 1895 (ice rink)
Opened—January 23, 1899 (ice rink)
Demolished—August 13, 1956
Owner—Christopher Lyman Magee
Ice surface dimensions—250 feet x 85 feet (original) /
    200 feet x 85 feet (shortened)
Construction cost—$500,000 (US)
Capacity—Ice hockey: 5,000
    Hockey (standing room): 5,657
    Unofficial capacity: 8,000
Teams—Pittsburgh Hornets (1936–1956)
    Fort Pitt Hornets
    Pittsburgh Athletic Club
    Pittsburgh Bankers
    Pittsburgh Duquesne
    Pittsburgh Keystones
    Pittsburgh Lyceum
    Pittsburgh Pirates
    Pittsburgh Pro HC
    Pittsburgh Shamrocks
    Pittsburgh Victorias
    Pittsburgh Yellow Jackets
    Pittsburgh Ironmen (basketball)
Firsts—First hockey rink to use glass above the dasher
    boards

Winter Garden
1916–1920

In the early part of the 20th century, hockey enjoyed a period of unprecedented popularity and growth in Pittsburgh. As the sport flourished, it became a challenge for the proliferation of amateur, college, and professional teams to secure ice time at the Duquesne Gardens, the city's preeminent indoor skating facility.

A solution would soon present itself. Noting the ever-increasing demand for ice, the Western Pennsylvania Exposition Society decided to convert the Main Hall of the Pittsburgh Exposition, which was located near the Point, into an indoor skating rink. An impressive structure, the Main Hall had been rebuilt following a fire that had devastated the Exposition in 1901. Constructed of steel, stone, and brick, it was built to withstand even the worst conditions. A city guidebook boasted "nothing short of an earthquake would cause it to even shake."

Following the Exposition of 1915, 125,000 feet of chiller pipe and a concrete floor were installed in the building. Using the latest technology of the day, a brine solution was pumped through the pipes from a refrigeration plant located in nearby Machinery Hall. The system maintained the floor temperature at a chilly minus 30 degrees and produced a dry, hard ice surface.

Completed in 1916, the new indoor rink was named the Winter Garden. Several teams from the former Western Pennsylvania Hockey League, including Pittsburgh Duquesne and Pittsburgh Lyceum, began playing their home games at the new facility. The Winter Garden also played host to one of the city's earliest women's hockey leagues.

The Winter Garden enjoyed its shining moment on March 24, 1917. The immortal Hobey Baker came to town with an All-Star team from Philadelphia to play an exhibition match. The former Princeton star scored a hat trick, including the game-winning goal in the third overtime, to best the local sextet.

It was the final game Baker would ever play. Enlisting in the U.S. Army as a pilot, he soon departed for France. After being awarded the Croix de Guerre for his service in World War I, he was killed just a few short weeks after the armistice when his newly repaired Spad crashed during a test flight. Orders to return home were found tucked inside his jacket.

The Winter Garden would meet an untimely end as well. Although truly a wonderful facility, it had its drawbacks. The ice sheet measured a massive 300 feet by 140 feet, compared to today's NHL standard of 200 feet by 85 feet. Playing on such a large expanse of ice was a test of even the hardiest player's spirit and endurance. A polio epidemic had forced the Exposition to close its doors in 1916, which left the Winter Garden as the lone attraction still open to the public. Located in an increasingly rough and seedy area of town, the Exposition became an undesirable place to visit.

After just four short years the Winter Garden ceased operations following the 1920 season. A sale of the Exposition properties was reported in the *Pittsburgh Post-Gazette* on April 9, 1920, but the transaction was never completed. With a white elephant on its hands, the city of Pittsburgh agreed to lease the property for an annual fee of $30,000. Soon it would serve as the city's auto pound.

In the mid-1930s a movement to revive the Expo site failed, and the city ended its lease agreement. One by one the monolithic old buildings were torn down. Machinery Hall was dismantled in 1942 to provide scrap metal for the war effort.

The Main Hall, which housed the Winter Garden, was the last building to be cleared, meeting with the wrecker's ball in 1951. Although it was an inglorious end for the city's third ice palace, it helped pave the way for the city's First Renaissance and the creation of scenic Point State Park.

Winter Garden Fast Facts

Full Name—The Winter Garden at Exposition Hall
Location—Site of Point State Park, Pittsburgh,
    Pennsylvania
Broke ground—1885
Built—1885–1889
Opened for expositions—1889
Renovated for hockey—1916
Closed—1920
Demolished—1942 (Machinery Hall)
    July 2, 1951 (Main Hall)
Owner—Pittsburgh Exposition
Operator—Pittsburgh Exposition, City of Pittsburgh
Ice surface dimensions—300 feet x 140 feet
Construction cost—$1 million (US)
Renovation cost—$600,000 (US)
Architect—Joseph Stillburg
Main contractors—Murphy and Hamilton, Marshall
    Foundry and Construction Company
Teams—Pittsburgh Duquesne
    Pittsburgh Lyceum
    Various Local Teams

Consol Energy Center
2010–

In the 1990s a wave of prosperity was sweeping over the National Hockey League. Seven new teams were added during the decade, swelling the circuit's ranks to 28 teams. To accommodate this unprecedented period of expansion and growth, older arenas throughout the league were being replaced. Fabled buildings such as Chicago Stadium, Boston Garden, Maple Leaf Gardens, and the Montreal Forum gave way to sparkling-new multipurpose facilities.

The oldest building in the league by half a decade, the Civic Arena had become antiquated. Despite numerous renovations over the years that increased the seating capacity from 10,732 to 16,940, the facility was woefully lacking in revenue-generating amenities such as luxury suites.

Entrepreneurial owner Howard Baldwin tried to find creative ways to increase profits. In the mid 1990s he installed

The brand-new Consol Energy Center (left) replaced iconic Mellon Arena as the Penguins' home in 2010.

luxury boxes (which were later removed) and ventured into the pay-per-view market with PenVision. Ultimately, however, Baldwin was stymied by the Civic Arena's limitations. Saddled with a hideous lease agreement, not to mention one of the league's highest payrolls, it was a recipe for financial ruin. With debt exceeding $100 million, he and his partner, Roger Marino, were forced to file for bankruptcy under Chapter 11 on October 13, 1998.

After gaining control of the Penguins in the fall of 1999, new owner Mario Lemieux immediately began to petition Pittsburgh mayor Tom Murphy and other local leaders for public funding for a new arena. However, the city coffers were strained following the construction of Heinz Field and PNC Park.

Undeterred, the Penguins purchased a tract of land on November 30, 2000, for $8 million. Located directly across Center Avenue from Mellon Arena, the site would be used for the construction of a new arena.

The Penguins had the land they needed, but they still lacked the necessary funding. In 2005 the Lemieux Group came up with an innovative solution. They struck a deal with Isle of Capri, a Biloxi, Mississippi, casino developer that was bidding on a state-granted slots license in Pittsburgh. Under the terms of the agreement, Isle of Capri pledged $290 million toward the construction of a new arena that would be located near the casino complex.

Remarkably, the Pennsylvania Gaming Control Board awarded the slots license to a competitor, Majestic Star, on December 20, 2006, killing the Penguins' deal with Isle of Capri.

Time was running short. With the Penguins' lease agreement with Mellon Arena set to expire the following summer, a clearly frustrated Lemieux decided to play hardball. He entertained offers from other cities including Kansas City, which was aggressively pursuing tenants for its state-of-the-art Sprint Center.

With the threat of losing the Penguins very real, the politicians finally sprang to action. After a series of grueling bargaining sessions with local and state officials—including Pennsylvania governor Ed Rendell—an arena deal was hammered out on March 12, 2007. Under the terms of the agreement, the new facility would be built with a combination of state and local funding. The team would contribute $4 million per year toward the construction costs and an additional $400,000 per year for capital improvements. Majestic Star would provide an additional $7.5 million per year in funding over 30 years.

Mario, who later confessed he never intended to move the team, addressed a sold-out crowd at the Mellon Arena the following evening. "I'm here to announce that your Pittsburgh Penguins will stay here in Pittsburgh, where they belong," he said.

The Penguins formally signed a 30-year lease agreement on September 20, 2007. With the team's future in Pittsburgh secured until 2040, planning for the new arena took center stage. Populous (formerly HOK Sport), the design firm that conceptualized Heinz Field and PNC Park, presented drawings to the Pittsburgh City Planning Commission on April 8, 2008. The initial design was rejected as being "too cold and uninviting." One month later Populous presented a second set of plans that featured a spectacular atrium facing downtown Pittsburgh. The design was unanimously approved.

"The atrium in the front allows everyone to see the energy and electricity inside the building during events," former Penguins CEO Ken Sawyer said. "When you're inside, you get to see the most beautiful city skyscape in the country."

Sawyer requested that the interior be modeled after Jobing.com Arena in Phoenix. "I was just taken aback by their seats," he said. "Even when I was up in a high level, I had a great view."

On August 14, 2008, Lemieux met with club officials and a group of local dignitaries at the future location of center ice for the groundbreaking ceremony. Using shovels crafted with the shafts from Sidney Crosby's old hockey sticks, the first clump of dirt was turned. The new arena was christened Consol Energy Center on December 15, 2008, when the Penguins signed a 21-year naming-rights agreement with Pittsburgh-based energy giant CONSOL Energy.

Slowly but surely the magnificent new building took shape. The structural steel was erected by August of 2009. Construction was completed on schedule in the summer of 2010.

A construction worker installs seats at the Consol Energy Center.

In honor of Sidney Crosby's No. 87, Consol Energy Center seats 18,087 for hockey. This includes 2,000 box seats and 66 suites—an homage to Mario Lemieux. To ensure the new facility offers the latest innovations, the Penguins partnered with the Pittsburgh Technology Council, a consortium of more than 1,400 local businesses. The luxury suites feature on-demand replays from touch screens. "Yinz Cam"—a system developed by Carnegie Mellon students—provides instant replays from any angle to fans on their cell phones. A Penguins All-Time Team zone, sponsored by Trib Total Media, features touch-screen displays, videos, photos, and bios about the team's greatest stars, executives, staff members, and personalities.

The Penguins officially moved into their new digs on August 1, 2010. Understandably proud of their beautiful new facility, the team held a series of open houses later in the month for season-ticket holders and the general public.

Consol Energy Center Fast Facts

Location—Downtown, bound by Washington Place, Centre Avenue, and Fifth Avenue, Pittsburgh, Pennsylvania
Broke ground—August 14, 2008
Built—August 2008–April 2010
Opened—August 2010
Owner—Sports and Exhibition Authority of Pittsburgh and Allegheny County
Ice surface dimensions—200 feet x 85 feet
Construction cost—$321 million (US)
Architect—Populous (formerly HOK Sport)
Project manager—Pittsburgh Arena Development, LP
Structural engineer—Thornton Thomasetti/Raudenbush
Capacity—Ice hockey: 18,087
    Basketball: 19,000
    Concert: End Stage 14,526, Center Stage 19,578
Teams—Pittsburgh Penguins

First Step

Tuesday, July 27, 2010, was a banner day in Penguins history. While team staff members and construction workers looked on, Pens owner Mario Lemieux and the club's reigning superstar, Sidney Crosby, christened the new arena by taking the very first skate on the virgin Consol Energy Center ice.

Mario and Sid planned to step onto the ice simultaneously from separate doors on the Penguins' bench. However, with a twinkle in his eye, Lemieux delayed his first step so that Crosby's skate would touch the ice first. It was his way of saying, "This is your building, Sid. Go out and make some new memories."

"It felt great to be able to skate for the first time with Sid," Lemieux said. "I think it was pretty special for all of us. It was a long time coming. We worked hard to get this accomplished. I'm glad we were able to do this today."

"That was pretty special," Crosby added. "There are going to be a ton of things that will happen here, so to go out there and be the first ones on the ice, that was pretty special. I feel very fortunate to have the opportunity to skate with Mario."

After the iconic duo enjoyed a leisurely skate, Lemieux once more displayed his generous spirit by inviting a group of youth hockey players to join them for an impromptu practice session. For the youngsters, sharing the ice with their heroes was the thrill of a lifetime.

Trades, Acquisitions, Sales, and Drafts

Since the team's inception in 1966, the Penguins have made hundreds of transactions through the years. This section includes a complete history of the trades, acquisitions, and sales of players who played in at least one game for the Penguins. It also includes a complete list of the players selected by the team in the NHL Amateur, Entry, and Supplemental Drafts, and players claimed or lost in the Expansion, Intra-League (Waiver), Inter-League, Reverse, and WHA General Player Drafts.

The section also features a list of the 10 best and 10 worst trades of all time. Some of the moves had an enormous impact on the team's on-ice performance. Others had less influence, but were no less noteworthy.

The Penguins' very first transaction occurred on August 11, 1966, more than a year before the team played its inaugural game. General manager Jack Riley acquired a trio of defensemen from the Cleveland Barons of the American Hockey League—Ted Lanyon, Dick Mattiussi, and Bill Speer—making them the first player purchases in team history.

Lanyon played five games with the Penguins before fading into obscurity. Mattiussi, who hailed from the colorfully named Smooth Rock Falls, Ontario, skated with the team for a season and a half before being dealt to Oakland in a big six-player trade. Speer was best known for serving as the team's barber.

Riley also purchased Barons goalie Les Binkley around this time, although he didn't officially sign with the Penguins until October of 1967. One of the team's earliest and brightest stars, Binkley posted a solid 3.12 goals-against average and 11 shutouts during his five seasons in Pittsburgh. He was inducted into the Penguins Hall of Fame in 2003.

Riley swung the team's first trade on June 6, 1967, immediately following the Expansion Draft. Seeking to add more depth to his fledgling club, he swapped Larry Jeffrey—whom he'd just selected from the Stanley Cup champion Maple Leafs—to the New York Rangers for Paul Andrea, Frank Francis, George Konik, and Dunc McCallum. Only McCallum, a rugged defenseman, had any impact. Konik later became the first Penguins player to be sold to another team.

A fellow by the name of Bill Lecaine was the club's first free-agent signee. An aggressive left wing, Lecaine had racked up 643 points during eight seasons in the International Hockey League, mostly spent with the Port Huron Flags. His career with the Penguins lasted all of four games.

The first notable player to leave Pittsburgh via free agency was Val Fonteyne. Selected from Detroit in the 1967 Expansion Draft, the veteran left wing served the Penguins with distinction while appearing in 349 games. A versatile and valuable performer, he skated on the speedy "Jet Line" with two of the team's all-time greats, Michel Briere and Jean Pronovost. Remarkably, Fonteyne drew only two minor penalties during his five seasons with the club. In 1972 he signed with the Edmonton Oilers of the World Hockey Association, making him the first Penguin to jump to the WHA.

Goaltender Steve Rexe was the first player selected by the Penguins in the Amateur Draft. Following a stint with the Canadian National Team, Rexe spent much of his career in the Ontario Senior League, backstopping teams like the Napanee Comets and the Lindsay Lancers before retiring in 1977.

Rugged Kevin McClelland (18) was acquired from Hartford in 1981 as part of a compensation package for Greg Millen.

The 10 Best Trades

1. March 4, 1991

Center John Cullen, left wing Jeff Parker, and defenseman Zarley Zalapski to Hartford for center Ron Francis and defensemen Grant Jennings and Ulf Samuelsson.

Known in Pittsburgh simply as "the Trade." The Whalers' all-time leading scorer at age 27, Francis was a superb two-way center and the perfect complement to Mario Lemieux. Samuelsson and Jennings provided backbone to a defense that was sorely in need of some. With one bold stroke, Craig Patrick had acquired the missing pieces to the Pens' Stanley Cup jigsaw puzzle.

2. November 24, 1987

Centers Dave Hannan and Craig Simpson and defensemen Chris Joseph and Moe Mantha to Edmonton for defenseman Paul Coffey and left wings Dave Hunter and Wayne Van Dorp.

Penguins fans had much to be thankful for on Thanksgiving Day. The arrival of the swift-skating Coffey at long last gave the Penguins a superstar to team with Lemieux, while trumpeting a turning point in the franchise's sorry history. In an instant, the club was transformed from loveable losers into legitimate Cup contenders.

Ron Francis helped lead the Pens to two Stanley Cups.

3. February 19, 1992

Defenseman Brian Benning, right wing Mark Recchi, and a first-round choice in the 1992 Entry Draft (acquired from Los Angeles) to Philadelphia for defenseman Kjell Samuelsson, right wing Rick Tocchet, goaltender Ken Wregget, and a conditional third-round choice in the 1993 Entry Draft.

Parting with Recchi was tough, but the return was even greater. Blessed with the wingspan of a jumbo jet, Samuelsson made life miserable for opposing forwards. Wregget was a solid backup goalie who proved to be worth his weight in gold. But the key to the deal was Tocchet, the rough-hewn warrior winger who willed the Penguins to their second Stanley Cup.

4. November 12, 1988

Defenseman Doug Bodger and left wing Darrin Shannon to Buffalo for goaltender Tom Barrasso and a third-round choice in the 1990 Entry Draft.

This was Tony Esposito's signature trade. At the time of the deal the Penguins were limping along with a collection of journeymen in goal. Suddenly, the team had a stud between the pipes. Supremely confident in his abilities, Barrasso solidified the club down the middle and was a linchpin on the Stanley Cup champions of the early 1990s.

5. September 9, 1983

Left wing Anders Hakansson to Los Angeles for the rights to left wing Kevin Stevens.

Few trades have received less fanfare and paid greater dividends. When it was announced, Stevens was a husky 18-year-old kid fresh out of high school. Over a four-year span in the early 1990s, he scored 190 goals while establishing himself as the best power forward in hockey. Perhaps general manager Eddie Johnston called the Psychic Hotline before swinging the deal.

6. December 11, 1990

Defensemen Chris Dahlquist and Jim Johnson to Minnesota for defensemen Larry Murphy and Peter Taglianetti.

One of the most overlooked trades in franchise history. Dahlquist and Johnson were diligent players, but they were hardly stars. Perhaps the most underrated player in the league, Murphy was a skilled, heady defenseman who controlled the flow of a game. As an added bonus the Penguins got Taglianetti, a reliable banger who filled a vital role during the team's first Cup run.

7. January 26, 1971

Left wing Glen Sather to the New York Rangers for center Syl Apps and defenseman Sheldon Kannegiesser.

In January of 1971 it seemed that an evil spell had been cast upon the Penguins. Michel Briere, the team's brilliant young center, lay in a coma in a Montreal hospital. The NHL had assumed control of the franchise from owner Donald Parsons. As if to dispel the gloom, Jack Riley stepped forward with his finest trade. Syl Apps would become the superstar Briere had promised to be.

8. June 14, 1978
Defenseman Dave Burrows to Toronto for defenseman Randy Carlyle and right wing George Ferguson.
Baz Bastien made his share of clunkers, but this trade was solid gold. He dealt Burrows, an All-Star whose skills were starting to fade, to Toronto for Ferguson and a kid defenseman named Randy Carlyle. A versatile forward, Ferguson would score 20-plus goals in each of his four seasons in Pittsburgh. But Carlyle was something special. In 1980–81 he won the Norris Trophy.

9. November 18, 1980
Center Kim Davis and left wing Paul Marshall to Toronto for defenseman Dave Burrows and center Paul Gardner.
This was another Bastien gem. Paul Gardner was a proven sniper who had scored 30 goals in each of his first three NHL seasons. He would tally 98 more over a three-year span with the Penguins, including the first four-goal game in franchise history. Meanwhile, Davis and Marshall combined for a total of three goals in 38 games with Toronto.

10. June 16, 1990
Second-round choice in the 1990 Entry Draft to Calgary for right wing Joe Mullen.
When Craig Patrick acquired Joe Mullen from Calgary for a second-round pick, the Flames thought he was washed up. It was a monumental blunder. Although a bit long in the tooth at 33 years of age, the American-born winger had plenty of gas left in the tank. Dubbed "Slippery Rock Joe" for the way he slithered past defenders, Mullen notched 153 goals and hoisted two Stanley Cups in Pittsburgh.

The 10 Worst Trades

1. July 11, 2001
Right wing Jaromir Jagr and defenseman Frantisek Kucera to Washington for centers Kris Beech and Michal Sivek, defenseman Ross Lupaschuk, and future considerations.
Nearing the end of his contract, Jaromir Jagr told Craig Patrick that he wanted out of Pittsburgh. Operating under strict financial constraints, Patrick did his best to oblige. However, the three prospects he received in return—Beech, Lupaschuk, and Sivek—came up woefully short. Only Beech, a fringe player at best, spent any significant time with the Penguins.

Clear the Track...Here Comes Shack

In the spring of 1972 the Penguins were struggling to keep pace with the Blues and the Flyers in the chase for a playoff berth.

Red Kelly and Jack Riley had injected a liberal dose of youth into the lineup. While the youngsters provided some fresh legs, Kelly felt the club lacked a veteran presence. He urged Riley to swing a deal with Buffalo for his old friend Eddie "the Entertainer" Shack. The price was promising young center Rene Robert.

One of the sport's true characters, Shack came by his nickname honestly. He acted on pure impulse, careening around the ice and barreling into foes as if they were tenpins on a bowling alley. Unable to read or write, he signed his contracts with an "X."

The trade provided an immediate spark, just as Kelly had hoped. Teamed with Ron Schock and Ken Schinkel on the tongue-twisting "Schink-Schock-Shack Line," the veteran winger caught fire and tallied five goals and nine assists in just 18 games.

However, Robert had enormous potential. He would blossom into a star as a member of the Sabres' famed "French Connection Line."

Eddie "the Entertainer" Shack

Markus Naslund blossomed into a big-time scorer with Vancouver.

2. March 20, 1996
Left wing Markus Naslund to Vancouver for right wing Alek Stojanov.

Perhaps the most lopsided one-for-one trade in hockey history. A productive power forward in junior hockey, Stojanov proved to be no more than a fourth-line mucker. Naslund blossomed into a perennial All-Star and team captain in Vancouver while racking up 395 career goals. An assist (or a raspberry) goes to head coach Eddie Johnston, who had soured on Naslund.

3. March 4, 1972
Right wing Rene Robert to Buffalo for left wing Eddie Shack.

At the behest of coach Red Kelly, Jack Riley sent promising young forward Rene Robert to Buffalo for Kelly's old friend and teammate Eddie Shack. While "the Entertainer" provided a spark during his season and change in Pittsburgh, he was nearing the end of the line. Robert would shine in Buffalo as a member of the deadly "French Connection Line."

4. October 28, 1982
Right wing George Ferguson to Minnesota for left wing Anders Hakansson, defenseman Ron Meighan, and an exchange of first-round choices in the 1983 Entry Draft.

Hakansson was big and fast, although he possessed flinty hands. Meighan was a highly touted former No. 1 pick who never panned out. The killer was the exchange of first-round picks. As the Penguins plummeted to the bottom of the standings it became all too apparent that Baz Bastien had traded away the first overall pick in the Entry Draft.

5. February 10, 2003
Right wing Alexei Kovalev, left wing Dan LaCouture, and defensemen Janne Laukannen and Mike Wilson to the New York Rangers for defensemen Joel Bouchard and Richard Lintner and right wings Rico Fata and Mikael Samuelsson.

Once again Craig Patrick dumped a superstar (and his salary) and got next to nothing in return. Of the grab-bag collection of players he received for Kovalev, only the speedy Fata experienced any success with the Penguins. Samuelsson would develop into a solid player, albeit with Detroit. Bouchard and Lintner were gone by the start of the 2003–04 season.

6. June 22, 1996
Defenseman Sergei Zubov to Dallas for defenseman Kevin Hatcher.

What looked like a swap of All-Star defensemen turned out to be a lopsided win for the Stars. Hatcher, fresh off a miserable year in Dallas, scored 45 goals during his three seasons with the Pens. But the big defender had lost all taste for physical play. The wondrously skilled Zubov emerged as an elite defenseman while anchoring a Stanley Cup winner in Dallas.

7. March 18, 1997
Right wing Glen Murray to Los Angeles for center Ed Olczyk.

Craig Patrick swapped an up-and-comer for a fading former star. While Olczyk was extremely popular with his new teammates, his production declined—especially after the arrival of defense-first coach Kevin Constantine. Murray struggled during his two seasons with the Pens, but found new life on the West Coast. The big winger would bang home 283 goals after leaving Pittsburgh.

8. July 8, 1995
Defenseman Larry Murphy to Toronto for defenseman Dmitri Mironov and a second-round choice in the 1996 Entry Draft.

Patrick thought he'd found a diamond in the rough when he acquired Dmitri Mironov for future Hall of Famer Larry Murphy. Mironov had all the tools. Big and mobile, he possessed a cannon of a shot. Too bad Patrick didn't heed the rest of the scouting report, which would've included the tag "underachiever." By season's end "Tree" was rooted to the bench.

Demolition Durby and Battleship

Rarely have a pair of tough guys had a greater hand in turning a team around than Bob "Battleship" Kelly and Steve Durbano.

When the duo arrived via a big trade with St. Louis in January of 1974 the Pens were being mauled on a nightly basis by the likes of Philly's "Broad Street Bullies" and the equally nasty Blues.

Almost overnight the club's fortunes took a turn for the better. Durbano and Kelly began to liquidate opposing goons who were still feeling their oats while creating a little mayhem of their own.

A case in point: in the spring of 1974 the Penguins were playing the New York Islanders. Garry Howatt, a scrappy little winger known as the "Toy Tiger," cruised in front of the Penguins' net, where he was confronted by Durbano. They clashed and Howatt flew into a rage.

The linesmen quickly separated the would-be combatants and escorted "Durby" to a safe haven behind the cage. Durbano took a step back and calmly rolled up his sleeves. It seemed that cooler heads would prevail. Suddenly, the swashbuckling defenseman bolted around the net and launched himself at Howatt.

A TV replay revealed why Howatt had become so infuriated: Durbano had speared him in the groin.

Kelly was the opposite of his volatile teammate. Like Clint Eastwood on skates, he oozed silent menace. Opponents were keenly aware of his fistic reputation and gave him a wide berth.

Steve Durbano

Occasionally a young gunslinger such as Toronto's "Tiger" Williams would test him. Battleship bloodied Williams with uppercuts and knocked him to the ice.

Kelly would play three and a half seasons with the club and develop into a highly effective scorer/enforcer, twice topping the 20-goal mark. However, Durbano's career was wrecked by a serious wrist injury and off-the-ice problems. Reduced to the role of a sideshow performer, he drifted from team to team.

Still, his wild-man reputation remained intact. Durby's friend and former teammate Steve Shutt pulled rookie Brian Engblom aside one night and offered him a sage bit of advice.

"There's a guy named Durbano out there tonight," he warned. "I don't know what his number is. Don't hit him. Don't slash him. Don't talk to him. Don't go near him!"

9. October 17, 1977
First-round choice in the 1979 Entry Draft to Washington for right wing Hartland Monahan.

This one had the critics scratching their heads. Monahan was a marginal player who enjoyed a career year (23 goals) in 1976–77. He'd scored a hat trick versus the Pens and had obviously made an impression. However, he wasn't worth a first-round pick. After watching his prized acquisition play, Baz Bastien must have agreed. Two weeks later he traded Monahan to the Kings.

10. October 18, 1978
First-round choice in the 1981 Entry Draft to Montreal for left wing Rod Schutt.

Baz Bastien was ecstatic when he made this deal, and for good reason. According to folklore, he thought he'd acquired Steve Shutt, the brilliant left wing who'd scored 60 goals in 1976–77. The player he actually received was *Rod* Schutt, a not-so-brilliant left wing who topped out at 25 goals. It was clearly an open-and-Schutt case of mistaken identity.

Major Player Trades

1967–68

June 6, 1967 – Left wing Larry Jeffrey to the New York Rangers for center Paul Andrea, Frank Francis, left wing George Konik, and defenseman Dunc McCallum.

Sept. 7, 1967 – Goaltender Roy Edwards to Detroit for goaltender Hank Bassen.

Oct. 11, 1967 – Center Jeannot Gilbert to Hershey (AHL) for left wing Gene Ubriaco.

Feb. 27, 1968 – Center Art Stratton to Philadelphia for right wing Wayne Hicks.

1968–69

May 21, 1968 – First-round choice in the 1969 Amateur Draft and cash to Boston for defenseman John Arbour and right wing Jean Pronovost.

June 11, 1968 – Left wing Ab McDonald to St. Louis for center Lou Angotti.

June 12, 1968 – Defenseman Al MacNeil to Montreal for center Wally Boyer.

Oct. 1, 1968 – First-round choice in the 1972 Amateur Draft to Minnesota for defenseman Bob Woytowich.

Oct. 1968 – Right wing Andy Bathgate loaned to Vancouver (WHL) for the 1968–69 season for future considerations.

Nov. 22, 1968 – Defenseman Larry Hillman to Montreal for defenseman Jean-Guy Lagace and cash.

Nov. 29, 1968 – Center Bob Dillabough to Oakland for center Billy Harris.

Jan. 24, 1969 – Defenseman Leo Boivin to Minnesota for defenseman Duane Rupp.

Jan. 30, 1969 – Center Earl Ingarfield, defenseman Dick Mattiussi, and left wing Gene Ubriaco to Oakland for defensemen Tracy Pratt and Bryan Watson and right wing George Swarbrick.

1969–70

May 20, 1969 – Center Paul Andrea, defenseman John Arbour, and the loan of Andy Bathgate for the 1969–70 season to Vancouver (WHL) for center Bryan Hextall.

June 6, 1969 – Center Lou Angotti and a first-round choice in the 1971 Amateur Draft to St. Louis for right wing Craig Cameron, center Ron Schock, and a second-round choice in the 1971 Amateur Draft.

Oct. 28, 1969 – Left wing Billy Dea to Detroit for defenseman Mike McMahon.

Nov. 1969 – Center Bob Rivard and cash to Baltimore (AHL) for defenseman Jim Morrison.

1970–71

May 22, 1970 – Defenseman Barry Ashbee to Philadelphia for defenseman Darryl Edestrand and left wing Larry McKillop.

June 11, 1970 – Right wing George Swarbrick to Philadelphia for defenseman Terry Ball.

Jan. 24, 1971 – Defenseman Terry Ball to Buffalo for defenseman Jean-Guy Lagace.

Jan. 26, 1971 – Left wing Glen Sather to the New York Rangers for center Syl Apps and defenseman Sheldon Kannegiesser.

1971–72

Jan. 11, 1972 – Defenseman Bob Woytowich to Los Angeles for right wing Al McDonough.

Mar. 4, 1972 – Right wing Rene Robert to Buffalo for left wing Eddie Shack.

Midseason acquisitions (left to right) Steve Durbano, Ron Stackhouse, Ab DeMarco, and Chuck Arnason at a 1974 practice session.

1972–73

Jan. 8, 1973 – Defenseman Joe Noris to St. Louis for left wing Jim Shires.

Feb. 25, 1973 – Third-round choice in the 1973 Amateur Draft and cash to Detroit for goaltender Andy Brown.

Mar. 2, 1973 – Defenseman Sheldon Kannegiesser to the New York Rangers for future considerations (right wing Steve Andrascik).

1973–74

Oct. 4, 1973 – Right wing Nick Harbaruk to St. Louis for goaltender Bob Johnson.

Oct. 25, 1973 – Defenseman Darryl Edestrand to Boston for defenseman Nick Beverley.

Jan. 4, 1974 – Right wing Al McDonough to Atlanta for right wing Chuck Arnason and defenseman Bob Paradise.

Jan. 17, 1974 – Left wing Greg Polis, defenseman Bryan Watson, and a second-round choice in the 1974 Amateur Draft to St. Louis for defensemen Ab DeMarco and Steve Durbano and left wing Bob Kelly. Defenseman Jack Lynch and goaltender Jim Rutherford to Detroit for defenseman Ron Stackhouse.

1974–75

May 27, 1974 – Defenseman Nick Beverley to the New York Rangers for left wing Vic Hadfield. Left wing Hank Nowak and a third-round choice in the 1974 Amateur Draft to Detroit for left wing Nelson Debenedet.

Sept. 13, 1974 – Right wing Blaine Stoughton and a first-round choice in the 1977 Amateur Draft to Toronto for right wing Rick Kehoe.

Nov. 4, 1974 – Defenseman Ab DeMarco to Vancouver for defenseman Barry Wilkins.

Dec. 14, 1974 – Center Ron Lalonde to Washington for right wing Lew Morrison.

Jan. 10, 1975 – Goaltender Denis Herron and defenseman Jean-Guy Lagace to Kansas City for goaltender Michel Plasse.

Jan. 20, 1975 – Right wing Bernie Lukowich to St. Louis for defenseman Bob Stumpf.

Jan. 21, 1975 – Defenseman Ron Jones to Washington for left wing Pete Laframboise.

1975–76

Nov. 26, 1975 – Defenseman Bob Paradise to Washington for a second-round choice in the 1976 Amateur Draft.

Dec. 16, 1975 – Left wing Harvey Bennett to Washington for left wing Stan Gilbertson.

Jan. 9, 1976 – Right wing Chuck Arnason, defenseman Steve Durbano, and an exchange of first-round choices in the 1976 Amateur Draft to Kansas City for center Ed Gilbert and right wing Simon Nolet.

Mar. 9, 1976 – Goaltender Gary Inness and cash to Philadelphia for goaltender Bob Taylor and defenseman Ed Van Impe.

Former 50-goal scorer and first-round pick Pierre Larouche skates for the Canadiens against his old team.

1976–77

Aug. 7, 1976 – Right wing Simon Nolet and goaltender Michel Plasse to Colorado as compensation for goaltender Denis Herron.

Aug. 11, 1976 – Third-round choice in the 1978 Amateur Draft to Montreal for defenseman Don Awrey.

Sep. 1, 1976 – Defenseman Colin Campbell loaned to Colorado for the 1976–77 season.

Oct. 8, 1976 – Fourth-round choice in the 1978 Amateur Draft to the New York Rangers for goaltender Dunc Wilson.

Oct. 18, 1976 – Fifth-round choice in the 1977 Amateur Draft to Los Angeles for left wing Mike Corrigan.

1977–78

Sept. 20, 1977 – Center Ron Schock to Buffalo for left wing Brian Spencer.

Oct. 1, 1977 – Rights to defenseman Don Awrey to Washington for defenseman Bob Paradise.

Oct. 17, 1977 – First-round choice in the 1979 Entry Draft to Washington for right wing Hartland Monahan.

Nov. 2, 1977 – Center Syl Apps and right wing Hartland Monahan to Los Angeles for center Gene Carr, left wing Dave Schultz, and a fourth-round choice in the 1978 Amateur Draft.

Nov. 29, 1977 – Center Pierre Larouche and the rights to right wing Peter Marsh to Montreal for right wing Peter Lee and center Pete Mahovlich.

Dec. 2, 1977 – Defenseman Dennis Owchar to Colorado for defenseman Tom Edur.

One of Baz Bastien's finest acquisitions, Paul Gardner averaged more than 30 goals per season for the Pens.

1978–79

June 14, 1978 – First-round choice in the 1978 Amateur Draft to Philadelphia for defenseman Tom Bladon, center Orest Kindrachuk, and left wing Ross Lonsberry. Defenseman Dave Burrows to Toronto for defenseman Randy Carlyle and right wing George Ferguson.

Sept. 6, 1978 – Right wing Jean Pronovost to Atlanta for center Gregg Sheppard.

Oct. 9, 1978 – Second-round choice in the 1980 Entry Draft to Chicago for defenseman Dale Tallon.

Oct. 18, 1978 – First-round choice in the 1981 Entry Draft to Montreal for left wing Rod Schutt.

Feb. 6, 1979 – Left wing Dave Schultz to Buffalo for left wing Gary McAdam.

1979–80

Aug. 3, 1979 – Center Pete Mahovlich to Detroit for left wing Nick Libett.

Aug. 30, 1979 – Goaltender Denis Herron and a second-round choice in the 1982 Entry Draft to Montreal for goaltender Rob Holland and right wing Pat Hughes.

Nov. 13, 1979 – Right wing Blair Chapman to St. Louis for defenseman Bob Stewart.

1980–81

Sept. 26, 1980 – Third-round choice in the 1983 Entry Draft to Montreal for defenseman Gilles Lupien.

Nov. 18, 1980 – Center Kim Davis and left wing Paul Marshall to Toronto for defenseman Dave Burrows and center Paul Gardner.

Jan. 2, 1981 – Fifth-round choice in the 1981 Entry Draft to Washington for left wing Gary Rissling.

Jan. 8, 1981 – Left wing Gary McAdam to Detroit for left wing Errol Thompson.

Feb. 20, 1981 – Defenseman Gilles Lupien to Hartford for a sixth-round choice in the 1981 Entry Draft.

Mar. 10, 1981 – Right wing Pat Hughes to Edmonton for defenseman Pat Price.

1981–82

Sept. 11, 1981 – Future considerations to Minnesota for goaltender Paul Harrison.

Sept. 28, 1981 – Goaltender Rob Holland to the New York Islanders for future considerations.

Dec. 29, 1981 – Defenseman Russ Anderson and an eighth-round choice in the 1983 Entry Draft to Hartford for center Rick MacLeish.

Feb. 3, 1982 – Sixth-round choice in the 1982 Entry Draft to Toronto for defenseman Greg Hotham.

Feb. 14, 1982 — Eighth-round choice in the 1984 Entry Draft to St. Louis for goaltender Gary Edwards.

Mar. 2, 1982 – Center Mark Johnson to Minnesota for a second-round choice in the 1982 Entry Draft.

1982–83

Sept. 15, 1982 – Third-round choice in the 1985 Entry Draft to Montreal for goaltender Denis Herron.

Oct. 28, 1982 – Right wing George Ferguson to Minnesota for left wing Anders Hakansson, defenseman Ron Meighan, and an exchange of first-round choices in the 1983 Entry Draft.

1983–84

Aug. 15, 1983 – Left wing Pat Graham and goaltender Nick Ricci to Toronto for right wing Rocky Saganiuk and goaltender Vincent Tremblay.

Sept. 9, 1983 – Left wing Anders Hakansson to Los Angeles for the rights to left wing Kevin Stevens.

Sept. 30, 1983 – Center Greg Malone to Hartford for a fifth-round choice in the 1985 Entry Draft.

Oct. 15, 1983 – Defenseman Marc Chorney to Los Angeles for a sixth-round choice in the 1985 Entry Draft and future considerations.

Oct. 23, 1983 – Right wing Rich Sutter and second and third-round choices in the 1984 Entry Draft to Philadelphia for left wing Andy Brickley, centers Ron Flockhart and Mark Taylor, and first- and third-round choices in the 1984 Entry Draft.

Oct. 24, 1983 – Center Andre St. Laurent to Detroit for future considerations.

Dec. 5, 1983 – Right wing Kevin McClelland and a sixth-round choice in the 1984 Entry Draft to Edmonton for center Tom Roulston.

Dec. 6, 1983 – Defenseman Randy Boyd to Chicago for defenseman Greg Fox.

Jan. 26, 1984 – Third-round choice in the 2004 Entry Draft to Vancouver for defenseman Kevin McCarthy.

Mar. 5, 1984 – Defenseman Randy Carlyle to Winnipeg for a first-round choice in the 1984 Entry Draft and future considerations (defenseman Moe Mantha).

1984–85

Oct. 15, 1984 – Fourth-round choice in the 1985 Entry Draft to Boston for defenseman Randy Hillier.

Nov. 9, 1984 – Center Ron Flockhart to Montreal for center John Chabot.

Nov. 16, 1984 – Left wing Pat Boutette to Hartford for the rights to defenseman Ville Siren.

Dec. 6, 1984 – Defenseman Tom Thornbury to Quebec for goaltender Brian Ford.

Mar. 12, 1985 – Center Mark Taylor to Washington for center Jim McGeough.

1985–86

Sept. 11, 1985 – Left wing Tim Hyrnewich, defenseman Marty McSorley, and future considerations (defenseman Craig Muni) to Edmonton for goaltender Gilles Meloche.

Oct. 4, 1985 – Future considerations (defenseman Mike Moller) to Edmonton for right wing Pat Hughes. Right wing Pat Hughes to Buffalo for left wing Randy Cunneyworth and defenseman Mike Moller. Defenseman Mike Moller to Edmonton.

Oct. 20, 1985 – Right wing Wayne Babych to Quebec for future considerations.

Mar. 11, 1986 – Right wing Doug Shedden to Detroit for right wing Ron Duguay.

1986–87

Nov. 12, 1986 – Center Mike Bullard to Calgary for center Dan Quinn.

Jan. 21, 1987 – Right wing Ron Duguay to the New York Rangers for left wing Chris Kontos.

Feb. 6, 1987 – Goaltender Roberto Romano to Boston for goaltender Pat Riggin.

1987–88

Nov. 24, 1987 – Centers Dave Hannan and Craig Simpson and defensemen Chris Joseph and Moe Mantha to Edmonton for defenseman Paul Coffey and left wings Dave Hunter and Wayne Van Dorp.

Dec. 17, 1987 – Future considerations to Montreal for right wing Perry Ganchar.

Feb. 5, 1988 – Left wing Chris Kontos and a sixth-round choice in the 1988 Entry Draft to Los Angeles for right wing Bryan Erickson.

Black Wednesday

March 20, 1996, is a date that will live in infamy among Penguins faithful. On that fateful day Craig Patrick, the brilliant general manager who'd made a living out of fleecing his front office brethren, engineered what is widely regarded as one of the worst hockey trades of all time. Looking to add size and toughness, he sent promising winger Markus Naslund to Vancouver for Alek Stojanov.

Alex Stojanov

It may be hard to believe in hindsight, but there was some justification for the trade. As undeniably talented as Naslund was, there were questions about his character. Coach Eddie Johnston, who had a keen eye for young talent, had soured on the speedy 22-year-old.

Stojanov did have some credentials. A tough, honest player, the husky 6'4", 220-pounder was selected one notch ahead of Naslund in the 1991 Entry Draft. Scouts felt he would develop into a decent if not prolific power forward.

When asked to evaluate the deal, Patrick readily admitted that the Penguins hadn't given Naslund enough ice time.

"I wouldn't say that Markus didn't succeed," he offered. "He's a gifted goal scorer. We couldn't—or didn't—allow him the playing time to accomplish what others have."

Regarding his new acquisition, Patrick was upbeat. "He's going to get better as time goes on. He scored well in junior, both playmaking and scoring goals." Then he added, rather prophetically, "One thing he'll need to improve to play on the top two lines is his skating."

Stojanov's skating never improved. His chances at even a modestly successful NHL career were snuffed out the following winter when he was injured in a car accident.

Naslund quickly dispelled any concerns about his heart. Serving as the Canucks' team captain, he blossomed into a perennial All-Star and 40-goal scorer.

Bryan Smolinski (left), Sergei Zubov (center), and Petr Nedved (right) were acquired in the summer of 1995.

1988–89

Sept. 1, 1988 – Third-round choice in the 1990 Entry Draft to Philadelphia for goaltender Wendell Young and a seventh-round choice in the 1990 Entry Draft.

Sept. 30, 1988 – Left wing Wayne Van Dorp to Buffalo for future considerations.

Nov. 1, 1988 – Rights to center Rob Gaudreau to Minnesota for right wing Richard Zemlak.

Nov. 12, 1988 – Defenseman Doug Bodger and left wing Darrin Shannon to Buffalo for goaltender Tom Barrasso and a third-round choice in the 1990 Entry Draft.

Dec. 17, 1988 – Center Steve Gotaas and defenseman Ville Siren to Minnesota for right wing Scott Bjugstad and defenseman Gord Dineen.

Jan. 9, 1989 – Goaltender Steve Guenette to Calgary for a sixth-round choice in the 1989 Entry Draft.

Mar. 7, 1989 – Defenseman Pat Mayer to Los Angeles for center Tim Tookey.

1989–90

June 17, 1989 – Left wing Randy Cunneyworth, center Dave McLlwain, and goaltender Rick Tabarraci to Winnipeg for center Randy Gilhen, defenseman Jim Kyte, and right wing Andrew McBain.

Sept. 14, 1989 – Right wing Lee Giffin to the New York Rangers for future considerations.

Oct. 24, 1989 – Defenseman Rod Buskas to Vancouver for a sixth-round choice in the 1990 Entry Draft.

Jan. 8, 1990 – Left wing Dave Capuano, right wing Andrew McBain, and center Dan Quinn to Vancouver for defenseman Rod Buskas, center Barry Pederson, and right wing Tony Tanti.

Mar. 6, 1990 – Future considerations to Chicago for goaltender Alain Chevrier.

1990–91

June 16, 1990 – Second-round choice in the 1990 Entry Draft to Calgary for right wing Joe Mullen.

Oct. 27, 1990 – Eleventh-round choice in the 1992 Entry Draft to St. Louis for defenseman Gordie Roberts.

Dec. 11, 1990 – Defensemen Chris Dahlquist and Jim Johnson to Minnesota for defensemen Larry Murphy and Peter Taglianetti.

Dec. 13, 1990 – Defenseman Jim Kyte to Calgary for center Jiri Hrdina.

Dec. 21, 1990 – Right wing Rob Brown to Hartford for right wing Scott Young.

Mar. 4, 1991 – Center John Cullen, left wing Jeff Parker, and defenseman Zarley Zalapski to Hartford for center Ron Francis and defensemen Grant Jennings and Ulf Samuelsson.

Mar. 5, 1991 – Right wing Tony Tanti to Buffalo for center Ken Priestlay. Left wing Brad Aitken to Edmonton for left wing Kim Issel.

1991–92

Feb. 19, 1992 – Defenseman Paul Coffey to Los Angeles for defensemen Brian Benning and Jeff Chychrun and a first-round choice in the 1992 Entry Draft. Defenseman Brian Benning, right wing Mark Recchi, and a first-round choice in the 1992 Entry Draft (acquired from Los Angeles) to Philadelphia for defenseman Kjell Samuelsson, right wing Rick Tocchet, goaltender Ken Wregget, and a conditional third-round choice in the 1993 Entry Draft.

Mar. 10, 1992 – Goaltender Frank Pietrangelo to Hartford for third- and seventh-round choices in the 1994 Entry Draft. Right wing Scott Young to Quebec for defenseman Bryan Fogarty.

1992–93

Nov. 6, 1992 – Defenseman Jeff Chychrun to Los Angeles for defenseman Peter Ahola.

Feb. 26, 1993 – Defenseman Peter Ahola to San Jose for future considerations.

Mar. 22, 1993 – Left wing Bob Errey to Buffalo for defenseman Mike Ramsey. Third-round choice in the 1993 Entry Draft to Tampa Bay for defenseman Peter Taglianetti.

1993–94

Aug. 27, 1993 – Right wing Shawn McEachern to Los Angeles for defenseman Marty McSorley.

Oct. 8, 1993 – Defenseman Paul Stanton to Boston for a third-round choice in the 1994 Entry Draft.

Feb. 16, 1994 – Defensemen Marty McSorley and Jim Paek to Los Angeles for right wings Shawn McEachern and Tomas Sandstrom.

Mar. 19, 1994 – Left wing Jeff Daniels to Florida for defenseman Greg Hawgood.

Mar. 21, 1994 – Right wing Mike Needham to Dallas for left wing Jim McKenzie.

1994–95

July 29, 1994 – Right wing Rick Tocchet and a second-round choice in the 1995 Entry Draft to Los Angeles for left wing Luc Robitaille.

Feb. 16, 1995 – Future considerations to Tampa Bay for goaltender Wendell Young.

Apr. 7, 1995 – Center Martin Straka to Ottawa for defenseman Norm Maciver and center Troy Murray. Defenseman Grant Jennings to Toronto for defenseman Drake Berehowsky.

1995–96

July 8, 1995 – Defenseman Larry Murphy to Toronto for defenseman Dmitri Mironov and a second-round choice in the 1996 Entry Draft.

Aug. 2, 1995 – Center Shawn McEachern and left wing Kevin Stevens to Boston for right wing Glen Murray, center Bryan Smolinski, and a third-round choice in the 1996 Entry Draft.

Aug. 31, 1995 – Left wing Luc Robitaille and defenseman Ulf Samuelsson to the New York Rangers for center Petr Nedved and defenseman Sergei Zubov.

Dec. 28, 1995 – Defenseman Norm Maciver to Winnipeg for defenseman Neil Wilkinson.

Mar. 1, 1996 – Eighth-round choice in the 1996 Entry Draft to Ottawa for center Dave McLlwain.

Mar. 20, 1996 – Fifth-round choice in the 1996 Entry Draft to San Jose for center Kevin Miller. Sixth-round choice in the 1996 Entry Draft to St. Louis for defenseman Jean-Jacques Daigneault. Left wing Markus Naslund to Vancouver for right wing Alek Stojanov.

1996–97

June 22, 1996 – Defenseman Sergei Zubov to Dallas for defenseman Kevin Hatcher. Seventh-round choice in the 1996 Entry Draft to Edmonton for center Tyler Wright.

Oct. 25, 1996 – Conditional choice in the 1997 Entry Draft to Los Angeles for right wing Petr Klima.

Nov. 17, 1996 – Center Bryan Smolinski to the New York Islanders for center Andreas Johansson and defenseman Darius Kasparaitis.

Nov. 19, 1996 – Left wing Shawn Antoski and defenseman Dmitri Mironov to Anaheim for left wing Alex Hicks and defenseman Fredrik Olausson. Center Chris Wells to Florida for center Stu Barnes and defenseman Jason Woolley.

Jan. 27, 1997 – Right wing Tomas Sandstrom to Detroit for center Greg Johnson.

Feb. 21, 1997 – Defenseman Jean-Jacques Daigneault to Anaheim for right wing Garry Valk.

Mar. 18, 1997 – Right wing Richard Park to Anaheim for right wing Roman Oksiuta. Future considerations to Vancouver for left wing Josef Beranek. Right wing Glen Murray to Los Angeles for center Ed Olczyk.

1997–98

Aug. 12, 1997 – Third-round choice in the 1998 Entry Draft to Edmonton for defenseman Jiri Slegr.

Sept. 24, 1997 – Defenseman Jason Woolley to Buffalo for a fifth-round choice in the 1998 Entry Draft.

Sept. 28, 1997 – Defenseman Francois Leroux to Colorado for a third-round choice in the 1998 Entry Draft.

Oct. 27, 1997 – Center Greg Johnson to Chicago for defenseman Tuomas Gronman.

Mar. 24, 1998 – Goaltender Patrick Lalime to Anaheim for center Sean Pronger.

1998–99

June 16, 1998 – Left wing Josef Beranek to Edmonton for defenseman Bobby Dollas and center Tony Hrkac.

June 17, 1998 – Left wing Dave Roche and goaltender Ken Wregget to Calgary for center Todd Hlushko and left wing German Titov.

Nov. 25, 1998 – Centers Petr Nedved and Sean Pronger and defenseman Chris Tamer to the New York Rangers for right wing Alexei Kovalev and center Harry York.

Mar. 11, 1999 – Center Stu Barnes to Buffalo for right wing Matthew Barnaby.

1999–00

Sept. 30, 1999 – Defenseman Kevin Hatcher to the New York Rangers for defenseman Peter Popovic.

Jan. 29, 2000 – Left wing Kip Miller to Anaheim for a ninth-round choice in the 2000 Entry Draft.

Mar. 13, 2000 – Defenseman Pavel Skrbek to Nashville for defenseman Bob Boughner.

Mar. 14, 2000 – Fifth-round choice in the 2000 Entry Draft to Anaheim for defenseman Dan Trebil. Defenseman Brad Werenka to Calgary for left wing Rene Corbet and goaltender Tyler Moss. Left wing German Titov to Edmonton for left wing Josef Beranek. Goaltender Tom Barrasso to Ottawa for defenseman Janne Laukkanen and goaltender Ron Tugnutt.

2000–01

Nov. 14, 2000 – Ninth-round choice in the 2001 Entry Draft to the New York Islanders for defenseman Dan Trebil.

Dec. 28, 2000 – Defenseman Dan Trebil to St. Louis for defenseman Marc Bergevin.

Jan. 13, 2001 – Center Roman Simicek to Minnesota for left wing Steve McKenna.

Jan. 14, 2001 – Defenseman Jiri Slegr to Atlanta for a third-round choice in the 2001 Entry Draft. Defenseman John Slaney to Philadelphia for left wing Kevin Stevens. Third-round choice in the 2001 Entry Draft to Columbus for right wing Krzysztof Oliwa.

Feb. 1, 2001 – Right wing Matthew Barnaby to Tampa Bay for center Wayne Primeau.

Mar. 12, 2001 – Defenseman Jeff Norton to San Jose for defenseman Bobby Dollas and goaltender Johan Hedberg.

Mar. 13, 2001 – Sixth-round choice in the 2001 Entry Draft to Columbus for defenseman Frantisek Kucera. Defenseman Sven Butenschon to Edmonton for left wing Dan LaCouture.

2001–02

July 11, 2001 – Right wing Jaromir Jagr and defenseman Frantisek Kucera to Washington for centers Kris Beech and Michal Sivek, defenseman Ross Lupaschuk, and future considerations.

Mar. 15, 2002 – Fourth-round choice in the 2003 Entry Draft to Columbus for defenseman Jamie Pushor.

Mar. 17, 2002 – Right wing Billy Tibbetts to Philadelphia for center Kent Manderville.

Mar. 19, 2002 – Defenseman Darius Kasparaitis to Colorado for defenseman Rick Berry and left wing Ville Nieminen. Right wing Stephane Richer to New Jersey for a seventh-round choice in the 2003 Entry Draft.

2002–03

June 23, 2002 – Right wing Krzysztof Oliwa to the New York Rangers for a ninth-round choice in the 2003 Entry Draft.

Feb. 9, 2003 – Defenseman Andrew Ference to Calgary for a third-round choice in the 2004 Entry Draft. Fifth-round choice in the 2003 Entry Draft to San Jose for defenseman Shawn Heins.

Feb. 10, 2003 – Right wing Alexei Kovalev, left wing Dan LaCouture, and defensemen Janne Laukannen and Mike Wilson to the New York Rangers for defensemen Joel Bouchard and Richard Lintner and right wings Rico Fata and Mikael Samuelsson.

Mar. 9, 2003 – Center Randy Robitaille to the New York Islanders for a fifth-round choice in the 2003 Entry Draft.

Mar. 11, 2003 – Defenseman Ian Moran to Boston for a fourth-round choice in the 2003 Entry Draft. Right wing Shean Donovan to Calgary for defenseman Micki DuPont and center Mathias Johansson. Center Jan Hrdina and defenseman Francois Leroux to Phoenix for left wings Ramzi Abid and Guillaume Lefebvre and defenseman Dan Focht. Center Wayne Primeau to San Jose for right wing Matt Bradley. Defenseman Marc Bergevin to Tampa Bay for center Brian Holzinger.

2003–04

May 12, 2003 – Ninth-round choice in the 2003 Entry Draft to Tampa Bay for defenseman Marc Bergevin.

June 21, 2003 – Right wing Mikael Samuelsson and first and second-round choices in the 2003 Entry Draft to

Georges Laraque and Gary Roberts (10) added muscle and leadership.

Florida for first- and third-round choices in the 2003 Entry Draft.

Aug. 25, 2003 – Goaltender Johan Hedberg to Vancouver for a second-round choice in the 2004 Entry Draft.

Nov. 30, 2003 – Center Martin Straka to Los Angeles for right wing Sergei Anshakov and defenseman Martin Strbak.

Feb. 11, 2004 – Defenseman Drake Berehowsky to Toronto for defenseman Ric Jackman.

Feb. 22, 2004 – Future considerations to Phoenix for right wing Landon Wilson.

Mar. 8, 2004 – Right wing Steve Webb to the New York Islanders for defenseman Alain Nasreddine.

Mar. 9, 2004 – Defenseman Marc Bergevin to Vancouver for a seventh-round choice in the 2004 Entry Draft. Center Brian Holzinger to Columbus for center Lasse Pirjeta.

2005–06

Aug. 10, 2005 – Fourth-round choice in the 2006 Entry Draft to Chicago for goaltender Jocelyn Thibault.

Sept. 9, 2005 – Center Kris Beech to Nashville for a fourth-round choice in the 2006 Entry Draft.

Dec. 9, 2005 – Defenseman Steve Poapst to St. Louis for center Eric Boguniecki.

Jan. 18, 2006 – Sixth-round choice in the 2006 Entry Draft to Florida for defenseman Eric Cairns.

Jan. 26, 2006 – Defenseman Dick Tarnstrom to Edmonton for defenseman Cory Cross and left wing Jani Rita.

Mar. 8, 2006 – Defenseman Cory Cross to Detroit for a fourth-round choice in the 2007 Entry Draft.

Mar. 9, 2006 – Right wing Mark Recchi to Carolina for center Krys Kolanos, right wing Niklas Nordgren, and a second-round choice in the 2007 Entry Draft. Defenseman Ric Jackman to Florida for center Petr Taticek.

2006–07

July 19, 2006 – Third-round choice in the 2007 Entry Draft to Nashville for center Dominic Moore and right wing Libor Pivko.

July 20, 2006 – Second-round choice in the 2007 Entry Draft to San Jose for goaltender Patrick Ehelechner and left wing Nils Ekman.

Feb. 27, 2007 – Defenseman Noah Welch to Florida for left wing Gary Roberts. Fourth-round choice in the 2007 Entry Draft to Florida for defenseman Joel Kwiatkowski. Center Dominic Moore to Minnesota for a third-round choice in the 2007 Entry Draft. Left wing Daniel Carcillo and a third-round choice in the 2008 Entry Draft to Phoenix for right wing Georges Laraque.

2007–08

June 22, 2007 – Center Chris Thorburn to Atlanta for a third-round choice in the 2007 Entry Draft.

June 23, 2007 – Center Stephen Dixon to Anaheim for center Tim Brent.

Feb. 26, 2008 – Right wing Colby Armstrong, centers Erik Christensen and Angelo Esposito, and a first-round choice in the 2008 Entry Draft to Atlanta for left wing Pascal Dupuis and right wing Marian Hossa. Second-round choice in the 2008 Entry Draft and a fifth-round choice in the 2009 Entry Draft to Toronto for defenseman Hal Gill.

2008–09

June 28, 2008 – Rights to left wings Ryan Malone and Gary Roberts to Tampa Bay for a third-round choice in the 2009 Entry Draft.

July 17, 2008 – Center Tim Brent to Chicago for defenseman Danny Richmond.

Oct. 9, 2008 – Future considerations to Phoenix for center Mike Zigomanis.

Nov. 16, 2008 – Defenseman Darryl Sydor to Dallas for defenseman Philippe Boucher.

Dec. 19, 2008 – Right wing Jonathan Filewich to St. Louis for a conditional sixth-round choice in the 2010 Entry Draft.

Jan. 17, 2009 – Goaltender Dany Sabourin, center Ryan Stone, and a fourth-round choice in the 2011 Entry Draft to Edmonton for goaltender Mathieu Garon.

Feb. 26, 2009 – Defenseman Ryan Whitney to Anaheim for left wings Chris Kunitz and Eric Tangradi.

Mar. 4, 2009 – Third-round choice in the 2009 Entry Draft to the New York Islanders for right wing Bill Guerin.

2009–10

Feb. 11, 2010 – Defenseman Nate Guenin to St. Louis for defenseman Steve Wagner.

Mar. 1, 2010 – Second-round choice in the 2010 Entry Draft to Florida for defenseman Jordan Leopold.

Mar. 2, 2010 – Left wing Luca Caputi and defenseman Martin Skoula to Toronto for left wing Alexei Ponikarovsky.

2010–11

May 30, 2010 – Exchange of sixth-round choices in the 2010 Entry Draft to Anaheim for goaltender Mattias Modig.

June 25, 2010 – Third-round choice in the 2011 Entry Draft to Philadelphia for the rights to defenseman Dan Hamhuis.

Major Purchases, Waiver Deals, and Free-Agent Signings

1966

Aug. 11, 1966 – Defensemen Ted Lanyon, Dick Mattiussi, and Bill Speer purchased from Cleveland (AHL).

1967–68

Aug. 1967 – Left wing Bill Lecaine signed as a free agent.

Sept. 1967 – Goaltender Marv Edwards signed as a free agent.

Oct. 1967 – Goaltender Les Binkley purchased from San Diego (WHL).

1968–69

Oct. 1968 – Defenseman Doug Barrie purchased from Detroit.

Nov. 22, 1968 – Defenseman Larry Hillman claimed on waivers from Minnesota.

1969–70

Jan. 27, 1970 – Defenseman Dunc McCallum purchased from Providence (AHL).

1970–71

July 1970 – Center Rod Zaine purchased from Baltimore (AHL).

Oct. 2, 1970 – Left wing Robin Burns purchased from Montreal.

1971–72

May 1971 – Center Bob Leiter purchased from Boston.

June 7, 1971 – Goaltender Roy Edwards claimed on waivers from Detroit.

Sept. 7, 1971 – Right wing Bill Hicke purchased from California.

1972–73

June 25, 1972 – Center Jim Wiley signed as a free agent.

1973–74

May 22, 1973 – Left wing Hank Nowak purchased from Hershey (AHL).

June 1973 – Goaltender Gary Inness signed as a free agent.

Aug. 1973 – Center Bob McManama signed as a free agent.

Oct. 1973 – Right wing Ted Snell signed as a free agent.

1974–75

June 25, 1974 – Left wing Harvey Bennett signed as a free agent.

July 15, 1974 – Right wing Kelly Pratt signed as a free agent.

Sept. 20, 1974 – Defenseman Colin Campbell signed as a free agent.

1976–77

Aug. 7, 1976 – Goaltender Denis Herron signed as a free agent.

Nov. 1976 – Right wing Steve Lyon signed as a free agent.

Feb. 28, 1977 – Defenseman Tom Price signed as a free agent.

1977–78

Oct. 11, 1977 – Center Tom Cassidy signed as a free agent.

Feb. 4, 1978 – Left wing John Flesch signed as a free agent.

Mar. 14, 1978 – Center Derek Sanderson signed as a free agent.

1980–81

Aug. 7, 1980 – Defenseman Paul Baxter signed as a free agent.

Highly touted collegian Dwight Mathiasen failed to produce for the Penguins.

1981–82

June 29, 1981 – Left wing Pat Boutette and right wing Kevin McClelland acquired from Hartford as compensation for goaltender Greg Millen.

June 30, 1981 – Goaltender Michel Dion signed as a free agent.

Sept. 4, 1981 – Right wing Paul Mulvey acquired from Washington as compensation for center Orest Kindrachuk.

Oct. 1, 1981 – Left wing Bobby Simpson signed as a free agent.

Feb. 23, 1982 – Center Andre St. Laurent claimed on waivers from Los Angeles.

1982–83

July 30, 1982 – Defenseman Marty McSorley signed as a free agent.

Oct. 4, 1982 – Left wing Phil Bourque and defenseman Ian Turnbull signed as free agents.

Nov. 8, 1982 – Left wing Stan Jonathan purchased from Boston.

Dec. 6, 1982 – Goaltender Roberto Romano signed as a free agent.

1983–84

July 22, 1983 – Defenseman Greg Tebbutt signed as a free agent.

Aug. 12, 1983 – Left wing Warren Young signed as a free agent.

Sept. 4, 1983 – Center Tom O'Regan signed as a free agent.

Sept. 12, 1983 – Defenseman Bob Gladney and center Tim Tookey signed as free agents.

Sept. 30, 1983 – Left wing Ted Bulley signed as a free agent.

Oct. 13, 1983 – Defenseman Bryan Maxwell claimed on waivers from Winnipeg.

Feb. 28, 1984 – Right wing Darren Lowe signed as a free agent.

1984–85

July 1984 – Defenseman Petteri Lehto signed as a free agent.

Dec. 30, 1984 – Defenseman Joe McDonnell signed as a free agent.

Mar. 1, 1985 – Defenseman Wally Weir claimed on waivers from Hartford.

Apr. 6, 1985 – Goaltender Steve Guenette signed as a free agent.

May 7, 1985 – Defenseman Chris Dahlquist signed as a free agent.

Free-agent signee Marty McSorley served two tours of duty with the Pens.

1985–86

Sept. 16, 1985 – Center Ted Nolan purchased from Buffalo.

Oct. 3, 1985 – Left wing Terry Ruskowski signed as a free agent.

Mar. 31, 1986 – Right wing Dwight Mathiasen signed as a free agent.

1986–87

July 23, 1986 – Left wing Carl Mokosak signed as a free agent.

July 24, 1986 – Center Mitch Wilson signed as a free agent.

Sept. 13, 1986 – Left wing Kevin Lavallee signed as a free agent.

Sept. 29, 1986 – Defenseman Neil Belland signed as a free agent.

Oct. 3, 1986 – Defenseman Craig Muni purchased from Buffalo.

Oct. 8, 1986 – Defenseman Dwight Schofield purchased from Washington. Left wing Warren Young purchased from Detroit.

Dec. 1986 – Center Alain Lemieux signed as a free agent.

1987–88

June 16, 1987 – Right wing Jimmy Mann signed as a free agent.

July 10, 1987 – Defenseman Pat Mayer signed as a free agent.

July 31, 1987 – Right wing Jock Callander signed as a free agent.

Aug. 31, 1987 – Left wing Mark Kachowski signed as a free agent.

Scorin' Warren

When Warren Young signed a four-year deal in the summer of 1985 with the Detroit Red Wings for $1 million, he did so with a heavy heart.

The rugged winger wanted nothing more than to stay in Pittsburgh. After years of bouncing around the minor leagues he'd found a home with the Penguins, scoring 40 goals while skating alongside fellow rookie Mario Lemieux. But Pens GM Eddie Johnston couldn't come close to matching the Red Wings' offer.

"I really didn't want to leave," Young said. "The situation was forced on me."

He soon found that life in Detroit was not all it was cracked up to be. The Red Wings were a bad team—even worse than the Penguins. If the big winger had harbored any illusions about the source of his success, they quickly evaporated. Minus Mario's picture-perfect setups, Young's scoring totals plummeted. With his fat contract he quickly became a lightning rod of discontent among the Red Wings faithful.

In the midst of his misery it just so happened that the Penguins were visiting the Motor City for a contest. Young snuck into the Penguins' locker room before game time and scrawled a simple message on the chalkboard to greet his former linemate—"Mario…help!"

Sept. 10, 1987 – Right wing Wilf Paiement signed as a free agent.

Dec. 3, 1987 – Center Glen Mulvenna signed as a free agent.

Dec. 14, 1987 – Left wing Scott Gruhl signed as a free agent.

1988–89

June 21, 1988 – Center John Cullen signed as a free agent.

1989–90

May 24, 1989 – Left wing Dave Michayluk signed as a free agent.

June 28, 1989 – Defenseman Gilbert Delorme signed as a free agent.

Feb. 26, 1990 – Center Doug Smith purchased from Vancouver.

1990–91

July 20, 1990 – Center Bryan Trottier signed as a free agent.

1991–92

July 6, 1991 – Goaltender Rob Dopson signed as a free agent.

1992–93

Aug. 25, 1992 – Center Dave Tippett signed as a free agent.

Sept. 30, 1992 – Center Mike Stapleton signed as a free agent.

Nov. 2, 1992 – Right wing Justin Duberman signed as a free agent.

1993–94

June 22, 1993 – Center Bryan Trottier signed as a free agent.

Sept. 28, 1993 – Right wing Doug Brown signed as a free agent.

Sept. 29, 1993 – Defenseman Greg Brown signed as a free agent.

Oct. 7, 1993 – Goaltender Roberto Romano signed as a free agent.

Mar. 9, 1994 – Left wing Larry DePalma claimed on waivers from the New York Islanders.

1994–95

Aug. 2, 1994 – Left wing Jeff Christian signed as a free agent.

Aug. 3, 1994 – Center John Cullen signed as a free agent.

Aug. 15, 1994 – Center Len Barrie signed as a free agent.

Apr. 7, 1995 – Center Ryan Savoia signed as a free agent.

1995–96

Aug. 7, 1995 – Defenseman Corey Foster signed as a free agent.

Aug. 10, 1995 – Defenseman Peter Allen and left wing Brad Lauer signed as free agents.

1996–97

July 10, 1996 – Center Kevin Todd signed as a free agent.

July 17, 1996 – Center Dan Quinn signed as a free agent.

July 31, 1996 – Left wing Shawn Antoski signed as a free agent.

Sept. 5, 1996 – Right wing Joe Mullen signed as a free agent.

Oct. 2, 1996 – Defenseman Craig Muni signed as a free agent.

1997–98

July 31, 1997 – Defenseman Brad Werenka signed as a free agent.

Aug. 6, 1997 – Center Martin Straka signed as a free agent.

Sept. 2, 1997 – Center Robert Lang signed as a free agent.

Sept. 25, 1997 – Goaltender Peter Skudra signed as a free agent.

Oct. 1, 1997 – Right wing Rob Brown signed as a free agent. Center Chris Ferraro and left wing Peter Ferraro claimed on waivers from the New York Rangers.

Oct. 25, 1997 – Center Robert Lang claimed on waivers from Boston.

1998–99

Aug. 11, 1998 – Defenseman Victor Ignatjev signed as a free agent.

Aug. 20, 1998 – Right wing Dan Kesa signed as a free agent.

Oct. 8, 1998 – Defenseman Jeff Serowik signed as a free agent.

Oct. 9, 1998 – Left wing Martin Sonnenberg signed as a free agent.

Oct. 18, 1998 – Left wing Patrick LeBeau signed as a free agent.

Mar. 19, 1999 – Defenseman Greg Andrusak signed as a free agent.

1999–00

Sept. 2, 1999 – Left wing Tom Chorske signed as a free agent.

Sept. 20, 1999 – Right wing Dennis Bonvie signed as a free agent.

Sept. 30, 1999 – Defenseman John Slaney signed as a free agent.

Oct. 19, 1999 – Right wing Stephen Leach signed as a free agent.

Feb. 4, 2000 – Right wing Pat Falloon claimed on waivers from Edmonton.

Apr. 10, 2000 – Right wing Billy Tibbetts signed as a free agent.

2000–01

Sept. 20, 2000 – Goaltender Rich Parent signed as a free agent.

Sept. 24, 2000 – Left wing Kip Miller signed as a free agent.

Oct. 10, 2000 – Goaltender Garth Snow signed as a free agent.

Nov. 14, 2000 – Defenseman Jeff Norton signed as a free agent.

2001–02

July 5, 2001 – Defenseman Mike Wilson signed as a free agent.

Oct. 2, 2001 – Right wing Stephane Richer signed as a free agent.

Oct. 3, 2001 – Defenseman John Jakopin claimed on waivers from Florida.

Jan. 4, 2002 – Center Randy Robitaille claimed on waivers from Los Angeles.

Mar. 15, 2002 – Right wing Shean Donovan claimed on waivers from Atlanta.

Mar. 16, 2002 – Center Jeff Toms claimed on waivers from the New York Rangers.

2002–03

July 12, 2002 – Left wing Steve McKenna signed as a free agent.

July 15, 2002 – Left wing Vladimir Vujtek signed as a free agent.

July 16, 2002 – Defenseman Francois Leroux signed as a free agent.

July 18, 2002 – Defenseman Marc Bergevin signed as a free agent.

Aug. 6, 2002 – Defenseman Dick Tarnstrom claimed on waivers from the New York Islanders.

Aug. 13, 2002 – Center Alexandre Daigle signed as a free agent.

2003–04

June 18, 2003 – Goaltender Tom Barrasso signed as a free agent.

July 31, 2003 – Right wing Kelly Buchberger and center Mike Eastwood signed as free agents.

Aug. 22, 2003 – Goaltender Martin Brochu signed as a free agent.

Aug. 28, 2003 – Defenseman Patrick Boileau signed as a free agent.

Aug. 29, 2003 – Defenseman Drake Berehowsky and left wing Reid Simpson signed as free agents.

Oct. 22, 2003 – Right wing Steve Webb claimed on waivers from Philadelphia.

Mar. 4, 2004 – Left wing Jon Sim claimed on waivers from Los Angeles.

Gifted defenseman Sergei Gonchar (right) arrived as a free agent in 2005.

2004–05

July 9, 2004 – Right wing Mark Recchi signed as a free agent.

July 12, 2004 – Right wing Ryan Vandenbussche signed as a free agent.

2005–06

Aug. 3, 2005 – Defenseman Sergei Gonchar signed as a free agent.

Aug. 4, 2005 – Right wing Andre Roy signed as a free agent.

Aug. 6, 2005 – Right wing Zigmund Palffy signed as a free agent.

Aug. 10, 2005 – Goaltender Dany Sabourin signed as a free agent.

Aug. 15, 2005 – Left wing John LeClair and defenseman Steve Poapst signed as free agents.

Sept. 2, 2005 – Defenseman Lyle Odelein signed as a free agent.

Mar. 9, 2006 – Left wing Andy Hilbert claimed on waivers from Chicago.

2006–07

June 15, 2006 – Defenseman Micki DuPont signed as a free agent.

July 3, 2006 – Defenseman Mark Eaton signed as a free agent.

July 4, 2006 – Right wing Jarkko Ruutu signed as a free agent.

July 24, 2006 – Right wing Ronald Petrovicky signed as a free agent.

July 25, 2006 – Right wing Mark Recchi signed as a free agent.

Aug. 9, 2006 – Right wing Connor James signed as a free agent.

Sept. 27, 2006 – Left wing Karl Stewart claimed on waivers from Anaheim.

Oct. 3, 2006 – Center Chris Thorburn claimed on waivers from Buffalo.

Mar. 22, 2007 – Center Mark Letestu signed as a free agent.

May 29, 2007 – Right wing Tim Wallace signed as a free agent.

2007–08

July 1, 2007 – Goaltender Dany Sabourin signed as a free agent.

July 2, 2007 – Defenseman Darryl Sydor and right wing Petr Sykora signed as free agents.

July 12, 2007 – Centers Chris Minard and Nathan Smith signed as free agents.

July 13, 2007 – Goaltender John Curry and center Jeff Taffe signed as free agents.

July 16, 2007 – Defenseman Deryk Engelland signed as a free agent.

July 19, 2007 – Goaltender Ty Conklin signed as a free agent.

Oct. 1, 2007 – Right wing Adam Hall signed as a free agent.

Jan. 26, 2008 – Center Kris Beech claimed on waivers from Washington.

2008–09

July 1, 2008 – Right wing Eric Godard signed as a free agent.

July 3, 2008 – Left wings Ruslan Fedotenko and Miroslav Satan signed as free agents.

July 6, 2008 – Left wing Matt Cooke signed as a free agent.

July 7, 2008 – Defenseman Ben Lovejoy and left wing Janne Pesonen signed as free agents.

July 15, 2008 – Right wing Bill Thomas signed as a free agent.

Mar. 4, 2009 – Right wing Craig Adams claimed on waivers from Chicago.

2009–10

July 1, 2009 – Center Mike Rupp signed as a free agent.

July 3, 2009 – Defenseman Nate Guenin signed as a free agent.

July 5, 2009 – Right wing Chris Conner signed as a free agent.

July 10, 2009 – Defenseman Jay McKee signed as a free agent.

July 21, 2009 – Goaltender Brent Johnson signed as a free agent.

Sept. 28, 2009 – Left wing Ryan Bayda signed as a free agent.

Sept. 29, 2009 – Defenseman Martin Skoula signed as a free agent.

Sept. 30, 2009 – Center Chris Bourque claimed on waivers from Washington.

2010–11

July 1, 2010 – Defensemen Paul Martin and Zbynek Michalek signed as free agents.

July 2, 2010 – Center Ryan Craig signed as a free agent.

July 3, 2010 – Left wing Brett Sterling signed as a free agent.

July 7, 2010 – Defenseman Andrew Hutchinson signed as a free agent.

July 16, 2010 – Defenseman Corey Potter signed as a free agent.

Players Released, Sold, or Lost to Other Teams

1966

Oct. 1966 – Defensemen Ted Lanyon and Bill Speer loaned to Buffalo (AHL) for 1966–67 season. Defenseman Dick Mattiussi loaned to Cleveland (AHL) for 1966–67 season.

1968–69

June 4, 1968 – Left wing George Konik sold to Oakland.

1969–70

Aug. 1969 – Left wing Mel Pearson sold to Portland (WHL).

1971–72

Oct. 3, 1971 – Defenseman Bob Blackburn sold to Vancouver.

Oct. 6, 1971 – Left wing Dean Prentice sold to Minnesota.

Nov. 22, 1971 – Right wing Bill Hicke sold to Detroit.

1972–73

Sept. 2, 1972 – Left wing Val Fonteyne signed as a free agent by Edmonton (WHA).

Oct. 1972 – Left wing Brian McKenzie sold to Atlanta.

Oct. 6, 1972 – Goaltender Roy Edwards sold to Detroit.

1973–74

May 18, 1973 – Goaltender Cam Newton signed as a free agent by Chicago (WHA).

June 1973 – Right wing Ron Snell sold to Hershey (AHL).

July 3, 1973 – Left wing Eddie Shack sold to Toronto.

Jan. 6, 1974 – Center Bryan Hextall claimed on waivers by Atlanta.

1974–75

June 1974 – Defenseman Duane Rupp signed as a free agent by Vancouver (WHA).

July 7, 1974 – Goaltender Andy Brown signed as a free agent by Indianapolis (WHA).

1975–76

May 1975 – Left wing Pete Laframboise signed as a free agent by Edmonton (WHA).

Aug. 28, 1975 – Right wing Kelly Pratt sold to Hershey (AHL).

Sept. 1975 – Goaltender Bob Johnson signed as a free agent by Denver (WHA).

Part-time defenseman Tony Feltrin (left) signed with the Rangers in 1995.

Dec. 1975 – Center Bob McManama signed as a free agent by New England (WHA).

1976–77

Sept. 2, 1976 – Defenseman Barry Wilkins signed as a free agent by Edmonton (WHA).

1977–78

Aug. 17, 1977 – Left wing Bob Kelly signed as a free agent by Chicago.

1978–79

June 6, 1978 – Center Gene Carr signed as a free agent by Atlanta.

Oct. 1978 – Center Ed Gilbert signed as a free agent by Cincinnati (WHA).

Nov. 17, 1978 – Goaltender Dunc Wilson sold to Vancouver.

1979–80

Jan. 13, 1980 – Left wing John Flesch signed as a free agent by Colorado.

1980–81

July 10, 1980 – Defenseman Tom Bladon signed as a free agent by Edmonton.

Aug. 7, 1980 – Defenseman Kim Clackson sent to Quebec as compensation for defenseman Paul Baxter.

1981–82

June 15, 1981 – Goaltender Greg Millen signed as a free agent by Hartford.

Sept. 4, 1981 – Center Orest Kindrachuk signed as a free agent by Washington.

Dec. 30, 1981 – Right wing Paul Mulvey claimed on waivers by Los Angeles.

Feb. 8, 1982 – Goaltender Paul Harrison claimed on waivers by Buffalo.

1982–83

Dec. 31, 1982 – Defenseman Pat Price claimed on waivers by Quebec.

1983–84

Aug. 15, 1983 – Right wing Peter Lee signed to play in West Germany.

Sept. 29, 1983 – Defenseman Paul Baxter signed as a free agent by Calgary.

Oct. 6, 1983 – Center Rick MacLeish signed as a free agent by Philadelphia.

1984–85

July 17, 1984 – Center Paul Gardner signed as a free agent by Washington.

Aug. 21, 1984 – Right wing Rocky Saganiuk signed as a free agent by Toronto.

Mar. 7, 1985 – Goaltender Vincent Tremblay signed as a free agent by Buffalo.

1985–86

July 10, 1985 – Left wing Warren Young signed as a free agent by Detroit.

July 11, 1985 – Center Tim Tookey signed as a free agent by Philadelphia.

July 19, 1985 – Defenseman Kevin McCarthy signed as a free agent by Philadelphia.

Versatile Kip Miller joined the Grand Rapids Griffins following his stay with the Penguins.

Oct. 3, 1985 – Left wing Rod Schutt signed as a free agent by Toronto.

Oct. 8, 1985 – Defenseman Tony Feltrin signed as a free agent by the New York Rangers.

1986–87

June 30, 1986 – Center Mitch Lamoureux signed as a free agent by Philadelphia.

July 3, 1986 – Defenseman Greg Hotham signed as a free agent by Toronto.

July 8, 1986 – Left wing Andy Brickley signed as a free agent by New Jersey.

Sept. 29, 1986 – Center Tom O'Regan signed as a free agent by Detroit.

1987–88

June 25, 1987 – Center John Chabot signed as a free agent by Detroit.

July 1987 – Left wing Terry Ruskowski signed as a free agent by Minnesota. Defenseman Dwight Schofield signed as a free agent by Winnipeg.

July 10, 1987 – Right wing Mike Blaisdell signed as a free agent by Toronto.

1988–89

Oct. 3, 1988 – Rights to left wing Dave Hunter transferred to Edmonton.

Oct. 4, 1988 – Left wing Carl Mokosak signed as a free agent by Boston.

1989–90

June 21, 1989 – Defenseman Todd Charlesworth signed as a free agent by Edmonton.

June 30, 1989 – Center Tim Tookey signed as a free agent by Philadelphia.

Aug. 24, 1989 – Right wing Scott Bjugstad signed as a free agent by Los Angeles.

Oct. 9, 1989 – Defenseman Steve Dykstra signed as a free agent by Hartford.

Mar. 2, 1990 – Right wing Bryan Erickson signed as a free agent by Winnipeg.

1990–91

July 5, 1990 – Goaltender Alain Chevrier signed as a free agent by Detroit.

Sept. 1990 – Right wing Dan Frawley signed as a free agent by Buffalo.

Nov. 8, 1990 – Right wing Richard Zemlak signed as a free agent by Calgary.

1991–92

July 30, 1991 – Defenseman Randy Hillier signed as a free agent by the New York Islanders.

Sept. 5, 1991 – Center Barry Pederson signed as a free agent by Hartford.

1992–93

July 11, 1992 – Center Glen Mulvenna signed as a free agent by Philadephia.

July 23, 1992 – Defenseman Gordie Roberts signed as a free agent by Boston.

July 29, 1992 – Right wing Jock Callander signed as a free agent by Tampa Bay.

Aug. 31, 1992 – Left wing Phil Bourque signed as a free agent by the New York Rangers. Defenseman Gord Dineen signed as a free agent by Ottawa.

Nov. 21, 1992 – Right wing Jamie Leach claimed on waivers by Hartford.

1993–94

Aug. 15, 1993 – Defenseman Todd Nelson signed as a free agent by Washington.

Aug. 30, 1993 – Center Dave Tippett signed as a free agent by Philadelphia.

Sept. 28, 1993 – Defenseman Bryan Fogarty signed as a free agent by Tampa Bay.

Feb. 19, 1994 – Center Mike Stapleton claimed on waivers by Edmonton.

1994–95

Aug. 3, 1994 – Defenseman Mike Ramsey signed as a free agent by Detroit.

Apr. 7, 1995 – Defenseman Greg Brown sold to Winnipeg.

1995–96

Aug. 2, 1995 – Left wing Jim McKenzie signed as a free agent by the New York Islanders.

Aug. 7, 1995 – Center Troy Murray signed as a free agent by Colorado.

Aug. 9, 1995 – Defenseman Peter Taglianetti signed as a free agent by Boston.

Aug. 31, 1995 – Defenseman Kjell Samuelsson signed as a free agent by Philadelphia.

Sept. 11, 1995 – Center John Cullen signed as a free agent by Tampa Bay.

Sept. 13, 1995 – Right wing Joe Mullen signed as a free agent by Boston.

Sept. 20, 1995 – Left wing Ladislav Karabin signed as a free agent by Buffalo.

Sept. 22, 1995 – Center Mike Hudson signed as a free agent by Toronto.

1996–97

July 18, 1996 – Center Kevin Miller signed as a free agent by Chicago.

July 29, 1996 – Center Dave McLlwain signed as a free agent by the New York Islanders.

Sept. 25, 1996 – Defenseman Greg Hawgood signed as a free agent by San Jose.

Oct. 4, 1996 – Center Kevin Todd claimed on waivers by Anaheim.

Feb. 26, 1997 – Right wing Petr Klima signed as a free agent by Edmonton.

1997–98

July 28, 1997 – Left wing Jeff Christian signed as a free agent by Phoenix.

Aug. 19, 1997 – Defenseman Peter Allen signed as a free agent by San Jose.

Sept. 30, 1997 – Defenseman Drake Berehowsky signed as a free agent by Edmonton.

Oct. 2, 1997 – Defenseman Craig Muni signed as a free agent by Dallas.

Jan. 9, 1998 – Left wing Peter Ferraro claimed on waivers by the New York Rangers.

1998–99

July 13, 1998 – Center Ron Francis signed as a free agent by Carolina.

Aug. 10, 1998 – Center Dominic Pittis signed as a free agent by Buffalo.

Aug. 13, 1998 – Center Chris Ferraro signed as a free agent by Edmonton.

Aug. 26, 1998 – Center Ed Olczyk signed as a free agent by Chicago.

Aug. 27, 1998 – Left wing Joe Dziedzic signed as a free agent by Phoenix.

Aug. 28, 1998 – Defenseman Fredrik Olausson signed as a free agent by Anaheim.

Sept. 29, 1998 – Center Andreas Johansson signed as a free agent by Ottawa.

Oct. 1998 – Left wing Alex Hicks signed as a free agent by San Jose.

Oct. 8, 1998 – Right wing Garry Valk signed as a free agent by Toronto.

Dec. 7, 1998 – Center Harry York claimed on waivers by Vancouver.

1999–00

July 9, 1999 – Center Len Barrie signed as a free agent by Los Angeles.

July 19, 1999 – Defenseman Greg Andrusak signed as a free agent by Toronto.

Aug. 10, 1999 – Defenseman Pat Neaton signed as a free agent by Utah (IHL).

Sept. 6, 1999 – Right wing Dan Kesa signed as a free agent by Tampa Bay.

Sept. 9, 1999 – Center Brian Bonin signed as a free agent by Vancouver.

Sept. 14, 1999 – Right wing Ed Patterson signed as a free agent by Grand Rapids (IHL).

Nov. 9, 1999 – Defenseman Bobby Dollas signed as a free agent by Ottawa.

Feb. 21, 2000 – Center Ryan Savoia signed as a free agent by HC Fribourg Gotteron (Switzerland).

2000–01

June 26, 2000 – Goaltender Philippe DeRouville signed as a free agent by Ayr Eagles (Britain).

July 2, 2000 – Defenseman Peter Popovic signed as a free agent by Boston.

Third Time's a Charm

Perhaps no single event shaped the Penguins' course in 2008–09—or contributed more greatly to the team's early season woes—than the defection of playoff hero Marian Hossa.

On the eve of free agency, the gifted winger stunned the club by spurning a lucrative long-term deal in favor of a one-year contract for less money with Detroit. When asked why he'd turned down a better offer from the Penguins, Hossa gave a simple yet surprising answer.

"When I compared the two teams," he said, "I felt like I would have a better chance to win the Cup in Detroit."

Although Hossa's reason for jumping ship was understandable if not admirable, it cut his former teammates to the bone.

"There's anger," Max Talbot said. "You can't forget about something like that because everybody in the organization… we expected him to come back. We thought he was comfortable here, and he was really good with Sid."

Paced by Hossa's 40 goals, the Red Wings cruised to another banner season, while the Penguins scrambled to qualify for the postseason. By the time the 2009 Stanley Cup Finals rolled around, however, the tables had turned.

Feeling added pressure to produce, Hossa failed to score during a hotly contested seven-game set against his ex-mates. Afterward it was revealed that he'd suffered a shoulder injury during the series.

"I tried to battle hard and couldn't get anything done offensively," he said.

While the Slovakian sniper languished, the unheralded Talbot popped in two goals in the series finale to help his team win the Cup.

And what about the postgame handshake? Were there any hard feelings?

"I just told him, 'Good job,'" Talbot said. "I think he knows he made the wrong choice, I don't have to tell him."

"It was his decision, a hard decision," Brooks Orpik added. "I've got nothing but respect for the guy. He was a great teammate. He's a really, really good person, too. He'll probably be a better person for it."

Hossa's story would have a happy ending. Following the Red Wings' ouster he signed a long-term deal with Chicago. In the spring of 2010 he became the first player in NHL history to appear in the Stanley Cup Finals three years in a row with three different teams. Buoyed by Hossa's superb two-way play, the Blackhawks ended a 49-year drought and captured the Stanley Cup.

July 4, 2000 – Goaltender Ron Tugnutt signed as a free agent by Columbus.

July 31, 2000 – Defenseman Dan Trebil signed as a free agent by the New York Islanders.

Aug. 25, 2000 – Right wing Pat Falloon signed as a free agent by HC Davos (Switzerland).

Oct. 3, 2000 – Goaltender Peter Skudra signed as a free agent by Boston.

Nov. 15, 2000 – Right wing Stephen Leach signed as a free agent by Louisville (AHL).

2001–02

May 31, 2001 – Left wing Kip Miller signed as a free agent by Grand Rapids (AHL).

June 16, 2001 – Center Rusty Fitzgerald signed as a free agent by Iserlohn (Germany).

July 1, 2001 – Goaltender Garth Snow signed as a free agent by the New York Islanders.

July 2, 2001 – Defenseman Bob Boughner signed as a free agent by Calgary.

July 12, 2001 – Goaltender Rich Parent signed as a free agent by Iserlohn (Germany).

Aug. 8, 2001 – Left wing Greg Crozier signed as a free agent by Boston.

Aug. 25, 2001 – Left wing Brad Lauer signed as a free agent by Sheffield (Britain).

Aug. 28, 2001 – Left wing Steve McKenna signed as a free agent by the New York Rangers.

Oct. 5, 2001 – Right wing Dennis Bonvie signed as a free agent by Boston.

Nov. 6, 2001 – Defenseman Marc Bergevin signed as a free agent by St. Louis.

2002–03

July 1, 2002 – Center Robert Lang signed as a free agent by Washington.

July 9, 2002 – Left wing Martin Sonnenberg signed as a free agent by Calgary.

July 11, 2002 – Center Jeff Toms signed as a free agent by Florida.

July 17, 2002 – Right wing Robert Dome signed as a free agent by Calgary.

Sept. 5, 2002 – Defenseman John Jakopin signed as a free agent by San Jose.

Nov. 15, 2002 – Left wing Vladimir Vujtek signed as a free agent by HC Vitkovice (Czech Republic).

Nov. 21, 2002 – Left wing Patrick LeBeau signed as a free agent by Frankfurt (Germany).

2003–04

July 14, 2003 – Defenseman Joel Bouchard signed as a free agent by Buffalo.

July 29, 2003 – Left wing Ville Nieminen signed as a free agent by Chicago.

Aug. 6, 2003 – Defenseman Micki DuPont signed as a free agent by Berlin (Germany).

Aug. 7, 2003 – Center Mathias Johansson signed as a free agent by Farjestad (Sweden).

Aug. 20, 2003 – Defenseman Richard Lintner signed as a free agent by Djurgarden (Sweden).

Sept. 10, 2003 – Defenseman Shawn Heins signed as a free agent by Atlanta.

Sept. 26, 2003 – Defenseman Hans Jonsson signed as a free agent by Modo (Sweden).

Sept. 30, 2003 – Center Alexandre Daigle signed as a free agent by Minnesota.

Nov. 1, 2003 – Defenseman Nolan Baumgartner claimed on waivers by Vancouver.

Nov. 18, 2003 – Defenseman Jamie Pushor signed as a free agent by Syracuse (AHL).

Nov. 21, 2003 – Center Kent Manderville signed as a free agent by Timra IK (Sweden).

2004–05

May 13, 2004 – Defenseman Patrick Boileau signed as a free agent by Lausanne (Switzerland).

May 19, 2004 – Center Michal Sivek signed as a free agent by Sparta Praha (Czech Republic).

June 23, 2004 – Right wing Landon Wilson signed as a free agent by Espoo (Finland).

July 14, 2004 – Right wing Eric Meloche signed as a free agent by Philadelphia.

July 30, 2004 – Center Toby Petersen signed as a free agent by Edmonton.

Sept. 2, 2004 – Left wing Jon Sim signed as a free agent by Phoenix.

Sept. 17, 2004 – Center Milan Kraft signed as a free agent by Plzen (Czech Republic).

Sept. 25, 2004 – Right wing Aleksey Morozov signed as a free agent by Kazan (Russia).

Oct. 2, 2004 – Defenseman Martin Strbak signed as a free agent by Kosice (Slovakia).

Oct. 26, 2004 – Left wing Steve McKenna signed as a free agent by Nottingham (Britain).

Mar. 13, 2005 – Left wing Reid Simpson signed as a free agent by Rockford (UHL).

2005–06

Aug. 1, 2005 – Right wing Tom Kostopoulos signed as a free agent by Los Angeles.

Aug. 8, 2005 – Left wing Ramzi Abid signed as a free agent by Atlanta.

Aug. 18, 2005 – Goaltender Jean-Sebastien Aubin signed as a free agent by Toronto. Right wing Matt Bradley signed as a free agent by Washington.

Aug. 26, 2005 – Defenseman Dan Focht signed as a free agent by Florida.

Aug. 29, 2005 – Defenseman Michal Rozsival signed as a free agent by the New York Rangers.

Jan. 20, 2006 – Center Lasse Pirjeta assigned to Kloten (Switzerland).

Jan. 31, 2006 – Right wing Rico Fata claimed on waivers by Atlanta.

Michel Ouellet signed with Tampa Bay following a 19-goal season in 2006–07.

2006–07

May 10, 2006 – Left wing Niklas Nordgren signed as a free agent by Rapperswil (Switzerland).

July 4, 2006 – Left wing Andy Hilbert signed as a free agent by the New York Islanders.

July 12, 2006 – Left wing Matt Murley signed as a free agent by Colorado.

July 13, 2006 – Center Matt Hussey signed as a free agent by Detroit.

July 17, 2006 – Center Shane Endicott signed as a free agent by Nashville.

July 30, 2006 – Defenseman Ross Lupaschuk signed as a free agent by Malmo (Sweden).

Aug. 8, 2006 – Goaltender Sebastien Caron signed as a free agent by Chicago.

Aug. 17, 2006 – Right wing Konstantin Koltsov signed as a free agent by Ufa (Russia).

Aug. 22, 2006 – Center Eric Boguniecki signed as a free agent by Columbus.

Sept. 26, 2006 – Right wing Ryan Vandenbussche signed as a free agent by Jokerit Helsinki (Finland).

Oct. 4, 2006 – Goaltender Dany Sabourin claimed on waivers by Vancouver.

Oct. 26, 2006 – Left wing Karl Stewart claimed on waivers by Chicago.

Dec. 2, 2006 – Right wing Andre Roy claimed on waivers by Tampa Bay.

Jan. 30, 2007 – Goaltender Andy Chiodo signed as a free agent by HPK Hameenlinna (Finland).

2007–08

July 1, 2007 – Right wing Michel Ouellet signed as a free agent by Tampa Bay.

July 3, 2007 – Defenseman Micki DuPont signed as a free agent by St. Louis.

July 5, 2007 – Goaltender Jocelyn Thibault signed as a free agent by Buffalo.

July 13, 2007 – Left wing Tomas Surovy signed as a free agent by Phoenix.

July 19, 2007 – Right wing Zigmund Palffy signed as a free agent by Skalica (Slovakia).

Aug. 12, 2007 – Left wing Nils Ekman signed as a free agent by Khimik Mytischi (Russia).

Aug. 30, 2007 – Defenseman Joel Kwiatkowski signed as a free agent by Atlanta.

Oct. 3, 2007 – Defenseman Joe Melichar signed as a free agent by Linkoping (Sweden).

Dec. 8, 2007 – Right wing Mark Recchi claimed on waivers by Atlanta.

2008–09

July 1, 2008 – Goaltender Ty Conklin signed as a free agent by Detroit. Right wing Adam Hall signed as a free agent by Tampa Bay.

July 2, 2008 – Right wing Marian Hossa signed as a free agent by Detroit. Right wing Jarkko Ruutu signed as a free agent by Ottawa.

July 3, 2008 – Right wing Georges Laraque signed as a free agent by Montreal.

July 14, 2008 – Center Nathan Smith signed as a free agent by Colorado.

Oct. 13, 2008 – Center Kris Beech signed as a free agent by HV71 Jonkoping (Sweden).

2009–10

July 1, 2009 – Goaltender Mathieu Garon signed as a free agent by Columbus. Defenseman Hal Gill signed as a free agent by Montreal.

July 2, 2009 – Defenseman Rob Scuderi signed as a free agent by Los Angeles.

July 6, 2009 – Center Jeff Taffe signed as a free agent by Florida.

July 13, 2009 – Center Chris Minard signed as a free agent by Edmonton.

Aug. 4, 2009 – Right wing Connor James signed as a free agent by Augsburger (Germany). Left wing Janne Pesonen signed as a free agent by Ak Bars Kazan (KHL).

Sept. 17, 2009 – Right wing Petr Sykora signed as a free agent by Minnesota.

Sep. 26, 2009 – Left wing Guillaume Lefebvre signed as a free agent by Boston.

Sept. 30, 2009 – Left wing Paul Bissonnette claimed on waivers by Phoenix.

Nov. 10, 2009 – Center Mike Zigomanis signed as a free agent by Djurgardens (Sweden).

Dec. 5, 2009 – Center Chris Bourque claimed on waivers by Washington.

Jan. 3, 2010 – Left wing Miroslav Satan signed as a free agent by Boston.

Jan. 20, 2010 – Right wing Bill Thomas signed as a free agent by HC Lugano (Switzerland).

2010–11

July 1, 2010 – Defenseman Sergei Gonchar signed as a free agent by Ottawa. Defenseman Dan Hamhuis signed as a free agent by Vancouver. Defenseman Jordan Leopold signed as a free agent by Buffalo.

July 2, 2010 – Defenseman Mark Eaton signed as a free agent by the New York Islanders.

July 27, 2010 – Left wing Alexei Ponikarovsky signed as a free agent by Los Angeles.

Aug. 20, 2010 – Right wing Arron Asham signed as a free agent.

Expansion Draft Selections

The NHL Expansion Draft was established as a way to stock expansion teams with big-league talent. The Penguins participated in the first Expansion Draft, which was held on June 6, 1967, in the ballroom of the Queen Elizabeth Hotel in Montreal. Subsequent drafts have been held with each new wave of expansion.

Under the rules of the draft, each expansion club is allowed to select a predetermined number of skaters and goaltenders from the established teams. If there is more than one expansion team during a given year, a lottery is held to determine draft order. The order is then reversed with each

Val Fonteyne was selected from Detroit in the 1967 Expansion Draft.

proceeding round. The league limits the number of players that can be selected from any particular team.

June 6, 1967 – Center Bob Dillabough and left wing Jeannot Gilbert selected from Boston. Left wings Billy Dea and Mel Pearson, goaltender Roy Edwards, and center Art Stratton selected from Chicago. Right wing Andy Bathgate, defenseman Leo Boivin, goaltender Joe Daley, and left wings Val Fonteyne and Ab McDonald selected from Detroit. Left wing Tom McCarthy, right wing Keith McCreary, defenseman Noel Price, and center Bob Rivard selected from Montreal. Defensemen Les Hunt and Al MacNeil, center Earl Ingarfield, and right wing Ken Schinkel selected from the New York Rangers. Left wing Larry Jeffery selected from Toronto.

June 10, 1970 – Defensemen Doug Barrie, Mike McMahon, and Tracy Pratt selected by Buffalo.

June 6, 1972 – Center Bob Leiter, right wing Keith McCreary, and left wing John Stewart selected by Atlanta.

June 12, 1974 – Left wing Robin Burns and right wing Ted Snell selected by Kansas City. Defenseman Yvon Labre selected by Washington.

June 13, 1979 – Left wing Wayne Bianchin and defensemen Colin Campbell and Tom Edur selected by Edmonton.

Defenseman Kim Clackson selected in the Reclaim Draft.

May 30, 1991 – Center Randy Gilhen selected by Minnesota.

June 18, 1992 – Defenseman Peter Taglianetti and goaltender Wendell Young selected by Tampa Bay.

June 24, 1993 – Defenseman Paul Laus selected by Florida. Left wing Troy Loney selected by Anaheim.

June 26, 1998 – Center Tony Hrkac selected by Nashville.

June 25, 1999 – Defenseman Maxim Galanov selected by Atlanta.

June 23, 2000 – Defenseman Jonas Junkka and center Tyler Wright selected by Columbus.

Intra-League (Waiver) Draft Transactions

The NHL Intra-League Draft was established as a means to ensure that talent would be spread evenly throughout the league.

The conditions of the draft were similar to the Expansion Draft. Each club was allowed to protect a predetermined number of skaters and goaltenders. Within certain guidelines, the unprotected players were eligible to be drafted by other clubs. Unlike the Expansion Draft, the Intra-League Draft did not call for a set number of rounds. The draft was completed when no claims were made during a particular round.

Due to the fact that so many amateur players were bound by sponsorship agreements, the Intra-League Draft was a useful tool for early expansion teams such as the Penguins to add additional talent. Over the years, however, participation in the draft dramatically decreased.

In 1977 the Intra-League Draft was renamed the Waiver Draft. The draft was discontinued in 2005 under the terms of the new collective bargaining agreement.

June 12, 1968 – Center Charlie Burns claimed from Oakland.

June 11, 1969 – Defenseman Bob Blackburn claimed from the New York Rangers. Left wing Dean Prentice claimed from Detroit. Left wing Glen Sather claimed from Boston. Goaltender Al Smith claimed from Toronto.

Center Charlie Burns claimed by Minnesota. Goaltender Marv Edwards claimed by Toronto. Defenseman Bill Speer claimed by Boston.

June 9, 1970 – Left wing Lowell MacDonald claimed from Los Angeles.

Right wing Craig Cameron claimed by Los Angeles. Goaltender Joe Daley claimed by Buffalo. Defenseman Jean-Guy Lagace claimed by Minnesota.

June 8, 1971 – Defenseman Dave Burrows claimed from Chicago. Defenseman Tim Horton claimed from the New York Rangers. Right wing Rene Robert claimed from Buffalo. Goaltender Jim Rutherford claimed from Detroit.

Goaltender Al Smith claimed by Detroit. Center Rod Zaine claimed by Buffalo.

June 5, 1972 – Defenseman Tim Horton claimed by Buffalo.

June 12, 1973 – Defenseman Ron Jones claimed from Boston.

June 10, 1974 – Center Jim Wiley claimed by Vancouver.

Oct. 4, 1982 – Left wing Doug Lecuyer claimed from Winnipeg.

Oct. 9, 1984 – Right wing Wayne Babych claimed from St. Louis. Right wing Bruce Crowder claimed from Boston.

Ex-Bruin Bruce Crowder arrived via the Waiver Draft in 1984.

Oct. 7, 1985 – Right wing Mike Blaisdell claimed from the New York Rangers. Right wing Dan Frawley claimed from Chicago. Right wing Willy Lindstrom claimed from Edmonton.

Oct. 5, 1987 – Left wing Charlie Simmer claimed from Boston.

Oct. 3, 1988 – Right wing Jay Caufield claimed from Minnesota. Defenseman Steve Dykstra and center Dave Hannan claimed from Edmonton.

Oct. 2, 1989 – Center Dave Hannan claimed by Toronto.

Oct. 1, 1990 – Defenseman Rod Buskas claimed by Los Angeles.

Jan. 18, 1995 – Center Mike Hudson claimed from the New York Rangers. Defenseman Chris Joseph claimed from Tampa Bay. Defenseman Francois Leroux claimed from Ottawa. Defenseman Wayne McBean claimed from Winnipeg.

Right wing Doug Brown claimed by Detroit.

Sept. 30, 1996 – Defenseman Corey Foster claimed by the New York Islanders. Defenseman Chris Joseph claimed by Vancouver.

Sept. 28, 1997 – Center Robert Lang claimed by Boston.

Oct. 5, 1998 – Defenseman Maxim Galanov claimed from the New York Rangers. Left wing Kip Miller claimed from the New York Islanders.

Oct. 4, 2002 – Defenseman Rick Berry claimed by Washington.

Oct. 3, 2003 – Defenseman Nolan Baumgartner claimed from Vancouver.

Inter-League and Reverse Draft Transactions

The NHL Inter-League Draft provided a way for teams to select a player who was under contract with another NHL club from that club's minor league affiliate. Conversely, the Reverse Draft allowed minor league teams to select unprotected players from NHL clubs. Like the Waiver Draft, the Inter-League and Reverse Drafts have been discontinued.

June 10, 1969 – Right wing Nick Harbaruk claimed from Vancouver (WHL).

June 12, 1969 – Defenseman Dunc McCallum claimed by Providence (AHL). Defenseman Noel Price claimed by Springfield (AHL).

June 10, 1971 – Right wing Andy Bathgate claimed by Providence (AHL).

June 13, 1973 – Center Rick Kessell claimed by Salt Lake City (WHL).

The WHA General Player Draft Selections

The World Hockey Association (WHA) General Player Draft was held over the course of two days, February 12 and 13, 1972, in Anaheim, California. The draft was established to provide an orderly process for the WHA teams to stock their rosters. Players from other professional leagues—most notably the National Hockey League—were eligible to be drafted.

The players were not under any legal obligation to sign with the drafting WHA club. However, after a player had been selected, the other WHA teams were prevented from negotiating with him.

Each Penguins player selected in the draft signed with his respective WHA team.

Feb. 12, 1972 – Right wing Yves Bergeron selected by Quebec. Goaltender Les Binkley selected by Ottawa. Center Wally Boyer selected by Winnipeg. Left wing Steve Cardwell selected by Ottawa. Goaltender Paul Hoganson selected by Los Angeles. Defenseman Dunc McCallum selected by Dayton-Houston. Center Garry Swain selected by Calgary-Cleveland.

Hard-checking Nick Harbaruk was claimed from Vancouver in the 1969 Inter-League Draft.

Amateur Draft Selections

The NHL Amateur Draft was created in 1963 by NHL president Clarence Campbell in an attempt to produce what he described as "a uniform opportunity for each team to acquire a star player."

Prior to the creation of the Amateur Draft, teams freely sponsored amateur teams and players, partly as a means to prevent other NHL clubs from acquiring their services. Amateur players were, for all intents and purposes, property of the NHL team that sponsored them.

The draft order was based on a reverse order of the standings. Initially, players under preexisting sponsorship agreements were not draft-eligible.

In 1969 the draft rules were amended to abolish all sponsorship agreements. Any amateur player under the age of 20, including non–North American players, was eligible for the draft.

June 7, 1967 – The Queen Elizabeth Hotel, Montreal, Quebec

Goaltender Steve Rexe from Belleville (OHA Sr. A), 1st round, 2nd pick overall.

Center Bob Smith from Sault Ste. Marie (NOJHL), 2nd round, 11th pick overall.

June 13, 1968 – The Queen Elizabeth Hotel, Montreal, Quebec

Center Garry Swain from Niagara Falls (OHA), 1st round, 4th pick overall.

Right wing Ron Snell from Regina (WCHL), 2nd round, 14th pick overall.

Defenseman Dave Simpson from Port Arthur (TBJHL), 3rd round, 21st pick overall.

June 12, 1969 – The Queen Elizabeth Hotel, Montreal, Quebec

Center Rick Kessell from Oshawa (OHA), 2nd round, 15th pick overall.

Center Michel Briere from Shawinigan (QMJHA), 3rd round, 26th pick overall.

Defenseman Yvon Labre from Toronto (OHA), 4th round, 38th pick overall.

Right wing Rusty Patenaude from Calgary (WCHL), 5th round, 50th pick overall.

Goaltender Paul Hoganson from Toronto (OHA), 6th round, 62nd pick overall.

June 11, 1970 – The Queen Elizabeth Hotel, Montreal, Quebec

Left wing Greg Polis from Estevan (WCHL), 1st round, 7th pick overall.

Left wing John Stewart from Flin Flon (WCHL), 2nd round, 21st pick overall.

Defenseman Larry Bignell from Edmonton (WCHL), 3rd round, 35th pick overall.

Left wing Connie Forey from Ottawa (OHA), 4th round, 49th pick overall.

Left wing Steve Cardwell from Oshawa (OHA), 5th round, 63rd pick overall.

Center Bob Fitchner from Brandon (WCHL), 6th round, 77th pick overall.

Defenseman Jim Pearson from St. Catharines (OHA), 7th round, 90th pick overall.

Goaltender Cam Newton from Kitchener (OHA), 8th round, 102nd pick overall.

Defenseman Ron Lemieux from Dauphin (MJHL), 9th round, 110th pick overall.

June 10, 1971 – The Queen Elizabeth Hotel, Montreal, Quebec

Left wing Brian McKenzie from St. Catharines (OHA), 2nd round, 18th pick overall.

Defenseman Joe Noris from Toronto (OHA), 3rd round, 32nd pick overall.

Left wing Gary Methe from Oshawa (OHA), 4th round, 46th pick overall.

Goaltender Dave Murphy from North Dakota (WCHA), 5th round, 60th pick overall.

Right wing Ian Williams from Notre Dame (WCHA), 6th round, 74th pick overall.

Defenseman Doug Elliot from Harvard (ECAC), 7th round, 88th pick overall.

June 8, 1972 – The Queen Elizabeth Hotel, Montreal, Quebec

Defenseman Jack Lynch from Oshawa (OHA), 2nd round, 24th pick overall.

Right wing Bernie Lukowich from New Westminster (WCHL), 2nd round, 30th pick overall.

Goaltender Denis Herron from Trois-Rivieres (QMJHL), 3rd round, 40th pick overall.

Center Ron Lalonde from Peterborough (OHA), 4th round, 56th pick overall.

Center Brian Walker from Calgary (WCHL), 5th round, 72nd pick overall.

Left wing Jeff Ablett from Medicine Hat (WCHL), 6th round, 88th pick overall.

Defenseman D'Arcy Keating from Notre Dame (WCHA), 7th round, 104th pick overall.

Right wing Yves Bergeron from Shawinigan (QMJHL), 8th round, 120th pick overall.

Left wing Jay Babcock from London (OHA), 9th round, 136th pick overall.

Goaltender Don Atchison from Saskatoon (WCHL), 10th round, 149th pick overall.

Jacques Cossette was a second-round pick in 1974.

May 15, 1973 – Mount Royal Hotel, Montreal, Quebec

Right wing Blaine Stoughton from Flin Flon (WCHL), 1st round, 7th pick overall.

Left wing Wayne Bianchin from Flin Flon (WCHL), 2nd round, 23rd pick overall.

Defenseman Colin Campbell from Peterborough (OHA), 2nd round, 27th pick overall.

Defenseman Dennis Owchar from Toronto (OHA), 4th round, 55th pick overall.

Defenseman Guido Tenesi from Oshawa (OHA), 5th round, 71st pick overall.

Left wing Don Seiling from Oshawa (OHA), 6th round, 87th pick overall.

Left wing Terry Ewasiuk from Victoria (WCHL), 7th round, 103rd pick overall.

Center Fred Comrie from Edmonton (WCHL), 8th round, 119th pick overall.

Defenseman Gord Lane from New Westminster (WCHL), 9th round, 134th pick overall.

Defenseman Randy Aimoe from Medicine Hat (WCHL), 10th round, 150th pick overall.

Center Don McLeod from Saskatoon (WCHL), 11th round, 164th pick overall.

May 28–30, 1974 – NHL Headquarters, Montreal, Quebec

Center Pierre Larouche from Sorel (QMJHL), 1st round, 8th pick overall.

Right wing Jacques Cossette from Sorel (QMJHL), 2nd round, 27th pick overall.

Defenseman Mario Faubert from St. Louis (CCHA), 4th round, 62nd pick overall.

Goaltender Bruce Aberhart from London (OMJHL), 5th round, 80th pick overall.

Left wing Buzz Schneider from Minnesota (WCHA), 6th round, 98th pick overall.

Left wing Robbie Laird from Regina (WCHL), 7th round, 116th pick overall.

Defenseman Larry Finck from St. Catharines (OMJHL), 8th round, 133rd pick overall.

Defenseman Jim Chicoyne from Brandon (WCHL), 9th round, 150th pick overall.

Right wing Rich Uhrich from Regina (WCHL), 10th round, 166th pick overall.

Right wing Serge Gamelin from Sorel (QMJHL), 11th round, 181st pick overall.

Defenseman Rich Perron from Quebec (QMJHL), 12th round, 195th pick overall.

Right wing Rick Hindmarch from Calgary (CWUAA), 13th round, 206th pick overall.

Defenseman Bill Davis from Colgate (ECAC), 14th round, 216th pick overall.

Defenseman J.D. Mathers from Northeastern (ECAC), 15th round, 223rd pick overall.

June 3, 1975 – NHL Headquarters, Montreal, Quebec

Goaltender Gord Laxton from New Westminster (WCHL), 1st round, 13th pick overall.

Defenseman Russ Anderson from Minnesota (WCHA), 2nd round, 31st pick overall.

Defenseman Paul Baxter from Winnipeg (WCHL), 3rd round, 49th pick overall.

Left wing Stu Younger from Michigan Tech (WCHA), 4th round, 67th pick overall.

Defenseman Kim Clackson from Victoria (WCHL), 5th round, 85th pick overall.

Left wing Peter Morris from Victoria (WCHL), 6th round, 103rd pick overall.

Slap Shot

During the early years the Penguins weren't known for their acuity at the draft table, especially in the later rounds. However, some of their lesser lights went on to gain notoriety.

Buzz Schneider, a sixth-round choice in 1974, earned lasting fame as a member of the 1980 "Miracle on Ice" U.S. Olympic team. Rugged rearguard Gord Lane, selected in the ninth round of the 1973 draft, won four Stanley Cups with the Islanders.

Perhaps the most famous under-the-radar pick was Guido Tenesi. The blond-haired blue-liner never played a game in the NHL. But he landed a key supporting role as narcissistic Charleston Chiefs defenseman Billy Charlesbois in the cult-classic movie *Slap Shot*.

Center Mike Will from Edmonton (WCHL), 7th round, 121st pick overall.

Defenseman Tapio Levo from Assat Pori (Finland), 8th round, 139th pick overall.

Left wing Byron Shutt from Bowling Green (CCHA), 9th round, 155th pick overall.

Goaltender Frank Salive from Peterborough (OMJHL), 10th round, 170th pick overall.

Defenseman John Glynne from Vermont (ECAC), 11th round, 185th pick overall.

Defenseman Lex Hudson from Denver (WCHA), 12th round, 196th pick overall.

Right wing Dan Tsubouchi from St. Louis (CCHA), 13th round, 202nd pick overall.

Left wing Brano Stankovsky from Fargo-Moorhead (MWJHL), 14th round, 206th pick overall.

Right wing Kelly Secord from New Westminster (WCHL), 18th round, 217th pick overall.

June 1, 1976 – NHL Headquarters, Montreal, Quebec

Right wing Blair Chapman from Saskatoon (WCHL), 1st round, 2nd pick overall.

Center Greg Malone from Oshawa (OMJHL), 2nd round, 19th pick overall.

Right wing Peter Marsh from Sherbrooke (QMJHL), 2nd round, 29th pick overall.

Left wing Morris Lukowich from Medicine Hat (WCHL), 3rd round, 47th pick overall.

Goaltender Greg Redquest from Oshawa (OMJHL), 4th round, 65th pick overall.

Defenseman Brendan Lowe from Sherbrooke (QMJHL), 5th round, 83rd pick overall.

Defenseman Vic Sirko from Oshawa (OMJHL), 6th round, 101st pick overall.

Perennial prospect Jim Hamilton served as the Penguins' entire farm system in the late 1970s.

The Other Mario

When hockey fans hear the name Mario, they automatically think of the Penguins' greatest star, Mario Lemieux. However, another player named Mario skated for the team in the pre-Lemieux era. He was a pretty good one, too.

In 1974 the Pens selected Mario Faubert in the fourth round of the Amateur Draft. A native of Valleyfield, Quebec, the right-handed-shooting defenseman was a fluid skater who displayed a flair for offense during his two seasons at St. Louis University. Faubert had a downside, however. Weighing barely 160 pounds, the lanky blue-liner was too light to be effective in the rough-and-tumble NHL.

For several seasons Faubert posted solid numbers while splitting time between the Penguins and the minors. Finally, by the 1980–81 campaign, he was ready for full-time duty. Now tipping the scales at a solid 185 pounds, Faubert enjoyed a terrific season. Manning the right point on the Pens' deadly power play, he tallied eight goals and 52 points. Remarkably, he developed into an excellent open-ice hitter, thanks to his skating and added bulk.

Faubert was poised to become a fixture on the Pens' blue line. However, on November, 18, 1981, he suffered a ghastly injury in a collision with the Blues' Mike Crombeen. Both the tibia and fibula bones in his leg were broken, bringing an abrupt and premature end to his promising career.

Mario Faubert

June 14, 1977 – NHL Headquarters, Montreal, Quebec

Right wing Jim Hamilton from London (OMJHL), 2nd round, 30th pick overall.

Center Kim Davis from Flin Flon (WCHL), 3rd round, 48th pick overall.

Center Mark Johnson from Wisconsin (WCHA), 4th round, 66th pick overall.

Goaltender Greg Millen from Peterborough (OMJHL), 6th round, 102nd pick overall.

June 15, 1978 – The Queen Elizabeth Hotel, Montreal, Quebec

Center Mike Meeker from Peterborough (OMJHL), 2nd round, 25th pick overall.

Left wing Shane Pearsall from Ottawa (OMJHL), 4th round, 61st pick overall.

Center Rob Garner from Toronto (OMJHL), 5th round, 75th pick overall.

Entry Draft Selections

In 1979 the NHL Amateur Draft became the NHL Entry Draft. The name was changed to reflect the eligibility of young players who had played professionally in the World Hockey Association, which had merged with the NHL. It also afforded NHL teams an opportunity to select non–North American players who were over the age of 20.

Aug. 9, 1979 – The Queen Elizabeth Hotel, Montreal, Quebec

Left wing Paul Marshall from Brantford (OMJHL), 2nd round, 31st pick overall.

Defenseman Bennett Wolf from Kitchener (OMJHL), 3rd round, 52nd pick overall.

Defenseman Brian Cross from Brantford (OMJHL), 4th round, 73rd pick overall.

Goaltender Nick Ricci from Niagara Falls (OMJHL), 5th round, 94th pick overall.

Defenseman Marc Chorney from North Dakota (WCHA), 6th round, 115th pick overall.

June 11, 1980 – Montreal Forum, Montreal, Quebec

Center Mike Bullard from Brantford (OMJHL), 1st round, 9th pick overall.

Defenseman Randy Boyd from Ottawa (OMJHL), 3rd round, 51st pick overall.

Defenseman Tony Feltrin from Victoria (WHL), 4th round, 72nd pick overall.

Center Doug Shedden from Sault Ste. Marie (OMJHL), 5th round, 93rd pick overall.

Left wing Pat Graham from Niagara Falls (OMJHL), 6th round, 114th pick overall.

Center Bob Geale from Portland (WHL), 8th round, 156th pick overall.

Defenseman Brian Lundberg from Michigan (WCHA), 9th round, 177th pick overall.

Defenseman Steve McKenzie from St. Albert (AJHL), 10th round, 198th pick overall.

June 10, 1981 – Montreal Forum, Montreal, Quebec

Right wing Steve Gatzos from Sault Ste. Marie (OMJHL), 2nd round, 28th pick overall.

Defenseman Tom Thornbury from Niagara Falls (OMJHL), 3rd round, 49th pick overall.

Defenseman Norm Schmidt from Oshawa (OMJHL), 4th round, 70th pick overall.

Defenseman Paul Edwards from Oshawa (OMJHL), 6th round, 109th pick overall.

Defenseman Rod Buskas from Medicine Hat (WHL), 6th round, 112th pick overall.

Right wing Geoff Wilson from Winnipeg (WHL), 7th round, 133rd pick overall.

Center Mitch Lamoureux from Oshawa (OMJHL), 8th round, 154th pick overall.

Left wing Dean DeFazio from Brantford (OMJHL), 9th round, 175th pick overall.

Center Dave Hannan from Brantford (OMJHL), 10th round, 196th pick overall.

June 9, 1982 – Montreal Forum, Montreal, Quebec

Right wing Rich Sutter from Lethbridge (WHL), 1st round, 10th pick overall.

Randy Boyd was the OHL's top defenseman in 1980–81.

Left wing Tim Hyrnewich from Sudbury (OHL), 2nd round, 38th pick overall.

Left wing Troy Loney from Lethbridge (WHL), 3rd round, 52nd pick overall.

Center Grant Sasser from Portland (WHL), 5th round, 94th pick overall.

Defenseman Grant Couture from Lethbridge (WHL), 7th round, 136th pick overall.

Left wing Peter Derksen from Portland (WHL), 8th round, 157th pick overall.

Center Greg Gravel from Windsor (OHL), 9th round, 178th pick overall.

Defenseman Stu Wenaas from Winnipeg (WHL), 10th round, 199th pick overall.

Right wing Chris McCauley from London (OHL), 11th round, 220th pick overall.

Goaltender Stan Bautch from Hibbing H.S. (Minn.), 12th round, 241st pick overall.

June 8, 1983 – Montreal Forum, Montreal, Quebec

Left wing Bob Errey from Peterborough (OHL), 1st round, 15th pick overall.

Defenseman Todd Charlesworth from Oshawa (OHL), 2nd round, 22nd pick overall.

Defenseman Mike Rowe from Toronto (OHL), 3rd round, 59th pick overall.

Goaltender Frank Pietrangelo from Minnesota (WCHA), 4th round, 64th pick overall.

Center Pat Emond from Hull (QMJHL), 6th round, 106th pick overall.

Defenseman Paul Ames from Billerica H.S. (Mass.), 7th round, 127th pick overall.

Right wing Marty Ketola from Cloquet H.S. (Minn.), 9th round, 169th pick overall.

Right wing Alec Haidy from Sault Ste. Marie (OHL), 10th round, 190th pick overall.

Left wing Garth Hildebrand from Calgary (WHL), 11th round, 211th pick overall.

Defenseman Dave Goertz from Regina (WHL), 12th round, 232nd pick overall.

June 9, 1984 – Montreal Forum, Montreal, Quebec

Center Mario Lemieux from Laval (QMJHL), 1st round, 1st pick overall.

Defenseman Doug Bodger from Kamloops (WHL), 1st round, 9th pick overall.

Center Roger Belanger from Kingston (OHL), 1st round, 16th pick overall.

Right wing Mark Teevens from Peterborough (OHL), 4th round, 64th pick overall.

Right wing Arto Javanainen from Assat (Finland), 5th round, 85th pick overall.

Defenseman Tom Ryan from Newton North H.S. (Mass.), 7th round, 127th pick overall.

Left wing John Del Col from Toronto (OHL), 9th round, 169th pick overall.

Right wing Steve Hurt from Hill-Murray H.S. (Minn.), 10th round, 189th pick overall.

Center Jim Steen from Moorhead Senior School (Minn.), 11th round, 210th pick overall.

Center Mark Ziliotto from Streetsville (Ont. Jr. B), 12th round, 230th pick overall.

June 15, 1985 – Metro Toronto Convention Centre, Toronto, Ontario

Center Craig Simpson from Michigan State (CCHA), 1st round, 2nd pick overall.

Right wing Lee Giffin from Oshawa (OHL), 2nd round, 23rd pick overall.

Goaltender Bruce Racine from Northeastern (Hockey East), 3rd round, 58th pick overall.

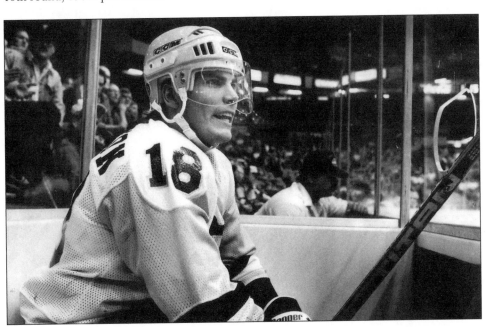

Top pick Craig Simpson cools his heels in the penalty box.

Center Steve Gotaas from Prince Albert (WHL), 5th round, 86th pick overall.

Left wing Kevin Clemens from Regina (WHL), 6th round, 107th pick overall.

Defenseman Stuart-Lee Marston from Longueuil (QMJHL), 6th round, 114th pick overall.

Goaltender Steve Titus from Cornwall (OHL), 7th round, 128th pick overall.

Defenseman Paul Stanton from Catholic Memorial H.S. (Mass.), 8th round, 149th pick overall.

Defenseman Jim Paek from Oshawa (OHL), 9th round, 170th pick overall.

Defenseman Steve Shaunessy from Reading H.S. (Mass.), 10th round, 191st pick overall.

Defenseman Doug Greschuk from St. Albert (AJHL), 11th round, 212th pick overall.

Left wing Gregory Choules from Chicoutimi (QMJHL), 12th round, 233rd pick overall.

June 21, 1986 – Montreal Forum, Montreal, Quebec

Defenseman Zarley Zalapski from Canada (Nat. Team), 1st round, 4th pick overall.

Left wing Dave Capuano from Mt. St. Charles Academy (R.I.), 2nd round, 25th pick overall.

Left wing Brad Aitken from Sault Ste. Marie (OHL), 3rd round, 46th pick overall.

Center Rob Brown from Kamloops (WHL), 4th round, 67th pick overall.

Right wing Sandy Smith from Brainerd H.S. (Minn.), 5th round, 88th pick overall.

Left wing Jeff Daniels from Oshawa (OHL), 6th round, 109th pick overall.

Defenseman Doug Hobson from Prince Albert (WHL), 7th round, 130th pick overall.

Left wing Steve Rohlik from Hill-Murray H.S. (Minn.), 8th round, 151st pick overall.

Center Dave McLlwain from North Bay (OHL), 9th round, 172nd pick overall.

Center Kelly Cain from London (OHL), 10th round, 193rd pick overall.

Right wing Stan Drulia from Belleville (OHL), 11th round, 214th pick overall.

Defenseman Rob Wilson from Sudbury (OHL), 12th round, 235th pick overall.

June 13, 1987 – Joe Louis Arena, Detroit, Michigan

Defenseman Chris Joseph from Seattle (WHL), 1st round, 5th pick overall.

Goaltender Rick Tabaracci from Cornwall (OHL), 2nd round, 26th pick overall.

Right wing Jamie Leach from Hamilton (OHL), 3rd round, 47th pick overall.

Left wing Risto Kurkinen from JyP HT Jyvaskyla (Finland), 4th round, 68th pick overall.

Defenseman Jeff Waver from Hamilton (OHL), 5th round, 89th pick overall.

Left wing Shawn McEachern from Matignon H.S. (Mass.), 6th round, 110th pick overall.

Center Jim Bodden from Chatham (SOJHL), 7th round, 131st pick overall.

Center Jiri Kucera from Dukla Jihlava (Czech.), 8th round, 152nd pick overall.

Right wing John MacDougall from New Prep School (Mass.), 9th round, 173rd pick overall.

Right wing Daryn McBride from Denver (WCHA), 10th round, 194th pick overall.

Mark Carlson from Philadelphia Jrs. (Pa.), 11th round, 215th pick overall.

Goaltender Ake Lilljebjorn from Brynas IF Gavle (SEL), 12th round, 236th pick overall.

June 11, 1988 – Montreal Forum, Montreal, Quebec

Left wing Darrin Shannon from Windsor (OHL), 1st round, 4th pick overall.

Left wing Mark Major from North Bay (OHL), 2nd round, 25th pick overall.

Left wing Daniel Gauthier from Victoriaville (QMJHL), 3rd round, 62nd pick overall

Right wing Mark Recchi from Kamloops (WHL), 4th round, 67th pick overall.

Defenseman Greg Andrusak from Minnesota-Duluth (WCHA), 5th round, 88th pick overall.

Left wing Troy Mick from Portland (WHL), 7th round, 130th pick overall.

Left wing Jeff Blaeser from St. John's Prep (Mass.), 8th round, 151st pick overall.

Right wing Rob Gaudreau from Bishop Hendricken H.S. (R.I.), 9th round, 172nd pick overall.

Defenseman Don Pancoe from Hamilton (OHL), 10th round, 193rd pick overall.

Left wing Cory Laylin from St. Cloud Apollo (Minn.), 11th round, 214th pick overall.

Defenseman Darren Stolk from Lethbridge (WHL), 12th round, 235th pick overall.

June 17, 1989 – Metropolitan Sports Center, Bloomington, Minnesota

Defenseman Jamie Heward from Regina (WHL), 1st round, 16th pick overall.

Defenseman Paul Laus from Niagara Falls (OHL), 2nd round, 37th pick overall.

Right wing John Brill from Grand Rapids (USS), 3rd round, 58th pick overall.

Defenseman Todd Nelson from Prince Albert (WHL), 4th round, 79th pick overall.

Center Tom Nevers from Edina (USS), 5th round, 100th pick overall.

Cold War

From the day the Penguins drafted Evgeni Malkin in 2004, they hoped to bring him to Pittsburgh. But prying the gifted young center loose from his Russian team proved to be a prickly proposition. With no agreement in place with the International Ice Hockey Federation for the transfer of players, Malkin's team—Metallurg Magnitogorsk—was demanding cash, and lots of it.

Still, the Penguins were confident that they could ink Malkin to a deal when his contract expired in the summer of 2006.

What followed was a development laced with all the intrigue of a Cold War spy novel. In early August the Penguins were shocked to learn that their prized prospect had signed a new contract with Magnitogorsk. Days later the situation escalated when Malkin fled his team's training facility in Finland, bound for North America.

A week later Malkin surfaced in Los Angeles. He explained that he had not intended to sign with Magnitogorsk, but that club officials had come to his home. In a "bargaining" session that would have done the KGB proud, they coerced him into signing.

"I was pressured very hard. I kept asking them, 'Why aren't you keeping your promise to let me play in America?' They did not want to listen. They just kept on with their arguments," Malkin said.

Evgeni Malkin

One future teammate was clearly impressed with Malkin's fortitude and determination.

"It showed a lot of guts for him to go through that and come over here," Sidney Crosby said. "I'm just looking forward to having him here and making him feel as comfortable as possible."

"Geno" would not disappoint. Although he spoke little English, Malkin bolted from the starting blocks with seven goals in his first six games—a scorching pace unmatched by any rookie since the days of Hall of Famers Cy Denneny, Newsy Lalonde, and Joe Malone.

Defenseman Mike Markovich from Denver (WCHA), 6th round, 121st pick overall.

Right wing Mike Needham from Kamloops (WHL), 6th round, 126th pick overall.

Defenseman Pat Schafhauser from Hill-Murray H.S. (Minn.), 7th round, 142nd pick overall.

Center Dave Shute from Victoria (WHL), 8th round, 163rd pick overall.

Defenseman Andrew Wolf from Victoria (WHL), 9th round, 184th pick overall.

Right wing Greg Hagen from Hill-Murray H.S. (Minn.), 10th round, 205th pick overall.

Defenseman Scott Farrell from Spokane (WHL), 11th round, 235th pick overall.

Center Jason Smart from Saskatoon (WHL), 12th round, 247th pick overall.

June 16, 1990 – BC Place Stadium, Vancouver, British Columbia

Right wing Jaromir Jagr from HC Kladno (Czech.), 1st round, 5th pick overall.

Left wing Joe Dziedzic from Edison H.S. (USHS-MN), 3rd round, 61st pick overall.

Defenseman Chris Tamer from Michigan (CCHA), 4th round, 68th pick overall.

Center Brian Farrell from Avon Old Farms (USHS-CT), 5th round, 89th pick overall.

Defenseman Ian Moran from Belmont H.S. (USHS-MN), 6th round, 107th pick overall.

Goaltender Denis Casey from Colorado College (WCHA), 6th round, 110th pick overall.

Center Mika Valila from Tappara (SM-Liiga), 7th round, 130th pick overall.

Defenseman Ken Plaquin from Michigan Tech (WCHA), 7th round, 131st pick overall.

Defenseman Pat Neaton from Michigan (CCHA), 7th round, 145th pick overall.

Center Petteri Koskimaki from Boston Univ. (Hockey East), 8th round, 152nd pick overall.

Left wing Ladislav Karabin from HC Slovan Bratislava (Czech.), 9th round, 173rd pick overall.

Left wing Tim Fingerhut from Canterbury H.S. (Conn.), 10th round, 194th pick overall.

Right wing Michael Thompson from Michigan State (CCHA), 11th round, 215th pick overall.

Defenseman Brian Bruininks from Colorado College (WCHA), 12th round, 236th pick overall.

June 22, 1991 – Memorial Auditorium, Buffalo, New York

Left wing Markus Naslund from Modo Hockey (Elitserien), 1st round, 16th pick overall.

Center Rusty Fitzgerald from Duluth-East H.S. (Minn.), 2nd round, 38th pick overall.

Defenseman Shane Peacock from Lethbridge (WHL), 3rd round, 60th pick overall.

Center Joe Tamminen from Virginia H.S. (Minn.), 4th round, 82nd pick overall.

Defenseman Rob Melanson from Hull (QMJHL), 5th round, 104th pick overall.

Center Brian Clifford from Nichols Academy (Mass.), 6th round, 126th pick overall.

Right wing Ed Patterson from Kamloops (WHL), 7th round, 148th pick overall.

Left wing Peter McLaughlin from Belmont Hill Prep. (Mass.), 8th round, 170th pick overall.

Goaltender Jeff Lembke from Omaha (USHL), 9th round, 192nd pick overall.

Defenseman Chris Tok from Greenway H.S. (Minn.), 10th round, 214th pick overall.

Defenseman Paul Dyck from Moose Jaw (WHL), 11th round, 236th pick overall.

Defenseman Pasi Huura from Ilves (Finland), 12th round, 258th pick overall.

June 20, 1992 – Montreal Forum, Montreal, Quebec

Center Martin Straka from Skoda Plzen (Czech), 1st round, 19th pick overall.

Defenseman Marc Hussey from Moose Jaw (WHL), 2nd round, 43rd pick overall.

Defenseman Travis Thiessen from Moose Jaw (WHL), 3rd round, 67th pick overall.

Defenseman Todd Klassen from Tri-Cities (WHL), 4th round, 91st pick overall.

Goaltender Philippe DeRouville from Verdun College Francais (QMJHL), 5th round, 115th pick overall.

Defenseman Artem Kopot from Traktor Chelyabinsk (Russia), 6th round, 139th pick overall.

Center Jan Alinc from Litvinov (Czech), 7th round, 163rd pick overall.

Center Fran Bussey from Duluth-East H.S. (Minn.), 8th round, 187th pick overall.

Center Brian Bonin from White Bear Lake H.S. (Minn.), 9th round, 211th pick overall.

Left wing Brian Callahan from Belmont Hill Prep. (Mass.), 10th round, 235th pick overall.

June 26, 1993 – Colisee de Quebec, Quebec City, Quebec

Defenseman Stefan Bergkvist from Leksands IF (Sweden), 1st round, 26th pick overall.

Center Dominic Pittis from Lethbridge (WHL), 2nd round, 52nd pick overall.

Left wing Dave Roche from Peterborough (OHL), 3rd round, 62nd pick overall.

Defenseman Jonas Junkka from Kiruna (Sweden), 4th round, 104th pick overall.

Defenseman Chris Kelleher from St. Sebastian's H.S. (Mass.), 5th round, 130th pick overall.

Goaltender Patrick Lalime from Shawinigan (QMJHL), 6th round, 156th pick overall.

Left wing Sean Selmser from Red Deer (WHL), 7th round, 182nd pick overall.

Center Larry McMorran from Seattle (WHL), 8th round, 208th pick overall.

Center Tim Harberts from Wayzata H.S. (Minn.), 9th round, 234th pick overall.

Center Leonid Toropchenko from Springfield (AHL), 10th round, 260th pick overall.

Defenseman Hans Jonsson from Modo (Sweden), 11th round, 286th pick overall.

June 28, 1994 – Hartford Civic Center, Hartford, Connecticut

Center Chris Wells from Seattle (WHL), 1st round, 24th pick overall.

Center Richard Park from Belleville (OHL), 2nd round, 50th pick overall.

Defenseman Sven Butenschon from Brandon (WHL), 3rd round, 57th pick overall.

Left wing Greg Crozier from Lawrence Academy (Mass.), 3rd round, 73rd pick overall.

Defenseman Alexei Krivchenkov from CSKA Moscow (Russia), 3rd round, 76th pick overall.

Defenseman Tom O'Connor from Springfield (NEJHL), 4th round, 102nd pick overall.

Left wing Clint Johnson from Duluth-East H.S. (Minn.), 5th round, 128th pick overall.

Center Valentin Morozov from CSKA Moscow (Russia), 6th round, 154th pick overall.

Center Serge Aubin from Granby (QMJHL), 7th round, 161st pick overall.

Defenseman Drew Palmer from Seattle (WHL), 7th round, 180th pick overall.

Center Boris Zelenko from CSKA Moscow (Russia), 8th round, 206th pick overall.

Defenseman Jason Godbout from Hill-Murray H.S. (Minn.), 9th round, 232nd pick overall.

Left wing Mikhail Kazakevich from Yaroslavl (Russia), 10th round, 258th pick overall.

Goaltender Brian Leitza from Sioux City (USHL), 11th round, 284th pick overall.

June 28, 1995 – Edmonton Coliseum, Edmonton, Alberta

Right wing Alexei Morozov from Krylja Sovetov (Russia), 1st round, 24th pick overall.

Goaltender Jean-Sebastien Aubin from Sherbrooke (QMJHL), 3rd round, 76th pick overall.

Center Oleg Belov from CSKA Moscow (Russia), 4th round, 102nd pick overall.

Center Jan Hrdina from Seattle (WHL), 5th round, 128th pick overall.

Center Alexei Kolkunov from Krylja Sovetov (Russia), 6th round, 154th pick overall.

Right wing Derrick Pyke from Hailfax (QMJHL), 7th round, 180th pick overall.

Defenseman Sergei Voronov from Dynamo Moscow (Russia), 8th round, 206th pick overall.

Goaltender Frank Ivankovic from Oshawa (OHL), 9th round, 232nd pick overall.

June 22, 1996 – Kiel Center, St. Louis, Missouri

Goaltender Craig Hillier from Ottawa (OHL), 1st round, 23rd pick overall.

Defenseman Pavel Skrbek from HC Kladno (Czech Extraliga), 2nd round, 28th pick overall.

Left wing Boyd Kane from Regina (WHL), 3rd round, 72nd pick overall.

Right wing Boris Protsenko from Calgary (WHL), 3rd round, 77th pick overall.

Defenseman Michal Rozsival from Dukla Jihlava (Czech), 4th round, 105th pick overall.

Center Peter Bergman from Kamloops (WHL), 6th round, 150th pick overall.

Right wing Eric Meloche from Cornwall (OCJHL), 7th round, 186th pick overall.

Center Timo Seikkula from Junkkarit (Finland), 9th round, 238th pick overall.

June 21, 1997 – Civic Arena, Pittsburgh, Pennsylvania

Right wing Robert Dome from Las Vegas (IHL), 1st round, 17th pick overall.

Center Brian Gaffaney from North Iowa (USHL), 2nd round, 44th pick overall.

Defenseman Joe Melichar from HC Ceske Budejovice (Czech Extraliga), 3rd round, 71st pick overall.

Center Alexandre Mathieu from Hailfax (QMJHL), 4th round, 97th pick overall.

Defenseman Harlan Pratt from Prince Albert (WHL), 5th round, 124th pick overall.

Left wing Petr Havelka from HC Sparta Praha (Czech Extraliga), 6th round, 152nd pick overall.

Defenseman Mark Moore from Harvard (ECAC), 7th round, 179th pick overall.

Defenseman Andrew Ference from Portland (WHL), 8th round, 208th pick overall.

Defenseman Eric Lind from Avon Old Farms (US Boarding School), 9th round, 234th pick overall.

June 27, 1998 – Marine Midland Arena, Buffalo, New York

Center Milan Kraft from Keramika Plzen (Czech Extraliga), 1st round, 23rd pick overall.

Left wing Alexander Zevakhin from CSKA Moscow (Russia), 2nd round, 54th pick overall.

Center David Cameron from Prince Albert (WHL), 3rd round, 80th pick overall.

Goaltender Scott Myers from Prince George (WHL), 4th round, 110th pick overall.

A first-round choice in 1997, Robert Dome had a hard time adjusting to the NHL.

Defenseman Rob Scuderi from Boston College (Hockey East), 5th round, 134th pick overall.

Center Jan Fadrny from Slavia Jr. (Czech), 6th round, 169th pick overall.

Center Joel Scherban from London (OHL), 7th round, 196th pick overall.

Goaltender Mika Lehto from Assat Jr. (Finland), 8th round, 224th pick overall.

Center Toby Petersen from Colorado College (WCHA), 9th round, 244th pick overall.

Center Matt Hussey from Avon Old Farms (US Boarding School), 9th round, 254th pick overall.

June 26, 1999 – Fleet Center, Boston, Massachusetts

Left wing Konstantin Koltzov from Severstal Cherepovets (Russia), 1st round, 18th pick overall.

Left wing Matt Murley from Rensselaer Polytechnic Institute (ECAC), 2nd round, 51st pick overall.

Defenseman Jeremy Van Hoof from Ottawa (OHL), 2nd round, 57th pick overall.

Goaltender Sebastien Caron from Rimouski (QMJHL), 3rd round, 86th pick overall.

Center Ryan Malone from Omaha (USHL), 4th round, 115th pick overall.

Center Tomas Skvaridlo from Zvolen Jr. (Slovakia), 5th round, 144th pick overall.

Defenseman Vladimir Malenkykh from Tolyatti (Russia), 5th round, 157th pick overall.

Left wing Doug Meyer from Minnesota (WCHA), 6th round, 176th pick overall.

Right wing Tom Kostopoulos from London (OHL), 7th round, 204th pick overall.

Defenseman Darcy Robinson from Saskatoon (WHL), 8th round, 233rd pick overall.

Left wing Andrew McPherson from Rensselaer Polytechnic Institute (ECAC), 9th round, 261st pick overall.

June 24–25, 2000 – Canadian Airlines Saddledome, Calgary, Alberta

Defenseman Brooks Orpik from Boston College (Hockey East), 1st round, 18th pick overall.

Center Shane Endicott from Seattle (WHL), 2nd round, 52nd pick overall.

Goaltender Peter Hamerlik from HK 36 Skalica (Slovakia), 3rd round, 84th pick overall.

Right wing Michel Ouellet from Rimouski (QMJHL), 4th round, 124th pick overall.

Defenseman David Koci from Sparta Praha Jr. (Czech), 5th round, 146th pick overall.

Left wing Patrick Foley from New Hampshire (Hockey East), 6th round, 185th pick overall.

Left wing Jim Abbott from New Hampshire (Hockey East), 7th round, 216th pick overall.

Right wing Steve Crampton from Moose Jaw (WHL), 8th round, 248th pick overall.

Center Roman Simicek from HPK (SM Liiga), 9th round, 273rd pick overall.

Goaltender Nick Boucher from Dartmouth (Hockey East), 9th round, 280th pick overall.

June 23–24, 2001 – National Car Rental Center, Sunrise, Florida

Right wing Colby Armstrong from Red Deer (WHL), 1st round, 21st pick overall.

Defenseman Noah Welch from St. Sebastian's H.S. (Mass.), 2nd round, 54th pick overall.

Defenseman Drew Fata from St. Michael's (OHL), 3rd round, 86th pick overall.

Defenseman Alexandre Rouleau from Val D'Or (QMJHL), 3rd round, 96th pick overall.

Left wing Tomas Surovy from Poprad (Slovakia), 4th round, 120th pick overall.

Center Ben Eaves from Boston College (Hockey East), 4th round, 131st pick overall.

Defenseman Andy Schneider from Lincoln (USHL), 5th round, 156th pick overall.

Goaltender Tomas Duba from HC Sparta Praha (Czech), 7th round, 217th pick overall.

Rangy Milan Kraft scored 19 goals for the Pens in 2003–04.

Goaltender Brandon Crawford-West from Texas (NAHL), 8th round, 250th pick overall.

June 22–23, 2002 – Air Canada Centre, Toronto, Ontario

Defenseman Ryan Whitney from Boston University (Hockey East), 1st round, 5th pick overall.

Defenseman Ondrej Nemec from Vsetin HC (Czech), 2nd round, 35th pick overall.

Center Erik Christensen from Kamloops (WHL), 3rd round, 69th pick overall.

Defenseman Daniel Fernholm from Djurgarden Jr. (Sweden), 4th round, 101st pick overall.

Left wing Andy Sertich from Greenway H.S. (Minn.), 5th round, 136th pick overall.

Center Cam Paddock from Kelowna (WHL), 5th round, 137th pick overall.

Goaltender Robert Goepfert from Cedar Rapids (USHL), 6th round, 171st pick overall.

Goaltender Patrik Bartschi from Kloten (Swiss), 7th round, 202nd pick overall.

Center Maxime Talbot from Hull (QMJHL), 8th round, 234th pick overall.

Defenseman Ryan Lannon from Harvard (ECAC), 8th round, 239th pick overall.

Goaltender Dwight Labrosse from Guelph (OHL), 9th round, 265th pick overall.

June 21–22, 2003 – Gaylord Entertainment Center, Nashville, Tennessee

Goaltender Marc-Andre Fleury from Cape Breton (QMJHL), 1st round, 1st pick overall.

Center Ryan Stone from Brandon (WHL), 2nd round, 32nd pick overall.

Right wing Jonathan Filewich from Prince George (WHL), 3rd round, 70th pick overall.

Left wing Daniel Carcillo from Sarnia (OHL), 3rd round, 73rd pick overall.

Defenseman Paul Bissonnette from Saginaw (OHL), 4th round, 121st pick overall.

Left wing Evgeni Isakov from Severstal Cherepovets (Russia), 5th round, 161st pick overall.

Defenseman Lucas Bolf from HC Sparta Praha (Czech), 6th round, 169th pick overall.

Goaltender Andy Chiodo from St. Michael's (OHL), 7th round, 199th pick overall.

Center Stephen Dixon from Cape Breton (QMJHL), 7th round, 229th pick overall.

Right wing Joe Jensen from St. Cloud State (WCHA), 8th round, 232nd pick overall.

Left wing Matt Moulson from Cornell (ECAC), 9th round, 263rd pick overall.

June 26–27, 2004 – RBC Center, Raleigh, North Carolina

Center Evgeni Malkin from Magnitogorsk (Russia), 1st round, 2nd pick overall.

Left wing Johannes Salmonsson from Djurgardens IF (Elitserien), 2nd round, 32nd pick overall.

Defenseman Alex Goligoski from Sioux Falls (USHL), 2nd round, 61st pick overall.

Right wing Nick Johnson from St. Albert (AJHL), 3rd round, 67th pick overall.

Center Brian Gifford from Moorhead Senior School (Minn.), 3rd round, 85th pick overall.

Center Tyler Kennedy from Sault Ste. Marie (OHL), 4th round, 99th pick overall.

Defenseman Michael Sersen from Rimouski (QMJHL), 5th round, 130th pick overall.

Right wing Moises Gutierrez from Kamloops (WHL), 6th round, 164th pick overall.

Defenseman Chris Peluso from Brainerd H.S. (Minn.), 7th round, 194th pick overall.

Defenseman Jordan Morrison from Peterborough (OHL), 7th round, 222nd pick overall.

Goaltender David Brown from Notre Dame (WCHA), 8th round, 228th pick overall.

Center Brian Ihnacak from Brown (ECAC), 9th round, 259th pick overall.

July 30–31, 2005 – Sheraton Hotel and Towers, Ottawa, Ontario

Center Sidney Crosby from Rimouski (QMJHL), 1st round, 1st pick overall.

Defenseman Michael Gergen from Shattuck St. Mary's H.S. (Minn.), 2nd round, 61st pick overall.

Defenseman Kris Letang from Val D'Or (QMJHL), 3rd round, 62nd pick overall.

Defenseman Tommi Leinonen from Karpat (Finland), 4th round, 125th pick overall.

Right wing Tim Crowder from South Surrey (BCHL), 5th round, 126th pick overall.

Defenseman Jean-Philippe Paquet from Shawinigan (QMJHL), 6th round, 194th pick overall.

Center Joe Vitale from Sioux Falls (USHL), 7th round, 195th pick overall.

June 24–25, 2006 – General Motors Place, Vancouver, British Columbia

Center Jordan Staal from Peterborough (OHL), 1st round, 2nd pick overall.

Defenseman Carl Sneep from Brainerd H.S. (Minn.), 2nd round, 32nd pick overall.

Defenseman Brian Strait from US National Team Development Program (NAHL), 3rd round, 65th pick overall.

Homegrown Ryan Malone was the first Pittsburgh native to be drafted by the Pens.

Goaltender Chad Johnson from Alaska Fairbanks (CCHA), 5th round, 125th pick overall.

Defenseman Timo Seppanen from HIFK (SM-Liiga), 7th round, 195th pick overall.

June 22–23, 2007 – Nationwide Arena, Columbus, Ohio

Center Angelo Esposito from Quebec (QMJHL), 1st round, 20th pick overall.

Center Keven Veilleux from Victoriaville (QMJHL), 2nd round, 51st pick overall.

Defenseman Robert Bortuzzo from Kitchener (OHL), 3rd round, 78th pick overall.

Center Casey Pierro-Zabotel from Merritt (BCHL), 3rd round, 80th pick overall.

Left wing Luca Caputi from Mississauga (OHL), 4th round, 111th pick overall.

Defenseman Alex Grant from St. John (QMJHL), 4th round, 118th pick overall.

Defenseman Jake Muzzin from Sault Ste. Marie (OHL), 5th round, 141st pick overall.

Center Dustin Jeffrey from Sault Ste. Marie (OHL), 6th round, 171st pick overall.

June 20–21, 2008 – Scotiabank Place, Ottawa, Ontario

Center Nathan Moon from Kingston (OHL), 4th round, 120th pick overall.

Goaltender Alexander Pechurski from Magnitogorsk (Russia), 5th round, 150th pick overall.

Goaltender Patrick Killeen from Brampton (OHL), 6th round, 180th pick overall.

Defenseman Nicholas D'Agostino from St. Michael's (OPJHL), 7th round, 210th pick overall.

June 26–27, 2009 – Bell Centre, Montreal, Quebec

Defenseman Simon Despres from St. John (QMJHL), 1st round, 30th pick overall.

Defenseman Philip Samuelssson from Chicago (USHL), 2nd round, 61st pick overall.

Right wing Ben Hanowski from Little Falls H.S. (Minn.), 3rd round, 63rd pick overall.

Right wing Nick Petersen from Shawinigan (QMJHL), 4th round, 121st pick overall.

Defenseman Alex Velischek from Delbarton School (N.J.), 5th round, 123rd pick overall.

Center Andy Bathgate from Belleville (OHL), 5th round, 151st pick overall.

Defenseman Viktor Ekbom from IK Oskarshamn (Allsvenskan), 6th round, 181st pick overall.

June 25–26, 2010 – Staples Center, Los Angeles, California

Right wing Beau Bennett from Penticton (BCHL), 1st round, 20th pick overall.

Right wing Bryan Rust from US National Team Development Program (NAHL), 3rd round, 80th pick overall.

Right wing Tom Kuehnhackl from Landshut (Germany), 4th round, 110th pick overall.

Left wing Ken Agostino from Delbarton High School (N.J.), 5th round, 140th pick overall.

Defenseman Joe Rogalski from Sarnia (OHL), 6th round, 152nd pick overall.

Defenseman Reid McNeill from London (OHL), 6th round, 170th pick overall.

Supplemental Draft Selections

The NHL Supplemental Draft was established in 1986 by the National Hockey League as an offshoot of the NHL Entry Draft. The Supplemental Draft was used by teams to select collegiate players who were not eligible for the standard Entry Draft. When a new collective bargaining agreement was signed in 1994, the Supplemental Draft was discontinued.

1986

Center Jeff Lamb from Denver (WCHA), 1st round, 17th pick overall.

Defenseman Randy Taylor from Harvard (ECAC), 1st round, 18th pick overall.

1987

Forward Dan Shea from Boston College (Hockey East), 1st round, 15th pick overall.

Defenseman John Leonard from Bowdoin College (NESCAC), 1st round, 16th pick overall.

1988

Center Paul Polillo from Western Michigan (CCHA), 1st round, 4th pick overall.

Tamer the Gamer

After serving a two-year apprenticeship in the minors, former University of Michigan standout Chris Tamer gradually worked his way into the Penguins' lineup.

He quickly established a reputation as a no-nonsense defender who would tangle with anyone. On the night of October 12, 1995, he earned his stripes. In the late stages of a 5–1 loss to Chicago, Tamer found himself nose to nose with Bob Probert, the league's reigning heavyweight champ. Standing 6'3" and weighing 225 pounds, the imposing Probert was hockey's answer to Mike Tyson.

In an instant the combatants dropped their sticks and gloves and began firing punches. Displaying boxing skills honed at Detroit's famed Kronk Gym, Tamer caught Probert flush with a left hook and dropped the burly Hawks winger to the ice.

The TKO victory earned the young Pens defenseman instant acclaim from hockey fight aficionados.

"I like that kid Tamer," said colorful *Hockey Night in Canada* commentator Don Cherry. "'Tamer the Gamer,' I call him. He did all right against Probert. He has no fear."

Forward Shawn Lillie from Colgate (ECAC), 1st round, 9th pick overall.

1989

Center John DePourcq from Ferris State (CCHA), 1st round, 21st pick overall.

1990

Center Joe Dragon from Cornell (ECAC), 1st round, 5th pick overall.

Center Savo Mitrovic from New Hampshire (Hockey East), 1st round, 9th pick overall.

1991

Forward Greg Carvel from St. Lawrence (ECAC), 1st round, 22nd pick overall.

Hornets Duke Harris (9), Irv Spencer (12), Aut Erickson (3), and goalie Hank Bassen fail to stop Buffalo's Len Lunde.

Other Pittsburgh Hockey Teams

In the fall of 1893 Pittsburgh power broker Christopher Magee decided to build a grand new gathering place for the city's residents. His proposal floundered until James Conant, an ice hockey enthusiast who had been hired to manage the facility, persuaded his boss to include an indoor ice skating rink. The result was the magnificent Schenley Park Casino.

Opened to the public on May 29, 1895, the Casino was a smash hit. Soon, hockey clubs began to form. Among the first was the Pittsburgh Hockey Club, which was comprised of players from nearby Carnegie Tech and Western University (later the University of Pittsburgh).

Almost overnight, the sport became wildly popular. Players and teams from across North America flocked to the Steel City to challenge the locals and skate on the Casino's artificial ice surface—the first of its kind.

Sadly, the Casino was destroyed by fire on December 17, 1896. Fortunately, a second arena, the Duquesne Gardens, was already in the works. The Gardens played host to its first hockey match on January 23, 1899.

Thanks to its brand-new home, Pittsburgh hockey enjoyed a period of unprecedented growth and popularity. With a glut of players flooding in from across the country and Canada, a new semiprofessional league was formed in 1900—the Western Pennsylvania Hockey League. It featured three teams—the Bankers, the Keystones (formerly the Pittsburgh Hockey Club), and the Pittsburgh Athletic Club.

According to extensive research compiled by Ernie Fitzsimmons, the WPHL was the first league to openly hire and trade players. By the start of the 1902–03 season, the WPHL—boasting future Hall of Famers such as Riley Hern, Alf Smith, and Hod Stuart—was a full-blown professional league. An imposing new team, the Victorias, joined the circuit and captured the league title in 1903–04. The Victorias challenged the Portage Lakes Hockey Club from Houghton, Michigan, for the United States Professional title, but lost two games to one.

In 1904 the WPHL ceased operations with the formation of the International Professional Hockey League, a new inter-city league. The Pittsburgh teams pooled their talent to form the Pittsburgh Pros. While the Pros failed to win a title, they were part of a thrilling three-team race in 1905–06.

Following the 1906–07 season professional leagues began to sprout up across Canada. Lured by the promise of bigger paychecks, many players returned to their native country. When the IPHL folded, the WPHL resumed operations. The four-team league was dominated by the Bankers, who won two consecutive titles. The WPHL disbanded for good in 1909.

Although there was no formal local professional league, teams like the Duquesne and Lyceum continued to compete in local amateur and senior circuits. In 1915 the Pittsburgh Athletic Association joined the United States Amateur Hockey Association. Boasting big-time players such as Lionel Conacher and Roy Worters, the PAA—renamed the Yellow Jackets—captured USAHA titles in 1924 and 1925.

The Yellow Jackets joined the National Hockey League the next year and renamed themselves the Pirates. The team enjoyed modest success before moving to Philadelphia in 1930.

Despite the loss of the Pirates, the decade of the Great Depression would usher in a second golden era in Pittsburgh hockey. The Yellow Jackets reformed and skated for several more seasons. The colorfully named Pittsburgh Shamrocks played in the International-American Hockey League in 1935–36.

In October of 1936 local theater owner John Harris purchased the Detroit Olympics and brought them to Pittsburgh. Rechristened the Hornets, the club would become a perennial American Hockey League power, capturing Calder Cups in 1952, 1955, and 1967.

Pittsburgh Keystones (WPHL)

The Pittsburgh Keystones was among the first hockey teams to form in the Pittsburgh area. Originally the Pittsburgh Hockey Club, the team drew its nickname from Pennsylvania's designation as the "Keystone State."

The Keystones were initially made up of college players from Carnegie Tech and Western University. They played their home games at the beautiful Schenley Park Casino, which boasted the first artificial ice surface in North America.

After the Casino burned to the ground in 1896, the Keystones moved to the city's newest facility, the Duquesne Gardens. They competed against other local amateur teams until 1901, when they joined the semiprofessional Western Pennsylvania Hockey League.

Like other clubs in the circuit, the Keystones began to pay players as a means of acquiring the best talent. This practice paid off handsomely in 1901–02, when the Keystones captured the first WPHL crown.

However, in the summer of 1902 the team became embroiled in a controversy that would besmirch its name and lead to its demise. A Keystones player, Harry Peel, admitted the club had paid him $35 per week. Stunned by the revelation, the Ontario Hockey Association—which staunchly fought against professionalism—immediately suspended Peel. The brouhaha hastened the transformation of the WPHL into a fully professional league.

The Keystones never recovered. After winning just two of 13 games in 1902–03, the team folded on January 17, 1904.

Record

Season	GP	W	L	T	GF	GA	PTS	Finish	
1895–01				NA					
1901–02	14	9	5	0	42	32	18	1st	WPHL
1902–03	13	2	11	0	19	71	4	4th	WPHL
1903–04	6	2	4	0	15	30	4	4th	WPHL

Pittsburgh Athletic Club (WPHL)

One of the earliest Steel City hockey teams, the Pittsburgh Athletic Club was also one of the finest. Formed in 1899, the Pittsburgh AC was a charter member of the Pittsburgh Hockey League—a forerunner of the Western Pennsylvania Hockey League.

The team had the distinction of skating in the first game ever played at Duquesne Gardens when it faced off against Western University on January 24, 1899.

Among the first teams to lure hockey players from north of the border, the Pittsburgh AC dominated local hockey at the turn of century. Boasting Canadian stars such as George "Pinky" Lamb, Bill Hamilton, Herb Reynor, and Billy Shields, the Pittsburgh AC captured three straight city championships from 1899 through 1901, garnering the coveted Trophy Cup and a $500 prize.

In 1901 the team joined the WPHL. Although future Hall of Famer Alf Smith joined an already star-studded lineup, the other teams in the circuit had caught on to the PAC's tactics and were heavily recruiting Canadian players as well. Unable to duplicate its early success, the PAC became one of the WPHL's weaker entries.

The PAC continued to play exhibition matches after the league folded in 1909.

Record

Season	GP	W	L	T	GF	GA	PTS	Finish	
1899–01				NA					
1901–02	14	8	6	0	46	28	16	2nd	WPHL
1902–03	13	7	5	1	36	32	15	2nd	WPHL
1903–04	14	4	10	0	44	62	8	3rd	WPHL
1907–08	17	3	12	2*	41	80	6	4th	WPHL
1908–09	14			NA				3rd	WPHL

* Tie games were replayed and are not reflected in total points

Pittsburgh Bankers (WPHL)

The aptly named Pittsburgh Bankers did not receive their nickname by accident. When the club formed in 1900, it consisted primarily of players drawn from a local banker's league.

According to Pittsburgh sportswriter Paul Sullivan, the Bankers League may have been one of the first circuits to actively recruit and pay its players.

"Some of the banks started a hockey league as a promotional stunt and brought Canadians down and gave them jobs in the banks," Sullivan recalled in an interview with Ed Bouchette of the *Pittsburgh Post-Gazette*. "They were down here to play hockey but in order to qualify and play for the bank they had to be an employee of the bank. I don't know what they gave them to do at the bank, but it wasn't much."

Charter members of the Pittsburgh-based Western Pennsylvania Hockey League, the Bankers captured three regular-season titles (1903, 1908, 1909)—the most of any team. In 1903 the Bankers faced off against the powerful Portage Lakes team from Houghton, Michigan, for the United States Pro title. Although Portage Lakes won the four-game set (2–1–1), they were outscored by the locals 11–6.

The Bankers were credited with making one of the first trades in professional hockey history. On January 28, 1908, they dealt Cliff Bennest, Joseph Donnelly, and a player named McGuire to the Pittsburgh Pirates for Edgar Dey, Jim MacKay, and Dunc Taylor.

Record

Season	GP	W	L	T	GF	GA	PTS	Finish	
1901–02	14	4	10	0	27	55	8	3rd	WPHL
1902–03	14	10	3	1	58	18	19	1st	WPHL
1903–04	15	8	7	0	45	45	16	2nd	WPHL
1907–08	19	12	4	3*	81	59	24	1st	WPHL
1908–09	15			NA				1st	WPHL

* Tie games were replayed and are not reflected in total points

Pittsburgh Victorias (WPHL)

The Pittsburgh Victorias had a relatively short life span of two years. However, the team would more than live up to its regal-sounding name during its brief appearance on the local hockey scene.

The Victorias joined the Western Pennsylvania Hockey League in 1902. Led by Hall of Fame center Bruce Stuart, the club tasted middling success in its inaugural campaign, sporting a record of 7–7. However, in their second season the Victorias became a power, rolling up an impressive 10–3 mark to capture the league title.

Three Pittsburgh teams challenged Portage Lakes for the U.S. Pro title in 1904. A true juggernaut, the Midwesterners had raided the WPHL prior to the season and landed some of its biggest stars, including Riley Hern, Bert Morrison, Billy Shields, and brothers Bruce and Hod Stuart. The Victorias gave the Portage Lakes squad the stiffest challenge from among the Steel City teams before bowing out in three games.

Following the 1903–04 season the WPHL teams merged into the Pittsburgh Pros, which competed in the new International Professional Hockey League. Although the WPHL resumed operations in 1907 following the demise of the IPHL, the Victorias never rejoined the league.

Record

Season	GP	W	L	T	GF	GA	PTS	Finish	
1902–03	14	7	7	0	47	40	14	3rd	WPHL
1903–04	13	10	3	0	56	23	20	1st	WPHL

Pittsburgh Pro HC (IPHL)

The Pittsburgh Pro Hockey Club, or Pittsburgh Pros for short, was created in 1904 to compete in the International Professional Hockey League. The new inter-city league included the Pros and four teams from the Midwest—Calumet-Larium, Houghton-Portage Lakes, Sault Ste. Marie (Canada), and Sault Ste. Marie (Michigan).

An amalgam of the top players from the WPHL, the Pros didn't fare too well in their first season, finishing a distant fourth. As was the custom of the day, players tended to hop back and forth to whichever team paid the most. In

1905–06, the Pros lured former WPHL standout and future Hall of Fame defenseman Hod Stuart back to town. The result was a strong third-place showing.

Featuring a lineup packed with stars such as Lorne Campbell, Jimmy Gardner, Horace Gaul, Tommy Smith, and goalie Jack Winchester, the Pros figured to make a strong bid for the title in 1906–07. Although they displayed plenty of dash, the Pros underachieved and finished third with a .500 record. On an individual basis Campbell and Smith were superb, outpacing future Hall of Famers Didier Pitre and Edouard "Newsy" Lalonde in the scoring race.

By 1907 the tide against professionalism in Canada had turned. With pro leagues proliferating all across the Dominion, Canadian players eagerly returned home, and for better pay to boot. The IPHL had little choice but to fold.

Record

Season	GP	W	L	T	GF	GA	PTS	Finish	
1904–05	24	8	15	1	82	144	17	4th	IPHL
1905–06	24	15	9	0	121	84	30	3rd	IPHL
1906–07	25	12	12	1	94	82	25	3rd	IPHL

Pittsburgh Pirates (WPHL)

Following a three-year hiatus due to the formation of the International Professional Hockey League, the Western Pennsylvania Hockey League resumed operations in 1907. However, only two of the league's original clubs, the Bankers and the Pittsburgh AC, rejoined the fold.

Hoping to have four teams in action, the WPHL admitted two new clubs, the Lyceum and the Pirates. Of the newcomers, the Pirates seemed far and away the most powerful. Stocked with a bevy of top-notch players including Edgar Dey, Charlie Mason, Harry McRobie, Ray Robinson, Ed Robitaille, Dunc Taylor, and goalie Jim MacKay, the Pirates were expected to provide stiff competition for the rest of the league. They fell far short of the mark, winning only five of 17 games.

Still, they were credited with one of the first player trades ever, swapping Dey, MacKay, and Taylor to the Pittsburgh Bankers for Cliff Bennest, Joseph Donnelly, and a player named McGuire.

The Pirates folded after just one season of play. However, their name would live on. In 1925 a second version of the Pirates joined the National Hockey League.

Record

Season	GP	W	L	T	GF	GA	PTS	Finish	
1907–08	17	5	10	2*	59	70	10	3rd	WPHL

* Tie games were replayed and are not reflected in total points

Pittsburgh Lyceum (WPHL)

With the Western Pennsylvania Hockey League seeking to return to a four-team format in 1907, the Pittsburgh Lyceum was invited to join the fold. Founded by the Reverend Lawrence A. O'Connell in 1903, the Lyceum would gain fame for producing boxing champions such as Billy Conn, Harry Greb, and Fritzie Zivic.

Paced by Jack Marks and Hall of Fame center Tommy Smith, who led the league with 33 goals, the Lyceum exceeded all expectations. They finished a strong second, narrowly missing out on the WPHL title by a scant two points.

The club did not fare as well in its second season. Decimated by the defections of their Canadian players who routinely jumped their contracts once the weather was cold enough to play on Canada's outdoor rinks, the Lyceum was unable to count on a set lineup. The team folded on December 23, 1908.

Known for producing championship boxers, the Catholic Lyceum sponsored a hockey team in the early 1900s. Pictured in front are Rev. Brennan (left) and Rev. L. A. O'Connell (right), who established the Lyceum in 1903.

When the WPHL disbanded following the 1908–09 season, the Lyceum reformed and competed in local amateur leagues.

Record

Season	GP	W	L	T	GF	GA	PTS	Finish	
1907–08	17	11	5	1*	77	49	22	2nd	WPHL
1908–09	8			NA				4th	WPHL

* Tie games were replayed and are not reflected in total points

Pittsburgh Duquesne (WPHL)

The Duquesne Athletic Club, or Pittsburgh Duquesne as they would come to be known, joined the Western Pennsylvania Hockey League in 1908 as a replacement for the Pittsburgh Pirates.

The Duquesne enjoyed a strong first season, finishing second to the league-champion Bankers. However, the WPHL was on its last legs. Plagued by the now constant defections of Canadian players, the league had an increasingly difficult time filling out its rosters. With the construction of artificial ice surfaces in Canada looming just around the corner, the WPHL ceased operations following the 1908–09 season.

Along with the Lyceum, the Duquesne soldiered on, competing in local amateur leagues. During the 1915–16 season they played exhibition games in a new circuit, the United States Amateur Hockey Association. At least three of the team's players—Arthur Brooks, Ed Gorman, and Alex Wellington—went on to play in the National Hockey League.

Record

Season	GP	W	L	T	GF	GA	PTS	Finish	
1908–09	15			NA				2nd	WPHL

Pittsburgh Yellow Jackets (USAHA, IAHL, EAHL)

By 1915 the halcyon days of Pittsburgh hockey had come to an end. Unable to secure top-drawer talent due to the growth of professional hockey in Canada, the Western Professional Hockey League had ceased operations in 1909. Although the sport was still immensely popular with the locals, the city boasted only a handful of amateur clubs.

That would soon change with the formation of the United States Amateur Hockey Association (USAHA). Roy Schooley, a lifelong hockey enthusiast and former referee, formed the Pittsburgh Athletic Association (PAA) to compete in the new league.

According to PittsburghHockey.net, the team was a dynamo. Sharing the Duquesne Gardens ice with Carnegie

Tech and the University of Pittsburgh during the 1919 season, the PAA ripped through the competition en route to a sterling record of 30–4.

The PAA changed its name twice, first to the Stars and then to the Yellow Jackets. The club wore yellow wool jerseys (which sportswriter John McMahon described as a "dingy mustard yellow") with the black felt letter "P" sewn onto the front—a color scheme that would become synonymous with Pittsburgh hockey.

In the early 1920s, Schooley hired an established coach, Dick Carroll, who had guided the Toronto Arenas to a Stanley Cup in 1918. He also recruited a host of promising young Canadians to play for his team. A pair of high-scoring forwards, Harry Darragh and Herbert "Hib" Milks, joined the club in 1922, followed in rapid succession by Lionel "Big Train" Conacher, Harold "Baldy" Cotton, Francis "Duke" McCurry, Roger Smith, Wilfred "Tex" White, and Roy "Shrimp" Worters.

The infusion of talent caused more than a few raised eyebrows among hockey pundits, who questioned the team's amateur status.

"They [the players] didn't come down from Canada because they thought Pittsburgh was a nice place," noted Paul Sullivan, who covered the local hockey beat for the *Pittsburgh Gazette-Times* and *Sun-Telegraph*. "They weren't exactly amateurs."

While the team's status may have been a dicey subject, there was little doubt about its ability. With rugged team captain Lionel Conacher leading the way, the Yellow Jackets rolled to the USAHA title in 1923–24. They were the first Pittsburgh hockey team to win a North American championship.

The city fell in love with its new heroes and the feeling was clearly mutual.

"This here's a real hockey town for sure," Conacher said. "The boys up north think they're in heaven after they get here."

Steel City fans were in for an even bigger treat in 1924–25. While the Yellow Jackets defeated the Eveleth Arrowheads in a three-game playoff to clinch the West Division crown, another local club—the Fort Pitt Hornets—snagged first place in the East.

The hometown rivals opened the four-game championship series on April 3, 1925, before a packed house at the Duquesne Gardens. Fort Pitt's captain, Paddy Sullivan, beat Worters six minutes into the first period to draw first blood. Darragh countered for the Yellow Jackets five minutes later, and the game settled into a knockdown, drag-out affair. Four minutes into overtime, Conacher sped into the Fort Pitt zone and beat Hornets goalie Joe Miller for the game winner.

Buoyed by their captain's heroics, the Yellow Jackets topped the Hornets 3–1 in Game 2 and battled them to a 2–2 tie in Game 3. On April 11, they eclipsed the East Division champs 2–1 to capture their second straight USAHA crown.

It appeared the Yellow Jackets would dominate the USAHA for years to come. However, the league folded over the summer.

Schooley encountered financial problems and was forced to sell the team to Pittsburgh lawyer James Callahan.

Callahan was convinced that his new team was ready for the big time. He secured a franchise in the National Hockey League, and the erstwhile Yellow Jackets—renamed the Pirates—turned pro.

The Pirates played in the NHL for five seasons with diminishing success. At the onset of the Great Depression the team moved across the state to Philadelphia, where they became the Quakers. With the Pittsburgh hockey market wide open, Roy Schooley reacquired the rights to the Yellow Jackets and secured a franchise in the International-American Hockey League, a relatively new minor pro circuit.

Stocked with former Pirates Gord Fraser, Mickey McGuire, Roger Smith, and Tex White, the recast Yellow Jackets performed reasonably well. However, keeping a hockey team afloat during the darkest days of the Depression was a difficult task, and the club withdrew from the IAHL following the 1931–32 campaign.

The Yellow Jackets were purchased by Pittsburgh theater owner John Harris in 1932. They competed as an independent team until 1935, when they joined the Eastern Amateur Hockey League. After two seasons in the EAHL, Harris merged them with the Pittsburgh Hornets.

As a final brush stroke to the team's enduring legacy, two of its bright young stars—goalie Frank Brimsek and right wing Gordie Drillon—would go on to Hall of Fame careers.

Record

Season	GP	W	L	T	GF	GA	PTS	Finish
1915-22				NA				USAHA
1922-23	20	10	10	0	–	–	20	3rd USAHA/W
1923-24	20	15	5	0	65	26	30	1st USAHA/W*
1924-25	40			NA				1st USAHA/W*
1930-31	48	21	18	9	101	108	51	4th IAHL
1931-32	48	17	22	9	91	118	43	4th IAHL
1932-35				NA				Independent
1935-36	40	22	16	2	108	74	46	2nd EAHL
1936-37	48	19	24	5	119	147	43	3rd EAHL

* Won USAHA Title

Fort Pitt Hornets (USAHA)

According to *Pittsburgh Post-Gazette* sportswriter Ed Bouchette, the Fort Pitt Hornets were spun off from another local amateur club, the Pittsburgh Yellow Jackets. This certainly seems plausible, given the fact that the powerful Yellow Jackets added no fewer than nine Canadians to their roster in the early 1920s, thus freeing up talent for other local teams.

The Hornets joined the United States Amateur Hockey Association for the 1924–25 season where they were paced by high-scoring defenseman Johnny McKinnon, who led the USAHA with 24 goals, and goalie Joe Miller, who recorded

17 wins and a sparkling 1.72 goals-against average. Many of the team's players, including Bernie Brophy, Charles "Bonner" Larose, Hec Lepine, player-coach Rennison "Dinny" Manners, McKinnon, and Miller went on to play in the NHL.

As if scripted, the Hornets captured the East Division title and the Yellow Jackets won the West to set up an all-Pittsburgh championship series. Sparked by their pepper-pot captain, Arthur "Paddy" Sullivan, the Hornets battled hard, but dropped a tight four-game set to their more seasoned rivals.

Unfortunately, the USAHA soon folded. While the victorious Yellow Jackets joined the NHL as the Pirates, the orphaned Hornets eventually disbanded.

They had made an impression during their brief existence. When the Pirates needed an infusion of new blood, they turned to former Hornets for help. On October 28, 1926, they purchased McKinnon from the Montreal Canadiens to bolster their defense. Two years later the Pirates acquired Miller from the New York Americans for holdout goalie Roy Worters.

Record

Season	GP	W	L	T	GF	GA	PTS	Finish
1924–25	22	17	5	0	–	–	34	1st USAHA/E

Pittsburgh Pirates (NHL)

In a roundabout way, the Pittsburgh Pirates hockey team owed its existence to football and the abilities of one extraordinary athlete.

Lionel Pretoria Conacher was born on May 24, 1901, in Toronto. The son of a teamster, he was one of 10 children. Times were tough for the Conachers, and young Lionel quit school after the eighth grade to help support his family.

A gifted athlete, he soon realized that sports were his ticket to a better life. As he matured, Conacher became Canada's answer to America's great multisport star Jim Thorpe.

There wasn't a sport he couldn't master. The strapping 6'1", 200-pounder excelled at football, lacrosse, and wrestling. An accomplished pugilist, he once fought a four-round exhibition with heavyweight champion Jack Dempsey. Although a bit crude in the outfield, he could also slug a baseball a country mile.

Having never laced on a pair of skates until he was 16, Conacher came relatively late to hockey. Yet in three years' time he led his junior team to the Memorial Cup title.

He was immediately courted by the Toronto St. Pats of the National Hockey League. But Conacher was determined to keep his amateur status so he could continue to play football—his first love. In 1921 he led the Toronto Argonauts to the Grey Cup title, scoring 15 of the Argos' 23 points.

It was Conacher's passion for the gridiron that brought him to Pittsburgh. In 1923 he accepted a scholarship from a local prep school, the Bellefonte Academy, to play football and hockey. He coaxed his good friends, Harold Cotton and Roy Worters, into joining him.

That winter they skated for the Pittsburgh Yellow Jackets, a local club that already boasted fellow Canadians Harry Darragh, Herbert Milks, Roger Smith, and Wilfred White. The Yellow Jackets had been a strong team prior to Conacher's arrival. With "the Big Train" serving as captain they became the scourge of the United States Amateur Hockey Association, cruising to two straight national titles.

Opportunity came knocking in the summer of 1925. The National Hockey League was seeking to add a third American team and the Steel City was deemed a prime location. Joined by his teammates, who each accepted offers to turn pro, Conacher agreed to play for a record salary of $7,500. On November 7, 1925, Pittsburgh was granted a franchise.

Little was expected from this bunch of amateurs. But the Pirates, as they were now called, had a few surprises in store. Their coach, former Montreal Canadiens scoring star Odie Cleghorn, was a true innovator. He made sure the youthful Pirates always had fresh legs on the ice by utilizing three forward lines, unheard of in those days. Cleghorn also was the first coach to change his players on the fly while the game was in progress.

The Pirates opened the season with a bang. On November 26, 1925, they defeated the Bruins at Boston Garden. Conacher scored the team's first-ever goal, beating Bruins goalie Charles Stewart at 17:50 of the second period to knot the score. Harry Darragh struck for the game winner midway through the final frame.

Two nights later the Pirates stunned the Canadiens 1–0 as Worters outdueled the Hab's legendary Georges Vezina. It was the last game Vezina would ever play; four months later he died of tuberculosis.

On December 2, Pittsburgh played host to its first NHL contest. A crowd of 8,200 packed the Duquesne Gardens to the rafters to watch the New York Americans down the Pirates 2–1 in overtime. Conacher, who had a flair for the dramatic, scored the lone goal for the home team.

Executing Cleghorn's fast-paced game plan to perfection, the Pirates edged out the Bruins for third place to grab the final playoff spot. Remarkably, they were the only team in the league not to have a player rank among the top 10 scorers. Hib Milks paced a balanced attack with 14 goals. The club also received solid production from Duke McCurry (13 goals) and Darragh (10 goals). Defensemen Conacher and Roger Smith chipped in with nine goals apiece. Worters was superb, finishing second among all goalies with a sparkling 1.90 goals-against average and seven shutouts.

The Pirates squared off against the second-place finishers, the Montreal Maroons, in the opening round of the playoffs. Led by future Hall of Famers Nels Stewart and Babe Siebert, the powerful Maroons beat the upstart Pirates 3–1 at the Duquesne Gardens to open the series. The Steel

City sextet battled the eventual Stanley Cup winners to a tie in Game 2 but lost the two-game, total-goals playoff by a margin of 6–4.

"They were an amateur team one year and in the Stanley Cup semifinals the next," sportswriter Paul Sullivan recalled. "And they were barely nudged out."

Buoyed by their surprising success, the Pirates eagerly awaited the start of the 1926–27 campaign. The club joined the newly formed American Division with the New York Rangers, Boston Bruins, Chicago Black Hawks, and Detroit Cougars.

The rival Western and Pacific Coast leagues folded over the summer, providing a fresh influx of talent. Aside from the acquisition of aging forward Ty Arbour, the Pirates curiously chose to stand pat. It was the first sign that all was not well in Pittsburgh.

"The Gardens only held about 5,000 people," Sullivan noted. "Nobody made very much money."

Nine games into the season the team was dealt a mortal blow. Desperate to trim his payroll, club president Horace Townsend pulled the trigger on a shocking trade. On December 16, 1926, he peddled Conacher and his hefty salary to the New York Americans for journeyman Charlie Langlois and $2,000 cash. With one swift stroke Townsend had ripped the heart out of the team. Shorn of their captain and leader the Pirates tumbled to a fourth-place finish.

Things looked even bleaker when the team opened the 1927–28 season on a 12-game winless skein. As was the custom of the day, the other clubs stepped forward to help a weaker squad. One year to the day after the Conacher trade, the Canadiens loaned promising young defender Marty Burke to the Pirates. Aggressive forward Bert McCaffrey arrived from Toronto in a three-way deal for Arbour.

The newcomers provided a desperately needed boost. Reinvigorated, the Pirates rallied to nail down third place in the American Division. Leading the way was Worters, who finished second to the Canadiens' scoring ace Howie Morenz in the voting for Most Valuable Player. The diminutive goalie posted a sparkling 1.66 goals-against average and 10 shutouts.

By virtue of their strong finish the Pirates appeared to have a legitimate shot at the Stanley Cup. However, once again they had the misfortune of facing the eventual champions, Lester Patrick's Rangers, in the opening round of the playoffs. Due to dwindling local fan support and limited seating capacity at the Duquesne Gardens, league president Frank Calder decided that both games would be played in New York's spacious Madison Square Garden. Predictably the Pirates were outclassed in a two-game, total-goals playoff.

It was all downhill from there. Prior to the 1928 training camp three of the team's top performers—Worters, Darragh, and Milks—held out for more money. While Darragh and Milks succumbed to pressure from Calder and new Pirates owner Benny Leonard (who served as a front man for reputed mobster "Big Bill" Dwyer), Worters refused to budge. On November 1, 1928, he was traded to the Americans for Joe Miller, joining his old pal Conacher in New York. The cash-strapped Pirates also received the princely sum of $20,000 in the exchange.

A former amateur star with the old Fort Pitt Hornets, Miller performed brilliantly and set a club record with 11 shutouts. But the Pirates barely mustered a goal a game and tumbled to a fourth-place finish.

Frustrated over his lack of input into trades and appalled by his players' poor work habits, Cleghorn resigned following the season to become an NHL referee. His successor was former Western League star and future Hall of Famer Frank Fredrickson. The change in leadership had little effect. The Pirates were atrocious in 1929–30, dropping into the American Division cellar while winning only five of 44 games.

One of the few bright spots of an otherwise dreary season occurred against Toronto on November 19, 1929. The Pirates' Johnny McKinnon scored four times to tie the league record for most goals in a game by a defenseman. Not to be outdone, Toronto blue-liner Hap Day tied the same record that night.

The onset of the Great Depression doomed professional hockey in Pittsburgh. Faced with sharply declining attendance, Leonard moved the franchise to Philadelphia for the 1930–31 season. The Quakers were every bit as bad as the Pirates and won just four games.

On September 26, 1931, the NHL Board of Governors announced that the Pittsburgh-Philadelphia franchise would suspend operations for the 1931–32 season. For each of the next four seasons the Pirates' owners were granted a stay of execution. But on May 7, 1936, the franchise was officially folded. Big-league hockey would not return to the Steel City for another 30 years.

As for the team's greatest player, Lionel Conacher would go on to a Hall of Fame career. After anchoring the defense for two Stanley Cup winners, he retired in 1937 while still at the top of his game.

The poor kid from Toronto entered the political arena and won a seat in the Canadian Parliament, where he served with distinction for several terms. In 1950 sportswriters named him Canada's "Outstanding Male Athlete of the First Half-Century."

Record

Season	GP	W	L	T	GF	GA	PTS	Finish
1925–26	36	19	16	1	82	70	39	3rd NHL
1926–27	44	15	26	3	79	108	33	4th NHL/Am.
1927–28	44	19	17	8	67	76	46	3rd NHL/Am.
1928–29	44	9	27	8	46	80	26	4th NHL/Am.
1929–30	44	5	36	3	102	185	13	5th NHL/Am.
Total	**212**	**67**	**122**	**23**	**376**	**519**	**157**	

Pittsburgh Shamrocks (IAHL)

Despite the ever-looming cloud of the Great Depression, Steel City hockey enjoyed somewhat of a resurgence in the 1930s. The Yellow Jackets re-formed following the departure of the Pirates, and in 1935 Pittsburgh was granted a franchise in the International-American Hockey League, a minor pro circuit.

Dubbed the Shamrocks, the team figured to be a popular draw at the Duquesne Gardens, which was located in the predominantly Irish neighborhood of Oakland. To ratchet up interest even further the team hired Sprague Cleghorn to serve as coach. The fiery older brother of former Pirates coach Odie Cleghorn, Sprague had literally bludgeoned his way into the Hall of Fame, spilling enough corpuscles to stock a blood bank.

Unfortunately, the club failed to display the same spit-in-your-eye intensity. The Shamrocks floundered to a fourth-place finish in the Western Division, well behind Detroit, Cleveland, and Windsor. They were a major disappointment at the box office as well, losing $36,000.

Still, the team made local history of sorts. Rookies Conrad and Jean Bourcier became the first brother tandem ever to skate together on a professional Pittsburgh hockey team.

Predictably, the Shamrocks folded. However, two of their better players—Bill Hudson and Red Anderson—joined another new Pittsburgh team, the Hornets, the following year.

Record

Season	GP	W	L	T	GF	GA	PTS	Finish
1935–36	46	18	27	1	137	170	37	4th IAHL/W

Pittsburgh Hornets (IAHL, AHL)

The decade of the 1930s was not especially kind to Western Pennsylvania. The Great Depression hit the steel-making region harder than most. Indeed, Pittsburgh would not fully recover its vitality until World War II, when it became the "Arsenal of Democracy."

Although the city had a long and storied love affair with hockey dating back to the turn of the 20th century, keeping a team in the Steel City during the lean years proved to be problematic. Pittsburgh lost its first National Hockey League team—the Pirates—to Philadelphia in 1930. Another club, the Yellow Jackets, competed in minor pro and amateur circuits through the early part of the decade before folding. The ill-fated Shamrocks skated for one season. They, too, were forced to shut down.

Into this bleak landscape stepped a man with a vision, as well as the financial wherewithal to back it up. John H. Harris was a local entertainment entrepreneur who owned a successful chain of theaters. He would later gain fame

The Hornets buzz the Quebec Aces net.

as the founder of the Ice Capades, a popular ice skating extravaganza.

Determined to re-establish hockey as a viable sport in Pittsburgh, he purchased the Detroit Olympics of the International-American Hockey League in the fall of 1936 and moved them to Pittsburgh. Harris named his new team the Hornets.

Unlike other Steel City clubs that always seemed to operate on a shoestring budget, the Hornets had a professional feel about them. A stern taskmaster, Harris made sure things were done the right way. He immediately purchased a new $5,000 sanitary soda fountain for the Duquesne Gardens, which served as the Hornets' home.

On November 7, 1936, the Hornets won their inaugural game, topping the Cleveland Falcons 4–2. The following night they drubbed the Falcons again 5–2 at the Gardens. With Mickey Drouillard (31 points) and Art Giroux (21 goals) pacing the attack, the Hornets finished a respectable second in the Western Division.

For the next decade the Hornets enjoyed fair to middling success while serving as the top farm team for the Detroit Red Wings. The 1938–39 squad featured IAHL scoring champ Don Deacon and two future Hall of Famers, center Sid Abel and rough-and-tumble defenseman "Black Jack" Stewart. A year later the Hornets made it all the way to the Calder Cup Finals before bowing to the Providence Reds. However, during the dismal 1943–44 season the club failed to win a single road game.

In 1945 the Hornets ended their affiliation with Detroit and joined the Toronto organization. For the championship-starved hockey fans of Pittsburgh, the timing couldn't have been better. The Maple Leafs, who would win five Stanley Cups over a glorious seven-year stretch, were loaded with top-drawer players. The Hornets became an integral part of the pipeline that funneled young talent to the parent club.

Featuring future NHL stars such as Fleming Mackell, Tod Sloan, and high-scoring Sid Smith, the Hornets reeled off consecutive seasons of 30, 35, 38, and 39 wins. Paced by

Smith's league-leading totals of 55 goals and 112 points, the 1948–49 version struck for an astonishing 301 goals in just 68 games.

It was a golden age for Pittsburgh hockey. Yet the Calder Cup remained an elusive prize. In the 1947 finals the club raced to a 3–1 series lead over Hershey only to collapse and lose the final three games by a combined score of 10–1. Four years later the Hornets fell short again, dropping a seven-game set to the Cleveland Barons.

Determined to bring home the American Hockey League title, the 1951–52 team rambled to a 46-win season to capture first place in the Western Division. Although the Hornets boasted future Hall of Famers George Armstrong, Leo Boivin, and Tim Horton, they were not the most talented bunch. But colorful coach Francis "King" Clancy instilled the tough, close-checking style of play that won championships.

Thanks to the brilliant goaltending of perennial All-Star Gil Mayer, the Hornets cruised past Hershey in the opening round of the playoffs. Once again, they rolled to a 3–1 series lead in the finals. Providence stormed back to win Game 5 at the Duquesne Gardens, but the Hornets would not be denied. Six minutes into the second overtime of Game 6, Ray Hannigan lashed a 15-foot wrist shot past Reds goalie Harvey Bennett. For the first time in their 16-year existence, the Hornets were Calder Cup champions.

Three years later they won their second AHL championship, besting the Buffalo Bisons in a six-game set. However, the creaky Duquesne Gardens was on its last legs. No longer "The Largest and Most Beautiful Skating Palace in the World," it was old, decrepit, and soon to be condemned.

"The building was not really heroic," said Frank Mathers, a defensive stalwart on the 1950s clubs. "It was an old car barn, but it was home. They claimed the rats there were the biggest in the league. [Trainer] Socko McCarey used to load up with pucks and fire away at the rats."

Following the 1955–56 season the Gardens was torn down to make way for an apartment building and restaurant, leaving the Hornets without a home. On February 4, 1956, a headline in *The Hockey News* blared that the city's new facility, the Civic Arena, could be ready in just over a year. It was wishful thinking. Construction of the new, space-age arena would not begin until 1958; it would not be completed until 1961.

Thus, the Hornets were put in cold storage for five years. Although it was widely reported that they became the Rochester Americans, this was not the case. One player, Gord Hannigan, went to the Amerks. Mathers and six of his teammates transferred to Hershey, while a dozen joined various NHL and AHL teams.

The Hornets, or "Wasps" as they were affectionately known, resumed play on October 14, 1961. With 9,317 in attendance, including owner John Harris and Pittsburgh mayor Joseph Barr, the Hornets dropped a tight 2–1 decision to Buffalo. The club would set many records that season:

most losses (58); most losses at home (27); most times shut out (9); fewest wins in team history (10); and fewest points in team history (22). The local die-hards didn't care. They were thrilled to have their beloved Hornets back.

Serving once more as the Red Wings' top farm club, the Hornets quickly improved, doubling their win total in each of the next two seasons. In 1963–64 slick center Art Stratton led the league in assists (65) and points (82), while flashy winger Yves Locas topped the circuit with 40 goals. The club qualified for postseason play three straight years, but was eliminated in the first round each time.

On February 4, 1966, came an announcement that would signal the end of the road for the Hornets. Pittsburgh was granted a new franchise in the National Hockey League. The 1966–67 season would be the Hornets' last.

As if penned by a Hollywood scriptwriter, the Hornets responded with a terrific year. Boasting a host of seasoned pros, including Gary Jarrett, Ab McDonald, and Don McKenney, the Hornets won 41 games to clinch first place in the West.

Backed by the superb goaltending of Hank Bassen, they steamrolled the Hershey Bears and swept aside Rochester to capture their third Calder Cup on a Billy Harris overtime goal. It was the perfect ending to a storybook season.

Although the Hornets were history, they would not be soon forgotten. Indeed, they cast a very long shadow over the city's new NHL team—the Penguins.

"This [the Penguins] was probably the hardest expansion franchise to sell due to the fact that we were the only

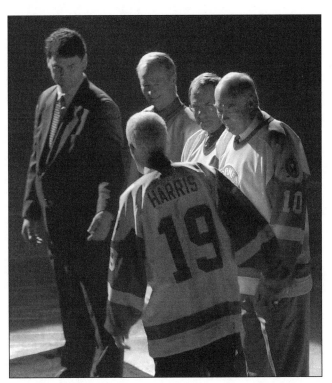

Billy Harris (19) is welcomed to center ice at Mellon Arena prior to a tribute game between Wilkes-Barre and Cincinnati on February 3, 2001.

Five new faces joined the Hornets for the 1965–66 season. They are (left to right): Bert Marshall, Bob Wall, George Gardner, Gary Doak, and Jim Cardiff.

expansion team that had an American League team," Penguins general manager Jack Riley said. "I don't think the fans were turned on by the Penguins like fans were in other new cities."

In time, the Penguins would establish a championship legacy of their own, while the Hornets faded from memory. But on the night of February 3, 2001, the Wilkes-Barre Scranton Penguins played a tribute game against Cincinnati at the Mellon Arena. Wearing replicas of the Hornets' old red-and-white jerseys, the players stood at center ice while a banner was raised in honor of the team's three Calder Cup championships.

John Harris would've been proud.

Record

Season	GP	W	L	T	GF	GA	PTS	Finish
1936–37	48	22	23	3	122	124	47	2nd IAHL/W
1937–38	48	22	18	8	100	104	52	2nd IAHL/W
1938–39	54	22	28	4	176	166	48	5th IAHL/W
1939–40	56	25	22	9	152	133	59	2nd IAHL/W
1940–41	56	21	29	6	156	170	48	3rd AHL/W
1941–42	56	23	28	5	210	223	51	5th AHL/W
1942–43	56	26	24	6	183	203	58	4th AHL
1943–44	52	12	31	9	140	181	33	3rd AHL/W
1944–45	60	26	27	7	267	247	59	3rd AHL/W
1945–46	62	30	22	10	262	226	70	2nd AHL/W
1946–47	64	35	19	10	260	188	80	3rd AHL/W
1947–48	68	38	18	12	238	170	88	2nd AHL/W
1948–49	68	39	19	10	301	175	88	4th AHL/W
1949–50	70	29	26	15	215	185	73	4th AHL/W
1950–51	71	31	33	7	212	177	69	3rd AHL/W
1951–52	68	46	19	3	267	179	95	1st AHL/W*
1952–53	64	37	21	6	223	149	80	2nd AHL
1953–54	70	34	31	5	250	222	73	4th AHL
1954–55	64	31	25	8	187	180	70	1st AHL*
1955–56	64	43	17	4	271	186	90	2nd AHL
1961–62	70	10	58	2	177	367	22	4th AHL/W
1962–63	72	20	48	4	200	317	44	4th AHL/W
1963–64	72	40	29	3	242	196	83	1st AHL/W
1964–65	72	29	36	7	228	256	65	3rd AHL/W
1965–66	72	38	33	1	236	218	77	3rd AHL/W
1966–67	72	41	21	10	282	209	92	1st AHL/W*
Total	1649	770	705	174	5557	5151	1714	

* Won Calder Cup

Pittsburgh Hornets Who Played for the Pittsburgh Penguins

Player	Position	Years with the Hornets	Years with the Penguins
Doug Barrie	Defense	1966–1967	1968–1969
Hank Bassen	Goaltender	1962–1965, 1966–1967	1967–1968
Andy Bathgate	Right Wing	1966–1967	1967–1968, 1970–1971
Leo Boivin	Defense	1951–1952	1967–1969
Joe Daley	Goaltender	1963–1964, 1966–1967	1968–1970
Bob Dillabough	Left Wing	1962–1965	1967–1968
Roy Edwards	Goaltender	1961–1962	1971–1972
Val Fonteyne	Left Wing	1965–1967	1967–1972
Nick Harbaruk	Right Wing	1961–1962	1969–1973
Billy Harris	Center	1965–1967	1968–1969
Tim Horton	Defense	1949–1952	1971–1972
Lowell MacDonald	Left Wing	1962–1965	1970–1971, 1972–1978
Pete Mahovlich	Center	1966–1967	1977–1979
Ab McDonald	Left Wing	1966–1967	1967–1968
Dick Mattiussi	Defense	1961–1962	1967–1969
Art Stratton	Center	1963–1964	1967–1968
Gene Ubriaco	Left Wing	1961–1962	1967–1969

Pittsburgh Forge (NAHL)

Following in the footsteps of the long-defunct Yellow Jackets, the Pittsburgh Forge established themselves as a top-notch amateur team in the early 2000s. The brainchild of former Penguins coach Kevin Constantine, the Forge joined the North American Hockey League—a Junior A Tier II circuit—in 2001.

The Forge exceeded all expectations during its inaugural season. Led by local stars Mike Handza, Pat Levendusky, and Dylan Reese, the Steel City sextet placed second in the tough East Division, trailing only the powerhouse Compuware Ambassadors. The Forge became the first expansion team in NAHL history to make it to the finals of the Robertson Cup tournament before bowing to the Ambassadors 2–0.

The following season the Forge was unstoppable. Although Constantine departed in January of 2003 to assume the coaching reins of the New Jersey Devils, they rolled to a league-record 43 victories to capture the East Division crown. Paced by a Jim Gehring hat trick, the Forge defeated the Texas Tornado 4–2 in Game 4 of the NAHL finals to claim the Robertson Cup. With future University of Denver star Peter Mannino providing stellar play between the pipes, the Forge won the Gold Cup at the U.S. Junior A National Championships in May.

Despite unparalleled success and a staggering .750 winning percentage over two seasons, the Forge was not a major gate attraction. Due to a lack of fan support, the club moved to Toledo in the summer of 2003.

While short-lived, the Forge produced a bevy of promising young skaters. No fewer than 18 former members went on to play for Division I college teams. Three Forge alumni—Mannino, Reese, and defenseman Grant Lewis—made it to the NHL.

Record

Season	GP	W	L	OT	GF	GA	PTS	Finish
2001-02	56	37	15	4	199	147	78	2nd NAHL/E
2002-03	56	43	9	4	208	111	90	1st NAHL/E*
Total	112	80	24	8	407	258	168	

* Won Robertson Cup and Gold Cup

The Hockey Hall of Famers

Through the years, no fewer than 27 former players, coaches, and members of the media associated with Pittsburgh's other hockey teams were inducted into the Hockey Hall of Fame. Some, including Frank Brimsek, Lionel Conacher, Tim Horton, Tommy Smith, and Roy Worters, were fixtures on the local hockey scene for several seasons. Others, such as Marty Barry, Gerry Cheevers, Fern Flaman, and Mickey MacKay, skated only a handful of games for Steel City clubs.

This section features a biography for every Hall of Fame inductee who played in or coached at least one game for Pittsburgh's other teams. Two of the featured inductees, Francis "King" Clancy and Sprague Cleghorn, coached Pittsburgh teams but were inducted into the Hockey Hall of Fame as players.

Frank Mathers, a long-time Hornets defenseman, and Bill Torrey, who served in the team's front office, were inducted as builders. Howie Meeker, who served the Hornets as both a player and a coach, received the Foster Hewitt Memorial Award for his 30-year career as a broadcaster. They are featured in this section as well.

Sidney Gerald Abel
Center
Hornets: 1938–39
Inducted into Hockey Hall of Fame: 1969 (Player)
Birthplace: Melville, Saskatchewan
B: February 22, 1918
D: February 7, 2000
Shoots: left

Sid Abel arrived in Pittsburgh fresh from the Flin Flon Bombers. For the 20-year-old Abel, the Steel City must have seemed a far cry from the rugged Manitoba mining town of 5,000 inhabitants. But the youngster adjusted beautifully. In just over half a season with the Hornets, Abel scored 22 goals and 24 assists to earn a call-up to the Red Wings.

He quickly established himself with Detroit as a play-maker. Nicknamed "Old Boot Nose" due to the size and shape of his most prominent facial feature, Abel centered the legendary "Production Line" for Gordie Howe and "Terrible" Ted Lindsay on the Red Wings' great Stanley Cup teams of the early 1950s.

	Regular Season					Playoffs				
	GP	G	A	PTS	PM	GP	G	A	PTS	PM
Hornets	41	22	24	46	27	-	-	-	-	-

George Edward Armstrong
Right Wing
Hornets: 1950–52
Inducted into Hockey Hall of Fame: 1975 (Player)
Birthplace: Skead, Ontario
B: July 6, 1930
Shoots: right

Nicknamed "the Chief" due to his Native-American heritage, George Armstrong began his long and eventful pro career in Pittsburgh. Skating for the Hornets, the 20-year-old Armstrong displayed all the attributes that would make him a great player—size, strength, consistency, and above all, leadership.

Following a solid first season, Armstrong blossomed into a top-notch right wing in 1951–52, scoring 30 goals in 50 games. Although he contributed greatly to the Hornets' success, he was not around to hoist the Calder Cup that spring. Instead, he was called up by Toronto for the stretch run.

As the captain of the Maple Leafs, Armstrong would sip champagne from Lord Stanley's coveted chalice four times. He retired in 1971 as one of the most beloved and revered players in team history.

	Regular Season					Playoffs				
	GP	G	A	PTS	PM	GP	G	A	PTS	PM
Hornets	121	45	62	107	111	13	4	9	13	6

Martin A. Barry
Center
Hornets: 1939–40
Inducted into Hockey Hall of Fame: 1965 (Player)
Birthplace: Quebec City, Quebec
B: December 8, 1905
D: August 20, 1969
Shoots: left

Among the players who have earned a spot in the Hockey Hall of Fame, few have been as highly regarded by teammates and foes alike as Marty Barry. One of the most productive players of his era, he was lauded for his work ethic, dedication, and stamina.

Barry was a second-line center on the powerful Boston clubs of the late 1920s and early 1930s that featured such all-time greats as Dit Clapper and Eddie Shore. A model of consistency, he scored at least 20 goals—roughly the equivalent of 40 goals today—in six straight seasons. In 1936–37 he was awarded the Lady Byng Trophy.

He arrived in Pittsburgh at the end of the 1939–40 season. Although his career was winding down, Barry helped spark the Hornets to a berth in the Calder Cup Finals.

	Regular Season					Playoffs				
	GP	G	A	PTS	PM	GP	G	A	PTS	PM
Hornets	6	2	0	2	0	7	2	1	3	4

Andrew James Bathgate
Right Wing
Hornets: 1966–67
Penguins: 1967–68, 1970–71
Inducted into Hockey Hall of Fame: 1978 (Player)
Birthplace: Winnipeg, Manitoba
B: August 28, 1932
Shoots: right

Following a brilliant 15-year career with the New York Rangers, Toronto Maple Leafs, and Detroit Red Wings, Andy Bathgate was demoted to the Hornets in 1966. The former Hart Trophy winner quickly proved that he was too good for the AHL. In six games with the Hornets, the classy old pro tallied four goals and 10 points to earn a quick recall by the Red Wings.

The following season Bathgate was back in Pittsburgh—this time as a member of the expansion Penguins. In 1967–68 he topped all West Division scorers with 59 points. Following a two-year hiatus, he returned in 1970–71 to score 44 points at the age of 38.

	Regular Season					Playoffs				
	GP	G	A	PTS	PM	GP	G	A	PTS	PM
Hornets	6	4	6	10	7	-	-	-	-	-
Penguins	150	35	68	103	89	-	-	-	-	-

Leo Joseph Boivin

Defense
Hornets: 1951–52
Penguins: 1967–69
Inducted into Hockey Hall of Fame: 1986 (Player)
Birthplace: Prescott, Ontario
B: August 2, 1932
Shoots: left

Leo Boivin was still a teenager when the Maple Leafs acquired his rights from Boston in 1950. Homesick, he briefly considered retiring from the game until Toronto owner Conn Smythe convinced him to give hockey another try.

The Hornets were glad he did. The 5'7", 190-pound "fireplug" quickly developed into a devastating open-ice hitter. After anchoring the defense for the Calder Cup–winning Hornets in 1952, Boivin made the Maple Leafs squad the following season.

Fifteen years later, Boivin returned to the Steel City to play for the expansion Penguins. Still popular with the Pittsburgh faithful, the rugged defender skated for a season and a half with the Pens before being dealt to Minnesota.

	Regular Season					Playoffs				
	GP	G	A	PTS	PM	GP	G	A	PTS	PM
Hornets	30	2	3	5	32	10	0	1	1	16
Penguins	114	14	26	40	100	–	–	–	–	–

Francis Charles Brimsek

Goaltender
Yellow Jackets: 1934–37
Inducted into Hockey Hall of Fame: 1966 (Player)
Birthplace: Eveleth, Minnesota
B: September 26, 1915
D: November 11, 1998
Catches: left

Following his graduation from famed Eveleth High School in Minnesota, Frank Brimsek came to Pittsburgh to tend goal for the Yellow Jackets. Cool and confident, he quickly established himself as a rising young star. At age 20, he led the Eastern Amateur Hockey League in 1935–36 with 20 wins and eight shutouts while posting a sparkling 1.95 goals-against average.

A classic standup goalie, Brimsek made his NHL debut with Boston in 1938. As a rookie he won the Calder Trophy and registered 10 shutouts to earn his enduring nickname— "Mr. Zero." Over the course of a brilliant 10-year NHL career, he backstopped the Bruins to two Stanley Cups.

	Regular Season					Playoffs				
	GP	MINS	GA	SH	AVE	GP	MINS	GA	SH	AVE
Yellow Jackets	101	6060	255	12	2.52	8	480	19	2	2.37

Gerald Michael Cheevers

Goaltender
Hornets: 1961–62
Inducted into Hockey Hall of Fame: 1985 (Player)
Birthplace: St. Catharines, Ontario
B: December 7, 1940
Catches: left

As debuts go, Gerry Cheevers' was somewhat less than auspicious. During a cup of coffee with the 1961–62 Hornets, "Cheesy" leaked for 21 goals in five games. Much to his credit, he won two of those games—one-fifth of the team's victory total for the season. It served to underscore the goalie's most enduring quality.

Gerry Cheevers was a winner. A selfless player, he didn't care how many goals he allowed as long as his team scored one more. And he won plenty of games—329 during the regular season and 60 more in the playoffs—over the course of a 14-year career spent mostly with Boston. One of the best money goalies of all time, Cheevers backstopped the Bruins to two Stanley Cups.

A gregarious sort, Cheesy possessed a good sense of humor. He was famous for painting stitches on his goalie mask to show where the puck would've hit him had his mug been exposed.

	Regular Season					Playoffs				
	GP	MINS	GA	SH	AVE	GP	MINS	GA	SH	AVE
Hornets	5	300	21	0	4.20	–	–	–	–	–

Francis M. Clancy

Coach
Hornets: 1951–53
Inducted into Hockey Hall of Fame: 1958 (Player)
Birthplace: Ottawa, Ontario
B: February 25, 1903
D: November 8, 1986

Francis "King" Clancy was one of the greatest players of his era, as well as one of the sport's most beloved figures. A skilled and rambunctious little defenseman, he excelled at rushing the puck and needling opponents to throw them off their game. Never giving an inch, he took on all comers, even though he lost most of the battles.

As a coach, the genial Irish Canadian was enormously popular. In 1951–52—his first season at the Hornets' helm— Clancy guided the team to a sterling 46–19–3 record and its first Calder Cup championship. The following year led the club back to the Calder Cup Finals, where it lost to Cleveland in a hotly contested seven-game set.

Clancy's fine work behind the Hornets bench earned him a promotion to Toronto. He coached for several seasons before moving into the front office. Serving as an assistant general manager, he helped to build four Stanley Cup winners.

	Regular Season						Playoffs			
	G	W	L	T	PTS	PCT	G	W	L	PCT
Hornets	132	83	40	9	175	.663	21	14	7	.667

Sprague Horace Cleghorn
Coach
Shamrocks: 1935–36
Inducted into Hockey Hall of Fame: 1958 (Player)
Birthplace: Montreal, Quebec
B: March 11, 1890
D: July 12, 1956

During his Hall of Fame playing career, Sprague Cleghorn cultivated a reputation as both a talented and violent competitor. One of the greatest defensemen of his era, Cleghorn wowed many a crowd with his daring end-to-end rushes. But it was his brutally efficient defensive play—not to mention his hair-trigger temper—that earned him lasting notoriety.

A treasured member of three Stanley Cup champions, Cleghorn tried his hand at coaching after hanging up his skates, with mixed results. In 1931–32 he guided the Montreal Maroons to the Stanley Cup semifinals. His next team, the Pittsburgh Shamrocks of the International-American Hockey League, didn't fare as well. With Cleghorn at the helm, the Shamrocks sputtered to a last-place finish in their only season.

	Regular Season						Playoffs			
	G	W	L	T	PTS	PCT	G	W	L	PCT
Shamrocks	46	18	27	1	37	.402	-	-	-	-

Lionel Pretoria Conacher
Defense
Yellow Jackets: 1923–25
Pirates: 1925–26
Inducted into Hockey Hall of Fame: 1994 (Player)
Birthplace: Toronto, Ontario
B: May 24, 1901
D: May 26, 1954
Shoots: left

Lionel "Big Train" Conacher came to Pittsburgh in the fall of 1923 on a football scholarship. One of Canada's greatest multisport athletes, he also starred as a defenseman for the Yellow Jackets hockey team. Although a lumbering skater, the burly 6'1", 200-pounder was a superb shot blocker and leader. He captained the Yellow Jackets to two straight United States Amateur Hockey Association titles.

The team joined the National Hockey League as the Pirates in 1925–26. Conacher enjoyed a strong first season, scoring nine goals and 13 points. However, on December

16, 1926, the Pirates sent the rugged defenseman to the New York Americans in a shocking trade.

Conacher would win Stanley Cups with Chicago and the Montreal Maroons before retiring in 1937. In 1950 he was named "Canada's Greatest Male Athlete of the First Half-Century."

	Regular Season					Playoffs				
	GP	G	A	PTS	PM	GP	G	A	PTS	PM
Yellow Jackets	60	26	4	30	-	21	11	3	14	-
Pirates	42	9	4	13	76	2	0	0	0	0

Gordon Arthur Drillon
Right Wing
Yellow Jackets: 1935–36
Inducted into Hockey Hall of Fame: 1975 (Player)
Birthplace: Moncton, New Brunswick
B: October 23, 1913
D: September 23, 1985
Shoots: right

A scout for the Toronto Maple Leafs discovered Gordie Drillon playing in his hometown of Moncton, New Brunswick, and signed him to a contract. The strapping winger was sent to Pittsburgh for the 1935–36 season, where he quickly made his mark. Skating for the Yellow Jackets, he popped in 22 goals in only 40 games. His production earned him a promotion to the Maple Leafs the very next season.

An early version of Bruins great Phil Esposito, Drillon parked himself in the slot and scored on rebounds and deflections. Although he was a big man, he wasn't especially physical, nor did he care for the nuances of defensive play. But he could score.

His career was remarkably brief. After racking up 155 goals in 311 games over seven seasons with Toronto and Montreal, Drillon enlisted in the Canadian Army in 1943. He never returned to the NHL, opting instead to play for various senior league teams.

	Regular Season					Playoffs				
	GP	G	A	PTS	PM	GP	G	A	PTS	PM
Yellow Jackets	40	22	12	34	4	8	3	2	5	0

Ferdinand Charles Flaman
Defense
Hornets: 1950–51
Inducted into Hockey Hall of Fame: 1990 (Player)
Birthplace: Dysart, Saskatchewan
B: January 25, 1927
Shoots: right

Ferdinand "Fernie" Flaman was already an established NHL defenseman when he came to Pittsburgh in November of 1950. Prior to his arrival via a big trade with Boston, Flaman spent three full seasons with the Bruins, where he developed a reputation as a tough, disciplined defender.

His stay with the Hornets was brief. Following a productive 11-game stint, Flaman was called up by the Maple Leafs. His rugged, stay-at-home play helped pave the way to a Stanley Cup victory.

Flaman returned to Boston in 1954, where he anchored the defense on the Bruins' Cup finalists later in the decade. To the end he remained a fearsome open-ice hitter, as well as a capable and ferocious fighter.

	Regular Season					Playoffs				
	GP	G	A	PTS	PM	GP	G	A	PTS	PM
Hornets	11	1	6	7	24	-	-	-	-	-

Sigurður Franklin Fredrickson
Center
Pirates: 1928–30
Inducted into Hockey Hall of Fame: 1958 (Player)
Birthplace: Winnipeg, Manitoba
B: June 11, 1895
D: May 28, 1979
Shoots: left

When he joined the Victoria Cougars of the Pacific Coast Hockey Association in 1920, Frank Fredrickson was regarded as the greatest amateur player in the world. He quickly reinforced his reputation with the Cougars, leading all PCHA scorers with 39 goals and 55 points in 1922–23. Two years later he led his team to a Stanley Cup triumph over the Montreal Canadiens.

The Pirates acquired Fredrickson on December 21, 1928, from Boston for Mickey MacKay and $12,000 cash. Following an uneventful first season the veteran center was named as the team's player-coach. Hoping to lead by example, the 34-year-old legend got off to a fast start in 1929, scoring four goals and 11 points in only nine games. However, a fractured ankle ended his season and the Pirates tumbled to a last-place finish.

	Regular Season					Playoffs				
	GP	G	A	PTS	PM	GP	G	A	PTS	PM
Pirates	40	7	14	21	48	-	-	-	-	-

James Henry Gardner
Left Wing
Pros: 1906–07
Inducted into Hockey Hall of Fame: 1962 (Player)
Birthplace: Montreal, Quebec
B: May 21, 1881
D: November 6, 1940
Shoots: left

Jimmy Gardner grew up playing for teams in his native Montreal. After winning the Stanley Cup with the "Little

Men of Iron" Montreal AAA in 1902, he jumped to a new team—the Wanderers.

With the formation of the International Professional Hockey League in 1904, Gardner moved on to the Calumet Miners. After two seasons in the Midwest, the rugged left wing signed to play for the rival Pittsburgh Pros. Gardner had a solid year in the Steel City, notching 10 goals in 20 games while helping the Pros to a third-place finish.

Following the 1906–07 season, Gardner returned to his hometown. In 1909–10 he served as a player and manager for the Montreal Wanderers and helped to form the National Hockey Association—a forerunner of the NHL.

	Regular Season					Playoffs				
	GP	G	A	PTS	PM	GP	G	A	PTS	PM
Pros	20	10	8	18	61	-	-	-	-	-

Douglas Norman Harvey
Defense
Hornets: 1967
Inducted into Hockey Hall of Fame: 1973 (Player)
Birthplace: Montreal, Quebec
B: December 19, 1924
D: December 26, 1989
Shoots: left

Prior to Bobby Orr's arrival in 1966, Doug Harvey was considered by many to be the finest defenseman ever to play the game. Beginning in 1955 he made the Norris Trophy his personal possession, winning the award seven out of eight seasons.

The 11-time NHL All-Star controlled the tempo of the game like few others have before or since. Harvey keyed the transition game and quarterbacked the power play for Montreal's Cup-winning dynasty of the late 1950s. Far from one-dimensional, he blocked shots and defended with authority.

The Doug Harvey who joined the Hornets in January of 1967 was a shell of his former self. Forty-two years old and overweight, he relied more on guile than ability. But he still could make a pretty first pass, and he still knew how to defend. Harvey became a valued member of the team, appearing in every playoff game during the Hornets' march to the Calder Cup.

	Regular Season					Playoffs				
	GP	G	A	PTS	PM	GP	G	A	PTS	PM
Hornets	28	0	9	9	22	9	0	0	0	2

William Milton Hern

Goaltender
Keystones: 1901–03
Inducted into Hockey Hall of Fame: 1962 (Player)
Birthplace: St. Mary's, Ontario
B: December 5, 1878
D: June 24, 1929
Catches: left

Like many Canadian stars of his day, William "Riley" Hern was lured to Pittsburgh for the opportunity to play for pay. Tending goal for the Keystones, he led the Western Pennsylvania Hockey League in victories while pacing his team to the league title. He was named to the WPHL All-Star Team.

The following year the Keystones fell on hard times, as did Hern. While the team plummeted from first to worst, he lost 10 of 11 games and posted an unsightly 7.96 goals-against average. Hern would rebuild his reputation as a premier goalie after leaving Pittsburgh, backstopping the Montreal Wanderers to four straight Stanley Cups.

	Regular Season					Playoffs			
	GP	MINS	GA	SH	AVE	GP	MINS	GA	SH	AVE
Keystones	31	1240	101	2	4.89	1	40	1	0	1.50

Miles Gilbert Horton

Defense
Hornets: 1949–52
Penguins: 1971–72
Inducted into Hockey Hall of Fame: 1977 (Player)
Birthplace: Cochrane, Ontario
B: January 12, 1930
D: February 21, 1974
Shoots: right

Following two terrific seasons with St. Michael's College in the Ontario Hockey Association, Miles "Tim" Horton turned pro at the age of 19. Labeled a can't-miss prospect, the husky teenage defenseman came to the Steel City to serve his apprenticeship.

Horton possessed all the tools to be a great one. However, his game needed some fine-tuning. During three seasons with the Hornets he showed steady improvement. In 1951–52 he paced the team's blue-liners with 12 goals while helping to lead the club to the Calder Cup. Horton's strong all-around play earned him a promotion to Toronto the following year. It was the start of a stellar 22-year NHL career.

In 1971–72 the rugged rearguard returned to Pittsburgh—this time as a member of the Penguins. Despite missing 34 games due to a broken ankle, he turned in a typically solid

season. Two years later he tragically died in an automobile accident.

	Regular Season					Playoffs				
	GP	G	A	PTS	PM	GP	G	A	PTS	PM
Hornets	192	25	63	88	358	24	1	12	13	32
Penguins	44	2	9	11	40	4	0	1	1	2

Duncan McMillan MacKay

Center
Pirates: 1928
Inducted into Hockey Hall of Fame: 1952 (Player)
Birthplace: Chelsey, Ontario
B: May 25, 1894
D: May 21, 1940
Shoots: left

Over the course of a sterling 16-year career, Duncan "Mickey" MacKay earned a reputation as one of the game's outstanding scorers and playmakers. A clean, gentlemanly player, MacKay was the all-time leading scorer in the Pacific Coast Hockey Association. During his time out West the "Wee Scot" led the Vancouver Millionaires to six PCHA titles and the Stanley Cup in 1915.

Hoping to add some leadership and scoring punch to a lackluster lineup, the Pirates purchased the 34-year-old center from Chicago in September of 1928. However, MacKay was clearly on the downside of his career. Following a brief 10-game trial, he was traded to Boston for another former star and future Hall of Famer, Frank Fredrickson.

	Regular Season					Playoffs				
	GP	G	A	PTS	PM	GP	G	A	PTS	PM
Pirates	10	1	0	1	2	-	-	-	-	-

Frank Sydney Mathers

Defense
Hornets: 1948–56
Inducted into Hockey Hall of Fame: 1992 (Builder)
Birthplace: Winnipeg, Manitoba
B: March 29, 1924
D: February 9, 2005
Shoots: left

Had he played in a different era, Frank Mathers would have enjoyed a long and successful NHL career. Unfortunately, his playing days coincided with the reign of the Original Six, which consigned many top-flight players to minor league careers.

A splendid all-around athlete who played professional football as well as hockey, Mathers joined the Hornets in 1948. Blessed with good size and offensive skills, he quickly developed into one of the American Hockey League's all-time great defensemen. He was named to the AHL All-Star team five straight seasons and helped lead the Hornets to two Calder Cups.

After the Hornets suspended operations in 1956, Mathers joined the Hershey Bears. He served the team for more than 30 years as a player, coach, general manager, and president, earning him an induction into the Hockey Hall of Fame in 1992.

	Regular Season					Playoffs				
	GP	G	A	PTS	PM	GP	G	A	PTS	PM
Hornets	490	61	253	314	429	50	7	21	28	46

Howard William Meeker
Coach/Right Wing
Hornets: 1954–56
Foster Hewitt Memorial Award: 1998
Birthplace: Kitchener, Ontario
B: November 24, 1924
Shoots: right

A true hockey legend, Howie Meeker enjoyed a multifaceted career that spanned all levels of the sport. He first gained notoriety in 1946–47 as a rookie right wing for Toronto, when he beat out another well-known first-year player, Gordie Howe, for the Calder Trophy. Settling into a checking role, he helped spark the Leafs to four Stanley Cups.

Following his playing career, Meeker assumed the Hornets' coaching duties from fellow Hall of Famer King Clancy. Under his guidance, "the Wasps" captured their second Calder Cup in 1955, besting Buffalo in six games. When injuries shortened his bench, Meeker returned to the ice for two games.

Meeker would earn lasting fame—and the Foster Hewitt Memorial Award—as an announcer on *Hockey Night in Canada*. He also operated Howie Meeker's Hockey School for a number of years.

	Regular Season						Playoffs			
	G	W	L	T	PTS	PCT	G	W	L	PCT
Hornets	128	74	42	12	160	.625	14	8	6	.571

Alfred E. Smith
Right Wing
PAC: 1901–02
Duquesne: 1908–09
Bankers: 1908–09
Inducted into Hockey Hall of Fame: 1962 (Player)
Birthplace: Ottawa, Ontario
B: June 3, 1873
D: August 21, 1953
Shoots: right

For at least one Hall of Famer, the Western Pennsylvania Hockey League offered a chance for redemption. In 1898 Ottawa HC star Alf Smith accepted a $100 bonus to play lacrosse for a hometown team. He was promptly barred from playing amateur hockey by the Amateur Athletic Association of Canada.

After coaching for several seasons, Smith jumped at the chance to resume his playing career. He enjoyed a strong season in 1901–02, potting 11 goals while helping the Pittsburgh Athletic Club to a second-place finish. Smith returned to Ottawa as a player-coach, leading the fabled "Silver Seven" to three straight Stanley Cups.

With his career winding down, Smith rejoined the WPHL in 1908–09. Although he stood only 5'7", he was a battler. Suspended for rough play by both the Duquesne and the Bankers, the veteran right wing finished his career in Ottawa.

	Regular Season					Playoffs				
	GP	G	A	PTS	PM	GP	G	A	PTS	PM
PAC	14	11	9	20	17	-	-	-	-	-
Duquesne	2	3	0	3	-	-	-	-	-	-
Bankers	3	2	0	2	-	-	-	-	-	-

Thomas J. Smith
Center
Pros: 1906–07
Lyceum: 1907–08
Bankers: 1909
Inducted into Hockey Hall of Fame: 1973 (Player)
Birthplace: Ottawa, Ontario
B: September 27, 1886
D: August 1, 1966
Shoots: left

Following in the footsteps of his older brother Alf, Tommy Smith came to Pittsburgh to start his pro career. Playing for the Pittsburgh Pros in the International Professional Hockey League, the 20-year-old phenom enjoyed an outstanding season, rolling up 31 goals and 44 points in only 23 games.

After the IPHL ceased operations in 1907, Smith joined the Pittsburgh Lyceum of the Western Pennsylvania Hockey

League. A feisty 5'6" buzz saw, Smith struck for a league-leading 33 goals in his first season.

The high-scoring center opened the 1908–09 campaign with 15 goals in six games. But on December 18, 1908, he jumped to Brantford of the OPHL, causing the Lyceum to fold. Smith returned to the WPHL in time for the playoffs, signing on with the Bankers. He scored three goals in the championship series.

	Regular Season					Playoffs				
	GP	G	A	PTS	PM	GP	G	A	PTS	PM
Pros	23	31	13	44	47	-	-	-	-	-
Lyceum	22	48	0	48	-	1	2	0	2	-
Bankers	-	-	-	-	-	3	3	0	3	3

John Sherratt Stewart
Defense
Hornets: 1937–39
Inducted into Hockey Hall of Fame: 1964 (Player)
Birthplace: Pilot Mound, Manitoba
B: May 6, 1917
D: May 25, 1983
Shoots: left

As a 20-year-old defenseman from the plains of Manitoba, Jack Stewart was eager to make his mark in Pittsburgh. Although a bit crude, the powerful farm boy displayed a penchant for hitting. His punishing bodychecks earned him the nickname "Black Jack."

Following a season and a half with the Hornets, Stewart was called up to the Red Wings. He gradually polished the rough edges from his game and developed into a capable, puck-rushing defender. But physical play remained his forte.

Stewart's strength was legendary. During a practice session his youthful Red Wings teammates, Gordie Howe and Ted Lindsay, decided to test him. Stewart pinned Howe against the boards with one arm and draped Lindsay over the boards with the other.

Following his Hall of Fame career, Stewart returned to the Steel City and coached the Hornets for part of the 1962–63 season.

	Regular Season					Playoffs				
	GP	G	A	PTS	PM	GP	G	A	PTS	PM
Hornets	69	0	1	1	36	2	0	0	0	0

Bruce Stuart
Center
Victorias: 1902–03
Inducted into Hockey Hall of Fame: 1961 (Player)
Birthplace: Ottawa, Ontario
B: November 30, 1882
D: October 28, 1961
Shoots: left

Bruce Stuart came to Pittsburgh in 1902 with his big brother Hod to play in the Western Pennsylvania Hockey League. While Hod signed on with the Bankers, Bruce joined a new club, the Victorias. During the 1902–03 season he skated in 10 games for the Victorias, piling up 16 goals and 22 points.

A gifted and versatile performer, Stuart could play rover or any forward position with equal ability. Standing 6'2" and weighing 180 pounds, he used his large frame to the fullest advantage. Adept at driving to the net and scoring in traffic, Stuart was considered by many to be one of hockey's original power forwards.

Stuart passed away in 1961, shortly after he was inducted into the Hockey Hall of Fame.

	Regular Season					Playoffs				
	GP	G	A	PTS	PM	GP	G	A	PTS	PM
Victorias	10	16	6	22	20	-	-	-	-	-

William Hodgson Stuart
Point
Bankers: 1902–03
Pros: 1905–06
Inducted into Hockey Hall of Fame: 1945 (Player)
Birthplace: Ottawa, Ontario
B: February 20, 1879
D: June 23, 1907

In 1902 William "Hod" Stuart came to Pittsburgh to play in the semipro Western Pennsylvania Hockey League along with his kid brother Bruce. As a member of the Bankers, he led the team to the WPHL title in his first season.

Stuart left the Bankers after one season, but returned to the Steel City in 1905 to play for the Pittsburgh Pros of the International Professional Hockey League. With Stuart playing the point and cover point positions, the Pros finished a strong third in the IPHL.

Like Lionel Conacher, Stuart was an exceptional all-around athlete. An outstanding skater for a big man, he was regarded as the finest two-way defender of his era.

Tragically, he died in an off-season diving accident in

1907. On January 2, 1908, the Hod Stuart Memorial Game, believed to be hockey's first benefit All-Star game, raised nearly $2,000 for his family.

	Regular Season					Playoffs				
	GP	G	A	PTS	PM	GP	G	A	PTS	PM
Bankers	13	7	8	15	29	4	1	2	3	2
Pros	24	12	3	15	69	-	-	-	-	-

William A. Torrey
Front Office
Hornets: 1960s
Inducted into Hockey Hall of Fame: 1995 (Builder)
Birthplace: Montreal, Quebec
B: June 23, 1934

Bill Torrey earned lasting fame and admiration as the architect of the great New York Islanders dynasty of the early 1980s. Through a combination of brilliant drafting and astute trades, he transformed the Islanders from a lowly 12-win expansion team to Stanley Cup champions in eight short years.

In many ways Torrey was the forerunner of today's modern hockey executive. He attended St. Lawrence University, were he studied business and psychology. Nicknamed "Billy Bow-Tie" for his signature apparel, he began his front office apprenticeship in the mid-1960s with the Hornets.

Following the NHL's first wave of expansion he served for two seasons as vice president of the Oakland Seals before moving on to the Islanders. In 1993 Torrey was named president and general manager of the expansion Florida Panthers, a position he held until his retirement in 2001.

Roy Worters
Goaltender
Yellow Jackets: 1923–25
Pirates: 1925–28
Inducted into Hockey Hall of Fame: 1969 (Player)
Birthplace: Toronto, Ontario
B: October 19, 1900
D: November 7, 1957
Catches: left

Roy "Shrimp" Worters arrived in Pittsburgh in the fall of 1923, joining his friend Lionel Conacher. Although he stood only 5'3", Worters was a giant in goal. He backstopped the Yellow Jackets to consecutive United States Amateur Hockey Association titles while establishing himself as the league's premier goalie.

The diminutive netminder continued to shine following the team's entry into the National Hockey League. In 1925–26 he finished second to Ottawa great Alex Connell in goals-against average and shutouts. Two years later he single-handedly lifted the Pirates to a playoff berth while posting a 1.66 goals-against average.

Seeking a hefty raise, Worters refused to report to training camp in 1928. The Pirates promptly dealt him to the New York Americans for Joe Miller and $20,000. His stellar play with the Americans earned him the Hart Memorial Trophy in 1928–29 and the Vezina Trophy two years later.

	Regular Season					Playoffs				
	GP	MINS	GA	SH	AVE	GP	MINS	GA	SH	AVE
Yellow Jackets	59	3120	59	24	1.13	21	1240	20	6	0.97
Pirates	123	7596	252	22	1.99	4	240	12	0	3.00

12

Statistics, Awards, and Honors

No book about the Penguins would be complete without a statistics section. This chapter features a comprehensive statistical overview, including important team and individual records and milestones.

In the first section we've provided an overview of the team's historical performance. It includes season-by-season records and finishes, career records for each coach and general manager, and game-by-game results. The Penguins' monthly performances and records against other NHL teams are detailed as well.

We've also included season-by-season statistics and career scoring and goaltending records for each Penguins player. Top-10 lists are provided for every major statistical category, including goals, assists, points, goals-against average, and shutouts. In addition, we feature a complete section on the team's Stanley Cup Playoff performance, including series-by-series results and team and individual statistics of note.

For true Penguins trivia buffs, we provided a catch-all section. It includes information such as regular-season and playoff attendance figures, minor league teams and coaches, assistant coaches, scouts, and club presidents. A list of the team's TV and radio affiliates also is provided, along with a compilation of Pens play-by-play announcers and color analysts.

The chapter also features an awards and honors section. It includes lists of the team's Hockey Hall of Fame and Penguins Hall of Fame inductees, retired numbers, All-Star selections, and award winners.

On a team blessed with so many once-in-a-generation players, the award winners merit special attention. Over the course of the team's 43-year history Penguins players have earned no fewer than 40 NHL trophies and awards. Indeed, Penguins have captured every major award except for the Vezina Trophy (top goalie) and the Jennings Trophy (fewest goals allowed).

The Pens' first award winner was Lowell MacDonald. Following a two-year absence due to knee surgery, MacDonald returned in 1972–73 to capture the Bill Masterton Trophy. Eight years later promising young defenseman Randy Carlyle garnered the Norris Trophy, while teammate Rick Kehoe was awarded the Lady Byng Trophy for gentlemanly play.

Through the years Penguins have won numerous other prestigious awards, including the Conn Smythe Trophy for the MVP of the playoffs (Mario Lemieux and Evgeni Malkin), the Maurice Richard Trophy (Sidney Crosby) for leading goal scorer, the Frank Selke Trophy for best defensive player (Ron Francis) and the Calder Trophy for top rookie (Lemieux and Malkin).

In recent seasons the Penguins have virtually annexed the Art Ross Trophy, which is awarded each year to the league's leading point scorer. Beginning in 1987–88, Pens superstars such as Lemieux, Jaromir Jagr, Sidney Crosby and Malkin have captured the award an astounding 13 times in 22 seasons—including a remarkable run of seven-straight years from 1995 through 2001. It is an achievement unparalleled by any other team in the annals of NHL history.

Likewise, the Penguins are well represented on the list of Hart Trophy winners. Lemieux (1988, 1993, 1995), Jagr (1999), and Crosby (2007) each have received the league's MVP trophy. In addition, the trio combined to win the coveted Lester B. Pearson Award seven times. A true measure of a player's worth, the award is bestowed each year to the league's top player by the NHL Players' Association.

ck Kehoe (left) and Randy Carlyle (right) show off
ir hardware at the 1981 NHL Awards Banquet. Kehoe
n the Lady Byng Trophy; Carlyle the Norris Trophy.

Penguins Season-by-Season Records

SEASON	GP	W	L	T	OTL	SOL	PTS	GF	GA	FINISH
1967–68	74	27	34	13	—	—	67	195	216	5th, West
1968–69	76	20	45	11	—	—	51	189	252	5th, West
1969–70	76	26	38	12	—	—	64	182	238	2nd, West
1970–71	78	21	37	20	—	—	62	221	240	6th, West
1971–72	78	26	38	14	—	—	66	220	258	4th, West
1972–73	78	32	37	9	—	—	73	257	265	5th, West
1973–74	78	28	41	9	—	—	65	242	273	5th, West
1974–75	80	37	28	15	—	—	89	326	289	3rd, Norris
1975–76	80	35	33	12	—	—	82	339	303	3rd, Norris
1976–77	80	34	33	13	—	—	81	240	252	3rd, Norris
1977–78	80	25	37	18	—	—	68	254	321	4th, Norris
1978–79	80	36	31	13	—	—	85	281	279	2nd, Norris
1979–80	80	30	37	13	—	—	73	251	303	3rd, Norris
1980–81	80	30	37	13	—	—	73	302	345	3rd, Norris
1981–82	80	31	36	13	—	—	75	310	337	4th, Patrick
1982–83	80	18	53	9	—	—	45	257	394	6th, Patrick
1983–84	80	16	58	6	—	—	38	254	390	6th, Patrick
1984–85	80	24	51	5	—	—	53	276	385	6th, Patrick
1985–86	80	34	38	8	—	—	76	313	305	5th, Patrick
1986–87	80	30	38	12	—	—	72	297	290	5th, Patrick
1987–88	80	36	35	9	—	—	81	319	316	6th, Patrick
1988–89	80	40	33	7	—	—	87	347	349	2nd, Patrick
1989–90	80	32	40	8	—	—	72	318	359	5th, Patrick
1990–91	80	41	33	6	—	—	88	342	305	1st, Patrick
1991–92	80	39	32	9	—	—	87	343	308	3rd, Patrick
1992–93	84	56	21	7	—	—	119	367	268	1st, Patrick
1993–94	84	44	27	13	—	—	101	299	285	1st, Northeast
1994–95	48	29	16	3	—	—	61	181	158	2nd, Northeast
1995–96	82	49	29	4	—	—	102	362	284	1st, Northeast
1996–97	82	38	36	8	—	—	84	285	280	2nd, Northeast
1997–98	82	40	24	18	—	—	98	228	188	1st, Northeast
1998–99	82	38	30	14	—	—	90	242	225	3rd, Atlantic
1999–00	82	37	31	8	6	—	88	241	236	3rd, Atlantic
2000–01	82	42	28	9	3	—	96	281	256	3rd, Atlantic
2001–02	82	28	41	8	5	—	69	198	249	5th, Atlantic
2002–03	82	27	44	6	5	—	65	189	255	5th, Atlantic
2003–04	82	23	47	8	4	—	58	190	303	5th, Atlantic
2005–06	82	22	46	—	8	6	58	244	316	5th, Atlantic
2006–07	82	47	24	—	5	6	105	277	246	2nd, Atlantic
2007–08	82	47	27	—	4	4	102	247	216	1st, Atlantic
2008–09	82	45	28	—	3	6	99	264	239	2nd, Atlantic
2009–10	82	47	28	—	5	2	101	257	237	2nd, Atlantic

Penguins Season-by-Season Home Records

SEASON	GP	W	L	T	OTL	SOL	PTS
1967–68	37	15	12	10	—	—	40
1968–69	38	12	20	6	—	—	30
1969–70	38	17	13	8	—	—	42
1970–71	39	18	12	9	—	—	45
1971–72	39	18	15	6	—	—	42
1972–73	39	24	11	4	—	—	52
1973–74	39	15	18	6	—	—	36
1974–75	40	25	5	10	—	—	60
1975–76	40	23	11	6	—	—	52
1976–77	40	22	12	6	—	—	50
1977–78	40	16	15	9	—	—	41
1978–79	40	23	12	5	—	—	51
1979–80	40	20	13	7	—	—	47
1980–81	40	21	16	3	—	—	45
1981–82	40	21	11	8	—	—	50
1982–83	40	14	22	4	—	—	32
1983–84	40	7	29	4	—	—	18
1984–85	40	17	20	3	—	—	37
1985–86	40	20	15	5	—	—	45
1986–87	40	19	15	6	—	—	44
1987–88	40	22	12	6	—	—	50
1988–89	40	24	13	3	—	—	51
1989–90	40	22	15	3	—	—	47
1990–91	40	25	12	3	—	—	53
1991–92	40	21	13	6	—	—	48
1992–93	42	32	6	4	—	—	68
1993–94	42	25	9	8	—	—	58
1994–95	24	18	5	1	—	—	37
1995–96	41	32	9	0	—	—	64
1996–97	41	25	11	5	—	—	55
1997–98	41	21	10	10	—	—	52
1998–99	41	21	10	10	—	—	52
1999–00	41	23	11	7	—	—	53
2000–01	41	24	15	2	—	—	50
2001–02	41	16	20	4	1	—	37
2002–03	41	15	22	2	2	—	34
2003–04	41	13	22	6	—	—	32
2005–06	41	12	21	—	5	3	32
2006–07	41	26	10	—	2	3	57
2007–08	41	26	10	—	2	3	57
2008–09	41	25	13	—	1	2	53
2009–10	41	25	12	—	3	1	54

Penguins Season-by-Season Road Records

SEASON	GP	W	L	T	OTL	SOL	PTS
1967–68	37	12	22	3	—	—	27
1968–69	38	8	25	5	—	—	21
1969–70	38	9	25	4	—	—	22
1970–71	39	3	25	11	—	—	17
1971–72	39	8	23	8	—	—	24
1972–73	39	8	26	5	—	—	21
1973–74	39	13	23	3	—	—	29
1974–75	40	12	23	5	—	—	29
1975–76	40	12	22	6	—	—	30
1976–77	40	12	21	7	—	—	31
1977–78	40	9	22	9	—	—	27
1978–79	40	13	19	8	—	—	34
1979–80	40	10	24	6	—	—	26
1980–81	40	9	21	10	—	—	28
1981–82	40	10	25	5	—	—	25
1982–83	40	4	31	5	—	—	13
1983–84	40	9	29	2	—	—	20
1984–85	40	7	31	2	—	—	16
1985–86	40	14	23	3	—	—	31
1986–87	40	11	23	6	—	—	28
1987–88	40	14	23	3	—	—	31
1988–89	40	16	20	4	—	—	36
1989–90	40	10	25	5	—	—	25
1990–91	40	16	21	3	—	—	35
1991–92	40	18	19	3	—	—	39
1992–93	42	24	15	3	—	—	51
1993–94	42	19	18	5	—	—	43
1994–95	24	11	11	2	—	—	24
1995–96	41	17	20	4	—	—	38
1996–97	41	13	25	3	—	—	29
1997–98	41	19	14	8	—	—	46
1998–99	41	17	20	4	—	—	38
1999–00	41	14	20	1	6	—	35
2000–01	41	18	13	7	3	—	46
2001–02	41	12	21	4	4	—	32
2002–03	41	12	22	4	3	—	31
2003–04	41	10	25	2	4	—	26
2005–06	41	10	25	—	3	3	26
2006–07	41	21	14	—	3	3	48
2007–08	41	21	17	—	2	1	45
2008–09	41	20	15	—	2	4	46
2009–10	41	22	16	—	2	1	47

Penguins Season-by-Season Openers

HOME (22–13–7)				ROAD (17–17–8)			
Oct. 2, 2009	**vs. NY Rangers**	**3–2**	**W**	Oct. 3, 2009	at NY Islanders	4–3	W*
Oct. 11, 2008	vs. New Jersey	1–2	L*	Oct. 20, 2008	at Boston	2–1	W*
Oct. 6, 2007	vs. Anaheim	5–4	W	**Oct. 5, 2007**	**at Carolina**	**1–4**	**L**
Oct. 5, 2006	**vs. Philadelphia**	**4–0**	**W**	Oct. 12, 2006	at NY Rangers	6–5	W
Oct. 8, 2005	vs. Boston	6–7	L*	**Oct. 5, 2005**	**at New Jersey**	**1–5**	**L**
Oct. 10, 2003	**vs. Los Angeles**	**0–3**	**L**	Oct. 11, 2003	at Philadelphia	3–3	T*
Oct. 10, 2002	**vs. Toronto**	**0–6**	**L**	Oct. 14, 2002	at Toronto	5–4	W
Oct. 10, 2001	**vs. Colorado**	**1–3**	**L**	Oct. 14, 2001	at Buffalo	1–4	L
Oct. 13, 2000	vs. Tampa Bay	3–2	W	Oct. 19, 2000	at Ottawa	3–3	T*
Oct. 8, 1999	vs. Colorado	3–3	T*	**Oct. 1, 1999**	**at Dallas**	**4–6**	**L**
Oct. 17, 1998	vs. NY Rangers	3–3	T*	**Oct. 10, 1998**	**at NY Islanders**	**4–3**	**W**
Oct. 1, 1997	**vs. Los Angeles**	**3–3**	**T***	Oct. 3, 1997	at Carolina	4–3	W
Oct. 5, 1996	**vs. Tampa Bay**	**3–4**	**L***	Oct. 8, 1996	at Hartford	3–7	L
Oct. 7, 1995	**vs. Toronto**	**8–3**	**W**	Oct. 9, 1995	at Colorado	6–6	T*
Jan. 27, 1995	vs. Ottawa	5–4	W	**Jan. 20, 1995**	**at Tampa Bay**	**5–3**	**W**
Oct. 7, 1993	vs. Montreal	2–1	W*	**Oct. 5, 1993**	**at Philadelphia**	**3–4**	**L**
Oct. 6, 1992	**vs. Philadelphia**	**3–3**	**T***	Oct. 10, 1992	at Montreal	3–3	T*
Oct. 6, 1991	vs. Philadelphia	2–2	T*	**Oct. 4, 1991**	**at Buffalo**	**5–4**	**W**
Oct. 7, 1990	vs. New Jersey	7–4	W	**Oct. 5, 1990**	**at Washington**	**7–4**	**W**
Oct. 10, 1989	vs. Winnipeg	5–1	W	**Oct. 5, 1989**	**at Boston**	**4–5**	**L**
Oct. 11, 1988	vs. Washington	8–7	W	**Oct. 7, 1988**	**at Washington**	**6–4**	**W**
Oct. 13, 1987	vs. Buffalo	8–3	W	**Oct. 8, 1987**	**at NY Rangers**	**4–4**	**T***
Oct. 9, 1986	**vs. Washington**	**5–4**	**W**	Oct. 12, 1986	at Chicago	4–1	W
Oct. 10, 1985	**vs. Montreal**	**3–5**	**L**	Oct. 16, 1985	at Chicago	5–5	T*
Oct. 17, 1984	vs. Vancouver	4–3	W	**Oct. 11, 1984**	**at Boston**	**3–4**	**L**
Oct. 8, 1983	vs. NY Rangers	1–6	L	**Oct. 4, 1983**	**at St. Louis**	**3–5**	**L**
Oct. 9, 1982	vs. NY Rangers	3–5	L	**Oct. 5, 1982**	**at New Jersey**	**3–3**	**T**
Oct. 10, 1981	vs. Quebec	2–1	W	**Oct. 6, 1981**	**at St. Louis**	**2–6**	**L**
Oct. 11, 1980	vs. Winnipeg	5–4	W	**Oct. 9, 1980**	**at Philadelphia**	**4–7**	**L**
Oct. 10, 1979	**vs. Winnipeg**	**4–2**	**W**	Oct. 14, 1979	at Boston	4–1	W
Oct. 11, 1978	**vs. Toronto**	**2–3**	**L**	Oct. 12, 1978	at Boston	2–8	L
Oct. 12, 1977	**vs. St. Louis**	**4–2**	**W**	Oct. 14, 1977	at Washington	1–2	L
Oct. 6, 1976	**vs. Vancouver**	**9–5**	**W**	Oct. 7, 1976	at Montreal	1–10	L
Oct. 11, 1975	vs. Washington	7–5	W	**Oct. 7, 1975**	**at Washington**	**4–2**	**W**
Oct. 12, 1974	vs. Detroit	7–2	W	**Oct. 9, 1974**	**at Minnesota**	**4–2**	**W**
Oct. 13, 1973	vs. NY Rangers	2–8	L	**Oct. 12, 1973**	**at Atlanta**	**4–3**	**W**
Oct. 7, 1972	**vs. Los Angeles**	**4–2**	**W**	Oct. 11, 1972	at St. Louis	5–2	W
Oct. 9, 1971	**vs. Philadelphia**	**3–2**	**W**	Oct. 10, 1971	at Buffalo	1–2	L
Oct. 10, 1970	**vs. Buffalo**	**1–2**	**L**	Oct. 15, 1970	at Minnesota	2–4	L
Oct. 11, 1969	**vs. California**	**2–2**	**T**	Oct. 19, 1969	at Boston	0–4	L
Oct. 12, 1968	**vs. Montreal**	**1–1**	**T**	Oct. 16, 1968	at Toronto	2–2	T
Oct. 11, 1967	**vs. Montreal**	**1–2**	**L**	Oct. 13, 1967	at St. Louis	3–1	W

Season Openers in Bold   * overtime game
Record in Season Openers (17–18–6)
2000 Season Opener played against Nashville in Japan (3–1 loss)
2008 Season Opener played against Ottawa in Sweden (4–3 OT win)

Penguins Month-By-Month Records

	OCT.	NOV.	DEC.	JAN.	FEB.	MAR.	APR.	MAY	SEASON
1967–68	3–6–1	6–3–2	4–8–2	4–7–2	4–5–3	6–5–3			27–34–13
1968–69	1–4–2	4–8–2	2–10–2	3–10–1	4–6–2	6–7–2			20–45–11
1969–70	1–4–3	5–6–2	5–7–0	3–7–3	8–5–0	3–7–4	1–2–0		26–38–12
1970–71	2–4–3	3–6–5	5–7–3	6–5–1	3–7–3	2–7–3	0–1–2		21–37–20
1971–72	5–5–2	3–9–0	3–7–4	1–8–3	7–6–0	6–3–4	1–0–1		26–38–14
1972–73	5–5–0	7–5–2	3–6–4	6–9–0	6–5–1	4–7–2	1–0–0		32–37–9
1973–74	4–4–1	3–7–2	2–10–2	5–8–0	5–6–1	7–4–3	2–2–0		28–41–9
1974–75	2–4–1	6–6–3	4–6–4	8–3–2	7–3–3	9–4–2	1–2–0		37–28–15
1975–76	4–2–1	6–8–1	5–7–2	4–7–3	8–2–4	7–6–1	1–1–0		35–33–12
1976–77	2–6–4	6–5–1	7–5–1	7–4–2	5–5–4	5–8–1	2–0–0		34–33–13
1977–78	3–5–1	4–6–3	4–6–4	5–5–3	4–2–5	2–11–2	3–2–0		25–37–18
1978–79	1–6–2	5–7–1	9–2–4	5–7–1	6–3–1	8–4–4	2–2–0		36–31–13
1979–80	4–4–1	5–4–3	5–3–7	5–10–0	4–7–0	6–7–2	1–2–0		30–37–13
1980–81	4–5–1	2–8–3	5–6–3	6–6–1	7–5–1	5–6–3	1–1–1		30–37–13
1981–82	5–7–2	7–1–2	4–7–2	5–8–2	3–8–2	5–5–3	2–0–0		31–36–13
1982–83	3–9–1	5–3–3	3–9–2	1–12–1	3–11–0	3–7–2	0–2–0		18–53–9
1983–84	3–9–0	3–7–3	3–8–2	1–11–0	3–10–1	3–12–0	0–1–0		16–58–6
1984–85	5–4–0	1–8–3	8–5–1	4–8–1	2–10–0	4–12–0	0–4–0		24–51–5
1985–86	3–5–2	5–7–1	8–6–1	7–4–2	7–4–1	3–9–1	1–3–0		34–38–8
1986–87	8–3–0	5–5–4	2–7–3	4–8–1	4–7–2	5–8–2	2–0–0		30–38–12
1987–88	3–6–3	6–4–2	7–4–2	5–9–2	4–7–0	9–5–0	2–0–0		36–35–9
1988–89	7–4–0	7–6–0	9–2–3	5–6–1	4–6–3	6–9–0	2–0–0		40–33–7
1989–90	3–7–2	6–7–0	7–5–1	6–6–1	8–5–1	2–10–3			32–40–8
1990–91	6–6–1	5–6–1	10–6–1	7–4–0	4–7–1	9–4–2			41–33–6
1991–92	5–5–2	8–3–2	9–5–0	3–7–1	3–7–3	10–3–1	1–2–0		39–32–9
1992–93	8–1–2	9–5–1	9–3–1	8–5–1	5–5–1	11–2–0	6–0–1		56–21–7
1993–94	7–4–1	5–3–5	6–4–2	6–3–3	7–6–1	9–5–1	4–2–0		44–27–13
1994–95				5–0–0	9–3–2	8–6–0	7–5–1	0–2–0	29–16–3
1995–96	4–2–2	10–3–1	10–4–0	7–7–0	6–5–1	9–5–0	3–3–0		49–29–4
1996–97	2–8–0	6–5–2	11–2–2	8–3–1	4–7–0	5–8–2	2–3–1		38–36–8
1997–98	7–5–2	7–4–3	7–3–3	8–3–2	1–2–3	6–3–4	4–4–1		40–24–18
1998–99	4–3–2	6–3–3	5–4–2	8–5–0	9–5–0	4–5–6	2–5–1		38–30–14
1999–00*	2–3–3–1	6–5–0–2	8–4–0–2	5–8–1–0	5–3–4–1	8–6–0–0	3–2–0–0		37–31–8–6
2000–01	5–4–1–0	6–4–2–1	6–6–3–0	8–5–0–1	7–3–1–0	8–5–2–0	2–1–0–1		42–28–9–3
2001–02	4–6–1–1	6–4–2–1	4–7–2–0	8–6–0–1	1–4–1–1	5–7–1–1	0–7–1–0		28–41–8–5
2002–03	6–2–2–0	5–4–1–3	4–9–0–2	6–7–1–0	4–8–0–0	1–13–2–0	1–1–0–0		27–44–6–5
2003–04	2–4–3–0	3–8–1–1	4–8–1–2	2–14–0–0	2–9–0–1	8–4–3–0	2–0–0–0		23–47–8–4
2005–06**	1–5–4–1	6–7–0–1	3–7–2–0	2–11–1–1	2–4–0–1	5–8–0–1	3–4–1–1		22–46–8–6
2006–07	6–3–0–0	5–5–3–1	5–7–0–2	8–2–0–2	9–3–1–0	12–3–1–1	2–1–0–0		47–24–5–6
2007–08	6–4–0–1	5–7–1–0	9–5–0–0	8–3–0–2	8–3–2–1	10–4–1–0	1–1–0–0		47–27–4–4
2008–09	5–4–1–1	9–2–0–1	5–8–0–1	5–8–1–0	7–4–0–1	10–1–0–2	4–1–1–0		45–28–3–6
2009–10	11–3–0–0	8–6–0–0	7–5–1–0	8–7–0–0	2–1–2–1	8–4–2–1	3–2–0–0		47–28–5–2
TOTALS***	172– 190– 55–7–3	225– 220– 72–12–3	236– 240– 76–9–3	226– 276– 43–4–5	211– 224– 56–8–4	262– 259– 71–5–5	75–69– 10–13–1	0–2–0 0–0	1,407–1,480– 383–48–24

* Seasons 1999–00 through 2003–04 display wins, losses, overtime ties, and overtime losses.

** Seasons 2005–06 through 2009–10 display wins, losses, overtime losses, and shootout losses.

*** Totals display wins, losses, ties (regulation and overtime), overtime losses, and shootout losses.

Penguins All-Time Coaching Records

Coach	Seasons	GP	W	L	T	OL	SL	PTS	PCT
Red Sullivan	1967–1969	150	47	79	24	—	—	118	.393
Red Kelly	1969–1973	274	90	132	52	—	—	232	.423
Ken Schinkel	1973–1974, 1976–1977	203	83	92	28	—	—	194	.478
Marc Boileau	1974–1976	151	66	61	24	—	—	156	.517
Johnny Wilson	1977–1980	240	91	105	44	—	—	226	.471
Eddie Johnston	1980–1983, 1993–1997	516	232	224	60	—	—	524	.508
Lou Angotti	1983–1984	80	16	58	6	—	—	38	.238
Bob Berry	1984–1987	240	88	127	25	—	—	201	.419
Pierre Creamer	1987–1988	80	36	35	9	—	—	81	.506
Gene Ubriaco	1988–1989	106	50	47	9	—	—	109	.514
Craig Patrick	1989–1990, 1997	74	29	36	9	—	—	67	.453
Bob Johnson	1990–1991	80	41	33	6	—	—	88	.550
Scotty Bowman	1991–1993	164	95	53	16	—	—	206	.628
Kevin Constantine	1997–1999	189	86	64	35	4	—	211	.558
Herb Brooks	1999–2000	57	29	21	5	2	—	65	.570
Ivan Hlinka	2000–2001	86	42	32	9	3	—	96	.558
Rick Kehoe	2001–2003	160	55	81	14	10	—	134	.419
Eddie Olczyk	2003–2005	113	31	64	8	8	2	80	.354
Michel Therrien	2005–2009	272	135	105	—	15	17	302	.555
Dan Bylsma	2009–present	107	65	31	—	6	5	141	.659
Totals		**3342**	**1407**	**1480**	**383**	**48**	**24**	**3269**	**.489**

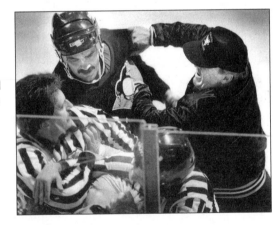

Pierre Creamer (right), seen breaking up a training camp fight, posted a winning record in his only season behind the Pens' bench.

Penguins All-Time General Manager Records

General Manager	Seasons	GP	W	L	T	OL	SL	PTS	PCT
Jack Riley	1967–1970, 1972–1974	375	130	190	55	—	—	315	.420
Red Kelly	1970–1972	126	33	64	29	—	—	95	.377
Jack Button	1974–1975	117	54	44	19	—	—	127	.543
Wren Blair	1975–1976	105	44	44	17	—	—	105	.500
Baz Bastien	1976–1983	527	193	248	86	—	—	472	.448
No GM	1983	8	2	5	1	—	—	5	.313
Eddie Johnston	1983–1988	400	140	220	40	—	—	320	.400
Tony Esposito	1988–1989	106	50	47	9	—	—	109	.514
Craig Patrick	1989–2006	1250	575	511	127	31	6	1314	.526
Ray Shero	2006–present	328	186	107	—	17	18	407	.620
Totals		**3342**	**1407**	**1480**	**383**	**48**	**24**	**3269**	**.489**

Penguins Game-by-Game Results

1967–68

RECORD: 27–34–13, 5th, West Division

DATE	RESULT	SCORE	OPPONENT	DATE	RESULT	SCORE	OPPONENT
Oct. 11	L	1–2	MONTREAL	Jan. 18	L	2–3	Los Angeles
Oct. 13	W	3–1	St. Louis	Jan. 20	W	8–5	DETROIT
Oct. 14	L	2–4	ST. LOUIS	Jan. 21	L	3–4	Minnesota
Oct. 18	T	3–3	MINNESOTA	Jan. 27	L	3–5	LOS ANGELES
Oct. 19	L	0–1	Philadelphia	Jan. 28	W	1–0	Boston
Oct. 21	W	4–2	CHICAGO	Jan. 31	L	4–9	St. Louis
Oct. 22	L	4–6	New York	Feb. 1	W	2–0	ST. LOUIS
Oct. 25	W	4–1	OAKLAND	Feb. 3	T	3–3	TORONTO
Oct. 28	L	3–5	LOS ANGELES	Feb. 7	W	4–1	Oakland
Oct. 29	L	2–4	Boston	Feb. 8	L	1–3	Los Angeles
Nov. 1	W	4–1	Minnesota	Feb. 10	T	2–2	NEW YORK
Nov. 4	W	1–0	Oakland	Feb. 14	W	6–3	MINNESOTA
Nov. 8	T	1–1	PHILADELPHIA	Feb. 16	L	1–3	ST. LOUIS
Nov. 9	L	1–5	Detroit	Feb. 17	L	3–4	Montreal
Nov. 11	L	1–5	ST. LOUIS	Feb. 21	T	1–1	PHILADELPHIA
Nov. 15	W	5–0	PHILADELPHIA	Feb. 24	L	1–3	OAKLAND
Nov. 18	W	5–3	St. Louis	Feb. 25	W	2–1	Philadelphia
Nov. 22	W	4–1	BOSTON	Feb. 27	L	3–5	BOSTON
Nov. 24	L	3–5	Los Angeles	Mar. 2	T	6–6	OAKLAND
Nov. 25	T	2–2	Oakland	Mar. 6	L	2–4	St. Louis
Nov. 29	W	6–1	OAKLAND	Mar. 7	T	2–2	Minnesota
Dec. 2	L	1–4	NEW YORK	Mar. 9	W	3–1	LOS ANGELES
Dec. 3	L	1–6	Detroit	Mar. 13	L	3–4	Chicago
Dec. 6	L	2–7	Chicago	Mar. 16	L	4–6	Montreal
Dec. 9	W	3–2	Minnesota	Mar. 17	L	0–3	New York
Dec. 10	L	4–7	MINNESOTA	Mar. 20	W	4–2	ST. LOUIS
Dec. 13	W	2–1	Toronto	Mar. 23	L	0–3	Minnesota
Dec. 16	T	1–1	CHICAGO	Mar. 24	T	4–4	MINNESOTA
Dec. 17	L	1–2	Philadelphia	Mar. 26	W	2–1	Los Angeles
Dec. 21	L	1–4	Los Angeles	Mar. 27	W	7–4	Oakland
Dec. 23	W	4–0	MINNESOTA	Mar. 30	W	2–0	Philadelphia
Dec. 25	W	4–3	LOS ANGELES	Mar. 31	W	5–1	PHILADELPHIA
Dec. 27	T	0–0	OAKLAND				
Dec. 29	L	1–2	St. Louis	Home games in CAPS			
Dec. 30	L	2–5	DETROIT				
Jan. 4	W	4–3	LOS ANGELES				
Jan. 6	T	2–2	PHILADELPHIA				
Jan. 7	L	1–3	Philadelphia				
Jan. 10	L	3–4	MONTREAL				
Jan. 12	W	4–3	TORONTO				
Jan. 13	L	0–7	Toronto				
Jan. 17	T	1–1	Oakland				

1968–69

RECORD: 20–45–11, 5th, West Division

DATE	RESULT	SCORE	OPPONENT	DATE	RESULT	SCORE	OPPONENT
Oct. 12	T	1–1	MONTREAL	Jan. 16	L	2–3	Detroit
Oct. 16	T	2–2	Toronto	Jan. 18	L	0–4	Los Angeles
Oct. 17	L	0–3	Philadelphia	Jan. 19	L	3–6	Oakland
Oct. 19	L	1–5	BOSTON	Jan. 23	L	1–3	MINNESOTA
Oct. 23	L	5–8	CHICAGO	Jan. 25	L	0–2	TORONTO
Oct. 26	W	4–2	ST. LOUIS	Jan. 26	L	3–5	Philadelphia
Oct. 30	L	3–7	New York	Jan. 29	L	1–2	ST. LOUIS
Nov. 2	L	2–3	Los Angeles	Feb. 1	T	2–2	PHILADELPHIA
Nov. 3	W	3–1	Oakland	Feb. 2	L	3–7	New York
Nov. 6	L	1–3	ST. LOUIS	Feb. 5	W	3–2	NEW YORK
Nov. 7	L	4–5	Montreal	Feb. 8	L	2–4	LOS ANGELES
Nov. 9	L	0–3	PHILADELPHIA	Feb. 9	L	1–3	Minnesota
Nov. 13	L	5–6	Chicago	Feb. 12	L	0–2	St. Louis
Nov. 14	L	4–6	CHICAGO	Feb. 15	T	4–4	OAKLAND
Nov. 16	L	1–2	NEW YORK	Feb. 16	L	0–4	MONTREAL
Nov. 20	L	2–5	Toronto	Feb. 19	W	3–0	BOSTON
Nov. 21	W	3–1	OAKLAND	Feb. 20	L	0–3	Detroit
Nov. 23	T	2–2	LOS ANGELES	Feb. 22	W	3–2	DETROIT
Nov. 27	T	3–3	TORONTO	Feb. 27	W	4–3	CHICAGO
Nov. 28	W	3–2	Chicago	Mar. 1	T	3–3	Toronto
Nov. 30	W	4–2	Los Angeles	Mar. 2	L	0–4	Boston
Dec. 1	T	4–4	Oakland	Mar. 5	W	4–2	ST. LOUIS
Dec. 4	L	2–7	DETROIT	Mar. 8	L	3–5	NEW YORK
Dec. 7	T	1–1	St. Louis	Mar. 12	L	3–4	New York
Dec. 8	L	1–4	TORONTO	Mar. 15	L	1–3	Los Angeles
Dec. 11	W	4–2	Minnesota	Mar. 16	L	2–7	Oakland
Dec. 14	L	1–2	LOS ANGELES	Mar. 19	L	2–3	BOSTON
Dec. 15	L	3–5	Boston	Mar. 20	L	3–5	Montreal
Dec. 17	L	2–8	Philadelphia	Mar. 22	W	2–1	St. Louis
Dec. 21	L	1–3	MINNESOTA	Mar. 23	W	5–0	MINNESOTA
Dec. 22	L	1–3	Chicago	Mar. 25	W	3–1	Minnesota
Dec. 25	W	6–3	DETROIT	Mar. 26	W	8–4	LOS ANGELES
Dec. 26	L	2–3	St. Louis	Mar. 29	T	3–3	Philadelphia
Dec. 28	L	3–4	OAKLAND	Mar. 30	W	2–1	PHILADELPHIA
Dec. 31	L	3–4	MONTREAL				
Jan. 2	W	5–2	Montreal				
Jan. 4	T	1–1	PHILADELPHIA	Home games in CAPS			
Jan. 5	L	1–2	Detroit				
Jan. 9	W	7–2	MINNESOTA				
Jan. 11	L	2–4	OAKLAND				
Jan. 12	L	4–8	Boston				
Jan. 15	W	3–1	Minnesota				

1969–70

RECORD: 26–38–12, 2nd, West Division

DATE	RESULT	SCORE	OPPONENT	DATE	RESULT	SCORE	OPPONENT
Oct. 11	T	2–2	OAKLAND	Jan. 24	W	4–2	LOS ANGELES
Oct. 16	T	3–3	PHILADELPHIA	Jan. 25	L	1–3	Boston
Oct. 18	T	3–3	BOSTON	Jan. 28	T	4–4	TORONTO
Oct. 19	L	0–4	Boston	Jan. 31	W	2–1	ST. LOUIS
Oct. 21	L	3–4	Oakland	Feb. 1	L	0–6	New York
Oct. 22	L	0–2	Los Angeles	Feb. 4	W	7–5	Minnesota
Oct. 25	W	4–1	Minnesota	Feb. 7	W	3–1	LOS ANGELES
Oct. 29	L	1–3	NEW YORK	Feb. 8	W	6–3	MINNESOTA
Nov. 1	W	6–3	MINNESOTA	Feb. 11	L	1–7	Chicago
Nov. 2	L	3–4	Detroit	Feb. 14	L	0–3	BOSTON
Nov. 5	L	2–4	DETROIT	Feb. 15	W	4–2	Detroit
Nov. 8	L	1–4	CHICAGO	Feb. 17	W	4–2	PHILADELPHIA
Nov. 12	W	3–0	Toronto	Feb. 19	W	6–1	Los Angeles
Nov. 13	L	0–4	St. Louis	Feb. 21	L	3–6	Oakland
Nov. 15	W	3–1	LOS ANGELES	Feb. 25	L	2–3	Montreal
Nov. 19	L	0–4	ST. LOUIS	Feb. 26	W	1–0	LOS ANGELES
Nov. 22	W	5–3	PHILADELPHIA	Feb. 28	W	3–2	OAKLAND
Nov. 23	L	2–3	Chicago	Mar. 4	W	2–1	MONTREAL
Nov. 26	T	4–4	Minnesota	Mar. 5	L	3–5	Detroit
Nov. 29	W	5–3	OAKLAND	Mar. 7	T	2–2	ST. LOUIS
Nov. 30	T	3–3	Philadelphia	Mar. 8	T	0–0	New York
Dec. 3	W	2–1	DETROIT	Mar. 11	T	2–2	Oakland
Dec. 6	L	0–5	Toronto	Mar. 12	L	1–4	Los Angeles
Dec. 7	W	3–2	TORONTO	Mar. 14	L	3–6	Minnesota
Dec. 10	W	2–0	Los Angeles	Mar. 18	L	0–2	NEW YORK
Dec. 12	L	1–4	Oakland	Mar. 19	L	1–3	St. Louis
Dec. 14	L	1–2	Boston	Mar. 21	L	3–5	CHICAGO
Dec. 17	L	2–5	MONTREAL	Mar. 22	L	4–5	Montreal
Dec. 20	L	4–6	BOSTON	Mar. 25	W	2–0	MINNESOTA
Dec. 21	L	0–4	Philadelphia	Mar. 28	W	2–1	Philadelphia
Dec. 26	W	3–2	New York	Mar. 29	T	5–5	ST. LOUIS
Dec. 27	L	0–3	CHICAGO	Apr. 1	W	4–1	PHILADELPHIA
Dec. 31	W	4–2	MONTREAL	Apr. 4	L	1–3	St. Louis
Jan. 3	L	0–6	St. Louis	Apr. 5	L	1–5	MINNESOTA
Jan. 4	T	4–4	TORONTO				
Jan. 7	L	3–5	NEW YORK	Home games in CAPS			
Jan. 8	L	1–3	Montreal				
Jan. 10	L	3–5	DETROIT				
Jan. 14	L	0–5	Chicago				
Jan. 17	L	0–4	Toronto				
Jan. 18	W	6–4	Philadelphia				
Jan. 21	T	3–3	OAKLAND				

1970–71

RECORD: 21–37–20, 6th, West Division

DATE	RESULT	SCORE	OPPONENT	DATE	RESULT	SCORE	OPPONENT
Oct. 10	L	1–2	BUFFALO	Jan. 14	T	2–2	Detroit
Oct. 15	L	2–4	Minnesota	Jan. 16	W	4–3	Vancouver
Oct. 17	T	0–0	PHILADELPHIA	Jan. 20	W	4–2	California
Oct. 18	T	1–1	Buffalo	Jan. 21	L	2–4	Los Angeles
Oct. 21	L	2–4	Los Angeles	Jan. 23	W	4–1	VANCOUVER
Oct. 23	W	3–1	California	Jan. 27	W	3–1	TORONTO
Oct. 25	T	1–1	Vancouver	Jan. 28	L	1–4	Chicago
Oct. 28	W	5–3	LOS ANGELES	Jan. 30	W	3–1	CHICAGO
Oct. 31	L	2–5	CHICAGO	Feb. 3	W	6–1	CALIFORNIA
Nov. 1	L	2–3	Philadelphia	Feb. 5	T	2–2	St. Louis
Nov. 4	W	8–3	VANCOUVER	Feb. 7	L	0–1	Chicago
Nov. 7	T	2–2	BOSTON	Feb. 9	L	1–4	Montreal
Nov. 8	T	3–3	Detroit	Feb. 10	W	5–3	PHILADELPHIA
Nov. 10	L	1–5	LOS ANGELES	Feb. 13	W	5–4	CHICAGO
Nov. 11	T	3–3	New York	Feb. 14	L	4–5	Minnesota
Nov. 14	W	6–1	CALIFORNIA	Feb. 17	L	3–4	Toronto
Nov. 19	L	0–1	ST. LOUIS	Feb. 18	T	6–6	Buffalo
Nov. 21	W	6–1	DETROIT	Feb. 20	L	0–2	NEW YORK
Nov. 22	L	2–4	Boston	Feb. 24	T	5–5	ST. LOUIS
Nov. 24	T	4–4	Toronto	Feb. 27	L	0–4	NEW YORK
Nov. 25	T	4–4	BUFFALO	Feb. 28	L	2–4	Detroit
Nov. 28	L	1–5	Montreal	Mar. 3	W	4–0	MONTREAL
Nov. 29	L	2–6	New York	Mar. 6	L	3–6	BOSTON
Dec. 2	T	3–3	MONTREAL	Mar. 7	T	3–3	CALIFORNIA
Dec. 5	W	3–1	VANCOUVER	Mar. 10	T	2–2	PHILADELPHIA
Dec. 6	L	3–6	Boston	Mar. 13	T	0–0	MINNESOTA
Dec. 8	W	4–0	TORONTO	Mar. 14	L	1–5	MONTREAL
Dec. 9	T	2–2	Minnesota	Mar. 17	L	2–5	California
Dec. 11	L	2–3	St. Louis	Mar. 19	L	4–6	Vancouver
Dec. 12	L	0–1	MINNESOTA	Mar. 20	L	4–8	Los Angeles
Dec. 16	L	2–4	TORONTO	Mar. 24	W	8–2	DETROIT
Dec. 19	W	9–1	DETROIT	Mar. 28	L	1–3	Philadelphia
Dec. 20	L	1–2	Chicago	Mar. 31	L	4–6	BUFFALO
Dec. 23	L	1–6	New York	Apr. 1	T	3–3	Buffalo
Dec. 25	L	4–8	Boston	Apr. 3	L	3–4	St. Louis
Dec. 26	W	4–2	BOSTON	Apr. 4	T	1–1	ST. LOUIS
Dec. 30	T	3–3	Montreal				
Dec. 31	W	4–1	MINNESOTA	Home games in CAPS			
Jan. 2	L	1–3	NEW YORK				
Jan. 6	L	3–4	Philadelphia				
Jan. 9	L	2–5	Toronto				
Jan. 13	W	4–2	LOS ANGELES				

1971–72

RECORD: 26–38–14, 4th, West Division

DATE	RESULT	SCORE	OPPONENT	DATE	RESULT	SCORE	OPPONENT
Oct. 9	W	3–2	PHILADELPHIA	Jan. 13	L	1–7	Montreal
Oct. 10	L	1–2	Buffalo	Jan. 15	W	4–2	PHILADELPHIA
Oct. 13	W	4–1	Los Angeles	Jan. 19	L	1–6	VANCOUVER
Oct. 16	W	2–1	Vancouver	Jan. 22	L	0–1	St. Louis
Oct. 17	W	4–2	California	Jan. 23	T	3–3	MONTREAL
Oct. 20	W	8–1	LOS ANGELES	Jan. 26	L	1–2	ST. LOUIS
Oct. 23	L	2–5	CHICAGO	Jan. 29	L	2–4	CHICAGO
Oct. 24	T	1–1	New York	Jan. 30	L	0–4	Philadelphia
Oct. 27	L	4–6	CALIFORNIA	Feb. 3	W	4–3	St. Louis
Oct. 28	L	0–2	Minnesota	Feb. 5	L	1–8	Los Angeles
Oct. 30	T	1–1	NEW YORK.	Feb. 9	W	4–1	Toronto
Oct. 31	L	1–3	Detroit	Feb. 10	W	6–1	LOS ANGELES
Nov. 3	L	3–5	California	Feb. 12	L	3–8	NEW YORK
Nov. 5	L	2–4	Vancouver	Feb. 13	W	6–4	VANCOUVER
Nov. 7	L	1–4	Chicago	Feb. 16	W	4–2	TORONTO
Nov. 9	W	4–1	St. Louis	Feb. 17	W	2–0	Buffalo
Nov. 10	W	3–1	VANCOUVER	Feb. 19	L	2–6	DETROIT
Nov. 13	W	6–4	LOS ANGELES	Feb. 20	L	0–2	Minnesota
Nov. 16	L	1–5	MINNESOTA	Feb. 23	L	0–2	Toronto
Nov. 18	L	3–4	Minnesota	Feb. 26	W	5–2	PHILADELPHIA
Nov. 20	L	2–4	ST. LOUIS	Feb. 27	L	3–5	Montreal
Nov. 21	L	3–7	Chicago	Mar. 2	W	7–4	DETROIT
Nov. 24	L	1–2	TORONTO	Mar. 4	W	4–2	MINNESOTA
Nov. 27	L	1–3	Montreal	Mar. 5	L	3–6	Detroit
Dec. 1	W	4–2	DETROIT	Mar. 8	L	4–5	MONTREAL
Dec. 4	W	4–2	NEW YORK	Mar. 11	W	6–4	BOSTON
Dec. 5	L	3–5	Boston	Mar. 12	T	4–4	Boston
Dec. 8	T	1–1	CALIFORNIA	Mar. 14	W	7–4	Vancouver
Dec. 11	T	3–3	BUFFALO	Mar. 18	T	4–4	Los Angeles
Dec. 12	L	1–6	New York	Mar. 19	T	3–3	California
Dec. 15	L	2–3	Toronto	Mar. 23	L	3–4	BUFFALO
Dec. 18	L	3–4	BOSTON	Mar. 25	W	3–2	MINNESOTA
Dec. 19	T	2–2	Boston	Mar. 26	T	2–2	Buffalo
Dec. 22	L	2–4	New York	Mar. 29	W	5–4	CALIFORNIA
Dec. 25	W	4–2	MONTREAL	Apr. 1	T	4–4	Philadelphia
Dec. 26	L	1–6	Philadelphia	Apr. 2	W	6–2	ST. LOUIS
Dec. 28	L	2–4	TORONTO				
Dec. 31	T	3–3	BUFFALO	Home games in CAPS			
Jan. 5	T	3–3	Chicago				
Jan. 8	L	0–4	CHICAGO				
Jan. 9	L	2–4	Detroit				
Jan. 12	T	2–2	BOSTON				

1972–73

RECORD: 32–37–9, 5th, West Division

DATE	RESULT	SCORE	OPPONENT	DATE	RESULT	SCORE	OPPONENT
Oct. 7	W	4–2	LOS ANGELES	Jan. 13	W	3–1	LOS ANGELES
Oct. 11	W	5–2	St. Louis	Jan. 14	L	2–3	Detroit
Oct. 14	W	5–2	CALIFORNIA	Jan. 17	L	4–6	Montreal
Oct. 15	L	4–8	Boston	Jan. 18	L	2–5	MONTREAL
Oct. 17	W	5–0	NY Islanders	Jan. 20	W	3–0	BOSTON
Oct. 18	L	3–4	Toronto	Jan. 21	L	3–9	Chicago
Oct. 21	L	2–4	BOSTON	Jan. 24	W	5–2	TORONTO
Oct. 24	W	4–0	Vancouver	Jan. 25	L	3–6	Philadelphia
Oct. 27	L	3–6	California	Jan. 27	L	3–5	PHILADELPHIA
Oct. 28	L	2–5	Los Angeles	Jan. 31	W	4–1	LOS ANGELES
Nov. 1	L	1–7	MONTREAL	Feb. 3	W	2–1	MINNESOTA
Nov. 2	L	2–4	Philadelphia	Feb. 4	L	3–4	Minnesota
Nov. 4	W	6–4	NY RANGERS	Feb. 7	L	2–5	Montreal
Nov. 5	T	1–1	Detroit	Feb. 10	L	3–6	Boston
Nov. 8	W	5–2	PHILADELPHIA	Feb. 14	W	6–2	VANCOUVER
Nov. 11	L	3–4	VANCOUVER	Feb. 17	T	3–3	BUFFALO
Nov. 12	L	0–1	Buffalo	Feb. 18	L	1–4	Buffalo
Nov. 15	W	7–1	MINNESOTA	Feb. 20	W	4–1	NY Islanders
Nov. 18	W	6–1	ATLANTA	Feb. 22	W	2–1	NY ISLANDERS
Nov. 19	W	5–3	NY Rangers	Feb. 24	W	2–0	CHICAGO
Nov. 22	W	10–4	ST. LOUIS	Feb. 25	L	1–2	Buffalo
Nov. 25	T	2–2	NY ISLANDERS	Feb. 28	W	4–2	ST. LOUIS
Nov. 26	L	2–6	Atlanta	Mar. 3	L	1–2	CALIFORNIA
Nov. 29	W	7–4	TORONTO	Mar. 4	L	2–5	MINNESOTA
Dec. 2	W	3–2	CHICAGO	Mar. 7	L	4–10	Minnesota
Dec. 3	L	2–4	Chicago	Mar. 10	L	4–5	NY RANGERS
Dec. 6	T	4–4	California	Mar. 11	L	2–3	Philadelphia
Dec. 9	L	1–3	Los Angeles	Mar. 14	W	3–2	Los Angeles
Dec. 13	W	9–1	NY ISLANDERS	Mar. 16	T	5–5	California
Dec. 16	W	5–3	ATLANTA	Mar. 17	L	1–6	Vancouver
Dec. 17	L	1–9	NY Rangers	Mar. 21	W	5–2	CALIFORNIA
Dec. 19	L	2–3	BOSTON	Mar. 24	T	4–4	BUFFALO
Dec. 23	L	3–6	Montreal	Mar. 25	W	4–2	Atlanta
Dec. 26	T	1–1	Detroit	Mar. 28	W	6–3	ATLANTA
Dec. 27	T	3–3	Toronto	Mar. 31	L	2–7	St. Louis
Dec. 29	L	0–4	TORONTO	Apr. 1	W	5–4	PHILADELPHIA
Dec. 30	T	2–2	DETROIT				
Jan. 2	L	4–5	St. Louis			Home games in CAPS	
Jan. 3	W	5–3	Chicago				
Jan. 6	W	4–2	VANCOUVER				
Jan. 7	L	0–3	NY Rangers				
Jan. 10	L	1–2	DETROIT				

1973–74

RECORD: 28–41–9, 5th, West Division

DATE	RESULT	SCORE	OPPONENT	DATE	RESULT	SCORE	OPPONENT
Oct. 12	W	4–3	Atlanta	Feb. 7	L	4–5	Philadelphia
Oct. 13	L	2–8	NY RANGERS	Feb. 9	W	3–2	NY Islanders
Oct. 17	W	4–2	Minnesota	Feb. 10	L	3–5	Chicago
Oct. 20	W	5–3	CALIFORNIA	Feb. 13	W	5–3	DETROIT
Oct. 21	L	2–8	Boston	Feb. 16	W	7–3	CALIFORNIA
Oct. 24	L	2–3	MONTREAL	Feb. 20	T	1–1	ST. LOUIS
Oct. 27	L	0–6	PHILADELPHIA	Feb. 23	L	2–6	BOSTON
Oct. 28	W	7–2	NY Rangers	Feb. 24	W	4–2	Chicago
Oct. 31	T	1–1	Montreal	Feb. 27	W	4–1	LOS ANGELES
Nov. 3	L	0–6	Toronto	Feb. 28	L	1–7	Montreal
Nov. 4	L	0–7	Philadelphia	Mar. 2	W	6–1	VANCOUVER
Nov. 7	T	1–1	NY ISLANDERS	Mar. 5	W	2–1	NY Islanders
Nov. 10	T	4–4	ATLANTA	Mar. 7	T	2–2	Toronto
Nov. 13	W	5–2	MINNESOTA	Mar. 9	W	7–5	St. Louis
Nov. 15	L	3–5	St. Louis	Mar. 10	L	4–5	MONTREAL
Nov. 17	L	1–4	CHICAGO	Mar. 13	L	1–5	Los Angeles
Nov. 18	L	0–7	NY Rangers	Mar. 15	W	6–1	California
Nov. 21	W	5–4	VANCOUVER	Mar. 16	W	8–6	Vancouver
Nov. 22	W	4–2	Toronto	Mar. 20	T	1–1	NY ISLANDERS
Nov. 24	L	2–5	MONTREAL	Mar. 23	L	1–5	Minnesota
Nov. 28	L	3–4	TORONTO	Mar. 24	W	8–0	DETROIT
Dec. 1	T	2–2	ATLANTA	Mar. 27	T	3–3	MINNESOTA
Dec. 2	L	1–2	Chicago	Mar. 31	W	4–2	ATLANTA
Dec. 5	L	1–4	Los Angeles	Apr. 2	L	2–3	NY Islanders
Dec. 7	L	3–4	California	Apr. 4	W	4–2	BUFFALO
Dec. 8	L	2–3	Vancouver	Apr. 6	W	6–1	PHILADELPHIA
Dec. 12	W	9–1	CALIFORNIA	Apr. 7	L	3–6	Atlanta
Dec. 15	L	0–2	DETROIT				
Dec. 16	W	2–1	Atlanta				
Dec. 20	L	5–6	Boston				
Dec. 22	L	1–4	NY RANGERS				
Dec. 23	L	2–3	Buffalo				
Dec. 26	T	2–2	Detroit				
Dec. 28	L	1–3	ST. LOUIS				
Dec. 29	L	2–4	CHICAGO				
Jan. 2	L	4–8	Minnesota				
Jan. 3	L	1–6	Buffalo				
Jan. 5	W	5–2	BUFFALO				
Jan. 9	L	4–6	TORONTO				
Jan. 12	W	5–2	BUFFALO				
Jan. 13	L	3–5	BOSTON				
Jan. 16	L	0–2	LOS ANGELES				
Jan. 18	W	6–2	Vancouver				
Jan. 20	W	5–3	Philadelphia				
Jan. 23	W	4–1	ST. LOUIS				
Jan. 26	L	0–2	LOS ANGELES				
Jan. 27	L	5–6	Detroit				
Jan. 30	L	2–4	NY RANGERS				
Feb. 2	L	1–3	CHICAGO				
Feb. 3	L	4–5	Boston				

Home games in CAPS

The Century Line of (left to right) Jean Pronovost, Syl Apps, and Lowell MacDonald powered the Pens to the playoffs in 1974–75.

1974–75

RECORD: 37–28–15, 3rd, Norris Division

DATE	RESULT	SCORE	OPPONENT	DATE	RESULT	SCORE	OPPONENT
Oct. 9	W	4–2	Minnesota	Jan. 18	T	4–4	BOSTON
Oct. 12	W	7–2	DETROIT	Jan. 19	W	3–2	Washington
Oct. 19	L	3–6	PHILADELPHIA	Jan. 22	W	7–5	CALIFORNIA
Oct. 20	L	1–5	Atlanta	Jan. 25	W	5–2	NY RANGERS
Oct. 23	T	5–5	BOSTON	Jan. 26	L	2–7	Montreal
Oct. 26	L	4–5	NY RANGERS	Jan. 29	W	6–1	CHICAGO
Oct. 29	L	0–2	Los Angeles	Jan. 30	L	2–5	Detroit
Nov. 1	L	4–7	Vancouver	Feb. 1	T	4–4	St. Louis
Nov. 3	T	3–3	Chicago	Feb. 4	W	3–2	Vancouver
Nov. 5	W	5–3	Kansas City	Feb. 5	W	3–2	Los Angeles
Nov. 7	L	3–5	LOS ANGELES	Feb. 7	W	4–1	California
Nov. 9	W	5–2	CALIFORNIA	Feb. 11	L	1–2	NY Islanders
Nov. 10	L	3–8	Buffalo	Feb. 12	T	3–3	BUFFALO
Nov. 13	W	8–2	NY ISLANDERS	Feb. 15	W	8–3	Toronto
Nov. 16	W	8–1	WASHINGTON	Feb. 16	W	3–2	NY ISLANDERS
Nov. 17	W	6–0	Washington	Feb. 19	T	2–2	LOS ANGELES
Nov. 19	L	3–4	NY Islanders	Feb. 22	W	3–2	ST. LOUIS
Nov. 20	W	8–5	Toronto	Feb. 23	L	1–3	DETROIT
Nov. 23	T	0–0	LOS ANGELES	Feb. 25	L	4–6	Boston
Nov. 24	L	5–7	NY Rangers	Feb. 26	W	3–1	WASHINGTON
Nov. 27	L	2–3	MONTREAL	Mar. 1	W	7–3	VANCOUVER
Nov. 30	T	5–5	BUFFALO	Mar. 2	W	8–6	NY Rangers
Dec. 1	L	3–6	Buffalo	Mar. 5	T	4–4	Kansas City
Dec. 4	W	4–2	TORONTO	Mar. 8	W	8–2	PHILADELPHIA
Dec. 7	L	2–5	Montreal	Mar. 9	L	4–8	Buffalo
Dec. 8	L	2–3	Boston	Mar. 12	W	5–3	BOSTON
Dec. 12	T	3–3	MONTREAL	Mar. 13	L	0–6	Philadelphia
Dec. 14	W	6–3	CHICAGO	Mar. 15	W	12–1	WASHINGTON
Dec. 15	W	3–2	Detroit	Mar. 16	W	6–3	KANSAS CITY
Dec. 18	L	4–6	Toronto	Mar. 18	L	2–5	St. Louis
Dec. 19	T	4–4	KANSAS CITY	Mar. 19	T	3–3	California
Dec. 21	L	7–8	Minnesota	Mar. 22	L	0–4	Los Angeles
Dec. 22	L	0–4	Philadelphia	Mar. 26	W	6–4	MONTREAL
Dec. 26	T	2–2	ST. LOUIS	Mar. 29	W	4–2	Detroit
Dec. 28	T	3–3	ATLANTA	Mar. 30	W	4–1	MINNESOTA
Dec. 30	W	7–5	TORONTO	Apr. 2	L	0–6	Montreal
Jan. 2	W	6–3	MINNESOTA	Apr. 5	W	7–1	DETROIT
Jan. 4	W	4–3	VANCOUVER	Apr. 6	L	4–8	Washington
Jan. 8	L	5–7	Chicago				
Jan. 10	T	3–3	Atlanta	Home games in CAPS			
Jan. 11	W	6–3	CALIFORNIA				
Jan. 15	W	5–3	ATLANTA				

1975–76

RECORD: 35–33–12, 3rd, Norris Division

DATE	RESULT	SCORE	OPPONENT	DATE	RESULT	SCORE	OPPONENT
Oct. 7	W	4–2	Washington	Jan. 15	L	1–4	Philadelphia
Oct. 11	W	7–5	WASHINGTON	Jan. 17	W	3–2	BUFFALO
Oct. 15	W	8–4	Toronto	Jan. 18	W	8–3	NY RANGERS
Oct. 18	W	6–1	DETROIT	Jan. 22	L	3–4	MONTREAL
Oct. 21	L	1–7	MONTREAL	Jan. 24	W	8–2	WASHINGTON
Oct. 25	T	4–4	PHILADELPHIA	Jan. 25	T	1–1	MINNESOTA
Oct. 30	L	0–4	Los Angeles	Jan. 29	W	6–2	KANSAS CITY
Nov. 1	L	3–7	Minnesota	Jan. 31	T	4–4	Kansas City
Nov. 2	L	2–7	Buffalo	Feb. 1	W	7–1	TORONTO
Nov. 5	W	7–6	NY ISLANDERS	Feb. 5	L	1–5	Boston
Nov. 6	W	5–3	St. Louis	Feb. 7	W	7–3	Los Angeles
Nov. 8	L	5–7	CHICAGO	Feb. 8	W	7–3	Vancouver
Nov. 9	L	4–6	Philadelphia	Feb. 11	T	4–4	California
Nov. 12	T	6–6	Washington	Feb. 14	T	4–4	NY Islanders
Nov. 13	L	4–5	MONTREAL	Feb. 15	W	6–4	LOS ANGELES
Nov. 15	L	2–5	BUFFALO	Feb. 17	W	6–1	KANSAS CITY
Nov. 18	L	3–5	CALIFORNIA	Feb. 19	W	7–5	TORONTO
Nov. 21	W	4–1	Atlanta	Feb. 21	W	10–1	CHICAGO
Nov. 22	W	6–3	LOS ANGELES	Feb. 22	T	2–2	Detroit
Nov. 26	W	5–2	DETROIT	Feb. 25	T	3–3	ATLANTA
Nov. 29	W	8–3	NY RANGERS	Feb. 28	W	5–4	VANCOUVER
Nov. 30	L	2–4	Boston	Feb. 29	L	3–5	ST. LOUIS
Dec. 3	T	3–3	Chicago	Mar. 2	W	6–2	Minnesota
Dec. 4	L	1–6	NY Islanders	Mar. 6	W	5–0	MINNESOTA
Dec. 7	W	6–3	TORONTO	Mar. 7	L	3–5	NY ISLANDERS
Dec. 9	L	2–3	Kansas City	Mar. 10	L	6–7	BUFFALO
Dec. 10	L	2–3	Detroit	Mar. 13	W	4–2	CALIFORNIA
Dec. 13	T	4–4	BOSTON	Mar. 14	W	7–1	ST. LOUIS
Dec. 14	L	4–7	Montreal	Mar. 16	L	4–5	Montreal
Dec. 17	W	9–2	California	Mar. 19	W	7–3	Washington
Dec. 19	L	1–5	Vancouver	Mar. 21	W	4–2	NY Rangers
Dec. 20	W	5–1	Los Angeles	Mar. 24	T	5–5	BOSTON
Dec. 23	L	3–4	NY Rangers	Mar. 25	L	2–5	St. Louis
Dec. 26	L	3–4	Atlanta	Mar. 28	W	3–0	DETROIT
Dec. 27	W	3–2	ATLANTA	Mar. 29	L	4–5	Toronto
Dec. 31	W	5–1	LOS ANGELES	Mar. 31	L	3–7	Montreal
Jan. 3	L	4–8	PHILADELPHIA	Apr. 3	L	4–5	WASHINGTON
Jan. 4	L	3–5	Chicago	Apr. 4	W	6–5	Detroit
Jan. 7	L	1–4	California				
Jan. 10	T	3–3	VANCOUVER	Home games in CAPS			
Jan. 11	L	0–6	Buffalo				
Jan. 13	L	2–6	Boston				

1976–77

RECORD: 34–33–13, 3rd, Norris Division

DATE	RESULT	SCORE	OPPONENT	DATE	RESULT	SCORE	OPPONENT
Oct. 6	W	9–5	VANCOUVER	Jan. 15	W	5–2	BUFFALO
Oct. 7	L	1–10	Montreal	Jan. 16	L	5–6	ATLANTA
Oct. 9	L	4–7	LOS ANGELES	Jan. 19	W	3–0	Vancouver
Oct. 13	L	1–4	Chicago	Jan. 20	L	3–5	Los Angeles
Oct. 15	L	1–2	Atlanta	Jan. 22	W	3–2	NY ISLANDERS
Oct. 16	W	4–3	DETROIT	Jan. 27	W	3–0	NY Rangers
Oct. 20	T	4–4	Toronto	Jan. 29	L	2–5	PHILADELPHIA
Oct. 23	L	1–9	MONTREAL	Jan. 30	W	5–2	BOSTON
Oct. 24	T	3–3	ATLANTA	Feb. 2	W	5–2	MINNESOTA
Oct. 27	T	4–4	Buffalo	Feb. 3	T	0–0	Cleveland
Oct. 28	L	0–3	Philadelphia	Feb. 5	W	3–1	DETROIT
Oct. 30	T	2–2	NY RANGERS	Feb. 6	L	2–5	Colorado
Nov. 2	W	7–1	LOS ANGELES	Feb. 8	L	3–6	St. Louis
Nov. 5	W	4–1	Colorado	Feb. 11	L	2–3	Vancouver
Nov. 7	T	2–2	Cleveland	Feb. 12	W	3–2	Los Angeles
Nov. 10	L	2–3	Minnesota	Feb. 16	T	4–4	MONTREAL
Nov. 13	W	1–0	PHILADELPHIA	Feb. 19	T	6–6	Toronto
Nov. 14	W	5–1	NY Rangers	Feb. 20	W	4–1	CLEVELAND
Nov. 20	L	2–5	COLORADO	Feb. 22	L	1–3	Washington
Nov. 21	W	5–0	CHICAGO	Feb. 24	L	2–3	Detroit
Nov. 24	L	0–4	BOSTON	Feb. 26	W	2–1	WASHINGTON
Nov. 26	W	3–1	Cleveland	Feb. 27	T	2–2	BOSTON
Nov. 27	L	1–3	NY ISLANDERS	Mar. 2	L	0–5	LOS ANGELES
Nov. 30	L	4–6	Washington	Mar. 3	L	1–5	Montreal
Dec. 2	W	4–2	NY Islanders	Mar. 5	T	3–3	Los Angeles
Dec. 4	L	1–3	Montreal	Mar. 6	W	2–1	St. Louis
Dec. 7	W	6–2	MINNESOTA	Mar. 9	W	3–0	COLORADO
Dec. 9	W	2–1	Buffalo	Mar. 12	W	3–2	BUFFALO
Dec. 11	L	3–6	NY Islanders	Mar. 13	L	0–4	Philadelphia
Dec. 12	W	5–3	ST. LOUIS	Mar. 15	L	3–7	Atlanta
Dec. 16	W	5–4	CLEVELAND	Mar. 16	W	7–3	ST. LOUIS
Dec. 18	L	3–5	WASHINGTON	Mar. 19	L	2–5	NY RANGERS
Dec. 19	L	3–6	Boston	Mar. 20	L	2–3	Chicago
Dec. 22	W	5–2	Toronto	Mar. 22	W	4–2	Minnesota
Dec. 23	L	2–5	Detroit	Mar. 27	L	0–3	Boston
Dec. 26	W	4–2	TORONTO	Mar. 30	L	3–4	WASHINGTON
Dec. 29	T	3–3	MONTREAL	Apr. 2	W	4–3	Detroit
Jan. 1	W	6–3	BUFFALO	Apr. 3	W	4–2	DETROIT
Jan. 4	T	2–2	VANCOUVER				
Jan. 6	T	3–3	Washington	Home games in CAPS			
Jan. 8	W	4–2	CHICAGO				
Jan. 11	L	0–2	TORONTO				

1977–78

RECORD: 25–37–18, 4th, Norris Division

DATE	RESULT	SCORE	OPPONENT	DATE	RESULT	SCORE	OPPONENT
Oct. 12	W	4–2	ST. LOUIS	Jan. 14	W	4–2	CLEVELAND
Oct. 14	L	1–2	Washington	Jan. 18	L	0–1	Atlanta
Oct. 15	L	2–8	PHILADELPHIA	Jan. 21	L	2–5	WASHINGTON
Oct. 19	T	3–3	NY Rangers	Jan. 22	W	3–1	NY RANGERS
Oct. 20	L	0–11	Philadelphia	Jan. 28	T	3–3	BUFFALO
Oct. 22	W	5–2	ATLANTA	Jan. 29	L	2–8	Boston
Oct. 23	W	3–2	Cleveland	Jan. 31	W	5–3	Detroit
Oct. 26	L	3–4	DETROIT	Feb. 1	W	6–1	MINNESOTA
Oct. 29	L	3–5	BOSTON	Feb. 4	L	1–8	BOSTON
Nov. 2	L	1–3	Detroit	Feb. 7	W	4–2	Colorado
Nov. 4	L	2–5	Atlanta	Feb. 11	T	3–3	Los Angeles
Nov. 5	L	3–4	NY Islanders	Feb. 14	W	2–1	CHICAGO
Nov. 9	W	5–3	CLEVELAND	Feb. 18	T	1–1	LOS ANGELES
Nov. 12	W	7–4	CHICAGO	Feb. 19	T	2–2	Chicago
Nov. 13	T	3–3	Buffalo	Feb. 21	W	5–4	St. Louis
Nov. 16	L	4–7	Minnesota	Feb. 22	T	2–2	ST. LOUIS
Nov. 19	T	5–5	NY RANGERS	Feb. 25	L	1–3	PHILADELPHIA
Nov. 22	T	3–3	Vancouver	Feb. 26	T	4–4	Buffalo
Nov. 24	L	3–5	Los Angeles	Mar. 1	L	2–5	MONTREAL
Nov. 26	W	5–2	NY ISLANDERS	Mar. 4	L	3–6	NY Islanders
Nov. 29	L	1–9	Montreal	Mar. 5	T	3–3	NY ISLANDERS
Nov. 30	W	6–4	DETROIT	Mar. 8	W	5–3	COLORADO
Dec. 3	T	4–4	BUFFALO	Mar. 11	L	1–3	VANCOUVER
Dec. 4	W	4–2	Washington	Mar. 12	L	1–7	TORONTO
Dec. 6	T	3–3	Colorado	Mar. 14	L	2–4	Los Angeles
Dec. 8	L	3–5	LOS ANGELES	Mar. 15	L	4–7	Vancouver
Dec. 10	L	2–6	Boston	Mar. 18	W	3–2	Toronto
Dec. 11	L	1–5	ATLANTA	Mar. 19	L	1–9	Chicago
Dec. 14	L	2–3	St. Louis	Mar. 21	L	1–7	Minnesota
Dec. 17	W	5–3	MONTREAL	Mar. 22	L	2–5	COLORADO
Dec. 22	T	3–3	Buffalo	Mar. 25	T	2–2	DETROIT
Dec. 23	L	2–6	TORONTO	Mar. 29	L	2–6	Montreal
Dec. 26	W	5–4	Toronto	Mar. 30	L	3–6	Boston
Dec. 28	T	2–2	WASHINGTON	Apr. 2	W	6–3	TORONTO
Dec. 29	L	3–4	Montreal	Apr. 5	W	7–2	MINNESOTA
Dec. 31	W	6–3	CLEVELAND	Apr. 6	L	4–6	Detroit
Jan. 2	L	2–3	Washington	Apr. 8	L	4–6	WASHINGTON
Jan. 4	W	8–3	VANCOUVER	Apr. 9	W	3–2	Cleveland
Jan. 7	T	3–3	LOS ANGELES				
Jan. 9	W	5–3	NY Rangers	Home games in CAPS			
Jan. 11	L	6–8	MONTREAL				
Jan. 12	T	4–4	Philadelphia				

1978–79

RECORD: 36–31–13, 2nd, Norris Division

DATE	RESULT	SCORE	OPPONENT	DATE	RESULT	SCORE	OPPONENT
Oct. 11	L	2–3	TORONTO	Jan. 14	W	5–4	Buffalo
Oct. 12	L	2–8	Boston	Jan. 16	W	5–0	MINNESOTA
Oct. 14	T	4–4	BOSTON	Jan. 17	L	1–4	Detroit
Oct. 18	L	3–5	NY ISLANDERS	Jan. 20	L	2–5	WASHINGTON
Oct. 19	L	1–3	Philadelphia	Jan. 24	L	1–4	Los Angeles
Oct. 21	W	5–1	WASHINGTON	Jan. 25	L	3–5	Colorado
Oct. 25	T	6–6	ST. LOUIS	Jan. 27	W	5–3	LOS ANGELES
Oct. 28	L	2–4	ATLANTA	Jan. 31	L	1–4	MONTREAL
Oct. 29	L	2–3	NY Rangers	Feb. 3	W	4–2	DETROIT
Nov. 1	L	4–6	Washington	Feb. 4	L	3–8	Detroit
Nov. 3	L	0–2	Atlanta	Feb. 15	W	6–5	MINNESOTA
Nov. 4	W	7–3	DETROIT	Feb. 17	W	6–3	BUFFALO
Nov. 8	W	6–3	COLORADO	Feb. 18	L	2–6	Detroit
Nov. 9	T	4–4	Buffalo	Feb. 21	W	3–1	MONTREAL
Nov. 11	L	1–2	NY RANGERS	Feb. 22	L	0–12	Montreal
Nov. 16	W	6–3	Vancouver	Feb. 24	W	5–1	CHICAGO
Nov. 18	W	3–1	Los Angeles	Feb. 25	T	2–2	Chicago
Nov. 22	L	2–3	MONTREAL	Feb. 28	W	5–3	COLORADO
Nov. 23	L	4–8	Montreal	Mar. 3	L	4–8	St. Louis
Nov. 25	L	1–3	PHILADELPHIA	Mar. 4	W	7–2	Colorado
Nov. 26	L	2–8	Toronto	Mar. 7	L	0–4	LOS ANGELES
Nov. 29	W	5–3	WASHINGTON	Mar. 10	W	3–2	PHILADELPHIA
Dec. 1	W	7–4	Washington	Mar. 11	L	0–4	Toronto
Dec. 2	W	5–2	CHICAGO	Mar. 13	W	9–3	Vancouver
Dec. 5	T	3–3	NY Islanders	Mar. 14	T	3–3	Los Angeles
Dec. 6	W	6–4	TORONTO	Mar. 17	W	5–2	Washington
Dec. 8	T	3–3	Montreal	Mar. 18	W	5–1	NY Rangers
Dec. 9	T	4–4	BUFFALO	Mar. 21	T	2–2	WASHINGTON
Dec. 13	W	3–0	ST. LOUIS	Mar. 22	W	3–1	Boston
Dec. 14	L	1–2	Philadelphia	Mar. 24	T	3–3	NY Islanders
Dec. 16	W	6–5	VANCOUVER	Mar. 25	T	2–2	NY ISLANDERS
Dec. 17	T	3–3	Chicago	Mar. 27	W	5–1	Minnesota
Dec. 21	W	4–1	Los Angeles	Mar. 23	W	7–1	NY RANGERS
Dec. 23	L	3–5	Minnesota	Mar. 31	L	3–5	Montreal
Dec. 27	W	5–2	LOS ANGELES	Apr. 1	L	2–7	ATLANTA
Dec. 30	W	3–1	DETROIT	Apr. 3	W	3–2	St. Louis
Dec. 31	W	5–4	Detroit	Apr. 7	W	4–3	DETROIT
Jan. 3	L	3–5	VANCOUVER	Apr. 8	L	2–5	Washington
Jan. 5	T	3–3	Atlanta				
Jan. 6	L	3–4	LOS ANGELES	Home games in CAPS			
Jan. 10	W	3–2	MONTREAL				
Jan. 13	W	5–3	BOSTON				

1979–80

RECORD: 30–37–13, 3rd, Norris Division

DATE	RESULT	SCORE	OPPONENT	DATE	RESULT	SCORE	OPPONENT
Oct. 10	W	4–2	WINNIPEG	Jan. 16	W	6–4	TORONTO
Oct. 13	T	3–3	HARTFORD	Jan. 18	L	1–7	Hartford
Oct. 14	W	4–1	Boston	Jan. 19	L	2–5	EDMONTON
Oct. 17	L	4–5	LOS ANGELES	Jan. 23	L	3–4	Edmonton
Oct. 20	W	5–1	WASHINGTON	Jan. 24	L	1–4	Colorado
Oct. 21	L	3–6	NY Rangers	Jan. 26	L	4–6	BOSTON
Oct. 24	L	3–7	Buffalo	Jan. 27	W	5–3	Boston
Oct. 25	L	5–8	Montreal	Jan. 30	L	3–4	ST. LOUIS
Oct. 31	W	4–2	COLORADO	Jan. 31	L	3–4	Detroit
Nov. 3	T	3–3	ATLANTA	Feb. 2	L	0–4	PHILADELPHIA
Nov. 7	T	3–3	MONTREAL	Feb. 7	L	0–9	Buffalo
Nov. 10	L	1–6	BOSTON	Feb. 9	L	2–5	MINNESOTA
Nov. 11	W	4–1	NY Rangers	Feb. 10	L	2–3	Chicago
Nov. 15	T	3–3	Los Angeles	Feb. 14	W	4–2	Toronto
Nov. 16	L	2–5	Vancouver	Feb. 16	L	1–8	Montreal
Nov. 18	W	3–2	Winnipeg	Feb. 17	L	5–6	Philadelphia
Nov. 21	W	5–2	ST. LOUIS	Feb. 20	W	7–5	DETROIT
Nov. 23	L	1–4	Atlanta	Feb. 23	W	2–1	QUEBEC
Nov. 24	W	5–3	NY RANGERS	Feb. 24	L	0–2	Quebec
Nov. 28	W	7–2	QUEBEC	Feb. 27	W	3–2	WINNIPEG
Nov. 30	L	5–7	Hartford	Mar. 2	T	0–0	NY ISLANDERS
Dec. 1	W	5–4	COLORADO	Mar. 3	L	1–5	St. Louis
Dec. 5	T	3–3	VANCOUVER	Mar. 5	L	3–5	TORONTO
Dec. 7	W	5–3	Washington	Mar. 8	W	5–4	EDMONTON
Dec. 8	T	3–3	CHICAGO	Mar. 9	L	2–6	Detroit
Dec. 11	T	3–3	St. Louis	Mar. 11	L	3–4	PHILADELPHIA
Dec. 12	T	3–3	NY ISLANDERS	Mar. 12	W	4–2	LOS ANGELES
Dec. 15	T	3–3	NY Islanders	Mar. 15	W	5–2	MINNESOTA
Dec. 16	L	1–4	Quebec	Mar. 18	L	3–4	Minnesota
Dec. 19	T	0–0	Chicago	Mar. 21	L	2–9	Edmonton
Dec. 20	T	1–1	Philadelphia	Mar. 23	W	4–2	Winnipeg
Dec. 22	L	3–4	NY RANGERS	Mar. 25	W	4–2	Vancouver
Dec. 26	W	6–4	DETROIT	Mar. 27	T	2–2	Los Angeles
Dec. 28	W	4–2	Atlanta	Mar. 28	L	0–5	Colorado
Dec. 29	W	3–2	ATLANTA	Mar. 30	W	4–0	WASHINGTON
Dec. 31	L	2–4	Minnesota	Apr. 1	L	2–6	Washington
Jan. 2	W	5–3	MONTREAL	Apr. 2	W	6–4	HARTFORD
Jan. 3	W	4–3	NY Islanders	Apr. 5	L	1–9	BUFFALO
Jan. 5	L	4–5	BUFFALO				
Jan. 7	L	5–9	Toronto	Home games in CAPS			
Jan. 9	W	4–2	VANCOUVER				
Jan. 12	L	2–3	CHICAGO				

1980–81

RECORD: 30–37–13, 3rd, Norris Division

DATE	RESULT	SCORE	OPPONENT	DATE	RESULT	SCORE	OPPONENT
Oct. 9	L	4–7	Philadelphia	Jan. 13	L	3–6	NY Islanders
Oct. 11	W	5–4	WINNIPEG	Jan. 14	W	6–3	ST. LOUIS
Oct. 12	W	6–3	NY Rangers	Jan. 17	W	5–4	LOS ANGELES
Oct. 15	L	2–5	HARTFORD	Jan. 21	L	0–5	PHILADELPHIA
Oct. 18	L	2–4	BUFFALO	Jan. 24	W	4–3	CALGARY
Oct. 21	L	5–8	Toronto	Jan. 27	L	1–7	St. Louis
Oct. 22	W	9–3	ST. LOUIS	Jan. 28	W	3–1	MINNESOTA
Oct. 25	L	2–8	CALGARY	Jan. 31	T	4–4	WASHINGTON
Oct. 29	T	1–1	Buffalo	Feb. 2	L	4–8	Chicago
Oct. 31	W	6–5	Winnipeg	Feb. 4	W	3–2	Winnipeg
Nov. 1	L	3–6	Minnesota	Feb. 6	L	4–6	Colorado
Nov. 3	T	4–4	Edmonton	Feb. 7	L	4–5	Calgary
Nov. 5	L	1–2	TORONTO	Feb. 12	W	5–3	NY ISLANDERS
Nov. 8	W	5–3	DETROIT	Feb. 14	T	2–2	VANCOUVER
Nov. 9	L	4–7	Boston	Feb. 17	L	1–4	Philadelphia
Nov. 12	L	1–3	WASHINGTON	Feb. 19	W	6–2	HARTFORD
Nov. 14	T	3–3	NY Rangers	Feb. 21	L	1–6	BUFFALO
Nov. 15	L	4–7	BOSTON	Feb. 22	W	9–4	COLORADO
Nov. 19	L	2–3	MINNESOTA	Feb. 25	W	4–3	WINNIPEG
Nov. 22	W	4–2	COLORADO	Feb. 26	W	7–5	Washington
Nov. 26	L	4–7	VANCOUVER	Feb. 28	W	6–4	NY RANGERS
Nov. 27	T	3–3	Boston	Mar. 2	W	5–4	Quebec
Nov. 29	L	2–4	NY RANGERS	Mar. 4	W	6–5	LOS ANGELES
Dec. 3	T	4–4	Toronto	Mar. 7	L	5–8	Minnesota
Dec. 4	W	3–2	Montreal	Mar. 8	W	6–4	EDMONTON
Dec. 6	W	6–4	CHICAGO	Mar. 11	L	1–2	MONTREAL
Dec. 7	L	1–10	Buffalo	Mar. 14	T	3–3	QUEBEC
Dec. 10	W	4–3	MONTREAL	Mar. 16	L	6–7	Edmonton
Dec. 12	W	6–2	Washington	Mar. 17	L	3–4	Vancouver
Dec. 13	L	5–6	PHILADELPHIA	Mar. 19	T	4–4	Los Angeles
Dec. 17	T	3–3	Los Angeles	Mar. 21	W	3–1	Colorado
Dec. 19	L	4–10	Vancouver	Mar. 25	W	5–2	TORONTO
Dec. 20	T	3–3	Calgary	Mar. 28	T	4–4	NY Islanders
Dec. 23	L	3–6	St. Louis	Mar. 29	L	2–5	EDMONTON
Dec. 26	L	7–9	Hartford	Mar. 31	L	1–5	Quebec
Dec. 27	W	6–4	QUEBEC	Apr. 2	T	1–1	Detroit
Dec. 31	L	1–3	Detroit	Apr. 4	L	2–5	BOSTON
Jan. 3	W	6–4	DETROIT	Apr. 5	W	5–4	Hartford
Jan. 4	L	2–3	Chicago				
Jan. 7	W	7–3	NY ISLANDERS	Home games in CAPS			
Jan. 8	L	2–4	Montreal				
Jan. 10	L	3–5	CHICAGO				

1981–82

RECORD: 31–36–13, 4th, Patrick Division

DATE	RESULT	SCORE	OPPONENT	DATE	RESULT	SCORE	OPPONENT
Oct. 6	L	2–6	St. Louis	Jan. 13	L	1–6	Winnipeg
Oct. 7	T	5–5	Chicago	Jan. 16	L	0–4	Calgary
Oct. 10	W	2–1	QUEBEC	Jan. 17	T	3–3	Vancouver
Oct. 11	L	2–8	Philadelphia	Jan. 20	W	5–4	BOSTON
Oct. 14	L	1–4	NY ISLANDERS	Jan. 21	L	1–6	NY Islanders
Oct. 17	W	5–2	MINNESOTA	Jan. 23	T	5–5	PHILADELPHIA
Oct. 18	L	2–3	Detroit	Jan. 26	L	2–9	NY Islanders
Oct. 20	W	5–3	COLORADO	Jan. 27	L	3–6	NY ISLANDERS
Oct. 22	T	3–3	Calgary	Jan. 30	W	2–1	WINNIPEG
Oct. 23	L	3–8	Edmonton	Jan. 31	L	3–8	Washington
Oct. 25	W	6–4	Vancouver	Feb. 2	L	6–9	MINNESOTA
Oct. 28	L	3–5	TORONTO	Feb. 6	L	4–6	WASHINGTON
Oct. 29	L	4–6	Philadelphia	Feb. 7	L	4–5	Philadelphia
Oct. 31	W	3–1	BUFFALO	Feb. 10	T	3–3	HARTFORD
Nov. 4	W	6–3	NY RANGERS	Feb. 11	L	2–4	Montreal
Nov. 7	W	7–2	PHILADELPHIA	Feb. 13	T	3–3	LOS ANGELES
Nov. 11	W	3–2	Washington	Feb. 16	L	2–6	NY Islanders
Nov. 14	T	3–3	Boston	Feb. 17	L	3–5	NY RANGERS
Nov. 18	W	6–1	ST. LOUIS	Feb. 20	W	6–5	PHILADELPHIA
Nov. 20	T	3–3	TORONTO	Feb. 21	W	4–3	NY ISLANDERS
Nov. 21	L	5–9	Montreal	Feb. 25	L	2–4	NY Islanders
Nov. 24	W	7–1	Quebec	Feb. 27	L	1–4	EDMONTON
Nov. 25	W	2–1	MONTREAL	Feb. 28	W	4–2	NY Rangers
Nov. 28	W	5–3	DETROIT	Mar. 3	L	2–3	BOSTON
Dec. 1	W	4–2	WINNIPEG	Mar. 6	W	6–4	Quebec
Dec. 5	L	1–3	St. Louis	Mar. 7	T	4–4	CALGARY
Dec. 6	L	4–7	Buffalo	Mar. 10	W	7–2	Washington
Dec. 9	L	1–4	PHILADELPHIA	Mar. 13	W	6–2	COLORADO
Dec. 12	W	7–4	WASHINGTON	Mar. 15	L	3–4	Minnesota
Dec. 14	L	4–5	NY Rangers	Mar. 17	L	4–10	Edmonton
Dec. 16	W	7–6	LOS ANGELES	Mar. 20	L	5–7	Los Angeles
Dec. 19	T	3–3	NY RANGERS	Mar. 21	W	6–0	Colorado
Dec. 20	L	1–3	Philadelphia	Mar. 24	L	2–7	NY RANGERS
Dec. 23	T	4–4	Toronto	Mar. 27	T	3–3	CHICAGO
Dec. 26	L	5–7	BUFFALO	Mar. 28	W	6–5	Washington
Dec. 27	L	3–5	NY Rangers	Mar. 31	T	4–4	WASHINGTON
Dec. 30	W	6–2	WASHINGTON	Apr. 2	W	7–5	NY Rangers
Jan. 2	W	9–4	HARTFORD	Apr. 4	W	7–2	NY ISLANDERS
Jan. 3	W	6–4	Hartford				
Jan. 6	L	3–6	Chicago	Home games in CAPS			
Jan. 7	L	4–5	Detroit				
Jan. 9	W	4–3	VANCOUVER				

1982–83

RECORD: 18–53–9, 6th, Patrick Division

DATE	RESULT	SCORE	OPPONENT	DATE	RESULT	SCORE	OPPONENT
Oct. 5	T	3–3	New Jersey	Jan. 12	L	0–7	MINNESOTA
Oct. 9	L	3–5	NY RANGERS	Jan. 13	L	1–8	Philadelphia
Oct. 10	L	3–4	Boston	Jan. 15	L	7–8	MONTREAL
Oct. 12	W	5–4	VANCOUVER	Jan. 19	T	1–1	NEW JERSEY
Oct. 14	L	0–9	NY Islanders	Jan. 22	L	3–7	QUEBEC
Oct. 16	L	5–6	NEW JERSEY	Jan. 24	L	2–8	Toronto
Oct. 20	L	3–5	ST. LOUIS	Jan. 26	L	2–6	WASHINGTON
Oct. 21	L	4–8	Quebec	Jan. 28	L	2–7	Washington
Oct. 23	W	4–2	PHILADELPHIA	Jan. 29	L	1–2	NY RANGERS
Oct. 27	W	7–5	WASHINGTON	Jan. 31	L	2–3	New Jersey
Oct. 28	L	2–9	Philadelphia	Feb. 2	L	4–7	Chicago
Oct. 30	L	1–4	CALGARY	Feb. 4	L	4–6	Winnipeg
Oct. 31	L	2–6	NY Rangers	Feb. 5	L	4–7	Calgary
Nov. 2	W	3–1	NY Islanders	Feb. 9	L	2–6	VANCOUVER
Nov. 4	T	4–4	New Jersey	Feb. 10	L	3–7	Boston
Nov. 6	L	2–6	Los Angeles	Feb. 12	W	6–4	LOS ANGELES
Nov. 10	W	5–4	EDMONTON	Feb. 15	L	3–7	DETROIT
Nov. 13	L	1–3	CALGARY	Feb. 17	L	1–4	NY Islanders
Nov. 14	T	6–6	Buffalo	Feb. 19	L	7–10	EDMONTON
Nov. 17	W	4–3	HARTFORD	Feb. 21	L	2–4	Toronto
Nov. 20	W	4–3	BOSTON	Feb. 23	W	6–4	WINNIPEG
Nov. 24	W	4–3	TORONTO	Feb. 24	L	3–6	Philadelphia
Nov. 26	T	6–6	Minnesota	Feb. 26	W	5–4	NEW JERSEY
Nov. 27	L	3–5	St. Louis	Feb. 28	L	3–9	NY Rangers
Dec. 1	L	2–4	CHICAGO	Mar. 1	T	3–3	NY RANGERS
Dec. 2	L	4–5	Washington	Mar. 4	L	2–10	Buffalo
Dec. 4	T	0–0	PHILADELPHIA	Mar. 6	L	3–5	PHILADELPHIA
Dec. 8	W	4–2	BUFFALO	Mar. 10	L	3–4	NY ISLANDERS
Dec. 11	L	4–7	QUEBEC	Mar. 12	W	7–2	Hartford
Dec. 12	L	3–4	Philadelphia	Mar. 13	L	3–4	CHICAGO
Dec. 15	T	4–4	DETROIT	Mar. 16	L	2–3	Minnesota
Dec. 18	L	1–3	WASHINGTON	Mar. 19	W	7–4	Los Angeles
Dec. 20	L	3–6	NY Rangers	Mar. 21	L	3–7	Vancouver
Dec. 21	W	3–2	Hartford	Mar. 26	T	4–4	Washington
Dec. 23	L	4–6	Detroit	Mar. 27	L	1–4	NY ISLANDERS
Dec. 26	W	4–3	NY RANGERS	Mar. 30	W	3–2	MONTREAL
Dec. 28	L	3–6	Washington	Apr. 2	L	3–6	NY Islanders
Dec. 29	L	5–6	ST. LOUIS	Apr. 3	L	3–5	NEW JERSEY
Jan. 1	W	2–1	NY ISLANDERS				
Jan. 2	L	1–5	Montreal				
Jan. 7	L	2–7	Edmonton	Home games in CAPS			
Jan. 9	L	3–4	Winnipeg				

The 1982–83 Penguins endured an 18-game winless streak—one shy of the NHL record.

1983–84

RECORD: 16–58–6, 6th, Patrick Division

DATE	RESULT	SCORE	OPPONENT	DATE	RESULT	SCORE	OPPONENT
Oct. 4	L	3–5	St. Louis	Jan. 14	L	3–7	Boston
Oct. 8	L	1–6	NY RANGERS	Jan. 15	L	0–2	Chicago
Oct. 9	L	1–7	Philadelphia	Jan. 18	L	4–5*	WINNIPEG
Oct. 12	L	3–4*	WINNIPEG	Jan. 20	W	6–3	NY Rangers
Oct. 14	W	4–0	Washington	Jan. 21	L	2–3	WASHINGTON
Oct. 15	L	4–6	HARTFORD	Jan. 25	L	3–6	NY RANGERS
Oct. 18	L	1–3	BUFFALO	Jan. 28	L	2–5	Montreal
Oct. 22	L	1–6	BOSTON	Jan. 29	L	3–7	Buffalo
Oct. 25	L	0–1	WASHINGTON	Feb. 1	W	4–0	MINNESOTA
Oct. 27	W	4–2	Chicago	Feb. 4	L	5–6	NY Islanders
Oct. 29	L	1–3	PHILADELPHIA	Feb. 5	L	4–5	NY ISLANDERS
Oct. 30	W	5–3	New Jersey	Feb. 8	L	5–6*	BUFFALO
Nov. 2	W	6–3	Winnipeg	Feb. 9	L	3–9	Detroit
Nov. 3	T	3–3*	Calgary	Feb. 11	W	3–2	NEW JERSEY
Nov. 5	L	3–7	Edmonton	Feb. 13	L	1–6	Quebec
Nov. 8	T	4–4*	CALGARY	Feb. 16	L	3–10	Calgary
Nov. 11	L	5–6	NY ISLANDERS	Feb. 17	W	4–1	Vancouver
Nov. 12	W	4–2	NY Islanders	Feb. 19	L	3–7	Edmonton
Nov. 16	L	2–3	TORONTO	Feb. 22	L	2–9	EDMONTON
Nov. 19	T	4–4*	ST. LOUIS	Feb. 25	T	3–3*	CHICAGO
Nov. 20	L	4–5	Philadelphia	Feb. 26	L	3–4*	NY Rangers
Nov. 23	W	4–1	NEW JERSEY	Feb. 29	L	5–9	VANCOUVER
Nov. 25	L	2–5	Detroit	Mar. 1	L	1–9	Washington
Nov. 26	L	4–7	DETROIT	Mar. 3	W	4–3	LOS ANGELES
Nov. 29	L	4–6	Minnesota	Mar. 5	L	2–5	WASHINGTON
Dec. 1	L	4–6	MINNESOTA	Mar. 6	L	5–6	New Jersey
Dec. 3	L	3–6	PHILADELPHIA	Mar. 8	L	6–8	QUEBEC
Dec. 6	L	3–5	BOSTON	Mar. 11	L	4–6	NY ISLANDERS
Dec. 11	T	3–3*	MONTREAL	Mar. 13	L	3–4	Vancouver
Dec. 13	W	3–2	HARTFORD	Mar. 14	L	6–7	Los Angeles
Dec. 15	L	1–3	Montreal	Mar. 17	W	4–2	Hartford
Dec. 17	L	5–6	LOS ANGELES	Mar. 21	W	3–1	TORONTO
Dec. 18	T	3–3*	Toronto	Mar. 22	L	4–13	Philadelphia
Dec. 20	L	3–11	NY Islanders	Mar. 24	L	0–6	Washington
Dec. 21	L	1–6	NY Rangers	Mar. 25	L	3–4	WASHINGTON
Dec. 23	W	6–5*	New Jersey	Mar. 28	L	3–5	PHILADELPHIA
Dec. 26	W	7–4	NY RANGERS	Mar. 29	L	4–6	NY Rangers
Dec. 31	L	0–2	St. Louis	Apr. 1	L	1–2	NY ISLANDERS
Jan. 3	L	5–7	PHILADELPHIA				
Jan. 6	L	1–3	New Jersey	Home games in CAPS			
Jan. 7	L	4–7	NEW JERSEY	*Overtime			
Jan. 10	L	1–7	Quebec				

1984–85

RECORD: 24–51–5, 6th, Patrick Division

DATE	RESULT	SCORE	OPPONENT	DATE	RESULT	SCORE	OPPONENT
Oct. 11	L	3–4	Boston	Jan. 19	W	5–4	CHICAGO
Oct. 13	L	3–4	Montreal	Jan. 21	L	6–7	Winnipeg
Oct. 17	W	4–3	VANCOUVER	Jan. 23	L	3–4	Minnesota
Oct. 20	W	3–1	PHILADELPHIA	Jan. 25	T	6–6*	Calgary
Oct. 21	L	2–4	Philadelphia	Jan. 26	L	3–6	Edmonton
Oct. 24	L	2–5	NEW JERSEY	Jan. 30	L	5–6	TORONTO
Oct. 27	W	6–5	MONTREAL	Feb. 2	L	0–4	NY ISLANDERS
Oct. 30	W	4–3	DETROIT	Feb. 7	L	3–6	New Jersey
Oct. 31	W	7–6	New Jersey	Feb. 9	L	1–4	NY Islanders
Nov. 3	L	5–7	NY RANGERS	Feb. 10	L	3–4	LOS ANGELES
Nov. 6	T	3–3*	EDMONTON	Feb. 14	L	4–5	Chicago
Nov. 8	L	2–6	ST. LOUIS	Feb. 16	L	1–8	QUEBEC
Nov. 10	L	4–5	NY Islanders	Feb. 18	L	2–8	Philadelphia
Nov. 14	W	4–3*	Winnipeg	Feb. 20	W	6–3	CALGARY
Nov. 16	L	6–7	Vancouver	Feb. 22	L	3–8	NY RANGERS
Nov. 17	L	3–5	Los Angeles	Feb. 23	W	3–1	Minnesota
Nov. 21	T	3–3*	WASHINGTON	Feb. 25	L	4–5	MINNESOTA
Nov. 22	L	3–9	Hartford	Feb. 27	L	4–6	WINNIPEG
Nov. 24	L	3–5	NEW JERSEY	Mar. 2	W	5–4	NY RANGERS
Nov. 27	T	2–2*	BUFFALO	Mar. 3	L	3–7	NY Rangers
Nov. 29	L	3–6	CHICAGO	Mar. 5	L	0–6	Los Angeles
Dec. 1	L	1–3	Philadelphia	Mar. 7	L	1–5	St. Louis
Dec. 2	L	1–9	Washington	Mar. 9	W	6–5*	Boston
Dec. 5	W	7–4	ST. LOUIS	Mar. 10	L	4–11	Philadelphia
Dec. 7	W	4–3*	NY Rangers	Mar. 13	L	3–7	BOSTON
Dec. 8	W	6–4	CALGARY	Mar. 16	W	5–0	NY RANGERS
Dec. 12	W	4–3	NY ISLANDERS	Mar. 17	L	3–4	Hartford
Dec. 15	W	5–2	Toronto	Mar. 19	L	3–5	PHILADELPHIA
Dec. 19	L	2–3	NEW JERSEY	Mar. 22	L	1–3	Buffalo
Dec. 21	W	4–2	PHILADELPHIA	Mar. 24	L	3–7	Washington
Dec. 22	L	2–5	NY Islanders	Mar. 26	L	4–5	NY Rangers
Dec. 26	W	6–5	NY ISLANDERS	Mar. 27	W.	4–3	NEW JERSEY
Dec. 28	W	4–0	HARTFORD	Mar. 30	L	4–6	New Jersey
Dec. 29	L	2–10	Quebec	Mar. 31	L	2–4	MONTREAL
Dec. 31	T	4–4*	Detroit	Apr. 2	L	3–4	NY Islanders
Jan. 2	W	2–1	Toronto	Apr. 3	L	2–3	DETROIT
Jan. 4	L	2–7	Buffalo	Apr. 6	L	4–7	WASHINGTON
Jan. 5	L	3–8	QUEBEC	Apr. 7	L	3–7	Washington
Jan. 9	W	7–4	VANCOUVER				
Jan. 12	W	4–3	EDMONTON	Home games in CAPS			
Jan. 16	L	4–5	WASHINGTON	*Overtime			
Jan. 17	L	2–6	Washington				

1985–86

RECORD: 34–38–8, 5th, Patrick Division

DATE	RESULT	SCORE	OPPONENT	DATE	RESULT	SCORE	OPPONENT
Oct. 10	L	3–5	MONTREAL	Jan. 11	T	3–3*	BUFFALO
Oct. 12	L	2–4	PHILADELPHIA	Jan. 16	W	6–3	NY ISLANDERS
Oct. 15	W	3–2	MINNESOTA	Jan. 18	W	5–2	St. Louis
Oct. 16	T	5–5*	Chicago	Jan. 19	W	3–2	MINNESOTA
Oct. 19	L	3–4	Quebec	Jan. 22	W	7–4	Edmonton
Oct. 23	W	5–4	Toronto	Jan. 24	L	3–4	Vancouver
Oct. 24	W	6–4	TORONTO	Jan. 25	L	2–5	Calgary
Oct. 26	T	4–4*	QUEBEC	Jan. 28	T	2–2*	PHILADELPHIA
Oct. 29	L	3–4	HARTFORD	Jan. 29	W	4–1	New Jersey
Oct. 30	L	3–6	Detroit	Feb. 1	L	3–4	NY Islanders
Nov. 2	T	4–4	Montreal	Feb. 2	L	2–3	Boston
Nov. 4	L	2–4	NY RANGERS	Feb. 8	W	4–0	NEW JERSEY
Nov. 6	L	1–4	WASHINGTON	Feb. 12	W	8–1	WASHINGTON
Nov. 8	L	3–5	New Jersey	Feb. 15	W	9–4	VANCOUVER
Nov. 9	W	3–1	CHICAGO	Feb. 16	T	5–5*	New Jersey
Nov. 13	W	6–3	Vancouver	Feb. 19	W	5–2	WINNIPEG
Nov. 16	L	3–4*	Los Angeles	Feb. 21	W	7–3	Detroit
Nov. 19	L	3–4	Washington	Feb. 22	L	3–5	ST. LOUIS
Nov. 20	L	1–3	WASHINGTON	Feb. 24	W	6–5*	LOS ANGELES
Nov. 22	W	8–1	WINNIPEG	Feb. 26	W	5–2	BUFFALO
Nov. 24	L	4–7	Philadelphia	Feb. 27	L	3–8	NY Rangers
Nov. 27	W	7–1	TORONTO	Mar. 1	W	5–1	HARTFORD
Nov. 30	W	5–4	NY RANGERS	Mar. 4	L	3–6	Calgary
Dec. 2	W	6–0	NY Rangers	Mar. 7	L	3–5	Edmonton
Dec. 4	W	5–2	DETROIT	Mar. 9	L	3–5	Winnipeg
Dec. 6	W	3–1	Buffalo	Mar. 11	L	3–5	Washington
Dec. 7	L	1–5	NEW JERSEY	Mar. 12	L	2–5	BOSTON
Dec. 10	L	4–7	NY Islanders	Mar. 15	T	2–2*	NY RANGERS
Dec. 11	T	4–4*	NY ISLANDERS	Mar. 17	L	3–5	WASHINGTON
Dec. 14	L	4–5	Hartford	Mar. 19	W	7–3	New Jersey
Dec. 15	W	5–2	NY Rangers	Mar. 20	L	1–5	Philadelphia
Dec. 17	W	4–3	CALGARY	Mar. 22	W	7–4	Quebec
Dec. 19	W	4–3*	Minnesota	Mar. 26	L	3–8	EDMONTON
Dec. 21	L	2–4	PHILADELPHIA	Mar. 29	L	3–4	Montreal
Dec. 22	L	2–3*	Philadelphia	Apr. 1	L	3–5	Washington
Dec. 26	W	4–3	BOSTON	Apr. 2	L	2–7	NY ISLANDERS
Dec. 28	L	2–4	NY ISLANDERS	Apr. 5	L	3–4*	PHILADELPHIA
Dec. 31	W	8–4	St. Louis	Apr. 6	W	5–4*	NY Rangers
Jan. 1	L	4–7	Chicago				
Jan. 6	W	4–3	NEW JERSEY				
Jan. 8	W	7–3	LOS ANGELES	Home games in CAPS			
Jan. 9	L	0–9	NY Islanders	*Overtime			

1986–87

RECORD: 30–38–12, 5th, Patrick Division

DATE	RESULT	SCORE	OPPONENT	DATE	RESULT	SCORE	OPPONENT
Oct. 9	W	5–4	WASHINGTON	Jan. 14	L	3–4	WINNIPEG
Oct. 11	W	6–5*	NY RANGERS	Jan. 17	L	2–4	Boston
Oct. 12	W	4–1	Chicago	Jan. 18	L	0–1	DETROIT
Oct. 14	W	4–3*	LOS ANGELES	Jan. 21	L	5–10	Los Angeles
Oct. 17	W	7–3	Buffalo	Jan. 23	W	6–0	Vancouver
Oct. 18	W	8–4	NEW JERSEY	Jan. 24	L	2–4	Edmonton
Oct. 22	W	5–4*	BUFFALO	Jan. 27	W	7–5	WASHINGTON
Oct. 23	L	3–5	Philadelphia	Jan. 29	L	3–5	Philadelphia
Oct. 25	W	4–2	PHILADELPHIA	Feb. 1	L	6–8	HARTFORD
Oct. 28	L	2–5	Hartford	Feb. 5	L	5–6	Boston
Oct. 29	L	6–8	NEW JERSEY	Feb. 7	W	4–1	CHICAGO
Nov. 1	T	3–3*	St. Louis	Feb. 8	W	2–1*	New Jersey
Nov. 4	T	2–2*	VANCOUVER	Feb. 14	T	3–3*	VANCOUVER
Nov. 8	W	4–2	Minnesota	Feb. 15	L	1–4	NY Rangers
Nov. 9	L	1–2	Detroit	Feb. 17	L	1–3	CALGARY
Nov. 12	W	2–1	BOSTON	Feb. 19	T	4–4*	Philadelphia
Nov. 14	L	4–5	New Jersey	Feb. 21	L	5–6	NEW JERSEY
Nov. 15	W	5–2	QUEBEC	Feb. 22	W	4–2	NY Rangers
Nov. 18	L	1–3	Winnipeg	Feb. 24	W	5–2	EDMONTON
Nov. 20	W	5–2	Calgary	Feb. 26	L	4–5	NY Islanders
Nov. 22	W	5–4	Washington	Feb. 28	L	1–2	CHICAGO
Nov. 25	L	1–5	NY Islanders	Mar. 1	T	5–5*	ST. LOUIS
Nov. 26	L	2–3	NY ISLANDERS	Mar. 3	W	8–1	Quebec
Nov. 29	T	5–5*	NY RANGERS	Mar. 5	L	2–7	Toronto
Nov. 30	T	2–2*	NY Rangers	Mar. 7	W	7–3	Minnesota
Dec. 5	L	2–4	EDMONTON	Mar. 8	W	5–3	Winnipeg
Dec. 6	W	5–2	MINNESOTA	Mar. 10	L	3–6	NY ISLANDERS
Dec. 10	L	4–6	CALGARY	Mar. 12	W	6–3	QUEBEC
Dec. 12	W	8–3	TORONTO	Mar. 14	L	2–3*	NY RANGERS
Dec. 13	L	2–3*	Toronto	Mar. 18	W	5–4	ST. LOUIS
Dec. 17	L	0–3	Los Angeles	Mar. 20	L	3–4	Washington
Dec. 20	L	4–6	PHILADELPHIA	Mar. 22	L	1–3	Philadelphia
Dec. 22	T	4–4*	Montreal	Mar. 24	T	3–3*	PHILADELPHIA
Dec. 23	L	3–4*	NY Islanders	Mar. 28	L	4–5	Hartford
Dec. 26	T	3–3*	Buffalo	Mar. 29	L	1–4	MONTREAL
Dec. 27	T	3–3*	NY ISLANDERS	Mar. 31	L	3–5	New Jersey
Dec. 30	L	3–5	NY RANGERS	Apr. 2	W	6–2	NEW JERSEY
Jan. 1	L	3–4*	Washington	Apr. 4	W	4–3*	DETROIT
Jan. 3	W	6–3	MONTREAL				
Jan. 7	W	5–2	WASHINGTON	Home games in CAPS			
Jan. 9	L	2–3	Washington	*Overtime			
Jan. 13	T	3–3*	NY Islanders				

1987–88

RECORD: 36–35–9, 6th, Patrick Division

DATE	RESULT	SCORE	OPPONENT	DATE	RESULT	SCORE	OPPONENT
Oct. 8	T	4–4*	NY Rangers	Jan. 10	L	5–7	Detroit
Oct. 9	L	3–6	New Jersey	Jan. 12	T	5–5	NY ISLANDERS
Oct. 13	W	8–3	BUFFALO	Jan. 15	L	4–5	PHILADELPHIA
Oct. 15	T	6–6	NY RANGERS	Jan. 16	W	4–3	Toronto
Oct. 17	L	2–3	Montreal	Jan. 19	W	6–4	NY Islanders
Oct. 18	L	2–3	Philadelphia	Jan. 20	W	8–3	Chicago
Oct. 21	L	4–5	NEW JERSEY	Jan. 23	W	4–3*	Montreal
Oct. 23	L	2–5	Detroit	Jan. 25	L	4–6	EDMONTON
Oct. 24	W	5–3	BUFFALO	Jan. 27	L	1–4	WINNIPEG
Oct. 27	T	4–4*	LOS ANGELES	Jan. 28	L	3–6	New Jersey
Oct. 29	L	0–4	TORONTO	Jan. 30	W	4–2	CHICAGO
Oct. 31	W	5–4*	Quebec	Feb. 2	W	3–2*	WASHINGTON
Nov. 3	W	5–1	PHILADELPHIA	Feb. 4	W	1–0	MINNESOTA
Nov. 5	W	4–2	NY Islanders	Feb. 6	W	5–4	HARTFORD
Nov. 7	L	1–4	Boston	Feb. 7	L	3–6	NY Rangers
Nov. 11	W	3–2	WASHINGTON	Feb. 13	W	7–5	Los Angeles
Nov. 12	L	2–5	Philadelphia	Feb. 17	L	0–5	Vancouver
Nov. 14	W	3–2*	NY RANGERS	Feb. 19	L	3–7	Edmonton
Nov. 17	L	4–6	Vancouver	Feb. 21	L	4–5	ST. LOUIS
Nov. 20	L	1–4	Edmonton	Feb. 23	L	3–4*	WINNIPEG
Nov. 21	T	4–4*	Calgary	Feb. 25	L	1–2	NY Rangers
Nov. 25	W	6–4	QUEBEC	Feb. 28	L	5–7	Chicago
Nov. 27	W	4–2	Washington	Mar. 1	W	8–3	MINNESOTA
Nov. 28	T	5–5*	WASHINGTON	Mar. 5	W	8–3	NY ISLANDERS
Dec. 2	L	1–7	NY ISLANDERS	Mar. 7	W	5–4	Calgary
Dec. 5	W	6–3	VANCOUVER	Mar. 10	L	4–6	St. Louis
Dec. 9	W	5–2	CALGARY	Mar. 12	L	3–6	Minnesota
Dec. 11	W	6–4	NY ISLANDERS	Mar. 13	W	5–4	Winnipeg
Dec. 12	L	2–5	St. Louis	Mar. 16	W	5–2	TORONTO
Dec. 15	L	2–5	PHILADELPHIA	Mar. 19	W	7–0	PHILADELPHIA
Dec. 17	W	7–4	New Jersey	Mar. 20	L	2–4	Philadelphia
Dec. 19	W	4–3	NY RANGERS	Mar. 23	W	7–1	WASHINGTON
Dec. 20	W	8–4	NY Rangers	Mar. 25	W	5–2	MONTREAL
Dec. 23	L	2–6	NEW JERSEY	Mar. 27	W	6–3	Quebec
Dec. 26	W	6–3	DETROIT	Mar. 29	L	0–4	New Jersey
Dec. 27	T	3–3*	Buffalo	Mar. 31	L	2–7	NEW JERSEY
Dec. 29	T	4–4*	BOSTON	Apr. 2	W	7–6*	Washington
Jan. 1	L	3–5	Washington	Apr. 3	W	4–2	HARTFORD
Jan. 2	L	2–3	NY Islanders				
Jan. 5	T	4–4	LOS ANGELES	Home games in CAPS			
Jan. 7	L	2–3	BOSTON	*Overtime			
Jan. 9	L	4–5*	Hartford				

1988–89

RECORD: 40–33–7, 2nd, Patrick Division

DATE	RESULT	SCORE	OPPONENT	DATE	RESULT	SCORE	OPPONENT
Oct. 7	W	6–4	Washington	Jan. 14	T	4–4*	NY RANGERS
Oct. 11	W	8–7	WASHINGTON	Jan. 15	L	4–6	NY Rangers
Oct. 12	L	5–8	Buffalo	Jan. 17	L	2–5	NY Islanders
Oct. 15	W	9–2	ST. LOUIS	Jan. 20	L	3–7	Winnipeg
Oct. 16	W	4–2	PHILADELPHIA	Jan. 21	W	7–4	Edmonton
Oct. 21	L	4–6	New Jersey	Jan. 25	W	5–4	WINNIPEG
Oct. 22	W	7–4	CHICAGO	Jan. 28	W	10–5	DETROIT
Oct. 25	W	6–1	CALGARY	Jan. 31	L	1–5	MONTREAL
Oct. 27	L	3–4	St. Louis	Feb. 2	W	5–3	Philadelphia
Oct. 29	W	5–4	Montreal	Feb. 3	T	3–3*	ST LOUIS
Oct. 30	L	2–9	NY Rangers	Feb. 5	W	5–2	Boston
Nov. 1	W	5–3	VANCOUVER	Feb. 9	W	5–2	QUEBEC
Nov. 3	L	2–6	QUEBEC	Feb. 11	L	1–8	Quebec
Nov. 6	L	4–5	Philadelphia	Feb. 12	L	2–4	CALGARY
Nov. 8	L	3–7	EDMONTON	Feb. 14	W	7–3	BUFFALO
Nov. 10	W	5–1	TORONTO	Feb. 17	L	1–5	Buffalo
Nov. 12	L	2–7	Los Angeles	Feb. 18	L	3–5	NY RANGERS
Nov. 13	W	4–2	Vancouver	Feb. 21	L	1–2	MINNESOTA
Nov. 16	L	5–8	Toronto	Feb. 23	T	6–6*	Detroit
Nov. 19	L	3–6	NY Islanders	Feb. 25	T	5–5*	NY Islanders
Nov. 23	W	8–2	NY RANGERS	Feb. 26	L	6–8	Hartford
Nov. 25	W	5–3	Washington	Mar. 1	W	4–1	NEW JERSEY
Nov. 26	W	4–3	PHILADELPHIA	Mar. 3	L	2–4	Washington
Nov. 30	W	6–4	WASHINGTON	Mar. 5	L	2–4	EDMONTON
Dec. 3	W	4–2	NY ISLANDERS	Mar. 7	L	2–3*	Los Angeles
Dec. 4	T	3–3*	Boston	Mar. 9	L	3–10	Calgary
Dec. 6	W	7–6	CHICAGO	Mar. 10	W	5–1	Winnipeg
Dec. 8	L	3–4	Philadelphia	Mar. 12	W	6–5	Chicago
Dec. 10	T	4–4	NEW JERSEY	Mar. 14	L	2–8	BOSTON
Dec. 14	W	5–4	LOS ANGELES	Mar. 16	W	2–1	New Jersey
Dec. 15	W	8–2	NY Islanders	Mar. 18	L	2–7	MONTREAL
Dec. 17	W	3–2	DETROIT	Mar. 20	L	2–7	Minnesota
Dec. 20	W	5–3	NY ISLANDERS	Mar. 22	L	4–5	WASHINGTON
Dec. 21	W	6–1	Toronto	Mar. 25	W	5–4	NEW JERSEY
Dec. 23	T	2–2*	New Jersey	Mar. 26	W	6–4	NY Rangers
Dec. 26	W	4–3*	Hartford	Mar. 30	L	5–9	HARTFORD
Dec. 29	L	2–3	PHILADELPHIA	Apr. 1	W	5–2	NY RANGERS
Dec. 31	W	8–6	NEW JERSEY	Apr. 2	W	6–5*	Philadelphia
Jan. 2	L	0–8	Washington				
Jan. 7	L	5–7	VANCOUVER	Home games in CAPS			
Jan. 10	W	5–3	NY ISLANDERS	*Overtime			
Jan. 12	W	9–2	Minnesota				

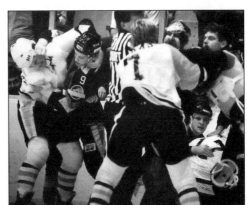

The Penguins led the NHL with 2,670 penalty minutes in 1988–89.

1989–90

RECORD: 32–40–8, 5th, Patrick Division

DATE	RESULT	SCORE	OPPONENT	DATE	RESULT	SCORE	OPPONENT
Oct. 5	L	4–5	Boston	Jan. 10	L	3–6	New Jersey
Oct. 7	T	4–4*	New Jersey	Jan. 12	W	6–4	Washington
Oct. 10	W	5–1	WINNIPEG	Jan. 16	W	4–3	PHILADELPHIA
Oct. 14	W	2–1*	MONTREAL	Jan. 18	T	3–3*	NY RANGERS
Oct. 15	L	2–4	NY Rangers	Jan. 23	L	2–4	NEW JERSEY
Oct. 17	W	7–5	TORONTO	Jan. 25	W	5–3	Detroit
Oct. 18	L	3–9	ST. LOUIS	Jan. 27	L	3–9	NY Islanders
Oct. 21	L	2–4	BUFFALO	Jan. 28	L	2–7	Buffalo
Oct. 25	L	6–8	TORONTO	Jan. 30	L	3–6	PHILADELPHIA
Oct. 26	T	3–3*	Detroit	Feb. 2	W	6–3	EDMONTON
Oct. 28	L	1–5	Montreal	Feb. 3	L	4–8	Toronto
Oct. 31	L	4–8	LOS ANGELES	Feb. 6	L	7–8*	NY ISLANDERS
Nov. 2	W	5–2	NY ISLANDERS	Feb. 8	W	7–5	WASHINGTON
Nov. 4	W	3–1	Edmonton	Feb. 10	W	7–6	LOS ANGELES
Nov. 5	L	3–5	Vancouver	Feb. 11	W	4–1	Philadelphia
Nov. 9	L	3–4	Chicago	Feb. 14	W	4–3*	NY Rangers
Nov. 11	L	3–8	St. Louis	Feb. 16	T	3–3*	Winnipeg
Nov. 14	W	6–0	NY RANGERS	Feb. 18	L	4–6	Chicago
Nov. 16	W	8–2	QUEBEC	Feb. 20	W	6–4	PHILADELPHIA
Nov. 18	W	5–3	NY ISLANDERS	Feb. 22	W	4–3*	NY ISLANDERS
Nov. 22	L	3–6	NEW JERSEY	Feb. 24	L	1–11	Montreal
Nov. 24	W	7–4	Washington	Feb. 26	L	2–3	Quebec
Nov. 25	L	1–4	WASHINGTON	Feb. 28	W	2–1	NEW JERSEY
Nov. 28	L	3–6	PHILADELPHIA	Mar. 2	L	5–6	New Jersey
Nov. 30	L	1–4	Philadelphia	Mar. 4	W	8–6	MINNESOTA
Dec. 2	W	7–4	Quebec	Mar. 6	L	3–4*	Edmonton
Dec. 6	W	5–3	WASHINGTON	Mar. 7	L	3–6	Calgary
Dec. 8	W	3–2	New Jersey	Mar. 10	L	2–8	Los Angeles
Dec. 9	L	4–6	CHICAGO	Mar. 11	L	3–5	Vancouver
Dec. 12	W	7–5	BOSTON	Mar. 15	W	6–1	DETROIT
Dec. 14	T	4–4*	Minnesota	Mar. 17	L	2–6	MINNESOTA
Dec. 16	L	3–4	Calgary	Mar. 18	T	2–2*	NY Islanders
Dec. 19	L	4–8	HARTFORD	Mar. 22	L	3–5	Philadelphia
Dec. 21	W	5–2	WASHINGTON	Mar. 24	T	3–3*	CALGARY
Dec. 23	L	6–8	NY Islanders	Mar. 25	L	2–4	Hartford
Dec. 26	L	3–6	Washington	Mar. 27	T	3–3*	HARTFORD
Dec. 27	W	7–4	NY RANGERS	Mar. 29	L	4–5	St. Louis
Dec. 31	W	5–4	NY Rangers	Mar. 31	L	2–3*	BUFFALO
Jan. 2	L	2–5	BOSTON				
Jan. 4	W	4–3	VANCOUVER	Home games in CAPS			
Jan. 6	W	5–3	WINNIPEG	*Overtime			
Jan. 8	W	7–5	NY Rangers				

1990–91

RECORD: 41–33–6, 1st, Patrick Division, Stanley Cup Champions

DATE	RESULT	SCORE	OPPONENT	DATE	RESULT	SCORE	OPPONENT
Oct. 5	W	7–4	Washington	Jan. 3	L	5–7	NY RANGERS
Oct. 7	W	7–4	NEW JERSEY	Jan. 5	W	5–2	NEW JERSEY
Oct. 9	L	3–4	St. Louis	Jan. 6	L	3–6	Montreal
Oct. 11	L	1–4	Chicago	Jan. 8	W	6–1	EDMONTON
Oct. 13	W	6–4	NY Islanders	Jan. 10	W	5–1	CALGARY
Oct. 16	L	1–5	PHILADELPHIA	Jan. 15	L	4–5	Philadelphia
Oct. 19	T	4–4*	Buffalo	Jan. 17	W	6–5*	Toronto
Oct. 20	L	3–4	NY RANGERS	Jan. 22	W	5–3	NEW JERSEY
Oct. 23	L	4–5	MONTREAL	Jan. 26	W	6–5	Quebec
Oct. 25	W	6–3	QUEBEC	Jan. 29	W	3–2*	WASHINGTON
Oct. 27	L	5–7	New Jersey	Jan. 31	L	2–4	Philadelphia
Oct. 28	W	8–3	NY ISLANDERS	Feb. 2	W	6–2	BOSTON
Oct. 30	W	6–2	Philadelphia	Feb. 3	L	3–6	Boston
Nov. 3	W	3–1	NY RANGERS	Feb. 8	L	2–6	Winnipeg
Nov. 6	W	6–5	CALGARY	Feb. 11	L	5–7	Edmonton
Nov. 8	L	2–3	ST. LOUIS	Feb. 14	W	5–2	NY ISLANDERS
Nov. 10	T	3–3*	Boston	Feb. 16	L	3–4	NY Islanders
Nov. 13	W	4–1	Minnesota	Feb. 19	W	6–3	BUFFALO
Nov. 14	W	6–4	Winnipeg	Feb. 21	W	11–4	TORONTO
Nov. 17	L	1–2*	Los Angeles	Feb. 22	L	2–5	New Jersey
Nov. 21	L	4–5	PHILADELPHIA	Feb. 24	T	5–5*	Washington
Nov. 23	L	3–7	Washington	Feb. 26	L	2–8	Los Angeles
Nov. 24	W	3–2*	WASHINGTON	Feb. 27	L	3–4	Vancouver
Nov. 27	L	3–7	EDMONTON	Mar. 1	L	2–6	Calgary
Nov. 29	L	4–6	HARTFORD	Mar. 5	W	4–1	VANCOUVER
Dec. 1	L	3–6	Minnesota	Mar. 7	W	3–2	LOS ANGELES
Dec. 3	W	9–4	NY Rangers	Mar. 9	W	5–2	Hartford
Dec. 5	L	1–3	WASHINGTON	Mar. 10	W	4–3	NY Islanders
Dec. 7	T	2–2*	VANCOUVER	Mar. 12	T	4–4*	MONTREAL
Dec. 8	L	1–3	Hartford	Mar. 16	W	6–3	QUEBEC
Dec. 11	L	1–4	CHICAGO	Mar. 17	W	4–2	NY Rangers
Dec. 13	W	9–5	NEW JERSEY	Mar. 19	L	4–5	New Jersey
Dec. 14	W	4–3	Buffalo	Mar. 21	W	5–4*	NY RANGERS
Dec. 16	W	4–1	DETROIT	Mar. 23	L	5–7	CHICAGO
Dec. 18	W	9–2	WINNIPEG	Mar. 26	W	3–1	Philadelphia
Dec. 20	W	4–3	MINNESOTA	Mar. 27	W	7–4	Detroit
Dec. 22	W	4–3	NY Islanders	Mar. 30	T	4–4*	PHILADELPHIA
Dec. 23	L	3–4*	NY ISLANDERS	Mar. 31	L	3–6	NY Rangers
Dec. 26	W	7–3	Washington				
Dec. 28	W	5–0	DETROIT	Home games in CAPS			
Dec. 29	L	3–6	Toronto	*Overtime			
Dec. 31	W	4–3	ST. LOUIS				

The 1990–91 team was led by "the Option Line" of John Cullen (11), Kevin Stevens (second from left), and Mark Recchi (right). Jim Johnson (6) joins in the celebration.

1991–92

RECORD: 39–32–9, 3rd, Patrick Division, Stanley Cup Champions

DATE	RESULT	SCORE	OPPONENT	DATE	RESULT	SCORE	OPPONENT
Oct. 4	W	5–4	Buffalo	Jan. 10	L	5–7	Calgary
Oct. 6	T	2–2*	PHILADELPHIA	Jan. 12	W	4–3	Vancouver
Oct. 10	W	6–3	Philadelphia	Jan. 16	T	3–3*	Detroit
Oct. 12	L	1–4	New Jersey	Jan. 23	L	4–5*	BUFFALO
Oct. 15	W	7–6*	NY Islanders	Jan. 25	W	5–3	NY Islanders
Oct. 17	W	8–5	NY ISLANDERS	Jan. 26	L	4–6	Washington
Oct. 19	L	4–5	NY RANGERS	Jan. 28	L	0–4	WINNIPEG
Oct. 22	T	4–4*	CHICAGO	Jan. 30	L	5–8	NY ISLANDERS
Oct. 24	L	2–4	NEW JERSEY	Feb. 1	W	4–1	ST. LOUIS
Oct. 26	L	1–4	Montreal	Feb. 3	T	4–4*	DETROIT
Oct. 29	L	0–8	WASHINGTON	Feb. 5	L	3–4	NY Rangers
Oct. 31	W	8–1	MINNESOTA	Feb. 8	L	3–4	LOS ANGELES
Nov. 2	L	5–6	HARTFORD	Feb. 9	L	3–6	Boston
Nov. 5	T	5–5*	BOSTON	Feb. 15	L	2–5	Minnesota
Nov. 8	W	3–1	Winnipeg	Feb. 16	T	3–3*	Philadelphia
Nov. 9	W	3–2	Minnesota	Feb. 18	W	7–1	TORONTO
Nov. 11	L	1–3	NY Rangers	Feb. 20	T	4–4	QUEBEC
Nov. 13	W	5–4*	EDMONTON	Feb. 22	L	1–2	Montreal
Nov. 15	L	2–6	Washington	Feb. 25	L	3–5	Washington
Nov. 18	W	7–3	Quebec	Feb. 27	L	4–8	HARTFORD
Nov. 20	W	5–2	PHILADELPHIA	Feb. 29	W	5–2	BUFFALO
Nov. 23	T	2–2*	NY ISLANDERS	Mar. 3	W	6–3	Calgary
Nov. 27	W	8–4	NEW JERSEY	Mar. 6	W	7–3	San Jose
Nov. 29	W	9–3	Philadelphia	Mar. 7	L	3–5	Los Angeles
Nov. 30	W	5–1	PHILADELPHIA	Mar. 10	W	5–2	CALGARY
Dec. 3	L	3–5	Edmonton	Mar. 12	W	6–4	NY ISLANDERS
Dec. 5	W	8–0	San Jose	Mar. 14	L	3–6	Toronto
Dec. 7	L	1–6	St. Louis	Mar. 15	W	4–3	Chicago
Dec. 10	W	5–3	NY RANGERS	Mar. 17	W	6–5	EDMONTON
Dec. 13	W	4–3	New Jersey	Mar. 19	W	6–3	QUEBEC
Dec. 14	L	2–7	WASHINGTON	Mar. 22	T	2–2*	Hartford
Dec. 17	W	10–2	SAN JOSE	Mar. 24	L	3–4	Detroit
Dec. 19	W	6–4	Boston	Mar. 26	W	7–3	VANCOUVER
Dec. 21	L	5–7	NY RANGERS	Mar. 28	W	6–3	MONTREAL
Dec. 23	W	6–3	NY Islanders	Mar. 31	W	6–5	PHILADELPHIA
Dec. 26	W	12–1	TORONTO	Apr. 13	L	1–5	New Jersey
Dec. 28	W	6–2	Washington	Apr. 15	W	4–1	WASHINGTON
Dec. 29	W	6–3	NY Rangers	Apr. 16	L	1–7	NY Rangers
Dec. 31	L	4–7	NEW JERSEY				
Jan. 2	L	0–4	New Jersey	Home games in CAPS			
Jan. 4	W	3–2	WINNIPEG	*Overtime			
Jan. 7	L	2–5	LOS ANGELES				

1992–93

RECORD: 56–21–7, 1st, Patrick Division, President's Trophy

DATE	RESULT	SCORE	OPPONENT	DATE	RESULT	SCORE	OPPONENT
Oct. 6	T	3–3*	PHILADELPHIA	Jan. 10	L	2–3	Winnipeg
Oct. 8	W	7–3	NY ISLANDERS	Jan. 14	L	0–7	Boston
Oct. 10	T	3–3*	Montreal	Jan. 16	W	6–1	OTTAWA
Oct. 13	W	6–5	BUFFALO	Jan. 19	W	5–2	Vancouver
Oct. 15	W	5–2	MONTREAL	Jan. 22	L	1–2	Edmonton
Oct. 17	W	7–3	Hartford	Jan. 23	W	4–3	Calgary
Oct. 20	W	5–1	VANCOUVER	Jan. 26	W	6–3	WASHINGTON
Oct. 22	W	9–6	DETROIT	Jan. 28	L	2–5	NY ISLANDERS
Oct. 24	W	4–3	New Jersey	Jan. 30	W	4–2	PHILADELPHIA
Oct. 27	W	7–2	Ottawa	Jan. 31	T	2–2*	Washington
Oct. 29	L	4–6	St. Louis	Feb. 8	W	4–0	BOSTON**
Nov. 1	W	5–4	Tampa Bay	Feb. 10	W	3–0	NY Rangers
Nov. 3	W	2–0	NY ISLANDERS	Feb. 13	W	4–1	CHICAGO
Nov. 5	W	8–4	ST. LOUIS	Feb. 14	L	4–7	Buffalo
Nov. 7	L	2–4	Toronto	Feb. 18	L	4–5	EDMONTON
Nov. 8	L	2–7	Chicago	Feb. 20	L	2–4	NY Islanders
Nov. 10	W	4–1	Minnesota	Feb. 21	W	4–3	Hartford
Nov. 12	T	4–4*	QUEBEC	Feb. 23	L	1–3	NEW JERSEY
Nov. 13	L	0–8	Detroit	Feb. 25	L	1–2	Ottawa
Nov. 17	W	4–2	BUFFALO	Feb. 27	T	3–3*	TAMPA BAY
Nov. 20	W	4–1	New Jersey	Feb. 28	W	4–2	Washington
Nov. 21	W	2–0	NEW JERSEY	Mar. 2	L	4–5	Philadelphia
Nov. 23	W	5–2	NY Rangers	Mar. 5	L	1–3	NY Rangers
Nov. 25	L	3–11	NY RANGERS	Mar. 9	W	3–2	BOSTON
Nov. 27	L	4–6	Washington	Mar. 11	W	4–3*	LOS ANGELES
Nov. 28	W	5–3	WASHINGTON	Mar. 14	W	3–2	NY Islanders
Dec. 1	W	7–3	NY Islanders	Mar. 18	W	7–5	WASHINGTON
Dec. 3	L	3–5	Los Angeles	Mar. 20	W	9–3	PHILADELPHIA
Dec. 5	W	9–4	San Jose	Mar. 21	W	6–4	Edmonton***
Dec. 8	W	5–2	WINNIPEG	Mar. 23	W	7–2	SAN JOSE
Dec. 11	L	1–2	New Jersey	Mar. 25	W	4–3	NEW JERSEY
Dec. 12	W	6–5	NEW JERSEY	Mar. 27	W	5–3	Boston
Dec. 15	W	6–2	PHILADELPHIA	Mar. 28	W	4–1	Washington
Dec. 17	W	5–4*	Philadelphia	Mar. 30	W	6–4	OTTAWA
Dec. 19	L	3–4	NY ISLANDERS	Apr. 1	W	10–2	HARTFORD
Dec. 21	W	7–4	QUEBEC	Apr. 3	W	5–3	Quebec
Dec. 23	W	4–0	Philadelphia	Apr. 4	W	5–2	New Jersey
Dec. 27	W	4–2	Buffalo	Apr. 7	W	4–3*	MONTREAL
Dec. 31	T	3–3*	TORONTO	Apr. 9	W	10–4	NY Rangers
Jan. 2	W	5–2	NY RANGERS	Apr. 10	W	4–2	NY RANGERS
Jan. 5	W	6–2	BOSTON	Apr. 14	T	6–6*	New Jersey
Jan. 7	L	3–6	MINNESOTA				
Jan. 9	W	3–2	CALGARY				

Home games in CAPS
*Overtime
**Game played in Atlanta
***Game played in Cleveland

1993–94

RECORD: 44–27–13, 1st, Northeast Division

DATE	RESULT	SCORE	OPPONENT	DATE	RESULT	SCORE	OPPONENT
Oct. 5	L	3–4	Philadelphia	Jan. 15	W	4–3	EDMONTON
Oct. 7	W	2–1*	MONTREAL	Jan. 18	L	3–6	Quebec
Oct. 9	W	3–2	NY RANGERS	Jan. 25	W	4–2	OTTAWA
Oct. 10	L	4–7	Quebec	Jan. 27	W	3–1	QUEBEC
Oct. 12	W	2–1	Florida	Jan. 29	T	4–4*	Toronto
Oct. 14	L	2–3	Tampa Bay	Jan. 31	L	3–5	NY Rangers
Oct. 16	W	5–3	HARTFORD	Feb. 1	W	2–1	FLORIDA
Oct. 19	W	3–2	NY Islanders	Feb. 4	W	6–3	Detroit
Oct. 22	W	4–2	Buffalo	Feb. 5	L	3–7	New Jersey
Oct. 23	T	3–3*	ST. LOUIS	Feb. 7	L	1–4	MONTREAL
Oct. 28	L	3–7	QUEBEC	Feb. 10	L	3–5	NY ISLANDERS
Oct. 30	W	4–3	CHICAGO	Feb. 12	L	3–9	DALLAS
Nov. 2	T	3–3*	San Jose	Feb. 13	W	3–0	Philadelphia
Nov. 3	W	6–2	BUFFALO**	Feb. 15	W	5–3	WINNIPEG
Nov. 6	L	3–8	Los Angeles	Feb. 17	W	6–4	HARTFORD
Nov. 7	W	5–4	Anaheim	Feb. 19	L	1–4	Montreal
Nov. 9	T	3–3*	St. Louis	Feb. 21	L	3–4*	NY Rangers
Nov. 11	L	1–4	Chicago	Feb. 24	T	2–2*	ANAHEIM
Nov. 13	L	3–7	DETROIT	Feb. 26	W	4–3	BUFFALO
Nov. 16	W	11–5	PHILADELPHIA	Feb. 28	W	4–3	Florida
Nov. 18	W	3–2	WASHINGTON	Mar. 4	L	1–2	Buffalo
Nov. 20	T	2–2*	Montreal	Mar. 6	W	5–3	Winnipeg
Nov. 24	W	7–3	BOSTON	Mar. 8	W	7–3	BOSTON
Nov. 26	T	4–4*	Washington	Mar. 10	L	2–4	TORONTO
Nov. 27	T	2–2*	OTTAWA	Mar. 12	W	6–2	NY RANGERS
Dec. 2	T	2–2*	NEW JERSEY	Mar. 13	W	3–2	Hartford
Dec. 4	W	7–6*	Hartford	Mar. 15	L	4–5*	WASHINGTON
Dec. 8	L	2–3	Dallas	Mar. 17	W	4–2	Boston
Dec. 11	W	6–3	Tampa Bay	Mar. 19	W	5–4	VANCOUVER
Dec. 14	W	4–2	LOS ANGELES	Mar. 20	W	2–1	NY Islanders
Dec. 16	W	2–1	BUFFALO	Mar. 22	T	2–2*	SAN JOSE
Dec. 19	L	3–6	NY ISLANDERS	Mar. 24	W	5–1	OTTAWA
Dec. 21	W	8–3	TAMPA BAY	Mar. 26	L	3–5	Calgary
Dec. 23	W	4–3	Boston	Mar. 27	L	3–5	Edmonton
Dec. 26	L	3–7	Washington	Mar. 30	W	3–1	Vancouver
Dec. 28	T	4–4*	PHILADELPHIA	Apr. 3	W	6–2	BOSTON***
Dec. 31	L	4–5	QUEBEC	Apr. 4	W	2–1	TAMPA BAY
Jan. 2	L	2–7	Hartford	Apr. 6	W	3–1	NEW JERSEY
Jan. 3	W	4–1	Ottawa	Apr. 8	L	2–7	New Jersey
Jan. 7	W	4–3*	Buffalo	Apr. 9	L	1–9	Montreal
Jan. 8	T	2–2*	CALGARY	Apr. 11	W	4–0	Ottawa
Jan. 11	W	5–4*	BOSTON				
Jan. 13	T	2–2*	FLORIDA				

Home games in CAPS
**Overtime
**Game played in Sacramento
***Game played in Cleveland

1994–95

RECORD: 29–16–3, 2nd, Northeast Division

DATE	RESULT	SCORE	OPPONENT	DATE	RESULT	SCORE	OPPONENT
Jan. 20	W	5–3	Tampa Bay	Mar. 24	W	5–2	NEW JERSEY
Jan. 23	W	6–5	Florida	Mar. 26	L	0–2	Florida
Jan. 25	W	3–2	NY Rangers	Mar. 28	W	6–3	NY ISLANDERS
Jan. 27	W	5–4	OTTAWA	Apr. 1	W	3–2	PHILADELPHIA
Jan. 29	W	4–1	Washington	Apr. 5	L	4–8	HARTFORD
Feb. 1	W	4–3	NY RANGERS	Apr. 8	L	1–2	Montreal
Feb. 4	W	6–3	TAMPA BAY	Apr. 10	W	4–3	Ottawa
Feb. 5	T	3–3*	New Jersey	Apr. 11	W	3–1	WASHINGTON
Feb. 7	W	7–3	FLORIDA	Apr. 15	W	5–2	OTTAWA
Feb. 9	W	5–2	NY Islanders	Apr. 16	L	3–4*	Philadelphia
Feb. 11	W	3–1	MONTREAL	Apr. 18	W	6–5	NY RANGERS
Feb. 14	W	5–3	BOSTON	Apr. 22	L	1–2	WASHINGTON
Feb. 16	W	5–2	HARTFORD	Apr. 23	W	4–2	Hartford
Feb. 18	L	2–4	Hartford	Apr. 26	T	3–3*	New Jersey
Feb. 19	T	3–3*	BUFFALO	Apr. 28	W	4–1	BOSTON
Feb. 21	W	5–4	QUEBEC	Apr. 30	L	2–5	Boston
Feb. 24	L	2–4	TAMPA BAY	May 2	L	2–7	Washington
Feb. 25	L	1–3	NY Islanders	May 5	L	3–4	FLORIDA
Feb. 27	W	7–5	Quebec				
Mar. 2	L	3–6	Buffalo				
Mar. 4	W	4–3*	Boston				
Mar. 5	L	2–6	Philadelphia				
Mar. 7	L	4–5	QUEBEC				
Mar. 9	W	4–2	NY ISLANDERS				
Mar. 11	W	6–2	BUFFALO				
Mar. 13	W	4–2	MONTREAL				
Mar. 15	L	5–8	Montreal				
Mar. 16	L	2–3	Quebec				
Mar. 19	W	4–3	Ottawa	Home games in CAPS			
Mar. 21	W	3–2	Buffalo	*Overtime			

1995–96

RECORD: 49–29–4, 1st, Northeast Division

DATE	RESULT	SCORE	OPPONENT	DATE	RESULT	SCORE	OPPONENT
Oct. 7	W	8–3	TORONTO	Jan. 16	L	2–5	COLORADO
Oct. 9	T	6–6*	Colorado	Jan. 17	W	1–0	Buffalo
Oct. 12	L	1–5	Chicago	Jan. 22	W	7–6*	BOSTON
Oct. 14	W	5–2	ANAHEIM	Jan. 24	W	4–3	Ottawa
Oct. 20	T	2–2*	Hartford	Jan. 27	W	7–4	PHILADELPHIA
Oct. 21	L	2–3*	LOS ANGELES	Jan. 29	L	1–2	Florida
Oct. 26	W	7–5	NY Islanders	Jan. 31	L	1–4	Tampa Bay
Oct. 28	W	5–3	New Jersey	Feb. 3	L	0–3	Detroit
Nov. 1	W	10–0	TAMPA BAY	Feb. 6	W	6–5	BOSTON
Nov. 3	T	3–3*	Buffalo	Feb. 7	T	1–1*	New Jersey
Nov. 4	W	7–4	PHILADELPHIA	Feb. 10	W	6–3	CHICAGO
Nov. 8	W	7–1	Ottawa	Feb. 12	L	1–4	Toronto
Nov. 10	W	9–1	San Jose	Feb. 16	W	1–0	Winnipeg
Nov. 11	L	2–3	Los Angeles	Feb. 18	W	4–3*	NY RANGERS
Nov. 14	W	4–2	DALLAS	Feb. 21	L	3–6	Buffalo
Nov. 17	W	3–2*	Washington	Feb. 23	W	5–4	HARTFORD
Nov. 18	W	3–0	WASHINGTON	Feb. 24	L	3–7	Montreal
Nov. 21	L	4–9	NY Rangers	Feb. 27	W	7–4	Vancouver
Nov. 22	L	3–4	NY RANGERS	Feb. 29	L	3–7	Calgary
Nov. 25	W	5–3	BUFFALO	Mar. 1	W	5–4	Edmonton
Nov. 28	W	7–2	OTTAWA	Mar. 5	W	9–4	WINNIPEG
Nov. 30	W	9–6	Boston	Mar. 7	W	5–1	OTTAWA
Dec. 1	W	2–1	FLORIDA	Mar. 9	L	3–4*	NEW JERSEY
Dec. 3	W	5–4	Tampa Bay	Mar. 13	L	2–3	Hartford
Dec. 5	W	6–3	NY Islanders	Mar. 14	L	2–4	Boston
Dec. 7	W	7–5	MONTREAL	Mar. 16	W	4–2	NY ISLANDERS
Dec. 9	W	6–0	HARTFORD	Mar. 21	W	5–4	EDMONTON
Dec. 13	L	3–6	Anaheim	Mar. 23	L	5–7	BUFFALO
Dec. 15	W	5–1	Dallas	Mar. 24	W	8–2	NY Rangers
Dec. 17	L	5–6	Philadelphia	Mar. 26	W	8–4	ST. LOUIS
Dec. 19	W	7–1	CALGARY	Mar. 28	W	3–2	Florida
Dec. 22	L	2–4	MONTREAL	Mar. 30	W	2–1	NEW JERSEY
Dec. 23	L	0–1	Montreal	Mar. 31	L	1–4	Philadelphia
Dec. 26	W	6–3	BUFFALO	Apr. 4	W	4–2	WASHINGTON
Dec. 28	W	9–4	HARTFORD	Apr. 6	W	2–1	TAMPA BAY
Dec. 30	W	6–5	FLORIDA	Apr. 8	L	4–5	Hartford
Jan. 1	L	2–4	Washington	Apr. 10	L	2–6	NY ISLANDERS
Jan. 3	W	4–1	OTTAWA	Apr. 11	W	5–3	Ottawa
Jan. 5	W	5–2	DETROIT	Apr. 14	L	5–6	Boston
Jan. 6	L	2–3	St. Louis				
Jan. 8	W	8–5	VANCOUVER				
Jan. 12	L	5–6	MONTREAL	Home games in CAPS			
Jan. 13	L	8–10	SAN JOSE	*Overtime			

1996–97

RECORD: 38–36–8, 2nd, Northeast Division

DATE	RESULT	SCORE	OPPONENT	DATE	RESULT	SCORE	OPPONENT
Oct. 5	L	3–4*	TAMPA BAY	Jan. 14	W	3–1	DALLAS
Oct. 8	L	3–7	Hartford	Jan. 15	W	3–0	Hartford
Oct. 11	L	2–3	Ottawa	Jan. 21	W	4–2	CALGARY
Oct. 12	W	3–2	OTTAWA	Jan. 23	L	3–4*	COLORADO
Oct. 16	L	1–8	NY Rangers	Jan. 25	L	4–7	NY RANGERS
Oct. 17	L	1–4	Buffalo	Jan. 26	W	5–2	Montreal
Oct. 19	W	2–1	WASHINGTON	Jan. 29	L	1–3	Buffalo
Oct. 22	L	2–5	Edmonton	Feb. 1	W	4–1	PHOENIX
Oct. 24	L	5–7	Calgary	Feb. 4	W	6–4	VANCOUVER
Oct. 26	L	1–2	Vancouver	Feb. 5	W	6–3	Montreal
Nov. 1	L	2–4	Washington	Feb. 8	L	5–6*	DETROIT
Nov. 2	W	7–3	OTTAWA	Feb. 12	L	1–5	NY ISLANDERS
Nov. 6	W	5–2	EDMONTON	Feb. 15	L	1–5	Philadelphia
Nov. 8	T	5–5*	Tampa Bay	Feb. 16	L	2–6	PHILADELPHIA
Nov. 9	L	2–4	Florida	Feb. 18	W	4–2	FLORIDA
Nov. 12	W	3–0	BUFFALO	Feb. 22	L	2–4	CHICAGO
Nov. 14	L	1–2*	Boston	Feb. 23	L	1–5	NY Islanders
Nov. 16	L	3–8	NY RANGERS	Feb. 27	L	1–4	Detroit
Nov. 19	W	4–2	ST. LOUIS	Mar. 1	L	3–6	New Jersey
Nov. 21	L	3–7	Philadelphia	Mar. 4	L	1–3	NEW JERSEY
Nov. 22	W	7–1	Hartford	Mar. 5	L	2–4	Buffalo
Nov. 27	T	2–2*	MONTREAL	Mar. 8	W	3–2*	PHILADELPHIA
Nov. 30	W	6–2	BOSTON	Mar. 10	T	2–2*	MONTREAL
Dec. 3	T	4–4*	HARTFORD	Mar. 12	T	5–5*	Phoenix
Dec. 4	W	4–2	Ottawa	Mar. 14	L	3–6	Colorado
Dec. 6	W	5–3	Washington	Mar. 16	L	2–6	Dallas
Dec. 7	W	5–3	ANAHEIM	Mar. 18	W	5–3	BUFFALO
Dec. 10	W	5–3	Los Angeles	Mar. 20	W	6–3	TORONTO
Dec. 11	W	7–3	Anaheim	Mar. 22	L	2–3	NEW JERSEY
Dec. 13	W	4–0	San Jose	Mar. 24	L	0–3	NY Rangers
Dec. 15	L	1–2	Chicago	Mar. 26	L	5–8	Montreal
Dec. 17	L	4–6	BOSTON	Mar. 29	W	4–1	LOS ANGELES
Dec. 19	W	4–0	St. Louis	Mar. 31	W	4–3	FLORIDA
Dec. 21	W	3–1	SAN JOSE	Apr. 3	T	5–5*	HARTFORD
Dec. 23	W	6–5	Toronto	Apr. 5	W	5–2	OTTAWA
Dec. 26	T	3–3*	MONTREAL	Apr. 8	W	3–1	BOSTON
Dec. 28	W	2–0	BUFFALO	Apr. 10	L	3–4	Tampa Bay
Dec. 30	W	5–3	WASHINGTON	Apr. 11	L	2–4	Florida
Jan. 2	W	6–1	New Jersey	Apr. 13	L	3–7	Boston
Jan. 4	W	7–3	TAMPA BAY				
Jan. 7	W	5–3	NY Islanders				
Jan. 10	W	5–2	NY ISLANDERS	Home games in CAPS			
Jan. 11	T	3–3*	Ottawa	*Overtime			

1997–98

RECORD: 40–24–18, 1st, Northeast Division

DATE	RESULT	SCORE	OPPONENT	DATE	RESULT	SCORE	OPPONENT
Oct. 1	T	3–3*	LOS ANGELES	Jan. 7	L	1–3	New Jersey
Oct. 3	W	4–3	Carolina	Jan. 10	W	4–1	NEW JERSEY
Oct. 4	L	3–5	FLORIDA	Jan. 12	W	4–1	Carolina
Oct. 8	L	0–3	MONTREAL	Jan. 14	L	2–5	Boston
Oct. 9	L	1–3	Philadelphia	Jan. 20	T	0–0*	OTTAWA
Oct. 11	W	4–1	CAROLINA	Jan. 22	W	3–2	New Jersey
Oct. 14	W	1–0	NY Rangers	Jan. 24	W	4–2	BOSTON
Oct. 15	T	1–1*	Montreal	Jan. 26	W	4–2	ST. LOUIS
Oct. 17	W	4–1	Tampa Bay	Jan. 28	T	2–2*	Washington
Oct. 19	W	4–1	Florida	Jan. 29	W	4–2	Boston
Oct. 22	W	5–2	San Jose	Jan. 31	W	4–2	DETROIT
Oct. 24	L	3–4	Edmonton	Feb. 2	L	2–4	NY ISLANDERS
Oct. 25	W	3–2*	Vancouver	Feb. 4	T	2–2*	WASHINGTON
Oct. 28	L	3–6	Calgary	Feb. 6	T	2–2*	Buffalo
Nov. 1	W	7–6*	VANCOUVER	Feb. 7	T	2–2*	Ottawa
Nov. 2	L	1–3	Chicago	Feb. 25	W	6–2	Montreal
Nov. 5	L	2–5	DALLAS	Feb. 28	L	2–6	Boston
Nov. 7	T	1–1*	Detroit	Mar. 2	W	3–1	TORONTO
Nov. 8	T	2–2*	BUFFALO	Mar. 5	T	2–2*	CHICAGO
Nov. 12	L	1–4	WASHINGTON	Mar. 7	W	6–4	PHILADELPHIA
Nov. 14	L	1–3	NY Rangers	Mar. 8	L	3–4*	Philadelphia
Nov. 15	W	5–0	Toronto	Mar. 11	W	4–1	CALGARY
Nov. 19	T	3–3*	BOSTON	Mar. 14	W	2–1	BUFFALO
Nov. 20	W	2–0	Ottawa	Mar. 15	L	0–3	Buffalo
Nov. 22	W	4–3*	NY RANGERS	Mar. 18	W	4–2	EDMONTON
Nov. 24	W	5–1	BUFFALO	Mar. 21	W	4–3	PHILADELPHIA
Nov. 26	W	3–2	CAROLINA	Mar. 22	T	0–0*	Dallas
Nov. 29	W	6–3	MONTREAL	Mar. 26	L	3–4	NY Islanders
Dec. 1	W	1–0	Montreal	Mar. 28	T	2–2*	NY RANGERS
Dec. 4	L	0–4	NEW JERSEY	Mar. 29	T	1–1*	OTTAWA
Dec. 6	W	5–2	ANAHEIM	Apr. 1	L	2–3	SAN JOSE
Dec. 9	W	2–1	Los Angeles	Apr. 4	W	4–1	Tampa Bay
Dec. 10	W	3–0	Anaheim	Apr. 5	L	1–3	Florida
Dec. 12	T	2–2*	Phoenix	Apr. 7	L	1–2	PHOENIX
Dec. 16	T	1–1*	TAMPA BAY	Apr. 9	L	1–4	Ottawa
Dec. 19	T	3–3*	Colorado	Apr. 11	T	3–3*	FLORIDA
Dec. 20	L	1–4	St. Louis	Apr. 15	W	5–1	TAMPA BAY
Dec. 26	W	4–1	Washington	Apr. 16	W	4–1	Carolina
Dec. 27	L	0–1	MONTREAL	Apr. 18	W	5–2	BOSTON
Dec. 29	W	5–1	NY ISLANDERS				
Dec. 31	W	3–2	CAROLINA				
Jan. 3	L	4–5*	COLORADO	Home games in CAPS			
Jan. 6	W	4–2	NY Islanders	*Overtime			

1998–99

RECORD: 38–30–14, 3rd, Atlantic Division

DATE	RESULT	SCORE	OPPONENT	DATE	RESULT	SCORE	OPPONENT
Oct. 10	W	4–3	NY Islanders	Jan. 30	W	5–2	BOSTON
Oct. 14	W	3–1	New Jersey	Jan. 31	W	5–3	Montreal
Oct. 17	T	3–3*	NY RANGERS	Feb. 2	W	5–3	BUFFALO
Oct. 21	L	0–5	Tampa Bay	Feb. 5	W	3–0	FLORIDA
Oct. 24	L	4–6	TORONTO	Feb. 7	W	2–1	DETROIT
Oct. 26	W	2–0	Toronto	Feb. 9	W	3–2*	MONTREAL
Oct. 28	W	5–2	Calgary	Feb. 11	W	6–5*	VANCOUVER
Oct. 30	T	2–2*	Vancouver	Feb. 13	W	3–2*	Nashville
Oct. 31	L	1–4	Edmonton	Feb. 15	W	7–3	WASHINGTON
Nov. 3	T	4–4*	PHILADELPHIA	Feb. 17	L	1–3	NY Islanders
Nov. 5	W	4–2	Ottawa	Feb. 19	L	1–6	NY Rangers
Nov. 7	T	0–0*	BOSTON	Feb. 21	L	1–2	Philadelphia
Nov. 10	W	3–2	NY ISLANDERS	Feb. 22	W	4–1	PHOENIX
Nov. 13	L	3–4	New Jersey	Feb. 25	W	3–2	Colorado
Nov. 14	W	4–0	FLORIDA	Feb. 26	L	4–6	Dallas
Nov. 17	L	1–4	PHILADELPHIA	Feb. 28	L	3–4	Washington
Nov. 19	W	5–1	Tampa Bay	Mar. 3	T	4–4*	MONTREAL
Nov. 21	W	5–2	TAMPA BAY	Mar. 5	T	2–2*	EDMONTON
Nov. 25	L	4–5	Washington	Mar. 7	L	1–3	COLORADO
Nov. 27	T	2–2*	NY RANGERS	Mar. 9	L	2–3	NEW JERSEY
Nov. 28	W	4–3	Montreal	Mar. 10	W	3–2*	Carolina
Dec. 1	T	4–4*	ANAHEIM	Mar. 13	W	4–0	PHILADELPHIA
Dec. 4	T	3–3*	Carolina	Mar. 16	T	2–2*	DALLAS
Dec. 5	L	1–2	Boston	Mar. 17	W	2–0	Tampa Bay
Dec. 12	W	4–3	St. Louis	Mar. 20	T	1–1*	NASHVILLE
Dec. 15	W	3–2*	TAMPA BAY	Mar. 21	T	2–2*	NY Rangers
Dec. 16	L	1–4	Florida	Mar. 23	W	5–2	CHICAGO
Dec. 19	W	3–0	WASHINGTON	Mar. 25	L	3–5	New Jersey
Dec. 21	L	1–7	Toronto	Mar. 27	T	1–1*	BUFFALO
Dec. 22	L	0–3	LOS ANGELES	Mar. 28	L	3–4*	Buffalo
Dec. 26	W	2–1*	OTTAWA	Mar. 30	L	4–6	OTTAWA
Dec. 30	W	7–4	FLORIDA	Apr. 1	T	3–3*	Ottawa
Jan. 2	W	4–2	Florida	Apr. 3	L	2–4	NEW JERSEY
Jan. 5	W	5–1	CALGARY	Apr. 5	L	1–3	Buffalo
Jan. 7	W	4–2	CAROLINA	Apr. 8	L	1–3	Philadelphia
Jan. 9	W	2–1	ST. LOUIS	Apr. 11	W	3–0	Detroit
Jan. 13	L	3–5	Phoenix	Apr. 15	L	2–4	Boston
Jan. 15	L	2–3	San Jose	Apr. 17	L	2–7	NY ISLANDERS
Jan. 16	W	5–1	Los Angeles	Apr. 18	W	2–1*	NY Rangers
Jan. 18	L	3–5	Anaheim				
Jan. 21	L	2–5	NY ISLANDERS				
Jan. 26	L	3–5	CAROLINA	Home games in CAPS			
Jan. 28	W	6–0	TORONTO	*Overtime			

1999–00

RECORD: 37–31–8–6, 3rd, Atlantic Division

DATE	RESULT	SCORE	OPPONENT	DATE	RESULT	SCORE	OPPONENT
Oct. 1	L	4–6	Dallas	Jan. 19	W	3–1	ST. LOUIS
Oct. 7	W	7–5	New Jersey	Jan. 22	L	2–4	Montreal
Oct. 8	T	3–3*	COLORADO	Jan. 23	T	4–4*	PHILADELPHIA
Oct. 14	W	5–2	NY Rangers	Jan. 25	L	3–4	NY RANGERS
Oct. 16	T	3–3*	CHICAGO	Jan. 27	W	4–1	ATLANTA
Oct. 23	L	2–3	CAROLINA	Jan. 29	L	1–7	ANAHEIM
Oct. 27	L	1–2*	Anaheim	Jan. 31	W	2–1*	Atlanta
Oct. 28	L	3–5	Los Angeles	Feb. 1	W	3–2	WASHINGTON
Oct. 30	T	1–1*	San Jose	Feb. 3	W	4–2	NY ISLANDERS
Nov. 2	L	4–5	LOS ANGELES	Feb. 9	W	5–2	ATLANTA
Nov. 4	L	1–2	Ottawa	Feb. 11	T	2–2*	EDMONTON
Nov. 6	L	4–7	TAMPA BAY	Feb. 12	L	1–5	NY Islanders
Nov. 10	W	5–4	MONTREAL	Feb. 14	W	3–0	VANCOUVER
Nov. 12	L	2–3*	Detroit	Feb. 16	T	1–1*	BUFFALO
Nov. 13	W	6–2	NASHVILLE	Feb. 19	W	2–1	Florida
Nov. 16	W	3–2	BUFFALO	Feb. 21	L	1–2	Tampa Bay
Nov. 18	L	1–2	Tampa Bay	Feb. 22	L	3–4	NY Rangers
Nov. 20	L	1–2*	Florida	Feb. 24	L	3–4*	Philadelphia
Nov. 23	W	3–1	TORONTO	Feb. 26	T	2–2*	BOSTON
Nov. 26	W	5–0	OTTAWA	Feb. 28	T	1–1*	OTTAWA
Nov. 27	L	3–5	Carolina	Mar. 1	L	2–8	Calgary
Nov. 30	W	4–1	Buffalo	Mar. 4	W	3–2	Edmonton
Dec. 2	L	2–5	SAN JOSE	Mar. 8	L	0–3	MONTREAL
Dec. 4	L	2–3*	Toronto	Mar. 9	L	0–7	Ottawa
Dec. 7	L	1–2	New Jersey	Mar. 11	W	3–1	NY RANGERS
Dec. 9	W	3–0	WASHINGTON	Mar. 13	L	2–3	NEW JERSEY
Dec. 11	W	4–2	PHOENIX	Mar. 16	W	4–2	FLORIDA
Dec. 14	W	4–2	BOSTON	Mar. 18	L	2–3	Boston
Dec. 15	W	6–3	Carolina	Mar. 19	W	5–4	NY RANGERS
Dec. 18	L	2–5	FLORIDA	Mar. 21	W	8–2	NY Islanders
Dec. 20	L	1–5	Montreal	Mar. 24	W	5–3	Atlanta
Dec. 21	W	4–0	NY Islanders	Mar. 26	L	1–3	Philadelphia
Dec. 23	W	4–3	TAMPA BAY	Mar. 28	W	3–2	NEW JERSEY
Dec. 26	W	4–2	Chicago	Mar. 30	W	4–3*	Washington
Dec. 29	L	2–3*	Washington	Apr. 1	L	2–3	PHILADELPHIA
Dec. 30	W	9–3	NY ISLANDERS	Apr. 3	W	3–2	CAROLINA
Jan. 2	W	4–3	DETROIT	Apr. 5	W	4–2	Toronto
Jan. 5	L	1–3	NEW JERSEY	Apr. 7	W	2–1*	Buffalo
Jan. 7	W	5–2	TORONTO	Apr. 9	L	1–3	Boston
Jan. 8	L	2–6	Philadelphia				
Jan. 12	L	1–3	Phoenix				
Jan. 13	L	3–4	Colorado	Home games in CAPS			
Jan. 15	L	2–4	Nashville	*Overtime			

2000–01

RECORD: 42–28–9–3, 3rd, Atlantic Division

DATE	RESULT	SCORE	OPPONENT	DATE	RESULT	SCORE	OPPONENT
Oct. 6	L	1–3	NASHVILLE**	Jan. 13	L	5–6	NY Islanders
Oct. 7	W	3–1	Nashville**	Jan. 15	W	3–2	ANAHEIM
Oct. 13	W	3–2	TAMPA BAY	Jan. 17	L	4–5	Phoenix
Oct. 14	W	8–6	NY RANGERS	Jan. 19	L	5–6*	Dallas
Oct. 18	L	2–3	CAROLINA	Jan. 21	W	4–0	Chicago
Oct. 19	T	3–3*	Ottawa	Jan. 24	W	3–1	MONTREAL
Oct. 21	W	5–2	COLUMBUS	Jan. 27	W	5–1	ATLANTA
Oct. 25	L	2–3	OTTAWA	Jan. 30	W	6–3	Atlanta
Oct. 27	W	4–1	NY Rangers	Jan. 31	L	1–5	PHILADELPHIA
Oct. 28	L	0–9	NEW JERSEY	Feb. 7	W	9–4	PHILADELPHIA
Nov. 1	L	2–3	San Jose	Feb. 10	W	5–4*	NEW JERSEY
Nov. 3	W	4–2	Vancouver	Feb. 11	L	2–4	Minnesota
Nov. 4	T	1–1*	Calgary	Feb. 14	W	2–1	MINNESOTA
Nov. 8	W	5–2	PHILADELPHIA	Feb. 16	T	4–4*	New Jersey
Nov. 10	W	4–2	New Jersey	Feb. 17	W	3–2*	Columbus
Nov. 11	W	5–2	EDMONTON	Feb. 19	L	1–5	Colorado
Nov. 13	L	2–3*	Colorado	Feb. 21	W	3–2*	FLORIDA
Nov. 16	L	3–4	St. Louis	Feb. 23	W	6–4	NY RANGERS
Nov. 18	W	3–1	ATLANTA	Feb. 25	W	6–1	NY ISLANDERS
Nov. 22	L	1–3	CAROLINA	Feb. 28	L	2–4	Montreal
Nov. 24	W	1–0	Philadelphia	Mar. 2	W	7–5	NY Rangers
Nov. 25	T	2–2*	LOS ANGELES	Mar. 3	L	3–4	Washington
Nov. 28	L	1–3	Boston	Mar. 7	L	3–4	WASHINGTON
Dec. 1	W	6–4	Buffalo	Mar. 8	W	5–3	Atlanta
Dec. 2	L	2–3	BUFFALO	Mar. 10	W	6–3	CALGARY
Dec. 5	W	4–2	Ottawa	Mar. 12	T	3–3*	NY Rangers
Dec. 6	L	2–3	BOSTON	Mar. 14	L	1–3	NY ISLANDERS
Dec. 9	L	1–5	Toronto	Mar. 16	W	6–3	Florida
Dec. 10	W	4–3	Detroit	Mar. 17	L	1–5	Tampa Bay
Dec. 13	L	4–7	TORONTO	Mar. 20	T	2–2*	BOSTON
Dec. 15	L	1–4	FLORIDA	Mar. 23	L	3–5	Carolina
Dec. 16	T	4–4*	Montreal	Mar. 25	W	4–2	New Jersey
Dec. 20	T	2–2*	Florida	Mar. 27	W	4–1	BUFFALO
Dec. 21	T	1–1*	Tampa Bay	Mar. 29	W	5–2	CHICAGO
Dec. 23	L	2–8	DALLAS	Mar. 31	W	5–3	ST. LOUIS
Dec. 26	W	5–3	Buffalo	Apr. 2	L	1–4	NY Islanders
Dec. 27	W	5–0	TORONTO	Apr. 4	W	4–2	TAMPA BAY
Dec. 30	W	5–3	OTTAWA	Apr. 7	L	3–4*	Philadelphia
Jan. 3	W	3–2	WASHINGTON	Apr. 8	W	6–4	Carolina
Jan. 5	L	3–4	MONTREAL				
Jan. 8	W	5–3	Washington				
Jan. 9	L	2–5	Boston	Home games in CAPS			
Jan. 12	W	4–3	NY ISLANDERS	*Overtime			
				**Game played in Tokyo, Japan			

2001–02

RECORD: 28–41–8–5, 5th, Atlantic Division

DATE	RESULT	SCORE	OPPONENT	DATE	RESULT	SCORE	OPPONENT
Oct. 3	L	1–3	COLORADO	Jan. 12	L	1–4	St. Louis
Oct. 6	L	2–4	ANAHEIM	Jan. 15	L	2–5	Vancouver
Oct. 10	L	3–6	NY ISLANDERS	Jan. 17	W	6–4	Calgary
Oct. 14	L	1–4	Buffalo	Jan. 19	W	1–0	Edmonton
Oct. 16	W	5–2	OTTAWA	Jan. 21	W	5–2	PHILADELPHIA
Oct. 18	W	3–0	Ottawa	Jan. 23	W	5–1	TAMPA BAY
Oct. 20	L	1–2*	St. Louis	Jan. 24	W	5–4*	NY Islanders
Oct. 23	W	4–2	Atlanta	Jan. 26	W	3–2*	ATLANTA
Oct. 24	W	3–2	DALLAS	Jan. 29	L	2–3*	Philadelphia
Oct. 27	L	0–4	Toronto	Jan. 30	L	3–6	SAN JOSE
Oct. 28	T	2–2*	FLORIDA	Feb. 5	T	3–3*	Carolina
Oct. 31	L	0–3	Philadelphia	Feb. 7	L	0–1	Montreal
Nov. 1	W	3–1	TORONTO	Feb. 9	L	1–2*	NEW JERSEY
Nov. 3	W	2–1*	TAMPA BAY	Feb. 10	L	3–4	NY RANGERS
Nov. 6	T	2–2*	Carolina	Feb. 12	L	1–5	Ottawa
Nov. 7	L	0–2	Florida	Feb. 27	L	4–5	LOS ANGELES
Nov. 10	L	2–3*	Tampa Bay	Feb. 28	W	4–3*	Columbus
Nov. 13	W	5–1	New Jersey	Mar. 2	L	2–4	DETROIT
Nov. 14	T	3–3*	NY ISLANDERS	Mar. 4	W	4–2	NY Islanders
Nov. 17	W	1–0*	NY RANGERS	Mar. 5	W	6–5*	FLORIDA
Nov. 21	L	1–4	VANCOUVER	Mar. 7	L	1–3	CAROLINA
Nov. 23	L	0–5	Nashville	Mar. 9	W	3–2*	NY RANGERS
Nov. 24	W	3–1	BUFFALO	Mar. 11	L	2–4	COLUMBUS
Nov. 27	W	6–0	NEW JERSEY	Mar. 13	L	2–4	Anaheim
Nov. 29	L	0–5	San Jose	Mar. 16	L	3–4	Los Angeles
Dec. 1	L	2–5	Phoenix	Mar. 18	W	4–2	Atlanta
Dec. 4	W	1–0	Toronto	Mar. 20	L	1–3	PHOENIX
Dec. 6	W	4–1	Boston	Mar. 23	T	4–4*	PHILADELPHIA
Dec. 8	W	6–3	ATLANTA	Mar. 24	W	6–2	WASHINGTON
Dec. 11	T	2–2*	Washington	Mar. 27	L	3–4	NEW JERSEY
Dec. 12	L	2–4	BOSTON	Mar. 30	L	1–2*	Montreal
Dec. 14	L	2–5	MINNESOTA	Apr. 1	L	0–3	MONTREAL
Dec. 16	L	0–7	CAROLINA	Apr. 3	L	2–3	Florida
Dec. 19	L	1–3	MONTREAL	Apr. 4	L	2–4	Tampa Bay
Dec. 21	W	4–3	WASHINGTON	Apr. 6	L	1–3	Philadelphia
Dec. 22	T	4–4*	Washington	Apr. 8	L	2–3	NY Rangers
Dec. 26	L	0–4	New Jersey	Apr. 10	T	4–4*	BUFFALO
Dec. 29	L	2–5	OTTAWA	Apr. 12	L	2–5	TORONTO
Jan. 3	L	2–4	NY Islanders	Apr. 13	L	1–7	Boston
Jan. 5	W	4–1	NY RANGERS				
Jan. 6	L	0–2	Chicago				
Jan. 8	L	2–3	BOSTON	Home games in CAPS			
Jan. 10	W	2–0	Buffalo	*Overtime			

2002–03

RECORD: 27–44–6–5, 5th, Atlantic Division

DATE	RESULT	SCORE	OPPONENT	DATE	RESULT	SCORE	OPPONENT
Oct. 10	L	0–6	TORONTO	Jan. 13	W	2–1	Boston
Oct. 12	W	6–0	NY RANGERS	Jan. 15	W	2–0	Carolina
Oct. 14	W	5–4	Toronto	Jan. 17	W	3–2	Tampa Bay
Oct. 16	W	3–2	ATLANTA	Jan. 18	L	0–3	Florida
Oct. 19	T	3–3*	TAMPA BAY	Jan. 21	T	0–0*	Buffalo
Oct. 22	T	3–3*	Montreal	Jan. 23	L	1–4	BOSTON
Oct. 25	L	3–7	Detroit	Jan. 25	W	5–3	CHICAGO
Oct. 26	W	5–2	BUFFALO	Jan. 28	L	2–5	NY Islanders
Oct. 28	W	3–2	WASHINGTON	Jan. 30	L	1–2	Washington
Oct. 30	W	4–1	Ottawa	Feb. 4	L	2–3	VANCOUVER
Nov. 2	W	5–3	TAMPA BAY	Feb. 6	L	0–6	FLORIDA
Nov. 6	L	3–4*	Florida	Feb. 8	W	5–2	Boston
Nov. 8	L	1–4	Tampa Bay	Feb. 12	L	0–3	OTTAWA
Nov. 9	L	2–3	Carolina	Feb. 14	L	0–1	NY Rangers
Nov. 14	T	1–1*	Minnesota	Feb. 15	W	4–1	New Jersey
Nov. 16	L	2–3	NY ISLANDERS	Feb. 18	W	4–3*	EDMONTON
Nov. 18	L	4–5*	Montreal	Feb. 20	L	2–5	COLORADO
Nov. 20	L	2–3*	MONTREAL	Feb. 22	W	2–1*	ST. LOUIS
Nov. 22	W	3–1	Atlanta	Feb. 23	L	3–4	NEW JERSEY
Nov. 23	W	4–1	SAN JOSE	Feb. 25	L	3–5	LOS ANGELES
Nov. 27	W	7–2	PHILADELPHIA	Feb. 27	L	0–6	Nashville
Nov. 29	W	4–1	Buffalo	Mar. 1	L	1–4	Colorado
Nov. 30	L	2–3	BOSTON	Mar. 2	L	1–3	Dallas
Dec. 3	L	1–4	WASHINGTON	Mar. 4	L	1–4	PHOENIX
Dec. 6	L	1–3	New Jersey	Mar. 6	L	0–4	CAROLINA
Dec. 7	L	3–6	NY ISLANDERS	Mar. 8	L	1–5	OTTAWA
Dec. 10	L	2–4	Toronto	Mar. 9	L	2–4	Ottawa
Dec. 12	L	2–5	San Jose	Mar. 12	T	2–2*	NASHVILLE
Dec. 14	L	2–3*	Los Angeles	Mar. 15	L	1–4	PHILADELPHIA
Dec. 15	L	0–5	Anaheim	Mar. 16	L	2–4	FLORIDA
Dec. 17	L	2–5	Phoenix	Mar. 18	L	1–5	DETROIT
Dec. 19	L	1–3	NEW JERSEY	Mar. 20	L	2–4	Philadelphia
Dec. 21	W	2–0	CALGARY	Mar. 21	L	1–3	New Jersey
Dec. 23	W	5–2	BUFFALO	Mar. 23	T	1–1*	Chicago
Dec. 26	W	6–1	NY Rangers	Mar. 26	W	3–1	NY Rangers
Dec. 28	W	3–2	MONTREAL	Mar. 29	L	0–3	Philadelphia
Dec. 30	L	2–3*	ATLANTA	Mar. 31	L	1–6	PHILADELPHIA
Dec. 31	L	2–5	Columbus	Apr. 2	W	3–2	CAROLINA
Jan. 3	W	4–1	Atlanta	Apr. 5	L	3–5	Washington
Jan. 4	W	3–2*	NY ISLANDERS				
Jan. 7	L	3–6	NY Islanders				
Jan. 9	L	2–4	TORONTO	Home games in CAPS			
Jan. 11	L	1–3	NY RANGERS	*Overtime			

2003–04

RECORD: 23–47–8–4, 5th, Atlantic Division

DATE	RESULT	SCORE	OPPONENT	DATE	RESULT	SCORE	OPPONENT
Oct. 10	L	0–3	LOS ANGELES	Jan. 12	W	2–1	Philadelphia
Oct. 11	T	3–3*	Philadelphia	Jan. 13	L	1–3	TAMPA BAY
Oct. 16	L	1–4	Montreal	Jan. 16	L	2–4	Minnesota
Oct. 18	W	4–3	DETROIT	Jan. 18	L	3–4	Washington
Oct. 22	T	1–1*	CAROLINA	Jan. 20	L	0–3	NEW JERSEY
Oct. 24	L	1–2	NEW JERSEY	Jan. 22	L	5–6	Ottawa
Oct. 25	L	2–7	NY Islanders	Jan. 24	L	3–5	COLORADO
Oct. 29	T	4–4*	NY ISLANDERS	Jan. 27	L	2–6	TAMPA BAY
Oct. 30	W	1–0	Chicago	Jan. 29	L	1–5	Tampa Bay
Nov. 1	W	3–2*	BOSTON	Jan. 31	L	3–5	PHILADELPHIA
Nov. 4	L	2–4	Toronto	Feb. 1	L	1–4	Boston
Nov. 7	L	3–6	Florida	Feb. 3	L	3–4	MONTREAL
Nov. 8	L	0–9	Tampa Bay	Feb. 10	L	3–6	BOSTON
Nov. 12	L	2–6	NY Rangers	Feb. 12	L	1–5	Florida
Nov. 14	W	2–1*	Buffalo	Feb. 14	L	2–3*	St. Louis
Nov. 15	L	2–3	FLORIDA	Feb. 16	L	4–8	TORONTO
Nov. 19	L	2–6	MINNESOTA	Feb. 18	L	3–4	NY Islanders
Nov. 21	L	1–2*	New Jersey	Feb. 20	L	0–2	FLORIDA
Nov. 22	W	2–1*	OTTAWA	Feb. 22	L	3–6	OTTAWA
Nov. 26	T	1–1*	PHILADELPHIA	Feb. 25	W	4–3*	Phoenix
Nov. 28	L	1–4	NY RANGERS	Feb. 27	L	2–4	San Jose
Nov. 29	L	3–4	Carolina	Feb. 29	W	3–2*	NY Islanders
Dec. 1	W	4–3	ATLANTA	Mar. 2	T	3–3*	NY ISLANDERS
Dec. 3	L	2–5	Philadelphia	Mar. 4	L	4–9	NASHVILLE
Dec. 6	L	3–4	Edmonton	Mar. 6	W	2–1	ANAHEIM
Dec. 7	L	1–6	Calgary	Mar. 7	W	7–4	NY RANGERS
Dec. 9	L	1–2*	Vancouver	Mar. 9	W	4–0	DALLAS
Dec. 12	L	3–6	Atlanta	Mar. 11	W	3–2	Toronto
Dec. 13	W	5–3	COLUMBUS	Mar. 14	T	3–3*	PHILADELPHIA
Dec. 16	W	2–1	BUFFALO	Mar. 16	W	4–1	WASHINGTON
Dec. 18	L	1–2*	Carolina	Mar. 17	L	1–6	New Jersey
Dec. 20	L	4–7	ATLANTA	Mar. 19	W	4–3*	CAROLINA
Dec. 22	L	1–4	Montreal	Mar. 21	W	4–3*	NY RANGERS
Dec. 26	T	3–3*	OTTAWA	Mar. 23	W	5–2	NY Rangers
Dec. 27	L	0–2	NEW JERSEY	Mar. 26	L	1–5	Buffalo
Dec. 29	W	1–0	CHICAGO	Mar. 27	T	2–2*	BUFFALO
Dec. 31	L	1–6	NY ISLANDERS	Mar. 30	L	2–4	Washington
Jan. 1	L	2–3	Nashville	Apr. 2	W	3–2	Atlanta
Jan. 3	L	1–4	NY RANGERS	Apr. 4	W	4–3	WASHINGTON
Jan. 5	L	0–5	TORONTO				
Jan. 7	W	4–2	New Jersey				
Jan. 8	L	1–3	Boston	Home games in CAPS			
Jan. 10	L	0–8	MONTREAL	*Overtime			

2005–06

RECORD: 22–46–8–6, 5th, Atlantic Division

DATE	RESULT	SCORE	OPPONENT	DATE	RESULT	SCORE	OPPONENT
Oct. 5	L	1–5	New Jersey	Jan. 13	L	1–4	Chicago
Oct. 7	SOL	2–3*	Carolina	Jan. 15	L	4–5	Nashville
Oct. 8	OTL	6–7*	BOSTON	Jan. 16	L	2–4	VANCOUVER
Oct. 10	OTL	2–3*	Buffalo	Jan. 19	L	2–4	NY RANGERS
Oct. 14	OTL	5–6*	Philadelphia	Jan. 21	L	1–2	PHILADELPHIA
Oct. 15	L	1–3	TAMPA BAY	Jan. 23	L	2–4	Philadelphia
Oct. 20	L	3–6	NEW JERSEY	Jan. 25	W	8–1	WASHINGTON
Oct. 22	L	3–6	Boston	Jan. 26	SOL	3–4*	NY Islanders
Oct. 25	OTL	3–4*	FLORIDA	Jan. 28	L	1–7	NY Rangers
Oct. 27	W	7–5	ATLANTA	Feb. 1	L	1–3	NY Rangers
Oct. 29	L	3–5	CAROLINA	Feb. 2	L	2–7	OTTAWA
Nov. 1	OTW	4–3*	New Jersey	Feb. 4	SOL	4–5*	NY ISLANDERS
Nov. 3	W	5–1	NY Islanders	Feb. 6	L	2–5	Ottawa
Nov. 5	L	3–6	Boston	Feb. 8	L	1–3	BOSTON
Nov. 7	W	3–2	NY Rangers	Feb. 10	W	4–3	Carolina
Nov. 9	L	0–5	Atlanta	Feb. 11	W	6–3	Washington
Nov. 10	SOW	3–2*	MONTREAL	Mar. 1	L	3–4	OTTAWA
Nov. 12	L	1–6	NY RANGERS	Mar. 4	L	5–7	CAROLINA
Nov. 14	SOL	2–3*	NY ISLANDERS	Mar. 7	SOL	4–5*	TAMPA BAY
Nov. 16	OTW	3–2*	Philadelphia	Mar. 8	L	3–6	Washington
Nov. 19	L	3–6	PHILADELPHIA	Mar. 11	W	6–3	NEW JERSEY
Nov. 22	W	5–4	WASHINGTON	Mar. 12	W	2–0	PHILADELPHIA
Nov. 25	L	3–6	Florida	Mar. 16	L	1–2	New Jersey
Nov. 27	L	1–4	Tampa Bay	Mar. 18	W	5–4	Montreal
Nov. 29	L	2–3	BUFFALO	Mar. 19	L	0–1	TORONTO
Dec. 1	L	1–2	NY Rangers	Mar. 21	L	2–5	Ottawa
Dec. 3	L	2–3	CALGARY	Mar. 24	OTW	4–3*	NY ISLANDERS
Dec. 8	L	0–5	MINNESOTA	Mar. 26	L	5–6	MONTREAL
Dec. 10	W	4–3	COLORADO	Mar. 29	L	3–5	FLORIDA
Dec. 12	L	1–3	Detroit	Mar. 31	W	4–0	NY Islanders
Dec. 13	L	0–3	St. Louis	Apr. 2	OTL	2–3*	NEW JERSEY
Dec. 16	OTL	3–4*	BUFFALO	Apr. 5	L	4–6	New Jersey
Dec. 17	L	3–4	Buffalo	Apr. 7	W	5–1	Florida
Dec. 23	L	4–5	PHILADELPHIA	Apr. 8	L	0–1	Tampa Bay
Dec. 27	OTL	2–3*	TORONTO	Apr. 11	L	3–4	Philadelphia
Dec. 29	W	6–2	NEW JERSEY	Apr. 13	W	5–3	NY RANGERS
Dec. 31	OTW	4–3*	NY RANGERS	Apr. 15	SOL	4–5*	NY Islanders
Jan. 2	OTL	2–3*	Toronto	Apr. 17	W	6–1	NY ISLANDERS
Jan. 3	W	6–4	Montreal	Apr. 18	L	3–5	Toronto
Jan. 6	L	4–6	Atlanta				
Jan. 7	L	3–4	ATLANTA	Home games in CAPS			
Jan. 10	L	1–3	EDMONTON	*Overtime			
Jan. 11	L	1–6	Columbus	OTW—Overtime Win		SOW—Shootout Win	
				OTL—Overtime Loss		SOL—Shootout Loss	

2006–07

RECORD: 47–24–5–6, 2nd, Atlantic Division

DATE	RESULT	SCORE	OPPONENT	DATE	RESULT	SCORE	OPPONENT
Oct. 5	W	4–0	PHILADELPHIA	Jan. 16	W	5–2	NY ISLANDERS
Oct. 7	L	0–2	DETROIT	Jan. 18	SOL	4–5*	Boston
Oct. 12	W	6–5	NY Rangers	Jan. 20	W	8–2	TORONTO
Oct. 14	L	1–5	CAROLINA	Jan. 26	SOW	4–3*	Dallas
Oct. 18	L	1–2	NEW JERSEY	Jan. 27	W	7–2	Phoenix
Oct. 19	OTW	4–3*	NY Islanders	Jan. 30	W	3–0	FLORIDA
Oct. 21	W	5–3	COLUMBUS	Feb. 1	SOW	5–4*	MONTREAL
Oct. 24	W	4–2	NEW JERSEY	Feb. 3	W	2–0	WASHINGTON
Oct. 28	W	8–2	Philadelphia	Feb. 4	OTL	3–4*	Montreal
Nov. 1	OTW	4–3*	Los Angeles	Feb. 6	W	4–1	NASHVILLE
Nov. 4	L	2–3	San Jose	Feb. 8	SOW	5–4*	Philadelphia
Nov. 6	OTL	2–3*	Anaheim	Feb. 10	OTW	6–5*	Toronto
Nov. 8	OTL	3–4*	TAMPA BAY	Feb. 14	SOW	5–4*	CHICAGO
Nov. 10	L	3–6	OTTAWA	Feb. 16	W	5–4	New Jersey
Nov. 11	L	2–6	Carolina	Feb. 18	W	3–2	WASHINGTON
Nov. 13	W	3–2	PHILADELPHIA	Feb. 19	L	5–6	NY Islanders
Nov. 17	L	2–4	Buffalo	Feb. 22	OTW	2–1*	Florida
Nov. 18	W	3–1	NY RANGERS	Feb. 25	L	1–5	Tampa Bay
Nov. 20	W	5–3	Philadelphia	Feb. 27	L	0–1	NEW JERSEY
Nov. 22	SOL	3–4*	BOSTON	Mar. 1	SOW	4–3*	NY Rangers
Nov. 24	L	1–3	NY Islanders	Mar. 2	L	2–3	Carolina
Nov. 25	OTL	1–2*	NY RANGERS	Mar. 4	SOW	4–3*	PHILADELPHIA
Nov. 28	W	3–2	NY ISLANDERS	Mar. 6	SOW	5–4*	OTTAWA
Dec. 1	L	2–5	New Jersey	Mar. 8	SOL	3–4*	NEW JERSEY
Dec. 2	L	3–5	NY ISLANDERS	Mar. 10	OTW	3–2*	NY RANGERS
Dec. 5	L	2–3	FLORIDA	Mar. 13	SOW	5–4*	BUFFALO
Dec. 7	SOL	2–3*	NY Rangers	Mar. 14	W	3–0	New Jersey
Dec. 9	OTW	4–3*	Atlanta	Mar. 16	W	6–3	MONTREAL
Dec. 11	SOW	5–4*	Washington	Mar. 18	SOW	4–3*	OTTAWA
Dec. 13	W	8–4	PHILADELPHIA	Mar. 19	L	1–2	NY Rangers
Dec. 15	W	7–4	NY ISLANDERS	Mar. 22	L	1–3	NY Islanders
Dec. 16	L	3–6	Montreal	Mar. 24	W	2–1	ATLANTA
Dec. 19	L	1–4	ST. LOUIS	Mar. 25	W	5–0	BOSTON
Dec. 21	SOL	3–4*	Atlanta	Mar. 27	W	4–3	Washington
Dec. 26	L	0–3	New Jersey	Mar. 29	W	4–2	Boston
Dec. 27	L	2–4	ATLANTA	Mar. 31	OTL	4–5*	Toronto
Dec. 29	W	4–1	TORONTO	Apr. 3	L	1–4	BUFFALO
Jan. 2	W	3–0	CAROLINA	Apr. 5	W	3–2	Ottawa
Jan. 5	W	4–2	Buffalo	Apr. 7	W	2–1	NY RANGERS
Jan. 7	SOL	2–3*	TAMPA BAY				
Jan. 9	L	2–3	Tampa Bay				
Jan. 10	L	2–5	Florida				
Jan. 13	W	5–3	Philadelphia				

Home games in CAPS
*Overtime
OTW—Overtime Win   SOW—Shootout Win
OTL—Overtime Loss   SOL—Shootout Loss

2007–08

RECORD: 47–27–4–4, 1st, Atlantic Division, Wales Conference Champions

DATE	RESULT	SCORE	OPPONENT	DATE	RESULT	SCORE	OPPONENT
Oct. 5	L	1–4	Carolina	Jan. 12	SOL	2–3*	Atlanta
Oct. 6	W	5–4	ANAHEIM	Jan. 14	W	4–1	NY RANGERS
Oct. 10	L	2–3	MONTREAL	Jan. 18	L	0–3	TAMPA BAY
Oct. 13	W	6–4	Toronto	Jan. 19	W	2–0	Montreal
Oct. 17	L	4–5	NEW JERSEY	Jan. 21	SOL	5–6*	WASHINGTON
Oct. 19	SOW	4–3*	CAROLINA	Jan. 24	L	3–4	Philadelphia
Oct. 20	W	2–1	Washington	Jan. 29	W	4–2	New Jersey
Oct. 23	W	1–0	NY RANGERS	Jan. 30	L	1–4	Atlanta
Oct. 25	L	2–5	TORONTO	Feb. 2	W	4–1	CAROLINA
Oct. 27	SOL	3–4*	MONTREAL	Feb. 4	OTL	3–4*	New Jersey
Oct. 30	W	4–2	Minnesota	Feb. 7	W	4–3	NY ISLANDERS
Nov. 1	L	2–3	Colorado	Feb. 9	W	4–2	LOS ANGELES
Nov. 3	L	2–3	NY Islanders	Feb. 10	W	4–3	PHILADELPHIA
Nov. 5	W	5–0	New Jersey	Feb. 13	L	1–2	BOSTON
Nov. 7	L	1–3	PHILADELPHIA	Feb. 14	L	2–4	Carolina
Nov. 8	L	2–4	NY Rangers	Feb. 17	W	4–1	Buffalo
Nov. 10	L	2–5	Philadelphia	Feb. 19	W	3–2	FLORIDA
Nov. 12	L	2–3	NEW JERSEY	Feb. 21	W	5–4	Montreal
Nov. 15	W	3–2	NY ISLANDERS	Feb. 23	OTL	3–4*	OTTAWA
Nov. 17	OTL	3–4*	NY RANGERS	Feb. 24	SOL	1–2*	SAN JOSE
Nov. 21	L	1–2	NEW JERSEY	Feb. 26	W	4–2	NY Islanders
Nov. 22	SOW	6–5*	Ottawa	Feb. 28	L	1–5	Boston
Nov. 24	W	5–0	ATLANTA	Mar. 1	L	4–5	Ottawa
Nov. 30	W	4–1	DALLAS	Mar. 2	SOW	3–2*	ATLANTA
Dec. 1	L	2–4	Toronto	Mar. 4	W	2–0	Tampa Bay
Dec. 3	W	3–1	PHOENIX	Mar. 6	L	2–5	Florida
Dec. 5	W	4–2	Edmonton	Mar. 9	W	4–2	Washington
Dec. 6	SOW	3–2*	Calgary	Mar. 12	W	7–3	BUFFALO
Dec. 8	SOW	2–1*	Vancouver	Mar. 16	W	7–1	PHILADELPHIA
Dec. 11	L	2–8	Philadelphia	Mar. 18	L	2–5	NY Rangers
Dec. 13	L	1–4	OTTAWA	Mar. 20	W	4–2	TAMPA BAY
Dec. 15	W	3–2	NY Islanders	Mar. 22	W	7–1	NEW JERSEY
Dec. 18	L	0–4	NY Rangers	Mar. 24	L	1–4	NY Islanders
Dec. 20	SOW	5–4*	Boston	Mar. 25	W	2–0	New Jersey
Dec. 21	L	2–4	NY ISLANDERS	Mar. 27	W	3–1	NY ISLANDERS
Dec. 23	W	4–2	BOSTON	Mar. 30	W	3–1	NY RANGERS
Dec. 27	OTW	4–3*	WASHINGTON	Mar. 31	OTL	1–2*	NY Rangers
Dec. 29	W	2–0	BUFFALO	Apr. 2	W	4–2	PHILADELPHIA
Jan. 1	SOW	2–1*	Buffalo	Apr. 6	L	0–2	Philadelphia
Jan. 3	W	6–2	TORONTO				
Jan. 5	W	3–0	FLORIDA	Home games in CAPS			
Jan. 8	W	3–1	Florida	*Overtime			
Jan. 10	W	4–1	Tampa Bay	OTW—Overtime Win		SOW—Shootout Win	
				OTL—Overtime Loss		SOL—Shootout Loss	

2008–09

RECORD: 45–28–3–6, 2nd, Atlantic Division, Stanley Cup Champions

DATE	RESULT	SCORE	OPPONENT	DATE	RESULT	SCORE	OPPONENT
Oct. 4	OTW	4–3*	Ottawa**	Jan. 13	W	4–2	Philadelphia
Oct. 5	L	1–3	OTTAWA**	Jan. 14	L	3–6	WASHINGTON
Oct. 11	OTL	1–2*	NEW JERSEY	Jan. 16	W	3–1	ANAHEIM
Oct. 14	OTW	3–2*	PHILADELPHIA	Jan. 18	W	3–0	NY RANGERS
Oct. 16	L	3–4	WASHINGTON	Jan. 20	L	1–2	CAROLINA
Oct. 18	W	4–1	TORONTO	Jan. 28	W	6–2	NY RANGERS
Oct. 20	SOW	2–1*	Boston	Jan. 30	OTL	3–4*	New Jersey
Oct. 23	W	4–1	CAROLINA	Jan. 31	L	4–5	Toronto
Oct. 25	SOL	2–3*	NY Rangers	Feb. 3	L	2–4	Montreal
Oct. 28	L	1–2	San Jose	Feb. 4	OTW	4–3*	TAMPA BAY
Oct. 30	L	1–4	Phoenix	Feb. 6	W	4–1	COLUMBUS
Nov. 1	W	6–3	St. Louis	Feb. 8	L	0–3	DETROIT
Nov. 6	W	5–4	EDMONTON	Feb. 11	SOW	2–1	SAN JOSE
Nov. 8	SOW	4–3*	NY Islanders	Feb. 14	L	2–6	Toronto
Nov. 11	OTW	7–6*	Detroit	Feb. 16	SOL	2–3*	NY Islanders
Nov. 13	SOW	5–4*	PHILADELPHIA	Feb. 19	W	5–4	MONTREAL
Nov. 15	W	5–2	BUFFALO	Feb. 21	W	5–4	Philadelphia
Nov. 18	SOL	1–2*	MINNESOTA	Feb. 22	L	2–5	Washington
Nov. 20	W	3–2	Atlanta	Feb. 25	W	1–0	NY ISLANDERS
Nov. 22	L	1–3	VANCOUVER	Feb. 27	OTW	5–4*	Chicago
Nov. 26	W	5–3	NY Islanders	Mar. 1	W	4–1	Dallas
Nov. 28	L	3–4	Buffalo	Mar. 3	W	3–1	Tampa Bay
Nov. 29	W	4–1	NEW JERSEY	Mar. 5	W	4–1	Florida
Dec. 3	SOL	2–3*	NY Rangers	Mar. 8	SOW	4–3*	Washington
Dec. 4	W	5–2	Carolina	Mar. 10	SOW	4–3*	FLORIDA
Dec. 6	L	2–3	Ottawa	Mar. 12	SOL	3–4*	Columbus
Dec. 8	L	3–4	BUFFALO	Mar. 14	SOL	3–4*	OTTAWA
Dec. 10	L	1–4	New Jersey	Mar. 15	W	6–4	BOSTON
Dec. 11	W	9–2	NY ISLANDERS	Mar. 17	W	6–2	ATLANTA
Dec. 13	L	3–6	Philadelphia	Mar. 20	W	4–1	LOS ANGELES
Dec. 18	W	6–3	Atlanta	Mar. 22	L	1–3	PHILADELPHIA
Dec. 20	L	3–7	TORONTO	Mar. 25	W	2–0	CALGARY
Dec. 22	OTW	4–3*	Buffalo	Mar. 28	W	4–3	NY RANGERS
Dec. 23	L	0–2	TAMPA BAY	Apr. 1	W	6–1	NEW JERSEY
Dec. 26	W	1–0	New Jersey	Apr. 4	OTL	2–3*	Carolina
Dec. 27	L	2–3	MONTREAL	Apr. 5	L	2–4	Florida
Dec. 30	L	2–5	BOSTON	Apr. 7	W	6–4	Tampa Bay
Jan. 1	L	2–4	Boston	Apr. 9	W	6–1	NY ISLANDERS
Jan. 3	L	1–6	FLORIDA	Apr. 11	W	3–1	Montreal
Jan. 5	L	0–4	NY Rangers				
Jan. 6	W	3–1	ATLANTA				
Jan. 8	L	3–5	Nashville				
Jan. 10	L	3–5	Colorado				

Home games in CAPS
*Overtime   ** Game played in Stockholm, Sweden
OTW—Overtime Win   SOW—Shootout Win
OTL—Overtime Loss   SOL—Shootout Loss

2009–10

RECORD: 47–28–5–2, 2nd, Atlantic Division

DATE	RESULT	SCORE	OPPONENT	DATE	RESULT	SCORE	OPPONENT
Oct. 2	W	3–2	NY RANGERS	Jan. 5	W	5–2	ATLANTA
Oct. 3	SOW	4–3*	NY Islanders	Jan. 7	L	4–7	PHILADELPHIA
Oct. 7	L	0–3	PHOENIX	Jan. 9	W	4–1	Toronto
Oct. 8	W	5–4	PHILADELPHIA	Jan. 11	L	3–4	Minnesota
Oct. 10	W	5–2	Toronto	Jan. 13	W	3–1	Calgary
Oct. 12	W	4–1	Ottawa	Jan. 14	W	3–2	Edmonton
Oct. 14	SOW	3–2*	Carolina	Jan. 16	L	2–6	Vancouver
Oct. 17	W	4–1	TAMPA BAY	Jan. 19	W	6–4	NY ISLANDERS
Oct. 20	W	5–1	ST. LOUIS	Jan. 21	L	3–6	WASHINGTON
Oct. 23	SOW	3–2*	FLORIDA	Jan. 24	W	2–1	Philadelphia
Oct. 24	L	1–4	NEW JERSEY	Jan. 25	W	4–2	NY Rangers
Oct. 28	W	6–1	MONTREAL	Jan. 28	L	1–4	OTTAWA
Oct. 30	SOW	4–3*	Columbus	Jan. 31	SOW	2–1*	DETROIT
Oct. 31	L	1–2	MINNESOTA	Feb. 1	W	5–4	BUFFALO
Nov. 3	W	4–3	Anaheim	Feb. 6	L	3–5	Montreal
Nov. 5	L	2–5	Los Angeles	Feb. 7	OTL	4–5*	Washington
Nov. 7	L	0–5	San Jose	Feb. 10	W	3–1	NY ISLANDERS
Nov. 10	L	0–3	Boston	Feb. 12	OTL	2–3*	NY RANGERS
Nov. 12	L	1–4	NEW JERSEY	Feb. 14	SOL	3–4*	NASHVILLE
Nov. 14	OTW	6–5*	BOSTON	Mar. 2	W	3–2	BUFFALO
Nov. 16	W	5–2	ANAHEIM	Mar. 4	OTW	5–4*	NY Rangers
Nov. 19	L	2–6	Ottawa	Mar. 6	W	6–3	DALLAS
Nov. 21	W	3–2	Atlanta	Mar. 7	W	2–1	BOSTON
Nov. 23	OTW	3–2*	Florida	Mar. 11	OTL	3–4*	Carolina
Nov. 25	W	3–1	MONTREAL	Mar. 12	L	1–3	New Jersey
Nov. 27	L	2–3	NY Islanders	Mar. 14	W	2–1	Tampa Bay
Nov. 28	W	8–3	NY RANGERS	Mar. 17	L	2–5	New Jersey
Nov. 30	W	5–2	NY Rangers	Mar. 18	W	3–0	Boston
Dec. 3	W	4–1	COLORADO	Mar. 20	OTL	2–3*	CAROLINA
Dec. 5	OTL	1–2*	CHICAGO	Mar. 22	L	1–3	Detroit
Dec. 7	L	2–3	CAROLINA	Mar. 24	SOL	3–4*	Washington
Dec. 10	W	3–2	Montreal	Mar. 27	W	4–1	PHILADELPHIA
Dec. 12	OTW	3–2*	FLORIDA	Mar. 28	SOW	5–4*	TORONTO
Dec. 15	W	6–1	PHILADELPHIA	Mar. 31	L	0–2	TAMPA BAY
Dec. 17	SOW	3–2*	Philadelphia	Apr. 3	OTW	4–3*	ATLANTA
Dec. 19	SOW	2–1*	Buffalo	Apr. 6	L	3–6	WASHINGTON
Dec. 21	L	0–4	NEW JERSEY	Apr. 8	W	7–3	NY ISLANDERS
Dec. 23	W	8–2	OTTAWA	Apr. 10	L	0–1	Atlanta
Dec. 27	L	3–4	TORONTO	Apr. 11	OTW	6–5*	NY Islanders
Dec. 29	L	3–4	Buffalo				
Dec. 31	L	0–2	New Jersey	Home games in CAPS			
Jan. 2	L	1–3	Tampa Bay	*Overtime			
Jan. 3	L	2–6	Florida	OTW—Overtime Win		SOW—Shootout Win	
				OTL—Overtime Loss		SOL—Shootout Loss	

Penguins All-Time Records vs. NHL Teams

Team	GP	W	L	T	OL	SL	PTS	GF	GA	PCT
Anaheim	22	12	6	2	2	0	28	72	69	.636
Atlanta	40	29	8	0	1	2	61	144	106	.763
Atlanta/Calgary	94	38	38	18	0	0	94	317	343	.500
Boston	178	57	97	21	1	2	138	554	698	.388
Buffalo	162	67	58	35	2	0	171	521	548	.528
Chicago	123	42	63	17	1	0	102	379	440	.415
Columbus	11	7	3	0	0	1	15	38	36	.682
Detroit	136	59	60	16	1	0	135	470	466	.496
Edmonton	64	25	35	4	0	0	54	228	286	.422
Florida	65	31	27	4	3	0	69	178	191	.531
Hartford/Carolina	114	51	47	11	4	1	118	417	412	.518
K.C./Colorado/New Jersey	196	82	90	17	6	1	188	652	666	.480
Los Angeles	146	58	69	18	1	0	135	462	509	.462
Minnesota	11	2	7	1	0	1	6	20	36	.273
Minnesota/Dallas	131	63	55	12	1	0	139	467	432	.531
Montreal	184	50	106	23	4	1	128	516	738	.348
Nashville	15	4	8	2	0	1	11	38	53	.367
New York Islanders	210	95	88	22	0	5	217	752	760	.517
New York Rangers	237	103	104	23	4	3	236	805	859	.498
Oak./California/Cleveland*	69	35	16	18	0	0	88	256	194	.638
Ottawa	74	38	25	9	1	1	87	247	214	.588
Philadelphia	248	85	129	30	4	0	204	763	907	.411
Quebec/Colorado	73	30	35	7	1	0	68	280	306	.466
San Jose	27	11	12	3	0	1	26	101	79	.481
St. Louis	132	49	63	18	2	0	118	421	448	.447
Tampa Bay	66	32	25	5	2	2	73	194	185	.553
Toronto	156	69	66	17	4	0	159	566	562	.510
Vancouver	104	57	35	11	1	0	126	421	365	.606
Washington	189	90	79	16	2	2	200	710	693	.529
Winnipeg/Phoenix	65	36	26	3	0	0	75	238	212	.577
Totals	**3342**	**1407**	**1480**	**383**	**48**	**24**	**3269**	**11227**	**11813**	**.489**

* Defunct

Penguins Preseason Records

YEAR	SITE	RECORD	YEAR	SITE	RECORD
1967–68	Brantford, Ont.	4–1–1	1989–90	Pittsburgh, PA	4–5–1
1968–69	Brantford, Ont.	1–5–2	1990–91	Pittsburgh, PA	7–2–0
1969–70	Brantford, Ont.	4–1–2	1991–92	Pittsburgh, PA/Denver, CO	4–3–2
1970–71	Brantford, Ont.	4–3–2	1992–93	Pittsburgh, PA	3–5–1
1971–72	Brantford, Ont.	3–2–3	1993–94	Pittsburgh, PA	5–4–0
1972–73	Brantford, Ont.	5–4–1	1994–95	Pittsburgh, PA	3–5–1
1973–74	Brantford, Ont.	4–2–3	1995–96	Canonsburg, PA	3–5–1
1974–75	Brantford, Ont.	5–4–0	1996–97	Canonsburg, PA	2–6–1
1975–76	Pittsburgh, PA	2–3–3	1997–98	Canonsburg, PA	4–4–0
1976–77	Pittsburgh, PA	7–3–0	1998–99	Canonsburg, PA	4–2–3
1977–78	Pittsburgh, PA	4–3–0	1999–00	Canonsburg, PA	2–3–0–1
1978–79	Pittsburgh, PA	3–5–0	2000–01	Canonsburg/Wilkes-Barre, PA	3–4–0–0
1979–80	Pittsburgh, PA	3–4–1	2001–02	Canonsburg/Wilkes-Barre, PA	1–2–3–0
1980–81	Pittsburgh, PA	1–3–2	2002–03	Canonsburg/Wilkes-Barre, PA	2–4–1–0
1981–82	Erie/Johnstown, PA	4–1–2	2003–04	Canonsburg, PA	2–4–1–0
1982–83	Johnstown, PA	1–3–3	2005–06	Pittsburgh/Wilkes-Barre, PA	2–6–2
1983–84	Johnstown, PA	3–4–1	2006–07	Pittsburgh, PA/Moncton, Nova Scotia	2–2–3
1984–85	Pittsburgh, PA	2–4–0	2007–08	Pittsburgh, PA	1–3–2
1985–86	Pittsburgh, PA	1–5–0	2008–09	Pittsburgh, PA	4–0–1
1986–87	Pittsburgh, PA	2–6–0	2009–10	Pittsburgh, PA	1–3–1
1987–88	Pittsburgh, PA	5–1–2			
1988–89	Pittsburgh, PA	6–3–0			

Former Boston great Bobby Orr (left) participates in a drill at the Pens' 1980 training camp.

Penguins Streaks

SEASON	OVERALL				HOME				ROAD			
	WIN	POINT	LOSS	WINLESS	WIN	POINT	LOSS	WINLESS	WIN	POINT	LOSS	WINLESS
1967–68	4	5	3	4	3	5	2	5	3	3	5	8
1968–69	4	6	7	9	4	4	4	6	2	5	8	14
1969–70	3	4	6	10	4	6	3	4	2	2	4	9
1970–71	2	4	4	8	7	7	2	5	2	3	15	18*
1971–72	4	5	6	9	3	4	3	4	3	6	6	14
1972–73	4	5	5	8	4	8	3	3	1	2	9	9
1973–74	3	4	6	8	3	6	4	4	2	3	4	5
1974–75	3	7	3	7	9	20*	2	4	3	4	4	6
1975–76	4	11	3	7	6	10	4	4	2	6	7	9
1976–77	3	6	4	6	3	7	2	3	2	2	3	6
1977–78	2	7	5	6	2	6	3	5	2	6	5	8
1978–79	4	10	4	5	6	8	3	3	3	7	6	8
1979–80	3	7	6	8	4	7	5	5	2	3	7	7
1980–81	6	6	3	6	5	6	3	3	2	4	8	11
1981–82	4	7	4	9	4	8	2	5	3	3	7	12
1982–83	3	5	11	18*	3	3	4	7	1	2	18*	18*
1983–84	2	3	8	8	1	2	7	11	4	5	6	7
1984–85	5	5	9	12	3	3	4	7	2	2	8	10
1985–86	5	6	5	7	4	10	4	6	2	2	5	5
1986–87	7	7	4	9	6	6	2	3	2	2	4	12
1987–88	4	4	6	10	6	6	3	7	4	4	4	5
1988–89	5	8	4	6	6	12	4	4	3	4	4	8
1989–90	4	5	4	8	7	7	4	4	2	3	8	13
1990–91	6	7	3	5	11*	14	3	5	3	4	6	10
1991–92	4	6	4	6	9	9	4	4	5	5	4	7
1992–93	17**	18*	3	3	10	11	2	3	7*	8*	3	2
1993–94	4	8	4	4	4	7	3	3	4	4	2	4
1994–95	7	13	3	3	7	9	2	2	4	6	3	3
1995–96	8	8	3	3	8	8	3	3	3	6	4	5
1996–97	6	14	6	6	6	8	3	3	6	7	8	13
1997–98	6	8	3	6	5	10	2	5	5	7	3	5
1998–99	10	10	3	8	9	11	3	4	2	3	3	6
1999–00	4	5	4	8	5	8	3	5	3	3	6	8
2000–01	4	5	2	6	4	5	5	7	2	6	4	4
2001–02	6	6	7	10	3	7	4	4	3	4	6	6
2002–03	4	5	9	16	3	6	5	10	3	3	6	7
2003–04	4	6	13*	18*	3	8	14*	16*	3	3	6	11
2005–06	2	5	10	10	2	3	5	6	2	3	5	9
2006–07	6	16	5	5	8	11	3	3	4	7	4	4
2007–08	8	10	4	4	8	11	2	2	4	6	2	3
2008–09	7	12	5	5	5	8	5	5	5	7	4	5
2009–10	7	9	5	5	4	11	2	2	6	6	4	4

* Club Record   ** NHL Record

Penguins Streaks—Continued

Longest Winning Streak	17	3/9/93–4/11/93
Longest Home Winning Streak	11	1/5/91–3/7/91
Longest Road Winning Streak	7	3/14/93–4/9/93
Longest Unbeaten Streak	18	3/9/93–4/14/93
Longest Home Unbeaten Streak	20	11/30/74–2/22/75
Longest Road Unbeaten Streak	8	3/14/93–4/14/93
Longest Losing Streak	13	1/13/04–2/12/04
Longest Home Losing Streak	14	12/31/03–3/22/04
Longest Road Losing Streak	18	12/23/82–3/4/83
Longest Winless Streak	18	1/13/04–2/22/04
Longest Home Winless Streak	16	12/31/03–3/4/04
Longest Road Winless Streak	18	10/25/70–1/14/71
		12/23/82–3/4/83
Consecutive Games Without Being Shutout	211	1/7/89–10/28/91
Consecutive Home Games Without Being Shutout	206	1/28/92–10/8/97
Consecutive Road Games Without Being Shutout	120	1/12/90–12/29/91
Consecutive Games Without Shutting Out Opponent	156	3/12/77–12/9/78
Consecutive Home Games Without Shutting Out Opponent	95	4/2/80–12/1/82
Consecutive Road Games Without Shutting Out Opponent	188	1/24/87–12/5/91
Consecutive Games Tied	4	12/8/79–12/15/79
Consecutive Games Going to Shootout	4	3/8/09–3/14/09

Penguins Season-by-Season Leaders

	GOALS			ASSISTS	
1967–68	22	Ab McDonald		39	Andy Bathgate
1968–69	25	Keith McCreary		38	Charlie Burns
1969–70	26	Dean Prentice		32	Michel Briere
1970–71	21	Keith McCreary, Dean Prentice, Jean Pronovost		32	Bryan Hextall
1971–72	30	Greg Polis, Jean Pronovost		44	Syl Apps
1972–73	35	Al McDonough		56	Syl Apps
1973–74	43	Lowell MacDonald		61	Syl Apps
1974–75	43	Jean Pronovost		63	Ron Schock
1975–76	53	Pierre Larouche		67	Syl Apps
1976–77	33	Jean Pronovost		43	Syl Apps
1977–78	40	Jean Pronovost		43	Greg Malone
1978–79	35	Greg Malone		42	Orest Kindrachuk
1979–80	30	Rick Kehoe		32	Greg Malone
1980–81	55	Rick Kehoe		67	Randy Carlyle
1981–82	36	Mike Bullard, Paul Gardner		64	Randy Carlyle
1982–83	29	Rick Kehoe		44	Greg Malone
1983–84	51	Mike Bullard		41	Mike Bullard
1984–85	43	Mario Lemieux		57	Mario Lemieux
1985–86	48	Mario Lemieux		93	Mario Lemieux
1986–87	54	Mario Lemieux		53	Mario Lemieux
1987–88	70	Mario Lemieux		98	Mario Lemieux
1988–89	85	Mario Lemieux		114	Mario Lemieux
1989–90	45	Mario Lemieux		78	Mario Lemieux
1990–91	40	Mark Recchi, Kevin Stevens		73	Mark Recchi
1991–92	54	Kevin Stevens		87	Mario Lemieux
1992–93	69	Mario Lemieux		91	Mario Lemieux
1993–94	41	Kevin Stevens		67	Jaromir Jagr
1994–95	32	Jaromir Jagr		48	Ron Francis
1995–96	69	Mario Lemieux		92	Ron Francis, Mario Lemieux
1996–97	50	Mario Lemieux		72	Mario Lemieux
1997–98	35	Jaromir Jagr		67	Jaromir Jagr
1998–99	44	Jaromir Jagr		83	Jaromir Jagr
1999–00	42	Jaromir Jagr		54	Jaromir Jagr
2000–01	52	Jaromir Jagr		69	Jaromir Jagr
2001–02	32	Alexei Kovalev		44	Alexei Kovalev
2002–03	28	Mario Lemieux		63	Mario Lemieux
2003–04	22	Ryan Malone		36	Dick Tarnstrom
2005–06	39	Sidney Crosby		63	Sidney Crosby
2006–07	36	Sidney Crosby		84	Sidney Crosby
2007–08	47	Evgeni Malkin		59	Evgeni Malkin
2008–09	35	Evgeni Malkin		78	Evgeni Malkin
2009–10	51	Sidney Crosby		58	Sidney Crosby

Penguins Season-by-Season Leaders—Continued

	POINTS		GAME-WINNING GOALS	
1967–68	59	Andy Bathgate	4	Andy Bathgate
1968–69	52	Ken Schinkel	4	Keith McCreary
1969–70	51	Dean Prentice	6	Jean Pronovost
1970–71	48	Bryan Hextall	3	Andy Bathgate, Keith McCreary
1971–72	59	Syl Apps	5	Bryan Hextall
1972–73	85	Syl Apps	5	Jean Pronovost
1973–74	85	Syl Apps	4	Al McDonough
1974–75	86	Ron Schock	9	Jean Pronovost
1975–76	111	Pierre Larouche	4	Syl Apps, Bob Kelly
1976–77	64	Jean Pronovost	6	Pierre Larouche, Jean Pronovost
1977–78	65	Jean Pronovost	5	Jean Pronovost
1978–79	65	Greg Malone	7	Peter Lee
1979–80	60	Rick Kehoe	5	Paul Marshall
1980–81	88	Rick Kehoe	5	Rick Kehoe, Rod Schutt
1981–82	85	Rick Kehoe	5	Mike Bullard
1982–83	67	Doug Shedden	4	Pat Boutette
1983–84	92	Mike Bullard	3	Rick Kehoe
1984–85	100	Mario Lemieux	3	Wayne Babych, Mike Bullard, Doug Shedden, Warren Young
1985–86	141	Mario Lemieux	7	Terry Ruskowski
1986–87	107	Mario Lemieux	5	Randy Cunneyworth
1987–88	168	Mario Lemieux	7	Mario Lemieux
1988–89	199	Mario Lemieux	8	Mario Lemieux
1989–90	123	Mario Lemieux	4	John Cullen, Mario Lemieux, Mark Recchi
1990–91	113	Mark Recchi	9	Mark Recchi
1991–92	131	Mario Lemieux	5	Mario Lemieux
1992–93	160	Mario Lemieux	10	Mario Lemieux
1993–94	99	Jaromir Jagr	9	Joe Mullen
1994–95	70	Jaromir Jagr	7	Jaromir Jagr
1995–96	161	Mario Lemieux	12	Jaromir Jagr
1996–97	122	Mario Lemieux	7	Mario Lemieux
1997–98	102	Jaromir Jagr	8	Jaromir Jagr
1998–99	127	Jaromir Jagr	7	Jaromir Jagr
1999–00	96	Jaromir Jagr	5	Jaromir Jagr, Robert Lang
2000–01	121	Jaromir Jagr	10	Jaromir Jagr
2001–02	76	Alexei Kovalev	6	Jan Hrdina
2002–03	91	Mario Lemieux	4	Jan Hrdina, Mario Lemieux, Martin Straka
2003–04	52	Dick Tarnstrom	5	Aleksey Morozov
2005–06	102	Sidney Crosby	5	Sidney Crosby
2006–07	120	Sidney Crosby	6	Evgeni Malkin
2007–08	106	Evgeni Malkin	6	Ryan Malone
2008–09	113	Evgeni Malkin	10	Petr Sykora
2009–10	109	Sidney Crosby	7	Evgeni Malkin

Penguins Season-by-Season Leaders—Continued

	POWER-PLAY GOALS			SHORTHANDED GOALS
1967–68	6	Ab McDonald	1	Earl Ingarfield, Ab McDonald
1968–69	8	Ken Schinkel	2	Jean Pronovost, Bob Woytowich
1969–70	12	Dean Prentice	1	Ron Schock
1970–71	7	Andy Bathgate, Dean Prentice	2	Ron Schock
1971–72	8	Greg Polis	2	Ron Schock
1972–73	8	Greg Polis, Eddie Shack	3	Ron Schock
1973–74	9	Lowell MacDonald	4	Syl Apps, Jean Pronovost
1974–75	11	Jean Pronovost	4	Vic Hadfield
1975–76	18	Pierre Larouche	2	Lew Morrison, Jean Pronovost
1976–77	8	Pierre Larouche	2	Syl Apps
1977–78	12	Jean Pronovost	2	Pete Mahovlich, Jean Pronovost
1978–79	10	Peter Lee	3	George Ferguson
1979–80	7	Rick Kehoe	3	George Ferguson
1980–81	20	Rick Kehoe	3	George Ferguson
1981–82	21	Paul Gardner	3	George Ferguson
1982–83	20	Paul Gardner	1	Pat Boutette, Randy Carlyle, Doug Shedden
1983–84	15	Mike Bullard	2	Kevin McClelland
1984–85	14	Mike Bullard	2	Mitch Lamoreux
1985–86	19	Doug Shedden	3	Dave Hannan
1986–87	19	Mario Lemieux	3	Dan Quinn
1987–88	22	Mario Lemieux	10	Mario Lemieux
1988–89	31	Mario Lemieux	13	Mario Lemieux
1989–90	14	Mario Lemieux	3	Mario Lemieux
1990–91	18	Kevin Stevens	4	Phil Bourque
1991–92	19	Kevin Stevens	4	Mario Lemieux
1992–93	26	Kevin Stevens	6	Mario Lemieux
1993–94	21	Kevin Stevens	2	Shawn McEachern, Joe Mullen
1994–95	8	Jaromir Jagr	3	Jaromir Jagr
1995–96	31	Mario Lemieux	8	Mario Lemieux
1996–97	15	Mario Lemieux	3	Mario Lemieux, Petr Nedved
1997–98	15	Stu Barnes	3	Martin Straka
1998–99	13	Stu Barnes	4	Martin Straka
1999–00	13	Robert Lang	2	Alexei Kovalev, German Titov
2000–01	16	Mario Lemieux	2	Alexei Kovalev
2001–02	8	Alexei Kovalev	1	Alexei Kovalev, Robert Lang, Dan LaCouture, Toby Petersen, Wayne Primeau
2002–03	14	Mario Lemieux	2	Ville Nieminen
2003–04	12	Dick Tarnstrom	3	Ryan Malone
2005–06	16	Sidney Crosby	5	Ryan Malone
2006–07	16	Evgeni Malkin	7	Jordan Staal
2007–08	17	Evgeni Malkin	2	Ryan Malone, Max Talbot
2008–09	14	Evgeni Malkin	2	Evgeni Malkin, Max Talbot
2009–10	13	Sidney Crosby, Evgeni Malkin	2	Sidney Crosby, Evgeni Malkin, Jordan Staal

Penguins Season-by-Season Leaders—Continued

	PENALTY MINUTES			SHOTS ON GOAL	
1967–68	74	Leo Boivin		293	Andy Bathgate
1968–69	81	Dunc McCallum		226	Ken Schinkel
1969–70	189	Bryan Watson		225	Ken Schinkel
1970–71	133	Bryan Hextall		225	Jean Pronovost
1971–72	212	Bryan Watson		214	Jean Pronovost
1972–73	179	Bryan Watson		285	Al McDonough
1973–74	138	Steve Durbano		260	Lowell MacDonald
1974–75	172	Colin Campbell		275	Jean Pronovost
1975–76	161	Steve Durbano		319	Pierre Larouche
1976–77	115	Bob Kelly		250	Rick Kehoe
1977–78	378	Dave Schultz		219	Jean Pronovost
1978–79	157	Dave Schultz		219	Peter Lee
1979–80	166	Kim Clackson		239	Rick Kehoe
1980–81	204	Paul Baxter		299	Rick Kehoe
1981–82	409	Paul Baxter		249	Rick Kehoe
1982–83	238	Paul Baxter		203	Rick Kehoe
1983–84	297	Gary Rissling		213	Mike Bullard
1984–85	209	Gary Rissling		209	Mario Lemieux
1985–86	174	Dan Frawley		276	Mario Lemieux
1986–87	218	Dan Frawley		267	Mario Lemieux
1987–88	206	Rod Buskas		382	Mario Lemieux
1988–89	285	Jay Caufield		342	Paul Coffey
1989–90	171	Kevin Stevens		324	Paul Coffey
1990–91	133	Kevin Stevens		253	Kevin Stevens
1991–92	254	Kevin Stevens		325	Kevin Stevens
1992–93	252	Rick Tocchet		326	Kevin Stevens
1993–94	199	Ulf Samuelsson		298	Jaromir Jagr
1994–95	114	Francois Leroux		192	Jaromir Jagr
1995–96	161	Francois Leroux		403	Jaromir Jagr
1996–97	155	Dave Roche		327	Mario Lemieux
1997–98	181	Chris Tamer		262	Jaromir Jagr
1998–99	93	Brad Werenka		343	Jaromir Jagr
1999–00	197	Matthew Barnaby		290	Jaromir Jagr
2000–01	168	Matthew Barnaby		317	Jaromir Jagr
2001–02	150	Krzysztof Oliwa		266	Alexei Kovalev
2002–03	128	Steve McKenna		235	Mario Lemieux
2003–04	127	Brooks Orpik		163	Rico Fata
2005–06	124	Brooks Orpik		278	Sidney Crosby
2006–07	125	Jarkko Ruutu		250	Sidney Crosby
2007–08	141	Georges Laraque		272	Evgeni Malkin
2008–09	171	Eric Godard		290	Evgeni Malkin
2009–10	120	Mike Rupp		298	Sidney Crosby

Dave "the Hammer" Schultz (center) led the NHL in penalty minutes in 1977–78.

Colorful Dunc Wilson topped the team with five shutouts in 1976–77.

German Titov was a plus 18 in 1998–99.

Penguins Season-by-Season Leaders—Continued

	PLUS/MINUS (Minimum of 60 games)			GOALS-AGAINST AVERAGE (Minimum of 25 games)	
1967–68	-2	Paul Andrea	2.86	Hank Bassen	
1968–69	-4	Jean Pronovost	3.23	Joe Daley	
1969–70	-1	Bryan Watson	3.03	Al Smith	
1970–71	10	Wally Boyer	2.86	Les Binkley	
1971–72	18	Syl Apps	3.22	Jim Rutherford	
1972–73	37	Lowell MacDonald	2.91	Jim Rutherford	
1973–74	21	Syl Apps	3.44	Jim Rutherford	
1974–75	29	Barry Wilkins	3.09	Gary Inness	
1975–76	27	Dave Burrows	3.45	Michel Plasse	
1976–77	13	Bob Kelly	2.94	Denis Herron	
1977–78	-5	Russ Anderson	3.57	Denis Herron	
1978–79	21	Ron Stackhouse	3.37	Denis Herron, Greg Millen	
1979–80	16	Ron Stackhouse	3.64	Greg Millen	
1980–81	4	Mark Johnson	4.16	Greg Millen	
1981–82	2	Pat Price	3.79	Michel Dion	
1982–83	-9	Peter Lee	4.26	Michel Dion	
1983–84	-19	Ron Flockhart	4.08	Denis Herron	
1984–85	-7	Wayne Babych	4.42	Roberto Romano	
1985–86	15	Mike Blaisdell	3.55	Roberto Romano	
1986–87	14	Randy Cunneyworth, Dan Quinn	3.43	Gilles Meloche	
1987–88	23	Mario Lemieux	4.09	Gilles Meloche	
1988–89	41	Mario Lemieux	4.04	Tom Barrasso	
1989–90	11	Randy Hillier	4.17	Wendell Young	
1990–91	18	Gordie Roberts	3.59	Tom Barrasso	
1991–92	33	Larry Murphy	3.53	Tom Barrasso	
1992–93	55	Mario Lemieux	3.01	Tom Barrasso	
1993–94	24	Martin Straka	3.36	Tom Barrasso	
1994–95	30	Ron Francis	3.21	Ken Wregget	
1995–96	37	Petr Nedved	3.24	Ken Wregget	
1996–97	27	Mario Lemieux	2.94	Patrick Lalime	
1997–98	17	Jaromir Jagr	2.07	Tom Barrasso	
1998–99	18	German Titov	2.55	Tom Barrasso	
1999–00	25	Jaromir Jagr	2.58	Jean-Sebastien Aubin	
2000–01	20	Robert Lang	2.98	Garth Snow	
2001–02	9	Robert Lang	2.75	Johan Hedberg	
2002–03	-9	Marc Bergevin	3.14	Johan Hedberg	
2003–04	-14	Tom Kostopoulos	3.74	Sebastien Caron	
2005–06	-1	Sidney Crosby	3.25	Marc-Andre Fleury	
2006–07	16	Jordan Staal	2.83	Marc-Andre Fleury	
2007–08	16	Evgeni Malkin	2.33	Marc-Andre Fleury	
2008–09	23	Rob Scuderi	2.67	Marc-Andre Fleury	
2009–10	19	Jordan Staal	2.65	Marc-Andre Fleury	

Penguins Season-by-Season Leaders—Continued

	SHUTOUTS			WINS	
1967–68	6	Les Binkley		20	Les Binkley
1968–69	2	Joe Daley		10	Les Binkley, Joe Daley
1969–70	3	Les Binkley		15	Al Smith
1970–71	2	Les Binkley, Al Smith		11	Les Binkley
1971–72	1	Jim Rutherford		17	Jim Rutherford
1972–73	3	Jim Rutherford		20	Jim Rutherford
1973–74	1	Andy Brown		13	Andy Brown
1974–75	2	Gary Inness		24	Gary Inness
1975–76	2	Michel Plasse		24	Michel Plasse
1976–77	5	Dunc Wilson		18	Dunc Wilson
1977–78	–	–		20	Denis Herron
1978–79	2	Greg Millen		22	Denis Herron
1979–80	2	Greg Millen		18	Greg Millen
1980–81	–	–		25	Greg Millen
1981–82	1	Gary Edwards		25	Michel Dion
1982–83	1	Denis Herron		12	Michel Dion
1983–84	1	Denis Herron, Roberto Romano		8	Denis Herron
1984–85	1	Denis Herron, Roberto Romano		10	Denis Herron
1985–86	2	Roberto Romano		21	Roberto Romano
1986–87	–	–		13	Gilles Meloche
1987–88	1	Steve Guenette, Frank Pietrangelo		12	Steve Guenette
1988–89	–	–		18	Tom Barrasso
1989–90	1	Wendell Young		16	Wendell Young
1990–91	1	Tom Barrasso		27	Tom Barrasso
1991–92	1	Tom Barrasso		25	Tom Barrasso
1992–93	4	Tom Barrasso		43	Tom Barrasso
1993–94	2	Tom Barrasso		22	Tom Barrasso
1994–95	–	–		25	Ken Wregget
1995–96	3	Ken Wregget		29	Tom Barrasso
1996–97	3	Patrick Lalime		21	Patrick Lalime
1997–98	7	Tom Barrasso		31	Tom Barrasso
1998–99	4	Tom Barrasso		19	Tom Barrasso
1999–00	2	Jean-Sebastien Aubin		23	Jean-Sebastien Aubin
2000–01	3	Garth Snow		20	Jean-Sebastien Aubin
2001–02	6	Johan Hedberg		25	Johan Hedberg
2002–03	2	Sebastien Caron		14	Johan Hedberg
2003–04	1	Jean-Sebastien Aubin, Sebastien Caron, Marc-Andre Fleury		9	Sebastien Caron
2005–06	1	Sebastien Caron, Marc-Andre Fleury		13	Marc-Andre Fleury
2006–07	5	Marc-Andre Fleury		40	Marc-Andre Fleury
2007–08	4	Marc-Andre Fleury		19	Marc-Andre Fleury
2008–09	4	Marc-Andre Fleury		35	Marc-Andre Fleury
2009–10	1	Marc-Andre Fleury		37	Marc-Andre Fleury

Penguins All-Time Scoring Leaders

GAMES

SEASON				CAREER	
Ron Francis	84	1992–93		Mario Lemieux	915
Shawn McEachern	84	1992–93		Jaromir Jagr	806
Joe Mullen	84	1993–94		Jean Pronovost	753
Larry Murphy	84	1993–94		Rick Kehoe	722
Martin Straka	84	1993–94		Ron Stackhouse	621
Kevin Stevens	83	1993–94		Ron Schock	619
Larry Murphy	83	1992–93		Dave Burrows	573
21 Players Tied with 82				Bob Errey	572
				Martin Straka	560
				Ron Francis	533

GOALS

SEASON				CAREER	
Mario Lemieux	85	1988–89		Mario Lemieux	690
Mario Lemieux	70	1987–88		Jaromir Jagr	439
Mario Lemieux	69	1992–93		Jean Pronovost	316
Mario Lemieux	69	1995–96		Rick Kehoe	312
Jaromir Jagr	62	1995–96		Kevin Stevens	260
Rick Kehoe	55	1980–81		Mike Bullard	185
Kevin Stevens	55	1992–93		Sidney Crosby	183
Mario Lemieux	54	1986–87		Martin Straka	165
Kevin Stevens	54	1991–92		Ron Francis	164
Pierre Larouche	53	1975–76		Mark Recchi	154

ASSISTS

SEASON				CAREER	
Mario Lemieux	114	1988–89		Mario Lemieux	1,033
Mario Lemieux	98	1987–88		Jaromir Jagr	640
Mario Lemieux	93	1985–86		Ron Francis	449
Ron Francis	92	1995–96		Syl Apps	349
Mario Lemieux	92	1995–96		Paul Coffey	332
Mario Lemieux	91	1992–93		Rick Kehoe	324
Mario Lemieux	87	1991–92		Sidney Crosby	323
Jaromir Jagr	87	1995–96		Kevin Stevens	295
Sidney Crosby	84	2006–07		Jean Pronovost	287
Paul Coffey	83	1988–89		Ron Schock	280
Jaromir Jagr	83	1998–99			

Penguins All-Time Scoring Leaders—Continued

POINTS

SEASON			CAREER	
Mario Lemieux	199	1988–89	Mario Lemieux	1,723
Mario Lemieux	168	1987–88	Jaromir Jagr	1,079
Mario Lemieux	161	1995–96	Rick Kehoe	636
Mario Lemieux	160	1992–93	Ron Francis	613
Jaromir Jagr	149	1995–96	Jean Pronovost	603
Mario Lemieux	141	1985–86	Kevin Stevens	555
Mario Lemieux	131	1991–92	Sidney Crosby	506
Jaromir Jagr	127	1998–99	Syl Apps	500
Mario Lemieux	123	1989–90	Martin Straka	442
Kevin Stevens	123	1991–92	Paul Coffey	440

EVEN-STRENGTH GOALS

SEASON			CAREER	
Mario Lemieux	47	1992–93	Mario Lemieux	405
Mario Lemieux	41	1988–89	Jaromir Jagr	320
Jaromir Jagr	41	1995–96	Jean Pronovost	233
Mario Lemieux	38	1987–88	Rick Kehoe	216
Jean Pronovost	37	1975–76	Kevin Stevens	150
Jaromir Jagr	37	2000–01	Sidney Crosby	126
Mike Bullard	36	1983–84	Martin Straka	126
Petr Nedved	36	1995–96	Mike Bullard	124
Sidney Crosby	36	2009–10	Bob Errey	119
Four Players Tied with 35			Greg Malone	113

POWER-PLAY GOALS

SEASON			CAREER	
Mario Lemieux	31	1988–89	Mario Lemieux	236
Mario Lemieux	31	1995–96	Jaromir Jagr	110
Kevin Stevens	26	1992–93	Kevin Stevens	110
Rob Brown	24	1988–89	Rick Kehoe	95
Mario Lemieux	22	1987–88	Jean Pronovost	69
Paul Gardner	21	1981–82	Rob Brown	68
Dan Quinn	21	1987–88	Mark Recchi	61
Kevin Stevens	21	1993–94	Evgeni Malkin	60
Four Players Tied with 20			Mike Bullard	59
			Paul Gardner	59

Jaromir Jagr leads the Penguins in game-winning goals.

Underrated Jan Hrdina is ninth on the club's all-time list in shooting percentage.

Penguins All-Time Scoring Leaders—Continued

SHORTHANDED GOALS

SEASON			CAREER	
Mario Lemieux	13	1988–89	Mario Lemieux	49
Mario Lemieux	10	1987–88	Jean Pronovost	14
Mario Lemieux	8	1995–96	Ron Schock	14
Jordan Staal	7	2006–07	George Ferguson	12
Mario Lemieux	6	1992–93	Syl Apps	11
Ryan Malone	5	2005–06	Ryan Malone	11
Eight Players Tied with 4			Jordan Staal	10
			Max Talbot	10
			Bob Errey	9
			Jaromir Jagr	9
			Martin Straka	9

GAME-WINNING GOALS

SEASON			CAREER	
Jaromir Jagr	12	1995–96	Jaromir Jagr	78
Mario Lemieux	10	1992–93	Mario Lemieux	74
Jaromir Jagr	10	2000–01	Jean Pronovost	42
Petr Sykora	10	2008–09	Kevin Stevens	27
Jean Pronovost	9	1974–75	Rick Kehoe	26
Mark Recchi	9	1990–91	Martin Straka	26
Jaromir Jagr	9	1992–93	Sidney Crosby	22
Joe Mullen	9	1993–94	Evgeni Malkin	22
Alexei Kovalev	9	2000–01	Joe Mullen	22
Three Players Tied with 8			Mark Recchi	22

SHOTS ON GOAL

SEASON			CAREER	
Jaromir Jagr	403	1995–96	Mario Lemieux	3,633
Mario Lemieux	382	1987–88	Jaromir Jagr	2,911
Jaromir Jagr	343	1998–99	Jean Pronovost	2,310
Paul Coffey	342	1988–89	Rick Kehoe	2,165
Mario Lemieux	338	1995–96	Kevin Stevens	1,631
Mario Lemieux	327	1996–97	Ron Stackhouse	1,342
Kevin Stevens	326	1992–93	Paul Coffey	1,306
Kevin Stevens	325	1991–92	Sidney Crosby	1,237
Paul Coffey	324	1989–90	Ron Schock	1,227
Pierre Larouche	319	1975–76	Ron Francis	1,201

Penguins All-Time Scoring Leaders—Continued

SHOOTING PERCENTAGE

SEASON			CAREER	
Warren Young	30.8	1984–85	Petr Nedved	19.8
Rob Brown	30.0	1987–88	Rob Brown	19.7
Rob Brown	29.0	1988–89	Mike Bullard	19.1
Terry Ruskowski	28.6	1985–86	Paul Gardner	19.0
Mario Lemieux	27.2	1988–89	Mario Lemieux	19.0
Mike Bullard	24.8	1981–82	Craig Simpson	18.8
Mario Lemieux	24.1	1992–93	Joe Mullen	17.8
Mike Bullard	23.9	1983–84	Mark Recchi	17.4
Martin Straka	23.1	1993–94	Jan Hrdina	17.0
Paul Gardner	22.9	1981–82	Rick Tocchet	16.9

PLUS/MINUS RATING

SEASON			CAREER	
Mario Lemieux	55	1992–93	Jaromir Jagr	207
Larry Murphy	45	1992–93	Mario Lemieux	115
Mario Lemieux	41	1988–89	Larry Murphy	102
Bob Errey	40	1988–89	Syl Apps	94
Lowell MacDonald	37	1972–73	Lowell MacDonald	77
Petr Nedved	37	1995–96	Ulf Samuelsson	76
Ulf Samuelsson	36	1992–93	Ron Francis	70
Larry Murphy	33	1991–92	Joe Mullen	64
Jaromir Jagr	31	1995–96	Ron Stackhouse	54
Jaromir Jagr	30	1992–93	Kjell Samuelsson	51
Ron Francis	30	1994–95		

PENALTY MINUTES

SEASON			CAREER	
Paul Baxter	409	1981–82	Kevin Stevens	1,048
Dave Schultz	378	1977–78	Troy Loney	980
Pat Price	322	1981–82	Rod Buskas	959
Gary Rissling	297	1983–84	Bryan Watson	871
Jay Caufield	285	1988–89	Paul Baxter	851
Kevin Stevens	254	1991–92	Mario Lemieux	834
Rick Tocchet	252	1992–93	Gary Rissling	832
Ulf Samuelsson	249	1992–93	Ulf Samuelsson	804
Paul Baxter	238	1982–83	Jay Caufield	714
Pat Boutette	230	1981–82	Russ Anderson	684

Penguins All-Time Goaltending Leaders

GAMES

SEASON			CAREER	
Marc-Andre Fleury	67	2006–07	Tom Barrasso	460
Marc-Andre Fleury	67	2009–10	Marc-Andre Fleury	302
Johan Hedberg	66	2001–02	Denis Herron	290
Greg Millen	63	1980–81	Ken Wregget	212
Tom Barrasso	63	1992–93	Les Binkley	196
Tom Barrasso	63	1997–98	Jean-Sebastien Aubin	168
Michel Dion	62	1981–82	Michel Dion	151
Marc-Andre Fleury	62	2008–09	Greg Millen	135
Denis Herron	60	1977–78	Roberto Romano	125
Gary Inness	57	1974–75	Johan Hedberg	116
Tom Barrasso	57	1991–92		

MINUTES PLAYED

SEASON			CAREER	
Marc-Andre Fleury	3,905	2006–07	Tom Barrasso	25,879
Johan Hedberg	3,877	2001–02	Marc-Andre Fleury	17,164
Marc-Andre Fleury	3,798	2009–10	Denis Herron	16,105
Greg Millen	3,721	1980–81	Ken Wregget	11,737
Tom Barrasso	3,702	1992–93	Les Binkley	11,046
Marc-Andre Fleury	3,641	2008–09	Jean-Sebastien Aubin	8,888
Michel Dion	3,580	1981–82	Michel Dion	8,477
Tom Barrasso	3,542	1997–98	Greg Millen	7,839
Denis Herron	3,534	1977–78	Roberto Romano	7,051
Tom Barrasso	3,329	1991–92	Johan Hedberg	6,832

WINS

SEASON			CAREER	
Tom Barrasso	43	1992–93	Tom Barrasso	226
Marc-Andre Fleury	40	2006–07	Marc-Andre Fleury	148
Marc-Andre Fleury	37	2009–10	Ken Wregget	104
Marc-Andre Fleury	35	2008–09	Denis Herron	88
Tom Barrasso	31	1997–98	Jean-Sebastien Aubin	63
Tom Barrasso	29	1995–96	Les Binkley	58
Tom Barrasso	27	1990–91	Greg Millen	57
Greg Millen	25	1980–81	Johan Hedberg	46
Michel Dion	25	1981–82	Roberto Romano	46
Tom Barrasso	25	1991–92	Jim Rutherford	44
Ken Wregget	25	1994–95		
Johan Hedberg	25	2001–02		

Penguins All-Time Goaltending Leaders—Continued

LOSSES

SEASON			CAREER	
Johan Hedberg	34	2001–02	Tom Barrasso	153
Les Binkley	31	1968–69	Denis Herron	133
Michel Dion	30	1982–83	Marc-Andre Fleury	106
Greg Millen	27	1980–81	Les Binkley	94
Marc-Andre Fleury	27	2005–06	Michel Dion	79
Denis Herron	25	1977–78	Jean-Sebastien Aubin	72
Les Binkley	24	1967–68	Ken Wregget	67
Michel Dion	24	1981–82	Roberto Romano	62
Denis Herron	24	1983–84	Johan Hedberg	57
Sebastien Caron	24	2003–04	Greg Millen	56

TIES/OVERTIME/SHOOTOUT LOSSES

SEASON			CAREER	
Denis Herron	15	1977–78	Tom Barrasso	53
Tom Barrasso	13	1997–98	Denis Herron	44
Denis Herron	12	1978–79	Les Binkley	34
Michel Dion	12	1981–82	Marc-Andre Fleury	32
Les Binkley	10	1967–68	Ken Wregget	21
Les Binkley	10	1970–71	Michel Dion	20
Gary Inness	10	1974–75	Greg Millen	18
Michel Plasse	10	1975–76	Gilles Meloche	17
Greg Millen	10	1980–81	Al Smith	17
Al Smith	9	1970–71	Michel Plasse	14
Tom Barrasso	9	1991–92	Jim Rutherford	14
Marc-Andre Fleury	9	2006–07		

POINTS

SEASON			CAREER	
Tom Barrasso	91	1992–93	Tom Barrasso	505
Marc-Andre Fleury	89	2006–07	Marc-Andre Fleury	328
Marc-Andre Fleury	80	2009–10	Ken Wregget	229
Marc-Andre Fleury	77	2008–09	Denis Herron	220
Tom Barrasso	75	1997–98	Les Binkley	150
Michel Dion	62	1981–82	Jean-Sebastien Aubin	137
Greg Millen	60	1980–81	Greg Millen	132
Tom Barrasso	60	1995–96	Michel Dion	104
Tom Barrasso	59	1991–92	Johan Hedberg	104
Gary Inness	58	1974–75	Jim Rutherford	102
Michel Plasse	58	1975–76		

Penguins All-Time Goaltending Leaders—Continued

POINTS PERCENTAGE

SEASON (Minimum of 25 games)			CAREER (Minimum of 75 games)	
Tom Barrasso	.734	1992–93	Ken Wregget	.596
Ken Wregget	.722	1994–95	Tom Barrasso	.584
Marc-Andre Fleury	.685	2006–07	Marc-Andre Fleury	.573
Ty Conklin	.661	2007–08	Michel Plasse	.563
Tom Barrasso	.647	1997–98	Frank Pietrangelo	.514
Marc-Andre Fleury	.645	2007–08	Gary Inness	.511
Marc-Andre Fleury	.642	2008–09	Greg Millen	.504
Tom Barrasso	.638	1995–96	Jim Rutherford	.477
Patrick Lalime	.629	1996–97	Wendell Young	.473
Marc-Andre Fleury	.625	2009–10	Jean-Sebastien Aubin	.469

GOALS AGAINST

SEASON			CAREER	
Greg Millen	258	1980–81	Tom Barrasso	1,409
Michel Dion	226	1981–82	Denis Herron	1,041
Denis Herron	210	1977–78	Marc-Andre Fleury	808
Michel Dion	198	1982–83	Ken Wregget	644
Tom Barrasso	196	1991–92	Michel Dion	605
Tom Barrasso	186	1992–93	Les Binkley	575
Marc-Andre Fleury	184	2006–07	Greg Millen	501
Denis Herron	180	1978–79	Roberto Romano	465
Michel Plasse	178	1975–76	Jean-Sebastien Aubin	432
Johan Hedberg	178	2001–02	Wendell Young	385

GOALS-AGAINST AVERAGE

SEASON (Minimum of 25 games)			CAREER (Minimum of 75 games)	
Tom Barrasso	2.07	1997–98	Marc-Andre Fleury	2.82
Marc-Andre Fleury	2.33	2007–08	Johan Hedberg	2.88
Ty Conklin	2.51	2007–08	Jean-Sebastien Aubin	2.92
Tom Barrasso	2.55	1998–99	Al Smith	3.07
Jean-Sebastien Aubin	2.58	1999–00	Les Binkley	3.12
Marc-Andre Fleury	2.65	2009–10	Jim Rutherford	3.14
Marc-Andre Fleury	2.67	2008–09	Tom Barrasso	3.27
Johan Hedberg	2.75	2001–02	Ken Wregget	3.29
Peter Skudra	2.79	1998–99	Gary Inness	3.34
Marc-Andre Fleury	2.83	2006–07	Sebastien Caron	3.49

Penguins All-Time Goaltending Leaders—Continued

SHUTOUTS

SEASON			CAREER	
Tom Barrasso	7	1997–98	Tom Barrasso	22
Les Binkley	6	1967–68	Marc-Andre Fleury	16
Johan Hedberg	6	2001–02	Les Binkley	11
Dunc Wilson	5	1976–77	Johan Hedberg	7
Marc-Andre Fleury	5	2006–07	Jean-Sebastien Aubin	6
Tom Barrasso	4	1992–93	Denis Herron	6
Tom Barrasso	4	1998–99	Ken Wregget	6
Marc-Andre Fleury	4	2007–08	Dunc Wilson	5
Marc-Andre Fleury	4	2008–09	Six Players Tied with 4	
Six Players Tied with 3				

SAVES*

SEASON			CAREER	
Denis Herron	1,920	1977–78	Tom Barrasso	12,076
Marc-Andre Fleury	1,770	2006–07	Denis Herron	8,072
Tom Barrasso	1,699	1992–93	Marc-Andre Fleury	7,837
Marc-Andre Fleury	1,688	2008–09	Ken Wregget	5,641
Johan Hedberg	1,673	2001–02	Les Binkley	5,022
Marc-Andre Fleury	1,604	2009–10	Michel Dion	3,998
Gary Inness	1,512	1974–75	Jean-Sebastien Aubin	3,937
Tom Barrasso	1,506	1991–92	Greg Millen	3,482
Michel Plasse	1,480	1975–76	Roberto Romano	3,407
Tom Barrasso	1,466	1995–96	Johan Hedberg	2,973

* Saves became an official NHL statistic in 1983–84.

SAVE PERCENTAGE*

SEASON (Minimum of 25 games)			CAREER (Minimum of 75 games)	
Ty Conklin	.923	2007–08	Marc-Andre Fleury	.906
Tom Barrasso	.922	1997–98	Jean-Sebastien Aubin	.901
Marc-Andre Fleury	.921	2007–08	Johan Hedberg	.901
Jean-Sebastien Aubin	.914	1999–00	Jim Rutherford	.899
Patrick Lalime	.913	1996–97	Al Smith	.899
Marc-Andre Fleury	.912	2008–09	Les Binkley	.897
Marc-Andre Fleury	.906	2006–07	Gary Inness	.897
Ken Wregget	.905	1995–96	Ken Wregget	.897
Marc-Andre Fleury	.905	2009–10	Tom Barrasso	.895
Gary Inness	.904	1974–75	Sebastien Caron	.892
Johan Hedberg	.904	2001–02		

* Save percentage became an official NHL statistic in 1983–84.

Jean-Sebastien Aubin
posted a 2.92 goals-against
average during his six
seasons with the Penguins.

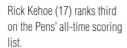

Rick Kehoe (17) ranks third
on the Pens' all-time scoring
list.

Penguins Career Scoring Statistics

RANK	PLAYER	GP	G	A	PTS	PIM
1	Mario Lemieux	915	690	1033	1723	834
2	Jaromir Jagr	806	439	640	1079	593
3	Rick Kehoe	722	312	324	636	88
4	Ron Francis	533	164	449	613	295
5	Jean Pronovost	753	316	287	603	306
6	Kevin Stevens	522	260	295	555	1048
7	Sidney Crosby	371	183	323	506	356
8	Syl Apps	495	151	349	500	241
9	Martin Straka	560	165	277	442	215
10	Paul Coffey	331	108	332	440	573
11	Ron Schock	619	124	280	404	201
12	Mark Recchi	389	154	231	385	300
13	Evgeni Malkin	309	143	238	381	338
14	Greg Malone	495	143	221	364	496
15	Mike Bullard	382	185	175	360	388
16	Alexei Kovalev	345	149	198	347	357
17	Ron Stackhouse	621	66	277	343	547
18	Rob Brown	414	150	192	342	392
19	Joe Mullen	379	153	172	325	101
20	Randy Carlyle	397	66	257	323	582
21	Lowell MacDonald	328	140	166	306	60
22	Larry Murphy	336	78	223	301	213
23	Doug Shedden	332	123	159	282	148
24	Dan Quinn	270	111	165	276	224
25	Bob Errey	572	132	140	272	651
26	John Cullen	262	88	184	272	399
27	Robert Lang	345	103	158	261	96
28	Sergei Gonchar	322	54	205	259	313
29	Pierre Larouche	240	119	134	253	99
30	Peter Lee	431	114	131	245	257
31	Ken Schinkel	371	93	143	236	86
32	Jan Hrdina	366	79	148	227	215
33	Aleksey Morozov	451	84	135	219	98
34	Randy Cunneyworth	295	101	115	216	513
35	Paul Gardner	207	98	105	203	105
36	George Ferguson	310	89	106	195	162
37	Bryan Hextall	335	71	115	186	498
38	Rick Tocchet	150	76	103	179	435
39	Pat Boutette	247	65	109	174	548
40	Petr Nedved	154	78	92	170	134
41	Ryan Malone	299	87	82	169	301
42	Rod Schutt	278	77	92	169	177
43	Troy Loney	532	69	100	169	980
44	Jordan Staal	327	84	84	168	173
45	Moe Mantha	232	37	131	168	223
46	Doug Bodger	299	35	132	167	292
47	Phil Bourque	344	75	89	164	435
48	Greg Polis	256	88	70	158	146
49	Tomas Sandstrom	172	71	84	155	168
50	Bob Kelly	250	69	85	154	462
51	Ryan Whitney	253	34	116	150	223

RANK	PLAYER	GP	G	A	PTS	PIM
52	Dave Hannan	355	60	88	148	530
53	Keith McCreary	292	82	59	141	199
54	Vic Hadfield	163	61	79	140	118
55	Kevin Hatcher	220	45	95	140	193
56	Stu Barnes	204	67	69	136	66
57	Zarley Zalapski	190	33	102	135	160
58	John Chabot	216	36	98	134	26
59	Dave Burrows	573	24	108	132	301
60	Al McDonough	152	56	74	130	46
61	Ross Lonsberry	236	56	73	129	150
62	Gregg Sheppard	241	50	73	123	113
63	Val Fonteyne	349	39	82	121	4
64	Orest Kindrachuk	144	38	80	118	181
65	Terry Ruskowski	143	40	74	114	307
66	Pete Mahovlich	117	39	75	114	76
67	Shawn McEachern	170	53	59	112	78
68	Mario Faubert	231	21	90	111	222
69	Wayne Bianchin	265	68	41	109	130
70	Petr Sykora	157	53	56	109	77
71	Jim Johnson	390	14	95	109	658
72	Craig Simpson	169	50	55	105	140
73	Duane Rupp	265	21	83	104	170
74	Andy Bathgate	150	35	68	103	89
75	Dick Tarnstrom	174	28	75	103	140
76	Warren Young	152	49	52	101	311
77	Nick Harbaruk	308	40	61	101	257
78	Blair Chapman	227	48	51	99	71
79	Colby Armstrong	181	37	61	98	175
80	German Titov	135	28	70	98	68
81	Wally Boyer	203	32	62	94	81
82	Paul Baxter	202	25	69	94	851
83	Ulf Samuelsson	277	11	83	94	804
84	Bob Woytowich	248	22	71	93	149
85	Russ Anderson	353	15	77	92	684
86	Randy Hillier	343	13	79	92	594
87	Dean Prentice	144	47	42	89	32
88	Max Talbot	306	44	43	87	258
89	Chuck Arnason	149	46	40	86	50
90	Jiri Slegr	252	24	62	86	337
91	Darius Kasparaitis	405	15	68	83	661
92	Milan Kraft	207	41	41	82	52
93	Michel Ouellet	123	35	45	80	46
94	Brooks Orpik	449	8	72	80	529
95	Tyler Kennedy	186	38	41	79	96
96	Kris Letang	217	21	58	79	102
97	Pascal Dupuis	168	32	46	78	54
98	Greg Hotham	170	11	63	74	118
99	Mark Taylor	106	31	41	72	43
100	Kip Miller	154	26	46	72	38
101	Darryl Edestrand	158	25	47	72	140
102	Bryan Trottier	156	24	48	72	114
103	Dan Frawley	240	33	37	70	610
104	Ruslan Fedotenko	145	27	42	69	94
105	Gary McAdam	140	27	40	67	95

RANK	PLAYER	GP	G	A	PTS	PIM
106	Markus Naslund	151	25	42	67	65
107	Dennis Owchar	168	18	49	67	146
108	Erik Christensen	143	33	33	66	88
109	Colin Campbell	243	14	52	66	517
110	Sergei Zubov	64	11	55	66	22
111	Michal Rozsival	237	18	47	65	161
112	Bryan Watson	304	8	57	65	871
113	Bryan Smolinski	81	24	40	64	69
114	Rod Buskas	431	16	48	64	959
115	Ian Moran	433	19	44	63	281
116	Mark Johnson	136	23	39	62	84
117	Matt Cooke	155	28	33	61	207
118	Mike Corrigan	98	22	39	61	46
119	Barry Wilkins	134	5	56	61	203
120	Andy Brickley	95	25	35	60	19
121	Earl Ingarfield	90	23	37	60	16
122	Fredrik Olausson	127	13	47	60	66
123	Pat Price	128	8	52	60	459
124	Gene Ubriaco	114	33	26	59	30
125	Eddie Shack	92	30	29	59	96
126	Tomas Surovy	126	27	32	59	71
127	Alex Goligoski	117	14	45	59	40
128	John LeClair	94	24	34	58	73
129	Bill Guerin	95	26	31	57	93
130	Norm Schmidt	125	23	33	56	73
131	Ville Siren	199	11	45	56	158
132	Doug Brown	77	18	37	55	18
133	Willy Lindstrom	131	24	30	54	36
134	Wayne Babych	67	20	34	54	35
135	Gene Carr	70	17	37	54	76
136	Brad Werenka	213	12	41	53	208
137	Noel Price	143	8	45	53	109
138	Ric Jackman	74	13	39	52	60
139	Pat Hughes	134	28	23	51	239
140	Glen Murray	135	25	26	51	81
141	Charlie Burns	76	13	38	51	22
142	Ron Flockhart	80	27	23	50	44
143	Chris Kunitz	70	20	30	50	55
144	Tony Tanti	83	20	30	50	66
145	Jock Callander	101	21	28	49	114
146	Dunc McCallum	185	14	35	49	228
147	Paul Stanton	206	11	38	49	199
148	Janne Laukkanen	125	11	37	48	82
149	Hans Jonsson	242	10	38	48	92
150	Rico Fata	120	21	26	47	74
151	Randy Robitaille	81	15	32	47	24
152	Dave Schultz	113	13	34	47	535
153	Billy Dea	139	26	20	46	10
154	Gary Rissling	184	20	26	46	832
155	Paul Andrea	90	18	27	45	4
156	Michel Briere	76	12	32	44	20
157	Ab McDonald	74	22	21	43	38
158	Dale Tallon	95	10	33	43	53
159	Tom Edur	58	5	38	43	18

RANK	PLAYER	GP	G	A	PTS	PIM
160	Luc Robitaille	46	23	19	42	37
161	Ziggy Palffy	42	11	31	42	12
162	Randy Gilhen	133	20	21	41	105
163	Leo Boivin	114	14	26	40	100
164	Alex Hicks	113	12	28	40	130
165	Bob Paradise	203	7	33	40	209
166	Josef Melichar	310	7	33	40	263
167	Dmitri Mironov	87	4	36	40	112
168	Kevin McCarthy	95	13	26	39	82
169	Gordie Roberts	134	5	34	39	157
170	Rob Scuderi	300	3	36	39	112
171	Nick Libett	121	20	18	38	18
172	Konstantin Koltsov	144	12	26	38	50
173	Chris Joseph	120	10	28	38	129
174	Andre St. Laurent	96	23	14	37	130
175	Glen Sather	122	20	17	37	210
176	Lou Angotti	71	17	20	37	36
177	Art Stratton	58	16	21	37	16
178	Stan Gilbertson	115	19	17	36	19
179	Miroslav Satan	65	17	19	36	36
180	Bob McManama	99	11	25	36	28
181	Andrew Ference	163	11	25	36	157
182	Barry Pederson	84	10	26	36	50
183	Chris Dahlquist	195	10	26	36	219
184	Jiri Hrdina	93	9	27	36	29
185	Jason Woolley	57	6	30	36	28
186	Josef Beranek	91	16	19	35	65
187	Steve Gatzos	89	15	20	35	83
188	Peter Taglianetti	167	7	28	35	338
189	Tom Bladon	135	6	29	35	99
190	Tyler Wright	238	17	16	33	317
191	Ed Olczyk	68	15	18	33	41
192	Matthew Barnaby	129	15	18	33	399
193	Wayne Primeau	131	9	24	33	127
194	Jim Hamilton	95	14	18	32	28
195	Jarkko Ruutu	152	13	19	32	263
196	Kjell Samuelsson	183	10	22	32	312
197	Norm Maciver	45	2	30	32	38
198	Mike Blaisdell	76	16	15	31	38
199	Bob Leiter	78	14	17	31	18
200	Ron Duguay	53	11	20	31	36
201	Mark Eaton	218	7	24	31	82
202	Tom Barrasso	460	0	31	31	251
203	Rick MacLeish	46	13	17	30	30
204	Ron Lalonde	106	10	20	30	16
205	Jim Morrison	132	5	25	30	72
206	Marty McSorley	134	5	25	30	378
207	Jim Paek	170	4	26	30	117
208	Dave Hunter	59	11	18	29	77
209	Chris Tamer	253	8	21	29	588
210	Dave McLlwain	108	14	14	28	48
211	Joe Dziedzic	128	14	14	28	131
212	Charlie Simmer	50	11	17	28	24
213	Tom Roulston	58	11	17	28	10

RANK	PLAYER	GP	G	A	PTS	PIM
214	Gary Roberts	57	10	18	28	66
215	Kevin LaVallee	33	8	20	28	4
216	Grant Jennings	210	7	21	28	357
217	Scott Young	43	11	16	27	33
218	Kris Beech	100	10	17	27	59
219	Steve Durbano	66	4	23	27	309
220	Lew Morrison	214	13	13	26	12
221	Tom Kostopoulos	79	10	16	26	76
222	Toby Petersen	91	10	16	26	8
223	Jack Lynch	64	1	25	26	61
224	Stephane Richer	58	13	12	25	14
225	Chris Kontos	67	9	16	25	18
226	Dave Tippett	74	6	19	25	56
227	Paul Marshall	59	12	12	24	13
228	Dave Roche	132	12	12	24	285
229	Mike Stapleton	136	11	13	24	28
230	Ville Nieminen	88	10	14	24	101
231	Brian Holzinger	70	7	17	24	44
232	Andreas Johansson	77	7	17	24	40
233	Jean-Guy Lagace	106	4	20	24	119
234	Jean-Jacques Daigneault	66	6	17	23	59
235	Marc Chorney	139	5	18	23	151
236	Bryan Maxwell	89	3	20	23	141
237	Ab DeMarco	42	9	13	22	8
238	Anders Hakansson	62	9	12	21	26
239	Dan LaCouture	137	8	13	21	157
240	Drake Berehowsky	52	5	16	21	63
241	Randy Boyd	84	4	17	21	126
242	Bill Speer	102	4	17	21	71
243	Marc Bergevin	157	4	17	21	89
244	Mitch Lamoureux	70	11	9	20	59
245	Steve Cardwell	53	9	11	20	35
246	Brian Spencer	86	9	11	20	81
247	Kevin McClelland	72	8	12	20	139
248	Bob Blackburn	124	8	12	20	105
249	Billy Harris	54	7	13	20	8
250	Pat Graham	62	7	13	20	71
251	Rick Kessell	84	2	18	20	2
252	Mike Rupp	81	13	6	19	120
253	Bobby Simpson	30	10	9	19	4
254	Lasse Pirjeta	38	10	9	19	18
255	Bernie Lukowich	53	9	10	19	32
256	Jeff Daniels	134	8	11	19	36
257	Bob Dillabough	61	7	12	19	20
258	Mike Eastwood	82	4	15	19	40
259	Rene Corbet	47	9	9	18	57
260	Andy Hilbert	19	7	11	18	16
261	Rene Robert	49	7	11	18	42
262	Pete Laframboise	35	5	13	18	8
263	Neil Wilkinson	122	4	14	18	169
264	Simon Nolet	39	9	8	17	2
265	Greg Johnson	37	8	9	17	16
266	Eric Meloche	61	8	9	17	32
267	Bob Rivard	27	5	12	17	4

RANK	PLAYER	GP	G	A	PTS	PIM
268	Tom O'Regan	61	5	12	17	10
269	Tracy Pratt	83	5	12	17	158
270	Matt Bradley	82	7	9	16	65
271	Ted Snell	55	4	12	16	8
272	Nick Beverley	67	2	14	16	21
273	Francois Leroux	165	2	14	16	356
274	George Konik	52	7	8	15	26
275	Nils Ekman	34	6	9	15	24
276	Dominic Moore	59	6	9	15	46
277	Georges Laraque	88	4	11	15	159
278	Darryl Sydor	82	2	13	15	28
279	Mike Needham	81	9	5	14	16
280	Jacques Cossette	64	8	6	14	29
281	Robert Dome	52	7	7	14	12
282	Jamie Leach	60	7	7	14	10
283	Errol Thompson	34	6	8	14	12
284	Tim Hrynewich	55	6	8	14	82
285	Andrew McBain	41	5	9	14	51
286	Jeff Taffe	53	5	9	14	10
287	Jim McGeough	42	4	10	14	20
288	Greg Fox	75	4	10	14	92
289	Martin Strbak	44	3	11	14	38
290	Len Barrie	53	3	11	14	84
291	Hal Gill	80	3	11	14	69
292	Steve McKenna	162	10	3	13	313
293	Rod Zaine	37	8	5	13	21
294	Pat Falloon	30	4	9	13	10
295	John Stewart	40	4	9	13	32
296	Don Awrey	79	1	12	13	40
297	John Flesch	29	7	5	12	19
298	Shean Donovan	65	6	6	12	34
299	Kim Davis	34	5	7	12	47
300	Todd Charlesworth	86	3	9	12	41
301	Jeff Norton	32	2	10	12	20
302	Al MacNeil	74	2	10	12	58
303	Gord Dineen	117	2	10	12	173
304	Kevin Miller	13	6	5	11	4
305	Mark Kachowski	64	6	5	11	209
306	Blaine Stoughton	34	5	6	11	8
307	Steve Gotaas	36	5	6	11	45
308	Eric Boguniecki	38	5	6	11	29
309	Wayne Hicks	15	4	7	11	2
310	Bruce Crowder	26	4	7	11	23
311	Richard Park	58	4	7	11	38
312	Greg Brown	36	3	8	11	28
313	Mike Hudson	40	2	9	11	34
314	Joe McDonnell	43	2	9	11	22
315	Tim Horton	44	2	9	11	40
316	Ken Priestlay	51	2	9	11	4
317	Craig Adams	91	0	11	11	72
318	Garry Valk	56	5	5	10	58
319	Marian Hossa	12	3	7	10	6
320	Gilbert Delorme	54	3	7	10	44
321	Bob Stewart	65	3	7	10	52

RANK	PLAYER	GP	G	A	PTS	PIM
322	Jay Caufield	194	3	7	10	714
323	Dan Kesa	67	2	8	10	27
324	Bobby Dollas	75	2	8	10	64
325	Jay McKee	62	1	9	10	54
326	Nelson Debenedet	31	6	3	9	11
327	Roman Simicek	29	3	6	9	30
328	Alexei Ponikarovsky	16	2	7	9	17
329	Billy Tibbetts	62	2	7	9	188
330	Tom Thornbury	14	1	8	9	16
331	Jordan Leopold	20	4	4	8	6
332	Martin Skoula	33	3	5	8	6
333	Roger Belanger	44	3	5	8	32
334	Kent Manderville	86	3	5	8	50
335	Wilf Paiement	23	2	6	8	39
336	Greg Hawgood	33	2	6	8	33
337	Ron Meighan	41	2	6	8	16
338	Matt Murley	59	2	6	8	38
339	Dan Focht	64	2	6	8	124
340	Sheldon Kannegiesser	75	2	6	8	76
341	Paul Mulvey	27	1	7	8	76
342	George Swarbrick	31	1	7	8	36
343	Dwight Mathiasen	33	1	7	8	18
344	Ed Van Impe	22	0	8	8	22
345	Alexandre Daigle	33	4	3	7	8
346	Maxim Galanov	51	4	3	7	14
347	Patrick Boileau	16	3	4	7	8
348	Tom Cassidy	26	3	4	7	15
349	Peter Ferraro	29	3	4	7	12
350	Jani Rita	30	3	4	7	4
351	Chris Ferraro	46	3	4	7	43
352	Mike Ramsey	77	3	4	7	30
353	Eric Godard	116	3	4	7	247
354	Perry Ganchar	33	2	5	7	36
355	Joe Noris	35	2	5	7	20
356	Dwight Schofield	25	1	6	7	59
357	Steve Dykstra	65	1	6	7	126
358	Wendell Young	111	0	7	7	14
359	Marc-Andre Fleury	302	0	7	7	26
360	Landon Wilson	19	5	1	6	31
361	Philippe Boucher	25	3	3	6	24
362	Ronald Petrovicky	31	3	3	6	28
363	Harvey Bennett	32	3	3	6	53
364	Tony Feltrin	38	3	3	6	44
365	Michal Sivek	38	3	3	6	14
366	Ed Patterson	68	3	3	6	56
367	Jamie Pushor	91	3	3	6	106
368	Guillaume Lefebvre	21	2	4	6	9
369	Mike Zigomanis	22	2	4	6	27
370	Noah Welch	27	2	4	6	24
371	Alek Stojanov	45	2	4	6	86
372	Adam Hall	46	2	4	6	24
373	Mathias Johansson	12	1	5	6	4
374	Bob Gladney	13	1	5	6	2
375	Tom Chorske	33	1	5	6	2

RANK	PLAYER	GP	G	A	PTS	PIM
376	Richard Zemlak	50	1	5	6	178
377	Peter Popovic	54	1	5	6	30
378	Kelly Pratt	22	0	6	6	15
379	Jeff Serowik	26	0	6	6	16
380	Denis Herron	290	0	6	6	67
381	Arto Javanainen	14	4	1	5	2
382	Brad Lauer	21	4	1	5	6
383	Ron Snell	7	3	2	5	6
384	Ramzi Abid	19	3	2	5	29
385	Richard Lintner	19	3	2	5	10
386	Ted Bulley	26	3	2	5	12
387	Chris Thorburn	39	3	2	5	69
388	Jon Sim	15	2	3	5	6
389	Chris Minard	35	2	3	5	14
390	Yvon Labre	37	2	3	5	32
391	Steve Leach	56	2	3	5	24
392	Martin Sonnenberg	58	2	3	5	19
393	Bob Boughner	69	2	3	5	216
394	Bryan Erickson	11	1	4	5	0
395	Doug Lecuyer	12	1	4	5	12
396	John Slaney	29	1	4	5	10
397	Alain Nasreddine	56	1	4	5	30
398	Krzysztof Oliwa	83	1	4	5	281
399	Greg Andrusak	19	0	5	5	12
400	Robin Burns	41	0	5	5	32
401	Greg Millen	135	0	5	5	20
402	Michel Dion	151	0	5	5	14
403	Ken Wregget	212	0	5	5	50
404	Derek Sanderson	13	3	1	4	0
405	Jim Kyte	57	3	1	4	127
406	Corey Foster	11	2	2	4	2
407	Jeff Christian	15	2	2	4	15
408	Matt Hussey	16	2	2	4	0
409	Rusty Fitzgerald	25	2	2	4	12
410	Chris Wells	54	2	2	4	59
411	Petr Klima	9	1	3	4	4
412	Mike McMahon	12	1	3	4	19
413	Wayne Van Dorp	25	1	3	4	75
414	Lee Giffin	27	1	3	4	9
415	Rocky Saganiuk	29	1	3	4	37
416	Kelly Buchberger	71	1	3	4	109
417	Bryan Fogarty	12	0	4	4	4
418	John Jakopin	19	0	4	4	42
419	Steve Poapst	21	0	4	4	10
420	Jim Wiley	26	0	4	4	2
421	Dick Mattiussi	44	0	4	4	32
422	Craig Muni	64	0	4	4	36
423	Scott Bjugstad	24	3	0	3	4
424	Chris Conner	8	2	1	3	0
425	Luca Caputi	9	2	1	3	6
426	Jeff Toms	14	2	1	3	4
427	Bill Thomas	16	2	1	3	2
428	Mitch Wilson	17	2	1	3	83
429	Andre Roy	47	2	1	3	128

RANK	PLAYER	GP	G	A	PTS	PIM
430	Jim McKenzie	50	2	1	3	79
431	Darren Lowe	8	1	2	3	0
432	Brad Aitken	11	1	2	3	25
433	Dustin Jeffrey	15	1	2	3	0
434	Jim Shires	18	1	2	3	2
435	Tuomas Gronman	22	1	2	3	25
436	Shane Endicott	45	1	2	3	47
437	Ben Lovejoy	14	0	3	3	2
438	Wally Weir	14	0	3	3	34
439	Stan Jonathan	19	0	3	3	13
440	Larry Bignell	20	0	3	3	2
441	Chris Bourque	20	0	3	3	10
442	Ron Jones	25	0	3	3	15
443	Kim Clackson	45	0	3	3	166
444	Michel Plasse	75	0	3	3	24
445	Frank Pietrangelo	87	0	3	3	30
446	Johan Hedberg	116	0	3	3	40
447	Jean-Sebastien Aubin	168	0	3	3	10
448	Hartland Monahan	7	2	0	2	2
449	Bill Hicke	12	2	0	2	6
450	Mikael Samuelsson	22	2	0	2	8
451	Nick Johnson	6	1	1	2	2
452	Brian McKenzie	6	1	1	2	4
453	Doug Barrie	8	1	1	2	8
454	Pat Neaton	9	1	1	2	12
455	Garry Swain	9	1	1	2	0
456	Doug Smith	10	1	1	2	25
457	Ted Nolan	18	1	1	2	34
458	Mike Wilson	21	1	1	2	17
459	Shawn Heins	27	1	1	2	33
460	Ed Gilbert	45	1	1	2	0
461	Frantisek Kucera	7	0	2	2	0
462	Tim Tookey	8	0	2	2	2
463	Deryk Engelland	9	0	2	2	17
464	Rick Berry	13	0	2	2	21
465	Troy Murray	13	0	2	2	23
466	John Arbour	17	0	2	2	35
467	Tim Wallace	17	0	2	2	7
468	Tom Price	19	0	2	2	8
469	Dean DeFazio	22	0	2	2	28
470	Greg Tebbutt	24	0	2	2	31
471	Dunc Wilson	66	0	2	2	21
472	Gary Inness	100	0	2	2	4
473	Gilles Meloche	104	0	2	2	22
474	Scott Gruhl	6	1	0	1	0
475	Larry DePalma	7	1	0	1	5
476	Sean Pronger	7	1	0	1	2
477	Patrick Lebeau	8	1	0	1	2
478	Mark Letestu	10	1	0	1	2
479	Connor James	14	1	0	1	2
480	Dan Trebil	19	1	0	1	7
481	Ryan Vandenbussche	20	1	0	1	42
482	Eric Cairns	28	1	0	1	92
483	Mel Pearson	2	0	1	1	0

RANK	PLAYER	GP	G	A	PTS	PIM
484	Neil Belland	3	0	1	1	0
485	Micki DuPont	3	0	1	1	4
486	Alain Chevrier	3	0	1	1	2
487	Vladimir Vujtek	5	0	1	1	0
488	Cory Cross	6	0	1	1	6
489	Joel Bouchard	7	0	1	1	0
490	Ryan Stone	8	0	1	1	7
491	Victor Ignatjev	11	0	1	1	6
492	Paul Bissonnette	15	0	1	1	22
493	Roy Edwards	15	0	1	1	0
494	Cam Newton	16	0	1	1	6
495	Jeff Chychrun	18	0	1	1	37
496	Peter Ahola	22	0	1	1	14
497	Brent Johnson	23	0	1	1	0
498	Lyle Odelein	27	0	1	1	50
499	Bennett Wolf	30	0	1	1	133
500	Gilles Lupien	31	0	1	1	34
501	Steve Guenette	32	0	1	1	2
502	Sven Butenschon	33	0	1	1	14
503	Ty Conklin	33	0	1	1	4
504	Pat Riggin	39	0	1	1	14
505	Peter Skudra	74	0	1	1	4
506	Sebastien Caron	90	0	1	1	12
507	Jim Rutherford	115	0	1	1	18
508	Roberto Romano	125	0	1	1	6
509	Les Binkley	196	0	1	1	2
510	Tim Brent	1	0	0	0	0
511	Martin Brochu	1	0	0	0	0
512	Greg Crozier	1	0	0	0	0
513	Marv Edwards	1	0	0	0	0
514	Rob Garner	1	0	0	0	0
515	Bob Geale	1	0	0	0	2
516	Joel Kwiatkowski	1	0	0	0	0
517	Alain Lemieux	1	0	0	0	0
518	Brian Lundberg	1	0	0	0	2
519	Pat Mayer	1	0	0	0	4
520	Glenn Mulvenna	1	0	0	0	2
521	Todd Nelson	1	0	0	0	0
522	Alexander Pechurski	1	0	0	0	0
523	Domenic Pittis	1	0	0	0	0
524	Greg Redquest	1	0	0	0	0
525	Rick Tabaracci	1	0	0	0	2
526	Eric Tangradi	1	0	0	0	0
527	Rob Dopson	2	0	0	0	0
528	Dave Goertz	2	0	0	0	2
529	Nate Guenin	2	0	0	0	0
530	Paul Hoganson	2	0	0	0	0
531	Lex Hudson	2	0	0	0	0
532	Reid Simpson	2	0	0	0	17
533	Bob Taylor	2	0	0	0	0
534	Harry York	2	0	0	0	0
535	Yves Bergeron	3	0	0	0	0
536	Philippe DeRouville	3	0	0	0	0
537	Ross Lupaschuk	3	0	0	0	4

RANK	PLAYER	GP	G	A	PTS	PIM
538	Steve Lyon	3	0	0	0	2
539	Carl Mokosak	3	0	0	0	4
540	Grant Sasser	3	0	0	0	0
541	Ryan Savoia	3	0	0	0	0
542	Karl Stewart	3	0	0	0	2
543	Bob Stumpf	3	0	0	0	4
544	John Curry	4	0	0	0	0
545	Justin Duberman	4	0	0	0	0
546	Mathieu Garon	4	0	0	0	0
547	Bill Lecaine	4	0	0	0	0
548	Mike Meeker	4	0	0	0	5
549	Pavel Skrbek	4	0	0	0	2
550	Vincent Tremblay	4	0	0	0	2
551	Nolan Baumgartner	5	0	0	0	2
552	Brian Bonin	5	0	0	0	0
553	Jonathan Filewich	5	0	0	0	0
554	Ted Lanyon	5	0	0	0	4
555	Steve Webb	5	0	0	0	2
556	Dave Capuano	6	0	0	0	2
557	Gary Edwards	6	0	0	0	2
558	Petteri Lehto	6	0	0	0	4
559	Ian Turnbull	6	0	0	0	4
560	Stefan Bergkvist	7	0	0	0	9
561	Roman Oksiuta	7	0	0	0	4
562	Rich Parent	7	0	0	0	0
563	Janne Pesonen	7	0	0	0	0
564	Ron Tugnutt	7	0	0	0	0
565	Peter Allen	8	0	0	0	8
566	Andy Chiodo	8	0	0	0	0
567	Brian Ford	8	0	0	0	0
568	Ladislav Karabin	9	0	0	0	2
569	Jimmy Mann	9	0	0	0	53
570	Rich Sutter	9	0	0	0	0
571	Mike Rowe	11	0	0	0	11
572	Bob Johnson	12	0	0	0	6
573	Shawn Antoski	13	0	0	0	49
574	Paul Harrison	13	0	0	0	0
575	Hank Nowak	13	0	0	0	11
576	Nathan Smith	13	0	0	0	2
577	Niklas Nordgren	15	0	0	0	4
578	Gord Laxton	17	0	0	0	0
579	Nick Ricci	19	0	0	0	2
580	Hank Bassen	25	0	0	0	8
581	Dennis Bonvie	31	0	0	0	80
582	Garth Snow	35	0	0	0	8
583	Joe Daley	38	0	0	0	2
584	Jocelyn Thibault	38	0	0	0	2
585	Patrick Lalime	39	0	0	0	0
586	Rob Holland	44	0	0	0	2
587	Dany Sabourin	44	0	0	0	4
588	Andy Brown	45	0	0	0	62
589	Al Smith	92	0	0	0	61

Penguins Career Goaltender Statistics

RANK	GOALTENDER	GP	MINS	GA	SO	GAA	W	L	T/OT	SAVES	SAVE %
1	Alexander Pechurski	1	36	1	0	1.67	0	0	0	12	.923
2	Martin Brochu	1	33	1	0	1.82	0	0	0	18	.947
3	Ron Tugnutt	7	374	15	0	2.41	4	2	0	182	.924
4	Ty Conklin	33	1866	78	2	2.51	18	8	5	935	.923
5	Roy Edwards	15	847	36	0	2.55	2	8	4	355	.908
6	Peter Skudra	74	3687	163	4	2.65	26	22	11	1374	.894
7	Brent Johnson	23	1108	51	0	2.76	10	6	1	490	.906
8	Marc-Andre Fleury	302	17164	808	16	2.82	148	106	32	7837	.907
9	Hank Bassen	25	1299	62	1	2.86	7	10	3	616	.909
10	Johan Hedberg	116	6832	328	7	2.88	46	57	12	2973	.901
11	Dany Sabourin	44	2252	108	2	2.88	16	18	3	965	.899
12	Mathieu Garon	4	206	10	0	2.91	2	1	0	84	.894
13	Jean-Sebastien Aubin	168	8888	432	6	2.92	63	72	11	3937	.901
14	Patrick Lalime	39	2058	101	3	2.94	21	12	2	1065	.913
15	Garth Snow	35	2032	101	3	2.98	14	15	4	913	.900
16	Marv Edwards	1	60	3	0	3.00	0	1	0	30	.909
17	Rich Parent	7	332	17	0	3.07	1	1	3	133	.887
18	Al Smith	92	5027	257	4	3.07	24	42	17	2777	.899
19	Les Binkley	196	11046	575	11	3.12	58	94	34	5022	.897
20	Jim Rutherford	115	6252	327	4	3.14	44	49	14	2915	.899
21	Joe Daley	38	2143	113	2	3.16	11	18	6	1094	.906
22	Philippe DeRouville	3	171	9	0	3.16	1	2	0	84	.903
23	Tom Barrasso	460	25879	1409	22	3.27	226	153	53	12076	.896
24	Ken Wregget	212	11737	644	6	3.29	104	67	21	5641	.898
25	Gary Inness	100	5366	299	2	3.34	39	37	13	2591	.897
26	Andy Chiodo	8	486	28	0	3.46	3	4	1	232	.892
27	Sebastien Caron	90	4933	287	4	3.49	24	47	12	2366	.892
28	Jocelyn Thibault	38	1908	112	1	3.52	8	17	5	944	.894
29	Dunc Wilson	66	3807	224	5	3.53	23	30	11	1750	.887
30	Michel Plasse	75	4190	251	2	3.59	33	24	14	2013	.889
31	Pat Riggin	39	2157	131	0	3.64	15	14	7	914	.875
32	Gilles Meloche	104	5726	348	0	3.65	34	43	17	2500	.878
33	Gary Edwards	6	360	22	1	3.67	3	2	1	171	.886
34	Steve Guenette	32	1779	110	1	3.71	17	15	0	834	.883
35	Cam Newton	16	814	51	0	3.76	4	7	1	360	.876
36	Andy Brown	45	2476	156	1	3.78	16	20	6	1126	.878
37	John Curry	4	174	11	0	3.79	2	2	0	72	.867
38	Greg Millen	135	7839	501	4	3.83	57	56	18	3482	.874
39	Denis Herron	290	16105	1041	6	3.88	88	133	44	8072	.886
40	Roberto Romano	125	7051	465	4	3.96	46	62	8	3407	.880
41	Rob Dopson	2	45	3	0	4.00	0	0	0	20	.870
42	Rob Holland	44	2513	171	1	4.08	11	22	9	1060	.861
43	Frank Pietrangelo	87	4478	308	1	4.13	34	32	3	2125	.873
44	Wendell Young	111	5576	385	1	4.14	42	47	5	2714	.876
45	Michel Dion	151	8477	605	0	4.28	42	79	20	3998	.855
46	Nick Ricci	19	1087	79	0	4.36	7	12	0	474	.857
47	Bob Johnson	12	476	40	0	5.04	3	4	1	237	.856
48	Alain Chevrier	3	166	14	0	5.06	1	2	0	75	.843
49	Bob Taylor	2	78	7	0	5.38	0	1	0	41	.837
50	Paul Harrison	13	700	64	0	5.49	3	7	0	288	.816
51	Gordie Laxton	17	800	74	0	5.55	4	9	0	359	.829
52	Vincent Tremblay	4	240	24	0	6.00	0	4	0	118	.831
53	Brian Ford	8	457	48	0	6.30	2	6	0	244	.836
54	Rick Tabaracci	1	33	4	0	7.27	0	0	0	17	.810
55	Paul Hoganson	2	57	7	0	7.37	0	1	0	21	.750
56	Greg Redquest	1	13	3	0	13.85	0	0	0	2	.400

Tomas Sandstrom (17) averaged nearly a point per game for the Pens.

Tom Barrasso leads the Penguins with 22 career shutouts.

Penguins Shutouts

GOALTENDER	DATE	OPP.	SCORE	SAVES
1967–68 (7)				
Les Binkley	11/4	at OAK	1–0	31
Hank Bassen	11/15	vs. PHI	5–0	27
Les Binkley (2)	12/23	vs. MIN	4–0	23
Les Binkley (3)	12/27	vs. OAK	0–0	24
Les Binkley (4)	1/28	at BOS	1–0	33
Les Binkley (5)	2/1	at STL	2–0	22
Les Binkley (6)	3/30	at PHI*	2–0	23
*Game Played in Quebec City				
1968–69 (2)				
Joe Daley	2/19	vs. BOS	3–0	41
Joe Daley (2)	3/23	vs. MIN	5–0	32
1969–70 (5)				
Les Binkley (7)	11/12	at TOR	3–0	31
Les Binkley (8)	12/10	at LA	2–0	29
Al Smith	2/26	at LA	1–0	30
Al Smith (2)	3/8	at NYR	0–0	33
Les Binkley (9)	3/25	vs. MIN	2–0	25
1970–71 (4)				
Les Binkley (10)	10/17	vs. PHI	0–0	24
Al Smith (3)	12/8	vs. TOR	4–0	29
Les Binkley (11)	3/3	vs. MTL	4–0	33
Al Smith (4)	3/13	vs. MIN	0–0	20
1971–72 (1)				
Jim Rutherford	2/17	at BUF	2–0	23
1972–73 (5)				
Denis Herron	10/17	at NYI	5–0	24
Denis Herron (2)	10/24	at VAN	4–0	23
Jim Rutherford (2)	1/20	vs. BOS	3–0	26
Jim Rutherford (3)	2/20	at NYI	4–0	34
Jim Rutherford (4)	2/24	vs. CHI	2–0	32
1973–74 (1)				
Andy Brown	3/24	vs. DET	8–0	23
1974–75 (2)				
Gary Inness	11/17	vs. WSH	6–0	26
Gary Inness (2)	11/23	vs. LA	0–0	30
1975–76 (2)				
Michel Plasse	3/6	vs. MIN	5–0	18
Michel Plasse (2)	3/28	vs. DET	3–0	29
1976–77 (6)				
Dunc Wilson	11/13	vs. PHI	1–0	25
Dunc Wilson (2)	11/21	vs. CHI	5–0	25
Dunc Wilson (3)	1/19	at VAN	3–0	21
Dunc Wilson (4)	1/27	at NYR	3–0	30
Dunc Wilson (5)	2/3	at CLE	0–0	22
Denis Herron (3)	3/6	vs. COL	3–0	32
1977–78 (0)				

GOALTENDER	DATE	OPP.	SCORE	SAVES
1978–79 (2)				
Greg Millen	12/3	vs. STL	3–0	33
Greg Millen (2)	1/16	vs. MIN	5–0	25
1979–80 (3)				
Greg Millen (3)	12/19	at CHI	0–0	29
Rob Holland	3/2	vs. NYI	0–0	24
Greg Millen (4)	3/30	vs. WSH	4–0	28
1980–81 (0)				
1981–82 (1)				
Gary Edwards	3/21	at COL	6–0	28
1982–83 (1)				
Denis Herron (4)	12/4	vs. PHI	0–0	34
1983–84 (2)				
Denis Herron (5)	10/14	at WSH	4–0	29
Roberto Romano	2/1	vs. MIN	4–0	34
1984–85 (2)				
Roberto Romano (2)	12/28	vs. HFD	4–0	34
Denis Herron (6)	3/16	vs. NYR	5–0	26
1985–86 (2)				
Roberto Romano (3)	12/2	at NYR	6–0	40
Roberto Romano (4)	2/8	vs. NJ	4–0	27
1986–87 (1)				
Meloche/Romano	1/23	at VAN	6–0	30
(Romano replaced Meloche at 10:11)				
1987–88 (2)				
Frank Pietrangelo	2/4	vs. MIN	1–0	31
Steve Guenette	3/19	vs. PHI	7–0	38
1988–89 (0)				
1989–90 (1)				
Wendell Young	11/14	vs. NYR	6–0	25
1990–91 (1)				
Tom Barrasso	12/28	vs. DET	5–0	27
1991–92 (1)				
Tom Barrasso (2)	12/5	at SJ	8–0	39
1992–93 (5)				
Tom Barrasso (3)	11/3	vs. NYI	2–0	19
Tom Barrasso (4)	11/21	vs. NJ	2–0	29
Tom Barrasso (5)	12/23	at PHI	4–0	20
Wregget/Barrasso	2/28	vs. BOS*	4–0	28
Tom Barrasso (6)	2/10	at NYR	3–0	30
(Barrasso replaced Wregget at 55:18, *Game Played in Atlanta)				

Penguins Shutouts—Continued

GOALTENDER	DATE	OPP.	SCORE	SAVES
1993–94 (3)				
Ken Wregget	1/27	vs. QUE	3–0	38
Tom Barrasso (7)	2/13	at PHI	3–0	22
Tom Barrasso (8)	4/11	at OTT	4–0	32
1994–95 (0)				
1995–96 (5)				
Ken Wregget (2)	11/1	vs.TB	10–0	27
Ken Wregget (3)	11/18	vs. WSH	3–0	32
Ken Wregget (4)	12/9	vs. HFD	6–0	35
Tom Barrasso (9)	1/17	at BUF	1–0	31
Tom Barrasso (10)	2/16	at WPG	1–0	32
1996–97 (5)				
Ken Wregget (5)	11/12	vs. BUF	3–0	25
Patrick Lalime	12/13	at SJ	4–0	20
Ken Wregget (6)	12/19	at STL	4–0	25
Patrick Lalime (2)	12/28	vs. BUF	2–0	21
Patrick Lalime (3)	1/15	at HFD	3–0	31
1997–98 (7)				
Tom Barrasso (11)	10/14	at NYR	1–0	36
Tom Barrasso (12)	11/15	at TOR	5–0	20
Tom Barrasso (13)	11/20	at OTT	2–0	27
Tom Barrasso (14)	12/1	at MTL	1–0	25
Tom Barrasso (15)	12/10	at ANA	3–0	26
Tom Barrasso (16)	1/20	vs. OTT	0–0	35
Tom Barrasso (17)	3/22	at DAL	0–0	28
1998–99 (9)				
Peter Skudra	10/26	at TOR	2–0	27
Jean-Sebastien Aubin	11/7	vs. BOS	0–0	18
Tom Barrasso (18)	11/14	vs. FLA	4–0	23
Tom Barrasso (19)	12/19	vs. WSH	3–0	24
Peter Skudra (2)	1/28	vs. TOR	6–0	21
Tom Barrasso (20)	2/5	vs. FLA	3–0	29
Peter Skudra (3)	3/13	vs. PHI	4–0	24
Jean-Sebastien Aubin (2)	3/17	at TB	2–0	16
Tom Barrasso (21)	4/11	at DET	3–0	20
1999–00 (4)				
Tom Barrasso (22)	11/26	vs. OTT	5–0	20
Jean-Sebastien Aubin (3)	12/9	vs.WSH	3–0	24
Peter Skudra (4)	12/21	at NYI	4–0	21
Jean-Sebastien Aubin (4)	2/14	vs. VAN	3–0	37
2000–01 (3)				
Garth Snow	11/24	at PHI	1–0	36
Garth Snow (2)	12/27	vs. TOR	5–0	40
Garth Snow (3)	1/21	at CHI	4–0	24

GOALTENDER	DATE	OPP.	SCORE	SAVES
2001–02 (6)				
Johan Hedberg	10/18	at OTT	3–0	29
Johan Hedberg (2)	11/17	vs. NYR	1–0	26
Johan Hedberg (3)	11/27	vs. NJ	6–0	39
Johan Hedberg (4)	12/4	at TOR	1–0	27
Johan Hedberg (5)	1/10	at BUF	2–0	36
Johan Hedberg (6)	1/19	at EDM	1–0	25
2002–03 (4)				
Jean-Sebastien Aubin (5)	10/12	vs. NYR	6–0	30
Johan Hedberg (7)	12/21	vs. CGY	2–0	23
Sebastien Caron	1/15	at CAR	2–0	26
Sebastien Caron (2)	1/21	at BUF	0–0	34
2003–04 (3)				
Marc-Andre Fleury	10/30	at CHI	1–0	20
Sebastien Caron (3)	12/29	vs. CHI	1–0	31
Jean-Sebastien Aubin (6)	3/9	vs. DAL	4–0	45
2005–06 (2)				
Marc-Andre Fleury (2)	3/12	vs. PHI	2–0	22
Sebastien Caron (4)	3/31	at NYI	4–0	29
2006–07 (6)				
Marc-Andre Fleury (3)	10/5	vs. PHI	4–0	40
Marc-Andre Fleury (4)	1/2	vs. CAR	3–0	31
Marc-Andre Fleury (5)	1/30	vs. FLA	3–0	32
Marc-Andre Fleury (6)	2/3	vs. WSH	2–0	30
Jocelyn Thibault	3/14	at NJ	3–0	25
Marc-Andre Fleury (7)	3/25	vs. BOS	5–0	29
2007–08 (8)				
Marc-Andre Fleury (8)	10/23	vs. NYR	1–0	36
Dany Sabourin	11/5	at NJ	5–0	20
Marc-Andre Fleury (9)	11/24	vs.ATL	5–0	28
Ty Conklin	12/29	vs. BUF	2–0	26
Ty Conklin (2)	1/5	vs. FLA	3–0	35
Dany Sabourin (2)	1/19	at MTL	2–0	31
Marc-Andre Fleury (10)	3/4	at TB	2–0	35
Marc-Andre Fleury (11)	3/25	at NJ	2–0	31
2008–09 (4)				
Marc-Andre Fleury (12)	12/26	at NJ	1–0	37
Marc-Andre Fleury (13)	1/18	vs. NYR	3–0	33
Marc-Andre Fleury (14)	2/25	vs. NYI	1–0	21
Marc-Andre Fleury (15)	3/25	vs. CGY	2–0	31
2009–10 (1)				
Marc-Andre Fleury (16)	3/18	at BOS	3–0	17

TOTAL-129   **HOME - 73**   **ROAD - 56**

Most All-Time – Tom Barrasso (22)
Most One Year (Individual) – Tom Barrasso (7) 1997–98
Most One Year (Team) – 9 in 1998–99

Penguins Single-Season Team Records

POINTS

Most Overall	119*	1992–93
Most Home	66	1992–93
Most Road	49	1992–93
Fewest Overall	38	1983–84
Fewest Home	18	1983–84
Fewest Road	13	1982–83

* Includes four points from neutral-site games

WINS

Most Overall	56	1992–93
Most Home	32	1995–96
Most Road	23	1992–93
Fewest Overall	16	1983–84
Fewest Home	7	1983–84
Fewest Road	3	1970–71

LOSSES

Most Overall	58	1983–84
Most Home	29	1983–84
Most Road	31	1982–83
Fewest Overall	21	1992–93
Fewest Home	5	1974–75
Fewest Road	14	1997–98

TIES

Most Overall	20	1970–71
Most Home	10	1967–68, 1974–75, 1997–98, 1998–99
Most Road	11	1970–71
Fewest Overall	4	1995–96
Fewest Home	0	1995–96
Fewest Road	1	1999–00

GOALS

Most For	367	1992–93
Most For Home	215	1995–96
Most For Road	162	1988–89
Most Against	394	1982–83
Most Against Home	182	1983–84
Most Against Road	224	1982–83
Fewest For	182	1969–70
Fewest For Home	95	2003–04
Fewest For Road	77	1969–70
Fewest Against	188	1997–98
Fewest Against Home	92	1970–71
Fewest Against Road	90	1997–98

ASSISTS

Most For	643	1995–96
Most Against	665	1982–83
Fewest For	294	1969–70
Fewest Against	298	1997–98

POINTS

Most For	1,005	1995–96
Most Against	1,049	1982–83
Fewest For	476	1969–70
Fewest Against	486	1997–98

PENALTIES

Most For	897	1988–89
Most Against	906	1988–89
Fewest For	248	1967–68
Fewest Against	330	1967–68

PENALTY MINUTES

Most For	2,670	1988–89
Most Against	2,702	1988–89
Fewest For	554	1967–68
Fewest Against	750	1967–68

MINOR PENALTIES

Most For	773	1987–88
Most Against	752	1987–88
Fewest For	237	1967–68
Fewest Against	315	1967–68

MAJOR PENALTIES

Most For	118	1988–89
Most Against	114	1988–89
Fewest For	1	1967–68
Fewest Against	6	1967–68

MISCONDUCT PENALTIES

Most For	69	1981–82
Most Against	87	1981–82
Fewest For	1	1968–69
Fewest Against	7	1976–77

Penguins Single-Season Team Records—Continued

SHOTS ON GOAL

Most For	2,760	1974–75
Most Against	2,908	1983–84
Fewest For	2,029	2003–04
Fewest Against	2,129	1998–99

POWER-PLAY PERCENTAGE

Highest For	26.0	1995–96
Highest Against	27.8	1982–83
Lowest For	13.6	1967–68
Lowest Against	13.6	1997–98

POWER-PLAY GOALS

Most For	119	1988–89
Most Against	120	1987–88
Fewest For	37	1967–68
Fewest Against	30	1967–68

SHORTHANDED GOALS

Most For	21	1988–89
Most Against	22	1984–85
Fewest For	2	1967–68, 1969–70
Fewest Against	4	1973–74, 1978–79, 1979–80

POWER-PLAY CHANCES

Most For	500	1987–88
Most Against	533	2005–06
Fewest For	261	1977–78, 1978–79
Fewest Against	195	1967–68

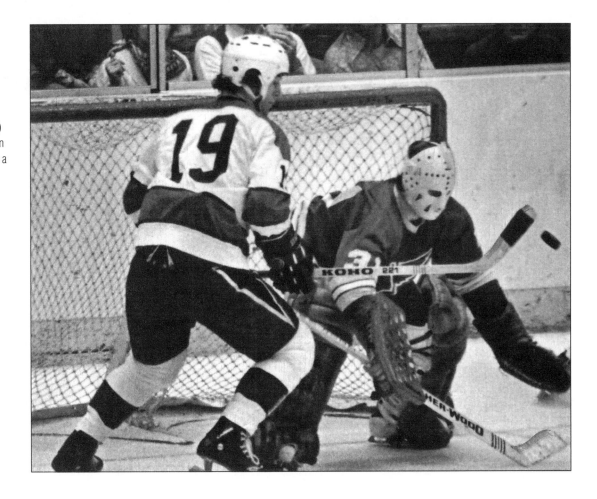

Jean Pronovost (19) was the first Penguin to score 50 goals in a single season.

Penguins Single-Season Team Records—Continued

80 OR MORE POINT PLAYERS

Most For	6	1992–93
Fewest For	0	13 times (last 2003–04)

90 OR MORE POINT PLAYERS

Most For	5	1992–93
Fewest For	0	18 times (last 2003–04)

100 OR MORE POINT PLAYERS

Most For	4	1992–93
Fewest For	0	22 times (last 2003–04)

20 OR MORE GOAL PLAYERS

Most For	9	1974–75
Fewest For	1	1968–69, 2003–04

30 OR MORE GOAL PLAYERS

Most For	5	1975–76, 1991–92, 1992–93
Fewest For	0	7 times (last 2003–04)

40 OR MORE GOAL PLAYERS

Most For	3	1991–92, 1992–93, 1995–96
Fewest For	0	19 times (last 2008–09)

50 OR MORE GOAL PLAYERS

Most For	2	1975–76, 1992–93, 1995–96
Fewest For	0	30 times (last 2008–09)

40 OR MORE ASSIST PLAYERS

Most For	7	1975–76
Fewest For	0	6 times (last 2003–04)

50 OR MORE ASSIST PLAYERS

Most For	6	1992–93
Fewest For	0	14 times (last 2003–04)

60 OR MORE ASSIST PLAYERS

Most For	5	1992–93
Fewest For	0	20 times (last 2009–10)

100 OR MORE PENALTY MINUTE PLAYERS

Most For	15	1988–89
Fewest For	0	1967–68, 1968–69, 1998–99

200 OR MORE PENALTY MINUTE PLAYERS

Most For	3	1981–82
Fewest For	0	30 times (last 2009–10)

Penguins Single-Game Records

GOALS

Most For, Home	12	Washington (3/15/75), Toronto (12/26/91)
Most For, Road	10	NY Rangers (4/9/93)
Most Against, Home	11	NY Rangers (11/25/92)
Most Against, Road	13	Philadelphia (3/22/84)
Most For, Two Consecutive Games	18	3/15/75–3/16/75, 12/23/91–12/26/91, 12/26/91–12/28/91
Most Against, Two Consecutive Games	19	3/22/84–3/24/84
Most For, Both Teams, Home	18	San Jose 10–Pittsburgh 8 (1/13/96)
Most For, Both Teams, Road	17	Philadelphia 13–Pittsburgh 4 (3/22/84)

ASSISTS

Most For, Home	20	Washington (3/15/75), Toronto (12/26/91)
Most For, Road	17	NY Rangers (12/3/90)
Most Against, Home	19	NY Rangers (11/25/92)
Most Against, Road	22	Philadelphia (3/22/84)
Most For, Both Teams, Home	28	Edmonton (2/19/83), NY Islanders (2/6/90)
Most For, Both Teams, Road	29	Hartford (12/26/80)

POINTS

Most For, Home	32	Washington (3/15/75), Toronto (12/26/91)
Most For, Road	25	NY Rangers (12/3/90)
Most Against, Home	30	NY Rangers (11/25/92)
Most Against, Road	35	Philadelphia (3/22/84)
Most For, Both Teams, Home	45	Edmonton (2/19/83)
Most For, Both Teams, Road	45	Hartford (12/26/80), Philadelphia (3/22/84)

POWER-PLAY GOALS

Most For, Home	6	Toronto (12/12/86), Atlanta (10/27/05)
Most For, Road	5	San Jose (12/5/91), NY Islanders (12/23/91), San Jose (12/5/92), Calgary (10/28/98)
Most Against, Home	6	Nashville (3/4/04)
Most Against, Road	5	Buffalo (10/12/88), Hartford (2/26/89), Boston (10/5/89)
Most For, Both Teams	10	New Jersey (10/29/89) (5–5)

POWER-PLAY CHANCES

Most For	12	NY Islanders (2/6/90), Florida (10/25/05)
Most Against	14	Washington (10/11/88)
Most For, Both Teams	22	at Washington (1/1/88) (PIT 9–WSH 13)
		vs. Philadelphia (3/19/88) (PIT 10–PHI 12)

SHORTHANDED GOALS

Most For	2	19 times (last 3/11/07)
Most Against	3	at Toronto (11/16/88), vs. Ottawa (2/2/06)
Most For, Both Teams	4	vs. Chicago (12/6/89) (2–2)

Penguins Single-Game Records—Continued

PENALTIES

Most For, Home	28	Edmonton (1/19/80)
Most For, Road	32	NY Rangers (10/30/88)
Most Against, Home	24	Edmonton (1/19/80), Washington (11/25/89)
Most Against, Road	27	NY Rangers (10/30/88)
Most For, Both Teams, Home	52	Edmonton (1/19/80)
Most For, Both Teams, Road	59	NY Rangers (10/30/88)

PENALTY MINUTES

Most For, Home	144	Edmonton (1/19/80)
Most For, Road	158	NY Rangers (10/30/88)
Most Against, Home	123	Edmonton (1/19/80)
Most Against, Road	134	NY Rangers (10/30/88)
Most For, Both Teams, Home	267	Edmonton (1/19/80), (PIT 144 – EDM 123)
Most For, Both Teams, Road	292	NY Rangers (10/30/88), (PIT 158–NYR 134)

SHOTS

Most For, Home	65	Washington (3/15/75)
Most For, Road	53	Montreal (12/16/00)
Most Against, Home	55	Montreal (10/23/76)
Most Against, Road	62	Chicago (3/12/89)
Fewest For, Home	11	Carolina (12/16/01), Los Angeles (10/10/03)
Fewest For, Road	11	Boston (3/27/77), Carolina (12/18/03), Ottawa (12/26/03)
Fewest Against, Home	11	Phoenix (12/11/99)
Fewest Against, Road	13	Phoenix (12/12/98)

SAVES

Most For, Home	51	Detroit (1/31/98)
Most For, Road	57	Chicago (3/12/89)
Most Against, Home	53	Montreal (3/10/74)
Most Against, Road	49	Montreal (12/16/00)
Fewest For, Home	9	Colorado (1/3/98), Phoenix (12/11/99)
Fewest For, Road	11	Vancouver (11/17/87), Phoenix (12/12/97), Edmonton (10/31/98), Carolina (12/4/98)
Fewest Against, Home	11	Philadelphia (3/21/98), St Louis (1/19/00)
Fewest Against, Road	9	Montreal (10/13/84)

LARGEST MARGIN OF VICTORY

Home	11	Washington (3/15/75) (12–1), Toronto (12/26/91) (12–1)
Road	8	San Jose (12/5/91) (8–0)

LARGEST MARGIN OF DEFEAT

Home	9	New Jersey (10/28/00) (9–0)
Road	12	Montreal (2/22/79) (12–0)

Penguins Single-Period Records

GOALS

Most For, Home	8	San Jose (12/17/91)
Most For, Road	7	Quebec (2/27/95)
Most Against, Home	6	7 times (last 11/16/96)
Most Against, Road	7	Philadelphia (3/22/84)
Most For, Both Teams, Home	8	9 times (last 11/1/97)

ASSISTS

Most For, Home	11	St. Louis (11/22/72)
Most For, Road	12	Quebec (2/27/95)
Most Against, Home	12	Quebec (2/16/85)
Most Against, Road	13	Philadelphia (3/22/84)
Most For, Both Teams, Home	15	Vancouver (10/6/76)
Most For, Both Teams, Road	16	Quebec (2/27/95)

POINTS

Most For, Home	18	St. Louis (11/22/72)
Most For, Road	19	Quebec (2/27/95)
Most Against, Home	18	Quebec (2/16/85)
Most Against, Road	20	Philadelphia (3/22/84)
Most For, Both Teams, Home	23	Vancouver (10/6/76)
Most For, Both Teams, Road	25	Quebec (2/27/95)

PENALTIES

Most For, Home	24	Edmonton (1/19/80)
Most For, Road	32	NY Rangers (10/30/88)
Most Against, Home	22	New Jersey (3/25/89)
Most Against, Road	33	Philadelphia (12/8/88)
Most For, Both Teams, Home	43	Edmonton (1/19/80)
Most For, Both Teams, Road	64	Philadelphia (12/8/88)

PENALTY MINUTES

Most For, Home	133	Edmonton (1/19/80)
Most For, Road	146	NY Rangers (10/30/88)
Most Against, Home	110	Edmonton (1/19/80)
Most Against, Road	141	Philadelphia (12/8/88)
Most For, Both Teams, Home	243	Edmonton (1/19/80)
Most For, Both Teams, Road	272	NY Rangers (10/30/88)

SHOTS

Most For, Home	27	Washington (3/15/75)
Most For, Road	25	San Jose (3/6/92)
Most Against, Home	25	Vancouver (1/7/89)
Most Against, Road	28	NY Islanders (12/5/78)
Fewest For, Home	0	San Jose (11/23/03)
Fewest For, Road	1	13 times (last 12/26/03)
Fewest Against, Home	0	Florida (2/21/01)
Fewest Against, Road	0	Florida (12/20/00)

SAVES

Most For, Home	23	Vancouver (1/7/89)
Most For, Road	25	3 times (last 3/11/04)
Most Against, Home	24	Hartford (2/19/81)
Most Against, Road	22	Minnesota (3/23/74)
Fewest For, Home	0	Florida (2/21/01), Boston (3/14/89)
Fewest For, Road	0	Florida (12/20/00), Phoenix (12/12/97)
Fewest Against, Home	0	San Jose (11/23/03)
Fewest Against, Road	0	Boston (12/15/68)

Penguins Fastest Goals

TEAM

FASTEST TWO GOALS
0:06   Mark Recchi and John Cullen, Feb. 16, 1990, in a 3–3 tie at Winnipeg.
0:06   Paul Coffey and Troy Loney, Feb. 22, 1993, in a 4–3 win vs. NY Islanders.

FASTEST THREE GOALS
0:27   Al McDonough, Ken Schinkel, and Ron Schock, Nov. 22, 1972, in a 10–4 win vs. St. Louis.

FASTEST FOUR GOALS
1:39   Alexei Kovalev (2), Jaromir Jagr, and Stu Barnes, Dec. 12, 1998, in a 4–3 win at St. Louis.

FASTEST FIVE GOALS
2:07   Bryan Hextall, Jean Pronovost, Al McDonough, Ken Schinkel, and Ron Schock, Nov. 22, 1972, in a 10–4 win vs. St. Louis.

FASTEST GOAL, START OF GAME
0:06   Jean Pronovost, Mar. 25, 1976, in a 5–2 loss at St. Louis.

FASTEST GOAL, START OF SECOND PERIOD
0:07   Lowell MacDonald, Feb. 10, 1973, in a 6–3 loss at Boston.

FASTEST GOAL, START OF THIRD PERIOD
0:11   Martin Straka, Oct. 18, 2003, in a 4–3 win vs. Detroit.

FASTEST GOAL, OVERTIME
0:13   Kevin Stevens, Mar. 21, 1991, in a 5–4 win vs. NY Rangers.

PLAYER

FASTEST TWO GOALS
0:07   Wally Boyer, Mar. 5, 1970, in a 5–3 loss at Detroit.
0:07   Martin Straka, Feb. 11, 2000, in a 2–2 tie vs. Edmonton.

FASTEST THREE GOALS
4:10   Nils Ekman, Nov. 8, 2006, in a 4–3 loss vs. Tampa Bay.

FASTEST FOUR GOALS
14:54   Mario Lemieux, Jan. 26, 1997, in a 5–2 win at Montreal.

Mellon Arena Regular-Season Records

TEAM RECORDS

MOST GOALS IN ONE GAME
12   March 15, 1975, in a 12–1 win vs. Washington
          Dec. 26, 1991, in a 12–1 win vs. Toronto

MOST SHOTS IN A GAME
65   March 15, 1975, in a 12–1 win vs. Washington

MOST PENALTY MINUTES IN A GAME
144   January 19, 1980, in a 5–2 loss vs. Edmonton

MOST GOALS IN A PERIOD
8   Dec. 17, 1991, in a 10–2 win vs. San Jose (2nd period)

PLAYER RECORDS

MOST GOALS IN A GAME
5   Mario Lemieux, Dec. 31, 1988, in an 8–6 win vs. New Jersey
          Mario Lemieux, March 26, 1996, in an 8–4 win vs. St. Louis

MOST ASSISTS IN A GAME
6   Ron Stackhouse, March 8, 1975, in a 8–2 win vs. Philadelphia
          Greg Malone, Nov. 28, 1979, in a 7–2 win vs. Quebec
          Mario Lemieux, Oct. 15, 1988, in a 9–2 win vs. St. Louis
          Mario Lemieux, Nov. 1, 1995, in a 10–0 win vs. Tampa Bay

MOST POINTS IN A GAME
8   Mario Lemieux, Oct. 15, 1988, in a 9–2 win vs. St. Louis
          Mario Lemieux, Dec. 31, 1988, in an 8–6 win vs. New Jersey

MOST PENALTY MINUTES IN A GAME
51   Russ Anderson, Jan. 19, 1980, in a 5–2 loss vs. Edmonton

MOST SAVES IN A GAME
51   Tom Barrasso, Jan. 31, 1998, in a 4–2 win vs. Detroit

Penguins Individual Player Records

SINGLE SEASON

GOALS
Overall	85	Mario Lemieux (1988–89)
Center	85	Mario Lemieux (1988–89)
Right Wing	62	Jaromir Jagr (1995–96)
Left Wing	55	Kevin Stevens (1992–93)
Defenseman	30	Paul Coffey (1988–89)
Rookie	43	Mario Lemieux (1984–85)
Rookie Defenseman	12	Zarley Zalapski (1988–89)

ASSISTS
Overall	114	Mario Lemieux (1988–89)
Center	114	Mario Lemieux (1988–89)
Right Wing	87	Jaromir Jagr (1995–96)
Left Wing	69	Kevin Stevens (1991–92)
Defenseman	83	Paul Coffey (1988–89)
Rookie	63	Sidney Crosby (2005–06)
Rookie Defenseman	33	Zarley Zalapski (1988–89)
Goaltender	8	Tom Barrasso (1992–93)

POINTS
Overall	199	Mario Lemieux (1988–89)
Center	199	Mario Lemieux (1988–89)
Right Wing	149	Jaromir Jagr (1995–96)
Left Wing	123	Kevin Stevens (1991–92)
Defenseman	113	Paul Coffey (1988–89)
Rookie	102	Sidney Crosby (2005–06)
Rookie Defenseman	45	Zarley Zalapski (1988–89)
Goaltender	8	Tom Barrasso (1992–93)

PENALTY MINUTES
Overall	409	Paul Baxter (1981–82)
Center	157	Dave Hannan (1988–89)
Right Wing	285	Jay Caufield (1988–89)
Left Wing	378	Dave Schultz (1977–78)
Defenseman	409	Paul Baxter (1981–82)
Rookie	285	Jay Caufield (1988–89)
Rookie Defenseman	172	Colin Campbell (1974–75)
Goaltender	60	Andy Brown (1973–74)

SHOTS
Overall	403	Jaromir Jagr (1995–96)
Center	382	Mario Lemieux (1987–88)
Right Wing	403	Jaromir Jagr (1995–96)
Left Wing	326	Kevin Stevens (1992–93)
Defenseman	342	Paul Coffey (1988–89)
Rookie	278	Sidney Crosby (2005–06)
Rookie Defenseman	156	Darryl Edestrand (1971–72)

Paul Baxter led the league with 409 penalty minutes in 1981–82.

Penguins Individual Player Records—Continued

POWER-PLAY GOALS

Overall	31	Mario Lemieux (1988–89, 1995–96)
Center	31	Mario Lemieux (1988–89, 1995–96)
Right Wing	24	Rob Brown (1988–89)
Left Wing	26	Kevin Stevens (1992–93)
Defenseman	13	Doug Bodger (1987–88) and Kevin Hatcher (1997–98)
Rookie	16	Sidney Crosby (2005–06) and Evgeni Malkin (2006–07)
Rookie Defenseman	5	Zarley Zalapski (1988–89)

POWER-PLAY ASSISTS

Overall	58	Mario Lemieux (1987–88)
Center	58	Mario Lemieux (1987–88)
Right Wing	34	Jaromir Jagr (1998–99)
Left Wing	27	Pat Boutette (1981–82)
Defenseman	53	Paul Coffey {1988–89)
Rookie	31	Sidney Crosby (2005–06)
Rookie Defenseman	23	Zarley Zalapski (1988–89)

POWER-PLAY POINTS

Overall	80	Mario Lemieux (1987–88, 1988–89)
Center	80	Mario Lemieux (1987–88, 1988–89)
Right Wing	51	Jaromir Jagr (1995–96)
Left Wing	44	Kevin Stevens (1992–93)
Defenseman	64	Paul Coffey (1988–89)
Rookie	47	Sidney Crosby (2005–06)
Rookie Defenseman	28	Zarley Zalapski (1988–89)

SHORTHANDED GOALS

Overall	13	Mario Lemieux (1988–89)
Center	13	Mario Lemieux (1988–89)
Right Wing	4	Jean Pronovost (1973–74) and Rick Tocchet (1992–93)
Left Wing	5	Ryan Malone (2005–06)
Defenseman	2	Bob Woytowich (1968–69); Moe Mantha (1985–86); Paul Coffey (1987–88); Grant Jennings (1991–92); Larry Murphy (1991–92, 1992–93); Darius Kasparaitis (1997–98) and Kevin Hatcher (1998–99)
Rookie	7*	Jordan Staal (2006–07)

* NHL Rookie Record

CONSECUTIVE GAME STREAKS

Goal	12	Mario Lemieux (10/6/92–11/1/92)
Assist	16	Jaromir Jagr (1/9/01–2/16/01)
Point	46	Mario Lemieux (10/31/89–2/14/90)
Goal (Rookie)	7	Mike Bullard (1/23/82–2/6/82)
Assist (Rookie)	6	Mario Lemieux (10/27/84–11/8/84 and 12/7/84–12/21/84); Sidney Crosby (10/5/05–10/15/05)
Point (Rookie)	11	Mike Bullard (12/12/81–1/3/82)

Known for his rugged play, Grant Jennings notched two shorthanded goals during the 1991–92 season.

Penguins Individual Player Records—Continued

GAME

Goals	5	Mario Lemieux (3 times) (vs. New Jersey, 12/31/88) (at NY Rangers, 4/9/93) (vs. St. Louis, 3/26/96)
Assists	6	Ron Stackhouse (vs. Philadelphia, 3/8/75) Greg Malone (vs. Quebec, 11/28/79) Mario Lemieux (3 times) (vs. St. Louis, 10/15/88) (at San Jose, 12/5/92) (vs. Tampa Bay, 11/1/95)
Points	8	Mario Lemieux (2 times) (vs. St. Louis, 10/15/88) (vs. New Jersey 12/31/88)
Shots	14	Ron Stackhouse (vs. Washington, 4/3/76)
Penalties	9	Russ Anderson (vs. Edmonton, 1/19/80)
Penalty Minutes	51	Russ Anderson (vs. Edmonton, 1/19/80)

Greg Malone recorded six assists versus the Nordiques on November 28, 1979.

PERIOD

Goals	4	Mario Lemieux (at Montreal, 1/26/97)
Assists	4	Syl Apps (vs. Detroit, 3/24/71) Ron Stackhouse (vs. Philadelphia, 3/8/75) Paul Coffey (vs. NY Islanders, 2/6/90) Mario Lemieux (vs. Tampa Bay, 11/1/95) Jaromir Jagr (at St. Louis, 12/19/96)
Points	4	22 times - last time Evgeni Malkin (at NY Islanders, 11/26/08)
Shots	9	Evgeni Malkin (at Phoenix, 10/30/08)
Penalties	8	Russ Anderson (vs. Edmonton, 1/19/80)
Penalty Minutes	46	Russ Anderson (vs. Edmonton, 1/19/80)

Penguins Goaltending Records

Single Season

GAMES

All-Time	460	Tom Barrasso
Season	67	Marc-Andre Fleury (2006–07, 2009–10)
Season, Home	37	Marc-Andre Fleury (2006–07)
		Johan Hedberg (2001–02)
Season, Road	32	Tom Barrasso (1997–98)

MINUTES PLAYED

All-Time	25,879	Tom Barrasso
Season	3,905	Marc-Andre Fleury (2006–07)
Season, Home	2,188	Marc-Andre Fleury (2006–07)
Season, Road	1,932	Tom Barrasso (1997–98)

WINS

All-Time	226	Tom Barrasso
Season	43	Tom Barrasso (1992–93)
Season, Home	24	Tom Barrasso (1992–93)
Season, Road	19	Tom Barrasso (1992–93)

LOSSES

All-Time	153	Tom Barrasso
Season	34	Johan Hedberg (2001–02)
Season, Home	18	Johan Hedberg (2001–02)
Season, Road	17	Les Binkley (1967–68)
		Michel Dion (1981–82)

TIES

All-Time	53	Tom Barrasso
Season	15	Denis Herron (1977–78)
Season, Home	9	Les Binkley (1967–68)
Season, Road	7	Denis Herron (1977–78)
		Denis Herron (1978–79)
		Greg Millen (1980–81)

SAVES

All-Time	12,076	Tom Barrasso
Season	1,920	Denis Herron (1977–78)
Season, Home	1,017	Marc-Andre Fleury (2006–07)
Season, Road	982	Denis Herron (1977–78)
All-Time Per Game	30.6	Joe Daley
Season Per Game	32.6	Denis Herron (1977–78)
Season Per Game, Home	31.2	Joe Daley (1968–69)
Season Per Game, Road	35.8	Denis Herron (1977–78)

SHUTOUTS

All-Time	22	Tom Barrasso
Season	7	Tom Barrasso (1997–98)
Season, Home	5	Marc-Andre Fleury (2006–07)
Season, Road	6	Tom Barrasso (1997–98)

Penguins Goaltending Records—Continued

WINNING PERCENTAGE
All-Time (Min. 75 games) .596 Ken Wregget (104–67–21)
Season (Min. 25 games) .734 Tom Barrasso (43–14–5) (1992–93)

GOALS AGAINST
All-Time 1,409 Tom Barrasso
Season 258 Greg Millen (1980–81)
Season, Home 128 Greg Millen (1980–81)
Season, Road 130 Greg Millen (1980–81)

GOALS–AGAINST AVERAGE
All-Time (Min. 75 Games) 2.82 Marc-Andre Fleury
Season (Min. 25 games) 2.07 Tom Barrasso (1997–98)
Season, Home 2.02 Al Smith (1970–71)
Season, Road 1.83 Tom Barrasso (1997–98)

SAVE PERCENTAGE
All-Time (Min. 75 Games) .906 Marc-Andre Fleury
Season (Min. 25 Games) .923 Ty Conklin (2007–08)

LONGEST CONSECUTIVE STREAKS
Games Played 26 Greg Millen (2/7/81–4/4/81) (11–10–5)
Wins 14 Tom Barrasso (3/9/93–4/9/93)
Wins, Home 13 Jim Rutherford (2/16/72–11/16/72)
Wins, Road 6 Tom Barrasso (3/14/93–4/9/93)
Unbeaten 16 Patrick Lalime (12/6/96–1/21/97) (14–0–2)
Unbeaten, Home 18 Michel Plasse (1/11/75–12/5/75) (14–0–4)
Unbeaten, Road 7 Denis Herron (3/13/79–3/27/79) (5–0–2)
    Tom Barrasso (2 times) (10/20/95–11/17/95) (5–0–2) and (11/15/97–12/19/97) (5–0–2)
Losses 9 Michel Dion (12/20/83–3/1/84)
Losses, Home 7 Sebastien Caron (12/31/03–2/10/04)
Losses, Road 10 Joe Daley (11/13/68 –3/20/69)
    Denis Herron (12/22/84–3/30/85)
Winless 15 Al Smith (1/28/71–4/1/71) (0–10–5)
Winless, Home 9 Les Binkley (11/6/68–12/21/68) (0–8–1)
Winless, Road 26 Al Smith (3/5/70–4/1/71) (0–18–8)

LONGEST SHUTOUT SEQUENCE
Individual 136:13 Jocelyn Thibault (3/6/07–3/19/07)
Team 187:30 Wregget/Barrasso (1/31/93–2/13/93)
Against 183:15 3/31/80–2/9/80

Penguins Special Teams

YEAR	POWER PLAY PPG/CHANCES	PCT.	NHL RANK	PENALTY KILLING PPGA/CHANCES	PCT.	NHL RANK
1967–68	37/273	13.6	11th	30/195	84.6	6th
1968–69	50/303	16.5	7th	39/231	83.1	5th
1969–70	53/315	16.8	9th	66/282	76.6	12th
1970–71	56/318	17.6	9th	48/276	82.6	8th
1971–72	46/286	16.1	11th	55/246	77.6	10th
1972–73	52/301	17.3	9th	49/264	81.4	8th
1973–74	47/276	17.0	11th	47/245	80.8	8th
1974–75	64/323	19.8	9th	63/324	80.6	8th
1975–76	75/307	24.4	6th	68/292	76.7	11th
1976–77	46/263	17.5	14th	47/209	77.5	15th
1977–78	53/261	20.3	11th	61/251	75.7	13th
1978–79	56/261	21.5	12th	57/250	77.2	11th
1979–80	52/262	19.8	14th	64/247	74.1	18th
1980–81	92/400	23.0	11th	99/370	73.2	21st
1981–82	99/404	24.5	7th	92/399	76.9	11th
1982–83	81/358	22.6	9th	110/396	72.2	21st
1983–84	70/340	20.6	16th	86/357	75.9	15th
1984–85	62/363	17.1	21st	74/311	76.2	14th
1985–86	93/425	21.9	12th	78/340	77.1	15th
1986–87	74/378	19.6	14th	72/318	77.4	15th
1987–88	110/500	22.0	6th	120/507	76.3	20th
1988–89	119/491	24.2	3rd	111/482	77.0	16th
1989–90	86/403	21.3	10th	94/372	74.7	20th
1990–91	89/388	22.9	3rd	73/351	79.2	16th
1991–92	92/423	21.7	4th	77/383	79.9	15th
1992–93	105/440	23.9	2nd	72/429	83.2	4th
1993–94	76/404	18.8	13th	72/401	82.0	10th
1994–95	42/221	19.0	10th	46/229	79.9	23rd
1995–96	109/420	26.0	1st	78/467	83.3	8th
1996–97	74/339	21.8	2nd	64/338	81.1	23rd
1997–98	67/407	16.5	11th	46/338	86.4	8th
1998–99	65/363	17.9	7th	56/302	81.5	23rd
1999–00	54/346	15.6	20th	56/321	82.6	19th
2000–01	76/375	20.3	5th	78/405	80.7	26th (tie)
2001–02	47/335	14.0	24th (tie)	57/352	83.8	18th (tie)
2002–03	66/360	18.3	7th	58/352	83.5	13th (tie)
2003–04	65/360	18.1	7th (tie)	84/369	77.2	30th
2005–06	94/495	19.0	6th	113/533	78.8	29th
2006–07	94/463	20.3	5th	75/419	82.1	17th
2007–08	77/378	20.4	4th	68/357	81.0	23rd
2008–09	62/360	17.2	20th	60/347	82.7	8th
2009–10	56/326	17.2	19th	52/327	84.1	9th
TOTALS	**2,983/15,014**	**19.9**		**2,915/14,184**	**79.4**	

Penguins Hat Tricks

PLAYER	DATE/OPPONENT	GOALIE(S)
1967–68 (2)		
Andy Bathgate	10/18 vs. MIN	Cesare Maniago (2), Garry Bauman
Ken Schinkel	10/21 vs. CHI	Denis DeJordy
1968–69 (0)		
1969–70 (1)		
Ken Schinkel (2)	2/4 vs. MIN	Cesare Maniago, Ken Broderick (2)
1970–71 (2)		
Glen Sather	12/19 vs. DET	Don McLeod (2), ENG
Duane Rupp	3/24 vs. DET	Jim Rutherford
1971–72 (1)		
Bob Leiter	12/1 vs. DET	Al Smith (2), Joe Daley
1972–73 (6)		
Al McDonough	10/11 at STL	Wayne Stephenson
Lowell MacDonald	11/5 vs. MIN	Gilles Gilbert
Al McDonough (2)	11/19 vs. ATL	Phil Myre
Al McDonough (3)	11/22 vs. STL	Wayne Stephenson
Eddie Shack	11/29 vs. TOR	Ron Low
Syl Apps	12/13 vs. NYI	Gerry Desjardins
1973–74 (3)		
Lowell MacDonald (2)	11/13 vs. MIN	Cesare Maniago
Bob Kelly	3/24 vs. DET	Doug Grant
Lowell MacDonald (3)	3/27 vs. MIN	Lorne Worsley
1974–75 (3)		
Rick Kehoe	2/15 at TOR	Doug Favell
Jean Pronovost	2/26 vs.WSH	Michel Belhemeur
Pierre Larouche	3/12 vs. BOS	Gilles Gilbert
1975–76 (9)		
Jean Pronovost (2)	11/12 at WSH	Bernie Wolfe
Syl Apps (2)	12/17 at CAL	Gilles Meloche
Bob Kelly (2)	12/17 at CAL	Gilles Meloche
Stan Gilbertson	1/18 vs. NYR	Dunc Wilson (2), Doug Soetaert
Pierre Larouche (2)	2/8 at VAN	Gary Smith (2), Ken Lockett
Jean Pronovost (3)	2/19 vs. TOR	Doug Favell
Pierre Larouche (3)	2/21 vs. CHI	Gilles Villemure
Lowell MacDonald (4)	2/21 vs. CHI	Gilles Villemure
Rick Kehoe (2)	3/10 vs. BUF	Al Smith
1976–77 (2)		
Rick Kehoe (3)	10/6 vs. VAN	Cesare Maniago (2), Curt Ridley
Pierre Larouche (4)	2/19 at TOR	Mike Palmateer, Wayne Thomas (2)

Penguins Hat Tricks—Continued

PLAYER	DATE/OPPONENT	GOALIE(S)
1977–78 (3)		
Blair Chapman	11/16 at MIN	Pete LoPresti
Pete Mahovlich	11/30 vs. DET	Ron Low
Wayne Bianchin	12/31 vs. CLE	Gary Edwards
1978–79 (3)		
Orest Kindrachuk	3/4 at COL	Michel Plasse
Ron Stackhouse	3/18 at NYR	Wayne Thomas
Greg Malone	3/28 vs. NYR	Doug Soetaert
1979–80 (1)		
Gary McAdam	11/28 vs. QUE	Michel Dion
1980–81 (5)		
Rick Kehoe (4)	11/26 vs. VAN	Richard Brodeur
Rick Kehoe (5)	12/3 at TOR	Jiri Crha
Paul Gardner*	12/13 vs. PHI	Phil Myre
Rick Kehoe (6)	1/14 vs. STL	Ed Staniowski
Gregg Sheppard	3/16 at EDM	Ed Mio
1981–82 (4)		
Paul Gardner (2)	11/7 vs. PHI	Pelle Lindbergh
Doug Shedden	1/2 vs. HFD	John Garrett
Rick Kehoe (7)	1/20 vs. BOS	Marco Baron
Andre St. Laurent	3/6 at QUE	Dan Bouchard

*Four Goal Game

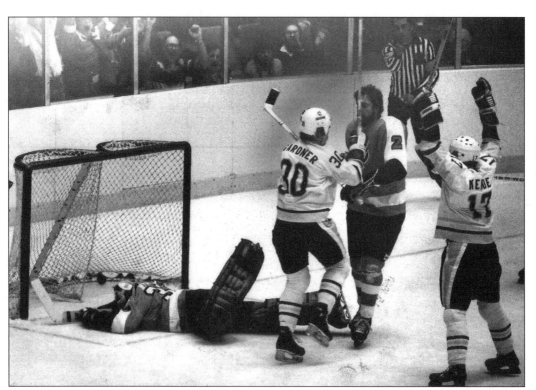

Paul Gardner (30) was the first Penguin ever to score four goals in one game.

Penguins Hat Tricks—Continued

PLAYER	DATE/OPPONENT	GOALIE(S)
1982–83 (3)		
Pat Boutette	10/12 vs. VAN	Richard Brodeur
Pat Boutette (2)	10/27 vs.WSH	Dave Parro
Rick Kehoe (8)	12/23 at DET	Greg Stefan
1983–84 (3)		
Andy Brickley	12/26 vs. NYR	Steve Weeks
Mike Bullard	1/18 vs. WPG	Mike Veisor
Mark Taylor	3/29 at NYR	John Vanbiesbrouck
1984–85 (2)		
Mike Bullard (2)*	12/5 vs. STL	Mike Liut
Mike Bullard (3)	12/26 vs. NYI	Kelly Hrudey
1985–86 (5)		
Mike Bullard (4)	12/31 at STL	Rick Wamsley
Mario Lemieux *	12/31 at STL	Rick Wamsley
Mike Bullard (5)	1/22 at EDM	Andy Moog
Doug Shedden (2)	2/15 vs. VAN	Richard Brodeur
Mike Bullard (6)	2/21 at DET	Greg Stefan, Mark LaForest (2)
1986–87 (12)		
Randy Cunneyworth	10/9 vs. WSH	Al Jensen
Mario Lemieux (2)	10/17 at BUF	Tom Barrasso
Terry Ruskowski	10/18 vs.NJ	Karl Friesen
Kevin LaVallee	10/29 vs. NJ	Alain Chevrier
John Chabot	12/6 vs. MIN	Don Beaupre
Mario Lemieux (3)*	12/12 vs. TOR	Ken Wregget (3), Allan Bester
Craig Simpson	12/22 at MTL	Patrick Roy
Mario Lemieux (4)	1/23 at VAN	Frank Caprice
Mario Lemieux (5)	2/5 at BOS	Bill Ranford
Randy Cunneyworth (2)*	3/3 at QUE	Mario Gosselin (3), Clint Malarchuk
Mario Lemieux (6)	3/8 at WPG	Pokey Reddick
Mario Lemieux (7)	3/12 vs. QUE	Mario Gosselin, ENG (2)
1987–88 (9)		
Dan Quinn	10/15 vs. NYR	Bob Froese
Mario Lemieux (8)	10/15 vs. NYR	Bob Froese
Mario Lemieux (9)	10/24 vs. BUF	Jacques Cloutier
Mario Lemieux (10)	1/5 vs. LA	Glenn Healy
Mario Lemieux (11)	1/10 at DET	Glen Hanlon
Paul Coffey	1/20 at CHI	Bob Mason (2), Darren Pang
Dan Quinn (2)	2/28 at CHI	Darren Pang
Dan Quinn (3)	3/7 at CGY	Mike Vernon
Mario Lemieux (12)	4/2 at WSH	Clint Malarchuk

*Four Goal Game

Penguins Hat Tricks—Continued

PLAYER	DATE/OPPONENT	GOALIE(S)
1988–89 (13)		
Mario Lemieux (13)	10/12 vs. WSH	Clint Malarchuk (2), Pete Peeters
Rob Brown	10/15 vs. STL	Vincent Riendeau
Mario Lemieux (14)	10/16 vs. PHI	Ron Hextall
Rob Brown (2)	11/25 at WSH	Clint Malarchuk
Mario Lemieux (15)	12/21 at TOR	Ken Wregget
Mario Lemieux (16)**	12/31 vs. NJ	Bob Sauve (3), Chris Terreri, ENG
Mario Lemieux (17)	1/10 vs. NYI	Kelly Hrudey
Rob Brown (3)	1/28 vs. DET	Greg Stefan (2), Glen Hanlon
Rob Brown (4)	2/5 at BOS	Andy Moog
Mario Lemieux (18)	2/14 vs. BUF	Jacques Cloutier
Mario Lemieux (19)	3/12 at CHI	Alain Chevrier
Mario Lemieux (20)	3/25 vs. NJ	Bob Sauve (2), Sean Burke
Mario Lemieux (21)*	3/30 vs. HFD	Kay Whitmore
1989–90 (10)		
Mario Lemieux (22)	10/17 vs. TOR	Allan Bester, ENG (2)
Kevin Stevens	10/31 vs. LA	Kelly Hrudey
Mario Lemieux (23)	12/2 at QUE	Ron Tugnutt
Rob Brown (5)	12/12 vs. BOS	Andy Moog (2), Reggie Lemelin
Mario Lemieux (24)*	1/8 at NYR	Bob Froese (2), John Vanbiesbrouck (2)
Tony Tanti	1/30 vs. PHI	Ken Wregget
Mario Lemieux (25)	2/2 vs. EDM	Randy Exelby (2), ENG
Rob Brown (6)	2/10 vs. LA	Kelly Hrudey, Mario Gosselin, ENG
John Cullen	2/20 vs.PHI	Ken Wregget (2), ENG
Rob Brown (7)	3/4 vs. MIN	Jarmo Myllys (2), ENG
1990–91 (5)		
Kevin Stevens (2)	10/25 vs. QUE	John Tanner, Ron Tugnutt (2)
Phil Bourque	12/3 at NYR	John Vanbiesbrouck, Mike Richter (2)
John Cullen (2)	1/17 at TOR	Peter Ing
Jaromir Jagr	2/2 vs. BOS	Norm Foster
Mario Lemieux (26)	3/26 at PHI	Pete Peeters
1991–92 (11)		
Mario Lemieux (27)	10/15 at NYI	Glenn Healy
Bob Errey	10/17 vs. NYI	Glenn Healy (2), ENG
Kevin Stevens (3)	11/13 vs. EDM	Bill Ranford
Mark Recchi	11/18 at QUE	Ron Tugnutt
Kevin Stevens (4)	11/18 at QUE	Ron Tugnutt
Kevin Stevens (5)	11/29 at PHI	Dominic Roussel (2), Ken Wregget
Kevin Stevens (6)	12/5 at SJ	Arturs Irbe, Brian Hayward (2)
Joe Mullen*	12/23 at NYI	Glenn Healy
Joe Mullen (2)*	12/26 vs. TOR	Grant Fuhr
Joe Mullen (3)	2/18 vs. TOR	Rick Wamsley
Rick Tocchet	3/6 at SJ	Jarmo Myllys

*Four Goal Game   **Five Goal Game

Penguins Hat Tricks—Continued

PLAYER	DATE/OPPONENT	GOALIE(S)
1992–93 (10)		
Kevin Stevens (7)*	10/17 at HFD	Sean Burke (3), Frank Pietrangelo
Mario Lemieux (28)	10/22 vs. DET	Tim Cheveldae
Kevin Stevens (8)	12/12 vs. NJ	Chris Terreri
Kevin Stevens (9)	1/26 vs. WSH	Don Beaupre
Mario Lemieux (29)*	3/18 vs. WSH	Don Beaupre (3), Jim Hrivnak
Mario Lemieux (30)*	3/20 vs. PHI	Tommy Soderstrom (3), Dominic Roussel
Rick Tocchet (2)	4/1 vs. HFD	Mario Gosselin, Frank Pietrangelo (2)
Rick Tocchet (3)	4/7 vs. MTL	Patrick Roy
Joe Mullen (4)	4/9 at NYR	Corey Hirsch, Mike Richter (2)
Mario Lemieux (31)**	4/9 at NYR	Corey Hirsch (3), Mike Richter (2)
1993–94 (2)		
Kevin Stevens (10)	1/11 vs. BOS	John Blue
Martin Straka	3/8 vs. BOS	Vincent Riendeau
1994–95 (2)		
Jaromir Jagr (2)	2/14 vs. BOS	Vincent Riendeau
Luc Robitaille*	2/16 vs. HFD	Pokey Reese
1995–96 (9)		
Mario Lemieux (32)	10/26 at NYI	Tommy Soderstrom
Mario Lemieux (33)	10/28 at NJ	Martin Brodeur
Ron Francis	11/10 at SJ	Arturs Irbe (2), Wade Flaherty
Markus Naslund	11/28 vs. OTT	Mike Bales
Mario Lemieux (34)*	11/30 at BOS	Scott Bailey (2), Craig Billington (2)
Mario Lemieux (35)	12/30 vs. FLA	John Vanbiesbrouck
Mario Lemieux (36)	1/27 vs. PHI	Garth Snow (2), Ron Hextall
Petr Nedved*	3/5 vs. WPG	Nikolai Khabibulin (2), Dominic Roussel (2)
Mario Lemieux (37)**	3/26 vs. STL	Grant Fuhr, Jon Casey (4)
1996–97 (4)		
Jaromir Jagr (3)	11/2 vs. OTT	Ron Tugnutt
Jaromir Jagr (4)	11/30 vs. BOS	Bill Ranford
Mario Lemieux (38)	12/19 at STL	Jon Casey
Mario Lemieux (39)*	1/26 at MTL	Jocelyn Thibault
1997–98 (3)		
Ron Francis (2)	12/29 vs. NYI	Eric Fichaud, Tommy Salo (2)
Stu Barnes	1/10 vs. NJ	Martin Brodeur
Martin Straka (2)	4/18 vs. BOS	Byron Dafoe (2), Robbie Tallas
1998–99 (2)		
Stu Barnes (2)	11/25 at WSH	Olaf Kolzig
Martin Straka (3)	11/28 at MTL	Jose Theodore (2), ENG
1999–00 (3)		
Aleksey Morozov	10/7 at NJ	Martin Brodeur
Jaromir Jagr (5)	11/26 vs. OTT	Patrick Lalime
Jaromir Jagr (6)	12/30 vs. NYI	Roberto Luongo

*Four Goal Game   **Five Goal Game

Penguins Hat Tricks—Continued

PLAYER	DATE/OPPONENT	GOALIE(S)
2000–01 (9)		
Jaromir Jagr (7)*	10/14 vs. NYR	Kirk McLean
Alexei Kovalev	11/8 vs. PHI	Brian Boucher
Jaromir Jagr (8)	12/16 at MTL	Jeff Hackett
Martin Straka (4)	1/8 at WSH	Olaf Kolzig (2), ENG
Mario Lemieux (40)	1/24 vs. MTL	Jose Theodore
Alexei Kovalev (2)	2/7 vs. PHI	Roman Cechmanek (2), Brian Boucher
Alexei Kovalev (3)	2/10 vs. NJ	Martin Brodeur
Alexei Kovalev (4)	2/23 vs. NYR	Vitali Yeremeyev
Jaromir Jagr (9)	3/10 vs. CGY	Mike Vernon (2), ENG
2001–02 (5)		
Toby Petersen	10/16 vs. OTT	Patrick Lalime
Alexei Kovalev (5)	11/13 at NJ	Martin Brodeur (2), ENG
Alexei Kovalev (6)	11/14 vs. NYI	Garth Snow
Alexei Kovalev (7)	1/5 vs. NYR	Mike Richter
Aleksey Morozov (2)	1/17 at CGY	Roman Turek
2002–03 (1)		
Alexei Kovalev (8)	1/25 vs. CHI	Jocelyn Thibault (2), Michael Leighton
2003–04 (0)		
2005–06 (1)		
Mark Recchi (2)	3/4 vs. CAR	Cam Ward
2006–07 (6)		
Sidney Crosby	10/28 at PHI	Antero Niittymaki (2), Robert Esche
Nils Ekman	11/3 vs. TB	Johan Holmqvist
Ryan Malone	12/15 vs. NYI	Mike Dunham (2), Rick DiPietro
Mark Recchi (3)	1/20 vs. TOR	Andrew Raycroft
Jordan Staal	2/10 at TOR	Andrew Raycroft
Ryan Malone	2/19 at NYI	Rick DiPietro
2007–08 (2)		
Evgeni Malkin	1/3 vs. TOR	Scott Clemmensen
Evgeni Malkin (2)	1/14 vs. NYR	Henrik Lundqvist
2008–09 (5)		
Jordan Staal (2)	11/11 at DET	Chris Osgood
Evgeni Malkin (3)	11/26 at NYI	Joey MacDonald
Sidney Crosby (2)	11/29 vs. NJ	Scott Clemmensen
Petr Sykora	12/11 vs. NYI	Yann Danis (2), Joey MacDonald
Pascal Dupuis	12/11 vs. NYI	Yann Danis (2), Joey MacDonald
2009–10 (6)		
Sidney Crosby (3)	10/28 vs. MTL	Jan Halak
Sidney Crosby (4)	11/28 vs. NYR	Steven Valiquette
Mike Rupp	11/30 at NYR	Henrik Lundqvist
Evgeni Malkin (4)	12/23 vs. OTT	Pascal Leclaire (2), Brian Elliot
Evgeni Malkin (5)	1/19 vs. NYI	Dwayne Roloson
Sidney Crosby (5)	2/1 vs. BUF	Ryan Miller

*Four Goal Game

Penguins Penalty Shots

PLAYER	OPPONENT	DATE	GOALTENDER	RESULT
George Konik	at STL	1/31/68	Glenn Hall	GOAL
Charlie Burns	vs. NYR	2/5/69	Ed Giacomin	No Goal
Keith McCreary	vs. NYR	3/18/70	Ed Giacomin	No Goal
Jean Pronovost	at DET	1/14/71	Roy Edwards	GOAL
Greg Polis	vs.STL	2/24/71	Ernie Wakely	No Goal
Syl Apps	at TOR	2/9/72	Bernie Parent	GOAL
Lowell MacDonald	at BUF	11/12/72	Roger Crozier	No Goal
Ron Schock	vs. DET	1/10/73	Roy Edwards	No Goal
Ron Schock	vs. NYR	3/10/73	Ed Giacomin	No Goal
Chuck Arnason	vs. CAL	2/16/74	Gilles Meloche	No Goal
Ron Schock	at WSH	11/30/76	Bernie Wolfe	No Goal
Blair Chapman	at WSH	12/4/77	Jim Bedard	No Goal
Pete Mahovlich	at WSH	1/21/78	Jim Bedard	No Goal
Blair Chapman	vs. COL	3/22/78	Bill McKenzie	No Goal
Ross Lonsberry	at NYI	12/5/78	Glenn Resch	No Goal
Ross Lonsberry	vs. MIN	2/9/80	Gilles Meloche	No Goal
Greg Sheppard	vs. STL	1/14/81	Ed Staniowski	No Goal
Dave Hannan	at WSH	10/14/83	Pat Riggin	GOAL
Andy Brickley	vs. CHI	11/29/84	Murray Bannerman	No Goal
Mario Lemieux	at QUE	12/29/84	Mario Gosselin	GOAL
Warren Young	at TOR	1/2/85	Tim Bernhardt	GOAL
Mario Lemieux	at NYI	1/19/88	Kelly Hrudey	GOAL
Mario Lemieux	vs. NJ	12/31/88	Chris Terreri	GOAL
Mario Lemieux	at LA	3/7/89	Kelly Hrudey	GOAL
Jock Callander	vs. MTL	3/18/89	Patrick Roy	GOAL
Mario Lemieux	at WSH	11/24/89	Bob Mason	GOAL
Bob Errey	vs. NJ	1/5/91	Chris Terreri	GOAL
Bob Errey	vs. MIN	10/31/91	Darcy Wakaluk	GOAL
Mario Lemieux	vs. EDM	3/17/92	Bill Ranford	No Goal
Jaromir Jagr	vs. WSH	1/26/93	Don Beaupre	No Goal
Martin Straka	at QUE	3/16/95	Jocelyn Thibault	No Goal
Mario Lemieux	vs. BUF	3/23/96	Dominik Hasek	No Goal
Jaromir Jagr	at FLA	11/9/96	Mark Fitzpatrick	No Goal
Mario Lemieux	at FLA	4/11/97	John Vanbiesbrouck	GOAL
Stu Barnes	at PHI	3/8/98	Ron Hextall	No Goal
Martin Straka	vs. STL	1/19/00	Roman Turek	GOAL
Martin Straka	at SJ	11/1/00	Evgeni Nabokov	No Goal
Martin Straka	at BOS	1/9/01	Byron Dafoe	No Goal
Martin Straka	at ATL	1/30/01	Damian Rhodes	GOAL
Wayne Primeau	at TB	11/10/01	Nikolai Khabibulin	GOAL
Eric Meloche	vs. NYR	1/3/04	Jussi Markkanen	No Goal
Brian Holzinger	vs. TB	1/27/04	John Grahame	No Goal
Ziggy Palffy	at NYR	11/7/05	Kevin Weekes	No Goal
Matt Murley	at TB	11/27/05	John Grahame	No Goal

Penguins Penalty Shots—Continued

PLAYER	OPPONENT	DATE	GOALTENDER	RESULT
Ryan Malone	vs.WSH	1/25/06	Olaf Kolzig	GOAL
Jordan Staal	vs. CBJ	10/21/06	Fredrik Norrena	GOAL
Jordan Staal	vs. NYR	11/25/06	Henrik Lundqvist	No Goal
Nils Ekman	at NYR	12/7/06	Henrik Lundqvist	GOAL
Jarkko Ruutu	vs. TOR	1/20/07	Andrew Raycroft	GOAL
Evgeni Malkin	at NYI	3/22/07	Rick DiPietro	No Goal
Jordan Staal	vs. NYR	10/23/07	Henrik Lundqvist	No Goal
Sidney Crosby	at VAN	12/8/07	Roberto Luongo	No Goal
Petr Sykora	at TB	3/4/08	Mike Smith	No Goal
Sidney Crosby	vs. NYR	1/18/09	Henrik Lundqvist	No Goal
Evgeni Malkin	vs. ATL	3/17/09	Johan Hedberg	No Goal
Evgeni Malkin	at CAR	4/4/09	Cam Ward	No Goal
Max Talbot	at ATL	11/21/09	Johan Hedberg	No Goal

Pittsburgh has scored on 21 of 57 attempts (8 for 27 at home, 13 for 30 on the road)

Opponents Penalty Shots

GOALTENDER	OPPONENT	DATE	PLAYER	RESULT
Les Binkley	vs. MIN	12/23/67	Bill Collins	No Goal
Andy Brown	at NYI	3/5/74	Ralph Stewart	No Goal
Gary Inness	at TOR	3/20/74	Dave Keon	GOAL
Dunc Wilson	at NYR	11/14/76	Bill Goldsworthy	No Goal
Dunc Wilson	vs. CHI	11/21/76	Alain Daigle	No Goal
Denis Herron	vs. CLE	12/16/76	Al MacAdam	GOAL
Dunc Wilson	vs. PHI	10/15/77	Orest Kindrachuk	GOAL
Paul Harrison	vs. PHI	10/11/81	Ilkka Sinisalo	GOAL
Denis Herron	at NYI	2/17/83	Bob Bourne	No Goal
Denis Herron	at MIN	3/16/83	Dino Ciccarelli	No Goal
Denis Herron	at HFD	3/17/84	Tony Currie	No Goal
Denis Herron	at QUE	12/29/84	Michel Goulet	No Goal
Roberto Romano	at LA	1/21/87	Dave Williams	No Goal
Pat Riggin	at NYI	2/26/87	Alan Kerr	No Goal
Pat Riggin	vs. STL	3/1/87	Doug Gilmour	No Goal
Pat Riggin	vs. QUE	3/12/87	Michel Goulet	No Goal
Pat Riggin	at NJ	10/9/87	Mark Johnson	No Goal
Gilles Meloche	at HFD	1/9/88	Dave Tippett	No Goal
Tom Barrasso	vs. WPG	10/10/89	Doug Smail	No Goal
Wendell Young	vs.WSH	12/16/89	Dale Hunter	No Goal
Wendell Young	vs. LA	2/10/90	Tomas Sandstrom	GOAL
Tom Barrasso	vs. QUE	3/16/90	Scott Pearson	GOAL
Wendell Young	at NYR	12/29/91	Darren Turcotte	No Goal
Ken Wregget	at CGY	1/23/93	Joe Nieuwendyk	No Goal
Ken Wregget	at NJ	2/7/96	Scott Niedermayer	No Goal
Tom Barrasso	at CGY	10/24/96	Robert Reichel	GOAL
Tom Barrasso	vs. CAR	1/7/99	Sami Kapanen	No Goal
Peter Skudra	vs. CHI	10/16/99	Doug Gilmour	No Goal
Jean-Sebastien Aubin	at ANA	10/27/99	Teemu Selanne	No Goal
Jean-Sebastien Aubin	at PHX	1/12/00	Keith Tkachuk	GOAL
Jean-Sebastien Aubin	at NYI	3/21/00	Tim Connolly	GOAL
Jean-Sebastien Aubin	at MTL	2/28/01	Martin Rucinsky	No Goal
Johan Hedberg	vs. OTT	10/16/01	Marian Hossa	No Goal
Johan Hedberg	vs. DAL	10/24/01	Mike Modano	No Goal
Marc-Andre Fleury	vs. LA	10/10/03	Esa Pirnes	No Goal
Sebastien Caron	vs. MIN	11/19/03	Marian Gaborik	GOAL
Sebastien Caron	at CAR	11/29/03	Erik Cole	No Goal
Marc-Andre Fleury	vs. TB	1/27/04	Dan Boyle	No Goal
Marc-Andre Fleury	vs. TOR	3/19/06	Chad Kilger	GOAL
Sebastien Caron	at NYI	3/31/06	Sean Bergenheim	No Goal
Marc-Andre Fleury	vs. NYI	4/17/06	Miroslav Satan	No Goal
Jocelyn Thibault	vs. WSH	2/18/07	Alexander Semin	No Goal
Marc-Andre Fleury	at BUF	12/29/09	Drew Stafford	GOAL
Marc-Andre Fleury	at TB	1/2/10	Vincent Lecavalier	No Goal
Brent Johnson	vs. NYI	1/19/10	Kyle Okposo	No Goal
Marc-Andre Fleury	vs. NJ	3/12/10	Ilya Kovalchuk	No Goal

Opponents have scored on 12 of 46 attempts (7 of 22 in Pittsburgh, 5 of 24 on the road)

Overtime and Shootouts

Penguins Season-by-Season Overtime Records

YEAR	OVERALL					HOME					ROAD				
	GP	W	L	T/SO	PTS	GP	W	L	T/SO	PTS	GP	W	L	T/SO	PTS
1983–84	12	1	5	6	8	7	0	3	4	4	5	1	2	2	4
1984–85	8	3	0	5	11	3	0	0	3	3	5	3	0	2	8
1985–86	14	3	3	8	14	7	1	1	5	7	7	2	2	3	7
1986–87	21	5	4	12	22	11	4	1	6	14	10	1	3	6	8
1987–88	16	5	2	9	19	9	2	1	6	10	7	3	1	3	9
1988–89	10	2	1	7	11	3	0	0	3	3	7	2	1	4	8
1989–90	14	3	3	8	14	7	2	2	3	7	7	1	1	5	7
1990–91	12	4	2	6	14	7	3	1	3	9	5	1	1	3	5
1991–92	12	2	1	9	13	8	1	1	6	8	4	1	0	3	5
1992–93	10	3	0	7	13	6	2	0	4	8	4	1	0	3	5
1993–94	19	4	2	13	21	11	2	1	8	12	8	2	1	5	9
1994–95	5	1	1	3	5	1	0	0	1	1	4	1	1	2	4
1995–96	9	3	2	4	10	4	2	2	0	4	5	1	0	4	6
1996–97	13	1	4	8	10	9	1	3	5	7	4	0	1	3	3
1997–98	23	3	2	18	24	13	2	1	10	14	10	1	1	8	10
1998–99	22	7	1	14	28	14	4	0	10	18	8	3	1	4	10
1999–00*	17	3	6	8	20	7	0	0	7	7	10	3	6	1	13
2000–01*	15	3	3	9	18	4	2	0	2	6	11	1	3	7	12
2001–02*	20	7	5	8	27	10	5	1	4	15	10	2	4	4	12
2002–03*	14	3	5	6	17	7	3	2	2	10	7	0	3	4	7
2003–04*	19	7	4	8	26	10	4	0	6	14	9	3	4	2	12
2005–06**	19	5	8	6	24	11	3	5	3	14	8	2	3	3	10
2006–07**	27	16	5	6	43	11	6	2	3	17	16	10	3	3	26
2007–08**	16	8	4	4	24	8	3	2	3	11	8	5	2	1	13
2008–09**	21	12	3	6	33	8	5	1	2	13	13	7	2	4	20
2009–10**	21	14	5	2	35	10	6	3	1	16	11	8	2	1	19
TOTALS	**409**	**128**	**81**	**200**	**504**	**206**	**63**	**33**	**110**	**252**	**203**	**65**	**48**	**90**	**252**

*Losses worth one point
**Wins include shootout win, ties/shootouts include shootout losses.

Penguins Overtime Records vs. Each Team

TEAM	GAMES	RECORD	TEAM	GAMES	RECORD
Anaheim	4	0–2–2	Nashville	4	1–0–3
Atlanta	8	5–1–2	New Jersey	22	4–7–11
Boston	20	8–2–10	NY Islanders	28	10–3–15
Buffalo	28	8–6–14	NY Rangers	38	16–6–16
Calgary	8	1–0–7	Ottawa	17	6–1–10
Chicago	9	2–1–6	Philadelphia	32	9–9–14
Columbus	4	3–0–1	Que./Colorado	10	1–3–6
Detroit	11	3–2–6	St. Louis	9	1–2–6
Edmonton	6	2–1–3	San Jose	5	1–0–4
Florida	14	7–3–4	Tampa Bay	14	3–3–8
Hart./Carolina	21	6–5–10	Toronto	11	3–5–3
Los Angeles	13	4–5–4	Vancouver	9	4–1–4
Minn./Dallas	6	2–1–3	Washington	24	9–4–11
Minnesota	1	0–0–1	Winn./Phoenix	8	2–3–3
Montreal	25	7–5–13	**TOTALS**	**409**	**128–81–200**

Penguins Overtime Wins

SCORER	DATE	TIME	OPPONENT	GOALIE	SCORE
Randy Carlyle	12/23/83	2:12	at New Jersey	Resch	6–5
Mario Lemieux	11/14/84	3:54	at Winnipeg	Behrend	4–3
Randy Hillier	12/7/84	1:35	at NY Rangers	Hanlon	4–3
Wayne Babych	3/9/85	1:06	at Boston	Peeters	6–5
Dan Frawley	12/19/85	0:38	at Minnesota	Casey	4–3
Doug Shedden	2/24/86	3:54	vs. Los Angeles	Melanson	6–5
Mario Lemieux	4/6/86	0:25	at NY Rangers	Hanlon	5–4
Doug Bodger	10/11/86	0:50	vs. NY Rangers	Vanbiesbrouck	6–5
Mario Lemieux	10/14/86	3:40	vs. Los Angeles	Melanson	4–3
Randy Cunneyworth	10/22/86	2:30	vs. Buffalo	Cloutier	5–4
Chris Kontos	2/8/87	2:12	at New Jersey	Chevrier	2–1
Mario Lemieux	4/4/87	1:26	vs. Detroit	Hanlon	4–3
Craig Simpson	10/31/87	4:05	at Quebec	Brunetta	5–4
Moe Mantha	11/14/87	2:04	vs. NY Rangers	Vanbiesbrouck	3–2
Charlie Simmer	1/23/88	0:24	at Montreal	Hayward	4–3
Mario Lemieux	2/2/88	4:11	vs. Washington	Peeters	3–2
Mario Lemieux	4/2/88	4:02	at Washington	Malarchuk	7–6
Rob Brown	12/26/88	1:39	at Hartford	Liut	4–3
Mario Lemieux	4/2/89	3:38	at Philadelphia	Empty Net	6–5
Randy Hillier	10/14/89	1:40	vs. Montreal	Roy	2–1
Troy Loney	2/14/90	3:33	at NY Rangers	Richter	4–3
Randy Gilhen	2/22/90	4:26	vs. NY Islanders	Fitzpatrick	4–3
Mark Recchi	11/24/90	1:11	vs. Washington	Liut	3–2
Scott Young	1/17/91	3:31	at Toronto	Ing	6–5
Paul Stanton	1/29/91	2:46	vs. Washington	Beaupre	3–2
Kevin Stevens	3/21/91	0:13	vs. NY Rangers	Vanbiesbrouck	5–4
Phil Bourque	10/15/91	2:30	at NY Islanders	Healy	7–6
Kevin Stevens	11/13/91	3:25	vs. Edmonton	Ranford	5–4

Penguins Overtime Wins—Continued

SCORER	DATE	TIME	OPPONENT	GOALIE	SCORE
Jaromir Jagr	12/17/92	2:50	at Philadelphia	Soderstrom	5–4
Jaromir Jagr	3/11/93	3:18	vs. Los Angeles	Stauber	4–3
Ulf Samuelsson	4/7/93	2:11	vs. Montreal	Roy	4–3
Joe Mullen	10/7/93	1:13	vs. Montreal	Roy	2–1
Jaromir Jagr	12/4/93	2:04	at Hartford	Reese	7–6
Ron Francis	1/7/94	4:54	at Buffalo	Hasek	4–3
Kevin Stevens	1/11/94	4:09	at Boston	Blue	5–4
Larry Murphy	3/4/95	4:36	at Boston	Riendeau	4–3
Jaromir Jagr	11/17/95	2:48	at Washington	Carey	3–2
Mario Lemieux	1/22/96	1:54	vs. Boston	Ranford	7–6
Mario Lemieux	2/18/96	2:17	vs. NY Rangers	Healy	4–3
Fredrik Olausson	3/8/97	0:19	vs. Philadelphia	Snow	3–2
Kevin Hatcher	10/25/97	0:41	at Vancouver	McLean	3–2
Rob Brown	11/1/97	3:52	vs. Vancouver	McLean	7–6
Jaromir Jagr	11/22/97	0:25	vs. NY Rangers	Richter	4–3
Kevin Hatcher	12/15/98	3:17	vs. Tampa Bay	Schwab	3–2
Jaromir Jagr	12/26/98	1:18	vs. Ottawa	Tugnutt	2–1
Alexei Kovalev	2/9/99	4:31	vs. Montreal	Chabot	3–2
Jaromir Jagr	2/11/99	1:21	vs. Vancouver	Hirsch	6–5
Kip Miller	2/13/99	3:39	at Nashville	Vokoun	3–2
Kip Miller	3/10/99	2:49	at Carolina	Irbe	3–2
Jaromir Jagr	4/18/99	1:22	at NY Rangers	Richter	2–1
Robert Lang	1/31/00	4:28	at Atlanta	Fankhouser	2–1
Hans Jonsson	3/30/00	2:25	at Washington	Kolzig	4–3
Jaromir Jagr	4/7/00	0:13	at Buffalo	Hasek	2–1
Alexei Kovalev	2/10/01	0:18	vs. New Jersey	Brodeur	5–4
Alexei Kovalev	2/17/01	1:19	at Columbus	Tugnutt	3–2
Mario Lemieux	2/21/01	2:10	vs. Florida	Luongo	3–2
Billy Tibbetts	11/13/01	1:51	vs. Tampa Bay	Khabibulin	2–1
Jan Hrdina	11/17/01	4:41	vs. NY Rangers	Blackburn	1–0
Aleksey Morozov	1/24/02	1:29	at NY Islanders	Snow	5–4
Randy Robitaille	1/26/02	4:02	vs. Atlanta	Hnilicka	3–2
Michal Rozsival	2/28/02	1:42	at Columbus	Tugnutt	4–3
Alexei Kovalev	3/5/02	3:23	vs. Florida	Luongo	6–5
Jan Hrdina	3/9/02	0:37	vs. NY Rangers	Richter	3–2
Martin Straka	1/4/03	0:42	vs. NY Islanders	Snow	3–2
Mario Lemieux	2/18/03	1:35	vs. Edmonton	Salo	4–3
Shawn Heins	2/22/03	4:33	vs. St. Louis	Johnson	2–1
Ryan Malone	11/1/03	2:10	vs. Boston	Raycroft	3–2
Aleksey Morozov	11/14/03	3.09	at Buffalo	Noronen	2–1
Ryan Malone	11/22/03	2:40	vs. Ottawa	Lalime	2–1
Ric Jackman	2/25/04	1:48	at Phoenix	Boucher	4–3
Ryan Malone	2/29/04	2:45	at NY Islanders	Snow	3–2
Aleksey Morozov	3/19/04	1:17	vs. Carolina	Weekes	4–3
Aleksey Morozov	3/21/04	4:52	vs. NY Rangers	Dunham	4–3
Sergei Gonchar	11/1/05	1:01	at New Jersey	Clemmensen	4–3
Sidney Crosby	11/16/05	4:13	at Philadelphia	Niittymaki	3–2

Penguins Overtime Wins—Continued

SCORER	DATE	TIME	OPPONENT	GOALIE	SCORE
Sidney Crosby	12/31/05	3:31	vs. NY Rangers	Lundqvist	4–3
Sidney Crosby	3/24/06	3:28	vs. NY Islanders	DiPietro	4–3
Sergei Gonchar	10/19/06	3:33	at NY Islanders	Dunham	4–3
Evgeni Malkin	11/01/06	2:45	at Los Angeles	Cloutier	4–3
Colby Armstrong	12/9/06	3:51	at Atlanta	Lehtonen	4–3
Jordan Staal	2/10/07	3:54	at Toronto	Raycroft	6–5
Colby Armstrong	2/22/07	2:39	at Florida	Belfour	2–1
Colby Armstrong	3/10/07	1:19	vs. NY Rangers	Lundqvist	3–2
Sergei Gonchar	12/27/07	1:33	vs. Washington	Kolzig	4–3
Tyler Kennedy	10/4/08	4:35	at Ottawa	Gerber	4–3
Pascal Dupuis	10/14/08	4:49	vs. Philadelphia	Niittymaki	3–2
Ruslan Fedotenko	11/11/08	3:49	at Detroit	Osgood	7–6
Sidney Crosby	12/22/08	0:43	at Buffalo	Miller	4–3
Evgeni Malkin	2/4/09	4:44	vs. Tampa Bay	McKenna	4–3
Evgeni Malkin	2/27/09	1:36	at Chicago	Niemi	5–4
Pascal Dupuis	11/14/09	1:24	vs. Boston	Thomas	6–5
Sidney Crosby	11/23/09	3:07	at Florida	Vokoun	3–2
Evgeni Malkin	12/12/09	0:37	vs. Florida	Vokoun	3–2
Evgeni Malkin	3/4/10	3:42	at NY Rangers	Lundqvist	5–4
Jordan Leopold	4/3/10	2:50	vs. Atlanta	Hedberg	4–3
Jordan Leopold	4/11/10	4:25	at NY Islanders	Roloson	6–5

Troy Loney scored an overtime winner against the Rangers on February 14, 1990.

Penguins Overtime Losses

SCORER	DATE	TIME	OPPONENT	GOALIE	SCORE
Lucien Deblois	10/12/83	1:34	vs. Winnipeg	Dion	4–3
Bobby Clarke	11/20/83	2:43	at Philadelphia	Herron	5–4
Paul MacLean	1/18/84	1:28	vs. Winnipeg	Dion	5–4
Dave Andreychuk	2/8/84	0:35	vs. Buffalo	Herron	6–5
Mark Osborne	2/26/84	2:18	at NY Rangers	Herron	4–3
Tiger Williams	11/16/85	3:10	at Los Angeles	Romano	4–3
Murray Craven	12/22/85	2:12	at Philadelphia	Meloche	3–2
Ilkka Sinisalo	4/5/86	1:59	vs. Philadelphia	Meloche	4–3
Steve Thomas	12/13/86	4:36	at Toronto	Romano	3–2
Mike Bossy	12/23/86	3:25	at NY Islanders	Romano	4–3
Mike Gartner	1/1/87	1:30	at Washington	Romano	4–3
Tomas Sandstrom	3/14/87	1:05	vs. NY Rangers	Riggin	3–2
Kevin Dineen	1/9/88	0:55	at Hartford	Meloche	5–4
Mario Marois	2/23/88	2:40	vs. Winnipeg	Pietrangelo	4–3
Dave Taylor	3/7/89	2:37	at Los Angeles	Barrasso	3–2
Don Maloney	2/6/90	4:28	vs. NY Islanders	Barrasso	8–7
Craig MacTavish	3/6/90	1:17	at Edmonton	Pietrangelo	4–3
Uwe Krupp	3/31/90	1:00	vs. Buffalo	Barrasso	3–2
Tony Granato	11/17/90	0:52	at Los Angeles	Pietrangelo	2–1
Patrick Flatley	12/23/90	4:29	vs. NY Islanders	Pietrangelo	4–3
Donald Audette	1/23/92	3:25	vs. Buffalo	Young	5–4
Tony Amonte	2/21/94	0:08	at NY Rangers	Barrasso	4–3
Randy Burridge	3/15/94	0:40	vs. Washington	Barrasso	5–4
Rod Brind'Amour	4/16/95	1:30	at Philadelphia	Wregget	4–3
Yanic Perreault	10/21/95	0:40	vs. Los Angeles	Wregget	3–2
Steve Thomas	3/9/96	0:21	vs. New Jersey	Barrasso	4–3
Shawn Burr	10/5/96	1:37	vs. Tampa Bay	Barrasso	4–3
Adam Oates	11/14/96	1:05	at Boston	Wregget	2–1
Valeri Kamensky	1/23/97	3:55	vs. Colorado	Lalime	4–3
Brendan Shanahan	2/8/97	2:01	vs. Detroit	Lalime	6–5
Valeri Kamensky	1/3/98	3:04	vs. Colorado	Skudra	5–4
Alexandre Daigle	3/8/98	4:03	at Philadelphia	Wregget	4–3
Dixon Ward	3/28/99	2:27	at Buffalo	Aubin	4–3
Teemu Selanne	10/27/99	3:38	at Anaheim	Aubin	2–1
Sergei Fedorov	11/12/99	0:36	at Detroit	Aubin	3–2
Mike Wilson	11/20/99	2:57	at Florida	Aubin	2–1
Mats Sundin	12/4/99	0:27	at Toronto	Barrasso	3–2
Adam Oates	12/29/99	4:32	at Washington	Aubin	3–2
Luke Richardson	2/24/00	4:51	at Philadelphia	Aubin	4–3
Joe Sakic	11/13/00	3:56	at Colorado	Snow	3–2
Darryl Sydor	1/19/01	0:42	at Dallas	Snow	6–5
John LeClair	4/7/01	4:39	at Philadelphia	Snow	4–3
Pavol Demitra	10/20/01	3:35	at St. Louis	Hedberg	2–1
Vaclav Prospal	11/10/01	4:29	at Tampa Bay	Aubin	3–2
Marty Murray	1/29/02	1:47	at Philadelphia	Aubin	3–2
Brian Rafalski	2/9/02	4:51	vs. New Jersey	Hedberg	2–1
Oleg Petrov	3/30/02	1:32	at Montreal	Hedberg	2–1
Valeri Bure	11/6/02	2:19	at Florida	Hedberg	4–3
Donald Audette	11/18/02	1:12	at Montreal	Hedberg	5–4
Andrei Markov	11/20/02	2:25	vs. Montreal	Aubin	3–2
Mathieu Schneider	12/14/02	4:22	at Los Angeles	Hedberg	3–2

Penguins Overtime Losses—Continued

SCORER	DATE	TIME	OPPONENT	GOALIE	SCORE
Ilya Kovalchuk	12/30/02	4:40	vs. Atlanta	Aubin	3–2
Patrik Elias	11/21/03	0:39	at New Jersey	Fleury	2–1
Markus Naslund	12/9/03	0:24	at Vancouver	Fleury	4–3
Jeff O'Neill	12/18/03	2:14	at Carolina	Caron	2–1
Eric Boguniecki	2/14/04	2:06	at St. Louis	Caron	2–1
Glen Murray	10/8/05	1:23	vs. Boston	Caron	7–6
Jochen Hecht	10/10/05	4:39	at Buffalo	Fleury	3–2
Mike Rathje	10/14/05	3:17	at Philadelphia	Caron	6–5
Stephen Weiss	10/25/05	0:53	vs. Florida	Thibault	4–3
Chris Drury	12/16/05	1:32	vs. Buffalo	Fleury	4–3
Tomas Kaberle	12/27/05	2:26	vs. Toronto	Fleury	3–2
Bryan McCabe	1/2/06	1:02	at Toronto	Thibault	3–2
Brian Gionta	4/2/06	2:22	vs. New Jersey	Fleury	3–2
Teemu Selanne	11/6/06	0:44	at Anaheim	Thibault	3–2
Vincent Lecavalier	11/8/06	2:41	vs. Tampa Bay	Fleury	4–3
Martin Straka	11/25/06	4:57	vs. NY Rangers	Fleury	2–1
Sheldon Souray	2/4/07	2:01	at Montreal	Fleury	4–3
Tomas Kaberle	3/31/07	3:55	at Toronto	Fleury	5–4
Jason Strudwick	11/17/07	1:40	vs. NY Rangers	Fleury	4–3
Zach Parise	2/4/08	0:37	at New Jersey	Conklin	4–3
Daniel Alfredsson	2/23/08	4:56	vs. Ottawa	Conklin	4–3
Chris Drury	3/31/08	1:46	at NY Rangers	Fleury	2–1
Zach Parise	10/11/08	4:22	vs. New Jersey	Fleury	2–1
Jamie Langenbrunner	1/30/09	4:00	at New Jersey	Fleury	4–3
Anton Babchuk	4/4/09	1:11	at Carolina	Fleury	3–2
Kris Versteeg	12/5/09	2:38	vs. Chicago	Fleury	2–1
Mike Knuble	2/7/10	2:49	at Washington	Fleury	5–4
Olli Jokinen	2/12/10	1:02	vs. NY Rangers	Fleury	3–2
Brian Pothier	3/11/10	0:23	at Carolina	Johnson	4–3
Jamie McBain	3/20/10	4:59	vs. Carolina	Fleury	3–2

Penguins Overtime Scoring

RANK	PLAYER	G	A	PTS
1	Mario Lemieux	11	11	22
2	Jaromir Jagr	9	5	14
3	Sidney Crosby	5	4	9
4	Evgeni Malkin	5	4	9
5	Sergei Gonchar	3	5	8
6	Alexei Kovalev	4	3	7
7	Martin Straka	1	6	7
8	Ron Francis	1	5	6
9	Dick Tarnstrom	0	6	6
10	Aleksey Morozov	4	1	5
11	Kevin Stevens	3	2	5
12	Larry Murphy	1	4	5
13	Jordan Staal	1	4	5
14	Colby Armstrong	3	1	4
15	Ryan Malone	3	1	4
16	Jan Hrdina	2	2	4
17	Paul Coffey	0	4	4
18	Rob Brown	2	1	3
19	Kevin Hatcher	2	1	3
20	Randy Hillier	2	1	3
21	Kip Miller	2	1	3
22	Doug Bodger	1	2	3
23	Phil Bourque	1	2	3
24	Ric Jackman	1	2	3
25	Michal Rozsival	1	2	3
26	Craig Simpson	1	2	3
27	Scott Young	1	2	3
28	Jiri Slegr	0	3	3
29	German Titov	0	3	3
30	Warren Young	0	3	3
31	Pascal Dupuis	2	0	2
32	Jordan Leopold	2	0	2
33	Randy Cunneyworth	1	1	2
34	Dan Frawley	1	1	2
35	Hans Jonsson	1	1	2
36	Robert Lang	1	1	2
37	Troy Loney	1	1	2
38	Moe Mantha	1	1	2
39	Mark Recchi	1	1	2
40	Paul Stanton	1	1	2
41	Billy Tibbetts	1	1	2
42	Stu Barnes	0	2	2
43	Kris Beech	0	2	2
44	John Cullen	0	2	2
45	Mike Eastwood	0	2	2
46	Darius Kasparaitis	0	2	2
47	Brooks Orpik	0	2	2
48	Tomas Sandstrom	0	2	2
49	Bryan Smolinski	0	2	2
50	Max Talbot	0	2	2
51	Zarley Zalapski	0	2	2
52	Ryan Whitney	0	2	2
53	Wayne Babych	1	0	1
54	Randy Carlyle	1	0	1
55	Ruslan Fedotenko	1	0	1
56	Randy Gilhen	1	0	1
57	Shawn Heins	1	0	1
58	Tyler Kennedy	1	0	1
59	Chris Kontos	1	0	1
60	Joe Mullen	1	0	1
61	Fredrik Olausson	1	0	1
62	Randy Robitaille	1	0	1
63	Ulf Samuelsson	1	0	1
64	Doug Shedden	1	0	1
65	Charlie Simmer	1	0	1
66	Marc Bergevin	0	1	1
67	John Chabot	0	1	1
68	Ron Duguay	0	1	1
69	Mark Eaton	0	1	1
70	Nils Ekman	0	1	1
71	Bob Errey	0	1	1
72	Rico Fata	0	1	1
73	Andrew Ference	0	1	1
74	Lee Giffin	0	1	1
75	Alex Goligoski	0	1	1
76	Bill Guerin	0	1	1
77	Dave Hannan	0	1	1
78	Rick Kehoe	0	1	1
79	Milan Kraft	0	1	1
80	Janne Laukkanen	0	1	1
81	Kris Letang	0	1	1
82	Norm Maciver	0	1	1
83	Josef Melichar	0	1	1
84	Tom O'Regan	0	1	1
85	Michel Ouellet	0	1	1
86	Wilf Paiement	0	1	1
87	Lasse Pirjeta	0	1	1
88	Steve Poapst	0	1	1
89	Stephane Richer	0	1	1
90	Gary Rissling	0	1	1
91	Gordie Roberts	0	1	1
92	Miroslav Satan	0	1	1
93	Ville Siren	0	1	1
94	Tony Tanti	0	1	1
95	Rick Tocchet	0	1	1

Penguins Season-by-Season Shootout Records

YEAR	OVERALL GP	W	L	HOME GP	W	L	ROAD GP	W	L
2005–06	7	1	6	4	1	3	3	0	3
2006–07	16	10	6	8	5	3	8	5	3
2007–08	11	7	4	5	2	3	6	5	1
2008–09	12	6	6	5	3	2	7	3	4
2009–10	10	8	2	4	3	1	6	5	1
TOTALS	**56**	**32**	**24**	**26**	**14**	**12**	**30**	**18**	**12**

Penguins All-Time Shootout Records vs. Each Team

TEAM	SHOOTOUTS AGAINST	W–L	TEAM	SHOOTOUTS AGAINST	W–L
Atlanta	3	1–2	Nashville	1	0–1
Boston	4	2–2	New Jersey	1	0–1
Buffalo	3	3–0	NY Islanders	7	2–5
Calgary	1	1–0	NY Rangers	4	1–3
Carolina	3	2–1	Ottawa	4	3–1
Chicago	1	1–0	Philadelphia	4	4–0
Columbus	2	1–1	San Jose	2	1–1
Dallas	1	1–0	Tampa Bay	2	0–2
Detroit	1	1–0	Toronto	1	1–0
Florida	2	2–0	Vancouver	1	1–0
Minnesota	1	0–1	Washington	4	2–2
Montreal	3	2–1	**TOTALS**	**56**	**32–24**

Penguins Shootout Wins and Losses

DATE	OPPONENT	W/L	WINNING GOAL	WINNING GOALIE	LOSING GOALIE	SHOOTOUT SCORE	FINAL SCORE
10/7/05	at Carolina	L	Stillman	Ward	Caron	0–1	2–3
11/10/05	vs. Montreal	W	Crosby	Thibault	Theodore	1–0	3–2
11/14/05	vs. NY Islanders	L	Blake	DiPietro	Thibault	2–3	2–3
1/26/06	at NY Islanders	L	Satan	Dubielewicz	Caron	0–1	3–4
2/4/06	vs. NY Islanders	L	Satan	DiPietro	Fleury	0–2	4–5
3/7/06	vs. Tampa Bay	L	Richards	Grahame	Fleury	0–2	4–5
4/15/06	at NY Islanders	L	Nilsson	DiPietro	Caron	3–4	4–5
11/22/06	vs. Boston	L	Sturm	Thomas	Fleury	0–1	3–4
12/7/06	at NY Rangers	L	Shanahan	Lundqvist	Fleury	0–1	2–3
12/11/06	at Washington	W	Malkin	Fleury	Kolzig	2–1	5–4
12/21/06	at Atlanta	L	Kozlov	Lehtonen	Thibault	0–2	3–4
1/7/07	vs. Tampa Bay	L	St. Louis	Holmqvist	Fleury	0–1	2–3
1/18/07	at Boston	L	Kessel	Toivonen	Fleury	1–2	4–5
1/26/07	at Dallas	W	Christensen	Fleury	Turco	1–0	4–3
2/1/07	vs. Montreal	W	Malkin	Fleury	Aebischer	2–1	5–4
2/8/07	at Philadelphia	W	Crosby	Fleury	Niittymaki	1–0	5–4
2/14/07	vs. Chicago	W	Christensen	Fleury	Khabibulin	2–0	5–4
3/1/07	at NY Rangers	W	Crosby	Fleury	Lundqvist	1–0	4–3
3/4/07	vs. Philadelphia	W	Christensen	Fleury	Biron	2–0	4–3
3/6/07	at Ottawa	W	Crosby	Thibault	Emery	2–1	5–4
3/8/07	vs. New Jersey	L	Elias	Brodeur	Fleury	0–1	3–4
3/13/07	vs. Buffalo	W	Crosby	Fleury	Miller	2–1	5–4
3/18/07	vs. Ottawa	W	Ruutu	Fleury	Emery	1–0	4–3
10/19/07	vs. Carolina	W	Crosby	Sabourin	Ward	3–2	4–3
10/27/07	vs. Montreal	L	Markov	Price	Sabourin	0–1	3–4
11/22/07	at Ottawa	W	Ruutu	Sabourin	Gerber	2–1	6–5
12/6/07	at Calgary	W	Letang	Sabourin	Kiprusoff	2–1	3–2
12/8/07	at Vancouver	W	Letang	Sabourin	Luongo	2–1	2–1
12/20/07	at Boston	W	Christensen	Conklin	Thomas	2–0	5–4
1/1/08	at Buffalo	W	Crosby	Conklin	Miller	2–1	2–1
1/12/08	at Atlanta	L	Recchi	Lehtonen	Conklin	0–1	2–3
1/21/08	vs. Washington	L	Semin	Kolzig	Conklin	1–2	5–6
2/24/08	vs. San Jose	L	Roenick	Nabokov	Conklin	2–3	1–2
3/2/08	vs. Atlanta	W	Letang	Fleury	Lehtonen	1–0	3–2
10/20/08	at Boston	W	Malkin	Sabourin	Thomas	2–1	2–1
10/25/08	at NY Rangers	L	Sjostrom	Lundqvist	Fleury	0–1	2–3
11/8/08	at NY Islanders	W	Sykora	Sabourin	MacDonald	1–0	4–3
11/13/08	vs. Philadelphia	W	Goligoski	Sabourin	Biron	1–0	5–4
11/18/08	vs. Minnesota	L	Zidlicky	Backstrom	Sabourin	0–1	1–2
12/3/08	at NY Rangers	L	Zherdev	Lundqvist	Sabourin	1–3	2–3
2/11/09	vs. San Jose	W	Crosby	Fleury	Boucher	1–0	2–1
2/16/09	at NY Islanders	L	Tambellini	MacDonald	Fleury	1–2	2–3
3/8/09	at Washington	W	Crosby	Fleury	Theodore	1–0	4–3
3/10/09	vs. Florida	W	Letang	Fleury	Vokoun	2–0	4–3
3/12/09	at Columbus	L	Huselius	Mason	Fleury	0–1	3–4
3/14/09	vs. Ottawa	L	Comrie	Elliott	Fleury	1–2	3–4
10/03/09	at NY Islanders	W	Letang	Fleury	Roloson	2–0	4–3
10/14/09	at Carolina	W	Kunitz	Fleury	Ward	2–1	3–2
10/23/09	vs. Florida	W	Crosby	Johnson	Vokoun	1–0	3–2
10/30/09	at Columbus	W	Crosby	Johnson	Mason	1–0	4–3
12/17/09	at Philadelphia	W	Letang	Fleury	Boucher	2–0	3–2
12/19/09	at Buffalo	W	Letang	Fleury	Lalime	1–0	2–1
1/31/10	vs. Detroit	W	Crosby	Fleury	Howard	2–0	2–1
2/14/10	vs. Nashville	L	O'Reilly	Ellis	Fleury	0–2	3–4
3/24/10	at Washington	L	Knuble	Theodore	Fleury	2–3	3–4
3/28/10	vs. Toronto	W	Crosby	Fleury	Giguere	2–0	5–4

Penguins All-Time Shootout Scoring

YEAR	GOALS	OVERALL SHOTS	PCT.	GOALS	HOME SHOTS	PCT.	GOALS	ROAD SHOTS	PCT.
2005–06	6	28	21.4	3	16	18.8	3	12	25.0
2006–07	17	47	36.2	9	24	37.5	8	23	34.8
2007–08	17	44	38.6	7	20	35.0	10	24	41.7
2008–09	11	40	27.5	5	20	25.0	6	20	30.0
2009–10	15	29	51.7	5	11	45.5	10	18	55.6
TOTALS	**66**	**188**	**35.1**	**29**	**91**	**31.9**	**37**	**97**	**38.1**

Penguins Shootout Scoring

PLAYER	G	S	PCT	PLAYER	G	S	PCT
Pascal Dupuis	1	1	1.0	Bill Guerin	0	3	0.0
Erik Christensen	14	23	60.9	Mario Lemieux	0	3	0.0
Jarkko Ruutu	4	8	50.0	Mark Recchi	0	3	0.0
Kris Letang	11	26	42.3	Ryan Malone	0	2	0.0
Sidney Crosby	20	48	41.7	Ziggy Palffy	0	2	0.0
Petr Sykora	5	15	33.3	Nils Ekman	0	1	0.0
Alex Goligoski	1	3	33.3	Andy Hilbert	0	1	0.0
Chris Kunitz	1	3	33.3	Konstantin Koltsov	0	1	0.0
Ryan Whitney	1	3	33.3	John LeClair	0	1	0.0
Michel Ouellet	1	4	25.0	Lasse Pirjeta	0	1	0.0
Evgeni Malkin	6	26	23.1	Jani Rita	0	1	0.0
Sergei Gonchar	1	5	20.0				
Miroslav Satan	0	4	0.0	**TOTALS**	**66**	**188**	**35.1**

Penguins Shootout Goaltending

PLAYER	RECORD	SHOTS	SAVES	GOALS	PCT.
Brent Johnson	2–0	6	6	0	1.000
Dany Sabourin	7–3	45	34	11	.756
Marc-Andre Fleury	19–13	92	67	25	.728
Jocelyn Thibault	2–2	17	11	6	.647
Ty Conklin	2–3	15	8	7	.533
Sebastien Caron	0–3	10	4	6	.400
TOTALS	**32–24**	**185**	**130**	**55**	**.703**

Stanley Cup Playoffs

Penguins Playoff Records

SERIES RESULTS

Season	Opponent	Series	Result
1969–70	Oakland	Stanley Cup Quarterfinals	Won 4 games to 0
	St. Louis	Stanley Cup Semifinals	Lost 4 games to 2
1971–72	Chicago	Stanley Cup Quarterfinals	Lost 4 games to 0
1974–75	St. Louis	Stanley Cup Preliminary Round	Won 2 games to 0
	NY Islanders	Stanley Cup Quarterfinals	Lost 4 games to 3
1975–76	Toronto	Stanley Cup Preliminary Round	Lost 2 games to 1
1976–77	Toronto	Stanley Cup Preliminary Round	Lost 2 games to 1
1978–79	Buffalo	Stanley Cup Preliminary Round	Won 2 games to 1
	Boston	Stanley Cup Quarterfinals	Lost 4 games to 0
1979–80	Boston	Stanley Cup Preliminary Round	Lost 3 games to 2
1980–81	St. Louis	Stanley Cup Preliminary Round	Lost 3 games to 2
1981–82	NY Islanders	Patrick Division Semifinals	Lost 3 games to 2
1988–89	NY Rangers	Patrick Division Semifinals	Won 4 games to 0
	Philadelphia	Patrick Division Finals	Lost 4 games to 3
1990–91	New Jersey	Patrick Division Semifinals	Won 4 games to 3
	Washington	Patrick Division Finals	Won 4 games to 1
	Boston	Wales Conference Finals	Won 4 games to 2
	Minnesota	**Stanley Cup Finals**	**Won 4 games to 2**
1991–92	Washington	Patrick Division Semifinals	Won 4 games to 3
	NY Rangers	Patrick Division Finals	Won 4 games to 2
	Boston	Wales Conference Finals	Won 4 games to 0
	Chicago	**Stanley Cup Finals**	**Won 4 games to 0**
1992–93	New Jersey	Patrick Division Semifinals	Won 4 games to 1
	NY Islanders	Patrick Division Finals	Lost 4 games to 3
1993–94	Washington	Eastern Conference Quarterfinals	Lost 4 games to 2
1994–95	Washington	Eastern Conference Quarterfinals	Won 4 games to 3
	New Jersey	Eastern Conference Semifinals	Lost 4 games to 1

Elvis (Scott Luff) and Phil Bourque celebrate the Pens' first Cup in 1991.

Stanley Cup Playoffs—Continued

Season	Opponent	Series	Result
1995–96	Washington	Eastern Conference Quarterfinals	Won 4 games to 2
	NY Rangers	Eastern Conference Semifinals	Won 4 games to 1
	Florida	Eastern Conference Finals	Lost 4 games to 3
1996–97	Philadelphia	Eastern Conference Quarterfinals	Lost 4 games to 1
1997–98	Montreal	Eastern Conference Quarterfinals	Lost 4 games to 2
1998–99	New Jersey	Eastern Conference Quarterfinals	Won 4 games to 3
	Toronto	Eastern Conference Semifinals	Lost 4 games to 2
1999–00	Washington	Eastern Conference Quarterfinals	Won 4 games to 1
	Philadelphia	Eastern Conference Semifinals	Lost 4 games to 2
2000–01	Washington	Eastern Conference Quarterfinals	Won 4 games to 2
	Buffalo	Eastern Conference Semifinals	Won 4 games to 3
	New Jersey	Eastern Conference Finals	Lost 4 games to 1
2006–07	Ottawa	Eastern Conference Quarterfinals	Lost 4 games to 1
2007–08	Ottawa	Eastern Conference Quarterfinals	Won 4 games to 0
	NY Rangers	Eastern Conference Semifinals	Won 4 games to 1
	Philadelphia	Eastern Conference Finals	Won 4 games to 1
	Detroit	Stanley Cup Finals	Lost 4 games to 2
2008–09	Philadelphia	Eastern Conference Quarterfinals	Won 4 games to 2
	Washington	Eastern Conference Semifinals	Won 4 games to 3
	Carolina	Eastern Conference Finals	Won 4 games to 0
	Detroit	**Stanley Cup Finals**	**Won 4 games to 3**
2009–10	Ottawa	Eastern Conference Quarterfinals	Won 4 games to 2
	Montreal	Eastern Conference Semifinals	Lost 4 games to 3

Penguins All-Time Playoff Records Against Opponents

OPPONENT	SERIES	W	L	GP	W	L	GF	GA
Washington	8	7	1	49	30	19	164	143
New Jersey	5	3	2	29	14	15	80	86
Philadelphia	5	2	3	29	14	15	89	91
NY Rangers	4	4	0	20	16	4	79	57
Boston	4	2	2	19	10	9	67	62
St. Louis	3	1	2	13	6	7	40	45
NY Islanders	3	0	3	19	8	11	58	67
Toronto	3	0	3	12	4	8	27	39
Buffalo	2	2	0	10	6	4	26	26
Chicago	2	1	1	8	4	4	23	24
Ottawa	3	2	1	15	9	6	50	42
Detroit	2	1	1	13	6	7	24	34
Carolina	1	1	0	4	4	0	20	9
Minn./Dal.	1	1	0	6	4	2	28	16
Oakland	1	1	0	4	4	0	13	6
Florida	1	0	1	7	3	4	15	20
Montreal	2	0	2	13	5	8	33	37
TOTAL	**50**	**28**	**22**	**270**	**147**	**123**	**836**	**804**

Penguins Playoff Records By Series

SERIES	PLAYED	W–L
Record in Stanley Cup Finals	4	3–1
Record in Semifinals/Conference Finals	7	4–3
Record in Quarterfinals/Division Finals/Conference Semifinals	16	7–9
Record in Preliminary Round/Division Semifinals/Conference Quarterfinals	23	14–9
Record in Two-Game Series	1	1–0
Record in Three-Game Series	3	1–2
Record in Four-Game Series	8	6–2
Record in Five-Game Series	13	6–7
Record in Six-Game Series	13	7–6
Record in Seven-Game Series	12	7–5

Penguins Playoff Records By Game

	OVERALL	HOME	ROAD
Game 1	23–27	16–11	7–16
Game 2	31–19	22–6	9–13
Game 3	31–18	12–10	19–8
Game 4	22–24	8–12	14–12
Game 5	20–18	13–6	7–12
Game 6	13–12	7–5	6–7
Game 7	7–5	2–5	5–0
TOTAL	**147–123**	**80–55**	**67–68**

Penguins Playoff Coaching Records

COACH	SERIES	W–L	GAMES	W–L
Dan Bylsma	6	5–1	37	23–14
Bob Johnson	4	4–0	24	16–8
Scotty Bowman	6	5–1	33	23–10
Michel Therrien	5	3–2	25	15–10
Ivan Hlinka	3	2–1	18	9–9
Eddie Johnston	8	3–5	46	22–24
Gene Ubriaco	2	1–1	11	7–4
Herb Brooks	2	1–1	11	6–5
Marc Bolieau	2	1–1	9	5–4
Kevin Constantine	3	1–2	19	8–11
Red Kelly	3	1–2	14	6–8
Johnny Wilson	3	1–2	12	4–8
Ken Schinkel	2	0–2	6	2–4
Craig Patrick	1	0–1	5	1–4
TOTAL	**50**	**28–22**	**270**	**147–123**

Penguins All-Time Playoff Scoring Leaders

GAMES

PLAYOFF		YEAR	CAREER	
22 Players Tied with 24			Jaromir Jagr	140
			Mario Lemieux	107
			Kevin Stevens	103
			Ron Francis	97
			Larry Murphy	74
			Troy Loney	66
			Ulf Samuelsson	66
			Martin Straka	65
			Sidney Crosby	62
			Evgeni Malkin	62
			Joe Mullen	62
			Brooks Orpik	62

GOALS

PLAYOFF		YEAR	CAREER	
Kevin Stevens	17	1991	Mario Lemieux	76
Mario Lemieux	16	1991	Jaromir Jagr	65
Mario Lemieux	16	1992	Kevin Stevens	46
Sidney Crosby	15	2009	Ron Francis	32
Evgeni Malkin	14	2009	Sidney Crosby	30
Kevin Stevens	13	1992	Evgeni Malkin	29
Mario Lemieux	12	1989	Martin Straka	19
Marian Hossa	12	2008	Joe Mullen	16
Jaromir Jagr	11	1992	Jordan Staal	16
Jaromir Jagr	11	1996	Larry Murphy	15
Mario Lemieux	11	1996	Rick Tocchet	15

Max Talbot (center) scored eight even-strength goals during the 2009 playoffs.

Penguins All-Time Playoff Scoring Leaders—Continued

ASSISTS

PLAYOFF		YEAR	CAREER	
Mario Lemieux	28	1991	Mario Lemieux	96
Mark Recchi	24	1991	Jaromir Jagr	82
Evgeni Malkin	22	2009	Ron Francis	68
Sidney Crosby	21	2008	Kevin Stevens	60
Ron Francis	19	1992	Larry Murphy	57
Larry Murphy	18	1991	Sidney Crosby	52
Mario Lemieux	18	1992	Evgeni Malkin	44
Kevin Stevens	16	1991	Sergei Gonchar	37
Mario Lemieux	16	1996	Mark Recchi	28
Sidney Crosby	16	2009	Martin Straka	27

POINTS

PLAYOFF		YEAR	CAREER	
Mario Lemieux	44	1991	Mario Lemieux	172
Evgeni Malkin	36	2009	Jaromir Jagr	147
Mark Recchi	34	1991	Kevin Stevens	106
Mario Lemieux	34	1992	Ron Francis	100
Kevin Stevens	33	1991	Sidney Crosby	82
Sidney Crosby	31	2009	Evgeni Malkin	73
Kevin Stevens	28	1992	Larry Murphy	72
Ron Francis	27	1992	Martin Straka	46
Mario Lemieux	27	1996	Sergei Gonchar	44
Sidney Crosby	27	2008	Mark Recchi	38

EVEN-STRENGTH GOALS

PLAYOFF		YEAR	CAREER	
Kevin Stevens	10	1991	Jaromir Jagr	44
Sidney Crosby	10	2009	Mario Lemieux	40
Jaromir Jagr	9	1992	Kevin Stevens	26
Kevin Stevens	9	1992	Ron Francis	24
Mario Lemieux	8	1991	Sidney Crosby	21
Max Talbot	8	2009	Joe Mullen	13
Ron Francis	7	1991	Martin Straka	13
Joe Mullen	7	1991	Evgeni Malkin	12
Jaromir Jagr	7	1995	Jordan Staal	12
Luc Robitaille	7	1995	Max Talbot	12
Mario Lemieux	7	1996		
Marian Hossa	7	2008		
Ruslan Fedotenko	7	2009		
Evgeni Malkin	7	2009		

Penguins All-Time Playoff Scoring Leaders—Continued

POWER-PLAY GOALS

PLAYOFF		YEAR	CAREER	
Mario Lemieux	8	1992	Mario Lemieux	29
Mario Lemieux	7	1989	Kevin Stevens	20
Kevin Stevens	7	1991	Jaromir Jagr	19
Evgeni Malkin	7	2009	Evgeni Malkin	16
Mario Lemieux	6	1991	Larry Murphy	10
Mark Recchi	5	1991	Sidney Crosby	9
Jaromir Jagr	5	1996	Ron Francis	8
Marian Hossa	5	2008	Kristopher Letang	6
Evgeni Malkin	5	2008	Five Players Tied with 5	
Sidney Crosby	5	2009		

SHORTHANDED GOALS

PLAYOFF		YEAR	CAREER	
Mario Lemieux	2	1991	Mario Lemieux	7
Mario Lemieux	2	1992	Bob Errey	2
Twenty-one Players Tied with 1			Jaromir Jagr	2
			Ed Olczyk	2
			Twelve Players Tied with 1	

GAME-WINNING GOALS

PLAYOFF		YEAR	CAREER	
Mario Lemieux	5	1992	Jaromir Jagr	14
Ron Francis	4	1991	Mario Lemieux	11
Kevin Stevens	4	1991	Kevin Stevens	9
Jaromir Jagr	4	1992	Ron Francis	8
Jaromir Jagr	4	2000	Evgeni Malkin	7
Michel Briere	3	1970	Sidney Crosby	5
Rob Brown	3	1989	Max Talbot	4
Kevin Stevens	3	1992	Michel Briere	3
Mario Lemieux	3	2001	Rob Brown	3
Evgeni Malkin	3	2008	Sergei Gonchar	3
Tyler Kennedy	3	2009	Tyler Kennedy	3
Evgeni Malkin	3	2009		

SHOTS ON GOAL*

PLAYOFF		YEAR	CAREER	
Evgeni Malkin	104	2009	Jaromir Jagr	461
Mario Lemieux	93	1991	Mario Lemieux	402
Kevin Stevens	86	1992	Kevin Stevens	296
Kevin Stevens	83	1991	Evgeni Malkin	247
Sidney Crosby	79	2009	Ron Francis	219
Mario Lemieux	78	1996	Sidney Crosby	199
Marian Hossa	76	2008	Larry Murphy	199
Evgeni Malkin	75	2008	Jordan Staal	129
Jaromir Jagr	74	1996	Tyler Kennedy	124
Bill Guerin	70	2009	Sergei Gonchar	119

*Shots on goal became an official NHL playoff statistic in 1983–84

Penguins All-Time Playoff Scoring Leaders—Continued

PENALTY MINUTES

PLAYOFF		YEAR	CAREER	
Phil Bourque	66	1989	Kevin Stevens	170
Gordie Roberts	63	1991	Ulf Samuelsson	123
Kevin Stevens	53	1991	Jaromir Jagr	121
Tracy Pratt	51	1970	Phil Bourque	107
Evgeni Malkin	51	2009	Troy Loney	97
Randy Hillier	49	1989	Gordie Roberts	95
Peter Taglianetti	49	1991	Evgeni Malkin	89
Bryan Trottier	49	1991	Mario Lemieux	87
Jim Johnson	44	1989	Peter Taglianetti	83
Larry Murphy	44	1991	Randy Hillier	73
			Larry Murphy	73
			Max Talbot	73

Rick Tocchet (left) and Kevin Stevens (right) revel with the Cup in 1992.

Ulf Samuelsson (shown roughing up Minnesota's Brian Bellows) is second in career playoff penalty minutes.

Penguins All-Time Playoff Goaltending Leaders

GAMES

PLAYOFF		YEAR	CAREER	
Marc-Andre Fleury	24	2009	Tom Barrasso	101
Tom Barrasso	21	1992	Marc-Andre Fleury	62
Tom Barrasso	20	1991	Ken Wregget	26
Marc-Andre Fleury	20	2008	Johan Hedberg	18
Johan Hedberg	18	2001	Ron Tugnutt	11
Tom Barrasso	13	1999	Denis Herron	10
Marc-Andre Fleury	13	2010	Greg Millen	10
Tom Barrasso	12	1993	Gary Inness	9
Tom Barrasso	11	1989	Les Binkley	7
Ken Wregget	11	1995	Michel Dion	5
Ron Tugnutt	11	2000	Frank Pietrangelo	5

MINUTES PLAYED

PLAYOFF		YEAR	CAREER	
Marc-Andre Fleury	1,447	2009	Tom Barrasso	5,918
Marc-Andre Fleury	1,251	2008	Marc-Andre Fleury	3,783
Tom Barrasso	1,233	1992	Ken Wregget	1,597
Tom Barrasso	1,175	1991	Johan Hedberg	1,123
Johan Hedberg	1,123	2001	Ron Tugnutt	746
Marc-Andre Fleury	798	2010	Greg Millen	625
Tom Barrasso	787	1999	Denis Herron	601
Ron Tugnutt	746	2000	Gary Inness	540
Tom Barrasso	722	1993	Les Binkley	428
Ken Wregget	661	1995	Michel Dion	310

WINS

PLAYOFF		YEAR	CAREER	
Tom Barrasso	16	1992	Tom Barrasso	56
Marc-Andre Fleury	16	2009	Marc-Andre Fleury	38
Marc-Andre Fleury	14	2008	Ken Wregget	13
Tom Barrasso	12	1991	Johan Hedberg	9
Johan Hedberg	9	2001	Ron Tugnutt	6
Tom Barrasso	7	1989	Les Binkley	5
Tom Barrasso	7	1993	Gary Inness	5
Ken Wregget	7	1996	Greg Millen	4
Marc-Andre Fleury	7	2010	Frank Pietrangelo	4
Tom Barrasso	6	1999	Denis Herron	3
Ron Tugnutt	6	2000		

Penguins All-Time Playoff Goaltending Leaders—Continued

LOSSES

PLAYOFF		YEAR	CAREER	
Johan Hedberg	9	2001	Tom Barrasso	42
Marc-Andre Fleury	8	2009	Marc-Andre Fleury	24
Tom Barrasso	7	1991	Ken Wregget	12
Tom Barrasso	7	1999	Johan Hedberg	9
Ken Wregget	6	1995	Denis Herron	7
Marc-Andre Fleury	6	2008	Greg Millen	6
Marc-Andre Fleury	6	2010	Ron Tugnutt	5
Denis Herron	5	1979	Gary Inness	4
Tom Barrasso	5	1992	Jim Rutherford	4
Tom Barrasso	5	1993	Michel Dion	3
Tom Barrasso	5	1996		
Ron Tugnutt	5	2000		

WIN PERCENTAGE

PLAYOFF (minimum of 3 games)		YEAR	CAREER (minimum of 5 games)	
Frank Pietrangelo	.800	1991	Frank Pietrangelo	.800
Ken Wregget	.778	1996	Les Binkley	.714
Tom Barrasso	.762	1992	Marc-Andre Fleury	.613
Les Binkley	.714	1970	Tom Barrasso	.571
Marc-Andre Fleury	.700	2008	Gary Inness	.556
Marc-Andre Fleury	.667	2009	Ron Tugnutt	.545
Tom Barrasso	.636	1989	Ken Wregget	.520
Tom Barrasso	.632	1991	Johan Hedberg	.500
Tom Barrasso	.583	1993	Michel Dion	.400
Gary Inness	.556	1975	Greg Millen	.400

GOALS AGAINST

PLAYOFF		YEAR	CAREER	
Marc-Andre Fleury	63	2009	Tom Barrasso	287
Tom Barrasso	58	1992	Marc-Andre Fleury	159
Tom Barrasso	51	1991	Ken Wregget	78
Johan Hedberg	43	2001	Johan Hedberg	43
Marc-Andre Fleury	41	2008	Greg Millen	40
Tom Barrasso	40	1989	Denis Herron	35
Marc-Andre Fleury	37	2010	Gary Inness	24
Tom Barrasso	35	1993	Michel Dion	22
Tom Barrasso	35	1999	Ron Tugnutt	22
Ken Wregget	33	1995	Les Binkley	15
Tom Barrasso	26	1996	Frank Pietrangelo	15

Penguins All-Time Playoff Goaltending Leaders—Continued

GOALS-AGAINST AVERAGE

PLAYOFF (minimum of 3 games)		YEAR	CAREER (minimum of 5 games)	
Ron Tugnutt	1.77	2000	Ron Tugnutt	1.77
Marc-Andre Fleury	1.97	2008	Les Binkley	2.10
Les Binkley	2.10	1970	Johan Hedberg	2.30
Ken Wregget	2.30	1996	Marc-Andre Fleury	2.52
Johan Hedberg	2.30	2001	Gary Inness	2.67
Tom Barrasso	2.60	1991	Tom Barrasso	2.91
Marc-Andre Fleury	2.61	2009	Ken Wregget	2.93
Gary Inness	2.67	1975	Frank Pietrangelo	3.12
Michel Plasse	2.67	1976	Denis Herron	3.49
Tom Barrasso	2.67	1999	Greg Millen	3.84

SHUTOUTS

PLAYOFF		YEAR	CAREER	
Marc-Andre Fleury	3	2008	Tom Barrasso	6
Tom Barrasso	2	1993	Marc-Andre Fleury	4
Ron Tugnutt	2	2000	Johan Hedberg	2
Johan Hedberg	2	2001	Ron Tugnutt	2
Michel Plasse	1	1976	Frank Pietrangelo	1
Frank Pietrangelo	1	1991	Michel Plasse	1
Tom Barrasso	1	1991	Ken Wregget	1
Tom Barrasso	1	1992		
Ken Wregget	1	1995		
Tom Barrasso	1	1996		
Tom Barrasso	1	1999		
Marc-Andre Fleury	1	2010		

SAVES*

PLAYOFF		YEAR	CAREER	
Marc-Andre Fleury	623	2009	Tom Barrasso	2,784
Tom Barrasso	578	1991	Marc-Andre Fleury	1,626
Marc-Andre Fleury	569	2008	Ken Wregget	826
Tom Barrasso	564	1992	Johan Hedberg	439
Johan Hedberg	439	2001	Ron Tugnutt	376
Ron Tugnutt	376	2000	Denis Herron	298
Tom Barrasso	349	1989	Greg Millen	297
Tom Barrasso	335	1993	Gary Inness	273
Ken Wregget	316	1995	Les Binkley	183
Tom Barrasso	315	1999	Michel Dion	164

* Saves became an official NHL statistic in 1983–84.

Penguins All-Time Playoff Goaltending Leaders—Continued

SAVE PERCENTAGE*

PLAYOFF (minimum of 3 games)		YEAR	CAREER (minimum of 5 games)	
Ron Tugnutt	.945	2000	Ron Tugnutt	.945
Marc-Andre Fleury	.933	2008	Les Binkley	.924
Ken Wregget	.930	1996	Gary Inness	.919
Les Binkley	.924	1970	Ken Wregget	.914
Tom Barrasso	.923	1996	Marc-Andre Fleury	.911
Gary Inness	.919	1975	Johan Hedberg	.911
Tom Barrasso	.919	1991	Tom Barrasso	.907
Ken Wregget	.915	1997	Frank Pietrangelo	.899
Johan Hedberg	.911	2001	Denis Herron	.895
Marc-Andre Fleury	.908	2009	Michel Dion	.882

* Save percentage became an official NHL statistic in 1983–84.

Penguins Season-by-Season Playoff Scoring Leaders

Season	Goals		Assists		Points	
1969–70	Michel Briere	5	Ron Schock	6	Michel Briere	8
1971–72	Bob Leiter	3	Darryl Edestrand	2	Bob Leiter	3
			Bryan Hextall	2		
			Greg Polis	2		
1974–75	Bob Kelly	5	Ron Stackhouse	6	Bob Kelly	8
					Ron Stackhouse	8
1975–76	Stan Gilbertson	1	Stan Gilbertson	1	Stan Gilbertson	2
	Vic Hadfield	1	Syl Apps	1		
	Lowell MacDonald	1	Pierre Larouche	1		
			Ron Schock	1		
			Ed Van Impe	1		
			Barry Wilkins	1		
1976–77	Jean Pronovost	2	Pierre Larouche	3	Jean Pronovost	3
	Ron Stackhouse	2			Ron Stackhouse	3
					Pierre Larouche	3
					Lowell MacDonald	3
1978–79	Orest Kindrachuk	4	Tom Bladon	4	Orest Kindrachuk	5
			Colin Campbell	4	Colin Campbell	5
1979–80	Rick Kehoe	2	Rick Kehoe	5	Rick Kehoe	7
	Mark Johnson	2				
	Ross Lonsberry	2				
	Rod Schutt	2				
1980–81	Randy Carlyle	4	George Ferguson	6	Randy Carlyle	9
1981–82	Pat Boutette	3	Paul Gardner	5	Paul Gardner	6
1988–89	Mario Lemieux	12	Paul Coffey	13	Mario Lemieux	19
1990–91	**Kevin Stevens**	**17***	**Mario Lemieux**	**28***	**Mario Lemieux**	**44***
1991–92	**Mario Lemieux**	**16***	**Ron Francis**	**19***	**Mario Lemieux**	**34***
1992–93	Mario Lemieux	8	Ron Francis	11	Mario Lemieux	18
			Larry Murphy	11		
			Kevin Stevens	11		
1993–94	Mario Lemieux	4	Larry Murphy	5	Mario Lemieux	7
1994–95	Jaromir Jagr	10	Ron Francis	13	Ron Francis	19
			Larry Murphy	13		
1995–96	Mario Lemieux	11	Mario Lemieux	16	Mario Lemieux	27
	Jaromir Jagr	11				
1996–97	Jaromir Jagr	4	Jaromir Jagr	4	Jaromir Jagr	8
1997–98	Jaromir Jagr	4	Jaromir Jagr	5	Jaromir Jagr	9
			Ron Francis	5		
1998–99	Martin Straka	6	Martin Straka	9	Martin Straka	15
1999–00	Jaromir Jagr	8	Martin Straka	9	Jaromir Jagr	16
2000–01	Mario Lemieux	6	Mario Lemieux	11	Mario Lemieux	17
2006–07	Sidney Crosby	3	Evgeni Malkin	4	Sidney Crosby	5
	Jordan Staal	3	Mark Recchi	4		
2007–08	Marian Hossa	12	**Sidney Crosby**	**21***	**Sidney Crosby**	**27****
2008–09	**Sidney Crosby**	**15***	**Evgeni Malkin**	**22***	**Evgeni Malkin**	**36***
2009–10	Sidney Crosby	6	Sidney Crosby	13	Sidney Crosby	19

* NHL Leader
**Tied for NHL Lead

Penguins Season-by-Season Playoff Goaltending Leaders

Season	Goals-Against Average[1]		Shutouts		Wins	
1969–70	Les Binkley	2.10	-	-	Les Binkley	5
1971–72	Jim Rutherford	3.50	-	-	-	-
1974–75	Gary Inness	2.67	-	-	Gary Inness	5
1975–76	Michel Plasse	2.67	Michel Plasse	1	Michel Plasse	1
1976–77	Denis Herron	3.67	-	-	Denis Herron	1
1978–79	Denis Herron	3.42	-	-	Denis Herron	2
1979–80	Greg Millen	4.20	-	-	Greg Millen	2
1980–81	Greg Millen	3.51	-	-	Greg Millen	2
1981–82	Michel Dion	4.26	-	-	Michel Dion	2
1988–89	Tom Barrasso	3.80	-	-	Tom Barrasso	7
1990–91	**Tom Barrasso**	**2.60***	**Tom Barrasso**	**1****	**Tom Barrasso**	**12***
			Frank Pietrangelo	**1****		
1991–92	Tom Barrasso	2.82	Tom Barrasso	1	**Tom Barrasso**	**16***
1992–93	Tom Barrasso	2.91	Tom Barrasso	2	Tom Barrasso	7
1993–94	Tom Barrasso	2.87	-	-	Tom Barrasso	2
1994–95	Ken Wregget	3.00	Ken Wregget	1	Ken Wregget	5
1995–96	Ken Wregget	2.30	Tom Barrasso	1	Ken Wregget	7
1996–97	Ken Wregget	3.64	-	-	Ken Wregget	1
1997–98	Tom Barrasso	2.71	-	-	Tom Barrasso	2
1998–99	Tom Barrasso	2.67	Tom Barrasso	1	Tom Barrasso	6
1999–00	Ron Tugnutt	1.77	Ron Tugnutt	2	Ron Tugnutt	6
2000–01	Johan Hedberg	2.30	Johan Hedberg	2	Johan Hedberg	9
2006–07	Marc-Andre Fleury	3.76	-	-	Marc-Andre Fleury	1
2007–08	Marc-Andre Fleury	1.97	**Marc-Andre Fleury**	**3****	**Marc-Andre Fleury**	**14****
2008–09	Marc-Andre Fleury	2.61	-	-	**Marc-Andre Fleury**	**16***
2009–10	Marc-Andre Fleury	2.78	Marc-Andre Fleury	1	Marc-Andre Fleury	7

* NHL Leader
** Tied for NHL Lead
(1) Minimum of 3 Games Played

Penguins Single-Season Playoff Records

	Player	Record	Season
Lowest goals-against average—goalie	Ron Tugnutt	1.77	1999–00
Most assists—center	Mario Lemieux	28	1990–91
Most assists—defenseman	Larry Murphy	18	1990–91
Most assists—goalie	Tom Barrasso	3	1992–93
Most assists—left wing	Kevin Stevens	16	1990–91
Most assists—right wing	Mark Recchi	24	1990–91
Most games—center	Ron Francis	24	1990–91
	Sidney Crosby	24	2008–09
	Evgeni Malkin	24	2008–09
	Jordan Staal	24	2008–09
	Max Talbot	24	2008–09
Most games—defenseman	Gordie Roberts	24	1990–91
	Mark Eaton	24	2008–09
	Hal Gill	24	2008–09
	Brooks Orpik	24	2008–09
	Rob Scuderi	24	2008–09
Most games—goalie	Marc-Andre Fleury	24	2008–09
Most games—left wing	Phil Bourque	24	1990–91
	Bob Errey	24	1990–91
	Troy Loney	24	1990–91
	Kevin Stevens	24	1990–91
	Matt Cooke	24	2008–09
	Chris Kunitz	24	2008–09
Most games—right wing	Jaromir Jagr	24	1990–91
	Mark Recchi	24	1990–91
	Craig Adams	24	2008–09
	Ruslan Fedotenko	24	2008–09
	Bill Guerin	24	2008–09
	Tyler Kennedy	24	2008–09
Most goals—center	Mario Lemieux	16	1990–91
	Mario Lemieux	16	1991–92
Most goals—defenseman	Larry Murphy	6	1991–92
Most goals—left wing	Kevin Stevens	17	1990–91
Most goals—right wing	Marian Hossa	12	2007–08
Most penalty minutes—center	Evgeni Malkin	51	2008–09
Most penalty minutes—defenseman	Gordie Roberts	63	1990–91
Most penalty minutes—goalie	Tom Barrasso	8	1988–89
	Tom Barrasso	8	1995–96
Most penalty minutes—left wing	Phil Bourque	66	1988–89
Most penalty minutes—right wing	Mark Recchi	33	1990–91
Most points—center	Mario Lemieux	44	1990–91
Most points—defenseman	Larry Murphy	23	1990–91
Most points—goalie	Tom Barrasso	3	1992–93
Most points—left wing	Kevin Stevens	33	1990–91
Most points—right wing	Mark Recchi	34	1990–91
Most shutouts—goalie	Marc-Andre Fleury	3	2007–08
Most wins—goalie	**Tom Barrasso**	**16****	1991–92
	Marc-Andre Fleury	**16****	2008–09

** Ties NHL Record

Penguins Individual Playoff Records

PERIOD

Goals	4*	4/25/89 vs. Philadelphia	Mario Lemieux
Assists	3	4/25/89 vs. Philadelphia	Mario Lemieux
		4/19/91 vs. Washington	Paul Coffey
		5/8/95 vs. Washington	Ron Francis
Points	4*	4/25/89 vs. Philadelphia	Mario Lemieux
		4/23/92 vs. Washington	Mario Lemieux
Shots	7	4/11/91 vs. New Jersey	Larry Murphy
		4/16/08 at Ottawa	Marian Hossa
Penalties	6	4/13/80 at Boston	Kim Clackson
PIM	26	4/13/80 at Boston	Kim Clackson
Saves	27	4/21/97 vs. Philadelphia	Ken Wregget

GAME

Goals	5	4/25/89 vs. Philadelphia	Mario Lemieux
Assists	4	Eight Times–Last Time 4/11/08 vs. Ottawa	Sidney Crosby
Points	8*	4/25/89 vs. Philadelphia	Mario Lemieux
Shots	12	4/29/92 vs. Washington	Kevin Stevens
		4/24/96 at Washington	Jaromir Jagr
Penalties	8	4/13/80 at Boston	Kim Clackson
PIM	32	4/19/70 at St. Louis	Tracy Pratt
Saves	70	5/4/00 vs. Philadelphia	Ron Tugnutt

SERIES

Goals	9	1989 vs. Philadelphia	Mario Lemieux
Assists	11	1995 vs. Washington	Ron Francis
Points	17	1992 vs. Washington	Mario Lemieux
PIM	43	1970 vs. St. Louis	Tracy Pratt
		1989 vs. NY Rangers	Randy Hillier

CONSECUTIVE GAME STREAKS

Goals	7	4/26/96–5/11/96	Mario Lemieux
		5/3/91–5/17/91	Mario Lemieux
Assists	10	4/19/91–5/11/91	Mario Lemieux
Points	15	4/13/91–5/17/91	Mario Lemieux

*NHL Record

Penguins Playoff Records

SERIES

MOST GOALS—BOTH TEAMS

2-Game Series	15	1975	PIT 9–STL 6
3-Game Series	23	1977	TOR 13–PIT 10
4-Game Series	30	1989	PIT 19–NYR 11
5-Game Series	41	1981	PIT 21–STL 20
6-Game Series	45	1991	PIT 27–BOS 18
7-Game Series	55	1989	PHI 31–PIT 24
	55	1995	PIT 29–WSH 26

MOST GOALS—PITTSBURGH

2-Game Series	9	1975	vs. St. Louis
3-Game Series	10	1977	vs. Toronto
4-Game Series	20	2009	vs. Carolina
5-Game Series	23	1993	vs. New Jersey
6-Game Series	28	1991	vs. Minnesota
7-Game Series	29	1995	vs. Washington

MOST GOALS—OPPONENTS

2-Game Series	6	1975	by St. Louis
3-Game Series	13	1977	by Toronto
4-Game Series	16	1979	by Boston
5-Game Series	22	1982	by NY Islanders
6-Game Series	20	1994	by Washington
7-Game Series	31	1989	by Philadelphia

FEWEST GOALS—BOTH TEAMS

2-Game Series	15	1975	PIT 9–STL 6
3-Game Series	11	1976	TOR 8–PIT 3
4-Game Series	19	1970	PIT 13–OAK 6
5-Game Series	24	2001	NJ 17–PIT 7
6-Game Series	24	2001	PIT 14–WSH 10
7-Game Series	31	2009	DET 17–PIT 14

FEWEST GOALS—PITTSBURGH

2-Game Series	9	1975	vs. St. Louis
3-Game Series	3	1976	vs. Toronto
4-Game Series	7	1979	vs. Boston
5-Game Series	7	2001	vs. New Jersey
6-Game Series	10	1970	vs. St. Louis
7-Game Series	14	2009	vs. Detroit

FEWEST GOALS—OPPONENTS

2-Game Series	6	1975	St. Louis
3-Game Series	8	1976	Toronto
4-Game Series	5	2008	Ottawa
5-Game Series	8	2000	Washington
6-Game Series	10	2001	Washington
7-Game Series	17	2001	Buffalo
		2009	Detroit

MOST POWER-PLAY GOALS

Pittsburgh	11	1992	vs. Washington
Opponents	9	1989	Philadelphia
Both Teams	19	1989	PIT 10–PHI 9

MOST POWER-PLAY CHANCES

Pittsburgh	42	1989	vs. Philadelphia
	42	1995	vs. Washington
Opponents	44	1995	Washington
Both Teams	86	1995	WSH 44–PIT 42

MOST PENALTIES

Pittsburgh	85	1989	vs. Philadelphia
Opponents	95	1989	Philadelphia
Both Teams	180	1989	PHI 95–PIT 85

FEWEST PENALTIES

Pittsburgh	9	1975	vs. St. Louis
Opponents	14	2009	vs. Detroit
Both	24	1975	STL 15–PIT 9

MOST PENALTY MINUTES

Pittsburgh	242	1989	vs. Philadelphia
Opponents	270	1989	Philadelphia
Both Teams	512	1989	PHI 270–PIT 242

FEWEST PENALTY MINUTES

Pittsburgh	18	1975	vs. St. Louis
Opponents	30	2001	by New Jersey
Both Teams	61	1976	TOR 36–PIT 25

Penguins Playoff Records—Continued

GAME

LARGEST MARGIN OF VICTORY
Home	7	4/20/93, 7–0 vs. New Jersey
Road	8	5/25/91, 8–0 at Minnesota

LARGEST MARGIN OF DEFEAT
Home	5	4/13/80, 8–3 vs. Boston
	5	4/25/92, 7–2 vs. Washington
	5	5/19/01, 5–0 vs. New Jersey
Road	7	4/7/82, 8–1 at NY Islanders

MOST GOALS
Both Teams, Home	17	4/25/89, 10–7 win vs. PHI
Both Teams, Road	12	5/12/93, 7–5 loss at NYI
Pittsburgh, Home	10	4/25/89, 10–7 win vs. PHI
Pittsburgh, Road	8	5/25/91, 8–0 win vs. MIN
Opponent, Home	8	4/13/80, 8–3 loss vs. BOS
Opponent, Road	8	4/7/82, 8–1 loss at NYI

MOST POWER-PLAY GOALS
For	4	4/29/92 vs. Washington
Against	3	Eight Times, Last 6/6/09 at Detroit
Both Teams	5	4/18/01, PIT 2–WSH 3
	5	4/29/92, PIT 4–WSH 1
	5	4/23/92, PIT 3–WSH 2
	5	4/19/91, PIT 2–WSH 3

MOST POWER-PLAY CHANCES
For	12	4/23/92 vs. Washington
Against	11	4/23/92 vs. Washington
Both Teams	23	PIT 12–WSH 11

MOST SHORTHANDED GOALS
For	2	4/23/97 vs. Philadelphia
Against	2	Five Times, Last 4/26/97 at Philadelphia

MOST SHOTS
Pittsburgh, Regulation	53	4/11/08 vs. Ottawa
Pittsburgh, Overtime	65	4/24/96 at Washington
Opponent, Regulation	61	5/4/96 at Florida
Opponent, Overtime	72	5/4/00 vs. Philadelphia

MOST SAVES
Pittsburgh, Regulation	56	5/24/96 at Florida
Pittsburgh, Overtime	70	5/4/00 vs. Philadelphia
Opponent, Regulation	49	4/26/70 by St. Louis
Opponent, Overtime	61	4/24/96 by Washington

FEWEST SHOTS
Pittsburgh	13	5/4/99 at New Jersey
Opponent	16	4/23/70 by St. Louis

FEWEST SAVES
Pittsburgh	14	4/23/70 vs. St. Louis
Opponent	9	5/4/95 at New Jersey

MOST PENALTIES
Both Teams, Home	48	4/6/89, PIT 25–NYR 23
Both Teams, Road	37	4/29/00, PIT 15–PHI 22
Pittsburgh	25	4/6/89 vs. NY Rangers
Opponent	23	4/6/89 by NY Rangers

FEWEST PENALTIES
Both Teams, Home	5	5/17/01 PIT 3–NJ 2
Both Teams, Road	3	5/1/92 PIT 2–WSH 1
Pittsburgh	0	5/13/09 at Washington
Opponents	1	5/22/01 by New Jersey
	1	5/4/99 by New Jersey
	1	5/1/92 by Washington

MOST PENALTY MINUTES
Both Teams, Home	125	4/25/89 PHI 79–PIT 46
Both Teams, Road	154	4/29/00 PHI 104–PIT 50
Pittsburgh	83	4/19/70 at St. Louis
Opponent	104	4/29/00 at Philadelphia

FEWEST PENALTY MINUTES
Both Teams, Home	10	5/17/01, PIT 6–NJ 4
Both Teams, Road	6	5/1/92, PIT 4–WSH 2
Pittsburgh	0	5/13/09 at Washington
Opponent	2	5/22/01 by New Jersey
	2	5/4/99 at New Jersey

Penguins Playoff Records—Continued

PERIOD

MOST GOALS

Both Teams, Home	7	4/6/89	PIT 5–NYR 2
	7	4/25/89	PIT 6–PHI 1
Both Teams, Road	8	5/8/93	PIT 4–NYI 4
Pittsburgh, Home	6	4/25/89	vs. Philadelphia
Pittsburgh, Road	4	4/9/81	at NY Rangers
	4	5/8/93	at St. Louis
Opponent, Home	5	4/13/80	vs. Boston
Opponent, Road	4	4/8/82	NY Islanders
	4	5/8/93	NY Islanders

MOST SHOTS

Pittsburgh, Home	21	4/15/75	vs. NY Islanders
Pittsburgh, Road	20	5/7/96	at NY Rangers
Opponent, Home	28	4/21/97	vs. Philadelphia
Opponent, Road	23	5/24/96	at Florida

MOST SAVES

Pittsburgh	27	4/21/97	vs. Philadelphia
Opponent	21	4/15/75	by NY Islanders

FEWEST SAVES

Pittsburgh	1	4/21/01	vs. Washington
	1	4/19/94	vs. Washington
Opponent	1	6/12/09	at Detroit

FEWEST SHOTS

Pittsburgh	1	5/19/92	vs. Boston
		6/12/09	at Detroit
Opponent	1	4/21/01	by Washington
	1	4/19/94	by Washington

MOST PENALTIES

Both Teams, Home	24	4/6/89	vs. NY Rangers
Both Teams, Road	24	4/29/00	at Philadelphia
Pittsburgh	15	4/29/00	at Philadelphia
Opponent	22	4/29/00	at Philadelphia

MOST PENALTY MINUTES

Both Teams, Home	84	4/25/89	PHI 51–PIT 33
Both Teams, Road	128	4/29/00	PHI 92–PIT 36
Pittsburgh, Home	35	5/17/91	vs. Minnesota
Pittsburgh, Road	40	4/19/70	at St Louis
Opponent, Home	51	4/25/89	vs. Philadelphia
Opponent, Road	92	4/29/00	at Philadelphia

FASTEST GOALS BY ONE PENGUINS PLAYER

Two	0:11	4/17/96	vs. Washington Petr Nedved

OVERALL BY PENGUINS

Two	0:07	4/13/80	vs. Boston Ron Stackhouse and Rick Kehoe
Three	1:29	5/10/93	vs. NY Islanders Mario Lemieux, Rick Tocchet, and Larry Murphy
Four	4:52	4/5/89	vs. Philadelphia Mario Lemieux (3) and Bob Errey

AT START OF GAME

Greg Malone	0:15	4/8/81	at St. Louis

AT START OF PERIOD OTHER THAN FIRST

Sidney Crosby	0:12	4/14/08	at Ottawa

Penguins Overtime Playoff Games

DATE	SCORER	TIME	OPPONENT*	GAME NO.	RESULT	SCORE
4/12/70	Michel Briere	8:28	Oakland	Game 4	W	3–2
4/9/72	Pit Martin	0:12	CHICAGO	Game 4	L	5–6
4/14/79	George Ferguson	0:47	Buffalo	Game 3	W	4–3
4/14/81	Mike Crombeen	25:16	St. Louis	Game 5	L	3–4
4/10/82	Rick Kehoe	4:14	NY ISLANDERS	Game 3	W	2–1
4/13/82	John Tonelli	6:10	NY Islanders	Game 5	L	3–4
4/21/89	Phil Bourque	12:08	Philadelphia	Game 3	W	4–3
4/5/91	Jaromir Jagr	8:52	NEW JERSEY	Game 2	W	5–4
4/19/91	Kevin Stevens	8:10	WASHINGTON	Game 2	W	7–6
5/3/91	Vladimir Ruzicka	8:14	Boston	Game 2	L	4–5
5/7/92	Kris King	1:29	NY RANGERS	Game 3	L	5–6
5/9/92	Ron Francis	2:47	NY RANGERS	Game 4	W	5–4
5/17/92	Jaromir Jagr	9:44	BOSTON	Game 1	W	4–3
5/14/93	David Volek	5:16	NY ISLANDERS	Game 7	L	3–4
5/14/95	Luc Robitaille	4:30	WASHINGTON	Game 5	W	6–5
5/26/95	Neal Broten	18:36	New Jersey	Game 4	L	1–2
4/24/96	Petr Nedved	79:15	Washington	Game 4	W	3–2
4/23/98	Benoit Brunet	18:43	MONTREAL	Game 1	L	2–3
5/2/99	Jaromir Jagr	8:59	NEW JERSEY	Game 6	W	3–2
5/13/99	Sergei Berezin	2:18	TORONTO	Game 4	L	2–3
5/17/99	Garry Valk	1:58	TORONTO	Game 6	L	3–4
4/15/00	Jaromir Jagr	5:49	WASHINGTON	Game 2	W	2–1
5/2/00	Andy Delmore	11:01	PHILADELPHIA	Game 3	L	3–4
5/4/00	Keith Primeau	92:01	PHILADELPHIA	Game 4	L	1–2
4/18/01	Jeff Halpern	4:01	WASHINGTON	Game 4	L	3–4
4/23/01	Martin Straka	13:04	WASHINGTON	Game 6	W	4–3
5/5/01	Stu Barnes	8:34	Buffalo	Game 5	L	2–3
5/8/01	Martin Straka	11:29	BUFFALO	Game 6	W	3–2
5/10/01	Darius Kasparaitis	13:01	Buffalo	Game 7	W	3–2
5/4/08	Marian Hossa	7:10	NY RANGERS	Game 5	W	3–2
6/2/08	Petr Sykora	49:57	Detroit	Game 5	W	4–3
4/17/09	Bill Guerin	18:29	PHILADELPHIA	Game 2	W	3–2
5/6/09	Kris Letang	11:23	WASHINGTON	Game 3	W	3–2
5/9/09	Evgeni Malkin	3:28	Washington	Game 5	W	4–3
5/11/09	David Steckel	6:22	WASHINGTON	Game 6	L	4–5
4/22/10	Matt Carkner	47:06	OTTAWA	Game 5	L	3–4
4/24/10	Pascal Dupuis	9:56	Ottawa	Game 6	W	4–3

* Home games in CAPS

Overall Overtime Record: 21–16
Home Overtime Record: 13–11
Road Overtime Record: 8–5

Penguins Playoff Leaders

SHUTOUTS

GOALTENDER	DATE	OPPONENT	SCORE	SAVES
Michel Plasse	4/8/76	vs. Toronto	2–0	21
Frank Pietrangelo	4/15/91	vs. New Jersey	4–0	27
Tom Barrasso	4/25/91	at Minnesota	8–0	39
Tom Barrasso	5/30/92	at Chicago	1–0	27
Tom Barrasso	4/20/93	vs. New Jersey	7–0	36
Tom Barrasso	5/4/93	vs. NY Islanders	3–0	26
Ken Wregget	5/18/95	vs. Washington	3–0	33
Tom Barrasso	5/28/96	vs. Florida	3–0	28
Tom Barrasso	5/7/99	at Toronto	2–0	20
Ron Tugnutt	4/13/00	at Washington	7–0	32
Ron Tugnutt	4/27/00	at Philadelphia	2–0	28
Johan Hedberg	4/16/01	vs. Washington	3–0	34
Johan Hedberg	4/26/01	at Buffalo	3–0	25
Marc-Andre Fleury	4/9/08	vs. Ottawa	4–0	26
Marc-Andre Fleury	4/27/08	vs. NY Rangers	2–0	26
Marc-Andre Fleury	5/18/08	vs. Philadelphia	6–0	21
Marc-Andre Fleury	5/4/10	at Montreal	2–0	18

HAT TRICKS

PLAYER	DATE	OPPONENT	GOALTENDER(S)
Ken Schinkel	4/11/70	at Oakland	Gary Smith
Mario Lemieux**	4/25/89	vs. Philadelphia	Ron Hextall
Mario Lemieux	4/23/92	vs. Washington	Don Beaupre
Ron Francis	5/9/92	vs. NY Rangers	Mike Richter/John Vanbiesbrouck (2)
Kevin Stevens*	5/21/92	at Boston	Andy Moog
Mario Lemieux	5/11/96	vs. NY Rangers	Mike Richter
Jaromir Jagr	5/11/96	vs. NY Rangers	Mike Richter
Martin Straka	4/25/99	at New Jersey	Martin Brodeur
Sidney Crosby	5/4/09	at Washington	Semyon Varlamov
Evgeni Malkin	5/21/09	vs. Carolina	Cam Ward

*Four goals, **Five goals (NHL Record)

PENALTY SHOTS

FOR PITTSBURGH

PLAYER	DATE	OPPONENT	GOALTENDER	RESULT
Jaromir Jagr	5/11/92	vs. NY Rangers	John Vanbiesbrouck	GOAL
Shawn McEachern	5/13/92	vs. NY Rangers	John Vanbiesbrouck	No Goal
Aleksey Morozov	4/23/98	vs. Montreal	Andy Moog	No Goal
Martin Straka	5/2/01	vs. Buffalo	Dominik Hasek	No Goal
Evgeni Malkin	5/1/08	at NY Rangers	Henrik Lundqvist	No Goal

FOR OPPONENTS

GOALTENDER	DATE	OPPONENT	PLAYER	RESULT
Tom Barrasso	5/10/95	at Washington	Michal Pivonka	No Goal
Ken Wregget	4/24/96	at Washington	Joey Juneau	No Goal

Penguins Playoff Scoring

	PLAYER	GP	G	A	PTS	PIM
1.	Mario Lemieux	107	76	96	172	87
2.	Jaromir Jagr	140	65	82	147	121
3.	Kevin Stevens	103	46	60	106	170
4.	Ron Francis	97	32	68	100	67
5.	Sidney Crosby	62	30	52	82	36
6.	Evgeni Malkin	62	29	44	73	89
7.	Larry Murphy	74	15	57	72	73
8.	Martin Straka	65	19	27	46	30
9.	Sergei Gonchar	60	7	37	44	26
10.	Mark Recchi	29	10	28	38	33
11.	Rick Tocchet	32	15	22	37	68
12.	Joe Mullen	62	16	15	31	20
13.	Maxime Talbot	59	13	16	29	73
14.	Alexei Kovalev	39	11	17	28	40
15.	Marian Hossa	20	12	14	26	12
16.	Paul Coffey	23	4	22	26	37
17.	Phil Bourque	56	13	12	25	107
18.	Chris Kunitz	37	5	20	25	27
19.	Jordan Staal	60	16	8	24	30
20.	Bill Guerin	35	11	13	24	17
21.	Jan Hrdina	40	10	14	24	22
22.	Petr Nedved	23	11	12	23	28
23.	Kristopher Letang	52	9	13	22	44
24.	Troy Loney	66	8	14	22	97
25.	Rick Kehoe	37	4	17	21	2
26.	Rob Brown	41	9	10	19	34
27.	Robert Lang	45	7	12	19	6
28.	Jean Pronovost	29	9	9	18	12
29.	Shawn McEachern	48	6	11	17	24
30.	Ryan Malone	25	6	10	16	25
31.	Ulf Samuelsson	66	4	12	16	123
32.	George Ferguson	22	4	11	15	13
33.	Pascal Dupuis	49	4	11	15	30
34.	Sergei Zubov	18	1	14	15	26
35.	Rod Schutt	22	8	6	14	26
36.	Ruslan Fedotenko	30	7	7	14	8
37.	Bryan Trottier	46	7	7	14	57
38.	Randy Carlyle	22	6	8	14	41
39.	Ron Schock	29	2	12	14	23
40.	Bob Errey	49	9	4	13	51
41.	Ron Stackhouse	32	5	8	13	38
42.	Matt Cooke	37	5	8	13	44
43.	Tyler Kennedy	54	5	8	13	19
44.	Jiri Slegr	29	3	10	13	33
45.	Tomas Sandstrom	36	7	5	12	50
46.	Paul Stanton	44	2	10	12	66
47.	Luc Robitaille	12	7	4	11	26
48.	Gregg Sheppard	17	4	7	11	2
49.	John Cullen	20	3	8	11	36
50.	John Callander	22	3	8	11	12
51.	Pierre Larouche	15	2	9	11	2
52.	Lowell MacDonald	15	6	4	10	8
53.	Petr Sykora	27	6	4	10	16
54.	Janne Laukkanen	29	4	6	10	24
55.	Mark Eaton	42	4	6	10	14
56.	Andrew Ference	18	3	7	10	16
57.	Alex Goligoski	15	2	8	10	2
58.	J.J. Daigneault	17	1	9	10	36
59.	Dan Quinn	11	6	3	9	10
60.	Bob Kelly	15	6	3	9	23
61.	Bryan Smolinski	18	5	4	9	10
62.	Aleksey Morozov	39	4	5	9	8
63.	Kip Miller	13	2	7	9	19
64.	Dave Roche	16	2	7	9	26
65.	Colin Campbell	19	2	7	9	51
66.	Zarley Zalapski	11	1	8	9	13

Mario Lemieux is the Pens' all-time leading playoff scorer.

Hall of Famer Joe Mullen ranks 12th in Pen's playoff scoring.

Penguins Playoff Scoring—Continued

	PLAYER	GP	G	A	PTS	PIM		PLAYER	GP	G	A	PTS	PIM
67.	Michel Briere	10	5	3	8	17	120.	Joe Dziedzic	21	1	3	4	23
68.	Craig Adams	37	5	3	8	31	121.	Francois Leroux	33	1	3	4	34
69.	Mike Bullard	9	4	4	8	4	122.	Fredrik Olausson	10	0	4	4	2
70.	Gary Roberts	16	4	4	8	34	123.	Keith McCreary	11	0	4	4	6
71.	Syl Apps	19	4	4	8	23	124.	Bob Leiter	4	3	0	3	0
72.	Kevin Hatcher	24	4	4	8	20	125.	Jim Hamilton	6	3	0	3	0
73.	Randy Cunneyworth	11	3	5	8	26	126.	Ed Olczyk	11	3	0	3	16
74.	German Titov	11	3	5	8	4	127.	Andre St. Laurent	5	2	1	3	8
75.	Greg Malone	18	3	5	8	32	128.	Blair Chapman	10	2	1	3	9
76.	Glen Murray	18	2	6	8	10	129.	Troy Murray	12	2	1	3	12
77.	Ryan Whitney	25	2	6	8	31	130.	Brad Werenka	19	2	1	3	14
78.	Peter Taglianetti	39	1	7	8	83	131.	Rene Corbet	24	2	1	3	21
79.	Rob Scuderi	49	1	7	8	10	132.	Chris Joseph	25	2	1	3	20
80.	Peter Lee	19	0	8	8	4	133.	Jarkko Ruutu	25	2	1	3	36
81.	Chris Tamer	37	0	8	8	52	134.	Wally Boyer	10	1	2	3	0
82.	Brooks Orpik	62	0	8	8	60	135.	Dunc McCallum	10	1	2	3	12
83.	Ken Schinkel	13	6	1	7	4	136.	Bob Woytowich	10	1	2	3	2
84.	Vic Hadfield	12	5	2	7	11	137.	Georges Laraque	17	1	2	3	4
85.	Mark Johnson	10	4	3	7	6	138.	Greg Hotham	5	0	3	3	6
86.	Stu Barnes	11	3	4	7	2	139.	Jason Woolley	5	0	3	3	0
87.	Paul Gardner	10	2	5	7	10	140.	Jim Morrison	8	0	3	3	10
88.	Dean Prentice	12	2	5	7	8	141.	Russ Anderson	10	0	3	3	28
89.	Scott Young	17	1	6	7	2	142.	Bryan Hextall	14	0	3	3	43
90.	Ian Moran	61	1	6	7	20	143.	Bob Boughner	29	0	3	3	37
91.	Kjell Samuelsson	44	0	7	7	72	144.	Hal Gill	44	0	3	3	18
92.	Tom Barrasso	101	0	7	7	38	145.	Mike Needham	14	2	0	2	4
93.	Gary McAdam	12	3	3	6	9	146.	Stan Gilbertson	3	1	1	2	2
94.	Chuck Arnason	9	2	4	6	4	147.	Nick Libett	5	1	1	2	0
95.	Jiri Hrdina	35	2	4	6	22	148.	Rick MacLeish	5	1	1	2	0
96.	Miroslav Satan	17	1	5	6	11	149.	Kevin McClelland	5	1	1	2	5
97.	Mike Ramsey	13	0	6	6	4	150.	Bob Stewart	5	1	1	2	2
98.	Orest Kindrachuk	7	4	1	5	7	151.	Dave Michayluk	7	1	1	2	0
99.	Jeff Daniels	12	3	2	5	0	152.	Pat Price	10	1	1	2	49
100.	Kevin Miller	18	3	2	5	8	153.	Brad Lauer	12	1	1	2	4
101.	Tyler Wright	30	3	2	5	40	154.	Grant Jennings	38	1	1	2	38
102.	Ross Lonsberry	17	2	3	5	13	155.	Darryl Edestrand	4	0	2	2	0
103.	Alexei Ponikarovsky	11	1	4	5	4	156.	Greg Polis	4	0	2	2	0
104.	Norm Maciver	12	1	4	5	8	157.	Michel Ouellet	5	0	2	2	6
105.	Dave Tippett	12	1	4	5	14	158.	Glen Sather	10	0	2	2	17
106.	Jim Paek	27	1	4	5	8	159.	Gord Dineen	11	0	2	2	8
107.	Gord Roberts	43	1	4	5	95	160.	Val Fonteyne	14	0	2	2	2
108.	Tom Bladon	8	0	5	5	2	161.	Matthew Barnaby	24	0	2	2	64
109.	Jim Johnson	11	0	5	5	44	162.	John Slaney	2	1	0	1	2
110.	Josef Beranek	29	0	5	5	8	163.	Len Barrie	4	1	0	1	8
111.	Pat Boutette	5	3	1	4	8	164.	Greg Johnson	5	1	0	1	2
112.	Nick Harbaruk	14	3	1	4	20	165.	Peter Laframboise	9	1	0	1	0
113.	Adam Hall	17	3	1	4	8	166.	Pat Falloon	10	1	0	1	2
114.	Mario Faubert	10	2	2	4	6	167.	Greg Andrusak	12	1	0	1	6
115.	Duane Rupp	10	2	2	4	8	168.	Bobby Dollas	13	1	0	1	6
116.	Darius Kasparaitis	38	2	2	4	50	169.	Dan Kesa	13	1	0	1	0
117.	Philippe Boucher	9	1	3	4	4	170.	Randy Gilhen	16	1	0	1	14
118.	Wayne Primeau	18	1	3	4	2	171.	Pete Mahovlich	2	0	1	1	0
119.	Dave Burrows	20	1	3	4	16	172.	Don Awrey	3	0	1	1	0

Penguins Playoff Scoring—Continued

	PLAYER	GP	G	A	PTS	PIM
173.	Wayne Bianchin	3	0	1	1	6
174.	Jacques Cossette	3	0	1	1	4
175.	Ed Van Impe	3	0	1	1	2
176.	Tim Horton	4	0	1	1	2
177.	Mark Letestu	4	0	1	1	0
178.	Al McDonough	4	0	1	1	0
179.	Eddie Shack	4	0	1	1	15
180.	Colby Armstrong	5	0	1	1	11
181.	Frank Pietrangelo	5	0	1	1	2
182.	Gary Rissling	5	0	1	1	4
183.	Greg Brown	6	0	1	1	4
184.	Barry Wilkins	6	0	1	1	4
185.	Marc Chorney	7	0	1	1	2
186.	Bob McManama	8	0	1	1	6
187.	Dennis Owchar	8	0	1	1	6
188.	Bob Paradise	8	0	1	1	17
189.	Dave Hannan	8	0	1	1	4
190.	Dave McLlwain	9	0	1	1	0
191.	Paul Baxter	10	0	1	1	42
192.	Tracy Pratt	10	0	1	1	51
193.	Alex Hicks	11	0	1	1	4
194.	Marc Bergevin	12	0	1	1	2
195.	Dmitri Mironov	15	0	1	1	10
196.	Randy Hillier	17	0	1	1	73
197.	Neil Wilkinson	20	0	1	1	18
198.	Ken Wregget	26	0	1	1	9
199.	Hans Jonsson	27	0	1	1	14
200.	Jean-Sebastien Aubin	1	0	0	0	0
201.	Drake Berehowsky	1	0	0	0	0
202.	Chris Conner	1	0	0	0	0
203.	Larry DePalma	1	0	0	0	0
204.	Steve Dykstra	1	0	0	0	2
205.	Nils Ekman	1	0	0	0	0
206.	Maxim Galanov	1	0	0	0	0
207.	Mathieu Garon	1	0	0	0	0
208.	Steve Gatzos	1	0	0	0	0
209.	Tuomas Gronman	1	0	0	0	0
210.	Greg Hawgood	1	0	0	0	0
211.	Victor Ignatjev	1	0	0	0	2
212.	Andreas Johansson	1	0	0	0	0
213.	Brent Johnson	1	0	0	0	0
214.	Paul Marshall	1	0	0	0	0
215.	Peter Skudra	1	0	0	0	0
216.	Jocelyn Thibault	1	0	0	0	0
217.	Wendell Young	1	0	0	0	0
218.	Richard Zemlak	1	0	0	0	10
219.	Mike Corrigan	2	0	0	0	0
220.	Chris Dahlquist	2	0	0	0	0
221.	Todd Hlushko	2	0	0	0	0
222.	Lex Hudson	2	0	0	0	0
223.	Michal Rozsival	2	0	0	0	4
224.	Bob Simpson	2	0	0	0	0
225.	Larry Bignell	3	0	0	0	2
226.	Brian Bonin	3	0	0	0	0
227.	Randy Boyd	3	0	0	0	11
228.	Kim Clackson	3	0	0	0	37
229.	Corey Foster	3	0	0	0	4
230.	Craig Muni	3	0	0	0	0
231.	Simon Nolet	3	0	0	0	0
232.	Ronald Petrovicky	3	0	0	0	2
233.	Michel Plasse	3	0	0	0	0
234.	Al Smith	3	0	0	0	0
235.	Stefan Bergkvist	4	0	0	0	2
236.	Steve Cardwell	4	0	0	0	2
237.	Erik Christensen	4	0	0	0	6
238.	Kim Davis	4	0	0	0	0
239.	Pat Graham	4	0	0	0	2
240.	Richard Park	4	0	0	0	2
241.	Jim Rutherford	4	0	0	0	0
242.	Mike Stapleton	4	0	0	0	0
243.	Darryl Sydor	4	0	0	0	2
244.	Dale Tallon	4	0	0	0	4
245.	Michel Dion	5	0	0	0	0
246.	Rusty Fitzgerald	5	0	0	0	4
247.	Pat Hughes	5	0	0	0	21
248.	Dan LaCouture	5	0	0	0	2
249.	Jay McKee	5	0	0	0	2
250.	Josef Melichar	5	0	0	0	2
251.	Krzysztof Oliwa	5	0	0	0	16
252.	Sean Pronger	5	0	0	0	4
253.	Bob Blackburn	6	0	0	0	4
254.	Doug Brown	6	0	0	0	2
255.	Les Binkley	7	0	0	0	0
256.	Martin Sonnenberg	7	0	0	0	0
257.	Milan Kraft	8	0	0	0	2
258.	Jordan Leopold	8	0	0	0	2
259.	Jim McKenzie	8	0	0	0	4
260.	Gary Inness	9	0	0	0	2
261.	Alek Stojanov	9	0	0	0	19
262.	Rod Buskas	10	0	0	0	23
263.	Denis Herron	10	0	0	0	5
264.	Greg Millen	10	0	0	0	0
265.	Peter Popovic	10	0	0	0	10
266.	Mike Hudson	11	0	0	0	6
267.	Mike Rupp	11	0	0	0	8
268.	Ron Tugnutt	11	0	0	0	2
269.	Lew Morrison	13	0	0	0	0
270.	Jay Caufield	14	0	0	0	30
271.	Bryan Watson	14	0	0	0	38
272.	Johan Hedberg	18	0	0	0	0
273.	Marc-Andre Fleury	62	0	0	0	6

Penguins Playoff Goaltending

RANK	PLAYER	GP	MINS	GA	SO	SAVES	SAVE%	GAA	W–L
1.	Mathieu Garon	1	24	0	0	8	1.000	0.00	0–0
2.	Jocelyn Thibault	1	8	0	0	1	1.000	0.00	0–0
3.	Jean-Sebastien Aubin	1	1	0	0	0	—	0.00	0–0
4.	Wendell Young	1	39	1	0	10	.909	1.54	0–0
5.	Ron Tugnutt	11	746	22	2	376	.945	1.77	6–5
6.	Brent Johnson	1	31	1	0	6	.857	1.94	0–0
7.	Les Binkley	7	428	15	0	183	.924	2.10	5–2
8.	Johan Hedberg	18	1123	43	2	439	.911	2.30	9–9
9.	Marc-Andre Fleury	62	3783	159	4	1626	.911	2.52	38–24
10.	Gary Inness	9	540	24	0	273	.919	2.67	5–4
11.	Michel Plasse	3	180	8	1	85	.914	2.67	1–2
12.	Tom Barrasso	101	5918	287	6	2784	.907	2.91	56–42
13.	Ken Wregget	26	1597	78	1	826	.914	2.93	13–12
14.	Peter Skudra	1	20	1	0	10	.909	3.00	0–0
15.	Frank Pietrangelo	5	288	15	1	133	.899	3.12	4–1
16.	Al Smith	3	180	10	0	79	.888	3.33	1–2
17.	Denis Herron	10	601	35	0	298	.895	3.49	3–7
18.	Jim Rutherford	4	240	14	0	131	.903	3.50	0–4
19.	Greg Millen	10	625	40	0	297	.881	3.84	4–6
20.	Michel Dion	5	310	22	0	164	.882	4.26	2–3

Marc-Andre Fleury
ranks second among
Pens goalies in
postseason games.

Awards and Honors

Hockey Hall of Fame Inductees/Honorees

Players Section	Years with Penguins	Inducted
Red Kelly[1]	1969–1973	1969
Tim Horton*	1971–1972	1977
Andy Bathgate	1967–1968, 1970–1971	1978
Leo Boivin	1967–1969	1986
Tony Esposito[2]	1988–1989	1988
Mario Lemieux	1984–1997, 2000–2006	1997
Bryan Trottier	1990–1992, 1993–1994	1997
Joe Mullen	1990–1995, 1996–1997	2000
Paul Coffey	1987–1992	2004
Larry Murphy	1990–1995	2004
Ron Francis	1991–1998	2007
Luc Robitaille	1995	2009

Builders Section	Years with Penguins	Inducted
Scotty Bowman	1990–1993	1991
Bob Johnson*	1990–1991	1992
Glen Sather[3]	1969–1971	1997
Craig Patrick	1989–2006	2001
Herb Brooks*	1995–2003	2006

Foster Hewitt Memorial Award	Years with Penguins	Honored
Mike Lange	1974–1975, 1976–present	2001

Elmer Ferguson Memorial Award	Years with Penguins	Honored
Dave Molinari	1983–present	2009

* Inducted posthumously
1. Red Kelly served the Penguins as a coach and general manager.
2. Tony Esposito served the Penguins as a general manager.
3. Glen Sather played for the Penguins.

Ron Francis was inducted into the Hockey Hall of Fame in 2007.

Penguins Hall of Fame Inductees

Inductee	Years with Penguins	Inducted
Bob Johnson	1990–1991	1992
Rick Kehoe	1974–1984	1992
Jean Pronovost	1968–1978	1992
Syl Apps	1971–1977	1994
Dave Burrows	1971–1978, 1980–1981	1996
Edward J. DeBartolo Sr.	1977–2001	1996
Elaine Heufelder	1967–2003	1996
Mario Lemieux	1984–1997, 2000–2006	1999
Jack Riley	1967–1975	1999
Joe Mullen	1990–1995, 1996–1997	2000
Anthony Caggiano	1967–2000	2001
Mike Lange	1974–1975, 1976–present	2001
Craig Patrick	1989–2006	2001
Les Binkley	1967–1972	2003
Vince Lascheid	1970–2003	2003
Ulf Samuelsson	1991–1995	2003
Paul Coffey	1987–1992	2007
Paul Sciulli	1967–2007	2007

Paul Coffey became a member of the Penguins Hall of Fame in 2007.

Penguins Retired Numbers

Number	Player	Career	Date Retired
21	Michel Briere	1969–1970	January 5, 2001[1]
66	Mario Lemieux	1984–1997, 2000–2006	November 19, 1997[2]

1. Briere's number was unofficially retired following his death on April 13, 1971
2. Lemieux's number was "unretired" when he began his comeback on December 27, 2000

Penguins All-Time Team

Players
Syl Apps
Tom Barrasso
Les Binkley
Dave Burrows
Paul Coffey
Ron Francis
Jaromir Jagr
Rick Kehoe
Pierre Larouche
Mario Lemieux
Joe Mullen
Larry Murphy
Jean Pronovost
Ulf Samuelsson
Kevin Stevens

Builders
John Barbero
Scotty Bowman
Herb Brooks
A.T. Caggiano
Edward J. DeBartolo Sr.
Elaine Heufelder
Bob Johnson
Eddie Johnston
Mike Lange
Vince Lascheid
Craig Patrick
Jack Riley
Frank Sciulli

Other Notable Penguins
Randy Carlyle
Lowell MacDonald
Ron Stackhouse
Martin Straka
Rick Tocchet

Superstars Jaromir Jagr and Mario Lemieux won the Art Ross Trophy 11 times.

Penguins Trophy and Award Winners

ART ROSS TROPHY
Mario Lemieux	1988, 1989, 1992, 1993, 1996, 1997
Jaromir Jagr	1995, 1998, 1999, 2000, 2001
Sidney Crosby	2007
Evgeni Malkin	2009

HART MEMORIAL TROPHY
Mario Lemieux	1988, 1993, 1996
Jaromir Jagr	1999
Sidney Crosby	2007

LADY BYNG TROPHY
Rick Kehoe	1981
Ron Francis	1995, 1998

CONN SMYTHE TROPHY
Mario Lemieux	1991, 1992
Evgeni Malkin	2009

CALDER MEMORIAL TROPHY
Mario Lemieux	1985
Evgeni Malkin	2007

JAMES NORRIS TROPHY
Randy Carlyle	1981

FRANK SELKE TROPHY
Ron Francis	1995

BILL MASTERTON TROPHY
Lowell MacDonald	1973
Mario Lemieux	1993

LESTER B. PEARSON AWARD
Mario Lemieux	1986, 1988, 1993, 1996
Jaromir Jagr	1999, 2000
Sidney Crosby	2007

NHL PLUS/MINUS AWARD
Mario Lemieux	1993
Ron Francis	1995

MESSIER LEADERSHIP AWARD
Sidney Crosby	2010

MAURICE RICHARD TROPHY
Sidney Crosby	2010

Penguins NHL All-Star Team Selections

NHL FIRST TEAM ALL-STAR

Randy Carlyle	Defense	1981
Mario Lemieux	Center	1988, 1989, 1993, 1996, 1997
Paul Coffey	Defense	1989
Kevin Stevens	Left Wing	1992
Jaromir Jagr	Right Wing	1995, 1996, 1998, 1999, 2000, 2001
Sidney Crosby	Center	2007
Evgeni Malkin	Center	2008, 2009

NHL SECOND TEAM ALL-STAR

Mario Lemieux	Center	1986, 1987, 1992, 2001
Paul Coffey	Defense	1990
Kevin Stevens	Left Wing	1991, 1993
Tom Barrasso	Goalie	1993
Larry Murphy	Defense	1993, 1995
Jaromir Jagr	Right Wing	1997
Sidney Crosby	Center	2010

Sebastien Caron was named to the NHL All-Rookie Team in 2003.

Penguins NHL All-Rookie Team Selections

Mario Lemieux	Center	1985
Warren Young	Left Wing	1985
Zarley Zalapski	Defense	1989
Jaromir Jagr	Right Wing	1991
Patrick Lalime	Goalie	1997
Sebastien Caron	Goalie	2003
Ryan Malone	Left Wing	2004
Sidney Crosby	Center	2006
Evgeni Malkin	Center	2007
Jordan Staal	Center	2007

Penguins NHL All-Star Game Selections

Season	Player	Team	G	A	PTS
1967–68	Ken Schinkel	NHL All-Stars	0	0	0
1968–69	Ken Schinkel	West Division	0	0	0
1969–70	Dean Prentice	West Division	1	0	1
	Bob Woytowich	West Division	0	1	1
1970–71	Greg Polis	West Division	0	0	0
1971–72	Greg Polis	West Division	0	0	0
1972–73	Lowell MacDonald	West Division	0	1	1
	Greg Polis (MVP)	West Division	2	0	2
1973–74	Dave Burrows	West Division	0	0	0
	Lowell MacDonald	West Division	1	1	2
	Al McDonough	West Division	1	0	1
1974–75	Syl Apps (MVP)	Wales Conference	2	0	2
	Jean Pronovost	Wales Conference	0	0	0
1975–76	Dave Burrows	Wales Conference	0	0	0
	Pierre Larouche	Wales Conference	0	0	0
	Jean Pronovost	Wales Conference	0	0	0
1976–77	Jean Pronovost	Wales Conference	0	0	0
1977–78	Jean Pronovost	Wales Conference	0	0	0
1978–79	No Penguins selected	NHL All-Stars			
1979–80	Ron Stackhouse	Wales Conference	1	0	1
1980–81	Randy Carlyle	Wales Conference	0	0	0
	Rick Kehoe	Wales Conference	0	0	0
1981–82	Randy Carlyle	Wales Conference	0	1	1
	Michel Dion	Wales Conference	30 minutes, 2 goals allowed		

Syl Apps (with his wife Anne) scored two goals at the 1975 All-Star Game to earn MVP honors…and a new car.

Penguins NHL All-Star Game Selections—Continued

Season	Player	Team	G	A	PTS
1982–83	Rick Kehoe	Wales Conference	0	0	0
1983–84	Mike Bullard	Wales Conference	0	0	0
1984–85	Mario Lemieux (MVP)	Wales Conference	2	1	3
1985–86	Mario Lemieux	Wales Conference	0	0	0
1986–87	Mario Lemieux	NHL All-Stars (2 games)	0	3	3
1987–88	Paul Coffey	Wales Conference	0	0	0
	Mario Lemieux (MVP)	Wales Conference	3	3	6
1988–89	Rob Brown	Wales Conference	0	0	0
	Paul Coffey	Wales Conference	0	0	0
	Mario Lemieux	Wales Conference	1	1	2
1989–90	Paul Coffey	Wales Conference	0	2	2
	Mario Lemieux (MVP)	Wales Conference	4	0	4
1990–91	Paul Coffey	Wales Conference	0	0	0
	John Cullen	Wales Conference	0	1	1
	Mark Recchi	Wales Conference	0	0	0
	Kevin Stevens	Wales Conference	1	0	1
1991–92	Paul Coffey	Wales Conference	0	0	0
	Jaromir Jagr	Wales Conference	0	1	1
	Mario Lemieux	Wales Conference	0	1	1
	Kevin Stevens	Wales Conference	1	0	1
	Bryan Trottier	Wales Conference	1	0	1

Wayne Gretzky (99) and Mario Lemieux (66) follow the action at the 1990 NHL All-Star Game in Pittsburgh.

Penguins NHL All-Star Game Selections—Continued

Season	Player	Team	G	A	PTS
1992–93	Mario Lemieux	Wales Conference	Did Not Play		
	Jaromir Jagr	Wales Conference	1	1	2
	Kevin Stevens	Wales Conference	1	2	3
	Rick Tocchet*	Wales Conference	2	0	2
1993–94	Jaromir Jagr	Eastern Conference	Did Not Play		
	Joe Mullen	Eastern Conference	1	1	2
	Larry Murphy	Eastern Conference	0	0	0
1994–95	No Game Played				
1995–96	Mario Lemieux	Eastern Conference	0	2	2
	Ron Francis	Eastern Conference	0	1	1
	Jaromir Jagr	Eastern Conference	1	0	1
1996–97	Kevin Hatcher	Eastern Conference	0	0	0
	Jaromir Jagr	Eastern Conference	Did Not Play		
	Mario Lemieux	Eastern Conference	2	1	3
1997–98	Jaromir Jagr	World	1	0	1
1998–99	Jaromir Jagr	World	0	1	1
	Martin Straka	World	0	0	0
1999–00	Jaromir Jagr	World	1	0	1
2000–01	Jaromir Jagr	World	Did Not Play		
	Alexei Kovalev	World	1	1	2
	Mario Lemieux	North America	1	1	2
2001–02	Mario Lemieux	North America	1	0	1
2002–03	Alexei Kovalev	Eastern Conference	0	0	0
	Mario Lemieux	Eastern Conference	Did Not Play		
2003–04	No Penguins selected	Eastern Conference			
2004–05	No Game Played				
2005–06	No Game Played				
2006–07	Sidney Crosby	Eastern Conference	0	0	0
2007–08	Sidney Crosby	Eastern Conference	Did Not Play		
	Sergei Gonchar	Eastern Conference	0	0	0
	Evgeni Malkin*	Eastern Conference	0	2	2
2008–09	Sidney Crosby	Eastern Conference	Did Not Play		
	Evgeni Malkin	Eastern Conference	1	0	1
2009–10	No Game Played				

* Replacement

Penguins Team Awards

MICHEL BRIERE MEMORIAL TROPHY (Rookie of the Year)

Season	Recipient	Season	Recipient
1967–68	Les Binkley	1988–89	Zarley Zalapski
1968–69	Jean Pronovost	1989–90	Mark Recchi
1969–70	Michel Briere	1990–91	Jaromir Jagr
1970–71	Greg Polis	1991–92	Jim Paek
1971–72	Dave Burrows	1992–93	Shawn McEachern
1972–73	No Winner	1993–94	No Winner
1973–74	Ron Lalonde	1994–95	No Winner
1974–75	Pierre Larouche	1995–96	No Winner
1975–76	No Winner	1996–97	Patrick Lalime
1976–77	Greg Malone	1997–98	Peter Skudra
1977–78	Peter Lee	1998–99	Jan Hrdina
1978–79	Greg Millen and Rod Schutt	1999–00	Jean-Sebastien Aubin
1979–80	Paul Marshall	2000–01	No Winner
1980–81	Mark Johnson	2001–02	Johan Hedberg
1981–82	Mike Bullard	2002–03	No Winner
1982–83	Dave Hannan	2003–04	Ryan Malone
1983–84	Roberto Romano	2005–06	Sidney Crosby
1984–85	Mario Lemieux	2006–07	Evgeni Malkin and Jordan Staal
1985–86	Jim Johnson	2007–08	Kris Letang
1986–87	No Winner	2008–09	No Winner
1987–88	Rob Brown	2009–10	No Winner

PLAYER'S PLAYER AWARD

Season	Recipient	Season	Recipient
1967–68	No Award	1988–89	Randy Hillier
1968–69	Val Fonteyne	1989–90	Randy Hillier
1969–70	Dean Prentice and Jean Pronovost	1990–91	Mark Recchi
1970–71	Jean Pronovost	1991–92	Joe Mullen
1971–72	Jean Pronovost	1992–93	Mario Lemieux
1972–73	Lowell MacDonald	1993–94	Ron Francis
1973–74	Jean Pronovost	1994–95	Ron Francis
1974–75	Ron Schock	1995–96	Ron Francis
1975–76	Jean Pronovost	1996–97	Joe Mullen
1976–77	Denis Herron	1997–98	Ron Francis
1977–78	Denis Herron	1998–99	Jaromir Jagr and Martin Straka
1978–79	Greg Malone	1999–00	Martin Straka
1979–80	Rick Kehoe	2000–01	Martin Straka
1980–81	Rick Kehoe	2001–02	Alexei Kovalev and Ian Moran
1981–82	Mike Bullard	2002–03	No Winner
1982–83	Pat Boutette	2003–04	Kelly Buchberger
1983–84	Denis Herron	2005–06	John LeClair
1984–85	Warren Young	2006–07	Mark Recchi
1985–86	Terry Ruskowski	2007–08	Ryan Malone
1986–87	Dan Quinn and Terry Ruskowski	2008–09	Eric Godard
1987–88	Mario Lemieux	2009–10	Jordan Staal

Penguins Team Awards—Continued

A.T. CAGGIANO MEMORIAL BOOSTER CLUB AWARD

Season	Recipient	Season	Recipient
1974–75	Vic Hadfield	1992–93	Mario Lemieux
1975–76	Dave Burrows	1993–94	Ron Francis
1976–77	Dunc Wilson	1994–95	Jaromir Jagr
1977–78	Denis Herron	1995–96	Mario Lemieux
1978–79	Randy Carlyle	1996–97	Mario Lemieux
1979–80	George Ferguson	1997–98	Jaromir Jagr
1980–81	Randy Carlyle	1998–99	Jaromir Jagr
1981–82	Michel Dion	1999–00	Jean-Sebastien Aubin
1982–83	Michel Dion	2000–01	Alexei Kovalev
1983–84	Mike Bullard	2001–02	Alexei Kovalev
1984–85	Mario Lemieux	2002–03	Mario Lemieux
1985–86	Mario Lemieux	2003–04	Ryan Malone
1986–87	Mario Lemieux	2005–06	Sidney Crosby
1987–88	Mario Lemieux	2006–07	Sidney Crosby
1988–89	Mario Lemieux	2007–08	Evgeni Malkin
1989–90	Mario Lemieux	2008–09	Evgeni Malkin
1990–91	Mark Recchi	2009–10	Sidney Crosby
1991–92	Mario Lemieux		

BADGER BOB JOHNSON MEMORIAL AWARD

Season	Recipient
1994–95	Ron Francis and Joe Mullen
1995–96	Jaromir Jagr
1996–97	Joe Mullen
1997–98	Ron Francis
1998–99	Martin Straka
1999–00	Jiri Slegr
2000–01	Darius Kasparaitis and Martin Straka
2001–02	Ian Moran

BAZ BASTIEN MEMORIAL AWARD (Good Guy Award)

Season	Recipient	Season	Recipient
1983–84	Gary Rissling	1996–97	Ken Wregget
1984–85	Gary Rissling	1997–98	Ron Francis
1985–86	Terry Ruskowski	1998–99	Jiri Slegr
1986–87	Dan Frawley	1999–00	Rob Brown
1987–88	Randy Cunneyworth	2000–01	Alexei Kovalev
1988–89	Jim Johnson	2001–02	Johan Hedberg
1989–90	Troy Loney	2002–03	Steve McKenna
1990–91	Phil Bourque	2003–04	Brooks Orpik
1991–92	Larry Murphy	2005–06	Sidney Crosby
1992–93	Kevin Stevens	2006–07	Pittsburgh Penguins team
1993–94	Joe Mullen	2007–08	Ryan Whitney
1994–95	Larry Murphy	2008–09	Sidney Crosby and Brooks Orpik
1995–96	Petr Nedved	2009–10	Sidney Crosby and Marc-Andre Fleury

Penguins Team Awards—Continued

DEFENSIVE PLAYER OF THE YEAR

Season	Recipient
2008–09	Jordan Staal
2009–10	Brooks Orpik

THE EDWARD J. DEBARTOLO COMMUNITY SERVICE AWARD

Season	Recipient	Season	Recipient
1991–92	Phil Bourque and Troy Loney	2001–02	Andrew Ference
1992–93	Shawn McEachern and Jim Paek	2002–03	Johan Hedberg and Steve McKenna
1993–94	Tom Barrasso and Ken Wregget	2003–04	Rico Fata and Steve McKenna
1994–95	Ron Francis and Bryan Trottier	2005–06	Colby Armstrong, Marc-Andre Fleury, Ryan Malone and Ryan Whitney
1995–96	Dave Roche		
1996–97	Joe Dziedzic and Chris Tamer	2006–07	Mark Recchi
1997–98	Chris Tamer and Tyler Wright	2007–08	Georges Laraque
1998–99	Rob Brown and Tyler Wright	2008–09	Eric Godard
1999–00	Matthew Barnaby and Ian Moran	2009–10	Sidney Crosby
2000–01	Bob Boughner		

MASTERTON NOMINEE (Comeback Player)

Season	Recipient	Season	Recipient
1982–83	Greg Malone	1996–97	Joe Mullen
1983–84	Denis Herron	1997–98	Rob Brown
1984–85	Gary Rissling and Warren Young	1998–99	Darius Kasparaitis
1985–86	Terry Ruskowski	1999–00	Darius Kasparaitis
1986–87	Randy Cunneyworth	2000–01	Ian Moran
1987–88	Randy Hillier	2001–02	Stephane Richer
1988–89	Phil Bourque	2002–03	Martin Straka
1989–90	Mario Lemieux	2003–04	Landon Wilson
1990–91	Mario Lemieux	2005–06	John LeClair
1991–92	Joe Mullen	2006–07	Alain Nasreddine
1992–93	Mario Lemieux	2007–08	Ty Conklin
1993–94	Kevin Stevens	2008–09	Mark Eaton
1994–95	John Cullen	2009–10	Bill Guerin
1995–96	Ron Francis		

Penguins Team Awards—Continued

MOST VALUABLE PLAYER AWARD

Season	Recipient
1967–68	Les Binkley
1968–69	Keith McCreary
1969–70	Jean Pronovost
1970–71	Ron Schock
1971–72	Jean Pronovost
1972–73	Dave Burrows
1973–74	Syl Apps, Dave Burrows, Lowell MacDonald, and Jean Pronovost
1974–75	Ron Schock and Ron Stackhouse
1975–76	Pierre Larouche
1976–77	Dunc Wilson
1977–78	Pete Mahovlich
1978–79	Orest Kindrachuk and Ron Stackhouse
1979–80	George Ferguson
1980–81	Randy Carlyle
1981–82	Michel Dion
1982–83	Doug Shedden
1983–84	Mike Bullard
1984–85	Mario Lemieux
1985–86	Mario Lemieux
1986–87	Mario Lemieux
1987–88	Mario Lemieux

Season	Recipient
1988–89	Mario Lemieux
1989–90	Mario Lemieux
1990–91	Mark Recchi
1991–92	Mario Lemieux
1992–93	Mario Lemieux
1993–94	Ron Francis
1994–95	Jaromir Jagr
1995–96	Mario Lemieux
1996–97	Mario Lemieux
1997–98	Ron Francis and Jaromir Jagr
1998–99	Jaromir Jagr
1999–00	Jaromir Jagr
2000–01	Mario Lemieux
2001–02	Alexei Kovalev
2002–03	Mario Lemieux
2003–04	Dick Tarnstrom
2005–06	Sidney Crosby
2006–07	Sidney Crosby
2007–08	Evgeni Malkin
2008–09	Evgeni Malkin
2009–10	Sidney Crosby

LEADING SCORER AWARD

Season	Recipient
1967–68	Andy Bathgate
1968–69	Ken Schinkel
1969–70	Dean Prentice
1970–71	Bryan Hextall
1971–72	Syl Apps
1972–73	Syl Apps

Season	Recipient
1973–74	Syl Apps
1974–75	Ron Schock
1975–76	Pierre Larouche
1976–77	Jean Pronovost
1977–78	Jean Pronovost
1978–79	Greg Malone

UNSUNG HERO AWARD

Season	Recipient
1969–70	Val Fonteyne
1970–71	Bob Blackburn
1971–72	Duane Rupp
1972–73	Lowell MacDonald
1973–74	Ron Schock
1974–75	Gary Inness

Season	Recipient
1975–76	Ron Stackhouse
1976–77	Wayne Bianchin
1977–78	Dave Schultz
1978–79	George Ferguson
1979–80	Russ Anderson

Miscellaneous

Penguins All-Time Uniform Numbers

No.	Player
1	Hank Bassen, Joe Daley, Paul Hoganson, Cam Newton, Roy Edwards, Jim Rutherford, Bob Johnson, Gord Laxton, Denis Herron, Richard Harrison, Steve Guenette, Pat Riggin, Wendell Young, Rob Dobson, Peter Skudra, Rich Parent, Johan Hedberg, **John Curry, Brent Johnson**
2	Leo Boivin, Duane Rupp, Bob Paradise, Ed Van Impe, Tom Edur, Tom Bladon, Pat Price, Giles Lupien, Brian Lundberg, Phil Bourque, Greg Fox, Joe McDonnell, Todd Charlesworth, Chris Dahlquist, Jim Paek, Chris Tamer, Josef Melichar, Hal Gill, Nate Guenin
3	Al MacNeil, John Arbour, Bob Woytowich, Tim Horton, Jack Lynch, Ron Stackhouse, Bennett Wolf, Norm Schmidt, Doug Bodger, Jim Kyte, Jim Paek, Grant Jennings, Sergei Zubov, Stefan Bergkvist, Dan Trebil, Marc Bergevin, Jamie Pushor, Steve Poapst, Mark Eaton, **Alex Goligoski**
4	Noel Price, Bob Blackburn, Dave Burrows, Dale Talon, Paul Baxter, Marty McSorley, Phil Bourque, Chris Dahlquist, Dwight Schofield, Larry Murphy, Gord Dineen, Greg Andrusak, Greg Hawgood, Corey Foster, Kevin Hatcher, Jeff Norton, Bobby Dollas, Mike Wilson, Jamie Pushor, Dan Focht, Cory Cross, Noah Welch, Rob Scuderi, Jordan Leopold
5	Dick Mattiussi, Ted Lanyon, Bryan Watson, Ab DeMarco, Barry Wilkins, Steve Lyon, Mario Faubert, Lex Hudson, Ron Meighan, Bryan Maxwell, Mike Rowe, Ville Siren, Gord Dineen, Ulf Samuelsson, Brad Werenka, Janne Laukkanen, Patrick Boileau, Rob Scuderi, Darryl Sydor, **Deryk Engelland**
6	Dunc McCallum, Tracy Pratt, Sheldon Kannegiesser, Ron Jones, Colin Campbell, Tom Price, Kim Clackson, Bennett Wolf, Errol Thompson, Greg Hotham, Jim Johnson, Todd Charlesworth, Scott Young, Jeff Chychrun, Peter Ahola, Mike Ramsey, Neil Wilkinson, Bob Boughner, Mike Wilson, Rick Berry, Richard Lintner, Nolan Baumgartner, Martin Strbak, Ryan Whitney, Joel Kwiatkowski, **Ben Lovejoy**
7	Art Stratton, Lou Angotti, Bryan Hextall, Steve Durbano, Russ Anderson, Rick MacLeish, Ian Turnbull, Rod Buskas, Joe Mullen, Andrew Ference, Kelly Buchberger, Matt Hussey, Michel Ouellet, Mark Eaton
8	Val Fonteyne, Jim Wiley, Rick Kehoe, Hartland Monahan, Dave Schultz, Mike Meeker, Bob Stewart, Dave Burrows, Randy Boyd, Tom O'Regan, Petteri Lehto, Terry Ruskowski, Perry Ganchar, Mark Recchi, Bryan Smolinski, Kevin Miller, Garry Valk, Bobby Dollas, Hans Jonsson, Matt Bradley
9	Andy Bathgate, Charlie Burns, Billy Hicke, Al McDonough, Chuck Arnason, Simon Nolet, Blair Chapman, Mark Johnson, Stan Jonathan, Rich Sutter, Ron Flockhart, John Chabot, Wilf Paiement, Andrew McBain, Tony Tanti, Ron Francis, Len Barrie, Dan Quinn, Greg Johnson, German Titov, Rene Corbet, Jeff Toms, Rico Fata, Andy Hilbert, **Pascal Dupuis**
10	Earl Ingarfield, George Swarbrick, Keith McCreary, Robin Burns, Ted Snell, Pierre Larouche, Peter Lee, Gary Rissling, Bob Errey, Wayne Babych, Ron Duguay, Dan Quinn, Barry Pederson, Ron Francis, Ville Nieminen, John LeClair, Gary Roberts
11	Gene Ubriaco, Tracy Pratt, Nick Harbaruk, Bernie Lukowich, Vic Hadfield, John Flesch, Tom Cassidy, George Ferguson, Anders Hakansson, Rocky Saganiuk, Tim Tookey, Troy Loney, Dwight Mathiasen, Lee Giffin, Alain Lemieux, Warren Young, John Cullen, Alek Stojanov, Shawn Antoski, Darius Kasparaitis, Alexandre Daigle, Lasse Pirjeta, Guillaume Lefebvre, **Jordan Staal**
12	Ken Schinkel, Blaine Stoughton, Kelly Pratt, Greg Malone, Mitch Lamoreux, Dean DeFazio, Tom O'Regan, Tom Roulston, Bob Errey, Larry DePalma, Troy Murray, Chris Wells, Richard Park, Sean Pronger, Martin Sonnenberg, Billy Tibbetts, Michal Sivek, Ryan Malone, Chris Bourque
13	Jim Hamilton, Charlie Simmer, **Alex Goligoski**, Bill Guerin
14	Billy Dea, Rick Kessell, Ron Snell, Lowell MacDonald, Rene Robert, Wayne Bianchin, Nick Libett, Doug Shedden, Dan Quinn, Chris Kontos, Bryan Erickson, Jock Callander, Gordie Roberts, Dave Tippett, Brad Lauer, Stu Barnes, Pat Falloon, Milan Kraft, Shane Endicott, Chris Minard, **Chris Kunitz**
15	Bob Dillabough, Billy Harris, George Swarbrick, Steve Cardwell, Yvon Labre, Brian McKenzie, Rick Kessell, Bob McManama, Stan Gilbertson, Pat Boutette, Gary Rissling, Randy Cunneyworth, Dave Capuano, Doug Smith, Randy Gilhen, Shawn McEachern, Dmitri Mironov, Josef Beranek, Robert Dome, Roman Simicek, Wayne Primeau, Brian Holzinger, Niklas Nordgren, Mike Zigomanis, **Dustin Jeffrey**
16	Wayne Hicks, Ron Snell, Glen Sather, Sheldon Kannegiesser, Ron Lalonde, Lew Morrison, Derek Sanderson, Kim Davis, Mike Meeker, Gary McAdam, Bennett Wolf, Marc Chorney, Mark Taylor, Jim McGeough, Kevin LaVallee, Charlie Simmer, Steve Gotaas, Jay Caufield, Mike Hudson, Joe Dziedzic, Eddie Olczyk, Jeff Serowik, Dennis Bonvie, Kris Beech, Erik Christensen, Paul Bissonnette
17	Billy Spear, Bill Lecaine, Ron Schock, Rick Kehoe, Lee Giffin, Brad Aitken, Tomas Sandstrom, Peter Ferraro, Brian Bonin, Tom Chorske, Toby Petersen, Matt Murley, Karl Stewart, Petr Sykora, **Mike Rupp**

18   George Konik, Wally Boyer, Lowell MacDonald, Ross Lonsberry, Kevin McClelland, Tom Roulston, Craig Simpson, Jimmy Mann, Mark Recchi, Richard Zemlak, Jeff Daniels, Ken Priestley, Francois Leroux, Garry Valk, Patrick Lebeau, Ryan Savoia, Josef Beranek, Shean Donovan, Steve Webb, Eric Boguniecki, Dominic Moore, Adam Hall, Marian Hossa, **Chris Conner**

19   Bob Rivard, Jean Pronovost, Dale Tallon, Greg Sheppard, Rick MacLeish, Grant Sasser, Arto Javanainen, Willy Lindstrom, Dave McLlwain, Randy Gilhen, Bryan Trottier, Vladimir Vujtek, Rico Fata, Ramzi Abid, Ryan Whitney

20   Ab McDonald, Bob Woytowich, Dean Prentice, Robin Burns, John Stewart, George Swarbrick, Steve Cardwell, Yvon Labre, Jacques Cossette, Yves Bergeron, Pete Mahovlich, Paul Marshall, Paul Gardner, Gary Rissling, Moe Mantha, Dave Hunter, Dave Hannan, Jamie Leach, Jeff Daniels, Luc Robitaille, Bryan Smolinski, Greg Johnson, Roman Oksiuta, Robert Lang, Mathias Johansson, Mike Eastwood, Colby Armstrong, Janne Pesonen

21   Keith McCreary, Michel Briere

22   Paul Andrea, Greg Polis, Bob Kelly, Brian Spencer, Kim Davis, Mike Bullard, Neil Belland, Dwight Mathiasen, Jim McGeough, Chris Joseph, Wayne Van Dorp, Steve Dykstra, Paul Stanton, Rick Tocchet, Norm Maciver, Jason Woolley, Sven Butenschon, Dan LaCouture, Randy Robitaille, Matt Murley, Ric Jackman, Chris Thorburn, Jeff Taffe

23   Mel Pearson, George Swarbrick, Jean-Guy Lagace, Doug Barrie, Rick Kessell, John Stewart, Bob Leiter, Eddie Shack, Larry Bignell, Nelson Debenedet, Ed Gilbert, Jim Hamilton, Rod Schutt, Gary Rissling, Doug Lecuyer, Rich Sutter, Andy Brickley, Wally Weir, Randy Hillier, Kjell Samuelsson, Paul Stanton, Chris Joseph, Domenic Pittis, Fredrik Olausson, Victor Ignatjev, Steve Leach, Dan Trebil, Steve McKenna, John Jakopin, Shane Endicott, Eric Boguniecki, **Chris Conner**, Alexei Ponikarovsky

24   Gary Swain, Rod Zaine, Tim Horton, Eddie Shack, Jean-Guy Lagace, Larry Bignell, Mario Faubert, Don Awrey, Bob Paradise, Pat Hughes, Marc Chorney, Pat Graham, Rob Garner, Ted Bulley, Kevin McCarthy, Roger Belanger, Dwight Mathiasen, Troy Loney, Doug Brown, Ian Moran, Lyle Odelein, Kris Beech, **Matt Cooke**

25   Robin Bums, John Stewart, Darryl Edestrand, Nick Beverly, Dennis Owchar, Greg Redquest, Tom Price, Randy Carlyle, Kevin McCarthy, Ted Nolan, Norm Schmidt, Kevin Stevens, Alek Stojanov, Dan Kesa, Jeff Norton, Marc Bergevin, **Max Talbot**

26   Dunc McCallum, Mike McMahon, Syl Apps, Pete Mahovlich, Orest Kindrachuk, Paul Mulvey, Steve Gatzos, Wayne Babych, Mike Blaisdell, Mark Kachowski, Mike Stapleton, Richard Park, Dave McLlwain, Petr Klima, Darius Kasparaitis, Garry Valk, Frantisek Kucera, Kent Manderville, Landon Wilson, Ronald Petrovicky, Ruslan Fedotenko

27   Jim Morrison, Joe Noris, Jim Shires, Hank Nowak, Yves Bergeron, Pete Laframboise, Mike Corrigan, Jacques Cossette, Rod Schutt, Todd Charlesworth, Gilles Meloche, Scott Bjugstad, Gilbert Delorme, Glen Murray, Eddie Olczyk, Alexei Kovalev, Georges Laraque, **Craig Adams**

28   Harvey Bennett, Mario Faubert, Gene Carr, Tom Price, Jim Hamilton, Bob Simpson, Tim Hrynewich, Bruce Crowder, Robert Geale, Steve Gatzos, Dan Frawley, Gordie Roberts, Kjell Samuelsson, Greg Andrusak, Jeff Christian, Craig Muni, Dan Kesa, Michal Rozsival, Matt Hussey, Jani Rita, Nils Ekman, Adam Hall, **Eric Godard**

29   Al Smith, Jim Rutherford, Denis Herron, Andy Brown, Gary Inness, Bob Stumpf, Dunc Wilson, Greg Millen, Michel Dion, Phil Bourque, Markus Naslund, Tyler Wright, Krzysztof Oliwa, Brooks Orpik, **Marc-Andre Fleury**

30   Les Binkley, Marv Edwards, Cam Newton, Andy Brown, Gary Inness, Bob Taylor, Gordon Laxton, Paul Gardner, Kim Davis, Gary Edwards, Roberto Romano, Steve Guenette, Alain Chevrier, Philippe DeRouville, Jean-Sebastian Aubin, Dany Sabourin

Craig Simpson wore No. 18 for the Pens.

Big Kjell Samuelsson wore No. 23 before switching to No. 28.

31	Michel Plasse, Nick Ricci, Vincent Tremblay, Brian Ford, Carl Mokosak, Rick Tabaracci, Tom Barrasso, Ken Wregget, Ron Tugnutt, Rich Parent, Sebastien Caron
32	Dave Hannan, Dave Goertz, Pat Mayer, Peter Taglianetti, John Slaney, Greg Crozier, Dick Tarnstrom, Alain Nasreddine, Chris Minard, Mathieu Garon
33	Tony Feltrin, Bob Simpson, Rocky Saganiuk, Bob Gladney, Doug Bodger, Mike Rowe, Mitch Wilson, Zarley Zalapski, Bryan Fogarty, Marty McSorley, Jim McKenzie, Stefan Bergkvist, Alex Hicks, Dan LaCouture, Guillaume Lefebvre, Reid Simpson, Zigmund Palffy, Eric Cairns, Ryan Stone
34	Andre St. Laurent, Tom Thornbury, Greg Tebbutt, Randy Hillier, Ted Nolan, Todd Charlesworth, Lee Giffin, Dwight Mathiasen, Scott Young, Dave Michayluk, Greg Brown, Rusty Fitzgerald, Jeff Christian, Peter Popovic, Garth Snow, Ross Lupaschuk, Ramzi Abid, Jonathan Filewich
35	Roberto Romano, Warren Young, Darren Lowe, Ron Duguay, Brad Aitken, Tom Barrasso, Ty Conklin
36	Jock Callander, Pat Neaton, Greg Andrusak, Corey Foster, Brad Lauer, J.J. Daigneault, Matthew Barnaby, Tom Kostopoulos, Andre Roy, Connor James, **John Curry**
37	Justin Duberman, Ladislav Karabin, Greg Andrusak, Kip Miller, Tom Kostopoulos, Mikael Samuelsson, Ryan VandenBussche, Jarkko Ruutu, Bill Thomas
38	Scott Gruhl, Jiri Hrdina, Peter Allen, Andreas Johansson, Jan Hrdina, Jeff Taffe, **Mark Letestu**
39	Mike Needham, Peter Allen, Joel Bouchard, Jon Sim, Chris Minard
40	Frank Pietrangelo, Patrick Lalime, Andy Chiodo, **Alexander Pechurski**
41	Shane Endicott, Jocelyn Thibault, Nathan Smith, Martin Skoula
42	Tuomas Gronman, **Dustin Jeffrey, Nick Johnson**
43	Jeff Daniels, Tomas Surovy, Philippe Boucher
44	Rob Brown, Todd Nelson, Drake Berehowsky, Ed Patterson, Stephane Richer, **Brooks Orpik**
45	Mike Needham, Glen Mulvenna, Rob Scuderi
46	Victor Ignatjev, Pavel Skrbek, Jeff Toms
47	Maxim Galanov, Kent Manderville, Michal Sivek, Micki DuPont, Tim Brent
48	Sven Butenschon, Jeff Serowik, Konstantin Koltsov, **Tyler Kennedy**
49	Greg Andrusak, Matt Hussey
50	Martin Brochu
51	Dave Roche
52	Rusty Fitzgerald
55	Larry Murphy, Drake Berehowsky, Ric Jackman, Sergei Gonchar
56	Sergei Zubov, **Eric Tangradi**
57	Chris Ferraro, Shawn Heins
58	**Kris Letang**
59	Robert Dome
61	Luca Caputi
63	**Tim Wallace**
65	**Ben Lovejoy**
66	Mario Lemieux
67	**Alex Goligoski,** Paul Bissonnette
68	Jaromir Jagr
71	Jiri Slegr, Konstantin Koltsov, **Evgeni Malkin**
72	Jeff Christian, Eric Meloche
74	Jay McKee
76	Richard Park
77	Paul Coffey
81	Miroslav Satan
82	Martin Straka
85	Petr Klima
87	**Sidney Crosby**
92	Rick Tocchet
93	Petr Nedved
95	Aleksey Morozov

Bold indicates current Penguin

GLEN SATHER   L. WING
PITTS. PENGUINS

Popular agitator Glen "Slats" Sather wore No. 16, but he was No. 1 in the hearts of Penguins fans.

Penguins Attendance—Regular Season

YEAR	ATTENDANCE	GAMES	AVERAGE	SELLOUTS	CAPACITY
1967–68	274,049	37	7,407	0	12,580
1968–69	228,285	38	6,008	0	12,580
1969–70	265,936	38	6,998	0	12,580
1970–71	377,182	39	9,671	3	12,580
1971–72	375,711	39	9,634	5	12,580
1972–73	436,601	39	11,195	7	12,866
1973–74	396,197	39	10,159	4	13,431
1974–75	448,977	40	11,224	11	13,404
1975–76	458,198	40	11,455	0	16,402
1976–77	401,580	40	10,040	1	16,404
1977–78	421,933	40	10,548	2	16,033
1978–79	457,209	40	11,430	3	16,033
1979–80	426,156	40	10,653	2	16,033
1980–81	413,407	40	10,335	0	16,033
1981–82	451,965	40	11,299	5	16,033
1982–83	336,300	40	8,408	1	16,033
1983–84	273,550	40	6,839	0	16,033
1984–85	400,711	40	10,018	4	16,033
1985–86	503,020	40	12,576	13	16,033
1986–87	598,614	40	14,965	26	16,033
1987–88	606,638	40	15,166	26	16,168
1988–89	629,345	40	15,734	34	16,025
1989–90	640,700	40	16,018	34	16,015**
1990–91	637,072	40	15,927	28	16,164
1991–92	639,736	40	15,993	32	16,164
1992–93	660,290	41	16,105	30	16,164
1993–94	685,589	41	16,714	11	17,537
1994–95	386,599	24	16,108	9	17,181
1995–96	665,790	41	16,239	20	17,181
1996–97	684,346	41	16,691	21	17,181
1997–98	617,815	41	15,069	7	16,958
1998–99	607,822	41	14,825	5	16,958
1999–00	636,199	41	15,517	13	16,958
2000–01	655,926	40	16,398	26	16,958
2001–02	641,641	41	15,650	18	16,958
2002–03	604,970	41	14,755	8	16,958
2003–04	486,961	41	11,877	1	16,940
2005–06	647,975	41	15,804	12	16,940
2006–07	673,422	41	16,424	30	16,940
2007–08	700,193	41	17,078*	41*	16,940
2008–09	682,298	40	17,058	40	16,940
2009–10	700,211*	41	17,078*	41*	16,940

* Club Record   ** Capacity increased to 16,236 in January

Penguins Attendance—Playoffs

YEAR	ATTENDANCE	GAMES	AVERAGE	SELLOUTS	CAPACITY
1969–70	53,592	5	10,718	2	12,580
1971–72	25,515	2	12,758	1	12,580
1974–75	66,833	5	13,367	4	13,404
1975–76	13,626	1	13,626	0	16,402
1976–77	25,967	2	12,984	0	16,404
1978–79	45,702	3	15,234	2	16,033
1979–80	26,901	2	13,451	0	16,033
1980–81	26,688	2	13,344	0	16,033
1981–82	25,457	2	12,729	0	16,033
1988–89	96,150	6	16,025	6	16,025
1990–91	210,132*	13*	16,164	13*	16,164
1991–92	161,640	10	16,164	10	16,164
1992–93	129,312	8	16,164	8	16,164
1993–94	46,412	3	15,471	0	17,537
1994–95	114,894	7	16,413	2	17,181
1995–96	171,597	10	17,159	9	17,181
1996–97	34,710	2	17,355*	2	17,181
1997–98	48,437	3	16,146	1	16,958
1998–99	99,787	6	16,631	4	16,958
1999–00	84,924	5	16,984	4	16,958
2000–01	137,184	8	17,148	8	16,958
2006–07	34,264	2	17,132	2	16,940
2007–08	188,452	11	17,132	11	16,940
2008–09	188,452	11	17,132	11	16,940
2009–10	119,924	7	17,132	7	16,940

*Club Record

Penguins Assistant Coaches

Mike Corrigan	1980–1984	Pierre McGuire	1990–1992
Mike Eaves	1997–1999	Lorne Molleken	2003–2004
Tom Fitzgerald	2009	Joe Mullen	2000–2005
Tony Granato	2009–	Rick Paterson	1988–1993
Randy Hillier	1997–1998, 2001–2005	Todd Reirden	2010–
Ivan Hlinka	2000	Jim Roberts	1984–1987
Fred Hucul	1973–1974	Andre Savard	2006–2009
Don Jackson	1997–1999	Barry Smith	1990–1993
Clement Jodoin	1987–1988	Bryan Trottier	1993–1997
Eddie Johnston	1999–2000	Troy Ward	1997–1999
Rick Kehoe	1987–1997, 1999–2001	Mike Yeo	2005–2010

Minor League Head Coaches

Coach	Team	Seasons Coached
Scott Allen	Johnstown	1997–1998
Lou Angotti	Baltimore	1982–1983
	Erie	1981–1982
Ed Bartolli	Dayton	1977
	Grand Rapids	1977–1979
Pat Bingham	Wheeling	2003–2005
Marc Boileau	Ft. Wayne	1971–1974
John Brophy	Hampton Roads	1995–1996
	Wheeling	2001–2003
Dan Bylsma	Wilkes-Barre/Scranton	2008–2009
Murray Eaves	Wheeling	1999–2000
Nick Fotiu	Johnstown	1996–1997
Chuck Hamilton	Hershey	1973–1977
Joe Hardy	Binghamton	1978–1979
Joe Harney	Wheeling	2001
Don Jackson	Knoxville	1990–1991
Ralph Keller	Ft. Wayne	1974–1975
Larry Kish	Binghamton	1977–1978, 1980–1981
Rick Ley	Muskegon	1984–1988
Blair MacDonald	Muskegon	1988–1991
Frank Mathers	Hershey	1971–1973
Jack McIlhargey	Syracuse	1997–1999
Rudy Migay	Amarillo	1968–1969, 1970–1971
	Baltimore	1969–1970
Rick Kehoe	Wilkes-Barre/Scranton	2005
Nelson LeClair	Grand Rapids	1979–1980
Alain Lemieux	Wheeling	2000–2001
Gerry Moore	Muskegon	1982
Joe Mullen	Wilkes-Barre/Scranton	2005–2006
Bill Nyrop	Knoxville	1991–1992
Michel Parizeau	Syracuse	1979–1980
Rick Paterson	Cleveland	1993–1997
Glenn Patrick	Wilkes-Barre/Scranton	1999–2003
	Wheeling	2005–2008
Poul Popeil	Muskegon	1981–1982
Greg Puhalski	Wheeling	2008–
Terry Reardon	Baltimore	1967–1968, 1970–1971
Todd Reirden	Wilkes-Barre/Scranton	2009–2010
Todd Richards	Wilkes-Barre/Scranton	2006–2008
Dick Roberge	Johnstown	1974–1975
Phil Russell	Cleveland	1992–1993
	Muskegon	1991–1992
Michel Therrien	Wilkes-Barre/Scranton	2003–2005
Gene Ubriaco	Baltimore	1983–1988
Ted Wright	Ft. Wayne	1974
Warren Young	Louisville	1993–1994

Presidents and Captains

Presidents		Captains	
1967–70	Jack E. McGregor	1967–68	Ab McDonald
1970–72	Jack Riley	1968–69	Earl Ingarfield
1973–74	No President	1969–73	No Captain
1975–77	Wren Blair	1973–77	Ron Schock
1977–81	Vince Bartimo	1977–78	Jean Pronovost
1981–88	Edward J. DeBartolo Sr.	1978–81	Orest Kindrachuk
1988–91	Denise DeBartolo-York	1981–84	Randy Carlyle
1991–92	Howard Baldwin	1984–86	Mike Bullard
1993–96	Jack Kelley	1986–87	Mike Bullard/Terry Ruskowski
1996–97	Donn Patton	1987–88	Dan Frawley/Mario Lemieux
1998–99	Craig Patrick	1988–94	Mario Lemieux
1999–01	Mario Lemieux	1994–95	Ron Francis
2001–02	Tom Rooney/Ken Sawyer	1995–97	Mario Lemieux
2002–07	Ken Sawyer	1997–98	Ron Francis
2007–Present	David Morehouse	1998–01	Jaromir Jagr
		2001–06	Mario Lemieux
		2006–07	No captain
		2007–Present	Sidney Crosby

Sidney Crosby was named captain in 2007.

Scouts

Edgar Brenchley	(1967–70, 1971–73)	Pierre McGuire	(1990–91)
Rudy Migay	(1967–68, 1971–75)	Mark Kelley	(1993–06)
Ken Carson	(1967–68)	Phil Russell	(1993–97)
Red Sullivan	(1969–70)	Glenn Patrick	(1994–06)
Dave Lucas	(1969–75)	Herb Brooks	(1996–03)
Clare Rothermel	(1969–75, 1977–84)	Wayne Daniels	(1999–05)
Ron Marlow	(1971–72)	Neil Shea	(1999–06)
Dick Coss	(1971–72)	Richard Rose	(2001–05)
Gerry Brown	(1971–74)	Chuck Grillo	(2001–present)
Jack Riley	(1974–75)	Bill O'Flaherty	(2006–07)
Ken Schinkel	(1974–76)	Matt Recchi	(2005–08)
Gerald Blair	(1976–77)	Kevin Stevens	(2005–present)
Billy Taylor	(1979–86)	Jim Madigan	(2006–present)
Albert Mandanici	(1981–88)	Dan MacKinnon	(2006–present)
Lou Angotti	(1984–86)	Patrik Allvin	(2006–present)
Bruce Haralson	(1984–89)	Wayne Meier	(2006–present)
John Gill	(1985–95)	Darryl Plandowski	(2006–08)
Paul Goulet	(1986–88)	Brian Fitzgerald	(2006–present)
Rick Kehoe	(1986–06)	Robert Neuhauser	(2006–present)
Doug Wood	(1986–88)	Derek Clancey	(2007–present)
Fred Gore	(1987–89)	David McNamara	(2007–present)
Greg Malone	(1988–06)	Luc Gauthier	(2008–present)
Les Binkley	(1989–99)	Ron Pyette	(2008–present)
Charlie Hodge	(1989–05)	Dan Allison	(2009–present)
Doug McCauley	(1989–91)	Andre Savard	(2009–present)
Ralph Cox	(1989–99)	Randy Sexton	(2010–present)
Gilles Meloche	(1990–06)		

Penguins Minor League Affiliates

1967–1970

Team	League
Amarillo Wranglers	Central Hockey League
Baltimore Clippers	American Hockey League

1970–1979

Team	League
Amarillo Wranglers	Central Hockey League
Baltimore Clippers	American Hockey League
Binghamton Dusters	American Hockey League
Dayton Owls	International Hockey League
Ft. Wayne Komets	International Hockey League
Grand Rapids Owls	International Hockey League
Hershey Bears	American Hockey League
Johnstown Jets	North American Hockey League
Syracuse Firebirds	American Hockey League

1980–1989

Team	League
Baltimore Skipjacks	American Hockey League
Binghamton Whalers	American Hockey League
Erie Blades	American Hockey League
Grand Rapids Owls	International Hockey League
Muskegon Lumberjacks	International Hockey League
Muskegon Mohawks	International Hockey League
Syracuse Firebirds	American Hockey League

1990–1999

Team	League
Cleveland Lumberjacks	International Hockey League
Hampton Roads Admirals	East Coast Hockey League
Johnstown Chiefs	East Coast Hockey League
Knoxville Cherokees	East Coast Hockey League
Louisville Ice Hawks	East Coast Hockey League
Syracuse Crunch	American Hockey League
Muskegon Lumberjacks	International Hockey League
Wheeling Nailers	East Coast Hockey League
Wilkes-Barre/Scranton Penguins	American Hockey League

2000–

Team	League
Wheeling Nailers	East Coast Hockey League
Wilkes-Barre/Scranton Penguins	American Hockey League

Penguins on Television

Seasons	Station Affiliation	Play-by-Play	Color
1967–1968	WTAE	Ed Conway	
1968–1969	WTAE	Ed Conway	
1969–1970	WTAE/WPGH	Joe Tucker	
1970–1971	WPGH	Bill Hamilton	John MacDonald
1971–1972	WIIC	Sam Nover	Jack Riley
1972–1973	WIIC	Sam Nover	Terry Schiffauer
1973–1974	WIIC	Sam Nover	Greg Benedetti
1974–1976	WIIC	Sam Nover	
1976–1977	WIIC	Sam Nover	Terry Schiffauer
1977–1978	WPGH	Bob Prince	Terry Schiffauer
1978–1979	WPGH	Jim Forney	
1979–1984	WPGH	Mike Lange	Terry Schiffauer
1984–1990	WPGH	Mike Lange	Paul Steigerwald
1990–1993	KDKA	Mike Lange	Paul Steigerwald
1993–1996	KDKA/KBL	Mike Lange	Paul Steigerwald
1996–1997	WPTT/WPGH	Mike Lange	Paul Steigerwald
1997–1999	FOX Sports Net	Mike Lange	Paul Steigerwald
1999–2000	FOX Sports Net	Mike Lange	Troy Loney
2000–2003	FOX Sports Net	Mike Lange	Ed Olczyk
2003–2004	FOX Sports Net	Mike Lange	Bob Errey
2004–2005	No games		
2005–2006	FOX Sports Net	Mike Lange	Bob Errey
2006–	FOX Sports Net	Paul Steigerwald	Bob Errey

Penguins on the Radio

Seasons	Station Affiliation	Play-by-Play	Color
1967–1968	WTAE	Ed Conway	
1968–1969	WTAE	Beckley Smith	Jim O'Brien
1969–1970	WEEP	Bill Hamilton	
1970–1973	KDKA	Jim Forney	
1973–1974	KDKA	Joe Starkey	
1974–1975	KDKA	Mike Lange	
1975–1976	KQV	Garry Morrell	
1976–1979	KDKA	Mike Lange	
1979–1981	WWSW	Mike Lange	Terry Schiffauer
1981–1984	KQV	Mike Lange	Terry Schiffauer
1984–1993	KDKA	Mike Lange	Paul Steigerwald
1993–1995	WTAE	Doug McLeod	Stan Savran
1995–1996	WTAE	Doug McLeod	Troy Loney
1996–1997	WTAE	Matt McConnell	Peter Taglianetti
1997–1999	WDVE	Matt McConnell	Peter Taglianetti
1999–2003	WWSW	Paul Steigerwald	Bob Errey
2003–2004	WWSW	Paul Steigerwald	Phil Bourque
2004–2005	No games		
2005–2006	WWSW	Paul Steigerwald	Phil Bourque
2006–	WXDX	Mike Lange	Phil Bourque

Bill Hamilton did play-by-play for the Pens in the early 1970s.

Sources

Books

Diamond, Dan, ed. *Total Hockey*. Andrews McMeel Publishing, 1998.

Fischler, Stan. *Bad Boys: Legends of Hockey's Toughest, Meanest, Most Feared Players!* McGraw-Hill Ryerson, 1991.

Fischler, Stan. *Boston Bruins: Greatest Moments and Players*. Sports Masters, 2001.

Fischler, Stan, and Fischler, Shirley. *Who's Who in Hockey*. Andrews McMeel Publishing, 2003.

Hart, Gene. *Score! My Twenty-Five Years with the Broad Street Bullies*. Bonus Books, Inc., 1990.

McMillan, Tom. *Pittsburgh Penguins: Cellar to Summit*. Ironist Press, 1995.

O'Brien, Jim. *Penguin Profiles: Pittsburgh's Boys of Winter*. James P. O'Brien—Publishing, 1994.

Schultz, Dave, with Stan Fischler. *The Hammer: Confessions of a Hockey Enforcer*. Summit Books, 1981.

Starkey, Joe. *Tales from the Pittsburgh Penguins*. Sports Publishing, LLC, 2006.

Magazines

Bechtel, Mark. "Lifting His Wings." *Sports Illustrated presents* (Special Commemorative Issue, 1997).

Creamer, Robert W., ed. "They Said It." *Sports Illustrated* (January 28, 1974).

Farber, Michael. "Stimulus Needed." *Sports Illustrated* (February 23, 2009).

Farber, Michael. "The Pens Are Mightier." *Sports Illustrated* (June 22, 2009).

Farber, Michael. "Where There's Smoke, There's Fire." *Sports Illustrated* (September 7, 1998).

Gelin, Dana. "Breaking Through." *Sports Illustrated presents* (Special Commemorative Issue, 1997).

Greenberg, Jay. "On Top at Last." *Sports Illustrated* (June 3, 1991).

Keteyian, Armen. "A Roundup of the Week of March 5-11." *Sports Illustrated* (March 19, 1984).

Mulvoy, Mark. "NHL" *Sports Illustrated* (October 21, 1974).

Mulvoy, Mark. "NHL" *Sports Illustrated* (October 20, 1975).

Mulvoy, Mark. "Who Said Penguins Can't Fly?" *Sports Illustrated* (April 28, 1975).

Scher, Jon. "Swept Away." *Sports Illustrated* (June 8, 1992).

Swift, E.M. "One of a Kind." *Sports Illustrated presents* (Special Commemorative Issue, 1997).

Swift, E.M. "Rare Bird." *Sports Illustrated presents* (Special Commemorative Issue, 1997).

Newspapers

Naples Daily News
Pittsburgh Press
Pittsburgh Post-Gazette
Pittsburgh Sun-Telegraph
Pittsburgh Tribune-Review
The Gazette Times
The Globe and Mail
The New York Times
The Toronto Sun
USA Today

Periodicals

The Sporting News

Team Publications

Pittsburgh Penguins Media Guide (2009-2010).

Videos

A Portrait of Courage: The Story of the 1992-93 Pittsburgh Penguins. The Pittsburgh Penguins with Ross Sports Productions, 1993.
Against the Odds: The Story of the 1991-92 Pittsburgh Penguins. KDKA Sports with Ross Sports Productions, 1992.
One from the Heart: The Story of the 1990-91 Pittsburgh Penguins. KBL with Ross Sports Productions, 1991.
Stanley Cup: 2009 Champions. Warner Home Video with the NHL, 2009.

Websites

azhockey.com
brainyquote.com
ceonfoosheys.wordpress.com
dropyourgloves.com
espn.com
fundinguniverse.com
greatesthockeylegends.com
hhof.com
hockey.ballparks.com
hockeydb.com
hockeydraftcentral.com
hockeygoalies.org
hockey-reference.com
hockeystoughguys.blogspot.com
legendsofhockey.net
letsgopens.com
mario-lemieux.com
nhl.com
nhlshootouts.com
penguinslegends.blogspot.com
penguins.nhl.com
pittsburghhockey.net
proicehockey.about.com
shrpsports.com
sportsbusinessjournal.com
sports.jrank.org
thehockeyblog.com
tmlfever.com